D1598315

China's environmental problems long predate the modern era. Official policies, sometimes local, sometimes on a massive scale, have often caused as many difficulties as they have solved. Yet the Chinese have always been aware of their environment. The Chinese written record on environmental matters is probably unique in its continuity and depth in time. Historically, Chinese conceptual representations of nature in official documents, literature, and popular thinking have both reflected patterns of human action in a changing environment and conditioned them.

This collection of essays is the first relatively comprehensive survey of the environmental history of China. Written by some of the world's leading Western and Chinese experts, *Sediments of Time* crystallizes a new and distinct field of scholarship that studies what happens when human social systems interact with the rest of the natural world. This book shows how deforestation, land reclamation, settlement, and water control, when combined with an ever-changing climate, shape a distinctive and often precarious environment. Pioneering essays explore new methodologies of historical environmental research; others offer comparative perspectives setting China in the context of the West and Japan, and describe the impact of the early modern ecological transformation on the spread of diseases such as cholera and tuberculosis. *Sediments of Time* is indispensable for anyone who wants to understand either the foundations of modern China or the deeper origins of many of China's most daunting contemporary challenges.

SEDIMENTS OF TIME

STUDIES IN ENVIRONMENT AND HISTORY

Editors

Donald Worster

University of Kansas

Alfred W. Crosby

University of Texas at Austin

OTHER BOOKS IN THE SERIES

Donald Worster *Nature's Economy: A History of Ecological Ideas*

Kenneth F. Kiple *The Caribbean Slave: A Biological History*

Alfred W. Crosby *Ecological Imperialism: The Biological Expansion of Europe, 900–1900*

Arthur F. McEvoy *The Fisherman's Problem: Ecology and Law in the California Fisheries, 1850–1980*

Robert Harms *Games Against Nature: An Eco-Cultural History of the Nunu of Equatorial Africa*

Warren Dean *Brazil and the Struggle for Rubber: A Study in Environmental History*

Samuel P. Hays *Beauty, Health, and Permanence: Environmental Politics in the United States, 1955–1985*

Donald Worster *The Ends of the Earth: Perspectives on Modern Environmental History*

Michael Williams *Americans and Their Forests: A Historical Geography*

Timothy Silver *A New Face on the Countryside: Indians, Colonists, and Slaves in the South Atlantic Forests, 1500–1800*

Theodore Steinberg *Nature Incorporated: Industrialization and the Waters of New England*

J. R. McNeill *The Mountains of the Mediterranean World: An Environmental History*

Elinor G. K. Melville *A Plague of Sheep: Environmental Consequences of the Conquest of Mexico*

Richard H. Grove *Green Imperialism: Colonial Expansion, Tropical Island Edens and the Origins of Environmentalism, 1600–1860*

Sediments of Time

ENVIRONMENT AND SOCIETY IN CHINESE HISTORY

Edited by

Mark Elvin
Australian National University

Liu Ts'ui-jung
Academia Sinica, Taipei

CAMBRIDGE
UNIVERSITY PRESS

PUBLISHED BY THE PRESS SYNDICATE OF THE UNIVERSITY OF CAMBRIDGE
The Pitt Building, Trumpington Street, Cambridge CB2 1RP, United Kingdom

CAMBRIDGE UNIVERSITY PRESS
The Edinburgh Building, Cambridge CB2 2RU, United Kingdom
40 West 20th Street, New York, NY 10011-4211, USA
10 Stamford Road, Oakleigh, Melbourne 3166, Australia

First published 1998

Printed in the United States of America

Typeset in New Baskerville

Library of Congress Cataloging-in-Publication Data
Sediments of time : environment and society in Chinese history /
edited by Mark Elvin, Liu Ts'ui-jung.
p.   cm. – (Studies in environment and history.)
Includes index.
ISBN 0-521-56381-X
1. Ecology – China.   2. Ecology.   3. Environmental sciences.
I. Elvin, Mark.   II. Liu, Ts'ui-jung, 1941–   III. Series.
QH540.83.C6S44   1998
333.7'0951 – dc20   96–22662
CIP

*A catalog record of this book is available from
the British Library*

ISBN 0-521-56381-X hardback

Peace does not become peace in a single day; a crisis does not become a crisis in a single day. Both become what they are through a gradual accumulation.

Jia Yi
Biography of Jia Yi, *j.* 48 of the *Han Shu* [History of the Han]

安者非一日而安也。危者非一日而危也。皆以積漸然。

漢書 卷四十八 賈誼傳

Contents

REPRESENTATIONS OF THE ENVIRONMENT – THE OFFICIAL MIND

REPRESENTATIONS OF THE ENVIRONMENT – LITERARY AND POPULAR SENSIBILITY

THE ENVIRONMENT AND EARLY MODERN ECONOMIC GROWTH IN TAIWAN AND JAPAN

Illustrations

MAPS

Preface

The chapters of this book are, with one commissioned addition, revised versions of the majority of the papers presented to the Conference on the History of the Environment in China held December 13–18, 1993, at the Silvermine Beach Hotel on Lantau, Hong Kong. This conference was jointly sponsored by the Research School of Pacific and Asian Studies of the Australian National University and by the Institute of Economics of the Academia Sinica. The greater part of the funding was provided by the Chiang Ching-kuo Foundation for International Scholarly Exchange, which has also made a generous grant toward the costs of publication. We would like to express our deep gratitude to the foundation and to our two institutional sponsors. Together they made possible an unprecedented event that may be reasonably described as the crystallization of a new field in Chinese and historical studies.

A somewhat fuller Chinese-language version is already in print, under the title 積漸所至。中國環境史論文集, edited by the same editors and published by the Institute of Economics of the Academia Sinica (1995). Reference should be made to this version for the four papers that, to our great regret, were precluded for reasons of space from inclusion in the present already massive volume. To the authors of these papers, our colleagues Professor Rhoads Murphey, Dr. Janice Stargardt, Professor Carney Fisher, and Dr. Alan Lu Yun, we should like to express our apologies and our continuing appreciation of their valuable and important work. For further information about initiatives stimulated by the conference and other current work in Chinese environmental history, readers should contact Professor Helen Dunstan 鄧海倫 at the School of Asian Studies, University of Sydney, Sydney, Australia 2006 (e-mail: helen.dunstan@asia. su.edu.au), with a request to subscribe to the *Chinese Environmental*

History Newsletter, specifying the English-language or Chinese-language version.

We should also like to thank all those who helped us at the conference. Special gratitude is due to Professor Wang Gungwu 王賡武, then Vice-Chancellor of Hong Kong University and an authority on the environmental problems faced by Hong Kong, who inaugurated our proceedings with a memorable opening address. Likewise, our two very knowledgeable doctoral students, Liu Shih-yun and Lewis Mayo, worked very hard at countless matters of detail on our behalf. Both the academic editors would like to pay tribute to Walter Havighurst, our press copy editor, for his painstaking but tactful reshaping of virtually every page of this book in the interests of increased clarity and internal consistency. We appreciate also the contributions of our production editor, Janis Bolster, in dealing with a book composed of exceptionally heterodox components. It is a pleasure to thank Mr. Andrew Johnson of the White Horse Press (UK) for kind permission to reproduce the photograph by Mark Elvin (Figure 10.12 herein) that originally appeared as the cover of the first issue of *Environment and History* (1995). Finally, our warmest thanks go to Keith Mitchell and his colleagues Ian Heyward and Neville Minch at the Cartography Unit of the Research School of Pacific and Asian Studies, who so expertly prepared our maps, and – of course – to Frank Smith, Executive Editor for the Social Sciences at Cambridge University Press, New York, who attended the Conference and provided us there and afterward with many useful comments and much encouragement.

Liu Ts'ui-jung
Mark Elvin
January 1997

Notes on Chinese Characters, Their Roman Transcription, and Terminology

The normal form of the Chinese characters used in the text and notes is the traditional or "full" form (*zhengti zi* 正體字, *fanti zi* 繁體字). The "simplified" forms (*jianti zi* 简体字) are used in the following cases: (1) for personal names of present-day authors who have customarily worked in the People's Republic of China, or who have to our knowledge expressed a preference for their names to be so written, and (2) for the titles of books and periodicals produced in the People's Republic of China since the changeover to the more or less general use of the simplified forms.

The transcription of Chinese characters into the Roman alphabet follows the *pinyin* system, with a handful of exceptions. Present-day place names in the Republic of China on Taiwan and in Hong Kong are kept in their customary contemporary forms throughout, as, for example, "Taipei." Personal names of living or recently deceased Chinese are initially given in their personally preferred form if this is known to us or can reasonably be inferred, with the pinyin form added in parentheses.

These rules work fairly consistently, but there are a few ambiguous areas where the editors have been obliged to make what may seem to be arbitrary choices. We hope that our readers will forgive us if they disagree with some of our decisions.

The rules for the joining, separating, and hyphenating of groups of pinyin syllables have never, to our knowledge, been satisfactorily systematized. Rather than try to invent such rules ourselves, we have therefore on the whole followed the preferences of our contributors in these matters. This has resulted in some minor inconsistencies between chapters from different hands; we trust these will not give offense to purists.

As regards the pronunciation of Chinese words, nonsinological readers may wish to note that, while the vowel sounds in standard modern Chinese are mostly close to those in Italian (with an *ü* that approximates the vowel in the French *rue* and an *ia* that is not far from "ye" as in English "yet"), the approximate values of some of the consonants are not immediately obvious:

> *c* is roughly "ts" and *z* roughly "dz"
>
> *q* is roughly "ch" before a yodized vowel (a vowel preceded by a brief *i*), the voiced form being *j*
>
> *zh* is roughly "dj" before a nonyodized vowel, the unvoiced form being *ch*,
>
> and *x* is roughly "sh" before a yodized vowel, with *sh* being used before the nonyodized vowels.

There are cases of ambiguity as to where a division should be made between syllables – an example being the bisyllabic name for the city "Xian" ("Shee-ahn"), which is transcribed (apart from the capital letter) like the monosyllabic word for "county," which is *xian* (roughly "shyen"). There is a (not wholly watertight) rule for the correct division of multisyllabic strings in pinyin: as a default option make the break at the first point in the string at which a valid Chinese syllable is complete; if this does not give the desired result, insert an inverted comma to indicate where the break should come. Thus the province "Henan" is composed of "He + nan." If it were "Hen + an" (both of which are also legitimate syllables) it would have to be transcribed "Hen'an." Using this rule requires a prior knowledge of which syllables are legitimate in Chinese; for the convenience of our nonsinological readers we have therefore inserted the inverted comma at points of apparent ambiguity where, for the sinologist, this is not strictly necessary. Hence the reader will find "Xi'an" for the city and "He'nan" for the province. The logically minded will note that the word for "county" would have to be transcribed as *xian'* to avoid ambiguity, something that, so far as we know, has never been done in practice.

This book follows the demographic convention that "immigration" and "emigration," and cognate terms, are reserved for movements of population across international political borders, while "inmigration" and "outmigration" designate movements within the same national political jurisdiction.

SEDIMENTS OF TIME

1

Introduction

MARK ELVIN

Environmental history is the historically documented part of the story of the life and death not of human individuals but of societies, and of species, both others and our own, in terms of their relationships with the world about them. The intellectual origins of modern environmentalism as a self-conscious domain of inquiry can probably be traced to the encounter of seventeenth- and eighteenth-century Western Europeans, especially colonial naturalists, medical officers, and administrators, with the unfamiliar environments of the tropics, and the damage done to these environments by Western Europeans.[1] From the mid-nineteenth century to the mid-twentieth an environmental history, founded on these ideas, developed primarily in the form of what we would tend to think of as historical geography,[2] culminating in the *summa, Man's Role in Changing the Face of the Earth*, published in 1956 under the general editorship of W. L. Thomas.[3] During the last few decades a number of historians have combined this approach with their own characteristic methods of documentary analysis and their characteristic concerns – the changing patterns of human economic, political, and intellectual structures – and, where possible, incorporated relevant scientific conceptions into their analyses.[4] The subject matter

---

[1] R. Grove, *Green Imperialism: Colonial Expansion, Tropical Island Edens and the Origins of Environmentalism, 1600–1800* (New York: Cambridge University Press, 1995).
[2] See the summary in A. Goudie, *The Human Impact on the Natural Environment*, 2d ed. (Oxford: Blackwell, 1986), pp. 1–7.
[3] Chicago: University of Chicago Press. Collaborators included C. O. Sauer, M. Bates, and L. Mumford. A partial sequel is B. L. Turner II, W. C. Clark, R. W. Kates. J. F. Richards, J. T. Mathews, and W. B. Meyer, eds., *The Earth As Transformed by Human Action: Global and Regional Changes in the Biosphere over the Past 300 Years* (New York: Cambridge University Press, 1990).
[4] See the summary "Doing Environmental History" by D. Worster, in Worster, ed., *The Ends of the Earth: Perspectives on Modern Environmental History* (New York: Cambridge University Press, 1988), pp. 289–307.

of the books now being published that could be described as "environmental history" has also become almost disconcertingly diverse. Thus, for
example, Keith Thomas's subtle essay on ideas, *Man and the Natural World:
Changing Attitudes in England, 1500–1800*,[5] and the cautious scientific
studies of land management in *Australian Environmental History – Essays
and Cases*, edited by Stephen Dovers,[6] would seem at first sight to be only
distantly related. In fact they define the two ends of the spectrum of topics
covered by the present collective volume, which may perhaps be defined –
we hope not immodestly – as the first relatively comprehensive coverage of
the environmental aspects of the Chinese historical experience.

What are its unifying themes?

Consider for a moment the following passage about the demonic figure
Kua Fu from the *Book of Master Lie*, a composite of Chinese Daoist materials
now about two millennia old:

> Kua Fu did not properly evaluate his own strength but pursued the brightness
> of the Sun. He chased it to the brink of the Valley of Sunset, becoming so
> thirsty that he wished for a drink. When he went and drank up both the
> Yellow River and the Wei River, the Yellow River and the Wei River proved
> insufficient. He was about to set off north to drink the Great Marsh, but
> before he arrived he had died of thirst on the road.[7]

The traditional Chinese literary use of this story is to describe someone who
has misjudged his own capacities and taken on a task that is beyond him.
Kua Fu is typically shown in woodblock prints striding the clouds with
furious energy, grasping a snake in one hand and scorpion in the other,
while the sun rolls away ahead of him.[8] We can redefine it for our present
purposes as an image that conjures up this question: Have the prodigious
and on the whole successful efforts of the Chinese over the last three
millennia to reshape their lands and waters, to clear their forests, and to
develop their economy in order to feed an ever-expanding population,
been a disaster in slow motion, one leading inexorably toward the weakening or even destruction of the systems of the natural infrastructure that
support life – here symbolized by the exhaustion of the great rivers, insufficient to satisfy Kua Fu's all-consuming thirst?[9]

[5] London: Allen Lane/Penguin, 1983/1984.
[6] Melbourne: Oxford University Press, 1994.
[7] *Liezi* 列子, 5, "Tang wen," in *Liezi xuanji san zhong* in the *Zhongguo zi-xue mingzhu jicheng*
(Taipei: Zhongguo zixue mingzhu jicheng bianyin jijinhui, 1978–80), pp. 151, 435, and 669.
[8] There is a reproduction in M. Elvin, "Tales of *Shen* and *Xin*: Body-Person and Heart-Mind in
China During the Last 150 Years," in T. P. Kasulis, ed., *Self as Body in Asian Theory and Practice*
(Albany: State University of New York Press, 1993), p. 220.
[9] See M. Elvin, "Three Thousand Years of Unsustainable Growth: China's Environment from
Archaic Times to the Present," *East Asian History* 6 (1993).

The purpose of the essays in this book is to provide some of the foundations for an answer, insofar as this answer can be drawn from the historical past. The present age poses different problems, related to the technologies of modern times, more powerful and productive and commensurately more dangerous, and so needs separate treatment.[10] But China's environmental crisis did not begin yesterday. Its roots are multimillennial. They reach back at least to that time when an archaic wisdom, sensitive to the need for a careful stewardship of the natural world, began to be abandoned in the pursuit of state military power built on a premodern economic development whose foundations were intensive agriculture and water control.[11] Even today many of the basic conditions of Chinese life and the physical milieu within which it functions are the demonstrable products of this history: the enormous population, the denuded mountains, the terraced fields, and even the anthropogenic land on which Shanghai, its greatest economic center, stands – tidal salt-marshes, like the *wadden* of the Netherlands, long ago reclaimed by the art of the medieval polder builders. Without the past the present is not fully comprehensible.

The scholars who have written the studies published here are drawn from many disciplines. J. R. McNeill is a comparative environmental historian whose first work was on the mountain systems around the Mediterranean. Wolfgang Holzner is a botanist, as is his colleague Monika Kriechbaum, specializing in the conceptual reconstruction of vanished landscapes, including the Himalayas. Nicholas K. Menzies is a sinological forester and forest historian who has worked as a rural development consultant in China with the Ford Foundation. Su Ninghu is a hydrologist, originally from the arid northwest of China, but now working in New Zealand. Zhang Yixia is an experimental microbiologist who previously served in the system for the prevention and cure of tuberculosis in the People's Republic.

The majority of the contributors are, as is to be expected, historians of China. Thus Pierre-Étienne Will is an authority on the Chinese bureaucracy and its role in the economy and in the provision of welfare, especially in late-imperial times. Christian Lamouroux is a hydraulic historian and analytic geographer specializing in the Song dynasty and the Huai River basin. Shiba Yoshinobu, having established himself as the world's

---

[10] See, for example, V. Smil, *The Bad Earth: Environmental Degradation in China* (New York: M. E. Sharpe, 1984); Smil, *China's Environmental Crisis* (Armonk, N.Y.: M. E. Sharpe, 1993); and He Baochuan, *China on the Edge: The Crisis of Ecology and Development* (San Francisco: China Books and Periodicals, 1991).

[11] For an introduction to this question, see M. Elvin, "Introduction," in M. Elvin, H. Nishioka, K. Tamura, and J. Kwek, *Japanese Studies on the History of Water Control in China: A Selected Bibliography* (Canberra and Tokyo: Institute of Advanced Studies, Australian National University, and Centre for East Asian Cultural Studies for Unesco, 1994), pp. 18–20.

leading expert on the economic history of the Song dynasty, has gradually moved into medieval Chinese environmental history, with a focus on the Jiangnan region. Liu Ts'ui-jung is a distinguished economic historian and historical demographer. Eduard B. Vermeer, who has made important contributions over many years to the study of irrigation, soil degradation, and internal frontier development in China, is one of the pioneers of the field of Chinese environmental history. Li Bozhong is an economic historian who has concentrated mainly on Jiangnan in Ming and Qing times, but with forays into earlier periods. Mark Elvin is an economic historian of China turned historical cartographer, then turned historian of hydraulic systems. Kerrie L. MacPherson is a specialist on the history of urban public health in China. Antonia Finnane has worked for many years in Chinese women's history and gender studies as they relate to late-imperial China. Robert B. Marks was originally a historian of rural revolution in south China but has now developed into a specialist on such environmental themes as the history of the south China climate and of tigers. Paolo Santangelo is the author of a number of pathbreaking books on the history of the emotions in late-imperial China and the real-life experience of the philosophic conceptions in the Chinese world of thought that relate to such issues as guilt, responsibility, desire, and passion. In the mid-1970s, Helen Dunstan was the first Western sinologist seriously to explore the history of diseases in late-imperial China, but her main work over the last decade has been on the theory and practice of statecraft in Qing-dynasty China, with special focus on economic issues. She now also edits the *Chinese Environmental History Newsletter*. An-Chi Tung is an economic historian of Taiwan. Kuo-tung Ch'en, who writes here on the history of forest use in the island, is a many-faceted historian of China who has moved back and forth between various aspects of economics and culture. Anne Osborne, a specialist in the mountain frontier zones in the interior of southeastern China, is a leader of the new generation, being one of the first Westerners to have written her doctoral dissertation in the domain of Chinese environmental history. Finally, an important comparative perspective is provided by Tessa Morris-Suzuki, who is best known for her work on the history of Japanese economic thought and modern Japan's technological transformation, but has written on a variety of topics with an environmental dimension, including the northern frontier in Japan's past expansion.

    All of these perspectives have a distinctive value, and they complement each other. One of the pleasantest surprises of our conferences was that there are no uncrossable barriers among colleagues from different disciplines who are concentrating on shared problems in environmental history. There is, on the contrary, a remarkable mutual appreciation and enrichment.

This book is appearing in both a Chinese-language and an English-language edition. This is appropriate for what has been a collaborative venture between two cultural worlds and an attempt to draw upon their respective strengths; but there is a deeper purpose. The writing of Chinese history will only achieve the full richness of which it is capable when the conceptions of the major scholarly traditions concerned with China – not only the traditions of the various components of the Chinese cultural world and of the West, but also the Japanese and perhaps even the Russian – are in continuous interaction. This is the motive for bilingual publication: to bridge what is perhaps the most important of the many divides between the intellectual cultures concerned. We have also done our best – with the same objective in mind – to find contributors from as wide a range of cultural perspectives as possible, even if we have been only relatively successful in this respect.

We hope that readers will find the ideas, methodologies, and materials presented here on China's environmental history, set in a world context by an initial comparative survey, as interesting as we did when first listening to their elaboration in the Silvermine Beach Hotel on the island of Lantau. On that occasion the hills rose above us, long stripped of their trees but still beautiful, and the harbor water lay at our feet – once unswimmable, but now, thanks to the efforts of the Hong Kong government's Environmental Protection Committee, at least partially restored – while in the distance appeared the city of Hong Kong, one of the world's more extraordinary examples of a modern built environment, as dynamic as it is precarious.[12] We were conscious of being at a meeting place of old and of new, and of continuing, environmental stories.

DEFINITIONS

Environmental history is more precisely defined as the study, through historical time, of the interface where specifically human systems meet with other natural systems. By "other natural systems" we mean, for the most part, climates, topographies, rocks and soils, water, vegetation, animals, and microorganisms, or, to put it another way, the biogeochemical systems on

---

[12] S. Boyden, S. Millar, K. Newcombe, and B. O'Neill, *The Ecology of a City and its People: The Case of Hong Kong* (Canberra: Australian National University Press, 1981).

and near the Earth's surface that produce and process energy and accessible resources and recycle waste products.[13]

Most, though not quite all, of these relationships are two-way interactions between humanity and some other part of nature. The domain of the pathogens provides illustrations of a typical spectrum of relations of this sort.[14] The domestication of animals (in some cases, as with dogs, possibly a two-way process of mutual evolutionary adaptation)[15] was almost certainly associated with the transfer of certain animal diseases to human beings. (An example is measles, which is a close relative of canine distemper.)[16] Settled farming and urbanization made possible densities of population that provided demographic pools of susceptible human hosts numerous enough for the so-called crowd diseases (like smallpox) to sustain themselves against acquired immunities and any possible shortage of new hosts due to mortality.[17] Improved transport, which reduced the cost of goods, also increased the mobility of pathogenic microorganisms. Thus it was that "true" cholera probably traveled to China from Bengal, on the ships of the emerging world trading system, early in the nineteenth century.[18] Typhus in military camps was often, in past times, a more lethal killer than enemy action, and could determine the outcome of campaigns.[19] Similarly, viruses and bacteria introduced by invaders into previously unexposed and hence immunologically unprotected populations, notably those in the New World and Oceania, frequently proved more destructive of life than the conqueror's weapons.[20] The historical expansion of wet-field rice farming in China not only expanded food supply; it also expanded the range of the helminthic disease schistosomiasis – because peasants used human excrement as fertilizer and worked in the snail-infested paddy-fields in their bare feet.[21] A person's occupation in a Chinese city in the first part of the present

[13] An elementary but useful textbook introduction may be found in G. Tylor Miller, *Living in the Environment: Concepts, Problems, and Alternatives* (Belmont, Cal.: Wadsworth, 1975).
[14] For an overview, see W. McNeill, *Plagues and Peoples* (Garden City, N.Y.: Anchor, 1976).
[15] D. F. Morey, "The Early Evolution of the Domestic Dog," *American Scientist* 82.4 (August 1994).
[16] R. Sollares, *The Ecology of the Ancient Greek World* (London: Duckworth, 1991), p. 288.
[17] F. MacFarlane Burnet and D. O. White, *Natural History of Infectious Disease*, rev. ed. (Cambridge: Cambridge University Press, 1972); and Major L. H. Greenwood, *Epidemics and Crowd Diseases* (New York: Macmillan, 1935).
[18] K. MacPherson, Chapter 13 of the present volume.
[19] H. Zinnser, *Rats, Lice, and History* (London: George Routledge and Sons, 1935).
[20] A. Crosby, *Ecological Imperialism: The Biological Expansion of Europe, 900–1900* (Cambridge: Cambridge University Press, 1986).
[21] Zhejiang Province Anti-Parasitic Diseases Committee, *Jishengchongbing-de fangzhi* 寄生虫病的防治 [The prevention and cure of parasitic worm diseases] (Shanghai: Renmin chubanshe [hereafter abbreviated as CBS], 1972), pp. 1–45; Miyashita Saburō 宮下三郎, "Sō-Gen no iryō" [Medical care under the Song and Yuan], in Yabuuchi Kiyoshi 藪内清, ed.,

century to a significant extent determined the probability that he or she would contract tuberculosis.[22] In recent times, modern hospitals have unintentionally become custom-built incubators for the rapid neo-Darwinian evolution of antibiotic-resistant strains of bacteria, and human host behavior directly affects the evolution of high or low microbial virulence.[23] In the early modern West and China, the perceived social experience of sexually transmitted diseases – above all, syphilis – may possibly have interacted with patterns of sexual behavior, including a reinforcement of puritanical values in the centuries before effective treatment for sexually transmitted diseases was available.[24] The general point behind these examples is that through economic and other activities, including the transformation of their own "natural" environments and the creation of new built and even of new somatic environments, humans have also changed the environment in which particular pathogens flourish, decline, or disappear. Hence they have altered the pattern of evolution of these pathogens, which replicate rapidly in comparison with large multicellular systems like ourselves. And thus, ultimately, there is a transitive impact, through microbial behavior, back upon human populations. The discovery and elucidation of such socionatural causal feedback loops is the most characteristic feature of environmental history as opposed to other branches of history, although not in itself enough to demarcate the subject.[25]

The long-term methodological objective of environmental history has to be the systematic combination of those of the natural sciences on the one hand and those of the social sciences on the other that are, in the case of each problem examined, appropriate to its needs. Handling this conceptual and analytical heterogeneity is the source of a significant part of the intellectual interest of environmental history, and most of its difficulty. It is not, however, entirely new. Archaeology and prehistory have covered some of the same terrain and met some of the same problems, a generation or more earlier. To give a precise definition of our subject, therefore, it is necessary also to stipulate the criterion that indicates the boundary line

---

Sō-Gen jidai no kagaku gijutsu [Science and technology under the Song and the Yuan] (Kyoto: Kyōto daigaku jimbun kenkyū-jo, 1976), pp. 130–31.

[22] See Zhang Yixia and M. Elvin, Chapter 14 of the present volume.

[23] Only a low-virulence strain of the HIV will, for example, keep its host alive long enough to have an odds-on chance of infecting another host in a population that practices "safe" sex. See P. Ewald, *Evolution of Infectious Disease* (New York: Oxford University Press, 1994).

[24] Mark Elvin, "The Environmental History of China: An Agenda of Ideas," *Asian Studies Review* 14.2 (1991), pp. 42–43.

[25] To some extent this idea is implicit in Gotō Akira's introduction to Gotō Akira 後藤明 et al., *Rekishi ni okeru shizen* [Nature in history] (Tokyo: Iwanami, 1989), pp. 1–13. We are grateful to Professor Shiba Yoshinobu for the gift of this book.

between it and archaeology and prehistory. This criterion is the central use of the historian's primary materials: written records. These materials also largely determine its characteristic time-scales: tens, hundreds, and occasionally thousands of years, since about 4000 B.P. at the earliest. Furthermore, because of its use of records, environmental history incorporates the human mind – its conceptions, representations, policies, and purposes – aspects that are at best only inferentially accessible to archaeology and prehistory. How the environment has been represented and valued at particular places and times, and religiously, philosophically, scientifically, and technologically understood, is thus – within the epistemological limits on any doubt-free access to "other minds" – an intrinsic part of the subject. What differentiates it in this dimension from cultural anthropology, which also handles such questions and is sensitive to environmental contexts and causes, is that environmental history is – in its essence, and not just incidentally – diachronic, that is to say, focused on change through time.

The present effort to open up this multidisciplinary domain with respect to China is indebted to many predecessors, Chinese, Japanese, and Western, who have pioneered individual aspects of our subject over at least the last two generations.[26] We think it is fair to say, however, that this is the first general attempt to crystallize Chinese environmental history, in most of its multiple dimensions, into a systematic and self-aware field of study. Like any such attempt it is preliminary and imperfect, and its success will to some extent have to be measured by the effectiveness of the assistance that it gives its successors to supersede it. It is also – to our regret, and in spite of our best efforts – unbalanced as regards its coverage in time, since, as fortune would have it, the last thousand years are disproportionately heavily represented. As regards the coverage of the subject matter, we would also have wished more on long-term climatic change and on long-term population dynamics, both topics of central importance. We believe, however, that, despite these inadequacies, this volume defines a new field for future work that is not only just as important as the political, economic, and intellectual histories of China but, more importantly, interacts with its older counterparts in such a way that it will end by transforming them.

LATE-IMPERIAL CHINA

Some awareness of what we would now call "environmental history" existed in late-imperial China even if, as Helen Dunstan pointed out at the confer-

---

[26] See Elvin, "Three Thousand Years of Unsustainable Growth," for an indication of some of these debts.

ence, there is no premodern Chinese word that properly corresponds to "environment." As an example we may take some passages from Xie Zhaozhe's 謝肇淛 *Wuzazu* 五雜組 [Fivefold miscellany] from late Ming times. Recounting how, in high antiquity, the Shang dynasty had repeatedly moved its capital because of the menace of the Yellow River, he observed, "I have not heard that *in those days* they sought out the methods of controlling waters, but merely moved in order to avoid them."[27] Later he commented that "the shifts of the Yellow River seem to be guided by some god, and not to be something in which human efforts can be involved; but if the installations are appropriate, and framed with ingenious single-mindedness of purpose, then they too can deflect its course."[28] He was also conscious of how political and economic considerations had gradually come over time to conflict with strictly hydrological ones:

> Those who are good at controlling water concentrate their plans on making it flow downhill. Moreover, those who controlled water *in ancient times* concentrated only on leading the water in the direction indicated by its position-power (*shi* 勢). Those who control water *these days*, besides being fearful of harming the farmland and cottages are also anxious not to damage the walled cities and their suburbs. As well as being apprehensive about blocking the Grand Canal they are also terrified of disturbing the imperial tombs. While afraid to take too long over the job, they also want to economize on expenditure. It can even happen that officials in charge of different territories struggle to safeguard their own domains, while functionaries in different parts of the empire each one of them competes for the advantages to be obtained. There are never any proposals in the discussions that take a comprehensive view.[29]

In other words, he was aware that the relations between human society and nature had changed as society had evolved.

There was a clear conception of the collective "management of the countryside" (*jingye* 經野) in late-imperial times. This can be seen in regulations issued for the maintenance of hydraulic systems to prevent flooding, which explicitly conceded that "what is of benefit to the great majority . . . may work to the detriment of certain individuals."[30] In some respects this management was, at least in intention, extremely precise, even indicating which species of trees might and which might not be planted along the tops of dikes.[31] This way of looking at the world extended to the

---

[27] Xie Zhaozhe, *Wuzazu* (1608. Reprinted, Taipei: Xinxing shuju, 1971), p. 171 (emphasis added).

[28] Xie Zhaozhe, *Miscellany*, p. 192.

[29] Ibid., p. 193 (emphasis added).

[30] Morita Akira 森田明, "Water Control in Zhehdong during the Late Mirng," *East Asian History* 2 (1991), p. 46. [31] Ibid., p. 60.

framing of policies aimed at protecting the habitats of valued vegetable and animal resources. Thus for fifty years the Qing attempted to "rest the hills by rotating collection" (*xieshan luncai* 歇山輪采) in order to safeguard stocks of wild ginseng in Manchuria.[32] The authorities likewise realized the effects of habitat destruction: "when the waste lands are gradually opened to farming, the prolongation of the existence of the sables and [other] animals is cut off (*huangwu jian pi, diao-shou jue yan* 荒蕪漸闢，貂獸絕延)."[33] The salinization of land that resulted from developing agriculture in arid areas not suited to it was also frequently described:[34]

Their forebears *in those times gone by* farmed on the built-up ridges.
Countless the spades that chopped the hills, till the hills' pulses shifted.
Like flowers on sprouts and early stems there opened saline flakes;
And mosquito larvae – big as cocoons – are spoken of in their tales.

One of the motives behind the building of the Qing-dynasty willow-wall boundary (*liutiao bian* 柳條邊) across southern Manchuria was to protect the environment beyond it, in effect the ginseng-producing areas, from Han migrants. According to a local ditty:

One gathers without exhausting supply –
    The trees on the mountains are many.
The plants in succession follow each other –
    Because of restrictions on human entry.[35]

The general sense of the potentially damaging impact of human activities on natural processes was thus developed to at least a first approximation.

It is understandable, then, that some Chinese of late-imperial times had a premonition of the coming exhaustion of resources, of the possible "wearing out of the world." An illustration of this is the poem by Wang Taiyue 王太岳, "Lament for the Copper-bearing Hills," written in the mid-eighteenth century.[36] As the ore grew scarcer and the wood needed for smelting was used up, winning a living became steadily harder for the miners:

[32] Cong Peiyuan 业佩远, *Dongbei san-bao jingji jianshi* 东北三宝经济简史 [A simple economic history of the "Three Treasures" of Manchuria] (Beijing: Nongye CBS, 1989), p. 148.
[33] Ibid., p. 222.
[34] From a poem by Zhou Xipu 周錫溥, partially translated in M. Elvin, "Skills and Resources in Late Traditional China," in D. Perkins, ed., *China's Modern Economy in Historical Perspective* (Stanford: Stanford University Press, 1975), p. 101 (emphasis added). The text is in Zhang Yingchang 張應昌, ed., *Qing shi-duo* 清詩鐸 [The Qing bell of poesy] (c. 1869. Reprinted, Beijing: Zhonghua shuju, 1960), pp. 174–75.
[35] Cong Peiyuan, *"Three Treasures,"* p. 127 (emphasis added).
[36] Zhang Yingchang, *Bell of poesy,* pp. 927–28 (emphasis added).

They gather, at dawn, by the mouth of the shaft,
Standing there naked, their garments stripped off,
Lamps strapped to their heads in carrying-baskets,
To probe in the darkness the fathomless bottom.

Grazed by the stones' teeth, by sharp-edged projections,
They grope down sheer cliffs, and across mossy patches,
The hot months torment them with harsh epidemics,
When poisonous vapors mix with hot gases.

In the chill of the winter, their bodies will tremble,
Hands blister with chilblains. Their feet will be chapped.
Down the mine, for this reason, they huddle together,
But hardly revive, life-force at a standstill.

. . . .

As the underground ways to the ores pierce new depths,
They fear, as they cut and they drill, to hit marble.
What took, *in times past*, a mere morning's efforts
Now needs ten full days of their work to be garnered.

The wood they must have is no longer available.
The woods are shaved bald, like a convict's head. Blighted.
Only now they regret – felling day after day
Has left them no way to provide for their firewood.

. . . .

The Dark Force and Bright Force contract, then dilate,
Like craftsmen unceasingly shaping their work.
If humans take all that there is, if they show no restraint,
Their force is enough to wear out both the Heaven and Earth.

These lines may serve to evoke the environmental crisis that several of the contributors to this book suggest was already weighing on China during the last centuries of the empire.

Observers in late-imperial times also focused on the lack of environmental resilience of the areas outside the traditional zone of Chinese economic exploitation when traditional farming technology was applied to them. Thus Fang Gongqian 方拱乾, who had been banished to Ninguta, wrote of the swift exhaustion of newly opened land in Jilin:[37]

> One can farm along the line of the hills . . . with no taxes levied. It costs dear [though] to develop this waste ground. When you hoe it the first year, it still

[37] Sutō Yoshiyuki 周藤吉之, *Shindai Manshū tochi seido seisaku no kenkyū* 清代滿州土地制度政策の研究 [Researches on land systems in Qing-dynasty Manchuria] (Tokyo. Kawade shobō, 1944), p. 322.

remains waste. The second year it becomes mature, and in the third, fourth,
and fifth years it is rich. In the sixth or the seventh year you abandon it, and
hoe some other area.

The practical dilemmas that confronted the late-imperial authorities concerned with the people's livelihood are summed up in the "Song of the
Timber Yards" by Yan Ruyi 嚴如熤.[38] He speaks both of the economic
usefulness of logging and of the environmental destruction that it causes.
He appreciates the employment that it affords, and fears the social disruption that can occur if it stops suddenly, as when wage costs, due to the
relatively rising price of food grain, make it uneconomical to employ
people. The following three stanzas illustrate his attitude:

> The loggers, who earned their food by toil, are scattered and dispersed.
> How can they now supply themselves, or themselves give orders for work?
> How can Ox Mountain's beauty return, that was lost so long ago,
> When a mere – bare – reflectance is the common state of the slopes?[39]

> Although it is sometimes said, when an age-old forest's cut down,
> It still remains easy enough to run a plowshare through in the ground,
> Are those who make such remarks aware that when lumber is taken out
> For every trunk that is cut some hundreds of men mill about?

> Down go the twisting roots, ten feet or more in depth.
> If you broadcast grain in such a place, just how many stalks will you get?
> Still in the stony soil there lingers the chill of the heights.
> Cereals for human use need quite other land and dikes.

Counterbalancing this, there was also, and had been from quite early times,
an enthusiasm for economic development. To take just one example, Lan
Dingyuan 藍鼎元 believed that the wild and often inhospitable landscape of
eighteenth-century Taiwan should be reshaped to suit Chinese requirements. He celebrated the process of opening it up for farming, and argued
that having had to suppress Zhu Yigui's rebellion was no reason for withdrawing agricultural settlements from areas close to the mountains, as some
officials had proposed:[40]

> Thereafter, little by little, malaria-stricken lands
> Were fashioned, and then refined, until they were resplendent.

---

[38] Zhang Yingchang, *Bell of poesy*, pp. 923–33.
[39] The reference is to a passage from the philosopher Mencius on the deforestation of Ox
Mountain, which he used to argue that such bareness was not its natural state, any more
than men's state in his time was their natural one.
[40] Chen Hanguang 陳漢光, ed., *Taiwan shilu* 台灣詩錄 [Records of Taiwan poetry] (Taipei:
Taiwansheng wenxian weiyuanhui, 1971), 1, p. 204.

The finer qualities of streams and plains showed forth in all their magic,
Nor could the thickset growth for long stay undeveloped.

The boundaries of their domain spread wider day by day,
Since withdrawing back again was not a long-term strategy,
Following, as appropriate, whatever was nature's way
With frontiers being negotiated as at each time seemed valid.

Just because Zhu Yigui's revolt had last year to be broken
Is no reason at all to go off food – just from the fear of choking!

Lan was a principled but determined believer in colonial settlement in a style that would have been understandable to the Europeans who settled North America or Australia. Writing after the third "eastern expedition" in which he had participated, he wrote of Han relations with the aborigines:[41]

> In the mountains in the interior there are "raw" savages who can little by little become "matured" [civilized]. If the effects of the Royal Transformation are not bestowed upon them, they will remain as barbaric as wild deer, stringing their bamboo bows and cutting off human heads, and adorning themselves with gold in order to vaunt the greatness of their tribes. . . . What crime has our people committed? If someone goes out in the morning to gather firewood, but in the evening fails to return, then, if [the criminal] is not brought to court, there should be a punitive expedition, and the mobilization of authority should impose peace upon the countless valleys.

So far as we have been able to discover, there was no counterbalancing sentiment among educated Chinese in late-imperial times that wilderness was beautiful or significant in itself,[42] or that the human beings who lived there could have a way of life that was as meaningful as, or even more meaningful than, that of the civilized world.[43]

Chinese attitudes to the environment during late-imperial times are thus – when sketched with the strokes of a sufficiently broad brush – not dramatically different from mainstream European ones at about the same time. There were of course a number of special features, such as geomancy, on which we have not touched here. But the important difference, insofar

---

[41] Ibid., p. 207. I have converted Lan's verses into prose here.

[42] Whether or not it was different in Nanbei-chao times is an interesting question. There is a useful collection of relevant materials in Obi Kōichi 小尾郊一, *Chūgoku bungaku ni arawareta shizen to shizenkan* [Nature and the conception of nature as they appear in Chinese literature] (Tokyo: Iwanami, 1962). A poet like Xie Tiao 謝朓 (464–99) might be thought to have come quite close to such a view on occasion. See Obi, pp. 305–07. The subject is, however, beyond the scope of the present introduction.

[43] See M. M. Rubel, *Savage and Barbarian: Historical Attitudes in the Criticism of Homer and Ossian in Britain, 1760–1800* (Amsterdam: North-Holland Publishing, 1978), for comments on the Northwestern European revaluation of primitive peoples.

as there was one, seems to have lain elsewhere. The range of Western experience presented sharper contrasts, especially because of voyages and settlement overseas, and the range of Western responses was correspondingly broader. There were Westerners – some Westerners – who increasingly found a value in wilderness, and, perhaps more importantly, some who began to see the environmental appropriateness of the ways in which people of quite different cultures gained and preserved their livelihoods.[44] This does not seem to have happened in China, at least among those who were literate and left records. Generally speaking, though, the accessible themes of the environmental history of premodern China emerge from premodern Chinese sources to a great extent in their own relatively explicit terms, and, it would seem, without any forced interpretation, even if – inevitably – we select and adapt them to fit our current categories of interest.

ENVIRONMENTAL HISTORY ON
THE CHINESE MAINLAND

Environmental history seems not quite to have crystallized into a distinctive field of study on the Chinese mainland as of the present date, but there are works by a number of scholars that approach it from a variety of directions. This is not the place to attempt a systematic survey of the bibliography, nor am I qualified to do so, but a number of illustrative examples – which are very far indeed from being exhaustive – may convey a preliminary idea of what has been done.

The last fifteen years or so have produced a rich scientific literature of articles in Mainland journals such as *Acta geographica sinica* (*Dili xuebao* 地理学报), *Agricultural archeology* (*Nongye kaogu* 农业考古), the *Journal of Water Control* (*Shuili xuebao* 水利学报), and others too numerous to list here, a substantial number of them on topics relevant to environmental history, including forests and river systems. Similarly useful contributions may also be found gathered into collections, such as those edited by Yan Qinshang 严钦尚 and Xu Shiyuan 许世远 on sedimentation processes in the Yangzi delta area,[45] or by Chen Jiyu 陈吉余 and his colleagues on the evolution of

---

[44] R. Grove, "Conserving Eden: The (European) East India Companies and their Environmental Policies on St Helena, Mauritius and in Western India, 1660–1854," *Comparative Studies in Society and History* 35.2 (1993), p. 350, has given an interesting example of this phenomenon in his account of Dr. Alexander Gibson.

[45] *Changjiang sanjiaozhou xiandai chenji yanjiu* 长江三角洲现代沉积研究 [Studies on present-day sediment deposits in the Yangzi delta] (Shanghai: Huadong Shifan-daxue, 1987).

China's coast.[46] Remote-sensing technology has been applied to archaeology and geography, notably by the Institute for the Technology and Applications of Remote Sensing at East China Normal University,[47] and shown to be a useful tool for the environmental historian. From the side of historical geography, a number of the articles in works such as *Jianhu yu Shaoxing shuili* 鉴湖与绍兴水利 [Mirror Lake and water control in Shaoxing], edited by Sheng Honglang 盛鸿郎,[48] may be classified as environmental history, in this particular case covering anthropogenic changes in the hydrology of the region. As regards particular topics, Tan Qixiang 谭其骧, who is best known as a historical cartographer,[49] has, for example, opened up a debate concerning the effect of the historical removal of the vegetation cover in the middle reaches of the Yellow River on the density of the river's sediment loading, and hence on the variable historical frequency of the breaching of dikes in the lower reaches caused by increased deposition on the bed of the river.[50] As regards the pioneering of regionally focused studies, Chen Qiaoyi 陳橋驛 [陈桥驿] has likewise laid the foundations of the environmental history of northern Zhejiang, documenting the stages of the loss of forest cover and changes in crop use. His work also relates the rise and fall of particular hydraulic systems to their internal logic (notably their interactions with other nearby systems), to sedimentation due to both natural and man-made causes, and to the shifting balance of power between farmers concerned with water supply and those eager to reclaim lake-bottom lands.[51]

---

[46] Chen Jiyu, Wang Baocan 王宝灿, and Yu Zhiying 虞志英, eds., *Zhongguo haian fayu guocheng he yanbian guilü* 中国海岸发育过程和演变规律 [The processes of coastal development in China and the [related] laws governing coastal evolution] (Shanghai: Shanghai kexue jishu CBS, 1989).

[47] See the two volumes of the recent special issue of *Huadong Shifan-daxue xuebao* 华东师范大学学报 on remote sensing (1992).

[48] Beijing: Zhongguo shudian, 1991. Sponsored by the Zhongguo shuili xuehui shuili-shi yanjiuhui and the Zhejiang-sheng Shaoxing-shi shuili dianli ju.

[49] He was the chief editor of the *Zhongguo lishi ditu ji* 中国历史地图集 [Historical maps of China], 8 vols. (Shanghai: Ditu CBS, 1982).

[50] Tan Qixiang, "Heyi Huanghe zai Dong-Han yihou hui chuxian yige changqi anliu-de jumian?" [Why was it possible for the Yellow River to manifest a long period of quiet flow after the Eastern Han dynasty?], *Xueshu yuekan* 学术月刊 2 (1962).

[51] 1. "Gudai Jianhu xingfei yu Shan-Gui pingyuan nongtian shuili" [The rise and disappearance of Mirror Lake, and agricultural land and water control in the Shanyin-Guiji plain in ancient times] in *Dili xuebao* 28.3 (Sept. 1962). 2. "Gudai Shaoxing diqu tianran senlin de pohuai ji qi dui nongye de yingxiang" [The destruction in ancient times of the natural forests of Shaoxing and its impact on agriculture], in *Dili xuebao* 31.2 (June 1965). 3. "Lishi-shang Zhejiang-sheng de shandi kenzhi yu shanlin pohuai" [The historical development of the mountain lands of Zhejiang province and the destruction of the mountain forests], in *Zhongguo shehui kexue* 中国社会科学 4 (1983). 4. "Lun lishi shiqi Ning-Shao pingyuan de hupo yanbian" On the changing distribution of lakes in the Ningbo-Shaoxing

Much Mainland research on environmental history has, however, tended to stay within the confines of a largely descriptive charting of environmental changes on the basis of traditional source material. Yuan Qinglin's 袁清林 useful overview *Zhongguo huanjing baohu shihua* 中国环境保护史话 [Historical discussion of the protection of the environment in China][52] is still a scissors-and-paste assemblage of materials. Cong Peiyuan's 丛丕远 *Dongbei san-bao jingji jianshi* 东北三宝经济简史 [Simple economic history of the "Three Treasures" of Manchuria (ginseng, sable, and deerhorn)][53] likewise consists mostly of extracts from historical texts that illustrate the rapid degradation of vegetable and animal habitats in Manchuria during the Qing dynasty under the pressure of intensified economic exploitation. As guides to sources of information, both are nonetheless extremely valuable.

At a more sophisticated level, Shi Nianhai 史念海 has shown how effectively historical materials can be combined with painstaking field observation. An example is his study of the transformation of the loess landscape – parts of it the heartland of ancient northern Chinese culture – as the result of large-scale gully erosion over the last few thousand years. He demonstrates how the use of the chronological anchor points provided by historically identified sites often permits exact dating and the calculation of average annual rates of gully back-cutting. He also proves human activities to have been the cause of a pronounced acceleration of gully formation: not only forest clearances and the opening of grasslands for farming, but also such less evident developments as the creation and then abandonment of large roads.[54] When he relies only on historical methods and the historian's materials, however, the conclusions are interesting rather than fully convincing. Thus he has used the feasibility of boat transport as a proxy variable for the volume of water in loess-region rivers. The sparse documentation – including that on the structure of bridges, indicating whether or not they were passable by boats – suggests, without really proving, a long-term historical decline, but his suggested explanation for what may or may not have been a fact is too simple to be conclusive, since it involves no hydrology either as theory or in the form of field investigation, and also ignores possible long-term large-scale climatic change that might have

plain in historical times], in *Dili yanjiu* 地理研究 3.3 (Sept. 1984). Co-authored with Lü Yichun 吕以春 and Yue Zumou 乐祖谋. (5) "Lun lishi shiqi Puyang-jiang xiayou de hedao bianqian" [Changes in the lower course of the Puyang River in historical times] in *Lishi dili* 历史地理 1 (1981).

[52] Beijing: Zhongguo huanjing kexue CBS, 1990.
[53] Beijing: Nongye CBS, 1989. See note 32 above.
[54] Shi Nianhai, "Lishi shiqi huangtu gaoyuan gouhe-de yanbian" [The evolution of gullies in the loess plateau during the historical period], *Zhongguo lishi dili luncong* 中国历史地理论丛 2 (1987).

affected average annual precipitation. (He concentrates solely on the loss of the original vegetation cover.)[55] When he turns to broader themes his approach becomes somewhat physiocratic, focusing on government revenues and the public welfare. In a study of the environmental changes that took place during the Sui and Tang dynasties, for instance, he discusses the shipping of firewood to the capital by a specially built canal, and the related decline of forests in the Southern Hills, together with the silting up of the canal along which grain supplies were brought to the capital, and how the rise of wet-field rice cultivation in the lower Yangzi valley led to this region replacing the lower Yellow River valley as the chief source of the court's cereals. He notes the pressure placed by cavalry pastures on arable land after the Tibetan conquests in the Northwest, and the building of the northern Jiangsu seawall, as well as such incidental points as the way in which the shape of the mouth of the Yangzi (unlike its shape today) allowed Yangzhou to be a major seaport at this period, and the need for some of the inhabitants of He'nan to live for a time in trees or on boats following the flooding of the Yellow River.[56] The result is a fascinating miscellany, but the structure is anecdotal.

A different sort of literature is exemplified by Liang Biqi 梁必骐 and Ye Jinzhao's 叶锦昭 *Guangdong-de ziran zaihai* 广东的自然灾害 [Natural disasters in Guangdong],[57] which offers something of a contrast. The term "natural" in the title is perhaps a misnomer, since the authors also deal with anthropogenic damage to the environment, and with degradation and pollution that occur slowly, not just "disasters" as commonly understood. It is scientifically informed, at a level appropriate for general policy formulation, and is motivated by the concern that environmental damage, both natural and man-made, obstructs and holds back economic growth, especially if this growth is ill-conceived. Socionatural causal feedback loops are identified and analyzed, an example being the spread of rats when cropping patterns are shifted toward fruit and sugarcane (which they particularly favor), the natural enemies of rats are exterminated or made extinct, and the rats themselves evolve resistance to rat poisons.[58] The historical section consists mostly of catalogs of events, but the crude data indicating a large long-term increase in the frequency both of droughts and of floods

---

[55] Shi Nianhai, "Huangtu gaoyuan zhuyao heliu liuliang-de bianqian" [Changes in the volume of flow in the most important watercourses in the loess plateau], *Zhongguo lishi dili luncong* 2 (1992).

[56] Shi Nianhai, "Sui-Tang shiqi ziran huanjing-de bianqian ji yu renwei zuoyong-de guanxi" [Changes in the natural environment during the Sui–Tang period, and their relationship with human activities], *Lishi yanjiu (Jing)* 1 (1990).

[57] Guangzhou (?): Guangdong renmin CBS, 1993.

[58] Liang Biqi and Ye Jinzhao, *Guangdong disasters*, p. 247.

in Guangdong from Song to early modern times are prima facie evidence
for continuing adverse effects from human interference with ecosystems.
The true statistical significance of the trends in these data – in the light of
a probably improved social recording system and a presumably increased
exposure of the population as it spread into relatively less favorable habitats
– is not, however, given the analysis it requires.[59]

In view of these extensive foundations it seems likely that the next few
years could see the emergence of a comparatively fully developed environmental history on the Mainland. The essential combination of natural-
scientific and historical methodology seems to present no inherent
problems, although it has so far only been imperfectly realized, and it is
probable that political considerations may make the incorporation of the
insights of the modern *social* sciences – for the analysis of patterns of
economic and political change, as well as of ideas and representations – a
relatively more difficult barrier to overcome.

THE PRESENT BOOK

The volume opens with J. R. McNeill's overview of Chinese environmental
history in the context of world environmental history. In comparative
terms, he sees China as having been for more than a thousand years "the
state with the greatest ecological complementarity" in the sense of incorporating a wide variety of different but mutually supplementing environments, and characterized by an "exceptional importance of state policy for
the environment." In spite of these and other special features, such as the
"thoroughly anthropogenic" landscape, he nonetheless sees the Chinese
pattern as having been broadly comparable with those of the other great
urban-agrarian civilizations. The particularities of China in an environmental perspective are thus, in the last analysis, more matters of relative scale or
of detail than of overall structure.

Two chapters on methodology follow. Their object is in no sense to aim
at a systematic coverage of what is desirable, or possible, but rather to widen
the conception of what historians can and should do in the domain of
enviromental history.

Wolfgang Holzner and Monika Kriechbaum thus show how one should
see a landscape through the eyes of what they call a "vegetation detective,"
using their fieldwork in the Himalayas as an illustration. By describing in
detail with their own photographs and line drawings some of the processes

---

[59] Liang Biqi and Ye Jinzhao, *Guangdong disasters*, pp. 36 and 50.

of deforestation that have taken place in Tibet, and how they relate to the different types of pastoral economy, they make it clear that many apparently "natural" mountain landscapes are nothing of the sort. They also raise the so-far unsolved question of why previous environmentally sustainable styles of stock rearing have recently tended to collapse in this area.

Nicholas Menzies next demonstrates how the recording and analysis of the collective memories of villagers, focused, under the investigator's guidance, on the cooperative drawing up of land-use maps, calendars of annual work, and historical time-lines, can reach back several or more generations and allow voices that are rarely heard in historical documents to become audible. These techniques are derived from the methods of participatory rural assessment used by some aid agencies, but they can also contribute, appropriately transformed, to a subtler and more finely grained history. Thus in the Yunnan villages in which Menzies worked, there can be shown to have been some recent regrowth of forest cover, and not just a linear pattern of deforestation.

We have had to omit, for reasons of space, the conference paper by Janice Stargardt on southern Thailand showing how a spectrum of archaeological techniques, including palynology, remote-sensing analysis, and the experimental reconstruction of a hydraulic system, can be used to produce a sharply patterned history even in the almost complete absence of written records. Her overall message for the field is an exciting but also sobering one: to make progress, we or our successors are going to have to become competent in a range of techniques, new to most historians, that are fascinating but often very difficult.

The historical pattern of human settlement in China – that culture of perpetual migrants – is the focus of the next two chapters. Shiba Yoshinobu focuses on the development of the southern shore of Hangzhou Bay and nearby areas from the middle of the Tang to the Qing dynasty. He distinguishes the various environmental subregions, demonstrating how the timing and pattern of agricultural exploitation and population growth differed in each one. He presents descriptions of how certain key water-control systems evolved, both technically and sociopolitically, in Shaoxing, Yuhang, and Ningbo. He concludes that the advanced hydraulic technology of this region was the underpinning of the later transformation of the lower Yangzi delta from Tang to early Ming times, and of its spectacular economic growth, and ends by noting the environmental crisis – evident in the attempted exploitation of the less fertile upland regions – looming over the area in the last few decades of the empire.

Liu Ts'ui-jung portrays Taiwan as a microcosm of Chinese processes of colonization and development, and one that is close to being unique for

Chinese history in that it is possible to document the entire sequence from the age of wilderness to that of modern economic growth. Her focus is on the steady expansion of Han population from the later seventeenth century to the nineteenth, and the accompanying growth of the water-control systems that were an integral part of the southern Chinese style of farming. She also establishes many aspects of the new society adapting its environment, both for worse and for better. Thus the lure of the overseas trade in deerskins, followed by the widespread conversion of grazing lands to arable, all but wiped out the once-enormous population of wild deer in less than a century. On the other hand, the Chinese-style transformation of the landscape (and no doubt a measure of selective survival and developing immunities among the colonists) seems to have reduced the incidence of the local diseases – of which malaria probably was the most important – to which the early settlers so often succumbed. Throughout there was a complex pattern of conflict and cooperation with the aboriginal people, which had its own distinctive impact on settlement, for example through the Chinese use of collective organizations for farming and defense in the more dangerous areas. The fascinating and almost brutally realistic account of early Taiwan seen through educated Chinese eyes that she quotes from the brush of Yu Yonghe 郁永河 also makes it clear why wilderness, zoologically dangerous and medically hazardous, was not seen as appealing.

The two chapters that follow examine the internal frontiers of economic development in late-imperial times.

Anne Osborne relates the mid-Qing environmental crisis in the highland borders between Zhejiang, Jiangxi, and southern Anhui provinces to the demographic pressures resulting from an "intensification [that] approached the limits of feasibility" in the neighboring lowland areas. She shows the destructive effects of deforestation and the upland cultivation of New World crops, often on a shifting basis: fuel rose in price, for example, and irrigation systems downstream of the stripping of vegetation cover became choked with an often sterile silt. She underscores the point that while many contemporaries had a lucid understanding of the unfolding tragedy and its causes, the strength of local political interests and short-term economic needs made it impossible to put into effect any appropriate long-term remedial policies.

Eduard Vermeer presents a critical examination of the now widely held view that the Qing, and especially the nineteenth century, was a period of environmental deterioration in China. Focusing mainly on newly developed areas in the arid northern and western regions, he comes to a cautious agreement with this position, tempered, however, by a number of serious reservations about the unreflective way in which at least some earlier scholars have interpreted the sources. He points out, for example, that the frequency of natural disasters appears to have been higher during the last two dynasties in part because the coverage of such events by the source material is much more fine-meshed than it is for earlier periods. Likewise he notes that, due to population pressure, there was more human settlement toward the end of the imperial age in what may be called "dangerous environments," another reason for the apparent increase in disasters. He also observes that, given the large-scale expansion of extensive farming in upland areas at this time, accurate land-use statistics ought to reveal an increasing ratio of farmed land to population; and that the historically available figures generally show the opposite suggests that they are unlikely to be a reliable guide to the situation. An additional feature of Vermeer's work is his discovery of an exceptional quantity of interesting but little-known Mainland scholarship and his finding ways of using it, in spite of biases that occur in some of this work due to the lingering traces of the ideology and images of the Maoist period, which he carefully and critically notes. Overall this chapter sets on a firmer basis than before what seems to be the emerging consensus on the Qing, namely that, in Vermeer's words, "within two centuries, the Chinese natural and economic environment had changed . . . beyond recognition."

We move on to water and to water control, arguably the environmental foundation of traditional Chinese civilization.

Pierre-Étienne Will reconstructs the story of the once-great Zheng-Bai irrigation system in southern Shaanxi over a period of more than two thousand years. Looking carefully at the complex loessial geological background, unraveling so far as is possible the puzzle of the often uncertain hydraulic technology employed, and maintaining a carefully critical attitude toward sources whose real content is often elusive, he shows how the constant downcutting of its bed by the Jing River, the main source of water supply, created in the system an instability that eventually defeated the ever more audacious efforts of engineers to repair or restore it. In the seventeenth and eighteenth centuries small-scale operations were finally explicitly accepted as being more reasonable, with leading officials decrying large projects as what Will terms "excesses of political mobilization for productivist ventures." A final section on the management structures under the Qing dynasty concludes that, in a sense, "the organization was part of the environment," but that, rather than the smooth cooperative functioning prescribed by the regulations, the reality was more likely to have been "a history of conflict and cheating" between the participating communities.

Mark Elvin and Su Ninghu present a more technical study, analyzing the impact of the sediments of the south-course Yellow River on Hangzhou Bay, via longshore-current transport, from the late twelfth to the mid-nineteenth century. Methodologically, this chapter is an attempt to link the findings of modern hydrology and geomorphology with the record in Chinese maps and documents. They show that a substantial proportion of the sediment carried into the bay even today derives from the erosion of the defunct south-course Yellow River delta in northern Jingsu, and suggest that both the absolute quantity of sediment and the percentage of Yellow River sediments in the total delivered to the bay were markedly higher when the southern course was in operation, approximately from 1194 to 1855. This was especially the case after the massive hydraulic operations of Pan Jixun had concentrated the flow of the river into a single course in the later sixteenth century. The timing of the changes in the river, both the initial shift to a southern course and its later anthropogenic concentration, indicates that these may have made a critical contribution to the rapid buildup of a new depositional coastline on the southern shore of the bay, strikingly different from what had existed there before.

We move on to two studies of regional climate, in which it turns out that climatic change is also an important, and often forgotten, "input" that has to be considered when explaining changes in agricultural productivity.

Robert Marks gives us a mathematically grounded analysis of "the historic relationships between climatic change and food production" in mid-Qing Guangdong, using the records of the imperial system for reporting on harvest levels and grain prices. He shows that "compared with periods before and after, the eighteenth century appears . . . warmer and wetter," and demonstrates that "climatic changes were the single most significant cause of harvest yield fluctuations during the eighteenth century." The analysis provides the important finding that "the expected inverse relationship between harvest yields and harvest prices . . . became weaker during the eighteenth century"; Marks suggests that this was because of the expansion of "an integrated market for rice." Overall, "while eighteenth-century South China rice prices were . . . sensitive to changes in harvest yields, there was less volatility in the relationship than in England," probably because of the added stability due to multicropping, irrigation, state grain-stocking policy, and effective large-scale markets. The evoking of this international comparative context enables the particularities of southern Chinese environmental history, including the impact of distinctively Chinese institutions, to emerge with remarkable clarity.

Li Bozhong examines the contribution made by various inputs, including the climate, to wet-rice farming in Jiangnan during the later Ming and the early and middle Qing. Much of his work is based on recent Chinese climatological and agronomic science, which has clarified, for example, the varying photosensitive response of different varieties of rice. Among his more important findings are the Qing-period fine-tuning of the seasonal cropping pattern, using varieties designed to "suit the different patterns of day-length," and, most notably, the greater use of slow-ripening "intermediate" rice. He also demonstrates a diffusion of the technically tricky use of supplementary fertilizer applied during the phase of inflorescence. The final section is an approximate calculation of rice consumption in Ming and Qing Jiangnan, and, taken together with the earlier findings, this points to "a significant increase in per-*mu* productivity in Jiangnan wet-rice farming during the Ming–Qing period," probably peaking in mid-Qing, when growing-season insolation was at its premodern maximum. This work both interlocks with other chapters, such as that of Osborne, which posits a Qing-dynasty intensification of lowland farming pushing toward its premodern limits, and to some extent qualifies while broadly confirming the older theory of the Elvin-Sinha late-imperial "high-level equilibrium trap."

We move on to two studies of disease in Chinese history.

Kerrie MacPherson's examination of cholera in China centers on two original and fundamental maps that are the result of the collection of new data. They show, with locations, that 1820, 1821, and 1822 were "three years of extraordinary epidemic activity that supports the contention that the disease was imported," presumably from eastern India. Analysis of earlier Chinese texts referring to cholera-like illnesses, and theoretical considerations, including Ewald virulence theory, combine to make this conclusion extremely plausible, if not wholly beyond question. Once established, cholera exacted a heavy toll in China for over a century, especially when there was "a dry season ending in heavy rains." Overall, MacPherson shows how the history of cholera, and especially that of the spread of the El Tor strain, which is both environmentally hardier and less virulent, can be used to illustrate the way in which changes in human host behavior can change the parameters of evolutionary competition among microorganisms.

In their chapter on tuberculosis, Zhang Yixia and Mark Elvin have assembled the available fragmentary information, most of it urban in origin, to sketch an approximative picture of the disease that caused the greatest number of deaths in China during the first half of the twentieth century. Their basic finding is that the most important single factor influencing the likelihood of infection was the character of the built environment in which a person worked and lived. In particular, as would be expected for a droplet-borne infection, working indoors or outdoors, density of exposure to other people, and the quality of the atmosphere for indoor workers were the crucial considerations affecting incidence of the disease in particular groups. In specific terms, these effects showed up most clearly in the sharply varying rates of infection for people in given occupations, whereas the more general categories of income level or social class had, in themselves, no explanatory or predictive power.

Following the consideration of these grim realities, the book shifts to four very different chapters on representations of the environment: how it was conceived, portrayed, and consciously experienced.

Christian Lamouroux's chapter is a subtle study, focused on the Yellow River during the Northern Song dynasty, of "how political and financial history was able to determine . . . decisions made with respect to the environment." He shows how the balance among the various components that constituted the official concept of the Yellow River – defense against floods and hydrological instability, transport, and the provision of a barrier against the Qidan and Jurchen invaders from the north – shifted steadily toward an emphasis on the military. By the middle of the eleventh century some realistic hydraulic proposals had become "unacceptable because [they] lacked a strategic perspective." After 1057 the Yellow River was no longer used for government transport. Overall, hydraulic issues, their terms defined by the slowly changing conceptual geography in the minds of the top policy makers, were resolved or left unresolved through a complex interplay of factional and bureaucratic special interests on the one hand, and, on the other, legitimate state concerns about reducing the costs of repairs and restructuring as well as the burden of labor service on the population. At times, as with some of the plans proposed for supplying the Bian Canal with water, hydrological reality was even completely ignored. Lamouroux thus reminds us, perhaps more than any other of the contributors, of the methodological difficulties of analyzing simultaneously the history of the social and the natural domains.

Helen Dunstan draws on her exceptional knowledge of Qing-period policy documents to select a small number of particular cases where a sort of intellectual X-ray diffraction can bring hidden structures of thought into view. She shows that officials were concerned to promote what she calls a "defensive expansion" in order to feed a steadily expanding population, rather than with improving wealth per person. There was in fact a strong desire to restrain "unnecessary popular consumption." At least one important bureaucrat had an "environmentalist social psychology," promoting a mass reforestation campaign, for example, not only because it offered a chance to reestablish the economic well-being of the population through the provision of income from fruit, building timber, and fuel, but because he believed in "a positive correlation between wind erosion and a decline in civilized behavior," which had to be reversed. She gives another case in which the permanent official closure of certain areas of southwestern forest was undertaken to preserve the supply of water, particularly interesting in that the insight into the causal connection was provided by a leader of a local non-Chinese community. In general, Chinese officials in the eighteenth century had numerous intelligent environmental perceptions, but they tended to be fragmentary, and were never joined together into a comprehensive and logically articulated set of views. Here and there, though, a foreshadowing of the premonitions of disaster that haunt the modern age can also be seen, and she quotes an observer of the disasters of the mid-seventeenth century as wondering if "the multiplication of creation" had reached such a point that "the Supreme Lord's heart, grown weary of them, has cast them off."

Paolo Santangelo, for his part, weaves a tapestry of insights and quotations to portray the conception of nature in Chinese imaginative literature, especially during the Ming and Qing dynasties. He distinguishes between the literary use of natural objects and phenomena as vehicles for expressing human emotions, and their complementary status as foci of contemplation that can draw the observer into a deeper intuitive understanding of the cosmos. These two aspects are linked, however, through the underlying unity of all that is. Hence there was an "identification of subjective consciousness with objective reality" that developed out of this process of contemplation. He devotes particular attention to gardens, creations with two creators, nature and the human mind, and suggests how the historical Chinese discussion of what was "natural" and what "artificial" about them is revealing of certain important polarities of Chinese thought. He also shows how the late-imperial obsession of the cultivated classes with flowers was rich with ambiguity: flowers can, for example, symbolize both the "uncorrupted life" and "women's seduction." Setting the late-imperial period in a longer-term perspective, he argues that this age saw the fading of the earlier sense that what was "wild" had magic powers, often fearsome ones, and the strengthening of an urbane and exclusively aesthetic appreciation that was more often than not directed at a natural world that was, so to speak, tamed.

Antonia Finnane explores differences in gender relationships with respect to their covariation with differences in environment. She takes as her domain of analysis the Jiangbei region, north of the mouth of the Yangzi River, from the later part of the nineteenth century down to the present day. This is a world that saw some major environmental changes in this period, such as the shifting of the Yellow River to a northern course in 1853–55, and the somewhat later decay of the Grand Canal that runs through the area and was once the key artery of the supply system of the capital at Beijing. Her interest is more directed, however, toward variations on a smaller scale: there were many fine-grained geographical subdivisions in Jiangbei, such as those between the old salt-producing areas along the coast and those lying inland, west of the main north-to-south seawall. Some of the differences that she identifies are relatively predictable: the women from fishing communities did not have bound feet (and seem to have tended even recently to go barefoot). The expressive forms of the marriage rituals for those who live on the land and those who live on the water in boats are quite different. Some customs have been elaborated around local specialties, such as the ducks of Gaoyou, which have served as the basis of a unique and delightful local ritual vocabulary for betrothals, weddings, and childbirths. Other lines of demarcation are, *per contra*, more subtle and difficult to decipher. Thus a disproportionate number of girls from Haimen have avoided marriage, in pre-Communist times most often by becoming nuns. Some of the patterns of differentiation have obscure historical foundations, and Finnane devotes particular attention to one of these, namely the geographically varied survival of the ancient custom of "the groom going to fetch the bride." Possibly the oddest environmental effect of all, however, is that which has over the centuries shifted Jingjiang from being an island near the south bank of the Yangzi to being adjacent to the north bank, where it still retains strong south-bank cultural and linguistic characteristics in sharp contrast with its immediate neighbors. The conservatism of human custom has outlasted topography.

The next two chapters are devoted to Taiwan, followed by a concluding chapter on Japan for comparative purposes.

Kuo-tung Ch'en presents a long-term analytical survey of deforestation occurring on the extensively wooded island of Taiwan since the earliest days of the Chinese settlement, with the emphasis on tree-cutting resulting from logging operations rather than from clearing the land for farming. During the Qing dynasty, the modest-sized state-controlled camphor-wood monopoly was the only source of pressure on resources apart from the demand for fuel, as most timber for construction was imported from the mainland, both for better-quality houses and for shipping. The Japanese occupation (1895–1945) did no more than marginally change this situation, as Taiwan remained a net importer of timber, and two-thirds of its area was still forested (and mostly owned by the state) on the eve of the Pacific War. Only during the first phase of the Nationalist government was there rapid stripping of timber, driven by the urgent need for foreign exchange and facilitated by improved over-the-ground transport technology that made it possible for logs to be removed easily from the forests, previously the main obstacle to expansion. Fortunately, by the later 1970s this process was slowing down, as industrial development matured, and today, the author concludes, "the nightmare . . . seems to have gone away."

An-Chi Tung tackles one of the classic questions in environmental history: the balance of economic, social, and environmental gains and losses in a large-scale dam- and reservoir-based hydroelectric project, focusing on the Zhuoshui complex of dams, of which that at Sun Moon Lake is the best known. She begins with the general background: on the positive side for hydropower, Taiwan has a high annual rainfall and steep river gradients, but also rapid erosion such that dense sediment loads tend to reduce the lifetime of both dams and generating equipment. She then shows how electricity from water power played an indispensable part in Taiwan's early industrial growth, under both the Japanese and the Nationalists, even if today it is of little account. Environmental restraints, in the form of limits on the supply of water, have made further expansion at the required rate impossible, in spite of technical refinements like recycling water in periods of low demand for power. (Since the later 1980s, Taiwan's power supply has been predominantly nuclear.) After looking at such negative factors as the aborigines who lost both lands and livelihood through displacement, alteration of disease patterns (as in the case of malaria), and the impairment of scenic beauty, biodiversity, and some water quality, she concludes that these effects have been, by world standards, on an extraordinarily small scale, and that because of the protection from the smaller upstream dams, which silt up relatively fast, and other technical measures, the main complex is assured of a future life in excess of two hundred years.

The book ends with a return to a comparative theme. Tessa Morris-Suzuki's study of the "perceptions of environmental disruption in Japan" shows how protests against industrial pollution, some of them starting in the later nineteenth century, drew on ideas that were significantly different from those in the West, most particularly that of *kōgai* 公害, that is, "public harm," as the essential criterion in validating opposition to a polluter. Even the leaders of protests were usually in favor of development, so long as it was balanced and fair to all interests. Moreover, as she says, in Japan "nature was identified not so much (as in the European tradition) with wilderness and freedom from social constraint, but rather with the very basis and origin of social order." In practical terms, the relative success of protests against pollution – characteristically, in the cases that she presents, that of soils, crops, and rivers from copper production – also seems to have depended on the solidarity of the higher and lower social classes in the locality that was protesting. If the better-off, who were needed for leadership and contacts, had themselves become involved in modern industrial development, this solidarity was unlikely to be present, and fragmentation of the protest movement and relative failure were the probable outcomes. It is difficult, in our view, to think of possible Chinese parallels, at least until very recent times, and also difficult to say why this should have been so.

Once more we are reminded that we are only at the beginning of our enterprise.

The Context

2

China's Environmental History in World Perspective

J. R. McNEILL

The point of this essay is to place Chinese environmental history in the global context.[1] In comparing the Chinese experience to that of other lands, I aim to show what is ordinary and what is exceptional. In many respects China appears a case apart, but in most such instances it may merely be that China was first or largest, not unique. In addition, I aim to exploit the outsider's perspective to suggest some opportunities that may await environmental historians of China.

2.1. CHINESE EXCEPTIONALISM

Historians of the United States have for decades argued about whether U.S. history followed its own unique trajectory.[2] Certain features of Chinese environmental history invite the judgment that China was exceptional. Most of these derive from the blessings of geography and the resilience of the Chinese state.

The Chinese have river systems as useful as any in terms of transport, and have tirelessly tried to improve upon nature's gift for more than three thousand years. China has a Nile in the north, a Ganges in the south, and a man-made Mississippi linking them. The Yellow River, like the Nile before the Aswan Dam, carries irrigation water and fertile silt through an arid

---

[1] Acknowledgments: S. A. M. Adshead, Tim Beach, Patrick Caffrey, Mark Elvin, J. Don Hughes, Liu Ts'ui-jung, Robert Marks, William McNeill, Peter Perdue, Jim Reardon-Anderson, Frank Smith, Howard Spendelow.
[2] See the forum of Ian Tyrell, "American Exceptionalism in an Age of International History," pp. 1031–55, and Michael McGerr, "The Price of the New Transnational History," pp. 1056–72, in *American Historical Review* 96.4 (1991).

land. It floods seasonally. It is navigable to about 600–800 kilometers
inland – as far from the sea as the first cataract of the Nile. The Yangzi flows
through the rice basket of China, providing irrigation water and cheap
transport, as the Ganges does in India. The Yangzi is navigable 2,700
kilometers upstream, as far as Chongqing (compared to only 1,600
kilometers on the Ganges-Jumna). But because of the difficulties of sailing
through the gorges, large traffic on the Yangzi goes only as far as Wuhan,
about 1,100 kilometers from the sea, about as far as the upstream limit for
large ships on the Ganges (Allahabad). Between the Yangzi and Yellow
rivers the Chinese state has built and for 1,400 years (usually) maintained
an artificial Mississippi, the Grand Canal, a transport artery linking the
north and south of the country. Taken together these waterways form a
gigantic fishhook, a huge fertile crescent united by cheap and safe transport. Countless capillaries – smaller rivers and feeder canals – connected
the main arteries to a broad hinterland. The system even extended to the
West/Pearl River in the far south via the Ling Qu canal (first built c. 230
B.C.).[3] No land-based transport network could rival this one for cheapness
until the railway age. No inland waterway system in world history approaches this one as a device for integrating large and productive spaces.

If the Indian subcontinent had had a canal linking the Indus and the
Ganges, then a system of the same power would have shaped Indian history.
But India never had a unitary state motivated to build such a canal – at least
not until the railway age had made long canals pointless. Geography and
political fragmentation kept Europe's many navigable rivers divided into an
Atlantic drainage system and a Mediterranean one until the seventeenth
century. Charlemagne in 793 had organized an attempt to dig a canal
linking the Danube and the Main, and thereby the Black and North seas
(and several fertile basins in between). But he gave up the effort and the
Mediterranean and Atlantic drainage systems remained discrete until the
completion of the Canal du Midi in 1681. Useful as that was, it did not unite
the Mediterranean with the commercially vibrant North or Baltic seas, but
only with the stormy Bay of Biscay. By the time the United States linked the
Mississippi, the Great Lakes, and the St. Lawrence, railroads had overshad-

---

[3] The cost of the Chinese system changed sharply with the course of the Grand Canal and the
path of the Yellow River. When the imperial capital was in the far north and the Yellow River
on a southerly course (Ming times), it cost more to maintain the system: the Canal had to
cross the Yellow River and the western flanks of the Shandong hills. The system was cheapest
to operate when the Yellow River was on a northerly course and the capital was at Kaifeng,
well to the west of the Shangdong hills. I owe this observation to Mark Elvin. The Ling Qu
canal is treated in a forthcoming book by Robert B. Marks (Prof. Marks kindly showed the
manuscript to me).

owed inland waterborne traffic. And in any case, the United States shared
this system with Canada. The Amazon, and the Zaire above Malebo Pool,
both fine arteries for transport, flow through much less fertile lands and
have yet to foster much economic integration, let alone political unity, in
their basins. The Niger from about the eighth century A.D. onward occasionally integrated a huge expanse of West Africa – but no truly rich basins.
It linked the western Sudan all the way to the Futa Jallon highlands with the
lower Niger and connected this whole system to North Africa and the
Mediterranean via Timbuktu, Gao, and the trans-Saharan caravan routes.
But despite the best efforts of ancient Ghana, Mali, and Songhai, no power
could enduringly unite the Sudanic belt with the forest zone to its south, so
the Niger system was both intrinsically poorer than the Chinese and impossible for any polity to capture fully. Perhaps the closest contender in the
convenient riverine geography sweepstakes was the Volga and the Don,
each greatly magnified in significance by flowing into easily navigable
inland seas, the Caspian and the Black seas respectively. But the rivers had
no canal connecting them until 1952 and not until the eighteenth century
were their upper and lower reaches politically united (Russia took control
of the Crimea in the 1780s). Interestingly, the Ottoman Grand Vizier
Mehmet Sokollu in 1569 tried to build such a canal to check the Russians
in their southern expansion. He wanted to retake Astrakhan (lost to Russia
in 1556) and get the Ottoman navy onto the Caspian Sea. Had this plan
succeeded, an Ottoman waterway system would have emerged to rival the
Chinese – and would have made the Ottomans much more formidable in
their confrontations with Persia, Russia, and, indirectly, with the Hapsburgs
and Venice.[4]

With its waterways the Chinese state from Song times forward kept under
its control (most of the time) a huge diversity of ecological zones with a
broad array of useful natural resources. The Song, who developed the
south, ruled over a belt of about twenty degrees of latitude, extending as far
south as Hainan, well into the tropics. The Ming and Qing, with Manchuria
and eventually (after 1760) Xinjiang, controlled a span of thirty degrees of
latitude and ecologies ranging from the tropical to the subarctic. Consequently the Chinese state had available great stocks and wide varieties of

[4] The project was abandoned when one-third complete. In the late sixteenth century the
Black Sea was an Ottoman lake, so control of the lower Don and Volga and the Caspian Sea
would have given the Ottomans control over all the western termini of Central Asian trade
as well as strategic advantages over their neighbors. The Ottoman navy might also have
extended Ottoman power north along the wide Volga. One of Alexander the Great's
generals and successors, Seleucus Nicator, planned but never built a Don–Volga canal. Peter
the Great tried and failed in 1697.

timber, grains, fish, fibers, salt, metals, building stone, and occasionally livestock and grazing land. This portfolio of ecological diversity translated into insurance and resilience for the state. It provided the wherewithal for war – except for horses, a constant concern resolved only by the Qing conquest of Mongolia. It assured that should crops fail and revenues dwindle in one part of the empire, the shortfall could be made good elsewhere. Forest fires, epizootics, or crop pests could devastate several localities without threatening the stability of the state. The role of ecological diversity as insurance helps explain the resilience of the Chinese state. No other state ever quite matched it – until the era of European overseas empire.

The Roman Empire at its apex in the first through third centuries A.D. extended from Britain to the Maghreb and the Red Sea, but it had no hold on tropical products. Its well-integrated zone extended east–west along the Mediterranean, and thus united zones of similar ecology. The Arab Umayyad caliphate also existed generally within ecologically similar zones. Its failure to take Constantinople (673–78) kept it from uniting the Black Sea's temperate ecosystems to the subtropical Mediterranean and Mesopotamian ones it did control. The Incas achieved a measure of ecological diversity through vertical integration,[5] ranging from the Pacific lowlands to the high Andean valleys, the altiplano, and occasionally to the eastern flanks of the cordillera. But 5,000 meters' difference in altitude is not a full substitute for thirty degrees of latitude. The Incas had just succeeded in uniting a narrow corridor of about thirty degrees of latitude at the time of the Spanish conquest (1532). Their roads had not yet integrated this territory nearly as well as the Chinese rivers and canals had united China. At its height in the sixteenth century, the Ottoman Empire enjoyed ecological diversity comparable although not quite equal to China's. Ottoman power extended from the Black Earth of the Ukraine to Egypt and Yemen, twenty-five degrees of latitude, and very much the same latitudinal belt as controlled by the Ming and Qing. The short-lived Mongol state of the thirteenth century united a huge expanse of grassland, but it had dissolved before it could consolidate control over the diverse portfolio of ecologies bordering the steppe.

Thus China was, from about A.D. 650 to 1800, almost always the most

---

[5] John Murra first explained the ecological complementarity of Andean societies organized in "vertical archipelagos." A recent reassessment of this idea appears in Murra, "El Archipélago Vertical Revisited," pp. 3–14, and Murra, "The Limits and Limitations of the 'Vertical Archipelago' in the Andes," pp. 15–20, in Shozo Masuda, Izumi Shimada, and Craig Morris, eds., *Andean Ecology and Civilization* (Tokyo: University of Tokyo Press, 1985). See also Charles Stanish, *Ancient Andean Political Economy* (Austin: University of Texas Press, 1992) for a more recent reconsideration.

ecologically resilient and resourceful state on earth.[6] Indeed, during this millennium China was probably the most ecologically diverse polity in the history of the world before Britain assembled its far-flung overseas empire. State and society gradually corroded China's diversity, simplifying ecosystems in the interest of maximizing the human crop, as this volume attests. Over the centuries China lost many of its ecological buffers, its forests, wetlands, wildlands. But it remained for more than eleven centuries the state with the greatest ecological complementarity.

Similarly, Chinese society was probably the most epidemiologically experienced. By virtue of its long urban tradition China had domesticated almost all the crowd diseases, such as measles and smallpox. By virtue of its animal husbandry, particularly the keeping of pigs and fowl, the Chinese had vast experience with those diseases humankind shares with animals – influenza for instance. By virtue of its great expanses of surface water, China had plenty of waterborne infections, mosquito breeding grounds, and parasites. By virtue of its hot south, many Chinese immune systems were familiar with malaria, dengue, and other tropical fevers.[7] These ecological circumstances amounted to a double-edged sword. Malaria and other tropical killers limited Chinese settlement and control over the far south. Illness and death haunted all of China, and the toll on children and other immunological naifs probably ranked among the highest anywhere in the world. But those who survived childhood, especially in southern China, where the variety of lethal infections was greatest, probably had the most alert and active (human) immune systems on earth. Consequently, the Chinese had less in the way of disease to fear from strangers than virtually anyone else, and strangers had much to fear from them. The Chinese were safe from the microbial imperialism of other peoples, and able to inflict its costs upon their less epidemiologically experienced neighbors. This probably helped China to expand at the expense of forest dwellers in the south, southwest, and northeast of modern China, and at the expense of Tibetans and the steppe peoples. Had the fifteenth-century Ming overseas voyages continued, had junks rather than caravelles linked

---

[6] The period of the Southern Song (1127–1279) excepted, as China was then divided.

[7] Not yellow fever, a lethal killer in the American and African tropics. Its absence in tropical Asia is unexplained. According to Mark Elvin (personal communication), in Tang times Chinese officials sent to the south from the north regarded this posting as a death sentence. In the Lingnan region (according to Robert Marks), malaria routinely killed northern immigrants and devastated northern armies, as in the era of the Qing conquest. Officials from the north died at such rates in eighteenth-century Guangxi that they petitioned for a relaxation of the "law of avoidance" whereby officials did not serve in their native districts. See Erhard Rosner, "'Gewöhning an die Malaria in chinesischen Quellen des 18 jahrhunderts," *Sudhoffs Archiv* 68.1 (1984), pp. 43–60.

the whole planet, China's brand of ecological imperialism presumably would have transformed landscapes and societies as thoroughly as Europe's did.[8]

The inland waterway system created in China a far more unified market, polity, and society than existed over comparably large and rich spaces elsewhere in the world. Consumer or government demand in one part of the empire influenced production patterns, land use, resource exploitation, in very distant provinces – wherever the capillaries of the waterway system reached. This was true not merely for expensive military and luxury goods, but for bulk goods – grain, timber, salt. So China's environmental history, like its economic history, is more integrated, less the mere sum of its local parts than is the case elsewhere. This integration, this cohesion, meant that state policy and the character of the prevailing economic system conditioned China's environmental history to an unusual degree.

The durability and resilience of the state depended in large part on Chinese geography, but Chinese ecology in turn depended on the state to an unusual degree. Without supposing a centralized hydraulic despotism of the sort Wittfogel imagined, in comparative perspective the Chinese state (here meaning imperial, provincial, and local authorities) appears remarkable for its ecological role. The Chinese imperial state was a meddlesome one, carefully looking after its own interests and, in keeping with cultural traditions, actively seeking to develop resources and rearrange nature so as to maximize tangible and taxable wealth. The Egyptian pharaohs and their minions did much the same, although in a far smaller area. The Inca Empire did it too, although for a much briefer time. Many smaller states have also pursued economic and political projects that implied thorough ecological change. In China the scale was greater and the duration longer than anywhere else. Here, more than elsewhere, the state served (often unsuccessfully) as the guarantor of ecological stability. The state took primary responsibility for building and maintaining many big waterworks, for

[8] For this concept, see Alfred W. Crosby, *Ecological Imperialism: The Biological Expansion of Europe, 900–1900* (New York: Cambridge University Press, 1986). For speculations along these lines, see J. R. McNeill, "Alfred Crosby and World History," paper delivered at the World History Association meetings, June 24–27, 1992, Philadelphia. Scarlet fever, diphtheria, and syphilis arrived in China only in the sixteenth century. Cholera followed (probably) in the nineteenth century. As Fisher's chapter in the Chinese-language version of this volume ("Zhongguo lishi-shang-de shuyi" [Taipei, 1995], vol. 2, pp. 673–745) shows, the arrival of plague in China cannot be dated reliably. Guesses range from the early seventh century to the late eighteenth. Angela Ki Che Leung, "Diseases of the Premodern Period in China," in Kenneth Kiple, ed., *The Cambridge World History of Human Disease* (New York: Cambridge University Press, 1993), pp. 354–62.

flood control, and (by late Qing times) for reforestation to preserve both fuel supply and hydrology.[9] Its bureaucrats were taught to see a link between natural events and imperial politics, and to propitiate, placate, manage, and manipulate nature in the state's interest.

The Chinese agricultural landscape, and eventually almost every hectare of inner China, was thoroughly anthropogenic. People chose (sometimes unwittingly) which animals and plants lived. People governed (as best they could) the paths of the waters. Even the soil was a human construct.[10] All agricultural landscapes are of course man-made (or in many cases woman-made). Rice paddies are more so than most. But even north China, the land of wheat and millet, was sculpted by human labor to an unusual degree.

Intensely anthropogenic landscapes require vigilant maintenance. China probably needed more than other lands. Peru, Rwanda, and ancient Hawaii, among other places, had terraces in need of regular attention; Holland had polders; Mesopotamia and the Indus had dikes and dams. But China's terraces, paddies, polders, dikes, dams, and canals needed massive and constant labor and investment. Should the supply of either of these fail, rapid and costly deterioration (from the human point of view) would inevitably follow. A sudden loss of population, whether deriving from epidemic or war, could easily lead to heightened erosion, flooding, waterlogging of fields, silting up of river beds and canals – damage that might take decades of favorable conditions (abundant labor and a strong state) to repair. Should the state crumble or merely withdraw its funding from waterworks, neglect and decay followed, with the same high ecological costs.[11] Equivalent demographic or political events in northern Europe or southern Africa – or any land without terracing and significant waterworks – would lead only to contractions in arable and resurgence of spontaneous vegetation. A single year of favorable conditions (adequate labor and a good burning season) could restore such lands to full production. Thus it is fair to say that the Chinese landscape was unusually dependent on demographic and political stability, and unusually vulnerable to disruption by neglect. In ecologists' language it was highly labile – susceptible to rapid and thorough change.

No other major society so locked itself into a situation demanding constant intensive maintenance to prevent sharp ecological degradation. Even the terraced slopes of Japan and Peru probably did not need the same

---

[9] See Kenneth Pomeranz, *The Making of a Hinterland: State, Society, and Economy in Inland North China, 1853–1937* (Berkeley: University of California Press, 1993).

[10] See the essay by Rhoads Murphey in the Chinese-language version of this volume: "Zai Yazhou bijiao guandian-xia-de Zhongguo huanjing shi" (Taipei, 1995), vol. 1, pp. 67–112.

[11] Kenneth Pomeranz shows how this happened in Huang-Yun; see *Making of a Hinterland.*

vigilance as China's landscapes. A more common parallel, which may have constricted other states and societies at least as much, is the intensive maintenance required of highly militarized states and empires. The Aztec, Russian, Roman, and Ottoman empires, to name a few, locked themselves into military situations from which there was no withdrawal. They needed frontiers of loot (or slaving) to support their expensive armies, and they needed their armies to generate and exploit the frontiers of loot. Such situations could be (and were) maintained for centuries, but in the very long run proved progressively more difficult to sustain as the cream was skimmed off the richer regions and borders and commitments were expanded. Military lability of this sort is fairly commonplace; the ecological lability of China much rarer.

The rapid and thorough ecological change provoked in China by neglect could be repaired in time. A new, strong, and solvent dynasty could restore waterworks, drain lowlands, and (least likely) reforest hills, thereby restoring high productivity until the next disruption. This situation gives the strong appearance of cycles, suggesting a long-term ecological equilibrium in which the hyperanthropogenic landscape deteriorated and recovered in an irregular rhythm defined by imperial finance, epidemics, and war.[12]

Such a cycle may well have existed over centuries, and if so it distinguished China from most other societies. But over millennia a deeper pattern asserted itself, more linear than cyclical: the slow drawdown of biological resources and elimination of ecological buffers. The progressive replacement of forests and wetlands by fields and people – progress most would say – put China in periodic crisis, necessitating either spatial expansions or technological revolutions permitting great leaps upward in agricultural productivity. In this, China's environmental experience is typical of the world at large.

2.2. CHINESE UNEXCEPTIONALISM

In several respects Chinese environmental history appears quite consistent with that of other societies around the world. Here I will briefly take up four themes: the power of belief systems, the fate of forests, water manipulation, and ecological sustainability.

[12] This view is partly based on Peter Perdue, *Exhausting the Earth: State and Peasant in Hunan, 1500–1850* (Cambridge, Mass.: Harvard University Press, 1987). See also Pierre-Étienne Will, "Un cycle hydraulique en Chine: la Province du Hubei du XVIe au XIXe siècle," *Bulletin de l'École Française de l'Extrême Orient* 68 (1980), pp. 61–87.

It seems a natural, if slightly Hegelian, assumption that what people believe about nature and their place in it should influence their behavior and the environmental history of their communities. A generation ago a historian of technology, Lynn White, ascribed the environmental crisis of the West to its Judaeo-Christian outlook.[13] Chinese belief, especially Daoism (but strains of Confucianism too), forms a clear contrast to the instrumentalist view of nature dominant in the West. But as far as anyone can tell, Chinese outlooks that cherish harmony between human beings and nature (or Indian ones such as Jainism) have had no appreciable effect in restraining the human tendency to transform environments. In the Mediterranean world there is no discernible difference in the behavior of Muslims and Christians with respect to the environment.[14] In China and elsewhere, belief and ideology have played a much smaller role in shaping environmental history than have other factors, notably population, economic structure, technology, and state action.[15] This, incidentally, should disconcert those who see attitude change as a sufficient step toward addressing current ecological dilemmas.

Probably the two greatest environmental changes in the last three thousand years of Chinese history have been the destruction of forests and the reorganization of surface waters. In both these matters the Chinese rank among the most enthusiastic and proficient of peoples, but their conduct, ambition, and motives are perfectly consistent with other societies'. Conversion of forests to arable and pasture is one of the hallmarks of civilization. Peoples round the world have used fire and ax to create landscapes capable of supporting (at least temporarily) the maximum human load. Sixteenth-century Amerindians probably burned more North American forests every year than the continent's current inhabitants do (although even after ten

---

[13] In "The Historic Roots of Our Ecologic Crisis," *Science* 155 (1967), pp. 1203–07.

[14] See Yi-Fu Tuan, "Discrepancies between Environmental Attitude and Behavior: Examples from Europe and China," *The Canadian Geographer* 12 (1968), pp. 176–91; J. R. McNeill, *The Mountains of the Mediterranean World: An Environmental History* (New York: Cambridge University Press, 1992).

[15] An opposing view argues that Hinduism did protect India's environment, and that India's environmental problems developed during the last 700 years of foreign cultural domination. O. P. Dwivedi, "*Satyagraha* for Conservation: Awakening the Spirit of Hinduism," in L. P. Pojman, ed., *Environmental Ethics* (Boston: Jones and Bartlett Publishers, 1994), pp. 187–93. Many scholars who regard Amerindians as careful stewards of the land also see an explanation for this in their religions. Of course belief and ideology may affect state action and prevailing economic structure to some degree. Historians who take the view that belief and culture are paramount variables (at least in certain contexts) include J. Donald Hughes, *Pan's Travail* (Baltimore: Johns Hopkins University Press, 1993), and Carolyn Merchant, *Ecological Revolutions: Nature, Gender and Science in New England* (Chapel Hill, N.C.: University of North Carolina Press, 1989).

thousand years they had more forest standing than today's North Americans have after four hundred years). Polynesians cut down and burned off lowland forests in virtually every island they settled. Europeans cleared 80 percent of their forests, Indians – with help from the British – somewhat more of theirs.[16] The denuded hills of Mencius's lament have their counterpart in the Attic hills whose condition saddened Plato.[17] China's replacement of trees by people easily fits the general pattern of the last ten thousand years. Its fuelwood and timber shortages resemble the experience of countless societies, ancient and modern, temperate and tropical.

China's record of water manipulation may involve more impressive technologies than found elsewhere (until 1750 at least). And certainly the scale of operations in China exceeded that elsewhere until the nineteenth century. But numerous other peoples have rerouted their waters with much the same aims and results as the Chinese. Dryland irrigation, channeling, and diking existed in Mesopotamia and Egypt before they did in China. In Central Asia the Syr Darya has been managed (off and on) since 2300 B.C. Finely articulated mountain irrigation systems existed in pre-Columbian Mexico and Peru, throughout the ancient Mediterranean and later Muslim worlds, and Ethiopia, not to mention Japan and China's southeast Asian neighbors. In most cases, states took a prominent role in building and operating these waterworks. In all cases, heightened production came at the cost of vulnerability to catastrophe in the form of disruption of the waterworks, which invariably led to food crises. In all cases, rearranging surface waters incurred ecological costs, although these varied in nature and severity. Mesopotamia perhaps paid most heavily – at least until the recent debacles in Soviet Central Asia. Again, there is nothing eccentric about the Chinese record as regards water manipulation. Only scale distinguishes it from others.

Much the same holds true for the other components of Chinese environmental history. The slow extension of arable into marginal environments, semi-arid grasslands, or ever steeper hillsides is a familiar tale with countless parallels. The doubling and redoubling of silt loads in the rivers, the progradation of deltas into the sea, the alteration of microclimates follow-

---

[16] Stephen J. Pyne, "Sky of Ash, Earth of Ash: A Brief History of Fire in the United States," in Joel S. Levine, ed., *Global Biomass Burning: Atmospheric, Climatic, and Biospheric Implications* (Cambridge, Mass.: MIT Press, 1991), pp. 504–11; Patrick V. Kirch, *The Evolution of the Polynesian Chiefdoms* (Cambridge, England: Cambridge University Press, 1984); H. C. Darby, "The Clearing of the Woodland in Europe," in W. L. Thomas, ed., *Man's Role in Changing the Face of the Earth* (Chicago: University of Chicago Press, 1956), vol. 1, pp. 183–215; Madhav Gadgil and Ramachandra Guha, *This Fissured Land: An Ecological History of India* (Berkeley, 1993).

[17] See *Critias* 111b–c.

ing vegetation change, even the modern crises of chemical pollution, in all these China's history is different only in detail, in timing perhaps, or in scale.

According to Elvin, China has pursued ecologically unsustainable patterns for three thousand years, avoiding total breakdown by periodically adapting to crisis with new technologies or new spatial expansions. This pattern too is a common one, although since no other societies can show three thousand years of cultural continuity it is not easy to see. But taken at the aggregate, global level it is clearer: two crucial ecological transitions have relaxed constraints on human population, allowing two distinct surges in population growth. Hunting and foraging societies may have invented agriculture out of necessity, in response to food crisis brought on by population pressure.[18] Even if invented for other reasons, the new technologies of food production allowed for far greater populations. But agriculture frequently entailed the slow (and sometimes fast) drawdown of fundamental resources, such as fertile soil, fresh water, and combustible fuel. In the eighteenth century, worldwide population growth brought matters of food and fuel to a head and in England produced the second great transmutation of the human condition, the intensive use of fossil fuels and machine power known as the industrial revolution. Through heightened agricultural productivity, better transport, and associated improvements, it not merely forestalled Malthusian crises, but allowed a further expansion of population and, in places, of wealth.

The industrial revolution now threatens a new crisis in the shape of mounting pollution loads and perhaps depletion of scarce resources too. Pollution loads are now occasionally great enough to damage human health directly, most widely perhaps in Russia and Eastern Europe, and to alter basic biogeochemical cycles on which all life depends. (I refer to the depletion of stratospheric ozone and the buildup of atmospheric carbon dioxide and other greenhouse gases.) Pollution (chiefly with organochlorides) has even begun to affect the biological capacity to reproduce among many species – ours included – by disrupting endocrine systems (these produce hormones that regulated metabolism and sexual development, among other things). A third transmutation awaits us. The past, Chinese and global, suggests – but cannot guarantee – that after much suffering we will find another clever but unsustainable solution.

---

[18] Mark Nathan Cohen, *The Food Crisis in Prehistory: Overpopulation and the Origins of Agriculture* (New Haven: Yale University Press, 1977). Bruce D. Smith, *The Emergence of Agriculture* (New York: American Scientific Library, 1995) argues against Cohen's thesis, preferring various mixes of opportunity and necessity as the driving forces behind the seven independent inventions of agriculture.

2.3. SOURCES AND METHODS

Chinese environmental historians, at least those interested in recent centuries, are blessed with a fine written record. The gazetteers produced by the imperial, provincial, and local gentry and bureaucracy provide abundant information on population, agriculture, waterworks, fishing, sometimes on forests and pastures, and more. These extend back (irregularly of course) to Song times. It is hard to find comparable information elsewhere. In Russia Peter the Great ordered a general inventory of his realm at the end of the seventeenth century, and for some provinces there are detailed land surveys from the mid-nineteenth, created in anticipation of the abolition of serfdom. In India systematic environmental data scarcely exist for the period before the establishment of British control. In southwestern Asia and southeastern Europe the Ottoman *defterler* provide a useful if irregular picture for the fifteenth and sixteenth centuries, and more frequent records from religious foundations offer agricultural data from the sixteenth to the nineteenth centuries. (The Ottoman records have yet to be interrogated from the point of view of environmental history.) In most of sub-Saharan Africa there are no systematic written records until the nineteenth century, and the accounts of Arab (and later European) geographers and travelers give at best a spotty picture.

In the Americas the modest record base remaining from pre-Columbian times sheds next to no light on environmental history. The bureaucracy of Spanish America generated a considerable written record, but it lacked Confucian training and showed little interest in ecology and the natural world. In North America after the sixteenth century the written record is even more abundant, and has permitted detailed and convincing work. In northwestern Europe too, the situation is favorable. In England, the Domesday Book of the late eleventh century provides an unrivaled account of the landscape. Switzerland and Germany also have considerable records appropriate for environmental history. The Mediterranean is of course comparatively strong for ancient times, but after that (with exceptions such as northern Italy) rather thin until the nineteenth century. In Oceania and Australia there is virtually nothing to go on until the end of the eighteenth century.

Environmental history in most of the world, then, is more difficult to reconstruct on the basis of written records than it is in China. In Africa, Oceania, the Americas, and much of Asia, historians interested in all but the latest periods must rely on the work of archaeologists, paleobotanists, palynologists, climatologists, geomorphologists, and others. Naturally, historians are well placed to interpret the findings of other scholars in light of social, economic, and political history. But for environmental change itself their own record base and expertise is worth very little. In China historians have a larger role to play, thanks to the diligence and sensibilities of Confucian-trained bureaucrats and scholars.

That is not to say that Chinese environmental historians do not have much to learn from their colleagues in natural sciences. Consider only palynology. China has more than its share of lakes and bogs with sediments full of fossilized pollen and spores. In them lies a history of forest clearance, settlement, crop introductions, cropping patterns, ecological successions, and more, that only palynologists can reveal. Much of the palynology done in China is aimed at reconstructing paleoclimates. But reading the pollen diagrams will cast additional light on many subjects of interest to Chinese environmental history. Palynology can help trace the moving boundaries of the desert and the sown. It can help determine whether a given foodstuff was imported or grown locally. If Chinese palynologists could afford fine-resolution techniques (very expensive), they could inform historians about probable harvest variations from year to year, which might help in agricultural as well as climate history.[19]

The promise of palynology is complemented by that of other techniques such as dendrochronology and coral analysis, both especially useful for climate history, and remote sensing, which has revealed long-abandoned irrigation networks in Egypt and southwestern Asia. The very richness of the Chinese written records means that these sciences are less crucial in the reconstruction of Chinese environmental history than they are elsewhere, but if armed with them, Chinese environmental historians could generate a picture of their subject as full and convincing as that available anywhere. The opportunities for collaborative interdisciplinary work seem especially promising.[20]

---

[19] Australians have done some of the pioneering work in fine-resolution palynology. I thank John Flenley of Massey University in New Zealand for acquainting me with the subject.

[20] The limitations of existing work in Chinese palynology, dendrochronology, coral analysis, and other paleoclimatic techniques are addressed in Raymond Bradley, ed., *High Resolution Record of Past Climate from Monsoon Asia: The Last 2,000 Years and Beyond*, PAGES Workshop Report 93-1 (Bern, 1993). Long-term climate history relies in part on ice-core analysis, which is under way in China (mostly Tibet). See L. G. Thompson et al., "Holocene–Late Pleistocene Climatic Ice Core Records from Qinghai–Tibetan Plateau," *Science* 246 (1989), pp. 474–77. James Reardon-Anderson, James Ellis, and their colleagues in the Grassland Ecosystem of the Mongolian Steppe (GEMS) project have pursued interdisciplinary investigations in a forthcoming book.

2.4. PATHS NOT YET TAKEN

Paths of inquiry taken by environmental historians elsewhere may help focus questions appropriate for China. Here I will briefly discuss eight.

Fire is humankind's oldest labor-saving device. It has played a conspicuous role in modifying ecologies in the Americas, Africa, the Mediterranean, Australia, and Oceania.[21] Its importance in China, at least in recent centuries, may well have been more modest, but it bears investigation.

China's aquatic environments surely deserve more attention, especially marine ecosystems. While further studies of waterworks, rivers, and lakes[22] would be welcome, the sea beckons. China has had the strongest role in modifying the great (nearly) inland sea that stretches from the Yellow Sea past Taiwan to the South China Sea. Silt, pollution, and fishing have no doubt made their marks. Work concerning Pacific America and Oceania show what can be done with these themes, with and without written sources.[23] The geomorphological history of Elvin and Su in this volume is but a start in these directions.

Biological invasion must also have affected Chinese environmental history. Typically lands with only recent or mild experience of humanity have been invaded by plants and animals that thrive in the disturbed environments that human effort creates. Thus recent centuries have brought many changes to the biota, and indirectly to the soils and the rest of the environment, in Oceania, the Americas, and southern Africa. Lands with long and intense histories of human occupation more typically export invasive species. But even the eastern Mediterranean, the first cradle of agriculture, has acquired new species in historical times: weeds, birds, rodents, fish, as well as pathogens and the American food crops. In China the consequences of

---

[21] See Stephen J. Pyne, *Fire in America: A Cultural History of Wildland and Rural Fire* (Princeton: Princeton University Press, 1988); Pyne, *Burning Bush: A Fire History of Australia* (New York: Henry Holt, 1991); Johan Goudsbloom, *Fire and Civilization* (London: Penguin, 1992); G. Kuhnholz-Lordat, *La Terre incendiée: Essai d'agronomie comparée* (Nîmes: Éditions de la Maison Carrée, 1939).

[22] E.g., R. Keith Schoppa, *Xiang Lake: Nine Centuries of Chinese Life* (New Haven: Yale University Press, 1989); Lyman Van Slyke, *Yangtze: Nature, History and the River* (Reading, Mass.: Addison–Wesley, 1988).

[23] E.g., P. V. Kirch, "Man's Role in Modifying Tropical and Subtropical Polynesian Ecosystems," *Archaeology in Oceania* 18 (1983), pp. 26–31; Ian W. G. Smith, "Maori Impact on Marine Megafauna: Pre-European Distributions of New Zealand Sea Mammals," in Douglas G. Sutton, ed., *Saying So Doesn't Make It So: Papers in Honour of B. Foss Leach* (Dunedin, New Zealand: New Zealand Archaeological Association, 1989), pp. 76–108; Arthur McEvoy, *The Fisherman's Problem: Ecology and Law in the California Fisheries, 1850–1980* (New York: Cambridge University Press, 1986).

American food crops have been studied (see Osborne among others in this volume) and the history of disease takes full account of the possibility of invasive microbiotic species (see MacPherson among others in this volume). What of sorghum, an African native, but important in northern Chinese agriculture for many centuries? What consequences have other biological invasions, intentional and otherwise, wrought?[24]

China, like the eastern Mediterranean, is presumably a great exporter of species and assemblages. Successful Chinese combinations, like mulberry trees and silkworms, which China has raised since the third millennium B.C., have found imitators far and wide, in Japan, India, Persia, Italy, and Moorish Spain – Thomas Jefferson even tried to establish silk culture in eighteenth-century Virginia. One insignificant plant, *Actinidia chinensis*, the Chinese gooseberry native to the Yangzi basin, when transplanted in the twentieth century became the kiwi fruit, an important New Zealand and minor California export. The peach and the wax gourd (Chinese watermelon) are among widely dispersed Chinese plants. Quite likely, a significant share of species exports accompanied overseas Chinese in their movements to Taiwan, Indonesia, Malaysia, the Philippines, and beyond. Like Polynesian, Norse, Spanish, and other settlers, they no doubt sought to create familiar and useful landscapes wherever they went – transported landscapes.[25] And, no doubt, they wrought many accidental changes as well. This too is a matter for Chinese environmental historians – or at least environmental historians who are familiar with Chinese culture and ecology. Taiwan (see Chapter 6 by Liu Ts'ui-jung, Chapter 19 by Kuo-tung Ch'en, and Chapter 20 by An-Chi Tung in this volume) is only the tip of this iceberg of overseas Chinese environmental impact.

Some of the most dramatic and revealing work in environmental history to date concerns frontier transformations, where one system of human ecology replaces another. Often, perhaps generally, frontier settlers have brought inappropriate techniques and tools with them, accelerating land

---

[24] See F. Di Castri, A. J. Hansen, and M. Debussche, eds., *Biological Invasions in Europe and the Mediterranean Basin* (Dordrecht: Kluwer Academic, 1990); R. H. Grove and F. Di Castri, eds., *Biogeography of Mediterranean Invasions* (Cambridge, England: Cambridge University Press, 1991); H. A. Mooney and J. A. Drake, eds., *The Ecology of Biological Invasions in North America and Hawaii* (New York: Springer-Verlag, 1986); I. A. W. MacDonald, F. J. Kruger, A. A. Ferrar, *The Ecology and Management of Biological Invasions in Southern Africa* (Cape Town: Oxford University Press, 1986); P. S. Ramakrishnan, ed., *The Ecology of Biological Invasions in the Tropics* (New Delhi: published for the National Institute of Ecology by International Scientific Publications, 1991); R. H. Grove and J. J. Burdon, *Ecology of Biological Invasions* (Cambridge, England: Cambridge University Press, 1986); J. A. Drake, ed., *Biological Invasions: A Global Perspective* (Chichester, England: John Wiley, 1989).

[25] The phrase of Edgar Anderson, *Plants, Man and Animals* (Boston: Little, Brown, 1952).

degradation. Portraits of North America (after 1492), Greenland (after c. A.D. 900), Australia (after 1788), and New Zealand (after 1840) especially emphasize this feature,[26] although it is equally valid in the history of Siberia (after 1600), the Maghreb (after A.D. 711), southern Africa after the Bantu migration and again after Dutch settlement (1652), southern Spain of the *reconquista*, and Moghul India, among others. It should be so in China as well: the overland Chinese had their impact too. This theme is recognized in this volume, especially by Holzner and Kriechbaum in their essay on the Himalayas (Chapter 3). Internal frontiers, the filling up of spaces amid islands of settlement, also get their due here (Chapter 4 by Menzies, Chapter 7 by Osborne, Chapter 8 by Vermeer). But the environmental transformations worked upon Manchuria, Inner Mongolia, Xinjiang, and Yunnan as they fell into the Chinese orbit – those pictures are yet to be drawn.[27]

War and political violence generally have at times led to notable environmental change.[28] In the Chinese case, the extensive waterworks were a sword of Damocles – and almost anyone could snip the thread.

Intentional inundations were a common feature of Chinese civil con-

---

[26] William Cronon, *Changes in the Land* (New York: Hill and Wang, 1983); Timothy Silver, *A New Face on the Countryside* (New York: Cambridge University Press, 1990); Gordon G. Whitney, *From Coastal Wilderness to Fruited Plain: A History of Environmental Change in Temperate North America from 1500 to the Present* (New York: Cambridge University Press, 1994); Richard Whyte, *The Roots of Dependency: Subsistence, Environment, and Social Change among the Choctaws, Pawnees, and Navajos* (Lincoln: University of Nebraska Press, 1983); Thomas McGovern, "The Arctic Frontier of Norse Greenland," in S. Green and S. Perlman, eds., *The Archaeology of Frontiers and Boundaries* (New York: Academic Press, 1985), pp. 275–323; Thomas McGovern, "Management for Extinction in Norse Greenland," in Carole L. Crumley, ed., *Historical Ecology: Cultural Knowledge and Changing Landscapes* (Santa Fe: School of American Research Press, 1994), pp. 127–54; Andrew Hill Clark, *The Invasion of New England by People, Plants, and Animals* (New Brunswick, N.J.: Rutgers University Press, 1949); Peter Holland and Sherry Olson, "Ecosystems in Transition: The Experience of Australia and New Zealand," *New Zealand Journal of Geography* 87 (1989), pp. 2–7; William J. Lines, *Taming the Great South Land* (Berkeley: University of California Press, 1991); Geoffrey Bolton, *Spoils and Spoilers: Australians Make Their Land* (Sydney, 1981); Tim Flannery, *The Future Eaters: An Ecological History of Australasia* (New York: Braziller, 1995).

[27] Steps in this direction are taken by James Reardon-Anderson, "Man and Nature in the West Liao River Basin During the Past 10,000 Years," forthcoming in the GEMS volume. See also the pioneering works of Owen Lattimore, notably *The Inner Asian Frontiers of China* (New York: American Geographical Society, 1951).

[28] A. H. Westing, *Warfare in a Fragile World* (London: Taylor and Francis, 1980); Westing, *Herbicides in War* (London: Taylor and Francis, 1984); Westing, ed., *Environmental Hazards of War* (Newbury Park, Calif.: Sage, 1990); Sven Rubenson, "Environmental Stress and Conflict in Ethiopian History: Looking for Correlations," *Ambio* 20.5 (1991), pp. 179–82; René Cintré, *Les marches de Bretagne au Moyen Age: économie, guerre, et société en pays de frontière, XIV–XVe siècles* (Pornichet: Éditions J.–M. Pierre, 1992); McNeill, *Mountains of the Mediterranean World*, pp. 260–70.

flicts, most famously in an episode (1938) in the anti-Japanese war. Ecological destruction during the Taiping Rebellion (1850–64) and the war against and occupation by Japan (1931–45) must surely have been considerable. But more broadly than the direct damages of war, there are the ecological effects of preparing for war and maintaining readiness – obtaining great quantities of timber and strategic metals, feeding men and horses at remote locations. The symbol of Chinese defense, the Great Wall – or more accurately the various northern walls, especially after their great reconstruction in Ming times[29] – must have interrupted and deflected the movements of steppe animals, wild and domestic, and disrupted the lives of people who depended on them, often all to the good from the Chinese point of view. Chinese defense policy against the steppe peoples, which involved varying proportions of alliance, trade, attack, and wall-building, had vast implications for land use, animal and human population sizes, disease prevalences, and much else in northern China and Mongolia. Several contributions to this volume touch on the destruction of war, but systematic investigation of the theme should be especially rewarding in the Chinese context.

In many parts of the world export trade has helped to shape environmental history. This tends to be true where trade accounts for a large share of production, such as in plantation societies. It is also true when and where small economies intersect with large ones: New Zealand with Britain in the nineteenth century for instance, or Fiji with China.[30] Within China, the role of foreign trade in environmental history was probably small until the nineteenth century, although the southern coast may at times have been an exception.[31] China's chief export in the seventeenth century was silk, but only a third of production (about 800 tons early in the seventeenth century) went for export.[32] The environmental consequences of raising silkworms and mulberry trees on this scale were surely modest indeed. Other frequent exports over the last thousand years, such as pottery, porcelain, copper, and gold, probably had some small environmental impact, especially through their fuel requirements. Linen, rice, sugar, and most of the other leading Chinese exports were produced in great quantity for domes-

---

[29] See Arthur Waldron, *The Great Wall of China: From History to Myth* (Cambridge, England: Cambridge University Press, 1990).

[30] These examples are treated in J. R. McNeill, "Of Rats and Men: A Synoptic Environmental History of the Island Pacific," *Journal of World History* 5.2 (1994), pp. 299–349.

[31] Robert Marks, in a forthcoming book, shows the importance of overseas trade to south China, especially in Ming times, but does not attribute much ecological impact to it.

[32] George B. Souza, *The Survival of the Empire: Portuguese Trade and Society in China and the South China Sea, 1630–1754* (Cambridge, England: Cambridge University Press, 1986), p. 46.

tic use; foreign trade had only the tiniest role in generating what environmental changes these products implied. But after 1842 (the Treaty of Nanjing) land-use decisions in coastal China increasingly came to reflect the relative profitability of various trade goods. Tea, for instance, inspired the clearing of new hillslopes. Since 1978 China has exported more and more, and the fields and factories of its coastal provinces, and thus their soils, air, and water, are indirectly affected by the structures and trends of the international economy. Taiwan's ecology has been strongly linked to export since 1960 – since 1895 if one includes the colonial relationship with Japan. While this theme may prove less central in China than it has elsewhere, since 1842 it is surely important enough to merit investigation.

Air pollution is another matter more prominent in the present than in the past, but not without a history. Chinese urban air is famously foul today. What is its history? Texts from the ancient Mediterranean and medieval England, combined with some ingenious atmospheric chemistry involving ice bubbles and old buildings, have permitted long-term sketched reconstructions of the pollution histories of major cities such as Rome and London.[33] Might Chinese texts and buildings, perhaps together with Tibetan and Tian Shan glaciers, reward similar researches?

Additional rewarding inquiries abound. There are large ones with potentially major implications for history and ecology: environmental comparisons between China and other hydraulic societies, Mesopotamia, Egypt, or the Indus. Or systematic studies of the role of population growth, flux, and even decline on local and regional ecosystems. Few doubt there is a relationship between population and environment, but fewer can say just what it is. China is a good place to try to find out, because population history is fairly clear, the contours of environmental change itself are becoming clear, and the role of additional important variables such as technology and state action are (comparatively speaking) very clear. And countless smaller inquiries, no less useful for bringing Chinese environmental history into focus, beckon to able researchers.

2.5. CONCLUSION

Environmental history as a self-conscious intellectual endeavor is only two decades old. So far its contribution has been strongest in North America,

---

[33] Hughes, *Pan's Travail*; Peter Brimblecombe, *The Big Smoke* (London: Methuen, 1987). Tibetan ice cores have begun to yield useful data for Chinese (and monsoon Asian) climate history. See Bradley, ed., *High Resolution of Past Climate from Monsoon Asia.*

Central Europe, and Australia, although Brazil and India are not so far behind. In another two decades Chinese environmental history will probably have as rich a harvest as anywhere. The necessary record base exists. The theme has obvious importance to Chinese history, and to the Chinese present. And, as this volume testifies, those with the necessary skills are hard at work.

Interpreting the Physical Environment

3

Man's Impact on the Vegetation and Landscape in the Inner Himalaya and Tibet

WOLFGANG HOLZNER AND MONIKA KRIECHBAUM

INTRODUCTION

When one is traveling from south to north in the Himalayas, three major regions can be distinguished according to the variation of the vegetation caused by changes in the climate, particularly the influence of the monsoon: the *Outer Himalaya*, with its lush monsoon vegetation; the semi-humid to semi-arid *Inner Himalaya*, where arborescent vegetation is potentially still possible – although actually great parts are treeless; and finally in the north the *Tibetan Himalaya*, where the climate is too harsh and dry for the growth of trees.[1]

This article is based on data collected during several geobotanical research expeditions to the arid and semi-arid landscapes of the Inner Himalaya and the adjacent areas to the north, including Ladakh, Zangskar, Rupshu, Spiti, Lahul, Dolpo, and Southern Mustang (Map 3.1).[2] These areas are situated in India and Nepal, neighboring the Chinese Autonomous Region Xizang (a part of former Tibet),[3] and there are strong ethnic, cultural, and biogeographical connections and similarities. Therefore observations on the vegetation of Tibet made during extensive travels in Xizang and Qinghai, which were of necessity superficial because of the huge areas covered, were usefully compared with results of the expeditions into the adjacent regions mentioned above. Extrapolations from one

---

[1] U. Schweinfurth, *Die horizontale und vertikale Verbreitung der Vegetation im Himalaya*, Bonner geographische Abhandlungen 3 (Bonn, 1957).

[2] The project was assisted by a grant from the Austrian "Fonds zur Förderung der wissenschaftlichen Forschung," project number P 8183.

[3] "Tibet" is used in this text not in a political but in a biogeographical sense.

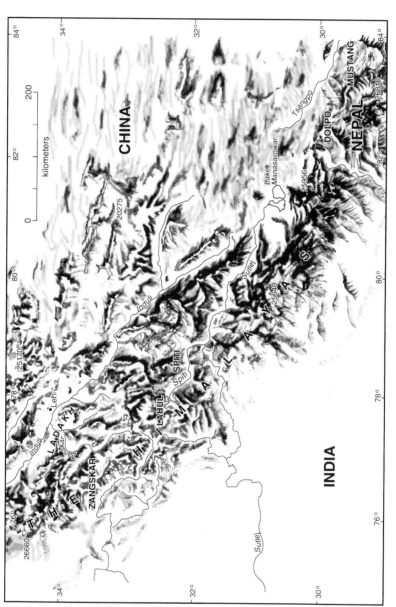

Map 3.1. The Himalayas, with places mentioned in the text. The mountains are only symbolic; they are drawn to make the situation of the Inner Himalaya behind the high peaks of the main range evident. Drawn by Cartography Unit (Ian Heyward), RSPAS, Australian National University.

Figure 3.1. Southeast of Mount Animaqing, Qinghai, China, above 4,000 m. The hill to the right bears a dark, dense rhododendron/willow scrub, while all the hills around – and this for hundreds of kilometers – are covered by open and short steppe vegetation. The climatic data for the area indicate the possibility of tree growth. All photographs and drawings in Chapter 3 by W. Holzner.

region to the other seem to be valid. They lead to a rough and sometimes hypothetical picture of the mutual relations between human beings and the natural landscape in this part of the world.

3.1. INDICATORS OF HUMAN IMPACT IN A LANDSCAPE

The methods used were appropriate to the huge areas covered: in addition to a phytosociological analysis of the vegetation, and hints coming from the plant cover itself, indicators and traces pointing to the activities of people and their livestock were collected. Direct information from the people or from literature was scarce. All this was put together as if in a jigsaw puzzle to construct the picture presented below. Before we start we would like to present a short introduction to the way vegetation ecologists "read" a landscape, and to describe some of the more common indicators of the presence of human beings in a seemingly untouched wilderness.

Figure 3.2. Juniper Krummholz north of Lhasa, c. 4,300 m. The rather sharp upper border may have natural reasons (long snow cover, which has also limited the growth of the shrubs in the hollow in the foreground). The patchy character of the slopes is anthropogenous, the result of cautious collection, particularly for incense, by the Tibetan nomads (tents in the foreground). As they have always preferred dung for heating, this shrub has been preserved until today. What can be noted on the picture only marginally (right) is the fact that, nowadays, these shrubs are recklessly cut for firewood (used in street construction and transported to Lhasa for the Chinese population). Once destroyed, they will never recover because of the difficult growing conditions.

"UNNATURAL" VEGETATION PATTERN. In this context "unnatural" means a pattern of vegetation that seems to be arbitrary, because none of the so-called abiotic factors, like fire or differences in soil humidity, geology or climate, can be imagined as being the underlying reason.[4] Figures 3.1 and 3.2 show examples of low- and high-scrub vegetation displaying such an isolated pattern within a vast high-altitude steppe area.

SHARP VEGETATION BOUNDARIES AND STRAIGHT LINES IN THE LAND-SCAPE. The "natural" parameters that cause changes in the pattern of vegetation very rarely show abrupt changes. The more or less gradual change of the environment is displayed in the landscape by transitions

---

[4] Human impact is considered "unnatural" in the sense given to it by ecologists.

Figure 3.3. Annapurna Sanctuary, Nepal, about 3,500 m. Though the area seems inaccessible, it is grazed by goats summer after summer. The conspicuous straight line on the opposite slope is the result of the incomplete burning of juniper scrub by herdsmen to increase the pasture area for goats. The line was probably caused by the wind conditions prevailing during the time of burning.

between plant communities. Related indicators are "straight lines" in a landscape, which are practically always a result of human impact (Fig. 3.3).

ISOLATED TREES OR SHRUBS. These or isolated groups of trees in a landscape bare of woody plants may be the sad remnants of the former plant cover (Figs. 3.4, 3.14, and 3.15). It is important to pay attention to the detailed circumstances under which the woody growth occurs: for example, whether the trees or shrubs are sparse because their very special growth conditions are only sparsely available (e.g., on shallow substrate where soil is sufficient for tree growth only here and there), or whether the single trees grow on large-scale homogeneous sites, which would make the growth of at least an open forest possible.

VEGETATION IN "INACCESSIBLE CORNERS." Though people and their cattle, sheep, and goats show astonishing climbing abilities in their search for food (Fig. 3.3), "corners" can be found that have been scarcely or not at all visited for various reasons, and give an impression of how landscape

Figure 3.4. Dunai, Dolpo, Nepal, 2,350 m. The growth conditions on this slope are obviously homogeneous, the dominant vegetation being a steppe of high tussock grasses. The single pine trees (and, higher up, cedars) tell us of a former forest (or steppe forest) cover.

and vegetation look like without a strong human impact. On a large scale this can be a valley inaccessible because of rocks at its entrance. But hints pointing to the potential vegetation also can be found on a very small scale: examples are remnants of trees in a rock face or grasses hidden within thorn scrubs (Fig. 3.5).

VEGETATION IN PROTECTED AREAS. Areas in a landscape may be protected for several reasons, for instance because they are private property. Particularly sacred areas, such as holy groves, may be the last reminder of a former forest cover (Figs. 3.6–3.8).

PREDOMINANCE OF UNPALATABLE PLANTS IN THE VEGETATION. Conclusions about the intensity of grazing can be drawn from the composition of the vegetation (see sections 3.2 and 3.3). As long as animals can choose, they will browse on the grasses and herbs they like best. Thus the number and cover of unpalatable species having mechanical (hard tissues or spiny organs) or chemical protection devices (bitter or acrid compounds, ethe-

Figure 3.5. *Stipa* grasses between the rocks within an overgrazed semi-desert in Ladakh. Are they the last witnesses of a former *Stipa* steppe, or do they grow in this sheltered place because the animals cannot reach them here, or because of the better water supply? Additional "indicators" will help to find the answer.

real oils, or poisonous substances) will increase, because these plants have a competitive advantage over the palatable ones.

Knowledge about the chemistry of plants is useful for this purpose but not necessary. Information on the palatability of plants in an area can be gathered by observations on the grazing habits of the animals, and by close attention to the vegetation, to determine which plants are browsed and which not.

PREDOMINANCE OF PIONEER PLANTS. If the grazing and/or trampling pressure becomes so intense that the vegetation is destroyed and the soil lies bare, plants that specialize in colonizing open soil invade. This development is the "natural" process for healing gaps in the vegetation. It is visible wherever wild or domestic animals abound, particularly in the places where they gather in greater concentration than elsewhere, for instance near watering places, or where they spend a long time resting. If a flora is not restricted to these heavily used places, but spreads over huge parts of a landscape, this may be an indicator of high grazing pressure.

At such places one has the opportunity to form an acquaintance with the

Figure 3.6. Fencing like this wall offers opportunities to compare vegetation with different grazing intensities. This special case in Hemis Shukpa, Ladakh, provided one of the examples showing that "hummock pastures" (foreground) are the result of destruction of *Kobresia* tussock bogs (behind the wall). For more details see section 3.3.4.

pioneer flora of an area. This is a method of botanizing suitable for the nonspecialist. Knowledge of how to recognize plants with high colonizing abilities is difficult to gather (see also section 3.3.2), and experience and "feeling" for the vegetation will always be necessary. One frequent feature of pioneer plants, for instance, is annual or biennial growth. Annuals can be recognized by their poor root system and the lack of nonflowering shoots; the life of the plant is dominated by the goal of producing flowers and setting seeds before the next disturbance, or frost or drought, occurs. A famous example is Shepherd's Purse. Biennials are very often plants producing a rosette of leaves pressed to the soil (see also Fig. 3.9) in the first year of growth, mullein being a well-known example. If they achieve flowering in one of the following years, they do this with a high, candle-like stalk and the whole plant dies after seed-set, leaving the dead stalks in the landscape. While most biennials are colonizing species, the predominance of annuals in a landscape can have causes quite different from large-scale disturbance. A Mediterranean-type climate, for instance, favors the growth of winter germinating annuals, which die before the summer drought, leaving the soil bare during the dry period. A similar phenomenon can be

Figure 3.7. The holy grove of *Juniperus macropoda* in Hemis Shukpa, Ladakh, India, 3,700 m, consists of trees that are more than a thousand years old. They are protected by religion and must not be cut down, but unfortunately the grove is grazed. This completely prevents the growth of young trees, so that the extinction of the "last forest of Ladakh" is inevitable.

observed in winter-dry desert areas with sparse and unreliable summer precipitation, where summer germinating annuals play a similar role. The occurrence of more than one of our indicators will help in deciding whether climate or overgrazing or both lead to the dominance of annuals in a particular area.

Often unpalatability and colonizing ability, particularly biennial growth or strong vegetative propagation in perennials, are combined. Additionally, fruits or seeds with devices that promote a distribution by animals, particularly hooks, indicate that the plant species concerned is adapted to dispersal by grazing animals.

COMPARISON WITH OTHER AREAS. If the vegetation of two adjacent valleys is different, though the "natural" environmental circumstances seem to be similar, a different intensity of human impact may be the cause. Besides the indicators mentioned, there are many other, sometimes minor, traces of human activities, like fireplaces, partly burned vegetation and soil, fuel stocks and roofs covered with plant materials, single tree stumps in a

Figure 3.8. These old and mighty trees are an impressive experience in a semi-desert landscape.

Figure 3.9. *Microula tibetica*, a biennial rosette plant with small, light blue flowers (resembling those of forget-me-nots); diameter, 10–20 cm.

treeless landscape, droppings and tracks of domestic animals, browsed forms of plants, and others, that can be observed by the "vegetation detective."

3.2. FORESTS (AND SCRUB) AND THEIR SUBSTITUTE COMMUNITIES

The slopes at altitudes between 3,000 and 4,000 meters in southern Tibet and the more humid part of the Inner Himalaya are covered by more or less dense forests. This original, "natural" state is also called *primary vegetation*. Species of the genera *Abies, Picea, Cedrus, Juniperus, Cupressus, Pinus, Betula,* and *Quercus* are dominants, depending on the geographical location, altitude, exposure, and other environmental parameters. In this chapter we have selected the forests of birch and those of juniper as examples. The vegetation prevailing after the forest has been removed by human beings is called *secondary*. The *tertiary* vegetation is the vegetation that prevails after heavy use or other causes have destroyed the secondary vegetation.

3.2.1. BIRCH FORESTS

3.2.1.1. Primary ("Natural") Vegetation

A characteristic tree at the upper limit of arborescent vegetation in the Himalayo-Tibetan region is the Himalayan Birch (*Betula utilis*), with its relatively short trunk and widely spreading treetop (Figs. 3.10 and 3.11). As it grows in high altitudes, frequently on slopes with unstable soils or under high snow pressure, it often shows "saber" growth. The distribution of this birch reaches from Nanga Parbat throughout the Himalayas to Yunnan. In the Outer Himalaya it occurs in a mixed forest at all exposures. In the drier Inner Himalaya pure stands of it are encountered on north-facing (shady) slopes. It grows at altitudes between 3,500 meters (locally on avalanche tracks down to 2,500 meters) and 4,200 meters.

The typical birch forests consist of three layers: birch trees are the main components; scattered conifers (fir, sometimes pine), singly or in small groups, rise above the birches; and the underlayer may be formed by shrubs, particularly evergreen *Rhododendron* species. (The importance of this famous genus increases from west to east: in the dry areas of the western or Inner Himalaya the dwarf shrub *R. lepidotum* plays this role; in the more humid regions *R. campanulatum*, a tall shrub with big leaves, becomes important; and in the eastern parts of the distribution range of

Figure 3.10. One of the last birch forests, Langtang, Nepal, 3,800 m, near the border with Tibet.

Figure 3.11. A look into the inside of this forest shows its characteristic growth form, with the long beards of lichens and an undergrowth of rhododendrons.

Betula utilis, the big-leaved rhododendrons finally dominate over the birches and gradually replace them.

Although the appearance of the birch forests could indicate a quite humid climate, actually the minimal precipitation under which birch forests are found is very low (200 mm, with a maximum of 2,000 mm). This is because these forests do not rely on the monsoon rains, but are supplied by snowmelt. There is a very intimate relation between snow and the Himalayan Birch. The typical bent growth of *Betula utilis* is caused by snow pressure. In avalanche tracks these birches grow like "Krummholz",[5] lying partly on the ground. The scientific name *Betula utilis* refers to the variety of uses of this plant. A striking feature of the Himalayan Birch is the outer bark, which consists of numerous paperlike layers exfoliating in broad horizontal rolls or belts. In former times it was a substitute for paper, mainly for the inscription of religious texts. Even today this "paper" is used as a packaging material (especially for butter), for roof construction, for making umbrella covers, as a bandage, as cigarette paper, to line the inside of the hookah tube, for wrapping amulets, and for various religious ceremonies. The wood is used for various building purposes; bridges are made of the branches, and the trees are lopped for fodder. But the main use of the birches is for fuel. Birch forests are the main source of firewood in the areas of their distribution – more accurately, it must be said that they have been. They have been used for this purpose, or been burned to be replaced by pastures, to such an extent that they have been practically eliminated from vast parts of their former area of distribution.

A common way of harvesting the wood is a kind of lopping. The whole tree is not cut, but only some of the branches; then in the following year another part is cut, until only the trunk is left, which is cut last of all (Fig. 3.12). This method has the advantage that the forest is more or less living (rather less than more) for several years while it delivers wood. The Himalayan Birch with its low trunk and spreading branches makes this style of cutting wood easy.

3.2.1.2. Secondary Vegetation Resulting from Extensive Human Impact

TALL RHODODENDRON SHRUBBERY. As mentioned above, tall (2–3 meters in height) rhododendrons are widespread as an undergrowth in *Betula* forests. As their wood is not considered as valuable for firewood as

---

[5] This German *terminus technicus*, usually not translated, indicates "crooked wood." It means a prostrate growth of bushes, or trees growing like bushes. On mountain slopes the twigs are often pointing downward; in this way they offer little obstacle to snow and avalanches.

Figure 3.12. As everywhere in the world, protection by law (in this case that covering a national park) is only theoretical, so long as there is no understanding by the people. This photo illustrates the piece-by-piece tree-cutting typical of the Himalayas. The forest is gradually getting lighter and the transition to secondary vegetation is smooth and more or less unnoticed.

that of birch, rhododendrons are the second choice and are only used after all the birches have gone to the fireplaces. After the removal of the competing trees the shrubs have a better growth. Thus in some places, high, dense, nearly impenetrable thickets of rhododendron are the remnants of former, probably rather open birch forests with rhododendron undergrowth (Fig. 3.13). More commonly the only remnants are some shrubs or a small rhododendron copse in the middle of a pasture (Figs. 3.14 and 3.15).

DWARF-SHRUB HEATH. On slopes with shallow soils a dense cover of 30–50 cm–high dwarf shrubs may mark the areas of former birch coverage (Fig. 3.16). Under "natural" conditions these dwarf shrubs either form their own

Figure 3.13. The result of the development started in Figure 3.12: secondary vegetation after the removal of all birches for campfires, a scrub of rhododendron and salix on the north-facing slopes in the Annapurna Sanctuary, Nepal, 3,500 m. After the cutting of the rhododendrons, the willows will remain; after they too have finally been burned, a dwarf shrub heath dominated by *Cassiope* (see Fig. 3.18) will be the last stage.

narrow belt above the (birch) tree-line or are restricted to particularly exposed sites within the subalpine forests, sites with shallow soils or poor snow cover where the competition with trees and other high-growing plants is not so severe. The anthropogenous removal of the subalpine forests has now enabled these dwarf shrubs to cover much larger areas than before.

This is a general pattern that can be observed on many mountains of the world: The alpine zone is lowered by the influence of cutting and burning and the grazing pressure of livestock (Fig. 3.17).[6] Vegetation that under natural conditions is restricted to extreme sites of very limited extension around the tree border can now cover huge areas at lower altitudes. This phenomenon is not restricted to dwarf-shrub heath but is also evident with other vegetation types, like tall herbs (primary on areas with extremely long-lasting snow cover, where trees have difficulties in growing because of

---

[6] The alpine zone is the area above the tree-line. The subalpine zone is the area of the highest forest belt under natural conditions.

Figure 3.14. Alpine dairy farm, South Dolpo, Nepal, 3,800 m, with Mt. Dhaulaghiri in the background. That there is practically no woody growth reminds us that the whole area was originally covered by birch forest. (See also Fig. 3.15.)

Figure 3.15. A single rhododendron bush amidst a flowering meadow is a witness of the potential natural vegetation.

Figure 3.16. Dwarf-shrub heath in southern Tibet near Nyalam, c. 3,800 m. Now a pasture, it probably replaced a birch forest.

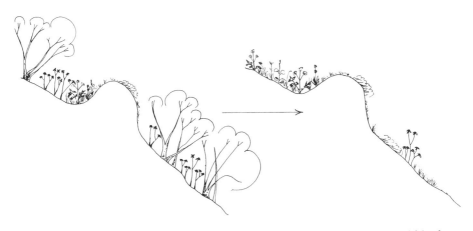

Figure 3.17. The vegetation above the tree-line and that of extreme sites within the subalpine forest spreads out after the removal of the trees and dominates the secondary landscape formed by (extensive) human impact.

Figure 3.18. *Cassiope tetragona*, a heather, about 20 cm high, with quadrangular twigs and bell-shaped white flowers. It is one of the components of dwarf-shrub heath, particularly on sites with deep and long-lasting snow cover.

the short vegetation period), the carpets of polygonum mentioned below (primary on very exposed ridges in arid regions), and alpine grassland.

Besides rhododendrons, other members of the heather family (Ericaceae) may also occur and form dense dwarf-shrub heath under special conditions; so does *Cassiope tetragona* (Fig. 3.18) under rather humid conditions and high snow cover (northern slopes) and *Gaultheria* on very shallow soils.

TALL-HERB VEGETATION. Tall herbs are high-growing but herbaceous perennials.[7] In the warm or cool temperate forest belts of the mountains of Eurasia they may form a conspicuous, characteristic dense vegetation on sites that are well supplied with water and nutrients but where a dense forest cover is prevented by a high and long-lasting snow cover or frequent avalanches.[8] Another characteristic feature of the tall-herb vegetation besides its herbaceous but luxuriant growth (up to 2.5 meters in the

---

[7] "Herbaceous" means nonwoody.

[8] W. Holzner and E. Hübl, *Vergleich zwischen Flora und Vegetation der subalpin-alpinen Stufe in den japanischen Alpen und in den Alpen Europas*, Veröff. Geobot. Inst. ETH, Stiftung Rübel, 98 (Zürich, 1988).

Himalayas, up to 5 meters in the Caucasus) is the predominance of plants with ways of protecting themselves from the teeth of large herbivores. These include mechanical protective structures like spines, but the most common means among tall herbs is poisonous and/or strong-tasting parts. Without these, the lush, soft, giant plants would be a preferred food for big mammals.[9] Thus lists of tall-herb communities read like the inventory of a chemist's shop.

Particularly important components of tall-herb thickets are members of the carrot family (Umbelliferae), particularly of the genera *Heracleum* and *Angelica* (Fig. 3.19); acrid-tasting or highly toxic genera of the buttercup family (Ranunculaceae, particularly *Aconitum*); the dock family (Polygonaceae), with their high content of oxalates; the daisy family (Compositae), including the liver-toxic genus *Senecio* and the thistles; and bitter plants of the Gentianaceae.

The tall herbs either already grow in the undergrowth of the birch forests and remain after the removal of the trees or grow adjacent to the forests on parts of the slope with extreme snow coverage and spread from there into the former forest soil. This development is furthered by the circumstance that already wet slopes get even wetter after the removal of the forest.

POLYGONUM CARPET. With the increasing aridity of the climate toward the west and north, the birch comes to its climatic limit, the aridity border of birch forests. The undergrowth of the forests here is low and poor in species. *Polygonum affine* (Fig. 3.20) grows on exposed sites above the "natural" tree-line, but also below on the horizontal faces of rocks and similar places. When the forests are removed the pink carpets may cover whole slopes, an impressive sight when they are flowering.

3.2.1.3. Tertiary Vegetation Resulting from Intensive Human Impact

The above-mentioned secondary vegetation types are sensitive to high grazing pressure and are replaced by lower and/or more open vegetation. Regular grazing promotes species with high regenerative capacity like grasses or rosette plants and creeping plants or plants with creeping shoots.[10] If the intensity or frequency of browsing exceeds the capacity for survival of even these plants, the result is bare soil that is colonized by plants

[9] M. Kriechbaum, *Die Verbreitung von Heil- und Giftpflanzen in verschiedenen Vegetationsformationen rund um den Attersee*, Diplomarbeit an der Universität für Bodenkultur (Wien, 1987).

[10] Rosette plants are those whose ground leaves are pressed close to the soil, avoiding being snapped up by browsing animals.

Figure 3.19. A giant member of the famous genus *Angelica*, nearly 3 m high, towering here above tall-herb vegetation replacing a fir forest (Nyalam, southern Tibet, c. 3,300 m).

Figure 3.20. With creeping underground stems, the knot-grass *Polygonum affine* may cover large areas. The conspicuous red carpets of the flowers, borne on an erect stem (6–30 cm long), may tinge whole slopes, particularly those facing north in late summer. Because of its decorative value it has been introduced as an ornamental in gardens in Great Britain and elsewhere.

that have not only colonizing abilities but also characteristics making them unpalatable.

In tall-herb communities a selection of plants with high regenerative capacity can lead to monocultures of giant polygonums. Under stronger impact a heterogeneous vegetation may develop with open patches of soil colonized by annual "stopgaps" of the genus *Impatiens*.

After the removal of rhododendron shrubbery under moderate grazing, a species-rich, about knee-high, meadowlike vegetation may develop, which we call *flower meadows*, because it is dominated not by grasses but by herbs. It is one of the most beautiful plant communities of the Himalayas, during the summer flowering a dream of fragile blooms in many sizes, forms, and colors often covered by sparkling drops of water from dew, mist, or rain. It is the flora of the fabulous "valley of flowers," polygonums small, pink- or white-spiked, white *Anaphalis*, very showy red or yellow species of the genus *Pedicularis*, and dark-red potentillas – all famous, like several other plants of

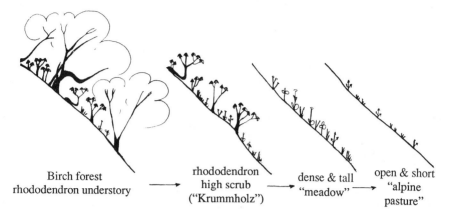

Birch forest
rhododendron understory   →   rhododendron
high scrub
("Krummholz")   →   dense & tall
"meadow"   →   open & short
"alpine
pasture"

Figure 3.21. This schematic example shows the gradual degradation of vegetation under medium-growth conditions. After the trees are cut, the undergrowth remains. The increasing impact of humans and their livestock (cutting, burning, grazing) will result in dense and tall flower meadows and finally in open and short alpine pastures.

this formation that have been gathered by "plant hunters" and brought to our gardens.

High grazing pressure may, under the favorable growth conditions of birch habitats, lead to *alpine pastures,* which not only in their appearance but also in the composition of plant genera and even species resemble their European or Caucasian counterparts.

Summarizing, we may say that very different vegetation types can replace the birch forests. Which of the secondary or tertiary vegetation types develop depends on climatic and soil conditions and on the quality and quantity of human impact (Figs. 3.21 and 3.22). After the removal of the forest, either the undergrowth remains more or less unchanged or adjacent vegetation of higher or more extreme habitats is able to spread. With increasing human impact the proportion of pioneer plants increases. With increasing grazing pressure the proportion of unpalatable species increases.

3.2.2. JUNIPER FORESTS AND JUNIPER SCRUB

3.2.2.1. Primary Vegetation

In dry areas and on southern slopes junipers form the *upper timberline,* often facing birches on the opposite slopes. In those parts of the Inner Himalaya

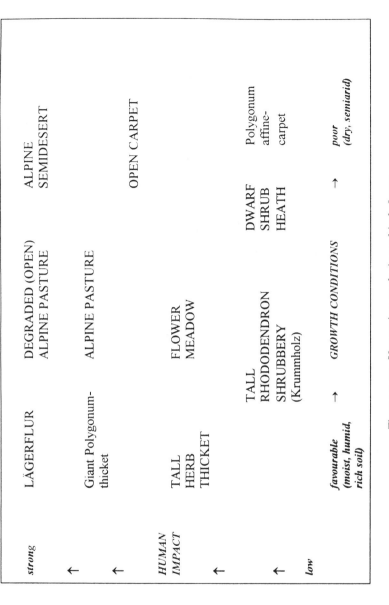

Figure 3.22. Vegetation replacing a birch forest.

Figure 3.23. Open *Cupressus torulosa* forest on a southwest-facing slope above the lower timberline (left) at Marpha, Nepal, 2,700 m. At the upper timberline birches can be seen indistinctly in the clouds. The bottom of the valley is too dry for tree growth but the irrigated land around the village makes afforestation possible (lower left corner). At the right side the dissolving of the lower timberline as a result of heavy human impact can be observed.

where, because of the dry climate, tree growth is near the subsistence level, the upper parts of the slopes may be better supplied with precipitation than the lower parts or the valley bottom. Under such conditions we find a *lower timberline*, which could be called the "aridity timberline," in contrast to the "frost timberline" higher up (Fig. 3.23).[11]

Several species of *Juniperus* can become trees. Taxonomy and systematics of *Juniperus* are still inadequate, so that we will not offer scientific names here.[12] Juniper forests occur at elevations between 2,000 meters and 4,000–4,200 meters; the upper limit is only reached on southern slopes, with a precipitation range of 300 mm to 800 mm per year.

[11] Temperature is just one of the limiting factors for tree growth here. Another one connected with it is the shortness of the vegetation period. The whole picture is too complex to be discussed here. See W. Tranquillini, *Physiological Ecology of the Alpine Timberline*, Ecol. Studies 31 (Berlin: Springer Verlag, 1979).

[12] We are very grateful to B. Dickoré, Göttingen, for discussions on this and other problems and his generous aid in the difficult work of identifying our specimens.

The term "steppe forest" gives an idea of this forest type: open, light, dry, the underlayer consisting of shrubs and steppe plants. More dense forests are found only in a protected location. At the lower and upper tree border *Juniperus* forests are replaced by different forms of steppe.[13] Particularly at the lower line a gradual transition from open forest to steppe can be imagined but seldom actually observed, because the human impact has been very strong here. Therefore it is also nearly impossible to find out the potential (or, in a sense, "natural") distribution range of juniper forest. Stands are known from northeastern Afghanistan, the Nanga Parbat area, the inner valleys of the northwestern Himalaya, the Karakorum, western and central Nepal, and the upper Tsangpo valley. The large areas in between have been obviously completely cleared of forests by human beings. Single trees in the vicinity of sacred places, which have been protected for religious reasons and are isolated occurrences, for example in Ladakh (see Figs. 3.7 and 3.8) and Spiti, indicate that the large geographical gaps of this forest zone were once smaller, or did not exist at all. At least they point to a more extensive distribution of juniper forests in former times, if one does not insist that these "holy groves" were planted long ago, which would be difficult to prove. We assume that they are the last remnants of the former vegetation cover; hints from the stories of the people of the region, from literature, and from our own observations support that assumption.

There are several reasons why juniper forests are the most damaged of all forest types. Vegetation in arid regions, particularly trees, is very sensitive to human interventions; trees growing already at their aridity limit are even more so. The quality of juniper as firewood is high; it burns quickly and with a peculiar smell. If people can choose, they prefer juniper. As already mentioned, the usual way to get fuelwood is not to cut down whole trees but to lop off small branches. Juniper wood is also used for building purposes, and is valued for making the supports of water channels because the heartwood is nearly imperishable in moist soils. *Shug-pa*[14] is used for religious purposes, the branches being collected for incense. In addition, the twigs are used for straw in stables.

It is difficult to estimate the extent of the practice of burning juniper forests to increase pasture area. The inflammable junipers are easily destroyed. Because they have a limited capacity to regenerate through seeding, they do not revegetate from burned sites easily.[15] A practice commonly

[13] Or semi-deserts, which are probably anthropogenous; see section 3.2.2.3.
[14] The Tibetan name for juniper.
[15] D. Schmidt-Vogt, *High Altitude Forests in the Jugal Himalaya (Eastern Central Nepal): Forest types & Human impact*, Geoecological Research, vol. 6 (Stuttgart: Franz Steiner, 1990).

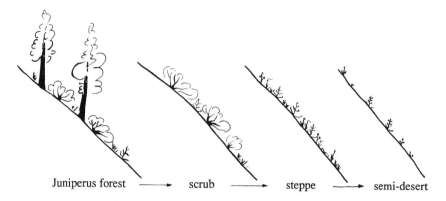

Juniperus forest ⟶ scrub ⟶ steppe ⟶ semi-desert

Figure 3.24. If the juniper trees are cut, a more or less species-rich shrubbery (depending on soil and climate conditions) replaces the forest vegetation in this example. The next step, after removal of all woody species, will be a steppe vegetation, which under high grazing pressure will degrade to pasture steppes and semi-deserts.

seen is the cutting of pieces from the lower part of the trunk for bonfires; the base of the trunk is used as a wind shelter for these fires, thus damaging the tree twofold. Even big trees will be killed sooner or later by such a treatment.

3.2.2.2. Secondary Vegetation

The general pattern of succession is about the same as with the birch forests (section 3.2.1.2). After the trees have been removed, the underlayer remains. If scrub remains, the extent to which it, too, is later exhausted depends on the availability of other sources of fuel. The next step in degradation (tertiary vegetation) is the result of the high intensity of pasturing usually imposed on the sites of the former juniper stands (Figs. 3.24 and 3.25).

SPECIES-RICH SHRUBBERY AND THORN SCRUB. In the semi-dry areas, shrubs of the genera *Cotoneaster, Rosa, Ribes, Potentilla, Berberis, Lonicera, Caragana, Rhamnus,* dwarf *Juniperus* (*J. squamata,* a small shrub, as well as tree junipers degraded to shrubs through cutting), and *Ephedra* (Fig. 3.26) dominate the undergrowth of *Juniperus* forests. Many of them are spiny; their spines protect them from being grazed and usually keep them from being gathered for firewood. Nevertheless, if there are no other sources of firewood, even the most prickly plants are cut. They are also used for roof construction and for building effective fences. Therefore the secondary

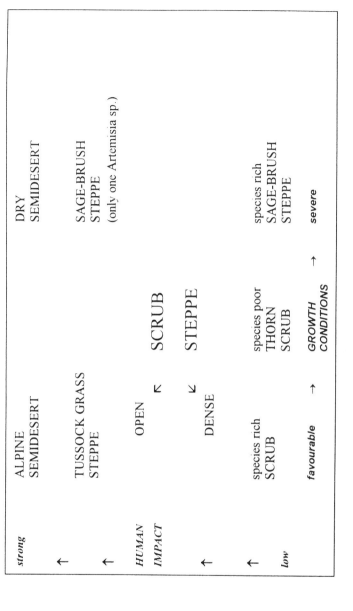

Figure 3.25. Vegetation replacing a juniper forest.

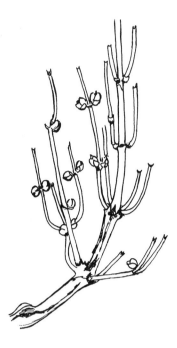

Figure 3.26. *Ephedra intermedia* resembles the well-known plant called Horsetail, but it is not related to it. It is a rigid, woody shrub without leaves – or more exactly, the leaves have been reduced to membranous two-lobed sheaths. This is an adaptation to dry areas. Assimilation is the duty of the green, articulated branches, which are browsed by herbivores, particularly by goats. The plants become conspicuous in autumn, when the orange-red, berrylike fruits bring shining dots of color into the desertlike landscape. The sweet fruits are in some places eaten by humans, though they contain alkaloids; together with the fruits of other species of the genus, they have been used as an important source of medicine, as by the Chinese, for the last 5,000 years. The woody parts of the plant are used as fuel.

scrub vegetation is rarely dense. The most widespread type is a steppe-like vegetation with scattered bushes, which look sheared because the tips of the twigs are browsed.

Depending on the geographical region and the local situation, more or less of the species of the above-mentioned shrub genera are involved. So we have, for instance, a scrub very rich in woody species in southern Tibet and a rather rich one in Spiti. The most widespread scrubs, consisting practically only of one species, particularly of the genera *Juniperus* and *Caragana*, are probably either primary vegetation or secondary thorn-scrub vegetation (in the case of *Caragana*) replacing overgrazed *Stipa* steppe.

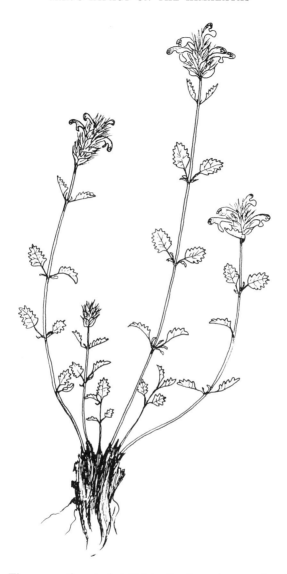

Figure 3.27. The aromatic catmint *Nepeta discolor*, a low-growing (c. 10–15 cm) perennial with spreading growth, is a very common plant of semi-deserts. The name comes from the leaves, which are grayish-green above but densely white and woolly beneath; the flowers are whitish or pale purple.

WORMWOOD STEPPE. In dry areas juniper forests are characterized by steppe undergrowth. These steppe types are composed of various grasses (*Stipa*, *Piptatherum*, *Festuca*, etc.) and herbs, many of them very aromatic ones like *Thymus* and *Nepeta* (Fig. 3.27), both members of the Labiatae.

Figure 3.28. The sad remains of a former *Juniperus* (steppe) forest near Darcha, Lahul, India, 3,700 m.

Various species of *Artemisia* (wormwood) also play an important role in this vegetation. If there are no shading and competition by junipers anymore, because the trees have been removed, *Artemisia* can expand – as long as the intervention of livestock leaves its mark on the vegetation. One example from a valley in Lahul illustrates this development (Figs. 3.28–3.31). The juniper forest has been almost completely removed here; only some tree stumps give evidence of the former vegetation. Substitute vegetation types cover the slopes. Over large areas two species of *Artemisia* (Fig. 3.31)

Figure 3.29. At this site, the secondary vegetation after juniper steppe forest was a wormwood steppe. This in turn has degenerated from heavy overuse into a semi-desert (tertiary vegetation) that is very poor in plant species and where colonizing plants play an important role.

dominate alternately, representing two stages of degradation of the vegetation. Originally both belonged to the undergrowth of juniper steppe forest, *A. brevifolia* (covered with gray hairs) growing on the drier ridges and *A. salsoloides* (shining green) restricted to the somewhat wetter habitats. Livestock disdains *A. salsoloides* but feeds on *A. brevifolia* if nothing better is available. The much more woody *A. brevifolia* is also taken for fuel, while *A.*

Figure 3.30. Detail of the landscape depicted in Fig. 3.29. The wormwood *Artemisia salsoloides* predominates because it is of no use as firewood and is despised by goats and sheep; other plants, like *Artemisia brevifolia* (in the foreground), are heavily browsed and are also reduced by being gathered for firewood.

salsoloides is not touched. In the long term, the result will be that the species untouched by people and their livestock will displace the other.

Steppe forest has been changed to a species-rich wormwood steppe mainly by removal of the trees. The steppe is again on the way to becoming a semi-desert with sparse and poor vegetation because of reckless overuse as pasture and for fuel collection. Desertification is proceeding.

TUSSOCK GRASS STEPPE. In some areas where conifer forests, or more commonly *Juniperus* Krummholz, have been removed, grass tussocks of various sizes replace them and form a characteristic "nature-like" steppe landscape (Figs. 3.32 and 3.33).

3.2.2.3. Tertiary Vegetation

If the woody species are removed and the vegetation is exposed to a high grazing pressure, the degradation to pasture steppes and further to semi-deserts and deserts is only a matter of time. The pastoral semi-deserts can be distinguished from the steppes by their extremely low vegetation cover (less than 20 percent) composed mainly of more or less unpalatable (e.g.,

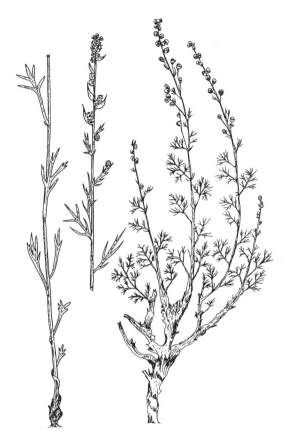

Figure 3.31. To the right, the "useful" *Artemisia brevifolia*, a low-growing (c. 15–40 cm) but heavily branched woody shrub (firewood) with pale gray to almost white, hairy, tender, aromatic leaves; to the left, the despised (but therefore successful) *A. salsoloides*, perennial but woody only at the base, with tough green leaves of disagreeable odor.

thistles, some *Artemisia* species, and *Nepeta* species, particularly *N. discolor*; see Fig. 3.27) or poisonous species and pioneer plants.

3.3. STEPPES AND SEMI-DESERTS

3.3.1. STEPPES ARE "NATURAL PASTURES"

In section 3.2.2.2 we have seen that steppes and semi-deserts and, under extreme human impact, even deserts can result from destruction of forests.

Figure 3.32. A dense *Juniperus* Krummholz (see footnote 5) covers the south-facing slope near the Xixabangma, southern Tibet, at about 4,500 m. The vegetation and landscape of this remote corner are practically untouched by humans; the nomads graze their yaks only on the flatter parts of the valleys.

Human beings act as a kind of amplifier of climatic severity, mainly aridity. When forests grow near their aridity limit, the lower tree border, the distances between the trees increase and the forest ground vegetation is formed more and more by plant species that are sensitive to shade but adapted to drought. The forest gradually changes to a steppe forest or forest steppe. If the trees are taken out, the ground vegetation does not change much – just the steppe remains.[16] Nevertheless many of the steppes and semi-deserts of Central Asia and the Tibetan Himalaya are natural ones, considering the climatic conditions of today, which do not permit the growth of trees except along the rivers (Fig. 3.34).

Steppes have always been a habitat and feeding basis for herds of large mammals. Therefore steppe vegetation has always been pasture, even before people and their livestock appeared. Adaptations to dry or poor grow-

---

[16] Thus it is even more difficult and hypothetical to establish the potential lower (aridity) tree-line than the upper (altitudinal) one.

Figure 3.33. A tussock steppe of wild, perennial oats grows as secondary vegetation after the burning of *Juniperus* Krummholz on the south-facing slopes of Annapurna Sanctuary, Nepal.

ing conditions also often prevent destruction by big herbivores. Such adaptations include the folding or rolling of the leaves of grasses so that leaf area is reduced; strong mechanical structures preventing wilting; the loss of leaves in the dry season with the ends of the twigs or the midrib remaining as thorns; a dense cover of hairs; and a high content of ethereal oils in the grasses, cooling the leaves on hot days but also deterring hungry animals. Because of the strong grazing pressure that must have always been imposed on the "natural" steppes of Tibet by wild yaks, wild sheep, kyang,[17] gazelles, and antelopes, the flora must have always been rich in plants adapted to grazing and trampling. These include plants with a high *regeneration ability* and rate, enabling them to grow up again quickly after having been browsed or otherwise damaged (typical example: many grasses). Other plants have low-growing green parts, trying to cower as close as possible to the ground and especially to keep the vegetation points near or under the ground level. Common and typical examples are plants with rosette leaves pressed to the ground surface, like daisies and plantains. Still other grazing-adapted steppe plants have hard tissues or spiny organs

[17] Wild donkeys.

Figure 3.34. A *Stipa* steppe at about 5,000 m on the north side of Mount Xixabangma, a vegetation maintained by nomadic pastoralism based on the principle of sustainability.

for *mechanical protection*, while others are poisonous or strong-tasting for *chemical protection*.

3.3.2. OVERGRAZING AND DESERTIFICATION

If large herbivores have used up a vegetation to such an extent that the palatable plants have become rare, the animals react by moving to another site; if this is not possible they react with reduced fertility and/or increased mortality. This allows the vegetation to re-create itself and we have the typical ecological equilibrium balanced by periodic fluctuations in both directions. If changes in the densities of herbivores are caused by other factors than the supply of edible plant biomass, the center of the equilibrium is a shifting one. If the animals are hunted so heavily that their reproductive capacity cannot replace the losses, or if their numbers are reduced by diseases or catastrophes, the vegetation will change in one direction, probably becoming higher and denser. Conversely, if the original, "natural" density of large herbivores is "artificially" raised, or if the free roaming of the animals is restricted by human herders, this impact can be detected in the composition of the plant cover, and in particular the proportion of plants with mechanical or chemical protective adaptations will increase. The result is the typical landscape with an abundance of "pasture weeds" that we find in many dry areas of the world. See Figures 3.35–3.39.

If the grazing pressure increases too fast, the vegetation cannot follow in the way described above. The same happens if the grazing pressure is kept too high over a period of several years, so that the fluctuating equilibrium described above changes to a process running in one direction. The result is an increasing ratio of open soil to vegetation, or of pioneer plants[18] to steppe plants, accompanied by a drying up of the soil and erosion by wind and water – in short by *desertification.*

As already mentioned, this process can be studied under moderate grazing intensities on the sites where the animals tend to stay for a longer time than on the rest of the pasture, or in places where they are herded overnight. *Overgrazing* occurs when the same process takes place on the whole grazing area and reaches an extent that makes the regrowth of vegetation impossible within the span of several human generations. Constant overgrazing results in desertification and is an *irreversible* process, at least under the climatic conditions of the Inner Himalaya and Tibet and seen in terms of human dimensions of time.[19]

Regarding the use of vegetation as a grazing area for livestock, two extreme modes can be distinguished.

SUSTAINABILITY. The grazing pressure per area is never raised above the point where irreversible degradation of the pasture starts. From an ecological point of view, we could say that the wild herbivores have been gradually, cautiously, and partially replaced by domesticated ones, so that the "natural" equilibrium has been kept. This way of herding livestock requires much understanding of, or perhaps rather a feeling for, animals, vegetation, and the optimal rhythm of grazing and wandering, a knowledge

---

[18] "Pioneer plants" are species with special abilities to recolonize soil opened by natural disasters or human activities. Various combinations of special features like short life-span, high seed output, long-living seeds that wait for centuries in the soil for their next chance, seed dispersal over far distances, and many others, make this possible. (See also section 3.1 and H. G. Baker and G. L. Stebbins, eds., *The Genetics of Colonizing Species* (New York: Academic Press, 1965).

[19] Of course, the equilibrium "is not destroyed or lost." But the amplitude of the fluctuation back to a former state of vegetation becomes so large that it is beyond our patience or possibility to wait for it.

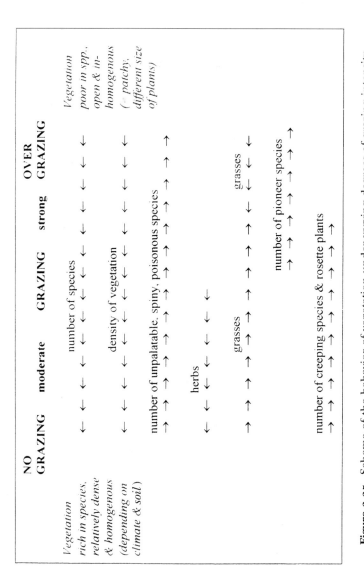

Figure 3.35. Scheme of the behavior of vegetation under varying degrees of grazing intensity.

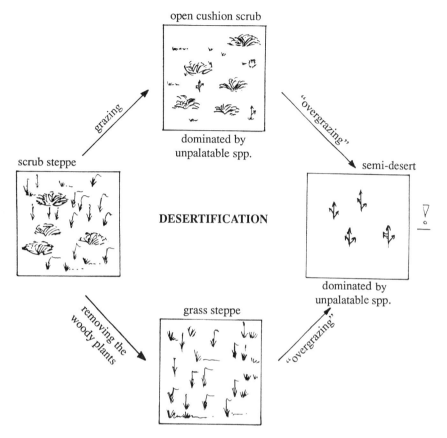

Figure 3.36. Depending on the kind and intensity of human impact, open cushion-scrub or grass steppe and finally semi-deserts will result. Grazing animals reduce the palatable species, particularly the grasses, and prune the scrubs to cushion form (or even poorer remains). If, on the contrary, the shrubs are burned and the grazing pressure is only moderate, grasses may dominate, conveying the impression of a natural steppe.

that has been handed down from one generation to the next since time immemorial.

In the parts of Tibet we have seen, we have formed the impression that until recently this mode was the predominating one, and that the vegetation seems to be in a kind of "natural" state, from a plant ecologist's point of view (Fig 3.34). Desertification could only be observed locally near camping grounds and settlements. This view is also supported by the fact that pastoralism is still the main livelihood there

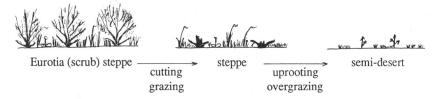

Eurotia (scrub) steppe $\longrightarrow$ steppe $\longrightarrow$ semi-desert
cutting   uprooting
grazing   overgrazing

Figure 3.37. Facing a semi-desert, one can hardly imagine that tall shrubs covered the soil in former times. In Tibet there are still large areas with *Eurotia* (scrub) steppe, whereas in other dry areas, e.g. in Ladakh, only some stumps, browsed or hacked to the ground (as in the middle drawing), remain for some time.

Figure 3.38. A short but rather dense *Kobresia pygmaea* steppe near the Nam-Tso lake, Tibet, at about 4,600 m. The whitish patches are carpets of a creeping Edelweiss species (probably *Leontopodium nanum*) that invades patches of soil opened by "natural" agents or livestock. The pikas (*Ochotona*) in the foreground also prefer open soil for their digging activities. High densities of these rodents may indicate the beginning of the destruction of vegetation, in which they later play their part too. The pikas may also indicate the recent overhunting of their predators (wolves, jackals, birds of prey) by humans.

Figure 3.39. A desertlike landscape and vegetation near the Nam-Tso lake, Tibet, a result of the overuse of *Kobresia pygmaea* steppe (see Fig. 3.38). The vegetation consists of the last patches of this vegetation, some unpalatable species or plants that avoid being grazed in other ways, e.g. the rosette-forming *Phlomis rotata*, and colonizers of bare soil like annual *Corydalis* species or *Microula tibetica* (Fig. 3.9). The reasons for the degradation may have been overgrazing and/or the cutting of the peaty turf for heating or for wall construction.

at the present time. Use of the natural resources in the mode described next would have led to the complete destruction of the pastures, because under the extreme environmental conditions of Tibet the vegetation is highly sensitive.

Our observations confirm the picture drawn by ethnologists who spent more than a year with the nomads of the Changtang and have described their strict regulations governing the amount of livestock per family and the duration and intensity of grazing.[20]

EXPLOITATION. In this mode the number of animals per area and the intensity and duration of grazing are not determined by "ecological" criteria but by social or political ones, or there are few or no rules at all. The results are overgrazing and desertification, which can be observed in nearly all the marginal areas of Tibet. The reasons for this phenomenon are not clear to us. Is the accessibility of many areas of Zangskar, Lahul, and Spiti to the herdsmen of the south responsible, or is it the influence of Hinduism and Islam, or is it both, or quite another reason? In recent decades exploitation of pastures has also occurred in areas where refugees from Tibet have taken shelter with their animals and in border areas where ancient seasonal migration routes of the herdsmen have been blocked for political reasons. The same has happened to the last remains of juniper forests in the Solu Khumbu.[21]

In Tibet the Chinese policy of trying to push up agricultural production has endangered the old system of sustainable pasture yields. According to official statistics the number of livestock has been multiplied. Because of the vast areas over which the nomads are moving, without roads and settlements, it is difficult to obtain exact information, like headcounts of livestock. Official statistics from the early period of Communist influence claim a doubling of livestock between 1959 and 1976.[22] Data from a case study at Nam-Tso suggest an increase in livestock of 25 percent between 1981 and 1988.[23] The results will be disastrous, because the destroyed pastures will never recover under the harsh climate of the Changtang, at least not in a time span that counts for human beings. We ourselves could observe indi-

[20] M. C. Goldstein and C. M. Beall, *Nomads of Western Tibet: The Survival of a Way of Life* (Hong Kong: Odyssey, 1990).

[21] C. von Fürer-Haimendorf, *The Sherpas Transformed: Social Change in a Buddhist Society of Nepal* (New Delhi: Sterling, 1984).

[22] I. Epstein, *Tibet Transformed* (Beijing: New World Press, 1983).

[23] G. E. Clarke, "China's Reforms of Tibet and Their Effects on Pastoralism," *Kailash* 14.1–2 (1988).

Figure 3.40. Wormwood steppe (*Artemisia persica*) at 3,800 m northwest of Leh, Ladakh.

cations of recent overgrazing, for instance in the vegetation in areas north of Lhasa where model pasture cooperatives have been established.

3.3.3. OTHER MODES OF HUMAN IMPACT BESIDES GRAZING LIVESTOCK

In addition to grazing there are other human impacts on steppe vegetation that may be at least locally of equal or even greater importance. In steppes with species that are somewhat woody at least at the base, like thornbrushes and wormwoods, the wood is cut and used as fuel and for fencing and roof coverings. The first result may be an "unnatural," heterogeneous pattern of woody growth that looks odd to the ecologist's eye. The complete removal of the shrubs will result in the development of a new vegetation type, for instance a grass steppe. This is particularly the case when the shrubs are chopped; sometimes they are burned first to dry them out and reduce their prickliness.

Some shrubs – we have witnessed this ourselves with *Artemisia persica* – are uprooted. This leads to a gradual thinning of this perennial, and thus slow-

Figure 3.41. *Artemisia* harvest near Yangtang, Ladakh, 3,700 m. After rain the wormwood can easily be pulled out of the soil. The practice of uprooting the plants prevents a regeneration. The result is various-sized patches of ground bare of any woody plant. Without knowledge of this mode of gathering firewood, it would be impossible for the ecologist to explain this vegetation pattern.

growing, species from the vegetation. The human impact can be only traced by holes in the soil (see Figs. 3.40–3.42).

The activities of burning, chopping, and especially uprooting clear the ground and make room for pioneer species. The regular occurrence of the biennial thistle *Cousinia thomsonii* at high densities together with other pioneer plants in the pastoral steppes in the valley of Spiti, for instance, could be interpreted as an indicator that harvesting brushes has a stronger impact on the vegetation there than grazing (Fig. 3.43).

Road construction in High Asia means destruction of the woody vegetation in a more or less broad belt along the roads, because huge masses of fuel for fires are needed. For this purpose even the shabbiest, prickliest woody growth is eradicated, for example *Caragana versicolor* in Ladakh (Fig. 3.44).

In the nonforested areas of Tibet the Chinese population (including the military and hundreds of thousands of workers employed in road construction living in tents) has increased the demand for heating fuel enormously. Chinese prefer wood to animal dung, the traditional Tibetan fuel. On the one hand this leads to the exploitation of the forests of southern and

Figure 3.42. *Artemisia* harvest near Yangtang, Ladakh, 3,700 m. Large amounts of this bush are carried home, stored on the roof, and used as fuel.

southwestern Tibet in addition to the export of wood to China, on the other to the removal of shrubs from areas where they had been preserved through cautious utilization by the inhabitants up till today.

3.3.4. "HUMMOCK PASTURES" AND THE CUTTING OF PEAT

Another way of destroying vegetation is a traditional one, restricted in its extent to certain relatively small areas: the removal of raw humus (or peat) together with vegetation for building walls and to provide combustible

Figure 3.43. Semi-desert dominated by *Cousinia thomsonii* in Spiti, c. 3,600m, a probably biennial pioneer thistle. We consider it an indicator for frequent soil disturbance resulting from the uprooting of small shrubs to obtain material for heating and roofs. Nowadays the landscape is practically free of woody growth.

material. This happens particularly with vegetation built up by species of *Kobresia* ("grasslike" Cyperaceae, Fig. 3.47), a very important genus with several species dominating the steppes at high altitudes. The dense turf formed by small species, or the thick tussocks of bigger ones, is cut, and the tussocks, after they have been dried by burning the vegetation, are used for the purposes mentioned. (See Figs. 3.45–3.49.)

On soils that are waterlogged at least in spring – a phenomenon that is quite common in Tibet, despite the climatic aridity, because permafrost makes the substrate impermeable – tussock bogs grow and peat may be formed. Intensive short-grazing of the tussocks dries them out, and leads finally to the death of the tussock-forming *Kobresia*. Slow decomposition of the peat surface is the result; mineral soil develops and the vegetation changes. The tussocks decompose gradually and partially, and become transformed into rounded hummocks – a small-scale but characteristic landscape that is often seen. This development is speeded up when nomads set fire to the dry tussocks. As the subsequent collection of peat is done on a small scale only and in an occasional, and arbitrary, way – not well organized as in Western Europe – patterns of vegetation and landscape result whose origin is difficult to discover.

Figure 3.44. Along the road from Leh to Manali the effects of road construction on the vegetation can be observed. Large amounts of fuel are needed for heating the asphalt, warming the tents of the workers, and cooking. Any woody plant is taken – in this case *Caragana versicolor*, an extremely prickly shrub (the dark patches in the background).

If the peat has been removed completely, as will be the case around campsites or along traveling routes used for millennia, the remains of the soil will soon be blown away and the vegetation (under the harsh climatic conditions prevailing here) will practically never recover (at least as seen from the narrow viewpoint of the human life-span). Only travelers who can "read" the landscape will guess that the resulting desertlike, barren landscape might once have borne a short but dense mat of dwarf *Kobresia*, providing tough but nutritious grazing for wild or domestic herbivores, or a lush, high tussock bog.

SUMMARY

The vegetation and landscape of the Inner and the Tibetan Himalaya have been strongly influenced by humans and their livestock, even in seemingly untouched, remote areas. Nowadays by far the greatest part of the vegeta-

Figure 3.45. "Hummock pasture" near Hemis Shukpa, Ladakh, 3,700 m. The bumpy vegetation is the result of overgrazing on a *Kobresia schoenoides* tussock bog. After the death of the tussock, the hills are invaded by other plants resistant to grazing. Animals trampling the soft soil between the tougher hummocks have contributed to the strange structure of the surface (resembling soil formations caused by frost). The north-facing slope to the left might long ago have borne a juniper forest. The sad remains seen nowadays can be called pastoral semi-desert. The sharp line at the bottom of the slope is a path running on the dry edge of the former bog and passing three stupas. The wall protects a small area used for the production of hay.

tion cover is formed by substitute communities. Pastoralism and the collection of firewood have been the main activities by which people have changed vegetation and landscape since time immemorial. In an arid climate plants and vegetation are particularly sensitive to human interventions. Where the conditions for tree growth are near the margins of their ecological amplitude, forests are easily destroyed. If this destruction is followed by intensive grazing, the destruction of the forests becomes an irreversible process.

The observation of traces (or indicators) in the vegetation of the more or less treeless landscapes of today, together with some evidence from literature and from native witnesses, supports the theory that huge areas in the Inner Himalaya originally bore forests but have been deforested by humans and their livestock.

Figure 3.46. Undisturbed *Kobresia* tussock on the foot of a mountain in Zangskar, 4,300 m, protected by large rocks blocking the access for animals.

Near the upper timberline, the vegetation originally covering extreme and therefore treeless sites spreads after the removal of the forests and dominates the secondary landscape. Near the lower timberline, steppe remains after the removal of the trees of the former steppe forest.

Extreme grazing pressure leads in an irreversible process toward a vegetation of low density dominated by unpalatable "pasture weeds" and plants adapted to the colonization of open soil, and further to soil erosion and changes in the water balance and mesoclimate of an area. This process,

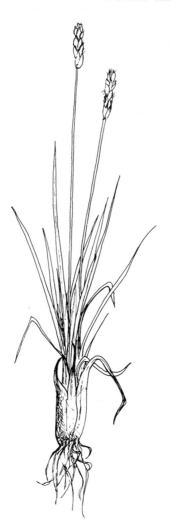

Figure 3.47. The grasslike or rushlike rigid leaves of *Kobresia schoenoides* are tough, but nevertheless a delicacy for domestic herbivores. The plant may form dense and high tussocks, consisting of the incompletely decomposed old parts of the plants. The species has a broad range of distribution and a wide ecological amplitude. Its size depends on growth conditions but can reach more than 50 cm in favorable places.

called desertification, can be observed in many areas of the Inner Himalaya.

In some other areas, particularly in Tibet, until recently a comparatively cautious use of the natural resources preserved a vegetation that could be called "natural." The original principle of sustainability observed since

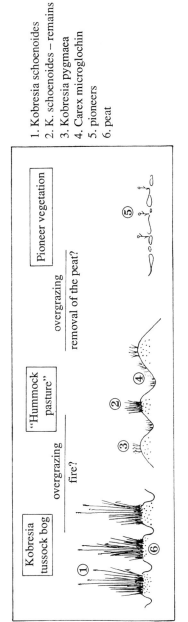

1. Kobresia schoenoides
2. K. schoenoides – remains
3. Kobresia pygmaea
4. Carex microglochin
5. pioneers
6. peat

Kobresia tussock bog → overgrazing fire? → "Hummock pasture" → overgrazing removal of the peat? → Pioneer vegetation

Figure 3.48. Degradation of *Kobresia* tussock bogs. Overgrazing and burning kills the *Kobresia* tussocks: "hummock pastures" are the result. The peat may be hacked away and used for buildings or as a fuel (the dry peat that is exposed to the air is naturally mineralized). Nothing remains but pioneer vegetation or wind-blown stone pavement.

Figure 3.49. A degraded state of *Kobresia* vegetation in Zangskar, 4,400 m. The hummocks have been burned and the peat has been partly removed.

ancient times in the pastoral system and the use of animal dung instead of wood as fuel has been partly replaced nowadays by the imported "philosophy of exploitation" to raise production. This system is obviously not adapted to the limited resources of High Asia and has led at least locally to an irreversible destruction of vegetation and pastures (desertification).

EPILOGUE

As already mentioned, our main source of information was the analysis of the actual vegetation in its present state. Information about the situation in the past was scarce. Therefore several of our extrapolations, in space and in time, and some of our conclusions are hypothetical. For some of them it will probably be impossible to find any reliable evidence at all. Nevertheless we think that our hypotheses can serve as a stimulus for discussion and further research.

One striking result only briefly touched on in this chapter is the observation that the intensity of human impact cannot be simply a function of population density, which seems to vary independently. The relatively densely populated Spiti valley has a much better-preserved vegetation, for instance, than adjacent areas with no permanent population at all. There are striking differences between the Changtang and other cold and arid areas as far as the preservation of natural vegetation is concerned, and there are similar differences in other areas that we could not explain.

One of the arguments frequently used to explain such phenomena is that the cultural background of the people, particularly their religion, is the main cause for the varying attitudes toward nature. In our region evidence for this opinion could be found: the Hindu-dominated population of the Outer Himalaya recklessly destroys the forests, and the huge herds of goats and sheep of the Muslim herdsmen in the east are the main agent in the accelerated process of desertification, while the Buddhist nomads of Tibet seem to treat the vegetation much more cautiously, as mentioned in section 3.3.2. But, as always with such generalizations and rough simplifications, more detailed investigations reveal a picture showing that things are more complicated, and for each of the above-mentioned examples evidence proving the contrary can be produced. The careful use of the vegetation by Tibetan nomads mentioned in section 3.3.2, for instance, is very likely much older than the history of Buddhism in that area and was probably induced by the barren landscape and harsh climate, which obliged the people to use the vegetation economically. The devastation of areas bordering the Tibetan Himalaya to the south and east by herdsmen may be the result of the lack of consideration of people coming in from other areas in summertime and taking out of the foreign country as much as possible. The lack of social integration together with a detailed regulation of pasture rights might also be responsible. The beginning of the destruction of the ancient pastoral system in Tibet and its result, the devastation of the pastures and the landscape, can be seen as an example of the negative impact of an imported system of agriculture not adapted to the environmental conditions of the new area and an imported philosophy of production growth, alien to the thinking of the nomads.

Another point is that the topic of our research has been the investigation of the impact of humans on nature, but we are aware that this is a one-sided point of view, because the human–nature relationship is a mutual one. An increasing scarcity of fodder, for instance, must be responded to by a reduction of livestock per area, a migration to other areas, or even a shifting to other possible ways of making a living if famines are not to follow. Changes induced by human beings change their own life conditions, both the physical as well as the psychical ones: people influence the landscape and the landscape has effects on them.

This is the point where we have to stop and leave the topic to scholars of other disciplines,[24] but we hope that our narrowly focused perceptions can serve as pieces in a puzzle providing an overall picture of the mutual relationships between people and their environment in the dry parts of the Himalayas.

---

[24] One view that we could not introduce or discuss at all, because our historical knowledge is insufficient, is the probable impact of migration of large groups of people, particularly military or civil expeditions. As we have explained, if a sensitive vegetation, like forests but also *Kobresia pygmea* turf-steppe, has been destroyed once, it is very likely that it is destroyed practically forever, because recovering, if it happens at all, will take centuries.

4

The Villagers' View of Environmental History in Yunnan Province

NICHOLAS K. MENZIES

Scholars in the field of environmental history face some unique challenges regarding their source material and research methodologies. The topic itself is, to a large extent, a recent construct. Although it has long been recognized that human activities affect the environment and are themselves shaped by environmental constraints,[1] it is only in the last thirty to forty years that scholars and historians have turned their attention to tracing the paths along which these interactions have played themselves out.[2] There is ample evidence that most societies have recognized the fact of linkages between themselves and their environment, but the analysis of these linkages and the attempt to follow their evolution over time is an activity that is still breaking new ground.

One of the most difficult challenges is the scarcity of reliable historical data. Treaties and charters are available to the political historian, while contracts and account books assist the economic historian. Until quite recently, few forest inventories, species counts, or air-quality indices existed to provide the raw information on which environmental history could be written. In the case of changes in vegetation or forest cover, the problem is compounded by geography. Over the centuries, changing patterns of settlement and land use have confined most remaining forest cover to remote

---

[1] See C. J. Glacken, *Traces on the Rhodian Shore: Nature and Culture in Western Thought* (Berkeley: University of California Press, 1967); George Perkins Marsh, *Man and Nature; or, Physical Geography as Transformed by Human Action* (1864. Reprinted, Cambridge, Mass.: Belknap Press, 1965).

[2] See William Cronon, *Changes in the Land: Indians, Colonists, and the Ecology of New England* (New York: Hill and Wang, 1983); Antoni Mączak and William N. Parker, *Natural Resources in European History, A Conference Report*, Resources for the Future Research Paper R-13 (Washington, D.C., 1978); James C. Malin, *History and Ecology: Studies of the Grassland*, ed. Robert P. Swierenga (Lincoln: University of Nebraska Press, 1984).

regions, far from political and economic centers. Difficult access to
these resources was one factor that preserved them, but being located so
far from the center, they were usually of little concern to government administrators, whose bureaucratic procedures and records constitute one of the richest sources of documentation for historians. These
peripheral areas often maintained distinct cultural identities poorly integrated into the mainstream of the country; they rarely produced prolific
writers, whose work might have provided alternative sources of historical
data.

China is no exception to this pattern. By the mid-nineteenth century, the
most extensive remaining tracts of forest were located in the northeast
(Manchuria), the subtropical and tropical southwest (Yunnan 云南,
Guangxi 广西, Hainan 海南), and some isolated "internal frontier" areas
such as the Qinling Mountains 秦岭 between Shaanxi 陕西, Hubei 湖北,
and Sichuan 四川. Extensive clearance and commercial logging had begun
in the northeast by the second half of the nineteenth century.[3] The Qinling
Mountains remained subject to periodic episodes of logging depending on
demand for timber in the cities of the Guanzhong 关中 region and the
developing industries of Hubei and the lower Yangzi River.[4] In the south,
meanwhile, pressure on resources increased with continuing migration
from other parts of the country, indigenous population growth, and
increasing demand for crops, timber, and other products from the border
regions.

While the overall picture of shrinking forest area is clear – if only from
the physical evidence of forest land converted to agricultural land and
degraded, eroded landscapes – the combination of ecological, social, and
economic forces that acted on forests and led to this process of change is
less well understood. For southwestern China in particular, primary documentary evidence is scarce and little of it is directly concerned with environmental issues.[5] To further complicate the task, most of the extant sources
were written by Han Chinese officials in a region where the primary resource users were members of some twenty to thirty ethnic groups, fre-

[3] Wang Xiliang 王希亮, "Jindai Dongbei Senlin Kaifa Shi Hua" 今代东北森林开发史话 [His-
torical words on the opening of the forests of the Northeast in modern times], *Heilongjiang
Linye* 11 (1983).
[4] N. K. Menzies, "Sources of Demand and Cycles of Logging in Pre-modern China," in
John Dargavel and Richard Tucker, ed., *Changing Pacific Forests: Historical Perspectives on the
Forest Economy of the Pacific Basin*, Proceedings of a conference sponsored by the Forest
History Society and IUFRO Forest History Group (Durham, N.C.; Forest History Society,
1992).
[5] Claudine Lombard Salmon, *Un example d'acculturation chinoise: la Province du Guizhou au
XVIIIème siècle* (Paris: École Française d'Extrême-Orient, 1972).

quently in conflict with the central authorities or with Han settlers. Piecing together a history of environmental change with these materials is an arduous and delicate task that could be facilitated by the cautious addition of any alternative sources of information. This chapter proposes the application of some field methodologies that have been devised recently to assist rural development workers develop a deeper understanding of the communities they work with. It describes some of these methodologies and gives some examples, mostly from Yunnan province, of the different perspectives such information can bring to the description and analysis of environmental change.

Before examining the use of nonconventional sources of historical data on environmental change, it is worth briefly reviewing the range of material that is already widely used, with some consideration of where additional information could yield useful insights.

Gazetteers are still probably the richest and most widely used source of information on local geography, land use, population change, and some of the other key variables affecting the environment. Their usefulness varies depending on the extent to which their compilers and editors were interested in nonagricultural land, often a problem given the traditional administrators' concern with agriculture as the bedrock of Chinese society. Another source, more commonly found in border areas than in the more settled agricultural lowlands, is the manuals prepared in connection with military campaigns against rebel forces, which describe the geography, economy, and land-use systems in otherwise poorly known outposts of the empire.[6] Official and semi-official publications such as these can be supplemented by scattered travelogues, including works by Western missionaries, botanists, and others who began to find their way into the interior by the second half of the nineteenth century.[7]

Local archives and collections of customary law and local histories in minority languages are two potential sources of data that remain largely unexplored, partly due to continuing restrictions on research in China and

---

[6] Yan Ruyu 嚴如熠. *San sheng bianfang beilan* 三省邊防備覽 [*A complete survey of the border defence in the Three Provinces*] (1806. Reprinted as *Chuan Shaan E bianfang ji* 川陜鄂邊防集, Nanchang: Guomindang Military Commission, 1934); Zhongguo Di Yi Lishi Dang'an Guan, Zhongguo Renmin Daxue Qing Shi Yanjiu Suo, and Guizhou Sheng Dang'an Guan 中国第一历史档案馆、中国人民大学清史研究所贵州省档案馆 *Qing dai qian qi Miao min qiyi dang'an shiliao* 清代前期苗民起义档案史料 [Historical materials on the Miao rebellions of the early Qing Dynasty] (Beijing: Guang Ming Ribao CBS, 1987).

[7] Père Armand David, *Abbé David's Diary*, trans. and ed. Helen M. Fox (Cambridge, Mass.: Harvard University Press, 1949); Robert Fortune, *A Residence among the Chinese: Inland, on the Coast, and at Sea* (London: John Murray, 1857); E. H. Wilson, *A Naturalist in Western China*, vols. 1 & 2 (London: Methuen, 1913).

partly due to practical problems of collection and translation. It is generally believed that local archives contain valuable collections of contracts and legal documents that could shed much light on how resources were managed at the local level. Work done with accessible archives in Baxian 巴縣 and Huizhou 徽州 suggests that this is indeed the case.[8] As for materials in minority languages, work is under way in some provinces to publish transcribed and translated collections from those ethnic groups that have a written script,[9] but there does not appear to be a systematic program for such work. Some basic ethnographic materials are also becoming available now with the publication of reports prepared by land-reform groups sent into minority areas in the early 1950s (the *Zhongguo shaoshu minzu shehui lishi diaocha ziliao* series).

Careful use of all these sources can produce a valuable account of environmental change in one area or region, and a few such works have appeared in English over the last few years.[10] The disadvantage, however, is that by their nature, these written documentary sources provide information about changes in the environment as seen by their authors. These local officials were usually more concerned with the governance of their district than with the changing landscapes at the margins of the productive agricultural lands for which they were responsible. With some exceptions, formulaic descriptions of wilderness and lists of trees drawn directly from the classics are more common than informed descriptions of vegetation and of the utilization of natural resources.

Even where credible descriptions are available, contemporary research in fields as different as forest management and rural sociology has shown that the priorities and concerns of resource-dependent communities or individuals may be quite different from those of officials or others respon-

[8] Madeline Zelin, "The Rights of Tenants in Mid-Qing Sichuan: A Study of Land-related Lawsuits in the Baxian Archives," *Journal of Asian Studies* 45.3, pp. 499–526; Joseph McDermott, *The Huizhou Documents – A Key to the Socio-economic History of Late Imperial China* (forthcoming).

[9] In the southwest, this means mostly the Dai, Naxi, Tibetans, and some branches of the many groups that have been classified together as the Yi. See, for example, Gao Lishi 高立士, *Dai zu yan yu* 傣族谚语 [*Proverbs of the Dai nationality*] (Chengdu: Sichuan Renmin CBS, 1990). See also Yunnan Minjian Wenxue Jicheng Bianji Ban Gong Shi 云南民间大学集编辑办公室, *Yunnan yi zu geyao jicheng* 云南彝族歌谣集成 [*Collected songs of the Yi nationality in Yunnan*] (Kunming: Yunnan Minzu CBS, 1985).

[10] Evelyn Sakakida Rawski, "Agricultural Development in the Han River Highlands," *Ch'ing-shih Wen-t'i* 3.4 (1975), pp. 63–81; Peter C. Perdue, *Exhausting the Earth: State and Peasant in Hunan, 1500–1850* (Cambridge, Mass.: Harvard University Press, 1987); R. Keith Schoppa, *Xiang Lake: Nine Centuries of Chinese Life* (New Haven: Yale University Press, 1989).

sible for representing the interests of the state or society at large in the protection or utilization of resources. Different perception of the "rational" use of forest resources frequently lead to the confrontation and conflict between forest management authorities and communities that are recurring themes in forest history.[11] Recently, well-publicized confrontations such as the "Chipko" movement in India, in which groups of village women hugged trees to protect them from loggers, have focused attention on the origins of these conflicts and the search for a solution. Part of the "problem" appears to be disagreement in the very definition of the "problem." Officials see environmental degradation causing flooding and siltation of water channels. Mountain farmers face daily choices about management of forests, rivers, and soils that have a critical bearing on the struggle for survival. A fuller understanding of the dynamics driving environmental change demands a better understanding of the priorities, concerns, and perceptions of all the different actors involved in taking decisions about the utilization of natural resources.

It is in this context that this chapter makes some tentative suggestions as to how to include the voices of farmers and villagers who depend on the natural resources surrounding them in the documentation of environmental change. The examples used come from exploratory work in Yunnan testing some of these methods. They shed some light on the history of this region, but the hope is that they will also suggest how the view from the village gives added depth to our understanding of the sources of pressure on the environment and the ways in which different communities have chosen to respond to them.

ORAL HISTORY

The first source of information is not particularly unconventional, although it does not appear to have been tapped as widely as it might be for environmental history. Oral histories are commonly used to document the

---

[11] For studies of such conflicts in Asia see Nancy Lee Peluso, *Rich Forests, Poor People: Resource Control and Resistance in Java* (Berkeley: University of California Press, 1991), on Indonesia; Ramachandra Guha, *The Unquiet Woods: Ecological Change and Peasant Resistance in the Himalaya* (Berkeley: University of California Press, 1989), on India; and Nicholas Menzies and Nancy Peluso, "Rights of Access to Upland Forest Resources in Southwest China," *Journal of World Forest Resource Management* 6.1 (1992), pp. 1–20, on China. Louise Fortmann, "Locality and Custom: Non-aboriginal Claims to Customary Usufructuary Rights as a Source of Rural Protest," *Journal of Rural Studies* 6.2 (1990), pp. 195–208, documents similar conflicts over forest management on national forests in the western United States.

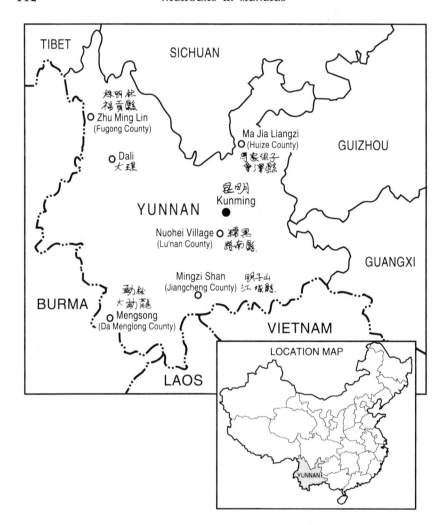

Map 4.1. Yunnan province, with places mentioned in the text.

roles of individuals in historical events, to document the movements of migratory people, and to add a human dimension to otherwise dry chronologies.

In the context of Yunnan, migration has been a key feature of settlement patterns and consequently of resource utilization. Many ethnic groups therefore attach great importance to the history of their journey to their present settlements, in some cases associating it with a spiritual quest. Shamans in Yao 瑤 villages along China's borders with Vietnam and Laos use a painted scroll as a visual prompt during ceremonial recitations of the community's history. Many of the scrolls were destroyed in the Cultural Revolution, but some survive with inscriptions in Chinese characters dating them to the Guangxu 光緒 period or earlier. The accounts of the migration do not refer to the condition of the environment through which the people traveled, but they give evidence for the length of time of the present settlement, and when linked to personal histories given by elderly residents, they can give a sense of the changing scarcity of different elements of the vegetation since settlement.

The semi-structured approach to interviewing, which is a hallmark of the methodology of oral history, lends itself to creative links with what little material evidence is available. One of the few and rare sources of primary evidence for village-level forest management is inscriptions, usually on stone stelae, extending protection to the forests under village control with lists of regulations and fines to be imposed on offenders. The texts of some stelae seen by this author in Guizhou 貴州, Yunnan, and Hu'nan provinces all tell a similar story of pristine forest degraded by a few greedy officials or threatened with destruction. The villagers recognized the importance of forests as a source of regular water flows and protection from flooding and so took action to protect them. The stelae usually commemorate the decision and list the rules and regulations adopted by the community to protect the forest.

The value of these stelae goes beyond the contents of the texts inscribed on them. As a symbol of action taken by the whole community, a stela can provide a focal point for interviews with village elders and other leaders who are often still responsible for implementing the regulations. Discussions that begin with questions about the origin of the stela quickly develop into a welcome opportunity to tell the story of the village and its forest. In the village of Nuohei 糯黑, Lu'nan 路南 county, in central Yunnan, an inscription dated the third year of the Republic (1914) lists the measures taken by the village to protect its forest. The stela stands in the courtyard of a large house that now acts as a center for community activities such as funeral and wedding banquets and meetings of the village committee. Most of the households in Nuohei are Sani 薩尼, an ethnic group classified as a branch of the Yi 彝 who have retained a strong sense of community identity. Being invited to a funeral banquet by a village elder, a former Party secretary, I found it possible to begin to ask about the stela, and to continue with a discussion about the history of Sani settlement in the area. The former Party secretary then offered to introduce me to the oldest resident in the village, who remembered some of the myths and legends about the sacred forest known as the Mizhi Lin 密枝林 and about individual sacred trees.

This conversation led in a natural fashion to reminiscences about changes in tree and forest cover, and finally the former Party secretary took me to his home, where he allowed me to look briefly at a document in the care of his family. Dated Qianlong 18 (1753), what remained of the badly damaged document showed it to be a land title granting rights to the land now occupied by Nuohei village to the newly arrived settlers.[12] The data confirmed, to an uncanny degree, the oral history of the village, which the earlier informant had said was settled "twelve generations ago" (or 240 years at an estimated twenty years per generation).

As the story of Nuohei was pieced together, it appeared that some twelve generations ago, a group of Black Yi (known through ethnographic sources to be one of the main branches of the Yi) moved into the area from Dali 大理 in northern Yunnan. The area apparently was well forested at the time. The Han name on the Qianlong documents is "Tengzi Xiao" 藤子哨 ("Rattan Lookout"), and the present Sani name of the village, "Nuohei," means "the Monkeys' Pool." There may well have been pressure on the forest since the earliest days of settlement. Modern Nuohei village is built around a pool at the foot of a south-facing hill. Between the village and the hill is a patch of forest no more than about one hectare in size, known as the sacred forest, "Mizhi Lin." Mizhi-Shima 什嫣[13] was the name of a young girl who was tending goats with a group of friends when a sudden hailstorm killed all the goats and goatherds except for Mizhi, who had taken shelter with her flock in a nearby patch of forest. It would be dangerous to read too much into this folk tale, but it suggests that from a very early time there was probably more open grassland than forestland.

The next period for which the oral history of Nuohei gives information is the early years of this century. The population of the village has increased from some 600 to over 1,000 during the eighty-five-year life-span of the oldest villager, whose grandfather "remembered seeing monkeys by the water," although the informant himself had not seen them. We may therefore assume that the monkeys' forest habitat disappeared approximately one hundred years ago. Some fifty to sixty years ago (during the childhood of the sixty-three-year-old former Party secretary) there were already no more trees left except on the hills to the south of the village. Most of the flat land that is now in maize fields belonged to an absentee landlord from the county town of Lu'nan who grew opium. By the mid-1950s land had been

---

[12] Since it was already a special privilege to be able to see the document, it would not have been appropriate to request further permission to copy the text.

[13] "Shima" is a diminutive added to the names of young Sani women.

redistributed and opium growing halted. The subsequent environmental history mirrors that of many other villages in the region, where remaining forest was devastated during the Great Leap Forward in 1959, most of the timber being used for mine props in the nearby Jiashan 圭山 coalmine. Since then, most villagers concur that there has been a slow recovery of forest and that there are now more trees than during the 1950s – though it is not clear whether this is due to the many officially sponsored reforestation campaigns or simply due to natural regeneration following the Great Leap Forward and to the village's recovery of some control over its own resources.[14]

I should note that this "history" is merely an initial sketch based on a brief visit of just two full days to Nuohei. It is not a carefully researched oral history, nor does it pretend to the depth of systematic interpretation that an anthropologist might bring, for example, to the story of the migration from Dali or the Mizhi-Shima legend. The various elements of the story would, of course need to be confirmed independently through other informants in the village. The uncanny match between the land-title document and the twelve generations of settlers, and the story of Mizhi-Shima, are two important questions that would need to be checked with other sources. The reconstructed story does, however, indicate the rich potential of combining information from oral history with existing evidence from inscriptions and documents and from observations of the existing environment.

METHODOLOGIES FROM
RURAL DEVELOPMENT

Rural development strategies have moved in the last twenty to thirty years from prescriptive, "top-down" planning and introduction of technologies to an approach that seeks first to understand the constraints faced by farmers and then to forge a partnership between villager, technical specialists, government agencies, and other concerned parties to design programs that correspond to the specific conditions faced by different communities. The participatory model of development is conceptually appealing but very difficult to implement. The challenge of opening channels of communica-

---

[14] For a more detailed history of changes in forest cover and utilization in a Yunnan village since 1949, also based largely on oral history, see Menzies and Peluso, "Rights of Access."

tion between the different worlds of the farmer, the technician, and the government official has generated a minor academic growth industry in "village assessment methodologies." Two of the more commonly used terms are "Rapid Rural Assessment" (RRA) or "Participatory Rural Assessment" (PRA). While both terms have their supporters and detractors, they share a commitment to interdisciplinary methodologies, semi-structured interviewing techniques, and the direct involvement of farmers in formulating and defining critical issues rather than acting simply as sources of information for specialists.[15]

The desire to involve farmers as active participants in the process of village assessment has led to the design of a number of simple but powerful graphic techniques to illustrate farmers' perceptions of their lives and agricultural system, as well as visual aids that encourage farmers to rank their preferences for crops, trees, livestock or other factors affecting their livelihoods. While these tools were not designed to collect historical data on the environment, the principle of using a visual or material aid to elicit farmers' reactions and perceptions promises to be a valuable complement to the more familiar methods of oral history outlined above. It is important to recognize that village assessment methodologies make no claim to constituting a formal, fixed body of knowledge. New techniques and ideas are constantly being devised and tested around the world, in fields as diverse as women's health care in North Africa, the management of grazing land in Mongolia, and irrigation management in Gujarat. Environmental history is perhaps a new area in which to apply these techniques, but in a field where conventional documentation is scarce, the villagers' view is likely at least to offer some insights into the dynamics of environmental change and contribute to the formulation of some new hypotheses to be tested with whatever other information is available.

A rough classification of the different components of "village assessment methodologies" might divide them into interviewing techniques and graphic or visual tools. Social scientists have long accepted that different interview formats will yield different kinds of information; this knowledge

---

[15] For more detailed information on Rapid Rural Assessment methodologies, see Khon Kaen University, *Proceedings of the 1985 International Conference on Rapid Rural Appraisal* (Khon Kaen, Thailand: Rural Systems Research and Farming Systems Research Projects, University of Khon Kaen, 1987); for Participatory Rural Assessment, see D'Arcy Davis Case, *The Community's Toolbox: The Idea, Methods and Tools for Participatory Assessment, Monitoring and Evaluation in Community Forestry*, Community Forestry Field Manual 2 (Rome: FAO, 1990). Robert Chambers, *Rural Appraisal: Rapid, Relaxed and Participatory* (Brighton, England: Institute of Development Studies, University of Sussex, 1992), is a useful review of both methodologies.

is deliberately applied in conducting individual interviews, focus group interviews (with small groups sharing a common characteristic such as gender, age, or occupation), and unstructured group interviews. The literature on this subject is extensive, so I will pursue it no further than to note that in the case of the preliminary environmental history of Nuohei village, different interview formats would be one way to flesh out the initial framework provided by the present two informants.

Of more interest here are the possibilities suggested by the use of visual tools. These tools are designed to involve informants in preparing graphic representations of time or space (especially with respect to land use) and relating them to village activities and social structures. The process is deliberately informal and usually involves the participation of several people, so there is considerable potential for inviting participants to compare the present situation with the past, piecing together a picture of the scale and pace of changes in the local environment. While the value of these methods to environmental history is only beginning to be explored, I will describe some experiments with the use of "time-lines" and participatory mapping that have already produced interesting results. I will also briefly note how one other visual tool, the agricultural calendar, could be useful, although it has not yet been tested as a source of historical data.

TIME-LINES AND CALENDARS

One simple technique that has immediate relevance to environmental history is the use of the time-line (Fig. 4.1). This involves drawing a vertical line, then noting important dates and events on it as they are referred to in interviews or conversations. One end of the line represents the most distant past that can be remembered, the other end represents the present. As a visual device, the time-line often encourages informants to try to fill in gaps by recalling more events. It is particularly effective when small groups of elderly people are building the time-line together, since the discussion generated during the activity serves to pool several sources of information and to check its accuracy.[16]

The simplicity of the time-line lends itself to refinements that can help build a fuller picture of how certain aspects of village life have changed, including its natural environment. Many researchers use the space on

---

[16] The paper presented at the conference by William Coaldrake presents a time-line for the history of the town of Matsushiro. The discussion here, however, refers to time-lines drawn by villagers themselves together with an outside researcher or "facilitator."

(Changes in village land use)	(Date)	(Political events)
Land clearance.	18th–19th century	
	1949	Liberation.
	1954	Mutual help groups set up. (*Hu zhu zu* 互助組)
Land belongs to the collective.	1955	Beginnings of the cooperatives.
Electricity reaches the village.	1956	"Higher level
Road construction.		cooperative" started.
Deforestation to provide fuel for collective canteens.	1958	Great Leap Forward People's Commune established.
Water channeled in through the Xiang Yang 向陽 aqueduct.	1972	
Increases in grain yields.		
Paddy fields and rainfed fields are allocated and managed differently.	1980	Implementation of the household responsibility system for agricultural land.
	1984	Implementation of
	1985	the family planning policy.
Repairs to the water storage tank.	1989	

Figure 4.1. Time-line for Ma Jia Liangzi village (Nagu township, Huize county, Yunnan province).

either side of the line for different forms of inforamtion. Dates and specific events might be listed on one side, for example, while the other is used to note processes of change or ecological observations ("Sacred forest still had monkeys"; "Trees cut for steel furnaces in the Great Leap Forward"). The line is also a convenient way to note and to order scattered comments in different interviews that are related to a date or an event or that have some other element of time involved.

The time-line in Figure 4.2 is a composite based on many interviews conducted since the winter of 1990 in the Hani 哈尼 (Akha) village of Mengsong 孟松 in Xishuangbanna 西雙版納. As the researcher became more familiar with the community, he was able to identify village elders who could recite detailed genealogies going back sixty generations, which told of a migration out of the Yuanyang 元阳 area of the Red River basin toward Xishuangbanna approximately one thousand years ago. The present site was settled 250 years ago, and it is at this point that the more detailed time-line begins. This particular study is now adding information about crops, cropping patterns, and marketing to the time-line in order to get a better understanding of the impact of economic changes on land-use patterns in this formerly forested border area.

Twelve generations ago, first group of Hani migrants settles in forested land in Mengsong.	(c. 240 yrs ago)
Other Hani groups migrate in from Burma.	1934–35
Another Hani group arrives bringing pear seedlings.	1942–45
Liberation.	1950
Land reform and prohibition of opium cultivation.	1952
The Great Leap Forward and establishment of the People's Commune.	1958
Road built into Mengsong.	1965
Dam construction.	1967
Hydroelectric power station built.	1969
Large expansion of swidden fields.	1979
155 households separated from original village to form a new administrative village.	1980
Revival of traditional resource management rules (such as protection for the Sangpabawa community forest).	1981
13 Lahu households migrate in from Burma.	
New policy on zoning of forest land.	1982
New policy defining swidden and forest land.	1984
Mining begins in the area.	1985
Rattan furniture mill begins operations.	1986
Death of traditional village chief (the "zoema").	1991
Border trade and local market boom.	1992

Figure 4.2. Time-line for Mengsong village (Da Meng Long county, Xishuangbanna Dai Autonomous prefecture). Adapted with permission from an original by Xu Jianchu, Pei Shengji, and Chen Sanyang, 徐建初、裴盛基、陈三羊. *From Subsistence to a Market-oriented System and its Impacts on Agroecosystem Biodiversity: The Case of the Hani (Akha) Swidden Cultivator in Mengsong, Southwest China*, paper presented at the 1993 SUAN workshop on biodiversity in swidden agricultural systems.

In identifying appropriate new technologies or other interventions to promote rural development, it is important to know whether or not they will fit into existing patterns of labor allocation and the timing of agricultural work. A graphic representation of the farmers' agricultural calendar is one aid that has been developed to do this (see Figs. 4.3 and 4.4). The calendar represents the various activities of a household over the year. It can be refined by varying the thickness of the bars representing specific tasks to indicate the intensity of labor needed or by subdividing the horizontal rows of the calendar to draw separate calendars for different members of the household (men, women, children, grandparents). It should be possible, for example, to ask older people as they draw up a calendar whether there have been changes in labor allocation since they were young.

Type of land	1	2	3	4	5	6	7	8	9	10	11	12
Home-garden and in the home	Plant vegetables. House repairs. Collect grass for animal bedding.	Feed pigs and livestock (done by women and children) *(bar spans months 2–12)*					Not enough food: carry subsidized rice up from Fugong (carried in baskets)	Short of cash. Earn money by doing odd jobs in village and in Fugong)				Plant potatoes
Rainfed land *(di)*	Weeding. Plant potatoes.	Hoeing *(spans 2–3)*		Plant maize. Men: plough. Women: spread fertilizer	Weeding and hoeing earth into mounds around potatoes (a)	Clear around maize stalks (keeps rats away). Keep weeding and hoeing further uphill	Dig up potatoes from upper fields. (Only a few days' work at a time) *(spans 7–8)*		Harvest maize (stored in a shed by the fields) (b)	Carry maize home *(spans 10–11)*; Plant rapeseed		
Paddy fields *(tian)*		Hoeing. Repair irrigation channels. *(spans 2–3)*		Prepare rice seedlings (when the rain starts). Men: plough. Women: apply fertilizer.	Transplant rice seedlings. Women: do the planting. Men: manage water flows with children.	Maintenance *(yang tian)* Mostly weeding *(spans 6–8)*				Harvest rice. Threshing on bamboo mats in the fields (c)	Plant rapeseed or potatoes (see note (d) below for decision rules about winter crops). *(spans 11–12)*	
Freehold mountain *(ziliu shan)*		Cut firewood and carry it home. (Everyone in the family participates).										
Collective mountain *(jiti shan)*		Plant *huang lian* in the forest (e) *(spans 2–3)*								Harvest tung oil *(spans 10–11)*		
"Other land"	Children herd cattle in the mountains *(spans 1–3)*					Children herd cattle in the mountains *(spans 6–12)*						

Lunar Month

120

Figure 4.3. Agricultural calendar for Zhu Ming Lin village (Fugong 福贡 county, Nujiang Lisu and Nu autonomous prefecture, Yunnan province). *Notes:* Zhu Ming Ling village is located at c. 1,600 meters elevation above the Nujiang 怒江 (Salween) River, linked to the county town of Fugong by a steep mountain trail. The administrative village of 200 households (all of the Lisu 傈僳 minority) is composed of three "natural villages" or hamlets. Village lands stretch from the banks of the river at an elevation of 1,300 meters to the ridge behind the village at an elevation of over 3,000 meters. The staple diet is potatoes supplemented on special occasions by rice. The village does not grow enough rice for its needs, and receives rice from the state at below-market, subsidized prices (*Fan xiao liang* 反消粮).

Irrigation is very limited. Most fields are rainfed. There is a small area of terraced paddy-fields on the relatively gentle slopes near the village. Management was described by informants: "Everyone works together to maintain the 'big sections' of the irrigation, then each family looks after its own channels. The "big section" consists of a stone-lined canal c. three kilometers long diverting water from the river to the village.

Livestock are mostly cattle. The cattle are kept in stalls in the home to collect their manure. Some families share livestock. Donkeys and horses are used for transport.

(a) Labor allocation at the busiest time of the year:
- Within each household, the head of household (usually the father) organizes the allocation of tasks to be done. This only happens at the busiest time of the year; otherwise different members of the family all know which job they will be doing.
- At the busiest time of the year several households will work together to share the workload. Religion is not a factor in the formation of family groups (the majority of the Lisu in the Nujiang area are evangelical Christians).

(b) The maize is divided into three categories:
- The best-quality maize is brought home immediately and stored for seed.
- Better-quality maize is carried down to the house as soon as possible and stored for eating (by humans, not livestock).
- The lowest-quality maize is stored for pig feed in a shed by the field. It is carried down to the house over several months whenever family members are not too busy with other jobs.

(c) Labor arrangements for rice harvest:
- Families work out labor exchange arrangements within family and among close friends.
- Exchange arrangements cover harvesting, threshing, and the use of livestock (cattle or horses) to carry the rice from the fields to the home.

(d) Decision-rules about which winter crops to plant in the paddy-fields:
- Potatoes and rapeseed are the most important crops. Wheat gives low yields and so is only planted on poor land.
- If the soil is waterlogged it is not good for potatoes. If it is too waterlogged to plant a winter crop, then it is used as the nursery bed for the next year's rice crop.

(e) *Huang lian* 黄连: a medicinal herb, "Chinese goldthread" (*Coptis chinensis*). A traditional variety has always been gathered and occasionally planted under the forest canopy. Since 1988, attempts have been made to introduce a higher-yielding variety from Hebei province, but the attempts have failed because of an oversupply of *huang lian* on the market.

Chinese terms used in Fig. 4.3:: *di shan* 地, *jiti shan* 集体山, *huang lian* 黄连, *shan* 山, *tian* 田, *yang tian* 苿田, *ziliu shan* 自留山.

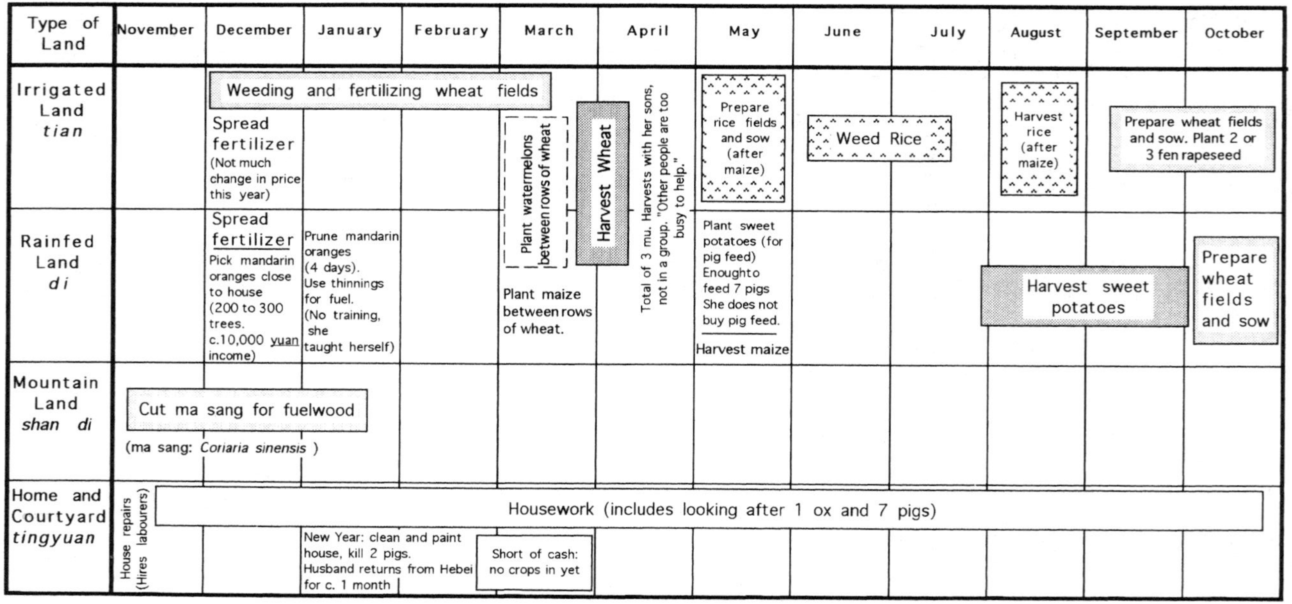

Type of Land

Type of Land	November	December	January	February	March	April	May	June	July	August	September	October
Irrigated Land *tian*		Spread fertilizer (Not much change in price this year) — Weeding and fertilizing wheat fields	Weeding and fertilizing wheat fields	Weeding and fertilizing wheat fields		Harvest Wheat	Prepare rice fields and sow (after maize)	Weed Rice	Weed Rice	Harvest rice (after maize)	Prepare wheat fields and sow. Plant 2 or 3 fen rapeseed	Prepare wheat fields and sow. Plant 2 or 3 fen rapeseed
Rainfed Land *di*		Spread fertilizer. Pick mandarin oranges close to house (200 to 300 trees. c.10,000 yuan income)	Prune mandarin oranges (4 days). Use thinnings for fuel. (No training, she taught herself)		Plant watermelons between rows of wheat / Plant maize between rows of wheat.	Total of 3 mu. Harvests with her sons, not in a group. "Other people are too busy to help."	Plant sweet potatoes (for pig feed) Enough to feed 7 pigs She does not buy pig feed. / Harvest maize				Harvest sweet potatoes	Prepare wheat fields and sow
Mountain Land *shan di*	Cut ma sang for fuelwood (ma sang: *Coriaria sinensis*)	Cut ma sang for fuelwood										
Home and Courtyard *tingyuan*	House repairs (Hires labourers)	New Year: clean and paint house, kill 2 pigs. Husband returns from Hebei for c. 1 month			Short of cash: no crops in yet	Housework (includes looking after 1 ox and 7 pigs)						

Figure 4.4. Agricultural calendar for Da Shi village (Quxian county, Sichuan province). Chinese terms used in Fig. 4.4: *masang* 麻桑, *tingyuan* 庭院.

122

More time spent on collecting firewood would be a fairly obvious indicator of changing forest cover, or a switch from a crop such as buckwheat (usually grown on recently cleared upland fields) to a more permanent crop such as maize would indicate intensification of land use due to changing population or markets.

SPACE: PARTICIPATORY MAPPING

While some training may be needed to produce maps with reliable cartographic accuracy, experience shows that farmers with little or no education do not find it difficult to visualize and record the spatial distribution of objects and features over the landscape they live in. With some initial assistance, farmers can become essential guides in mapping different categories of land, present land use, the distribution of resources critical to the community, and changes over time. As with the time-line, the process of working together and the finished map itself both prompt informal discussion, during which much can be learned about environmental change.

In the first example shown here (Map 4.2), I spent a morning on a hill overlooking the village of Nuohei (referred to above) with the former Party secretary of the village. Although I did the drawing myself, the notes inscribed on the map suggest how the act of drawing any one feature of the landscape was the starting point for a conversation about what makes it distinctive, how it relates to other features, and whether or not it is new. Drawing the map revealed, for example, the extent of land formerly planted to opium (all the land now designated as *Di* 地 to the east of the village), and that the village had preserved a number of unusual traditional tenure arrangements on "fodder mountains" (*Yang cao shan* 養草山) with separate tenure over the hill itself, the grass, and the trees on the hill.

In India, rural communities have been eager to prepare three-dimensional models of the land surrounding their village using sand, stones, and other readily available materials. Where participatory mapping has been tried in Yunnan, farmers seem to prefer to leave the actual drawing of the map to the visiting investigator. More lively discussions have been generated, however, when villagers do the work themselves, often with younger people drawing a map of the present land use while elders and others watching the process comment on where there have been changes and when they took place (Map 4.3 shows a land-use history map drawn in this way in Huangbo 黃柏村, a Miao village in Hu'nan province).

In another example (Map 4.4) the informants from the Hani (Akha) village of Mingzi Shan 明子山 in Jiangcheng 江城 county, southern Yunnan, had access to a base map being used for an ongoing rural development

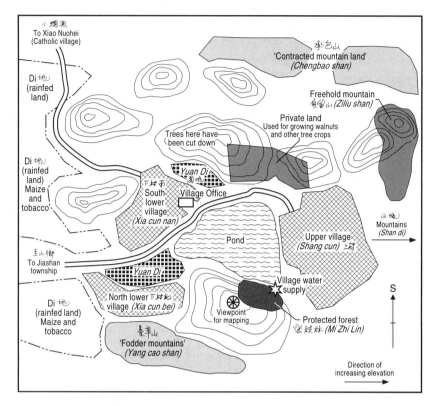

Map 4.2. Nuohei village (Jiashan township, Lu'nan county, Yunnan province). This map was drawn on August 28, 1993, by Nick Menzies, instructed and assisted by the former Party secretary of Nuohei village (63 years old).

Each mountain surrounding the village has a name that is used to identify the location of plots of land and fields.

Categories of land

Yuan di 园地	Plots of land close to the village. Mostly used for growing vegetables. Individually allocated, not collectivized during the Cultural Revolution.
Di 地	Rainfed fields. Now grows mostly maize and tobacco (tobacco was introduced in the 1950s, but only became common after the road was improved in 1967). Most of the *di* to the east and north of the village used to belong to the landlord (a Han who lived in Lu'nan). "He owned all the land as far as a horse could gallop in one day." The landlord grew mostly opium, as did some individuals in the village. Opium growing stopped in the 1950s.
Shan di 山地	Mountain land. *Shan di* used to grow potatoes intercropped with buckwheat. Also wheat and barley. No fertilizer used, only green manure.

program in the village. A group of three men recognized by the rest of the village as "knowing a lot about the past and about village traditions" spent one evening talking about the history of the village, using colored felt-tip pens to indicate where the first settlement had been, where they first cleared land for cultivation, and what had been there when the first settlers arrived. One of the group was the village shaman, who had spent a morning during a previous visit on the hillside explaining the rituals and significance of the village's sacred forest, providing relatively independent corroboration for the discussions during the mapping. The history that emerged from these visits will be described below as an example of the surprising richness of detail that can be pieced together using these participatory methods.

Caption to Map 4.2 *(cont.)*

Ziliu shan 自留山	"Freehold mountain." Allocated to households in 1983 on the basis of the number of people in each household. Mostly used for cutting firewood.
	Two plots of mountain land near the village are private plots used for growing walnuts and tree crops. This was private land before Liberation (it did not belong to the landlord). It was collectivized in the 1950s, but reprivatized in the 1960s. Technically should be *ziliu shan* but people in the villages prefer to call it "private mountain land" (*ge ren shan di* 各人山地).
Chengbao shan 承包山	"Contracted land." Also allocated to households in 1983. Mostly forest land. Some natural, some planted (pines). People can cut shrubs for fuel without permission, but not trees. Harvesting is regulated by the county department of forestry. "It is getting easier to get permission to cut now because there are more trees than there used to be."
Yang cao shan 养草山	"Fodder mountains." To grow fodder for livestock. The mountain is allocated as *chengbao shan* or *ziliu shan* with respect to the trees. The grass under the trees is common property. In August or September, the village committee allocates an area of grass to every family in the village (i.e., allocated separately from the trees). The committee announces a period of three days during which families may cut the grass on the plot allocated to them. The allocation is only valid for that period of time; the grass then becomes common property again.

Vegetation

When the informant was a child, most of the trees were in the hills to the south of the village. They were cut during the Great Leap Forward to make props for the Jiashan coalmine (no one in Nuohei village works in the coalmine).

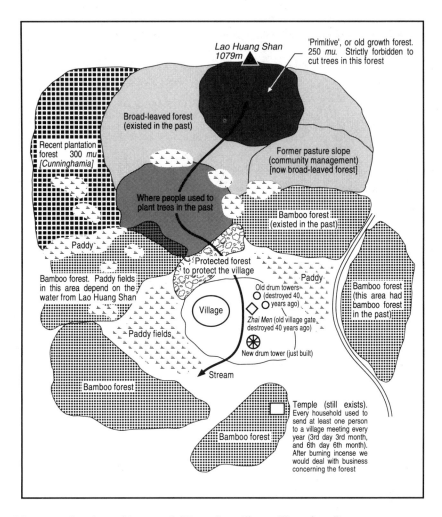

Map 4.3. Land-use history of Huangbo village (Tongdao Dong autonomous county, Hu'nan province).

It is important to remember that all these techniques are no more than tools. The time-line, the map, and the agricultural calendar rarely give direct answers to questions about environmental change. Asking farmers to create them, however, initiates a dialogue in which the outside researcher can learn about how and when environmental changes have affected farmers' lives and the relative importance they assume compared to other factors such as national and local policies or increasing access to markets.

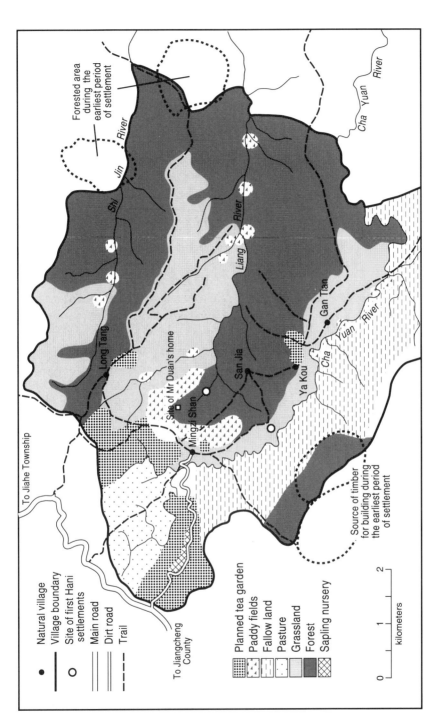

Legend:

- Natural village
○ Site of first Hani settlements
— Village boundary

||| Main road
||| Dirt road
- - - Trail

Planned tea garden
Paddy fields
Fallow land
Pasture
Grassland
Forest
Sapling nursery

Forested area during the earliest period of settlement

Source of timber for building during the earliest period of settlement

To Jiahe Township

To Jiangcheng County

Jin River
Shi River
Liang River
Cha Yuan River
Cha Yuan River

Long Tang
Site of Mr Duan's home
Mingzi Shan
San Jia
Ya Kou
Gan Tan

0 1 2
kilometers

Map 4.4. Mingzi Shan (Jiangcheng Hani and Yi autonomous county, Yunnan province).

THE STORY OF MINGZI SHAN

The village of Mingzi Shan is located about fifty kilometers from the county seat of Jiangcheng in Simao 思茅 prefecture, southern Yunnan province, one of the thirty poorest counties in China in 1987. Until a tractor road was built in 1992, the village was a one-hour walk through the hills from the nearest road, which links Jiangcheng to the small township of Jiahe. The administrative village consists of four settlements – Mingzi Shan itself, Yakou 丫口, San Jia Cun 三家村, and Long Tang 龙塘 – spread along a ridge forming two arms of a horseshoe-shaped valley with its opening facing eastward toward the Laotian border. The 130 households in the administrative village refer to themselves as belonging to the Bi-yo branch of the Hani ethnic group, although the term "Hani" is a Han word for the people known as the Akha in northern Thailand and Laos.

In 1989, sparse forest covered the hilltops surrounding the village and persisted along the main watercourses. Extensive areas behind the ridge to the west of the village were used for swidden (shifting) cultivation, whereby upland rice was grown for two to three years after clearance and the land was then left fallow for up to eight years. Although crop yields were declining, rapid natural regeneration of the nitrogen-fixing alder *Alnus nepalensis* helped maintain this agricultural system. In the valley to the east of the village, farmers managed a mixed farming system with some terraced paddy rice and maize, vegetable plots near their homes, and scattered clumps of bamboo used for food and for sale as timber. This landscape began to change in 1990 when an internationally funded aid program began to assist farmers to diversify their cropping system and to experiment with perennial cash crops such as timber trees and rattan. More dramatic changes have taken place since 1992, when the county established a tea plantation on the former swidden fields and moved an additional seventy families into the area from neighboring villages to provide the supplementary labor needed to build terraces and manage the plantation.

While there is documentary evidence for future historians to trace the transformation of Mingzi Shan's environment since 1989, there is nothing to tell of what had shaped it from the time of settlement until that date. Interviews and visits to remaining patches of forest accompanied by older members of the village indicated that customary law enforces strict protection of individual sacred trees on some areas of forest, especially along the watercourses and in designated sacred forests behind settlements. Further informal conversations revealed that the present sacred forest was new, consisting of regenerating natural forest protected when the village of

Mingzi Shan moved to its present location from farther down the hill about twenty years ago, and that most people believed that there was more forest surrounding the village now than there had been when they were young.

In the course of an evening spent with village elders in the participatory mapping exercise referred to above, the map of the village provided a framework on which the three participants could focus their discussions, stimulating further questions about what had changed and why. Together with earlier anecdotal information, in was then possible to establish at least the initial outlines of the environmental history of Mingzi Shan and to identify issues deserving further research.

The Bi-yo families who now live in Mingzi Shan began to migrate there from Lüchun 綠春 county in what is now Mojiang 墨江 district (about two hundred kilometers northeast of Mingzi Shan) seventy to eighty years ago. The village is now made up of four main families: the Bai 白, who were the first to arrive; the Li 李; who followed; the Hu 胡; and finally the Ma 馬, who came as late as 1944.[17] The settlers moved here because of land shortages in Mojiang and first built their homes by the river at the bottom of the valley; they soon moved farther up the hill as easily irrigated land was converted to fields. When they moved into the area, there was only grassland with very few trees, although there was still a lot of wildlife. One informant said, "We could not leave pigs out at night because the leopards would kill them," and another added that it was dangerous to graze cattle because the leopards were so large, "up to three hundred *jin* in weight if you could shoot one."

In addition to the dangers posed by wild animals, the migrants were harassed by bandits: "We had to carry our plows back from the fields – otherwise the bandits would take them." This observation led to the discovery that there had been at least one family resident in the area before the arrival of the Hani settlers, the Duan 端 household. When the first Hani arrived, wooden pillars and stone foundations from the Duan mansion could still be seen (and are marked on the map). Duan himself was known as "Duan Fei 匪" (Bandit Duan). He had had all the land in the valley cleared for cultivation but skirmished frequently with the bandits. At one point he was captured and about to be killed but escaped during the confusion caused by a sudden rainstorm and flood. It seems that in the end the bandits did kill him, but not before he warned in a curse that after he was killed, the grain would not ripen and big trees would topple over: "After he died, the dragons from the eight dragon pools in this area all flew away,

---

[17] There is some dispute about the order in which the four families came, but general agreement on the time frame in which the migration took place.

and the trees did topple over, which is why there were no trees left when we arrived." To this day, parents invoke the name of Bandit Duan to keep naughty children quiet with the terrible phrase, "Be careful or the Duans will get you!"

When this colorful and dramatic story is combined with what is known from more conventional sources about this border region in the early years of this century, it would seem that Duan was an opium grower involved in illicit smuggling either toward the Chinese interior or to what was then French Indochina (now Laos). The normal processes of ecological succession would make it quite likely that after his death, the land that had been cleared and planted to poppies would revert to grassland, and that the forest cover would slowly regenerate where land was under the customary protection extended to river banks and sacred forests.

Since the land reform that took place there in 1955, Mingzi Shan has continued to see a small increase in the land under forest cover, but the wildlife has nearly all disappeared. There appears to have been an officially inspired campaign to eliminate such "pests" at the time of land reform and now there are only a very few wild pigs left for hunters. The three informants agreed, however, that there is less grassland now than there used to be and that wood for building is more abundant and more accessible than it had been when they were young. In addition to natural regeneration, some trees had been planted in 1960 and 1961 so that it was no longer necessary to fetch timber from the remaining natural forest behind the settlement of Long Tang. It would be of interest to pursue this point, since in another meeting, village women were unanimous that they now had to spend more time collecting firewood than in the past. Further investigation might show that this contradictory evidence is related to the species used for different purposes. Oak is preferred for fuelwood but is almost never planted, whereas alder, which grows readily in fallow fields, and Toona sinensis (Xiang Chun 香椿), which is commonly planted, are preferred for timber. This point is also a reminder that environmental change does not always affect men and women in the same way, and that efforts must be made to corroborate information from many different sources.

CONCLUSIONS: LESSONS FROM THE "VILLAGE VIEW" OF ENVIRONMENTAL HISTORY

The history of Mingzi Shan outlined above is not a full and accurate account of change over the last century. There are many gaps and inferences that need to be supplemented and corroborated through further interviews. It is detailed enough, however, to show how the perceptions of those whose lives depend on the natural resources surrounding them can add depth and shed new light on environmental history. The commonly accepted pattern of change is a Malthusian view of demographic pressure driving a slow but inexorable expansion of agriculture and the consequent destruction of natural ecosystems. The view from the village is a contrasting one of change affected by commercial opportunities, conflict, migration, changing technologies, custom or tradition, and interventions driven by policies formulated far from the resources themselves. The long-term direction of change may be toward a reduction in the area of natural vegetation, but it is often punctuated by periods of rapid transformation and even reversals of the trend, as in Mingzi Shan.

This discussion of nonconventional sources of information for environmental history does not represent a comprehensive review of available methodologies, nor have the examples cited come out of a coherent research design. It has served, however, to question the universal validity of a linear model of change. It has served, too, to provide evidence for the proposition that different people perceive environmental change or degradation in different ways – a point made by other papers at the conference. If this is the case, then it would be logical to expect different responses to environmental change and, by extension, to measures taken to mitigate its effects. Given the conspicuous lack of success of most government-sponsored efforts all over the world to slow environmental degradation and to rehabilitate degraded ecosystems, the methods described in this chapter might contribute in the future to helping to understand more about the view from the village.

Human Settlement

5

Environment versus Water Control

THE CASE OF THE SOUTHERN HANGZHOU BAY AREA FROM THE MID-TANG THROUGH THE QING

SHIBA YOSHINOBU

INTRODUCTION

This chapter is an attempt to illustrate in considerable detail the historical process of the interplay between the progressive movement of colonization and the eventual change in environmental settings, both of which took place in the lower Yangzi 揚子江 region in China.

From the earliest times the Chinese were distinguished for their pervasive tendency to settle in lowland areas, while they proved themselves to have a genius for developing both the advanced technology and the organization needed for draining and taming wild lowlands. A superb illustration of such Chinese skills in water control may be found in the extensive reclamation of the lower Yangzi delta. Its fundamental works were carried out from the eighth to the thirteenth century. How was such a difficult, large-scale project feasible in the rather short span of time of only a few hundred years? In dealing with this question, I first survey the subject within a wider context that includes the lower Yangzi delta and its neighbor, the southern Hangzhou Bay 杭州灣 littoral, and over a longer span of time. I then examine the distributional patterns of ecology shared by both areas. Next, basing myself on the known fact that the southern Hangzhou Bay littoral historically preceded the lower Yangzi delta in developing systems of re-claiming swampy floodplains, I analyze the essentials of the methods of water control that emerged in the bay littoral, and infer that these essential elements were mobilized on an extensive scale when the opening up of the land in the lower Yangzi Lowlands was later pressed forward.

The southern Hangzhou Bay littoral also preceded the lower Yangzi delta in reaching the worsening balance between resources and population characteristic of late-imperial times. In the last section of this chapter, I conclude by examining how the people of the bay area responded to the intensifying crisis of their environment.

5.1. THE LOWER YANGZI REGION

5.1.1 FORMATION AND SETTLEMENT OF THE DELTA

The Chinese preference for low-lying locations as their sites of settlement was a traditional feature of their society. Professor Chang Sen-dou once argued as follows:[1]

> Among the 1276 county capitals in the eighteen provinces of China Proper in the 1890's, 913, or well over 70 percent, were located at elevations below 400 meters. Even those cities situated above that level were largely concentrated in the lowest-lying portions of each province. Yet areas below 400 meters account for less than a quarter of the total territory in the eighteen provinces.
>
> The Chinese preference for low-lying urban sites is closely associated with the heavy concentration of their predominantly agrarian population in the lowlands – in flood plains, river valleys, intermontane basins, and small oases along the foothills. As a result, upland areas, marginal for Chinese agriculture, remained largely unsettled and undeveloped.

Indeed, the drainage basins provided colonists with higher levels of agricultural productivity and crucial transport advantages.

By the eighth century, the feasibility of expanding intensive rice culture, salt production, and commercial tea planting in South China became widely known throughout the empire. Inmigrants from distant areas, the Northerners in particular, arrived in the southeastern provinces to fill the open spaces and tried to settle in the unsettled lowlands of the lower Yangzi

[1] Chang Sen-dou 章生道, "The morphology of walled capitals," in G. William Skinner, ed., *The City in Late Imperial China* (Stanford, Calif.: Stanford University Press, 1977), pp. 85–86. See also Chang, "Some Aspects of the Urban Geography of the Chinese *Hsien* Capitals," *Annals of the Association of the American Geographers* 51 (1961), p. 309; Ho Ping-ti 何炳棣, *Studies on the Population of China: 1368–1953* (Cambridge, Mass.: Harvard University Press, 1959), p. 147.

delta, among other areas. This ushered in the advent of the massive reclamation movement that occurred in this delta during the succeeding several
centuries.

In a long-run perspective, the land formation of the lower Yangzi delta
was basically the product of natural processes.[2] Prior to the Neolithic Age,
Lake Tai 太湖 in the center of the present-day delta was a bay, directly open
to the sea. At that time the whole Yangzi valley was covered with thick forest
and vegetation. The amount of sediment carried by the Yangzi River was
small, and some portion of this settled as mud on the bottom of natural
reservoirs existing here and there along the course of the river. In time, a
thin headland of sandy elevation developed from the northern part of the
bay of the later Lake Tai, advanced eastward, and then – being blocked by
oceanic tides and currents – made a bend southeastward. Meanwhile, the
silt that had flowed out of the mouth of the Qiantang River 錢塘江 facilitated the accretionary development of flat plain to the south of the later
Lake Tai. The headland of this flat plain also moved eastward, finally
joining the other headland coming from the northeast to form the earliest
historical shorelines of the delta. The easternmost coastlines ran parallel
with those of the present day, but they were more than ten kilometers to the
interior of the site of the later city of Shanghai 上海. With the emergence of
these coastlines, Lake Tai became a lagoon. A long elevated belt with a
width of 1.5 to 8.0 kilometers, and running closely parallel with the easternmost coastlines, was formed by the forces of the oceanic tides and currents.
The central area between this elevated stretch and Lake Tai for a long while
remained as a vast marshy lowland throughout which numerous small
islands were interspersed.

Human habitation in the deltaic area started in the Neolithic Age. At
first colonists preferred to settle in the areas around Lake Tai. The further
direction of colonization seems to have moved from there to the flat plain
to the south and southeast of the lake, and to the elevated belt along the
eastern coastlines. Until the fourth century A.D. the formation of land by
alluvium seaward of the easternmost shorefront remained minimal, having
a rate of one kilometer per several hundred years. The delta's southern
coastlines facing Hangzhou Bay were unstable because they were open to
erosion by currents and tides. During the fourth through the seventh

---

[2] Tan Qixiang 谭其骧, "Shanghai shi dalu-bufen di hailu bianqian he kaifa guocheng" 上海市
大陆部份的海路变迁和开发过程 [The process of land formation along the coastlines and of
the reclamation of such alluvium in the vicinity of present-day Shanghai], *Kaogu* 考古 1
(1973), pp. 2–10.

centuries, the eastern shorelines of the delta advanced for about ten kilometers, at the rate of one kilometer per forty years. Nevertheless, there continued to be only a thin distribution of population in the eastern section of the delta. During the Former Han 前漢 through the mid-Tang 唐 period, we can ascertain the establishment of three county capitals therein. However, two of them were abolished in the late sixth century due to administrative restructuring.³

A dramatic change in the colonization of the delta took place during the eighth through thirteenth centuries. The construction of long earthen seawalls along the eastern shorelines in the early eighth century showed the arrival of the age of intensified reclamation of the delta. The lines of these seawalls ran parallel with the eastern edges of the sandy elevation about ten kilometers seaward of it. At one point they passed the site of modern Shanghai. Soon the seawalls were extended along the delta's shoreline facing Hangzhou Bay so that they reached Hangzhou 杭州. The final step of this construction was taken during the time of the Wuyue Kingdom 吳越國 (907–78). This was the building of stone seawalls at the mouth of the Qiantang River 錢塘江 where Hangzhou, the capital of that kingdom, was located. Reflecting the sudden progress in reclamation in the delta areas as a whole, the eastward advance of the land was accelerated in the eastern coastlines. Hence a second line of seawalls had to be built at a distance of around seven kilometers seaward of the Tang seawalls in the first half of the tenth century, and again a third line at a distance of around six kilometers seaward of the second line in 1172. Thus during the fifth through twelfth centuries the total gain in distance of eastward land advancement in this section came to approximately thirty kilometers, a pace of one kilometer per twenty-seven years. Formerly, the areas bordering the southern and eastern coastlines of the delta had had only one county-level capital, Haiyan 海鹽, which had been maintained since Han times. This was the site of the superintendancy of salt production, located near the southern end of the elevation. In 751 the capital of Huating 華亭 county was inaugurated to the east of Haiyan. In order to administer these two counties, Xiuzhou 秀州 prefecture (later Jiaxing 嘉興) was established to the southeast of Lake Tai.⁴ We may conclude from these facts that the colonization of the eastern part of the lower Yangzi delta belongs to relatively recent times.

³ Ibid., pp. 3–4.
⁴ Ibid., pp. 4–7; Akiyama Motonobu 秋山元信, "Shanghai-ken no seiritsu" 上海縣の成立 [The formation of Shanghai county], in Umehara Kaoru 梅原郁, ed., Chūgoku kinsei no toshi to bunka 中國近世の都市と文化 [The city and urban culture in early modern China] (Kyoto: Kyōto Daigaku Jinbunkagaku Kenkyūsho, 1984), pp. 455–84.

5.1.2. THE PHYSIOGRAPHY OF THE LOWER YANGZI REGION

In advance of the detailed description that follows, it would be useful to take a look at the physiographic features of the lower Yangzi region. Map 5.1 shows, in simplified manner, a distributional pattern of various ecological zones that together form the region's overall topography.[5]

We can make a sixfold zonal subdivision of the region in terms of its ecological differences. These are, in order of elevation, (1) hills, (2) fan/slope complexes, (3) elevated plains, (4) low-lying plains, (5) sandy elevations, and (6) lowlands.[6] Remember that the rice culture in the region has been practiced throughout historical times. It goes without saying that for their large scale of rice production, the "lowlands" areas stand out among the rest. But the region's history indicates that the conversion of the lowlands into paddies by the construction of enclosures did not occur until the tenth through fourteenth centuries. This was because a sustained and regulated supply of fresh water into paddies was not available in these areas in earlier times.

When people were scarce and the technology of water control was not well developed, agriculturists were primarily concerned with safe production and safe living. The upland areas abounded in small separated basins, surrounded by forests, that could fill these needs. When people came to exert severe pressure on the resources in these upland basins, those outnumbered found the areas of "fan/slope complex" to be their second-best locations for production and settlement. While people enjoyed the occupancy of a larger area here, the physical surroundings were less favorable than those in the hills. In the wet season, torrents of water ran down

---

[5] Map 5.1 was drawn with reference to the discussions and the accompanying map in "Taihu diqu tudileixing tezheng" 太湖地区土地类型特征 [The characteristics of types of physiography in the Lake Tai area] by Gong Chunsheng 宫春生, in *Taihu liuyu shuitu ziyuan ji nongye fazhan yuanjing yanjiu* 太湖流域水土资源及农业发展远景研究 [The study of the water and land resources in the Yangzi valley and a long-term trend of agrarian development in the area] (Beijing: Zhongguo Kexueyuan Nanjing Dili Yu Hubo Yanjiusuo, 1988), pp. 60–69. See also Shiba Yoshinobu 斯波義信, *Sōdai Kōnan Keizaishi no Kenkyū* 宋代江南經濟史の研究 [Studies on the economic history of the Jiangnan region in Song times] (Tokyo: Tōkyō Daigaku Tōyōbunka Kenkyūsho, 1988), pp. 167–79; Takaya Kōichi 高谷好一, "Tai inasaku no shizen kōzō: chikei to inasaku" タイ稲作の自然構造: 地形と稲作 [The physical structure of rice culture in Thailand: geomorphology and rice culture], in Ishii Yoneo 石井米雄, ed., *Taikoku: hitotsu no inasaku shakai* クア國: ひとつの稲作社會 (Thailand: a society of rice culture) (Tokyo: Sōbunsha, 1975), pp. 215–39; Takaya, *Nettai deruta no nōgyō hatten* 熱帶デルタの農業發展 [Agrarian development in tropical deltaic area] (Tokyo: Sōbunsha, 1982), pp. 10–19.

[6] Refer to Takaya, "The physical structure" pp. 216–39, and *Agrarian development*, pp. 10–19.

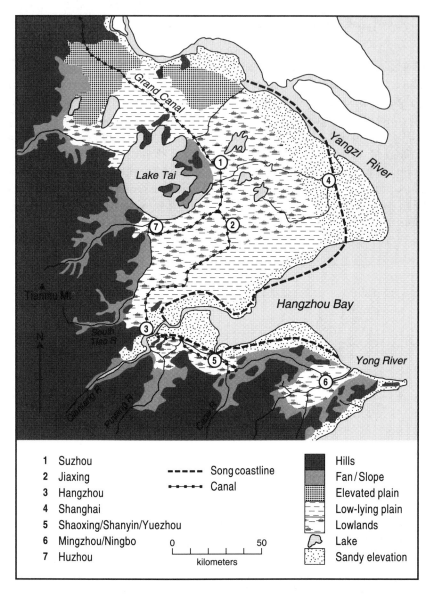

Map 5.1. Ecological zones of the lower Yangzi region.

through the area. Furthermore, since the surface water percolated into the ground water through the loamy soil, the areas at large tended to be characterized by their arid topography. The building of artificial reservoirs at the heads of alluvial fans in this category of land was indispensable for the people there to sustain their livelihood. The reservoirs had multiple functions: for defense against seasonal inundation, for the supply of regulated irrigation water, and for the provision of fresh drinking water.

As stated above, the "lowlands" resisted the access of settlers over a long period. Though they were very extensive in their dimensions, these areas in earlier times were covered with brackish water. The amount and the level of such water fluctuated considerably either in response to the seasonal variations in the amount of stream water from the uplands or in accordance with the ebb-and-flow movement of the tide. The conditions for settlement and production in the areas of "elevated plains," "low-lying plains," and "sandy elevations" in earlier times were somewhat better than those in the "lowlands." People in the elevated plains could sustain their lives by their production of dry and wet crops, while those in the low-lying plains near Hangzhou Bay and the sandy elevations along the eastern coast enjoyed good access to salt production and fishing.

All in all, if we assume that the lines delineated by the Grand Canal and the Zhedong Canal 浙東河 (parallel with the southern Hangzhou Bay littoral) are indicative of the boundary between the old and the new deltas, we may infer that the region's colonization in earlier centuries took place in the old delta, its centers being the areas of "fan/slope complex."[7]

5.2. THE PROTOTYPE OF WATER CONTROL IN THE SOUTHERN HANGZHOU BAY AREA

5.2.1 MIRROR LAKE IN THE SHAOXING PLAIN

The size of the Shaoxing 紹興 plain was but moderate, with an area of about 700 square kilometers, mostly under ten meters above sea level. In earlier times there was no peninsula-like salient of sandy sedimentation projecting northward into Hangzhou Bay from the shoreline of the area's western half. The plain lay between the shorelines of the bay and the foothills at the base of mountain ranges (300 to 700 meters high) to the south. The northern half of the plain was low, two to three meters above sea level. The plain's eastern end was bounded by the Caoe River 曹娥江, while its western end was demarcated by the Xixiao River 西小江 or the lower reaches of the Puyang River 浦陽江. The Caoe and the Puyang rivers formerly joined together, forming a common estuary at the seashore near where the Caoe still flows. Later, in the middle of the fifteenth century, an artificial diver-

---

[7] Shiba, *Studies on the economic history*, pp. 169–79.

sion of the Puyang River into the Qiantang River 錢塘江 was made at the
point where the Puyang flowed into the plain. Prior to that, the river water
was drained off into the bay by way of the Xixiao River. Thus before the
mid-Ming 明 the runoff from the southern mountains, which was collected
by these two rivers, came down to the plain, causing chronic seasonal
flooding there. In addition, the currents and tides in the bay transported
the brine up into the interior of the plain, leaving salt deposits there to
form countless saline marshes. It is known that in the time of the ancient
Yue Kingdom 越國 (which existed for several centuries from a date of
foundation that is unknown until its end in 222 B.C.) its capital was relocated from the rim of southern foothills to the site of modern Shaoxing
city, and that at that time people lived mostly in upland basins or in the
fan/slope areas and their vicinity (see Map 5.2a).

Under the rule of the Qin 秦 and the Former Han 前漢 dynasties, the
plain remained little utilized for colonization. At that time the Shaoxing
area was a part of the Guiji Commandery 會稽郡, a very extensive jurisdic-
tional unit including the Yangzi delta and the later provinces of Zhejiang 浙
江 and Fujian 福建, with its capital at Wu county 吳縣 (later Suzhou 蘇
州). In A.D. 129, the Guiji Commandery was subdivided into the Wu 吳 and
the new Guiji commanderies. At the same time the capital of the latter was
set up at the seat of the Shanyin 山陰 county (later the city of Shaoxing).
The jurisdiction of this new Guiji Commandery was still extensive, covering
the territories of the later provinces of Zhejiang and Fujian, but excluding
the areas equivalent to the two drainage basins of the Qiantang 錢塘江 and
the Tiao rivers 苕溪.

In A.D. 140, soon after this subdivision, the first large-scale project of
water conservancy in the area was undertaken in the center of the plain at
the initiative of Ma Zhen 馬臻, the governor of the new commandery. An
artificial reservoir appeared there, with an area of 20,600 hectares and a
circumference of 148 kilometers. The most important portions were the
massive earthen embankments running from west to east and serving as the
linear northern flank of the reservoir. They were designed to store the water
from the southern hills on a level, up to four to five meters higher on
average than the surface land in the northern part of the plain. Further, as
the level of the bottom of the eastern half of the reservoir was a bit higher
than that of the western half, an earthen partition was made in the middle
of the reservoir so as to make the regulation of the water within the reservoir
more efficient. The proper name of the reservoir was Jianhu 鑑湖 (Mirror
Lake), but it was popularly called Yuehu 月湖 (Moon Lake) after its shape.

In order to regulate the water within and outside of the lake, elaborate
systems of sluices and lockgates were installed along the embankments,

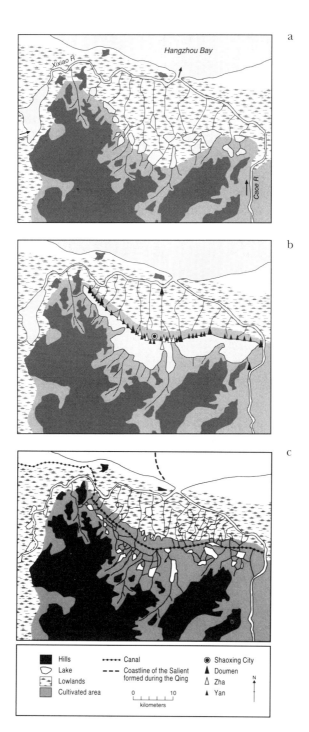

Map 5.2. The Shaoxing plain during three periods: (5.2a) before A.D. 140; (5.2b) from the later Han dynasty through the Tang dynasty; (5.2c) during the Southern Song dynasty.

though it is hard to identify the exact time when each regulation facility was installed. Their total number came to forty-three. The largest, and of great importance, were eight *doumen* 斗門 (floodgates) built at key positions on the embankments, through which the excess water within was to be drained off into the bay through several channels. Next to them in size were seven *zha* 閘 (lockgates) and twenty-eight *yan* 堰 (mini-watergates). There were also thirty-three *yin'gou* 陰溝 (tunnels) at the interstices of the *doumen* 斗門. The lesser lockgates functioned as facilities for the supply of irrigation water and to provide passage for the waterborne traffic in the northern part of the plain. Around the year 300, a canal was constructed from the port town of Xixing 西興 (located on the shore opposite the city of Hangzhou 杭州 at the mouth of the Qiantang River) to the lower reaches of the Caoe River. This canal was for commercial traffic, and its course through the plain ran closely parallel with the embankments of the lake (see Maps 5.2b and 5.2c).[8]

The second-century record of the lake boasts that the acreage of plowland thus irrigated by the lake amounted to 4,122,000 hectares. This figure must be an exaggeration or else be the aggregation of the acreages of paddies and of the salt-fields along the beachfront. We have evidence to show that concurrently with the creation of the lake, crude earthen seawalls were built along the shorelines, while a few floodgates were built for the first time at the junction of the Caoe and the Xixiao rivers.[9] But, as will be discussed later, full regulation of the water in the northern part of the plain was not undertaken until Ming 明 times. For centuries since the creation of the lake, the prime beneficiaries of the lake were the agriculturists who lived immediately to the south of it. When the lake was filled, some houses and tombs of the people living in the southern part of the plain were submerged under the surface of the lake water. Governor Ma Zhen, the creator of the lake, was accused by them of causing the loss of their estates, and sentenced to death by the authorities.[10] Nevertheless the lake protected the southern plain both from seasonal flooding and from inroads of brine from the sea. After it had been built the colonists settled at the foot of the hills could extend their farmland down to the shores of the lake, enjoying stabilized yields and the benefit of improved communications.

---

[8] Chen Qiaoyi 陈桥驿, "Gudai Jianhu xingfei yu Shan-Gui pingyuan nongtian shuili" 古代鉴湖兴废与山会平原农田水利 [The rise and fall of ancient Mirror Lake and water control in the Shaoxing plain], *Dilixuebao* 28.3 (Sept. 1962), pp. 187–202; and "Lishi shiqi Shaoxing diqu julo de xingcheng yu fazhan" 历史时期绍兴地区聚落的兴废与发展 [The rise and later development of the settlements in Shaoxing through historical times], *Dilixuebao* 35.1 (March 1980), pp. 14–23.

[9] Chen Qiaoyi, "The rise and fall," p. 193.

[10] Ibid., p. 193, footnote 1.

The records of the Shaoxing area in the first quarter of the fifth century indicate that the southern section of the plain was already affected by the ever-worsening trend of overpopulation, and that the local government forced the landless people who now composed a third of the population of Shanyin 山陰 county to emigrate to Yuyao 餘姚 (an area immediately to the west of later Yuyao county), Yin 鄞, and Mao 鄧 (both located near later Ningbo 寧波) counties to reclaim land by applying the Mirror Lake method.[11] Other evidence from the same period also testifies to the creation of more than a few small reservoirs, all replicas of Mirror Lake, in Shangyu 上虞 county near the Shaoxing plain.[12] In other words, the physiographic similarity of these other areas to the Shaoxing plain allowed people there to expand their farmland by using the method first tested and developed in the Shaoxing plain.

5.2.2. SOUTH LAKE IN YUHANG COUNTY TO THE NORTH OF HANGZHOU

In A.D. 173, thirty-three years after the building of Mirror Lake and forty-four years after the subdivision of the former Guiji Commandery into the Wu 吳 and the new Guiji 會稽 commanderies, another important water-control project in the region occurred in Yuhang 餘杭 county, located in the heart of the small drainage basin of the South Tiao River 南苕溪. This was the construction of a man-made reservoir known as South Lake 南湖 (794 hectares). Though it was only one-third as large as Mirror Lake, its creation gave the people there great assistance not only in securing the stability of their production and livelihood but also eventually in expanding their agricultural and other activities down to the low-lying plains in present-day Huzhou 湖州, Jiaxing 嘉興, and Hangzhou 杭州, lying to the east and the northeast of the basin.

As previously mentioned, in the western sector of the Yangzi delta (i.e.,

---

[11] Amano Motonosuke 天野元之助, "Chūsei nōgyō no tenkai" 中世農業の展開 [The growth of medieval agriculture in China], in Kiyoshi Yabuuchi 清藪內, ed., Chūgoku chūsei Kagakugijutsushi no Kenkyū 中國中世科學技術史の研究 [Studies on the history of science and technology in medieval China] (Tokyo: Kadokawa Shoten, 1963), p. 417; Nakamura Keiji 中村圭爾, "Rikuchō jidai Sango chihō ni okeru kaihatsu to suiri ni tsuite no jakkan no kōsatsu" 六朝時代三吳地方にまける開發と水利について若干の考察 [Some investigations into development and water control in the Lower Yangzi region during the Six Dynasties period], in Chūgoku Suiri-shi Kenkyūkai 中國水利史研究會, ed., Satō hakushi kanreki kinen: Chūrvgoku suiri-shi ronsō 佐藤博士還曆記念中國水利史論業 [Collected works on the history of water control in China: a festschrift celebrating the sixtieth anniversary of Dr. Satō Taketoshi 佐藤武敏] (Tokyo: Kokushokankōkai, 1981), pp. 43–84.

[12] Nakamura, "Some investigations," pp. 63–99.

the old delta) the areas of human habitation were largely limited to zones
of upriver basin or of fan/slope complex, and to some elevations around
Lake Tai. The major source of water supply for these areas was the runoff
from Tianmu Mountain 天目山 (794 meters) to the west. The water drained
into the systems of the West and South Tiao rivers 苕溪 and then flowed
down into Lake Tai. This lake was surrounded by sizable plains lying to its
west, south, and southeast. Their altitudes were quite low, only three to four
meters above sea level, and it was not until the eleventh century that the
successful regulation of water was achieved here.

The altitude of the riverbed of the South Tiao River at the foot of
Tianmu Mountain was 35 meters above sea level. When the river passed
along the southern walls of the city of Yuhang, it grew wider (114 meters),
descending to 30 meters above sea level. Soon after passing the city, the
course of the river was blocked by a chain of low hills, against which it made
a sharp bend northward, continuing its journey toward Lake Tai. Near the
city, the river's water level fluctuated widely from highs of 2.7 meters in the
wet season to lows of 1.5 meters in the dry season. When the volume of
water from the mountain became too much to be contained by the riverbed, the excess was liable to cause inundation not only in the small basin
around the city but also in the wide, low-lying neighboring plains to the
west and south of Lake Tai.[13]

Prior to the building of the lake in A.D. 173 at the initiative of Chen Hun
陳渾, the magistrate of Yuhang county, the city of Yuhang was moved from
its former site on the river's southern bank to the opposite bank. Along the
southern bank of the river and close to the city, twin lakes, known as Upper
South Lake and Lower South Lake, were created, sharing a common partition between them. Upper South Lake, which was the shallower, was designed to contain excess water in the wet season, while Lower South Lake,
which was deeper, was mostly for the provision of a regulated amount of
irrigation water to the paddies lying to its southeast. A loose demarcation of
the twin lakes' outer periphery was drawn by the local authorities, defining
it as officially owned land to protect both the twin lakes and their banks
from arbitrary encroachment by local families (see Map 5.3).

The circumference of Lower South Lake was embanked. An intake of
the river water, equipped with a stone sluice, was built at the Shimen Qiao

---

[13] Shiba, "The history of water conservancy: the South Lake in northern Zhejiang province" in
Zhongguo jinshi shehui-wenhuashi lunwenji 中國近世社會文化史論文集 [Papers on the history
of the society and culture of early modern China] (Taipei: Institute of History and Philology, Academia Sinica, 1992), pp. 563–85, esp. p. 569; Zheng Zhaojing 郑肇经, ed., *Taihu
shuili jishushi* 太湖水利技术史 [The history of technology for water control in the Lake Tai
area] (Beijing: Nongye CBS, 1987), pp. 49–61.

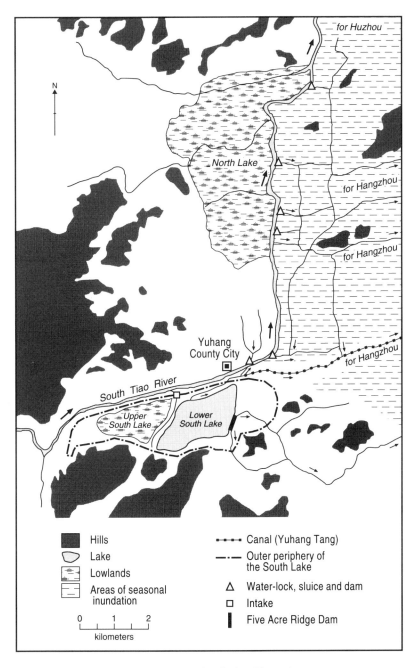

Map 5.3. South Lake during Tang times.

Bridge 石門橋, situated at the northern edge of the partition. One of the two outlets for water from Lower South Lake was built on its northern bank so as to let the excess water run back into the river through a drainage channel. The other outlet was built at the lake's southeastern and deepest corner. Close to this and outside of the embankments stood the Wumucheng 五畝塍 (Five Acre Ridge) Dam, an earthen construction 148.5 meters in length and 2 meters in height. When the amount of water within Lower South Lake approximated its normal capacity, the excess water flowing through the outlet would find its way into the open reserved space behind the dam, at first detouring along the foot of the dam, and then spilling over both of the dam's lowered ends. All in all, South Lake was a device to relieve the basin from its seasonal suffering of inundation and simultaneously to encourage the growing of rice in the basin.[14]

However, aside from repair work done in A.D. 436, South Lake sank into obscurity for about five centuries. Then, in 816, during the Tang 唐 dynasty, water conservancy in this basin saw considerable improvement. Gui Yao 歸珧, the magistrate of the county, took the initiative in resurrecting water control in Yuhang. Basing his work on a close survey of the original plan by Chen Hun, he reconstructed the twin lakes just as they had been in 173. Furthermore, he directed the embanking of the course of the South Tiao River for about eight kilometers from its bend near the city to the northern boundary of the county. Several floodgates were installed here and there in these new embankments. This work turned the arid plain to the north of the city into a reserve that received the excess water in the wet season, and was called North Lake 北湖. While this work indicated the growing malfunctioning of Upper South Lake due to siltation, it eventually facilitated the movement of colonization and reclamation not only in the plains to the east of the north-bound course of the river but also in the lower reaches of the river. In 1122, Gui's project was followed up in a more sophisticated manner by county magistrate Jiang Zhi 江峽.

As a result of these improvements the effectiveness of South Lake reached its peak in the twelfth century. The total dimensions of the farmland in the Yuhang basin that came to enjoy the benefits of a regulated supply of water grew to 5,800 hectares cultivated by about 7,000 households. Ironically South Lake at its zenith saw the first sign of incipient deterioration. During Song 宋 times (960–1279), concurrently with the growing stabilization of farming in the Yuhang basin, reclamation was progressing in the much smaller upriver basins along the South Tiao River. The amount of silt flowing into South Lake thus tended to grow. In 1122, Jiang Zhi witnessed the appearance of a cross-patterned shallow over the

---

[14] Shiba, "The history of water conservancy," pp. 569–74.

middle of the surface of Lower South Lake. This natural process was followed by the beginning of the encroachment on the peripheral zone as well as the shallower parts of the lake by powerful private persons. Hereafter, the history of the lake was mostly concerned with how to rejuvenate the lake to its former condition and how to protect it from the greedy inroads of these persons.[15]

Be that as it may, from the eighth century onward the major focus of reclamation and colonization in the old delta moved from the fan/slope complex areas to the low-lying plains around Lake Tai. The basic technology, used widely for this stage of the reclamation of these plains, was the building not of reservoirs but of a dense network of channels. Regardless of differences in size, these channels were generally called *tang* 塘. In most cases each *tang* was a line of embanked channel for the multiple purposes of water traffic and land traffic, drainage, and irrigation. We have some evidence of the development of the web of such channels in the southern shorelines of Lake Tai in the later half of the Tang 唐 dynasty. In 810 a bypass of the Grand Canal was built along the shorelines to link the Grand Canal with the South Tiao River. In time, several lines of channels were built so as to run parallel with this bypass. This was followed by the concurrent creation of numerous smaller channels that not only linked larger channels but also had the function of discharging excess water into the lake. By the eleventh century the southern and western shorelines of the lake were circumscribed by massive walls with thirty-six floodgates in them.[16] The lakeshore walls and the network of channels played the key role in converting low-lying plains into plowland. Needless to say, a plot of land partitioned by such channels became the basis of polder land (*weitian* 圍田, *yutian* 圩田, fields within an enclosure). But here again, we can see the precedent of this kind of water control in the drainage basins of the southern Hangzhou Bay littoral in the mid-Tang 唐 dynasty.

5.3. WATER CONTROL IN THE LOWLANDS

5.3.1. THE YONG RIVER VALLEY IN THE MINGZHOU/NINGBO AREA

In the middle of the Tang 唐 dynasty, lowlands in the southern Hangzhou Bay littoral were reclaimed by introducing a web of channels (*tang*) in the central part of the drainage basin of the Yong River 甬江, the immediate

---

[15] Ibid., pp. 576–78.
[16] Shiba, *Studies on the economic history*, pp. 373–74.

hinterland of what was later to be the city of Ningbo. The first known mass inmigration of the landless people from the Shaoxing area into this basin took place in the early fifth century. At this time three county cities existed in this area. All of them were located at the ecological boundaries between the foothills and the low-lying plain, the latter still being largely saline due to the subsurface intrusion of seawater. Settlement was limited to the seashores and the upriver basins, and hence the area's industries were represented by fishing, salt making, the pottery industry, and hill products. With the unification of the empire by the Sui 隋, the former territory of Guiji Commandery was reduced to the geographic area of the southern Hangzhou Bay littoral. Then, in 738, the Tang dynasty subdivided Guiji Commandery 會稽郡 into the two prefectures of Yue 越 (Shaoxing 紹興) and Ming 明 (Ningbo 寧波). In response to this, the work of building the prefectural capital in the center of the lowlands was started, being completed in 821. This city building necessitated the reclamation of the central lowlands.[17]

The external factor prompting this change was the rise in the seaborne trade along the eastern coast of China at the time. Yangzhou 揚州, a leading port in the lower Yangzi region, was losing its locational advantage of direct access to the Yangzi River because of siltation in or around 738. But the Yong River in Mingzhou 明 /Ningbo 寧波 was deep enough (from five to eight meters in depth depending on the tide) in its lower reaches to allow large oceanic junks to navigate thirteen miles from the river mouth to the confluence of its tributaries (the Yuyao 餘姚江 and the Fenghua rivers 奉化江). It was at this confluence that the prefectural capital was located. Further, in expectation of the rise in commercial wealth in this new outport of the delta, an extension of the Zhedong Canal 浙東河 in Shaoxing was built, so as to link it with the city of Mingzhou by way of the Yuyao River. In brief, this was the extension of the Grand Canal up to Mingzhou.

The reclamation of Mingzhou's central lowlands started with the draining of brackish marshy land in the southeastern sector. In 744 an old reservoir at the foot of hills to the east of the city was transformed into a larger one (5,660 hectares). It was renamed the Dongqianhu 東錢湖 (East [Plentiful] Coins Lake or East Lake 東湖). It was circumscribed by massive embankments, along whose western side three major outlets were installed in the form of large sluices. Three major drainage channels (*tang* 塘) were

---

[17] Shiba, "Ningbo and its Hinterland," in G. William Skinner, ed., *The City in Late Imperial China* (Stanford: Stanford University Press, 1977), pp. 391–439, esp. pp. 395–96; Shiba, *Studies on the economic history*, p. 469. Also refer to *Minguo Yin-xian tongzhi* 民國鄞縣通志 (1935 edition of the Local Gazetteer of Yin county, Ningbo), Yudizhi, Ji-bian, hequ 輿地志 已編河渠, pp. 63–104.

built, running across the lowlands westward and emptying into the Yong River or the Fenghua River. The northern one, called the Front Channel, was 18 kilometers in length, 30 meters in width, and 1.9 meters in depth; the middle one, called the Middle Channel, was 9 kilometers in length, 24 meters in width, and 1.5 meters in depth; the southern one, called the Rear Channel, was 18 kilometers in length, 30 meters in width, and 1.4 meters in depth. As it flowed along these channels the fresh water from the lake was distributed by numerous auxiliary smaller channels to reclaimed paddies. Along the Yong and Fenghua rivers embankments were built to protect the lowlands from the inroads of the brine. Several floodgates were installed on the embankments at important points for water control, which included the junctions of three major channels and two rivers. Both the drying out and the desalination of this sector of lowlands progressed thenceforth (see Map 5.4).

Meanwhile, the improvement of the western sector of the lowlands was of vital importance not only for production there but also for the growth of the city itself. Due to the existing topography, a rich and constant supply of fresh water to the farmland and citizens in this sector was only obtainable by diverting water from the Zhangxi 章溪 Stream, which collected runoff from Siming 四明 Mountain (916 meters) in the westernmost part of the area. However, the stream, after it passed the foothills, flowed into the Yin River 鄞江 (a tributary of the Fenghua River 奉化江). The force of the tide on the course of the Yong River 甬江 was so strong that brine was able to reach the confluence of the Yin River and the Zhangxi Stream. Hence the diversion of the stream water before it reached this confluence was crucial for the later development of the western plain as well as of the city. In the years between 713 and 741, pivotal work was done to solve the problem. A huge stone dam, named Tashan Yan 它山堰, was constructed at a site 1.6 kilometers short of the stream's influx into the Yin River. This was a trapezoidal stone dam 131 meters in width, consisting of thirty-six terraces apart from its upper-middle section, which was left open in the form of a channel of rectangular cross-section. Soon after that, a large channel, 23 kilometers in length, 34 meters in width, and 1.5 meters in depth, was built along the southern rim of the western lowlands, reaching the South Gate of the city. It was called the South Channel. This channel received the stream water at an intake 500 meters upstream of the dam site where the stream took an abrupt bend to the south. In the wet season, three-tenths of the stream water flowed into the channel, letting the rest of the water be received by the Yin River. In the dry season the ratio of the distribution of water was reversed. Water flow was regulated by means of a sluicegate installed in the upper-middle part of the dam. A final touch was added in

1242 with the construction of a waterlock at a point about 100 meters upstream of the dam. Since the flow of the stream was blocked by this lock, the sediment carried by the stream settled on the stream bed there. Here the speed of the flow was slow due to the partial discharge of water into the South Channel at its intake 500 meters upstream, and hence the dredging of silt was easy.

Before long embankments were made along the courses of the Fenghua 奉化江 and the Yuyao rivers 餘姚江. These were followed by the construction of the second and third channels: the Middle Channel, 12 kilometers in length, 30 meters in width, and 1.5 meters in depth; and the West Middle Channel, 12 kilometers in length, 20 meters in width, and 1.5 meters in depth. They were laid down across the lowlands, both of them reaching the West Gate of the city. The reclamation of the lowlands progressed following the building of these three channels and the development of subchannels alongside them. As early as 773, Guangde Lake 廣德湖 (Lake of Extensive Virtue), or the area in the central part of the western sector of the lowlands, which contained brackish water throughout all seasons, underwent an initial conversion into plowland around its periphery. By the end of the twelfth century the lake itself had vanished as the result of reclamation. In the Southern Song 南宋 dynasty and in the early Yuan 元 dynasty, farming in the western lowlands became highly productive. The rice fed the city and the straw mats of that area were renowned even in Cambodia among the Chinese goods traded there. In some year between 1225 and 1227, Wu Qian 吳潛, prefect of Mingzhou and a provincial military commissioner, who had done much to improve the water-control system of the area, took a boat trip from the city to the Tashan Dam. On his return he had a stone slab erected in the canal at the center of the city with the character *ping* 平 (equitable level) carved on it to show the level of water there appropriate for the city's water supply as well as for irrigation in the western plain. From this episode we also learn that the city was freely accessible to plain dwellers by boat via channels. By this time the rest of the lowlands in the area had largely been converted into the farm land (see Map 5.4).[18]

5.3.2. THE SEAWALLS AND THE ENCLOSED WET-FIELDS

The Yangzi delta in the eighth century saw a marked transition in the mode of its water control. Spatially, the region's reclamation was moving from the upriver areas to the lowlands. Along with this, the dominance of the reser-

[18] Shiba, *Studies on the economic history*, p. 471.

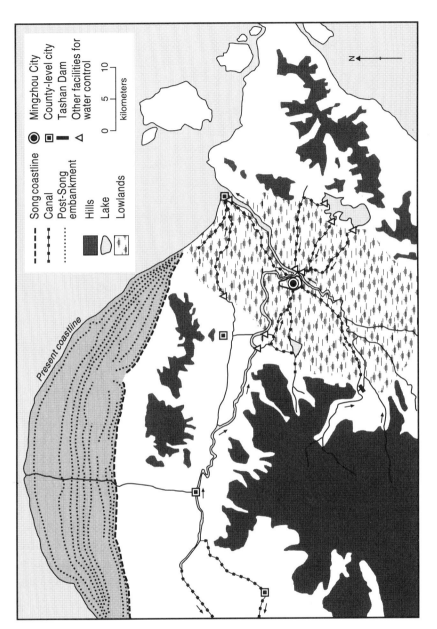

Map 5.4. The Yong River basin during Tang–Song times.

voir in water conservancy in the upriver areas was tending to be supplanted by the dissemination of a new technology for reclamation in the lowlands: a combination of seawalls, channels, and enclosed wet-fields (bearing a resemblance to the polders of Holland in Europe). The use of the reservoir did not, however, come to an end. It was still proving its efficacy for the opening up of the terraced fields in the hilly areas at large. Nevertheless the aggregate dimensions of lands served by reservoirs were no match for those opened by the new methods. Furthermore, the old reservoirs of considerable size, such as Mirror Lake, were in the process of losing their former size mostly because of the irresistible demand of local people to convert them into paddies (see Map 5.2c).[19]

Meanwhile, the adoption of the aforementioned new technological facilities in the taming of the wild lowlands was hardly feasible without the state's involvement in the process. What attracted the attention of the central government to the reclamation of lowlands in the region was the emergence of commercial salt production along the coastlines. In 758 the government set up a new monopoly on the salt industry centered in the lower Yangzi region. This was designed to meet the state's financial need for coping with the menace of the centrifugal power of the military governors. Under the system the areas of salt production were densely distributed along the coastlines of what were later to be the provinces of Jiangsu 江蘇 and Zhejiang 浙江. Among them major centers of salt production existed in the Hangzhou Bay area: Hangzhou 杭州, Jiaxing 嘉興, Shaoxing 紹興, and Mingzhou 明州. Production was carried on by licensed producers under the officials' supervision. Licensed merchants purchased the salt at the assigned center of production, also paying customs duties in advance for trading in a monopoly product. The merchants then distributed the salt to officially designated market areas in the Yangzi River valley.[20]

Before monopolization, a long stretch of seawalls running from the vicinity of what was later to be Shanghai to Hangzhou along the northern shorelines of the Hangzhou Bay had been built in the first quarter of the eighth century. Simultaneously, the construction of seawalls from Shaoxing

---

[19] Chen Qiaoyi, "The rise and fall," pp. 195–201.

[20] Seo Tatsuhiko 妹尾達彦, "Tōdai kōhan-ki ni okeru Kōwai enzei-kikan no ritchi to kinō" 唐代後半期にまける江淮鹽税機關の立地と機能 [The geographic locations of the intendancies of salt production in Jiangsu and Zhejiang provinces and the functions of these official organs during the later half of the Tang dynasty], *Shigaku-zasshi* 91.2 (Feb. 1982), pp. 1–37; Saeki Tomi 佐伯富, *Chūgoku ensei-shi no kenkyū* 中國鹽政史の研究 [A study of the history of governmental policies concerning the production and exchange of salt in China] (Kyoto: Hōritsubunka-sha, 1987), pp. 88–110.

to Mingzhou along the southern coastlines of the bay had been undertaken. In 910, the king of the Wuyue Kingdom 吳越國 (907–78), who ruled
over the region during the interregnum of the Five Dynasties period (907–
60), had also rebuilt the seawalls at the mouth of the Qiantang River near
the city of Hangzhou (the capital of the kingdom) into solid stone ones.[21]
Thus the initial construction of seawalls in the Hangzhou Bay area was for
hydraulic defense as well as for the encouragement of the salt industry
emerging within the walls. Meanwhile, in the Mingzhou area, the lowlands
to the west of the Yong River 甬江 were converted into farmland from the
later Tang 唐 to the Northern Song 北宋 dynasty. Here, the seawalls along
the seashores, the river embankments with their sluices, and the installation
of skeletal channels were made to work in combination in order to drain
away the saline water stored in the lowlands.

In the deltaic lowlands the pace of the reclamation seemed to progress
more gradually. Some specialists have suggested that the overall reclamation there got started during the Wuyue Kingdom 吳越國.[22] But this would
be a bit of an exaggeration. The evidence suggests that farming in the
central lowlands in the delta remained unstable till the mid-Northern Song
dynasty 北宋.[23]

For an assessment of the long-term process of reclamation in the delta
lowlands, we have reliable statistics as of 1377 on land utilization in
the prefecture of Huzhou 湖州. Huzhou prefecture, located south and west
of Lake Tai, consisted of six counties. Of these, Anji 安吉 occupied a large
hilly area to the west of the lake, while Wukang 武康, lying to its southeast,
was an area with a mixture of hills and slopes known for its being the area
of the oldest settlement within the prefecture. The other four counties of
Wucheng 烏程, Guian 歸安, Deqing 德清, and Changxing 長興 were together located in the lowlands south and west of the lake. As mentioned
above, the first reclamation of the lowlands in Huzhou took place along the
southern shorelines of the lake in the early eighth century, in the vicinity of
the prefectural capital, which was also the seat of Wucheng county.[24]

Let us first examine the pattern of the distribution of each of four
categories of land in the prefecture as a whole. It was as follows.

---

[21] Zheng Zhaojing, ed., *The history of technology*, pp. 189–90.

[22] Ibid., pp. 82–86.

[23] Shiba, *Studies on the economic history*, pp. 137, 138; Ōsawa Masaaki 大澤正昭, "So-Ko
      jukusureba tenka taru: kyozō to jitsuzō" 蘇湖熟すれば天下足る虚像と實像 [A rethinking of
      the saying that when Suzhou and Huzhou reap a good crop, the supply of food throughout
      the empire will be sufficient: was it true or not?], *Atarashii Rekishigaku no Tameni* 新しい歴史
      學のために 179 (June 1985), pp. 1–10.

[24] Shiba, *Studies on the economic history*, pp. 376–99.

Categories of Land	Percentage (%)
paddy 田	51
dry field 地	11
hill 山	34
marsh 蕩	4
	100%

Next, let us take a look at the patterns of the same kind of distribution by county.

	烏程 Wucheng (WC)	歸安 Guian (GA)	德清 Deqing (DQ)	長興 Changxing (CX)	武康 Wukang (WK)	安吉 Anji (AJ)
paddy	69	66	71	50	46	15
dry field	8	10	15	12	20	8
hill	19	16	6	36	21	77
marsh	4	8	8	2	13	0
	100%	100%	100%	100%	100%	100%

Let us also look at the patterns of distribution of each category of land by county across the prefecture as a whole.

	WC	GA	DQ	CX	WK	AJ	
paddy	27	25	16	23	3	6	100%
dry field	15	18	17	26	7	17	100%
hill	11	9	2	25	2	51	100%
marsh	19	36	20	12	11	2	100%

Finally, let us take a look at the pattern of percentage distribution of the numbers of the enclosed wet-fields (i.e., polders) counted by county. It is safe to assume that these statistics show the aggregation by county of larger-sized wet-fields in the prefecture.

WC	GA	DQ	CX	WK	AJ	
45	25	14	13	3	0	100%

An explanation is in order here for the reason for the very low percentage of hilly land held by Wukang (2%) in the prefecture-wide comparison. A partial explanation can be found in the smallness of this county. Once it held extensive territory, including the county of Deqing to its east, but in 691 a subdivision of the territory made Deqing independent. Secondly, Wukang long remained the central area where the earlier colonists had settled. The opening of the hillside by the construction of reservoirs and terraced fields is documented in earlier records. In other words, we may infer that a considerable part of the former "hills" had been converted into dry-fields by 1377.

The higher percentages of paddies shared equally by the counties of Wucheng, Guian, Changxing, and Deqing suggest the successful reclamation of wet-fields in the lowlands there. This observation will be reconfirmed if we look into the pattern of density distribution of the numbers of the enclosed wet-fields in the prefecture. By the way, the original data on this density distribution give the numbers from village to village. Meanwhile, the pattern of distribution of marshy lands in Wukang, Guian, Deqing, and Changxing helps us to identify these as counties with a surplus of untapped lowlands. In prefecture-wide comparison, Guian (36%) stood out above all others.[25] Let us next consider how things may have been with the overall lowlands at the center of the delta (see Map 5.1). The gaps in our knowledge are still too wide to make a reasonable assessment. We may speculate that a full reclamation of the lowlands there probably occurred by the middle of the Ming dynasty.

Before closing this section, let us also take a brief look at the aftermath of the building of the seawalls in the Hangzhou Bay area.[26] While the building of seawalls was a great benefit to the productivity and livelihood of the people there, it also left an unexpected result, the changeable flow of water from the Qiantang River 錢塘江 into the bay. Partly blocked by solidified seawalls along the shorelines of the bay and partly blocked by the influx of oceanic currents from the outside since Song times, the muddy

---

[25] Ibid.

[26] For the details of this environmental change, refer to Mark Elvin and Su Ninghu 苏宁浒, "Man against the Sea: Natural and Anthropogenic Factors in the Changing Morphology of Harngzhou Bay, circa 1000–1800," in *Environment and History* (Feb. 1995), pp. 3–54.

water discharged from the mouth of the Qiantang River made sharper meanders within the bay than before. The result was changeability in gaining and losing accretionary land along the shorelines, which occurred from place to place in accordance with the frequent changes in the course of the Qiantang River. A wide inward curve of the northern coastline of the bay to the east of Hangzhou, caused in the past by the force of the river discharging into the bay, was now replaced by a reverse jutting out of accretionary shallows there. This change in turn led to the gradual enlargement of an islet located in the middle of the bay to the north of Shaoxing. This caused a further slowing down of the flow of muddy water discharged from the mouth of the river, facilitating the enhancement in the amount of sedimentation in the vicinity of the mouth. Finally, by Qing 清 times, a peninsula-like salient of alluvium was formed from the western coast of Shaoxing, extending into the bay for about forty kilometers. These changes within the bay worsened the menace of wet-season inundation in the plains in Shaoxing and to the west of it.[27]

Some portion of the sedimentation near the mouth of the Qiantang River floated eastward along the southern coastlines of the bay, and formed another wide salient of land into the bay to the north of Mingzhou 明州. The total area of this extension of alluvium was about 600 square kilometers, with a width of 17.5 kilometers at its widest part and a length of about 70 kilometers at its outer shorelines. From the mid-Tang 唐 through the mid-Northern Song 北宋 dynasties the jutting of land toward the sea in this area remained minimal. But after the construction of solid earthen seawalls in 1047 to cover the shorefront without break, the pace of salient accretion progressed with increased speed. From 1047 to the present, the area saw the creation of nine separate lines of seawalls, one after another (see Map 5.4).[28]

5.4. THE EXHAUSTION OF OPEN SPACE IN THE REGION

5.4.1. THE DELTAIC LOWLANDS

During the Song dynasty, the eastern half of the delta remained to be incorporated into a single prefecture of Xiuzhou 秀州 / Jiaxing 嘉興, which administered its extensive territory through the three counties belonging to it. But the area underwent gradual progress in production and com-

[27] Zheng Zhaojing, ed., *The history of technology*, pp. 178–84.
[28] *Cixi Shuili-shi* 慈溪水利史 [The history of water control in Cixi county, Zhejiang province] (Zhejiang Renmin CBS, 1991), pp. 41–51. See also the discussion of this process in Elvin and Su, Chapter 10 of the present volume.

merce in that period. Aside from the growth in production of rice and salt, the impact of maritime trade played a considerable role. One of five offices of the Liangzhe commissioner of overseas trade 兩浙市舶使 was set up at the capital of Huating 華亭 county from 1113 to 1166. The hydraulic improvement alongside the Wusong 吳淞江 River and the Grand Canal at its section in Suzhou 蘇州 in the 1040s brought about an unexpected trend toward overall siltation of the river systems in Huating and threatened the capital's position as an important port of trade; its role was eventually taken over by the rise of the port of Qinglong Zhen 青龍鎮, and then by that of Shanghai. During the Southern Song, seven such local economic centers grew within the territory of Huating county.

In 1277, or two years before the final collapse of the Southern Song dynasty, Huating county in the former Xiuzhou 秀州/Jiaxing 嘉興 prefecture became an independent prefecture. It was renamed Songjiang 松江 in the next year. During the Yuan and the early Ming dynasties, it was enlarged to include the two counties of Huating and Shanghai (newly established in 1290) within its jurisdiction. Spatially, the prefectural territory covered most of the eastern half of the delta. We may infer that the subdivision was an indication of the progress in reclamation and colonization in it. This inference is supported by a glance at the increase in the amount of taxed grain shouldered by Xiuzhou/Jiaxing in the late Southern Song and that in Songjiang in the early Ming. In late Southern Song times, the figure for Jiaxing was 67,000 Song *shi* (6,357 kiloliters), but the figures for Songjiang alone rose to 199,755 Yuan *shi* (27,293 kiloliters) in Yuan times and to 878,377 Ming *shi* (833,377 kiloliters) in early Ming times.[29] Such a sudden rise in figures must be regarded with some suspicion.

From 1263 through the early decades of the Ming, official revenue from grain in six prefectures (Suzhou 蘇州, Hangzhou 杭州, Huzhou 湖州, Jiaxing 嘉興, Changzhou 常州, and Zhenjiang 鎮江), all of which were located in the vicinity of Lake Tai, had two sources: official land and private land. In 1263, the Southern Song regime, in its desperate effort to cope with a diminishing income from taxed grain owing to growing landlordism, introduced the system of the state demesne in the above six prefectures. The official estates were the aggregation of many plots of land formed by purchase or by confiscation. By the early Ming 明 the total area of this category of land in Suzhou had doubled, comprising two-thirds of the sum of plowlands in these six prefectures. Interestingly, the management of the state demesne did not preclude the existence of private landlordism within it. Only a handful of landlords and a mass of poor peasants were occupants of such official estates, but they were regarded by the government as its

---

[29] Shiba, *Studies on the economic history*, pp. 154–55.

"tenants" 佃戶 without distinction. The rate of "rent" 租 on the official estates was most commonly about twofold that of the taxation rate charged on privately owned land, customarily set at one-tenth of the yield per acre; but in some cases it rose to tenfold or more, the distribution being sharply skewed. In a long-run perspective, the system worked for the redistribution of land resources in the area, while as a short-term fiscal measure it was a powerful relief to the regimes of the late Yuan 元 and the early Ming 明. For example, in Yuan times the official income from grain from the Jiangnan 江南 region at large amounted to 37 percent of empire-wide income, and 40 percent of it was from the state demesne there.[30]

The sociopolitical unrest that characterized the lower Yangzi region in the transition from the Yuan to the Ming was successfully removed within a century or so after the founding of the Ming dynasty. This was followed by a resumption of traffic on the Grand Canal in 1415, by the relocation of the state capital from Nanjing (Nanking) to Beijing (Peking) in 1421, and by a simultaneous revival of interprovincial traffic, transactions, and silver diffusion. By the sixteenth century, the lower Yangzi region had gained its advantageous position as the central hub of the empire-wide economy. In consequence, people in the region could feel the advantages of the division of labor and the specialization of production. Cotton production and the making of cotton cloth grew in the prefectures of Songjiang 松江 and Suzhou 蘇州, while sericulture and the silk industry became the specialties of those of Hangzhou 杭州, Huzhou 湖州, Suzhou 蘇州, and Jiaxing 嘉興. In the latter prefectures, people tried to subsist by combining sericulture and riziculture, dividing their paddies into 60 percent for mulberry planting and the rest for rice production.[31]

These economic changes in the region attracted an ever-increasing influx of people from without. Owing to the spread of intensive cultivation of the surface soil and the worsening deforestation and denudation of the region, the bottom of Lake Tai became shallow. Reductions in the lake's discharge of water in turn caused the intensifying dysfunction of the Wusong

[30] Mori Masao 森正夫, *Mindai Kōnan tochiseido no kenkyū* 明代江南土地制度の研究 [A study of the land system in Jiangnan in Ming times] (Kyoto: Dōhōsha, 1988), pp. 45–69; Otagi Matsuo 愛宕松男, "Gen no Chūgoku shihai to Kanminzoku shakai" 元の中國支配と漢民族社會 [The Yuan rule over China and Chinese society], in *Sekai-Rekishi* 9 (Tokyo: Iwanami Shoten, 1970), pp. 304–08. It should be noted that Mori's table on p. 140 mistakenly gives the units as *dou*, rather than *shi*.

[31] Li Bozhong 李伯重, "Sang zheng daotian yu Ming-Qing Jiangnan nongye shengchan jiyuechengdu de tigao" 桑争稻田与明清江南农业生产集约程度的提高 [The production of two crops of mulberry trees and rice in the same field in the same growing season as evidence of intensifying farming in the Jiangnan area during the Ming and Qing periods], *Zhongguo Nong-shi* 1 (1985).

River 吳松江, a major drainage system that received its water from Lake Tai and drained the excess water in the central lowlands into the sea to the east. We have plenty of qualitative evidence indicating the crisis of overpopulation felt throughout the region.[32] Shortages of arable land as well as food were relieved to some extent by the gravitation of lowlands reclamation from the Yangzi delta to drainage basins in the provinces of Jiangxi 江西, Hu'nan 湖南, Hubei 湖北, and eastern Sichuan 四川 and by the transshipment of surplus rice from there to the lower Yangzi region.[33] The shortage of fuel also became a serious problem, for the producers of salt in particular. As early as in the middle of the Northern Song dynasty, producers along the southern shorelines of Hangzhou Bay became involved in murders and lawsuits over their access to firewood on nearby hills.[34] The scarcity of fuel supplies finally forced salt producers on both the north and south side of the bay to adopt the solar evaporation method by the Yuan period.

5.4.2. THE DISAPPEARANCE OF MIRROR LAKE

Mirror Lake had vanished from sight by Southern Song times (see Map 5.2c) on account of private encroachment. In time, the plain lying between the southern lines of foothills and the former northern banks of the lake turned into the area of the richest paddy-fields in Shaoxing. According to a local history of Shaoxing edited in 1587, local authorities gave the area premier rank in their fourfold classification of taxable lands under control, the second rank being the zones of "hill" land, the third "shorefront," and the lowest one "lowlands."[35]

In the meantime, the overpopulation in Shaoxing became undeniable during the Ming and Qing dynasties. According to 1820 statistics, the population density in the area was 510 persons per square kilometer, which was the second highest among the thirty most populous prefectures in the empire, following 838 persons in Suzhou 蘇州 prefecture in Jiangsu 江蘇.[36] In response to this pressure, attention was given to the improvement of nature in the area's nearby periphery. Such attempts dated back to 1112. At that time, Xiaoshan 蕭山 county, the western neighbor of Shaoxing, suffered from the

[32] Ho Ping-ti, *Studies on the Population of China*, pp. 217–21.

[33] Ibid., pp. 136–58; Wang Yeh-chien 王業鍵, "Food Supply and Grain Prices in the Yangzi Delta in ca. Eighteenth Century," *Proceedings of the Second Conference on Modern Chinese Economic History* (Taipei: Academia Sinica, 1989), pp. 424–29.

[34] Guo Zhengzhong 郭正忠, *Songdai yanye jingjishi* 宋代盐业经济史 [The economic history of the salt industry in Song times] (Qinhuangdao Renmin CBS, 1990), p. 123.

[35] Xiao Lianghan 蕭良翰 et al., ed., *Wanli Shaoxing-fu-zhi* 萬曆紹興府志 (1587 edition), ch. 14.

[36] Gilbert Rozman, *Population and Marketing Settlements in Qing China* (Cambridge: Cambridge University Press, 1982), pp. 12–14.

floods of the Puyang River 浦陽江 and occasional droughts. An artificial
reservoir (2,094 hectares), called Xianghu 湘湖, was created in 1112 to the
south of the county capital. It lay between two lines of hills. With the install-
ment of additional embankments and eighteen stone tunnels for the discharge of water, the reservoir was capable of irrigating the paddy-fields
around it over an area of 8,312 hectares. A very elaborate method was
thought out to distribute an equal amount of water in each sector of these
paddies.[37]

In the middle of the fifteenth century, the Shaoxing 紹興 and Xiaoshan
蕭山 areas saw a final but noteworthy project of water control. The first step
of this work was to divide the flow of the Puyang River into two. A small hill
lying to the west of the point where the river ran into the low-lying plain was
excavated so as to let a new westward branch of the river flow into the
Qiantang River 錢塘江. A sluice was built just upstream from where the hill
was cut and on the northern bank, right at the place where the hill had
been, with double functions of blocking the inroads of brine from the
Qiantang River and regulating the amount of the water to be sent to the
Xixiao River 西小江, or the former lower course of the Puyang River. Near
the forking point of the river, three auxiliary sluices were built to regulate
the influx of water in the Xixiao River more efficiently. The final work of
this project was the construction in 1536 of a huge sluice with twenty-eight
gates at the end of the Xixiao River near the shore of Hangzhou Bay. The
sluice was called Sanjiangzha 三江閘 (Three Rivers Sluice). In the dry
season, water from the Puyang River was taken into the Xixiao River
through upriver sluices and was stored in the channels connected with the
river. In the wet season, the upriver sluices were closed and the gates of
Three Rivers Sluice were opened to drain the excess of water.

5.4.3. SOUTH LAKE

South Lake in Yuhang county 餘杭縣 (present-day Yuhang Zhen 鎮) has
managed to survive up to now, but not without considerable reduction in its
former size. The degeneration of its overall functions, first witnessed in
1122, could not be effectively reversed during the Ming 明 and the Qing 清
periods. In 1149 we find the last record of the lake's recovery to its size in
1122. This was a reaction to an extensive inundation of the South Tiao

---

[37] Shiba, *Studies on the economic history*, pp. 558–83; Keith Schoppa, *Xiang Lake: Nine Centuries
of Chinese Life* (New Haven: Yale University Press, 1989); Schoppa, *Chinese Elites and Political
Change: Zhejiang Province in the Early Twentieth Century* (Cambridge, Mass.: Harvard University
Press, 1982); Chen Qiaoyi 陈桥驿, "Lun lishi shiqi Puyangjiang xiayou de hedao bianqian"
论历史时期浦阳江下游的河道变迁 [The changes in the courses of the Puyang River during
historical times), *Lishidili* 1 (1981), pp. 65–79.

River 南苕溪 that victimized the paddy-fields alongside it not only in the vicinity of Yuhang but also in the prefectures of Huzhou, Hangzhou, and Jiaxing. Except during such large-scale floods, the importance of South Lake in the regulation of water was apt to dwindle in the eyes of people in the downstream areas, where the development of the network of enclosures protected them from the ordinary fluctuations of the flow of the river.[38]

In 1544, the central government dispatched Fu Fengxiang 傅鳳翔, a touring censorial inspector, to Yuhang county to investigate the situation at South Lake. During his stay there, he made a survey of the lake and confiscated illegally reclaimed land within the lake, totaling 473.28 hectares. Meanwhile he drew a new boundary for the lake, including its periphery. The area enclosed by the new boundary was much smaller than those in the past. Further, his survey excluded North Lake, most of Upper South Lake, and a fair area of the former periphery zone from the new measurement of South Lake. During the years of 1609–10, a last vigorous effort was made to restore the size of the lake to its boundaries as redrawn by Fu.[39]

The final blow paralyzing South Lake was dealt by the cultivation of the upriver highlands to the west of Yuhang by the "shack people" (*kemin* 客民 or *pengmin* 棚民) in the Qing 清 period. They were mostly people from the land-scarce southeastern provinces, who were invited in by the owners of hilly districts in the Yangzi valley to serve as their labor forces for the production of such goods as lumber, jute, indigo, lacquer, charcoal, and tobacco. On the hillsides they sustained themselves by planting maize, sweet potatoes, and peanuts. With their settlement in the hilly districts in northwestern Zhejiang 浙江 province, deforestation spread everywhere beginning in the 1720s. Then, during the late phase of the Taiping Rebellion, when the hilly portion of the two provinces of Jiangsu 江蘇 and Zheziang 浙江 was under attack by the rebels, the depopulation in such areas prompted a reinforced influx of these shack people. They tilled the slopes intensively, causing chronic erosion of the surface soils.[40]

By the late nineteenth century, Upper South Lake had been fully trans-

<hr>

[38] Shiba, "The history of water conservancy," pp. 580–82.

[39] Ibid., pp. 582–83.

[40] Morita, Akira, 森田明 "Shinmatsu Sekkō Yokō-ken no Nanko suiri to kyakumin mondai" 清末浙江餘杭縣の南湖水利と客民問題 [Water control in South Lake and the problems of the shack people in Yuhang county, Zhejiang, in the late Qing period], in Morita, ed., *Chūgoku suiri-shi no kenkyū* 中國水利史の研究 [Studies in the history of water control in China] (Tokyo: Kokushokankokai, 1995), pp. 493–513; Morita, "Shinmatsu Sekkōshō Yokoken Nanko suiri ni tsuite: kaishun jigyō wo chūshin to shite" 清末浙江省餘杭縣南湖水利について開濬事業と中心として [Water control in South Lake in Yuhang county, Zhejiang, in the late Qing: with a particular focus on dredging], *Kyūshū Sangyōdaigaku Kiyō*, 29.3 (1993). On the problem of the shack people in Zhejiang, see Ho Ping-ti, *Studies on the Population of China*, pp. 146–48, and Anne Osborne in Chapter 7 of the present volume.

formed into paddies by the shack people, who now took the lead in en-croachment. Fortunately, Lower South Lake survived as the result of offi-cials' enthusiasm for its maintenance. Finally, in 1901, the Bureau of Commerce in Beijing made a shift in its policy from the traditional upkeep of Lower South Lake to the encouragement of its reclamation. Under the regime of the People's Republic of China, the construction of countless modern reservoirs in the upriver basins of the South Tiao River has contrib-uted to the reduction of flooding along the river. The former South Lake has now been transformed into a state farm.

CONCLUSION

Several findings can be drawn from the above discussion. First, the history of water control in the lower Yangzi region confirms the general assump-tion that the Chinese by cultural preference were traditionally plains and valley people. The flat deltaic plain was the area where the Chinese cultural repertoire, particularly the technology and social organization of produc-tion and exchange, developed maximally. Second, the technological de-vices that were used in the reclamation and colonization movement in the deltaic lowlands on a wide scale and with increasing sophistication since the eighth century were not so much new ones as traditional ones. They had been accumulated and tested in the process of human settlement in the areas of higher elevation immediately south of the delta.

Third, in the earlier stage of lowlands reclamation in the Yangzi delta from the eighth through thirteenth centuries, the government played an important role in the laying down of the network of channels and in the building of the seawalls. The climax of such official enthusiasm in the work of water control occurred during the periods of the Northern and South-ern Song 宋. Fourth, the siting of the state capitals of the Southern Song 南宋 (Hangzhou) and the early Ming 明 (Nanjing) along with the establish-ment of their metropolitan provinces in the Lower Yangzi region also did much to promote the overall development of the region.

Fifth, be that as it may, there was an apparent secular decline in the up-keep of water-control systems in the region after the formation of their origi-nal skeletal structures. In other words, from the Ming 明 dynasty onward the officials' effort to maintain key facilities for water control was challenged by the will of local people to privatize them. Sixth, the trend of diminishing official involvement in water control in the region was paralleled by an increasing imbalance between natural environmental resources and human activities.

6

Han Migration and the Settlement of Taiwan

THE ONSET OF ENVIRONMENTAL CHANGE

LIU TS'UI-JUNG

This essay takes human settlement as its subject of study within the context of the environmental history of Taiwan. The aim is to understand the process and significance of the changes occurring from about 1600 to 1900. The environment of any locality is no doubt affected by both natural and human conditions, but it is the people who construct the settlement; thus a main concern of environmental history is to see how people form and transform their settlements. The physical features and climate of Taiwan changed very little during this period.[1] Taiwan was converted, however, from a wasteland to a cultivated island. This environmental transformation was mainly caused by Han migrants who settled down to farm the land. This essay looks into this process by focusing on the increase in Han settlements and the expansion of cultivated lands through the construction of irrigation works. Other related aspects, such as the issue of deforestation, are examined in a later chapter by my colleague Kuo-tung Ch'en. The discussion is chronological; the administrative divisions and rivers concerned are shown on Map 6.1.

6.1. THE SIXTEENTH AND SEVENTEENTH CENTURIES (THE LATE MING, THE DUTCH, AND THE ZHENG PERIODS)

Before the seventeenth century, the Han Chinese came to Taiwan mainly for fishing and trading. The Southern Song records suggest that there were

[1] Chen Zhengxiang 陳正祥, *Taiwan dizhi* 台灣地誌 [A geography of Taiwan] (Taipei: Fumin Geographical Institute of Economic Development, 1959–61), pp. 45–62.

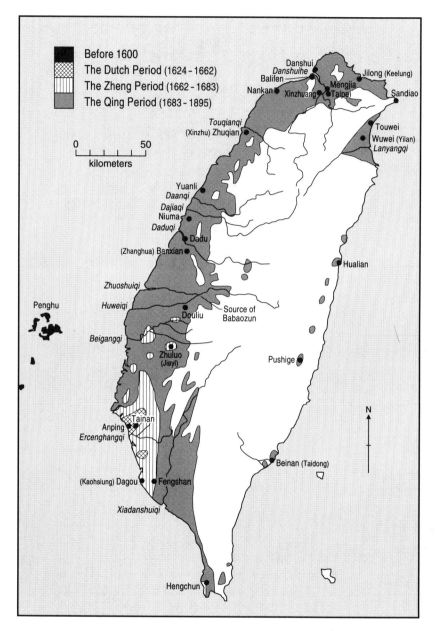

Map 6.1. Expansion of Han reclamation on Taiwan, 1600–1895.

Han settlers in Penghu 澎湖 (the Pescadores) by the end of the twelfth century. The Ming literature reveals that the Han people came to Taiwan at latest in the mid-sixteenth century. At that time the international maritime trade route in the Far East had to pass by Taiwan, and traders and fishermen from southern Fujian visited the island frequently. The traders and fishing boats landed on the west coast of Taiwan at various ports, from Dagou 打狗 (today's Kaohsiung) in the south to Jilong 雞籠 (today's Keelung) in the north. Besides fishing, most fishermen also traded with the aborigines. They obtained deerskin, dried venison, and firewood for the cargoes of their return trips. It is also possible that some fishermen settled down in Taiwan.[2]

The activities of these traders and fishermen must have modified Taiwan's landscape to some extent as regards environmental change. Their impacts, however, were certainly not as significant as those of migrants who came later and settled down to open up new lands.

The number of Han settlers in Taiwan was still very small at the beginning of the seventeenth century.[3] During the first half of that century, a larger number of the Han Chinese began to migrate to Taiwan. Lian Heng has noted two streams of this early migration. The first stream came around 1624–26: more than 3,000 people affected by droughts and famines in Zhangzhou 漳州 and Quanzhou 泉州 moved to Taiwan following the landing there of some pirates, among them Zheng Zhilong 鄭芝龍 (Nicholas Iquan in the Dutch literature).[4] The second stream came around 1628–31 when Xiong Wencan 熊文燦 governor of Fujian, accepted Zheng Zhilong's advice to ship the people pressed by droughts to Taiwan. This group consisted of "several tens of thousands" of starving people; they were provided with three taels of silver per person and one head of cattle for every three.[5] The scale of the second migration stream is, however, rather suspect.[6] It is not clear where these migrants settled down and how they were

[2] Cao Yonghe 曹永和, "Mingdai Taiwan yuye zhilüe" [A study on fishing in Taiwan in the Ming dynasty], *Taiwan yinhang jikan* 台灣銀行季刊 [Quarterly of the Bank of Taiwan] 6.1 (1953), pp. 169–75; "Mingdai Taiwan yuye zhilüe bushuo" [A further study on fishing in Taiwan], *Taiwan jingjishi siji* 台灣經濟史四集 [The fourth collection on the economic history of Taiwan] (Taipei: Bank of Taiwan, 1956), pp. 16–47; Chen Zhengxiang, "Sanbainianlai Taiwan dili de bianqian" [Geographic changes in Taiwan in the last three hundred years], *Taiwan wenxian* 台灣文獻 [Reports on Historiographical Studies of Taiwan] 12.1 (1961), pp. 77–85.

[3] Wen-hsiung Hsu, "From Aboriginal Island to Chinese Frontier," in R. Knapp, ed., *Chinese Island Frontier* (Honolulu: University of Hawaii Press, 1980), p. 10.

[4] Lian Heng 連橫, *Taiwan tongshi* 台灣通史 [General history of Taiwan] (Taipei: Bank of Taiwan, 1962), pp. 168, 727–28. For records of drought and famine, see *Zhangzhou fuzhi* 漳州府誌 [Gazetteer of Zhangzhou prefecture] (1877), *j.* 47, p. 9b; *Fujian tongzhi* 福建通誌 [Gazetteer of Fujian province] (1871), *j.* 271, p. 49b; Peng Sunyi 彭孫貽, *Jinghaizhi* 靖海誌 [A treatise on pacification on the sea] (Taipei: Bank of Taiwan, 1959), p. 2.

[5] Lian Heng, *General history*, pp. 168, 647; Fang Hao, "Chongzhen chunian Zheng Zhilong yimin jutai shi" [On the event of moving people into Taiwan by Zheng Zhilong during the early Chongzhen reign], in *Fang Hao liushi ziding gao* 方豪六十自定稿 [The collected works of Fang Hao on his sixtieth birthday] (Taipei: published by the Author, 1969), pp. 659–62.

[6] Chen Shaoxing 陳紹馨 et al., *Taiwansheng tongzhi* 台灣省通誌 [Gazetteer of Taiwan province] (Taipei: Historical Research Commission of Taiwan Province, 1972), section on population,

organized to cultivate the land, although Lian Heng states that the first group was not sent by any official order and the second one paid rents to Zheng Zhilong; this suggests that these migrants were not under the control of the Dutch who had built Fort Orange (renamed Fort Zeelandia in 1627) on a sandbank nearby Anping 安平.[7]

During the period of Dutch rule (1624–62), the Dutch East India Company promoted agriculture in Taiwan to achieve the company's mercantile goals. As the aborigines still engaged only in primitive agriculture, the company encouraged Chinese peasants to move to the island. The company provided land and capital, such as money and cattle, to Chinese peasants who tilled their fields as "Crown land." Partly due to the company's promotion and partly to the disorder in China during the dynastic transition, many people moved to Taiwan.

By the end of the Dutch period, the Han population in Taiwan was recorded by various authors to be 25,000 households, 30,000 households, or 100,000 people. Modern scholars tend to agree that the most plausible figure should be below 50,000 people. The total cultivated acreage was about 10,000 jia 甲 (1 jia is approximately 11 mu, 1 morgen, or 1 hectare). The area already reclaimed centered on today's Tainan 臺南 and in scattered fashion reached north to Beigang 北港 and south to Gangshan 岡山. The company paid much attention to building irrigation and drainage systems. The main crops were rice and sugarcane, but the company also introduced others, such as garden peas and tobacco, and promoted cultivation of indigo and medicinal herbs. In sum, the Dutch India Company left a legacy of crops, domestic animals, irrigation, and a land system for Taiwan's agriculture.[8]

vol. 1, pp. 40–41. Chen contends that if the transport cost and reported numbers of people and cattle at that time are taken into consideration, it is incredible that all of them were moved with such a scale of provisions.

[7] Lian Heng, General history, p. 168. For relations between Zheng Zhilong and the Dutch, see Yang Yanjie 楊彥傑, Hejushidai Taiwanshi 荷據時代台灣史 [History of Taiwan under the Dutch rule] [Nanchang: People's Press, 1992], pp. 66–67, 155–56; Yang Xuxian 楊緒賢, "Zheng Zhilong yu Helan zhi guanxi" [The relationship between Zheng Zhilong and the Dutch], Taiwan wenxian 27.3 (1976), pp. 164–65.

[8] Okuda Iku 奧田彧 et al., "Heling shidai zhi Taiwan nongye" [Taiwan's agriculture under Dutch rule], Taiwan jingjishi chuji [The first collection on the economic history of Taiwan] (Taipei: Bank of Taiwan, 1954), pp. 38–53; Nakamura Takashi 中村孝誌, "Heling shidai zhi Taiwan nongye ji qi jiangli" [Taiwan's agriculture and its promotion under Dutch rule], Taiwan jingjishi chuji, pp. 54–69; Cao Yonghe, "Hejushiqi Taiwan Kaifa shilüe" [A brief history of Taiwan's development during the Dutch period], Taiwan wenxian 26.4–27.1 (1975–76), p. 200; Yang Yanjie, History of Taiwan under the Dutch, pp. 170–80; Chen Shaoxin, Gazetteer of Taiwan province, section on population, vol. 1, pp. 46–48; Wen-hsiung Hsu, "From Aboriginal Island," pp. 12–18; John Shepherd, Statecraft and Political Economy on the Taiwan Frontier 1600–1800 (Stanford, Calif.: Stanford University Press, 1993), p. 86.

In 1661, Zheng Chenggong 鄭成功 (known as Koxinga in the West), son of Zheng Zhilong, landed on Taiwan with his army and in the next year took over control from the Dutch. A new phase of the Han settlements in Taiwan thus began. Shortly after the landing of Zheng's forces, he issued a decree commanding the army to undertake military colonization. To solve the problem of labor supply, Zheng ordered his officers and soldiers to move their families to Taiwan and encouraged inmigration. At the same time, the Qing government coerced the people living along the southeastern coast of China to move inland to make it difficult for Zheng to survive on Taiwan. Nevertheless, many people, mostly male adults, still took the risk of moving to Taiwan.

Among regulations announced for agricultural colonization, the following two, concerning land acquisition and resource utilization, are the most notable:

(1) All officials and officers might enclose lands for permanent holding according to the number of people under their command. They should not enclose the land already reclaimed by the aborigines and the early Han settlers.

(2) They might have rights over the forests and ponds situated within their enclosures as long as maps were presented to the authorities for fixing the tax; these resources should be used sparingly, trees should not be cut without limitations as to the time of year and the water should not be drained just for fishing, so that later generations could enjoy the benefits forever.

The task of opening up new lands began to bear fruit by 1666. The Crown land previously under Dutch control was transferred to the Zheng government and known as "official land" (*guantian* 官田); the lands enclosed by officials and officers were known as "civil and military official land" (*wenwu guantian* 文武官田) or "private land" (*sitian* 私田); and the lands cultivated by soldiers at garrison posts were known as "garrison land" (*yingpan* 營盤). Besides these categories of official land, it is also known that there were twelve and a half private villages (*minshe* 民社) and other settlements founded by migrants from Zhangzhou and Quanzhou. These settlements were mostly scattered along the southwest coast. During the Zheng period (1661–83), although new assarts were still scattered, the scale was larger than before. Rice and sugarcane remained the main crops, and more than twenty irrigation works were built. By the end of this period, total cultivated acreage was about 18,000 *jia* and the Han population was estimated to be 120,000.[9]

---

[9] For details of agricultural expansion see, Cao Yonghe, "Zhengshi shidai zhi Taiwan kenzhi" [Agricultural expansion in Taiwan in the Zheng period], *First collection*, pp. 70–85; Chen Hanguang 陳漢光, "Zhengshi futai yu qi kaiken" [Restoration and reclamation of Taiwan by

Throughout the seventeenth century, the primitive landscape of Taiwan had not been changed very much despite more lands being opened up. The best eyewitness can be found in *Pihai jiyou* 裨海紀遊 [Travel over a small sea], written by Yu Yonghe 郁永河, who visited Taiwan in 1697.[10] This was only fourteen years after Taiwan was conquered by the Qing navy led by Admiral Shi Lang 施琅. The purpose of Yu's journey was to obtain sulfur for the Fujian provincial government. On March 17, 1697, he landed on Taiwan at Luermen 鹿耳門, then the harbor for reaching the prefectural city (today's Tainan). After gathering equipment, he took the land route northward.[11] On May 26, 1697, Yu and his followers and servants, altogether fifty-five people, departed from the prefectural city. His vehicle was a carriage harnessed to a young yellow ox and driven by the aborigines; the oxcart was changed at every aboriginal village on the way. It took them twenty days to reach their destination. A few landmarks reflecting comparative degrees of development in Taiwan can be gathered from his observations.

On the first day, they passed through three aboriginal villages; Yu comments, "Houses in these villages are tidy and they are not very different from those in the interior of China" (p. 17). This demonstrated the acculturation of the aborigines residing near the prefectural city. Four days later, they arrived at Banxian She 半線社 (later the site of Zhanghua Xian 彰化縣) in central Taiwan. Beyond this place, the road became stony and the surroundings were "Wildernesses of trees and bushes, and high grasses that bury one's shoulders, as if it is under a different heaven from places south of Banxian" (p. 19). This suggests that Banxian was then at the edge of the developed area. Two days later, they arrived at Niuma She 牛罵社 (today's Chingshui 清水); they had to stay there for ten days because of heavy rain. Then they crossed the Dajiaqi 大甲溪 to reach Yuanli She 宛里社. Yu notes: "The villages are all empty along this way, we are not able to obtain even a ladle of water; we will be happy if we meet anybody. From here northward, the situation is about the same" (p. 21). In other words, the Dajiaqi River was another demarcation line of development.

Two more days later, they arrived at Zhuqian She 竹塹社 (later the site of

---

the Zheng regime], *Taiwan wenxian* 12.1 (1961), pp. 39–54; Chen Zhengxiang, "Geographic changes," pp. 80–81. For estimates of the population, see Chen Shaoxin, *Gazetteer of Taiwan province*, section on population, vol. 1, pp. 51–52.

[10] The page numbers cited below are those of the edition published by the Bank of Taiwan (Taipei, 1959).

[11] Originally, Yu had planned to take the sea route and bought two boats. He later accepted a suggestion from a fellow countryman and took the land route, but his equipment was still carried in two boats, one of which was damaged in a storm halfway. See *Travel over a small sea*, pp. 16, 20–22.

Danshui Ting 淡水廳 and Xinzhu Xian 新竹縣) and the next day, Nankan She 南嵌社. Yu records:

> From Zhuqian to Nankan was a distance about eighty to ninety *li* 里 [1 *li* is approximately 0.5 kilometer]. We saw nobody and no house and there was not a single tree to give us a shade. We dug a hole in the ground and on top of it cooked the food with an earthen pot; under the fierce heat of the sun we were satisfied with a meal enriched by the water obtained from a torrent. On the way, we came across groups of elks, deer, female elks, and does; my aboriginal followers were able to catch three deer. Upon arriving at Nankan, we entered into deep rushes and our caps and shoes were all broken after going through. This was just a cave for animals and not a place suitable for human beings to visit! (p. 22)

Finally, they arrived at Balifen She 八里坌社, then canoed across the river to Danshui She 淡水社. The headman welcomed them and had some twenty thatched huts built in five days about ten *li* upstream from Gandamen 甘答門 (today's Kuantu 關渡) for the group to shelter in during their sojourn (pp. 22–23). In late June, Yu went up to the mountain to investigate the sulfur mine. He passed through stiff rushes that were more than ten feet high. He entered into a deep forest of small and large trees that he could not name; he saw old rattans climbing up trunks like dragons and huge trees that his guide identified as *nan* 楠 (*Phoebe formosana Hayata*). He heard for the first time a tremendous variety of birds' songs, although he could see no birds. The wind was cool and he almost forgot that it was in hot summer (pp. 24–25). In short, he vividly described a scene of the forest in northern Taiwan.

Moreover, Yu Yonghe had some comments on the hardships of living in the natural environment of Taiwan. First, the "miasma" (*zhangli* 瘴癘) was dreadful.

> It was said that the climate of this place was harmful. Once one fell ill, the only outcome was death. Gentlemen at the prefectural city had talked about this carefully but I did not believe it. After only a short stay, however, the servants fell ill; nine out of the ten helpers were sick! Even the cook was sick and nobody could help with the cooking. . . . In my opinion, the mountains and the rivers are not different from those in China and there is no evidence for evil spirits; once one has arrived here, however, one suddenly falls ill. This is just because the deep mountains and the great rivers are still in the condition of wilderness; grasses and woods are dark and thick; there are not yet many people, and accumulated pestilential vapors can be easily sucked into the lungs and bowels. Thus one falls ill suddenly and the same symptom is found for thousands. (p. 26)

Next, it was a hardship to travel long distances under rough and primitive conditions. Yu describes what it was like to go along the west coast of
Taiwan, then mostly uncultivated:

> When I look across the plain, I see nothing but flourishing grasses; the strong
> ones rise above my head and the weak ones reach to my shoulders; the
> carriage going through the grasses is as if it were underneath the ground; the
> tips of the grasses cut my face and neck, mosquitoes and flies suck my skin and
> body and cannot be driven away, as if they were hungry eagles and tigers.
> Moreover, the flaming sunshine blazes and my neck and back are almost split
> open. This, indeed, is the greatest toil and suffering on this world. (p. 26)

Furthermore, simple hovels and natural surroundings not to any degree
improved were rather inconvenient and dangerous:

> The four walls and the roof of the thatched hut are all covered with rushes;
> the wind comes in from all directions as if it were arrows, and whenever I lie
> down I see the sky. Grasses grow up on top of the bed and after being
> plucked, grow up again quickly. When it rains, the room becomes a torrent,
> and after the rain, I have to get on to the bed with my wooden shoes for at
> least ten days. There are always the lutes of cicadas and flutes of earthworms
> underneath the bed, and the morning and evening tides always arrive at the
> front of the stairs. Out of the house, grasses cover my shoulders, old trees
> tangle together, bamboos cluster, and I cannot see through them over a short
> distance. The big adders which have swelling necks have a strength to swallow
> a deer; they can be heard every night nearby my pillow and sometimes
> the sound is as loud as the snore of a cow; small snakes glide after the people
> as fast as flying arrows. Once it gets dark, I dread to got out of the door. (pp.
> 26–27)

Yu's observations reveal that at the end of the seventeenth century the
Han people in Taiwan still felt threatened by miasma and had to endure
extreme hardship when traveling over a long distance, and the aboriginal
houses in natural surroundings were inconvenient and dangerous. These
conditions changed gradually in the next century as more migrants settled
in.

Before going on to trace the agricultural expansion led by these Han
inmigrants, a problem of environmental protection in seventeenth-century
Taiwan should be mentioned here: the protection of the deer. As mentioned earlier, since the mid-sixteenth century traders and fishing boats
carried deerskin and dried venison back to Fujian. It seems that up to the
early seventeenth century such commercial activity had not sounded any
warning of a decrease in the numbers of deer. For instance, in 1603, Chen
Di 陳第 visited Taiwan and recorded the customs of the aborigines in his

Dongfanji 東蕃記 [A note on the eastern tribes]. Chen mentions that there were hundreds and thousands of deer, and among the aborigines, "It is prohibited to catch a deer privately. When winter comes and herds of deer appear, then a hundred more men are gathered to hunt; as soon as they catch up with a herd, they make a circle and drive the herd into it and then spear them." In this way, "Deer are caught year after year but they are not exhausted."[12]

The situation changed in the first half of the seventeenth century when the Dutch East India Company shipped a large number of deerskins to Japan. The company purchased deerskins from the aborigines and the Han people who had hunting licenses. The price paid by the company for one piece of deerskin was four pence, but it was sold for three shillings in Japan, nine times the original price! The profit was high, but the volume of trade could not grow in sustained fashion; the main reason for this was that the number of deer was decreasing. Available statistics show that during 1634–61, the annual quantity of deerskins shipped to Japan was over 100,000 pieces in 1634, 1638, and 1655; in most other years, it was over 50,000 pieces. Since a doe can produce only one fawn at a time, a natural outcome of large-scale hunting is thus a sharp decline in the deer population. To maintain the trade, the Dutch decided in 1640 to prohibit the Han people from using traps and nets. In 1645, the Dutch again decided to protect the deer by prohibiting the use of traps and by allowing hunting for two years and then enforcing a rest in the third year. These measures, however, had no effect. By the end of the seventeenth century, herds of deer were rarely seen in southern Taiwan. During the eighteenth century, most grasslands for deer were reclaimed by Han settlers. The Qing government also prohibited the use of traps, but in vain.[13] From the point of view of today's environmentalism, the story of Taiwan's deer may be counted as one

---

[12] The two citations are from *Liuqiu yu Jilongshan* 流求與雞籠山 [A collection of essays on early Taiwan] (Taipei: Bank of Taiwan, 1964), p. 91. On Chen Di's visit to Taiwan and the value of the *Dongfanji* 東番記, see Chen Zhengxiang, "Geographic changes," pp. 78–79.

[13] For various aspects of deer in Taiwan, see Nakamura Takashi, "Shiqi shiji Taiwan lupi zhi chuchan ji dui-Ri maoyi" [The production of deerskins in seventeenth-century Taiwan and their trade to Japan], *Taiwan jingjishi baji* [The eighth collection on the economic history of Taiwan] (Taipei: Bank of Taiwan, 1959), pp. 24–42; Zhou Minghong 周鳴鴻, "Lu zai Taiwan" [Deer in Taiwan], *Taiwan jingjishi jiuji* [The ninth collection on the economic history of Taiwan] (Taipei: Bank of Taiwan, 1963), pp. 104–16; Cao Yonghe, "Brief history," pp. 217–19; Yang Yanjie, *History of Taiwan Under the Dutch*, pp. 200–13; Shepherd, *Statecraft and Political Economy*, pp. 74–75, 79–80. It may be noted that Zhou mentions that *Cervus swinhoe* deer (*shuilu* 水鹿) were raised domestically at a few places in Taiwan in the 1960s. It may also be noted that on January 23, 1994, ten Formosan sika deer raised in Kenting National Park were sent back to the wild; see *The Free China Journal*, January 28, 1994.

among numerous failures to afford protection in the history of human-kind's exploitation of nature.[14]

6.2. THE EIGHTEENTH AND NINETEENTH CENTURIES (THE QING PERIOD)

In the eighteenth century, more and more Han Chinese crossed the Taiwan Strait, and the cultivated lands on the island also expanded from scattered points to connected areas. This section will first summarize the Qing policies regarding inmigration and the opening up of new land in Taiwan, then trace the process of reclamation from south to north and then to the east.

6.2.1. THE POLICY BACKGROUND

In 1683, the Qing government took over control of Taiwan. Its policy of ruling this new frontier was rather cautious in the beginning. A passport was required for inmigration, and the migrant could not bring his family along. Before 1790, the rule about bringing one's family was loosened four times and tightened five times; altogether it was loosened for forty-five and tightened for sixty-one years. Finally, in 1790 this prohibition was abolished. A passport was still required, however, and this control was not relaxed until 1875. Moreover, at Shi Lang's suggestion, people from Chaozhou 潮州 and Huizhou 惠州 were initially forbidden to move to Taiwan; this restriction was gradually loosened only after Shi's death in 1696. Despite the prohibitive regulations, the Qing government was not able to prevent people from going to Taiwan illegally.[15]

It is difficult to determine the exact number of Han migrants because

---

[14] For a debate on the environmental problem since the 1960s, see B. Harvey and J. Hallett, *Environment and Society* (Cambridge, Mass.: MIT Press, 1977), pp. 76–85.

[15] See Chen Shaoxin, *Gazetteer of Taiwan province*, section on population, vol. 2, pp. 99–103; Huang Fusan 黃富三, "Qingdai Taiwan yimin de gengdi qude wenti ji qi dui tuzhu de yingxiang" [The problem of immigrants' land acquisition in Qing Taiwan and its impact on the aborigines], *Shihuo Monthly* 食貨 11.1 (1981), pp. 20–22; Shi Tianfu 施添福, *Qingdai zai Tai Hanren de zuji fenbu he yuanxiang shenghuo fangshi* 清代在台漢人的祖籍分布和原鄉生活方式 [The distribution of the Han people in Taiwan as reflected by their native places and way of life] (Taipei: National Normal University, 1987), pp. 36–37, 44–45; Lin Renchuan 林仁川 and Wang Puhua 王蒲華, "Qingdai Fujian renkou xiang Taiwan de liudong" [The flow of population from Fujian to Taiwan in Qing times], *Lishi yanjiu* 历史研究 [Historical studies] 162 (1983), pp. 132–37.

of a lack of reliable statistics. An investigation of the Baojia 保甲 (local policing system) in 1811 reported 1,944,737 people in Taiwan; this figure can be taken as a comparatively reliable one for the Han population. If we compare this with the 120,000 estimated for the Han population around 1680, the mean annual growth rate during these 131 years can be seen to be 2.1 percent. As mentioned above, before 1790 inmigrants were not allowed to bring their families for most of these years, and thus the sex ratio was unbalanced. It is quite obvious that during the eighteenth century, the rapid increase of population in Taiwan was due mainly to the influx of migrants. Another relatively comprehensive investigation of the population in Taiwan was taken during 1892–94. The result showed that there were 2,546,000 people, most of them Han Chinese, except that aborigines were also included in Taidong Zhou 臺東州. Thus, from 1811 to 1893, the mean annual growth rate of the Han Chinese in Taiwan was about 0.3 percent. This suggests that during the nineteenth century, the population in Taiwan was gradually reaching a point of saturation; little room was left for new inmigrants and the growth rate was much restrained by the frequent occurrences of riots and natural calamities.[16]

The Qing government also adopted a prohibitive policy on land to prevent Han migrants from entering the mountain areas freely. This prohibitive policy was meant to have three aspects: to guard against the Han people occupying strategic locales for stirring up revolts, to restrict the Han people from encroaching upon aboriginal land, and to prevent violent conflict between mountain aborigines and Han inmigrants. To carry out this policy, stones were set up as boundary markers and guards were posted at strategic passes along the mountains. The first boundary was set up in 1722 after the suppression of the revolt of Zhu Yigui 朱一貴. In the 1740s, ditches were dug at places where boundary stones were set up. In 1760–61, the boundary was reinforced by digging deep ditches and building earthen mounds at places where there were no rivers to serve as natural boundaries. Since the mounds looked like oxen lying on the ground, they were called "earthen oxen" (*tuniu* 土牛), and the ditches next to them, *tuniugou* 土牛 溝. In 1790, the Qing government allotted the grassland east of the ditch to the acculturated aborigines who served as post guards, and stones were set up for a new boundary. A general opinion held by scholars is that these boundaries served no effective purpose, in no way preventing the Han people from going beyond them. Nevertheless, the deep ditches with

[16] For population estimates, see Chen Shaoxin, *Gazetteer of Taiwan province*, section on population, vol. 1, pp. 53–57.

earthen oxen lying nearby did form a peculiar anthropogenic landscape in the mountain areas of northern Taiwan.[17] From the viewpoint of environmental change, the prohibitive policy and the existence of these boundaries may to some extent have held back the speed with which the mountain areas were exploited, and hence delayed deforestation.

For the acquisition of land, one had to apply for a license from the local government for opening up ownerless wasteland; and for opening up aboriginal land, one had to negotiate a contract, usually through mediation of an interpreter, with the aboriginal landowner.[18] Basically, the Qing government recognized aboriginal land rights and issued several decrees to protect them; the goal of this policy was, however, to maintain order in the frontier society and to reduce conflicts between ethnic groups rather than to secure the interests of the aborigines.[19] Thus, from the eighteenth century on, aboriginal lands gradually changed hands. Of course, during the process of agricultural expansion, Han inmigrants took various means to obtain land. Cases of cooperation, conflicts, intermarriage, and shameless contractual tricks all occurred, but the aborigines lost land rights mainly through the mechanisms of "leasing the land to Han people" and "borrowing money at a long-term low interest rate."[20] When it was a matter of

[17] Wang Shiqing 王世慶, "Taiwan aizhi kao" [On the system of pass guards in Taiwan], *Taiwan wenxian* 7.3-4 (1956), pp. 7-25; Shi Tianfu, "Taiwan lishi dili yanjiu zhaji (I): shishi tuniu hongxian" [A note on Taiwan's historical geography (I): an explanation of earthen oxen and red lines], *Taiwan fengwu* 台灣風物 [Taiwan Folkways] 39.2 (1989), pp. 95-98; Shi Tianfu; "Qingdai Taiwan Zhuqian diqu de tuniugou he quyu fazhan" [The earthen oxen ditches and development in Zhuqian area in Qing Taiwan], *Taiwan fengwu* 40.4 (1990), pp. 1-68; Shepherd, *Statecraft and Political Economy*, pp. 182-91.

[18] For instance, a license dated 1685 was issued to Shen Shaohong 沈紹宏 for opening up Luyecao 鹿野草 (in today's Chiayi); a contract dated 1730 was signed between Yang Daohong 楊道弘 (who had obtained a license in 1727 to open up Xingzhipu 興直埔 in today's Hsinchuang in Taipei county) and the aboriginal owner of Wulaowan She 武嘮灣社 to cultivate the aboriginal surplus land. See *Qingdai Taiwan dazu diaochashu* 清代台灣大租調查書 [Investigation records of major rent in Qing Taiwan] (Taipei: Bank of Taiwan, 1962), p. 1, pp. 5-7; Liao Hanchen 廖漢臣, *Taiwansheng kaipi ziliao xubian* 台灣省開闢資料續編 [Second collection of materials on the opening up of Taiwan province] (Taichung: Historical Research Commission of Taiwan Province, 1977), pp. 65, 74, 109-12.

[19] Shepherd, *Statecraft and Political Economy*, pp. 239-307.

[20] Huang Fusan, "Qingdai Taiwan de tudi wenti" [Land problems of Taiwan in the Qing period], *Shihuo Monthly* 4.3 (1974), pp. 13-34; Chen Qiukun 陳秋坤, "Pingpuzu Anlishe Panxing jingying dizhu de jueqi, 1699-1770" [The formation of an aboriginal landlord in central Taiwan], *Bulletin of the Institute of Modern History, Academia Sinica* 20 (1991), pp. 1-35; and "Shijiu shiji chuqi tuzhu diquan wailiu wenti: yi Anlishe de tudi jingying weili" [The outflow of aboriginal land ownership in the early nineteenth century: the case of Anlishe], in Chen Qiukun and Xu Xueji 許雪姬, eds. *Taiwan lishishang de tudi wenti* 台灣歷史上的土地問題 [The land issues in Taiwan history] (Taipei: Taiwan History Field Research Office, Academia Sinica, 1992), pp. 29-53.

obtaining a license or negotiating a contract, usually only powerful people could do it. These powerful people customarily rented land to tenants, who were obliged to pay rent deposit or open up new land at their own expense, including investments in irrigation works, as the conditions upon which they obtained permanent contracts. These tenants, in turn, rented land to their own tenants, and thus the system of "two owners of one field" was formed.[21] The consequence was that the land system became very complicated and serious land problems were created.

6.2.2. THE AREA SOUTH OF THE HUWEIQI

By 1725, most Han settlements being formed were in the area south of the Huweiqi 虎尾溪. After taking over Taiwan, the Qing government established Taiwan as a *fu* 府 (prefecture) of Fujian province to govern this new frontier. Under Taiwan Fu, three *xian* 縣 (counties), Taiwan 台灣, Fengshan 鳳山, and Zhuluo 諸羅, were set up. The jurisdiction area of Taiwan Xian included Penghu and the area between two rivers: the Ercenghangqi 二層行溪 and the Beigangqi 北港溪. The jurisdiction area of Fengshan Xian extended south of the Ercenghangqi; that of Zhuluo Xian, north of the Beigangqi. These three counties extended only along the west coast; eastern Taiwan beyond the mountains was still rather unknown to Han settlers at this time.[22]

The 1696 gazetteer of Taiwan prefecture provides a record of settlements existing at the end of the seventeenth century. In the *fu* city, there were 4 *fang* 坊 (urban wards); Taiwan Xian, surrounding the city, had 15 *li* 里 (villages); Fengshan Xian had 10 *li*, 3 *bao* 保 (rural wards), 5 *zhuang* 莊 (villages), and 12 *she* 社 (aborigine villages); Zhuluo Xian had 4 *li*, 14 *zhuang*, and 40 *she*. In urban wards of the *fu* city, there were already some streets (*jie* 街) and markets (*shi* 市). Streets also existed in some villages: two in Taiwan Xian, three in Fengshan, and one in Zhuluo. These streets and markets were places where commercial activities took place and were the

[21] Matsuda Yoshirō 松田吉郎, "Shindai Taiwan chūhokubu no suiri jigyō to 'Yi tian liang zhu' sei no seiritsu katei" [Hydraulic enterprises in central-north Taiwan under the Qing and the process whereby the system of "two owners of one field" was established], in *Chū goku suirishi ronsō* 中國水利史論叢 [Collected articles on the history of water control in China: Dr. Satō retirement commemoration volume] (Tokyo: Kokushokankokai, 1984), pp. 411–17; and Matsuda Yoshirō "Taiwan no suiri jigyō to 'Yi tian liang zhu' sei" [Hydraulic enterprises and the system of "two owners of one field" in Taiwan], in Chen Qiukun and Xu Xueji, eds., *Land issues*, pp. 105–38. I would like to thank Prof. Elvin for providing the first article.

[22] Gao Gongqian 高拱乾, *Taiwan Fuzhi* 台灣府誌 [Gazetteer of Taiwan prefecture] (Taipei: Bank of Taiwan, 1960), pp. 5–7; Zhou Wenyuan 周文元, *Chongxiu Taiwan fuzhi* 重修臺灣府誌 [Revised gazetteer of Taiwan prefecture] (Taipei: Bank of Taiwan, 1960), pp. 6–8.

original form of cities developed later. In *fang, li, bao,* and *zhuang,* the residents were predominantly Han people; in the *she* of Fengshan Xian, the Han people mostly lived intermingled with the aborigines; while in the *she* of Zhuluo, the aborigines were predominant.[23]

The area of the jurisdiction of Taiwan Xian was changed during the Yongzheng reign (1723–35). In 1727, Penghu was divided off from the county and set up as a *ting* 廳 (subprefecture); during 1731–34, some adjustments in the areas of villages were made along the boundaries with the two other counties.[24] From then until 1887, when Taiwan Fu was renamed as Tainan Fu and Taiwan Xian as Anping Xian, the area of Taiwan Xian remained more or less the same.[25] The increase of settlements in this area is summarized in Table 6.1.

Thus, during 1720–1830, the number of streets in the prefectural city increased 277 percent, and the number of *jie* in the villages increased 57 percent. In other words, the prefectural city grew quite remarkably.

As for the system of land utilization, during the Zheng period, since land was still abundant, it was possible to adopt shifting cultivation at some places, as noted in the *Zhuluo zashi* 諸羅雜識 [Miscellaneous notes on Zhuluo]: "The nature of the soil was light and loose, and after three years its fertility declined and the harvests decreased, so that many people abandoned their old farms and tilled somewhere else."[26] In the early eighteenth century, however, almost all available land around the prefectural city was cultivated and the natural fertility of the land was almost exhausted. For instance, the 1720 gazetteer of Taiwan Xian records that rice paddies and sugarcane fields in this county had mostly been reclaimed during the Zheng period: "As this is already a long time ago and the fertility of the land is exhausted, the farmers have to apply night soil. It is not as in Fengshan and Zhuluo where lands are newly opened and harvests are ample with no need of weeding."[27] In 1722, Huang Shujing 黃叔璥, who came to Taiwan as a censor, observed: "In recent years, the cultivated land in Taiwan Xian has become less fertile due to destruction by floods; some people already apply night soil to nourish their lands."[28] This shows the effect of population density on land utilization.

[23] Gao Gongqian, *Gazetteer of Taiwan prefecture,* pp. 35–38; Zhou Wenyuan, *Revised gazetteer,* pp. 41–44.
[24] Wang Bichang 王必昌, *Chongxiu Taiwan xianzhi* 重修台灣縣誌 [Revised gazetteer of Taiwan county] (Taipei: Bank of Taiwan, 1961), pp. 26–28.
[25] *Taiwan tongzhi* 台灣通誌 [Gazetteer of Taiwan] (Taipei: Bank of Taiwan, 1962), p. 29.
[26] Cited in Huang Shujing 黃叔璥, *Taihai shichalu* 台海使槎錄 [A record of rafting over the sea to Taiwan] (Taipei: Bank of Taiwan, 1957), p. 20.
[27] Chen Wenda, *Gazetteer of Taiwan county,* p. 56.
[28] Huang Shujing, *Record of rafting,* p. 53.

Table 6.1. *Settlements in Taiwan Xian, 1720–1830*

	fu city		Taiwan Xian	
	No. of *jie*[a]	No. of *li*	No. of *zhuang*	No. of *jie*
1720	22	15	1	7
1752	45	0	0	(4?)
1807	56[b]	20	2	8
1830	83	0	0	11

[a] These *jie* (streets) existed in the villages.
[b] There were also 20 *jie* in suburbs.
Sources: Chen Wenda 陳文達, *Taiwan xianzhi* 臺灣縣志
[Gazetteer of Taiwan county] (Taipei: Bank of Taiwan,
1961), pp. 85–86, 91–92; Wang Bichang, *Chongxiu Tai-
wan xianzhi* [Revised gazetteer of Taiwan county], p. 29;
Xie Jinluan 謝金鑾, *Xuxiu Taiwan xianzhi* 續修臺灣縣志
[Additional gazetteer of Taiwan county] (Taipei: Bank
of Taiwan, 1962), pp. 9–11; Chen Guoying 陳國瑛 et al.,
Taiwan caifangce 臺灣采訪冊 [Records of inquiries in
Taiwan] (Taipei: Bank of Taiwan, 1959), pp. 16–17.

Moreover, population density also changed the environment adjacent to
the prefectural city. The 1720 gazetteer describes conditions there:

The habitations are dense. There are thousands of households. Heavy dew
becomes scarce and miasma cannot enter; this is different from Fengshan in
the far south, where the dew falls right after sunset and the fog disappears
after sunrise. . . . Nearby the prefectural city, the plain is wide and flat with
only some small mounds; this is different from Jilongshan 雞籠山 [in the far
north], where the threatening mountain vapors are most dreadful.[29]

This suggests that around the prefectural city the threat of miasma had
diminished because of population density.

It should be noted that in the early eighteenth century, there was no
Hakka village in Taiwan Xian. But to the north of Zhuluoshan 諸羅山 and
south of the Xiadanshuiqi 下淡水溪, farmers came mostly from Chaozhou;
each village had several hundred, even the smallest one had a hundred-odd
people.[30] In short, as land fertility had declined and the population density

[29] Chen Wenda, *Gazetteer of Taiwan county*, p. 62.
[30] Ibid., p. 57.

was rather high in Taiwan Xian, the newcomers could only go southward to Fengshan or northward to Zhuluo.

In Fengshan Xian, villages of migrants were mostly located along the Xiadanshuiqi and the Donggangqi 東港溪 valleys. The 1720 gazetteer of Fengshan recorded that this county had 9 *li*, 2 *bao*, 6 *zhuang*, 1 *zhen* 鎮 (town), and 12 *she;* moreover, there were 10 *jieshi* 街市 (market streets).[31] Compared with twenty-five years earlier, the number of villages had changed slightly, but the market streets had increased from 3 to 10.

In 1721, when the Zhu Yigui uprising occurred, more than 12,000 "righteous people" from thirteen large and sixty-four small villages in Fengshan Xian gathered to assist the Qing army in suppressing the revolt. These people were migrants from both Guangdong and Fujian provinces.[32] This event showed that there were already quite a number of Han settlements in this county. After suppression of the revolt, Manbao 滿保, the governor-general of Fujian and Zhejiang, suggested that a boundary should be set up along the mountains (as discussed above). He also suggested that all houses at the place where Zhu had risen in revolt should be burned down, the people should all be driven back to their native places, and those engaging in gathering rattans, sawing boards, burning charcoal, cutting firewood, and tilling the surrounding land should all be driven away. In response to Manbao's suggestions, Lan Dingyuan 藍鼎元 wrote a long letter expressing different opinions. He warned that the abandoned villages might become resorts of robbers and the supply of timber and firewood would also be affected. Moreover, as Taiwan gained large profits from rice and sugar, there was little reason to draw back the frontier after it had been expanded.[33] The Qing government finally favored Lan's viewpoints.

In 1731, there was a minor boundary adjustment between Taiwan and Fengshan Xian.[34] In 1875, when the area south of the Shuaimangqi 率芒溪

[31] Chen Wenda, *Fengshan xianzhi* 鳳山縣誌 [Gazetteer of Fengshan county] (Taipei: Bank of Taiwan, 1962), pp. 25–26.

[32] Fan Xian 范咸, *Chongxiu Taiwan fuzhi* 重修台灣府誌 [Revised gazetteer of Taiwan prefecture] (Taipei, 1961), p. 360; Yu Wenyi 余文儀, *Xuxiu Taiwan fuzhi* 續修台灣府誌 [Additional gazetteer of Taiwan prefecture] (Taipai: Bank of Taiwan, 1962), p. 450. Chen Shaoxin, *Gazetteer of Taiwan province*, section on population, vol. 2, p. 106, cited the study of Inō Yoshinori, who did not mention that among the 12,000 people there were some from Fujian.

[33] Lan Dingyuan, *Dongzhengji* 東征集 [Recollections on the eastern expedition] (Taipei: Bank of Taiwan, 1958), pp. 33–40. Lan Dingyuan also wrote some poems that carried similar ideas; see Chen Hanguang 陳漢光, ed., *Taiwan shilu* 台灣詩錄 [Collection of poems on Taiwan], (Taichung: Historical Research Commission of Taiwan Province, 1971), pp. 204–06. I would like to thank Prof. Elvin for calling my attention to these poems.

[34] Wang Yingzeng 王瑛曾, *Chongxiu Fengshan xianzhi* 重修鳳山縣誌 [Revised gazetteer of Fengshan county] (Taipei: Bank of Taiwan, 1962), pp. 8–9; Lu Dejia 盧德嘉, *Fengshanxian*

was divided to set up Hengchun 恆春 Xian, the area of Fengshan was changed once again.[35] There is no record of the number of villages in Fengshan Xian during the second half of the eighteenth century. However, in 1764, among the settlements of this county, 16 were named as *jie*; most of the *jie* had only one street, but the county seat at Xinglongzhuang 興隆莊 had 6 and Xiapitoujie 下陂頭街, located 20 Chinese "miles" east of the county seat, had 4 streets.[36] Compared with forty years earlier, the number of *jie* again increased from 10 to 16.

The 1894 records show that Fengshan Xian was divided into 14 *li*, which consisted of 948 *zhuang* and 8 *jieshi* where markets were convened daily.[37] As for Hengchun Xian, the 1889 investigation records 13 *li* with 89 *zhuang*.[38] These numbers at least suggest that south of the Ercenghangqi, villages became more densely distributed and market streets were increasing during the eighteenth and nineteenth centuries.

At the same time, together with the expansion of settlements, the number of irrigation works also increased. The 1720 gazetteer of Fengshan recorded water conservancy as follows: 17 reservoirs (of which 15 were constructed during the Zheng period, and 6 had springs and 11 had not), 5 pools (of which only one had a spring), 2 creeks, 1 lake, and 1 gully. Those bodies of water that were fed by springs, including the reservoirs, the pool, and the lake, did not dry up during times of drought; both the creek and the gully had springs and flowed over a long distance. Generally speaking, the reservoirs were built, while the lake, pool, creek, and gully were simply utilized for their natural water, including rain water.[39] In 1722, Huang Shujing visited the area south of the Xiadanshuiqi and saw that the villagers were all Hakkas. "They built reservoirs for the supply of irrigation water and tilled very hard on their farms," he reported.[40] Again, the 1764 Fengshan gazetteer records that there were 27 reservoirs; 10 of them had existed since the Zheng period, one had been built by Admiral Shi Lang, and the remaining 16 had been newly built after 1722. In addition, there were 10 pools, of which 7 were new and some were not natural but constructed by the villagers; one was even built by the

caifangce 鳳山縣採訪冊 [Records of inquiries in Fengshan county] (Taipei: Bank of Taiwan, 1960), p. 1. The two records are slightly different.
[35] *Gazetteer of Taiwan*, pp. 11–12.
[36] Wang Yingzeng, *Revised gazetteer of Fengshan*, pp. 31–32.
[37] Lu Dejia, *Records of inquiries*, pp. 1–14, 136–39.
[38] Tu Jishan 屠繼善, *Hengchun xianzhi* 恆春縣誌 [Gazetteer of Hengchun county] (Taipei: Bank of Taiwan, 1960), pp. 125–29.
[39] Chen Wenda, *Gazetteer of Fengshan*, pp. 29–31.
[40] Huang Shujing, *Record of rafting*, p. 53.

aborigines. There were also 2 creeks and 2 gullies, but the old lake no longer existed.[41]

Finally, the 1894 investigation produced detailed records and classified water conservancy in Fengshan Xian into five categories. Only a summary will be given here. The irrigation ditches were organized into three systems, which together consisted of at least 140 ditches and irrigated 10,161 *jia*. These ditches were mostly completed after 1838, with the magistrate Cao Jin 曹謹 initiating construction. There were 135 reservoirs that actually functioned; they irrigated 4,374 *jia*. Moreover, 22 deep pools irrigated 835 *jia*, 18 ponds irrigated 116 *jia*, and 305 water pits irrigated 577 *jia*. Thus, the five categories irrigated a total of 16,481 *jia*, or about one-fourth of the cultivated acreage (80,314 *jai*) in Fengshan Xian.[42] It is also notable that there were only 4 artificial fishing ponds around 1720 but the number had increased to 96 around 1890.[43] In sum, the increasing number of irrigation works and fishing ponds indicated changes in the rural environment of Fengshan.

In Zhuluo Xian, the early stages of agricultural expansion by Han inmigrants proceeded as follows:

(1) "When the county was first established, the county seat was situated among wild grasses and civil and military officials all stayed at Jialixing 佳里興; the crowd of migrating cultivators did not go farther beyond Douliumen 鬥六門."

(2) In 1704, "the crowd of migrating cultivators gradually moved north of Douliumen."

(3) In 1710, "the crowd of migrating cultivators gradually moved beyond Banxian and north to the Daduqi 大肚溪. From now on, there were more and more migrants and some of them arrived at Rinan 日南, Houlong 後龍, Zhuqian, and Nankan."

(4) In 1717, the area between Banxian and Danshui was still a wilderness of trees, streams, and fertile lands, but migrating cultivators took boats to go back and forth and already knew that there were strategic locales by land and water routes around Dajia 大甲, Houlong, and Zhuqian.[44]

Thus, by 1720 the plain south of Banxian had almost all been reclaimed by Han inmigrants, while to the north, apart from some points scattered along the coast, it was still a wilderness.

As for the irrigation systems constructed in the process of reclamation, the 1717 gazetteer of Zhuluo lists 75 reservoirs and ditches with the year of

[41] Wang Yingzeng, *Revised gazetteer of Fengshan*, pp. 35–39.

[42] Lu Dejia, *Records of inquiries*, pp. 65–112. For the total cultivated acreage, see Chen Shaoxin, *Gazetteer of Taiwan province*, section on population, vol. 1, pp. 61–63.

[43] Chen Wenda, *Gazetteer of Fengshan*, p. 32; Lu Dejia, *Records of inquiries*, pp. 112–16.

[44] Chen Menglin 陳夢林, *Zhuluo xianzhi* 諸羅縣誌 [Gazetteer of Zhuluo county] (Taipei: Bank of Taiwan, 1962), pp. 110, 112, 114.

construction. The earliest one was Xinpi 新陂 (New Reservoir), constructed in 1692. A simple distribution over time shows that 9 works were built before 1701, 27 between 1702 and 1711, and 39 between 1712 and 1717. Among the last 39 works, 36 were completed during 1714–17 when Zhou Zhongxuan 周鍾瑄 was the magistrate, and he contributed silver or grain to assist the construction of 28 works. As for the location of the reservoirs, the northernmost was located at Maowushu 貓霧捒 (in today's Taichung 臺中) and was built in 1717 with a contribution of grain by Magistrate Zhou. Next, five reservoirs located near Huweiqi and Banxian were also supported by Zhou's contributions. These six reservoirs were all given to Zhanghua Xian later.[45] Because the plain south of Banxian was almost all opened up, the author of the Zhuluo gazetteer suggests that "the area north of Banxian should be divided to establish another county and allow the people to open up new land freely."[46]

In fact, it was only after Zhu Yigui's revolt had been suppressed that Zhuluo Xian was divided to form Zhanghua Xian in 1723 and Danshui Ting in 1731. Thus, the new Zhuluo extended south of the Huweiqi. Zhuluo was renamed Jiayi 嘉義 in 1787 by the Qianlong Emperor to compliment the people for their resistance to the rebel Lin Shuangwen 林爽文. In 1887, the area north of the Niuchouqi 牛稠溪 and south of the Zhuoshuiqi 濁水溪 was taken from Jiayi to establish Yunlin 雲林 Xian.[47] New administration divisions implied to some extent the increase of new settlements.

There seems to be no record of the number of settlements in Zhuluo (Jiayi) from the 1720s to the 1890s. Scholars often used the names of jie and zhuang listed in the Jiayi guannei caifangce 嘉義管內採訪冊 [Records of inquiry in the jurisdiction of Jiayi] to discuss the situation in the late Qing. However, this record was compiled during 1897–1901, when Taiwan was under Japanese rule, and should only be used as a reference for the period before Yunlin Xian was established. According to this source, Jiayi Xian had 5 bao 堡 (rural subdivisions), under which there were 166 zhuang and 4 jie.[48]

[45] Ibid., pp. 34–41; Zhou Xi 周璽, Zhanghua xianzhi 彰化縣誌 [Gazetteer of Zhanghua county] (Taipei: Bank of Taiwan, 1962), p. 56.

[46] Chen Menglin, Gazetteer of Zhuluo, p. 112.

[47] Lian Heng, General history, pp. 110–11, 115, 121–22; Chen Yan 陳衍, Taiwan tongji 台灣通紀 [A chronology of Taiwan] (Taipei: Bank of Taiwan, 1961), pp. 138–39.

[48] Jiayi guannei caifangce 嘉義管內採訪冊 [Records of inquiry in the jurisdiction of Jiayi] (Taipei: Bank of Taiwan, 1960), pp. 1–2, 15–16, 23–27, 49–51, 55–59. For an example of work based on the use of this material, see Chen Shaoxin, Gazetteer of Taiwan province, section on population, vol. 1, pp. 69–71; Hong Cannan 洪燦楠, "Taiwan diqu juluo fazhan chi yanjiu" [A study on development of settlements in Taiwan], Taiwan wenxian 29.2 (1978), p. 38.

It is also not clear whether new irrigation systems were added during this period. If we compare the records in the Zhuluo gazetteer and Lian's *General History of Taiwan,* we see that all thirty-four works included in the latter already existed in the former.[49] It is notable that Lujuegoupi 鹿堀溝 埤, Shisijiazun 十四甲圳, and Meizikengzun 梅子坑圳 were not included in previous records, but the dates of their construction are not clear.[50]

As for Yunlin Xian, in 1894 this county was divided into 15 *bao,* with a total number of 708 *zhuang* and 18 *jie.* In regard to water conservancy, there were 34 reservoirs, 25 irrigation ditches, and 1 drainage ditch.[51] In sum, increases in settlements and irrigation works in Jiayi and Yunlin can still be roughly seen on the basis of these limited records.

6.2.3. THE AREA SOUTH OF THE DAJIAQI

As mentioned above, Zhanghua Xian was established in 1723. This county comprised the area north to the Huweiqi and south to the Dajiaqi. The western part of this area was situated along a cliff from which abundant springs flow; this made it an ideal location for inmigrants to establish new settlements.[52] As late as 1735, Zhanghua was still a place where Han inmigrants lived intermingled with the aborigines.[53] But new settlements increased rapidly. Around 1745, there were 110 *zhuang;* around 1830, there were 1,089 *zhuang.*[54] During the same period, the number of *jie* increased from 9 to 41.[55] In other words, in eighty-five years, *zhuang* increased 890 percent and *jie* 355 percent. It is notable that *jie* did not increase as fast as *zhuang;* this may imply that some *jie* had gradually become larger centers.

[49] Chen Menglin, *Gazetteer of Zhuluo,* pp. 34–41; Lian Heng, *General history,* pp. 673–75.

[50] *Records of inquiry in Jiayi,* pp. 16, 29, 52, 61.

[51] Ni Zanyuan 倪贊元, *Yunlinxian caifangce* 雲林縣採訪冊 [Records of inquiries in Yunlin county] (Taipei: Bank of Taiwan, 1959), pp. 2–200.

[52] Wen Zhenhua 溫振華, "Qingdai Taiwan zhongbu de kaifa yu shehui bianqian" [Development and social changes in central Taiwan during the Qing period], *Shifan daxue lishi xuebao* 師範大學歷史學報 [Historical Journal of Normal University], 11 (1983), p. 43.

[53] "Guandimiao beiji" 關帝廟碑記 [A stela of the Temple of the God of War], in *Taiwan zhongbu beiwen jicheng* 台灣中部碑文集成 [Collection of stelae texts of central Taiwan] (Taipei: Bank of Taiwan, 1962), pp. 1–2. The inscription was written in 1735.

[54] Liu Liangbi 劉良璧, *Chongxiu Fujian Taiwan fuzhi* 重修福建台灣府誌 [Revised gazetteer of Taiwan prefecture in Fujian] (Taipei: Bank of Taiwan, 1960), pp. 77–80; Fan Xian, *Revised gazetteer of Taiwan,* pp. 67–68. The records of these two sources are the same; the year 1745 is taken as approximate, for Liu's gazetteer was compiled in 1741 and Fan's gazetteer in 1747. As for the number of *zhuang* in 1830, Wen Zhenhua counted it to be 983; see his "Development and social changes," p. 69. The number 1089 is a calculation from Zhou Xi, *Gazetteer of Zhanghua* (Taipei: Bank of Taiwan, 1962), pp. 43–51.

[55] Wen Zhenhua, "Development and social changes," pp. 73–74. The number given by Zhou Xi, *Gazetteer of Zhanghua,* pp. 39–42, is 34 in addition to the county city.

In respect to water conservancy, Babaozun 八堡圳, the most important irrigation system related to the development of central Taiwan, was initiated as early as in 1709 by Shi Shibang 施世榜, a migrant from the south. This system was completed ten years later with the assistance of a Mr. Lin, who solved the difficult technical problem of leading water from the Zhuoshuiqi into irrigation ditches.[56] The 1807 gazetteer of Zhanghua records 27 reservoirs and ditches, but mostly without giving the time of construction. There were 9 exceptions, including the aforementioned 6 reservoirs built originally in Zhuluo Xian during 1714–17 and 3 others built in 1721, 1735, and 1751. In addition, rivers and mountain springs were utilized for irrigation; it was only the coastal land that had not yet been irrigated.[57] As reconstructed by modern geographers, settlements were formed along irrigation ditches in this area during the process of reclamation.[58]

The area of today's Taichung city and county roughly runs between the Daduqi on the south and the Daanqi 大安溪 on the north; this area was under the jurisdiction of Zhanghua Xian by 1887 when a new county was established.[59] The opening up of this area by Han migrants mostly occurred after 1700. Some studies have been done recently on this subject; it will suffice to summarize findings related to settlements below.

After about 1700, migrants with origins in Fujian and Guangdong came to this area. The two groups arrived at about the same time, and at the beginning, there was no distinction on the lines that Fujianese tended to settle on the plain while Hakkas took to the hillsides. This differentiation appeared only after 1782, when feuds among the local groups took place more frequently.

When Han migrants first arrived, they tended to select a place that was well drained but accessible to the water. In most cases, such localities had already been chosen by the aborigines. Thus, whether Han migrants could smoothly acquire the land depended on how well they could get along with and negotiate with the aborigines. The most famous example here was the

---

[56] Zhou Xi, *Gazetteer of Zhanghua*, p. 56. For studies on Babaozun, see Morita Akira 森田明, *Shindai suirishi kenkyū* 清代水利史研究 [Studies on history of water conservancy in Qing times] (Tokyo: Aki shobo, 1974), pp. 498–562; Wang Sung-hsing, "Pa Pao Chun: An 18th Century Irrigation System in Central Taiwan," *Bulletin of the Institute of Ethnology, Academia Sinica* 33 (1972), pp. 165–76; and "Babaozun yu Taiwan zhongbu de kaifa" [The Babao irrigation canal system and the opening up of central Taiwan], *Taiwan wenxian* 26.4–27.1 (1976), pp. 42–49.

[57] Zhou Xi, *Gazetteer of Zhanghua*, pp. 55–58; Wen Zhenhua, "Development and social changes," pp. 60–64.

[58] Shi Zaitian 石再添 et al., "Zhuo-Da liuyu de juluo fenbu yu dixing zhi xiangguan yanjiu" [A geographical quantitative study on the distribution of communities in the Zhuoshui and Dadu river drainage basins in central Taiwan], *Taiwan wenxian* 28.2 (1977), pp. 83, 87.

[59] Lian Heng, *General history*, p. 119.

case of Zhang Dajing 張達京, who signed contracts with the aborigines of Anli She 岸裡社 to open up the land with the construction of the irrigation system at the area around present-day Fengyuan.

The establishment of new assarts spread from the coastal plain up to the mountains. During the Qianlong reign, except for the mountain areas, cultivable lands were mostly reclaimed. In the coastal plain, reclamation was mostly done by individual farming households, while near the mountain area, large-scale cooperative organizations were formed to promote cooperation in cultivation and armed guards were posted at mountain passes to provide defense against the mountain aborigines. This type of organization was commonly found in the reclamation of mountain areas in Taiwan.[60]

6.2.4. THE AREA NORTH OF THE DAJIAQI

The area north of the Dajiaqi was under the jurisdiction of Danshui Ting after 1731. The *ting* site was located at Zhuqian, but the office of the subprefect was first built at Zhanghua; a new office was built at Zhuqian only in 1756.[61] The jurisdiction area of Danshui Ting changed four times in the nineteenth century. In 1826, the area beyond Yuanwangkeng 遠望坑 at Sandiao 三貂 was given to Gemalan Ting 噶瑪蘭廳. In 1875, Taibei Fu 台北府 was set up to supervise Danshui Ting, Gemalan Ting, and the newly established Jilong Ting 基隆廳. In 1878, Danshui Ting was divided into Xinzhu 新竹 and Danshui Xian. Finally, in 1889, Miaoli 苗栗 Xian was established.[62] This section discusses the area lying west to Gemalan.

---

[60] Hong Liwan 洪麗完, "Qingdai Taizhong difang Fu-Ke guanxi chutan: jian yi Qingshui pingyuan sanshan guowangmiao zhi xingshuai weili" [A preliminary study on relations between Fujianese and Hakka in Central Taiwan in the Qing period: the case of the three mountain Kings' temple at the Qingshui plain], *Taiwanshi yanjiu lunwenji* 台灣史研究論文集 [Symposium of studies on Taiwan history] (Taipei: Research Center of Taiwan Historical Landmark, 1988), pp. 135–85; Wen Zhenhua, "Development and social changes," pp. 43–95; Chen Yanzheng 陳炎正, *Xinguangzhuang: yige Taiwan xiangcun de shehui fazhanshi* 新廣莊：一個台灣鄉村的社會發展史 [A study of social development of a village in Taiwan] (Taichung: Taichung Research Association on Poetry, 1984), pp. 32–60; Zhang Longzhi 張隆誌, *Zuqun guanxi yu xiangcun Taiwan: yige Qingdai Taiwan pingpu zuqunshi de chongjian he lijie* 族羣關係與鄉村台灣：一個清代台灣平埔族羣史的重建和理解 [Ethnicity and rural Taiwan: an ethnohistorical study of the Pazeh in Qing times] (Taipei: National Taiwan University, 1991), pp. 122–52.

[61] Yu Wenyi, *Additional gazetteer*, pp. 4, 67; Chen Peigui 陳培桂, *Danshui tingzhi* 淡水廳誌 [Gazetteer of Danshui subprefecture] (Taipei: Bank of Taiwan, 1963), p. 51.

[62] Zheng Pengyun 鄭鵬雲 et al., *Xinzhu xianzhi chugao* 新竹縣誌初稿 [Draft gazetteer of Xinzhu county] (Taipei: Bank of Taiwan, 1960), p. 1; Shen Maoyin 沈茂蔭, *Miaoli xianzhi* 苗栗縣誌 [Gazetteer of Miaoli county] (Taipei: Bank of Taiwan, 1962), p. 17. *Xinzhuxian caifangce* 新竹縣採訪冊 [Records of inquiries in Xinzhu county] (Taipei: Bank of Taiwan, 1962), p. 2, records that Xinzhu and Danshui were divided in 1879.

In the early eighteenth century, most parts of Danshui Ting still remained a wilderness. In 1697, when Yu Yonghe traveled between Zhuqian and Nankan, he saw groups of deer but not a single man. Han migrants moved gradually to Rinan, Houlong, Zhuqian, and Nankan after 1710. In 1721, however, Lan Dingyuan still noted, "The sphere of Zhuqianpu 竹塹埔 was about 100 *li*, walking through it all day long one saw no habitation."[63] In addition, there are two often-cited passages. One is a poem entitled "Zhuqian," written by Ruan Caiwen 阮蔡文 in 1715, one line of which reads, "The deer fields are now half opened up by migrants."[64] The other is a statement made by Huang Shujing in 1722: "Previously, all the lands near the mountains were aboriginal deer fields; now, Han settlers till them, good farm lands extend as far as one can see, and deer can be hunted only in the deep mountains."[65] Shi Tianfu has pointed out that these two passages are misunderstood most of the time. He says that Huang's statement is applicable not to Zhuqian but to the area south of the Dajiaqi, or perhaps south of the Daduqi. Ruan's poem refers to Zhuqian or at most to its vicinity, not to the entire Zhuqianpu. The pioneer cultivator of Zhuqian, Wang Shijie 王世傑, came around 1711, while the opening up of Zhuqianpu mostly occurred after 1723.[66]

By 1735, new assarts in the coastal plain were found only in the Zhuqian area. Inmigrants came mostly during the Qianlong reign (1736–95) and new arrivals appeared almost every year; farmlands were mostly reclaimed from the wilds and Han inmigrants cooperated quite well with the aborigines. In the Jiaqing reign (1796–1820), cultivators gradually moved into the mountain areas, and during the Daoguang period (1821–50), reclamation was speeded up.[67] For opening up the mountain areas, at least eighteen large-scale cooperative organizations were formed; the most famous among them was the Jinguangfu 金廣福. Besides farming, they also engaged in gathering the sap from camphor trees for the manufacture of camphor, and cutting camphor wood for the building of warships. Tremendous

[63] Lan Dingyuan, *Collection of writings*, p. 87.

[64] Chen Peigui, *Gazetteer of Danshui*, p. 434.

[65] Huang Shujing, *Record of rafting*, p. 65.

[66] Shi Tianfu, "Taiwan lishi dili yanjiu zhaji (II): Zhuqian, Zhuqianpu he luchang banwei liuminkai" [A note on Taiwan's historical geography (II): Zhuqian and Zhuqianpu and the deer fields being half opened up by the migrating crowd], *Taiwan fengwu* 39.3 (1989), pp. 73–82; Shi Tianfu, "Qingdai Zhuqian diqu de kenquzhuang: Cuifengzhuang de sheli he yanbien" [The reclamation village of the Zhuqian area in Qing times: the establishment of and changes in Cuifengzhuang], *Taiwan fengwu* 39.4 (1989), pp. 33–69.

[67] For a chronology of the arrival of new inmigrants, see Sheng Qingyi 盛清沂, "Xinzhu, Taoyuan, Miaoli san xian diqu kaipishi" [A history of the opening up of the three counties of Xinzhu, Taoyuan, and Miaoli], *Taiwan wenxian* 31.4 (1980), pp. 168–76; 32.1 (1981), pp. 136–49.

progress was made in the development of the mountain area. By the
Tongzhi period (1862–74), almost all cultivable lands in the near mountain areas had been reclaimed.[68]

After 1875, the Qing government started to adopt the positive policy of
"open the mountains and soothe the aborigines" (kaishan fufan 開山撫番).
Old guards at strategic passes were abolished and new bureaus in charge of
the task known as fukenju 撫墾局 (pacification and reclamation bureaus)
were set up. At the same time, some large-scale private organizations,
among which the most famous was Guangtaicheng 廣泰成, were also
formed to undertake the opening up of the mountain areas. The cooperation between official and private organizations in this process seems to have
been quite effective.[69]

The effect of the preventive boundaries along the mountains should be
noted here. Recently, Shi Tianfu has been able to reconstruct the locations,
distributions, and patterns of tuniugou in the Zhuqian area by matching
materials from the local gazetteers and old contracts with findings from
fieldwork. He contends that the existence of tuniugou and the new 1790
boundary helped create three distinctive human geographical zones that
had different land systems and social organizations but one common feature, namely, that the pattern of settlements was predominantly scattered
hamlets of individual farms of tenants, who used their own labor and
capital to open up new lands. Among such scattered hamlets, some com-

[68] Shi Tianfu, "Earthen oxen ditches," pp. 30–33; Wu Xueming 吳學明, Jinguangfu ken'ai yu
Xinzhu dongnan shanqu de kaifa, 1834–1895 金廣福墾隘與新竹東南山區的開發 (1834–1895)
[The opening up of Jinguangfu and the development of the southeastern mountain areas
in Xinzhu county, 1834–1895] (Taipei: National Normal University, 1986), pp. 121–265;
Zhuang Yingzhang 莊英章 and Chen Yundong 陳連棟, "Wan Qing Taiwan beibu Hanren
tuoken xingtai de yanbian: Yi Beipu Jiangjia de kenpi shiye weili" [The changing pattern of
reclamation by the Han Chinese in northern Taiwan during the late Qing: the case of the
Jiang family at Beipu], in Taiwan shehui yu wenhua bianqian 台灣社會與文化變遷 [Social and
cultural change in Taiwan] (Taipei: Institute of Ethnology, Academia Sinica, 1986), pp. 1–
43; Matsuda Yoshirō 松田吉郎, "Gōkon soshiki 'Kinkōfuku' ni tsuite" [On the cooperative
cultivation organization: the Jinguangfu], Taiwanshi kenkyū 台灣史研究 9 (1991), pp.
1–18.

[69] Huang Zhuoquan 黃卓權, "Taiwan caiai hou de zhuming ken'ai: Guangtaicheng kenhao
chutan" [A famous cultivation organization in Taiwan after the abolition of official posts:
the case of Guangtaicheng], in Taiwanshi yanjiu ji shiliao fajue yantaohui lunwenji 台灣史研究
暨史料發掘研討會論文集 [Proceedings of a conference on Taiwan history and the discovery
of historical materials] (Kaohsiung: Research Center for Taiwan Historical Landmarks,
1987), pp. 105–40; Huang Zhuoquan, "Cong Shitan shanqu de tuoken kan wan Qing
Taiwan neishan kenwu de yanbian" [Changes in reclamation in the inner mountain areas
of Taiwan in the late Qing as viewed from the case of the Shitan mountain area], in
Proceedings of a conference, pp. 103–31.

pact villages also developed, centered on places where the Han and aboriginal landlords or headmen of tenants collected rents.[70]

As for the opening up of the area that is today Taipei, though a few scattered Han settlements might have been founded during the Zheng period, the earliest document related to the reclamation of the Taipei plain was a proclamation of reclamation at Dajiala 大佳臘 (in today's Taipei city). In 1709 this document was given to a cooperative reclamation household (kenhu 墾戶) known as Chen Laizhang 陳賴章 by the acting magistrate of Zhuluo county. From then on, small and large cooperative households were formed; more than twenty of them left valuable documents. Lands were reclaimed either from grassland or woodland. Among these households, there were competition, cooperation, lawsuits, and transfers relating to land acquisition. Only those who managed the reclamation in the manner of an "enterprise" were likely to be successful.[71] During the Qianlong reign, almost all cultivable lands of the Taipei plain were reclaimed and migrants began to open up the nearby mountain areas, such as Shiding 石碇 and Dakekan 大嵙崁. In 1886 a Fukenju was set up at Dakekan and in 1894 Nanya Ting 南雅廳 was established to govern the nearby area.[72] It is to be noted that the commercial center of the Taipei plain was located at Xinzhuang 新莊 in the mid-eighteenth century; it was only around 1820 that Mengjia 艋舺 (Wanhua 萬華 in today's Taipei city) rose to take its place.[73]

The increase of settlements in Danshui Ting was at first quite rapid. In 1747, Danshui Ting was divided into 2 bao: Danshui Bao with 25 zhuang and Zhuqian Bao with 10 zhuang; moreover, there were 2 jie, Zhuqian and Balifen.[74] Around 1774, Danshui Ting included 132 zhuang, of which 29 were south of the ting city and 103 north of it. As for the jie, 6 more were added; Zhonggang 中港, Houlong, Yuanli, Xinzhuang, Mengjia, and Bazhilanlin 八芝蘭林 (today's Shihlin 士林 in Taipei city).[75] This shows that

---

[70] For details see Shi Tianfu, "Reclamation village," pp. 33–69; Shi Tian fu, "Earthen oxen ditches," pp. 1–68; and Shi Tianfu, "Qingdai Zhuqian diqu de juluo fazhan he xingtai" [The development and pattern of settlements in the Zhuqian area], in Land issues, pp. 71–82.

[71] Yin Zhangyi 尹章義, Taiwan kaifashi yanjiu 台灣開發史研究 [Studies on the opening up of Taiwan] (Taipei: Lianjing, 1989), pp. 29–150.

[72] Mitsuura Yūshi 三浦祐之, "Taihoku heiya no kaitaku ni tsuite" [On the reclamation of Taipei plain], Taiwan nō jihō 台灣農事報 [Journal of agriculture in Taiwan] 29.11 (1933), pp. 46–56; 30.2 (1934), pp. 58–62; Chen Shaoxin, Gazetteer of Taiwan province, section on population, vol. 2, pp. 106, 116; Chen Zhengxiang, Geography of Taiwan, pp. 1015–1020.

[73] Yin Zhangyi, Studies on the opening up, p. 393.

[74] Fan Xian, Revised gazetteer, pp. 69, 78.

[75] Yu Wenyi, Additional gazetteer, pp. 75–78, 89–90.

during twenty-seven years, *zhuang* increased 277 percent and *jie* by 300 percent. Furthermore, the 1871 gazetteer recorded that there were 6 streets in the *ting* city; outside the city, there were 6 *xiang* 廂 (suburbs) with a total number of 80 *zhuang*. North of the *ting* city (in today's Taoyuan and Taipei counties), there were 8 *bao* with 160 *zhuang* and among them 10 *jie*. South of the *ting* city (today's Hsinchu and part of Miaoli counties) there were 4 *bao* with 137 *zhuang* and among them 5 *jie*. Altogether, there were 297 *zhuang* and among them 15 *jie*.[76] These figures show that between 1774 and 1871, the number of settlements was more than doubled (*zhuang* increased 125 percent and *jie* 150 percent).

The 1894 *Xinzhuxian caifangce* 新竹縣採訪冊 [Records of inquiry for Xinzhu county] recorded the situation after Danshui Ting was divided. According to this source, Xinzhu Xian included three *bao*: Zhuqian, Zhu'nan 竹南, and Zhubei 竹北. It is quite difficult to compare these divisions precisely with those in 1871. Roughly speaking, the area of Zhuqian Bao included the city and suburbs around it; besides the original six suburbs, two more were added. As for the number of *zhuang*, there were 9 outside the four city gates and 201 in the eight suburbs. It should be noted that the village names listed under the original six suburbs were not all listed again in the 1894 record. In terms of the total number, between 1871 and 1894, *zhuang* increased from 80 to 210, a rate of increase of 163 percent or 7 percent per annum. Zhu'nan Bao (the former Zhonggang Bao) had 26 *zhuang* in 1871 and 66 in 1894, an increase of 154 percent or 6.7 percent per annum. As for Zhubei Bao, there were 281 *zhuang* in 1894, but most of them cannot be compared with earlier records.[77] In any case, it is obvious that during the last quarter of the nineteenth century, the number of villages in Xinzhu Xian was increasing faster than it had in the previous one hundred years.

Also around 1894, the gazetteer of Miaoli Xian recorded that the county included 3 *bao* with 198 *zhuang*.[78] This figure may be compared with the 111 *zhuang* of the 3 *bao* in 1871; thus there was an increase of 78 percent during twenty-three years of about 3 percent per year. The increase of settlements in what is today Taoyuan and Taipei counties during the same period cannot be discussed here because of a lack of comparable documents.

Concerning water conservancy in Danshui Ting, the gazetteers of Taiwan prefecture, revised in 1747 and 1774, provided no record. But this does not imply that Han inmigrants did not build irrigation works along

---

[76] Chen Peigui, *Gazetteer of Danshui*, pp. 57–64.

[77] *Xinzhuxian caifangce* [Records of inquiries], pp. 68–83.

[78] Shen Maoyin, *Gazetteer of Miaoli county*, pp. 36–48.

with reclamation in this area. The 1871 gazetteer of Danshui Ting records 42 items under the category of reservoirs and ditches, among which was one built by the pioneer cultivator Wang Shijie. Obviously, irrigation works were constructed here along with the opening up of new lands, just as in other areas. The location of these irrigation ditches showed that 2 were near the *ting* city, 22 north of the *ting* city and 18 south of it. With available information related to builders and time, it is possible to figure out that 2 were built in the Yongzheng period and 15 in the Qianlong period.[79]

The 1894 *Records of Inquiries for Xinzhu County (Xinzhu caifangce)* stated that since the Qianlong and Jiaqing periods, numerous reservoirs and ditches had been built: Zhuqian Bao had 46 irrigation ditches and one natural ditch, Zhu'nan had 12 irrigation ditches, and Zhubei had 16 irrigation ditches and one natural big water pit. Moreover, the three *bao* each had 4 reservoirs; those at Zhuqian and Zhu'nan were built during the Daoguang and Guangxu periods, while those in Zhubei were the big ones that had springs as water sources.[80]

In Miaoli, there were 27 irrigation ditches around 1894. One of them, located six Chinese "miles" north of the county capital, had been destroyed by a flood.[81] Since 1871 there had been an increase of 10 ditches. It is notable that among the existing 26 ditches, 12 were old, but the irrigation acreage had increased. This suggests not only that new works were added but that old ones were expanded.

6.2.5. THE AREA BEHIND THE MOUNTAINS

The area east of the Central Mountain Range is usually referred to as the area "behind the mountains" in the Qing literature. The first administrative division set up in this area was Gemalan Ting in 1810; it was upgraded to Yilan Xian 宜蘭縣 in 1875.[82] The earliest venturers to try to open up

[79] Chen Peigui, *Gazetteer of Danshui*, pp. 73–80; see also Mitsuura Yūshi, "On the reclamation", pp. 54–56.

[80] *Xinzhuxian caifangce* [Records of inquiries], pp. 141–63.

[81] Shen Maoyin, *Gazetteer of Miaoli*, pp. 51–54.

[82] For the opening up of this area, see Chen Shujun 陳淑均, *Gemalan tingzhi* 噶瑪蘭廳誌 [Gazetteer of Gemalan subprefecture] (Taipei: Bank of Taiwan, 1963), pp. 3, 329–30; Lian Heng, *General history*, pp. 853–55; Li Luping 李鹿苹, *Taiwan xiaoquyu dili yanjiuji* 台灣小區域地理研究集 [A collection of geographic studies on small areas in Taiwan] (Taipei: National Institute for Compilation and Translation, 1984), pp. 16–19; Zhuang Yingzhang 莊英章 and Wu Wenxing 吳文星, "Qingdai Toucheng de tuoken yu fazhan" [The exploitation and development of Toucheng under the Qing dynasty], *Taiwan wenxian* 36.3–4 (1984), pp. 215–23; Liao Fengde 廖風德, *Qingdai zhi Gemalan: yige Taiwanshi de quyu yanjiu* 清代之噶瑪蘭：一個台灣史的區域研究 [Gemalan in Qing times: a regional case study in the history of Taiwan] (Taipei: Zhengzhong, 1990), pp. 79–109.

Gemalan dated back to 1768, but they were killed by the aborigines. Some tried again but all failed. It was not until 1796 that Wu Sha 吳沙, a resident at Sandiao and a trader experienced in dealing with the aborigines, decided to open up the fertile land of Gemalan. Wu Sha recruited vagrants from Zhangzhou, Quanzhou, and Guangdong to serve as vanguards to lead village braves to go ahead, with tenants to follow later; and they built the first settlement at Touwei 頭圍. The encroachment of outsiders stirred up the resistance of the aborigines, toward whom Wu Sha took measures of both compromise and intimidation. It was, however, by curing the aborigines of an epidemic of smallpox that he was able to win their trust.[83] In 1797, Wu Sha went to Danshui Ting to obtain a license and recruited more tenants. The reclamation was quickly extended to Erwei 二圍. At the end of that year Wu Sha died, and the leadership was entrusted to his nephew Wu Hua 吳化. Wu Hua negotiated with the aborigines for a cease-fire. He also mediated feuds among different Han inmigrant groups. In 1802, the reclamation was extended to Wuwei 五圍 (Yilan city). From then on, more and more migrants arrived; in 1809, they crossed the Lanyangqi 蘭陽溪 to open up the south bank of this river. During 1821–50, the fertile lands on both banks of the Lanyangqi were almost all cultivated and new migrants moved toward the hillside area. The opening up of these hillsides was led by Chen Huihuang 陳輝煌, and more than 800 jia of land was reclaimed by 1874. Among the Han Chinese, the Zhangzhou group constituted the majority; they settled on the rich soils in the middle of the plain, the Quanzhou group on the two sides of the plain, and the Guangdong group on the hillsides. Hamlets in this area were mostly as scattered as those in northern Taiwan. However, the land tenancy system did not play a significant role in shaping the settlement pattern here.[84]

The number of settlements increased very rapidly in the beginning. The 1832 gazetteer recorded that the ting capital had 22 streets and that outside the city, there were 11 bao with 97 zhuang and 3 jie.[85] This shows that the number of Han settlements increased from one to one hundred in thirty-five years. Comparing these figures for 1832 with the 276 zhuang and jie that existed in 1898, over that period the increase averaged 2.7 percent per year.[86]

[83] See Wen Zhenhua 溫振華, "Taiwan tuzhu tianhua chuanbo chutan" [Preliminary study on infection by smallpox among Taiwan aborigines], in Liao Yunfan 廖運範 et al., eds., Chen Shengkun Yishi jinianji 陳勝崑醫師紀念集 [Essays in memory of Dr. Chen Shengkun] (Taipei: Jujing, 1992), pp. 82–94.

[84] Cho-yun Hsu, "The Chinese Settlement of the I-lan Plain," in R. Knopp, ed., China's Island Frontier (Honolulu: University of Hawaii Press), pp. 69–86.

[85] Chen Shujun, Gazetteer of Gemalan, pp. 25–28. Ke Peiyuan 柯培元, Gemalan zhilüe 噶瑪蘭誌略 [A short gazetteer of Gemalan] (Taipei: Bank of Taiwan, 1961), pp. 27–28, listed 12 bao.

[86] Liao Fengde, Gemalan in Qing times, pp. 34–36.

With regard to water conservancy, the 1832 gazetteer recorded 19 irrigation ditches, 5 dikes, and 8 reservoirs with no reference to the date of construction.[87] A later estimate suggested that in the Qing period, Gemalan had more than 80 reservoirs and irrigation ditches; they were all privately owned and the earliest work could be dated back to the time of Wu Sha. In other words, just as in other areas, irrigation works were undertaken simultaneously with reclamation. It is notable that the Lin family of Banqiao (板橋林家) was deeply involved in investment in water conservancy and in the camphor trade of this area beginning in the Daoguang period.[88]

Although some earlier venturers went to the area south of Gemalan, the opening up of eastern Taiwan mostly proceeded after 1875 under the policy of *kaishan fufan*. In that year, Beinan Ting 卑南廳 was established; it was upgraded to Taidong Zhou in 1887.[89]

Two measures were taken to open the mountains: (1) the army was dispatched to build roads and to provide defense and (2) people were recruited to open up new lands. To begin with, three roads were constructed in 1875 to connect west and east, and people who were willing to follow were recruited. In 1886, three bureaus (*fukenju*) were set up at Beinan, Pushige 璞石閣, and Hualian 花蓮. Moreover, bureaus for recruiting cultivators (*zhaokenju* 招墾局) were set up in Amoy, Swatow, and Hong Kong. The recruits were provided with rations and one *jia* of land per person; they were also assisted with cattle, seeds, and implements; and it was ruled that the land reclaimed would be exempted from tax for three years. However, most migrants went to southeast Asia rather than Taiwan. Thus, Huang Yanzhao 黃延昭, magistrate of Hengchun, suggested that farmers already in Taiwan be recruited to move east on the same terms. In the 1880s, more people did move east and cultivated lands were somewhat expanded. But not many movers actually settled down, for some of them died and most of them left because of maladjustment to the local climate.[90] In 1894, Taidong Zhou had 32 Han settlements: the smallest one had only 2 or 3 households and the largest one no more than 90 households.[91]

The area behind the mountains was opened up much more slowly than the west coast. Lian Heng has two comments on this situation. According to

[87] Chen Shujun, *Gazetteer of Gemalan*, pp. 17, 36–41. Ke Peiyuan, *Short gazetteer of Gemalan*, pp. 36–42, listed the same number.
[88] Liao Fengde, *Gemalan in Qing times*, pp. 190–202.
[89] Lian Heng, *General history*, pp. 125–27, 417; Chen Xianzhong 陳顯忠, "Tan Taiwan houshan zhi kaifa" [Discourse on the opening up of the area behind the mountains in Taiwan], *Taiwan wenxian* 32.1 (1981), p. 187.
[90] Chen Zhengxiang, *Geography of Taiwan*, p. 1215.
[91] *Taidongzhou caifangce* 台東州採訪冊 [Records of inquiries in Taidong district] (Taipei: Bank of Taiwan, 1960), pp. 18–21.

him, eastern Taiwan remained a wilderness and agriculture had not been extended after twenty years of administration, for there was a lack of transportation facilities and "miasma" was still dreadful.[92] Herein lay the environmental problems to be tackled for further development of this area.

6.2.6. PENGHU

Finally, let us take a look at Penghu, where the Han Chinese had settled earlier than on the island of Taiwan itself. Penghu was established as a *ting* in 1727, and this status did not change until the end of the Qing period.

The unit of settlement at Penghu was known as the *ao* 澳 (bay); the local gazetteer describes it as follows: "The houses are all built in the hollows of the hills or at the bays, and so a place is called an *ao*."[93] This shows the influence of particular natural conditions on the pattern of settlement in Penghu. During the Kangxi period, there were only 9 *ao*; from the Yongzheng period on, the population increased and 4 more were added; during the Qianlong period, there were 13 *ao* and under them some 75 *she* 社 (villages).[94] The 1893 gazetteer recorded that there were 13 *ao* and 82 *she*, but among them only Magong She 媽宮社 was densely populated. Furthermore, only 6 *she* had 300 to 1,000 households, while the rest were very small villages scattered on isolated small islands.[95] Again, this shows that the pattern of settlement in Penghu was rather peculiar. Because of its special geographical conditions, Penghu had no water conservancy; some concerned local officials tried, however, to promote it by paying much attention to digging wells.[96]

The residents in Penghu came mainly from Quanzhou.[97] The genealogical records show that from the late Ming to the early Qing, the majority of inmigrants were from Jinmen 金門.[98] From the Qianlong period on, the population of Penghu increased rapidly, but famines occurred frequently (during 1762–1892, on the average, there was one famine every 4.1 years),

---

[92] Lian Heng, *General history*, p. 126, p. 447.

[93] Lin Hao 林豪, *Penghu tingzhi* 澎湖廳誌 [Gazetteer of Penghu subprefecture] (Taipei: Bank of Taiwan, 1963), p. 322.

[94] Hu Jianwei 胡建偉, *Penghu jilüe* 澎湖紀略 [Notes on Penghu] (Taipei: Bank of Taiwan, 1961), p. 33.

[95] Lin Hao, *Gazetteer of Penghu*, pp. 78–82.

[96] Hu Jianwei, *Notes on Penghu*, p. 46; Lin Hao, *Gazetteer of Penghu*, p. 309.

[97] Du Zhen 杜臻, *Penghu Taiwan jilüe* 澎湖台灣紀略 [Notes on Taiwan and Penghu] (Taipei: Bank of Taiwan, 1961), p. 2.

[98] Chen Shaoxin, *Gazetteer of Taiwan province*, section on population, vol. 1, pp. 19–20; Xu Xueji 許雪姬, "Penghu de renkou qianyi: yi Baisha Wadongcun weili" [Migration of the population in Penghu: The case of Wadongcun at Baisha], in *Zhongguo haiyang fazhanshi lunwenji* 中國海洋發展史論文集 [Essays on the history of Chinese maritime development] (Taipei: Institute of Three People's Principles, Academia Sinica, 1988), pp. 61–92.

and thus there were outmigrations to Taiwan.[99] Outmigrations were mostly seasonal prior to 1850, and most people went to the Hengchun area to work on farms or to make charcoal; after 1850, most of them went to the Tainan area to engage in commerce or to learn handicrafts; and after 1900, most went to the Kaohsiung area.[100] In short, Penghu was no longer a fisherman's island group as the Portuguese saw it in the sixteenth century.

6.2.7. DIFFERENT PATTERNS OF RURAL SETTLEMENTS

As mentioned above, in the process of reclamation in the Zhuqian area the isolated farmhouses of tenants gradually formed scattered settlements. Researches in this area touch on the issue of the relationship between reclamation and the pattern of settlement. Tomita Yoshirō, the first scholar to do fieldwork on this problem, published his findings in 1933. He pointed out that there were different forms of rural settlements in Taiwan: villages in the south were compact while those in the north were dispersed. The dividing line between these two regional patterns was marked by the Zhuoshuiqi, with a transitional area between this river and the Daduqi. This general viewpoint was repeated in Tomita's later works.[101] In 1951, Chen Zhengxiang also did fieldwork in many places. He used the number of main houses in a village as a criterion of classification and showed once again that a regional pattern did exist.[102] Both Tomita and Chen contended that the regional pattern was a result of interactions between natural and human conditions, and that the most relevant factors were the limitation of water sources, differences in natural geographic features, the necessity of defense, and the organization of the land system. Most scholars who have dealt with this issue have accepted this generalization about regional differences; even when quantitative geographical methods are applied to measure the distribution of settlements more precisely, the basic regional pattern is not changed.[103] With regard to the relevant factors, some scholars

---

[99] Chen Shaoxin, *Gazetteer of Taiwan province*, section on population, vol. 2, pp. 21–30.

[100] Cited in Xu Xueji, "Migration of the population," p. 62.

[101] Tomita Yoshirō 富田芳郎, "Taiwan ni okeru nōson shuraku no keitai ni tsuite" [On the rural settlement forms in Taiwan], *Taiwan chigaku kiji* 臺灣地學記事 [Description of Taiwan's geography] 4.2–4.3 (1933), pp. 11–14, 18–24. I have not yet collected all of Tomita's works that relate to this topic, but fortunately, Shi Tianfu has collected twenty-nine works and reviewed Tomita's theory and methodology. See his "The development and pattern," pp. 58–62. To save space, this chapter will not list all Tomita's works.

[102] Chen Zhengxiang, *Geography of Taiwan*, pp. 256–60.

[103] For examples, Chen Fanghui 陳芳惠, "Taoyuan taidi juluoxing de jiliang dili" [A geographical quantitative study on the distribution of communities on the Taoyuan plateau], *Taiwan wenxian* 27.2 (1976), pp. 311–18; Shi Zaitian et al., "Geographical quantitative study," pp. 91–92.

have tended to reiterate the above four;[104] others have emphasized the applicability of certain factors at certain localities.[105] On this issue further study should be done case by case, and more attention should be paid to changes in the twentieth century, particularly those taking place during the process of Taiwan's industrialization, but these are beyond the purview of this chapter.

6.3. FURTHER REMARKS

To sum up, in the seventeenth century, more Han settlements laid the foundation for further development in Taiwan; in the eighteenth century, despite the prohibitive policies of the Qing government, agricultural expansion proceeded rapidly from south to north; by 1895, when Taiwan was ceded to Japan, the plains, the uplands, and the hillsides in the west and northeast of the island were almost all cultivated, and the opening up of the eastern longitudinal valley was already initiated. Total cultivated acreage in Taiwan at that time was 600,000 hectares, more than thirty-three times that at the end of the Zheng period.[106] The legacy of agricultural expansion by the Han people is summed up succinctly by Lian Heng: "Taiwan was indeed but an island of wasteland, [our ancestors] lived in a humble way and opened up the mountains and forests, [their achievements are] what we have relied on until today."[107] Here I will only propose a few points for further study of the environmental history of Taiwan.

First, there is the problem of "miasma," or endemic disease. When Taiwan was first opened up, its bad climate was a great source of dread that deterred inmigrants. As mentioned above, in 1697, Yu Yonghe accepted that accumulated "miasma" was the reason for the illness of his followers; he observed that the patients quivered, but he had no idea that chills were a symptom of malaria.[108] Before the twentieth century, a common idea of

---

[104] For example, Hong Cannan, "Study on development," pp. 37–42.

[105] For example, Ronald Knapp, "Settlement and Frontier Land Tenure," pp. 55–68, has pointed out that the land-tenancy system was a major factor in the Taoyuan alluvial plain. Cho-yun Hsu, "Chinese Settlement of the I-lan Plain," pp. 69–86, has argued *per contra* that the land system was not a significant factor for the I-lan region. Shi Tianfu, "The development and pattern," pp. 63–64, has suggested that the organization of reclamation was the major factor influencing the original pattern of the settlement, but that the maintenance of the pattern was affected by natural conditions such as climate, physical features, and hydrology as well as human factors such as the style of agricultural management.

[106] Chen Zhengxiang, *Geography of Taiwan*, p. 30.

[107] Lian Heng, *General history*, p. 15, author's preface.

[108] Yu Yonghe, *Travel over a small sea*, p. 26. For the identification of *zhangqi* 瘴氣 as malaria, see Chen Shengkun 陳勝崑, *Zhongguo jibingshi* 中國疾病史 [History of disease in China] (Taipei:

those who talked about climate in Taiwan was that "miasma" would diminish with the spread of human habitations. As mentioned earlier, the 1720 gazetteer of Taiwan Xian claims that "miasma" was no longer harmful there, for habitations were already quite dense. A few more examples are given below.

The 1717 gazetteer of Zhuluo states:

> The vapors of mountains and rivers have accumulated to become "miasma"; once human beings have brought them under their management, these vapors have a means of being dissipated and what is closed up is gradually opened; this is a common rule of nature. When garrisons are numerous, villages dense, roads opened, and trees uprooted, then insects, serpents, and other harmful species are gradually driven away, and as soon as the darkness and viciousness have disappeared, the pestilence ceases of its own accord. On top of this, as long as the people manage to have clean houses and food, and with supplement of medicine, they do not have to worry about bad environment any more.[109]

In the early nineteenth century, Xie Jinluan held this opinion:

> Taiwan was originally a place of poisonous "miasma." . . . After the administration was set up, the people gathered and the population increased, the epidemic vapors disappeared and the fogs, the dews, the winds, and the rains no longer had anything to pick up to become "miasma." Thus we know when the *yin* and the *yang* are in harmony, the cold and the warm weather will be in right season. Ever since the ancient time, many people have held this view; isn't it due to the efforts of man?[110]

Similarly, in the mid-nineteenth century, Ding Shaoyi commented. "We know that the local climate [*diqi* 地氣, literally 'the energy-vitality of the earth'] will be changed by man. . . . When Gemalan was first opened up, there were more rainy days than sunny ones; now, however, cold and warm are both the same as in the interior, and there is no more poisonous 'miasma.' "[111]

In short, the above statements all carry the same idea that "miasma" would disappear with human management, although none of these authors

---

Jujing Publishing, 1992), pp. 159–69. For a further discussion of this point see Ts'ui-jung Liu and Shi-yung Liu, "Disease and Mortality in the History of Taiwan," presented at the Conference on Asian Population History, Jan. 4–8, 1996 (Institute of Economics, Academia Sinica, Taipei), publication forthcoming.

[109] Chen Menglin, *Gazetteer of Zhuluo*, p. 113.

[110] Xie Jinluan, *Additional gazetteer*, p. 47; the same words were also cited in Zhou Xi, *Gazetteer of Zhanghua*, p. 30.

[111] Ding Shaoyi 丁紹儀, *Dongying shilüe* [A note on the eastern ocean] (Taipei: Bank of Taiwan, 1957), p. 56.

recognized it as malaria. As a matter of fact, it was not until 1965 that malaria was eradicated in Taiwan as the result of great human efforts.[112]

The fact is that "miasma" was still quite dreadful in Taiwan at the end of the nineteenth century. When the Huai 淮 and the Japanese armies landed on Taiwan at different expeditions, they were infected by epidemics (*yili* 疫癘).[113] Some of these have been identified as malaria, cholera, or other diseases.[114] But the issue of *yili* needs further study. Moreover, studies should also be done on the effects of converting grassland into rice paddies. Was the style of paddy rice cultivation in Taiwan also related to certain kinds of disease introduced by parasitic insects, such as hookworm?[115] Further studies are required to look into the relationship between environment and health in Taiwan.

Next, there is the problem of the living environmemt. As mentioned above, Yu Yonghe talked about how inconvenient and dangerous the thatched huts and their natural surroundings were. According to a study by Fang Hao, the roofs of houses in southern Taiwan had been gradually changed from thatch to tile in the Kangxi period, but in the Yilan area, the same change started only in the Daoguang reign.[116] Because of the limited availability of building materials, most houses in rural Taiwan were still thatch-roofed until the end of the nineteenth century. For example, an observation on Yunlin Xian around 1894 reported:

> This place does not have many cryptomeria, the columns and pillars of houses in the county city are mostly made of bamboo (the kind is *cizhu* 莿竹, *Bambusa stenostachya Hack*) and on top are tile-roofed; but in the villages most houses are thatch-roofed. Even though the simple ancient style is thus still preserved, it is apt to catch fire. Recently, houses have been roofed by split Makino's bamboos (*guizhu* 桂竹, *B. makinoi Hayata*), which is not as durable as tile, but can last for seven to eight years.[117]

The materials and forms of houses are important components of the environmental scene; it is thus important to study changes in houses. Some

---

[112] Chen Shengkun, *History of disease*, p. 169. Wang Jinmao 王金茂 et al., *Nüe'ji chengyin yu kongzhi ji qi genchu fazhan zhixiang* 瘧疾成因與控制及其根除發展指向 [The cause and control of malaria and the direction of its eradication in Taiwan] (Taichung: Taiwan Provincial Government, 1974), pp. 85–103.

[113] See Chen Yan, *Chronology of Taiwan*, pp. 203–56, for records by year.

[114] Chen Shengkun, *History of disease*, pp. 46, 168.

[115] Jacques May, "The Ecology of Human Disease," in Jack Bresler, ed., *Environment of Man* (Reading, Mass.: Addison-Wesley Publishing, 1968), p. 79.

[116] Fang Hao, "Taiwan shishang de yimao yiwa" [On changing thatch to tile in the history of Taiwan], in *Collected works*, vol. I, pp. 738–43.

[117] Ni Zanyuan, *Records of inquiries*, p. 27.

fieldwork has recently been done, but more is needed.[118] Scholars interested in the built environment have paid much attention to the concept of space as reflected in vernacular houses.[119] More important, studies should be undertaken not only on the spatial structure of individual houses, but also on the built environment of entire settlements; this kind of study is still rather rare.[120] It seems that only architects can handle the topic of the built environment with ease;[121] however, if the subject concerned is not limited to the spatial structure of buildings, then many aspects related to human habitation, such as water supply, garbage disposal, and so on, still require further studies.[122] In particular, during recent decades, houses in Taiwan have been undergoing great changes, and the living environment is certainly an important topic for future study.

This chapter only traces changes in the number of settlements and irrigation works, using very rough approximations. Further studies are required on the growth and decline of settlements and irrigation systems, and these studies should be done with meaningful specific cases.[123]

Finally, it should be noted that this chapter does not deal with issues in the twentieth century. From the 1930s onward, Taiwan has been gradually changing from an agricultural society into an industrial one; thus, new environmental issues relating to settlements are emerging, and with a greater urgency. These issues will have to be dealt with by other studies.

[118] For example, see Xu Xueji et al., *Taizhong xian jianzhu fazhan: minzhai pian* 台中縣建築發展 —民宅篇 [Development of vernacular houses in Taichung county] (Fengyuan: Cultural Center of Taichung County, 1991 and 1993).

[119] For example, Guan Huashan 關華山, "Taiwan chuantong minzhai suo biaoxian de kongjian guannian" [Spatial concept presented in the vernacular houses in Taiwan], *Bulletin of the Institute of Ethnology, Academia Sinica* 49 (1980), pp. 175–215.

[120] For example, Lin Huicheng 林會承 and Qiu Yongzhang 邱永章, "Wugoushui shizhi huanjing zhi xingcheng yu jiegou" [Formation of material environment and its structure: the case of Wugoushui], *Taiwanshi yanjiu xueshu yantaohui lunwenji* 台灣史研究學術研討會 論文集 [Symposium of studies on the history of Taiwan] (Taipei: Research Center of Taiwan Historical Landmark, 1989), pp. 127–75.

[121] For the theory of built environment, see Amos Rapoport, *The Mutual Interaction of People and Their Built Environment* (The Hague: Mouton, 1976).

[122] For example, see Liu Ts'ui-jung and Liu Shi-yung 劉士永, "Jingshui zhi gongji yu wushui zhi paifang: Taiwan juluo huanjingshi yanjiu zhi yi" [Water supply and water drainage: a study on the history of environmemt in Taiwan], *Academia Economic Papers* 20.2 (1992), pp. 459–504.

[123] For example, a study on spatial changes in harbors in Taiwan has just been completed by Lin Yuru 林玉茹, "Qingdai Taiwan gangkou de kongjian jiegou" [The spatial structure of harbors in Taiwan during the Qing period], M.A. thesis, National Taiwan University (1993). Further studies still need to be done to relate environmental change with the growth and decline of harbors.

The Frontiers

7

Highlands and Lowlands

ECONOMIC AND ECOLOGICAL INTERACTIONS IN THE LOWER YANGZI REGION UNDER THE QING

ANNE OSBORNE

In the lower Yangzi region during the late-imperial period, a basic conflict existed between pressures for economic intensification on one hand and the necessity to preserve ecological and social stability on the other. Rice farming was reaching saturation point and yields were stagnating, while silk and cotton production approached the limit as well. Production increases often came at the cost of diminishing marginal returns to labor, and sometimes to capital as well. More threatening in the long run, intensification through encroachment on the waterways infringed on the areas of slack that gave the ecological and social systems their resilience – that is, on the ability of these systems to absorb significant fluctuations in the natural world without being jolted into a new configuration.[1] At first, opening the highlands seemed a way out of this trap, providing an underexploited niche where returns to capital and labor were initially quite high. But mountain and forest resources were rapidly depleted, through direct exploitation and land clearance for food production to support a burgeoning work force. The irreversible impoverishment of the natural world – destruction of forests, erosion of topsoil, damage to water systems, and depletion of natural resources – not only made this intensification unsustainable over the long term within the highlands, it also threatened the agricultural ecology of the valleys. This environmental degradation undermined the resilience of the ecological and social systems in the late-imperial period,

I would like to thank Mark Elvin, Liu Ts'ui-jung, Robert Marks, Pierre-Étienne Will, and the other participants in the Conference on the History of the Environment in China for their comments and suggestions. I am grateful to Rider College for financial support for this research.

[1] C. J. Krebs, *Ecology*, 4th ed. (New York, 1985), pp. 586–88. I am grateful to Mark Elvin for valuable suggestions on this point.

and it continues to limit possibilities for development even under a modern technological regime.[2]

This study is a preliminary examination of this issue in the lower Yangzi region from the eighteenth to the mid-nineteenth century. The plains and the upland valleys in the hills on the lower Yangzi periphery had long been settled, but the steeper slopes, which rise from near sea level to elevations of several hundred meters, with peaks jutting up to 1,000 to 2,000 meters, remained a wilderness until the eighteenth century. The process of reclamation and intensification there, its environmental costs, and the dilemmas it posed are relatively well documented.

This intensification was stimulated by demographic growth that had begun in the sixteenth century, retreated in the seventeenth, and then recovered and accelerated from the eighteenth to the mid-nineteenth century. It was accompanied and partly supported by a significant increase in the commercialization of the economy. Both led to pressures for reclamation of more land in lowlands and highlands alike. These trends, of course, long antedated the eighteenth century: already in the Song dynasty (960–1279) there were fears that excessive reclamation was undermining the ecological stability of the region, and there was a wave of highland reclamation in the late Ming (1368–1644). Nevertheless, the eighteenth century saw the beginning of a new assault upon the highlands, which combined with the cumulative effects of old trends in the lowlands to increase instability and undermine resilience in the region as a whole. And although demographic recovery, continuing commercialization, and environmental degradation were powerful forces in the late nineteenth century as well, the Taiping Rebellion (1850–64) is a watershed in the history of the region that this study cannot cross. The environmental destruction of the war must be evaluated separately from the effects of demographic and economic growth.

After discussing evidence for heightened pressure on the land, we shall describe the economic expansion of the eighteenth and early nineteenth centuries and the ecological damage it produced. We shall examine the dilemma of economic alternatives that undermined ecological or social stability, growth in one area often being offset by losses elsewhere, with few unambiguous gains. And finally we shall turn to an evaluation of government regulation and elite management.

[2] See Vaclav Smil, *The Bad Earth* (Armonk, N.Y., 1984), and *China's Environmental Crisis: An Inquiry into the Limits of National Development* (Armonk, N.Y., 1993); He Baochuan, *China on the Edge: The Crisis of Ecology and Development* (San Francisco, 1991).

PRESSURE ON THE LAND

Because concerns about reclamation are analyzed below as the effects of pressure on the land, they are not cited here to prove its existence. But there is other evidence of a full landscape. Cultivated acreage figures stagnated while the population boomed; land prices rose from the mid-eighteenth century until the mid-nineteenth; farms were tiny, forcing reliance on income from by-employments and wage labor, and labor-intensive production of cotton and silk and their handicrafts. The waters themselves were more intensively exploited. Scattered but consistent evidence tells of increasing conflict over the land as well. Intensified exploitation of land indicates that it was the limiting factor: greatly increased expenditures of labor, and sometimes of capital, were lavished on static land holdings, while heavy investments of labor and capital created new land through diking and draining water margins and terracing slopes. Highland resources like timber and bamboo came under greater pressure, and land once considered wasteland was brought into production through the adoption of new crops and new techniques.

The population in certain core counties of the Yangzi delta in 1816 was more than two and a half times that of 1393, yet not only was there no significant increase in officially registered cultivated acreage in these counties, it actually decreased by almost 7 percent. Registered acreage for the lower Yangzi region as a whole fell from around 3–5 *mu* per capita in the early Ming dynasty to less than half that in the early nineteenth century.[3] Rice yields appear to have stagnated, despite a growing use of oilcake fertilizers, suggesting that under the existing technology, an upper limit to increases in productivity per acre had been reached.[4]

In the upland valleys between southern Anhui and northern Zhejiang,

---

[3] Philip C. C. Huang, *The Peasant Family and Rural Development in the Yangzi Delta, 1350–1988* (Stanford, Calif., 1990), appendix B. See also Liang Fangzhong, *Zhongguo lidai hukou, tiandi, tianfu tongji* [Historical statistics on the population, cultivated area and land tax of China], (Shanghai, 1980), table 77. In 1820, the provincial averages were: Anhui, 1.2 *mu* per capita; Jiangsu, 2.4; and Zhejiang, 1.7.

[4] Li Bozhong, "Ming Qing shiqi Jiangnan shuidao shengchan jiyue chengdu de tigao" [Intensification of wet-rice production in Jiangnan during the Ming and Qing periods], *Zhongguo nongshi* 1 (1984), pp. 25–28. Kang Chao, *Man and Land in Chinese History: An Economic Analysis* (Stanford, Calif., 1986), p. 214, argues for stagnating or slightly declining rice yields after the eighteenth century. Huang also finds no clear indication of rising yields, despite growing use of fertilizer in the Qing. *Peasant Family and Rural Development*, pp. 88–90. For a slightly different perspective, see Chapter 12 by Li Bozhong in the present volume.

land prices rose steadily for a century after 1740. They began to decline by 1850, perhaps indicating that there, too, limits to increases in productivity had been reached. Although the data are scattered, analysis of the holdings of individual families indicates a very low rate of turnover, great reluctance to alienate more land than was absolutely necessary, and eagerness to acquire whatever scraps of land might enter the market – conditions consistent with land scarcity.[5] Even in the highlands limits to exploitation were being reached. In Xiuning in Huizhou, "It takes ten or more terraces just to make a single *mu*. Though [the people] diligently use the land, they can get barely half a year's needs."[6] In Taiping county in Ningguo, the mountains were terraced from the spring line to the bottom, "in orderly rows like the scales of a fish, like layered clouds, but yield less than several catties of grain from a whole hillside." Further terracing was impossible, so some farmers tilled unterraced slopes, climbing up and down "like apes and monkeys," practicing slash-and-burn agriculture and moving on every three years.[7]

Tension increased between rival claimants to the land and its resources, and was particularly acute where lineages held land in common. In the lowlands, Jiangsu governor Zhuang Yougong in 1756 discovered widespread fraud and misappropriation of lineage lands by some lineage members acting in collusion with outsiders.

> In recent years, the price of grain has increased and gets more expensive every day. If there are some fellows who for the sake of riches are prepared to act in inhumane fashion, they create schemes through bribery to entice one or two unfilial sons and grandsons within the lineage to take the land they want to get, and illicitly set up a sale contract.[8] They pay half price and then immediately [the sellers] take flight far away. The buyer then relies on force to usurp and occupy the land, and obstinately collects rents. When an accusation is brought before the officials, because the one who received the price cannot be caught, there is no time limit for deciding the case, and the one who bought it illegally retains the property.[9]

---

[5] Chao, *Man and Land in Chinese History*, ch. 6.

[6] *Xiuning xianzhi* [History of Xiuning county], Fang Chongding et al., eds. (1815), preface 1a.

[7] *Ningguo fuzhi* [History of Ningguo prefecture], Lu Quan, ed. (1815), j. 9, pp. 26b–27a.

[8] Presumably as if they had an individual right to the land, rather than merely a claim on group property as lineage members. See other cases of fraudulent sales and rentals in Qingtian and Huizhou, below.

[9] Zhuang Yougong, "Zou wei qing ding daomai daomai sichan yitian zhi li" [Memorial requesting fixed regulations on the illegal selling and buying of sacrificial property and charity fields], in Renhe Qinchuan (pseud.), ed., *Huang Qing Zouyi* (Taipei, 1967), pp. 4181–87; *Da-Qing huidian shili* [Collected statutes and substatutes of the great Qing dynasty], ed. Li Hongjiang et al. (1899 ed.), j. 755, pp. 4b–5a.

Lineage members also cut cemetery trees and dismantled "graves, houses, gravestones, bricks, tiles and timbers" for illicit sale. Although problems with lineage lands were by no means new, during the eighteenth and early nineteenth century they were considered to be increasingly acute. Noting that the absence of a law specifically forbidding such conduct made prosecution difficult, Zhuang Yougong proposed stiff penalties for the misappropriation of lineage property. These were adopted and entered into the *Huidian shili.*

Similar tensions appeared in the highlands in Wenzhou.

> Under the pretext of repairing the ancestral hall, some appropriate and usurp the sacrificial rents. There are also those who squat under the eaves of the ancestral hall and summon bandit-types [presumably as tenants], and foment trouble and implicate everyone. There are old sacrificial fields or small sacrificial fields, which produce several tens or over one hundred *shi*; [lineage members] take turns receiving them and offering the sacrifices. Degenerate sons' and grandsons' mouths water over them and they fraudulently sell them or illicitly appropriate them for themselves, pretending to public spirit but working for their own ends. The result is that the members of one household are at daggers drawn and multitudes of lawsuits arise.[10]

This sort of conflict appears to have been a perennial problem in Huizhou as well.[11] In the 1780s, and again about twenty years later, lineage toughs illicitly recruited outside tenants for jointly held lineage land.[12] They kept the large advance rents as personal income. When the lineage leaders accused the tenants of encroachment, the existence of rental contracts cleared them of the charges. The disreputable poor relations had disappeared with the money. Unwilling to use their own resources to rebate the advance rents, the lineages turned to litigation and violence to try to drive out the interlopers. On several other occasions during the first half of the nineteenth century, outsiders in collusion with "unfilial sons" from the lineages illicitly opened coalmines or burned lime on lineage property in the hills of Huizhou.[13] In response to such incidents throughout the region, severe penalties were adopted for those who "took common mountain land and without notifying those with whom they share ownership," illicitly

---

[10] *Qingtian xian xuzhi* [Continuation of the history of Qingtian county], Wu Chuchun et al., eds. (1777), *j.* 4, p. 3a.

[11] Anne Osborne, "The Local Politics of Land Reclamation in the Lower Yangzi Highlands," *Late Imperial China* 15.1 (June 1994), pp. 1–46.

[12] *Zuyi gongye.* Yang Maotian, "Daoxian Yang Maotian chajin pengmin an'gao" [Draft report of His Excellency Intendant Yang Maotian on the shack people] (1807), in *Huizhou fuzhi* [History of Huizhou], Ma Buchan et al., eds. (1827), *j.* 4B, pp. 39b–45b. The phrase appears on p. 42b.

[13] *Yixian san zhi* [Three histories of Yi county], Xie Yongtai, ed. (1872), *j.* 11, pp. 17a–20a.

recruited outsiders as tenants.[14] Although they had never been monoliths with only a single interest, the internal fragmentation of the lineages seems to have intensified in the late-imperial period in response to the rising value of their land.

ECONOMIC EXPANSION

Lowland land use adapted to demographic growth by making every square inch as productive as possible. Grain fields were double-cropped or converted to higher-value cash crops, water margins were enclosed, and terraces were built to make new fields. Reeds, aquatic plants, fish, and turtles were harvested from streams and ponds. In the hills, the pace of extraction quickened for timber, bamboo, and other highland resources, mines and handicraft workshops spread, while slopes were cleared to plant industrial crops such as dyestuffs and fiber plants, as well as new food crops like maize and sweet potatoes, both for local subsistence and as commercial crops for the expanding highland work force. Eventually these kinds of intensification approached the limits of feasibility, and if pushed further might have become counterproductive, undermining the ecological stability of the region. The mobility of labor required by the expansion of the highland economy also posed new challenges to social control.

In the mid-Ming, the Yangzi delta still produced a major rice surplus. By the late Ming dynasty, population had grown and cash cropping had expanded to such an extent that the region imported grain. Rising prices encouraged enclosing water margins to create new fields, and terracing to expand paddy-fields up low hillsides. Both required significant investments of labor and capital, not only for the initial creation of the fields, but also for long-term maintenance of the polders, terraces, and irrigation systems. This process has so transformed the landscape of the Yangzi delta that it is estimated that approximately 25 percent of the paddy land in the region was created by such enclosures. Rice paddies were subject to minimal erosion and efficiently used both water and fertilizer. These reclamations could significantly increase productivity without seriously disrupting the ecological balance of the region.

Despite enormous ingenuity and prodigal expenditures of labor, however, reclamation of rice land eventually approached the limit. For example, 199 lakes dotted the Ning-Shao plain at the beginning of the Ming

---

[14] *Jiang gonggong shanchang bu gaozhi heye zhi ren. Da Qing huidian shili, j.* 158, pp. 28b–29a. The phrase appears on 29a.

dynasty. By the twentieth century, all but 44 had been entirely reclaimed, and those that remained had reduced surface area and water storage capacity.[15] By the Qianlong reign (1736–95), some paddy reclamations registered under the previous reign were removed from the tax registers because they could not be kept permanently productive. Furthermore, small odd-shaped parcels of lower-quality land were permanently exempted from taxation.[16] There was little room for new enclosures.

Cotton could be grown on dry land difficult to convert to paddy-fields, and mulberries for silk production yielded significantly more value per unit area than rice, although labor, fertilizer, and other requirements were also heavier. Intensification in these areas, despite diminishing marginal re- turns to labor and sometimes to capital, allowed for fuller employment of the whole farm family, and therefore supported an ever-increasing popula- tion on a declining acreage per capita. This sort of growth without develop- ment has been dubbed "agricultural involution."[17] Although condemning farm families to unrelenting labor, it need not lead to ecological disruption and it may even increase social resilience by diversifying the crops and ecological zones that support the population. Eventually, in the lowlands, conversion of almost all suitable land and severely diminishing marginal returns to labor limited further intensification of this kind as well.

As the lowland economy filled the landscape more completely, became more highly commercialized and diversified, and became more involuted under the pressure of population growth, economic transformation af- fected the highlands as well. Hillsides had produced timber, bamboo, charcoal, and tea for centuries. These continued to be harvested in ever more remote and inaccessible areas, as prices rose with demand. Extraction of these resources, however, often outstripped natural regrowth or reforestation.

Timber became increasingly scarce and expensive: it was said that a man with a thousand *shan* 杉 trees was the equal of a feudal lord.[18] Paradoxically, this did not necessarily encourage investment in timber production. Forest fires could devastate a district.[19] Timber rustling was a concern, and usurpa- tion or litigation over rights to a mature stand of trees could consume the

---

[15] Chen Qiaoyi et al., "Lun lishi shiqi Ning-Shao pingyuan de hupo yanbian" [The historical evolution of the lakes of the Ning-Shao plain], *Dili yanjiu* 3.3 (1984), p. 32.

[16] Peng Yuxin, *Qingdai tudi kaiken shi* [A history of land development in the Qing period], (Beijing, 1990), p. 146.

[17] Huang, *Peasant Family and Rural Development*, following Clifford Geertz, *Agricultural Involu- tion: The Process of Ecological Change in Indonesia* (Berkeley, 1963).

[18] *Huaining xianzhi* [History of Huaining county], Wang Yufang et al., eds. (1827), *j.* 7, p. 5a.

[19] For this reason, local government sometimes tried to prohibit field preparation by burning. *Qimen xianzhi* [History of Qimen county], Wang Rang et al., eds. (1827), *j.* 16, p. 3b.

profits of decades of care. At times this meant that no one was willing to contract to produce timber on mountain land.

> Although the price of timber is excellent, planting it is not easy. In all the mountains where the timber has already been sold, one must again register to plant and open it, clear it, and raise and nurture it to be the land for future [production]. But the expenditures and meals for the workers year after year are many and very troublesome, and the longest take forty to fifty years; the earliest twenty to thirty years. Only then can one ask a price from someone. Now the mountain landlords mostly are poor. When they get the price for the timber, immediately it is used up. Either they abandon [the land] and do not plant it again, or they plant it but do not weed the thorns and brambles that cover and shade the trees, and they will not grow. Nine out of ten families are like this. The future profit from *shan* trees will be minuscule.[20]

> If by good fortune they grow into a forest, either there will be false usurpation and incitement of lawsuits, or struggles over boundaries will begin. The benefit is the longest delayed and the most difficult.[21]

Thus the incentive of high prices could not always make up for relatively heavy production costs and long-delayed returns, as well as significant risks.

Overcutting also led to a shortage of fuel. In the mid-eighteenth century, demand was so strong in the neighboring lowlands that entrepreneurs rented hillsides and used hired labor to scythe off the grass to sell as cooking fuel.[22] At the turn of the nineteenth century, fuel prices rose steeply in the highlands. It was said that firewood sold like precious cassia wood.[23] In the southern Anhui hills, people combed up the fallen needles of deciduous conifers and sold the bundles in the villages.[24] There was a growing incidence of the illicit dismantling of houses for the fuel their timbers would provide.[25]

The tea industry expanded significantly in the mountains of Fujian, Zhejiang, and southern Anhui. Although environmentally more benign than annual crops, the establishment of tea plantations required deforesta-

[20] *Xi'an xianzhi* [History of Xi'an county], Fan Chongkai et al., eds. (1810), j. 20, p. 2a–b.

[21] Chen Jingchao, "Kaizhong baolu lihai lun" [On the advantages and disadvantages of reclamation and planting maize] (n.d.), in *Fenshui xianzhi* [History of Fenshui county], Zang Chengxuan et al., eds. (1906), j. 1, pp. 41b–42a.

[22] Li Min, "Qianlong xingke tiben zhong youguan nongye zibenzhuyi mengya de cailiao" [Materials on the sprouts of capitalism in agriculture in routine judicial memorials of the Qianlong period], *Wenwu* 9 (1975), p. 72.

[23] *Jixi xianzhi* [History of Jixi county], Qing Kai et al., eds. (1810), j. 3, *tu tian* (Taibei, 1985) pp. 58–59.

[24] *Huaining xianzhi*, j. 7, p. 5a.

[25] Fang Chun, *Chusong shanfang zaju* [Miscellaneous writings from the Chusong studio] (n.d.), in *Huizhou fuzhi*, j. 4B, pp. 45b–46a.

tion, and tea bushes did not hold the soil as well as forest cover. Some tea was terraced, but much was not, or was grown on terraces without stone facing, which eroded badly in the region's heavy downpours. The spread of tea also brought in outsiders to work the plantations, upsetting the balance between local food supply and local demand, and driving up prices. The bands of strong, unattached workers were feared as potential bandits.

> More and more mountains have been planted over. Verdant cliffs have been cut down to the red soil, and clear streams in the valleys have become yellow-flowing [because of] the reckless cultivation. In the mountains good and bad people mingle together in the tea workshops. Not only are they unprepared for drought and floods, but [they are] also exposed to bandits.[26]

Paper production expanded in the eighteenth century, but was already in decline in some places by the mid-nineteenth century, due to overcutting of bamboo and paper mulberry. In Yushan, "only the old are able to point out the places where the paper-making factories used to be."[27] Elsewhere in Guangxin, paper production depended on supplies of bamboo imported from neighboring Fujian.[28]

New commercial crops such as hemp, ramie, indigo, and tobacco, as well as the New World food crops, were introduced into much of the area at this time by people from Guangdong, Fujian, Jiangxi, and Anhui. For the first few years after the removal of forest cover, the thin highland soils remained productive, their fertility boosted by the elements released in the burning of the clearance debris. Maize and sweet potatoes were much more productive than the traditional dry grains, especially on unimproved land, and were typically grown without fertilizer, weeding, or irrigation. Local people rapidly adopted maize, and it soon spread throughout the lower Yangzi hills.

Describing maize, a local history from Zhejiang noted:

> It is only necessary to remove the grass, there is no need to use fertilizer. . . . But when it is planted among the mountains, then the earth is

---

[26] Cited in Robert P. Gardella, *Harvesting Mountains: Fujian and the China Tea Trade, 1757–1937* (Berkeley, 1994), pp. 177–78. See also James Polachek, "Economic Diversification, Seasonal Migration, and Social Conflict in the Kiangsi–Fukien Border Area in the Mid-Ch'ing," paper presented at the Annual Meeting of the Association for Asian Studies, Washington, D.C., March 21–23, 1980. I am grateful for permission to cite these two studies. An earlier examination of the ecological costs of expanded tea cultivation appears in Hatano Yoshihiro, *Chūgoku kindai kōgyō-shi no kenkyū* [Studies on the modern industrialization of China] (Kyoto, 1961), pp. 111 and 199, n. 43a. I am indebted to Mark Elvin for this reference.

[27] *Yushan xianzhi* [History of Yushan county], Wu Huachen et al., eds. (1873), *j.* 1B, pp. 24a–b.

[28] *Guangxin fuzhi* [History of Guangxin prefecture], Li Shufan et al., eds. (1872), *j.* 1B, p. 97a.

loosened and the rocks emerge. Whenever there is heavy rain the water and rocks accordingly wash down in mudslides. The streams and torrents are silted up and blocked. Since the floods of 1801, Xuanping's streams and pools have been filled in with sand, and rocks pile up and accumulate. This is the only reason that water cannot be stored. Thus when maize is planted, after ten years or so, the mountain is necessarily ruined, and moreover, one can no longer plant bamboo and timber. The benefits are completely exhausted and evil follows.[29]

Likewise in Fenshui in Yanzhou, migrants from Anhui and Fujian "remove the grass and do not use fertilizer, but the harvest is good. Local people imitate them." Yet because of environmental problems, "the gains cannot offset the losses."[30]

By providing cheap, reliable staple foods for locals and inmigrants, the New World crops supported the expansion of established mountain enterprises like logging and tea and paper production, as well as new ventures like growing hemp and indigo, quarrying, and mining.[31] Lime burning was an innovation of the early nineteenth century in Yixian in Huizhou, where burnt lime replaced the traditional wood ash as fertilizer, perhaps as an adaptation to deforestation. Kilns employed "several hundred" outside workers hired by a few Huizhou men.[32]

Because returns to labor were quite high and it could use land previously considered worthless, commercial agriculture in the hills was profitable even on rented land with hired labor. Managerial agriculture appears to have remained viable in the hills after it was squeezed out by family production in the valleys. Yet this depended on abandoning fields when the temporary fertility of newly cleared land was exhausted, and clearing and burning over a new hillside – production techniques that damaged soil and water resources both locally and farther downstream.

Opening the highlands at first increased opportunities for handicrafts and petty trade based on mountain and forest products. For example, in

[29] *Xuanping xianzhi* [History of Xuanping county], Pi Xirui et al., eds. (1878), *j.* 17, pp. 5a–b.
[30] *Fenshui xianzhi, j.* 3, p. 41a.
[31] Chen Qiaoyi, "Lishishang Zhejiangsheng shandi kenji you shanlin pohuai" [The opening of mountain land and destruction of forests in the history of Zhejiang Province], *Zhongguo shehui keshui* 4 (1984), pp. 212–15; Chen Shuping, "Yumi he fanshu zai Zhongguo chuanbo qingjuang yanjiu" [A study of the circumstances of the diffusion of maize and sweet potatoes in China], *Zhongguo shehui kexue* 3 (1980), pp. 200–3.
[32] Hu Yuanxi, "Yishan jin wamei shaohui shuo" [On prohibiting digging coal and burning lime in the mountains of Yixian] (1845), in *Yixian san zhi, j.* 15.3, pp. 70b–72b; "Biyang Shuyuan shoushu chanmei geshanye gongyiji" [Record of the public discussion on the contribution of coal-producing mountains to the Biyang Academy] (1845), in *Yixian san zhi, j.* 5.3, pp. 35b–36b.

Taiping county, local people peddled "paper, knives, flowers, scissors, varnish, fans, floss, umbrellas, and various items to the four corners of the Empire."[33] People in Xi'an turned to production for the market or to petty trade to eke out a living as population expanded beyond the carrying capacity of local agricultural land.

> Xi'an has not many profitable products. Merchants from other districts are extremely few. Recently the population has been growing and people are rather distressed for food and taxes, clothing and rent. Therefore people rush to compete and hasten to wrangle to become merchants, and the number of merchants is increasing daily.[34]

The scale of development is suggested by the statement that the inmigrants who planted tobacco, indigo, hemp, and maize were "as numerous as quills on a hedgehog"; "in all the deep mountains and secluded places, their shacks and worksheds adjoin each other like the scales of a fish."[35] In western Huzhou, where "the mountains extend far into inaccessible gullies and lonely precipices," after the arrival of inmigrants growing sweet potatoes, "deep in the mountains there was almost no wasteland."[36]

The dynamism of the highland economy is also suggested by the involvement of outsiders, as entrepreneurs, as tenants, and as hired labor.[37] This appears to rest on three main factors. The first is that sometimes the capital came from the outside, and the entrepreneurs might bring their own work force with them. For example, in Huizhou in the late eighteenth and early nineteenth centuries, lowland entrepreneurs invested hundreds or thousands of taels in long-term leases of hillsides, which they reclaimed for maize production using hundreds of hired workers from outside.[38] In Guangxin, paper factories were founded by outsiders: "Rich merchants

---

[33] *Ningguo fuzhi,* j. 9, p. 27a.

[34] *Xi'an xianzhi,* j. 20, pp. 2a–b.

[35] *Xuancheng xianzhi* [History of Xuancheng county], Li Yingtai, ed. (1888), j. 2, pp. 7b–8a.

[36] *Wucheng xianzhi* [History of Wucheng county], Zhou Xuejun et al., eds. (1881), j. 35, pp. 28a–b.

[37] It is difficult to get any conclusive estimate of the numbers of people involved. According to what appears to be an actual count in 1807, there were 8,681 resident shack people in Huizhou alone, as well as "innumerable" itinerants, presumably significantly more than the residents. Another estimate at that time suggests there were 200,000 such itinerants, but the source exaggerates in reporting other figures. Yang, "Chajin pengmin an'gao," p. 42a; Gao Tingyao, *Huanyou jilüe* [Records of a roaming official] (1908), Shang 39b. James Polachek, "Economic Diversification," reports early nineteenth-century estimates from the neighboring Wuyi Mountains of over 100,000 itinerant workers (p. 22), and in the 1840s of "several tens of thousands" (p. 12).

[38] Anne Osborne, "Barren Mountains, Raging Rivers: The Ecological and Social Effects of Changing Landuse on the Lower Yangzi Periphery in Late Imperial China," Ph.D. thesis, Columbia University (1989), ch. 4.

and big traders come bringing capital under their arms. The majority are people from Huizhou and Fujian."[39]

The second factor in the involvement of outsiders in the highland economy was their specialized knowledge. Although the local people rapidly adopted maize and participated in much of the rest of the diversification of the economy, hemp and indigo remained inmigrants' specialties generations after their first introduction into the highlands.[40] Specialized mushroom production for a gourmet market was something that local people "had no knowledge of."[41] Finally, the local population probably could not supply all the labor needed at peak seasons, because of conflicts with other agricultural tasks, such as the transplantation of rice in the spring, which coincided with the optimum time for gathering the first crop of tea leaves; local labor might also have been drawn away by other strategies such as peddling, which took some of the local population out of the region for extended periods. Fang Chun notes the apparent paradox of a region so poor in paddy land that its population is forced into petty trade, yet which also attracts investment capital and labor from the outside.[42]

Despite the influx of outside labor, several sources note that wages and meals for workers were a heavy expense. In the timber industry, this made it impossible for poorly capitalized families to make the investments necessary for successful reforestation.[43] In agriculture, hired workers were portrayed as lazy and spoiled, lying abed in the morning and expecting delicacies like tea and *dianxin* 點心, while handicraft workers were said to be even more demanding.[44] However exaggerated this may be, it suggests a sellers' market for labor, which would have been even more pronounced without a supply of seasonal migrants. Before the spread of the New World crops and the development of the highland economy, it was common for highlanders to go down to the valleys to work during the agricultural busy season.[45] In the later eighteenth and nineteenth century, by contrast, the flow of workers seems to have been reversed.

Perhaps in part because they were not local people, the outsiders often did not manage their enterprises for sustained yields, but rather expanded quickly and collapsed just as fast when the local resources were depleted.

[39] *Guangxin fuzhi, j.* 1B, pp. 97a–b.
[40] Wu Qian and Wang Yuanji, *Chun'an huangzheng jilüe* [Outline of famine relief in Chun'an] (1824), p. 37a.
[41] *Guangde zhouzhi* [History of Guangde department], Hu Youcheng et al., eds. (1881), *j.* 22, p. 3b.
[42] Fang Chun, *Chusong shanfang zaju.*
[43] *Xi'an xianzhi, j.* 20, pp. 2a–b.
[44] *Ningguo xianzhi* [History of Ningguo county], Liang Zhongfu, ed. (1825), *j.* 12 *fu*, p. 5a.
[45] Chen Qiaoyi, "Zhejiangsheng shandi kenji," p. 213.

Their investments often did not lead to sustained economic growth, and might even leave the locality more deeply impoverished than before.

> Areas opened up near the mountains in the Yongzheng reign provided timber to Hangzhou. Recently, as the population has multiplied and the fertility of the soil has been exhausted, they do not wait until [the trees] that remain are a handspan in diameter and the sound of axes rings "zheng! zheng!"[46]

> People from other districts without local registration form bands to dig up [*mao* 毛 bamboo]. They eradicate it completely. This is greatly harmful to the local people, and deeply grieves the elders.[47]

Inmigrant tenants in the highlands inspected the thickness of the soil, and set the term of rental contracts according to how long the soil would take to erode.[48]

Natural resources were often depleted, as in the case of overcutting timber and bamboo, declining paper production, or the erosion of topsoil that made grain production unsustainable. Open-ended expansion was also hindered by competition for scarce land between different factors of production, or between them and food for the work force. An example is the cloth-dyeing industry. Its regional center shifted from Songjiang to Suzhou after the mid-seventeenth century. One reason for this was the scarcity of fuels in the lowlands, and the advantage to Suzhou of proximity to the wooded hills of Zhexi, to provide the charcoal for the dyeing process.[49] Demand from Suzhou also encouraged reclamation of these hills for indigo production. Ironically, the deforestation that cleared the mountains for commercial farms for dyestuffs, and also for the provision of staple foods for the workers, made charcoal increasingly scarce and expensive and hindered the expansion of the industry.

Mining expanded during this period as well. Iron mines developed in this region, but iron required enormous amounts of fuel for smelting. Coal mining, which might have ameliorated the fuel shortage and thereby promoted economic growth, also contributed to limits on such growth. It led

---

[46] *Yushan xianzhi, j.* 1B, pp. 20a–b.

[47] *Yuhang xianzhi* [History of Yuhang county], Zhang Ji'an et al., eds. (1808), *j.* 38, p. 5b.

[48] Wang Yuanfang, "Qing jin pengmin kaishan zushui yi du fuhuan shu" [Memorial requesting a prohibition on the shack people's reclaiming mountains and obstructing waterways in order to prevent future calamities] (1850), p. 1487, in *Huangchao Dao-Xian-Tong-Guang Zouyi,* Wang Yanxi, ed., pp. 1486–88. Reprinted in *Jindai Zhongguo shiliao congkan* (Taipei, 1969), vol. 331a–d.

[49] Li Bozhong, "Ming Qing Jiangnan gong nongye shengchan zhong di ranliao wenti" [On the problem of fuels in industrial and agricultural production in Jiangnan in the Ming and Qing], *Zhongguo shehui jingjishi yanjiu* 4 (1984), p. 46.

to deforestation and erosion, directly for mining operations and indirectly through encouraging reclamation of slopelands for grain production to feed the workers. Strip-mining of shallow seams of coal also might spread pollution from mine tailings to irrigation water and agricultural land. Both erosion and water pollution increased the risks to agriculture downstream.

UNSUSTAINABLE DEVELOPMENT: ECOLOGICAL AND SOCIAL COSTS

The ecological damage caused by lowland enclosures and highland reclamation was mutually reinforcing, while the tighter economic ties linking highlands and lowlands encouraged the exchange of capital and labor, but undermined social stability. Contemporaries argued that the gains in production did not offset the increased ecological risk, while the benefits of increased employment had to be weighed against the dangers of concentrations of drifters outside of government control.

Enclosure of water margins to create new paddy-fields cut off some fields from direct access to irrigation, and could reduce their productivity. The need for irrigation water rose while storage capacity fell. This contributed to a rising risk of drought, as well as the danger that in wet seasons runoff could exceed capacity and lead to floods. Intensified production of reeds and aquatic grasses, and placement of weirs to trap fish and shrimp, hastened the eutrophication of ponds and waterways. Water-control experts had been aware of these problems for centuries, constantly struggling to balance intensification with preservation. In the early nineteenth century, these perennial problems were exacerbated by intensification of production in the highlands, which further disrupted the hydrology of the whole region.[50]

Highland deforestation was significant in itself, as we have seen, leading to shortages of timber, bamboo, and fuel. It also initiated a chain reaction of further destruction, contributing to erosion, silting of waterways, and the danger of flood and drought when water-storage capacity was reduced. The connections were very clear to contemporaries.

Fang Chun, a native of Huizhou, described the results of reclamation on Huizhou's periphery.

> The location of this prefecture is in the midst of myriad mountains. To begin with, arable land is limited, and the topography is high and steep. In violent

[50] Wang Fengsheng, *Zhexi shuili beikao* [Report on water control in western Zhejiang] (1824), vol. 4, pp. 4.4a–b; vol. 1, pp. 1b–2a.

rainstorms, there are severe floods. If for ten days there is no rain, then there is a severe drought. All depend on ravines and mountain torrents as drains and dikes to store or drain off water, and to use for irrigation. Ever since the shack people have rented and farmed all the places with steep and precipitous terrain, there are none that are not opened up. When the grass cover is completely removed, then the sand and earth cannot remain in place. Each time there is heavy rain, sand and mud then wash away with the water, and streams and mountain torrents, drainage channels and dikes are gradually stopped up. The technique of the farmers for collecting and draining water for irrigation cannot be continued, with the result that year after year there are bad harvests. Now the fields near the mountains all have been flooded and covered. If this situation continues many decades, how can this problem be solved? This is the first problem, that [reclamation] damages the people's fields.

Another problem is that the daily necessities of the prefecture all are obtained from the outside. For the item of grain, in this area, even a year of bumper harvest barely supplies three months' [necessities]: we especially depend on the outside supplement. On one thread of a stream, truly a million lives depend. When the sand from the mountains flows down and silts up the streams and drainage channels, it then bursts through into the main rivers. The riverbeds are higher every day, and the flow is daily shallower. Hauling the boats becomes harder. If it stops raining for ten days together, then commodity prices soar and grain cannot be supplied. The people's hearts go into a panic. There is no year when this does not happen. This is the second problem, that it damages water-control networks.

In the prefecture there are range upon range of mountains. The people all dwell near the mountains. When the brooks and streams are silted up, then the drainage system is not able to conduct the water. Whenever there is excessive rain, the situation of the water is that mud and sand block it up and it overflows in four directions and rushes against the houses and they collapse in ruins. This is the third problem, that it is harmful to people's dwellings.

The graves of the people of this prefecture all are dug in the mountains. Everywhere they are strung together as in a necklace. For all of them, since the shack people have opened and planted the mountains, they hoe the mounds and fill in the depressions, and gradually the traces of their shape are lost. I fear that if this goes on the bones will not be preserved. This is the fourth problem, that it is harmful to graves.

In the prefecture, firewood was just barely sufficient for use. Now that the shack people have opened up the mountains, not only do they not plant or maintain [trees for] firewood, but even the roots and stumps are completely dug up. It even goes so far that grass and herbs are repeatedly burned and hoed and the sprouts give up hope; with the result that the price of firewood compared to several years ago has suddenly increased several-fold. The benefit to the local people of gathering fuel has been destroyed. As a result there are innumerable cases of dismantling people's dwellings and unauthorized cutting of cemetery trees. This harm to firewood is the fifth problem.

The shack people are all people from outside without proper registration. Their background cannot be known. They are enduring and work hard: in this they seem very poor. They come bringing their capital: they also seem very rich. This prefecture's soil is basically very barren, and the people go out to seek humble employment; but the shack people on the contrary come here from native places that are far away. Those who come to the mountains are comparatively strong and vigorous. The shacks that they build mostly are in secluded mountain areas. The people of one shack are not less than several tens of people. This is also a source of anxiety about the unexpected. We cannot but prepare for untoward eventualities.[51]

An essay by Mei Zengliang indicates a rather sophisticated understanding of the role of forest cover and leaf litter in protecting the ground from the force of raindrops, slowing the speed of runoff, replenishing the water table, and maintaining stream flow.

When I was writing a biographical sketch for Dong Wenke I looked at all his memorials. When he was governor of Anhui province (1807) he memorialized on the subject of permission for the shack people to reclaim the mountains. Forcefully he stated his main thought.

"Those who bring charges and countercharges against the shack people all are given over to the theories of geomancy. At the extreme, a mountain of several hundred *mu* is the land that protects a single grave. . . . The wasting of natural resources cannot be allowed. The shack people are able to work painstakingly, suffering a dreary existence in the crowded mountain ranges and inaccessible places, reclaiming the land and planting dryland grains. They thereby supplement rice and millet. Then among the people there is no one who is idle, and there is no land that is unprofitable. The plan [to allow reclamation] is most appropriate: it must not be prohibited and thereby start disturbances."

I examined his view and approved it.

When I came to Xuancheng [in Ningguo prefecture] and asked the various local people, they all said that before the mountains were reclaimed, the soil was firm and the rocks were solid. The grass and trees grew closely, rotten leaves accumulated, and in several years it could reach a depth of two or three inches. Whenever it rained, it fell from the trees to the fallen leaves, from the leaves to the earth and rocks, it passed through the cracks in the rocks and trickled and formed a spring. The flow of the water was slow: it flowed down, but the earth did not wash down with it. Its downflow always was slow. Therefore the fields below received it, but it was not a disaster, and if for half a month there was no rain, the high fields still were watered by the water

---

[51] Fang Chun, *Chusong shanfang zaju.*

[retained in this way]. Now they lay bare the mountains with axes and clear the earth with hoes and plows. Even before each shower is finished, the sand and rocks wash down and quickly flow into the mountain streams, which are all filled in and silted up. They are unable to store water. The water flows straight down to the bottom fields, and only then it stops. The bottom fields are ruined, and there is no way to water the mountain fields. This amounts to harming fields that produce grain in order to open up sterile soil, impoverishing tax-paying households in order to benefit laborers who pay no taxes!

I heard this viewpoint and approved it. Alas! It is not possible for either benefit or harm to be unmixed.[52]

Other texts note that reclaimed land often could not be kept productive, nor could it always revert to earlier uses: "The soil is exhausted so that not even an inch of grass will grow."[53] "Roving people reclaimed the mountains and planted maize. Several years later the soil was loosened, causing flooding, and submerging fields and irrigation ditches. The mountains fell into disuse."[54]

Contemporaries had a clear understanding of the impact of highland reclamation on the ecology of the region. When deforestation in the hills reduced the ability of the soil to absorb water, it increased the speed and volume of runoff. The water table fell, springs dried up, and rivers and streams fluctuated violently between periods of spate and reduction to a trickle. Erosion not only stripped the thin topsoil from the mountain fields, it silted up the waterways in the hills and valleys. Irrigation and transportation suffered as waterways were choked with sand and gravel washed down from the barren mountains; fields were covered by debris transported by flood waters. "Rich land became stones and bones, there were mudslides and erosion, and fields that produced rice were covered with sand and gravel. Innumerable ones have been eaten up and are gone."[55]

---

[52] Mei Zengliang, "Ji pengmin shi" [Record of the shack people] (1823), in his *Bojian shanfang wenji* [Collected works of the Bojian studio] (1855), *j.* 10, pp. 5a–6a.

[53] *Jixi xianzhi*, pp. 58–59.

[54] *Xi'an xianzhi, j.* 21, pp. 2b–3a.

[55] *Changhua xianzhi* [History of Changhua County] Wang Zhaoxing, ed. (1823), "Shuili," p. 6a. For other problems in Zhexi alone, see *Yuqian xianzhi* [History of Yuqian county], Jiang Guangbi et al., eds. (1812), *j.* 10, pp. 14a–5b; Wang Fengsheng, *Zhexi shuili beikao*, "Yuhangxian shuidao tushuo," pp. 28b–29b; *Wukang xianzhi* [History of Wukang county], Shu Lang et al., eds. (1829) *j.* 4, p. 24b; *Wucheng xianzhi, j.* 29, p. 4b; *j.* 35, p. 28b; *Fenshui xianzhi, j.* 3, p. 41a. Even when production continued, long-term – perhaps permanent – damage could result from this flooding. For example, an agricultural manual from the lowlands noted that after the great flood of 1823, rice yields around Songjiang rarely attained the levels that previously had been expected in a good year. Jiang Gao, *Pu Mao nongzi* [Report on agriculture in the (Huang) Pu river and Mao (hu) Lake area] (1834), pp. 11a–b, cited in Huang, *Peasant Family and Rural Development*, pp. 68–69.

In the highlands, deforestation threatened production based on mountain resources. We have seen that when the raw materials they depended on were exhausted, local industries sometimes disappeared as well. This not only raised the cost of living and limited opportunities for by-employments and petty trade, it may have hindered larger-scale commercial activity as well. For example, the deterioration of the environment in the highlands may have contributed to the decline of the Huizhou merchants. Increasing exactions from the government and the decline of the tea trade certainly were significant. But one advantage that had allowed Huizhou to gain prominence was access to highland resources. Some merchants began their careers using local timber and sometimes uncompensated labor by the tenant-servants, the *dianpu* 佃僕, to acquire capital, and then went on to invest in other enterprises such as the tea trade or the salt monopoly.[56] Perhaps the degradation of the environment around Huizhou, combined with gradual loss of control over the *dianpu*, removed the advantages of their position in the natural and social ecology, and helps to explain their decline. It is also intriguing that the decline of Jingdezhen in the eighteenth century coincides with the deforestation of the surrounding territory and a serious shortage of charcoal and fuelwood, as well as deterioration of river transport because of siltation and disruption of streamflow. Perhaps environmental degradation played a role in destroying the economic viability of that great porcelain-manufacturing city.[57]

Shifting cultivation preserved productivity on marginal highland soils, but spread the damage of deforestation and erosion in an ever-widening zone. It circumvented the problem of the thinness and fragility of mountain soils, but at the cost of exacerbating environmental problems, and social control problems as well. With a shifting population, it was impossible to guarantee that no "bandits" found shelter among the honest workers, and if incidents occurred, it was difficult to investigate and capture those implicated.

One partial solution to social control problems was to minimize the conditions likely to lead to open conflict: local production of cheap, flood- and drought-resistant staple foods helped to protect the locality from the

---

[56] Harriet Zurndorfer, "Merchant and Clansman in a Local Setting in Medieval China: A Case Study of the Fan Clan of Hsiu-ning Hsien, Hui-chou, 800–1600," Ph.D. thesis, University of California, Berkeley (1977), pp. 19–21; Ye Xian'en, *Ming-Qing Huizhou nongcun shehui yu dianpu zhi* [Rural society and the tenant-servant system in Ming-Qing Huizhou] (Anhui, 1983), pp. 106–10.

[57] Liang Miaotai indicates that fuel was a major cost of production, but does not show secular trends of prices. "Qingdai Jingdezhen yichu lucun yaohao de shouzhi yingli" [The income and expenses and profit of a porcelain kiln at Jingdezhen in the Qing dynasty], *Zhongguo shehui jingjishi yanjiu* 4 (1984), p. 16.

price spikes and panics that arose when flood, drought, or bad harvests in the lowlands interrupted the importation of food from the valleys. The New World crops were produced for just these reasons, but while addressing one problem related to social control, their widespread adoption exacerbated environmental degradation.

Another problem was the use that was already made of the mountains and water margins by those seeking to survive in difficult times. Government policy eventually rejected the legitimacy of entrepreneurial reclamation as a greedy search for personal profit at the public expense, but the poor and weak were apparently considered to have a claim on these resources. Even after new enclosures on the water margins was forbidden, for example, propertyless people were allowed to have small-scale reclamations; after prohibitions on outside reclamation in the mountains, it was still accepted that in bad years refugees would rely on crops planted in the mountains to eke out a living, and should be allowed to stay until conditions improved.[58] This traditional use of the lake shores and the highlands preserved a margin within the dense landscape of the lower Yangzi region in which people could survive temporary dislocations and fluctuations in the natural and social worlds. But this depended on these lands not being incorporated into routine use. When they were reclaimed, their productivity would rise, at least temporarily, but the "safety net" function would be lost. This threat to the survival of the indigent endangered social stability. "If the powerful families [around Lake Tai] stick in the tip of an awl, then the livelihood of the poor people will become more desperate every day. If the livelihood of the people is more desperate every day, how can this be beneficial to the nation?"[59]

Here was yet another trade-off: intensification could lead to a rise in average productivity, but at the price of reducing the resilience of the ecological and social system as a whole.

It thus seems that in the lower Yangzi region, expansion in one area often led to constriction in another, rather than producing net growth. As contemporaries put it, "The gains do not offset the losses." The constraints were a combination of ecological and social factors. As the state was well aware, one essential foundation of social order was the provision of a livelihood for unemployed men, yet the expanding mountain economy of

---

[58] *Huangchao jingshi wenbian* [Collected essays on statecraft], He Changling, ed. (1826. Reprinted, Taipei, 1963), *j.* 38, pp. 9a–b (pp. 1375–76). Tao Zhu, *Tao wenyi gong quanji* [Complete works of Tao Zhu] (1840), *j.* 36, p. 9a (p. 2099). For similar findings in the middle Yangzi, see Peter Perdue, *Exhausting the Earth: State and Peasant in Hunan, 1500–1850* (Cambridge, Mass., 1987), p. 224.

[59] *Huangchao jingshi wenbian, j.* 38, pp. 9a–b.

the early nineteenth century put these men outside the control networks of local society, and furthermore threatened the ecological as well as social stability of the region. Social control could hardly be more seriously threatened than by a subsistence crisis brought on by ecological destruction.

COPING STRATEGIES

Not all intensification of land use need lead to environmental degradation. Up to a point, the enclosure of rice paddies, the building of terraces, and the production of cash crops could significantly increase production without destabilizing the ecology of the region. But that point appears to have been reached by the end of the eighteenth century.

Other kinds of development sometimes explicitly tried to combine economic growth with environmental preservation or even improvement. In the Yongzheng reign (1723–35), for instance, entrepreneurs proposed raising a grass-eating fish in West Lake in Hangzhou. The fish would help to keep the lake clear, while the entrepreneurs would harvest the fish commercially. A rather unusual element in this case is that the entrepreneurs applied to use official capital to start up their business.[60] In a similar vein, after serious flooding in 1823, it was proposed that kiln households be recruited to set up brick and tile works in the vicinity of silted-up South Lake in Hangzhou. Excavating clay for the kilns would open up water storage capacity without the expense of dredging. An improved local supply would lower the price of bricks and tiles, and facilitate their use in construction, which would reduce fire danger in Hangzhou. The ambitious strategy tried to achieve three objectives with a single proposal: economic growth, improved water control, and reduced fire danger.[61]

There was widespread awareness of the value of trees, bamboo, and perennial crops in holding the soil while providing income from sloping lands too vulnerable to erosion for annual cropping to be sustained. Ruan Yuan,[62] Wang Fengsheng, Tao Zhu, and others urged that the creation of economic plantations of such crops would provide employment, make immediate expulsion of migrant workers unnecessary, and protect the waterways. In one case, a local degree holder also advocated planting indigo and hemp among the saplings: for the first few years, these would

---

[60] *Huangchao jingshi wenbian*, j. 116, p. 23a–b (pp. 4107–08).

[61] Wang Fengsheng, *Zhexi shuili beikao*, c. 1, *Yuhang xian zhi nanhu shuo*, 25a.

[62] "Jin pengmin shi" [Proclamation of prohibition of the shack people] (1802), in *Deqing xian xuzhi* [Continuation of the history of Deqing county], Xu Yangyuan et al., eds. (1808), j. 4, pp. 2a–b.

provide an income. When the trees had grown up enough to shade the ground, cash-crop production would be abandoned. If the saplings were economic trees like tung or lacquer rather than timber trees, they might already be on the verge of production by the time cash cropping ceased.[63] In other cases, where deforestation had already led to erosion and the destruction of the adjacent lowland fields, if the drainage patterns did not affect a wider area, some advocated allowing even maize cultivation to proceed: the damage it could do was already done, so no purpose would be served by depriving the people of its contribution to local subsistence.[64]

Other strategies tried to address the institutional weakness caused by the prevalence of lineage landholding in the hills of southern Anhui and Zhejiang. The government tried to protect these lands from short-sighted exploitation by individuals by establishing severe penalties for illicit private appropriation. Dissatisfied with this, local elites who feared environmental and social disruption sometimes took such land out of group ownership. For example, in Yuqian on the periphery of Hangzhou, in order to quiet litigation over boundaries and land rights, they advocated division of common holdings under the leadership of a respected elder.[65] In Yixian, in the hills of Huizhou, a group of landlords, including lineage members and individual owners, despaired of maintaining control over their high-land holdings against the greed of unfilial sons and grandsons. They contributed the whole coal-bearing upland to a local academy, to be rented out exclusively for charcoal production so that the hillsides could recover.[66]

When encroachment on waterways and silting led to drought or flooding, one response was to use public works for improving water control in place of outright relief. For example, when a drought in 1814 led to soaring grain prices the following spring, a censor from Renhe in Hangzhou advocated setting the needy to work dredging West Lake, to improve water-storage capacity while providing public employment that would enable them to survive until the next harvest.[67]

As this sampling indicates, there were a number of ways in which late traditional Chinese society sought to accommodate pressures for intensification while balancing them against the rival claims for preservation.

[63] Chen Jingchao, "Kaizhong baolu."

[64] Wu and Wang, *Chun'an huangzheng beilan*, p. 37a–b.

[65] *Yuqian xianzhi*, j. 10, pp. 14a–15a.

[66] *Yixian san zhi* [Three histories of Yi county], Xie Yongtai et al., eds. (1872), j. 11, pp. 17b–18a.

[67] *Da-Qing shichao shengxun* [Sacred edicts of ten reigns of the Great Qing dynasty], Wenhai CBS, ed. (1880. Reprinted, Taipei, 1965), vol. 4b, j. 46, p. 3b (4b, p. 858).

Their ingenuity was impressive, but these ad hoc measures could not resolve the broader dilemma. For that a more comprehensive approach was required.

GOVERNMENT REGULATION
AND ELITE MANAGEMENT

By the mid-eighteenth century, some observers feared that further reclamation in the lowlands would threaten the ecological stability of the region, endangering both economic productivity and social order. Soon highland reclamation became controversial as well: although continued reclamation undermined ecological and social stability, it was feared that blocking it would also disrupt the economy and trigger unrest. Environmentally sound policies were devised to address these dilemmas, but their economic and political realism is questionable. No realistic way was found to channel the pressures for economic intensification generated by population growth and commercialization. For implementation of its policies, the state relied on partnership with local elites, yet the short-term interests of these elites often lay with intensification. These failures allowed environmental degradation to proceed unchecked.

In the lowlands, at first in piecemeal fashion, then in a regional context, proposals were made to control, halt, or even reverse reclamation where pressure on the waterways was especially intense. In 1745 the finance commissioner of Zhejiang province requested a prohibition on encroachment on official lakes.[68] In 1758, an edict forbade further encroachment around West Lake in Hangzhou.[69] In 1763, Governor Zhuang Yougong requested a prohibition on further enclosures in the whole of Jiangsu province, and the destruction by the state of dikes that obstructed water flows.[70] In 1770, further reclamation around South Lake in Hangzhou was forbidden.[71] In 1824 Wang Fengsheng offered comprehensive proposals for improving water control in Zhexi, including prohibition of further enclosures, abandonment of some recently reclaimed land, and regulation of agricultural and silvicultural practices in the upland watershed.[72] In 1828, Zhejiang authorities ordered confiscation of all new alluvial deposits so the state could dredge them if they blocked waterways. Four years later, noting that

---

[68] *Huangchao jingshi wenbian*, j. 38, pp. 9b–10a (pp. 1376–77).
[69] *Da-Qing shichao*, vol. 3c, j. 137, p. 3a (vol. 3c, pp. 1739–40).
[70] Huang, *Peasant Family and Rural Development*, p. 39.
[71] *Da-Qing shichao*, vol. 3c, j. 147, p. 4a (vol. 3c, p. 1741).
[72] Wang Fengsheng, *Zhexi shuili beikao, passim.*

over time, "negligence is born, and crafty villains acting illicitly encircle the land with dikes," an edict ordered local officials to undertake annual personal inspections of these deposits and threatened impeachment if encroachments occurred. Regulations were elaborated on when and whether dikes were to be destroyed. If dikes and enclosures blocked important water flows, and threatened serious destabilization of water control, they were to be destroyed. Less damaging dikes could be left in place, but repairs might be forbidden; dikes that did no harm could be retained and repaired, but not extended.[73] By the middle of the nineteenth century, Wei Yuan advocated sweeping measures to protect the whole course of the Yangzi River from Dongting Lake in the middle Yangzi downstream to the sea.[74]

In the highlands, saturation was reached somewhat later, but a regional perspective was quickly adopted to address the problems. Although there were earlier efforts to tighten control over migrant workers, and local expulsions of inmigrants because of environmental damage, it was not until the first decade of the nineteenth century that further reclamation was generally perceived to be too dangerous to be permitted. Environmental destruction and social control were both subjects of concern. Governor Ruan Yuan in 1802 prohibited further highland reclamation by outsiders throughout Zhejiang, where disastrous flooding had followed deforestation.[75] A few years later, an imperial edict forbade such reclamations in Anhui, and a general policy was enacted for the whole lower Yangzi region. In 1815, Censor Fu Tang warned,

> In Zhejiang in each prefecture with deep and dangerous mountains, most places have roving people from outside, who rent fields, chop the brushwood, turn over and dig out the roots, and bank up [the soil] and plant maize. This causes the earth and stones to be loose and light. Whenever the mountain waters suddenly burst forth, they enter the rivers and waterways, and silt and block them up. The riverbanks and dikes burst open, and they overflow and flood the fields and crops. It is greatly harmful to the farmers. These roving people mostly have come from Fujian, Jiangxi, and Anhui provinces. They form groups and join with companions, from several tens up to over a hundred. In scattered places amidst the mountains, there is no one to investigate them. It is not possible not to strictly forbid this.[76]

The court ordered an investigation, adapting to local conditions the regulations developed a few years earlier for Anhui. In 1850 Wang

[73] *Da-Qing shichao*, vol. 5d, j. 118, p. 5b (vol. 5d, p. 2092).
[74] Perdue, *Exhausting the Earth*, pp. 219–33; Wei Yuan, *Guweitang neiwaiji* [Collected writings of Wei Yuan] (1878), *waiji*, j. 6.5a–7b.
[75] Ruan Yuan, "Jin pengmin shi."
[76] *Da-Qing shichao*, vol. 4b, j. 46, p. 3b (vol. 4b, p. 858).

Yuanfang, a censor from Yuhang county in Hangzhou, offered proposals to tighten up regulations on land transfers and tax collection, so that their own self-interest would force local landlords to refuse to rent their land for uses that would destroy its productive capacity. It was hoped that this would prevent destructive highland reclamation and thereby safeguard the waterways of Zhejiang and Jiangsu.[77]

The goals for policy enacted in the early nineteenth century, and reiterated in succeeding decades, may be summarized as follows: prohibition of further reclamation around water margins in most of the lower Yangzi region; prohibition of any new highland reclamation by outsiders or renewal of outsiders' existing contracts; prohibition of maize production by locals or inmigrants and its replacement by crops that would hold the soil; blanket expulsion of short-term migrant labor. The increased production on newly reclaimed land, whether lowland paddies and reedbeds, or hillside converted to cash-crop or maize production, did not compensate for the ecological destruction it caused. In the case of lowland reclamations, it was argued that the additional tax revenue they generated was only a fraction of the potential cost of tax remissions and relief over the much wider area they endangered.[78] In the hills the costs outweighed the benefits even more heavily. The migration of labor was also seen as a threat to social stability.

These goals were environmentally reasonable but economically naive. No staple food was promoted to replace maize, no incentives were offered to encourage investment in tree crops and perennials, no provision was made for the livelihood of repatriated workers and tenants. Politically these goals were undermined by the basic contradiction of the state's reliance on elite management to implement its policies. The policy goals accommodated the interests of some elites but contradicted those of others. For some landowners, high rents for seemingly worthless land were an unlooked-for bonanza; for others, the reclamations threatened the destruction of existing fields.[79] Those who hired the migrants profited from labor and expertise that the local population could not supply. Yet bands of men whose "comings and goings were not fixed" were an anomaly not easily dealt with by the standard social control system based on the *baojia* 保甲 system. An awareness of the inevitable influx of outsiders, as well as environmental destruction, underlay opposition in many highland localities to tea production, tobacco growing, lime burning, and coal mining. Yet for those

[77] Wang Yuanfang, "Qing jin pengmin kaishan."
[78] *Da-Qing shichao*, vol. 3c, j. 147, p. 4a (vol. 3c, p. 1741).
[79] Mei Zengliang, "Ji pengmin shi," eloquently expresses the dilemma.

who received rents sometimes double the purchase price for land once considered worthless,[80] the temptation to violate the regulations was irresistible.

In the lowlands, the attempts to restrict or reverse reclamation clashed directly with the interests of powerful local families. Around Lake Tai,

> They do not stop at encroachment on fields; they go further and encroach on the water. What is more oppressive than this one device of the strongmen? Our prefecture is number one in the benefit of edible aquatic grasses, water lilies, reeds, fish, and turtles. . . . Now the great majority goes to the powerful families. When people catch fish, first the benefit goes to the powerful, then [the people] eat what is left over. It begins with strongmen who bribe evil clerks and runners to pay taxes on the water surface. This is called "to request a tenancy." Afterward they recklessly annex it, and those who govern this locality do not know.[81]

Even the actions of an effective governor did not long outlast his tenure in office. Zhuang Yougong ordered the restoration of Lake Tai in 1764, and the accumulated sediment was cleared out, the grasses and rushes along the banks uprooted. "How much this cost the national treasury and the labor of the people!" Several years later, when Zhuang had been transferred,

> The powerful, by bribing corrupt yamen underlings, first encroached on fields along the lake shore and again paid taxes on the lake surface and allowed others to plant aquatic grasses in it. These spread out and filled the lake. It was silted up twice as much as before, and those who governed the locality again did not know it.[82]

The resources of the lake should have served to support the poor and propertyless, yet they were monopolized by the powerful, who were seen as predators:

> The wild beasts born on a mountain are supported by the mountain, and fish born in [a stretch of] water are supported by the water. The hearts of the living things of heaven and earth must be like this. But if everything is taken by the strongmen, it is as if the mountain has a fierce tiger, and so is empty, or the water has a crocodile, and so is exhausted.[83]

Proposals for comprehensive dredging that would have destroyed diked fields carved out of South Lake near Hangzhou aroused such opposition

---

[80] *Wucheng xianzhi, j.* 35, p. 28b.
[81] *Huangchao jinshi wenbian, j.* 38, p. 9a–b (pp. 1375–76).   [82] Ibid.
[83] Ibid. See also the centuries-long battle over Xiang Lake chronicled by R. Keith Schoppa, *Xiang Lake: Nine Centuries of Chinese Life* (New Haven, 1989).

from powerful local families that the official who offered them was slandered and driven from office and the proposals were dropped. Some years later a much more modest proposal was put forward for limited dredging and repair of sluicegates, together with redoubled efforts to control reclamation in the hills of South Lake's watershed. If that were to be achieved (the proposal continued), it would ease pressure downstream and create a resolution in accord with public sentiment.[84]

We thus see that those with political clout tried to protect their own short-term economic interests, while attempting to displace the burden of sacrifices required to maintain ecological stability onto others. Despite the fact that local elites sometimes gave lip service to the prohibitions on reclamation, and even sometimes instigated investigations to prevent or roll back reclamation, officials in 1807 and 1837 in Anhui, in 1802 and 1824 in Zhejiang, and 1850 for Zhejiang and Jiangsu, all emphasized the short-sighted greed of local landlords, which caused them to ignore their own longterm interest as well as the interest of society as a whole.[85]

There was clearly adequate knowledge of the environmental factors involved, and the ability to trace environmental impacts across ecological zones and regional boundaries. The prime weakness seems to have been a lack of comprehension of or adaptation to economic and demographic changes which generated pressures too strong simply to block, but which conceivably could have been diverted into environmentally and socially more benign if not cost-free channels. Although officials did at times attempt such diversion, for example in encouraging slopeland production of perennials and other crops which would hold the soil, this was undercut by less appropriate attempts at simple blockage. For example, the order for across-the-board expulsion of short-term migrant workers took no account of their importance to the highland economy, nor of the difficulty of settling them peacefully in the home districts they had presumably left for lack of work. The order was practically unenforceable, and making their presence in the highlands illegal only made it more difficult to maintain social control. Similarly, the absolute prohibition on renewal of outsiders' rent contracts, a cornerstone of government policy in the nineteenth century, can only rarely have been enforced. Yet it must have increased the

---

[84] *Huangchao jingshi wen xubian* [Continuation of the collected essays on statecraft under the present dynasty], Ge Shijun, ed. (1898. Facsimile reprint, Taipei, 1964), *j.* 98, pp. 8a–b (pp. 2533–34); *Da-Qing shichao*, vol. 6b, *j.* 99, p. 4a (vol. 6b, p. 1207).

[85] Ruan Yuan, "Jin pengmin shi," p. 2a; Yang Maotian, "Chajin pengmin angao," p. 42b; Tao Zhu, *Tao wenyi gong quanji* [Complete works of Tao Zhu] *j.* 26, p. 10b (p. 2102); Wang Fengsheng, *Zhexi shuili beikao* [Report on water control in western Zhejiang], "Yuhangxian shuidao tushuo," p. 28b; Wang Yuanfang, "Qing jin pengmin kaishan," p. 1487.

insecurity of tenure, and therefore encouraged ruthless mining of the soil and destruction of natural resources, rather than husbanding them for sustained yields over the long term. Just such cynical calculation is described in an account of the rent strategy adopted by inmigrants in the hills of Zhexi around 1850: "[They consider that] the most hateful thing is that with the contract not yet expired, the land is already exhausted, and they have to move on; or alternatively, that with the time limit already completed, the land is not yet exhausted."[86]

Since any incentive for stewardship of the land had been removed, leaving the tenants in place until their contracts expired was the option most likely to lead to natural disaster, however necessary to prevent social unrest.

CONCLUSION

Much of the Chinese scholarship on the agents of economic change in the late-imperial period has interpreted objections to intensification as the obstruction by "feudal" or "backward" elements of progressive forces that threatened their dominance.[87] No doubt a good deal of the hostility was based on just such conservative attitudes. But the ecological processes described by local people and officials are real, and the disasters of the nineteenth century force us to take their objections seriously. Some scholarship has also seen the use of rented land and hired labor by entrepreneurs in the highlands as signs of protocapitalism.[88] Yet in many cases this entrepreneurship does not seem to have been the beginning of open-ended growth, but extraction that rapidly consumed its own resource base.

We might tentatively conclude that the expansion of the highland economy was probably not a zero-sum game in most instances: usually the gains probably offset the losses at least in the short term. Yet from a long-term perspective, economic growth based on highland reclamation was clearly unsustainable, depending on the consumption of forests, topsoil,

---

[86] Wang Yuanfang, "Qing jin pengmin kaishan," p. 1487.

[87] E.g., Feng Erkang, "Shilun Qingzhongye Wannan fuyou pengmin di jingying fangshi" [A preliminary exploration of the mode of production of the rich shack people of southern Anhui in the mid-Qing] *Nankai daxue xuebao* 2 (1978), pp. 92–96; Dai Yifeng, "Lun jindai Minjiang shang yu shanqu shangpin jingji fazhan de zhiyue yinsu" [On the restrictive factors in the development of a commodity economy in the mountain area of the upper Min River in modern times], *Zhongguo shehui jingjishi yanjiu* 3 (1987), pp. 89–98. On the other side, we might note Chen Qiaoyi's work.

[88] E.g., Li Min, "Xingke tiben zhong youguan zibenzhuyi mengya de cailiao."

water, and other resources faster than they could be replaced, and at an ever-accelerating rate. Environmental degradation limited the transformative potential of the mountain- and forest-led growth of the eighteenth and nineteenth centuries.

Attempts at greater intensification did not utilize empty niches external to the resilience of the existing system, but rather encroached on reservoirs of resources, cushions of ecological and social stability, that played an essential part in buffering the entire system from the fluctuations of the natural world. In lowlands and highlands alike, as these buffers disappeared, the long-term effect appears in some instances to have been a continual scramble for further intensification in a deteriorating environment, so that people had to run harder just to stay in place. Heroic effort could hold off declining yields for a long time, only to have them suddenly crumble from a major shock, such as the flooding of 1823 or 1850, leaving a permanently impoverished environment, a legacy of restricted opportunities for the future. It seems to me likely, although not at this point provable, that the lower population in this region in 1953, compared to 1850,[89] may be an indication of the crossing of such an environmental threshold.

REFERENCES

Changhua xianzhi 昌化縣志 [History of Changhua county]. 1823. Wang Zhaoxing 王兆杏, ed.

Chao, Kang. 1986. *Man and Land in Chinese History: An Economic Analysis* (Stanford, Calif.).

Chen Jingchao 陳景潮. n.d. "Kaizhong baolu lihai lun" 開種苞蘆利害論 [On the advantages and disadvantages of reclamation and planting maize], in *Fenshui xianzhi* [History of Fenshui county], ed. Zang Chengxuan et al. (1906), *j.* 1, pp. 41b–42a.

Chen Qiaoyi 陈桥驿. 1984. "Lishishang Zhejiangsheng shandi kenji you shanlin pohuai" 历史上浙江省的山地垦殖与山林破坏 [The opening of mountain land and destruction of forests in the history of Zhejiang Province], *Zhongguo shehui keshui* 4, pp. 207–17.

Chen Qiaoyi et al. 1984. "Lun lishi shiqi Ning-Shao pingyuan de hupo yanbian" 论历史时期宁绍平原的湖泊演变 [The historical evolution of the lakes of the Ning-Shao plain]. *Dili yanjiu* 3.3, pp. 29–43.

Chen Shuping 陈树平. 1980. "Yumi he fanshu zai Zhongguo chuanbo qingkuang yanjiu" 玉米和番薯在中国传播情况研究 [A study of the circumstances of the diffusion of maize and sweet potatoes in China], *Zhongguo shehui kexue* 3, pp. 187–204.

[89] P. T. Ho, *Studies on the Population of China, 1368–1953* (Cambridge, Mass., 1959), p. 246.

Dai Yifeng 戴一峰. 1987. "Lun jindai Minjiang shang yu shanqu shangpin jingji fazhan de zhiyue yinsu" 近代闽江上游山区商品经济发展的制约因素 [On the restrictive factors in the development of a commodity economy in the mountain area of the upper Min River in modern times], *Zhongguo shehui jingjishi yanjiu* 3, pp. 89–98.

Da-Qing huidian shili 大清會典事例 [Collected statutes and substatutes of the Great Qing Dynasty]. 1899. Li Hongzhang 李鴻章 et al., eds.

Da-Qing shichao shengxun 大清十朝聖訓 [Sacred edicts of ten reigns of the Great Qing dynasty]. 1880. Wenhai CBS, ed. (Reprinted, Taipei, 1965).

Deqing xian xuzhi 德清縣續志 [Continuation of the history of Deqing County]. 1808. Xu Yangyuan 徐養原 et al., eds.

Fang Chun 方椿. n.d. *Chusong shanfang zaju* 楚頌山房雜著 [Miscellaneous writings from the Chusong studio], in *Huizhou fuzhi* (1827), j. 4B, pp. 45b–46a.

Feng Erkang 冯尔康. 1978. "Shilun Qingzhongye Wannan fuyou pengmin di jingying fangsi" 试论清中皖南富裕棚民的经营方式 [A preliminary exploration of the mode of production of the rich shack people of southern Anhui in the mid-Qing], *Nankai daxue xuebao* 2, pp. 92–96.

Fenshui xianzhi 分水 [History of Fenshui county]. 1906. Zang Chengxuan 臧承宣 et al., eds.

Gao Tingyao 高廷瑤 *Huanyou jilüe* 宦遊紀略. 1908. [Records of a roaming official].

Gardella, Robert P. 1994. *Harvesting Mountains: Fujian and the China Tea Trade, 1757–1937* (Berkeley, Calif.).

Geertz, Clifford. 1963. *Agricultural Involution: The Process of Ecological Change in Indonesia* (Berkeley, Calif.).

Guangde zhouzhi 廣德州志 [History of Guangde department]. 1881. Hu Youcheng 胡有誠 et al., eds.

Guangxin fuzhi 廣信府志 [History of Guangxin prefecture]. 1872. Li Shufan 李樹藩 et al., eds.

Hatano Yoshihiro 波多野善大. 1961. *Chūgoku kindai kōgyō-shi no kenkyū* 中國近代工業史の研究 [Studies on the modern industrialization of China] (Kyoto).

He Baochuan. 1991. *China on the Edge: The Crisis of Ecology and Development* (San Francisco).

Ho, P. T. 1959. *Studies on the Population of China, 1368–1953* (Cambridge, Mass.).

Hu Yuanxi 胡元熙. 1845. "Yishan jin wamei shaohui shuo" 黟山禁挖煤燒灰説 [On prohibiting digging coal and burning lime in the mountains of Yixian], in *Yixian sanzhi* [Three Histories of Yi county] (1872), j. 15.3, pp. 70b–72b.

1845. "Biyang Shuyuan shoushu chanmei geshanye gongyiji" 碧陽書院收輸產煤各山公議記 [Record of the public discussion on the contribution of coal-producing mountains to the Biyang Academy], in *Yixian sanzhi* j. 15.3, pp. 35b–36b.

Huaining xianzhi 懷寧縣志 [History of Huaining county]. 1827. Wang Yufang 王毓芳 et al., eds.

Huang, Philip C. C. 1990. *The Peasant Family and Rural Development in the Yangzi Delta, 1350–1988* (Stanford, Calif.).

Huangchao Dao-Xian-Tong-Guang Zouyi 皇朝道咸同光奏議. [Memorials of the Daoguang, Xianfeng and Tongzhi Reign-periods of the present dynasty]. 1969. Wang Yanxi 王延熙, ed., in *Jindai Zhongguo shiliao congkan* 近代中國史料叢刊 (Taipei), vol. 331a–d.

Huangchao jingshi wenbian 皇朝經世文編 [Collected essays on statecraft]. 1826. He Changling 賀長齡, ed. (reprinted, Taipei, 1963).

Huangchao jingshi wen xubian 皇朝經世文續編 [Continuation of collected essays on statecraft]. 1898. Ge Shijun 葛士濬, ed. (reprinted, Taipei, 1963).

Huizhou fuzhi 徽州府志 [History of Huizhou prefecture]. 1827. Ma Buchan 馬步蟾 et al., eds.

Jiang Gao 姜皋. 1834. *Pu Mao nongzi* 浦泖農咨 [Report on agriculture in the (Huang) Pu River and Mao (hu) Lake area].

Jixi xianzhi 績溪縣志 [History of Jixi County]. 1810. Qing Kai 清愷 et al., eds.

Krebs, C. J. 1985. *Ecology*, 4th ed. (New York).

Li Bozhong 李伯重. 1984. "Ming Qing Jiangnan gong nongye shengchan zhong di ranliao wenti" 明清江南工农业生产中的燃料问题 [On the problem of fuels in industrial and agricultural production in Jiangnan in the Ming and Qing], *Zhongguo shehui jingjishi yanjiu* 4, pp. 34–49.

———. 1984. "Ming Qing shiqi Jiangnan shuidao shengchan jiyue chengdu de tigao" 明清时期江南水稻生产集约程度的提高 [Intensificantion of wet-rice production in Jiangnan during the Ming and Qing period], *Zhongguo nongshi* 1, pp. 24–37.

Li Min 黎民. 1975. "Qianlong xingke tiben zhong youguan nongye zibenzhuyi mengya de cailiao" 乾隆刑科題本中有关农业资本主义萌芽的材料 [Materials on the sprouts of capitalism in agriculture in routine judicial memorials of the Qianlong period]. *Wenwu* 9, pp. 69–75.

Liang Miaotai 梁淼泰. 1984. "Qingdai Jingdezhen yichu lucun yaohao de shouzhi yingli" 清代景德镇一处炉寸窑号的收支盈利 [The income and expenses and profit of a porcelain kiln at Jingdezhen in the Qing dynasty]. *Zhongguo shehuijingjishi yanjiu* 4, pp. 1–16.

Mei Zengliang 梅曾亮. 1823. "Ji pengmin shi" 記棚民事 [Record of the shack people], in his *Bojian shanfang wenji* 柏梘山房文集 [Collected works of the Bojian studio] (1855), *j.* 10, pp. 5a–6a.

Ningguo fuzhi 寧國府志. 1815. [History of Ningguo Prefecture]. Lu Quan 魯銓, ed.

Ningguo xianzhi 寧國縣志 [History of Ningguo County]. 1825. Liang Zhongfu 梁中孚, ed.

Osborne, Anne. 1989. "Barren Mountains, Raging Rivers: The Ecological and Social Effects of Changing Landuse on the Lower Yangzi Periphery in Lake Imperial China," Ph.D. thesis, Columbia University.

———. 1994. "The Local Politics of Land Reclamation in the Lower Yangzi Highlands," *Late Imperial China* 15.1 (June), pp. 1–46.

Peng Yuxin 彭雨新. 1990. *Qingdai tudi kaiken shi* 清代土地开垦史 [A history of land development in the Qing period] (Beijing).

Perdue, Peter. 1987. *Exhausting the Earth: State and Peasant in Hunan, 1500–1850* (Cambridge, Mass.).

Polachek, James. 1980. "Economic Diversification, Seasonal Migration, and Social Conflict in the Kiangsi-Fukien Border Area in the Mid-Ch'ing," paper presented at the Annual Meeting of the Association for Asian Studies, Washington, D.C., March 21–23.

Qimen xianzhi 祁門縣志 [History of Qimen county]. 1827. Wang Rang 王讓 et al., eds.

Qingtian xian xuzhi 青田縣續志 [Continuation of the history of Qingtian county]. 1777. Wu Chuchun 吳楚椿 et al., eds.

Ruan Yuan 阮元. 1802. "Jin pengmin shi" 禁棚民示 [Proclamation of prohibition of the shack people], in *Deqing xian xuzhi, j.* 4, pp. 2a–b.

Schoppa, R. Keith. 1989. *Xiang Lake: Nine Centuries of Chinese Life* (New Haven, Conn.).

Smil, Vaclav. 1984. *The Bad Earth* (Armonk, N.Y.).

——— 1993. *China's Environmental Crisis: An Inquiry into the Limits of National Development* (Armonk, N.Y.).

Tao Zhu 陶澍. 1840. *Tao wenyi gong quanji* 陶文毅公全集 [Complete works of Tao Zhu].

Wang Fengsheng 王鳳生. 1824. *Zhexi shuili beikao* 浙西水利備考 [Report on water control in western Zhejiang].

Wang Yuanfang 汪元方. 1850. "Qing jin pengmin kaishan zushui yi du fuhuan shu" 請禁棚民開山阻水以杜復患疏 [Memorial requesting a prohibition on the shack people reclaiming mountains and obstructing waterways in order to prevent future calamities], in *Huangchao Dao-Xian-Tong-Guang Zouyi*, ed. Wang Yanxi, pp. 1486–88. Reprinted in *Jindai Zhongguo shiliao congkan* (Taipei, 1969), vol. 331a–d.

Wei Yuan 魏源. 1878. *Guweitang Neiwaiji* 古微堂內外集 [Collected writings of Wei Yuan] (n. p.).

Wu Qian 吳嶔 and Wang Yuanji 王元基. 1824. *Chun'an huangzheng jilüe* 淳安荒政紀略 [Outline of famine relief in Chunan] (n.p.).

Wucheng xianzhi 烏程 [History of Wucheng county]. 1881. Zhou Xuejun 周學濬 et al., eds.

Wukang xianzhi 武康 [History of Wukang county]. 1829. Shu Lang 疏筤 et al., eds.

Xi'an xianzhi 西安 [History of Xi'an county]. 1810. Fan Chongkai 范崇楷 et al., eds.

Xiuning xianzhi 休寧 [History of Xiuning county]. 1815. Fang Chongding 方崇鼎 et al., eds.

Xuancheng xianzhi 宣城 [History of Xuancheng county]. 1888. Li Yingtai 李應泰 et al., eds.

Xuanping xianzhi 宣平 [History of Xuanping county]. 1878. Pi Xirui 皮錫 et al., eds.

Yang Maotian 楊懋恬. 1807. "Daoxian Yang Maotian chajin pengmin an'gao" 道憲 ... 查禁棚民案稿 [Draft report of His Excellency Intendant Yang Maotian on the shack people], in *Huizhou fuzhi*, ed. Ma Buchan et al. (1827), *j.* 4B, pp. 39b–45b.

Ye Xian'en 叶显恩. 1983. *Ming-Qing Huizhou nongcun shehui you dianpu zhi* 明清徽州农村社会佃仆制 [Rural society and the tenant-servant system in Ming-Qing Huizhou] (Anhui).

Yixian san zhi 黟縣三志 [Three histories of Yi county]. 1872. Xie Yongtai 謝永泰 et al., eds.

Yuhang xianzhi 餘杭縣志 [History of Yuhang county]. 1808. Zhang Ji'an 張吉安 et al., eds.

Yuqian xianzhi 於潛縣志 [History of Yuqian county]. 1812. Jiang Guangbi 蔣光弼 et al., eds.

Yushan xianzhi 玉山縣志 [History of Yushan county]. 1873. Wu Huachen 吳華辰 et al., eds.

Zhuang Yougong 莊有恭. "Zou wei qing ding daomai daomai sichan yitian zhi li" 奏為請定盜賣盜買祀產義田之例 [Memorial requesting fixed regulations on the illegal selling and buying of sacrificial property and charity fields], in Renhe Qinchuan (pseud.) ed., *Huang Qing zouyi* [Memorials of the Qing dynasty] (Taipei, 1967), pp. 4181–87.

Zurndorfer, Harriet 1977. "Merchant and Clansman in a Local Setting in Medieval China: A Case Study of the Fan Clan of Hsiu-ning Hsien, Hui-chou, 800–1600." Ph.D. thesis, University of California, Berkeley.

8

Population and Ecology along the Frontier in Qing China

EDUARD B. VERMEER

INTRODUCTION

In premodern societies, population numbers in both core and peripheral areas tended to fluctuate considerably, as a result of climatic changes, changes in trade and other economic ties, the quality of government and other forms of organization, and warfare and internal violence. During the Qing dynasty, China entered a new phase of definite and irreversible change. Its population numbers, starting from a considerably reduced base, almost tripled, leading to an increased demand for food, textiles, industrial crops, timber, and minerals. Commercialization, extension of transport, technological improvements, the introduction of new crops such as maize and tobacco, and the growing foreign demand for tea, silk, and other products all contributed to a rapid growth in demand for, and exploitation of, China's resources. Its territory almost doubled, to include many ecologically vulnerable mountain and steppe areas. Many forms of exploitation were unsustainable, and within two centuries the Chinese natural and economic environment had changed, for better or worse, beyond recognition. In the east and south, China had become treeless, with denuded hills and very productive paddies, while floods and droughts continuously threatened the dense human settlements and crops in the river valleys. The northwestern prairies had been significantly reduced by conversion to arable and by the quickening pace of desertification processes. It seemed as if humans had set out to reduce their original natural environment to only two types of land: carefully maintained, productive, private farmland, and ruthlessly exploited, unproductive, common wasteland.

Because of China's size and great variety of climate, altitude, soil, population, land use, level of development, crops, and so forth, it is impossible to provide more than a patchy impression of how population growth and the use of land and other natural resources changed the physical and economic environment during this period. So far, scholarly research into these questions has been rather limited, and has concentrated on some major, usually rather large, areas. The resurgence of interest in local history and an increasing sensitivity to environmental issues such as the conservation of resources have resulted in a still-modest but increasing number of articles in historical journals, and even some books. Most still rely heavily on traditional, and for the Qing, abundant, literary and local gazetteer sources of a rather general nature. Recently, some very thorough and detailed studies have been written on the Han Chinese organization of land reclamation and resource use at the village and household level in Taiwan in the eighteenth and nineteenth centuries.[1] Taiwan is exceptional in having conserved rather abundant source materials and in having historians who have gone deeply into the social and economic organization of their frontier society. In this chapter, for reasons of space, I will not venture into Taiwan, but take my examples from elsewhere, mainly from the ecologically most vulnerable, semi-arid or mountainous regions in the north and west of China.

I will treat, successively, the belated opening up of the areas beyond the Great Wall and the minority areas, postwar reconstruction, deforestation, the ecological effects of agricultural and tax policies, the encroachment on public or communal land, reservations, the spread of new crops, population growth, the recognition of environmental deterioration by the Chinese bureaucracy, and the increased vulnerability of settlements. Our most fundamental question will be how properly to assess the ecological effects of population growth, government policies, and economic organization, and the linkages among these three factors.

---

[1] See, e.g., Liao Hanchen 廖漢臣, *Taiwansheng kaipi ziliao xubian* 台灣省開闢資料續編 [Collection of materials on the opening up of Taiwan province] (Taichung, 1977); Sheng Qingyi 盛清沂, "Xinzhu, Taoyuan, Miaoli sanxian diqu kaifa shi" 新竹，桃園，苗栗三縣地區開闢史 [History of the opening up of the region of the Xinzhu, Taoyuan, and Miaoli counties], *Taiwan wenxian* 台灣文獻 31.4 (1980), pp. 154–76, and 32.1 (1981), pp. 136–57; John Shepherd, *Plains Aborigines and Chinese Settlers on the Taiwan Frontier in the 17th and 18th Centuries*, Ph.D. diss., Stanford, 1981; Song Zengzhang 宋增璋, *Taiwan Fuken Zhi* 台灣撫墾志 [Record of the protection of aborigines and land reclamation in Taiwan], 2 vols. (Taipei: Taiwansheng wenxian weiyuanhui, 1980); Yin Zhangyi 尹章義, *Taiwan kaifa shi yanjiu* 台灣開發史研究 [Research on the history of the development of Taiwan] (Taipei: Lianjing CBS, 1989); and Cheng Daxue 程大學, *Taiwan kaifa shi* 台灣開發史 [History of the development of Taiwan] (Taipei: Zongwen tushu CBS, 1991).

8.1. THE DATING OF DESERTIFICATION IN THE NORTHERN BORDER AREAS

Ma Zhenglin has surveyed the historical progress of desertification in China. Historical sources and place names provide ample evidence. He observes that in the historical period, desertification has usually been caused by irrational economic activities that destroyed the local ecological balance. In the *Gansu corridor*, during the early Han dynasty when animal husbandry flourished, there were ample grasslands, the mountains were covered with forests, and deserts were very small. In Han, Tang, and subsequent dynasties, it became a major traffic artery and part of the "Silk Route." Population increased and all suitable land was colonized and converted to arable. As a result, the deserts began to expand during the Han, and this process proved irreversible. The contraction of the Dunhuang oasis is a good example of this process. In the *Taklamakan desert*, the loss of oases such as Loulan was primarily caused by shifts in river courses and wind action; human influence was only a secondary cause. The *Horqin desert* in Inner Mongolia is mainly a product of forest felling and land reclamation by the Kitan during the Liao dynasty and government-supported land reclamation in the mid- and late Qing. The *Mu Us (Maowusu) desert* in northern Shaanxi may have already existed in the Han, but the receding frontier line of the (mostly military) settlements of the Han, Tang, and Ming dynasties indicate its subsequent expansion. The *Ordos plateau* was originally covered with grass and forest; desertification only occurred after the large-scale land reclamation projects of the mid-Qing, and particularly in the first decade of the Republic, when Suiyuan's farmland area roughly quadrupled in size. The Ming Great Wall, which runs through what now is the Ordos desert, is proof of the change of soil type. "Where else could the Ming have obtained all this clay needed for building the Wall?"[2] One should add that already from a very early date, the destruction of forests for fuel and timber along the Inner Asian trade routes by passing merchants, armies, and colonists negatively affected the local microclimate, water supplies, and soils, resulting in lasting damage to pastures and agriculture.

[2] Ma Zhenglin 马正林, "Renlei huodong yu Zhongguo shamo diqudi kuoda" 人类活动与中国沙漠地区的扩大 [Human activities and the enlargement of desert areas in China], *Shaanxi shida xuebao* 陝西師大學報 3 (1984), pp. 38–47; Zhao Yongfu 赵永复, "Lishishang Maowusu shadidi bianqian wenti" 历史上毛乌素沙地的变迁问题 [The problem of historical shifts of the Maowusu desert], *Lishi dili* 歷史地理 1 (1981), pp. 34–47; Chen Yuning 陈育宁, "Ordossu diqu shamohuadi xingcheng he fazhan shulun" 鄂尔多斯地区沙漠化的形成和发展述论 [A discussion of the formation and development of desertification of the Ordos area], *Zhongguo shehui kexue* 中國社會科學 2 (1986), pp. 69–82.

In recent years, ideas about the original vegetation of northwestern China have changed. A lesser role is now assigned to the human impact on the processes of desertification, and the original vegetation of the Han times is now thought to have been rather poor and desertlike. However, most textual research awaits archaeological corroboration, for instance through pollen analysis. On the basis of coin finds, Zhu Zhenda 朱震達 has concluded that the pastoral population and economy flourished during the Tang and Northern Song, but greatly contracted in subsequent dynasties, probably because of land reclamation. Zhao Yongfu has noted that in the Mu Us, between the Han and early Qing, desertification was very slow and the human impact minor. Human activities were to become an important factor only at the end of the Qing and during the early Republic, when foreign missionaries acquired land and led cultivation projects on the desert fringe, which resulted in serious desertification of pastures. Most of the desertification in the 100-*li* zone south of the Ming Great Wall occurred after the Qing government had introduced its policies of "filling the border regions with migrants" (*yi min shi bian* 移民實邊) and "supporting the people by giving out land" (*jie di yang min* 借地養民) in the mid-eighteenth century.[3] Thus, at least until the end of the Qing, climatic changes rather than human activities may have been the more important factor in the shifts between agricultural and pastoral areas.

8.2. ECOLOGICAL EFFECTS OF BORDER POLICIES IN THE NORTH OF CHINA

During the Ming dynasty, the Great Wall marked the border between the Chinese civilization and the nomadic and forest-dwelling peoples. One of the methods used in its defense symbolized the conflict between agricultural, sedentary China and the pastoral, nomadic cultures of Inner Asia: the Chinese garrisons were ordered to set fire to a 50-to-100-*li* stretch of wasteland on the northern side of the wall (at least in strategic areas) every year, in order to deprive barbarian cavalries of feed for their horses. The method was still advocated by Gu Yanwu in the final years of the Ming – "although it takes a considerable effort, one may have a peaceful winter"[4] – but it is unclear to what extent the method was actually practiced.

[3] Yuan Qinglin 袁清林, ed., *Zhongguo huanjing baohu shihua* 中国环境保护史话 [Talks on the history of environmental protection in China] (Beijing: Zhongguo Huanjing Kexue CBS, 1989), p. 54, quoting Zhu Zhenda.

[4] Gu Yanwu 顧炎武, *Rizhilu* 日知錄 [Record of knowledge day by day] (Canton: Shugutang, 1834), "Shao huang."

Some decades after the conquest, the Qing formally separated the Han Chinese and the nomadic peoples again. While the former were forbidden to leave China proper, the latter were forbidden to remain within 50 *li* of the Great Wall, a distance that was later reduced (not for settlement, but only for herding cattle) to 40, 30, or even 20 *li* in 1682 and 1719, but increased back to 50 *li* in 1740. "These rules had a certain positive effect on the restoration of the vegetation cover in West Mongolia and on [prevention of] desertification."[5]

After the Qing conquest, many Manchus left the Northeast and the resulting labor shortage and neglected farmland created a vacuum that attracted Han Chinese inmigrants. After several decades of support for Han Chinese migration, the Manchu court decided to close off Manchuria. Land beyond the Great Wall was to be issued to bannermen and soldiers only. This decision was based on a perceived need to maintain the Manchu identity and lifestyle. The Manchu rulers feared that their tribes would be swamped by droves of Chinese colonists. By preserving their homeland, they sought to protect the livelihood of the bannermen and maintain their military prowess. Moreover, some areas, such as Shanhaiguan and the Changbai mountains, were declared forbidden territory, not just to Han Chinese migrants, but for all people, in order to protect the monopoly supply (in the form of tribute) of ginseng, hides, and other precious forest products.[6] As for the Mongol territories, they were closed to Han Chinese in order to prevent collision or collusion with the natives. Within Manchuria, the natives' access to forests and permission to open up land for agriculture was more strictly controlled in some places than in others. From the Kangxi period till the early Qianlong, the government established a limited number of bannermen colonies (*qitun* 棋屯), government farms (*guanzhuang* 官莊) and government farmland (*gongtian* 公田). Their main purposes were to guard the region against the Russians and secure the area and its postal routes. These establishments had to be self-supporting in food grain.[7] Because many bannermen and their officers were unwilling to move from Beijing back to Manchuria, they preferred to invite Han Chinese migrant workers to work the land for them. Apart from these pull factors, there was the push of famines in northern China. Though inmigration was

---

[5] Cheng Chongde 成崇德, "Qingdai qianqi dui Menggudi fengjin zhengce yu renkou, kaifa ji shengtai huanjingdi guanxi" 清代前期对蒙古的封禁政策与人口，开发及生态环境的关系 [The closure policy for Mongolia in the early Qing period and its relation to population, development, and ecology], *Qingshi yanjiu* 清史研究 2 (1991), pp. 26–31.

[6] Cong Peiyuan 丛佩远, *Dongbei sanbao jingji jianshi* 东北三宝经济简史 [Short economic history of the "Three Treasures" of the Northeast] (Beijing: Nongye CBS, 1989), p. 65.

[7] Sutō Yoshiyuki 周藤吉之, *Shindai manshū tochi seisaku no kenkyū* 清代清州土地政策の研究 [Land policies in Qing-dynasty Manchuria] (Tokyo: Kawade shobō, 1944), p. 403.

illegal, it was sometimes tolerated or even expressly approved by the authorities.

The interdiction of Han Chinese migration into northeastern China and Mongolia checked the advance of agriculture for one or two centuries. There was limited access on the basis of official permits until 1740, interdiction (with some exceptions) until 1860, unchecked private inmigration (of over half a million people per year) until 1880, and finally, government encouragement of inmigration. For Inner Mongolia and Chahar, the initial phase of recruitment lasted till 1740, and the lifting of the ban and official encouragement only started in 1898.[8]

Some authors believe that the effect of famines and population pressure at the end of the eighteenth and the beginning of the nineteenth century was so strong that the government could no longer control outmigration to the Northeast; they take this as proof that there was overpopulation in China proper. In fact, however, large-scale migration was successfully prevented until the second half of the nineteenth century. By the time the ban was partially lifted in 1860, population numbers had already dropped substantially because of the Taiping Rebellion, and the motive for allowing Han Chinese to settle in certain frontier areas was strategic reinforcement, or "filling" the frontier, not the emptying of China proper. In Manchuria, because of its size and the often-difficult conditions, agricultural settlements spread only slowly, from the south. Public land was issued first, and Mongol land only much later. It was estimated in 1914 that only one-fifteenth of Manchuria's wasteland had been reclaimed.[9] Most of this was dry farming in the plains. Thus, the environmental impact of colonization was still rather limited.

The shortage of agricultural farmland in the early nineteenth century, together with a reduction in army activities, led to the conversion of many army horse-farms into arable. Most of these horse-farms were located in semi-arid areas in the North and Northwest. Once the government had agreed to lift their special status, their population of bannermen and Han Chinese colonist-tenants rapidly increased. In some cases, investments in dams and irrigation canals yielded great economic benefits. In other cases, the agricultural land dried out and turned into dustbowls, for example along the upper reaches of the Daling River in West Liaoning. Because of

[8] Tian Fang 田方 and Chen Yiyun 陈一筠, eds., *Zhongguo yimin shilüe* 中国移民史略 [A short history of Chinese migrants] (Beijing: Zhishi CBS, 1986).
[9] Liu Jialei 刘家磊, "Lüelun Qingji dongbei yimin shibian zhengce" 略论清季东北移民实边政策 [A short discussion of the policy of strengthening the borders with migrants during the Qing period], in Lü Yiran 吕一燃 et al., eds., *Zhongguo bianjiang shidi lunji*. 中國邊疆史地論集 (Harbin: Heilongjiang CBS, 1991), pp. 195–209.

prior illegal reclamation, erosion had increased. In 1827, a flood of the Daling River had deposited silt on a huge stretch of land along its lower reaches, thereby creating suitable soil conditions for rice farming.[10] Already in 1789, serious floods were reported to have destroyed 11,000 *mu* of bannerman lands in Jinzhou;[11] they may have been partly caused by land reclamation and erosion in the upper reaches of Josoto League.

When land was issued for agricultural land reclamation, the rent and tax obligations of the colonists and the size of their farmland were spelled out in detail. For instance, when in 1832 land was surveyed in the Kuduli area of Horqin (northwestern Liaoning) for the accommodation of more than 300 additional Chinese colonist households, it was stipulated that they should pay 5,000 cash per *qing* for the permanent land lease (*dazu* 大租), to be paid after five years, and 320 cash of annual rent (*xiaozu* 小租) for the tenant farmer. As for the native Mongols: "each of the 57 Mongol settlements in this area should continue to hold 2 to 3 or 6 to 7 *li* of pasture and cropland, depending on its population, to be used for grazing or agriculture. . . . Land already reclaimed by them will be left alone." The boundaries were to be marked with earthen walls and inspected annually.[12] However, much of the agricultural expansion went unregistered, and its environmental effects have been recorded in a few cases only. The natural grass area of Horqin, which used to support large flocks of animals, was sold to Han Chinese grain farmers by the Qing government and Mongol nobility in the late nineteenth and early twentieth century. As it turned out, after only a few years of cultivation the loose topsoil was blown away, and wind erosion had reduced the cultivated areas to a desert; pastures deteriorated as well, since herds had to be accommodated on an ever-shrinking territory.[13] One may assume that in most areas, agricultural reclamation went on at the expense of pastoral farming, although cultivation of fodder crops might contribute to animal husbandry. In Inner Mongolia as elsewhere, the traditional systems of pastoral farming were very vulnerable to the vagaries of climate and often disrupted by warfare. At different times of the year, small flocks owned by local herdsmen used the same lands as large flocks, owned by the nobles, that migrated over the entire territory of one banner.

---

[10] 1856 Memorial by the Liaoning Finance Department Councillor Shu Yuan 書元, *Dao Xian Tong Guang sichao zouyi* 道鹹同光四朝奏議 [Memorials of the reigns of Daoguang, Xianfeng, Tongzhi, and Guangxu] (Reprinted, Taipei: Commercial Press, 1970), p. 1203.

[11] Sutō Yoshiyuki, *Land policies*, p. 236.

[12] *Li fan yuan zeli* 理藩院則例 [Rules of the Court of Colonial Affairs] (1832), vol. 10, *dimu* 地畝, pp. 1–9, 13–15, 19–22, 30–41.

[13] *Zhongguo ziran dili: Lishi ziran dili* 中国自然地理：历史自然地理 [Natural geography of China: historical natural geography] (Beijing: Kexue CBS, 1982), p. 250.

Once the Banner Chiefs (*jasagh*) began to receive additional income from rents from newly settled farmers, they might reduce the size of their flocks, which in turn would benefit the common herdsmen. Thus, the relation between agricultural land reclamation and pastoral farming was rather complex, and differed as between areas and periods.[14]

The Court of Colonial Affairs (*Li Fan Yuan* 理藩院) had stipulated that when farmers were recruited to reclaim Mongol land for agriculture, part of the proceeds from sales of wasteland and rents was to be used to compensate the resultant losses suffered in animal husbandry or to reduce the taxes and corvées of the bannermen. According to Tian Zhihe, this rule remained a dead letter, all proceeds going into the pockets of the feudal leaders, and neither the animal husbandry sector nor individual herdsmen received one cash. When rules were laid down for recruitment of farmers, it had been stipulated that pastures for grazing cattle and sheep should be preserved. In the Guangxu period, it was specified that four *fang* 方 ("squares," each measuring one by one *li* 里, or about 45 *xiang* 向) should be left for members of the Mongol nobility (*taiji* 太吉), and half that amount for male adults. Moreover, all landless Mongols should be granted some cattle. It is clear from this rule that the Qing government tried to use legal means to maintain the pastoral lifestyle and economy of the Mongols. However, in spite of this, many Mongols abandoned animal husbandry for agriculture at this time. Because they lacked experience, their productivity and income were low, and many eventually had to mortgage or sell their land to the Mongol princes, monasteries, merchants, or Chinese colonists.[15]

Around 1900, the Qing government's motives for allowing, and even encouraging, Han Chinese settlers to colonize Mongol territories were both political and economic. First, China's national defense against Russia and Japan would be strengthened, and second, the expansion of economic activities and grain production would benefit Mongols and Chinese alike, and land sales would bring much-needed state revenue. Not all Mongols saw it that way, and although opposition (mainly from the lower Mongol nobility) against land sales and Han Chinese encroachment was repressed by legal and military means, colonization schemes met with little success.

[14] See my article "Checks without Balances: Manchu State Building and Chinese Agricultural Expansion on the Inner Mongolian Frontier," in James Reardon-Anderson, ed., *Continuities and Change on the Mongolian Steppe: Implications for Land Use* (GEMS Project, forthcoming).

[15] Tian Zhihe 田志和, "Qingdai Dongbei Mengdi kaifazhongdi maodun he douzheng" 清代东北蒙地开发中的矛盾和斗争 [Conflicts and struggle in the development of Mongol land in northeast China during the Qing period], *Dongbei shida xuebao* 东北师大学报 4 (1986), pp. 56–61.

Nevertheless, the newly established counties became centers of Han Chinese presence, from which agricultural techniques and cultural influence slowly spread.[16] Owen Lattimore has provided us with a fascinating history and first-hand account of the plight of the Mongols and frontier life at the end of the nineteenth and the early twentieth century. He stressed that many early Chinese settlers in Mongol territories "went native," and that later many Mongols became agriculturalists.[17] However, there is insufficient evidence for an estimate of the numbers involved.

8.3. THE POSITIVE IMAGE OF THE "UNIFICATION OF CHINA"

Recent Chinese authors are somewhat ambiguous about how to evaluate the Han Chinese expansion into minority territories during the Qing. On the one hand, nationalist and communist ideas and Han Chinese chauvinism all contribute to their very positive image of the integration of border areas into the Chinese empire and civilization. Thus, the Qing prohibition of Han Chinese entering Miao and Mongol/Tibetan territories for trading and settlement "harmed the interests of all peoples. It was a reactionary measure hampering their economic and cultural exchange. . . . Because all the people concerned resisted, this prohibition was gradually eroded and destroyed."[18] "The Qing policy of separating peoples went against the historical trend and the interests of the Mongol and Han peoples; it gave an opportunity for foreign enemies."[19]

In the early Qing, the nomad regions were underdeveloped and production was insecure; Chinese farmers were recruited to help create a more secure basis of food grain.

> The flourishing of the Mongol pastoral economy in the 18th and mid-19th centuries proves that ecological and economic benefits could be combined. Of course, the Qing dynasty did not reckon with ecological factors. However, its restrictive policy towards migration reflected a certain consciousness of the

---

[16] He Yaozhang 何耀彰, *Man-Qing zhi Meng zhengcezhi yanjiu* 滿清治蒙政策之研究 [Research into the Qing Manchu policy of ruling the Mongols] *Guoli shifan daxue lishi yanjiusuo* 國立師範大學歷史研究所 special Issue 2 (1978), pp. 154–56.

[17] Owen Lattimore, *Manchuria: Cradle of Conflict* (New York: Macmillan, 1935), pp. 55–56.

[18] Tian Fang and Chen Yiyun, eds., *A short history*, p. 135.

[19] Ma Yongshan 马永山 and Zhao Yi 赵毅, "Qingchao guanyu neimenggu diqu jinken fangken zhengcedi yanbian" 清朝关于内蒙古地区禁垦放垦政策的演变 [Changes in the Qing dynastic policy toward the interdiction or permission to reclaim land in the Inner Mongolian areas], *Shehui kexue jikan* 社会科学辑刊 5 (1992), pp. 86–91.

characteristics of the Mongolian natural environment, of the conflict between indiscriminate reclamation and the interests of animal husbandry,
desertification of pastures, etc.[20]

On the other hand, the resulting damage to the fragile environment of
the pastures has been gaining recognition in recent years. One way out of
the moral dilemma felt by Marxist Chinese historians has been to blame
environmental destruction in the border regions during this period on
imperialist, missionary, or capitalist exploitation. Such moral verdicts have
not been very helpful to our understanding of the many issues involved.
What one would like to see now from Chinese historians is more detailed
studies of local change, also from the perspective of the minority peoples,
which should be based not only on written evidence (missionary records,
travelogues, and early Republican draft histories have been neglected so
far, partly for political reasons) but also on oral tradition and physical data.
The official county histories written during the past few years provide
ample contemporary data, but usually do not cover the Qing period and
the Republican period, or do so in a perfunctory manner only.

8.4. DESTRUCTION OF PEOPLE, PROPERTY, AND RESOURCES BY THE QING CONQUESTS, AND EFFORTS AT REBUILDING

Internal and external wars conducted by the Qing government took many
lives and destroyed property and natural resources. Urban centers and
other accessible areas where armies passed through were affected most
severely. People fled to the mountain forests and deserts, and many per-
ished. Existing systems of cultivation and trade were destroyed, and could
not always be restored because of lack of people and beasts of burden.
Apart from reducing population pressure on land, it also brought a temporary change in resource use. In some areas, particularly those where Chinese civilization was newly introduced, the postwar reconstruction effort
created new methods of exploitation of land. The most important long-
term effect of all was the integration of the border regions into the Chinese
state and economy, which led to the creation of new frameworks for economic activity and social development.

Population losses and migration because of war and war-related famine
can only be estimated, because the wars caused a breakdown of the admin-

---

[20] Cheng Chongde, "Closure policy for Mongolia," pp. 26–31.

istrative system. After the Ming–Qing transition, Sichuan's registered population had dropped to 16,000 taxpayers, and the actual population may have dropped by five-sixths to about half a million. Repopulation and reclamation of wasteland in such areas were major elements of the postwar government's reconstruction effort, which is often well documented. However, the undocumented private undertakings of returning refugees and new inmigrants were much larger. A recent article concludes that Sichuan had between half a million to one million inmigrants until the end of the Kangxi period (when the migration wave had virtually ended); another article estimates that by 1800, "at least 85 percent" of Sichuan's twenty million inhabitants were inmigrants or their descendants.[21] As could be expected, both inmigrant numbers and the natural rates of increase in population were very high, but our data are insufficient for more precise estimates.

The loss of life and destruction of property among the minority peoples caused by the Qing army campaigns are particularly difficult to establish. The Qing commanders tended to exaggerate the number of enemies or "rebels" killed, but could have no idea of the indirect losses caused by the war. The defeated minority people or rebels did not keep records either. Some campaigns resulted in their almost complete extermination; for instance, by 1759 only 10 percent or so of the more than 600,000 Zungars had survived the Qing campaigns in Xinjiang. Their fate was not typical. Less organized resistance against the Qing by more scattered and diverse peoples such as the Miao might last for decades; some yielded to Chinese pressure and moved into higher mountain areas, others were sinicized, and only the confident or desperate stood their ground to offer battle. Without archaeological evidence, which is still very rare in most regions, it is usually impossible to establish whether newly established Chinese farms and settlements took the place of older native ones. Textual evidence is mainly limited to the establishment of military colonies (*tuntian* 屯田, *qitun* 棋屯), or government-supported colonies of Han Chinese (*mintun* 民屯), convicts (*fantun* 犯屯), or minority peoples (*miaotun* 苗屯, *huitun* 回屯, etc.). After campaigns against minority "rebels," the Qing military commanders and civil government often confiscated privately owned farmland to establish colonies of soldier-colonists that could support the garrisons and even the costs of local administration (e.g., in the Miao areas in Hu'nan after

---

[21] Lan Yong 蓝勇, "Qian-Jia kenzhi dui Sichuan nongye shengtai he shehui fazhan yingxiang chutan" 乾嘉垦殖对四川农业生态和社会发展影响初探 [Preliminary investigation of the influence of land reclamation and colonization during the Qianlong and Jiaqing reign-periods on Sichuan's agricultural ecology and social development], *Zhongguo nongshi* 中国农史 12.1 (1993), pp. 19–28.

1800).[22] It is clear, though, that even if the confiscated farmland had been in use before, the Chinese colonist-farmers brought new and more intensive farming techniques and crops, which required more labor, fertilizer, water, and other inputs. Insofar as these techniques were copied by the native population and supported by improvements in infrastructure and trade, newly conquered areas became capable of supporting a larger population than before.[23]

Initially, the environmental impact of the Han Chinese land reclamation was rather limited. Much more destruction was caused by logging and mining (iron, copper, silver, tin, etc.) conducted by Chinese merchants and by the government monopolies following, and sometimes preceding, the Qing occupation of southwestern China. Apart from wanting to reinforce strategic control over their territories, one of the major reasons for the court and Governor Ortai establishing a more direct administration over the minority areas was to gain control over such resources. "The Miao regard their splendid forests only as a source of fuel. But the trees and bamboos should be used for timber, and their resources are inexhaustible."[24] Claudine Salmon's study of eighteenth-century Guizhou shows the variety of ways in which the Qing government and Chinese merchants and farmers invaded and sinicized the Miao territories. Initial containment was followed by repeated efforts to subjugate and incorporate the various groups of Miao, establishment of guardhouses, and "search and destroy" campaigns, but also slow integration by intermarriage. The traditional Miao were marginalized and their habitat destroyed.[25] Of course, this went in the

[22] Yan Ruyi 嚴如煜, *Miaofang beilan* 苗防備覽 [An overview of defense against the Miao] (An. pref. dated 1820), ch. 13; Wu Xinfu 伍新福, "Shilun Qingdai 'tunzheng,' dui Xiangxi Miaozu shehui fazhandi yingxiang" 試論清代 '屯政' 对湘西苗族社会发展的影响 [Discussion of the influence of the "colonial policy" of the Qing period on the social development of the Miao people in West Hu'nan], *Minzu yanjiu* 民族研究 3 (1983), pp. 32–40; Guo Songyi 郭松義, "Qingdai Xiangxi Miaoqu tuntian" 清代湘西苗区屯田 [Colony fields in the Miao areas in west Hu'nan during the Qing period], *Minzu yanjiu* 民族研究 2 (1992), pp. 89–95.

[23] See, e.g., Hua Li 华立, "Qianlong nianjian yimin chuguan yu Qingqianqi Tianshan beilu nongyedi fazhan" 乾隆年间移民出关与清前期天山北路农业的发展 [The outmigration beyond the Great Wall during the Qianlong period and agricultural development of the district north of the Tianshan during the early Qing], *Xibei shidi* 西北史地 4 (1987), pp. 119–31.

[24] Wang Lüjie 王履階, "Gaitu guiliu shuo" 改土歸流説 [An explanation of "Change the native [headmen] and return to rotating [Chinese officials]"], in Wang Xiqi 王錫祺, *Xiaofanghu zhai yudi congchao* 小方壺齊輿地叢鈔 [Collected geographical documents from the Small Pot Studio] (Shanghai, 1891), vol. 8, p. 154.

[25] Claudine Lombard-Salmon, *Un exemple d'acculturation chinoise: la province du Guizhou au XVIII*-siècle* (Paris: EFEO, 1972).

name of economic and cultural progress, which it mostly was, but it was also very painful and destructive for humankind and nature.

8.5. DEFORESTATION BECAUSE OF INCREASED DEMAND FOR TIMBER AND WOOD FUEL

The deforestation of China has been a long-term process. Early data are best for the surroundings of Chang'an: the Qinling mountains.[26] Before the Ming dynasty established its capital at Beijing, the Western Hills had already lost their original forest to the construction works of the Liao and Yuan dynasties. Most of the large pines went in the Jiajing and Wanli periods, and the Ming emperors had to take the timber for their palaces from provinces as far away as Sichuan and Guizhou (spending almost 10 million silver taels in the latter period.[27] This felling of trees for imperial use has received much attention in Chinese sources. In the Ming, most provinces had been assigned a delivery quota. The Kangxi emperor reduced the felling of imperial timber. He was also forced to resort to using pines instead of the precious *nanmu* 楠木 (*Phoebe nanmu*), because provincial governors had had to report that the latter could no longer be supplied. However, in 1726 another imperial request to Sichuan for *nanmu* could be met with the supply of 1,738 standard logs.[28] According to some sources, the giant trees needed for the Ming and Qing imperial palaces could only be found in remote mountain areas, which had never been commercially exploited because of the high transport costs and absence of local demand. The impact of imperial requisitioning was greatest on original forests; large quantities of timber were involved, which were felled in a limited number of specific areas.

Traditional Chinese thought exhibited a definite bias against forests and the cultivation of trees. Forest areas were seen as hideouts for bandits and rebels, beyond the reach of government authority, where uncivilized people lived their wretched lives without observing the rules of propriety. In this view, the clearance of forests and agricultural reclamation brought

[26] Ma Zhenglin, "Renlei huodong yu Zhongguo shamo diqudi kuoda" [Human activities and the enlargement of desert areas in China], *Shaanxi Shida xuebao* 3 (1984), pp. 38–47.
[27] *Mingshi: Shihuozhi* 明史：食貨志 [Ming history: record of food grain and goods], 6.
[28] See Sichuan governor Zhang Dedi's 張德地 1668 memorials and later supplies in Ping Han 平翰 et al., *Zunyi fuzhi* 遵義府志 [Gazetteer of Zunyi prefecture] (1841), ch. 18, "Timber administration," pp. 12 and 15.

safety and political and cultural progress. Such ideas were not only put forward after the quelling of uprisings by minority peoples, miners, migrants, bandits, or other inhabitants of mountain forests, but were commonly held by local magistrates. However, the main argument for conversion of forest to arable was an economic one: farmland was much more economically productive than forest. A late Ming handbook for local magistrates summed up the reasons given by farmers (in Shandong) for not liking to grow (elm) trees:

> One: saplings are hard to come by and farmers cannot afford them. Two: trees grown at roadsides and on wasteland are not guarded and may be stolen by thieves or eaten by cattle and goats. Three: there is not enough water even for irrigation of the rice fields. Four: once trees along the public roads have grown tall, they become public property, and landowners are not allowed to cut them down. Five: the roots of elms [and such trees] are superficial and, once grown, they take water away from the paddy rice. Six: trees planted on sandy or saline soils do not grow.

However, the author, Lü Kun, then went on to argue that each of these objections might be overcome:

> Trees are better able to withstand drought or flood; they will provide timber, fuel, and cash income; they grow well on plots where only the topsoil is saline and drainage ditches are dug; they may be located along field borders; their size may be cut back to keep competition with grain crops in check; saplings may be thinned out and young trees cut back to enhance their chance of survival; a ditch with stakes may make things difficult for thieves and cattle.

Moreover, a stone inscription had been put up in front of the yamen, stating that from 1587 on, all trees planted along public roads would forever remain private property, that their felling by others was forbidden, and that all trees grown on land that was not subject to grain tax before would forever be exempt from taxes. According to Lü, all these arguments were even stronger for other, more profitable trees such as persimmons, pears, mulberries, and jujubes.[29]

These and other late Ming recommendations imply that intensification of farmland use and diversification were held to be more productive than the expansion of agriculture into wasteland.

> With less farmland, it is easier to apply fertilizer. . . . One *mu* of fertile soil is better than ten times as much poor soil. One *mu* of fine land is better than ten times as much wasteland. However, stupid farmers, who want more, often

[29] Lü Kun 呂坤, *Lügong shizheng lu: minwu* 呂公實政錄：民物 [Record of the administrative actions of Mr. Lü], vol. 2, pp. 8–11.

think that with an expansion of farmland there will not be any lean harvests. They do not realize that more farmland brings heavier grain taxes.[30]

In the late Ming and again in the mid- and late Qing, officials were convinced that population growth had led to a serious shortage of farmland and other resources. However, there was a big difference between the two periods. Under the Qing, political and social controls had been loosened and mobility was greater than ever before. Local administration was spread thinly, particularly in less productive mountain areas, and rather weak. Felling of forest, reclamation of wasteland and lakes, and other forms of environmentally destructive activity were of minor concern to the authorities. The location of these areas (far from county seats), their land status (not subject to taxation), type of crop (not rice, wheat, or millet), and lack of market access made them look unimportant in the eyes of government. Of course, that fact itself attracted adventurous private developers and migrants, who appreciated the economic and social opportunities of unchecked development of this frontier.

For the Qing government and economy, the gains from cutting down forests and conversion to arable were both short-term (the provision of timber) and long-term (the creation of income and employment for poor farmers and the increase in food grain). During the mid-Qing, land reclamation was stimulated by a number of economic conditions: (1) the new crops such as maize and sweet potatoes raised the food production potential of sloping, unirrigated, and high-altitude farmland; (2) because of the growth of population and market opportunities, more labor was available for investment in soil improvement and farming activities; (3) rising prices and greater demand for commercial crops, such as tea and tobacco, which were grown at higher altitudes, increased the land values in mountain areas; and (4) after 1740, the Qing government lost its interest (namely, tax revenue) and its administrative control over almost all farmland that had been privately reclaimed.

In addition to slash-and-burn farming and conversion to arable, the burgeoning industries, as of porcelain, iron smelting, paper, shipbuilding, salt, and lime, used up most forests in their immediate surroundings for fuel and timber.[31] Probably because of their late date, the rise and fall

---

[30] Ibid., p. 5.

[31] Bao Hongchang 暴鸿昌 and Hu Fan 胡凡, "Ming-Qing shiqi Changjiang zhongshangyou senlinzhi pohuaidi lishi kaocha" 明清时期长江中上游森林植被破坏的历史考察 [A historical investigation of forest vegetation destruction along the middle and upper reaches of the Yangzi River in the Ming and Qing periods], *Hubei Daxue xuebao* 湖北大学学报 1 (1991), pp. 72-77.

of such industries along the fringes of the original forests in the mountains
of southern Shaanxi has been documented rather well, by Lü Kun, Yan
Ruyi, and local gazetteers. As the original forests receded and became
few in number, more and more investments were needed to obtain large
logs.

> The large timber factories fell trees in the old forests further than 200 *li* away
> [from the Han River plain]. One has to build slides first. Small roundwood is
> cut, with a length of about 10 feet, and placed as sleepers to form a bed for
> an easy slide, with planks 7 to 8 feet wide. . . . In uneven terrain, protruding
> parts are covered with stone slabs, and hollow parts are propped up with
> piles. . . . The constructions look like bridges. This is the largest item of
> expenditure. The slides may run across valleys for tens of *li*, to the waterfront.
> For crossing steep hills and mountains, pulleys are used with oxen, mules or
> coolies. . . . This is where the large timber factories employ most of their
> labor . . . no less than three to five thousand [each].[32]

Moreover, felling for fuel and other private household uses took its toll.
Once the original forest had been felled, after some years secondary forest
stands might be exploited for charcoal burning. However, in most cases the
forest was lost for good. Eighteenth-century local sources indicate rapidly
dwindling supplies of both wood fuel and charcoal. For instance, in the
vicinity of Chongqing,

> Recently, the mountain timber has been felled completely, and charcoal has
> become scarce. Prices have shot up, and three [out of seven] charcoal-
> burning firms have stopped their business and changed trade . . . now two
> more have stopped.[33]

> We found that in Chongqing, the smelting of the lead [ore] from Guizhou,
> which is destined for Beijing, requires more than six hundred thousand *jin* of
> charcoal every [year]. . . . Formerly, wood fuel was easy to get, but recently, its
> price has more than doubled.[34]

Once the supply of wood fuel or charcoal had become uneconomic because of increasing transportation costs, some smelters and other factories
turned to coal as an alternative source of fuel, while others had to close
down and move.

The minority areas were not spared, even those where land sales to Han

---

[32] Yan Ruyi 嚴如煜, *Sansheng bianfang beilan* 三省邊防備覽 [An overview of defense in the
border region of the Three Provinces] (1830), ch. 9, pp. 2–4.

[33] Petition to the magistrate by Yang Mei 楊美 et al., dated May 18, 1760, *Baxian Archives*, in
Qingdai Qian-Jia-Dao Baxian dang'an xuanbian 清代乾嘉道巴縣檔案選編 (Chengdu, 1989),
pp. 318–19.

[34] Proposal by the Baxian government to raise the official price of charcoal, dated July 13,
1761, ibid.

Chinese had been forbidden and access had been limited. For instance, the governor-general of Huguang introduced regulations that continued to forbid land sales by Yao to Han Chinese, after their uprising had been quelled, and warned Chinese traders in forestry products that they should give the Yao their fair share of profits. Yet they also permitted Han Chinese to buy timber stands in the Yao mountains, for a maximum period of twenty years. Only one felling was allowed during that period, after which the plot had to be returned to the Yao owner.[35] Of course, this would have seriously reduced the value of such a plot, and the land would have subsequently become subject to greater erosion even if covered with secondary vegetation.

> Han and Yao people in the mountain areas in the west do not engage in farming, but only fell timber. The natives want to receive the land rent for one season [of felling], but do not think of the subsequent disaster. They recruit migrant workers from Hu'nan . . . who cut down all trees, or plant maize. Even if the fields were fertile originally, they will still be eroded and become unfit for further cultivation of rice and millet. We should evict these people . . . except for those who have been living there for a long time already. . . . Mountain areas should be reclaimed by local residents only, and recruitment of migrants should be forbidden.[36]

Nevertheless, as timber prices rose, commercial growing of timber became a viable option in some minority areas. In Liping 黎平 county, a thinly populated Miao area in Guizhou, the technique was described as follows:

> The mountains are suitable for growing China fir (shan 杉). The local people say that before one plants these firs, one should grow wheat and maize for one or two years in order to loosen the soil and make tree planting easy. The trees bear seeds after 15 or 16 years, and one should select seeds from the upward-pointing branches. . . . In spring, one should fertilize the soil, overturn the grass, and let it dry and burn it. Then one puts the seeds into the soil and protects them with tree branches, in order to increase their vitality and slow down their sprouting. Once they have grown into saplings, they are transplanted and put at a distance of one foot from each other. They receive fertilizer to promote their growth. When they have grown somewhat, the crooked ones are removed and the resulting gaps filled up with other saplings. . . . At twenty years, they may be cut.[37]

[35] 1833 Memorial by the Governor-General of Huguang Narjing'e 訥爾經額, *Memorials of the reigns*, p. 281.

[36] 1848 Memorial by Governor-General Xu Guangjin 徐廣縉 and Governors Zeng Zutan 鄭祖琛 and Ma Dianjia 馬殿甲 of Guangxi, ibid., p. 815.

[37] Luo Raodian's 羅繞典 1847 revised edition of Ai Bida 愛必達, *Qiannan Zhilüe* 黔南識略 [Synopsis of Guizhou] (1749), ch. 21, pp. 8–9.

However, insufficient protection of ownership against felling by the military or bandits and against government requisitioning, and the long period of investment, were major impediments to commercial timber growing. At the end of the Qing, the few remaining forests were located either in the most inaccessible places or in the natural preserves or minority areas that ordinary Han people were forbidden to enter, or, as isolated stands of trees, on the hilly slopes of temple properties and in graveyards. At that time, a western forester criticized the scarcity of timber, the ruthless exploitation of forests, and the denudation of hills and mountains through-out China. He noted that "the most destructive influence to the forests is the tendency of the Chinese to encroach on the land of the aborigines" and accused them of "unfair dealings with the savages in southwest China."[38]

The Russian and Japanese exploitation of the Manchurian forests early in this century was the most extensive and best organized ever undertaken. A recent publication estimates that China's forest cover was reduced by almost one-half between 1840 and 1947, and sums up six causes of forest losses:

(1) "Imperialist plunder," including the ceding of Chinese territory in northeast-ern China to Russia in 1860 and the construction of the Manchurian railways and consequent exploitation of the Daxing'an forests, first by the Russians, thereafter by the Japanese, who also started to exploit the Yalu's timber resources.

(2) Wanton felling and increased exploitation of forests after the lifting of the ban on migration into northeastern China in 1878. The late Qing and warlord governments considered the public forests a resource that should be ex-ploited quickly for their revenue, and issued many permits. It was only in 1930 that a law was adopted aiming at forest protection and conservation.

(3) Clearance of forests for agricultural land reclamation.

(4) Cutting of trees for fuel, the need for which increased with population growth and industrialization (including traditional industries such as porcelain, salt, and metals).

(5) Forest fires.

(6) The burning down of rebel hideouts in the mountains during internal wars, such as that against the Taiping, as in Nanzheng and Zhouzhi in southern Shaanxi, and in World War II.[39]

---

[38] Norman Shaw, *Chinese Forest Trees and Timber Supply* (London: Fisher and Unwin, 1914), pp. 58 and 169.

[39] Xiong Datong 熊大桐 et al., eds., *Zhongguo jindai linye shi* 中國近代林業史 [A modern history of forestry in China] (Beijing: Zhongguo Linye CBS, 1989), pp. 56–78.

8.6. ECOLOGICAL EFFECTS OF AGRICULTURAL AND LAND POLICIES

8.6.1. THE BLAME FOR ECOLOGICAL DESTRUCTION ACCORDING TO MARXIST AND NATIONALIST VIEWS

During the 1970s, historians in the People's Republic of China liked to blame environmental deterioration on the "ruling class," while praising the "laboring masses" for their development of agriculture, water control, and so on. For instance, in a 1977 handbook on water and soil conservation referred to by Ma Zongshen, the three main causes of forest destruction in Chinese history were claimed to have been the felling of timber for use in the construction of imperial palaces and graves, the quelling of peasant uprisings by destroying the forests in which the rebels used to hide, and the burning of vegetation to the north of the Great Wall for reasons of defense.[40] Although dynastic histories, with their primary interest in central government activities, contain references to these causes, their effects must actually have been minimal. Moreover, these historians blamed wanton felling and reclamation of wasteland on feudal society, in which peasants were driven from their land by the high rents charged by landlords and forced to seek a living in the hills and mountains. This argument runs counter to logic. Higher rents reflect intensification of farming practices, hence higher productivity and income, and thus high-rent land accommodates and provides income for more, not less, people than does low-rent farmland. Sometimes, Marxist historians have put forward the argument that because the ruling class feared the rebellions of the landless migrants, it deflected them to the felling of forests and land reclamation. This runs counter to the historical fact that the Ming and at first also the Qing government did their best to stop people from migrating to mountain and border areas.

In the modern period, imperialist exploitation (notably by the Russians and Japanese) took a heavy toll of the forest resources of northeastern China: during World War II, the Japanese plundered 70 million cubic meters of timber, or one-tenth of China's entire timber reserves at that

---

[40] Ma Zongshen 马宗申, "Woguo lishishangdi shuitu baochi" 我国历史上的水土保持 [Water and soil conservation in our country's history], *Nongshi yanjiu* 农史研究 3 (1983), pp. 61–74.

time, with serious consequences for the loss of water and soil.[41] Nevertheless, when Manchuria and Siberia were opened up by the construction
of railroads, China, as a sovereign power, concluded a treaty for the supply
of sleepers, and set up two joint forestry companies.[42] The exploitation of
forest resources, which was made possible by the railroad, did not just
further the "capitalist," "colonialist" and "imperialist" interests of these
foreign powers; it also furthered China's strategic aims and interests.

8.6.2. NINETEENTH-CENTURY
CHANGE: FUNDAMENTAL OR NOT?

Since the loosening of the Marxist-Leninist straitjacket, historical explanations are no longer that simple. However, certain images persist. For instance, China's development in the nineteenth century has always been put
in a bad light, both for external reasons (its weakness against Western
imperialism and the great contrast with the rapidly evolving European
political and economic systems of that age) and on account of internal
conditions such as bureaucratic corruption and rebellions attributed to
famines due to overpopulation. This is not the place to go into the validity
of this image. I would like to note that there seems to be no reason to
believe that ecological destruction caused by land reclamation in the nineteenth century was worse than in the eighteenth (and certainly not than in
the twentieth!). The fact that in the early nineteenth century, historical
sources began to refer more explicitly to the problems of deforestation,
erosion, and overpopulation does not mean that the level and scope of
destruction had become significantly higher than before. It primarily
meant that in China proper what one might call the "forest clearance zone"
had begun to come to its end, with the loss of natural vegetation on the
higher hills and even in remote mountain areas. During the Qing, the
technology of exploitation along this frontier did not change; it just
moved higher and further away from the traditional centers of population
and river plains, driven by population growth and increased economic
demands.

In the early nineteenth century, the Bashan mountains on the border of
Shaanxi and Sichuan were one of the last remaining original forest areas in
China proper, which may have been why at that time Yan Ruyi and Lu Kun
described their felling and exploitation in great detail. Another reason may

---

[41] Ibid.
[42] Liu Jinzao 劉錦藻 ed., *Qingchao xuwenxian tongkao* 清朝續文獻通考 (1921. Reprinted, Shanghai, 1936), ch. 378, p. 11, 274.

have been that these forests and local factories had been viewed by officials as hiding places of the Taiping rebels.[43] Suzuki Chūsei has pointed to the weakness of government control in this region as a major cause of the White Lotus rebellion, and provided an elaborate description of its socio-economic background.[44] However, one might also argue the opposite: the extension of government control in this "Wild West" area in the late eighteenth century produced a violent reaction. Felling may have been carried out in a manner quite similar to earlier exploitation of mountain forests elsewhere. There was a dual onslaught. Migrant farmers cleared land for cultivation, often moving on as soon as the soil lost its fertility (sources mention three to five years) or after their plots had been damaged by floods. Entrepreneurs employed tens of thousands of loggers, felling trees for timber and to provide fuel for mines, salt wells, iron and paper factories, and so on. As these enterprises were critically dependent on wood for their source of energy, they had to close down as soon as the supply of cheap wood fuel was exhausted, or find a supply of coal. Agricultural and industrial exploitation went hand in hand. Many mountain farmers' sons worked in factories on a seasonal basis, particularly in years when grain prices were low, in order to supplement their family income.[45] Contemporary observers gave enthusiastic descriptions of these industrial activities (which are still reflected in Fu Yiling's demonstration of "capitalist sprouts" in this area),[46] but most industries were basically temporary, self-limiting, and detrimental to the conservation of water and soil.

8.6.3. AGRICULTURAL RECLAMATION OF PUBLIC FORESTS AND WASTELAND AND ENCROACHMENT ON COMMON PROPERTY

Before the Ming dynasty, hilly and mountain areas had few settlements, and most terraces for agriculture were found along rivers and near cities. One survey in northern Jiangxi found that in the river valleys, hills, and mountains, only 22 percent, 15 percent, and 11 percent, respectively, of natural

---

[43] Yan Ruyi, *Overview of defense*, ch. 14, pp. 47–54; Lu Kun 盧坤, *Qinjiang zhilüe* 秦彊治略 [A summary of administration of the Shaanxi border area] (Taipei, 1970).

[44] Suzuki Chūsei 鈴木中正, *Shinchō chūki-shi kenkyū* 清朝中期史研究 [Studies on the Mid-Qing period] (1952), pp. 77–79.

[45] Eduard B. Vermeer, "The Mountain Frontier in Late Imperial China: Economic and Social Developments in the Dabashan," *T'oung pao* 77. 4–5 (1991), pp. 306–35.

[46] Fu Yiling 傅衣凌, "Qingdai zhongye Chuan-Shaan-Hu-sansheng bianqu shougongye xingtai jiqi lishi yiyi" 清代中叶川陕湖三省边区手工业形态及其历史意义 [Form and historical significance of handicraft industry in the Sichuan-Shaanxi-Hubei border region in the mid-Qing], *Ming-Qing shehui jingjishi lunji* 明清社会经济史论集 (Beijing, 1982).

villages dated back to before the Ming.[47] In most areas in China, cultivation of hilly and mountainous farmland did not begin until the late Ming or mid-Qing. As I have discussed elsewhere, one may distinguish five basic forms of agricultural land reclamation: (1) postwar or post-famine socio-economic reconstruction; (2) government-supported military or civil colonization; (3) illegal or unsupported agricultural settlements of migrants (often refugees) in hitherto uncultivated or sparsely populated mountain and border areas; (4) medium- or large-scale land-development projects aimed at the expansion or intensification of (usually irrigated) agricultural land; and (5) gradual encroachment of the village arable lands into the surrounding wasteland and forests, by either individual or collective efforts on the part of the peasants.[48] These types are different in economic context, organizational scale, soil quality and productivity, the presence of infra-structure, and movement of the farming population. Several forms might coexist in the same area. For instance, the original colonizers of Urumqi were garrison soldiers and their children, private entrepreneurs, poor migrants relocated from Gansu, convict laborers, and Muslim auxiliaries, and all operated under different conditions.[49]

In the Ming and early Qing, government-sponsored land reclamation schemes had often been located on fertile land fallen into disuse because of a loss of population or flood disaster. At that time, ample natural resources were available to colonists. A quote from advice given about Fengyang county, north of the Yangzi River in Anhui (where much wasteland belonging to the military had been abandoned because of disputes over ownership and tenancy rights) may suffice to illustrate this early era of low population densities and extensive land use:

> I recommend growing trees and raising animals north of the Yangzi, where this is much more easily done than to its south. In Jiangnan, not an inch of soil is left unused, sheep are tended individually, and every pig has its own stye. Farmers feed their oxen and horses with rice gruel, hay, and beans. North of the Yangzi River, there are many forests and grass is abundant; the marshes have a variety of water plants, and one can leave horses and oxen free

[47] Cao Shuji 曹树基, "Ming-Qing shiqidi liumin he Ganbei shanqudi kaifa" 明清时期的流民和 赣北山区的开发 [Migrants of the Ming and Qing periods and the opening up of the mountain areas in north Jiangxi], *Zhongguo nongshi* 中国农史 2 (1986), pp. 12–37.

[48] Eduard B. Vermeer, "Ch'ing Government Concerns with the Exploitation of New Farm-land," in L. Vandermeersch, ed., *La société civile face à l'État* (Paris: EFEO, 1994), pp. 203–48.

[49] Wang Xilong 王希隆, "Qingdai Wulumuqi tuntian shulun" 清代乌鲁木齐屯田述论 [A discussion of colony fields in Urumqi during the Qing period], *Xinjiang shehui Kexue* 新疆 社会科学 5 (1989); Wang Xilong 王希隆, *Qingdai xibei tuntian yanjiu* 清代西北屯田研究 [Research on the colony fields in the Northwest in the Qing period] (Lanzhou: Lanzhou Daxue CBS, 1990).

without having to tend them in a stable. . . . In Jiangnan, land is very expensive . . . and people fight over the use of marshes. However, north of the Yangzi River, orchards have been abandoned and fields lie fallow, wasteland is overgrown with grasses . . . empty prairies as far as the eye can see. . . . I recommend that families with several people should reap the benefit from keeping chickens, pigs, oxen, and sheep. Apart from the reclaimed wasteland [for grain crops], each should plant a field with vegetables, fruits, cotton, and hemp. If there is spare wasteland, one might plant trees like pears, jujubes, mulberries and willows.[50]

In the Qing period, the usage rights (if not ownership) of forests, marshes, and wasteland in China proper ultimately rested with the state. Though state ownership had not been expressly stated, once people started to exploit land resources and disputes arose between various users, the government would allocate usage rights, begin levying taxes, and by implication establish its ownership. People could rent such lands against payment of a tax or fee.[51] One could also apply for a permit to open up and reclaim such land. However, in actual fact the rights to many forests and wasteland areas had been appropriated by local families. Projects to open up state-owned or privately owned forests or wasteland, or to reclaim farmland from river banks or lakes, often infringed on existing utilization rights of communities or individuals in the area. In the past as today, the project agency and entrepreneur might preempt potential conflicts by engaging local people as workers and giving them tenancy rights. Even so, local farmers often protested to the magistrate, and with success. Landowners might try to maintain exclusive riparian or water rights, but the government did not necessarily recognize such rights. "Native farmers should not be allowed to prevent colonists from using water from canals and streams. When irrigation ponds or dams are built, costs should be borne according to the acreage 'benefited,' and the colonist-reclaimers should not have to pay more."[52] Even if the ownership rights to wasteland were purchased from the state or private persons, its occupants, whether illegal or not, could not be easily removed. The magistrate might invoke the public or common interest, particularly when new projects threatened the supply of irrigation water.

---

[50] Zhu Gesheng 諸葛昇, "Kentian Shiyi" 墾田十議 [Ten proposals for reclamation of farmland], quoted by Xu Guangqi 徐光啟 in *Nongzheng quanshu* 農政全書, ch. 8.

[51] Huang Liuhong 黃六鴻, *Fuhui quanshu* 福惠全書 [The complete book on fortune and favor] (1684), tr. Djang Chu (Tucson, 1984).

[52] 1870 Rules for land reclamation in Yan 嚴 prefecture in Zhejiang, in Xi Yufu 席裕福 and Shen Shixu 沈師徐, eds., *Huangchao zhengdian leizuan* 皇朝政典類纂 (Shanghai, 1903), Tianfu 田賦 3, p. 14.

When (which was rather exceptional) existing uses of public forests were of considerable benefit to the local population, local officials were told to protect the interests of these users and not offer these forests for sale for conversion to arable. "All land now in use for tapping lacquer trees, chopping bamboos, gathering tree bark and tree fungi, etc., should not be designated as wasteland, and local officials should not force people to reclaim and cultivate it, nor should they tax it."[53] However, this quote is from a 1741 edict, which was directed at thinly populated southern Shaanxi. The main concern of government continued to be food grain production, and even more so after the great increase in population during the Qianlong reign. It is difficult to establish how much influence government policies toward land use and crop choice ever had. At least in the eighteenth and the first half of the nineteenth century, forest clearance and conversion to arable (land reclamation forms 3 and 5 mentioned above) were largely undertaken privately.

However, particularly during the post-Taiping reconstruction and again at the end of the Qing and during the Republic, the provincial governments' position changed. They became much more actively involved in land reclamation schemes, and therefore gave more support to actual developers and users of land, and less consideration to the claims, whether legally confirmed or not, of previous owners. Also, partly because of improvements in transport and trade and partly for personal gain, local officials began to support diversification, commercial crops, and capitalist land developers to whom they began to sell exclusive land rights.[54] The influence of foreign examples of plantation agriculture brought to China by Overseas Chinese was strongest in the South and Southeast. In 1901, two governors-general memorialized that tree planting should be stimulated in mountain areas, and coarse grains and grasses along the coast. People who purchased titles to state-owned wasteland should not be obliged to grow rice, but should also be allowed "to grow cotton, sugarcane or other crops, or have cattle ranges like those in Western countries and America."[55]

The ecological effects of greater capitalist exploitation of land resources were mixed. Generally, development projects led to a more intensive, but also more rational and productive land use. The investments made in irrigation, diking, or terracing usually increased the capacity of the land to retain water and fertilizer, and more intensive use of land and other re-

---

[53] Ibid., Tianfu 2, p. 2.

[54] Vermeer, "Exploitation of New Farmland."

[55] Memorial by Liu Kunyi 劉坤一 and Zhang Zhidong 張之洞, in *Huangchao zhengdian leizuan*, Tianfu 3, p. 20.

sources might relieve the pressure on resources elsewhere. The vulnerability of crops, livestock, and humans to floods and droughts might be reduced in the project area, but this was sometimes at the expense of other areas. While the immediate benefits may have been easy to spell out, the external costs were only considered in part, if at all. More often than not, the traditional system of land use was less exploitative of nature. However, its carrying capacity was low, and it could not maintain itself under conditions of population growth. Keeping this in mind, one should not condemn *a priori* the new organizations, such as land reclamation companies, for their ecological destructiveness, or for the more intensive and exploitative methods of land use introduced during the late Qing and Republic. More often than not, these land reclamation companies (labeled "feudal organizations in capitalist clothes" by Sun Jiashan)[56] purchased the type of land that individual households had not been able to develop in the past, because it required major improvements before agriculture could become rewarding. There were great advances in investment, organizational scale, techniques, and choice of crops over earlier periods.

8.6.4. ENCLOSURES AND PRESERVES

The Ming dynasty had declared many mountain and forest areas to be forbidden territory. The Qing government was less obsessed by control over the population, and after its defeat of the Southern Ming only a limited number of interior mountain areas and coastal areas remained "closed off" to human settlement for security reasons. Gradually, most such areas were eventually illegally settled in the eighteenth century, despite the interdiction. In almost all cases, such settlements were subsequently sanctioned by the government, and their status as closed-off areas was lifted. As a provincial governor noted:

> In this closed-off area [of Pucheng-Zongan] there are hardly any old trees left. Most mountain slopes have been reclaimed and are now cultivated, with maize and millet around the trunks of trees. . . . We have found that, in the past few years, floods in Jiangxi have driven the poor people into the mountains to make a temporary living; they have not been bandits or outlaws. In spite of the interdiction and guards, groups of people have felled trees and reclaimed farmland, going in and out secretly. Thus, this area was closed off in name only.[57]

---

[56] Sun Jiashan 孙家山, *Subei yanken shi chugao* 苏北盐垦史初稿 [A preliminary draft history of reclamation of salt fields in North Jiangsu] (Beijing: Nongye CBS, 1984), p. 116.

[57] 1835 Memorial by Governor-General of Fujian/Zhejiang Zheng Zuluo 程祖洛 et al., *Memorials of the reigns*, p. 345.

No doubt, the closure of such areas had a retarding effect on their exploitation. In most cases, farming was only a part of a much wider range of economic activities, which included salt production, timber felling, fishery, forestry, smuggling, and so forth. For instance, an 1823 survey showed that the closed area of the Nantian Peninsula had 6,400 illegal colonists, who had reclaimed 6,000 *mu.* Considering the lack of irrigation facilities, more than twice as much farmland would have been needed per capita for them to make a living from agriculture alone. The rice crop was harvested with the use of migrant labor.[58] One does not find any arguments of an ecological nature in the court's deliberations about maintaining their closed status.

The imperial hunting grounds were a special case. Here, court officials could not but be aware of the loss of wildlife because of destruction of the natural habitat.

> The Jilin hunting grounds were originally used for raising animals for the hunt. They were staked off with piles and signs, and access was strictly forbidden. Yet migrants secretly entered the area under the pretext of land reclamation, in order to poach game and fell trees. The animals became extinct or fled elsewhere. . . . The benefits which the land produced during several centuries of closure were finally squandered in this way, and nothing was left. In 1861, Jing Lun's 景綸 memorial said that there were still twenty-one hunting parks. Now they measure only 17 to 18 *li* by a little over 80 *li*, and are completely devoid of trees or wildlife. Everywhere one sees encroachment by migrants.[59]

A similar story might be told for the imperial Mulan hunting park established in Chengde, Hebei, in 1681. Encroachment by poachers, cattle thieves, and loggers started before 1800, and imperial hunting stopped around 1820. Four decades later, over 4,000 *qing* had already been converted into farmland. In 1905 its special status was lifted, and within a few decades, its forest cover was reduced to a mere 5 percent.[60]

8.6.5. THE ENVIRONMENTAL EFFECT OF FARMLAND TAX POLICIES

The Qing dynasty promoted land reclamation in several ways. First, positive incentives were given by granting several years' (during most of the Qing,

---

[58] Memorial by the Governor-General of Fujian/Zhejiang Zhao Shenzhen 趙慎畛 and the Governor of Zhejiang Shuai Chengying 帥承瀛, ibid., pp. 93–103.

[59] 1868 Edict, *Qingchao xuwenxian tongkao,* ch. 2, p. 7525.

[60] Nie Zhongxun 鈕仲勛 and Pu Hanxin 浦汉昕, "Qingdai shouliequ Mulan weichangdi xingshuai he ziran ziyuandi baohu yu pohuai" 清代狩猎区木兰围场的兴衰和自然资源的保护与破坏 [The rise and fall of the Mulan Park hunting grounds in the Qing period and the conservation and destruction of natural resources]. *Ziran ziyuan* 自然資源 1 (1983), pp. 51–57.

six or ten years') initial tax exemption for newly reclaimed farmland. In practice, this applied mainly to highly productive irrigated land. From 1740 onward, most newly reclaimed farm plots were exempt from taxes, if their soil or location were not very favorable or plot size was small. Second, sloping farmland used for crops other than grain was as a rule not taxed at all. Third, the Qing tax registers were not revised in a substantial way, but basically followed the acreages given in the late Ming *Fu yi quan shu* 賦役全書 [Complete book of taxation]. The effect of these policies was that the highest tax burdens continued to fall on the traditionally highly productive irrigated farmland in the plain areas.

These tax policies were detrimental to the environment in certain ways. They stimulated an uncontrolled squandering of land and forest resources through reclamation projects, a piecemeal, small-scale development of new farmland, and the exploitation of sloping, stony plots with a thin soil layer. The six- or ten-year tax-free period encouraged perverse economic behavior. Colonists abandoned their new plots after some years to avoid taxation; the same plot might be reclaimed again later. On the one hand, because farmland taxes (and often rents as well) had been fixed at a precise amount of grain or money, increases in output were not taxed. This stimulated a more intensive use of farmland and the planting of a second crop. Investments in the improvement of farmland that had previously been classified and taxed as low-output farmland were particularly rewarding. Farmland that had been improved through government-supported irrigation schemes would generally have its taxes increased, while privately financed improvements were reflected only in the rents. On the other hand, the fact that taxes continued to be levied on registered farmland that had become less productive (whether from natural or human causes) was a disincentive for a continued use of such land; its owners and tenants often tried to escape their obligations by fleeing their land and letting it go to waste. While this might at first be detrimental to conservation of water and soil, the vegetation cover and water-holding capacity might slowly improve again later.

8.7. INVESTMENT POLICIES IN LAND IMPROVEMENT, IRRIGATION, AND FLOOD CONTROL

Though hydrological engineers such as Pan Jixun and Chen Huang had recognized the causes for riverbeds, canals, and reservoirs silting up, remedial anti-erosion measures were beyond the scope of traditional government.[61] Xu Guangqi recognized both natural and man-made factors responsible for the floods in his day. Quoting Song and Ming authors, he particularly blamed the occupation of marshes, lakes, and river floodplains by local powerful families for short-term profit; reclamation of water bodies for agriculture increased the danger of floods and hurt the entire community.[62] There is a wealth of source materials about the various conflicts of interests between short-term profit and occasional flood damage, between irrigation and drainage of high- and low-lying fields and upstream and downstream areas, and between old and new polders. The government had an important function here as an equitable mediator and protector of long-term interests of flood control, irrigation, and shipping. A number of studies have concluded that the Qing government did not fulfill this function very well, but others such as Morita Akira and Mark Elvin are more positive.[63] Probably, the verdict should be different for different regions and spheres of activity. Of course, both national and local governments in China as elsewhere are inclined to yield to pressures for short-term profit or cheap solutions. The Chinese government did not acknowledge riparian rights or exclusive rights to water, and when addressing water-conservancy disputes officials were motivated by considerations of distributive justice rather than of ownership; thus, there often was no firm policy against encroachment on irrigation systems. In any case, when irrigation systems deteriorate slowly over time for reasons other than lack of maintenance, the government may not be able to do very much, given the limited traditional level of knowledge, technology, and scale of construction.

In semi-arid or arid regions and along the Chinese coast, land reclamation projects were completely dependent on the construction of irrigation canals. Historical sources usually mention how much farmland benefited from such projects, but rarely consider the loss of water to users in adjacent areas. For instance, all sources agree that the irrigation canals constructed in the early 1840s under Lin Zexu in what was later to be Xinjiang resulted

[61] E. B. Vermeer, "P'an Chi-hsün's Solutions for the Yellow River Problems of the late 16th Century," T'oung pao 70.3 (1987), pp. 33–67; Zhongguo gudai dilixue shi 中国古代地理学史 [A history of China's ancient geography], ed. by the Geography Group of the Institute for the History of Natural Sciences of the Chinese Academy of Sciences 中国科学院自然科学史研究所地学史组 (Beijing: Kexue CBS, 1984), p. 161.

[62] Nongzheng quanshu, vols. 12, 13, and 16.

[63] Peter C. Perdue, Exhausting the Earth: State and Peasant in Hunan, 1500–1850 (Cambridge, Mass.: Harvard University Press, 1987); R. Keith Schoppa, Xiang Lake: Nine Centuries of Chinese Life (New Haven: Yale University Press, 1989); E. B. Vermeer, "The Decline of Hsinghua Prefecture in the Early Ch'ing," in E. B. Vermeer, ed., Development and Decline of Fukien Province in the 17th and 18th Centuries (Leiden: Brill, 1990), pp. 101–62; Morita Akira 森田明, Shindai suirishi kenkyu 清代水利史研究 (Tokyo, 1974).

in a fuller exploitation for agricultural use of the water running down the Tian Shan mountains, which was channeled into well-organized irrigation districts. However, to a certain extent they also restricted the area of water use, to the detriment of existing agricultural and pastoral uses of the land. Along the coast, new polder projects had to take most if not all of their water from the same sources as existing paddies, and the latter suffered as a consequence.[64] In this type of case, the local magistrate acted as a mediator between different interests, and therefore local gazetteer sources describe both sides of the conflicts. In the previous case, the government (whether military or civil) was itself an interested party, and the Chinese sources are silent about whether there was a negative impact on non-Han parties. When forests in Chinese border and mountain areas had to be burned down in order to clear the land, immediate losses of resources were suffered.

A number of techniques for the improvement of saline-alkaline soils had been in use at least since the Han dynasty. In marshy and coastal areas, such as those near Tianjin, salts were flushed out by the improvement of drainage and the cultivation of paddy rice. Heavy irrigation was used to keep down salty underground water, and drainage ditches were built to remove salts. Along rivers, salinized or sandy land was flooded with silt-laden water to cover the infertile soil with a top layer of silt. Green fertilizers such as alfalfa were sown to improve soil structure and nitrogen content. Trees and grasses might be planted to reduce excess groundwater. The salty topsoil layer might be plowed under (or even scraped away) in order to bring less salinized soil to the surface.[65] Not all these techniques were effective in the long term, and some conflicted with other interests of flood control or shipping, or had very large labor requirements. Without any doubt, the most effective way to improve soil was to create paddy-fields. Within their tightly controlled environment, water, soil, and fertilizers were maximally conserved, and the fields were most productive. Of course, they depended on a reliable and controlled supply of irrigation water. Thus, water conservation and irrigation became the most important concerns of rural communities.

During the late Ming and Qing, several large-scale state projects were

---

[64] Lin Tingshui 林汀水, "Cong dixue guandian kan Putian pingyuandi weiken" 從地學觀點看 莆田平源的圍墾 [Reclamation of polders in the Putian plain as seen from a geological perspective], *Zhongguo shehui jingji shi yanjiu* 中國社會經濟史研究 1 (1983), pp. 49–58; Vermeer, "Decline of Hsinghua Prefecture," pp. 101–62.

[65] Min Zongdian 闵宗殿, "Woguo gudaidi zhili yanjiantu jishu" 我国古代的治理盐碱土技术 [Our country's ancient techniques of saline-alkaline soil treatment], *Nongshi Yanjiu* 农史研 究 8 (1989), pp. 104–12.

undertaken to drain marsh lands, such as the mostly state-owned ones near Tianjin, and to develop rice farming, with partial success. Memorials refer to opposition to such projects from the owners and users of wastelands and lakes, who exploited them for collecting reeds, fish, and fowl. Local government officials who had been the recipients of "wasteland use fees" or "reed taxes" often protected the existing users.[66] However, the official ideology held that food grain was of overriding importance. Provincial officials and the court maintained that grain production should dominate all other crops such as cotton or fruit, and *a fortiori* less intensive forms of land use. Expansion of grain production was held to be in the public interest.[67]

The impetus to implement projects of land reclamation or flood control was only partly due to a changed socioeconomic situation and the organizational power of the government. Usually, projects had simply become viable or even been dictated by natural or man-made changes elsewhere. For instance, though reclamation of parts of the Dongting Lake had already started during the early Ming, this project was greatly expanded in the late Ming and Qing.[68] This was due to a huge increase in water inflow and sedimentation from the Yangzi River, because the outlets along its left bank leading into the Jianghan plain had been virtually closed during the mid-sixteenth century, as a consequence of which the farmers along the lakeshores had to protect and dike their fields. Yang Xifu distinguished three types of polder: (1) government polders that had resulted from state-constructed dikes, built primarily for flood protection; (2) civilian polders, built by private initiative, that had been reported to and sanctioned by the authorities; and (3) unreported private polders, which were illegal. From the Qianlong period onward, the government tried to keep the second and third categories in check. However, because of the subsequent great increase (possibly a tripling) of sediment deposits in the lake, during the

---

[66] Huang Liuhong, *Fortune and favor*, vol. 8.

[67] For a good example of this attitude see the 1842 memorial by the Minister of Works Xu Shifen 徐士芬, *Memorials of the reigns*, p. 543; Gao Wangling 高王凌, "Kang-Yong-Qian shiqidi renkou zengzhang he nongye duice" 康雍乾时期的人口增长和农业对策 [Population increase and agricultural remedies during the Kangxi-Yongzheng and Qianlong periods], *Nongcun jingji shehui* 农村经济社会 2 (1985), pp. 357–76.

[68] Zhang Guoxiong 张国雄, "Qingdai Jianghan pingyuan shuihan zaihaidi bianhua yu yuantian shengchan di guanxi" 清代江汉平原水旱灾害的变化与垸田生产的关系 [The relation between changes in the flood and drought disasters and production of polder fields in the Jianghan Plain in the Qing period], *Zhongguo nongshi* 中国农史 3 (1990), pp. 91–102; Zhang Jianmin 张建民, "Qingdai Jianghan – Dongtinghu qu tiyuan nongtiande fazhan jiqi zonghe kaocha" 清代江汉 – 洞庭湖区堤垸农田的发展及其综合考查 [Development of diked polder fields in the Jianghan and Dongting lake areas during the Qing period and their comprehensive investigation], *Zhongguo nongshi* 中国农史 2 (1987), pp. 72–88.

second half of the nineteenth century most of the lake was reclaimed anyway; reportedly, there were more than a thousand polders totaling more than 5 million *mu*. Floods became much more serious and frequent as a consequence.[69] Along the Yangzi River and its tributaries in northern Anhui, in the Ming Wanli period several large polders, each of more than a thousand hectares, were created, and the same happened in Lujiang and Huaining counties in the nineteenth century. By the 1930s, this area also had some 5 million *mu* of polders.[70]

As a result of the constriction of riverbeds and the reduction of natural flood catchment areas, flood levels rose, and heights and standards of dike building had to be raised. A Ming (Jiajing reign-period) handbook pre-scribed that polders that were at par with the (low) water level should have dikes with a height of 8 feet and a top and bottom width of 8 and 14 feet, respectively. This contrasts with a height of 7.5 feet and a top width of 5 feet prescribed for such polders in the Song. Dikes should be one foot higher than the historical highest flood-water level.[71] How much protection a particular height offered could only be estimated; historical high-water levels had always been reduced by multiple dike breakthroughs over large areas. New, higher dikes diverted the flood problem to less well protected flood-prone areas. The city walls might offer protection for county capitals, but the countryside was left to its own devices. Although polders were built with drainage ditches for every few hectares, during the flood period waterlogging might easily occur because of the impossibility of draining water from the polder.

In their early stages, large polders had often been constructed to incor-porate some existing water bodies, which served both for interior drainage and as sources of water supply. Typically, these low-lying areas were subse-quently reclaimed, giving rise to a variety of problems and conflicts. For one, such reclamation was often illegal. Even if official authorization had been obtained, the prior agreement or consent of other landowners in the polder might not have been obtained. Second, irrigation water supply and drainage of the existing polder fields might be affected, causing an in-creased vulnerability to droughts and floods and a reduction of yields and the quality of soil. Third, the original organization, management, and cost-

---

[69] Wang Jialun 汪家伦 and Zhang Fang 张芳, *Zhongguo nongtian shuili shi* 中国农田水利史 [History of agricultural water conservation in China] (Beijing: Nongye CBS, 1990), pp. 380–82; (Daoguang) *Dongtinghu zhi* 洞庭湖志, ch. 4; Yang Xifu 楊錫紱, "Chakan tiyuan tiaoyi," (Qianlong) *Changshafu zhi* 查勘堤垸條議，長沙府志, ch. 22.

[70] Wang Jialun and Zhang Fang, *History of agricultural water conservation*, pp. 386–90.

[71] Ibid., pp. 390–92, quoting the late Ming *Songjiangfu zhi* 松江府志; Yao Wenhao's 姚文灝 "How to build polders" in the (Jiajing) *Jiangyinxian zhi* 江陰縣志; and Geng Ju's 耿橘 *Changshuxian shuili quanshu* 常熟縣水利全書.

sharing arrangements within the polder were upset. The building of such interior polders is a classic example of the externalization of costs, as the entire community has to carry the burden of the increased costs of flood protection and water control. Of course, the government gradually became aware of this, and took action. But it was hardly ever capable of stopping the long-term process of reclamation of lakes, marshes, and riverine land.

8.8. THE SPREAD OF NEW CROPS

Maize and tubers have been of tremendous importance in expanding and changing the agricultural and economic environment of the Chinese farmer. Their origins and spread in China are not very clear, partly because of the great variety of names adopted for them in different regions. As both crops were primarily suited to dry, sloping farmland, they did not command the attention of farmers and authorities in the existing high-yield irrigated areas. Some Chinese believe that maize was introduced by the Arabs and reached northwestern China first, through India and Tibet. In recent years, Cao Shuji has espoused this view, and maintains that Ho Ping-ti's and Chen Shuping's ideas that maize and potatoes both reached China by several different routes at different times are based on a misreading of Chinese terms in local gazetteers. For instance, Yunnan references in the late Ming to "pearl wheat" (yumai 玉麥) are to a wheat variety, not to maize.

Likewise the various early gazetteer names for tubers should not be interpreted as "sweet potatoes," but as "yams." If this is true, the route by which sweet potatoes first reached China was from the Philippines into Fujian and Guangdong, at the end of the sixteenth century. Local gazetteers do testify to their spread into almost all other Chinese provinces during the 1730s and 1740s.

Cao believes, moreover, that in most areas maize became a major crop much later than Chen has suggested. Having been promoted as a famine crop in the late Qianlong period, the sweet potato only thereafter spread further. By the early nineteenth century, however, a maize belt had taken shape, stretching across six provinces in central-west China, from Shaanxi to Guangxi, and in the southeast, there was a sweet potato belt. The two belts overlapped in Hu'nan. A lesser and later role should be attributed to these two crops in most areas of Sichuan and Yunnan. Both crops were spread mainly by migrant farmers, who brought their familiar staples to new reclamation areas. Because northern China had less land available for reclamation and less inmigration and population growth, the spread of maize in particular was much slower there. Thus, Ho Ping-ti may have exaggerated the mutually reinforcing effect of the revolution in food production because of the sweet potato and maize, on the one hand, and the population explosion during the Qing, on the other, at least with respect to northern China.[72] Because of a lack of quantitative data, scholars still hold rather different opinions about the size and importance of their contribution to the Chinese food supply in the course of the eighteenth and nineteenth centuries.

The population decline during the Ming–Qing transition may have been responsible for the belated spread of the sweet potato, which was seen as a crop to be cultivated on poor, unirrigated soils to stave off famine. Only when reclamation of virgin soils was resumed in the early eighteenth century did the crop once again command the attention of the gazetteer writers. Sweet potatoes were cultivated with success first in Taiwan (from whence at a later date the Irish potato also spread), in the hills of Shandong and Jiangsu, and on the sandy coastal soils of the Southeast. Maize gave high yields on the mountain and hill slopes of central China. The two crops created the conditions necessary not only for a large-scale expansion of the food-crop acreage, but also for considerably higher unit-yields. They barely competed with other food grains for water or land (except for low-yield food grains such as buckwheat, millet, and sorghum), and served as a stabilizing supplement. Moreover, because they could be cultivated almost anywhere, they greatly facilitated food supply to miners, loggers, tobacco and indigo growers, tea pickers, and other laborers in mountain and forest areas. Thus they were a main factor in the booming exploitation of mountain and forest resources in the mid- and late eighteenth century. As pig feed they contributed significantly to an increase of pork in the Chinese diet, and in turn the pig manure helped to raise soil fertility and yields of rice, wheat, and other main crops. A general improvement in the Chinese diet may have been one factor in the waning of epidemic diseases and the development of a population explosion in the eighteenth century. I should point out here that many Chinese historians have a less positive view: they see the rapid spread of maize and particularly that of sweet potatoes as evidence of the overpopu-

---

[72] Cao Shuji 曹树基, "Yumi he fanshu chuanru Zhongguo luxian xintan" 玉米和番薯传入中国路线新探 [A new probe into the routes of introduction of maize and potatoes into China], *Zhongguo shehui jingji shi* 中国社会经济史 4 (1988), pp. 62–66, 74; Cao Shuji, "Qingdai yumi, fanshu fenbudi dili tezheng" 清代玉米，番薯分布的地理特征 [Characteristics of the geographical spread of maize and potatoes during the Qing period], in Fudan Daxue Zhongguo Lishi Dili yanjiusuo 复旦大学中国历史地理研究所, ed., *Lidai dili yanjiu* 历代地理研究, vol. 2. (Shanghai: Fudan Daxue CBS, 1990), pp. 287–303; Chen Shuping 陈树平, "Yumi he fanshu zai Zhongguo chuanbo qingkuang yanjiu" 玉米和番薯在中国传播情况研究 [The situation of the spread of maize and potatoes in China], *Zhongguo shehui kexue* 中国社会科学 3 (1980), pp. 187–204.

lation of China at the end of the eighteenth century. According to Zhou Yuanhe, in spite of overpopulation there was no serious social disorder during the Jiaqing period (*sic* – he was forgetting the White Lotus uprising), "because it was postponed by the ameliorating effects of the wide-spread cultivation of high-yield crops. The Jiaqing foodgrain crisis was mitigated by the sweet potato."[73] This more negative view of the role of maize and the sweet potato seems to reflect the dominant cultural (and administrative) view of these food crops as inferior to rice and wheat.

8.9. POPULATION GROWTH, SETTLEMENTS, AND EXPANSION OF FARMLAND

The reasons for China's rapid population growth during the eighteenth century have not yet been sufficiently explained. The most common explanations are: the vigor of the new dynasty and a sustained period of peace and political stability under its three emperors; the spread of new, high-yielding crops such as maize and New World tubers, which could be cultivated on slopes and at higher altitudes; improvements of climatic conditions; and the rather sudden disappearance of epidemic diseases. One might add to this the increased mobility of the rural (and urban) population due to the relaxation of Ming controls, and territorial expansion and the increased income and employment derived from trade (including international trade). However, the demographic effects of each of the various factors have not yet been quantified. It is generally accepted that by 1800, China had become overpopulated and a period of stagnation or even decline had set in, but there is less agreement about subsequent demographic and economic developments.

At the same time, it is commonly agreed that the expansion of farmland during these centuries did not keep pace with population growth. Even if some of the increased population found alternative employment and sources of income, the ratio of farmland to population worsened. Some quantifications have been made for China as a whole or for specific regions, but most are based on rather shaky data. Contemporary reports about overpopulation and increasing land shortages do not mean very much; one might interpret such reports as healthy signs of an expanding economy (e.g., during the Yongzheng period). The perceptions of what constituted available farmland and reclaimable wasteland shifted over time, following,

---

[73] Zhou Yuanhe, "A Study of China's Population During the Qing Dynasty,' *Social Sciences In China* 3 (1982), p. 95.

among other things, changes in available crops, agricultural technologies, prices for agricultural products, and availability of labor.

The concern about population pressure on limited resources was put forward most strongly in a Malthusian way by Hong Liangji 洪亮吉 at the end of the eighteenth century. As he saw it, under conditions of peaceful government, population about doubled every generation, but

> Heaven and earth can only supply so much . . . and those who plan for the welfare of the people can only do so much. . . . One adjustment is by nature: floods and droughts and pestilences, but only 10 or 20 percent of the people die from these. The other is by government. It should make sure that no land is waste, no labor is unused. When new land is opened up in border areas, one should move farmers there and settle them. When taxes are oppressive, one should consider their present and past (amount) and reduce them. . . . In case of flood and drought disaster, one should open relief granaries, and all prefectural treasuries should provide relief funds.

However, he noted that farmland and housing were in short supply. Food-grain prices were bound to soar. There was widespread unemployment. Thus he was worried that overpopulation would result in uprisings.[74] Such ideas could also be found among court officials. In 1773 a court edict stated that apart from Urumqi, China had run out of land suitable for reclamation, and provincial governors should drop the subject.[75] Above, I mentioned the general pardon given by the court to the illegal Han Chinese settlers in Mongolia, many of whom had fled famines such as the one in Zhili in 1792. This famine had deeply impressed the court, which issued an edict saying that "one should not stop refugees going to Mongolia in search of a living;" the court later announced that due to more than a century of peace, the population of the empire had increased more than tenfold (*sic*), creating problems of subsistence. "Luckily, since we came to power, land has been developed and border regions opened up; . . . the common people may reclaim land in the border regions, and use it for maintaining their livelihood."[76] The perceived link between population increase, high grain prices, and the vagrancy of the landless in the mid- and late Qianlong period may be demonstrated from a variety of national and local sources.[77]

---

[74] *Hong Beijiang shiwenji* 洪北江詩文集, vol. 1, *Yiyan: Zhipingpian, Shengjipian* 意言：治平篇，生計篇, pp. 8–11.

[75] *Qing Gaozong shilu* 清高宗實錄, vol. 998 (1773), 12th month *wuzi* 戊子.

[76] *Qing Gaozong shilu* 清高宗實錄, vol. 1408, 7th month *xinsi* 辛巳, p. 6, and vol. 1441, 11th month *wuwu* 戊午, p. 15.

[77] Guo Songyi 郭松义, "Qingdaidi renkou zengzhang he renkou liuqian" 清代的人口增长和人口流迁 [Population increase and migration during the Qing period], *Qingshi luncong* 清史论丛 5 (1985), pp. 113–38.

However, they usually consider only the push factors, and not the pull from economic opportunities in the new areas.

There is an obvious link between a worsening land/population ratio, higher agricultural prices, the exploitation of hilly and poor farmland, and soil degradation. Yet none of these links is straightforward. For one thing, national aggregates of population and farmland are almost meaningless. Once disentangled and subjected to a closer scrutiny, regional and local factors are difficult to establish because of defective local historical data; thus, often, no firm conclusions can be drawn. Yet many historians have concluded that the nineteenth century was a period of environmental deterioration, caused by overpopulation and overexpansion of farmland in the preceding century.

Let me give one example. According to the official registers, farmland in Sichuan province increased from 46 million *mu* in 1766 and 1783 to 78 million *mu* in 1812. The population may have increased from about 9 million to 21 million between 1783 and 1812, and risen to 38 million by 1840. On the basis of this and Luo Erkang's (somewhat high) estimate that during the Qing, in southern China 4 *mu* of farmland per capita was a minimum for survival, recent authors have calculated that in Sichuan the average farmland per capita, which dropped from 4.9 *mu* in 1783 to 3.76 *mu* in 1812 and to about 2 *mu* in 1840, was much below the subsistence line. At the same time, the continuous and rapid expansion of farmland reclamation "made clear that large-scale land reclamation of slopes had begun, which had surpassed the limits of maintaining a good agro-ecological environment." By the mid-Qianlong period, all potential low-land farmland in the Sichuan basin had been reclaimed, and subsequent expansion had to be in the mountain areas.[78] The general conclusions of these scholars may be correct (migration *from* Sichuan into southern Shaanxi after 1800 also suggests a relative overpopulation of Sichuan in that period), but all their figures about population and farmland are dubious. Skinner has expressed his confidence in the 1812 census figures recorded in the *Jiaqing huidian* 嘉慶會典, ch. 11, and referred to above, but Li Shiping believes them (and later Qing figures) to be inflated.[79] This

---

[78] Lan Yong 蓝勇, "Qian-Jia kenzhi dui Sichuan nongye shengtai he shehui fazhan yingxiang chutan" 乾嘉垦殖对四川农业生态和社会发展影响初探 [Preliminary investigation of the influence of land reclamation and colonization during Qianlong and Jiaqing on Sichuan's agricultural ecology and social development], *Zhongguo nongshi* 中国农史 12.1 (1993), pp. 19–28; Meng Mo 蒙默 et al., *Sichuan Gudai Shigao* 四川古代史稿 [Draft ancient history of Sichuan] (Chengdu: Sichuan Renmin CBS, 1989), pp. 444–55.

[79] Li Shiping 李世平, *Sichuan Renkou Shi* 四川人口史 [A demographic history of Sichuan] (Chengdu: Sichuan Daxue CBS, 1987), pp. 167–85.

census gave Sichuan 6 percent of China's total population of 362 million, as against 9.3 percent in 1840 and about 10 percent during this century; this seems to contradict the idea of overpopulation of Sichuan by 1800. The dramatic drop in farmland per capita also seems difficult to reconcile with expansion into hilly and less productive mountainous farmland. Because of lower unit-yields in such areas, one should expect an increase instead of a decrease of farmland per capita. The best effort so far to reconcile Sichuan's population, farmland, and food-grain data is that of Wang Di. His conclusion that by the end of the Qing, Sichuan's annual per capita food-grain output fell short of the minimum requirement (defined as 300 kilograms, for food, clothing, housing, and other living needs) by 26 to 29 percent, and that this was the fundamental cause of the societal disorder, depends critically on his assumption of 600 *jin* (revised downward from 365 kilograms) as a minimum requirement.[80] "Overpopulation" is a relative concept. One might conclude that at the end of the Qianlong period Sichuan was perceived as being overpopulated because its previous relative abundance of farmland was rapidly dwindling, but that it still had an advantage over most other areas in China until the 1840s.

While felling original forest is an obvious form of environmental destruction, not all land reclamation and conversion to arable is. Earlier slash-and-burn types of agriculture were sustainable only as long as population numbers were very low. Most went unnoticed by government, and Chinese sources tell us little or nothing. There was a clear correlation between the intensity of use, productivity, and official registration. This correlation was much stronger in relation to irrigated rice than to other crops. More intensive use of slopes, particularly in the form of rice paddies, was registered much more accurately. Farming in paddies, though more intensive, does not necessarily cause more erosion than dry farming, as terraced fields conserve water, soil, and fertilizer much better than extensively cultivated sloping lands sown to maize, wheat, millets, or tubers. Dry cultivation of maize and tubers on steep slopes was most damaging, because it left the soil bare for much of the year. The mountain soil might be eroded and become unusable within a few decades, and downstream areas were also affected. Tea bushes and other commercial crops could hold the soil together for considerably longer. In many areas of China the exhaustion and erosion of mountain soils have resulted in unusable thin soils with a secondary vegetation cover that offers inadequate protection against further erosion. The

[80] Wang Di 王笛, "Qingdai Sichuan renkou, gengdi ji liangshi wenti" 清代四川人口，耕地及粮食问题 [Problems of population, farmland, and food grain in Sichuan during the Qing period], *Sichuan Daxue xuebao* 四川大学学报 3 (1989), pp. 90–105, and 4 (1989), pp. 73–87.

construction of polders along the coast and lake shores produced much new land suitable for sustaining high-yield agriculture, and drainage and amelioration of saline soils contributed to a new man-made agriculturally productive environment. This serves as a reminder that although some forms of land reclamation during the Qing were environmentally destructive, forms of land usage could differ greatly in their effects.

8.10. RECOGNITION OF ENVIRONMENTAL DETERIORATION BY THE CHINESE BUREAUCRACY AND LITERATI

As early as in the Southern Song, the erosion problems following irrigation projects were attributed to the destruction of the forest cover upstream. The Tuoshan Ditch is an often-cited example.[81] In the Ming period, there are some isolated examples of concern about deterioration of farm soil. For instance, a 1622 memorial about Gansu says: "the people lead a bitter life, without provision for their food. Their only recourse is to reclaim the hills and open up the forbidding cliffs for farmland. Alas! The Eastern Hills cannot withstand the flow of water, and their thin soils cannot be irrigated. As soon as the rain pours down, there are disastrous floods, the soil is swept away and rocks appear."[82] However, it was only around 1800 that the erosion problems became so serious and widespread that high officials began to pay attention to them. They noted the correlation between forest destruction, erosion and increased flood problems, and loss of soil quality. In Anhui:

> When Dong Wenke was governor of Anhui [1807–11], he wrote a memorial about the granting of permission for shack people to open up the mountains. Its gist was that... "Wasteland cannot be made profitable, yet the shack people are capable of attacking it. They can put up with the jungle and steepness of the mountains, and open up remote places for cultivating dry grains, as a supplement to rice and millet. Nobody is idle, and all soils are fully used. Since this is so advantageous from the point of view of policy, one cannot stop them, because it would give cause to trouble." When I saw these words I thought they were quite correct.

---

[81] Wei Xian 魏峴, *Siming Tuoshan shuili beilan* 四明陀山水利備覽 [An overview of water control relating to the Tuoshan in Siming (Ningbo)] ch. 1, pp. 6–7, 10, in *Siming congshu* 四明叢書 (Taipei, 1966), vol. 3, pp. 95–128.

[82] Gao Tui 高推, Memorial about the difficulty of paying new grain taxes, *Yuxuan mingchen zouyi* 御選明臣奏議 [Memorials and proposals by Ming officials selected by the emperor] (1781. Reprinted, Taipei, 1968), ch. 36, p. 24.

When I came to Xuancheng, I asked the villagers, and they said: "When the mountains had not yet been opened up, the soil was firm and stones were fixed. There was a thick growth of grasses and trees, and the rotten leaves accumulated for several years, forming layers of two or three inches. When it rained, the drops fell from the trees onto the leaves, and from the leaves to the soil. . . . The runoff was gentle, and the water did not take soil with it. Because the runoff was gentle, it did not create disaster in the 'receiving' fields below. Even after two weeks without rain the upper paddy-fields were still able to receive their irrigation water. However, at present axes have laid the mountains bare, and plows have loosened the soil, so as soon as it rains, sand and stones are swept down into the streams. They are filled up with dirt and water cannot be stored any more. Moreover, as soon as the rain is over, the water flows down to the lower paddies and stops there. Once the lower paddies have dried up, there is no followup of water from the mountain paddies."

This is a case of opening up sterile soil while ruining productive rice paddies at the same time. It benefits the hired laborers, who do not pay tax, at the expense of tax-paying families. I had already heard it said, and found it to be true. Alas! Profits and losses are never totally one way or the other.[83]

And in the Hanzhong area in southern Shaanxi:

Along the Wulongjiang and Xushui rivers people have the practice of building weirs and canals for the irrigation of their paddies. However, the old forests have now been cleared for several decades, and the mountain soil has been upturned and become loose. Every summer and autumn, the torrents rage violently, carrying sand and stones with them, and the riverbeds fill up and gradually rise. Sand and gravel are swept into the irrigation ditches, dikes and canals are eroded and the water intakes of the irrigation canals are clogged. . . . People suffer greatly because of this![84]

Yan Ruyi also described how, four to five years after the felling of forests and reclaiming of land, "the soil gets loose and is swept away by the monsoon rains, and only stones remain."[85] Lu Kun reported erosion in the Qinling mountains as follows:

In the past few decades, migrants have moved in from Sichuan and Guangdong. They rent mountains and open up the land, sow maize, and fell trees and shrubs. They burn timber and make charcoal. . . . Now, serious erosion has occurred in places near the mountains and the Wei river; and farmland has been flooded as a result.[86]

[83] Mei Zengliang 梅曾亮, *Baijian shanfang wenji* 柏梘山房文集 [Collection of writings from the Baijian mountain lodge] (1823, 1856. Reprinted, Taipei: Huawen Shuju, n.d.), ch. 10, pp. 5–6: "Ji Pengmin Shi" 記棚民事 [Record of the shack people affair].
[84] Yan Ruyi, *Sansheng bianfang Beilan*, ch. 8, p. 3.
[85] *Hanzhongfu Zhi* 漢中府志, ch. 21, p. 6.
[86] Lu Kun 盧坤, *Qinjiang zhilüe* 秦疆治略, *Huazhou* 華州.

The Jiangsu governor Tao Shu, in a 1832 memorial, recommended confis-
cating illegally occupied riverine silt flats and handing them over to tax-
paying tenants to cultivate; he pointed out that new silt deposits and islets
were blocking the waterways and causing floods in the lower Yangzi basin.
The fundamental reason for this was that in the upper and middle basin of
the river,

> too much land has been opened up, the jobless migrants fell mountain forests
> everywhere in order to cultivate miscellaneous grains. With heavy rains, the
> soil and stones are carried down with the flow, and when they settle, the
> sediment deposits rise above the water. It is difficult to stop poor people who
> try to make their living this way, but as the opening up for agriculture
> increases, landslides and obstructions get worse, and once the sediment has
> formed islets, it is even harder to remove. Considering that the construction
> of one canal or one dam already costs tens of thousands of taels, how much
> more would treatment of the entire Yangzi River cost?[87]

Nevertheless, although the loss of timber resources, increased siltation of
irrigation systems, and vulnerability to floods were occasionally deplored,
there is no doubt that the creation of farmland and particularly rice paddies was considered to be of overriding importance. Feeding the people
continued to be a priority, in spite of occasional concerns about ecological
deterioration. Thus, Tao Shu's recommendations all aimed at improving
state control over and intensifying the agricultural use of these new lands,
but did not take account of the destruction of the natural vegetation
upstream.

As for Yan Ruyi, around 1810 he had hailed the clearance of the original
forests of southern Shaanxi in unambiguous terms:

> Now that the forests have been cleared and the reclaimed land cultivated, all
> has become fertile soil . . . which can feed countless human beings. It is
> estimated that all old forests will have been reclaimed in twenty years, the land
> will then have harvests every year, and this is the benefit of a century! As soon
> as the old forests have been reclaimed, the true face of the mountain will
> appear. No longer will the bush create danger and bandits be able to hide.
> Thus, benefits will come and evils be removed automatically.[88]

In the early nineteenth century, provincial officials began making recommendations that any further reclamation and cultivation in the hills of

---

[87] *Tao Wenyi gong quanji* 陶文毅公全集 [Complete works of Tao Wenyi (= Tao Shu)], vol. 10,
p. 15. (Taipei reprint of 1840 edition, *Jindai Zhongguo shiliao congkan* 近代中國史料叢刊 29,
p. 281.)

[88] Yan Ruyi 嚴如熤, *Sansheng shannei fengtu zazhi* 三省山內風土雜誌 [Miscellanea on the
customs in the mountains of Three Provinces), p. 28.

southern and eastern China should be forbidden, in order to reduce the damage from water and soil erosion. These recommendations were specifically directed at the uncontrollable "shack people" (*pengmin* 棚民), and motivated by sociopolitical reasons (a generally hardening attitude toward migrants and vagrants) as well as by concerns about siltation and the flooding of high-yield farmland in the lower reaches of many rivers. In 1802, a Zhejiang governor issued rules forbidding any further contracts with shack people for land reclamation; their number (he said) should be reduced step by step. Local residents were forbidden to grow maize. He urged landlords to try to break their contracts and refund their money, and to order their tenants to switch to indigo, sweet potatoes, or tea. His major concern, according to Anne Osborne, was to forestall environmental destruction.[89] In 1815, the court agreed that all shack people who had lived in Zhejiang, for more than twenty years, owned farmland, and had their homes and wives there, should be registered as residents. Others in the same position, who had not been there so long, might apply in due time. Those without such ties were allowed to stay only till their lease had expired, or, if it had no specified expiry date, within five years (three years longer than the original time limit proposed by Yang Maotian in 1807).[90] However, they might then be registered as hired laborers. "Nobody is allowed to continue the cultivation of maize." Local people who recruited shack people to reclaim common (*gonggong* 公共) mountain land without having obtained prior permission from their co-owners (*heye zhi ren* 合業之人) would be punished according to the rules for stealing and selling ancestral property, and so would the tenants, according to the rules on appropriation of public or private mountain land.[91] Provincial officials soon began to ask for stricter measures (e.g., in Zhejiang, Wang Yuanfang 汪元方 requested that shack people be stopped from "opening up the mountains and obstructing watercourses in order to prevent later disasters").[92] There is no indication that local government regulations were effective in this respect. However, they did create a legal framework and social justification for growing opposition to outsiders and migrants, and a strengthening of village and clan ties, such as those seen in the conflicts between the Punti and the Hakka. This gave a larger degree of organized control over local natural resources, both for conservation and for exploitation. It also increased the financial resources available for projects of water control,

---

[89] Anne Osborne, *Barren Mountains, Raging Rivers*, Ph.D. diss., Columbia University, p. 251.
[90] (1827) *Huizhou fuzhi* 徽州府志, ch. 4b, p. 38.
[91] (1899) *Da Qing Huidian Shili* 大清會典事例, ch. 158, *hukou, liuyu yidi* 戶口，留餘義地.
[92] *Memorials of the reigns*, p. 903.

improvement of farmland, road building, cutting and transporting timber, and so on.

Half a century later, the geographical historian Wang Shiduo 汪士鐸 noted in his diary what the damaging effects of China's huge population had been:

> Mountain tops have been brought under cultivation with grains. In the [Yangzi] River, people have constructed islets of paddies. In Sichuan, the original forests have been cleared. In the Miao regions, the dense bamboo forests have been cleared. Nevertheless, there is not enough food and nature's strength, *tiandi zhi li* 天地之力, has been exhausted. . . . In spite of the most careful methods of cultivation . . . there is still not enough. The power of human doings has ended. . . . Division of property has made people poor. . . . People are told to return to farming, but there are no more fields to cultivate, and to return to trades, but there aren't any that need people. Everybody says that with so many people, one cannot increase prosperity. One *mu* can only have one farmer, and one home only a few people. Now how can one wish to live off one *mu* with a hundred farmers and to live in one home with a thousand people? All people want children and grandchildren . . . but where can they find a living? . . . The population doubles every thirty years, so one person at the beginning of the Qing has multiplied to 128 persons by now. In Huizhou . . . people marry at sixteen years of age, and thus its population doubles every twenty years![93]

8.11. INCREASED VULNERABILITY OF SETTLEMENTS IN THE MOUNTAINS, MARSHES, AND FLOODPLAINS

It is quite common for Chinese historians to cite the increasing number and severity of floods and droughts recorded in Ming and Qing sources as proof of the negative influence of human action on the environment. Simply put, forest felling and agricultural land reclamation increased run-off, erosion, and siltation, and reduced the holding capacity of natural water bodies, leading to an increase in natural calamities. This idea is only partly valid. There were at least three other additional factors at work. One is methodological; sources for the late Ming and Qing are considerably more abundant than those for earlier periods, thus providing greater coverage of floods and droughts than was the case in previous dynasties.

---

[93] *Wang Huiweng yibing riji* 汪悔翁乙丙日記 [Wang Huiweng's diary of 1855–56], ed. Deng Zhicheng 鄧之誠, vol. 3, pp. 26–28, reprinted in *Jindai Zhongguo shiliao congkan* 近代中國史料叢刊 126.

Second, the concept of calamity usually referred to extraordinarily large losses of food crops, followed by famine. In less intensive systems of food cropping (particularly with dry farming), large annual fluctuations were accepted as normal. However, intensified cultivation of high-yielding crops was more dependent on ideal conditions of weather and irrigation; thus, they were perceived to be more vulnerable to flood or drought. The population increase since the eighteenth century may have increased the danger of famine, but improvements in communications and trade at the same time helped to reduce it. Thus, during the Qing period it was not only changes in food crops that redefined the "natural calamities," but also economic changes and changed expectations. Third, it goes without saying that the growth of population, the number of human settlements, and the area of farmland increased the damage done by floods or droughts in terms of the numbers and areas affected. Most important of all, most of the expansion of human settlements took place in dangerous environments: mountain gullies, semi-arid areas with marginal rainfall, riverbanks and floodplains, polders inadequately protected by dikes, urban centers next to rivers, and so forth. For instance, in the nineteenth and twentieth centuries the higher flood levels and increased number of calamities in the Dongting Lake area were the result of the mutually reinforcing processes of land reclamation and siltation: the natural water bodies became smaller and smaller, and their beds higher and higher. The raising of dikes offered some degree of protection to some areas, but shifted the flood danger to other areas, particularly to the old polders, which had by then become low-lying.[94] The increasing incidents of "natural calamities" referred to in our sources were products of human settlement in unsafe locations just as much as of natural changes in the environment.

8.12. CONCLUSION

In the absence of archaeological and farm-level data, conclusions about population, settlements, and land use in the various regions of China can only be tentative.

During the Qing period, the frontier of forest exploitation, human

---

[94] Zhang Xiugui 张修桂, "Dongtinghu yanbiandi lishi guocheng" 洞庭湖演变的历史过程 [The historical process of change of the Dongting Lake], *Lishi dili* 历史地理 1 (1981), pp. 99–116; Bian Hongxiang 卞鸿翔 and Gong Xunli 龚循礼, "Dongtinghu qu weiken wentidi chubu yanjiu" 洞庭湖区围垦问题的初步研究 [Preliminary research on the problem of land reclamation in the Dongting Lake area], *Dili xuebao* 地理学报 40.2 (1985), pp. 131–41.

settlement, and agricultural land reclamation moved across China proper slowly at first, but more rapidly during the eighteenth and early nineteenth century, when shortages of timber and farmland became more acute. The main accelerating factors were the increasing demand for timber and fuel, food-grain shortages, and the expansion of the cultivation of commercial crops. Although all three were stimulated by China's population growth as such, there were considerable local variations. Until after the mid-nineteenth century, the remarkably effective government limitation of access to non-Han areas set entirely different socioeconomic conditions of exploitation for a very large part of the Qing territory. By the end of the Qing period, the environmental impact of state-supported inmigration into the Northeast, "filling the frontiers," was still quite limited. The minority areas in southwestern China, where soils were more vulnerable and timber resources had been exploited for a longer time, suffered more serious degradation. On the positive side, Chinese colonists in or near minority areas brought new and more intensive farming techniques and crops, and invested heavily in irrigation, terracing, transport, and other infrastructural improvements.

Deforestation was primarily the result of the increasing demand for timber and fuel. The shortage of quality timber and fuel became more serious during the Qianlong period, and after 1800, some high-ranked officials began to express their concern about the erosion problems caused by deforestation. This marked the end of a long-drawn process of unchecked expansion and destruction of the original mountain forests in China proper. In the nineteenth and twentieth centuries, the opening up of secondary forests (usually with poor stands of trees) was "pushed" by the need for farmland that could be sown with maize or sweet potatoes, rather than "pulled" by a demand for timber, tea, or tobacco, as had been the case in the eighteenth century. The more explicit references of nineteenth-century sources to environmental destruction do not necessarily imply a higher level of destructive activities; rather, they demonstrate the increasing scarcity of forest resources and good farm soils. The new human settlements and high-yield crops were also particularly vulnerable to "natural" calamities in the form of floods and droughts (and the worsening nineteenth-century climate also played a role).

Qing tax policies favored both land reclamation and the more intensive use of existing farmland. The legal protection enjoyed by original, extensive users of land (whether communal or private) was rather weak. Mongol herdsmen, Yao foresters, Han Chinese reed cutters, varnish tappers, and charcoal burners were pressed to give way to intensive grain cultivation. The increasing shortage of timber and some other forest products and rising prises should have led to a greater official recognition of the need to protect forest resources and their use, but no such signs can be found. Probably the administrative concern for and involvement in the supply of food grain, and the traditional bias against forests and their unruly inhabitants and exploiters, stood in the way of such a change in official attitude. At the end of the Qing period, under the influence of Western ideas and overseas Chinese investors, the government gave greater legal protection to the interests of land reclamation companies and other investors in land development, which worked against the claims of previous users. The environmental effects of large-scale capitalist exploitation of resources were different from earlier uses, which had been more local, unsystematic, gradual, and less intensive, but not necessarily less destructive in the long run. Ultimately, once the restrictions on migration had been lifted, economic factors such as improvements in transportation and population growth had a decisive impact on the relative exhaustion of natural resources and the pace of environmental change in the various regions of China.

Water

9

Clear Waters
versus Muddy Waters

THE ZHENG-BAI IRRIGATION
SYSTEM OF SHAANXI
PROVINCE IN THE LATE-
IMPERIAL PERIOD

PIERRE-ÉTIENNE WILL

Instability and change seem to be among the main characteristics of Wei 渭 River valley hydrology. The chapters devoted to waterways and irrigation in the local gazetteers abound in lengthy descriptions of canals and irrigation devices ending with words like "all the above canals have disappeared" – and quite often, have been gone for centuries.[1] As in most alluvial basins in China, this style of presentation does not simply result from the peculiarities of gazetteer writing; it reflects the problems raised by a specific environment. What we have is a landscape whose larger structure and main features in terms of water availability and distribution, determined as they were by the relief, the geology, and the climate, can only have changed very gradually in the *longue durée*, but within which smaller systems of irrigation were repeatedly being set up and then left to decay.

How and why this apparently unavoidable process of decay took place, and, more especially, in which terms it was understood and dealt with by

---

Abbreviations commonly used in notes to this chapter: JQTS *Jingqu tushuo* 涇渠圖説, JQZ 涇渠志, JYXZ 涇陽縣志, JYXA/JQZ the 涇渠志 contained in the JYXZ (not the same as the preceding JQZ), and XAFZ 西安府志. See footnote 8 for bibliographical details. Memorials are dated in the order: reign-period/year/lunar month/day.

[1] As an example among many others: *Xi'an fuzhi* 西安府志 [Gazetteer of Xi'an prefecture, hereafter *XAFZ*] (1779), *j.* 6, p. 3a. I wish to thank Mr. Huo Datong 霍大同, my research assistant during the year 1992–93, who ably located gazetteer and *Veritable Records* evidence for me. I must also thank Mark Elvin, Christian Lamouroux, and Charles Le Blanc, who directed my attention to several valuable secondary studies of Guanzhong hydrology and irrigation. Helen Dunstan's discussion at the Hong Kong conference as well as Mark Elvin's remarks on the first version of this essay have been both a challenge and an inspiration.

the people experiencing it in the field, is what I shall try to discuss in this essay: I see it as a problem of environment in the larger sense of the term, referring not only to natural factors and phenomena, but also to their mutual interaction with economic activity and social organization – in this respect, "ecology" might perhaps be a more appropriate term.

In the Wei valley, what I have called the larger hydrological structure included, potentially at least, and since the middle of the third century B.C., an artificial waterway that branched off the Jing 涇 River – the main tributary of the Wei – on the territory of Jingyang 涇陽 county. This waterway ran in a course north of the Jing and then of the Wei River, and helped feed the smaller irrigation systems of the plain in between, before flowing into the Wei or certain of its tributaries farther east (which ones depended on the period). This was the famed Zheng Guo Canal 鄭國渠, completed in 246 B.C., and its later variants down to the present day. The Zheng Guo and its successors formed the backbone of the more important irrigation enhancement programs designed under the successive dynasties in the Guanzhong 關中 plain. What follows is devoted to these programs.[2]

My remarks will be concentrated on the Qing dynasty, more particularly the eighteenth century, both because sources dealing with the perception of the "environmental" aspects that interest us are more substantial at that time, and for internal reasons. As we shall see, over the centuries the technical prowess that was responsible for the original Zheng Guo Canal became more and more difficult and costly to maintain, while at the same time it yielded ever-smaller returns. If the infrastructure appears already to have fitted less and less easily in its environment even from an early date, clearly the problems that it raised had come to a head by the beginning of the Qing dynasty. As a result, and in spite of their claims to revive the achievements of prestigious ancient dynasties, the Qing authorities were eventually compelled to adopt a new, much less ambitious approach: in effect, what was at that time known as the Longdong Canal 龍洞渠 ceased to be a diversion canal feeding on a natural stream and became instead a comparatively modest infrastructure fed by mountain springs and irrigating a reduced area of land.

---

[2] There were a few other sizable irrigation systems in the northern half of the Wei valley (feeding on the Wei itself or on some of its tributaries like the Qian 汧 and the Luo 洛). Only small-scale irrigation was possible on the right bank of the Wei, however. For a rapid overview see Huang Shengzhang 黃盛璋, "Guanzhong nongtian shuili de lishi fazhan ji qi chengjiu" 关中农田水利的历史发展及其成就 [The historical development of water control for agriculture in Guanzhong, and its achievements], in his *Lishi dili lunji* 历史地理论集 [Studies in historical geography] (Beijing: Renmin CBS, 1982), pp. 111–46 (here p. 113).

However, even though Qing-period developments and debates are our main concern here, an overview of the history of what is often called the Zheng-Bai 鄭白 irrigation system – from the names of its two earliest creators – appears necessary: not only was the system as it existed during the Qing the product of a continuous two-thousand-year evolution, but in late-imperial discussions constant reference was made to earlier problems, earlier approaches, and earlier figures. Before embarking on such an overview, however, a word must be said of the main relevant geographic features of the area in which the system operated.[3]

Roughly, the terraces forming the northern half of the Wei valley *graben* consist of comparatively recent river deposits covered with loess; due to the subarid climate of the region, the largely alkaline surface can only be made fertile through irrigation. One difficulty in doing this is morphological: the Wei River and its tributaries are cutting their course deep into the alluvial layers (what some texts describe as "the rivers are deep and the soil is thick"), making it impossible simply to open their banks and divert water into irrigation channels. Hence the technique, used with the Zheng-Bai and a few other canals in the region, of tapping the river flow at a higher place, near the fault marking the limit between the alluvial plain and the rocky ranges (like those traversed by the Jing River) or loess plateau overlooking it to the north. In the case that interests us, however, several other problems are in evidence in historical sources from a fairly early date.

One is the scouring of the Jing riverbed in the ancient (Pleistocene) alluvial cone at the exit of the rocky gorge and, lower, in the more recent deposits of the valley proper, which gradually lowered the water level until the flow could no longer be brought into the canal intake – hence the necessity of opening new intakes upriver in ever harder and more difficult terrain.[4] Scouring occurs especially during the periods of summer spate – corresponding to the precipitation maxima in the continental monsoon regime – when the Jing discharge and velocity are liable to increase severalfold. Another problem is the extremely high silt content of the Jing River, whose higher course flows through an area of the northern Shaanxi loess plateau that is among the thickest and most severely eroded found anywhere.[5] This content can reach up to 50 percent at the time of the July

---

[3] My colleague Pierre Gentelle's help has been crucial in putting together the excessively schematic paragraph that follows.

[4] Pending a detailed field investigation, it would seem that the Song and post-Song intakes (see below) were opened in the conglomerate of sand and stones forming the ancient cone and in the hard rock of the gorge higher up.

[5] See, for an illustration, the map of soil erosion on the loess plateau in the middle Yellow River course in Chen Yongzong 陈永宗, "Huangtu gaoyuan goudao liuyu chansha guocheng de chubu fenxi" 黄土高原沟道流域产沙过程的初步分析 [A preliminary analysis of the

and August peaks, which account for the larger part of the siltation, followed by the fall months.[6] We shall see in due time that, while the alluvium brought along by the Jing was celebrated for its fertilizing power in the very first accounts of the canal, during the late-imperial period it was basically considered to be a problem insofar as it tended to clog the system without bringing any benefit to the fields it was irrigating at its periphery. A change in the nature of the materials carried by the flow is one possibility; another is that the changes brought to the design of the higher parts of the system, hence in the quantity and velocity of the water entering it, increased siltation directly in the canal bed.[7]

Our first question, then, is: How did the Chinese hydraulic engineers who tried to maintain the Zheng-Bai Canal for more than two millennia cope with all of these difficulties?

9.1. A BRIEF HISTORY OF THE ZHENG GUO CANAL AND ITS CONTINUATIONS UP TO THE SEVENTEENTH CENTURY

Retracing the history of the system in the wake of the many authors who discussed it over the centuries is not an easy task. The difficulty is first of all historiographical, as a close examination of the datable sources reveals numerous uncertainties or even obscurities in most of them, and equally numerous contradictions among them, not to mention the tendency of several important authors to project contemporary realities and problems onto poorly documented earlier periods.

process of erosion in the river basins of the loess plateau], *Dili yanjiu* 2.1 (1983), p. 36: the higher reaches of the Jing and, especially, the course of its tributary the Huanjiang, are part of what is defined there as the area with the next-to-highest recorded rate of erosion (10,000–20,000 tonnes/km^2/yr). See also Liu Tungsheng, *Loess in China*, 2d. ed. (Beijing: China Ocean Press, 1985), pp. 192–93.

[6] See *Huanghe zhi* 黄河志 [A treatise on the Yellow River], comp. Zhang Hanying 张含英, (Shanghai: Guoli bianyiguan, 1937), vol. 3, pp. 23, 142–45. This study provides a detailed description of the seasonal cycle of discharge, including a monthly table for the years 1922, 1923, 1930, and 1931. While the winter and spring discharge is fairly constant from one year to the next, the summer peaks are unpredictable and can be extremely violent and sudden. In summer 1936, the highest peak reached a discharge of 3,000 m^3/s, the Jing level at the head of the canal rising by 30 (English) feet within ten minutes. See also Nie Shuren 聂树人, *Shaanxi ziran dili* [Natural geography of Shaanxi] 陕西自然地理 (Xi'an: Shaanxi renmin CBS, 1981), pp. 192–95.

[7] Another type of change, which can only be surmised at this point, is neotectonics, as the region is subjected to a continuing process of warping due to the upthrust of the massif of which the rocky range traversed by the Jing is one part.

I have not been able to examine directly the entire stock of historical sources on the Zheng-Bai system. Much of it, however, has been retrieved by the scholars who compiled the eighteenth- and nineteenth-century gazetteers of the region;[8] as far as pre-Qing developments are concerned, at least, it is to the evidence collected in these works – with some additions which will be duly noted – that I have turned first of all. I have looked, however, for the original sources whenever possible – an exercise that, it has to be said, does not always speak in favor of the thoroughness and precision of the work done by the gazetteer compilers. Other types of literature will be more systematically used in my considerations of Qing problems.

There exist secondary studies offering a general outline of the history of the Zheng Guo Canal and its successors,[9] but few of them really attempt to

---

[8] Information on the Zheng-Bai system appears in gazetteers of Shaanxi province, of Xi'an prefecture (within whose borders the system entirely lay), and principally of Jingyang county (where its most crucial parts are still located). Of eight recorded Shaanxi provincial gazetteers (starting in 1522), I have consulted those of 1735 and 1827. The only late-imperial edition of the Xi'an prefectural gazetteer (*Xi'an fuzhi*) dates from 1779; it had, however, a famed ancestor, the 1069 *Chang'an zhi* 長安志 [Gazetteer of Chang'an], many later editions of which were published with an appendix entitled *Chang'an zhi tu* 圖 [Gazetteer of Chang'an with maps], of which *juan* 3 is an important treatise on the Zheng-Bai system, the *Jingqu tushuo* 涇渠圖説 [Maps and explanations on the Jing Canal] (hereafter *JQTS*) by Li Weizhong 李惟中 (Li Haowen 好文), with a preface of 1342. The edition used here is that edited in 1784 by Bi Yuan 畢沅 (then governor of Shaanxi). Among the seven recorded Jingyang county gazetteers (*Jingyang xianzhi* 涇陽縣志, hereafter *JYXZ*), I was able to use the last three, the 1778, 1842, and 1910 editions. The 1842 *JYXZ* is by far the most complete on our subject: in addition to the information recorded in its hydraulics (*shuili* 水利) chapter (*juan* 13), it has a three-chapter annex entirely devoted to the Zheng-Bai system, entitled *Jingqu zhi* 涇渠志 [Treatise on the Jing Canal] (hereafter *JYXZ/JQZ*; the third chapter includes important parts of the *JQTS* text). What sets this annex apart from other gazetteer accounts of the canal is that it is much clearer in distinguishing between history and contemporary description; moreover, its history of the canal takes into account the discussions found in an important critical study of the subject bearing the same title (*Jingqu zhi*, hereafter *JQZ*), published in 1767 by Wang Taiyue 王太岳, a local official, whose 1804 reprinting I was able to use.

[9] All the general histories of water conservancy in China include a section on the topic. See, for example, the classic Zheng Zhaojing 鄭肇經, *Zhongguo shuili shi* 中國水利史 [A history of water control in China] (Changsha: Shangwu jinshuguan, 1939), pp. 269–72. "Zhongguo shuili shigao" bianxie zu [a group constituted within the Wuhan Hydraulic and Hydroelectric Institute], comp., *Zhongguo shuili shigao* 中国水利史稿 [A draft history of water control in China], vol. 1 (Beijing: Shuili dianli CBS, 1979), pp. 118–37, gives a much more detailed account for the ancient periods (I have not been able to see vol. 2). See also Joseph Needham, *Science and Civilisation in China*, vol. 4, part 3 (Cambridge: Cambridge University Press, 1971), pp. 228, 285–87, who ignores the Ming and Qing periods altogether. Huang Shengzhang, "Guanzhong nongtian shuili de lishi fazhan," considers the canal's history in the larger context of Guanzhong irrigation, but is rather short on this same Ming-Qing period. For a technical study taking the results of field investigations into account (which the above-mentioned Wuhan study also does), see Ye Yuchun 叶遇春, "Yin Jing guangai jishu chutan – cong Zheng Guo qu dao Jinghui qu" [Preliminary considerations on the techniques

sort out the numerous and sometimes considerable contradictions that subsist among primary sources, nor do they bring out sufficiently the history-conscious (or should I say history-obsessed) approach that was common to all the authors and officials who reflected on the system's problems.[10] In short, an exhaustive study still remains to be done, which of course what follows does not attempt to be.

The romantic story of the engineer Zheng Guo being sent to Qin by his employer, the king of Han, with the idea of wearing the war-inclined Qin out with a pharaonic project of irrigation is too well known to need retelling. When unmasked by the future Qin Shihuangdi and threatened with execution, Zheng Guo is reported in the *Hanshu* to have extricated himself by convincing the angry king that, once completed, the new canal's contribution to Qin prosperity would last ten thousand generations. It did not: even though, reportedly, in its first decades of operation it enormously increased the economic might of the Qin kingdom by irrigating more than 40,000 *qing* (or 4 million *mu*) of land,[11] problems of maintenance and

of irrigation feeding on the Jing: from the Zheng Guo Canal to the Jing Canal] 引泾灌溉技术初探 — 从郑国渠到泾惠渠, in *Shuili shi yanjiu hui chengli dahui lunwen ji* 水利史研究会成立大会论文集 [Collected papers from the inauguration meeting of the Society for Research in the History of Water Control] (Beijing: Shuili dianli CBS, 1984), pp. 35–42. Ye Yuchun is also the chief editor of a recent general history of the canal, *Jinghuiqu zhi* 泾惠渠志 (Xi'an, Sanqin CBS, 1991), which I have seen only after completing the present chapter, but which does not adduce any critically new material or interpretation. A short and fairly uncritical account of an archaeological survey done in 1973 is Qin Zhongxing 秦中行, "Qin Zheng Guo qu qushou yizhi diaocha ji" 秦郑国渠渠首遗址调查记 [Record of an investigation of the remains of the head of the Zheng Guo Canal of the Qin], *Wenwu* (1974), pp. 33–38.

[10] The most careful examination of sources is to be found in the Wuhan volume referred to in the previous note.

[11] What this means in modern units remains open to debate. The conversions one encounters in the literature would range from less than 74,000 ha (Ye Yuchun, table on p. 39, given in present-day *mu*), to c. 187,000 ha (*Zhongguo shuili shigao*, pp. 124–25), to almost 270,000 ha (Needham's 667,000 acres, p. 285). The problem is, what did the Qin *mu* amount to, or, to be more precise: was it the old, pre-imperial 100-pace (small) *mu*, or the large 240-pace *mu* first created by Shang Yang, but only generalized at the time of emperor Wu of the Han? Authors like Kang Chao in *Man and Land in Chinese History* (Stanford: Stanford University Press, 1986) (table of traditional units of measure on p. 231) put it at the same value as the Han *mu*, or 461 m² (which would yield about 184,000 ha); others like Ye Yuchun posit a much smaller Qin *mu*, worth 0.29 modern *mu*, or 193 m², less than half his Han *mu* (that is to say, the old "small *mu*"). This would be in accord with the conclusion of Wang Taiyue in his 1767 study of the Zheng-Bai Canal (*JQZ*, pp. 36b–37a), who states that the Qin used the old Zhou 100-pace *mu* in order to get more revenue – hence a Zheng Guo-irrigated area much smaller than is usually said in terms of Han and post-Han measures. In fact, the opposite view seems to be correct: although before the empirewide generalization of the large 240-pace *mu* under Han Wudi the small *mu* was still used in eastern China, in Qin-dominated Shaanxi the Shang Yang 240-pace *mu* was definitely the one in use. On these problems see, for example, Wu Hui 吴慧, *Zhongguo lidai liangshi muchan yanjiu* 中国历代粮食亩产研究 (Beijing, 1985), pp. 1–20. My thanks to Professor Guo Zhengzhong 郭正忠 of the Chinese Academy of Social Sciences for enlightening me on these tricky issues. One may

silting up such as those I will mention in more detail later soon diminished its efficiency, until in the end the last traces of its course had become completely obliterated.[12]

But the idea endured, and across the centuries canals were dug or reopened that bore different names[13] but played the same function as the original Zheng Guo, albeit on a smaller scale. The essentially similar basic design they all followed consisted of three components: (1) an intake device located near the place where the Jing River enters the Guanzhong plain, or, later, higher up the gorge that cuts between the Zhongshan 中 (or 仲) 山 mountain to the east and the Jiuzong 九嵕 mountain to the west;[14] (2) what might be called the feeder (as opposed to irrigation) canal: from the Song onward its higher portion was partly cut into the rock and ran along the hillside, following a course parallel and extremely close to that of the Jing itself, from which it separated when entering the Guanzhong plain; and finally (3) the irrigation canal proper, which distributed water through systems of irrigation gates (*dou* 斗 or *doumen* 斗門, also written 陡 in other systems) discharging into distribution canals irrigating the fields.[15]

---

also note that, according to *Zhongguo shuili shigao* (pp. 124–25), based on the present-day discharge of the Jing River its waters diverted into the canal cannot have irrigated more than one-fifth of the 184,000 ha they calculate. But then we need to define what exactly "irrigation" means.

[12] See note 16 of this chapter. The Zheng Guo story is recounted in *Shiji* 史記 [Historical records] j. 29, p. 1408, and almost identically in *Hanshu* 漢書 [The Han dynastic history], j. 29, p. 1678 (all dynastic histories citations in this essay are from the Zhonghua shuju ed.). For translations, see Derk Bodde, *China's First Unifier: A Study of the Ch'in Dynasty as Seen in the Life of Li Ssu (280?–208 B.C.)* (Leiden: E. J. Brill, 1938), pp. 59–60, and Needham, *Science and Civilisation*, vol. 4, part 3, p. 285. I discovered afterward that Bodde uses the same phrase, "romantic story," that I had used in my conference paper.

[13] The generic name Jing qu 涇渠 seems to make its appearance with the fourteenth-century *JQTS*. The combined appellation Zheng-Bai qu 鄭白渠, referring to the original Zheng Guo Canal and to the Baigong Canal of the Han, continued to be used as a generic name long after the former had disappeared.

[14] As we shall see later, after 1737 this intake device was blocked up and the canal was fed by local springs instead.

[15] The system of *dou* irrigation gates is explicitly mentioned from the Tang period onward (see, e.g., *JYXZ/JQZ*, j. 3, pp. 66–79). A field investigation of 995 or 996 stated that "the 176 gates that had been set up in the past were all in disrepair" (*Songshi* 宋史 [The Song dynastic history], j. 94, p. 2346): this figure may have dated back to the Tang, even though the *Chang'an zhi* of 1069 (j. 17, p. 56) cited a figure of 48; there were 135 irrigation gates during the Yuan (*JQTS*, p. 11a–b), and 106 in the nineteenth century (calculated from the enumeration in *JYXZ/JQZ*, j. 2, pp. 3a–18b). Based on the step-by-step descriptions of the system given both in *JQTS* and in some late-imperial gazetteers, what I call the irrigation canal proper could be further analyzed into several levels, namely, main canals (*ganqu* 干渠), branch canals (*zhiqu* 支渠), and sublateral canals (*douqu* 斗渠, i.e., those controlled by the above-mentioned *dou*). On these notions and terms, which are found in traditional sources as well, see James E. Nickum, ed., *Water Management Organization in the People's Republic of China* (Armonk, N.Y.: Sharpe, 1981), p. xv.

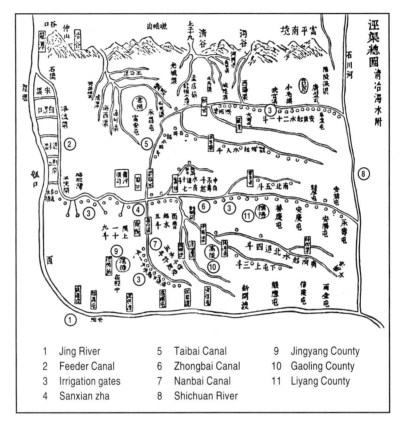

Map 9.1. The Zheng-Bai irrigation system in Song and Yuan times. From *Jingqu tushuo*, original ed., 1342.

(See Map 9.1 for a Yuan representation of the entire system showing the location of the irrigation gates; see Maps 9.2a–c and 9.4. for Qing representations.)

It is unclear when the original Zheng Guo Canal finally fell out of use.[16] But after it did the more or less definitive pattern for this last section

---

[16] The wording of the *Hanshu* implies that the Bai Canal (opened a century and a half later; see below) and the Zheng Guo functioned simultaneously. This is what many (if not all) later authors understood. An example is the two officials sent out in 995 to inspect how various irrigation sites in the empire might be rehabilitated. They started their tour with the Zheng-Bai and, in their historical overview of the system, simply added the figures of irrigated areas given for the two canals in order to get the total prevailing under the Han. See Huangfu Xuan 皇甫選 and He Liang 何亮, as quoted in *Song huiyao jigao* 宋會要輯稿 [A draft compilation of the Song Collection of Important Documents] (1936 ed.), *shihuo* 食貨, j. 7, pp. 2b–3a; also *Songshi*, j. 94, p. 2346, quoted in *JQZ*, p. 9a, and most gazetteers, but wrongly attributing this calculation to Chen Yaosou 陳堯叟 and Liang Ding 梁鼎, the two

was that set by the Bai Canal 白渠, opened in 95 B.C. by the Lord Bai 白公, most likely as an adjunct to the Zheng Guo, which probably branched off the Jing at or near the same "mouth,"[17] ran along a more southerly course, and went much less far. (See Map 9.3 for a conjectural map of the Zheng Guo and Bai canals.) Whereas the total length of the original Zheng Guo Canal was reported as "more than three hundred *li*" (or 126 kilometers according to modern surveys), that of the Bai Canal was said to be only two hundred *li* (possibly including secondary branches). The difference in the irrigated area reported in the ancient sources is still more dramatic, since the figure given in the *Hanshu* is only 4,500 *qing*, or about one-tenth the original acreage serviced by the Zheng Guo (one-fifth if one accepts the very small value of the Qin *mu* assumed by some modern authors).

After the original Zheng Guo Canal had definitely disappeared and, apparently, from the Tang period onward, the successive versions of the system, down to the Longdong Canal of the Qing, basically followed the same course, dividing into three branches at a place named Sanxian zha 三限閘.[18] These branches were called Taibai 太白, Zhongbai 中白, and Nanbai 南白, respectively (sometimes Shangbai or Beibai, Zhongbai, and Xiabai), hence the frequent appellation for the entire system, Sanbai qu 三白渠. (See Maps 9.1 and 9.2 for representations of the Sanbai system during the Yuan and Qing, respectively.) Topography suggests that, in the beginning, the middle branch may have serviced the largest irrigated area of the three;[19] indeed, according to some authors, under the Tang the Zhongbai

court officials whose memorials were the cause of Huangfu's and He's being sent on tour. One may note that the only detailed description of the course of the Zheng Guo is to be found in the late fifth- or early sixth-century *Shuijingzhu* 水經注 [The annotated classic of waterways], Yang Shoujing 楊守敬 et al., eds. (Nanjing, 1989), vol. 2, pp. 1455–60. Tang evidence implies that at least parts of the Zheng Guo were still being used alongside the Bai Canal, albeit with a much lower yield than in antiquity (see, e.g., *JQZ*, pp. 37a–b, or *JYXZ* [1778], *j.* 4, pp. 5a–b). The above-mentioned report by Huangfu Xuan and He Liang (dated 996) provides an apparently *de visu* description of the vestiges of the Zheng Guo as they stood at the beginning of the Song; the authors state that this once most impressive work had been in ruins and out of use "for a long time" (*Songshi, j.* 94, p. 2346, featuring details absent from the *Song huiyao jigao* version). Ultimately – at some point during the Song dynasty – its course became impossible to trace.

[17] See *Zhongguo shuili shigao*, pp. 127–29.

[18] Or Sanqu kou 三渠口, Sanxian kou 三限口, Sanzha kou 三閘口. See, e.g., *JYXZ/JQZ, j.* 2, pp. 19a, 36b; or *Zhongguo shuili shigao*, pp. 129–30. The description of the Bai Canal in the *Shuijingzhu* (vol. 2, pp. 1644–48) mentions two secondary canals branching off the Bai qu, but they do not seem to be the same as the later branches of the Sanbai system.

[19] Downstream from Sanxian zha, at the limit between Jingyang and Gaoling counties, the Zhengbai had another sluicegate called the Pengcheng zha 彭城閘, established in 825, which apportioned water between the main branch and four subbranches.

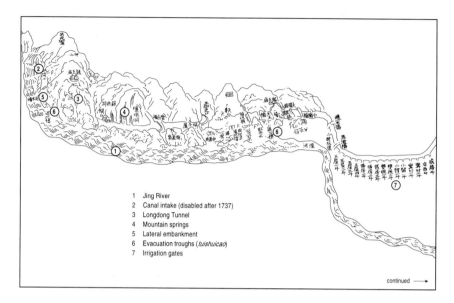

1   Jing River
2   Canal intake (disabled after 1737)
3   Longdong Tunnel
4   Mountain springs
5   Lateral embankment
6   Evacuation troughs (*tuishuicao*)
7   Irrigation gates

continued ⟶

a

Map 9.2a–c. The Zheng-Bai (or Longdong) irrigation system in the eighteenth century. From *Shaanxi tongzhi*, 1735.

branch flowed beyond the Shichuan 石川 River and into the Wei;[20] at the end of the empire, by contrast, two-thirds of a severely reduced irrigated area were serviced by the section of the canal upstream of Sanxian zha, about one-sixth by the north branch of the Sanbai proper, and the rest by the south branch and by the middle branch with its several subbranches.[21] The main change from the Bai Canal as it had developed by the Tang to each one of its Song, Yuan, Ming, and Qing successors was the exact place and technique of intake upstream of the system, and the course of the highest part of the feeder canal.

The original Han version of the Bai Canal seems to have functioned throughout the first millennium of imperial history and beyond – or at

---

[20] See *Zhongguo shuili shigao*, pp. 129–30; Ye Yuchun, "Yin Jing guangai jishu chutan," pp. 39–40. But even this was significantly less than the original Zheng Guo canal, whose more northerly course ran much farther east, crossing several natural streams and reaching to the Luo River.

[21] See the 1842 *JYXZ/JQZ, j.* 2, pp. 3a–18a, which is the first source to give figures of irrigated area for each irrigation gate; the total ran to about 640 *qing*. A comparison between the Yuan description of the system in *JQTS* and that in *JYXZ/JQZ* also shows that in between several important subbranches of the north and middle branches had disappeared; see, e.g., *JYXZ/JQZ, j.* 2, p. 20a.

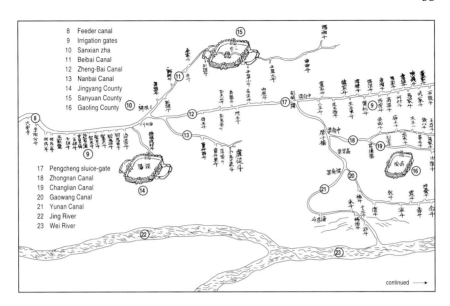

8   Feeder canal
9   Irrigation gates
10 Sanxian zha
11 Beibai Canal
12 Zheng-Bai Canal
13 Nanbai Canal
14 Jingyang County
15 Sanyuan County
16 Gaoling County

17 Pengcheng sluice-gate
18 Zhongnan Canal
19 Changlian Canal
20 Gaowang Canal
21 Yunan Canal
22 Jing River
23 Wei River

continued ——▶

b

least, to have been regularly put back into operation, and still under this name, after periods of neglect or political turmoil. The Bai Canal and its management are frequently discussed in Tang sources, at a time when, as in the Qin and Han, the Guanzhong plain was the hinterland of the capital of a large empire, and therefore its economy a matter of high priority. Reported figures of land irrigated by the system shrink from over 10,000 *qing* in the middle of the seventh century to a low 6,200 *qing* during the Dali era (766–79).[22] One interesting point in these discussions is the oft-mentioned competition of watermills (*nianwei* 碾磑) operated by rich people, aristocrats, and monasteries (and even a princess) in the upper reaches of the canal, which according to one report took up to 70 percent of the water away from agricultural use, so that emperors and officials repeatedly had to order their destruction.[23]

[22] Cf. *Zhongguo shuili shigao*, pp. 129–30. The first figure may have included areas irrigated by what remained of the Zheng Guo Canal. The second figure is sometimes given as a mere 6,000 *mu* (60 *qing*): see, e.g., the Song encyclopaedia, *Yuhai* 玉海 [The jade sea] (Beijing, 1987, reprint of the 1883 Zhejiang shuju ed.), *j.* 22, p. 11b, or *JQZ*, p. 37b, quoting from the Tang dynastic history. According to Wang Taiyue, the author of *JQZ*, this low figure fits with indications suggesting that by these years – which one should recall were the immediate aftermath of the An Lushan and Shi Siming upheaval – agricultural production in the region had come to a virtual standstill, and should therefore be accepted.

[23] See, e.g., the sources quoted in *XAFZ*, *j.* 7, pp. 7b–8b, or in *Yuhai*, *j.* 22, pp. 6b–7b, 11a–b. Also Jacques Gernet, *Les aspects économiques du bouddhisme dans la société chinoise du Ve au Xe*

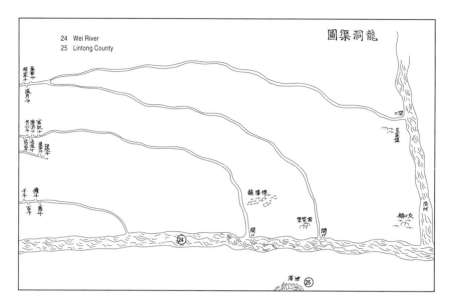

24 Wei River
25 Lintong County

龍洞渠圖

C

At the beginning of the Song the system appears to have been in a sorry
condition; late tenth- and eleventh-century reports speak of increasing
difficulties in harnessing the flow of the Jing to feed it into the canal,
while the area actually benefiting from irrigation seems never to have
exceeded (depending on the period and the author) 2,000 or possibly
3,000 *qing*.[24] And yet, even though the imperial capital was no longer
located in Guanzhong and the vital economic areas were now in the south,
because of its strategic importance in facing the Xixia state, enhancing the
agricultural productivity of the region was still considered to be of the
utmost urgency.

The breakthrough came with the construction of what was to be the first

siècle (Paris: École Française d'Extrême-Orient, 1956), pp. 140–42. One cannot fail to note
the economic conundrum presented by the competition for a resource (water) that was
needed both to help produce the cereal and to activate the machinery – the *meunerie
automatique*, to use Gernet's phrase – that processed it. There is a convenient overview of the
water-mills problem under the Tang in Zhou Kuiyi 周魁一, "'Shuibushi' yu Tangdai de
nongtian shuili guanli" 水部式与唐代的农田水利管理 [The Ordinances of the Depart-
ment of Waterways and the Management of Irrigation under the Tang], *Lishi dili* 4 (1986),
pp. 88–101, here pp. 95–96.

[24] See, among others, the 996 report by Huangfu Xuan and He Liang (note 16 of this
chapter). The accounts of the construction of the Fengli Canal (on which see below) claim
that, before its opening in 1108, the Sanbai system downstream was irrigating no more than
(according to the author) 2,000 or 2,700 *qing*.

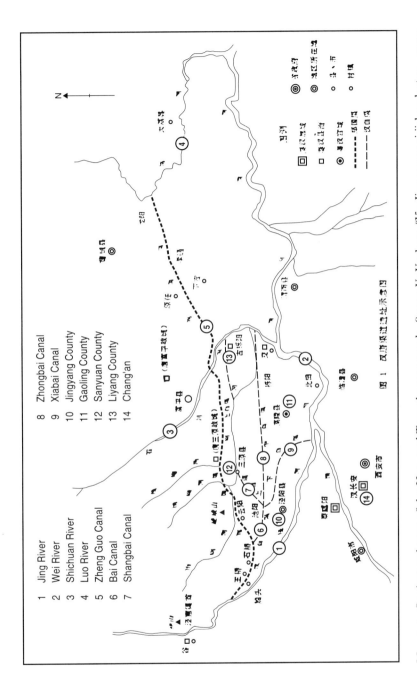

1 Jing River 8 Zhongbai Canal
2 Wei River 9 Xiabai Canal
3 Shichuan River 10 Jingyang County
4 Luo River 11 Gaoling County
5 Zheng Guo Canal 12 Sanyuan County
6 Bai Canal 13 Liyang County
7 Shangbai Canal 14 Chang'an

Map 9.3. Conjectural map of the Han- and Tang-dynasty canals. *Source*: Ye Yuchun, "Yin Jing guangai jishu chutan – cong Zhengguo qu dao Jinghui qu," p. 38.

in a series of new intake systems that were located each time higher in the Jing River gorge, and for that reason necessitated the cutting of new feeder canals, or sections thereof, going deeper in the mountain. (It was in fact these new additions that gave their names to the system considered as a whole, even though the three-branch pattern described above stayed unchanged and continued to be called Sanbai all along.)[25]

The Song version of the upper section of the canal, called the Fengli Canal 豐利渠, was built in 1108–10 in the wake of several unsuccessful efforts at rehabilitating the old Bai Canal intake, starting in the very first years of the dynasty,[26] and then of an aborted attempt at cutting a new feeder canal above the old one. This last attempt, interestingly, occurred sometime between 1072 and 1075, at a time when Emperor Shenzong 神宗 and his prime minister, Wang Anshi 王安石, were inquiring about "neglected benefits" 遺利 that might be brought to realization by government projects. Its main promoter, Hou Ke 侯可, was then Jingyang magistrate, and he seems to have successfully "sold" his project to the dignitaries sent down by the court to evaluate it.[27] While it is unclear why the work started by Hou Ke and his colleagues had to be interrupted after only about 30 percent had been completed,[28] its precedent was duly invoked when the decision to create what would be known as the Fengli Canal was eventually taken.[29]

[25] The principal source on the Song and Yuan canals is *JQTS*, which, as we have seen, dates back to 1342.

[26] Conveniently surveyed in *Songshi*, j. 94, pp. 2345–48.

[27] See *Song huiyao jigao, shihuo*, j. 7, pp. 24b–25b, quoting from the evaluation by Zhou Liangru 周良孺, and from an interview where we see Wang Anshi convincing the emperor of the importance and feasibility of launching major construction on the Sanbai site. There is some hesitation in the sources as to the exact date when the work was started. Curiously, 1074 is the last date for "works of importance" in the entire Zheng-Bai history given by Needham (*Science and Civilisation*, vol. 4, part 3, p. 286, note f).

[28] Depending on the account, the cause was a famine in Shaanxi, political attacks against Hou Ke, or Hou Ke's dismissal for some administrative fault. Interestingly, the first two versions seem to be attributable to the same person, Hou Ke's grandson Hou Meng 蒙, the author of one of the two stelae celebrating the completion of the Fengli Canal (see note 29), where he mentions a famine as the cause of the interruption of the work in 1073. But Hou Meng was also the signatory of a letter ghostwritten by one of the two famous philosopher brothers, Cheng Hao 程顥 (1032–85) and Cheng Yi 頤 (1033–1107) (which one depends on the source), addressed to an unidentified minister and former Chang'an prefect, which insists on the "hate" (*hen* 恨) felt by the Guanzhong populace, by his grandfather in the other world, and by himself at the thought that this occasion of accomplishing Emperor Shenzong's will had been spoiled because of political maneuvers. See *JYXZ* (1778), j. 10, p. 1a–b, "Dai ren shang zaixiang lun Zheng-Bai qu shu" 代人上宰相論鄭白渠書, here attributed to Cheng Yi. Cheng Hao might be a better choice since he started his career as an assistant magistrate in Shaanxi, and was for a time an associate of Wang Anshi.

[29] The major source on the construction of the Fengli Canal (which is not even mentioned in the *Songshi*) is a couple of stelae that could be seen near the Hongyan 洪堰 dam during the

The project was started in the ninth month of 1108 after a careful process of investigation and discussion, and completed in the intercalary eighth month of 1110. A new intake was built higher in the gorge, and a new feeder canal leading to the lower Bai qu system was cut through the rock for its upper part, and dug through the earth for its lower part. While most later sources say that the system irrigated between 30,000 and 35,000 *qing*, according to the stelae engraved at the time the figure was 20,000 to 25,000 in seven counties (Jingyang 涇陽, Liquan 醴泉, Gaoling 高陵, Yaoyang 櫟陽, Yunyang 雲陽, Sanyuan 三原, and Fuping 富平).[30] Whatever the case may have been, it was obviously a dramatic improvement over the previous situation when, says one source, 80 or 90 percent of the irrigation supposed to be done through the Sanbai system existed only in name, even though the people of the entire area reached by the canal still had to bear the cost and to endure the sufferings of the annual works at the intake dam.

Indeed, one crucial advantage of the new canal, duly advertised in the two stelae celebrating its opening, was that it did not need a dam: its elevation had been calculated in such a way that its bottom at the intake would be five feet below the surface of the Jing's waters, so that "one could avoid the abuses of dam maintenance" (*ze wu xiu yan zhi bi* 則無修堰之弊).[31]

This certainly was solving an old problem, although apparently not as old as the canal itself. There is no evidence that the original Zheng Guo intake featured any system of dam built across the river and aimed at raising the level of the flow to the canal entrance, or even that part of the flow was diverted by an embankment laid in the middle of the riverbed.[32] Indeed, in

---

Yuan (Hongyan or Hongkou 洪口 being a common appellation for the intake by that time) and whose texts are reproduced in *JQTS*, pp. 4b–8a. One is attributed to Hou Meng (see note 28), the other (dated 1110) to a military officer by the name of Cai Pu 蔡溥. They are not without contradictions between them. Nishioka Hiroaki 西岡弘晃, "Sōdai ni okeru Sansai no suiri kaihatsu – Hōrikyo no kōchiku o chūshin to shite" 宋代における陝西の水利開發 — 豐利渠の構築を中心として [The development of water control in Shaanxi during the Song, centering on the construction of the Fengli Canal], *Chūgoku suiri shi kenkyū*, no. 6 (1974), pp. 20–36, is a convenient introduction, but it hardly discusses the numerous technical difficulties involved in the texts and at places seriously misreads the sources.

[30] According to the conversion table in Kang Chao, *Man and Land*, p. 231, the *mu* equaled 576.6 m² in the Song, as against 461 m² in the Han (and, according to him, the Qin), 693.6 m² from the Yuan through the Qing, and 666.5 m² in Republican times. The figures for the length of the Song feeder canal also vary. The Hou Meng stela, which seems to be the most reliable in this case, gives the equivalent of about 12 km.

[31] Cai Pu's text, *JQTS*, p. 6a.

[32] On this point, see in particular *Zhongguo shuili shigao*, p. 121. A Ming author, Yuan Huazhong 袁化中, states that back in the third century B.C. Zheng Guo had built his dam

spite of the affirmation of many authors, some even presenting photo-graphs,[33] it may well be that all traces of the original "mouth" (or mouths) or the Zheng Guo and Bai have been completely obliterated by erosion, since they were dug in earth, not in rock like those of the later versions.[34] But obviously, at some point during the following centuries the scouring effect that we mentioned earlier, plus, possibly, silting up in the canal bed, made the building of a dam to raise the water level up to the canal intake unavoidable.

The first reliable mention of a dam – described as a sturdy stonework permanent structure sometimes called the "General-in-chief dam" (*Jiangjun sha* 將軍翣) – is to be found in a memorial dated 991, attributed to a local inhabitant by the name of Du Siyuan 杜思淵. This memorial states that the dam had been in ruins "for a long time," without, however, giving any indication of when it was built or when it went out of service.[35] According-ing to the next source mentioning it, the Jiangjun sha was 100 paces long and 100 paces wide,[36] and most probably it was a dam laid across the entire width of the river (which would better accord with the word *yan*, also used in connection with it), rather than an embankment diverting part of the flow into the canal.[37] An attempt in the wake of the 991 memorial to rebuild a permanent stone structure that would stay on for "several tens of years" failed; and for the entire duration of the Song, Yuan, and Ming dynasties, when the level of the Jing River had to be raised – that is, most of the time – it was in effect dammed with structures of various descriptions that I would suggest be called "disposable," inasmuch as they had to be replaced

by piling up 112 rows of a hundred gabions (see below on this technique), but this is pure imagination, even if some modern authors like to quote the passage as a "tradition" and take it at face value (Qin Zhongxing, "Qin Zheng Guo qu qushou yizhi diaocha ji," pp. 34–35). Yuan's text appears in *JYXZ* (1902), pp. 884–88, under the title "Kai Diaoerzui yi" 開弔兒嘴議 [A discussion on the opening of the Diaoer mouth], and in a somewhat abridged form in *XAFZ, j.* 7, pp. 13b–14a, under the title "Jingqu yi" 涇渠議 [A discussion of the Jing Canal].

[33] See, e.g., Needham, *Science and Civilisation*, vol. 4, part 3, p. 287; Qin Zhongxing, "Qin Zheng Guo qu qushou yizhi," pp. 34, 37; or, more recently, *Zhongguo wenming da tuji* 中國文明大圖集 [Illustrated encyclopaedia of Chinese civilization] (Taipei: Yixin wenhua shige gongsi, 1992), vol. 2, p. 159.

[34] The point is made in particular by Ye Yuchun, "Yin Jing guangai jishu," p. 35.

[35] See *Songshi, j.* 94, p. 2345. The text is reproduced in all the gazetteers and in *JQZ*, pp. 9b–10a.

[36] Cf. the memorial by Huangfu Xuan and He Liang, sent to inspect the site in or just after 995 (see above), as quoted in the same sources. These dimensions may evoke the square shape of the ancient sort of fan known as the *sha* (see, e.g., the Morohashi dictionary at no. 28739 for an illustration).

[37] See Ye Yuchun, "Yin Jing guangai jishu," p. 36 (according to whom the reported width is practically that of the river), and *Zhongguo shuili shigao*, p. 129.

almost every year, at great cost for the riparians, after the summer floods had damaged them beyond repair.[38]

The first mention of such a technique dates back to the Qiande era (963–68), when a local official is reported to have dammed the Jing with a combination of wooden materials that, although it was fairly efficient, was washed away whenever the summer rainstorms caused the river to swell.[39] The same was apparently the case with the "wooden dams" (*muyan* 木堰) made of thousands of poles, possibly fitted into holes drilled in the bed-rock, which continued to be used after the above-mentioned attempt to rebuild a permanent dam made of stones had foundered at the end of the tenth century: they had to be reassembled "year after year" after the summer floods had swept them away.[40] This situation still prevailed on the eve of the opening of the Fengli Canal in 1110, when, reportedly, every year during the eighth month thousands of corvée laborers had to bring in quality materials to erect a "huge dam" (*ji liangcai qi juyan* 集良材起巨堰) that would only be destroyed in the following summer.[41]

As we saw, the Fengli Canal, whose intake was located a few kilometers upstream, did not use a dam at first. It is unclear how long this remained possible. What is sure is that, when a new intake was built higher in the

---

[38] A couple of quotations from a capital official named Wang Yan 王沿, set far apart and out of context in the *Yuhai* (*j.* 22, pp. 13a and 36a), has led several gazetteer compilers to state that a permanent diversion embankment made of big rocks fastened with iron and laid in the middle of the current was set up in 1036 (see in particular *JYXZ* [1842], *j.* 13, p. 2b). Nishioka, "Sōdai ni okeru Sansei no suiri kaihatsu," p. 22, makes the same affirmation, even calling it an illustration of the technical advances made at the time (p. 27), but without the excuse of not having had access to the more complete Wang Yan text as quoted in the *Song huiyao jigao, shihuo, j.* 7, pp. 6b–11a, dated 1026, of which he does not seem to have understood the thrust. Wang, then a censor, was lengthily and passionately refuting the arguments of some of his colleagues who opposed the revival of a canal using the water of the Zhang 漳 River in present-day He'nan, an infrastructure that like the Zheng-Bai had its origin in the Warring States period. Wang adduced the example of the Zheng-Bai and of the techniques it reportedly used, obviously based on hearsay, to bolster his argument, but nowhere is it stated that such a structure was *actually* built during the eleventh century. In 1036 Wang Yan, then a tribute-grain official (*caochen* 漕臣), did advocate rehabilitating the Zheng-Bai intake, but we know that the official who was put in charge of it continued to use wooden posts that had to be replaced every year.

[39] See Du Siyuan's 991 memorial referred to above. The text mentions twigs and stems (*shaorang* 梢穰), bamboo fences (*bali* 笆籬), and beams or planks (*muzhan* 木棧), but the way all of this was assembled is unclear.

[40] See the 996 report of Huangfu Xuan and his colleagues as given in *Songshi, j.* 94, pp. 2346–47. The text speaks of 11,300 poles (*shaochun* 梢椿) that had to be annually contributed by the riparians; it suggests taking down the dam every year *before* the summer spates and storing the materials along the river, which would allow them to be used for at least two or three years.

[41] See Cai Pu's stela in *JQTS*, p. 5b.

gorge in the fourteenth century, due to the secular lowering of the Jing bed, "disposable" dams, but now of a different type, had been for an unknown amount of time a regular feature of the system. The operating cost and technical difficulty of feeding the Sanbai with the water of the Jing – in other words, of continuing a pattern that was claimed to have made massive irrigation possible since ancient times – was to remain a permanent feature of the Zheng-Bai system until the very idea was abandoned in 1737.

One should also at least mention at this point another type of difficulty that appeared with the construction of the new Song feeder canal: cramped as they were between a river prone to violent floods and steep, gullied slopes with unpredictable torrents, the Fengli Canal and its later additions were extremely vulnerable to environmental hazard, and this made it necessary to devise new technical responses to protect them. How this was attempted we will discuss in some detail in the last part of this chapter.

According to all indications, after the Mongols had conquered Guanzhong from the Jin 金 dynasty the system was in ruins, the entire region laid waste, and, most importantly in the eyes of the new regime, the armies could not be fed. Efforts at reconstruction came in as early as 1240;[42] a "General administration of military land development" (*tuntian zongguan fu* 屯田總管府) was established in 1291 to manage the system;[43] and later during the dynasty rules for water use (most certainly inspired by Song-Jin precedents) were laid down that were still in use, with few variants, as late as the nineteenth century (see section 9.3 below).

As far as infrastructures are concerned, the person who is inseparably associated with this period is a certain Wang Ju 王琚 (with a variant Wang Chengde 王承德), whose name was given to a new section cut still higher in the Jing gorge and opened in 1339; the Censor-Wang Canal (Wang yushi qu 王御史渠), also called the "New Canal" (*xinqu* 新渠). Wang Ju had earlier, as Jingyang magistrate, taken part in an effort to put the system back into shape after it had been damaged by a flood in 1304.[44] In 1308, now a censor, he proposed to extend the Song feeder canal 51 *zhang* (or about 150 meters) upstream in order to catch the flow of the Jing at a higher, narrower, and thus more convenient place. If we are to believe the chronology given in an editor's note to the 1342 *Jingqu tushuo*, about four-fifths of the work was done in the years 1314–16, while the remainder had to wait

---

[42] See *Yuanshi* 元史 [The Yuan dynastic history], *j.* 65, pp. 1629–30.

[43] *Yuanshi, j.* 66, p. 1658; see *JQTS*, pp. 16b–19a, for details on its personnel. This bureau was the successor of a *Hequ yingtianshisi* 河渠營田使司 established in 1264.

[44] See *Yuanshi, j.* 66, p. 1658, and Wang Ju's biography in *JYXZ* (1842), *j.* 19, pp. 2b–3a.

until 1337 and 1339, when the dam was at last transferred to the "new mouth" (*xin qukou*).[45] However protracted and costly,[46] the undertaking must not have been very efficient, since Song Bingliang 宋秉亮, a Shaanxi censor who toured the site in 1343, spoke of a rapidly diminishing water supply and of the necessity of thoroughly overhauling (and indeed, it seems, completing) a system that according to him was going to be shortly "of no benefit to the people."[47] Song's program of repairs, which he formulated after a field visit and interviews with the locals, was three-pronged: (1) completing the work at the dam and intake, (2) putting back in order the system of twin overflow sluicegates established in the Song (on which see below), and (3) reopening the paths that made it possible to remove from the canal the dirt dug out during dredging. To this he added putting competent officials in charge and not being stingy with expenses. It seems that at least the third part of the program was implemented in 1344. The last, terse document we have before the fall of the Yuan dynasty is one reporting that in 1360 an official was sent by the provincial authorities to repair the system and that the rather improbable figure of 45,000 *qing* of land could thereafter be irrigated.

The techniques used for the intake as they are described in Yuan sources differ from those mentioned above, which we remember antedated the opening of the new Fengli intake in 1110. As we saw, while the Fengli as it had been conceived was supposed to work without a dam, at some unknown point during the two hundred years that followed – but possibly relatively early – the scouring of the river made it necessary again to find ways to "block the water" (*yan shui* 堰水 or *yong shui* 壅水), that is to say, to raise its level up to that of the canal entrance.

What is described in the fourteenth-century *Jingqu tushuo* and later texts is dams consisting of rows of what might be translated as "stone containers" (*shidun* 石囤),[48] or perhaps gabions,[49] laid down across the flow. The most

---

[45] *JQTS*, pp. 8a–b. In some versions (e.g., *Yuanshi, j.* 66, pp. 1658–59) the work was completed in 1318, not 1339.

[46] It would seem that in 1331 a flood completely destroyed the intake and that exceptional funding had to be found for the repairs because the riparians normally mobilized for the work had been decimated by drought and epidemics during the preceding years. See *Yuanshi, j.* 65, p. 1631.

[47] The fullest version of Song's lengthy analysis of the problems of the intake and of the feeder canal, together with his proposals, is to be found in *JYXZ* (1778), *j.* 10, pp. 3a–5b.

[48] Several texts use *jun* 囷 instead of *dun*, or even use them interchangeably.

[49] This is the term used by Needham, *Science and Civilisation*, vol. 4, part 3, pp. 339–41. Needham's description, a "sausage-shaped open-work crate of bamboo packed with stones," may evoke what is described in the sources on the Zheng-Bai intake, but bamboo is not among the wooden materials mentioned in Shaanxi, and the various descriptions seem to suggest that the gabions were set up vertically – not horizontally as in the illustration

straightforward definition is that found in the Yuan dynastic history concerning repairs done in 1304: shrubs were woven and stuffed with stones to make gabions, the gaps being then filled in with grass and earth.[50] The description in the *Jingqu tushuo* mentions rafters, kaoliang stalks, jujube-tree branches, stones, grass, and ropes, and is complete with figures of the quantities of labor required to procure each sort of material and to assemble it; exactly what the description means is much more difficult to figure out.[51]

Sources differ as to the dimensions and layout of the Jing River "stone-container" dam. The main *Jingqu tushuo* text, which apparently describes the pre-Wang yushi situation – specifying that the system has been inherited from the previous (Song or Jin) dynasty – speaks of a structure 850 feet long (from bank to bank) and 85 feet wide, made up of 1,116 containers laid out in eleven rows; a footnote states that the new (Wang yushi) dam stands at a place that is narrower, and consists of only two rows of gabions. Song Bingliang in his 1343 memorial gives fairly different figures: in order to block the course of the Jing and raise it a few feet up to the intake of the old Fengli Canal, 380 containers had been required, corvée workers being sent onto the site each year to "erect" them after the summer floods had destroyed the previous year's dam; but now, in the new canal built by Censor Wang, which branched off the Jing at a narrower place, only 110 were needed, hence significant savings in labor and materials. He also mentioned that because of a three-foot difference in elevation between the Jing River and the bottom of the canal, the height of the containers at the deepest part of the bed had to reach 15 feet, which made them unsteady and easily damaged when the river was in spate: in fact he considered the Song-type dam, maintained by posts fitted in holes dug in the rock, to be more sturdy.[52]

Whatever the difficulties encountered by the managers of the system during the Mongol period may have been, the Ming engineers still strove to

---

and other materials (in his description Song Bingliang uses the term "to erect," *qili* 起立).

[50] *Yuanshi*, quoted in *JQZ*, pp. 15a–b. "Bound gabions" (*zajun* 紮囷) of a similar description are mentioned at the mouth of the Tongli 通利 Canal, opened in the early thirteenth century, which diverted part of the flow of the Fen 汾 River in Shanxi. See Morita Akira 森田明, *Shindai suiri shakai shi no kenkyū* 清代水利社會史の研究 (Tokyo: Kokushi kankōkai, 1990), p. 273.

[51] Editor's note to *JQTS*, p. 10a, abstracted in most gazetteers.

[52] *JYXZ* (1778), *j.* 10, pp. 3a–4b. Song's solution would have been to depress the bottom of the canal by eight feet and build a thicker and lower dam, but obviously nothing such as this was ever done.

keep access to the Jing River in order to revive a system that was periodically reported as being in a state of decay. Large-scale work on the Jing Canal is mentioned as early as 1375, when more than 100,000 laborers of military status are said to have been mobilized to "dredge the Hongyan" (perhaps meaning to rebuild the dam and dredge the feeder canal), and in 1405, when, reportedly, over 29,000 civilian and military laborers were sent to work on the Jing Canal.[53] Other projects of rehabilitation are mentioned as having been undertaken in 1398 and 1427, but it is unclear exactly what they may have achieved.[54] Only a century after the founding of the Ming, in fact, after putting the Wang yushi intake back into shape had definitely proved to be hopeless, a new project was launched that attempted, once again, to catch up with the changes in the elevation of the Jing riverbed.

The technical novelty in this last version of the feeder canal (before modern times) was, if we are to believe some of the sources, the boring of a tunnel one *li* in length through the Xiaolongshan 小龍山 and the Dalongshan 大龍山, which once again made it possible to bring in the water of the Jing from still higher up the gorge.[55] The Ming system was called the Guanghui Canal 廣惠渠, but as in the Song and the Yuan only the intake and the higher part of the feeder canal were new. It was started in 1465 under the direction of Vice Censor-in-Chief and Grand Coordinator Xiang Zhong 項忠, who had been in the region since the late 1450s and reportedly was very popular there.[56] The new infrastructure was not, however, operational until eighteen years later. Xiang was soon promoted to a court

---

[53] For 1375, cf. Tang Binggang (see below on this author) in *XAFZ, j.* 7, p. 4b, and *Mingshi* 明史 [The Ming dynastic history], *j.* 88, p. 2146 (which does not give a figure, and is considered an error in *JQZ*, p. 23b); for 1405, Tang Binggang, *XAFZ, j.* 7, pp. 4b and 13a (the *Mingshi* has no mention of this).

[54] *Mingshi, j.* 88, pp. 2146, 2152; and see the discussions in *JQZ*, pp. 23b–24b.

[55] For the length of one *li*, see Tang Binggang, "Longdong qu shuili yi" 龍洞渠水利議, in *XAFZ, j.* 7, pp. 3b–6a, *passim*. It would seem, in fact, that only part of this new feeder canal was a tunnel, the rest being a deep trench cut across the rocky slope. Yuan Huazhong's (see above) and other descriptions (e.g., Chen Hongmou in a directive of 1751, in *Peiyuantang oucun gao* 培遠堂偶存稿 [Remaining drafts of the Peiyuan Hall], *j.* 30, p. 23a) speak of a narrow ditch 50 to 100 feet deep and 4 feet wide, from whose bottom the workers could not see the light of day. Other sources unambiguously speak of a tunnel (or tunnel sections) in which openings called "dragon's eyes" (*longyan* 龍眼) or "windows" (*chuang* 窗) were opened (see *JYXZ/JQZ, j.* 2, p. 1a–b). Later pictures of the Longdong Canal suggest that at least the section where the Longdong "spring" flowed in was a tunnel (hence its name): see Maps 9.2a and 9.4. Wang Taiyue (*JQZ*, p. 30a) explains that a succession of vertical wells called *Shigezi* 石隔子 were bored, from the bottom of which the workers would dig horizontally.

[56] See his *Mingshi* biography, *j.* 178, pp. 4727–31.

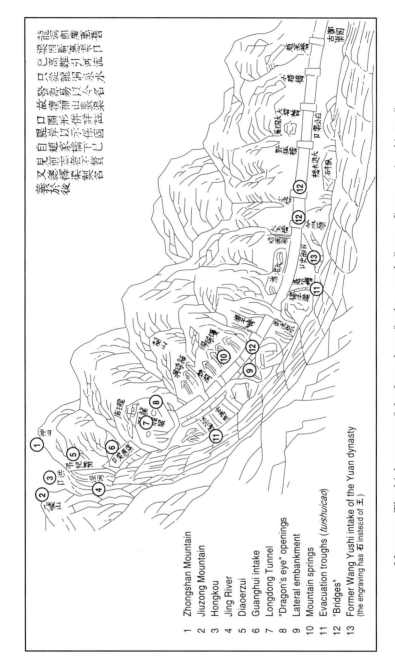

1 Zhongshan Mountain
2 Jiuzong Mountain
3 Hongkou
4 Jing River
5 Diaoerzui
6 Guanghui intake
7 Longdong Tunnel
8 "Dragon's eye" openings
9 Lateral embankment
10 Mountain springs
11 Evacuation troughs (*tuishuicao*)
12 "Bridges"
13 Former Wang Yushi intake of the Yuan dynasty
   (the engraving has 石 instead of 王)

Map 9.4: The higher part of the Longdong feeder canal. *Source: Jingyang xianzhi*, 1778.

position and left leaving the work unfinished. But he was sent back to the Northwest in 1468 and, when passing through Shaanxi, had the work completed – or so he claimed.[57] The new canal was not yet connected to the Jing, however, and much more had to be done under a succession of officials (among others, Yu Zijun 余子俊 in 1475–77 and Ruan Qin 阮勤 in 1481–82) in order to fix what seems to have been a rather hastily conceived project. According to reports, water was successfully admitted into the new canal, "flowing like a river," in the first month of 1482.[58]

Were all these efforts worth the trouble? While they all insist on the extreme difficulty of the work, when it comes to the benefits that it may have brought the different accounts of the Guanghui Canal present strong discrepancies. The source just mentioned claims that the new infrastructure made it possible to irrigate a total of more than 8,000 *qing*. Xiang's own stela text cites a figure of 8,022.8 *qing* (civilian land) plus 289.5 *qing* (garrison land). Yu Zijun's biography is much more modest, since it speaks only of "more than 1,000 *qing*,"[59] and indeed, even though the figure of 8,000 *qing* may have been reached at the start, according to the detailed account we owe to late-Ming Jingyang magistrate Yuan Huazhong,

> After the completion of the [Guanghui] Canal officials and people were exhausted and obstruction by silt only grew worse by the day; compared with the Song and Yuan, the benefits from irrigation (*shuili*) were less than one-tenth. Therefore Fuping county was deprived of its supply of water, while in Jingyang and the other four counties it was greatly reduced. Later it was established that the [quota of] irrigated fields would be only 800 *qing*.[60]

[57] See Xiang's own very triumphant account in *Jingyang xianzhi* (1910), pp. 850–55, under the title "Guanghui qu ji" 廣惠渠記 [An account of the Guanghui Canal]; also in Gu Yanwu's 顧炎武 *Tianxia junguo libing shu* 天下郡國利病書 [Advantages and disadvantages of the prefectures and kingdoms of the empire] (1879 ed.), *j.* 57, pp. 1b–4a. This is apparently the text of the stela that according to Wang Taiyue (writing in the 1760s) could still be seen by an "abandoned water bureau" (*shuisi feizhai* 水司廢宅) on the west slope of the Zhongshan, and on which Xiang recorded that he had christened the new canal "Guanghui."

[58] See the fairly detailed account by Peng Hua 彭華, a high official who introduces himself as a *tongnian* and friend of Ruan Qin (the latter being the son of a Vietnamese immigrant), entitled *Chongxiu Guanghui qu ji* 重修廣惠渠記 [An account of the reconstruction of the Guanghui Canal] (in *JYXZ* [1910], pp. 856–60). Although it ends on a festive note – the text is strangely reminiscent of Hou Meng's 1110 stela in its description of the populace's enthusiasm and awe at the water pouring in – Peng's account strongly insists on the technical difficulties overcome and the hardships endured by the workers.

[59] *Mingshi, j.* 178, p. 4738.

[60] Yuan Huazhong, "Kai Diaoerzui yi" (*JYXZ* [1910], pp. 884–88); also Yuan's biography in *JYXZ* (1842), *j.* 19, p. 4a. Yuan is among the most eloquent on the extreme difficulty of the excavation: the stone inside the hill was "as hard as iron" – hence the nickname "Iron Tunnel" (*tiedong* 鐵洞) given to the Guanghui – and "charcoal-burning and vinegar-

This is indeed within the range of figures reported from the Wanli period onward.[61]

The history of the system during the second half of the Ming is a rather confused one. A 42-*zhang* shortcut called the Tongji qu 通濟渠 was carved in the rock between 1516 and 1532, apparently to avoid a section of the old Fengli Canal of the Song that ran along the river and whose embankment was being constantly destroyed by the summer floods. Stelae studied by Wang Taiyue in the 1760s detail considerable reconstruction and dredging on various sections of the feeder canal in 1576–77. The same author concludes his section on the Ming period by stating that no regime since the Qin and the Han had devoted so much energy and effort to the system; but the situation, he adds, had become so different that in the later period the water was each day more difficult to get into the canal, and the canal was each day more in danger of being destroyed.[62]

An important novelty introduced by the Ming works must be mentioned before proceeding further. This is the harnessing of a number (often said to be "several tens") of "mountain springs" (*shanquan* 山泉) that were opened in the course of the excavation and gushed forth from cracks in the rock.[63] A frequent term for these underground waters is *dongquan* 洞泉; they included the important Longdong 龍洞 spring, which was to give its name to the Qing version of the canal. In fact, several later authors claim that for much of the time the Guanghui Canal did not take in the flow of the Jing at all and could only rely on the water of these "springs," which until then had seeped through to the river underneath the mountain slope on its left bank.[64]

---

soaking" (*tanzhi cucui* 炭炙醋淬) techniques had to be resorted to (mention of such techniques is already found in the accounts on the Censor-Wang Canal; contrary to Needham's suggestion [p. 287] *Science and Civilisation*, vol. 4, part, 3, it is clear that no gunpowder was involved).

[61] In his discussion of these discrepancies (*JQZ*, pp. 26b–27b), Wang Taiyue concludes that the 8,000-*qing* figure found both in Peng Hua's account and in the Xiang Zhong stela was in fact a "programmatic" figure based on hearsay going back to the Mongol period, not a description of the current reality. While this seems obvious in the case of Xiang Zhong (who dropped out long before the actual completion of the work), it remains that Peng's account claims to describe what effectively occurred in 1482.

[62] See *JQZ*, pp. 28a–29a. In the context, the word *shi* 勢, which I have translated "situation," might well be translated "the environment."

[63] Workers cutting the Censor-Wang Canal in the Yuan had already hit such underground waters, which are characteristic of the geological structure of the Pleistocene cone mentioned above. See, e.g., *JQZ*, p. 29b.

[64] E.g., Chen Hongmou, *Peiyuantang oucun gao, j.* 30, p. 23a; and in a memorial of the same period (*Gongzhongdang Qianlong chao zouzhe* 宮中檔乾隆朝奏摺 [Palace memorials of the Qianlong period], Taipei, Old Palace Museum, vol. 1, p. 389). For these documents see below.

9.2. QING ATTEMPTS AT REHABILITATING THE ZHENG-BAI IRRIGATION SYSTEM

Even in the seventeenth century irrigating the plain lying north of the Wei River by diverting part of the discharge of the Jing continued to be seen as the *raison d'être* of the Zheng-Bai system. In order to achieve this, as we have just seen, the officials and engineers who struggled dynasty after dynasty to keep it functioning, or to revive it, had to move the water intake ever higher in the gorge and to extend the feeder canal accordingly. The canal inherited by the Qing thus presented itself as the addition of all the previous versions since the Han. This pattern is nicely summed up by Tang Binggang 唐秉剛 at the beginning of an important text dating from the very first years of the Qianlong period,[65] where he describes the course of the canal from upstream to downstream by enumerating its successive sections in reverse chronological order: it starts from the "rock tunnel" (*shidong* 石洞) bored in the Xiaolongshan, followed by the so-called iron tunnel (*tiedong*), these two sections corresponding to the Guanghui of the Ming; then it flows through the "rock canals" (*shiqu*) of the former Wang Yushi and Fengli sections,[66] then through the part-rock, part-earth feeder section of the Bai Canal, until it enters the plain and the Sanbai distribution system.

The major cause for the successive opening of new intakes, each located higher upstream than the previous one, had been the continuous eroding and lowering of the bed of the Jing, which eventually brought its flow out of reach of the successive "mouths" of the feeder canal.[67] The phenomenon was compounded by the continuous silting up of the latter, making

---

[65] "Longdong qu shuili yi" 龍洞渠水利議 [A discussion of Longdong Canal water control], in *XAFZ* (*j.* 7, pp. 3b–6a). Tang Binggang was the magistrate of Jingyang county (where the crucial parts of the system are located) from 1736 to 1746 and seems to have been a particularly active and enterprising official; see his biography in *JYXZ* (1842), *j.* 19, p. 6b. Like Chen Hongmou, who arrived in the province as governor in 1744 and whom we shall meet later, he was from Guilin in Guangxi province. His text is not dated, but internal evidence suggests that it was part of a debate around Governor Cui Ji's projects in 1737–38 (see below). That its argument became the orthodoxy in the eighteenth century is suggested by the fact that it is quoted in full, but without credit, as an editor's comment in the hydraulics chapter of *JYXZ* (1778), *j.* 4, pp. 14b–23a.

[66] Of which only the intakes had been put out of use. A text from the very end of the Ming suggests that in periods of flooding the Jing water still threatened to enter the canal laterally through the ancient "mouths" (see *JYXZ* [1778], *j.* 10, p. 9b).

[67] Various authors, from Song Bingliang in 1343 to the present, give figures the precision of which is certainly open to some doubts prior to verification. The widest elevation differential cited is fifty feet above the Jing for the old Zheng Guo Canal entrance (which in fact is now lost).

the circulation of water yet more difficult, until it became completely impossible.

To counterbalance this trend by means of fetching the water from higher up in the gorge, the canal builders devised engineering feats each time more audacious, but which were also at a higher cost, both financially and in terms of the "people's sufferings." Besides, in the long term they yielded drastically diminished returns: even though the figures of acreage of irrigated land (whatever that notion exactly means)[68] given in the sources, and of which we have quoted several in the above account, raise all sorts of problems of interpretation, and present many highs and lows, the trend is unmistakable.

The Qing inherited a system that had reached (and in effect exceeded) its limits, and a number of later Ming and Qing authors writing on the subject were well aware of this. Even the high officials who promoted their programs by celebrating the miraculous efficiency of the Qin and Han canals – whose name the contemporary system still bore – admitted that the history of canal irrigation in Shaanxi was essentially one of a downward trend, the end result of which lay before their eyes: numerous canals, big and small, that were out of use, or even completely obliterated, and the main elements of the Longdong/Sanbai system in a dilapidated, or, at best, endangered, condition. Wang Jiyou 王際有 (a Jingyang magistrate who did repairs on the system in 1669), for example, reporting on a field visit, spoke of "innumerable" spots where the Zheng-Bai Canal was clogged and water was spilling over, of overflow systems that did not work, of leaking or ruined embankments, and so on; and he mentioned his colleagues' discouragement at the idea that nowadays, even though you do not have to create everything from scratch like the people of old, you can only expect results ten and a hundred times less than theirs.[69]

What strikes one when reading in succession the Song, Yuan, Ming, and Qing authors whose essays and proposals on the Zheng-Bai irrigation system have been preserved in local gazetteers and other sources, is the deep change that seems to have occurred during the seventeenth and eighteenth centuries, both in the discourse and in what was actually attempted in the field. Not only did the canal definitively cease to feed on the water of the Jing River – as it had done, with increasing difficulty, since the third century B.C. – but the officials who discussed irrigation improvement in the Guanzhong plain progressively dropped any idea of acting once again as

---

[68] Irrigated acreages per se are not an absolute measure of irrigation, since the quantity of water per year (or season) brought to a given acreage may vary considerably.

[69] See Wang's stela text in *JYXZ* (1910), pp. 865–69.

the men of antiquity had done, and operating a large-scale infrastructure with the same spectacular results;[70] this in the event had to be left to modern engineering in the twentieth century. More than that, most eighteenth-century authors dealing with the topic evince, or so it seems to me, a new attitude of cautiousness insofar as the environmental and human costs of a revival of the ancient system are concerned. But it took some time and, apparently, some debate before such cautiousness became the standard approach of Shaanxi officials.

This should not surprise us. For a devoted eighteenth-century official posted in Shaanxi, the question whether the present dynasty, equipped as it was with its virtue and presiding over an age of Great Peace, could restore the ancient systems, or at least to what point, was not academic or routine. From the early decades of the century (or, to speak more appropriately, from the last two decades of the Kangxi reign), increasing agricultural productivity in the face of a population that was rapidly growing upon a severely limited land base had become a sort of national priority,[71] and in most of the writings I am about to mention due reference was made to this aspect of the question. As a result – and, after all, in a strikingly modern way – there existed a dilemma between encouraging productivist adventures with promises of spectacular benefits "forever," and, at the same time, caring for an endangered environment and a precarious balance between people and land, as well as maintaining a realistic sense of what could be asked from the population in terms of labor and contributions. In what follows I shall try to show how this dilemma was approached and, occasionally, expressed by the eighteenth-century officials of Shaanxi, both high and low, who wrote on the problem.

YONGZHENG-STYLE ACTIVISM: YUE ZHONGQI'S REHABILITATION PROGRAM

The first overall plan of rehabilitation of the Zheng-Bai system during the Qing[72] was presented by Yue Zhongqi 岳鍾琪 (1686–1754), a famous gen-

---

[70] This ambition was still forcefully expounded by Xiang Zhong, the initiator of the Guanghui Canal in the Ming.

[71] See my essay, "Développement quantitatif et développement qualitatif en Chine à la fin de l'époque impériale," *Annales: Histoire, Sciences Sociales* no. 4 (1994), pp. 863–902.

[72] Following local attempts at dredging and rebuilding the existing canal and streamlining the organization of maintenance and water distribution by magistrates Jin Handing 金漢鼎 and Wang Jiyou 王際有, in 1652 and 1669 respectively. See their biographical sketches in *JYXZ* (1842), *j.* 19, pp. 5b–6a. Like Yuan Huazhong in the Wanli period, Jin Handing was an early advocate of relying exclusively on the water of the "springs."

eral who descended from Yue Fei – another famous general – and who became a governor-general of Sichuan and Shaanxi in 1725. Yue's intervention in the Zheng-Bai irrigation system is not recorded in much detail in the printed sources,[73] but, fortunately, the Qing archives hold at least two memorials of his that give a vivid account of his efforts, and, more generally, of how things were discussed and handled in the higher echelons of the state apparatus in the early eighteenth century.[74] For these reasons it may be interesting to follow them closely.

In the first memorial, dated YZ [i.e., Yongzheng] 4/9/22 (1726), Yue begins by recalling the past glory of the Zheng Guo Canal, which – according to him – still renders some service. In fact, among other canals in the region as well, "there still are some which have not disappeared, and which can somehow be used for irrigation." Then Yue refers to an audience he had the year before with the emperor, who had ordered him to investigate the local potential for land-opening and canal repair. Such instructions were representative of the Yongzheng emperor's obsessive concern, exemplified in a large body of edicts, with developing agricultural production in the face of a growing population, and more particularly with "opening land" (kaiken 開墾) and taking advantage of "neglected benefits" (yili 遺利). Equally typical of the period was Yue's response: he had ordered local officials in the Xi'an and Fengxiang prefectures (in other words, the core of the Wei valley) to conduct exhaustive field investigations of all the canals of the region, of the topography, of what sources of water could be harnessed, of what should be dredged, of where new ditches should be dug and new wells should be drilled, and so on, and, presumably, to submit the results of their inquiries in the form of detailed reports and "registers."

The results of these investigations are now coming in, says Yue. According to the local officials, the old canals have long been neglected and are progressively getting clogged with silt, most of them, as a result, being no more than rivulets useless for irrigation; they should be properly dredged. As for those that have virtually disappeared, or are located too far from the sources of water, or have their courses running too low, so that it is difficult or impossible to raise their water to the fields, they should be abandoned and well irrigation should be energetically promoted instead. With these recommendations Yue generally agrees, noting in particular that "the rules for each canal already exist" (ge qu chenggui ju zai 各渠成規具在), and that if

---

[73] There is only one entry in the Yongzheng Veritable Records (see below); see also JYXZ (1842), j. 13, p. 56, JQZ, p. 31a–b. One short biographical sketch in JYXZ (1910), p. 496, cites Yue's active interest in the revival of the Zheng-Bai Canal. His official biography in the Qingshi 清史 [The dynastic history of the Qing] does not mention the project.

[74] No. 1 Historical archives, Beijing, Palace memorials, Box 337.

something is not done as rapidly as possible it will become definitively impossible to lead the water available in the natural streams into the fields. In other words, he is not contemplating any technological or organizational breakthrough: what he wants to do, like so many before him, is to combat the process of environmental decay and managerial entropy that threatens most irrigation systems, particularly in northern China.

In any case – and this is again typical of the style of government encouraged at this time – he would not dare to make final recommendations and ask for funding before he has made a field investigation himself, which he plans to do within the year. The emperor's long rescript notes, among other things, that owing to the peaceful condition of the empire and the abundance of funds in public coffers it is the right time to launch operations of this sort everywhere in the provinces.[75]

Yue's second preserved memorial, dated YZ 5/1/29, reports on the results of his travels, in the course of which he has concentrated on the major source of "benefits" in the region – the Zheng-Bai Canal. He begins by giving a brief historical sketch of this system. The last version of the canal – the one fed by the tunnel dug under the direction of Xiang Zhong, which Yue calls the Longdong instead of the Guanghui Canal – had been, according to him, a success, with more than 8,000 *qing* irrigated at the start and assessed at the highest tax rate; but again, with the passing of the years, dredging became neglected and now "the Longdong and the Zheng-Bai" (meaning the Ming feeder canal, or Guanghui, and the Sanbai distribution system downstream) are completely obstructed with mud and alluvium, most embankments have collapsed, and the water from the "mountain springs," instead of being channeled into the feeder canal, is leaking down into the Jing River. The "water registers" (*shuice* 水冊) of the five counties concerned indicate a total of no more than 1,000 *qing* of irrigated land. In years of drought, there is not one drop of canal water available, and yet the people continue to pay the higher tax rate attached to "irrigated fields" (*shuitian*).[76]

Yue has duly inspected the site in person, "climbing on top of the ridges

---

[75] Yongzheng is clearly alluding to the "public funds" being made available by his well-known fiscal reforms. Indeed, when discussing funding the next documents use terms like *gongxiang* 公項 or *gongyong yin* 公用銀.

[76] Yue's phrasing implies that a field should be considered as "irrigated" when the canal system ensures a supply of water even in dry years – in other terms, when one has "guaranteed irrigation," as opposed to the situation where permanent irrigation facilities exist but do not operate in dry years. On these notions, see, for instance, Eduard B. Vermeer, *Water Conservancy and Irrigation in China* (Leiden: Leiden University Press, 1977), pp. 183–87. In the situation described by Yue, where there should be "guaranteed irrigation," it has ceased to exist.

and leaning over precipices," and has concluded that it is urgent to dig out the clogged parts of the Longdong feeder canal and reestablish water circulation, to dredge thoroughly the Zheng-Bai system, and to do all the necessary repairs. But he has been ordered to move to Sichuan just at the time when he was calculating the budget. Consequently, he has expedited the work: he has mobilized a provisional sum of 1,000 taels from public funds and has commissioned the Xi'an prefect to start the dredging in time and to evaluate the funding needed to rebuild the embankments and sluicegates. The prefect has now reported that the households (potentially) benefiting from irrigation – here called the *shoushui minhu* 受水民戶 – are dredging the distribution canals in the five counties concerned; that, as far as the "big work" on the Longdong and Zheng-Bai is concerned, he is hiring laborers to do the dredging and repairs (*shuxiu* 疏修), some of which have already been completed; and that a sum of 7,000 taels would be needed for labor and materials on the construction sites (*jianzhu gongliao* 建築工料). According to Yue, there is still enough to pay for this from the previous year's public funds in the provincial treasury, and he now asks for the emperor's authorization to use it.

Yongzheng's positive answer appears in an edict to the grand secretaries dated two weeks later and quoted in the *Veritable Records*.[77] It also appears in the vermilion rescript to Yue's memorial, which has the extra interest of illustrating the Yongzheng emperor's idiosyncratic approach to such projects. While he is accepting Yue's plans, the emperor reminds him that they will meet success only if enough people are sent to the field to take charge of them; indeed, he indicates that he has already ordered two court dignitaries (their exact positions are not specified) to recruit "people whom they know and who are close to them, including possibly board officials now serving in the capital, or expectant appointees, or unassigned personnel from their own locale or banner," whom they would recommend for serving as supervisors on the Zheng-Bai rehabilitation program. The dignitaries' answer is contained in a memorial dated YZ 6/3/16,[78] in which they announce that they have selected fifteen circuit intendants and prefects and sent them to work on the site, plus thirteen officers and military degree holders hailing from the province, because "the military are used to hardship" and "locals are more conversant with local conditions and prices."

---

[77] *Shizong shilu* 世宗實錄, j. 53, pp. 22b–23b, dated YZ 5/2/16.

[78] Or more than one year later, which seems unlikely; it cannot be excluded that "6" is an error for "5" either in my notes or on the memorial itself, which is in the same box at the Beijing archives as Yue Zhongqi's two pieces.

I mention such details because this way of strengthening (if not altogether bypassing) the administrative manpower locally available with ad hoc personnel carefully selected through networks of councillors enjoying the emperor's personal trust, and therefore considered more dependable than the average bureaucrat, was characteristic of Yongzheng's methods when it came to carrying out important and difficult tasks.[79] That the reviving of the Zheng-Bai system was a project of the utmost significance in his eyes is confirmed by an incident that occurred in the wake of the 1732 provincial examinations in Xi'an. For one of the so-called policy essays (*ce* 策) required from the candidates, the examiners had chosen Shaanxi irrigation as the topic. Unfortunately for them, the "question" they handed down to the aspiring licenciates mentioned the works of many great men of the past but did not say one word of the programs just completed in the province by order of Yongzheng himself, beginning with the rehabilitation of the "Zheng-Bai and Longdong." This obviously infuriated the emperor, and the chief examiners were duly referred to the Board for punishment.[80]

CUI JI'S REHABILITATION ATTEMPT

What the experienced officials and tough military officers specially sent to the site achieved is indicated in only general terms in the sources. It must not have been impressive even in the short term, since despite Yue Zhongqi's and Yongzheng's interest in the project (Yue had left to lead a military expedition into western Mongolia in the spring of 1729) the condition of the Zheng-Bai irrigation system at the beginning of the Qianlong reign, only a few years later, appears to have been once again appalling. In a memorial that must date from the end of 1737, Governor Cui Ji 崔紀 said that the construction done under Yue Zhongqi had indeed been beneficial to irrigation in the four counties then fed by the system (Jingyang, Liquan, Sanyuan, and Gaoling), but that it did not endure because "rules for annual maintenance had not been fixed." As a result, the mud and sand discharged by the Jing River at times of flood had not been dredged, and had obstructed the canal, water was spilling over, and in spite of some dredging done later at the suggestion of his predecessor Shuose 碩色, much of the water provided by the "mountain springs" was being lost

---

[79] As a contrast, one may note that earlier Jingyang magistrates like Jin Handing and Wang Jiyou, who did try to fix the Zheng-Bai irrigation system inherited from the Ming, would invite two or three local worthies from the concerned counties to help them in their projects: the scale of manpower mobilization at the top echelon is much more modest.

[80] See Yongzheng's edict in *Da Qing huidian shili* 大清會典事例 (1899 ed.), *j.* 331, p. 2a. My thanks to Mr. Philippe Favre for bringing this entry to my attention.

because of leaky banks. Indeed, the water of the Longdong spring (the one at the head of the system and one of the most abundant) was flowing backward north into the Jing River, which suggests that the feeder canal was hardly functioning at all.[81]

Cui Ji (a 1718 *jinshi*), whose occupancy of the Xi'an gubernatorial yamen spanned the short period from the seventh month, 1737, to the third month, 1738, apparently was a devoted if little-experienced activist in matters regarding the people's welfare. In fact he seems to have been somewhat too much of an activist, since he had to be hastily moved to another province in the face of the opposition and, it seems, popular unrest provoked by the forceful campaign of well drilling he launched in the drought-stricken Wei River valley during the winter of 1737 and spring of 1738.[82] Whatever the exact causes of the agitation – insufficient planning, hastiness, perhaps even outright coercion – and in spite of the limitations of the technique,[83] well irrigation was obviously the best option in at least parts of the Guanzhong plain. This is illustrated by the fact that Cui's campaign did have lasting results, even though not quite as impressive as he had claimed, and that in several areas the drive for drilling wells seems to have continued spontaneously.[84]

[81] This assessment of Yue Zhongqi's efforts is not without its problems. According to several gazetteers the decisions taken in 1727–29 marked a crucial improvement in the management of the system. For the authors of the 1884 Gaoling county gazetteer (*Gaoling xian xuzhi* 高陵縣續志), *j.* 1, p. 12b, while during the Ming irrigation in the county via the Sanbai system had been "but an empty name," thanks to the 1727 works and the posting of a Xi'an assistant prefect in charge of hydraulics (*shuili tongpan* 水利通判) on the site, "for the first time [Gaoling] could get its fair share of the benefits of irrigation (*de jun qi li* 得均其利) together with Jingyang, Liquan, and Sanyuan." We find similar considerations in the 1880 Sanyuan county gazetteer (*Sanyuan xian xinzhi* 三原縣新志), *j.* 3, p. 18b (quoting from an earlier edition).

[82] Cui's inspiration for this program was Wang Xinjing 王心敬 (1660–1744), a statecraft scholar from Shaanxi and the author of a manifesto entitled "Of the advantages of wells" (*Jingli shuo* 井利説), reproduced in several collections including the *Huangchao jingshi wenbian* (1873 ed., Taipei, Shijie shuju reprint, 1964), *j.* 38, pp. 4a–6a. See also *Gaozong shilu* 高宗實錄 [Veritable Records of the Qianlong emperor], *j.* 45, pp. 14b–17a, *j.* 57, p. 19b, 20b, *j.* 58, p. 21b–22b, *j.* 63, p. 20b, *j.* 64, pp. 8a–9b. On Cui's career, see *Qingshi* 清史, *j.* 310, pp. 4180–81; *Beizhuan ji* 碑傳集, *j.* 70, pp. 8a–13a.

[83] The short section on well irrigation in *Xingping xianzhi* 興平縣志 (1923), *j.* 1, p. 4a–b, insists on the tediousness of drawing water and transporting it to the fields for watering: only a minority of rich have wells equipped with "water-wheels" (*shuiche* 水車, a device for pumping up well water – also mentioned in Wang Xinjing's pamphlet as a specialty of Shanxi and Shaanxi – whose exact description remains unclear and that was presumably powered by humans, perhaps by animals in some cases). As a result, the difference with the areas fertilized by the Zheng-Bai Canal, or benefiting from "natural irrigation," is "like that between Heaven and earth."

[84] A little more than a decade later, Chen Hongmou launched a new, but more cautious, drive for well drilling. See *Peiyuantang oucun gao*, *j.* 26, pp. 41a–42b, *j.* 29, pp. 48a–50a.

Cui was also a proponent of large-scale canal irrigation. Not only did he report on the sorry condition of the Longdong Canal, as we have just seen, but he proposed to do serious work on it and got the Board of Works' approval as well as the emperor's authorization. To be sure, the information available on this aspect of his activity during his short tenure in Shaanxi is scarce. The only dated document I have found so far is a *Veritable Records* entry mentioning the Board of Works' discussion of his request for more funding of the project, which is dated from the end of winter, 1737–38: in addition to a previous estimate of 1,022 taels, a further 5,375 taels now appear to be necessary.[85] Cui's memorial itself is only briefly abstracted in the board's discussion, but we find a somewhat fuller quotation of it (or possibly of a slightly earlier one on the same subject) in an editor's note in the *Huangchao jingshi wenbian*.[86] Cui began with one more reminder of the history of the Zheng-Bai Canal, then gave the above-mentioned assessment of its current condition. What he proposed to do was a thorough cleaning of the Longdong itself, and of all the canals of the system, in order to reestablish the circulation of the waters of the Longdong and other springs. The most urgent matter, according to him, was to build a stone dam inside the Longdong in order to prevent the water of the springs from flowing into the Jing, and to reinforce the southern embankment of the feeder canal as a defense against silting up by muddy waters flowing in laterally from the Jing River, where the Jing ran parallel to the canal, in times of spate. In addition, dams were to be built along the mountain springs downstream so as to lead them into the canal. Finally, he proposed to appoint thirty "water workers" (*shuifu* 水夫) who would open and close the sluicegates (probably, those at the head of the overflow troughs in the higher part of the feeder canal).

We have no means of knowing exactly what Cui Ji was able to achieve before being transferred to Hubei. Some of his biographers state that he did do considerable construction work on the parts of the canal that had collapsed, that he opened or reopened more than seventy canals, and that the quantity of land that could be irrigated thanks to his efforts was, depending on the author, "several tens of thousand *qing*" (an extreme exaggeration) or "innumerable" (which is less risky).[87] The record in the

---

[85] See *Gaozong shilu, j.* 59, p. 8b, dated QL 2/12/19. One may note that the amounts are of the same order of magnitude as those suggested by Yue Zhongqi a decade earlier.

[86] This note is appended to the text of Wang Xinjing's "Of the advantages of wells," referred to earlier; its principal subject is Cui's well-drilling project. See *Huangchao jingshi wenbian, j.* 38, pp. 5b–6a.

[87] See *Beizhuan ji, j.* 70, pp. 8b, 11a, 12b. Generally speaking, the authors of these stelae do not appear to be very dependable as far as precise detail is concerned.

Jingyang gazetteer indicates that the crew of laborers was assembled in the eleventh month of 1737, and that the work was completed in the tenth month of 1739, in other words, well after Cui's departure. The renovated canal, now officially called the Longdong, irrigated a total, rather modest 740 *qing* of land.[88]

The principal fact about the 1737–39 works is that they definitively – that is to say, until the 1930s – put an end to the ambition of maintaining, or reviving, what had been the main feature of the system since its creation, namely, that it irrigated the fields with water transferred from the Jing River. All the sources give 1737 as the year when the Zheng-Bai ceased to be fed by the Jing, whose flow was now blocked by a dam built at the entrance of the Longdong tunnel;[89] the canal would only use the underground waters harnessed from the "springs" gushing forth from between the rocks in its higher section.

The debate on the appropriateness of taking such a move had been developing since the late Ming dynasty; and, even though Governor Cui Ji does not allude to it in any of his very few preserved statements on the rehabilitation of the Zheng-Bai, in 1737 it had apparently come to a head. If we are to believe our sources, it was during the Wanli period that it was first proposed to alleviate the problems posed by the now century-old Guanghui Canal by moving the intake still higher in the gorge, to a place named Diaoerzui 弔兒嘴.[90] Reportedly, the suggestion was made by an inhabitant of Sanyuan county by the name of Wang Siyin 王思印, who sent a memorial to the capital to that effect; but the idea was dropped after magistrate Yuan Huazhong's intervention, following a protracted period of hesitation on the part of the Board of Works. Yuan, say the sources, "was the first who advocated relying exclusively on water from the springs."[91]

---

[88] E.g., *JYXZ* (1910), p. 259. The gazetteers have several detailed descriptions of the post-1737 canal, taking it step by step from the now disabled Guanghui intake through the easternmost irrigation gates of the Sanbai system. The most exhaustive is in the 1842 *JYXZ/JQZ*, *j.* 2, pp. 1a–18b. See also the representations of the feeder canal in Maps 9.2 and 9.4.

[89] See, e.g., *JYXZ* (1910), p. 259. This was the solution advocated by Tang Binggang, then the magistrate of Jingyang, rather than building a dam inside the tunnel as proposed by Cui Ji. Tang argued that his own solution, with some fixing up inside the tunnel, would make it possible to harness some more springs flowing in north of the Longdong spring. See *XAFZ*, *j.* 7, p. 5b.

[90] There are variant names, such as Yaoerzui 銚兒嘴, Dunzuier 鈍嘴兒, and others.

[91] See *JYXZ* (1842), *j.* 13, p. 4a–b; *JYXZ* (1910), pp. 255–56. For Yuan's rebuttal of the plan, see his "Kai Diaoerzui yi" mentioned above. We may note, by way of contrast, that a Sanyuan magistrate of the Chongzhen period (the last reign of the Ming) concluded a very technical proposal on what to do with the canal by stating that, indeed, if one went upriver to fetch the water the bed of the Jing would be higher and higher, and when one arrived at Diaoerzui there would be no further difficulty (in harnessing enough of the flow). See Zhang Jinyan 張縉彥, "Tiaochen xiu qu ba ce" 條陳修渠八策 [Eight policies to repair the canal], in *JYXZ* (1778), *j.* 10, pp. 8b–10a; also *JYXZ* (1842), *j.* 13, p. 4b.

While the debate is mentioned in the early Kangxi period, even at the time of the Yongzheng works trying to harness the Jing still continued to be the orthodoxy: the Jingyang gazetteers clearly imply that the sluicegates set up at the demand of Chalang'a 查郎阿, Yue Zhongqi's successor, were intended to control the inflow of the Jing into the canal, which therefore "had not yet been entirely cut from the Jing."[92] At some point after 1729, when the system was evidently continuing to encounter grave problems, the river still bringing in mud and gravels when it was in spate, and the local officials being reluctant to organize serious maintenance, the provincial authorities once again sent investigators who, reportedly, advocated resuscitating the Diaoerzui project. We know of two responses to this: one is by a Hanlin academician named Shichen 世臣, whose connection to Zheng-Bai problems is unclear;[93] the other is the already mentioned text by Jingyang magistrate Tang Binggang, which is from beginning to end a lengthy and passionate plea against any project of the sort – using arguments some of which I will comment on in the last section of this essay. As we saw, Shichen's and Tang's arguments apparently won the day.

CHEN HONGMOU'S CONSERVATIVE APPROACH

That from now on things would have to remain in this state is made eloquently clear in the statements of the next governor to launch serious work on the system. In 1751, the already illustrious Chen Hongmou (1696–1771), who was about to complete the second (1748–51) of his four terms as Shaanxi governor, personally visited the site[94] and decided on a thorough cleaning and reinforcing of the Longdong Canal. We have at least two pieces of his on the topic, one a directive written for his subordinates in the province, and one a memorial sent in to the throne some three months later.[95] Both allude to the works directed by Yue Zhongqi and Cui

---

[92] *JYXZ* (1842), *j.* 13, p. 5b; *JYXZ* (1910), p. 258. See also the comparatively clear account in *JQZ*, pp. 31a–b: Chalang'a's sluicegate at the intake would allow the Jing in only during winter and spring, whereas it was to be closed during the "dangerous" summer months; he also (re)established sluicegates at the head of all the overflow troughs.

[93] See *JQZ*, pp. 31b–32b; *JYXZ* (1842), *j.* 13, p. 5b; *JYXZ/JQZ, j.* 3, pp. 5a–6a. These texts state that Shichen's proposals were forwarded to the Shaanxi governor (presumably, Cui Ji), who approved them and put them in effect.

[94] Chen claims to have combined a detailed visit to the canal works, interviews with local "old commoners," and an examination of the written sources, which was of course good statecraft and "evidential" (*kaozheng* 考證) practice. Wang Taiyue, the author of the *Jingqu zhi*, did the same, with perhaps more thoroughness on the evidential side; but so apparently did several statesmen of the Song, Yuan, and Ming periods.

[95] The directive, entitled "Xiuli Zheng-Bai qu shiti xi" 修理鄭白渠石堤橄 [Instruction on the repair of the Zheng-Bai Canal stone embankment], dated from the intercalary fifth month

Ji. In the memorial, which once again states that this canal is the most important of the irrigation systems in the province, Chen says that Cui not only obtained the authorization to do construction, but also fixed regulations on annual repairs (*suixiu* 歲修) and on the funding of a team of "water workers" (*shuifu gongshi* 水夫工食), thanks to which water was again circulating for the benefit of the people's fields.[96]

This was insufficient, however. The stone dikeworks built during the previous decades were too thin, and not strong enough to perform what was the essential task now that "there is no more point in discussing ways of using the water of the Jing for irrigation." This was keeping the turbid flow (*zhuoshui* 濁水) of the Jing away from the clear water (*qingshui* 清水) of the mountain springs running in the canal, and preventing silting up in the system. In his directive of the intercalary fifth month, Chen ordered his administration to send experienced officials to prepare a thorough plan of rehabilitation and reinforcement together with the local officials.

A few days after the directive had been sent, the Jing River swelled as it had rarely done, its flow rising more than one *zhang* (ten feet) higher than the dike that separated it from certain sections of the feeder canal. There was much destruction and the canal was again filled up with alluvium and debris, not a drop of water flowing through the lower part of the system. Major work was more urgent than ever, and the budget Chen asked the emperor's permission to mobilize amounted to a total of 6,710 taels for construction, dredging, tools, and materials – a sum of which about one-third, however, corresponding to the labor and tools for the dredging, would be paid for by the people benefiting from irrigation.

In short, in the situation prevailing at that time as well as in the ensuing decades, even though the feeder canal cut parallel to the course of the Jing was no longer supposed to take in part of the flow of the river, it remained in constant danger of being damaged and made useless by the river's periodic floods. The environment was as dangerous as ever, and the sort of solution that Chen advocated to preserve the irrigation water flowing in from the springs was the purely defensive one of building still-higher dikes and sturdier stonework.

---

of 1751, is in *Peiyuantang oucun gao, j.* 30, pp. 23a–24b. The original memorial, dated from the eighth month of the same year, is reproduced in *Gongzhongdang Qianlong chao zouzhe*, vol. 1, pp. 389–91. (No abstract appears in the *Veritable Records.*)

[96] The gazetteers specify that after the 1737–39 works the thirty *shuifu* entrusted with removing the water-plants growing in the canal bed and checking the dikes and sluicegates were each paid an annual salary of six taels. Annual repairs done in the ninth month would also be funded by the government. Chen Hongmou's memorial indicates that by 1751 this annual repair budget amounted to around 290 taels.

Was this the correct approach? One note in the Jingyang gazetteer states that the dike built on the right bank of the canal by Xiang Zhong in the fifteenth century was seven feet wide and only two feet high – enough to hold the canal water flowing inside, not enough to contain the Jing floods coming in from outside – and that it had held good for more than a century. By contrast, the trend toward heightening this partition between the feeder canal and the river had started with Yue Zhongqi's campaign of works, reaching a maximum of nine feet in the early Qianlong period, but without a corresponding thickening. As a result, the dikeworks were more and more easily damaged or even destroyed. For the authors of this note, even making higher *and* wider walls was not the solution, since they would be eaten into by the current anyway. They advocated a low and sturdy dike that, even though it could not contain the higher waters of the Jing, would not have to be rebuilt after only a few years; the dredging inside the canal that would have to be done instead was much less expensive.[97] One wishes one had more evidence and knew whether there was any public debate on this sort of alternative between head-on resistance to environmental risk and a more flexible approach yielding to the consequences of unavoidable natural phenomena – but always in order to preserve an infrastructure that was acknowledged to be "unnatural."

BI YUAN: MAINTENANCE AND SEARCH FOR LOCAL IMPROVEMENT

The next reported personal visit to the site by a Shaanxi governor after Chen Hongmou's was that of Bi Yuan 畢沅 (1730–97) in 1775: once again, what he saw testified to the fragility of the Longdong upper system, and hence the difficulty of maintaining irrigation downstream.[98] According to a memorial he sent in a few years later, in 1782,[99] he had found the Longdong Canal in bad repair, blocked up by silt and irrigating no more

---

[97] See *JYXZ* (1842), *j.* 13, p. 6a; also in *JYXZ* (1910), p. 259.

[98] Bi was a governor of Shaanxi from 1773 to 1785. His 1775 visit to the Longdong, and the program of rehabilitation he launched after lengthy discussions back in Xi'an, are related in *XAFZ, j.* 7, p. 19a–b, which allowed the editors of this work, published in 1779, to close the chapter on the Zheng-Bai system on a note of reasonable hope. Their remarks are also quoted in the 1842 and 1910 Jingyang gazetteers.

[99] Reproduced in the *Huangchao jingshi wenbian* (*j.* 36, pp. 4a–5a) under the title "Shaan sheng nongtian shuili muxu shu" 陝省農田水利牧蓄疏 [Memorial on water control for agriculture and animal husbandry in Shaanxi province]. The text was apparently composed in response to an imperial circular (one more) asking the governors for suggestions on how to improve popular customs (*fengsu* 風俗) and bureaucratic discipline (*lizhi* 吏治). It dealt with the economic and environmental problems of the three main subregions of Shaanxi and suggested some solutions.

than about 10,000 *mu* (or 100 *qing*). Such a figure suggests how pale a replica of its predecessors this infrastructure had become – one that Bi, after innumerable others, said had been the main source of prosperity in the region since the Qin and the Han; or, to use the words of the editor of the Xi'an gazetteer, how "the benefits of several thousand years were about to be progressively engulfed."[100] Reportedly, the 2,394 *zhang* of canal that Bi reopened allowed the water to flow for a distance of 134 *li* and to irrigate a thousand *qing*, which certainly was a serious improvement.[101]

At the same time, his memorial of seven years later said that there still was much to do in the region, and, like several of his predecessors, he suggested yet another general investigation into the potential of the Wei River valley for irrigation: what rivers could be dredged and diked up, what canals could be dug, what old infrastructures could be put back to full use, or simply revived, and so forth.[102] Indeed, it is interesting to note that, while he was advocating this new investigation in 1782, Bi himself apparently had already done much in the same domain only a few years earlier, probably at the same time as, or in the wake of, the Longdong works. An entry in the *Veritable Records* mentioning water-conservancy work in Shaanxi under him points to an undeniable thoroughness of approach:

> The governor of Shaanxi, Bi Yuan, has memorialized that he has pressed for the dredging (*shujun* 疏濬) of a total of 1,171 canals (*qu*) in forty-seven departments and counties attached to Xi'an and other prefectures, taking advantage of the dry period during last winter. All the dikes and embankments (*tiyan* 堤堰) have been thoroughly and solidly rebuilt.[103]

In any case, it is apparent (and, occasionally, explicitly mentioned) that such general campaigns of irrigation enhancement in the province as those launched by Chen Hongmou, Bi Yuan, and others in the eighteenth century, not to mention a variety of local efforts, were predicated on the idea that grandiose programs with hopes of enormous benefits, like restoring the Zheng-Bai system to its ancient glory, were outdated. A multiplication of small-scale operations, like restoring or, possibly, creating local contour

---

[100] *XAFZ*, j. 7, p. 19a. The text does not speak of 100 *qing*, but states that by that time the irrigation registers mentioned only 567 *qing*.

[101] Intriguingly, while the accounts of the previous rehabilitation drives mention budgets and funding, the only indication in the case of Bi's efforts is a note in *JYXZ* (1842), j. 13, p. 6a (and p. 259 of the 1910 edition) saying that the work was entirely funded by a 5,000-tael private contribution from a local inhabitant, one Meng Jiwu 孟輯五.

[102] Chen Hongmou in 1751 had launched such an investigation: see his memorial in *Gongzhongdang Qianlongchao zouzhe*, vol. 1, pp. 385–87 (dated QL/16/8/11), and several related directives in *Peiyuantang oucun gao*.

[103] *Gaozong shilu*, j. 1005, p. 40b, dated third month, 1776.

canals, and encouraging the drilling of wells, was seen as the more reasonable solution in the face of growing population pressure on the land and increased environmental fragility. As a matter of fact, it might well be that such insistence, on the part of the more activist officials, upon getting the best out of existing possibilities, provided they could be translated into reality without too much disruption or risk, did help the region to experience the eighteenth-century demographic growth without presenting the symptoms of a grave Malthusian crisis.

THE NINETEENTH-CENTURY ROUTINE

To be sure, more research is necessary to know as precisely as possible what was done, and when, in terms of local irrigation improvement.[104] As far as the Longdong site and the irrigation system that depended on it are concerned, several interventions are mentioned in the nineteenth century.[105]

Typically, a new campaign of construction and dredging, usually directed by the Jingyang magistrate, would be made necessary by the destruction of embankments and accumulation of mud in the feeder canal in the wake of one of the Jing River's periodic floods. This is what occurred in 1787, 1806, 1816, 1821, and 1823, for example. What can also be noted about these episodes is that the budgets reported for repairs that certainly do not seem to have been more important than those mentioned above, were, on several of these occasions, considerably higher than in the earlier period, ranging from over 10,000 taels in 1806 to 21,000 taels in 1821.[106]

Nothing of importance is mentioned thereafter,[107] until in 1869 Grand Secretary Yuan Baoheng 袁保恆 (1826–78), who had recently joined the staff of Zuo Zongtang and was in charge of the supplies for Zuo's armies in the Northwest, proposed to build a dam made of wooden posts, iron fittings, and piled stones across the Jing River, and put the old Guanghui Canal (which, we remember, dated back to the fifteenth century and had definitely ceased functioning in 1737) once more into operation. The attempt was abandoned after a year of unsuccessful effort. One would of course want to know more about this resurgence of a type of project that

---

[104] For a first impression, see the table on pp. 141–46 in Huang Shengzhang, "Guanzhong nongtian shuili."

[105] The most accessible source is the 1910 Jingyang gazetteer, pp. 259ff, using in part information drawn from the more detailed 1842 edition, j. 13, p. 6a–b.

[106] A variable mix of treasury funds, treasury loans, private contributions, and surtaxes (this last system started in 1787, at the rate of 5 fen [hundredths of a tael] per mu) is mentioned.

[107] But see some unsuccessful and even naive attempts by Gaoling magistrates in the 1860s, as recorded in the 1884 Gaoling county gazetteer (Gaoling xian xuzhi), j. 1, p. 13a.

had been considered definitely unfeasible more than a century earlier. What is sure is that the context was different, the Shaanxi core area being now exposed to rebellion and war, with the accompanying disruption and depopulation and, at the same time, a high demand for military supplies, for the first time since the Ming–Qing transition.

Campaigns of repairs to the canal in the wake of floods, most of them with comparatively low budgets, are mentioned for the ensuing years. The idea of again directing the flow of the Jing into the Longdong Canal surfaced once more after destructive rainstorms in 1901; this time, interestingly, it came from an English missionary (of whom we know only his Chinese name, Dun Chongli 郭崇禮) who suggested paying for the operation with half the relief funds sent by his country. The proposal came to nothing.

It is well known that the eventual revival of the old technique of diverting the Jing River for irrigation, inaugurated with the Zheng Guo Canal and abandoned during the early eighteenth century, occurred at the beginning of the 1930s, when a combination of provincial and especially foreign funding, on the one hand, and of scientific planning and modern technology, on the other, led to the construction of what was called the Jinghui Canal 涇惠渠. This new system (which was only the first part of a more ambitious project) fed in the water of the Jing at a narrow pass higher in the gorge than previously. A dam 68 meters long at the top and 9.20 meters high at the deepest part of the river was built in concrete, and a tunnel 359 meters long and 16.8 square meters in section was bored through the mountain; and parts of the old feeder canal were reused and enlarged so that they would transmit a much larger discharge than before. This discharge was, for the first time in the history of the system, expressed in a rational unit: 16 cubic meters per second, of which 14 came from the Jing River and only 2 from the mountain "springs."[108]

These last figures suggest how modest the output of the Qing Longdong Canal, which was fed entirely by the springs, must have been when compared with that of the more ancient systems. Compared with the situation at the end of the empire (c. 800 *qing* or less), the area irrigated by the new canal was eventually increased by almost an order of magnitude: the figure of land effectively irrigated was about 1,200 *qing* in 1932, 2,000 in 1933, and 5,000 in 1934, and was further brought to 6,000 *qing* in the following

---

[108] The Jinghui Canal was inaugurated in June 1932. Plans had been made as early as 1921, but civil war cut them short. This and other information can be found in the already mentioned *Huanghe zhi*, vol. 3, pp. 139–58. See also Nickum, *Water Management Organization*, p. 26, and Needham, *Science and Civilisation*, vol. 4, part 3, p. 287.

years.[109] The entire distribution area was also reorganized, the old Sanbai pattern being partly replaced with a new pattern articulated along two main branches. The Jinghui canal system was further enlarged under the PRC (it was rechristened the People's Yinjing 引涇 canal during the Cultural Revolution), and in the end irrigated an area about twice that of the 1930s, which necessitated tapping further sources of water, like groundwater by means of tube wells.[110] (See Map 9.5 for the Republican and PRC pattern.) Twentieth-century developments are beyond the scope of this essay, however.

9.3. THE NATURAL, SOCIAL, AND ADMINISTRATIVE ENVIRONMENT: SOME GENERAL REMARKS

What I would like to attempt in this last section is a brief recapitulation of several problems that can be called "environmental" in the wider sense – including the human and political dimension. Although several of them have already been alluded to in the foregoing account, they deserve a closer, even if in this case a somewhat unsystematic, consideration.

The technical problems raised by the periodic attempts at reviving the Zheng-Bai hydraulic system of old were clearly intractable, and for want of some technological breakthrough they could only grow more so over the centuries, inasmuch as the fragile combination of topographical and hydrological features that had made it possible to devise the intake system in the first place was bound to deteriorate – the main cause being, as we saw, the downcutting of the Jing riverbed. Similarly, problems like erosion in the catchment areas and silting up were ultimately beyond control (and in fact, are still a major difficulty for all damming and irrigation projects set up in comparable geological and hydrological contexts).

Such natural factors, to which a highly variable rainfall and the sometimes violent changes in the Jing River discharge should of course be added, were not the only ones in play. That contemporary observers were aware of the intricate relationship between natural givens and demographic, social, and political factors is well illustrated – to give only one example – by an editor's comment in the chapter on "Large Waterways"

[109] The Republican *mu* (0.01 *qing*) was slightly smaller than the Qing *mu* (666.5 m² as against 693.6 m²).
[110] See Nickum, *Water Management Organization*, pp. 26–28, and the 1973 document (replete with Maoist flourishes) translated on pp. 201–13. A new dam built in the 1950s is reported to have brought the potential discharge to 46 m³ per second.

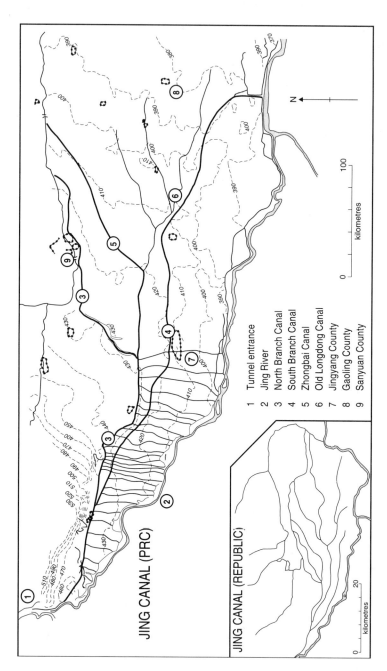

JING CANAL (PRC)

JING CANAL (REPUBLIC)

N

kilometres
0   100

kilometres
0   20

1   Tunnel entrance
2   Jing River
3   North Branch Canal
4   South Branch Canal
5   Zhongbai Canal
6   Old Longdong Canal
7   Jingyang County
8   Gaoling County
9   Sanyuan County

Map 9.5. The Jing Canal in Republican and PRC times. *Source*: Huang Shengzhang, "*Guanzhong nongtian shuili de lishi fazhan ji qi chengjiu*," p. 126.

(*dachuan* 大川) of the Xi'an prefectural gazetteer.[111] Among other considerations, the passage notes that, since the present dynasty, in contradistinc-
tion to earlier regimes, is no longer interested in using the canal system for
transportation,[112] all the important rivers should be fully available for agricultural development (*gengtun* 耕屯) through irrigation; but then,

> Why is it that all the canals and embankments bequeathed by antiquity are
> day after day getting obstructed by silt, and that once they have disappeared
> it is impossible to bring them back into service? It all comes from the fact that
> the terrain in Shaanxi is high in elevation, and that the weather is frequently
> hot and dry, [so that] those of humble status struggle to make a profit out of
> every foot and inch of soil: as soon as they see that a canal or ditch has dried
> out, they plant the space [thus freed]. Their superiors [*weishangzhe* 為上者,
> meaning either the officials or the irrigation officers] occasionally appropri-
> ate the rent for their own profit and do not care to enforce the prohibitions.
> Once one canal has been obstructed, the flow is cut upstream and down-
> stream, and the main waterways all become useless. This is why crops can only
> avail themselves of rainwater.

This process of overoccupation of the land initiates a sort of vicious
environmental cycle since (according to this author) the more dry land
there is, the less rainfall one can expect. The problem is seen in the first
place as one of balance between land and water. The gazetteer quotes from
a Ming author by the name of Wei Chengrun 魏呈潤, according to whom
"the rain results from the transformation of the *qi* of water. To keep water
conservancy in good condition (水利修) is the secret (術) of bringing about
rain."[113] This problem is then compounded by the low productivity of the
region, and by a sociopolitical system wherein the necessary discipline to
maintain the irrigation infrastructures is not enforced.

To give just another example of how social organization and political
management, and the changes they undergo, are crucial elements in defining the way a human infrastructure fits in its environment and interacts
with it, we may recall that the sort of large-scale conscription of labor that
the states of antiquity – or the first Ming emperors, for that matter – were
able to resort to through sheer coercion was no longer politically acceptable in late-imperial China: labor had to be paid its due value. Of these and

---

[111] *XAFZ, j.* 5, pp. 12b–13b.

[112] 漕輓之利不復取給於茲. The remark is interesting in that it does not consider the possibility that the former infrastructures for government provisioning of an imperial capital or (as
in the Northern Song) of a standing frontier army be turned over to commercial transportation. Development is seen exclusively in terms of agricultural production.

[113] The same sentences are found in Gu Yanwu's *Rizhi lu* 日知錄, in the section on water
conservancy.

other problems, some eighteenth-century critics of the rehabilitation programs laid out by activist governors (or their advisers) appear to have been
remarkably aware. What seems to me interesting in the considerations of an
author like Tang Binggang in the 1730s, for example, is a sense of the
evolution of the environment and of the opportunities for economic development (here, irrigation) it offered within the available technology, knowing, besides, that there were political limits to conscripting the populace
the way former regimes had done.

FACING A DANGEROUS ENVIRONMENT

I have already mentioned the problems caused by the sudden swellings of
the Jing in the summer months and by the large quantities of silt, sand, and
other debris it carried along, as did the mountain streams that rushed down
from the gullies on the east side of the feeder canal and intersected with it
at several points along its course. Ever since the Song version of the canal,
the feeder section, compressed as it was between the course of a capricious
and occasionally violent river and unstable rocky slopes, was under constant
threat of being badly damaged, or clogged with sand and gravel, or both.

As I mentioned in the first section, the Song engineers who built the
Fengli Canal at the beginning of the twelfth century seem to have been the
first to devise techniques to protect the higher and more fragile parts of
the system against this dangerous environment. To control the impact of
the seasonal floods of the Jing River they built systems of overflow at the
head of the canal, such as the two sluicegates called Jinglang 靜浪 and
Pingliu 平流 ("quiet waves" and "stable flow," respectively), or the two
evacuation tunnels (*dong* 洞) called Huilan 迴瀾 and Dengbo 澄波 ("turning
back the flow" and "pure waves," respectively). As far as I can understand
the descriptions, the tunnels evacuated the water entering the canal when
it rose above seven feet, and the sluicegates when it rose above six feet.[114] In
1343 Song Bingliang advocated rehabilitating the Jinglang and Pingliu
gates of the Song, still visible in his time, of which he said that they used to
be lowered either to evacuate the overflow and prevent siltation or to empty
the canal during repair time; they were fifty paces apart, and emptied into
an "evacuation trough" (*tuishuicao* 退水槽) located in between them and
leading to the Jing.[115] In spite of such lateral devices the problem of

---

[114] See the Cai Pu stela in *JQTS*, p. 7a, or *JYXZ* (1842), *j.* 13, pp. 2b–3a. The Hou Meng stela,
ibid., only speaks of "drain holes" (*tongdou* 通竇).

[115] See Song Bingliang in *JYXZ* (1778), *j.* 10, pp. 4a–b. Qing representations (e.g., Map 9. 4)
show several *tuishuicao* along the higher course of the feeder canal.

overflow control seems to have been a perennial one. It should be recalled that the swelling of the Jing to unmanageable levels could happen in a matter of a few hours. What remains unclear, in particular, is the sort of device (if any) that may have existed at the "mouth" of the Song and post-Song canals: indeed, the possibility of closing it altogether to prevent sand and gravels from accumulating in the narrow channel at the head of the feeder canal does not seem to be mentioned in the sources.

Other installations were meant to protect the canal against rocks and other materials being swept along downhill during the heavy summer rains and getting deposited in its bed. The risk seems to have been particularly great at the so-called gullies (gou 溝), some of which collected the runoff of vast catchment areas. Four of them, visible on Qing representations, are already mentioned in Song sources (called Dawang 大王, Xiaowang 小王, Toucao 透槽, and Fankeng 樊坑, respectively). The technique that was apparently adopted in 1107–10 consisted in erecting sturdy fences as grids across the gullies, made of tree trunks fastened to wooden pillars driven deep into the ground: during the rainstorms, water would pass through, but the bigger pieces of rock would be stopped.[116]

The efficiency of this method (of which I have found no mention in post-Song literature) had to be enhanced by structures that isolated the canal flow from runoff water, sand, and gravel at the points where the gully channels intersected its course. These devices were known either as "stone tents" (shipeng 石棚, referring to their shape; also written 硼 in some sources), or as 'bridges' (qiao 橋), sometimes "concealed bridges" (anqiao 暗橋): the "tent" description referred to the part underneath the "bridge", that is, the tunnel of stonework covered with earth through which the canal flowed; while the "bridge" was the structure above, on which the gully runoff passed on its way to the river beyond.[117] According to some sources the concave shape of the upper "bridges," with their high edges making them look like stone troughs (shicao 石槽) and preventing sand and gravel from spilling over into the canal, was a creation of the Jin period.[118] A number of them are visible on Qing representations, and the Jinghui Canal of the 1930s also had several of them – only one, reportedly, going back to the old imperial canal.[119]

---

[116] JQTS, p. 7a–b.

[117] The first description is in the Cai Pu stela, JQTS, p. 7b; it is reproduced in most later sources, e.g. a list of technical terms with explanations entitled Longdong qu tushuo 龍洞渠圖説 [Plates and explanations on the Longdong Canal], by Tang Binggang, in XAFZ, j. 7, p. 6a (the plates are, regrettably, nowhere to be seen). For a comparatively clear account, see JQZ, p. 34b. We do not have any indication of the dimensions of these works.

[118] See, for example, XAFZ, j. 7, p. 10b.

[119] See Huanghe zhi, vol. 3, p. 149.

These techniques, and others mentioned in the same sources, aimed at protecting a man-made infrastructure cutting across the natural lines of a rugged and unstable terrain from the natural consequences of precipitation and erosion. These are environmental hazards, and the descriptions of the precarious situation of the intake and feeder system of the Zheng-Bai Canal in the sources cannot be read without evoking our own mountains, where walls against avalanches, tunnels, and other engineering feats aim at isolating roads, settlements, or even ski slopes, from ordinary climatic or geologic events that seem to take on cataclysmic proportions only because they come in the way of human activities that were not (in a sense) supposed to occur there in the first place.

THE IDEA OF "NATURALNESS"

In contrast with the audacious designs and technical ingenuity displayed by the engineers working in the Jing gorge – at the same time creating an environmental hazard and trying to control it – many sources put forward a notion of "naturalness" (*ziran* 自然) that would seem to deserve a close examination. As this is not the place to elaborate on the idea of nature in the Chinese philosophical tradition, I will limit myself to mentioning a few places where the notion comes up in writings discussing the technical problems of the Zheng-Bai irrigation system.

Several Song and Yuan authors speak of the desirability of being able to tap the "natural flow" of the Jing, as opposed to the flow raised by a jetty (i.e., the solution that had virtually always to be adopted). In 1343, Censor Song Bingliang, who had toured the site and inquired about local opinions, advocated a combination of a low but sturdy dam made of several layers of stone containers, and a lowering of the bottom of the intake canal by eight feet (to be dug in the rock!) so as to put the "mouth" five feet below the level of the Jing, the jetty serving to increase the intake over the five feet of "natural water" (*ziran zhi shui* 自然之水).[120] As we saw, the idea of digging deep enough not to need a jetty was supported, and indeed put into practice, at the time of the building of the Fengli Canal under the Song. Zhao Quan 趙佺, the official in charge of the project in 1107, also said that at the "mouth" the bed of the canal should be five feet below the level of the Jing, so that one could make do without a dam.[121] As such

---

[120] Speaking of the Fengli canal of 200 years earlier, Song Bingliang uses the term *zilai zhi shui* 自來之水, which is more explicit: the water enters the canal without having to be helped, as it were.

[121] This notion of a natural flow five feet deep as the ideal canal discharge comes up in other writings as well. Tang Binggang (*XAFZ, j.* 7, p. 5b) cites an anonymous Yuan writer to the

options were hardly realistic during most periods, the reasons for advocating them seem to have been, more often than not, ideological as well as technical.

There was, first, the argument of the plight of the corvée laborers who had to be mobilized every year by the irrigated communities and sent up the gorge of the Jing to rebuild the jetty under extremely arduous conditions. Beyond this "Confucian" sort of argument (to which I will come back in a moment) – or perhaps related to it – the argument of "naturalness" implied a sort of harmony, or smooth interaction, between nature and man. The sufferings and disruption experienced by the laborers toiling on the construction sites only enhanced the fact that the spectacular engineering realizations of the builders of the more recent canal intakes and upper sections did violence (in some sense) to nature itself. The ideal, projected by several authors backward onto the Qin and Han versions of the system, would have been to harness hydrological resources in such a way that the infrastructures thus created could function without any further intervention – as components, as it were, of the natural landscape.

This view did not condemn large-scale man-made engineering. Jingyang magistrate Yuan Huazhong in the Wanli period of the Ming claimed that the original Zheng Guo Canal was "natural" even though (he said) it used a dam made of more than 1,000 stone containers (shidun) to "dam up the river" (yong shui 壅水). Not only was the jetty supported by big rocks lying in the riverbed – it was "borrowing the strength of the natural rocks for its framework" (jie tiansheng zhongshi zhi li yi wei yan gu 借天生眾石之力以為堰骨) – but at that time the canal was still dug in earth and "followed the nature of the water" (shun shui zhi xing 順水之性), there being no "boring through the mountains and trying to fight with the water" (fei chuan shan er yu yu shui zheng ye 非穿山而欲與水爭也).[122] The fact that Yuan's description of the original Zheng Guo intake is total fiction – there is not a word on the technique of water diversion used at that time in any pre-Song source – does not detract from the ideological representativeness of his interpretation.

The phrase "the nature of water" (shuixing) also occurs in Tang Binggang's discussion, but with different implications. Whereas in this phrase "water" should rather be rendered as "flow," in Tang's section

---

effect that "A natural flow of five feet can irrigate more than 30,000 qing of land (五尺自然之水，灌田三萬餘頃)."

[122] See JYXZ (1910), pp. 884–85. The notion of "struggling" (or competing) with the water, or, conversely, "following" it – or, as the case may be, constricting it between dikes or allowing it to expand – of course informs much of the reflection and policy debates on water control in China.

devoted to it[123] it is the very nature of the element that is discussed. In considerations that are not always easily translated (that is, understood), Tang contrasts the nature of the water of the Jing and that of the "springs." The former is laden with silt, and, while its fertilizing power was celebrated in Qin and Han times, nowadays the plants growing on land exposed to it are literally destroyed. We do not know how far Tang's description should be taken at face value – even though he puts forth the testimony of "peasants from the mountains and old people from the wilderness" (*shannong yelao* 山農野老) – but in any case he explains the contrast by the fact that, in antiquity, the slowness of the flow ensured both irrigation and fertilization thanks to a harmonious combination of earth and water; whereas, ever since the Jing has been harnessed higher in the gorge, the nature (*xing*) of its water has become colder (*kuhan* 苦寒), its texture (*zhi* 質) coarser (*cuzhong* 粗重), since it carries along only sand and gravel, and there is "no earth energy whatsoever to enrich it" (*quan wu tuqi yi zi zhi* 全無土氣以滋之). The water from the mountain springs, by contrast, is perfectly clear and fresh, and the warmth or coolness of its "energy" (*qi* 氣) is well adapted to irrigating the crops.[124]

As we saw, comparable considerations can be found in Chen Hongmou's two texts mentioned above, where he elaborates on the unequal struggle between the clear water of the springs and the alluvial mud carried along by the Jing when the river is in spate: "Whenever the mud (*zhuoni* 濁泥) meets clear water, the clear cannot stand up to the muddy (*qingzhuo bu di* 清濁不敵), and silting up immediately results." Clear water (from the springs), says Chen, means free flowing (*changliu* 暢流); muddy water (from the Jing) means destruction and blockage (*chongsai* 沖塞).

. One can only wonder to what physical reality these considerations may possibly correspond, and, more specifically, to what *change* in the environment over the centuries. They contrast strikingly with the celebration of the Jing water's fertilizing power over poor alkaline soils that was mentioned as early as the *Shiji* and is confirmed by a famous popular rhyme reproduced in the *Hanshu*, according to which "One picul of the water of the Jing contains several pecks of mud" (*Jingshui yi shi, qi ni shu dou* 涇水一石 其泥數斗), so that "it both irrigates and fertilizes" (*qie gai qie fen* 且溉且糞).[125]

---

[123] Entitled "One has to discriminate what is appropriate concerning the nature of the water" (*Shuixing bu ke bu bian suo yi* 水性不可不辨所宜), no. 4 of the "One has to" items structuring Tang's plea (this passage in *XAFZ*, *j.* 7, pp. 4b–5a).

[124] The same celebration of the qualities of the water from the springs (in winter it "does not chap the hands") is repeated in many other sources of the period: e.g. *JYXZ* (1842), *j.* 13, p. 5b, *JYXZ/JQZ*, *j.* 2, p. 1b, and *j.* 3, p. 6a.

[125] See *Hanshu*, *j.* 26, p. 1685; and Needham, *Science and Civilisation*, vol. 4, part 3, p. 228, for a translation.

Did the nature of the silt carried by the Jing change, or was it the evolution in the design of the canal and in irrigation techniques that made a difference?

Possibly both. According to one recent author,[126] what was done with the Qin and Han canals was alluvial irrigation based on seasonal flooding (or "warping" – in Chinese, *yinhong yuguan* 引洪淤灌), which was made possible by the discharge and regularity of flow of the ancient canals. By contrast, the Song and post-Song canals provided continuous irrigation (except during the months assigned to repairs), but with their narrower intakes they had a much smaller outflow; as a result, during the high-water season when the silt content of the Jing was at its maximum, the silt would be deposited on the canal bed instead of being brought to the fields.[127]

Did the very nature of the silt content of the Jing change? One hypothesis[128] would be that with the passing of the centuries, due to the stripping of the vegetation cover the upper catchment of the Jing had been eroded down below the soil layer into the loess proper, that is, the untransformed and therefore virtually sterile loess, which was now being washed into the river by runoff. But at this point the chronology remains unclear: more research is needed to refine this contrast and better understand the process of change that led from one extreme (the reported alluvial bounty that multiplied the productivity of the region in ancient times) to the other (the Qing situation wherein the system provided only "lifesaving water" [*jiuming shui* 救命水] from "mountain springs" flowing into the feeder canal, which had now to be cut from the infertile waters of the river). Regrettably, so far as I can tell there is no discussion of the nature of the Jing water in any source during the nearly two millennia separating the two periods.

---

[126] Ye Yuchun, "Yin Jing guangai jishu chutan," p. 41.

[127] For example, Yuan Huazhong in the late Ming said that the flow of the Jing rushed into the Guanghui Canal entrance, obstructing it with mud and stones, but that even when the passage had been cleared the current would slow down after less than a hundred paces and deposit sand and gravel in the canal bed. This in itself, let us note, is not necessarily a problem: in a well-calculated system the diminution of slope, and therefore of velocity, ahead of the irrigation section allows the infertile sands to be deposited in the bed of the feeder canal (to be regularly dredged, of course), whereas the finer loess soil particles are brought to the fields (Pierre Gentelle, personal communication). What may have happened with the later versions of the Zheng-Bai is that, as a result both of the content of the Jing water and of the profile given to the feeder canal, the slowing down of the flow resulted in excessive sand deposits in one short section and therefore in obstruction. Compare, too, Tang Binggang's hypothesis that in the ancient situation (i.e., a slow and regular flow) "the coarse [particles] would sink down" (*culi xiachen* 粗糲下沉) while "the mud [literally, the juice] would float up" (*jiangzhi shangfu* 漿汁上浮).

[128] Suggested to me by Mark Elvin.

MANAGEMENT AND MAINTENANCE

In a way, what we have with all the above theorizing about "naturalness" is an effort to understand the causes of the environmental instability and, more often than not, low performance of the later versions of the Zheng-Bai system. Yet, since there was no escape from the difficulties of the natural environment in which the canal, in particular its higher sections, operated, it remained necessary not only to devise technical means of protection such as those mentioned above, but also to set up structures of maintenance and methods of management that would ensure the proper functioning and durability of the system as it existed. In a sense, organization was part of the environment, or at least it was indispensable to dealing with it: the canal was periodically in a state of decay both because of the attacks of nature and because of human neglect and administrative sloppiness.

There were two sorts of organizational tasks: one was the maintenance itself, which included both the annual repairs and major construction in the wake of exceptional disasters; the other was ensuring a smooth and proper distribution of irrigation water in the subsystems. Maintenance and distribution were in fact closely related, in the sense that the quality of maintenance all along the system was dependent on the social harmony and economic well-being of the irrigation communities downstream, which in turn relied on an adequate functioning of institutions handling the distribution of the water.

These last are comparatively well documented and described in the sources, at least from the Yuan period onward – but it is easy to imagine that from the start such a large-scale and complex infrastructure must have been subjected to detailed and constraining regulations.[129] The fourteenth-

---

[129] The first mention of "water regulations" (*shuiling* 水令) in historical sources seems to go back to 111 B.C., when a canal called the Liufu qu 六輔渠, whose exact location remains unclear (it is sometimes said to have been a branch of the Zheng Guo), was opened in Guanzhong by an official named Er Kuan 兒寬: see *Zhongguo shuili shigao*, pp. 125–26. We know that the Tang had a body of regulations, called the *shuibushi* 水部式, that concerned irrigation, water transportation, bridges, fisheries, and so on, in various places across the empire, and whose updated versions were regularly circulated by the Department of Waterways (*shuibu*) of the Board of Works. The only surviving fragment of some length, discovered among the Dunhuang manuscripts and dating from 737, includes several entries devoted to the personnel and rules of the Bai Canal. See Denis Twitchett, "The Fragment of the T'ang Ordinances of the Department of Waterways Discovered at Tunhuang," *Asia Major* n.s. 6.1 (1956), pp. 23–79 (providing a full translation); and Zhou Kuiyi, "'Shuibushi' yu Tangdai de nongtian shuili guanli"; see also Twitchett, "Some Remarks on Irrigation under the T'ang," *T'oung Pao* 48. 1–3 (1960), pp. 175–94. Some quotations from the *shuibushi* in literary works are reproduced in the irrigation chapters of gazetteers, notably one to the effect that they "indicated the time for opening irrigation" (*juexie you shi* 決洩有時) and "fixed [the layout of?] the irrigation ditches" (*quankuai you du*

century regulations detailed in the *Jingqu tushuo* under the heading "Yongshui zeli" 用水則例, which clearly followed earlier models, remained in use, with some adaptation, and in spite of changes in the quantity of land irrigated and in the pattern of irrigation gates and ditches, through to the end of the imperial period; they can be found in most gazetteers.[130] A crucial set of data that is found only in the 1842 Jingyang gazetteer is an extraordinarily detailed timetable indicating the day and hour (precise to the minute) for the opening and closing of each one of the 106 irrigation gates then in service within the system, plus the quota of irrigated fields and of "cultivators benefiting [from irrigation]" (*lifu* 利夫) per gate (see Fig. 9.1).[131] The evidence clearly suggests that exacting patterns of the same sort had been in existence during the five centuries since the compilation of the *Jingqu tushuo*, and indeed, in earlier periods as well.

According to these texts, the irrigation season opened on the first day of the tenth lunar month and continued through to the seventh month of the next year; the eighth and ninth months were reserved for repairs and maintenance.[132] In the above-mentioned 1842 document, the distribution of water from gate to gate follows a monthly cycle starting at the eastern-

畝澮有度). We also know that enforcement was supervised by the Chang'an vice-prefect (*shaoyin* 少尹). See, e.g., *Yuhai*, j. 22, pp. 12b–13a; *JYXZ/JQZ*, j. 3, p. 7b; *Gaoling xianzhi* [1541], j. 1, p. 6a. Song regulations, reportedly, dated back to 1028, when an official by the name of Li Tong 李同 stated that it was necessary to "establish a covenant to regulate [literally, to limit] the use of water in the Sanbai Canal" (*Sanbai qu yi li yue yi xian shui* 三白渠宜立約以限水) (see *Yuhai*, j. 22, p. 13a; *JYXZ/JQZ*, j. 3, p. 7b). None of these texts has been preserved.

[130] Thus *XAFZ*, j. 7, p. 3a–b; *JYXZ* (1778), j. 4, pp. 2b–3a; *JYXZ* (1910), pp. 271–72. On the fact that the Qing regulations were "basically" those inherited from the Yuan, see the remark in *JYXZ/JQZ*, j. 3, pp. 7b–8a. The original Yuan regulations in *JQTS*, pp. 13a–16b, are reproduced (with some misprints) in *JYXZ/JQZ*, j. 3, pp. 11b–14a; they include, in fact, both the rules currently enforced and a number of (usually more complicated) "old rules" (*jiuli* 舊例) whose exact date is unclear.

[131] See *JYXZ/JQZ*, j. 2, pp. 3a–18b (which is not a section on regulations, but a step-by-step description of the system); more or less the same data are found in *JYXZ* (1910), pp. 264–71, for those parts of the system located on the Jingyang territory; an editor's note on p. 277 suggests that at the very end of the Qing the timetable was still in force, and that its stipulations were engraved on a stela (or several stelae). "Benefiting cultivators" (*lifu*) are also called "benefiting households" (*lihu* 利戶). A *fu* was in fact a corvée-labor unit: inseparable from the benefits of irrigation was the obligation to work at maintenance at the prescribed periods.

[132] In the Yuan regulations (when in addition to canal maintenance there was the heavy burden of dam maintenance at the canal intake) irrigation was stopped on the 15th day of the seventh month, the "beneficiaries" being then sent to dredge the distribution canal. Irrigation could also be suspended in the sixth month when the Jing River was in spate. Song descriptions of the system prior to the opening of the Fengli Canal indicate an irrigation period running from the tenth to the fourth month.

most extremity of the system on the fourth day at 3:00 a.m. and ending at the first gate upstream on the first day of the next month (or second day in the case of a twenty-nine-day "short month," *xiaojian* 小建) at 9:30 a.m. The three (or two) days left were, presumably, devoted to replenishing the canal through its extremity. The Zhongbai Canal and two of its subbranches downstream of Pengcheng zha (lock) were served first; then its two other subbranches; then its section between Sanxian zha and Pengcheng zha; then (after an interval of 16 hours left to fill it from Sanxian zha) the Beibai; then (after 3.15 hours to fill it) the Nanbai; and finally the trunk canal upstream of Sanxian zha (see Fig. 9.1). This pattern of a monthly cycle of irrigation from downstream to upstream is also found in the fourteenth-century regulations. These specify, in addition, that beginning in the tenth month fields planted with summer crops – what we call "winter wheat" – would be watered; then in the third month the still bare fields for hemp and autumn grains; then in the fourth month the fields with hemp sprouts; and finally, in the fifth month, people would be free to allocate water between hemp and autumn grains.[133]

The Qing gazetteers indicate a quota of one *qing* of irrigated land per beneficiary/corvée laborer – meaning, concretely, that for every *qing* irrigated the landowners had to contribute one laborer-unit, with a possibility of dividing this *pro rata* if their individual properties were too small; but the detailed 1842 data show that by that time in the lower parts of the system the figure could be as low as about 50 *mu* – obviously a result of the drastic constriction of the system since the eighteenth century, if not earlier.[134]

Prior to opening irrigation, the "irrigation gate officers" (*douli* 斗吏) – apparently one per gate – were to submit a form indicating the numbers of benefiting households and the types of crops within each gate, in exchange for which the officials would give them a certificate (*youtie* 由帖) authorizing them to open the gate. After having used the water, they were to present a "declaration of used water" (*poshuizhi* 破水直) stating the time during which they had opened the gate, the area watered, and the types of crops.[135] As soon as a gate had been closed after its allotted time period, the use of the water was to be passed on to the next one upstream, without allowing for any

---

[133] *JQTS*, p. 13b. Apparently the overall evolution was from even more constraining rules (in the Song or early Yuan) as to how much land sown to which crop could get water during which month, to more flexible systems (at the end of the imperial period) whereby people were left free to irrigate what and where they wished within the time period allowed every month to each gate.

[134] Higher figures, up to 260 *mu* at the beginning of the Yuan when population density was at its lowest, are mentioned for earlier periods. See *JQTS*, pp. 14a–15a.

[135] A footnote reproduced in all the gazetteers states that *shuizhi* means *shuicheng* 水程. One also finds the variant *bao* 報 *shuizhi*.

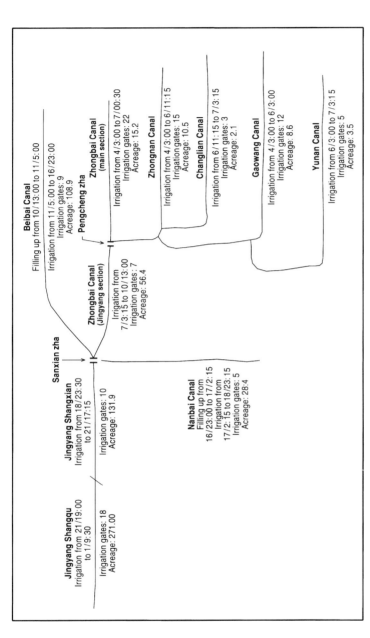

Figure 9.1. The monthly cycle of irrigation among the different sections of the Longdong Canal in the 1840s. *Source: Jingyang xianzhi/Jingqu zhi, j.* 2, pp. 3a–18b. The source indicates the date and hour authorized for irrigation within each month, plus the figure of irrigated acreage and number of corvée laborers for every one of the system's 106 irrigation gates, then abstracts the information for each larger section. Only the data pertaining to the larger sections have been retained for this chart. For each section the following information is given:

Name of the section.   Day/hour of opening the first irrigation gate to day/hour of closing the last one.

Number of gates.   Acreage irrigated (in *qing*).

interruption day or night. The users within each gate were to share the water among the ditches reaching to their fields according to equally strict time-tables; beyond that general statement, however, we have no detailed data on intragate organization. Various fines were stipulated for people who over-stepped their rights or were neglectful in maintaining the embankments, and for irrigation officers who concealed or encouraged irregularities.

The task of checking on the regularity of operations was entrusted to various officials and/or representatives of the irrigated communities, and the list of these appears to have varied significantly according to period. The fourteenth-century regulations, for example, say that each of the counties concerned was to send a ranking official to the head of the branch canals (*xianshou* 限首), who together with his colleagues would check that there was no cheating; but they also cite "old regulations" in which this task was entrusted to "controlling households" (*jianhu* 監戶) from the different counties together with a chief controller (*dujian* 都監), who had in addition to report every day to the officials on the quantity of water that had passed through.[136] Constant surveillance of the individual irrigation gates and their opening and closing at the proper time was incumbent on the irrigated communities; for example, there is one fourteenth-century regulation about punishing the water user in charge of closing a gate on time who falls asleep in the middle of a cold night.

This said, it has to be acknowledged that we lack essential information on the personnel who ran the Zheng-Bai system at the local level, and that, paradoxically, this is still more the case when the Qing period is concerned. For a few decades in the eighteenth century (from 1729 to the 1770s) the canal was placed under the control of a Xi'an assistant prefect in charge of hydraulics stationed in Baigu zhen 百谷鎮, at the head of the system, but thereafter his functions were split among the individual magistrates. These officials could only act as overseeers, however, and we do not have the detailed information on lower, nonofficial personnel that exists for other comparable infrastructures.[137] The only scrap of evidence I have found so

---

[136] See *JQTS,* pp. 10b, 11b. A complex editor's note on p. 13a shows that the quantity was reckoned by the section (width times depth) of the flow passing through a canal or gate, the unit being one square foot, called *jiao* 徼. Velocity was not taken into account, which would mean that it was considered a constant during a given period of irrigation.

[137] I am thinking here of the Tongli 通利 and other canals in the Fen River valley in nearby Shanxi, studied by Morita Akira in his *Shindai suiri shakai shi no kenkyū,* pp. 268–95 (this source was pointed out to me by Mark Elvin). Morita was able to use published "canal registers" (*quce* 渠冊) providing extremely detailed evidence on irrigation management down to community level. Note, however, that even the Tongli Canal, which encompassed three counties, was a system with a significantly smaller range than the Longdong of the Qing, the latter itself a much-reduced replica of its predecessors under older dynasties.

far is one eighteenth-century text indicating that "water elders" (*shuilao* 水老) from Sanyuan county were sent every month to the Sanxian zha distribution lock to oversee its opening at the right time together with their Jingyang colleagues.[138] What we would like to know, of course, is the exact status of these water elders, and how they were chosen. It is perfectly possible that the same process of "publicly selecting" (*gongju* 公舉) that is described in other sites was at work, both for such people with an apparently countywide competence and for those operating at gate (or village) level,[139] but pending the discovery of further evidence we cannot say for sure.

The question, in fact, is that of the inscription of the system in its sociopolitical environment. During its entire history the Zheng-Bai system was first of all a large-scale infrastructure created (or rebuilt) by the state and managed according to bureaucratic principles and rules – as opposed to an alternative "community" model wherein both the infrastructure and its management would be the creation and shared responsibility of the community of its users, officials acting only as legitimizers and as the ultimate resort in case of conflict.[140] To be sure, a large part of the responsibility for maintaining and running the system *had* to be delegated to the village communities located within the irrigation gates and to their chiefs – whoever these last might be – but it is a telling indication that, according to texts that the eighteenth- and nineteenth-century gazetteers claim to be still in force, the people in charge of the gates should be called *li*,[141] that they

---

[138] See *Sanyuan xian xinzhi* (1880), *j.* 3, pp. 18b–19a.

[139] For the Shanxi example see Morita, *Shindai suiri shakai shi, passim*, especially pp. 275–76 for the three "canal chiefs" (*quzhang* 渠長) of the Tongli Canal, and pp. 301ff for the managers of various canals in Hongdong 洪洞 county. See also, concerning irrigation in the Dunhuang oasis during the Tang period, the Pelliot and Stein manuscripts cited by Twitchett, "Some Remarks on Irrigation under the T'ang," *art. cit.*, pp. 183–86, which mention various types of managers chosen from among the local users.

[140] This is the model at work in Morita's above-mentioned study. According to this author, socioeconomic developments from the late Ming onward led to a gradual breaking up of the canal communities (the term is of course the theory-laden *kyōdōtai* 公同體), answered by efforts, supported by the state, at reaffirming the inseparability of landowning, access to irrigation, participation in maintenance, and tax paying.

[141] The managers at village level in the Tongli system described by Morita were called *goushou* 溝首, and their deputies were the *jiashou* 甲首. Late-imperial sources on the Zheng-Bai do not mention nonofficial positions at system level (which is what the term *quzhang* would indicate), but at the very end of the period we do find one intriguing and perhaps revealing mention of a "member of the gentry in charge of the canal by the name of Yu Tianci" (*guan qu Yu shen Tianci* 管渠于紳天賜) to whom were entrusted in 1900 some contribution and corvée funds levied by the administration that he was to deposit with merchants, the interest being intended for the maintenance of the "people's" part of the canal (*minqu* 民渠, that is, everything downstream from the first irrigation gate): see *JYXZ* (1910), pp. 273–74.

should get certificates from the officials before being authorized to open the gates and report to them afterwards, and so forth. What we have, at least in these sources, does not resemble a self-contained and self-governed system following a set of customary rules. To this it might be added that they leave one with a strange impression of permanency over a period of many centuries that was not lacking in military upheavals and social change.[142]

Indeed, what the real practices and actual power relations may have been at any given time is not easy to know. One thing seems sure, however: for much if not most of the time, the exacting and constraining set of rules for Zheng-Bai water distribution and infrastructure maintenance promulgated by the state gave a mainly theoretical and extremely optimistic image of the existing situation in the field. To cite but one example, if we are to believe the editors of the 1884 Gaoling gazetteer, during the nineteenth century at least, water was hardly ever seen in the various subbranches downstream from Pengcheng zha that constituted the easternmost extremity of the system on the territory of Gaoling: such a statement stands in stark contrast with the superbly precise and ingenious timetable of irrigation (in Gaoling and elsewhere) provided in the above-mentioned 1842 description of the Longdong Canal.[143] Indeed, what the Gaoling texts suggest is a history of conflict and cheating in which the upstream communities were in the better position to deprive the downstream communities of access to water. One finds mentions of episodes to that effect ever since the Song, and even the Tang, period. During the Qing, after the 1727–29 reforms had, reportedly, brought some order and fairness in the functioning of the system, the old abuses soon cropped up again.[144] In Sanyuan, similarly, it apparently did not take much time until the northern branch of the Sanbai, which was supposed to irrigate parts of the county, was again reduced to receiving "only a thread of water" because the Jingyang users deliberately

[142] Concerning this last factor, we are reduced to suppositions and a few impressionistic data. It is obvious that the ideal model of a peasantry essentially composed of small independent taxpayers, which was a precondition for the smooth operation of this sort of system, cannot have prevailed at all times. I mentioned earlier the encroachments of aristocrats and entrepreneurs in the Tang; on various occasions under the following dynasties we find allusions to powerful people and/or uncontrollable evil types disrupting the orderly and disciplined functioning of irrigation. Nothing, however, permits us to do more than hypothesize the sort of class differentiation and development of big landowning that Morita posits as a major cause for the breakdown of the "irrigation communities" from the Ming-Qing transition onward.

[143] See Gaoling xian xuzhi (1884), pp. 12b–13a.

[144] The crucial event, reportedly, was the suppression in the 1770s of the post of assistant prefect in charge of the entire system that had been instituted in 1729.

allowed silt to accumulate where the canal entered Sanyuan territory; in 1765 a local subaltern official had the deposit dug out, however, so that the flow could be reestablished.[145] As the editors of the Gaoling gazetteer noted, even though irrigation was supposed to proceed from downstream to upstream of the system, water flows from upstream to downstream: while those who are far from the source of water stay powerless (literally, "they can't reach it with their whip"), those who are close to it are able to use their connections to practice knavery (*yinyuan wei jian* 因緣為姦).

There would be much more to say concerning the way environmental, social, and political forces are likely to play havoc with perfectly conceived regulations and blueprints. Thus it is known to be a quasi-universal law in irrigation matters that water-conservancy infrastructure maintenance and operation at the periphery – that is, in the subsystems — is the weakest link in any large system. Problems of coordination, of enforcement, and of funding are all involved. It is there that conflicts over water distribution and labor allocation are the most likely to occur, and that "free rider" types of behavior are the most to be expected, especially when the system's output is inferior to its theoretical levels, meaning more competition for a scarcer resource.[146] At the same time, troubles occur primarily in the subsystems because of the dispersion of settlements and infrastructures, which makes centralized government monitoring and enforcement the most difficult to achieve. To this we should add, for the Chinese case, the way in which the horizontal division between administrative units encouraged up-stream–downstream rivalries espoused by magistrates pressed by their constituencies.[147]

Economic constraints are also in evidence in the case of the Zheng-Bai system. Whereas dredging and repairs at higher levels were directed and funded by the bureaucracy, the local beneficiaries of irrigation were supposed to organize themselves at community level, and to provide their labor for free. In the second of Yue Zhongqi's memorials cited above, for

---

[145] See Sanyuan xian xinzhi (1880), *j*. 3, pp. 18b–19a. The same source tells us (p. 19a–b) that by 1866 water had not reached Sanyuan for twenty years because Jingyang users upstream were stealthily cutting it off. In this year the Sanyuan officials and elite were able to trade their participation in the rehabilitation work ordered by the governor against the reinstatement of their water rights.

[146] At different periods of the history of the Zheng-Bai canal we find mentions of "innumerable lawsuits" associated with the fact that, because of its bad condition, the system could service only "one or two tenths" of the theoretical irrigated area.

[147] I have developed this theme at length concerning another context – the Jiang-Han plain in Hubei – in my study, "State Intervention in the Administration of a Hydraulic Infrastructure: The Example of Hubei Province in Late-Imperial Times," in Stuart Schram, ed., *The Scope of State Power in China* (London: SOAS, 1985), pp. 295–347.

example, we see that for the "large works" (*dagong* 大工) on the Longdong
feeder canal and on the trunk canals of the Bai system the government
would "hire laborers" (*mu fuyi* 募夫役) and draw money from provincial
funds, whereas in the subsystems "each household benefiting from irrigation [would] put forth its own efforts to the utmost (*ge jie ji li* 各竭己力) and
enthusiastically do the dredging (*yongyue tiaojun* 踴躍挑濬)." The pattern
was apparently similar for regular maintenance. According to the governor's plans formulated at the time of the 1737–39 works, a team of thirty
"water workers" (*shuifu* 水夫) with government salaries was to exert continuous surveillance over the canal bed and embankments in the "official"
section of the system (that is, from the Longdong spring down to the first
irrigation gate), and to do the necessary repairs every year during the ninth
month at government expense, whereas it was incumbent on the riparians
themselves to meet the costs of the maintenance downstream, including
the planting of trees to maintain the embankments.[148]

Of course, one would like to know more about the people's above-
mentioned "enthusiasm" for making their "own efforts." The phrase is
commonplace (and indeed, a must) in Qing documents reporting on
official efforts at mobilizing their constituents on public projects supposed
to ensure their well-being for generations to come: it implies a spirit of
cooperation and trust between officials and people that is a sure indication
of sage government and Great Peace. The reality must have been, more
often than not, decidedly more conflictual, especially when labor and
contributions were solicited from people whose fields were located in parts
of the system that were no longer receiving their due part of the water – in
other words, when they considered that there were no benefits to balance
the costs (or "hardships"). This situation appears to have been fairly common in the lower parts of the Sanbai irrigation network (on the territories
of Sanyuan and Gaoling) during the Qing and probably earlier.

More generally, even when a community willingly contributes exceptional efforts to the building of a new irrigation infrastructure (or the
rehabilitation of an old one, as in all post-Tang Sanbai projects) from which
fast returns can be expected, the momentum can rarely be maintained for
long periods. Once the mobilization and even exhilaration of the beginning give way to the drudgery of everyday maintenance and management,
a process of entropy almost inevitably takes place whereby enforcing even
carefully laid-down rules, combating negligence, and resolving conflicts
become more and more difficult.

[148] See, e.g., *JQZ*, p. 32b; *JYXZ* (1910), pp. 273–74. The last source specifies that the county
administrations have no funds earmarked for exceptional repairs, so that special contributions or surtaxes have to be levied.

Thus a combination of social, economic, political, and organizational problems added itself to the objective difficulties and constant pressure from the natural environment in which a system like the Zheng-Bai operated, and participated in the recurring process of decay that was described and deplored by so many authors in so many periods. In what follows I will concentrate on how these contradictions were sometimes emphasized using the politically sensitive notion of the "sufferings of the people."

THE HUMAN COST

Concern with the human cost is to be found, more specifically although not exclusively, with respect to the higher sections of the system, whose technical hazards have been described earlier in this chapter. It is here that we find, at least until the 1737 decision to cut off the canal from the Jing River, a particular combination of factors that resulted in what several authors denounced as an unacceptable human burden. Indeed, this helps explain the vehemence with which certain late Ming and early Qing authors attacked any project whatsoever of opening a new intake to bring the Jing water anew into the system.

A quantity of literature could be cited in this regard. As we saw, Yuan Huazhong in the Wanli period, recalling the seventeen years of toil in a hostile environment that had been needed eventually to open the Guanghui Canal, said that in the end "the strength of officials and people was exhausted," and that "[as] the river was directed into the canal, the problem of silting up and clogging got worse day after day." If a new, similar project were to be launched, not only would it be useless (for the technical reasons discussed above), but it would "squander the wealth [of the people] for nothing" (*xu mi zhigao* 虛糜脂膏).

Jin Handing, a magistrate of Jingyang at the very beginning of the Qing, noted, for his part, that the Han king in the third century B.C. had wanted to "wear Qin out" in the short term with the construction of the Zheng Guo Canal, but did not realize that future generations would be still more "worn out" by the costs of maintaining the canal that was eventually dug.[149]

But the one author who was perhaps the most eloquent in denouncing the human cost of such enterprises was Tang Binggang in the first years of the Qianlong reign. Indeed, his plea against suggestions of opening a new "mouth" upriver at Diaoerzui resumes all the technical, economic, and political arguments formulated by other authors since Song times. According to him, the quantity of water harnessed and the returns in terms of

---

[149] See, e.g., *JYXZ* (1910), pp. 861–62.

irrigated area, if the Diaoerzui project were to be implemented, would be even smaller than in the earlier periods (possibly no Jing water at all would be tapped in the end). At the same time, the duration of the work on the site would have to be even more than the seventeen years of toil that had been necessary to open the inefficient Guanghui intake and feeder canal under the Ming.

This brings him to a section on the necessity of "relieving the energies of the people" (xu minli 恤民力), which he begins with an enumeration of the very large numbers of corvée laborers mobilized in the downriver communities and sent to the site since the Yuan dynasty, of the huge numbers of "work-units" (gong 工) needed each time to rebuild the infrastructure, and so forth.[150] Worse than that, the damming devices used since at least the Song (more specifically, the so-called stone containers) were unable to withstand the summer floods of the Jing and had to be rebuilt every year. Like other authors before him, but with more rhetorical flourish, Tang insists on the sufferings endured year after year by the laborers sent to the site in the eighth and ninth months: they had to travel up to more than a hundred li in the heat and cold to get to an inhospitable gorge with overhanging cliffs and no place to rest; and then they had to enter the tunnel, lift pieces of rock and crawl in the mud; in performing the annual maintenance of the jetty they had to fell trees, dig out the gravel, split rocks, and walk into the current of the Jing to put the stone containers in place . . . Tang's conclusion, as we saw, is that opening a new intake on the same pattern would lead to still higher human and financial costs for a smaller result, or possibly no result at all.

We find the same sort of considerations with other eighteenth-century authors. Among the most interesting of these is Wang Taiyue (1722–85), the author of the Jingqu zhi, who spent long stretches of time in Shaanxi posts.[151] Wang's approach is in fact still more negative than that of most other critics, since according to him a close reading of even the ancient historical texts reveals hidden warnings against large-scale irrigation projects that seem successful at first but rapidly fall into decay. But people do not care, says Wang; they only see the bright aspect of things, which they bring forth to further their own ambitions. Indeed, Wang's texts are a denunciation of the excesses of political mobilization for productivist ven-

---

[150] Tang says that the pre-Yuan figures are not known, but we do have very detailed Song figures in JQTS.

[151] Wang's considerations on "contemporary" Zheng-Bai problems appear in the "general comments" (zonglun 總論) and in the postface of JQZ; the postface was anthologized in Xu Dong's 徐棟 Muling shu 牧令書 (1838), j. 9. See also the quotation from a long memorial of his on the same subject in his Beizhuan ji biography (j. 86, pp. 1a–3b).

tures, of their native optimism, and of the corruption and abuse they foster in the lower administrative levels.

In any case, Wang Taiyue comes up with conclusions similar to those of Tang Binggang some years earlier – some of his considerations are actually borrowed directly from Tang's text. Proponents of a revival of the methods used since the Song on the upper Zheng-Bai system, he says, only see the benefits (*li*) and ignore the negative impact (*hai*), even though in the present situation the negative aspects have definitely outstripped the potential benefits. And, if such is the case, it is because the overall combination of environmental, technical, economic, social, and political factors entering the Zheng-Bai equation have been thrown out of balance by centuries of attempts at harnessing a resource that could no longer be "naturally" brought into the service of agriculture.

In short, what we see in the eighteenth century – in a context of mounting anxiety about the gradual imbalance between population and food production – is a growing awareness, in Shaanxi political circles, that theirs was a time when trying to emulate, even on a smaller scale, the glorious technical achievements of the past, with all the ambitions of heightened productivity they carried along, could only go against the opportunities offered by the environment and be gravely counterproductive. That this sort of conservative approach had become generally accepted in the nineteenth century is suggested by a comment of the editors of the treatise appended to the 1842 Jingyang gazetteer,[152] to the effect that relying exclusively on irrigation water from "mountain springs" definitely saves incalculable costs, which in any case would have only brought diminishing returns; but, they add, it is less likely than ever that the benefits brought by the system will even approach those of the more ancient periods. It was only in late-imperial times that such wisdom made its appearance in the discourse on the Zheng-Bai.

---

[152] See *JYXZ/JQZ, j.* 3, pp. 6a–b.

Action at a Distance

THE INFLUENCE OF THE YELLOW
RIVER ON HANGZHOU BAY
SINCE A.D. 1000

MARK ELVIN AND SU NINGHU

OVERVIEW

In a previous paper on Hangzhou Bay 杭州灣 on the eastern coast of China,[1] we suggested that the infilling of the inner part of the estuary and its changing geometry between the thirteenth and eighteenth centuries, most notably the formation of the Nansha 南沙 Peninsula, were in significant measure due to the reduction of the peak discharge of all but its two largest rivers as a result of man-made seawalls, locks, and irrigation systems. In general terms this may be considered the reverse side of the conclusion of Verger, namely that the reason that many estuaries along the French coast have not filled in faster over the last millennium or so is probably due to the peak discharge of rivers.[2] In the present essay, which is a review and analysis of the modern scientific literature[3] and premodern historical docu-

---

[1] M. Elvin and N. Su, "Man Against the Sea," in *Civilization and Environment* (Kyoto: International Center for Japanese Studies, September 1992), special issue on the conference "Nature and Humankind in the Age of Environmental Crisis." Revised version, "Man Against the Sea: Natural and Anthropogenic Factors in the Changing Morphology of Hangzhou Bay, circa 1000–1800," *Environment and History* 1 (1995), pp. 3–54. A fuller version may be found in our "Engineering the Sea: Hydraulic Systems and Pre-Modern Technological Lock-In in the Harngzhou Bay Area circa 1000–1800," in Ito Shuntarō and Yasuda Yoshinori, eds., *Nature and Humankind in the Age of Environmental Crisis* (Kyoto: International Research Center for Japanese Studies, 1995). Both this paper and the present chapter owe a major debt to the criticisms of Professor John Chappell, and we should like to express our thanks to him for his generosity with his time and expertise.

[2] F. Verger, *Marais et wadden du littoral français* [Marshes and tidal flats of the French coasts], 3d ed. (Caen: Paradigme, 1988), p. 234.

[3] The numerical data from Chinese papers cited in the text are on occasion difficult to assess. Details of experimental procedures are often inadequately specified – for example, the locations examined, the number of samples analyzed, the spatial profile of these samples

ments available to us, we concentrate on the possible role played by the sediment derived from the Yellow River (Huanghe 黄河) during the period from 1194 to 1855, when it followed a southern course and debouched south of the Shandong Peninsula, both in accelerating the infilling of the inner bay, a process (described in the earlier paper) that seems to have been at its maximum during the seventeenth century, and in the creation of the coastal salient north of Yuyao 餘姚 in the outer bay after about 1400, and especially after 1579. Maps 10.1a and 10.1b provide geographical orientation, and Plate 10.1, a LandSat image taken in early 1984, shows the present form of the salient.

Present-day patterns of sediment movement from the defunct and now eroding Yellow River delta in northern Jiangsu province suggest that a substantial percentage of the finer fraction ($d < 10\mu$) was transported southward along the coast, mixed with Yangzi River 楊子江 sediments, and carried into Hangzhou Bay, at a time when the sediment volume can be estimated to have been greater than it is today. Although in open water the entrainment velocity of such finer sediments is directly proportionate to grain size, at shorelines settling is accelerated on account of settling lag (that is, forward motion on an incoming tide that continues beyond the point where the velocity of the water drops below that required for deposition) and scour lag (the gap between the deposition and re-entrainment velocities).

We focus on the period from 1579 to 1591, when the seaward extension of the south-course Yellow River delta (1.54 kilometers per year) and its vertical accretion (16.6 cm per year) temporarily reached extraordinary levels as the result of the concentration of the flow of the Yellow River and the Huai River 淮河 into a single channel by Pan Jixun 潘季馴, a measure of flood control that proved unsuccessful and had to be reversed by Yang Yikui 楊一魁. We also raise the alternative or complementary possibility that the mid-bay sandbar (*shadan* 沙潬) that was a feature in Song 宋 and Ming 明 times, according to the historical documents, but is not referred to in Qing-dynasty sources, may have been a source of the materials for the peninsula and salient. Since Yellow River materials, which derive mainly from the northwestern loess (*huangtu* 黃土), are identifiable by their distinctive percentages of clays (especially, abundant montmorillonite) and mineral tracers, it is suggested that examining cores from the peninsula and salient

(surface and depth coordinates), and the time profile of the samples (time of year taken, number of years covered, etc). The quantitative picture that we present is therefore a preliminary sketch that will have to be revised. Studies of the sediment balance of estuaries and the determination of the sources of the materials deposited are notoriously difficult. Verger, *Marais et wadden*, pp. 167, 169, 173–4, gives an illustration of this.

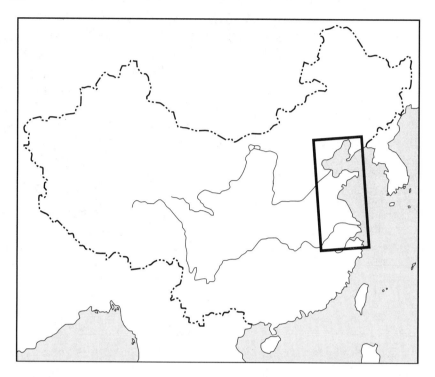

Map 10.1a. General location of the East China coast and Hangzhou Bay.

might indicate whether sediment input from the south-course Yellow River or a redistribution of mid-bay bar sediments played a greater role in the creation of these two features.

10.1. HANGZHOU BAY

Hangzhou Bay lies between 30° and 31°N latitude and 120° and 122°E longitude. Its outer section covers 5,000 square kilometers. The apex, at Ganpu 澉浦 on the northern shore at the western end, has a cross-section of 25 kilometers; the base, between Luchaogang 蘆潮港 on the northeast and Zhenhai 鎮海 on the southeast, has a cross-section of 100 kilometers.[4] The average tidal range is 5.47 meters at Ganpu, and the maximum range

[4] Cao Peikui 曹沛奎, Gu Guochuan 谷国传, Dong Yongfa 董永发, and Hu Fangxi 胡方西, "Hangzhou-wan nisha yundong-de jiben tezheng" [The basic characteristics of sediment transport in Hangzhou Bay], *Huadong Shifan Daxue xuebao* 华东师范大学学报 3 (1985).

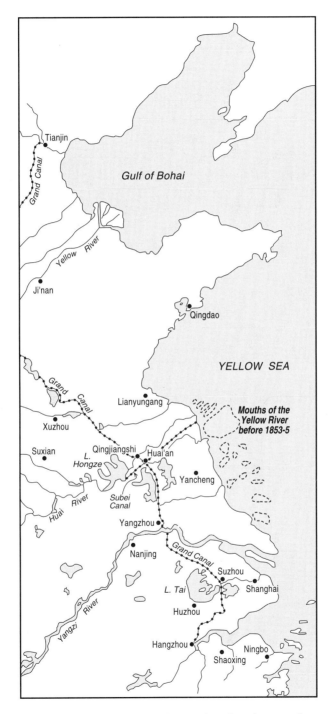

Map 10.1b. The East China coast and Hangzhou Bay (present-day coastlines).

is 8.93 meters.[5] Tidal currents are of the order of 2 meters per second. Mean annual temperature at present is between 15.5°C and 16°C; and the mean annual rainfall is between 1,114 and 1,260 mm. Southwest shifting to southeast winds prevail as late spring moves into summer, with a period of intense precipitation from mid-June to mid-July known as the "plum rains" (*meiyu* 梅雨) due to warm southern airflows meeting the cold polar airmass; mostly northeast to northerly winds prevail in autumn and winter. In other words, there is a monsoon regime.[6]

The inner estuary upstream of Ganpu consists of the mouth of the Qiantang River 錢塘江, which has a catchment area of 49,000 square kilometers, and discharges 2.905×10^{10} cubic meters per year of water and 6.68×10^{6} tonnes per year of sediment as measured at Lucibu 蘆茨埠, where the tides become insignificant. Total sediment influx into the bay from riverine and marine sources is 5.328×10^{7} tonnes per year.[7] The tidal bore today forms near the two Jianshan 尖山 hills, and moves at speeds ranging from 4.8 to 9.6 meters per second.[8]

During the last ice age, at maximal marine withdrawal, about 15,000 years B.P., the rivers of eastern China flowed across the continental shelf into a sea that was more than 100 meters below its present level. The pattern of the valleys formed by these rivers at different times is shown in Map 10.2. It is evident that they moved about much as they have done in recent centuries on the northern China plain. Thus the paleo-Yellow River had two main former courses, one north and one south of the Shandong Peninsula. These joined again to the southwest of present-day Korea. The paleo-Yangzi River had three main former courses. One joined the paleo-Yellow; one went due east; and the third took a variety of routes to the south. The Qiantang estuary and Hangzhou Bay were formed later by the postglacial rise of the sea, which reached a maximum about 7,000 B.P., a

[5] Zhou Sheng 周胜 Ni Haoqing 倪浩清, Zhao Yongming 赵永明, Yang Yongchun 杨永春 Wang Yifan 王一凡, Lü Wende 吕文德, and Liang Baoxiang 梁保祥, "Qiantangjiang shuixia fanghu gongcheng-de yanjiu yu shijian" [Research and practice relating to the protective underwater engineering on the Qiantang River], *Shuili xuebao* 1 (1992), p. 20.

[6] Ding Yihui, *Monsoons over China* (Dordrecht/Boston/London: Kluwer, 1994), pp. 19–22, 128, 134, and 195 et seq.

[7] Lin Chengkun 林承坤, "Changjiang-kou nisha-de laiyuan fenxi yu shiliang jisuan-de yanjiu" [Analysis of the sources and quantities of sediments at the estuary of the Yangzi River], *Dili xuebao* 44.1 (1989); Lin Chengkun, "Changjiang-kou yu Hangzhou-wan-de nisha yu hechuang yanbian dui Shanghai-gang ji qi tonghai hangdao jianshe-de yingxiang" [The influence of the sediment in the Yangzi River estuary and Hangzhou Bay, and changes in the riverbed, on the port of Shanghai and the construction of shipping channels giving access to the sea], *Dili xuebao* 45.1 (1990), p. 80; and also Cao Peikui et al., "Basic characteristics of sediment transport," p. 75.

[8] Zhou Sheng et al., "Research and practice," p. 23.

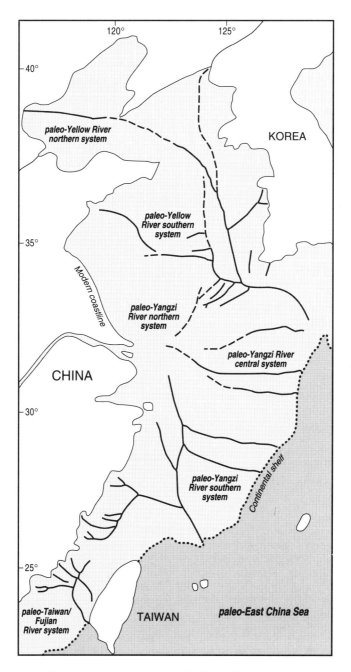

Map 10.2. The paleo-river system off the East China coast, c. 15,000 B.P.

few meters above the present level, when mean annual temperature may
have been almost 4°C above its value today.[9]

This picture is confirmed by archaeological findings of human relics that
suggest that Lake Tai 太湖 and the northern coastline of Hangzhou Bay
both took on recognizable shape around 6,000 years B.P. as the sea began
to withdraw. Maps 10.3 and 10.4 show the coastlines in 7,000 B.P. and
6,000 B.P. based on C^{14} dating of artifacts, and the emergence of the funnel-
or horn-shaped estuary.[10]

We begin by analyzing the movements of river and coastal sediments at
the present day, and then, assuming the mechanisms at work to have been
effective over the last millennium, use this analysis in an interactive interpretation with the premodern documents and maps referring to the bay.

10.2. THE SEDIMENT BALANCE IN THE BAY TODAY

Hangzhou Bay is one of a limited number of estuaries whose sediment is
primarily supplied not by its rivers but by the sea retransporting along the
coast materials brought down elsewhere by other rivers.[11] Sediment leaving
the Yangzi River moves southward toward the bay because of the Coriolis
pseudo-force and the southward ocean currents in winter, while a
longshore current carries a load of fine-grained material south from the
eroding abandoned delta of the south-course Yellow River on the coast
some 350 kilometers to the north of the mouth of the Yangzi.[12] As Table
10.1 shows, the percentage contribution made by the abandoned Yellow
River delta varies with particle size.

Sources were identified on the basis of the different percentages of clays
(especially montmorillonite, kaolinite, and chlorite) and fifteen mineral

---

[9] Geng Xiushan 耿秀山, "Zhongguo dongbu lujia-de haidi gu hexi" [The ancient river system on the sea floor of the continental shelf of East China], *Haiyang kexue* 海洋科学 16.2 (1981).

[10] Wu Weitang 吴维棠, "Cong xin-shiqi-shidai wenhua yizhi kan Hangzhou-wan liang-an-de quanxinshi gu dili" [Holocene paleogeography of Hangzhou Bay reconstructed from Neolithic cultural remains], *Dili xuebao* 地理学报 38.2 (1983).

[11] Thus the Loire probably supplies the Bay of Bourgneuf to its south. Verger, *Marais et wadden*, pp. 157–58.

[12] Lin Chengkun, "Analysis of the sources"; Lin Chengkun, "Influence of the sediment"; Lin Chengkun, "Changjiang-kou ji qi linjin-haiyu nianxing nisha-de shuliang yu shuyi" [The quantity and transport of cohesive sediments in the Yangzi River estuary and the nearby sea], *Dili xuebao* 47.2 (1992); Cao et al., "Basic characteristics of sediment transport"; and Cao Peikui, Dong Yong, and Zhou Yueqin 周月琴, "Hangzhou-wan beibu chaoliu chongshua-cao yanbian-de fenxi" [An analysis of the scouring channels in northern Hangzhou Bay], *Dili xuebao* 44.2 (1989).

Table 10.1. *Variation in percentage contribution to Yangzi estuary sediment by different sources according to particle size*

Sources	Particle size (diameter)		
	$d > 50\mu$	$50\mu > d > 10\mu$	$d < 10\mu$
Yangzi River	92.1	93.1	96.4
Yellow River delta (abandoned)	9.9	10.4	30.9
Hangzhou Bay (*outflow received from Yangzi estuary*)	−2.0	−3.5	−27.3

Source: Lin Chengkun, "Analysis of the sources."

tracers (magnetite, titanomagnetite, horneblende, epidote, biotite, muscovite, etc.) found in the parent materials of Yangzi and Yellow River sediments. Proportionately more fine sediment is transported to Hangzhou Bay (row 3 in Table 10.1), as would be expected from the inverse correlation between grain size and distance traveled. Table 10.2 shows the total quantities of sediments moved each year. It must be assumed that the residue not accounted for in Table 10.2, namely $[(4.750 + 0.6659) − 4.605] \times 10^8$ tonnes per year, that is, 8.109×10^7 tonnes per year, is circulating or being deposited in the estuary. During the 246 years from 1733 to 1979 the triangular peninsula southeast of the mouth of the Yangzi has grown 9 kilometers eastward and 3 kilometers southward. In recent years (1973 to 1979) the rate of growth of the eastern face has been 60 meters per year and that of the southern face 100 meters per year.[13]

Table 10.3 shows, by percentages, the grain-size distribution of the sediment delivered each year by the Yangzi to Hangzhou Bay $[(A_i/A) \times 100]$, and the percentage represented by each fraction of the total annual turnover of that fraction at the Yangzi estuary $[(A_i/B_i) \times 100]$. The distribution in Table 10.3 is what would be expected, the finer sediments being

[13] Shao Xusheng 邵虚生 and Yan Qinshang 严钦尚, "Shanghai chaoping chenji" [The sediments of intertidal flats in the coastal region of Shanghai], *Dili xuebao* 37.3 (1982); Ling Shen 凌申, "Huanghe nantu yu Subei haianxian-de bianqian" [The southward course of the Yellow River and changes in the coastline of northern Jiangsu], *Haiyang kexue* 5 (1988); Li Yuanfang 李元芳, "Fei-Huanghe sanjiaozhou-de yanbian" [The development of the abandoned Yellow River delta], *Dili yanjiu* 10.4 (1991).

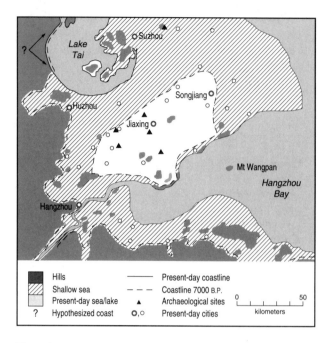

Map 10.3. Hangzhou Bay, c. 7,000 B.P., showing coastlines and archaeological sites.

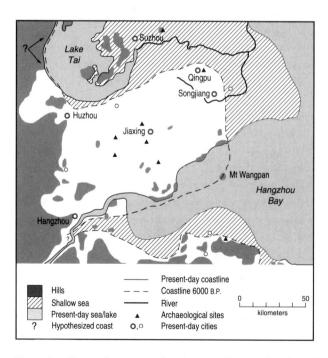

Map 10.4. Hangzhou Bay, c. 6,000 B.P., showing coastlines and archaeological sites.

Table 10.2. *Sediment exchange at the Yangzi River estuary (in 10^8 tonnes per year)*

	V_i From Yangzi valley	Y_i From former Yellow River delta	B_i Turnover at Yangzi estuary	A_i From Yangzi estuary to Hangzhou Bay
Grain diameter				
$d > 50\mu$	1.297	0.1366	1.380	0.028
$50 > d > 10\mu$	2.199	0.2370	2.279	0.083
$d < 10\mu$	1.254	0.2923	0.946	0.355
Totals	4.750	0.6659	4.605	0.466

Note: Yangzi sediment measures were made at Datong 大通 hydrometric station.
Source: Calculated from Lin Chengkun, "Analysis of the sources."

Table 10.3. *Distribution by grain size of Yangzi estuary sediments delivered to*
Hangzhou Bay

	$A_i/A \times 100$ (fraction$_i$ as a % of Yangzi sediment delivered to bay)	$A_i/B_i \times 100$ (% of fraction of total estuary turnover)
Grain size		
$d > 50\mu$	6.01	2.03
$50\mu > d > 10\mu$	17.81	3.64
$d < 10\mu$	76.18	37.53
Totals	(100.00)	10.12 (A/B)

Source: Calculated from Table 10.2.

transported in greater proportionate quantity. Figure 10.1 shows the contribution to suspended load made by particles of different diameter.

Table 10.4 shows the contribution made by the abandoned delta of the Yellow River to the sediment of the estuary of the Yangzi River at the present day. These figures indicate that the abandoned Yellow River delta delivers over 66 million tonnes of sediment each year to the Yangzi estuary.[14] It follows that the delta contributes 14.46% of the total Yangzi estuary sediments (0.66595/4.605). If the materials are well mixed before being

---

[14] Lin (1992) himself gives a lower total figure (2.73×10^7 tonnes per year), which we believe is incorrect.

Table 10.4. *Annual contribution of sediment to the estuary of the Yangzi River by the abandoned delta of the Yellow River*

	% of supply	Total sediment at Yangzi estuary (in 10⁸ tonnes per year)	Total supply from abandoned Yellow River delta (in 10⁸ tonnes per year)
Grain size			
$d > 50\mu$	9.9	1.380	0.13662
$50\mu > d > 10\mu$	10.4	2.279	0.23702
$d < 10\mu$	30.9	0.946	0.29231
Totals		4.605	0.66595

Source: Lin Chengkun, "Analysis of the sources."

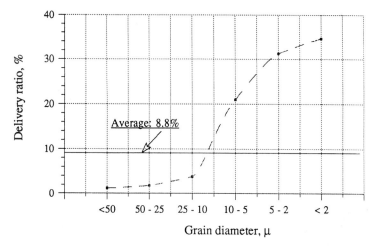

Figure 10.1. The contribution to suspended load made by particles of different grain size moving from the mouth of the Yangzi to Hangzhou Bay. *Source*: Lin Chengkun, "Quantity and transport."

retransported, the weights of sediments of various grain sizes delivered to Hangzhou Bay are as shown in Table 10.5. The more than 12 million tonnes a year of sediments transported from the abandoned delta of the Yellow River into Hangzhou Bay amount to almost 26 percent of the sediment provided by the Yangzi River estuary (12.1099/46.60).

The overall pattern of sedimentary inputs into Hangzhou Bay is summarized in Table 10.6 from data previously cited. The relative insignificance

Table 10.5. *Sediment transported to Hangzhou Bay from the abandoned delta of the Yellow River, via the Yangzi estuary*

Grain size	% of sediment supplied to Yangzi estuary from Yellow River delta	Total sediment moving from Yangzi estuary to Hangzhou Bay (in 10^6 tonnes per year)	Yellow River delta sediment moving to Hangzhou Bay (in 10^6 tonnes per year)
$d > 50\mu$	9.9	2.80	0.2772
$50\mu > d > 10\mu$	10.4	8.30	0.8632
$d < 10\mu$	30.9	35.50	10.9695
Totals		46.60	12.1099

Sources: Table 10.4 and Lin Chengkun, "Analysis of the sources."

Table 10.6. *Sedimentary inputs into Hangzhou Bay*

Source	Sediment delivered (in 10^6 tonnes per year)	Percentage
(Total Yangzi River estuary)	46.60	87.46
Yangzi River catchment	34.49	64.73
Abandoned Yellow River delta	12.11	22.73
Qiantang River catchment	6.68	12.54
Total	53.28	100.00

of the contribution of the Qiantang River is evident. External inputs dominate.

10.3. THE PRESENT-DAY GEOMETRY OF HANGZHOU BAY AND ESTUARINE DYNAMICS

Hangzhou Bay is at the extreme upper end of the distribution of the twenty-three major Chinese rivers studied by Jin Yuanhan et al. (1990)[15] both as

---

[15] Jin Yuanhan 金元欢, Shen Huanting 沈焕庭, and Chen Jiyu 陈吉余, "Zhongguo ruhai hekou fenlei chuyi" [Preliminary discussion of the classification of river estuaries in China], *Haiyang yu huzhao* 21.2 (1990).

regards its estuary coefficient and its tidal discharge ratio. The estuary coefficient E_c is defined as the increase in the width of an estuary per unit length. Thus

$$E_c = (B_1 - B_2)/L$$

where B_1 and B_2 are, respectively, the widths of the mouth and of the apex of the estuary, and L is the midcourse distance from B_1 to B_2. The tidal discharge ratio T_d is defined as the ratio between the mean discharge rate (in cubic meters per second) of the rising tide and the annual mean discharge rate (in cubic meters per second) of the river into the sea (usually written as QF/QR). The relationship between the two rates has been found to be

$$T_d = 3.8437 \ \mathbf{exp}[6.632 \ E_c]$$

This exponential relationship is shown in Figure 10.2. The Qiantang River is the point in the upper right-hand corner, and the Yellow River the point nearest to the origin. Historical maps discussed in our three previous papers on the bay and later in the present chapter suggest a smaller E_c a millennium ago (as B_2 was greater) and hence a lower T_d, and lower sediment delivery ratio S_d (commonly written SF/SR and defined as the ratio between the mean sediment delivery rate of the rising tide (measured in kilograms per second) and the annual mean sediment delivery rate of the river into the sea (likewise in kilograms per second)). The relationship between the tidal discharge ratio T_d and S_d is a power function and has been found to have the form

$$S_d = 0.3133 \ T_d^{1.9677}$$

The graphic form of this function is shown in Figure 10.3.

Given these two equations, it follows that there is a relationship between the estuary coefficient E_c and the sediment delivery ratio S_d. It has been found to be

$$S_d = 5.2913 \ \mathbf{exp}[11.541 E_c]$$

This is shown in Figure 10.4. Gu Guochuan and Hu Fangxi[16] have also shown an approximately linear relationship between the size of the catchment area of a river A (measured in square kilometers) and its annual se-

---

[16] Gu Guochuan and Hu Fangxi, "Woguo yanhai jin'andai shuiyu-de xuansha fenbu tezheng" [Characteristics of the distribution of near-shore sediment in China], *Dili yanjiu* 8.2 (1989).

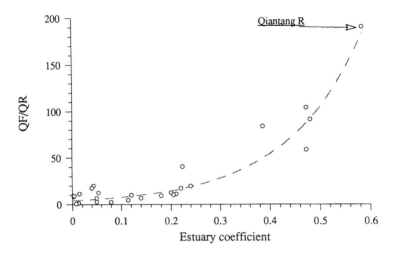

Figure 10.2. The relationship between the estuary coefficient E_c and the tidal discharge ratio T_d for major Chinese rivers. *Source*: Jin Yuanhuan et al., "Preliminary discussion."

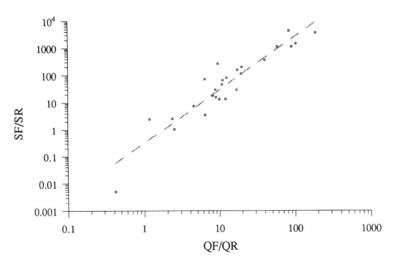

Figure 10.3. The relationship between the tidal discharge ratio T_d (QF/QR) and the sediment delivery ratio S_d (SF/SR) for various Chinese rivers (log/log scale). *Source*: Jin Yuanhuan et al., "Preliminary discussion."

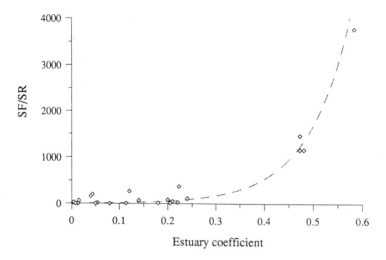

Figure 10.4. The relationship between the estuary coefficient E_c and the sediment delivery ratio S_d (SF/SR). *Source*: Jin Yuanhuan et al., "Preliminary discussion."

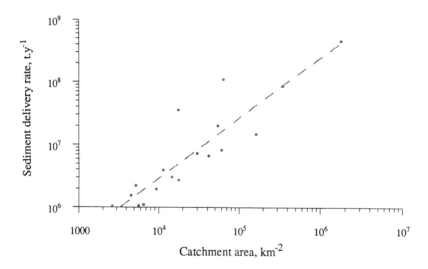

Figure 10.5. The relationship between the catchment area and the sediment delivery rate for the major Chinese rivers, except the Yellow River. *Source*: Gu and Hu, "Characteristics of the distribution of sediment."

diment delivery rate D_s (measured in tonnes per year) for twenty rivers with a delivery rate of over 1 million tonnes per year in China, with the exception of the Yellow River. For these units of measurement, the equation is

$$D_s = 398.47\, A^{0.964}$$

See Figure 10.5. Hence the tidal discharge ratio (T_d) and the sediment delivery ratio (S_d) increase exponentially with the estuarine coefficient (E_c), roughly speaking the angle at which the estuary opens. The sediment delivery ratio is related to the tidal discharge ratio by a power law. The annual sediment delivery rate (D_s) increases approximately linearly with the area of the catchment.

10.4. SEASONAL FLUCTUATIONS

Systematic data for annual patterns of sediment transport in Hangzhou Bay are not available at present. It is evident, however, that there are significant differences among seasons. To illustrate this point we reproduce figures from Cao Peikui et al. (1985) in Table 10.7 showing the different net movement of sediments onto and off the shoreline of the bay at different times of the year. Note the difference made by whether the tide is a spring tide or a neap tide. It should be noted that these figures are only illustrative. The excess of outflow over inflow shown in the fourth column of the first row of Table 10.7 results from the contribution of the Qiantang River, the month of July falling in its period of peak discharge. It seems, however, that the sediment in the bay is approximately in balance over the year, notwithstanding its continuous large-scale in-bay redistribution. There is also some movement out of the bay and down the coast of eastern Zhejiang province, compensated for by inflow.

The annual variation in suspended load in Hangzhou Bay is shown in Figure 10.6, as measured at Tanhushan 灘滸山, a small island in the middle of the bay. The density declines from a maximum of just under 2.42 kilograms per cubic meter in January to a minimum of about 0.75 in June. This decline is probably due to dilution resulting from an increased flow of fresh water from the rivers during the summer.

Cao Peikui et al. also measured sediment concentrations on the north side of the bay at Jinshanzui 金山嘴, where the southward flow from the Yangzi River was significant. They found 0.54 kilograms per cubic meter in the spring, 0.35 kilograms per cubic meter in the summer, 0.71 kilograms per cubic meter in the autumn, and 1.08 kilograms per cubic meter in the winter. These levels were probably affected by the shift in the ocean currents, which flow south in the period beginning in October, bringing longshore sediment with them, but north after January.

We may note here, for our later discussion of the earlier period when the Yellow River was following a southern course, that, apart from a minor peak in April due to snowmelt discharges, the present-day period of high dis-

Table 10.7. *Seasonal and spring/neap tidal variation in sediment transport in Hangzhou Bay*

	Rising Tide			Ebbing Tide			
Date	Water (10^9 m^3)	Sediment (10^4 tonnes)	Sediment/ water (kg·m^{-3})	Water (10^9 m^3)	Sediment (10^4 tonnes)	Sediment/ water (kg·m^{-3})	Balance (10^4 t)
July 21, 1982	36.6	5,100	1.393	36.7	6,200	1.689	−1100
Dec. 8, 1982 (neap tide)	21.1	3,074	1.457	21.0	2,703	1.287	+371
Dec. 16, 1982 (spring tide)	33.7	8,220	2.439	32.4	7,300	2.262	+881

Note: The minus figure in the last column indicates a net outflow of sediment.
Source: Cao Peikui et al., "Basic characteristics of sediment transport."

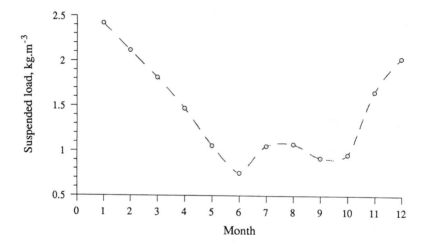

Figure 10.6. The monthly variation in suspended sediment load measured at Tanhushan in the middle of Hangzhou Bay. *Source*: Gu and Hu, "Characteristics of suspended sediment."

charge, high sediment delivery, and high sediment concentration in the Yellow River is from approximately July to October, the lagged consequence of monsoon stormbursts. This pattern is complementary in seasonal terms to that of the present Hangzhou Bay, except that both patterns share a low point in June. The quantities are substantial: discharge in early August is about 7.8×10^9 cubic meters per month, sediment delivery at this time is about 3.5×10^8 tonnes per month, and sediment concentration is 45 kilograms per cubic meter. It is possible that when the Yellow River was exiting south of the Shandong Peninsula the effect was to flatten out somewhat the curve of seasonal variations in suspended sediment concentration in Hangzhou Bay.

10.5. SALINITY DENSITIES

Salt concentration variations, both spatial and temporal, can act as guides to patterns of flow. Studies of Hangzhou Bay[17] have shown that rising tides increase the salt content in the bay, due to the intrusion of salt water, while the reverse process occurs during ebb tides. The flow of fresh or mildly saline water southward from the Yangzi may also trap saline "patches" in the bay. In the Yangzi estuary itself there is a freshwater "plume" that flows seaward, while below it the denser seawater flows landward, resulting in a mixing process that reduces the salinity of the seawater that moves into Hangzhou Bay from the north.

This southward flow from the area around the mouth of the Yangzi is also the primary cause of the salt concentration gradient that runs across Hangzhou Bay from a minimum in the northwest to a maximum in the southeast. In any given place, the vertical distribution of the salt concentration is usually uniform, however, because of the mixing due to turbulence.

10.6. THE SOUTHERN COURSE OF THE YELLOW RIVER

The foregoing sections have provided a picture of the hydrological relations between Hangzhou Bay and the Yellow River at the present day. We now consider the past. In crude terms, the Yellow River followed a southern course from 1194 to 1855, emptying into the Yellow Sea east of historical Huaian. In fact it took a variety of different routes downstream of the Kaifeng region during this period, and usually multiple ones at any given time, interacting in a variety of ways with the Huai River, whose mouth it had captured. In the present section we summarize the approximate picture that emerges from the available sedimentological data, not attempting

[17] We rely here on Han Cengcui 韩曾萃 and Cheng Hangping 陈杭平, "Qiantang jiangshui hanyandu jisuan-de yanjiu" [The calculation of the concentration of salt in the water of the Qiantang River], *Shuili xuebao* 6 (1981), and Hu Fangxi, Gu Guochuan, et al., "Hangzhou-wan erwei yandu kuosan wenti-de yizhong shuzhi jiefa" [A numerical solution to the problem of two-dimensional salt density diffusion in Hangzhou Bay], *Haiyang yu huzhao* 17.4 (1986).

to fine-tune for these minor changes, with the exception of distinguishing the periods before and after 1578.

Table 10.8 shows the past pattern of land formation in what is now the abandoned delta compared with the recent pattern of land formation in the Gulf of Bohai since the river moved back north. Ren Mei'e 任美鍔 (1990) has estimated that the Huai coastal plain was growing at about 2.55 square kilometers per year before 1194.[18] The Yellow River's shift to the southern course was thus to more than double this rate.

The most important point is the shift in the scale of delta deposition after the later sixteenth century, which we shall later show was at least initially an anthropogenic effect due to a change in hydraulic technology. Since it was also a long-term phenomenon, and there was at least some reversion at times to an earlier hydraulic approach, there were probably other contributing causes. We suspect the intensified stripping of the vegetation cover of the middle course of the river under the Qing dynasty. To the extent that this was so, the crucial factor in increasing the supply of sediment to Hangzhou Bay (assuming that this is what happened) was not so much the southward shift of the course of the Yellow River in itself in 1194, though this probably had some effect, as suggested by Ren's findings, so much as the combination of this shift with the increase, after the later sixteenth century, in the sediment load carried to the sea mouth due to a change in the methods used to try to control the river, plus the intensified erosion caused by human developmental activities in the middle part of the catchment area.

Table 10.9 presents a set of estimates, made by Ye Qingchao (1986) and Xu Hailiang (1990),[19] for the advance of land in the Yellow River delta and the accretion of sedimentary deposits during the period of the southern course. The effect of Pan Jixun's hydraulic engineering is visible in row 2 of Table 10.9. By unifying the course of the river and eliminating multiple channels, and then constricting the channel that remained, he unintentionally raised the level of the bed of the channel at the mouth (where the current, after scouring the lower course, had then to slow down) by more than two meters in thirteen years. The figures, which are all linear in this table, do not fully convey the volumetric increase in sediment that was required for this to happen.

It seems likely that while the Yellow River was emptying into the sea south of the Shandong Peninsula, its supply of sediment to Hangzhou Bay

[18] Cited in Li Yuanfang, "Development of the abandoned Yellow River delta," p. 38, n. 39.
[19] On the basis of Guo Ruixiang 郭瑞祥, *Jiangsu haian lishi yanbian* [Historical changes in the coastline of Jiangsu province] (1980), to which we have not had access.

Plate 10.1. LandSat image of outer Hangzhou Bay, Feb. 27, 1984 (processed by ACRES), showing surface-layer suspended sediments.

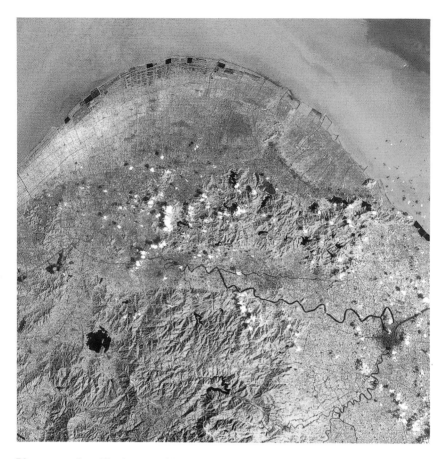

Plate 10.2. LandSat image of Yuyao salient, compressed 2 : 1 along the east–west axis, Feb. 27, 1984 (processed by ACRES), showing water channels associated with successive seawalls.

Table 10.8. *Land formation by the Yellow River on its southern and northern courses from 1194 to 1983*

Course	Period	Years	Land formed (km²)	Rate of land formation (km²·y⁻¹)
South	1194–1577	384	2,300	5.99
South	1578–1854	277	6,700	24.19
North	1855–1908	54	1,239	22.94
North	1909–53	45	588	13.07
North	1954–70	17	270	15.88
North	1976–83	8	261	32.63
Total (excluding 1971–75)	1184–1983	785	11,358	14.47

Note: The calculations have been adjusted to avoid double-counting of the years at the boundaries between periods.
Source: Li Yuanfang 李元芳, "Fei-Huanghe sanjiaozhou-de yanbian" [Changes in the deltas of the abandoned Yellow River], *Dili xuebao* 10.4 (1991), p. 37.

Table 10.9. *The speed of advance and rate of accretion of the Yellow River delta from 1195 to 1854*

Period	Years	Advance (km)	Speed of advance (m·y⁻¹)	Rate of accretion (cm·y⁻¹)	Total accretion (m)
1195–1579	384	15.0	33.0	0.4	1.536
1579–91	13	20.0	1,540.0	16.6	2.158
1592–1700	109	13.0	119.0	1.75	1.908
1701–47	47	15.0	320.0	3.4	1.598
1748–76	29	5.5	190.0	2.0	0.580
1777–1803	27	3.0	111.0	1.2	0.324
1804–10	7	3.5	500.0	5.4	0.378
1811–55	45	14.0	300.0	3.1	1.395
Total	660	90.0	136.0	4.24	9.877

Note: For slightly different figures, see Wan Yansen 万延森, "Subei gu Huanghe sanjiaozhou-de yanbian" [Changes in the old delta of the Yellow River in northern Jiangsu], *Haiyang yu huzhao* 20.1 (1989). The terminal dates of the periods have been adjusted for consistency.
Source: Ye Qingchao 叶青超, "Shilun Subei fei-Huanghe sanjiaozhou-de fayu" [A provisional discussion of the development of the abandoned Yellow River delta in northern Jiangsu], *Dili xuebao* 41.2 (1986); and Xu Hailiang 徐海亮, "Huanghe xiayou-de duiji lishi he fazhan qushi" [The history and trends of development of the sediments in the lower course of the Yellow River], *Shuili xuebao* 7 (1990).

was greater than before the change of course. The supply of fresh sediment to the sea would have been continuous during this period, whereas the present contribution depends solely on scouring by the sea that cuts back the abandoned delta by about 80 meters per year (a loss that still represents some tens of millions of cubic meters of material). Is it possible to be more precise? Perhaps. From the seasonal pattern of sediment delivery by the present Yellow River observed at the Lijin hydrometric station 利津水文站 from 1950 to 1977, and shown in Figure 10.7, it appears that the peak delivery in August represents about 3.75 times the overall monthly average. The concentration of suspended load off the coast of the present-day Yellow River ranges from a minimum of 0.4 kilograms per cubic meter to a maximum of 3.5 kilograms per cubic meter, as shown in Figure 10.8. On the assumption that the Lijin seasonal pattern can be applied, this suggests an average concentration of suspended load in the present Yellow River's coastal waters of 0.933 kilograms per cubic meter. The present-day concentrations in the coastal waters off the abandoned delta of the former south-course Yellow River, measured at two points, range today from 0.1 to 0.2 kilograms per cubic meter and from 0.2 to 0.5 kilograms per cubic meter respectively. Since seasonal variations are slight here, because variations in inland snowmelt and precipitation have no effect, we may take a simple average of 0.25 kilograms per cubic meter. On the further assumption that the processes of sediment transport along the Jiangsu and Zhejiang coasts functioned prior to 1855 as they do today, the suspended sediment moving from the south-course Yellow River to Hangzhou Bay at this earlier time can be estimated as having been 3.732 times greater than it is from the abandoned delta at the present. Since at least[20] 84.5 percent of the abandoned delta was deposited after 1578, this estimate cannot be taken as applying to the period before this date. In terms of quantity, the multiplier 3.732 indicates 45.194×10^6 tonnes per year entering Hangzhou Bay from the south-course Yellow River prior to 1855, which would have been 33.084×10^6 tonnes per year more than the present rate for this component, an increase of approximately 71 percent in total sediment delivery from the Yangzi estuary area, and of approximately 62 percent in total sediment delivery from all sources, including the Qiantang River. That this result is reasonable does not imply that it is correct. What it does suggest is that the effect may have been big enough to show up in cores of material taken from

[20] Because this percentage is based on the linear measure of delta advance as shown in Table 10.9, which underestimates the volume of sediment per unit of distance in the later period, which would have been deposited in deeper water. Li Yuanfang's estimate, however, in "Development of the abandoned Yellow River delta," gives about 86% of the volume as having been deposited after 1578.

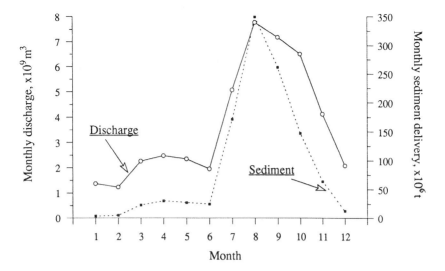

Figure 10.7. The monthly discharge and sediment delivery at Lijin hydrometric station, 1950–77, near the mouth of the Yellow River. *Source*: Pang Jiazhen 庞家珍 and Si Shuheng 司书亨, "Huanghe hekou yanbian" [Changes in the mouths of the Yellow River], *Haiyang yu huzhao* 11.4 (1980).

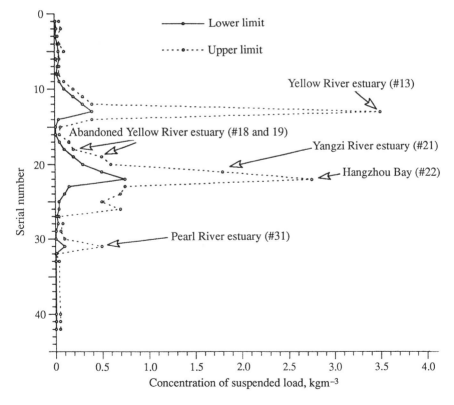

Figure 10.8. Concentrations of suspended sediment load along China's eastern coast. *Source*: Gu and Hu, "Characteristics of the distribution of sediments."

areas known to have been built up mainly since the sixteenth century, such as the Yuyao salient, and we propose that such cores should be examined (and, if necessary, taken) with this question in mind.

10.7. THE EFFECTS OF LONG-TERM FLUCTUATIONS IN CLIMATE

Since long-term variations in precipitation, and hence in runoff, cause variations in erosional forces on the soil surface, it is important to consider the possible effects of long-term changes in climate on sediment transport by the Yellow, Yangzi, and Qiantang rivers. Historical studies suggest that during the last five hundred years there have been approximately three *relatively* wet periods in northern and central China: (1) the later sixteenth century, which as we show below corresponded to a phase of intensified hydraulic difficulties in the lower course of the Yellow River; (2a) the seventeenth-eighteenth-century transition (northern China only) and (2b) the very late eighteenth century; and (3a) the late nineteenth century (especially central China) and (3b) the early twentieth century (mainly northern China).[21] Apart from period (1), there are no unambiguous correlations with speed of Yellow River delta growth. Several investigators have also detected periodicities in Chinese climatic patterns,[22] but our data do not have fine enough resolution for possible correlations to be detected.

10.8. THE TIDAL BORE IN HANGZHOU BAY DURING THE SONG AND YUAN DYNASTIES

Observation and chronological measurement of the tides, skepticism toward earlier explanations, and a modicum of hydrological experimentation were already developed in Song China. Outstanding as both an observed and theorist was Yan Su 燕肅, a Northern Song official with a talent for

---

[21] Ding, *Monsoons over China*, p. 298.

[22] For example, Ding, *Monsoons over China*, pp. 297–98; Chen Jiaqi 陈家其, "Huanghe zhongyou diqu jin 1500-nian shui-han bianhua guilü ji qi qushi fenxi" [Analysis of the laws and trends governing the changes in floods and droughts in the last 1,500 years in the middle reaches of the Yellow River], *Renmin Huanghe* 5 (1983). See also Wang Shaowu 王绍武 and Zhao Zongci 赵宗慈, "Jin wubai-nian woguo hanlao shiliao-de fenxi" [Analysis of Chinese historical materials relating to droughts and floods during the last 500 years], *Dili xuebao* 34.4 (1979).

hydraulic clockwork and other mechanical devices, who wrote the *Haichao [tu]lun* 海潮[圖]論 [An (illustrated) theory of tides], which illustrates the level of understanding that had been achieved about a millennium ago, including the concept of superimposed phases.[23] He was also intrigued by the unusual behavior of the Qiantang bore. We will not quote his views *in extenso*, although they contain many interesting points,[24] but confine ourselves to his discussion of the mid-bay sandbar:

(5) Someone may ask: "In all the seas the full tide comes slowly. Only on the Zhe River 浙江 [i.e. the Qiantang and Hangzhou Bay] does the wave arrive in a horizontal line like a range of mountains, as impetuous as thunder, flying crosswise between the two shores, with its snowy banks spurting forth at the side, roaring and rising up, overflowing in its haste, and hissing fearfully. [This was the celebrated tidal bore, a sort of shock wave that advanced like a wall of water.][25] Is it possible to be told the reason for its thus swelling up in anger?"

(6) Some people say that there are mountains on the coasts that constrict its side. That to the south is called Mount Kan 龕山, and that to the north Mount Zhe 赭山. Where the two mountains face each other is called the "Sea Gate" (*haimen* 海門).[26] It is simply that the coasts are narrow and the situation forces there to be a wave. – If it is maintained that narrowness is responsible for the forcing, then the Eastern Sea swallows two rivers in Yuyao 餘姚 and Fenghua 奉化 counties [on the south coast of the bay] after it passes in from Dinghai 定海 [present-day Zhenhai 鎮海 in Ningbo prefecture], and these are even narrower than the Qiantang. But when the tide comes one does not hear any sound from the waves [in these places].

(7) Now, if one looks across the mouth of the Qiantang River [i.e. Hangzhou Bay] from Zuanfeng Pavilion 纂風亭 [in present-day Shaoxing prefecture near Lihai 瀝海] northward to the large hills 大山 in Jiaxing prefecture the water is more than 200 *li* 里 across.[27] Thus the ships of seagoing merchants are afraid of the [underwater] sandbar [*sha-dan* 沙潬], and merely

[23] On tidal theory in China, see J. Needham with Wang Ling, *Science and Civilisation in China*, vol. 3, "Mathematics and the Sciences of the Heavens and the Earth" (Cambridge: Cambridge University Press, 1959), pp. 483–94.

[24] Paragraphs 2 and 3 are also translated in Needham, *Science and Civilisation*, III, p. 491, but do not resolve all the difficulties. An older version is in A. C. Moule, "The Bore on the Ch'ien-t'ang River in China," *T'oung pao* 22 (1923).

[25] Since shallow-water waves naturally move at a celerity determined by the depth (namely, $c = \sqrt{gd}$), when the rising tide in a sharply narrowing channel or steepening gradient in the bed forces a wave front to reach or exceed this speed, a shock wave is created that forms a wall of water.

[26] This mouth of the Qiantang River silted up by the early years of the seventeenth century. Today both mountains are part of the Nansha Peninsula on the south shore.

[27] The correct conversion ratio for the *li* varies with the date of composition and other factors (the range being from about 420 to 600 meters). Jiaxing is on the order of 100 kilometers distant from Lihai, looking north-northeast.

sail as far as the small river in Yuyao, where they change vessels and proceed along the canal to Yuezhou 越州 [modern Shaoxing] and Hangzhou. The reason for this is that under the water there is a sandbar stretching from north to south that presents an intervening obstacle to the waves, and abruptly blocks the force of the tide. The fact of the matter is that when the moon is passing through the [phases of the cycle represented by] the trigrams *zhen* 震 and *dui* 兌,[28] another tide is already rising, but in the Qiantang alone the water has still not come to a stop. When the moon passes through the [phases of the diurnal cycle represented by the] trigrams *sun* 巽 and *qian* 乾, the tide has half-arrived. The waves, turbid [with sediment], hold themselves back and become congested. More water comes from behind them, and they thereupon overflow across the sandbar with fierce anger and a sudden surge. The power of the sound radiates outward. Thus it is that it rises up and becomes the wave [of a tidal bore]. It is not a phenomenon caused by the shallowness and constriction of the river and the [coastal] hills.[29]

It does not seem that the abrupt and clearly defined way in which the tide crossed the sandbar that is described by Yan Su was in evidence by the later seventeenth century. The gazetteer for Shaoxing prefecture for the Kangxi reign (1662–1722) states that "when the men of past times said that, when there was a high tide (*ping* 平) at Yuyao, the tide coming on to Xiaoshan had to 'mount the sandbar' before it arrived," they were "in error."[30] Nor can it be anywhere observed at the present day. One possibility is that the previous bar submerged at high tide has, in a sense, been transformed over the centuries, partly into the Nansha Peninsula, which now blocks most of the inner bay, and partly into the Yuyao salient. However this may have been, we have a preliminary picture for Song times of a shallow estuary in which the tide was constantly moving and reworking a large quantity of mid-estuary sediment.

[28] The trigrams can be ordered in several ways. We would guess that the pattern used for the eight main cardinal points on the diviner's board and compass is the most likely here. If this is correct, then *zhen* and *dui* are East and West respectively, and *sun* and *qian* Southeast and Northwest respectively. See J. Needham with Wang Ling and K. G. Robinson, *Science and Civilisation in China*, vol. 4, part 1, "Physics and Physical Technology," pp. 263, 266, and plate 116 facing p. 286. This layout was not invariable (see plate 120 facing p. 294, for example). The presumption must be that "East" and "West" represent low water in a twice-daily cycle, and the phase arrow is thought of as rotating clockwise, so that the "Northwest" and "Southeast" mentioned later are the phases immediately preceding the two high tides at "North" and "South."

[29] Quoted in Shi Su 施宿 et al., eds., revised by Shen Zuobin 沈作賓, *Jiatai Guiji zhi* 嘉泰會稽志 [Jiatai reign gazetteer for Guiji], in *Song-Yuan fangzhi congkan* 宋元方志叢刊 [Collection of Song- and Yuan-dynasty local gazetteers] (1201–04. Reprinted, Beijing: Zhonghua shuju, 1992), vol. 7, p. 7065.

[30] *Shaoxing fuzhi* [Gazetteer for Shaoxing prefecture] (1719. Reprinted, Taipei: Chengwen, 1983), p. 649.

Around 1224 Zhu Zhongyou 朱中有, who had spent fifty years of his life beside the Qiantang, wrote the *Chaozhe* 潮磧 [Mysteries of the tides], a prose poem prefaced by a series of questions and answers. His discussion of the part played by the sandbar in causing the tidal bore invokes a simple form of experiment:

> Would you now like to look into the matter in detail? Let me try testing it with you by examining what goes on in a ditch. If you put in water until the ditch is full, the water in it will invariably enter smoothly (*ping jin* 平進) until the ditch is half full. [Next] pile fragmented stones so that they form a rough and irregular surface (*juyu* 齟齬). Let water flow in from the upper end and then out in such a way that it has to pass over this roughness before draining away through a sluice below. There will be nothing surprising in the turbulent flow of the water (*jiyong* 激湧). What Mr. Yan called a "bar" is sand under the water. The Qiantang sea-gate bar stretches across 200 *li*. The fact of the matter is that the water has to make up the difference in level (*ying ke* 盈科) before it flows on in. When the tide is increasing but has not yet reached the bar, the Qiantang River (upstream) is still quite empty (*kongkong* 空空). After the tide has grown and confronted it head on, it discharges from the bar as through a sluice (*douxie* 斗寫) into the river. Furthermore, the sand banks above the surface in the river (*jiang-sha zhi zhang* 江沙之漲) sometimes shift east and sometimes west, without having any constant location. The tide is displaced and constricted by these sands and gravels[31] (*shaqi* 沙圻), so that its turbulent flow that "shakes the skies and makes the earth tremble" comes on like a high cliff. This is the pattern principle of water. Is it anything to wonder at? That which I called the "rough and irregular surface" [in the experimental ditch] was simply like the bar.
>
> Thus it is that the schedule of the tides in the Qiantang estuary is behind that for the tides at Dinghai. At Dinghai the sea comes in smoothly (*ping jin*) but that in the Qiantang estuary has to wait to climb the bar before it enters the river. . . . When the tide ebbs, it either passes through the low point(s) in the bar, or else it floods over the two tail-ends of the bar, so as to reach the sea. The explanation for this is that the bar is high in the middle but its two ends become gradually lower. The midpoint confronts the onrush of the Qiantang [River]. The slightly lower places to the east confront the debouchments of the Qianqing River 錢清江 and the Cao'e River 曹娥江 [which flow in close together from the south coast]. The bar is very low at the mouth of the Qianqing, and the tidal bore (*chaotou* 潮頭) [on this river] is extremely slight. The bar off the Cao'e is somewhat higher than that off the Qianqing, and therefore its tidal bore shows a greater difference in height.[32]

---

[31] *Qi* 圻 means "the stones on the side of a mountain," like scree.

[32] Zhang Hao, ed., *Baoqing Guiji xu-zhih* [Baoqing reign-period continuation of the gazetteer for Guiji], in *Song-Yuan fangzhi congkan* (1225. Reprinted, Zhonghua shuju: Taipei, 1992), vol. 7, p. 7180.

Zhu Zhongyou had correctly observed the different courses that are often taken by the flood and ebb tides, but present-day theory tends to regard a high coefficient of friction on the estuary bed as tending to inhibit rather than facilitate the formation of a bore.[33] Although transient sandbanks that are exposed at low water are still a feature of the inner bay today, there is at the present time no single semisubmerged transverse barrier, presenting the clear, steplike discontinuity of which Zhu Zhongyou speaks, visible either on Admiralty charts of this or the nineteenth century or on satellite images. Map 10.5, for example, which is part of a chart surveyed in 1840–44, shows the bay north of Yuyao 餘姚, where such a bar might be expected to be. The Yuyao salient (most of which is post-Song, as shown later) is evident, but the soundings (which are in fathoms, a fathom being c. 2 meters) show a channel running round it to the north. The mid-bay island designated "Pe-yu-shan" (far left) appears on no other chart that we have seen to date, and is presumably a transient. There is reason to suspect that the bay has changed in both geometry and tidal processes since the thirteenth century.

10.9. THE YUYAO SALIENT

Why did part of the coastline north of Yuyao 餘姚 and Ciqi 慈溪[34] grow so rapidly after about 1400? A preliminary geographical orientation is provided by Map 10.6, based on maps at a scale of 1 : 50,000 made by the Japanese Army,[35] which gives an overall view of the salient as it had developed by the early 1930s. To the south is what was once a typical sunken coastline, with the land more than 25 meters above sea level indicated by the solid black areas, but which has now been filled in with deposited sediments to form a nearly level plain between the hills and mountains.

---

[33] J. J. Stoker, *Water Waves: The Mathematical Theory with Applications* (New York: Interscience, 1957), p. 468; and R. Silvester, *Coastal Engineering*, 2 vols. (Amsterdam: Elsevier, 1974), vol. 2, pp. 163, 166 et seq. See also Du Yong 杜勇 "Hekou junyunliu-zhong yongchao-de xingshi" [The formation of tidal bores in constant flow at a river mouth," *Haiyang yu huzhao* 22.1 (Jan. 1991), p. 83, who argues that "friction wearing off energy" tends to inhibit bore formation.

[34] Note that present-day Ciqi is the former Hushan, and that the old Ciqi, referred to here, has become Ciqicheng 慈溪城.

[35] Rikugun, *Chūgoku Tairiku 1 : 50,000 chizu shūsei* [1 : 50,000 maps of the Chinese mainland], 3 vols. (c. 1938. Reprinted, Tokyo: Kagaku shoin, 1991). These maps, like those from premodern Chinese sources discussed later, have been scanned and then redrawn, and some detail removed, in order to render them easily visually intelligible. No alterations have been made to the basic structures but important symbols have been standardized and important names transcribed into English.

Seaward of this area is an arc enclosed by a complex system of seawalls that uses outlying hills as anchorage points, where these are available, and that consists not of a line or lines so much as of a sequence of linked cells that resemble bulkheads. These walls are the 1930s incarnations of structures that in earlier times ran to the landward side of these modern defenses, and whose approximate positions can be estimated from older literary and cartographic sources. The fragments of surviving seawall near Hushansuo 滸山所 city and near Linshanwei 臨山衛 city, for example, indicate an earlier line of dikes that ran close up against the mountains. Plate 10.2, a satellite image of the salient compressed east-to-west by a ratio of 2 to 1, shows the general pattern of successive outward progression, though the clearest features are the drainage channels beside the dikes, the dikes themselves not being visible as such.

The structure of the northern coast is complex (see Map 10.7). The lack of a satisfactory legend for the Japanese maps makes their interpretation speculative, but what they would seem to show is (1) an infratidal zone normally submerged even at low tide (the banks whose seaward edge is indicated by a dotted line); (2) a lower intertidal zone or *slikke*, made of relatively fine-grained sediments (and hence to be distinguished from coarse-grained sandy beaches), but without vegetation cover or the development of soil (a zone whose outer limits are indicated by a double continuous line, which reproduces a dashed line in the original map); (3) an upper intertidal zone or *schorre*, only covered by spring tides or during storm surges, with some soil development and substantial halophytic vegetation cover (a zone whose outer limits are shown by a double broken line, which again reproduces a solid line in the original); (4) diked paddy-fields seaward of the seawalls proper (a zone whose outer edge is indicated by a heavy broken line, but whose status is certain because of the land-use symbols in the original); and (5) the seawall complex (indicated by a single beaded line, and again of certain status).[36] The pattern in space (moving from sea to land) represents a sequence in time (moving back from the present toward the past) through which infratidal deposits have more or less continuously developed into *slikke*, then into *schorre*, and then into reclaimed agricultural land.

Present-day aerial photography and satellite photographs show that the tidal flats north of Andong 安東, near the center of the Yuyao salient, today reach out for about 13 kilometers, but much less far to the east and west. These are in the main fine sands and silts, with a slightly more clayey

---

[36] The definitions of the Flemish terms *slikke* and *schorre* are based on Verger, *Marais et wadden*, esp. pp. 54 and 63.

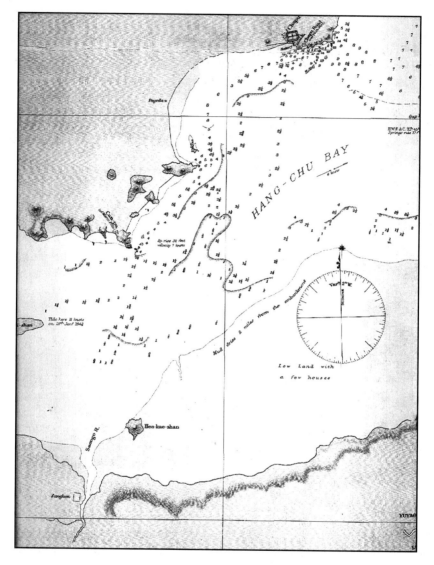

Map 10.5. Section of British Admiralty Chart showing Hangzhou Bay, surveyed 1840–44, with later additions (issued 1883: China, East Coast #1199).

character along the eastern shore of the salient and a more sandy one along the western flank. In general the grain diameter lies in the range of 10μ to 100μ, and particles can be entrained by currents of 30 to 40 cm per second. The flats on the southwestern side of the salient, near the mouth of the Caoe River 曹娥江, are unstable, and cut by numerous tidal channels. The

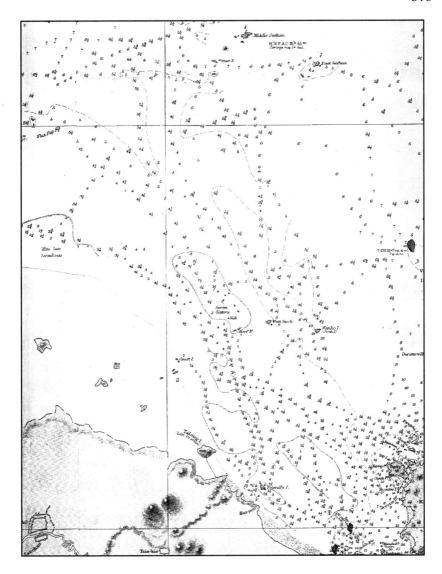

northern "cap" is wider and increasing in size, while the eastern side is fairly stable. Bands of the club-rush *Scirpus xmarigueter* in the upper part of the intertidal zone (i.e., above the mean level of the tide), from about 10 meters to 200 meters wide, tend to damp the waves, and promote the deposition of sediment and the buildup of organic matter. They can serve as food for cattle and fish but are not widely employed for this purpose. The club-rushes are succeeded, after a transitional zone, by narrower bands of the reed

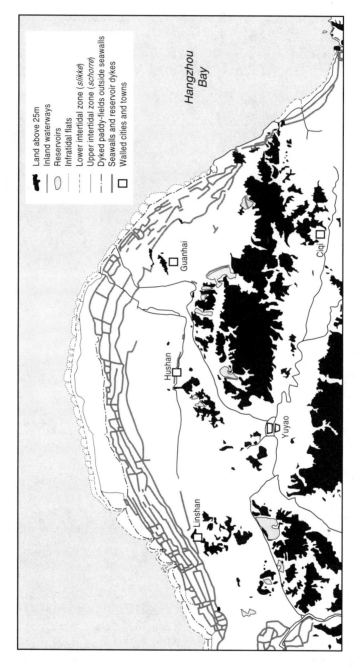

Map 10.6. Yuyao salient, c. 1938. Based on sheets from the Rikugun (Japanese Army) 1 : 50,000 maps of China.

Legend:
- Land above 25m
- Inland waterways
- Reservoirs
- Infratidal flats
- Lower intertidal zone (*slikke*)
- Upper intertidal zone (*schorre*)
- Dyked paddy-fields outside seawalls
- Seawalls and reservoir dykes
- Walled cities and towns

Hangzhou Bay

Guanhai

Hushan

Yuyao

Ciqi

Linshan

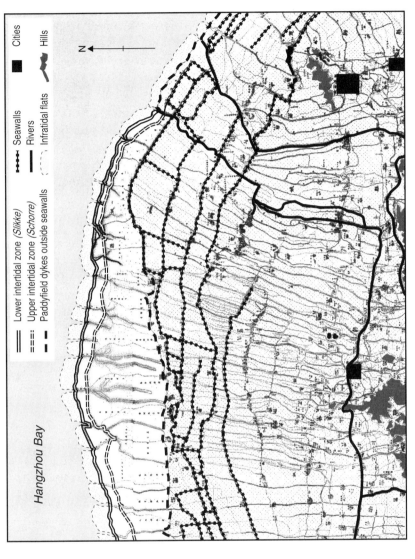

Map 10.7. Part of the Yuyao salient north of Hushan, c. 1938, showing seawalls and drainage.

Lower intertidal zone *(Slikke)*
Upper intertidal zone *(Schorre)*
Paddyfield dykes outside seawalls

Seawalls
Rivers
Infratidal flats

Cities
Hills

Hangzhou Bay

N

Phragmites australis, a plant that does have economic uses, such as serving as material for the manufacture of paper, and is hence to some degree planted deliberately. The *Phragmites* zone is also used for grazing cattle and sheep. Further inland is land being prepared for enclosure and farming, its transformation often accelerated by the building of spur dikes (*dingba* 丁埧) and longitudinal dikes (*shunba* 順埧).[37] Maps 10.8 and 10.9, which are based on a combination of aerial and satellite photographs and field examination, respectively show (Map 10.8) the distribution of particle sizes in the flats around the perimeter of the salient, and (Map 10.9) the distribution of *Scirpus* and *Phragmites*. They give broad support to our interpretation of the Japanese map, though it is evident that the correspondence is approximate, possibly because of changes over the intervening fifty years.

The part played by vegetation in the transformation of new *slikke* to *schorre* is hinted at by a Yuan-dynasty writer quoted in the late Qing gazetteer for Yuyao:

> Places that in times past were gnawed away by the [sea's] impact and drowned have been subsequently filled by muddy sediment (*shatu*); and thickets of reeds (*luwei* 蘆葦) have grown here, in unbroken succession for several tens or a hundred *li*. With the help of Heaven, even such uncanny events can occur.[38]

The gazetteer for Changguo 昌國 department (that is, Ming- and Qing-dynasty Dinghai 定海, at the eastern end of the southern coast of the bay) in the Dade reign-period (1297 to 1307) noted that

> the commoner-civilians (*min*) provide themselves with the money to build shores of gently sloping dikes (*nati*[39] 捺提), which cause the mudflats (*tu* 塗) to turn into farmland. If they fail to repair them in good time, the dike walls collapse or leak, and the farmland reverts once more to being mudflats.[40]

The processes observed in modern times, both natural and anthropogenic, appear to have been at work – broadly speaking – a millennium ago.

---

[37] Shi Jiqing 施纪青 and Yan Weiyun 严蔚云, "Yaogan tuxiang zai Hangzhou-wan tantu diaocha-zhong de yingyong" [The function of remote-sensing images in investigations of the mudbanks in Hangzhou Bay], in Zheng Quanan et al., eds., *Yaogan jishu zai haiyang huanjing yu ziyuan diaocha-zhong de kaifa yanjiu* [Studies on remote-sensing techniques in marine environments and investigation of resources] (n.p.: Guojia haiyang-ju keji si, 1987), pp. 47–60.

[38] Honda Osamu, "Sō-Gen jidai Settō no kaitō ni tsuite" [On the seawalls in Zhedong under the Song and the Yuan], *Chūgoku suiri-shi kenkyū* (1979), p. 12.

[39] This translation is speculative. *Na* 捺 is the name for a downstroke in Chinese calligraphy that slopes, rather like a dune, to the right. The suspicion is that it is analogous to our "T-junction" or the Chinese term for a pyramid, namely 金字塔 *jinzita*, "*jin*-character tower."

[40] Honda Osamu, "Seawalls in Zhedong," p. 7.

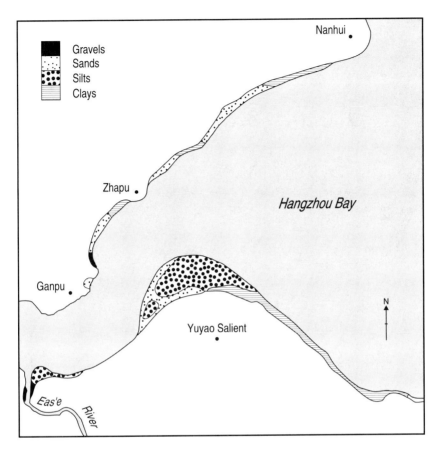

Map 10.8. Distribution of surface-layer deposits around Hangzhou Bay, by grain size.

Mudflat fields (*tutian* 塗田), shown in Fig. 10.9, are depicted and described in generic terms in the mid-eighteenth-century encyclopedia *Qinding shoushi tongkao* 欽定授時通考 [Imperially commanded comprehensive examination of the seasonal allocation of work]:

The lands along the seashore also make use of this method for fields. The sediment in the tides either accumulates in islands or fills up submerged sinuosities. . . . Saltwater vegetation grows in thickets on their upper parts. When in due course a tide comes [over them] they little by little encourage the deposition of mud. One first of all plants *Panicum crus-corvi* [*shuibai* 水稗]. Once the salinity has been entirely removed, they can be made into fields for cereals. . . . On coastlines that have been filled up one either builds walls or implants stakes in order to resist the tides. Ditches are cut at the sides of the

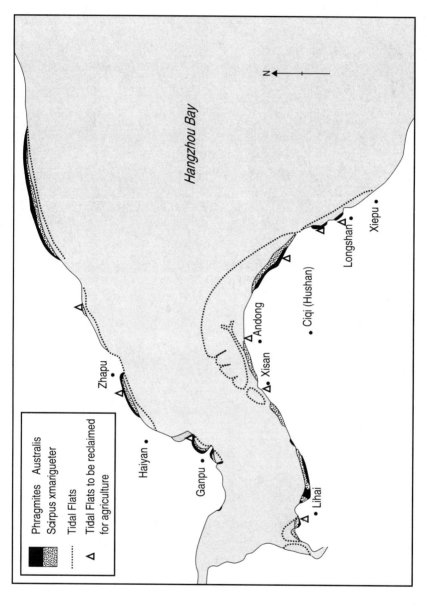

Map 10.9. Distribution of club-rush (*Scirpus xmarigueter*) and reeds (*Phragmites australis*) around the shoreline of present-day Hangzhou Bay.

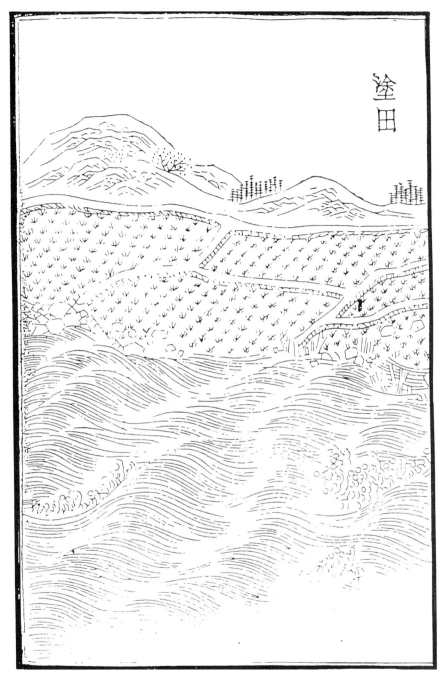

涂田

Figure 10.9. Mudflat fields. Woodblock print from E'ertai et al., *Comprehensive examination of seasonal work, j.* 14, p. 11b.

fields for the rainwater to run off. In dry periods one can irrigate from them. They are called "freshwater ditches."[41]

We may note in passing that most sea embankments (*haishi* 海澨) on the south coast of the mouth of the Yangzi had a mile or more of reeds and mudflats on their seaward side, and where this was not the case they needed the exceptional protection of stone seawalls, and even this was not necessarily adequate.[42] Morita also quotes a passage from the late Qing gazetteer for Nanhui county 南匯縣 at the end of the promontory on the south side of the mouth of the Yangzi to the effect that

> East [that is, outside] of the outer seawall, if there is some swamp among the profusion of aquatic grasses and reeds that can be opened for agriculture, they build an additional polder-dike (*yutang* 圩塘) that serves as a protection for the outer seawall.[43]

In general, the man-made defenses of this period functioned best in conjunction with more or less natural organic defenses. Otherwise, as was reported of Qingcun 青村 and Zhelin 柘林, which had only hastily planted trees and improvised earthen walls once their exposed stone dike had been breached, "they successively built [defenses], only [to see them] successively broken and breached, and have had in succession to take flight."[44]

The subsection of Yuyao shown in Map 10.7 is that to the north of Hushansuo 滸山所 city. The most striking feature is the alignment of the minor waterways that now lie immediately *within* the main complex of seawalls, on the landward side. They run approximately parallel in a north–south direction, at right angles to the seacoast, but they are separated from the coast and are shown as flowing *south* into the small river that runs west-to-east just north of the little city and on the north side of the remnants of the seawall. These channels were probably once the ebb tide runoff channels for earlier *schorres* and *slikkes*, though their direction of flow has now reversed, and in all likelihood is similar to the channels that can be seen along the coast to the north (at the date at which this map was compiled), none of which in this sector are linked to the inland drainage system. South

---

[41] E'ertai 鄂爾泰 et al., eds., *Qinding shoushi tongkao* 欽定授時通考 [Comprehensive examination of the seasonal allocation of work, compiled by imperial command] (1742), "Tu yi," Tianzhi-tu *xia, j.* 14, p. 15a.

[42] Ye Mengzhu 葉夢珠, *Yueshi bian* 閱世編 [An examination of the age] (late seventeenth century), reprinted in *Shanghai Zhanggu congshu* (Shanghai: Shanghai tongshe, 1934), *j.* 1, p. 7a.

[43] Morita Akira 森田明, *Shindai suiri-shi kenkyū* 清代水利史研究 [Research on the history of water control in Qing times] (Tokyo: Aki shobō, 1974), p. 285.

[44] Ye Mengzhu, *Examination of the age, j.* 1, p. 7a.

of the west–east river (and of the residual seawall) the pattern made by the minor waterways changes: their courses bear relatively little relation to those immediately to the north, and they drain into a separate west-to-east river running south of the old seawall, and/or south into the main Yuyao River (at the extreme south of the map).

The traditional terms used in Yuyao for the various parts of the *wadden* (to adopt the Flemish term for areas subject to morphological modification by the tides, cognate with the Latin *vadum*, "shallows") were as follows: (1) *haitu* 海塗 – "seaborne sediments" (literally "sea mud"), either in suspension or deposited; (2) *shatu* 沙塗 – "sedimentary mud" or "sandy mud," the section next to the sea, and perhaps approximately *slikke*; (3) *liudi* 溜地 – "land marked by the flow of water," the next section in a landward direction, approximately *schorre*; and (4) *shadan* 沙潭 – usually "midwater banks of deposited sediment" (in the bay), but also used for shore areas flanked by two creeks or, sometimes, just land next to the sea. The last three terms may be seen in Map 10.10, which is reproduced from a late nineteenth-century gazetteer for Yuyao county.[45] The four main seawalls in the central section are, from south to north, the Profitable Dike (*liji-tang* 利濟塘), the Old Polder Dike (*lao yu-tang* 老圩塘), the Old New Polder Dike (*lao xin yu-tang* 老新圩塘), and the New Polder Dike (*xin yu-tang* 新圩塘). The two dikes outside this line in the west are, respectively, the Fifth Polder Dike and the Sixth Polder Dike. The four streams (in the northeast sector) that traverse the tidal flats are safeguarded where they cross the seawalls either by locks (*zha* 閘) or by sluices (*dong* 洞). The two roads, marked by dotted lines that cross the diked area as far as the edge of the mudflats, are both described as "new roads" (*xinjie* 新街). The names often betoken a sense of change. Between about 1400 and 1900 the sea seems to have withdrawn from being 35 *li* north of Yuyao city to "more than 80 *li* north" of it, over 45 *li* in 500 years (or just under one *li* per decade).[46] In the present century the process has continued,[47] two further lines of seawalls being added under the Communist government.[48] As we discovered in our visit to the area in 1994–95, it is now all but impossible on the ground to identify the older seawalls of times past, since they resemble any other modest-sized dike, but the local inhabitants still remember which they are and willingly point them out to the visitor.

[45] Shao Youlian and Sun Dezu, eds., *Yuyao xianzhi* [Yuyao county gazetteer] (1899. Reprinted, Taipei: Chengwen, 1983), Huazhong #500, 2 vols., pp. 40–41. The "sea mud" is referred to as an area from which the submerged stones of a destroyed seawall were on one occasion successfully recovered (see p. 110), but it could also be reclaimed for farming (see p. 113).
[46] Shao and Sun, *Yuyao*, p. 64.
[47] Shi Jiqing and Yan Weiyun, "Function of remote-sensing images."
[48] Honda Osamu 本田治, "Seawalls in Zhedong."

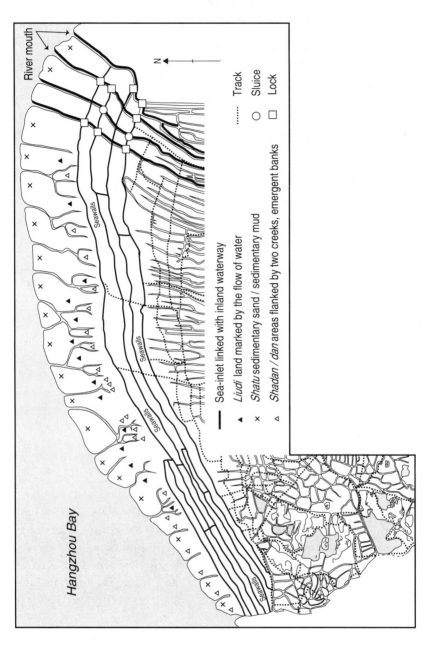

Map 10.10. Part of the coast of the Yuyao salient, showing terms traditionally used for different types of shore terrain.
Source: Gazetteer for Yuyao county (1899).

We have not found a map of the salient from Song or Yuan times. Map 10.11, which shows coastal defenses and is taken from the seventeenth-century anthology of documents compiled by Gu Yanwu 顧炎武, gives an idea of the coastline before the rapid accumulation of sedimentary deposits.[49] Tidal inlets run in between the coastal mountains, several widening into lakes, with locks preventing the entry of the tides except for the shipping channel leading to Yuyao, shown near the center of the map. There are offshore islands not yet joined to the mainland, or, like Mount Sheng 勝山, sticking out into the sea on a promontory and in the process of being joined. The walled cities along the coast are the headquarters of military Guards (*wei* 衞) and Stations (*suo* 所); and the flags flying from staffs mostly mark shoreline beacons (*fengdun* 烽墩), but also some of the Police Offices (*xunsi* 巡司). The walled county capitals of Ciqi, Yuyao, and Shangyu are visible in east-to-west order along the bottom margin. Remarks in cartouches that have been removed from the original, being too smudged to be legible in reproduction, refer to measures taken against the "Japanese"[50] pirates who attacked between the years 1553 and 1556, and more especially to patrols at the time of the "spring floods" (*chunxun* 春汛). The contrast with the modern shoreline is striking. Map 10.12, published in 1624,[51] presents a 45°-angle view of Ciqi showing how the mountains rose up out of the depositional plain. The locks (*zha* 閘) protecting the inlets east of Guanhai Guard 觀海衞 are also indicated. Map 10.13 comes from an even later source, the 1730 gazetteer for Ciqi,[52] but (likewise anachronistically) shows the shoreline before the salient had built up. Ciqi is central, while Zhenhai county 鎮海縣 (previously Dinghai county 定海縣) is at the extreme right, Ningbo prefecture 寧波府 slightly to the west and inland, and Yuyao county at the exteme left. No appreciable extension of the salient is shown, although (as demonstrated below) it had begun to be important at least two centuries earlier. In other words, there was a marked cartographic lag behind reality.

The chronology of seawall construction was as follows. According to an account quoted by the Yuyao county gazetteer for the later sixteenth or early seventeenth century, "there used in the past to be a long dike that

---

[49] Gu Yanwu, ed., *Tianxia junguo libing shu* 天下郡國利病書 [Documents on the advantageous and disadvantageous aspects of the commanderies and principates of the empire] (Siku shanben MS facsimile edn., Zhejiang), *shang, ce* 32. pp. 82–12b. The map was already somewhat out of date at the time it was put into the form shown here.

[50] By this date most of the pirates were Chinese, but the name had stuck.

[51] Yao Zongwen 姚宗文, ed., *Ciqi xianzhi* 慈溪縣志 [Ciqi county gazetteer] (1624. Reprinted, Taipei: Chengwen, 1983. Huazhong #490), pp. 20–21.

[52] Yang Zhengsun 陽正荀, ed., *Ciqi xianzhi* 慈溪縣志 [Ciqi county gazetteer] (1730. Reprinted, Taipei: Chengwen, 1975. Huazhong #191), pp. 48–53.

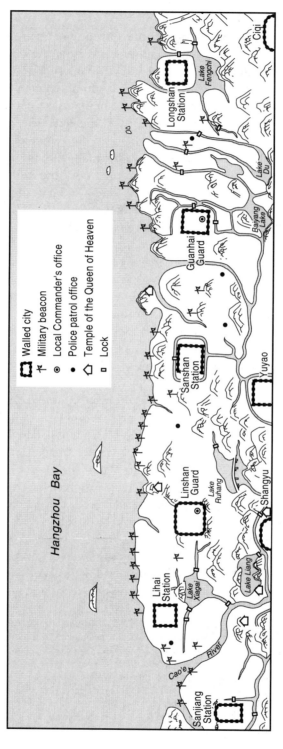

Map 10.11. Southern shoreline of outer Hangzhou Bay north of Yuyao, prior to the development of the salient, showing walled cities, military beacons, and locks.

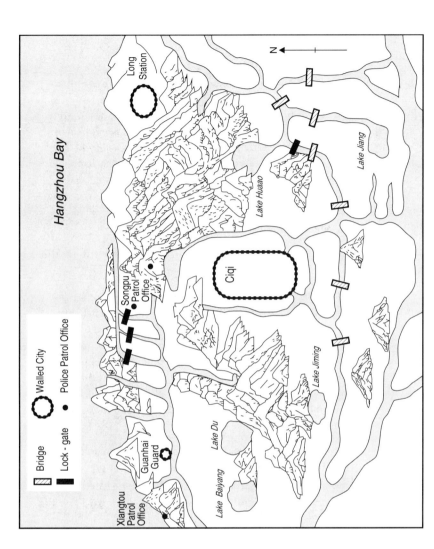

Map 10.12. Oblique-angled local gazetteer map/view of Ciqi and the southern shore of Hangzhou Bay (published in 1624, but illustrating the coastal topography at least 200 years previous).

protected the farmlands of the commoner-civilians" in the period before the eleventh century.[53] The same account goes on to say,

> The three rural districts of Xiaoyi 孝義, Longquan 龍泉, and Yunke 雲柯 had mounting deposits of sediment and hence [relatively] high-lying land [at this time]. They had no threat of breaches caused by storm surges or tides. In the five rural districts of Kaiyuan 開原, Dongshan 東山, Lanfeng 蘭風, Meichuan 梅川, and Shanglin 上林 [to the west] there were open gaps (*querang* 缺壤), and these it was that were a source of anxiety to the commoner-civilians. In 1047 the county magistrate Xie Jingchu 謝景初, built a seawall of 28,000 feet from Yunke to Shanglin.... A hundred and fifty years later, in 1196, the county magistrate Shi Su 施宿 further built a dike of 42,000 feet from Shanglin to Lanfeng, of which 5,700 feet were in stone.[54]

The late Qing-dynasty gazetteer gives the following background to this eleventh-century seawall:

> There were salt-lands to the south of the water of the sea, several tens of *li* from north to south and 80 to 90 *li* from east to west. They produced fish, salt, crabs, bivalves, rice, millet, pulses, wheat, melons, cotton, and reeds. The humbler people of all rural districts made a living therefrom. The seaside land was salty and brittle (*lucui* 鹵脆); the tidal currents broke in torrents; and several tens of *li* of land were soaked through by the sea, which came into the interior, submerged the people's houses, and killed off the crops. Earlier generations had suffered from this. It was for this reason that a dike was built to resist the sea.[55]

The epitaph of Xie Jingchu, architect of the first seawall in Yuyao in Song times, notes that the people "took delight in the profits to be had from the illegal boiling of brine to make salt," that is, outside the government's salt-monopoly system. Xie, it says, stopped them doing this, and paid for his dike from increased salt-monopoly profits.[56]

A number of earthen dikes were also built some way inland "to prevent the tides overflowing." These secondary dikes "followed the lie of the land, going up and down in irregular fashion without forming a unified system, being known as scattered dikes (*santang* 散塘)."[57] We are also told that "from the Baoqing reign-period [1225–27] to the Dade reign-period of the

[53] *Xinxiu Yuyao xianzhi* [Newly revised county gazetteer for Yuyao] (no compilers given) (Wanli reign of the Ming dynasty [1573–1619]. Reprinted, Taipei: Chengwen, 1983), p. 109. Pages are missing from this book, and some of the characters are illegible.
[54] *Revised gazetteer for Yuyao*, p. 109.
[55] Shao and Sun, *Yuyao*, pp. 141–42.
[56] Honda Osamu, "Seawalls in Zhedong," p. 7.
[57] *Revised gazetteer for Yuyao*, p. 101.

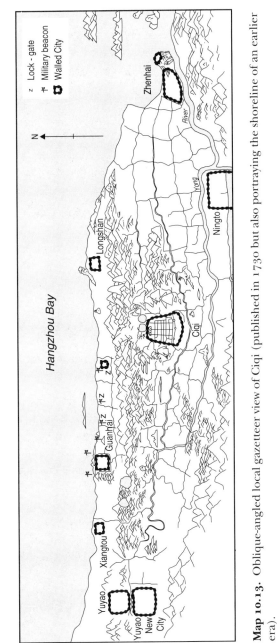

Map 10.13. Oblique-angled local gazetteer view of Ciqi (published in 1730 but also portraying the shoreline of an earlier era).

Yuan dynasty [1297–1307] there were repeated breaches [in the seawalls], and the lands of all eight rural districts were soaked through by the sea. In 1341 the departmental vice-magistrate Ye Heng 葉恆 therefore built 21,211 feet of stone dike, 90 feet wide at the base, half that width at the top, and 15 feet in height."[58] Thus the rapid buildup of the salient had not yet begun by the mid-fourteenth century.

Prior to vice-magistrate Ye, people had simply "looked at where the water came to a stop, and had built [the seawall] in sections as convenient, in mutually incompatible dimensions and forms." Ye constructed a unified system that was said to have prevented major disasters for more than a hundred years. Around this time

> the seaside land grew like a heap, and could be cultivated. In the Yongle reign-period [1403–24] *for the first time a seawall was built to the north of the old seawall* in order to protect the salt-lands.... The sediment-derived seaside fields (*sharuan* 沙壖) grew still more, while the waters of the sea moved more than 10 *li* further to the north, and all that lay in between could be farmed and harvested. In the Chenghua reign-period [1465–87] the ministerial secretary for water control Hu Fu 胡復 built a dike at the sea mouth to guard against the tides, which was called "The New Anti-Tidal Seawall." From this time on, the profits from the salt-lands gave good harvests, but the salt workers in the important state salt-production system experienced difficulties in boiling down their brine.[59]

Clearly, rapid growth of the salient started a little before 1400.

The farmers, some of them "powerful and rich," were now in conflict with the salt producers over the conversion of the saline wetlands to arable. Around 1460 the government tried demarcating saltern land and agricultural land "in perpetuity"; when this was not effective, they levied a tax on farmed acreage, the "wetland price" (*dangjia* 蕩價), to supplement in cash the falling supplies of salt provided by the brine boilers. Around 1470 Zhou Jinlong 周進隆 carried out an inquiry ordered by Shaoxing prefecture. "After scrutinizing the physiognomy of the topographical relief (*xiang di qian-shen* 相地淺深), he built a dike below [that is, seaward of] the New Dike in order to form a boundary line. To the south of the dike, soldiers and commoner-civilians were to share the profit, but to its north the salt households were to treat [the land] as their property. With this, it was possible to put an end to the causes of quarrels."[60]

The late Qing county gazetteer quotes a certain Ye Xianzu 葉憲祖, whose

---

[58] Shao and Sun, *Yuyao*, p. 142.
[59] Ibid. Emphasis added.
[60] *Revised gazetteer for Yuyao*, pp. 101–2; Shao and Sun, *Yuyao*, p. 142.

date is not given but is probably late Ming, and who stressed the changed nature of the coastline:

> I have myself seen the *slikke* (*shatu* 沙塗) north of the Antitidal Dike (*yuchao tang* 禦潮塘) slowly growing, covering a distance that removes it far from the sea. *It is not like past times* when huge waves appeared at the foot of the stone seawall and major incursions took place. For this reason the area to the south of the seawall has become fertile soil.
>
> The districts of Meichuan and Shanglin have heavy soils suited to cereal crops [rice], whereas the districts of Xiaoyi and Kaiyuan do best with cotton, beans, and wheat. Having different crops, they likewise have different water-control systems. To the east of Hushan people have dredged new creeks deeper and deeper in various places, and stored water in barrage-and-reservoir systems that they regard as their own property. To the west of Hushan *there used to be* channels that linked with each other in a north–south direction, supplying each other if there was a shortage of water, and draining it away when there were floods. Crops like cotton, beans (*dou* 豆), are twice as profitable as rice, but the sources of water seem to be inadequate and sluggish, *since the way in which the land is laid out is entirely different from what it was in the past* (*yin di-zhiyi guihua yi jin fei fu nangshi bi yi* 因地制宜規畫已盡非復曩時比矣).
>
> A waterway has been excavated below the old seawall in a crosswise east–west alignment for water transport. Both merchants and commoner-civilians benefit from it. [The reason for its existence is that] in 1555 the ships of the "Japanese" pirates dropped anchor off the seacoast and the northern districts were the principal sufferers. The county magistrate Li Bosheng 李伯生 asked permission to cut a new waterway below the old seawall as a defense against the "Japanese," running from Guanhai 觀海 in the east to Linshan 臨山, a distance of over 100 *li*. It was 20 feet wide and more than 10 feet deep. . . . Once the threat had passed, however, precautions grew slack, and the rich and powerful have filled it in, without having any authorization to do so, in order to extend their private acreage. The old course of the waterway has still not entirely vanished, though, and it would be of advantage to open it up in order to irrigate the fields, drain off floods due to prolonged or violent rains, and provide for boat transport. If threats should suddenly appear from the sea, the long channel will be adequate to provide an obstacle to such contingencies.[61]

There was thus also a military aspect of hydraulic works.

The seawalls surviving into the twentieth century, and shown on the Japanese Army map, were only a proportion of those ever built. An unnamed – and undated – writer, quoted in the late Ming gazetteer for the

---

[61] Shao and Sun, *Yuyao*, p. 143. Emphasis added.

county, said: "I have walked around the old seawalls, and sighed [in admi-
ration] at the achievements of Xie, Shi, and Ye [their builders]. They
should all have temple sacrifices [as deities]. I have also looked at the New
Antitidal Dike, which had a close connection with extracting profit from
the salty land. *Today all of them are in ruins.* If the high tides of autumn were
to break in, the profit from the land would certainly be lost."[62] It is not clear
if this refers to a period before, during, or after the six disastrous irruptions
of the tides between 1471 and 1582, which the late Qing gazetteer attributes to the people having become accustomed to "doing well without
exerting themselves, and to settling the seashore lands, with the seawalls
day by day becoming defective and incomplete."[63] What is important is that
these late Ming disasters seem to be *the last recorded* as caused by the tides at
the Yuyao salient, and the timing suggests that this was connected with the
shift of the Qiantang River to a northern outlet on the other side of the bay
in the course of the seventeenth century.

The building of extra dikes farther and farther out accelerated during
the mid-Qing. According to the late Qing gazetteer:

> By the time of the present [Qing] dynasty, the "Lotus Flower Dike" (*lianhua
> tang* 蓮花塘)[64] and the various seawalls built in addition to the seaward side of
> it had become ever more delapidated. The seven dikes along the sea men-
> tioned in the previous gazetteer have all become far removed from the sea. In
> 1724 the "Elms-and-Willows Dike" (*yu-liu tang* 榆柳塘) was built in addition
> below Zhou's Dike (*Zhou tang* 周塘). In 1737 a further request was made for
> public funds to add to it and consolidate it. Prior to this the seaborne
> sediment (*haitu*) had been piling up as *slikke* (*zhangsha* 漲沙) for year after
> year, and it had become necessary to built in addition a Sediment-Protection
> Dike (*husha tang* 護沙塘). In 1734 both commoner-civilians and salt house-
> holds subscribed cash according to the number of adult males to construct
> the Profitable Dike (*liji tang* 利濟塘) outside the Elms-and-Willows Dike. In
> 1747 a request was submitted for more than 24,000 ounces of silver, on the
> principle of "using public works as a substitute for [famine] relief (*yi gong dai
> zhen* 以工代振)" to build in addition the Feng Donggan Beacon Straight Dike
> at Liangxia Granary 梁下倉馮東干墩直塘.... In 1761 the order was given to
> levy money in order to set up a line of 1,554 pottery oxen to safeguard [in
> supernatural fashion] the foundations of the wall. Today, of the dikes along
> the seacoast, only the Large Old Dike (*dagu tang* 大古塘), Zhou's Dike, the
> Elms-and-Willows Dike, and the Profitable Dike are of strategic importance.[65]

---

[62] *Revised gazetteer for Yuyao*, p. 103. Emphasis added.

[63] Shao and Sun, *Yuyao*, p. 142

[64] The formal name for the main Song-dynasty dike. It was also known as the Inner-Sea Dike
(*Houhai tang* 後海塘), with reference to the alternative name for Hangzhou Bay.

[65] Shao and Sun, *Yuyao*, p. 145.

Figure 10.10. Yuyao salient tidal flats north of Andong at low water, with seawall and bicycle in the foreground. *Photograph*: M. Elvin, 1994.

Figure 10.11. Yuyao salient tidal flats north of Andong at low water, with hovercraft in the middle distance. *Photograph*: M. Elvin, 1994.

Figure 10.12. Most recent seawall, near Wugong Lock, eastern side of Yuyao salient, Hangzhou Bay, 1994. Looking south, the outline of the hills that ran along the coast a thousand years ago can just be detected. The tidal flats lie to the east side of the seawall, and the reclaimed fields to the west. *Photograph*: M. Elvin, 1994. Reprinted by permission of *Environment and History* 1.1 (Feb. 1995), cover.

A present-day report on the soils of Ciqi to which we have had access lists five more seawalls built after this time: in 1796–1819, 1815–1918, 1945, 1952, and 1970–73.

In summary, the northward growth of the salient started in the later

Figure 10.13. Ebb channel at low tide on the western side of Nansha peninsula, Hangzhou Bay, 1994. The removal of such sediment deposits, which are mostly of marine origin, requires the combination of ebb flows and periods of peak river discharge. The latter were increasingly blocked during the Ming and the Qing dynasties by hydraulic works along the south coat of the bay. *Photograph*: M. Elvin, 1994.

fourteenth century, not long after the partial shift of the Yellow River to a south course; it accelerated in the late sixteenth century, at the time Pan Jixun unified and concentrated the lower part of this course. Today, in total contrast to the hills and inlets that formed the coast a thousand years ago, the growing edge of the salient beyond the seawall is a vast, bleak, horizontal expanse of tidal flats traversed by sinuous ebb-flow channels, broken by occasional pools and edged with salt-resistant grasses, where the sound of the rising tide can be heard rumbling more than an hour before it arrives, and where only the hovercraft that shuttles back and forth to the north shore of the bay is really at home.

10.10. HYDRAULIC WORKS ON THE YELLOW RIVER IN THE MING AND EARLY QING

The southward shift of the Yellow River and its maintenance on this course were partly due to human action (and inaction). The change in the rates of seaward advance of delta land and the accretion of sediment in the sea-mouth section of the river channel were primarily due to the effects of human action. A full reconstruction of the complicated history of the southern course of the Yellow River will not be attempted here, but only an outline of aspects relevant to these points. Map 10.14 (oriented with west in the usual north position) was published in the mid-seventeenth century, and shows the geographical relation between the lower Yellow River on its southern course, the coastline to the south with its fringe of mudflats (*sha* 沙), its Fan Gong seawall (*Fan-gong ti* 范公隄, shown by a heavy line), and its salterns (*chang* 場) just inland, and the mouth of the Yangzi River. The Grand Canal crosses the center of the map from south to north (i.e., left to right), and the Huai River joins the Yellow River near the top right-hand corner. Map 10.15 (oriented toward the north) gives a close-up of the mouth of the south-course Yellow River after the cutting of the new exit channel in 1595, discussed in subsection (10) below. It was here that the sediment that was to end in Hangzhou Bay first entered the sea.

The pattern of events, considerably oversimplified, was as follows.[66]

(1) In 1077 the Yellow River broke temporarily into two branches, one going south of the Shandong Peninsula along the Southern Qing River 南清河 (the old course of the Si River 泗河, and sharing a mouth with the Huai 淮), while the other continued to go north along the Northern Qing River 北清河 (the old course of the Ji River 濟河). The full northern course was restored the following year, but this was the shape of events to come. In 1168, the *History of the Jin* relates, "the River broke out at Li Gu's Ford 李固渡, its waters invading the city of Caozhou 曹州, and dividing its course to flow through the region of Shanxian 單縣 [in southwestern Shandong].... [The director of waterways Liang] Su 梁肅 further observed: "The new river's waters have taken 60 percent and the old river's waters 40 percent. If we now block off the new river, the two rivers will again join together to form a single one."[67] When this was done there was again a single course. Before long, though, the Yellow River's pressure on the state's resources and manpower intensified to the point that in 1193 the regional commandant Wang Rujia 王汝嘉 and others observed: "The Great River in the past had branch streams and debouchments off its southern bank. If it were possible to lead it off in such a way that it spread out (*sudao*

---

[66] This account is based mainly on Tani Mitsutaka 谷光隆, *Mindai Kakō-shi kenkyū* 明代河工史研究 [Studies on the hydraulics of the Yellow River in the Ming dynasty] (Kyoto: Dōhōsha, 1991). We are most grateful to Professor Tani for the gift of his book.

[67] Tuotuo 脫脫 et al., eds., *Jin shi* 金史 [History of the Jin] (Beijing: Zhonghua shuju, 1975), "Hequ zhi," *j.* 27, p. 670.

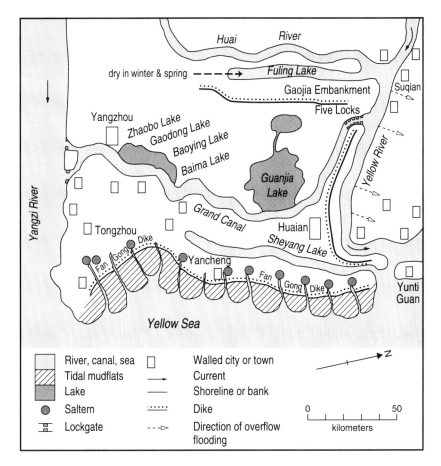

Map 10.14. The mouths of the south-course Yellow River and the Yangzi in the middle of the sixteenth century. *Source*: Gu Yanwu, *Advantageous and disadvantageous aspects of the empire*, "Huai-Xu."

疏導), this would be enough to drain away the position-power (*shi* 勢) [of the water]."[68]

(2) In 1194 debates continued in the Jin government as to how best to subdivide the river while avoiding heavy expenses on hydraulic works, or

[68] Tuotuo et al., *History of the Jin, j.* 27, p. 674. It was usual to distinguish *shi* ("position-power") from *li* ("strength"). Thus Wang Chong 王充 argued that while cattle and horse had greater strength than the mosquitoes and gnats who pestered them, they had less position-power. See his *Lun-heng jiaoshi* 論衡校釋 ["Discourses weighed in the balance" corrected and explained], ed. Huang Hui 黃暉, 4 vols. (Taipei: Shangwu yinshuguan, 1964), p. 145. The translation of *su* is based partly on lexicographical grounds (Couvreur: "faire diverger"), partly on the sense of the context, and partly on parallels such as Sima Guang 司馬光 's

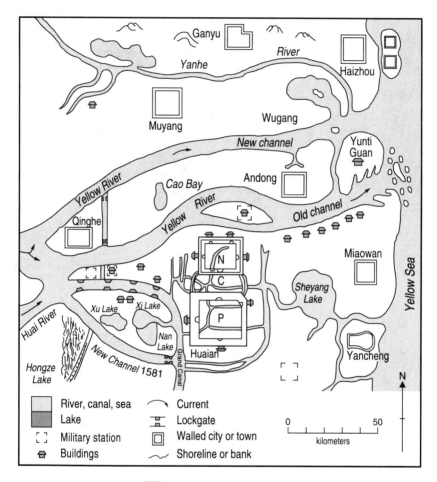

Map 10.15. The mouths of the south-course Yellow River after 1595. *Source*: Gu Yanwu, *Advantageous and disadvantageous aspects of the empire*, "Huai."

damaging cities and farmland that lay in the path of possible routes both north and south, especially since their course could not be exactly determined before the dikes were breached. The objective hoped for was to "nullify [the water's] position-power by means of subdivision (*fen-sha qi shi* 分殺其勢)." In the fall the river broke out southward from north of Kaifeng,

Duleyuan ji 獨樂園集, where it describes the laying out of the streams in his garden: "In the midst was a pond. . . . I made the waters diverge (*sushui* 疏水) in the form of five 'flows' [using an archaic character for *liu* 流] and pour into this pond, having the form of a tiger's claw (*hu zhua* 虎爪)." See *Wenyuange Siku quanshu* [Wenyuange edition of the "Four Treasuries of Literature"] (Taipei: Shangwu, 1986), "Chuanjia ji," 1094–1653.

and the report of the Department of Affairs of State asserted that Wang Rujia and other officials "took no care at all, but, since they saw that the water was tending in a southerly direction, made no plans in advance to deal with it."[69] In the event, the flow was divided between the same two rivers (the two *Qing he* 清河) as before, but also using the Bian River 汴水 for its southern route after 1351.

(3) Only after the floods of 1391, according to the *Baoying tujing* 寶應圖 經, did "the Yellow River *in its entirety* enter the old course of the Huai 淮," which it reached via Xiangcheng 項城 and Shouzhou 壽州 along the Ying River 潁河, with a lesser branch exiting to the sea via Xuzhou 徐州.[70]

(4) Between 1416 and 1448, the dominant southern course took the bed of the Guo River 渦水, but between 1448 and 1455 there was again a substantial northern course, via the Northern Qing River, which was eventually closed off.

(5) After the floods in the late 1480s and early 1490s, up to 70 percent of the water went north again. In 1492 a decree directed Chen Zheng 陳政 to make an inspection:[71]

> We have heard that the Yellow River, which passes through a wide expanse of land in He'nan, Shandong, and North and South Zhili, moving its course in irregular fashion, has been a menace for a long time past, and has recently grown significantly worse. The general explanation for this is that previously it flowed southeast from Kaifeng into the River Huai, but today its old course has silted up and become shallow, so that it has gradually shifted north, joining with the Qin River 沁水 [i.e the *Qin he* 沁河 in Handan 邯鄲 in northern Zhili], its situation becoming more and more unmanageable.

Proposals were made at court to give up the effort to control the Yellow River and to cease maintaining the Grand Canal, because of the expense in money and manpower, on the grounds that it was preferable to transport the state's tax-grain by sea instead.[72] The critical point is that during this period the greater part of the sediment carried by the Yellow River was deposited *on the plain* through which it ran. It was only transported to a limited degree all the way to the sea mouth.[73]

---

[69] Tuotuo et al., *History of the Jin, j.* 27, p. 678.

[70] Cited in Tani, *Studies on the hydraulics of the Yellow River*, introduction, p. 20, n. 24, and main text pp. 5–6. Emphasis added.

[71] Cited in Wu Qihua [Wu Chi-hua] 吳緝華, "Huanghe zai Mingdai gaidao qianxi hejue Zhangqiu de niandai" [On the date of the breach at Zhangqiu just prior to the change of course of the Yellow River in the Ming dynasty], in Wu Qihua, *Mingdai shehui jingji shi luncong* 明代社會經濟史論叢 [Collected historical essays on the society and economy of the Ming dynasty] (Taipei: Taiwan xuesheng shuju, 1970), p. 368.

[72] Wu Qihua, "On the date of the breach at Zhangqiu," p. 375.

[73] Li Yuanfang, "Development of the abandoned Yellow River delta," p. 30.

(6) In 1493 Liu Daxia 劉大夏 rebuilt the dikes in such a way that an *exclusive* southern course was assured after this date. This increased the quantity of sediment coming down to the river mouth and there forming "mounds" (*fu* 阜).[74] In 1534, according to Zhu Shang 朱裳, director-general of the Yellow River,

> In times past the waters of the Huai flowed into the sea on their own, and there were also curved channels (*tao* 套) at the sea mouth, for the flow upstream and downstream at Andong 安東. There were in addition the Jian River 澗河 [which flowed past Huaian and was at one time used for transport to Yancheng 鹽城], and the Maluo Creek 馬邏港, whereby the waters were divided and so entered the sea. Today the Yellow River has joined with the Huai, and the position-power of the water is not as it was before, with the Jian River, the Maluo Creek, and all the curved channels at the sea mouth having become blocked up, so that they are unable to drain the water swiftly. The way through downstream is blocked, and there are floods upstream, which obstructs the grain transport [to the capital]. The creeks should be dredged one after the other, and the sediment in the curved channels [dealt with] by installing numerous "dragon-claw boats" (*longzhua-chuan* 龍爪船 = dredgers) to go backward and forward so as to scour and scrape (*patang* 爬盪) and widen the way to the sea.[75]

(7) During the first three-quarters of the sixteenth century, the Yellow River took a *multiplicity of paths* across the Huai valley, often simultaneously. An illustration of this is cited by the historical geographer Gu Zuyu 顧祖禹 for 1558:[76]

> The old [south] course of the Great River (*da He* 大河) was from Xinji 新集 [in Guide 歸德] . . . to Jimenji 薊門集 in Xiao county 蕭縣, from which it came out at Xiaofu Bridge 小浮橋 in Xuzhou. This was the old course of the river that was restored by Jia Lu 賈魯 [in 1344],[77] its configuration being like that of an overturned jar (*jian ling* 建瓴) flowing easily from above to below. Later, because the disasters caused by floods in He'nan had become a matter of some urgency, a separate lesser river was opened [by Bai Ang 白昂 in the late fifteenth century] with the intention of destroying the position-power of the water by subdividing it. The river would not, however, follow two courses. The original main course became ever shallower and more obstructed. Over 250

[74] Tani, *Studies on the hydraulics of the Yellow River*, p. 54.
[75] Fu Zehong 傅澤洪, ed., *Xingshui jinjian* 行水金鑒 [The golden mirror of the passing streams] (*c.* 1725. Reprinted, Taipei: Wenhai CBS, 1969), in Shen Yunlong 沈雲龍, ed., *Zhongguo shuili yaoji congbian* 中國水利要籍叢編, *j.* 23, p. 958.
[76] Gu Zuyu, ed., *Dushi fangyu jiyao* 讀史方輿紀要 [Essential geography for the reading of history] (1667. Reprinted, Taipei, Xinxing, 1972) *chuandu* 3, "Da He" *xia*, *j.* 126, p. 6b, p. 2363; also cited in Tani, *Studies on the hydraulics of the Yellow River*, p. 12. Emphasis added.
[77] Tani, *Studies on the hydraulics of the Yellow River*, p. 53.

li of it thus became silted up between Xinji and the Xiaofu Bridge. The river flowed north [of the previous line] . . . and further split into six branches (*gu* 股) . . . all of which followed [the course of] the Grand Canal to the rapids at Xuzhou. A further branch separated off from the town of Jiancheng 堅城集 . . . and then split again into five small branches . . . and these likewise went from the Xiaofu Bridge to join the Xuzhou rapids. The Yellow River was *divided into eleven streams* and its position-power was weakened. When its position-power had been weakened it deposited sediment on a vast scale; and the breaches of dikes, and the floods, thus became even worse.

In 1565 there were sixteen channels.[78] A Yellow River of this sort can hardly be considered hydrologically the "same river" as that which was to emerge after the hydraulic transformation of 1578–79.

(8) After the mid-sixteenth century, the sea mouths shared by the Yellow River and the Huai became blocked by sediment. According to Wu Guifang 吳桂芳, then in charge of the imperial grain transport, "the general cause is that for many long years the way through the branching creeks (*chagang* 汊港) along the coast has been blocked by dams (*dao yin* 道湮). Entry to the sea relies wholly on the single route via Yunti 雲梯 [the customs station on an island off the main mouth]. When [the river] reaches the sea it is obstructed in a transverse fashion, and its entire current has become an overflow of mud."[79] The seawall along the coast between the mouth of the Yellow River and the mouth of the Yangzi may be seen in Map 10.14 with tongues of sand (*sha* 沙) lying seaward and salterns (*chang* 場) situated inland. By 1578 the width of the central sea mouth had narrowed from 14 or 15 *li* downstream of Yunti in early Ming to from 7 to 8, or perhaps 10, *li*.[80]

In 1577 Wu Guifang opposed proposals to divide the Huai and the Yellow rivers and divert them into the Yangzi. He contrasted the earlier channel pattern whereby the greater part of the Yellow River had joined the Huai in *midcourse* with that of his own day where the two rivers only joined *close to the sea*:

The Yellow River is laden with silt to an extreme degree. If the clear Huai is not used to cleanse it, the sea mouth will be nothing but turbid mud. This will inevitably cause a worsening of the blocking of the lower course, and breaches of the dikes along the banks, and irruptions of water, will become an ever more menacing threat. . . .

Since the Song and the Yuan dynasties, and down to the Zhengde reign of our present dynasty [1506–21], a period of almost 500 years, the Yellow River

[78] Ibid., p. 24, n. 29.
[79] Ibid., p. 64.
[80] Li Yuanfang, "Development of the abandoned Yellow River delta," p. 30.

has [in great measure] entered the sea via the Huai without the sea mouth becoming blocked up. When the Yellow River reached the province of He'nan it joined with the Huai and they proceeded together, passing by Ying 穎, Shou 壽, Feng 鳳, and Si 泗 to the [Southern] Qing River, and thus the clear [water] cleansed the turbid, and it was made possible for the muddy dregs (*nizi* 泥滓) not to be deposited. So it was that for several hundred years there were no disasters. The general explanation for this is that during this time 70 percent of the water of the Yellow River was passing by way of Ying and Shou, and only 30 percent by way of the branch stream that flowed via the Xiaofu Bridge in Xuzhou.

Recently, though, since some time in the Jiajing reign-period [1522–66], the flow past the Xiaofu Bridge in Xuzhou has become insufficient, and the two sets of rapids, at Xuzhou and at Lü, have often dried up. Those in authority have not set their minds upon the long view, but have struggled to divert the Yellow River so that all of it flows through Xuzhou and Peizhou 邳 州 to the [Southern] Qing River. *For the first time there has been no [midcourse] juncture with the Huai.* Thus the position-power of the Yellow River is [now] strong, but the flow of the Huai is weak, and its contribution to the cleansing process minimal. Thus it is that the sea mouth is gradually growing higher, and every year the threat of floods overflowing becomes more urgent. . . . If the flow of the Huai is now to be permanently cut off, and it is no longer to join with the Yellow River, then only mud will flow down, and day after day the deposition of sediment will increase. "The ocean will turn into mulberry fields" between Yunti, Cao Bay 草灣, Jincheng 金城, and the mouth of the Guan 灌口. To an ever-increasing extent, the Yellow River will have nowhere to go.[81]

Thus concentrating the Yellow River in the Xuzhou branch began before the time of Pan Jixun's main work, and the effects of this were already visible at the sea mouth, and understood as being such.

In fact, the Yellow River also had a number of smaller exits both to the north and to the south of the main mouth. Gu Yanwu, working in the seventeenth century, quotes a source that describes how in recent times the minor mouths on the southern side had become silted up as the result of the tides washing back the sediment flushed by the Yellow River into the sea:

In the old days none of these [supplementary] sea mouths was silted up. That they have silted up in recent times has been due to the yellow sediment (*huangsha* 黃沙). . . . The general explanation is that the seawater is subject to

[81] Gu Yanwu 顧炎武, comp., *Tianxia junguo libing shu* 天下郡國利病書 [Documents on the advantageous and disadvantageous aspects of the principates and commanderies of the empire] (1659) (Siku shanben reprint) "Huai" [original] *c.* 10, [reprint] *c.* 13, p. 56ab (emphasis added).

tides twice a day. . . . The seawater blocks the lake water for two double hours when it comes in, so that the latter cannot flow. This happens for four double hours during every day. How can the yellow sediment fail to be deposited?[82]

The supplementary sea mouths to the north, in the direction of Haizhou 海州, were in the same situation, having been "in recent days" blocked by the yellow sediment, and the main mouth there had shrunk to half its former width. This source is not dated, but is probably from just before Pan Jixun's main period of activity, as it advocates the view that "if the position-power of the waters of the Yellow River and the Huai is not divided as they come south, but their strength is joined as they approach the sea, then the new sediment will not remain and the old sediment will automatically be removed."[83]

(9) Pan Jixun (1511–95) put this prescription into practice.[84] He set forth his hydrological views as follows:

> When waters divide, then their position-power is weakened; and when their position-power is weakened, the [suspended, saltating, and bedload] sediments come to a standstill. When the sediments come to a standstill, then the river becomes [as it were] bloated with food, with a foot or [a few] inches of water passing above the surface of the [deposited] sediments. One only perceives how high [the channel bed] has become.
>
> When waters join, their position-power is fierce, and when their position-power is fierce, then the sediments are scoured away. When the sediments are scoured away, the river becomes deep, with fathoms of water passing above the bed of the channel. One only perceives how low [the channel bed] has become.
>
> One builds dikes to confine the water and one uses the water to attack the sediments. If the water does not precipitately overflow the two banks, then it has to scour in a straight line along the bottom of the river. There is here a fixed pattern-principle (li 理) and a position-power that is inexorable.
>
> This is why joining [the river channels] surpasses dividing them.[85]

Although Pan's views were not quantified, they approximated to the modern hydraulic theory whereby the capacity of water to carry sediment, S_c, is proportional to the fourth power of the velocity of the current, V, and the velocity is determined by the square root of the slope, S, defined as an angular measure (radians), the inverse of the roughness of the bed expressed by the roughness coefficient n, and the 2/3 root of the "hydraulic

---

[82] Ibid., c. 10 [13], p. 44b.
[83] Ibid.
[84] For an introduction to Pan's work, see E. Vermeer, "P'an Chi-hsün's Solutions for the Yellow River Problems of the Late 16th Century," *T'oung Pao* 73 (1987).
[85] Tani, *Studies on the hydraulics of the Yellow River*, p. 373.

radius" of the channel, R, defined as the cross-sectional flow area divided by the wetted perimeter (A/P):

$$S_c \propto kV^4$$

and

$$V = (1/n)R^{2/3}S^{1/2}$$

where k is a scaling constant. Sediment-carrying capacity is thus sensitive to small changes in velocity, and velocity is sensitive to changes in the depth of the channel. For a given cross-sectional flow area A, a larger wetted perimeter P implies a smaller hydraulic radius A/P. A smaller hydraulic radius $A/P = R$ implies a smaller velocity, other things being equal, as is shown in the foregoing formula. In the simple case of a channel with a given rectangular cross-section A, and having the width ch, where h is the depth, the highest value for A/P is where $dA = P$, i.e. for $c = 2$. It falls as the ratio of depth h to width ch decreases after this point. Hydraulic engineering can make a major difference.

From 1578 to 1579 Pan restructured the Yellow River. In round numbers, he built 1.2 million feet of earthen embankment and 30,000 feet of stone embankment, stopped 139 breaches, constructed four stone spillways of 300 feet each, dredged 115,000 feet of riverbed, planted 830,000 willow trees to stabilize the tops of the dikes, drove in a large but unrecorded number of tree trunks as pilings under the embankments, and spent almost 500,000 ounces of silver and nearly 127,000 piculs of rice.[86] He unified the channel and confined it within so-called thread dikes (lüti 縷提) close to the banks, but backed these up in most places with "set-back dikes" (yaoti 遙堤) that were 2 or even 3 li removed from the river. The purpose of these was the contain any overflow that broke through or came over the top of the thread dikes during the peak discharge period of the late summer and autumn.[87]

One difficulty with this strategy was that the more rapid flow of the Yellow River past the junction with the Huai at Qingkou 清口 tended to block off the weaker Huai and even force reverse flow up the latter, so causing siltation. The traces of this, the so-called Threshold Sediments (menxian sha 門限沙), are visible today.[88] Figure 10.14 shows the junction of

[86] Ibid., p. 374.
[87] Ibid.
[88] Ibid., p. 392. On the name "Menxian Sediments" see Zhang Tingyu 張廷玉, ed., Ming shi 明史 [History of the Ming dynasty] (Beijing: Zhonghua shuju, 1974), "Hequ zhi er," "Huanghe xia," j. 84, p. 2059.

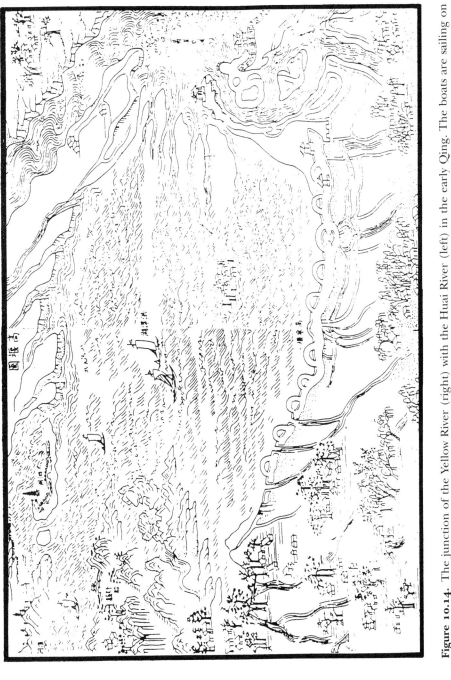

Figure 10.14. The junction of the Yellow River (right) with the Huai River (left) in the early Qing. The boats are sailing on the Hongze lake. Woodblock print from Fu Zehong, *Golden Mirror*, pp. 62–63. Compare Map 10.14, top right.

the Yellow River and the Huai in the early Qing dynasty. The miscalculation was Pan's belief, in the words of the *Ming History*, that "if we can bring it about that the Yellow River and the Huai exert their full strength, and that every drop of water goes into the sea, then the force will be immense and concentrated. The accumulated sediments in the lower course will be automatically removed, and the sea [mouth] will be opened without dredging.[89] More specifically,

> The old [sea]mouth is all accumulated sediment, but although human power is incapable of dredging it, the power of the water itself is capable of scouring it away by impact. There is no pattern-principle [in nature] that permits the sea to be dredged. When, however, the river is led to make its way to the sea, then one is using water to control water, in other words a strategy for [indeed] dredging the sea. Likewise the Yellow River cannot be led by human power. If we keep the dike defenses in good repair, on the other hand, so that there are no breaches of the banks, then the water will pass through the midst of the land and the sediment will be removed by being entrained by the water. In other words, this is [indeed] a strategy for leading the Yellow River.[90]

The effect of this strategy was, however, to increase deposition at the sea mouth and reduce the gradient of the lower course.

(10) Flooding returned in a decade. In 1591 the capital city of Sizhou 泗州 was inundated to a depth of three feet and it was said that "90 percent of the inhabitants were drowned."[91] An official observer, Zhang Zhenguan 張貞觀, described the city wall in the floods as being "like a cup floating on the water, the cup itself also being full."[92] He recommended "that clearing the sediment accumulated at the sea mouth be made the first priority."[93] Later, with two colleagues, he added that "since there is no hope of dredging the sea [mouth] sediment, the channel bed grows higher every day; and since the Yellow River constantly flows in a reversed direction, Qingkou becomes more obstructed by the day." They suggested clearing Qingkou and then dividing the Yellow River there, but rejoining the branches lower down so that the water "strikes the sea with concentrated force."[94] The debate over what to do about the sea mouth "growing ever more obstructed" continued, some critics of Pan pointing out that too much constriction had in fact caused flooding. The majority inclined to revert to the policy of multiple channels.[95]

[89] Zhang Tingyu, *History of the Ming, j.* 84, p. 2052.
[90] Ibid., p. 2051.
[91] Ibid., p. 2056.
[92] Ibid.
[93] Ibid.
[94] Ibid., p. 2057.
[95] Ibid., pp. 2060–62.

In 1593 the emperor put Yang Yikui 楊一魁 in charge of hydraulic operations, and during 1595–96 he basically implemented this majority view, which he had himself contributed to forming. "The waters of the Yellow River were divided and drained into the sea, in order to repress the power of the Yellow River. Seven *li* of sediments were cleared at Qingkou, . . . and the Huai was drained into the sea by three channels, and its branches diverted into the Yangzi."[96] Yang's efforts were moderately successful, but only in the short run. What is important in the context of the present discussion is that we have a hydraulic explanation for some part of the reduction in the rate of growth of the Yellow River delta after the early 1590s.

(11) The next surge in the rate of advance of the delta, and of sediment accretion, from 1701 to 1747 (shown in Table 10.9), was slighter than that associated with Pan Jixun's policies (about 21 percent of the 1579–91 rate of advance and 20 percent of the rate of accretion, as measured from deposits still in position today). There is a possible, though perhaps tenuous, connection here with the shift in hydraulic policies effected by Jin Fu 靳輔, who was in charge of the Yellow River almost continuously from 1677 until his death in 1692.[97] Jin broadly agreed with Pan's ideas,[98] and he built an earthen extension to the levees along the lower course of the river downstream of Yunti Guan for about 180,000 feet (about 64.5 kilometers)[99] in order to concentrate the flow, and so scour away the accumulated sediment. Thereafter, it was said, "the water was constricted within the levees, being swift all the way, and having the force to scour the sediment. The undesirable accumulation of silt in the sea mouth was removed and a sink for drainage thereupon cleared."[100] The date of this was before 1690, by which time, according to an official report, the divided lower course had been unified again and was cutting a wider and deeper channel.[101]

The lower course of the Yellow River had silted up rapidly during the third quarter of the seventeenth century.[102] This may have been due to the (alleged) cutting of dikes by the rebels in the last years of the Ming

[96] Ibid., p. 2062.
[97] See the life of Jin Fu in A. Hummel, ed., *Eminent Chinese of the Ch'ing Period* (Washington: U.S. Government Printing Office, 1943), pp. 161–63.
[98] Fu Zehong, *Golden mirror, j.* 47, pp. 1718–19. See also *j.* 51, pp. 1836–37.
[99] Converting at 1 Chinese foot (*chi* 尺) = 0.35814 meter, according to *China Proper* (Edinburgh: [British] Naval Intelligence Division, 1945), vol. 3, p. 610.
[100] Fu Zehong, *Golden mirror, j.* 52, p. 1875.
[101] Ibid., *j.* 50, pp. 1818–19.
[102] Jin Fu thought that the river mouth had still been large enough to carry the peak discharge in mid-century. See ibid., *j.* 48, pp. 1749–50, and also Jin's comment in 1677 that the lowest section of the main course had "all silted up and become land" for "more than 10 years," in ibid., *j.* 48, p. 1725.

dynasty,[103] and/or the Ming government's breaching of dikes to drown the rebels,[104] and what Jin Fu called the "division of drainage" caused by floods such as those of 1676 that were unable to reach the sea.[105] By this time "only a thread (*xian* 線)" of the main course through the sea mouth remained, and "in addition, [he noted], coarse grasses and thickets of reeds intertwine [there], and are not something to which human strength can [usefully] be applied."[106] The deposits also hardened with time:

> There is, moreover, a difference between old and new deposits of sediment. In the case of those newly deposited within the last three years, although their outside is as hard as a board (*bantu* 板土) the sediment inside has not yet dried out and it is easy to scour them by means of the impact [of water]. Before five years have elapsed, though, the sediment inside will have become dried into a clod of boardlike sediment (*bansha* 板沙), and scour by impact will have become very difficult.[107]

Besides building the constricting earthen levees mentioned above, he increased the height of the dikes in two reservoirs upstream (the Zhai Barrage 翟壩 and the Gaojia embankment 高家堰, which retained the Hongze Lake) "to assist in the storage of water that may be used to have an impact on the sea mouth [when released],"[108] and to cut a large dry channel in the dried-up sediment of the main course – which latter he described as now being "299 parts out of 300 of the [former] exit to the sea" – close enough to the remaining trickle of current that when the peak discharge was directed into it the boundary layer between the two would collapse, making a single enlarged course.[109] After difficulties with floods that occurred before the planned scouring was complete,[110] the scheme seems to have been successful.

Thus the period of rather more than a hundred years during which the geometry of Hangzhou Bay was most dramatically transformed (from the late sixteenth to the mid-eighteenth century) coincided with two efforts to transform the hydraulics of the lower course of the south-flowing Yellow

[103] Ibid., *j.* 49, p. 1783.
[104] Wang Zhibin 王质彬, "Huanghe wenti-de jidian kanfa – dui Wei. Jin. Nanbeichao" [Some understanding of the issue of the Yellow River during the Wei, the Jin, and the Northern and Southern Dynasties], *Renmin Huanghe* 5 (1980), and Wang Zhibin, "Kaifeng Huanghe jueyi mantan" [A general discussion of the breaking of the Yellow River dikes at Kaifeng], *Renmin Huanghe* 4 (1984).
[105] Fu Zehong, *Golden mirror, j.* 47, p. 1721
[106] Ibid., *j.* 48, p. 1751, and *j.* 49, p. 1767.
[107] Ibid., *j.* 48, pp. 1725–26.
[108] Ibid., *j.* 49, pp. 1768–69.
[109] Ibid., *j.* 48, p. 1726.
[110] Ibid., *j.* 49, p. 1775.

River some 300 or so kilometers to the north. Both of these concentrated the flow, and carried an increased quantity of sediment to the sea mouth and beyond. We would therefore argue that, when this is taken in conjunction with the southward longshore transport of suspended sediment demonstrated by data in recent Chinese studies, there is a prima facie case for believing that human intervention in the hydrology of the Yellow River played a significant part first in triggering and then in accelerating the growth of the Yuyao salient in Hangzhou Bay, and perhaps in the blocking of the south and central exits of the Qiantang River in the inner bay by the sands of the Nansha Peninsula, regarded as irreversible by 1765–80.[111]

DISCUSSION

Cases of shoreline change in one location due to the effects of engineering works undertaken in another are well known in the literature.[112] The case discussed here is unusual, certainly for the premodern period, both as regards the suggested principal mechanism and the long distance (c. 300 kilometers) over which it operated. It is also unusual in that the historical documentation allows a span of close to one thousand years to be examined in conjunction with the scientific evidence. The hypothesis requires testing through the examination of cores taken from the Yuyao salient to determine whether or not there were in fact marked increases in the proportion of materials originating from the Yellow River first after about 1200 and then, on a larger scale, after about 1580.

[111] Elvin and Su, "Man Against the Sea," section 2, "The Shifting Landscape: Hangzhou Bay from +500 to +1800."

[112] R. W. G. Carter, *Coastal Environments: An Introduction to the Physical, Ecological and Cultural Systems of Coastlines* (London and New York: Academic Press, 1988), pp. 516–28.

Weather and Climate

11

"It Never Used to Snow"

CLIMATIC VARIABILITY AND HARVEST
YIELDS IN LATE-IMPERIAL
SOUTH CHINA, 1650–1850

ROBERT B. MARKS

"The climate has changed," China's Kangxi emperor declared near the end of his sixty-one-year reign in 1717.

> I remember that before 1671, there was already new wheat [from the winter wheat crop] by the eighth day of the fourth month. When I was touring in Jiangnan, by the eighteenth day of the third month new wheat was available to eat. Now, even by the middle of the fourth month, wheat has not been harvested. . . . I have also heard that in Fujian, where it never used to snow, since the beginning of our dynasty, it has.[1]

To the Kangxi emperor, the climate not only seemed to have turned colder during his lifetime, but the cooler climate had noticeably delayed the wheat harvest. The emperor's observations, though, were not merely impressionistic musings. At least since 1693, he had been collecting weather reports from Jiangnan; he thus had some knowledge upon which to base

Preparation of this essay has been supported in part by NEH fellowship FB-28715-91. Many people have read and commented upon various versions of it, and I have benefited from their observations. I want to thank the participants of the Conference on the History of China's Environment, especially Pierre-Étienne Will and Mark Elvin, for their critiques, and likewise acknowledge the participants in a February 1993 UCLA Center for Chinese Studies seminar, in particular R. Bin Wong, James Lee, Cao Shuji, Philip Huang, Joseph Esherick, and Chen Chunsheng, for their critiques. I also wish to thank G. William Skinner, William Atwell, Mary Rankin, and John D. Post, all of whom commented upon earlier versions. Special thanks go to Gordon Jacoby and Rosanne D'Arrigo for sharing with me their reconstruction of northern hemisphere temperature trends, and then reading a draft that incorporated their findings. Needless to say, I alone am responsible for whatever errors or lapses in interpretation remain.

[1] *Da Qing sheng zu (Kangxi) shi lu* 大清聖祖康熙實錄 [The Veritable Records of the Qing Dynasty – Kangxi period], j. 272, pp. 9–10, reprinted in *Qing shi lu Guangxi ziliao ji lu* 清实录广西资料辑录 [Source Materials on Guangxi compiled from the Veritable Records of the Qing Dynasty] (Nanning: Guangxi Renmin CBS, 1988), vol. 1, p. 208.

his conclusion.[2] And although he was incorrect about it never having snowed in Fujian,[3] he was an astute observer of the connection between changes in the climate and the quality of the harvests.

This chapter thus takes the Kangxi emperor's observation seriously, and examines the question of whether climatic change in late-imperial China affected harvest yields, food supplies, and rice prices. Such a simple question, though, prompts other questions and thus yields a complex answer. To begin with, what was the historic climate of China, and did it change? Second, how can historic harvest yields be determined? And finally, what were the linkages and relationships among climatic change, harvest yields, and food supplies?

These questions are interesting and important both because they are critical to understanding the dynamics of a preindustrial economy and because they help illuminate the conditions under which ordinary people lived and died. As Fernand Braudel observed: "[T]he world between the fifteenth and eighteenth centuries consisted of one vast peasantry, where between 80% and 90% of people lived from the land and from nothing else. The rhythm, quality and deficiency of harvests ordered all material life."[4] Whatever one may think of such grand generalizations,[5] Braudel certainly was right that for most people most of the time, the size and quality of the harvest was an important, if not critical, annual event in their lives.

Historians of Europe have long probed the question of the impact of climatic change upon the European economy, and several impressive studies have resulted. Surprisingly though, few if any Western historians of China have examined the linkages between climatic change and the economy of late-imperial China. This chapter takes a first step in that direction by focusing not upon all of China but upon the climate, harvests, and people of the South China province of Guangdong during the period

---

[2] See Xie Tianzuo 谢天佐, "Qihou, shoucheng, liangjia, minqing – du 'Li Xu zouzhe'" 气候收成粮价民情—读李煦奏摺 [Climate, harvests, grain prices, and popular sentiment – a reading of Li Xu's palace memorials] *Zhongguo shehui lishi* (1981), pp. 17–20.

[3] Local gazetteers for Fujian, Guangdong, and Guangxi provinces contain numerous references to snow and frost, several instances of which will be examined later in this chapter.

[4] Fernand Braudel, *The Structures of Everyday Life*, vol. 1 of *Civilization and Capitalism 15th–18th Century*, Sian Reynolds, trans. (New York: Harper and Row, 1979), p. 49.

[5] Jan deVries characterized Braudel's statement as a "banalization of agrarian history," whereby "economic history, or at least agrarian history, is reduced to being 'one damn thing after another.'" DeVries argued that the problem for historians was to demonstrate the linkages between climate and agrarian history, rather than just assume them. See Jan deVries, "Measuring the Impact of Climate on History: The Search for Appropriate Methodologies," in R. I. Rotberg and T. K. Rabb, eds., *Climate and History: Studies in Interdisciplinary History* (Princeton: Princeton University Press, 1981), pp. 21–22.

from 1650 to 1850. The chapter is organized into three sections. Section 11.1 examines the issue of climatic change and locates Qing-era South China in terms of climate history. Section 11.2, "Harvest Yields," discusses the system by which Qing officials reported estimates of harvest yields to the imperial court, assesses the reliability and uses of these estimates, reconstructs eighteenth-century harvest yields, and links harvest yields to climatic factors. Section 11.3, "Harvest Yields and Rice Prices," proposes a model for relating harvest yields to grain prices and food supplies. The chapter concludes with a comparison of harvest yields in China and England and a brief discussion of the historical significance of the observed differences.

11.1. CLIMATE AND CLIMATIC CHANGE IN SOUTH CHINA

The present climate of South China is subtropical; Guangdong province straddles the Tropic of Cancer, while the more southerly-positioned Leizhou 雷州 Peninsula and Hainan Island 海南島 have a tropical climate.[6] Current monthly mean temperatures range from about 10° C to 30° C, and plentiful rainfall (about 1,600 mm annually) falls mostly during the growing season for rice. Although the region is not frost-free, the growing season ranges from 250 to 320 days (15° C is the minimum temperature for growing rice).[7] Figure 11.1 summarizes present climatological data for Guangzhou 廣州.

Much can be said about climatic change in China over the past five thousand years, but our discussion here will be limited to the period from the seventeenth century on in order to place the climate regime of early- to mid-Qing South China into broader historical perspective. Climate of course is more than just temperature and rainfall, including as well solar radiation, humidity, and wind, among other elements. But temperature and rainfall, the two critical elements for which historical data are most readily available, will be used here to characterize climate and climatic changes.

---

[6] For a classification and description of China's "agro-ecological regions," see Li Xiaofang, "Supplement to the Preliminary Standard Classification System for Land Evaluation in China," in Kenneth Puddle and Wu Chuanjin, eds., *Land Resources of the People's Republic of China* (United Nations University, 1983), pp. 25–26; and Zhang Jiacheng and Lin Zhiguang, *Zhongguo qixiang* 中國氣象 (Taipei: Ming Wen Book Co., 1987), pp. 513–31.

[7] In northern Guangdong province, because of higher altitudes and exposure to cold currents in the winter, there are only about 225 frost-free days, and the growing season is hence shorter. See International Rice Research Institute, *Rice Research and Production in China* (Los Banos, Philippines: IRRI, 1979), p. 25.

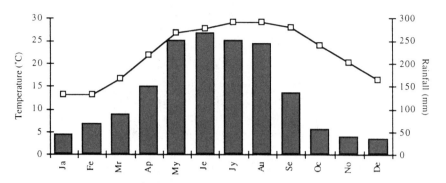

Figure 11.1. Mean monthly temperature and rainfall at Guangzhou. *Source:* International Rice Research Institute, *Rice Research and Production in China* (Los Banos, Philippines: IRRI, 1979), p. 25.

TEMPERATURE

Historical temperatures before the time of modern instrumentation (c. 1880) have been reconstructed using different kinds of proxy evidence – oxygen isotopes preserved in ice core samples or annual tree-ring growth, for example.[8] In his classic study of China's historic temperatures, Zhu Kezhen used phenological evidence and the dates of lakes freezing in the lower Yangzi region to estimate the onset of colder temperatures.[9] More recently, Zhang De'er combed through local gazetteers for evidence of cold weather to reconstruct nearly five hundred years of winter temperatures in South China.[10] By quantifying literary comments from local gazetteers and then averaging those indicators by decade, Zhang identified several periods as having colder winters than others (see Fig. 11.2), in particular the 1610s, 1650s, 1680s, 1710s, 1760s, 1830s, and 1850s–70s.

Data specifically from Guangdong province paint a similar picture. A comprehensive search of Guangdong local gazetteers for the two centuries

---

[8] For a listing and discusion of the various kinds of proxy data, see H. H. Lamb, *Climate, History and the Modern World* (London: Methuen, 1982), ch. 5.

[9] See especially Zhu Kezhen 竺可桢, "Zhongguo wuqian nian lai qihou bianqian de chubu yanjiu" 中国五千年来气候变迁的初步研究 [A preliminary study of climate change in China over the past 5,000 years], *Kaogu xuebao* 1 (1972); and Zhang Peiyuan and Gong Gaofa, "Three cold episodes in the climatic history of China," in Ye Duzheng et al., eds., *The Climate of China and Global Climate: Proceedings of the Beijing International Symposium on Climate* (Berlin: Springer-Verlag, 1987), pp. 38–44.

[10] Zhang De'er 张德二, "Zhongguo nanbu jin 500 nian dongji wendu bianhua de ruogan tezheng" 中国南部近500年冬季温度变化的若干特征 [Some special points about winter temperature change in South China over the past 500 years], *Kexue tongbao* 6 (1980), pp. 270–72.

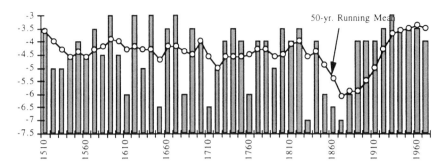

Figure 11.2. South China winter temperature reconstruction, 1510–1979. *Source*: Zhang De'er, "Winter temperatures", pp. 270–72. The meaning of the scale is unclear from the text of the article, but the vertical axis probably indicates degrees C° below the mean annual temperature.

from 1650 to 1850 produced 202 citations that can be classified as indicative of cold winters. If the number of counties reporting cold weather is a rough guide to the severity of the cold, and if reports in two or more consecutive years can be taken as indicative of something like a trend, then the coldest periods as recorded in the gazetteers occurred in the 1680s and the 1830s, with shorter cold spells in other decades.[11] Furthermore, volcanic eruptions in the 1680s and 1830s provide reasonable explanations for cooling trends that link the temperatures in South China to global trends: in 1680 Krakatoa erupted, followed by several years of other eruptions, and in 1831 a series of eruptions cooled global temperatures sufficiently to cause massive harvest failures in Japan in 1832 and 1833.[12]

China is unique in the world in having such a long-term historical record from which to extract relevant climatological data; scientists elsewhere have had to develop and calibrate other proxy records from which to reconstruct global temperature trends. Given the length of China's written record and its contribution to reconstructing past climates – as the work by Zhu Kezhen and Zhang De'er has demonstrated – an important question is the extent to which temperature trends are global (or at least hemispheric) rather than merely local. This question is important not merely for those scientists now pondering the connection between climate

[11] *Guangdong sheng ziran zaihai shiliao* 广东省自然灾害史料 [Historical source materials on natural disasters in Guangdong province] (Guangzhou: Guangdong sheng wen shi yanjiu guan, 1963), pp. 171–80.

[12] H. H. Lamb, "Volcanic Dust in the Atmosphere; with a Chronology and Assessment of Its Meteorological Significance," *Philosophical Transactions of the Royal Society of London* 266 (series A) (July 1970), pp. 425–550.

change and the prospects for global warming, but also for historians (like me) trying to uncover the historic relationships between climate change and food production. Significantly, recent studies have answered these questions by demonstrating that temperatures in different places in the northern hemisphere are highly correlated.[13] This finding is important because temperatures based on proxy rather than documentary evidence can be reconstructed on an annual basis, thereby allowing for more precise dating of temperature changes and their effects upon harvest yields and prices.

A recent reconstruction of annual temperatures for the northern hemisphere since 1671, based on the work by Jacoby and D'Arrigo, is plotted in Figure 11.3. The Jacoby-D'Arrigo temperature reconstruction shows that from the extremely cold decades at the end of the seventeenth century, temperatures rose significantly for the first three decades of the eighteenth century, varied within a similar range for the rest of the century, and finally plunged beginning around 1800 to new lows by the middle of the nineteenth century. Comparing the Jacoby-D'Arrigo reconstruction with Zhang De'er's, both series identify as cold decades the 1680s, 1710s, 1760s, and 1830s, and as warm decades the 1720s, 1730s, and 1810s, indicating a substantial amount of agreement. The two series point in opposite directions for the 1740s and the 1840s, though, and are inconclusive about the 1870s.

In summary, whether literary evidence from China's written sources or tree-ring growth in North America is used, the best available evidence all points to the same general conclusion about Qing-era temperature trends in South China: after unusually cold temperatures in the 1680s and early 1690s, temperatures warmed in the eighteenth century, plunged in the first half of the nineteenth century with the coldest temperatures probably being reached in the 1830s, and then warmed again in the second half of the nineteenth century.

---

[13] China's temperatures for the period since 1880 show a 0.95 correlation with northern hemisphere temperatures; see R. S. Bradley et al., "Secular Fluctuations of Temperature over Northern Hemisphere Land Areas and Mainland China since the Mid-19th Century," in Ye Duzheng et al., eds., *Climate of China*, p. 84. Zhang Peiyuan and Gong Gaofa conclude that eighteenth-century European and North American temperature "trends are the same as in China." See "Three Cold Episodes in the Climatic History of China," in Ye Duzheng et al., eds., *Climate of China*, p. 43. For graphic depictions of the correlation, see Zhang Jiacheng and Thomas B. Crowley, "Historical Climate Records in China and the Reconstruction of Past Climates," *Journal of Climate* 2 (Aug. 1989), p. 843. See also J. M. Lough et al., "Relationships between the Climates of China and North America of the Past Four Centuries: A Comparison of Proxy Records," in Ye Duzheng et al., eds, *Climate of China*, pp. 89–105.

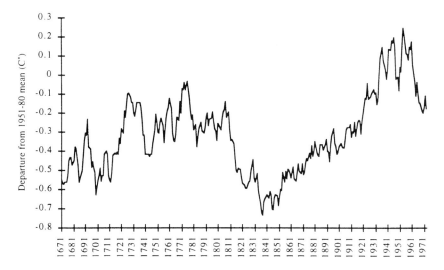

Figure 11.3. Northern hemisphere temperatures, 1671–1973. *Source*: Gordon C. Jacoby and Rosanne D'Arrigo, "Reconstructed Northern Hemisphere Annual Temperature since 1671 Based on High-Latitude Tree-Ring Data from North America," *Climatic Change* 14 (1989), pp. 39–59. Their data are used here not just because they constitute the most reliable reconstruction of northern hemisphere annual temperatures, but also because they most kindly made their database available to me. The chart plots the deviation of temperatures from "present," defined as the mean for 1950–79.

RAINFALL

Unlike temperature trends, which exhibit a clear hemispheric regularity, rainfall patterns are particular to the various continents. Thanks to the published results of an important climatological project headed by China's Bureau of Meteorology to quantify and map meteorological data contained in China's written historical records, China's historic rainfall and drought patterns can be analyzed.[14] Since the publication of this work in 1981,

---

[14] Zhongyang qixiang ju 中央气象局, *Zhongguo jin wubai nian han lao fenbutu ji* 中国近五百年旱涝分布图集 [Yearly charts of droughts and floods in China for the past 500 years] (Beijing: Kexue CBS, 1981). Both the data and the mapped results from this project must be used carefully. Researchers combed through hundreds of local gazetteers, compiling qualitative comments about the weather, and then quantified those comments on a scale of 1 to 5, with 3 repesenting "normal" rainfall; reports of extensive drought were quantified as a 5, while reports of extensive flooding were quantified as a 1, with lesser degrees of drought or flood assigned a 2 or a 4. Certainly, there are limitations inherent in this method, but I can think of no better way of mapping the vast quantity of data culled from the gazetteers and of obtaining a rough sense of changes in rainfall patterns over both time and space.

Table 11.1. *Climatic changes in South China, 1650–1859*

Period	Years wet[a]	Years dry[b]	Climate
1650–64	13	2	cool and wet
1665–99	11	24	cool and dry
1700–36	28	9	warming and wet
1737–88	25	27	warm and variable
1789–1801	11	2	warm and wet
1802–38	18	19	cooling and variable
1839–59	17	5	cool and wet

[a] Defined as types 1a, 2, or 4.
[b] Defined as types 1b, 3, or 5.

researchers have analyzed the data for periodicities and regularities in the patterns of floods and droughts,[15] and have classified the characteristic patterns into six types.[16] An examination of the frequency of those flood and drought types (see Table 11.1) for the two centuries beginning in 1650 (chosen to include fifty years on either side of the eighteenth century) shows definable periods marked by general wet or dry conditions, with two periods equally divided between types (1737–88 and 1802–38).

Combined with the temperature trends discussed earlier, the classification of flood and drought types allows a general characterization of the climatic regimes in South China from 1650 to 1850 as summarized in Table 11.1. Overall, seven distinct periods can be identified.

Compared with the periods before or after, the eighteenth century appears generally warmer and wetter. But even within the eighteenth century, three distinct periods can be discerned: 1700–36 was warm and wet,

[15] See especially Gong Gaofa 龚高法 et al., "Ying yong shiliao feng qian jizai yanjiu Beijing diqu jiang shui liang dui dong xiaomai shoucheng de yingxiang" 应用史料丰歉记载研究北京地区降水量对冬小麦收成的影响 [The use of historical records of deficient and bumper harvests to study the influence of rainfall on wheat harvests in the Beijing region] *Qixiang xuebao* 气象学报 41.4 (Nov. 1983), pp. 444–51; S. Hameed et al., "An Analysis of Periodicities in the 1470 to 1974 Beijing Precipitation Record," *Geophysical Research Letters* 10.6 (June 1983), pp. 436–39; and Huang Jia-you and Wang Shao-wu, "Investigations on Variations of the Subtropical High in the Western Pacific during Historic Times," *Climatic Change* 7 (1985), pp. 427–40.

[16] Wang Shao-wu and Zhao Zong-ci, "Droughts and Floods in China, 1470–1979," in T. M. L. Wigley et al., eds., *Climate and History: Studies in Past Climates and their Impact on Man* (Cambridge: Cambridge University Press, 1981), pp. 271–88. The types are: (1a) flood in most of China; (1b) drought in most of China; (2) drought in the Yangzi valley, flood in other parts; (3) flood in the Yangzi valley, drought in other parts; (4) flood in South China, drought in North China; and (5) drought in South China, flood in North China.

1737–88 generally was warm with alternating flood and drought types, and 1789–1801 once again was characterized by a warm and wet climate. Even though I have characterized the eighteenth-century South China climate as generally warm, cold air masses did penetrate the Nanling Mountains and settle over Guangdong; sometimes the cold winter was an isolated occurrence, but at other times the local gazetteers reported consecutive years of cold weather and drought.[17]

CLIMATE AND AGRICULTURE

The ways in which variations in temperature, rainfall, humidity, and solar radiation affect the growth rates and yields of particular food crops, especially cereal grains, are more complex than can be detailed here. Suffice it to say that like other plants, cereal grains have certain requirements for warmth, moisture, and sunshine during their growing period if they are to come to fruition and be harvested.[18] Too little or too much of any of these factors affects yields, but not necessarily in a linear way.[19] Climatic variability and change thus affect agriculture and harvest yields. Historical studies of the impact of climatic change on European and Japanese agriculture have focused on temperature variations, since cool summers and cold winters in temperate regions have had a greater adverse impact on harvest yields than variations in rainfall.[20] However, in studies of subtropical South China with its dependence on the summer monsoon to bring rainfall, additional attention must be paid to drought and flood.

In eighteenth-century South China, the main crop was rice; wheat was a secondary crop. Throughout much of Guangdong province, the annual cropping pattern consisted of two crops of rice followed by wheat or vegeta-

[17] The relationship between changes in average annual temperatures and precipitation is not uniform and varies considerably around the world. In Northern and Western Europe, cold summers tended also to be wet; a similar pattern apparently holds for North China too. For central and South China, though, cooler periods have been related to increased frequency of drought. For a discussion, see Zhang Jiacheng and Thomas J. Crowley, "Historical Climate Records," pp. 842–44.

[18] Lamb, *Climate, History and the Modern World*, p. 282.

[19] Richard W. Katz, "Assessing the Impact of Climatic Change on Food Production," *Climatic Change* 1 (1977), pp. 85–96.

[20] See especially M. L. Parry and T. R. Carter, "The Effect of Climatic Variations on Agricultural Risk," *Climatic Change* 7 (1985), pp. 95–110; and two works by John D. Post, *Food Shortage, Climatic Variability and Epidemic Disease in Preindustrial Europe* (Ithaca, N.Y.: Cornell University Press, 1985), and *The Last Great Subsistence Crisis in the Western World* (Baltimore: Johns Hopkins University Press, 1977). For Japan, see Junsei Kondo, "Volcanic Eruptions, Cool Summers, and Famines in the Northeastern Part of Japan," *Journal of Climate* 1 (Aug. 1988), pp. 775–88.

bles. In some areas, because either higher elevation or a more northerly location shortened the frost-free growing season to 220–40 days, one crop of rice (rather than two) was followed by wheat or vegetables.

Based upon documentary materials for 1764–65 (two years without any discernible climatic abnormalities such as drought, flood, or extreme cold),[21] I have reconstructed the annual agricultural cycle and charted it underneath a curve of current mean monthly temperatures at Guangzhou (see Fig. 11.4). The first, or early, rice crop, started around February 1 as seeds germinated; it then grew for two months in a nursery before being transplanted to the main field around April 1 (the Qing Ming festival – held April 4 or 5 – was generally considered to be the time of transplanting); the crop was then harvested in the first two weeks of July. In June, while the first crop was ripening in the field, the second, or late, rice crop started in the nursery beds, being transplanted into the field about two weeks after the first crop was harvested. The late rice crop was then harvested in late October or early November; two weeks later the wheat crop was planted directly in the field without any prior time sprouting in nursery beds. With just two or three weeks between the harvesting of one crop and the planting of the next, there was hardly an agricultural slack season in the "rice-rice-wheat" cycle.

Modern researchers have found that the favorable temperature range for the growth of rice is 15°–18°C to 30°–33°C, and that within that range, temperatures of 20°–22°C generally favor the growth and development of the rice plant; at temperatures below 15°C rice seeds either do not germinate or they rot.[22] Under "normal" temperature conditions, then, in January and early February temperatures in Guangdong are below those required for rice; after daily mean temperatures rise to 15°C in mid- to late February, seeds could be sprouted in nursery beds. The first crop then is transplanted into the main field just at the optimum temperature – 22°C – and harvested in July at the peak of both temperature and rainfall. For the first rice crop, the critical periods thus were first in the early stage of nursery or transplanting when unusual cold could kill the plants, and then during ripening when lack of water could desiccate the plants. For the second

---

[21] The documents are all palace memorials published in *Gong-zhong dang Qianlong-chao zouzhe* 宮中檔乾隆朝奏摺 [Palace memorials of the Qianlong period], Gugong bowuyuan 古宮博物院, comp. (Taipei: Guoli gugong bowuyuan, 1982–86), dated QL29.3.4 (vol. 20, p. 733); QL29.7.4 (vol. 22, p. 104); QL29.11.9 (vol. 23, p. 152); QL30.2i.25 (vol. 24, p. 247); QL30.7.11 (vol. 25, p. 476); and QL30.10.24 (vol. 26, p. 424). Referred to hereafter as *Qianlong memorials*. An intercalary month is denoted by an "i".

[22] I. Nishiyama, "Effects of Temperature on the Vegetative Growth of Rice Plants," in *Proceedings of the Symposium on Climate and Rice* (Los Banos, Philippines: IRRI, 1974), pp. 159–85.

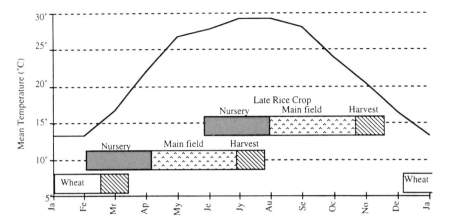

Figure 11.4. Annual cropping cycle. The temperature curve here is based upon current mean temperatures. The mean annual temperature in 1764–65 might have been about 0.3 °C lower than represented in the chart, which would shift the curve somewhat lower.

crop, the critical periods were following transplanting when drought would pose problems, and in September or October when unusual cold could kill the ripening crop. The double cropping of rice thus increased the riskiness of farming by pushing the sprouting time of the first crop and the ripening of the second crop into times of the year when frost was possible.

Cold temperatures affected rice in three ways.[23] First, spring frost could kill the early crop, and fall frost could kill the standing second crop. Both could and did happen. In 1832 in Xingning county 興甯縣 in eastern Guangdong, according to the local gazetteer, "spring snow harmed the rice sprouts." And perhaps more commonly than might be expected for a "semitropical" climate, frost and snow in September or October killed the standing crop, as was recorded in 1681 in both Hua 化 and Maoming counties 茂名縣. Both of these examples are from decades already identified as especially cold, but early fall frost killed rice crops in other years as well, as in 1712, 1757, 1763, and 1784.[24]

Second, cold temperatures in the early spring, below 15°C, could delay

---

[23] S. Yoshida and F. T. Parao, "Climatic Influence on Yield Components of Lowland Rice in the Tropics," in *Proceedings of the Symposium on Climate and Rice* (Los Banos, Philippines: IRRI, 1974), pp. 471–94; K. Munakata, "Effects of Temperature and Light on the Reproductive Growth and Ripening of Rice," in *Proceedings of the Symposium on Climate and Rice* (Los Banos, Philippines: IRRI, 1974), pp. 187–210.

[24] See the comments recorded for those years and compiled in *Natural disasters in Guangdong*, pp. 174–77.

transplanting, forcing peasant farmers either to forgo the spring planting altogether or to compromise with a rice strain for the second crop that had a shorter growing season but lower yields as well. I have not found a specific reference to this happening, but all gazetteers listed early-ripening rice strains whose express purpose was to fend off food shortages when harvests failed.

The final way in which cold temperatures affected the rice crop was indirectly, by "precipitating" drought. Even if the spring temperatures proved warm enough to germinate seeds, a cold air mass might disrupt the normal circulation of the North Pacific subtropical high, and with it the arrival of the rain-giving summer monsoon.[25]

Freezing cold and snow in a subtropical region like South China affected more than just the cereal crops. Indeed, comments in the local gazetteers indicate that frost or snow killed trees and grasses, as in 1636, 1690, and 1815. Plum trees, fruit trees, and other trees of commercial value all suffered, spreading economic hardship to those who relied upon them for their livelihood. Sometimes farmyard animals – chickens, pigs, and perhaps water buffalo – also died, and in a few cases (as in 1532) water froze so deep that fish died. Finally, people froze to death too. The effects of unusual cold in South China thus could be rather widespread, and the broader consequences for the people and the economy should not be overlooked.

11.2. HARVEST YIELDS

While the Kangxi emperor was interested in the impact of colder temperatures on harvest yields, I have not seen any evidence to indicate that either of his successors, the Yongzheng emperor (reigned 1723–35) or the Qianlong emperor (reigned 1736–95), was aware that the climate during their reigns was warmer than in Kangxi's time, or appreciated the fact that conditions had turned more favorable for agriculture. They were nonetheless mindful of the importance of monitoring the food supplies of the empire: building upon innovations begun during the Kangxi emperor's reign, they developed bureaucratic systems by which local officials routinely

---

[25] The mechanism by which cold temperatures created drought conditions is associated with the annual movement of the North Pacific subtropical high pressure system, and the relationship of the movement of this high-pressure system to the summer monsoon. For a lucid explanation of this complex phenomenon, see Zhang Jiacheng and Thomas J. Crowley, "Historical Climate Records in China and the Reconstruction of Past Climates," *Journal of Climate* 2 (Aug. 1989), p. 835.

reported grain harvest estimates, rainfall amounts, and grain prices to the central government.[26] Vast numbers of these memorials are extant and available in archives in Beijing and Taipei, making possible a reconstruction of the history of eighteenth-century harvest results.

The memorials reporting harvest yields were of two types: detailed county-level reports for each of the three main harvests (the winter wheat, early rice, and late rice harvests), and provincewide harvest figures.[27] The provincial figures probably were averages (how precise is another question) of the county-level estimates, and all were reported in terms of decile blocks (*fen* 分), which I have chosen to translate as percentages (e.g., a harvest rated at "eight *fen*" is translated as 80 percent, and one at "over eight *fen*" as 85 percent). As stipulated in the *Collected Statutes of the Qing Dynasty*, "all estimates of harvest rates are to be memorialized" and rated according to the following definitions:

> Harvest ratings: 80 percent (eight *fen*) and above are plentiful (*feng*); 60 percent (six *fen*) and above are average (*ping*); 50 percent (five *fen*) and below are deficient (*qian*). The reality [of the harvest size] is to be investigated thoroughly and reported. Each year the provincial [authorities] are to estimate the wheat, early-rice, and late-rice harvests. The governor-general is to memorialize the facts. . . .[28]

How the harvest estimates were made, or who actually did the estimating, is not at all clear. What seems to have been the case is that estimates were developed first at the county level, and then aggregated at the prefectural and provincial levels. Presumably, harvest estimates were expected to be based upon actual inquiry at the county level, but that kind of investigation did not always occur. How did the county magistrate make the estimates? By sending runners into the countryside to look at the crops standing in the fields? By asking landowners? Tillers of the fields? A military commander en route to his new post in Guangxi in 1725 wrote that "according to various

---

[26] The grain-price reporting system is well known, and thus will not be discussed here. See Wang Yeh-chien 王業鍵, "Qing dai de liang jia chenbao zhidu" 清代的糧價陳報制度 [The Qing grain price reporting system], *Taibei gugong likan* 13.1 (1978).

[27] The provincial estimates as reported in the routine memorials may have been produced as a result of a bureaucratic struggle over control of information at the beginning of the Qianlong reign, while the county-level estimates became part of the secret palace memorial system. See Beatrice S. Bartlett, *Monarchs and Ministers: The Grand Council in Mid-Ch'ing China, 1723–1820* (Berkeley and Los Angeles: University of California Press, 1991), pp. 164–65.

[28] *Da Qing huidian* 大清會典 [Collected statutes of the Qing code], 1899 ed. (Shanghai: Shangwu yinshu guan, 1911), *j.* 21, p. 17a.

villagers," fields near water would harvest 90 percent or so; those in the hills would harvest about 60–70 percent.[29] Was asking "the villagers" common practice?[30] At this point we simply do not know. But the estimates clearly were of uneven quality. Even as early as 1729, officials such as finance commissioner Wang Shijun 王士俊 commented, "I fear that some [harvest] reports are not factual."[31]

Finally, it should be clear that harvest ratings based on deciles (*fen*) and translated here as percentages were blunt, probably impressionistic, estimates. A harvest of eight or nine *fen* tells us nothing about how much grain actually was harvested.[32] Indeed, as population increased and more land was brought into cultivation, higher levels of productivity were achieved, and hence larger amounts of grain were produced, the harvest ratings remained based on percentages: an eight-*fen* harvest in 1780 certainly was larger than an eight-*fen* harvest in 1736, yet both were glossed as "plentiful" relative to the supply and demand at the time.

Despite the limitations of the harvest ratings estimates, Qing officials used them to manage the food supply of the empire, and to administer the state granary system.[33] Furthermore, the harvest ratings apparently also became public information, for tenants used the ratings to reduce the amount of rent they were expected to pay landlords.[34] Far from being

---

[29] Memorial dated YZ2.11.7 in *Gong zhong dang Yongzheng-chao zouzhe* 宮中檔雍正朝奏摺 [Palace memorials of the Yongzheng period] (Taipei: Guoli gugong bowuyuan, 1977–88), vol. 3, pp. 426–27. Hereafter referred to as *Yongzheng memorials* with volume number and page number.

[30] In England, W. G. Hoskins noted, "the annual harvest was the perennial subject of conversation in town and country, from landowner down to cottager." He also cites an American colleague who claimed that "even in Kansas City, a town of a quarter million people in the 1920's, the quality of the harvest was the staple of conversation." See Hoskins, "Harvest Fluctuations and English Economic History, 1480–1619," *Agricultural History Review* 12 (1964), pp. 28–29.

[31] *Yongzheng-chao hanwen zhupi zouzhe huibian* 雍正朝漢文朱批奏摺会编 [Collected Chinese-language palace memorials of the Yongzheng period] (Nanjing: Jiangsu guji CBS, 1989), vol. 15, p. 528 (YZ7.6.11). Hereafter referred to as *Yongzheng Chinese memorials*.

[32] During the eighteenth century, yields for the first rice harvest averaged about 4 *shi* per *mu*. If that yield corresponded to an 85% harvest (i.e., the mode for the series), then the "abundant" (*feng*) or "deficient" (*qian*) harvests yielded somewhat more or somewhat less than 4 *shi* per *mu*. For a discussion of harvest yields in the lower Yangzi and an attempt to quantify the per *mu* changes over a very long period of time, see Chen Jiaqi 陈家其, "Ming Qing shiqi qihou bianhua dui Tai hu liuyu nongye jingji de yingxiang" 明清时期气候变化对太湖流域农业经济的影响 [The influence of climate change in the Ming and Qing on the agrarian economy of the Tai lake drainage basin], *Zhongguo nongshi* 中国农史 3 (1991), pp. 30–36.

[33] See Pierre-Étienne Will, *Bureaucracy and Famine in Eighteenth-Century China* (Stanford, Calif.: Stanford University Press, 1990), pp. 110–13.

[34] For the practices in Jiangnan, see Kathryn Bernhardt, *Rents, Taxes, and Peasant Resistance: The Lower Yangzi Region, 1840–1950* (Stanford, Calif.: Stanford University Press, 1992), pp. 37–39.

merely bureaucratic busy work, the Qing officials' harvest ratings estimates influenced the way the empire was governed, and even entered into private contractual arrangements. Clearly, people at the time put substantial stock in these estimates; what might they tell us today about the size and quality of eighteenth-century harvests?

Within the county-level ratings, the range for both the early- and late-harvest estimates was largely between 70 percent and 100 percent, implying that officials mostly chose one of four different ratings for the harvest: 70, 80, 90, or 100 percent. In just five cases (out of about 13,000 reports) did officials report countywide harvests of less than 60 percent. The reason for the few cases of ratings below 60 percent may lie with the regulations and procedures for providing relief payments to families stricken by natural disaster and crop loss. According to Pierre-Étienne Will, "no relief payments were to be made when the damage was below or at 50 percent."[35] Natural disasters prompted investigations of villages, with preliminary and final surveys determining the crop loss on a field-by-field and case-by-case basis. Families that harvested less than 50 percent of their crop thus were eligible for monetary relief payments to enable them to purchase food and seed. This being the case, a countywide harvest rating of less than 50 percent meant that every person in the county would have been eligible for relief, and no county magistrate was about to make that claim. Did the county-level harvest rating estimates of 60–70 percent in 1787 thus mean that in some places the harvest was less than 50 percent, triggering the relief payments, while harvests of more than 50 percent in other parts of the county raised the countywide average to 60–70 percent? Some "areas" or "fields" had harvests of less than 50 percent, but never entire counties.

The early-harvest ratings averaged 82–83 percent and the late-harvest ratings 84–85 percent, both within the range defined by the Qing *Statutes* as "plentiful" (*feng* 豐).[36] If officials' harvest ratings estimates are a rough guide to harvests, then one can conclude that for most of the Qianlong period, Guangdong harvests were good. Given the generally favorable climatic conditions, this conclusion is not unexpected, but it is worth noting that the officials' harvest ratings are consistent with the climatological data.

Although the *Collected Statutes* stipulated that harvest ratings between 60 and 80 percent were "average" (*ping* 平), the historical record in Guangdong indicates that recorded harvests in that range coincided with serious food shortages and conditions described by local officials as "dearth" (*ji* 饑). In 1726, for instance, a typhoon hit eastern Guangdong

[35] Will, *Bureaucracy and Famine*, p. 113.
[36] *Qing statutes, j.* 21, p. 17a.

just before the fall harvest, destroying much of the crop. The governor-general reported the fall harvest in Chaozhou and Huizhou prefectures at 60–70 percent,[37] but in the winter substantial relief operations were begun to provide food to the affected areas. Besides purchasing additional grain from Guangxi for sales at reduced prices (*pingtiao* 平糶), officials exhorted merchants to donate money and grain for free distribution to the hungry.[38] Even then, refugees turned up begging in Guangxi.[39]

Similarly, in 1786, when a drought prompted Governor-general Sun Shiyi 孫士毅 to memorialize that "there is no soil that isn't dry and parched,"[40] the worst harvest reports were in the 60–70 percent range.[41] When the drought continued into 1787 and eighteen county gazetteers glossed the year with comments of "major drought" (*da han* 大旱), "dearth" (*ji* 饑), or "famine" (*da ji* 大饑), the provincial authorities rated county harvests no lower than 60 percent.[42]

GUANGDONG PROVINCE HARVEST RATINGS, 1707–1800

Like the county-level harvest ratings, the provincial ratings ranged narrowly between 70 and 100 percent (seven to ten *fen*), with the mode being in the 80–85 percent range (see Fig. 11.5). Even within that range, though, variations are apparent, and, I think, meaningful. If a deficient harvest is defined as one that is at least one standard deviation below the mean, then Guangdong experienced deficient harvests in thirteen out of the ninety-four years covered by the time series. Moreover, climatic conditions caused each of those deficient harvests (see Table 11.2).[43] To explore the connections between climate and harvest yields in more detail, I have chosen three case studies with the best available documentation to illustrate the effects of cold (in 1757–58), drought (in 1786–87), and floods (in 1725–27) upon harvest yields.

---

[37] Memorial dated YZ4.11.15, *Yongzheng memorials*, vol. 8, p. 437.

[38] Memorials dated YZ5.3.22, YZ5.i3.25, *Yongzheng memorials*, vol. 9, pp. 309–10, 500.

[39] Memorial dated YZ5.4.8, *Yongzheng memorials*, vol. 9, pp. 598–99.

[40] Memorial dated QL51.10.18, *Qianlong memorials*, vol. 62, p. 16.

[41] Memorials dated QL51.7.4 and QL51.10.7, *Qianlong memorials*, vol. 61, pp. 71, 731–32.

[42] Guangdong and Fujian officials' time, energy, and attention in 1787 were taken up with the Lin Shuangwen uprising on Taiwan. See David Alan Ownby, "Communal Violence in Eighteenth Century Southeast China: The Background to the Lin Shuangwen Uprising of 1787," Ph.D. dissertation, Harvard University (1989).

[43] Disease also adversely affected harvest yields, but insect damage tended to be less frequent and was limited to a county here or there. Only climate had the power to destroy crops over a wide enough area to be reflected in the provincial-level harvest ratings.

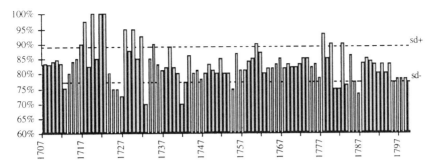

Figure 11.5. Guangdong province harvest ratings, 1707–1800. This chart has been constructed using three sources: (1) the reported provincial figures gleaned from more than one hundred volumes of published palace memorials in *Kangxi memorials*, *Yongzheng memorials*, and *Qianlong memorials* provided data for 42 years; (2) for another 32 years, a provincial figure was computed by averaging the county-level estimates; and (3) for 20 years the missing data were reconstructed using a rice-price series.

The last source requires some explanation. European economic historians interested in assessing harvest yields, for instance, have not had harvest yield estimates such as those produced by Chinese officials, but have had to rely upon grain-price series to deduce harvest qualities. W. G. Hoskins reasoned that annual grain prices substantially above or below what might be considered "normal" reflected harvest conditions. The methodology developed by Hoskins to characterize English harvests based on grain-price behavior can be adopted here to bridge the gaps in our series of Chinese officials' harvest ratings: first, we determine the departures of mean annual rice prices from "normal" prices, and then we estimate what Chinese officials might have reported for those years for which memorials are missing and thus fill in the gaps in the time series. Hoskins characterized English harvests from 1480 to 1759 as "abundant, good, average, deficient, bad, or dearth" depending on how far annual grain prices deviated from a 31-year moving average. Hoskins used the 31-year moving average on the assumptions that this was the average length of a human generation and that such a long-term average eliminated the effect of monetary changes and population growth from the series. Since Hoskins wrote, a centered 11-year moving average has become the accepted standard for detrending a price series, and thus is used here. The lacunae in the harvest estimates were calculated from the regression equation of the extant ratings on average annual prices: $y = -0.001x + 0.911$, where y is the harvest rating and x is the price (price is actually the dependent variable, but this equation is the easiest form to solve for the harvest rating). Since this regression equation had an r^2 value of .102, it is probable that the actual ratings varied from the predicted values.

For a full discussion of this methodology, see W. G. Hoskins, "Harvest Fluctuations and English Economic History, 1480–1619," *Agricultural History Review* 12 (1964), pp. 28–46; and "Harvest Fluctuations and English Economic History, 1620–1759," *Agricultural History Review* 16 (1968), pp. 15–31. Hoskins's work was critiqued by C. J. Harrison, "Grain Price Analysis and Harvest Qualities, 1465–1634," *Agricultural History Review* 19 (1969), pp. 135–55.

Table 11.2. *Deficient harvests in Guangdong province*

Year	Cause
1713	Cold
1725–27	Floods, typhoon
1733	Floods
1742–43	Drought
1755	Drought and flood
1781–82	Drought
1784	Cold
1787	Drought

The 1757–58 Frosts

In searching through the county-level harvest ratings for long periods of consecutive reports, I was fortunate to discover the eight-year period from 1755 to 1762, for which good documentation illustrates the relationships among cold temperatures, drought conditions, harvest ratings, and grain prices. The chart in Figure 11.6 relates harvest yields estimates as reported for Shunde county 順德縣 in the Pearl River delta (the bars at the bottom of the chart), with monthly rice prices recorded for Guangzhou prefecture (the line). (The year and month are along the horizontal axis, with "1755. 11" meaning, for instance, "November 1755.")

The story begins with the early and late harvests for 1755, rated at 75 percent and 80 percent respectively, continuing a run of poor harvests from the early 1750s; rice prices thus had reached a relatively high level of around 2 taels 兩 per *shi* 石, and remained there throughout 1755 and into the first half of 1756. The early harvest in 1756 was excellent (92 percent); rice prices started to fall in June, and continued to do so after a good late harvest (85 percent) in November, reaching a low of about 1.5 taels after the late harvest was in. Prices in the spring of 1757 began edging up, as they normally would, until March 3, 1757. Then, on the night of March 4, a killing frost was reported in Xin'an county 新安縣 (the area just north of what is now Hong Kong). The early-rice crop was then growing in nursery beds in preparation for transplanting into the fields, which, under normal circumstances, would have taken place about one month later.

Immediately after the March 4 frost, rice prices shot up and continued climbing until the early harvest came in. When it did, officials rated it at 70 percent, a "deficient" harvest, but even so, sufficient rice was harvested for prices to level off. But then sometime in October – our sources are not specific – frost in Guishan county 歸善縣 (just east of Guangzhou) "killed

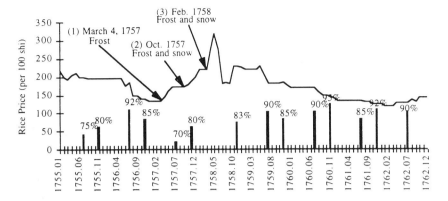

Figure 11.6. Frost, harvest ratings, and rice prices in the Pearl River delta, 1755–62.

rice plants,"[44] and rice prices shot up again, leveling off in January 1758 at the peaks reached in 1755–56. And then once again, this time in February 1758, frost and snow were reported in many areas throughout the Pearl River delta, and rice prices skyrocketed to 3.15 taels per *shi*, the highest prices recorded during the Qianlong reign. Presumably this frost came too early in February to affect the early harvest, for rice prices plummeted after the early harvest came in. Unfortunately, the officials' early-harvest rating estimate for 1758 is missing, but we can imagine it to have been relatively high. The late harvest in 1758 again was good (83 percent), beginning a string of excellent harvests that continued for another four years, resulting in steadily declining rice prices.

The unexpected cold snap in early 1757 affected harvest yields through-out Guangdong province, all the way from the Leizhou 雷州 Peninsula in the south to Kaijian county 開建縣 in the northwest, where the local gazetteer reported for 1757 that "the early crop was completely lost; the late harvest was deficient."[45] Counties throughout the province re-ported high rice prices in both 1757 and 1758; some reported "dearth" (*ji*) and some "famine" (*da ji*). And in Gaoyao county 高要縣, up the West River from Guangzhou, the local gazetteer reported that "on June 2, hungry villagers stole grain from wealthy households."[46] But whether or not elevated mortality levels accompanied the highest rice prices in the eigh-teenth century is unclear, since the documentary sources do not speak to the issue. As we will see in the other cases, though, higher mortality levels did accompany the climatic shock to harvest yields and rice prices.

[44] Excerpted in *Natural disasters in Guangdong*, p. 175.
[45] Excerpted in ibid., p. 206.
[46] Excerpted in ibid.

This brief account of the 1757–58 cold snap reveals much about the relationships among climatic changes, the harvest ratings, and rice prices. First, prices shot up immediately after the frosts, considerably in advance of the actual harvests. Rice wholesalers and retailers no doubt played on people's fears that the frost would severely constrict food supplies to push prices up significantly in advance of the harvests. But the behavior of prices following each of the three harvests – leveling off or falling – indicates that the harvest was not as deficient as had been feared. The 1757 early-harvest rating of 70 percent in Shunde was followed not by increasing prices, but by steadying prices. The same phenomenon can be observed after the 1757 late harvest. Second, when the series of good harvests began in 1758, harvest ratings ranging from 85 percent to 95 percent were accompanied by generally declining prices, but none that could be directly correlated with the harvest rating. In 1759, for instance, a 90 percent early harvest was followed by a lower-rated late harvest (85 percent), and yet prices continued to decline. While as a general rule it might be expected that better rice harvests are correlated with declining prices, the specifics of the cases (like this one) will make statistical correlations weaker than might be assumed. The explanation undoubtedly is that families, rice wholesalers, and the state all began storing rice, so that runs of good harvests – even if some were slightly smaller than the previous one – nonetheless added to the stocks in storage. Third, the literature on subsistence crises would lead one to suspect that high rice prices are an indicator of elevated mortality. If so, in this instance – when prices reached the highest recorded levels in the eighteenth century – the record is silent. The absence of evidence, of course, cannot be construed to mean that mortality did not increase. In other cases the documentary sources do speak to the question; in this case, they do not.

Finally, this case also demonstrates the connection between cold and drought in South China, for nine counties reported drought conditions in 1758. Apparently, if the cold snap did not kill off the early crop, the ensuing drought decreased the yields. While it is not possible now to sort out which had a greater adverse impact on harvest yields, the combination of cold and drought certainly reduced the harvests in 1757. And that was not the only time such a "one-two punch" hit harvest yields.

The 1786–87 Guangdong Drought and Famine[47]

Beginning with observations of "little rain" just before the 1786 autumn harvest, drought continued through to the end of 1787, probably having

---

[47] For maps, see Zhongyang qixiang-ju, *Atlas of droughts and floods* (Beijing: Kexue CBS), pp. 164–65.

been occasioned by the significant global cooling of 2–3°C caused by massive volcanic eruptions casting a thick veil over the atmosphere and preventing solar radiation from reaching the surface of the earth.[48] The cooler temperatures blocked the North Pacific subtropical high from its usual path, disrupting the summer monsoon and bringing drought to South China. The areas affected by the drought included the populous, centrally located prefectures in Guangdong most dependent upon imports for their food supplies.

The effect of the drought on food supplies in and around Guangzhou was magnified by two additional factors. First, after six months of the drought, rivers so shriveled that the grain boats normally bringing rice into Guangzhou could not navigate the shoals, so market supplies began to dry up.[49] Second, worried provincial officials conducted an audit of granary stocks and discovered, somewhat to their alarm, massive deficits.[50] Without granary stocks or imports from Guangxi, by the spring of 1787 the food supply in Guangdong – and especially to Guangzhou – was precarious at best. Officials sent emissaries to the Yangzi valley to purchase rice, and called upon merchants to do the same. The officially purchased rice did not arrive until the fifth month, and then it was distributed not through the ever-normal granaries but at specially established "depots" (*chang* 廠), and then probably only in Guangzhou.[51] In the meantime, spring rains raised water levels in the West River so Guangxi grain boats could navigate, and a moderate winter-wheat harvest hit the market.[52]

Moderate rainfall in the spring resulted in a poor early-rice harvest, but then little rain fell during the summer of 1787. The provincial authorities appeared unaware that a disaster was building, and only in the ninth month declared a disaster (*zai*). The drought continued through 1787, resulting in the worst late-rice harvest in years. Rains came in the spring of 1788, leading to a decent winter-wheat harvest and then to "plentiful" early- and late-rice harvests. The drought was over.

Compared with the energetic response to harvest failure earlier, the response of the state bureaucracy to the 1786–87 drought was anemic. A perusal of the *Qing shi lu* [*Veritable records of the Qing dynasty*] for those years

---

[48] Major volcanic eruptions in Iceland and then in Japan in 1783 were followed by a series of smaller eruptions in 1785–86, lowering global temperatures for as long as six years afterward. See Lamb, "Volcanic Dust," pp. 508–09. For a discussion of the impact in Japan, see Junsei Kondo, "Volcanic Eruptions, Cool Summers," pp. 775–88.

[49] Memorial dated QL52.2.13, *Qianlong memorials*, vol. 63, p. 347.

[50] Memorial dated QL51.11.5, *Qianlong memorials*, vol. 62, pp. 192–93.

[51] Memorial dated QL52.5.27, *Qianlong memorials*, vol. 64, pp. 524–25.

[52] Memorials dated QL52.3.15, *Qianlong memorials*, vol. 63, pp. 635–36; QL52.6.13, *Qianlong memorials*, vol. 64, p. 670.

also reveals no attention on the part of the central government, although note is made in the spring of 1788 of a palace memorial from the governor of Guangxi discussing rice prices, granary operations, harvest estimates, and weather reports.[53] The absence of provincial reports to the central government about the drought and the impending disaster, and the lack of central government attention to routine matters in South China, are partially explained by the fact that the state apparatus was absorbed with the crisis caused by the Lin Shuangwen rebellion on Taiwan, which coincidentally spanned almost exactly the same time frame as the Guangdong drought. Liang-Guang governor-general Sun Shiyi was in Taiwan for much of 1787 engaged in military actions, and the *Veritable records* reflect that concern by being filled with reports about Taiwan. Significantly, the Qianlong emperor did not reprimand Sun for his lack of attention to the drought, but instead rewarded him for his role in the suppression of the Lin Shuangwen rebellion.[54] Thus to the provincial authorities and the central government, the drought, investigations to determine the extent of crop losses, the declaration of a disaster, state relief efforts, the condition of the ever-normal granaries, and the numbers of poor and hungry affected, were minor matters requiring little of their attention. The result was a disaster of historic proportions, the record of which is found not in the palace memorials, but in terse entries in local gazetteers: "famine" (*da ji*), noted several, while others acknowledged that "many died of starvation."[55]

In the final case study, we turn our attention from colder temperatures and their effect upon harvest yields through killing frosts and droughts, to the impact of warmer temperatures and floods.

The 1725–27 Floods and Typhoon[56]

If in South China colder-than-normal temperatures tended to create atmospheric conditions conducive to drought, then with warming trends the reverse tended to be true as well: warming trends brought more than the usual amounts of rain, sometimes causing floods. This relationship held true during a two-year period from 1725 to 1727, and the documentation exists to chart what happened.

The crop failures and disaster relief operations in 1725–27 were the

[53] *Gaozong Qing shi lu* 高宗清實錄 [Veritable records of the Qing–Qianlong period], *j.* 1302, pp. 13b–15a.
[54] Hummel, *Eminent Chinese of the Ch'ing Period*, p. 680.
[55] For example, see *Xin'an xianzhi* 新安縣志 (1820 edition), *j.* 2, p. 51; *Guangzhou fuzhi* 廣州府志 (1864 edition), *j.* 81, p. 7a. All told, I have counted 41 separate references to famine and/or high prices in Guangdong local gazetteers for the 1786–88 drought.
[56] For maps, see Zhongyang qixiang-ju, *Atlas of droughts and floods*, pp. 133–34.

result of two separate natural disasters: a flood on the West River in late 1725, followed a year later by a typhoon in eastern Guangdong, both of which occurred after more than a decade-long warming trend. Beginning in 1711 and 1712, when (as later in 1757) frost in late October killed the standing rice crop in western Guangdong and central Guangxi provinces, temperatures rose steadily into the mid-1720s (see Fig. 11.3), bringing more moist air masses flowing into South China. Then, in November 1725, flooding along the West River in Guangdong destroyed a significant portion of the standing rice crop in Gaoyao, Sihui, Gaoming, Nanhai, and Sanshui counties. Except for these counties, Governor-general Kong Yuxun 孔毓珣 reported, the rest of the province had a plentiful autumn harvest.[57] The counties affected by the flood were classified into two groups: those with fields without a harvest and those with a loss but "not a disaster (*bu cheng zai* 不成災)."[58]

State relief operations spanned the time from the flooding until the spring of 1726. When a good early harvest came in and rice entered the market, provincial officials believed the crisis over. But in September, a typhoon struck eastern Guangdong, destroying the standing rice crop in eleven counties. An investigation determined that six counties had a "disaster (*zai*)."[59] Rising to the challenge, provincial officials distributed granary stocks,[60] imported more rice from Guangxi for reduced-price sales, and exhorted the wealthy to contribute money and grain.[61]

Certainly disaster relief operations on this scale reduced the human suffering that otherwise would have come in the wake of the typhoon.[62] Even so, belletristic literature described the disaster as a major famine, and explicitly mentioned deaths. In Chaozhou 潮州 the disaster was described as a famine with many deaths. Denghai county 澄海縣 also registered "countless dead," and in Guangzhou there were "people dying one on top of the other along the roads."[63] The governor of Guangxi, Han Liangfu, 韓良輔 reported "wandering, hungry people from Guangdong" arriving in Guangxi.[64]

---

[57] Memorial dated YZ3.11.15, *Yongzheng memorials*, vol. 5, p. 379.

[58] Memorial dated YZ4.4.22, *Yongzheng memorials*, vol. 5, p. 843.

[59] Memorial dated YZ4.9.20, *Yongzheng Chinese memorials*, vol. 8, pp. 139–40.

[60] Chen Chunsheng 陈春声, *Shichang jizhi yu shehuibianqian: shiba shiji Guangdong mi jia fenxi* 市场机制与社会变迁：十八世纪广东米价分析 [Market mechanism and social change: an analysis of rice prices in 18th-century Guangdong] Ph.D. thesis (1987), Xiamen University, p. 34.

[61] Memorials dated YZ5.3.22; YZ5.13.25; and YZ5.4.21, *Yongzheng Chinese memorials*, vol. 9, pp. 309–10, 501, 696–97.

[62] Memorial dated YZ5.5.20, *Yongzheng Chinese memorials*, vol. 9, pp. 832–33.

[63] Quoted in Chen Chunsheng, *Market mechanism and social change*, pp. 262–64.

[64] Memorial dated YZ5.4.8, *Yongzheng Chinese memorials*, vol. 9, pp. 598–99.

For the state, one consequence of the double disaster was to deplete Guangdong's granary stocks. By the time the early-rice harvest came in and officials could cease relief operations, just 200,000 *shi* remained in the granaries for the entire province. Adding to the officials' woes was the fact that since so much of the grain had to be provided as relief rather than sold, there were just 200,000 taels in the provincial treasury to purchase grain to restock the granaries.[65] As late as 1728 the granaries had not yet been restocked, and the governor's orders to local officials to replenish the deficits had not been followed. Fortunately, the 1728 harvests were the best in years, and rice prices fell to their lowest recorded levels. So good were harvests in the next two years as well that in 1729, for the only recorded time in the eighteenth century, Guangdong was self-sufficient in rice supplies.[66]

Summary

These three case studies document the linkage between climatic variability and harvest yields: freezing cold in 1757–58, drought in 1786–87, and floods in 1725–27 all resulted in smaller-than-usual harvests. Certainly these are not the only instances of climatic factors adversely affecting harvest yields, but they are the ones for which the best documentation exists. Moreover, the officials' harvest rating estimates corresponded to this documentary record, leading to the conclusion not only that the harvest ratings were reasonable estimates of the direction of harvest fluctuations from year to year, but also that climatic changes were the single most important cause of harvest yield fluctuations during the eighteenth century.[67] The reconstructed time series of Guangdong provincial harvest ratings thus provides a useful summary of very broad changes in harvest yields and food supplies during the course of the eighteenth century.

---

[65] Memorial dated YZ5.5.24, *Yongzheng Chinese memorials*, vol. 9, p. 845.

[66] Memorial dated YZ7.9.1, *Yongzheng Chinese memorials*, vol. 16, p. 580.

[67] Asking similar questions about the relationship between climate and harvest yields, the Chinese geographer Zheng Sizhong classified and statistically analyzed over 11,000 citations on climate and harvest from Guangdong gazetteers covering a 500-year period. Zheng's data show: (1) that the incidence of colder-than-normal temperatures is significantly correlated both with drought and with dearth; (2) that warmer temperatures are significantly correlated with floods; and (3) that typhoons generally are correlated with bumper harvests (by bringing additional rain inland to upland fields). Zheng's conclusions support those reached here. Zheng Sizhong 郑斯中, "1400–1949 nian Guangdong-sheng de qihou zhendong ji qi dui liangshi fengqian-de yingxiang" 1400–1949 年广东省的气候振动及其对粮食丰歉的影响 [Climate change in Guangdong from 1400 to 1949 and its impact on grain harvests]. *Dili xuebao* (*Acta Geographica Sincia*) 地理学报, 38.1 (1983), pp. 25–32. Zhang also found (using power spectrum analysis) that droughts tended to exhibit a thirty-year recurring cycle.

Not all deficient harvests, of course, resulted in food shortages, rising prices, and dearth conditions. The state-managed granary system, private storage of grain, and the smooth operation of the market ensured adequate supplies in most years,[68] even when climatic factors caused isolated years of deficient harvests, as in 1713, 1733, and 1755. The state and society encountered real problems, though, when one deficient harvest succeeded another. In these instances, the stocks of grain in state granaries or private hands were insufficient to carry people through two bad years, and then food shortages, dearth, and famine resulted. During the course of the eighteenth century, instances of successive years of poor harvests occurred just three times – in 1725–27, 1742–43, and 1781–82 – each of which produced harvest ratings one standard deviation below the mean for the entire series.

11.3. HARVEST YIELDS AND RICE PRICES

The price of rice, like that of other commodities, was a function of market supply and demand. Demand for rice was of course conditioned by population size and consumer preferences, and while consumers could switch to sweet potatoes when the price of rice rose too high (and vice versa),[69] in the short run demand for rice was more or less inelastic.[70] With demand constant, variation in supply caused primarily by fluctuation of harvest yields was the primary factor accounting for changes in annual rice prices. When harvests failed and the food supply contracted, rice prices rose; conversely, bumper harvests depressed prices.

---

[68] For a discussion of rice markets, population size, and demand for rice, see Robert B. Marks, "Rice Prices, Food Supply, and Market Structure in Eighteenth-Century South China," *Late Imperial China* 12.2 (Dec. 1991).

[69] Following the 1756 harvest, the governor of Guangdong reported: "Throughout the province the price of sweet potatoes and taro is low. For a few coppers (*wen* 文), the people (*xiao min* 小民) can eat till they are full. This hasn't been the case for years." Memorial dated QL21.8.24, *Qianlong memorials*, vol. 15, 237. The reason for the decline in sweet potato prices most likely had less to do with the sweet potato than the rice harvest: as the price of rice came down, those who had been consuming sweet potatoes feasted on rice.

[70] As Slicher van Bath wrote of grain prices in premodern Europe: "The need for agricultural produce, and especially of bread grain, is practically constant. Since the human stomach has a limited capacity, the consumer does not eat more bread because the price has fallen. The money saved on bread is spent in other ways; the poorer people may spend it on more expensive food . . . or on all sorts of industrial goods. . . . When corn [i.e., wheat] is scarce, everyone is afraid of not getting enough; hence the familiar readiness to pay high prices in times of scarcity." B. H. Slicher van Bath, *The Agrarian History of Western Europe, 500–1800* (London, 1963), pp. 118–19.

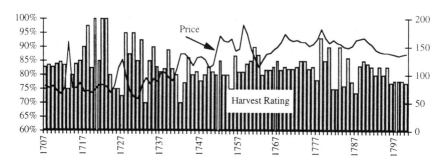

Figure 11.7. Harvest ratings and rice prices, 1707–1800. The data graphed here are averages: the rice price is the average high price of common rice as reported in the ten prefectures and three independent *zhou* that constitute Guangdong province; the harvest rating is the average of the early and late harvest ratings. Since most of the rice in Guangdong was produced by two crops annually, it is prudent to distinguish between the yield of a single harvest and total annual crop yield produced by two harvests. The bars depict the latter. I thank Mark Elvin for helping me sharpen this distinction.

The relationship between annual crop yields and rice prices in eighteenth-century Guangdong province is summarized in Figure 11.7. When the officials' harvest ratings are correlated with the price series,[71] the results, as expected, indicate an inverse relationship (see Table 11.3): better harvests tended to depress rice prices, and poorer harvests tended to increase rice prices.

Although this statistical test does demonstrate the expected inverse rela-

---

[71] The correlation of the harvest ratings series with the price series presents two methodological problems. First, it is necessary to remove the trend from the price series. Although it might be assumed that the trend in rice prices in the eighteenth century was to increase more or less in a linear fashion ($y = 1.026x + 76.493$; $R^2 = 0.613$) because of the growing population, the trend actually is best expressed as a wave ($y = 82.571 - 1.116x + 0.079x^2 - 0.001x^3$; $R^2 = 0.775$). (The shape of the wave was determined using standard statistical routines running on the Statview software package.) Several factors account for this shape of the trend line, including population growth, changing monetary exchange rates, and political decisions regarding stocks in the state-managed granary system; but the most important was the development of an integrated market for rice, linking the vast, rice-producing hinterland of Guangxi province to the growing demands of Guangdong province. Detrending the price series eliminates these influences on the movement of prices from one year to the next, making it possible to isolate the impact of annual variation in harvest size upon prices.

    Second, if harvest yields influenced rice prices, then harvest yields and rice prices from the same year cannot be used, since the impact of a deficient harvest would be felt in the following year's prices. Thus to obtain a more accurate reading of the impact of harvest yields on prices, the proper method is to correlate harvest yields with the following year's price. The resulting correlation, then, is between the harvest ratings and the lagged, detrended price series.

Table 11.3. *Correlation of harvest rating with price*

Period	r
1707–1800	−0.353
1707–31	−0.413
1731–58	−0.275
1762–78	−0.203
1778–1800	−0.157
1762–1800	−0.223

tionship between harvest yields and rice prices, it also shows that the relationship became weaker during the course of the eighteenth century.[72] The explanation for this gradual delinking of grain prices from harvest yields, I think, has to do with the growing power and importance of an integrated market for rice, with grain merchants from Guangzhou overseeing the importation of rice from Guangxi. Until the late 1750s, officials supervised the grain trade through the regulation of rice brokerage firms (*mi yahang* 米牙行), creating conditions for profiteering, corruption, and restriction of the rice market. To combat rising grain prices, sometimes in the late 1750s the governor-general abolished the brokerage system, thereby opening the grain market more widely, lowering prices, and increasing the importation of rice from Guangxi.[73] From that time on, deficient harvests in Guangdong sparked price increases in Guangxi, with large imports of rice weakening the connection between the harvest ratings and prices in Guangdong. Nonetheless, though weakening, the relationship between the annual crop yield and rice prices remained inverse.

Not surprisingly, this inverse relationship was so obvious that everyone knew it, and officials commented on it continually in their palace memorials. In 1756, for example, the Liangguang governor-general reported that the early harvest was rated "better than 90 percent." He noted that harvests the two previous years had been rated much lower, with some counties having harvests rated only 60 percent, and then observed: "This truly is a bountiful year. The granary bins are overflowing, and grain prices moder-

---

[72] For an explanation of the periodization in Table 11.3, see Robert B. Marks and Chen Chunsheng, "Price Inflation and Its Social, Economic, and Climatic Context in Guangdong Province, 1707–1800," paper pesented at the 34th International Congress of Asian and African Studies, Hong Kong, August 1994.

[73] Palace memorial from Yang Jingju 楊應琚 dated QL28.6.11, Taipei Palace Museum *Gongzhongdang* 宮中檔 Archives, document #QL015160. I am indebted to Pierre-Étienne Will both for bringing this memorial to my attention and for then making a copy available to me.

ate daily."[74] The Guangdong governor confirmed: "Throughout the province rice prices are moderating, and there is not a village or a neighborhood with shortages. Truly this is the most abundant harvest year in several."[75]

Given Qing officials' knowledge of how the agrarian economy worked, and the fact that officials had their hands on vast mounds of rice price data, harvest ratings estimates, granary stock reports, and even population figures, what is surprising is that no official at the time, at least as far as I am aware, tried to establish with more precision the relationship between the size of the rice harvest and the price of rice.[76] After all, officials were collecting and reporting both harvest ratings and rice prices on a regular basis: would not some ability to predict price behavior have enhanced their bureaucratic effectiveness?

This is not an idle question, for Europeans tried to demonstrate not just a relationship between harvest size and grain prices, but that the relationship could be expressed in mathematical terms. Gregory King (1650–1710), a keen observer of economic activity and population changes in England, sought to establish a regular relationship between an inadequate harvest and cereal prices. "Gregory King's law" posited a geometrical increase in prices for each tenth by which the harvest was below normal. Later economists (Jevons and Bouniatian)[77] refined the relationship between harvest yield and grain prices that King had observed, and expressed it mathematically as an equation of the kind $y = a/(x-b)^2$, where y is the index of the price, x is the harvest as a proportion of normal, and a and b are constants.[78]

---

[74] Memorial dated QL21.6.17, *Qianlong memorials*, vol. 14, p. 647.

[75] Memorial dated QL21.6.17, *Qianlong memorials*, vol. 14, p. 650.

[76] The best candidates would have been Li Xu, one of the Kangxi emperor's most trusted officials, and the Kangxi emperor himself. As mentioned earlier, since at least 1693, the emperor had Li Xu report on climate, harvests, and rice prices. Later, in 1715, the emperor appointed Li Xu to oversee an experiment to introduce a second rice crop into the Suzhou area. When Li Xu reported that the results of the second harvest were less than stellar, the emperor reminded him that he had planted both the first and second crops too late. In subsequent years the experiment yielded better results, and Li Xu reported specific harvest yields, both in terms of seed-to-harvest ratios and per *mu*. See Jonathan D. Spence, *Ts'ao Yin and the K'ang-hsi Emperor: Bondservant and Master* (New Haven: Yale University Press, 1966), pp. 278–81.

[77] For a discussion of King's law, see Slicher van Bath, *Agrarian History of Western Europe*, p. 119; Wilhelm Abel, *Agricultural Fluctuations in Europe from the Thirteenth to the Twentieth Centuries* (New York: St. Martin's Press, 1980), pp. 1–13; and E. A. Wrigley, "Some Reflections on Corn Yields and Prices in Pre-Industrial Economies," in E. A. Wrigley, *People, Cities, and Wealth* (New York: Basil Blackwell, 1987), pp. 92–130.

[78] The equations are: Jevons, $y = 0.824/(x - 0.12)^2$; Bouniatian, $y = 0.757/(x - 0.13)^2$. Bouniatian's formulation is now taken to be more elegant, and will be used in later calculations. For the reasons, see E. A. Wrigley, "Some Reflections on Corn Yields," pp. 92–130.

Table 11.4. *King's law*

Harvest yield	Prices predicted by	
	King	Bouniatian
100%	≈1.00	≈1.00
90%	1.30	1.28
80%	1.80	1.69
70%	2.60	2.33
60%	3.80	3.43
50%	5.50	5.53

The results of calculations from these formulas can be seen in Table 11.4. The table shows, for example, that a harvest 90 percent of normal would result in prices about 130 percent of normal, while a harvest just 50 percent of normal would be accompanied by prices approximately five times normal. What these equations model are situations where grain prices changed at rates different from the changes in harvest size. The reason, according to Slicher van Bath, is that "very slight over-production can make the price drop considerably; the least shortage can drive it up."[79]

King's insight about the mathematical relationship between the size of harvests and changes in grain prices has not only informed classic studies of European agricultural history (such as those by Slicher van Bath and Wilhelm Abel), but has prompted a recent reexamination of the relationship between harvest yields and grain prices by E. A. Wrigley. In his essay, Wrigley uses King's law to examine numerous issues, including the relationship between consumption and sale of grain, the influence of carryover and storage on prices, the variable impact of rising prices on farmers and consumers, the riskiness of farming strategies, the calculation of harvest yields from price series, and the declining marginal returns to labor.[80] Although Wrigley regarded his essay as "speculative," he did argue that the issue of harvest yields was critically important for understanding the dynamics of European economic history. Clearly, then, modern historians have used King's insights to illuminate aspects of European economic and demographic history. What might King's model tell us about eighteenth-century Guangdong?

[79] Slicher van Bath, *Agrarian History of Western Europe*, pp. 118–19.
[80] E. A. Wrigley, "Some Reflections on Corn Yields," pp. 92–130. Wrigley attributes the articulation of King's law to the economist Davenant, who published works based upon King's unpublished papers.

Table 11.5. *Price changes following abundant or deficient harvests*

Year	Rating	Price
1723	100%	79
1726	73%	127
Change (%)	−27%	61%
1739	89%	95
1742	70%	138
Change (%)	−21%	45%
1758	81%	189
1761	90%	128
Change (%)	11%	−32%
1776	83%	156
1777	78%	165
Change (%)	−6%	6%
1784	90%	151
1787	73%	162
Change (%)	−19%	7%

GREGORY KING'S LAW APPLIED TO CHINA'S HARVEST YIELD ESTIMATES

The fact that Chinese officials did not produce mathematical models of the relationship between harvest size and rice prices does not mean that such models cannot apply to China's agrarian history. The question is: How well do the models suggested by King compare to actual rice-price behavior in Guangdong during the eighteenth century? The results for five periods are shown in Table 11.5. What these data show is that harvest failures in Guangdong did not cause prices to increase as much as predicted by King's law. In the first two cases, for example, harvest deficiencies of 27 and 21 percent produced price increases of 61 and 45 percent respectively, not the 80–160 percent increases modeled by King's law. Nonetheless, if King's law does not fit the Chinese case in its details, the general point is well taken: deficient (or good) harvests tended to have a more or less predictable effect upon rice-price behavior. How predictable can be statistically analyzed in terms of a regression equation relating harvest yields (as reflected in the officials' harvest ratings estimates) and rice prices.

In Nanhai county, the price of common rice in Guangzhou tended to decline by 25 taels per 100 *shi*, or something on the order of 10–15 percent, for each one *fen* increase in the harvest rating (e.g., from 7 to 8 *fen*, or 70 to 80 percent).[81] The slope of the regression line, in other words, is a rough guide to how much rice prices could have been expected to decline with each *fen* increase in the officials' harvest rating estimates. To be sure, the regression equation accounts for only some of the variability of the prices ($R^2 = 0.211$), and the regression equation paints a linear rather than a geometric relationship between harvest quality and prices. But the regression equation nonetheless demonstrates two important points: (1) as harvest yields increased, rice prices decreased (and vice versa); and (2) the decline (or increase) in prices in Guangdong was substantially less than that suggested by King's law.

Eighteenth-century Guangdong was not England, after all, and while the general relationship between harvests and prices holds for China, the specific proportions suggested by King's law do not. These data suggest that while rice prices in eighteenth-century South China were indeed sensitive to changes in harvest yields, there was less volatility in the relationship than in England. Moreover, after 1761, rice prices tended to become even less variable than in the preceding decades, accentuating the difference with the English record (see Table 11.6). It will also be recalled that just three times in the eighteenth century did Guangdong experience two consecutive years of deficient harvests.

Compared with England, this record is rather remarkable. According to W. G. Hoskins's reconstruction of English harvests, during the first sixty years of the eighteenth century (his study ends with 1759), England already had four periods of two or more years of consecutive deficient harvests during which prices increased 25–50 percent over "normal," and he suggests that the remaining forty years of the century were about the same.[82] In England, in short, there were perhaps six or more times of at least two consecutive years of deficient harvests, twice the incidence recorded in Guangdong. Thus not only did South China experience fewer deficient harvests than England, when the harvest was deficient grain prices tended to increase less than suggested by King's law.

Besides the lower frequency of deficient harvests in the eighteenth century, other differences between Guangdong and England are apparent. Despite a common doubling of the population during the eighteenth century (from 10 to 20 million in Guangdong province and from less than 5 to 9 million in England), grain prices in England rose 250 to 300

---

[81] The regression equation is $y = 25x + 379$.

[82] W. G. Hoskins, "Harvest Fluctuations and English Economic History, 1620–1759," p. 16. The consecutive years of deficient harvests were 1707–11 (a four-year run), 1727–28, 1739–40, and 1756–57.

Table 11.6. *Variation of rice prices in Guangdong*

Period	Mean	St. dev.	Coef. var.
1707–31	0.81	0.22	27.2
1731–58	1.22	0.32	25.9
1762–1800	1.52	0.14	9.0
1707–20	0.81	0.23	28.0
1721–40	0.81	0.21	26.0
1741–60	1.42	0.21	14.9
1761–80	1.53	0.16	10.5
1781–1800	1.49	0.11	7.1

percent,[83] while in Guangdong prices increased just 100 percent. According to Abel, with grain prices outstripping wages, European farmers rapidly accumulated capital and reinvested substantial amounts in expanding the cultivated land area and improving productivity. By contrast, in Guangdong, as I have argued elsewhere,[84] the increase in grain prices after 1762 did not keep pace with population growth, leading one to suspect that the incentive for investing in agricultural improvements began to evaporate.

What accounts for the differences in the harvest record and price histories of South China and England? Although this chapter is about climate, climatic factors are not a likely explanation. As we have already seen, temperature variations are highly correlated around the northern hemisphere, so that both England and China probably experienced similar temperature variations. As a common factor, climatic variability thus is an unlikely candidate to account for differences. Explanations thus should look to different institutional arrangements for producing, distributing, and consuming food. Without delving into the English case, I would like to highlight a few features of the agricultural economy in South China that strike me as relevant to the comparison.

The first and perhaps most important difference is that South China peasant farmers produced two harvests in one year, while English farmers produced just one. While it is true that the warmer climate in South China was a necessary condition for peasant farmers to produce two crops, it was

---

[83] See Abel, *Agricultural Fluctuations in Europe*, ch. 7. Abel points out that the price increases sparked a debate over the causes, much as the grain price increases in the early 1740s prompted the Qianlong emperor to initiate a similar debate. To my knowledge, no one has yet studied this potentially interesting comparison.

[84] Marks and Chen, "Price Inflation and Its Social, Economic, and Climatic context."

not a sufficient condition: technological improvements coupled with larger labor supplies (a larger, more dense population) pushed the development of double cropping. With the innovation of double cropping, then, over the course of two years Chinese farmers had four harvests, thereby significantly decreasing the risk of losing an entire year's output, while their English counterparts had just two.

Further reducing the risk of farming in South China, where harvest output was so dependent on rainfall levels and grain price so sensitive to harvest yield, peasant farmers and state bureaucrats took whatever mitigating measures they could to smooth out the impact of weather on rice production and market supplies. For farmers, managed and manageable irrigation lessened the impact of drier years, which were more usual in the second half of the eighteenth century, while excess rainfall (but not destructive typhoons) had little impact on irrigated fields but certainly improved the yield of dry fields. During the Qianlong period, the state also encouraged and supported water-control projects, and evidence from local gazetteers suggests that the amount of irrigated land doubled during the course of the eighteenth century.[85]

Grain supplies also improved not only as a function of better control of harvest yields through irrigation, but also because of public and private storage of grain. Not much is known about the extent of private storage of grain, but the Chinese state, primarily through the granary and famine relief system, did what it could to mitigate the harmful effects of food shortages caused by drought or flood, selling granary stocks at discounted prices in the spring before the first harvest came in, and providing relief to areas devastated by drought or flood. Clearly, massive state intervention into the grain markets prevented prices from going as high as they otherwise might have in bad times.[86] And over and above better technology and active state intervention into management of the food supply, by the middle of the eighteenth century an integrated market for rice had emerged in South China, linking the economically advanced but chronically food-

---

[85] The story of land reclamation, the spread of irrigation works, and the construction of water-control projects obviously is larger than can be told here. For a general overview of Qing period land reclamation policies and programs, see Peng Yuxin 彭雨新, *Qing-dai tudi kaiken shi* 清代土地开垦史 [A history of opening new land under the Qing dynasty] (Beijing: Nongye CBS, 1990). For an extensive bibliography of works on irrigation and water control, see Mark Elvin et al., *Japanese Studies on the History of Water Control in China: A Selected Bibliography* (Canberra: Institute of Advanced Studies, Australian National University, 1994).

[86] For a discussion of the granaries and their impact on grain prices, see Pierre-Étienne Will and R. Bin Wong, *Nourish the People: The State Civilian Granary System in China, 1650–1850* (Ann Arbor: University of Michigan Press, 1991), esp. ch. 13.

deficient region in the Pearl River delta to a vast rice-producing hinterland in Guangxi province.[87]

All of these factors – improved technology as represented by the extension of irrigation works, the state granary system, and an efficient market mechanism – served to lessen the impact of climatic changes upon harvest yields and rice prices in South China. A detailed examination of similar arrangements in England (or more broadly in Europe) would go well beyond the scope of this chapter, but I doubt that the agrarian economies there were as protected from climatic fluctuations. But even without a more rigorous comparison, the observed difference in price behavior in South China as opposed to England suggests that the relationships among climatic changes, harvest yields, and grain prices are complex and cannot readily be reduced to universal formulas. The significant differences – between the incidence of deficient harvests, the variability of prices, and the increases in grain prices – cannot be attributed directly to climatic differences, but rather to the different institutional responses of the people of South China and England to the challenges posed to agriculture by climatic change. And in creating this response, the peasant farmers, state bureaucrats, and grain merchants of South China managed better than their English counterparts to even out the adverse effects of climate upon their respective agricultural economies.

CONCLUSION

By way of conclusion, I would like to comment on the significance of my findings for three other aspects of Chinese history. First, the linkage of climatic change to grain prices is relevant to our understanding of the theories of subsistence and demographic crises[88] and their application to China's demographic history. Whether in the classical model (which excludes the effects of epidemic disease) or in the modified form proposed by Dupâquier, both begin with "climatic shocks" to the system and conclude with elevated mortality.[89] Certainly the evidence from late-imperial South

---

[87] See Marks, "Rice Prices, Food Supply, and Market Structure."

[88] For a discussion of the linkages to the economy, see especially Andrew Appleby, *Famine in Tudor and Stuart England* (Stanford, Calif.: Stanford University Press, 1978), ch. 1.

[89] In the classical model, as summarized by Dupâquier, "demographic crises are caused by poor harvests which are produced by climatic shocks (a rainy spring as in 1693, a 'Siberian' winter as in 1709)." Critiquing the classical model, Dupâquier includes the role of epidemic disease and fungal plant infections as causal agents in elevating mortality levels. Jacques Dupâquier, "Demographic Crises and Subsistence Crises in France, 1650–1725," in John Walter and Roger Schofield, eds., *Famine, Disease and the Social Order in Early Modern Society* (New York and Cambridge: Cambridge University Press, 1989), pp. 189–99.

China presented here supports these general models of demographic crises: climatic shocks did decrease harvest yields, which in turn elevated grain prices and contributed to increased mortality. But the comparative perspective offered by the South China case demands that the model be modified to take account of the institutional arrangements that lessened the impact both of climatic shocks upon harvest yields and of deficient harvests upon grain-price increases, and it suggests too that not all price peaks were accompanied by increased mortality.

Nonetheless, if the model of demographic crises as suggested both by the classical model and by Dupâquier is fundamentally sound – and I think it is – and if the agricultural economy of South China had developed in such a way as to lessen the impact of climatic shocks upon harvest yields and rice prices, then South China most likely experienced fewer and less severe mortality crises than England or France. Since comparable demographic data are virtually nonexistent for China, a full testing of this hypothesis may never be possible. Nonetheless, it does suggest that in South China at least, the linkage between climatic shocks and mortality crises as mediated through the agrarian economy had been substantially weakened, if not altogether severed, earlier than in Europe, and without the concurrent creation of an industrial economy. On the one hand, this difference may be seen as a substantial achievement. But the irony, of course, is that the subsequent growth in China's population may well have precluded the emergence of self-sustaining economic growth based on industrial development.

Second, the impact of climate on agriculture and food supplies is significant for understanding China's late-imperial economy. In his work on China's macroregional cycles of economic development, G. William Skinner speculated that "in an agrarian society where agriculture accounts for the bulk of the national product, it is hardly unreasonable to suppose that a cooling climate could lead to economic distress and depress economic activity," and vice versa.[90] As a variation on the Labrousse thesis regarding eighteenth-century French trade cycles, this connection is broadly true, for the long-term temperature trend during the Qing – rising from the cold 1680s to a peak around 1800 and then dropping to new lows in the 1840s – corresponds to Lingnan's regional economic cycle. Certainly all the evidence I have marshaled here supports the idea that harvest yields and grain prices fluctuated less in the last half of the eighteenth century than the first. But as I have shown in this chapter, the linkages among hemispheric temperature fluctuations, harvest yields, and rice prices are more complex than can be modeled in a simple causal model. As a consequence

---

[90] G. William Skinner, "Presidential Address," *Journal of Asian Studies* 44.2 (Feb. 1985), p. 285.

of the relative success in sheltering harvest yields from adverse climatic influences, by the end of the eighteenth century, rice prices in Guangdong underperformed the growth of population, providing disincentives for any further investment in improving the productivity of fields devoted to rice. If this can be interpreted as a major turning point in Lingnan's regional economic cycle, it was reached around 1800, coincident with the downturn in temperatures. The links between climate and regional economic cycles thus may be more complex than those hypothesized by Labrousse and Skinner, with declines in agricultural productivity coming even in periods of relative warmth.

Finally, the story of the linkage of climatic change to grain prices as mediated through harvest yields is significant for our conception of the role of the Qing state. In reflecting on the nature of the primary sources used in this chapter – the harvest ratings estimates and the monthly grain-price series – I am struck by how bold the Chinese state was not merely in deciding early in the eighteenth century that it would routinely and systematically collect data regarding harvest yields and grain prices to better assess the condition of the empire's food supply, but also in implementing the system. To appreciate the magnitude of the Qing state's accomplishment, one need only think about the vast flooding of the American Midwest in the summer of 1993 and the attempts of the U.S. government to assess the extent of crop damage by the use of remote-sensing satellites and its agricultural extension agent. And then how did Secretary of Agriculture Mike Espy convey his findings to the American people and the commodity markets? By estimating that the corn harvest would be just 6 percent below expectations, and concluding that with the grain in storage the deficient harvest should not affect grain prices. One is tempted to conclude that with regard to estimating harvest yields and monitoring grain prices, the Chinese state was positively modern. Or would it be more correct to think of the modern state as positively Chinese?

Changes in Climate, Land, and Human Efforts

THE PRODUCTION OF WET-FIELD RICE IN JIANGNAN DURING THE MING AND QING DYNASTIES

LI BOZHONG

PRELIMINARY REMARKS[1]

Farm output results from a combination of human exertions and the natural environment, the most relevant aspects of the latter being climate and land. Traditional Chinese agricultural theorists referred to climate as "Heaven" (*Tian* 天), "the seasons of Heaven" (*Tianshi* 天時), or "the Way of Heaven" (*Tian Dao* 天道). Land was "Earth" (*Di* 地), "benefits drawn from the Earth" (*Di li* 地利), or "the way of the Earth" (*Di Dao* 地道). Human efforts were "man" (*ren* 人), "the coordination of the people" (*renhe* 人和),[2] "human doings" (*renshi* 人事), or "the Way of men" (*ren Dao* 人道). Together they constituted the three basic elements of farm production.

With this doctrine of the "Three Powers" (*san cai* 三才) as its nucleus,

---

For valuable criticisms of my original paper presented to the 1993 Conference in Hong Kong on the History of the Environment in China, I would like to offer my thanks to Professor You Xiuling of the Agricultural History Unit of Zhejiang University of Agriculture; Professor Li Genpan of the Institute of Economics of the Chinese Academy of Social Sciences; Professor Guo Songyi of the Institute of History of the Chinese Academy of Social Sciences; Professor Mark Elvin of the Research School of Pacific and Asian Studies of the Australian National University; and Professor Liu Ts'ui-jung of the Institute of Economics of the Academia Sinica.

[1] Please note that units for the volume of grain (*shi* 石) used during the Song, Ming, and Qing dynasties varied in the ratios 0.6185, 1.000, and 0.9644, respectively, while the unit for the area of farmland varied in the ratios 0.8313, 1.000, and 0.9610. See Gang Deng, *Development Versus Stagnation: Technological Continuity and Agricultural Progress in Pre-modern China* (Westport, Conn.: Greenwood, 1993), p. xxv. Thus *shi* per *mu* varied in the ratios 0.744, 1.000, and 1.004, which is significant for comparisons between late medieval and late traditional times, but not as between Ming and Qing.

[2] An alternative rendering is "appropriate human action," to indicate the aspect of adaptation to natural circumstances. [Trans.]

traditional Chinese agricultural theorists produced penetrating explanations of the interactions between the three elements just mentioned and farm output.[3] By the Ming and Qing dynasties, the thinkers
and agronomists of the lower Yangzi valley ("Jiangnan") had elucidated
this further. It was the view of Zhang Lüxiang 張履祥 that "the essential concern of agriculture and sericulture is to make use of the Way of
Heaven, to depend on human labor power, and to promote the benefits
provided by the Earth. This is an absolute truth."[4] According to Lu Shiyi 陸
世儀:

> It is not only in military matters that one must take into account seasons and
> weather, the advantages afforded by terrain, and appropriate human action.
> This applies to everything, and with particular force to farmland. "Seasons
> and weather" refer to flood and drought, "advantages afforded by terrain" to
> whether the soil is fertile or barren, and "appropriate human action" to the
> opening up of land and its good management. . . . We have to place the
> greatest weight [of practical concern] on appropriate human action, with
> land in second place, and the weather last. But [climate and] the weather is
> the element of the greatest [ultimate] importance among the three, followed
> by land, and with human action last. Thus, if rainfall and sunshine are
> appropriate, poor-quality land can give as good a yield as top-quality land. If
> the land is richly fertile, a low-level farmer can get as good a yield as a top-level
> farmer. The reason for this is that there are big differences in labor inputs in
> the above cases (*lao-yi dun shu gu ye* 勞逸頓殊故也). Nonetheless, if one has
> the advantage of [good] weather and of [good] land, and adds to them (*ji zhi*

[3] Li Genpan 李根蟠, *Zhongguo gudai nongye* 中国古代农业 [China's premodern agriculture in
antiquity] (Tianjin: Tianjin jiaoyu CBS, 1991), ch. 3, sec. 5, provides a complete analysis:
" 'Heaven' and 'Earth' indicate the weather and the soils, the topography, and suchlike
elements of the natural environment of farming, while 'man' indicates its core productive
component. Farming represents the unification of natural reproduction and economic
reproduction. Insofar as they reproduce naturally, farm products (or, in other words, the
harvests) are inseparable from their circumambient natural environment. Insofar as they
constitute economic reproduction, they are inseparable from those in charge of farming.
Agriculture consists of the mutual interdependencies – the ecological system of mutual
control, and the economic system – that link farm products, the natural environment, and
human beings. This intrinsic character of farming is already touched on in the propositions
of the *Shenshi* 審時 [Agricultural timing] in the *Lü-shi chunqiu* 呂氏春秋 [The 'Springs and
Autumns' of Mr. Lü] (third century B.C.) relating to the interconnections between the farm
crops and the 'Three Powers.' "
[4] Zhang Lüxiang, *Bu nongshu* 補農書 [Supplement to the agricultural encyclopedia (of Mr
Shen)], "zonglun," in Chen Hengli 陈恒力 and Wang Da 王达, eds., *"Bu nongshu" jiaoshi* 补
农书校释 [The "Supplement to the agricultural encyclopedia," annotated and translated],
rev. ed. (Beijing: Nongye CBS; 1983), p. 152. An alternative rendering of the last clause (*zui
shi zhi-cheng wu-wei* 最是至誠無偽) would be "The activities farming and sericulture are the
most practical." [Trans.]

濟之) with appropriate human action, one will even so always reap more than others. This is why we must honor appropriate human action.[5]

This provides a relatively correct explanation of the roles of climate and weather, land, and human efforts, while further elucidating, at least to a first approximation, the existence of certain types of mutual dependence, control, and substitutivity among them.

These elements are always in a process of ongoing change. Thus if one of them changes, this induces changes in the others, leading to changes in agriculture. In this sense there is no "stagnation" in agriculture, and traditional Chinese farming provides no exception to this rule. Since China has long been an agrarian country, agriculture has occupied the most important position in the national economy; an inquiry into the changes in the three main elements that constitute agriculture, and the influences these changes have had, is of special significance for its socioeconomic history.

The present story focuses on Jiangnan during Ming-Qing times because of the comparative abundance of historical documentation. The period may be more precisely defined as the late Ming, from the Jiajing reign (1522–66) until the end of the dynasty, and the early and middle Qing, from the Manchu conquest until the end of the Daoguang reign in 1850. In other words, from the early sixteenth century to the middle of the nineteenth. This starting point has been chosen partly because prior to this date documentation is comparatively sparse, and partly because, in the view of many scholars, the development of the Jiangnan economy went through a turning point broadly around the Jiajing reign, so that it was clearly different afterward from what it had been before.[6] The reason for placing the terminus in the Daoguang reign (1821–50) is that this reign was followed by the most extensive socioeconomic destruction witnessed by the region for two millennia, in the form of the Taiping Rebellion.[7] These points of chronological demarcation are clearly broadly identical with the period that most Mainland historians call "the sprouts of capitalism." I shall leave this latter question to one side, but it may be affirmed that the development of the Chinese economy during this period, especially in this

---

[5] Lu Shiyi, *Sibian-lu jiyao* 思辯彔輯要 [Summary of the "Record of Thinking"] (N.p.: Jiangsu shuju, 1877), *j.* 11, "Lun qu-tian."

[6] Fu Yiling 傅衣凌, *Mingdai Jiangnan shimin jingji shitan* 明代江南市民經濟試談 [An exploration of the economy of the urban residents of Jiangnan in the Ming dynasty] (Shanghai: Shanghai renmin CBS, 1957), p. 1.

[7] The population of Jiangsu, Anhui, and Zhejiang may have been reduced to almost half its previous level. See Dwight Perkins, *Agricultural Development in China, 1368–1968* (Chicago: Aldine, 1969), pp. 210–12.

region, has its own particularity, and constituted a distinctive phase, which makes this periodization a rational one.

The term "Jiangnan" used in this chapter is another name for the Yangzi delta or the drainage basin of Lake Tai. It comprises the eight Ming-Qing prefectures of Suzhou (plus the Taicang department, which was split off from Suzhou), Songjiang, Changzhou, Zhenjiang, Yingtian (or Jiangning), Hangzhou, Jiaxing, and Huzhou. The principal reason for selecting these boundaries is that these prefectures are cut off from the areas outside them by the Yangzi River to their north, the Qiantang River to their south, the ocean to their east, and several lines of mountains to their west. Internally they form a dense network of waterways consisting of a lake (Lake Tai), two streams (the Jing 荆溪 and the Tiao 苕溪, the main sources of Lake Tai), "Three Rivers" (*san jiang* 三江),[8] "Five Lakes" (*wu hu* 五湖),[9] and numerous creeks, canals, lakes and marshes, and dammed reservoirs. In consequence, this region not only has a high degree of hydrological and ecological unity, but is also an economic area with unusually dense internal interrelationships. In Ming-Qing times people saw its characteristic economic and cultural traits as setting it apart from the other areas of Jiangsu and Zhejiang provinces, hence the term "Jiangnan," and the justification for treating these eight prefectures as a distinct unity.[10]

CHANGES IN CLIMATE, LAND, AND HUMAN ACTION IN JIANGNAN DURING THE MING-QING PERIOD

Climate should not be confused with weather, and refers to the state of the long-term macroclimate of the earth. The most important components of climate that have a close connection with agriculture are the energy of solar radiation, duration of sunlight, temperature, and precipitation. When the present chapter (somewhat metaphorically) speaks of "earth," this not only includes such external characteristics as geology, geomorphology, and hydrology, but also such internal properties as the nature of soils, their structure, composition, fertility, depth of arable layer, permeability, and acidity or alkalinity. Mainland Chinese agronomists normally consider the

---

[8] A term whose identification is debated but which most ancient historians regard as indicating the main waterways once draining Lake Tai into the sea.

[9] Again debatable as regards identification, but all lakes on the Jiangnan plain.

[10] See Li Bozhong, "Jian lun 'Jiangnan diqu'-de jieding" 简论 "江南地区" 的界定 [A simple discussion of the demarcation of the "Jiangnan region"], in *Zhongguo shehui-jingji-shi yanjiu* 中国社会经济史研究 4 (1990).

key elements of climate and land as light, heat, oxygen and carbon dioxide, soil, water, and fertility.[11] By combining with each other in determinate patterns these elements collectively constitute the basic natural environment of agriculture. Our inquiry into the changes in the environment of wet-field rice production in Jiangnan during the Ming-Qing period will essentially concentrate on the changes in these elements. When we speak of changes in "human efforts" we shall likewise focus on such aspects as large-scale improvements in hydraulics and land management, and advances in cultivation technology and their diffusion.

CHANGES IN CLIMATE

Zhu Kezhen 竺可楨 did the initial work on changes in the climate in China (and particularly in Jiangnan) during the last five hundred years.[12] This field of research has flourished during the last ten years but seems to have concentrated on fluctuations in temperature and on disasters due to floods and droughts.

In 1972 Zhu Kezhen showed that between 1400 and 1900 China had two periods of warm winters (1550–1600 and 1720–1830) and three periods of cold winters (1470–1520, 1620–1720, and 1840–90). The seventeenth century was the coldest of these latter, especially between 1650 and 1700. Zhu's sources were mainly local gazetteers from eastern and central China, and thus his conclusions may be taken as representing the general trend of changes in temperature in Jiangnan.[13] Research undertaken from a different angle during the 1980s confirmed that the trends signaled by Zhu were in the main correct.[14] Minor divergences aside, researchers agreed that the seventeenth century and the middle of the nineteenth

---

[11] Fang Zaihui 方载辉 et al., *Zhejiang-de gengzuo zhidu* 浙江耕作制度 [The system of farming in Zhejiang] (Hangzhou: Zhejiang kexue-jishu CBS, 1984), pp. 2–3; Guo Wentao 郭文韬 et al., *Zhongguo nongye keji fazhan shiluë* 中国农业科技发展史略 [A short history of the development of agricultural science and technology in China] (Beijing: Zhongguo kexue-jishu CBS, 1988), p. 87.

[12] Zhu Kezhen, "Lishi shidai shijie qihou-de bodong" 历史时代世界气候的波动 [Fluctuations in world climate during the historical period], *Renmin ribao* 人民日报 (Beijing), May 7, 1961.

[13] Zhu Kezhen, "Zhongguo jin-wuqian-nian-lai qihou bianqian-de chubu yanjiu" 中国近五千年来气候变迁的初步研究 [Preliminary researches on the changes in climate in China during the last five thousand years], *Kexue tongbao* 1 (1972).

[14] Ren Zhenqiu 任振球, "Zhongguo jin-wuqian-nian-lai qihou-de yichang-qi ji qi tianwen chengyin tantao" 中国近五千年来气候的异常期及其天文成因探讨 [An inquiry into the abnormal periods in China's climate during the last five thousand years and contributing astronomical factors], *Nongye kaogu* 农业考古 1 (1986); Wang Zichun 汪子春 and Gao Jian'guo 高建国, "Zhongguo jin-erqianwubai-nian-lai zhiwu chonghua lishi jilu-zhi wuhou

century were cold periods in China (including Jiangnan), and that the later sixteenth century and the eighteenth century were warm periods. It also became apparent from some of their work that the mean annual temperature in Jiangnan during the eighteenth century was about 1°C warmer than it had been in the seventeenth.[15]

On the basis of many years of meteorological records it is broadly true to say that for every additional 100 meters in height the mean annual temperature falls by 0.45°C (about 0.42° in winter and 0.51° in summer), while precipitation increases and hours of sunlight and radiant energy decrease. Thus, if the mean annual temperature were to fall by 1°C, the climate of the present-day Jiangnan plain would be close to, or slightly worse than, that of the present-day hill country in southern Zhejiang. In other words, the mean annual temperature would fall from above 16°C to below 15.5°C; the total annual warmth received in the range between 10° and 20° would decrease from 4,100°C to below 4,000°C; the mean quantity of radiation would decline from above 110–14 to below 101–05 kilocalories per square centimeter; the annual hours of sunshine would diminish from in excess of 2,000 hours to under 1,900; while annual precipitation would increase from less than 1,200mm to more than 1,500mm.[16] The climate in the eighteenth century was marginally cooler than it is today, from which it may be deduced that the climate of the Jiangnan plain in the seventeenth century was slightly more cold and overcast, and more humid, than that of the hilly districts in the mountains of southern Zhejiang is at the present time.

Zheng Zhaojing's 郑肇经 research on floods and droughts in Jiangnan during the Ming-Qing period suggests that floods, and hence a rainy climate, were predominant in the four hundred years from the sixteenth to the nineteenth century, apart from 1523–68 and 1625–62, which were dominated by droughts, and hence a dry climate. During the last flood-dominated period, however, namely that from 1663 to 1900, the relative annual frequency of floods was only 60 percent, whereas in the two preceding rainy (flood-dominated) periods the corresponding rates were 85 percent and 90 percent. Likewise the percentage of "major floods" out of all floods in the final period was 29 percent, lower than the 36 percent and 32

---

yanjiu" 中国近二千五百年来值物重花历史记录之物候研究 [Phenological researches on historical records relating to the reflowering of plants in China during the last two thousand five hundred years], *Nongye kaogu* 1 and 2 (1985); and Wang Yejian [Yeh-chien Wang] 王業鍵, "Secular trends of rice prices in the Yangtze delta, 1632–1935," in T. Rawski and L. Li, eds., *Chinese History in Economic Perspective* (Berkeley: University of California Press, 1992), citing the work of Zhang Peiyuan [Piyuan] 張丕遠 et al.

[15] Ren Zhenqiu, "Abnormal periods in China's climate," fig. 1.

[16] Fang Zaihui et al., *Zhejiang farming*, pp. 48, 50, 53, 61, and table 2-2.

percent levels for the two preceding periods. The frequency of floods during the Ming dynasty (1368–1644) was one in 3.7 years, while during the Qing dynasty (1644–1911) it was one in 4.0 years.[17] The same trend of falling frequency from the Ming to the Qing is shown by Fang Zaihui's figures on floods in the three prefectures of Hangzhou, Jiaxing, and Huzhou, namely one flood every 1.3 years under the Ming, and one in every 1.7 years under the Qing.[18] Exceptionally severe floods and droughts, defined as those affecting more than two-thirds of the entire area, had the following pattern: in the sixteenth century there were three such floods and two droughts; in the seventeenth century there were two such floods and two droughts, both types of disaster manifesting on these occasions the greatest severity for the entire period; in the eighteenth century there was one such flood; and in the nineteenth century there were two such floods and two droughts.[19]

There was thus a degree of correlation[20] in Jiangnan between the changes in rainfall implied by Ming-Qing flood and drought statistics and the changes in temperature discussed earlier. Floods to some extent varied inversely with the temperature. The main reason for this is that the climate of eastern China belongs to the regime of the East Asian monsoon: rain falls when northward-moving water vapor from the tropical southwest Pacific meets cold air moving south from northern Asia. If the temperature falls, the warm air over southeastern China lacks the strength to continue on northward once it has reached the lower Yangzi valley, and is obliged to remain here, where for a long period it forms an unstable sawtooth-shaped front with the cold northern air, causing prolonged rains and continuing overcast skies. Since the main part of Jiangnan, the Jiangnan plain, is low-lying and easily inundated, a slight increase in precipitation can cause flooding. Floods have historically been the main natural disaster in the region, and prolonged rains their chief cause.[21] Rains and overcast weather for an extended period have a serious impact on both the number of hours

---

[17] Zheng Zhaojing, ed., *Taihu shuili jishu shi* 太湖水利技术史 [A history of the technology of water control on Lake Tai] (Beijing: Nongye CBS, 1987), p. 255.

[18] Fang Zaihui et al., *Zhejiang farming*, p. 90.

[19] Zheng Zhaojing, *Lake Tai water control*, ch. 10.

[20] Limited by periods of cold winters (e.g., 1620–1720) partially overlapping with dry spells (e.g., 1625–62).

[21] In the Lake Tai region, from A.D. 300 to 1900, the frequency of floods was about twice that of droughts. Of the floods, some 70% of those for which the causes have been recorded were the result of prolonged rains. See Zheng Zhaojing, *Lake Tai water control*, p. 240. Since there is an abundance of groundwater in Jiangnan and a fully developed irrigation system, droughts caused by an insufficiency of rainfall have not on the whole been severe, with the exception of those in a few high-lying areas, and in a few years in which rain has been especially short.

of sunshine and the intensity of the radiation. In Jiangnan they normally occur between the fifth and eighth months of the traditional lunar calendar,[22] when the hours of sunlight and intensity of radiation reach a potential maximum.[23]

CHANGES IN THE LAND

There were both natural and anthropogenic changes in the Jiangnan terrain. Among the former were the silting up of the exits of Lake Tai to the sea, and the reduction of the zone affected by the tide. Among the latter were projects for water control and land management.

Most of those who have studied water control in Jiangnan under the Ming and Qing have not valued its achievements highly. The prevailing view is that even if the officials of this time did to some degree exert themselves, what they were able to do was constrained by the lack of unified objectives and a long-term unified strategy. As a result, it is maintained, the entire water-control system fell into disorder, and the capacity to handle disasters declined.[24]

There is a certain rationale for this view, but it would seem that it is hard to say that it is soundly based. There were limits to the technical capacity of the period to prevent major natural changes in the terrain, such as whether the exits to the sea of Lake Tai flowed freely or were silted up or changed their courses, or the zone under tidal influence altered. Deeper study is needed to determine if the reasons for any disorder in the Jiangnan water-control system were ultimately natural or anthropogenic. Whether the major natural changes in the terrain in the last analysis harmed Jiangnan agriculture or benefited it also needs reexamination. Thus, changes in the zone under tidal influence (which were linked with changes in Lake Tai's exits to the sea) may have been detrimental to the cultivation of wet-field rice in the coastal districts in northeastern Jiangnan, such as Taicang and the northern parts of Suzhou and Songjiang, but possibly beneficial to the coastal districts along the Qiantang River in the Southeast, that is, the

---

[22] Zheng Zhaojing, *Lake Tai water control*, pp. 242–43.

[23] Fang Zaihui et al., *Zhejiang farming*, p. 61, compare the present-day Hang-Jia-Hu plain with the hill country in the mountainous region of southern Zhejiang, finding that the plain enjoys more hours of sunlight, "richer illumination," and a comparatively greater intensity of solar radiation. The main reason for the difference is that there is relatively less rain, and that the dry period in the second half of the year is relatively prolonged.

[24] Zheng Zhaojing, *Lake Tai water control*, pp. 94–95; Philip Huang [Huang Zongzhih 黃宗智], *The Peasant Family and Rural Development in the Yangzi Delta, 1350–1988* (Stanford, Calif.: Stanford University Press, 1990), pp. 34–35 and 38–40.

eastern part of Hangzhou prefecture. Overall, these changes may have helped wet-field rice cultivation in the region more than they hurt it.[25] What is more, the theory that the capacity of the Jiangnan water-control system to handle disasters declined does not fit with the lower frequency of floods in Jiangnan under the Qing as compared with the Ming. Even if this lower frequency was the consequence of the climatic factors recounted above, there is no doubt that the water-control system still played an important function. The historical record also shows that advances in the system also brought about a manifest reduction in the frequency of floods in certain areas that were particularly susceptible to them. A typical example is the county of Qingpu 青浦縣, one of the lowest-lying areas in Jiangnan. After the method of building polders by "circumvallation" (wei 圍) and "striking head-on" (qiang 搶) advocated by Sun Jun 孫峻 had been put into effect, the county suffered no more floods for the next thirty years.[26] In summary, we have to a large degree to attribute the credit for improvements in water control in Jiangnan during the period under consideration to the water-control system.

Important improvements in the land took place in Ming-Qing times, although the scholarly community has not in the past assigned much importance to them. Recently, Hamashima Atsutoshi 浜島敦俊 has expressed the view that while the opening up of lowland fields in Jiangnan was already basically complete by the early Ming, large-scale improvement began in the middle of the fifteenth century, reaching what was by and large completion by the middle of the seventeenth.[27] Kitada Hideto's investigation into the ecology of Jiangnan farmland has shown that even at the beginning of the nineteenth century, in certain areas, particularly along the eastern seaboard, there was still a fairly large quantity of land awaiting improvement.[28] In Morita Akira's 森田明 view, the key to improving farmland was drainage, and the method most widely relied on was the collective

[25] Kitada Hideto 北田英人, "Chūgoku Kōnan sankakusu ni okeru kanchō chiiki no hensen" [Changes in the tidal zone in the Jiangnan delta in China], Tōyō gakuhō 63 (1982).

[26] Sun Jun, Zhu-yu tushuo 築圩圖説 [Illustrated explanation of how to build polders], 1869 ed., preface by Chen Qiyuan 陳其元.

[27] Hamashima Atsutoshi, "Tudi kaifa yu keshang huodong – Mingdai zhongqi Jiangnan dizhuzhi touzi huodong" 土地開發與客商活動 — 明代中期江南地主之投資活動 [Land development and the activities of nonlocal merchants – the investment activities of the landlords of Jiangnan during the mid-Ming], in Zhongyang yanjiu-yuan di-er-jie guoji Hanxue huiyi lunwen-ji 中央研究院第二屆國際漢學會議論文集 (Taipei: Academia Sinica, 1989).

[28] Kitada Hideto, Sō-Gen-Min-Shin-ki Chūgoku Kōnan sankakusu no nōgyō no shinka to nōson shukōgyō no hattatsu ni kansuru no kenkyū [A study of agricultural progress and the development of village handicrafts in the Jiangnan delta during Song, Yuan, Ming, and Qing times], Report on the results of research (Tokyo: mimeographed by Sutaa shōkai, 1988).

operation of square-pallet chain-pumps (*longgu-che* 龍骨車 or *dapeng-che* 大棚車) in large numbers.[29] Although this method of operation had appeared long before, it became widespread only in Qing times. My view is therefore that the process of improving farmland only reached completion by the middle of the nineteenth century.

Prior to the middle of the fifteenth century, the main objective in the development of land in Jiangnan was to increase the cultivated acreage, or what Hamashima calls "extensive development." The principal method was the establishment of polders (*yutian* 圩田 or *weitian* 圍田 – there being no great difference in meaning between these two terms by Ming-Qing times), in other words the transformation of low-lying, wet, uncultivated land by surrounding it with a man-made dike. These polders were usually fairly large. Down to the Xuande reign of the Ming (1426–35) it was still the case in Suzhou prefecture that polders might have "as many as 6,000 to 7,000 *mu*, and, where these were fewer in number, still 3,000 to 4,000 *mu*."[30] Even in the Wanli reign (1573–1619) there were still places in Jiangnan where polders were above 1,000 *mu*.[31] An example is Xiushui county 秀水縣 in Jiaxing prefecture, which in the Wanli reign still had 17 polders over 5,000 *mu*, 34 of 3,000 to 5,000 *mu*, 104 of 1,000 to 3,000 *mu*, 47 of 500 to 1,000 *mu*, and 30 below 500 *mu*.[32] The larger a polder the worse its shortcomings were. Because of the inequalities in elevation in its interior, the considerable enclosed low and swampy areas could not be effectively utilized, and Hamashima has pointed out that large polders contained a lot of uncultivated land and lakes and ponds.[33] Further, while the large polders were effective at preventing the incursion of water from outside, because of the limited capacity of the machines used at that time for drainage, if there were prolonged rains or an extended drought, the situation would be that described by Zhao Menglin 趙夢麟, who was the county magistrate of Wujiang 吳江 during the Wanli reign: "If a large polder meets with heavy rains, then the pumps and bailers will not be up to the task, and one will have to sit and watch it become submerged. If there is a drought then the

[29] See Morita Akira's speech in Watabe Tadayo 渡部忠世 and Sakurai Yūmio 桜井由躬雄, eds., *Chūgoku Kōnan no inasaku bunka – sono gakusaiteki kenkyū* [The rice-growing culture of Jiangnan in China – researches on the frontiers of scholarship] (Tokyo: Nihon Hōsō shuppan kyōkai, 1984), p. 198.
[30] Kuang Zhong 況鍾, *Ming Kuang-taishou zhi-Su zhengji quanji* 明況太守治蘇政績全集 [Complete collection of documents on the achievements of Prefect Kuang in governing Suzhou during his time in office under the Ming] (1764 ed.), j. 9, "Xiu-jun tian-yu ji jianghu shuili zou."
[31] Hamashima Atsutoshi, "Land development and nonlocal merchants."
[32] Watabe Tadayo and Sakurai Yūmio, *Rice-growing culture of Jiangnan*, pp. 194–95.
[33] Hamashima Atsutoshi, "Land development and nonlocal merchants."

water brought in by the pumps and bailers will not reach [everywhere it should], and this amounts to standing by and waiting for it to become dried out."[34] In the 1810s, Sun Jun, a local hydraulics expert in Qingpu county, also pointed out the shortcomings of large polders:

> Some of the land in the field plots in a large polder may differ in height by from one to 1.4 or 1.5 feet (*chi* 尺), or even two to three feet. Although the dikes can protect the polder against the tides from outside, the water inside will drain downward, and the rice sprouts still be drowned. If one wants to remedy the situation by bailing, [this is not feasible because] there is a flooded expanse across [internal] interlinked dike paths covering several hundred *mu*.[35]

Since large polders thus had many undrainable flooded fields in the rainy climate of Jiangnan, it was common – from Song to the early Ming – for much of the farmland to be under water.[36] Prolonged submersion is not good for the soil of rice fields, severely reducing its productive capacity.[37]

Hamashima has called the improvement of farmland that took place from the mid-fifteenth century "intensive development." Its main objectives were to do away with the "internal frontier" by opening up the extensive wastelands inside the polders, and to "dry out the fields," by transforming arable areas that were low-lying and wet, and increasing the degree of maturation of their soils.[38] The method most commonly used was the increased "subdivision of polders" (*fen yu* 分圩), or in other words splitting a large polder into a multiplicity of smaller ones. The criterion defining a "small" polder decreased in consequence: from 500 *mu* in the Xuande reign to a 100 *mu* in Wanli.[39] These smaller polders were appropriate for the draining and irrigating capacities of the machinery of those times, making it possible both to open up the wasteland in their interiors and to dry them out by pumping out water that had ponded in their fields. The control of the larger polders was also rationalized, by such means as subdividing them into smaller areas for management, and restructuring their

[34] Dong Fen 董份, *Biyuan ji* 泌園集 [Collection of [the Master of] the Bi garden], "Wujiang Ming fu Zhao-hou yizheng bian xu" [Preface to the collection on the exceptional governance of His Excellency Zhao, Prefect of Wujiang], in Liu Chenggan 劉承幹, ed., *Wuxing congshu* 吳興叢書 [Collection of works on Wuxing].

[35] Sun Jun, *How to build polders.*

[36] Kitada Hideto, *Study of agricultural progress*, ch. 2.

[37] Gao Liangzhi 高亮之 and Li Lin 李林, *Shuidao qixiang shengtai* 水稻气态象生态 [The climatic ecology of wet-field rice] (Beijing: Nongye CBS, 1992), p. 391.

[38] Hamashima Atsutoshi, "Land development and nonlocal merchants."

[39] Hamashima Atsutoshi, "Guanyu Jiangnan 'yu'-de ruogan kaocha" 关于江南 "圩" 的若干考察 [Some investigations into the Jiangnan "polder"], *Lishi yanjiu* 7 (1988).

water systems both internally and externally, with substantial progress resulting between late Ming and mid-Qing.[40] This also improved the soils. By
the middle of the nineteenth century it had become possible to grow winter
dry-field crops in what had previously been low-lying and wet land occupying a large proportion of the arable area of Jiangnan.[41] It needs stressing
that when this alternation of wet and dry conditions became feasible, it had
a very positive effect on the improvement of the fields.

Thus, even if hydrological changes and various kinds of problems with
hydraulic installations had some damaging effects, overall the condition
of the land in Jiangnan during the Ming-Qing period was continually
improving.

CHANGES IN THE PATTERNS OF HUMAN EFFORT

Jiangnan farmers during the Ming-Qing mainly used the following methods
to raise productivity per *mu* in wet-rice agriculture: (1) improvement of
hydraulic installations and farmland; (2) fine-tuning spatial cropping patterns, as by growing commercial crops like cotton and mulberry trees in
areas unsuited to wet-field rice; (3) the heavy application of fertilizers; (4)
improvement of the techniques of cultivation; and (5) extending the use of
the best cropping systems. Since the first of these has been discussed above,
and I have dealt with the second and third elsewhere,[42] the following
analysis will be confined to developments in the fourth and fifth of these
approaches.

Techniques of Cultivation

Tang Qiyu 唐啟宇 has taken the position that from the mid-sixteenth to the
mid-nineteenth century no new techniques, procedures, or types of seeds

---

[40] Zheng Zhaojing, *Lake Tai water control*, pp. 120–36.

[41] Up to about 1850 there was still a small quantity of land in Jiangnan that was either too low-
lying or subject to too much rainfall, or both, for the alternation of wet-field rice and dry-
field "spring-flowering crops" (*chunhua* 春花). The counties in the western part of Songjiang
prefecture are a case in point. After the severe floods of 1823 the weather continued to be
abnormal, and very few low-lying fields were planted with "spring-flowering crops." See
Jiang Gao 姜皋, *Pu Mao nong zi* 浦泖农咨 [Report on agriculture in the Huangpu and Mao
(lake) area (i.e., Songjiang)] (Shanghai: Shanghai tushuguan, 1963).

[42] Li Bozhong, "Ming-Qing shiqi Jiangnan shuidao shengchan jiyue chengdu-de tigao" 明清时
期江南水稻生产集约程度的提高 [The intensification of wet-field rice cultivation in Jiangnan
in the Ming-Qing period], *Zhongguo nongshi* 1 (1984); and Li Bozhong, "Ming-Qing
Jiangnan nongye ziyuan-de heli liyong" 明清江南农业资源的合理利用 [The rational utilization of agricultural resources in Ming-Qing Jiangnan], *Nongye kaogu* 2 (1985).

were introduced into wet-field rice farming (and more particularly not in Jiangnan).[43] That no new techniques were discovered does not mean, however, that technology was stagnant. Mark Elvin has pointed out that in studying technological progress it is necessary to distinguish (1) invention (or the initial discovery of a technique), (2) innovation (or the first incorporation of this newly discovered technique into the structure of actual production), and (3) dissemination (the generalization of the use of the technique).[44] The use of this approach is important for the accurate evaluation of changes in technology in Qing-dynasty Jiangnan. In this context, it should not be overlooked that certain important techniques invented and/or innovated in Ming times were widely disseminated in Qing times. Nor should we, however, ignore the invention and innovation in Qing-dynasty Jiangnan of some techniques in wet-field rice agriculture – and their diffusion.

There were two main subspecies of rice in Jiangnan, long-grained or *indica* (*xiandao* 籼稻) and round-grained or *japonica* (*jingdao/gengdao* 粳稻). *Indica* has comparatively high requirements for warmth and does not endure low temperatures, whereas *japonica* has lower requirements for warmth and is relatively resistant to cold.[45] The *indica* and *japonica* subspecies may each of them be further subdivided into "early" and "late" varieties, on the basis of their seasonal pattern of growth. The main environmental factor distinguishing them is the effect of the length of the day, which can be the result either of latitude or of the time of year – the latter being more significant in Jiangnan. The "early" rices are either sluggishly responsive to the length of the day or not responsive at all: given suitable warmth, their growing period is much the same whether the days be short or long. The late rices are sensitive to day length, and are typical short-day crops. To put it generally, *indica* and *japonica* are subspecies primarily developed to suit different regimes of temperature, and their "early" and "late" varieties are secondary developments to suit different patterns of day length. Furthermore, there is a transitional variety midway between the "early" and the "late," namely "intermediate rice" (*zhongdao* 中

---

[43] Tang Qiyu, *Zhongguo zuowu zaipei shigao* [A draft history of Chinese cultivation of crops] (Beijing: Nongye CBS, 1986), p. 39.

[44] Communication to the author, May 1, 1994.

[45] Gao Liangzhi and Li Lin, *Ecology of wet-field rice*, pp. 11 and 201; You Xiuling 游修龄, "Taihu diqu daozuo qiyuan ji qi chuanbo han fazhan wenti" 太湖地区稻作起源及其传播和发展问题 [The questions of the origins of rice cultivation in the Lake Tai area, and of its dissemination and development], in Zhongguo nongye kexue yuan and Nanjing nongye daxue Zhongguo nongye yichan yanjiushi, eds., *Taihu diqu nongshi lunwen-ji* 太湖地区农史论文集 [Collected essays on the agriculture of the Lake Tai region] 1 (Nanjing: Nanjiang daxue, 1985).

稻).⁴⁶ The slowly maturing strains of intermediate rice have a relatively strong photosensitivity and in this are close to late rices; but the early-maturing strains of intermediate rice have weak photosensitivity or none, and are close to the early rices.⁴⁷ One key factor in raising wet-field rice production has been matching the biological differences of these various types and varieties with their varying needs as regards temperature and the length of the day. Over a long period of natural and artificial selection that has lasted at least since the Song dynasty, the main strains of early rice in Jiangnan have come to be *indicas*, and those of intermediate and late rice to be *japonicas*.⁴⁸ The understanding of both farmers and agronomists in Jiangnan regarding the particular characteristics of early, intermediate, and late rices was, however, far from clear and exact over a long period of time.

Suzhou farmers already knew about the difference between early and late rice by Northern Song times; and by the Southern Song Hangzhou farmers could distinguish between early, intermediate, and late *japonica* rice (as could those of nearby Mingzhou, the present-day Ningbo). By the late Yuan or early Ming at the latest the same was true for the Suzhou region: in the Suzhou prefectural gazetteer for the Hongwu reign (1368–98), *juan* 42, which is on local products, contains part of a work called the *Wumen shilei* 吳門事類 [Matters concerning the Suzhou area, arranged by categories], which for the first time in Jiangnan gives the criteria for distinguishing the three strains. The gazetteer for the Jiajing reign (1522–66) for Taicang department, which was under the jurisdiction of Suzhou, also cites this passage, suggesting the same criteria were in use there.⁴⁹ What is surprising is that after this time and until the end of the Ming, even agricultural theorists in Jiangnan had no very clear understanding of early, intermediate, and late rice. Thus the mid-Ming *Bian min tuzuan* 便民圖纂 [Collected illustrations on matters of convenience for the common people] as well as the late-Ming *Shen-shi nongshu* 沈氏農書 [Mr. Shen's agricultural

---

⁴⁶ The quotation marks around the terms "early," "intermediate," and "late" are dropped after this point, but the reader is asked to bear in mind that these are technical terms, somewhat variable in sense, and usually having a meaning that is not accurately conveyed by the simple dictionary definitions.

⁴⁷ Nanjing nongxue-yuan and Jiangsu nongxue-yuan eds., *Zuowu zaipei-xue* 作物栽培学 [Crop cultivation], southern series, *shang ce* (Shanghai: Shanghai kexue-jishu CBS, 1979), pp. 26–28.

⁴⁸ You Xiuling, *Rice cultivation in the Lake Tai area.*

⁴⁹ Sutō Yoshiyuki 周藤吉之, *Sōdai keizai-shi kenkyū* [Researches on the economic history of the Song dynasty] (Tokyo: Tōkyō daigaku shuppansha, 1962), pp. 146–47; Amano Motonosuke 天野元之助, *Chūgoku nōgyō-shi kenkyū* [Researches on the agricultural history of China], augmented ed. (Tokyo: Ochanomizu shobō, 1979), pp. 212–13.

encyclopedia],[50] two important agricultural encyclopedias, both style rice maturing and harvested in the ninth month of the old lunar calendar as "*early* rice,"[51] whereas, according to the definition provided by the *Wumen shilei*, this ought to be a typical *late* rice. By the mid-Qing, the conception of early rice had become clear and exact, and knowledge of the intermediate and late strains had also deepened. Not only were the criteria used by the *Wumen shilei* to differentiate the three strains widely disseminated in areas outside Suzhou,[52] but Jiangnan farmers also had precise knowledge of the basic biological dissimilarities deriving from early rice being an *indica* and the other two being *japonicas*, as well as the principal other differences deriving from a long or short growing season, and not just from whether the seasons for transplanting and harvesting were early or late in the year. They also had a clearer perception of differences in yields and quality.[53]

---

[50] Shi Shenghan 石声汉 and Kang Chengyi 康成懿, eds., *Bian min tuzuan* (Beijing: Nongye CBS, 1982), and the *Shen-shi nongshu in Cheng Hengli and Wang Da, Supplement to the agricultural encyclopedia* (see note 4 of this chapter).

[51] Chen Hengli and Wang Da, *Supplement to the agricultural encyclopedia*, pp. 21, 38.

[52] *Qingpu xianzhi* 青浦縣志 [Gazetteer for Qingpu county], 1788 ed., *j.* 11, "Chanwu"; Bao Shichen 包世臣, *Qimin si-shu* 齊民四術 [Four arts for the governance of the common people], in Bao Shichan *Anwu Si-zhong*, Daoguang reign ed., *j.* 1, Nong 1 *shang*, "Bian gu."

[53] It seems to have been already known in the Southern Song that most early rices were *indicas* and most late ones *japonicas*. See Kawakatsu Mamoru 川勝守, *Min-Shin Kōnan nōgyō keizai-shi kenkyū* [Researches on the economic history of farming in Jiangnan in Ming and Qing times] (Tokyo: Tōkyō daigaku shuppansha, 1992), pp. 20–21. In mid-Ming, Huang Shengceng 黄省曾 had a relatively clear appreciation of these sorts of differences, observing that "*Indica* ripens early; hence it is called 'early rice.' *Japonica* matures late; hence it is termed 'late rice.'" See his *Lisheng yujing daopin* 理生玉鏡稻品 [Jade mirror of the varieties of rice for making a living], in Wang Wenlu 王文祿, ed., *Bai ling xueshan ji* 百陵學山集: Wanli reign–period. But he was unaware of the most important differences; otherwise he could not have said (as he did), "The smaller *japonicas* are called '*indicas*.'" By the mid-Qing few agronomists confused subspecies in this way. For example, in Bao Shichen's *Four arts*, we read that "*Japonica* (*jingdao* 粳稻) is today the common source of food grain. The early-ripening type is called *indica*. Its harvest is finished by the solar period 'Autumn Begins' [August 7–22]. The most slowly-ripening type is called 'late rice,' being white, long-grained, and of a beautiful fragrance. It is especially good for people's health, and the ears mature in the ninth month. The variety that ripens in the eighth month is given the special name of *jing* 粳 [or *geng*] rice, and it is considered that its red color is of benefit to people's well-being. Its yield is about the same. Only the early rice is somewhat more meagerly productive. Advantage is taken of its earliness to bridge the gap between harvests, and to avoid the droughts of the fall." Likewise the Jiang Gao, *Report on agriculture in the Huangpu and Mao [lake] area*, says: "Early rice: . . . Here they call it red 'rice' (*chi mi* 赤米) and also *xian* rice [*indica*]. It is planted in the fifth month and is ripe by the seventh. Even in years of plenty, however, its yields per *mu* do not exceed 1.4 to 1.5 *shi*. The labor and capital expended do not give comparable returns to those on late rice." Or again: "The mid-autumn rice matures in the eighth month, and the late rice at about the time that the frosts are first falling. There is a popular saying, 'If the green rice sprouts are not up when the dew grows cold [the solar period approximately equivalent to October 8–22], when the frosts fall [the period from

Tang Qiyu holds the view that the most important achievement in the technology of rice cultivation in Ming-dynasty Jiangnan was the introduction of the application of supplementary fertilizer (*zhuifei* 追肥).[54] The term "supplementary fertilizer" principally indicates fertilizer applied during the growth of the inflorescence. The fertilizer applied before transplanting, or "basic fertilizer" (*jifei* 基肥), was called "banking up the foundation" (*diandi* 墊底), hence the later top-dressing was seen as a supplement. In *Mr. Shen's agricultural encyclopedia*, it says in the section "Yun tiandi fa" [How to manage the fields] that once the period Autumn Begins has arrived (August 7–22), the effect of the basic fertilizer will have been exhausted, hence supplementary fertilizer is applied to provide continuity. For this reason, another name for supplementary fertilizer in Ming-Qing Jiangnan was the figurative one of "carrying on the power" (*jie li* 接力).

The technique of adding supplementary fertilizer appeared early in China,[55] and as early as the Song dynasty the peasants of Yuqian county 于潛縣 in the mountainous region of western Jiangnan were using it on their seedling plots.[56] But even by the late Ming this technique had not been generally mastered for the period of production in the main fields. The *Zhi fu qi shu* [Wonderful book for making you rich],[57] which dates from the mid-Ming, although it mentions the application of supplementary fertilizer on the main rice fields, does not indicate the quantity, though it is very precise about this as regards the "basic fertilizer." Both Li Le's 李樂 *Wuqing zhi* 烏青志 [Gazetteer of Wu-Qing town][58] from the Wanli reign and *Mr. Shen's agricultural encyclopedia* from the Chongzhen reign (1628–44), which develops its discussion of this point from the preceding treatise,[59] talk about the heavy application of supplementary fertilizer and the quantities. The latter, however, emphasizes the great difficulty of using the method:

October 23 to November 6] they will all lodge [i.e., collapse].'" The *jing/geng* rice referred to in the first of these works as ripening in the eighth month, and the "autumn rice" referred to in the second, are intermediate rices. It may be seen from these that by the first half of the nineteenth century Jiangnan people had a full knowledge of the biological characteristics of the three types of rice.

[54] Tang Qiyu, *Chinese food crops*, p. 29.

[55] Cao Longgong 曹隆恭, "Woguo daozuo shifei fazhan shilüe" 我国稻作施肥发展史略 [An outline history of the development of the application of fertilizer in rice cultivation in our country], in *Zhongguo nongshi* 1 (1989).

[56] Lou Shou 樓璹, *Geng-zhi tu* 耕織圖 [Pictures of farming and weaving (with poems)], fig. 7, "Yu yin," as discussed in Amano Motonosuke, *Agricultural history*, pp. 226–28.

[57] *Zhifu qi shu* 致富奇書 (Kimura kendō 木村兼堂 ed. in Nihon Naikaku Bunko).

[58] Parts of this now-lost work are cited in the *Wucheng xianzhi* 吳城縣志 [Wucheng county gazetteer] (1879). See also the following note.

[59] You Xiuling, "'Shen-shi nongshu' he 'Wuqing zhi'" "沈氏農書" 和 "烏青志" [*Mr. Shen's Book on Farming and the Wuqing zhi*], *Zhongguo ke-ji shiliao* 4 (1989).

The general explanation is that, while all the [other] tasks of the farming life are easy, in the single case of the application of supplementary fertilizers for "carrying on the power" you must scrutinize the season and the weather, and examine the appearance [of the crops]. This has the most serious implications for the farmer. Families that lack resources will suffer from meager harvests due to insufficient fertilizer; and families with an abundance of fertilizer will always be menaced by grain that only consists of husks because of an excess of [this] fertilizer.[60]

Thus the application of supplementary fertilizer on main rice fields was not generally mastered by Jiangnan peasants even by the late Ming, as may also be seen from the absence of any reference to it in Xu Guangqi's 徐光啓 *Nongzheng quanshu* 農政全書 [Complete treatise of farm administration][61] and the rarity of references in late Ming local gazetteers from the region.

The Qing period was very different. The application of supplementary fertilizer on main fields in wet-field rice cultivation is repeatedly referred to in the agricultural encyclopedias, and is far from infrequent in the local gazetteers. Not only was the practice widespread by the early mid-Qing, but quantities had become by and large uniform: on the order of 40 *jin* per *mu* of beancake or its equivalent,[62] indicating technological standardization. Tang Qiyu has pointed out that "mastery of the circumstances and timing for the application of supplementary fertilizer on wet-land fields is exceedingly difficult."[63] The diffusion of this technique represents major technical progress in the Qing period.

It should be stressed at this point, however, that supplementary fertilizer has relatively little effect in increasing the yield of early rice but is highly important for raising that of intermediate and late rices.[64] Thus supplementary fertilizer was closely linked to the more widespread use of intermediate and late rices.

Cropping Systems

A cropping system is a technological complex with many facets. Here we shall only touch on multiple cropping rotations.

The alternation of rice and wheat that lies at the heart of the system of two crops per year had already appeared in Jiangnan in Tang times,[65] after which it gradually spread to become the dominant system in ever

[60] *Mr. Shen's agricultural encyclopedia*, "Yun tiandi fa."
[61] Shi Shenghan, ed. (Shanghai: Shanghai guji CBS, 1985).
[62] Li Bozhong, "Increased intensification of rice production."
[63] Tang Qiyu, *Chinese cultivation of crops*, p. 29.
[64] Gao Liangzhi and Li Lin, *Ecology of wet-field rice*, pp. 377–78; Nanjing nongxue-yuan et al., *Crop cultivation*, p. 77.
[65] Li Bozhong, "Rice-wheat multicropping."

more localities. It was only around the Ming–Qing transition, however, that (in Kitada's words) it acquired a "commanding" position in the Jiangnan plain.[66] It is Kitada's view that the Ming-Qing system of two crops per year was different from its Song predecessor in two respects: (1) the earlier system was mostly practiced on the "high-lying fields" of western Jiangnan, whereas the late one was practiced in the "low-lying fields" of the plain; and (2) the earlier system took early rice as its principal crop, and wheat as its secondary one, whereas the new system took late rice as its main crop and wheat, rape, and beans as its subsidiary crops.[67] What needs to be emphasized at this juncture is that, even if the two-crops-per-year system had already taken a dominant position in the Jiangnan plain by the Ming–Qing transition, the process of its generalization was still far from finished. It may be seen from Kitada's work that down to the turn of the eighteenth and nineteenth centuries the one-crop-per-year system was still being practiced in a considerable number of wet-fields. It would seem that only by the middle of the nineteenth century was the diffusion process complete.[68]

[66] While it must be pointed out that there were a considerable number of fields in Jiangnan in Tang times that were under a system in which wet conditions alternated with dry and gave two crops a year (Li Bozhong, *Tangdai Jiangnan nongye-de fazhan* 唐代江南农业的发展 [The development of agriculture in Jiangnan under the Tang] (Beijing: Nongye CBS, 1990), pp. 118–19), and that this area clearly expanded under the Song, the work of Ashitatsu Keiji 足立啟二 and Ōsawa Seishō 大沢正昭 has shown that the greater part of such land at this time was on the hills in the river valleys. Most of Jiangnan is of course a low-lying plain and at this period gave one crop of rice a year, or even one every two years, being under a "cultivation system for excessively wet land." See Ashitatsu Keiji, "Sōdai Ryōsetsu ni okeru suitō no seisanryoku suijun" [The level of productivity of wet-field rice in the Liang-Zhe under the Song], *Kumamoto daigaku bungakubu ronsō* 17 (1985); Ōsawa Seishō, "'So-Ko juku, Tenka soku' – kyozō to jitsuzō no aida" ['When there is a full harvest in Suzhou and Huzhou, the Empire has enough to eat' – midway between a myth and a reality], *Atarishii rekishigaku no tame ni* 179 (1985); and Kitada Hideto, *Agricultural progress and village handicrafts in the Jiangnan delta*. This corresponds with the model of historical agricultural progress in Jiangnan advocated by Shiba Yoshinobu 斯波信義, *Sōdai Kōnan keizai-shi no kenkyū* [Studies on the economic history of Jiangnan under the Song] (Tokyo: Tōkyō daigaku Tōyō bunka kenkyūjo, 1988), pp. 169–74), and so we may take it as correct.

[67] Kitada Hideto, *Agricultural progress and village handicrafts in the Jiangnan delta*, chs. 2 and 3. It is my opinion, however, that the "early" rice of which Kitada speaks here should be "intermediate" rice. This is because the main-field growing periods of early rice and of the secondary crop overlap, which makes a yearly cycle of rotation impossible. See Li Genpan, "Zhongguo gudai gengzuo zhidu-de ruogan wenti" 中国古代耕作制度的若干问题 [Certain questions relating to the cultivation system used in premodern China], *Gu-jin nongye* 1 (1989). As indicated above, down to the end of the Ming, and even in such a major work dedicated to agricultural technology as *Mr. Shen's agricultural encyclopedia*, early-ripening strains of late rice were still being taken to be "early rice." Kitada may thus have used Ming technical terminology to describe the situation under the Song.

[68] Li Bozhong, *Agricultural Development in Jiangnan, 1620–1850* (London: Macmillan, forthcoming), ch. 2.2.

Anthropogenic changes in wet-field rice cultivation during the Ming-Qing period may thus be epitomized as the spread of a new system of two crops per year, closely linked with the diffusion of the cultivation of late-ripening intermediate rice and early-ripening late rice, and the extension of the use of supplementary fertilizer.

THE INTERRELATIONS BETWEEN THESE CHANGES IN CLIMATE, LAND, AND HUMAN ACTIVITIES

Last of all, we briefly consider the interrelationships between the changes in the climate, the land, and human activities. They had two manifest particularities: climatic changes played the leading role in such interrelationships; and changes in climate and human activities, especially the former, had a major influence on changes in the land.

Shifts in precipitation and temperature have a decisive effect on the aridity or moistness of the soils. Speaking with respect to the present-day situation in the Jiangnan plain, the aridity index, or in other words the ratio of evapotranspiration to precipitation over a given period of time, lies between 1.0 and 1.3 from April through June, and thus falls in the humid to semi-humid range, while from July through September it lies between 1.5 and 2.0, which indicates semi-aridity.[69] Since most of the Jiangnan plain is low-lying, with abundant surface water, once the semi-arid conditions of July through September have passed away and the aridity index is down, there is an excess of water over the year as a whole. An excess of water over a long period can damage the structure of the soil, and lead to an increase in toxicity and stronger redox reactions, which reduces the fertility of the soil. If, to the contrary, the temperature is comparatively elevated and precipitation comparatively slight, the aridity index climbs, and the water stored in the soil diminishes, which improves the soil condition. In a manner of speaking one might say that climate was also to be thanked for achievements in the efforts to dry out the rice fields in Jiangnan during the Qing dynasty, and especially the eighteenth century.

Further, different meteorological environments can have different effects on activating the latent fertility of soils. This latter is dependent on weather conditions. When the temperature is high, microbial activity increases, the organic content of the soil is more swiftly decomposed, the

[69] Fang Zaihui et al., *Zhejiang farming*, p. 79.

level of activation of the latent fertility is high, and the supply of nutrients that can be effectively absorbed by crop growth – hence the efficiency of fertilizer – is also high. If the contrary holds, then the level of absorbable nutrients is low, and the efficiency of fertilizer is reduced. If water stands for a long time in a paddy-field, then even if the latent fertility in the soil is high, the very low proportion of the total nutrients that are in an effectively usable state will result in a very low capacity to supply fertility. The same line of argument holds good as regards organic fertilizers that are applied to farmlands. Hence, given a certain level of latent fertility in a soil, comparatively more organic fertilizer has to be applied to a rice field under conditions of low temperature and high water content in order to produce the same yield as in one with high temperature and low water.[70]

Human efforts also played a considerable part in effecting changes in the land at a more modest level. This was done through improving water systems and soil quality, increasing the input of fertilizers, and rotating alternate wet-field and dry-field crops in the paddies. According to the Ming-dynasty Jiangnan agronomist Ma Yilong 馬一龍, "there are two [types of] methods of increasing soil fertility: those that take effect through human efforts include irrigation, hoeing out weeds, and making fields and reed-beds;[71] and those that take effect through the powers of material things include mud, ordure, lime, oil-cake (*shen* 粃), straw, and vegetable matter."[72] Han Mengzhou 韓夢周, who lived in the Qianlong reign (1736–95), wrote that "in Jiangsu and Zhejiang the land is rich, cultivating is done properly, and beancake and ordure are applied to increase the fertility.... The rice that they bring to fruition is all bursting with plumpness, and every *mu* has a harvest of from 800 to 900 *jin*."[73] From these we may derive an impression of the part played by the farmers of Jiangnan during Ming-Qing times in improving the fecundity of their lands.

---

[70] Gao Liangzhi and Li Lin, *Ecology of wet-field rice*, pp. 364, 375, 377, 378.

[71] The last is a tentative reading of *tudang* 塗蕩. [Trans.]

[72] Ma Yilong, *Nongshuo* [A discussion of farming], cited in Xu Guangqi, *Complete treatise, j.* 2 "Nong ben," p. 47.

[73] Han Mengzhou, *Litang wenji* [Collection of Li Tang's works], 1823 ed., waiji, "Quanyu yedian jitian jia fen wen." A *jin* is a measure of weight, historically variable, and strictly speaking incommensurable with units of capacity. Gang Deng, *Development Versus Stagnation*, p. xxv, and Chen Hengli and Wang Da, *Supplement to the agricultural encyclopedia*, indicate that in modern times one modern *shi* (of husked rice) weighs, on average, 140–50 modern *jin*.

THE IMPACT OF THESE CHANGES IN WEATHER, LAND, AND HUMAN ACTIONS ON WET-FIELD RICE PRODUCTION IN JIANGNAN DURING THE MING-QING PERIOD

Jiangnan agronomists were conscious of the importance of the effects of variations in the climate, soil conditions, and human inputs on the growth of rice. Thus Ma Yilong wrote:

> While it pertains to human beings to nourish [rice], bringing it to maturity pertains to Heaven. The inflorescence must be exposed to the sunlight before it will open. If rain continues for a long time it will close its apertures and not flower. If the winds are rough, the inflorescence will be damaged and not fruit. Both are threats to the as yet immature grain. When the ripened grain is about to be harvested, too dry a soil will cause the rice-kernels to be damaged by dryness; excessive immersion due to an abundance of water will produce black rot. These latter two are also afflictions that destroy the harvest. How can it be within the power of human beings to cause overcast or sunny weather, or arid or humid conditions?

He also said of paddy-fields: "If they are constantly under cropping, their energy-vitality (qi 氣) will invariably weaken. (By 'weakening' I mean that the power of the soil weakens. . . . The rice sprouts draw their resources from the soil in order to grow, and when the power of the soil is lacking, it becomes weak. [Original note.])."[74] Bao Shichen said: "No matter whether there is flood or drought, when one is managing farmland an additional dressing of manure will increase the grain by two dou[75] per mu, and the addition of one [man's] working day ($yi\ gong$ 一工) will likewise augment it by two dou."[76] There is an excessive simplicity in the analysis by these two authors, such as Bao's view of the effect of incremental human labor inputs on productivity, and a certain lack of clarity in respect to certain important concepts, an example being the failure to distinguish between climate and weather. There may also perhaps be an excessive narrowness, as in their restricting the concept of "land" to one of fertility. While we may take exception to this, however, they did realize that the weather, the land, and

---

[74] Ma Yilong, *Discussion of farming*, p. 51.

[75] 10 *dou* = 1 *shi*.

[76] Bao Shichen, *Four techniques for the governance of the common people*, j. 2, Nong er.

human labor were all variable inputs, changes in which had a major impact on wet-field rice production.

The nature of these impacts is a complex question, and only two aspects will be discussed in what follows: (1) The effect of changes in climate and land, with the technique of cultivation held constant; and (2) The effect of changes in cultivation technology, with climate and land held constant. On this foundation we shall then be able to examine what the consequences of these effects were on productivity of rice fields per *mu* in Jiangnan during the Ming-Qing period.

THE IMPACT OF CHANGES IN WEATHER AND LAND ON WET-FIELD RICE PRODUCTION

Climate has decisive effects on the rearing of rice seedlings, transplantation, application of fertilizer, and irrigation. We give a résumé of these below, on the basis of the work of Gao Liangzhi and Li Lin.[77]

CLIMATE AND SEEDLING GROWTH. The environmental conditions required during the period of seedling growth relate to temperature, water content of the soil, oxygen, sunlight, and nutrients.

The lowest temperature at which *Oryza sativa japonica*, the main subspecies of rice used in Ming-Qing Jiangnan, will sprout is about 10°C, and the lowest temperature at which seedlings will grow is 12°C, with the range most suitable to sturdy shoots being between 20° and 25°C. Speeds of germination, emergence, and growth are all positively correlated with temperature.

Speed of uptake of water, a sufficient quantity of which is essential for germination, rises with temperature from a point below 10°C, but this effect vanishes above 15°C.

Sprouting and growth demand adequate oxygen, which is necessary for the materials stored in the endosperm to be metabolized, the leaves and roots to grow well, and the sprout to be healthily nourished. Insufficient oxygen causes weakly seedlings that may rot if the weather is unfavorable. For this reason the soil of the seedling plot needs good ventilation for the maintenance of a sufficient supply of oxygen. This implies good irrigation and drainage.

Before the seedling reaches the three-leafed stage, organic nutrients are mainly supplied by the endosperm, but afterward it relies on photosynthesis by the leaves to make them. Hence adequate sunlight is indispensable.

---

[77] Gao Liangzhi and Li Lin, *Ecology of wet-field rice*, ch. 8.

At the same time, after leaving the embryo stage it relies on its roots to absorb inorganic nutrients; hence the presence of effective nutrients in the soil is a key factor.

CLIMATE AND TRANSPLANTATION. Given a high temperature and enough sunshine, a single stalk of rice will rapidly sprout numerous tillers,[78] which will result in numerous ears of grain. The high temperature also facilitates the activation of the fertility latent in the soil. If, under such conditions, the spatial density of the transplanted seedlings is reduced, a dense growth of stalks and ears may be obtained while economizing on seeds, seedling plots, fertilizers, and labor.[79]

CLIMATE AND FERTILIZATION. The quantity of fertilizer that should be applied is commonly approximated by the formula

$$\left(F_a - S_f\right)\big/u_f$$

where F_a is the total quantity of a given fertilizing nutrient needed for the anticipated yield, S_f is the quantity of fertilizing nutrient supplied by the soil, and u_f is the rate of utilization of the fertilizing nutrient supplied in both forms.

---

[78] A tiller is the shoot of a grass, usually lateral and at or near the base, and more or less erect.

[79] The question of whether to transplant seedlings at a high density on rich soils was for long a topic of debate in China. With suitable seeds and techniques, dense transplanting will indeed give high yields per *mu*. The advantages and disadvantages, however, depend on the type of rice. During the Ming-Qing period, the principal wet-field rice was long-stalked: if this was densely transplanted, the growth of stalks and leaves would consume a relatively large proportion of fertilizer, and the lack of space between stalks, which impeded the circulation of air, would make the prevention of insect pests difficult. Hence widely spaced transplanting was comparatively better, as those alive at this time were aware. According to Ma Yilong, "A low or high density is a concomitant of rich or poor soil [respectively]. . . . If the soil is rich, high density is particularly inappropriate" (see *Discussion of farming*, p. 50). Xu Guangqi leveled the following criticism against dense transplanting: "The way in which people today make use of seeds is to plant more than a *dou* per *mu*, to [trans]plant densely but apply little fertilizer, which makes it difficult to weed, with the result that harvests are meager" (*Complete treatise*, *j.* 25, Shuyi zhong). The *Wuxing zhanggu ji* 吳興掌故集 [Collection of historical records on Wuxing] (in the *Wuxing congshu* 吳興叢書, 1914 ed.), *j.* 13, Wuchan lei, pointed out that "In Huzhou they plow deeply but transplant seedlings at a low density. Their land is essentially very fertile, and many of those who do not transplant at a low density suffer from insect pests in the autumn." An agricultural handbook from Huzhou in the Daoguang reign (1821–50) also said: "In general, the grain sprouts delight in the wind passing through them. Insects are comparatively rare in places where there is wind." See *Nongshi youwen* 農事幼聞 [What I heard in my youth about farming], partially preserved in *Nanxun zhenzhi* 南潯鎮志 [Gazetteer of Nanxun town] (1863), *j.* 21, Chuchong. Low-density transplanting in rich soils was common knowledge to many agronomists in Jiangnan in this period.

The relationship between the capacity of the soil to provide fertilizing nutrients and the weather has already been discussed. Here we will only touch on two further points:

(a) During the phase of vegetative growth, the capacity of the root system to absorb nutrients is greatly influenced in a positive sense by temperature and humidity. During the middle and final phases of growth the root system tends to decay, its capacity to produce oxygen little by little declines, and it often depends upon oxygen obtained from the aeration of the soil to maintain its regular vital functions. If there are heavy rains at this time, and the paddy-fields are full of standing water for a long period, this can impede the root system's absorptive function and ingestion of nutrients.

(b) Solar radiation is the most evident of the many factors affecting the rate of utilization of fertilizer. If radiation diminishes, so does photosynthesis in the rice plant. In cases where the level of the nitrogen compounds so necessary to a good yield is low, the production of constituent elements is not sufficient, the rate of seed formation low, and the yield small. Even if a large quantity of nitrogenous fertilizer is applied, it will be of no help, but merely a self-created waste of fertilizer.

CLIMATE AND IRRIGATION. An adequate water content in the soil is necessary throughout the process of the growth of wet-field rice, but irrigation is not required at every phase. On the contrary, in South China it is common, when the rice plants sprout tillers, to dry out the fields (*kaotian* 烤 田), so that for a time the soil is short of water. This has two effects: (1) It reduces the absorption of water and nutrients by the main stalk, and also photosynthesis, so that the soil only meets the needs of the main stalk and of the tillers that branched off early, so preventing an ineffective proliferation of further tillers. (2) It causes a large quantity of oxygen to enter the soil surface, so that there are fewer products of reduction processes, the activities of aerobic bacteria and the mineralization of organic matter are increased, and the number of black stalks is reduced, while the development of the root system is promoted, so that after the water has returned it will have a strong capacity for absorbing fertilizer and water, with substantially enhanced photosynthesis. In this way the plant's resistance to lodging[80] can be increased, and the material basis for the formation of large ears augmented. The period when single-crop rice in a wheat-stubble field (*maicha* 麥茬) sprout tillers is often at the late-spring–early-summer season of the "plum rains" (or "rotting rains") when the weather is mostly overcast

---

[80] Falling over.

and rainy with little sunshine, which has an adverse effect on the drying out of the fields and hence serious implications for rice production.

OTHER EFFECTS OF CLIMATE. Changes in climate had many other effects on rice production. For example, it was mentioned above that each further 100 meters above sea level reduces the mean annual temperature by about 0.45°C, while rainfall increases and hours of sunlight and intensity of solar radiation diminish. Investigation has shown that for each further 100 meters in altitude, the growing season for wet-field rice shortens by four to seven days, and the accumulated temperature at above 10°C diminishes by from 100° to 150°C, with consequences for the spatial distribution of the crop.[81] On this basis, since the mean annual temperature in the seventeenth century was about 1°C less than in the eighteenth century, the growing season for wet-field rice would have been one to two weeks shorter.[82] The same effect would also have made itself felt in some degree on the secondary crops. Falling temperature means an increased frequency of damage from cold, to which wet-field rice is highly vulnerable in Jiangnan. Low temperatures at seedling time may cause the stalk to grow poorly, clearly with reduction of the number of ears in consequence; and it may delay the heading stage, with the renewed risk of meeting with cold. In the growing stage there is a direct effect on yield. For example, in the summer of 1976 the temperature was abnormally chilly, and the wet-field rice yields in Jiangsu were 46.5 kilograms less per *mu* than they had been the year before. In 1980, when it was again cold, overcast, and rainy, the decline in the per-*mu* yields of single-crop late rice and second-crop late rice were 17 and 101.5 kilograms respectively. Although excessive heat can also have a bad effect on the growth of wet-field rice, this cannot easily happen in Jiangnan because of its proximity to the ocean, a body of water that exercises a moderating effect and keeps the air humidity high, so that temperatures rise slowly and extremes of heat are out of the usual run of things.[83]

To sum up, when climatic factors reduce the water content in the soil, then environmental conditions are favorable for the growth of wet-field rice. A hypothetical analysis by Zhang Jiacheng 张家诚, based on

---

[81] Gao Liangzhi and Li Lin, *Ecology of wet-field rice*, p. 418.

[82] This effect is not confined to rice. Yeh-chien Wang has pointed out, on the basis of research by A. B. Appleby and others, that in sixteenth- and seventeenth-century Europe whenever the mean annual temperature fell by 1°C, this could shorten the cropping season by three to four weeks, which was equivalent to increasing the altitude of cultivation by 500 English feet. See Yeh-chien Wang, "Rice prices."

[83] Gao Liangzhi and Li Lin, *Ecology of wet-field rice*, pp. 425–26 and 447–48.

macrotheory, argues that a change of 1°C in mean annual temperature would alter accumulated annual temperature in South China by up to 365°C. This would amount to a difference in accumulated annual temperature of from 100° to 200°C for each major crop, depending on its period of maturation. Hence for every change of 1°C in temperature, the corresponding change in the "category of ripening" (in other words, from "early-ripening" to "middle-ripening" or vice versa, and so on) will by and large be two grades for each of the crops. According to the economics of agricultural production, a difference of one "category of ripening" implies a change of about 10 percent in output, or 20 percent for two degrees, as here.[84] More research will be needed to establish whether this analytical finding applied to Ming-Qing Jiangnan, but there are a few records that show that the categories of ripening of wet-field rice varied with changes in climate.[85] Thus relatively good yields can be obtained under conditions of unchanging practice in cultivation, and with comparatively small inputs of labor, seeds, and fertilizer, provided that climate and soils are favorable.

THE IMPACT OF CHANGES IN THE PATTERN OF HUMAN EFFORTS

In this section we explore the effects of changes in the style of farming, with the focus on varieties of seeds, the application of supplementary fertilizer, and the cultivation system.

As has been recounted, the much-enhanced understanding of the different types of wet-field rice in the Ming-Qing period was accompanied by a wider use of slow-ripening intermediate rice and early-ripening late rice, these being better suited to the present-day natural conditions of Jiangnan, especially climate. The slowness of the return of warmth in the early spring and the wide range of temperatures encountered at this period created a damaging insecurity in the cultivation of early rice.[86] Since early rice was

[84] Zhang Jiacheng, *Qihou yu renlei* 气候与人类 [Climate and humankind] (Zhengzhou: He'nan kexue-jishu CBS, 1988), pp. 123–25.

[85] For example, in the eastern part of Huzhou toward the end of the Ming, late-ripening late rice was the main crop. By the Kangxi reign (1662–1722), however, the villagers here were harvesting in the ninth lunar month, and "did not dare to go past the solar period 'Falling Frosts' [commonly in the latter half of the ninth lunar month, or from October 23 to November 6.]" A local saying described the ninth month as "the busy month" or the "month when gold is put in baskets and jewels obtained." See the *Wuqing wenxian* [Records from Wu-Qing], cited in the *Wuqing zhenzhi* [Gazetteer of Wu-Qing town], 1746 ed., *j.* 2; and *Huzhou-fu zhi* 湖州府志 [Gazetteer for Huzhou prefecture], 1874 ed., *j.* 29, "Si-shi su, shang," and *j.* 32, "wuchan, shang." Thus the category of ripening for late rice in the eastern part of Huzhou changed from a late-ripening to an early-ripening variety.

[86] Fang Zaihui et al., *Zhejiang farming*, pp. 71–72.

grown early in the year, and the temperature at the time of growth was somewhat low, a comparatively heavier dressing of fertilizer was needed.[87] The short growing period of early rice meant that yields were low and the quality of the grain was poor, while there was also a conflict in the timing of its cultivation with that of the previous year's secondary crop that ripened in the summer. Although late rice gave high yields per *mu* and was of good quality, the long duration of the growing season required a relatively large input of fertilizer.[88] There was also a clash with the timing of the cultivation of the secondary crop that would ripen in the summer of the following year. Hence it was that slow-ripening intermediate rice and early-ripening late rice were varieties better suited to Jiangnan conditions.

In Southern Song times, according to the *Siming zhi* 四明志 [Ningbo gazetteer] for the Baoqing reign (1225–27),[89] in Mingzhou, which was to become modern Ningbo, and was next door to Jiangnan, most of the rice grown was an intermediate rice that ripened in the solar period Limit of Heat (roughly equivalent to the middle ten-day period of the seventh month of the lunar calendar, approximately August 23 to September 7), with an early rice that ripened in the solar period Autumn Begins (roughly equivalent to the first ten-day period of the seventh lunar month) in second place. Of the late rice that ripened in the eighth lunar month there was very little. The situation was much the same in Yuezhou, which was to become the present-day Shaoxing prefecture.[90] There is something of a difference of opinion between Kawakatsu and You Xiuling, the former thinking that late rice was dominant in northern Zhejiang (southern Jiangnan) and the latter that the Lake Tai area (or Jiangnan plain) resembled southern Zhejiang (in which Ningbo and Shaoxing are located).[91] According to the criteria in the *Wumen shilei* (cited above), "intermediate rice" in Song times belonged to the category of "early rice," while Song "late rice" belonged to that of "intermediate rice." On this account it would appear that during the Song dynasty, early rice or early-ripening intermediate rice predominated, and that early rice continued to hold a considerable place in Jiangnan until the middle Ming. According to the list of 21 important varieties of non-glutinous Jiangnan rice given in Huang Shengceng's sixteenth-century *Varieties of rice*, there are still 9 in the "early" group, and only 5 in the "intermediate" and 7 in the "late."[92] Although the

[87] Gao Liangzhi and Li Lin, *Ecology of wet-field rice*, p. 377.
[88] Nanjing nongxue yuan et al., *Crop cultivation*, p. 136.
[89] *Siming zhi* [Ningbo gazetteer] (1854), j. 4, "Wuchan."
[90] Kawakatsu Mamoru, *Farming in Jiangnan in Ming and Qing*, p. 20.
[91] You Xiuling, *Rice cultivation in the Lake Tai area*, pp. 10–41.
[92] J. 21. See also Amano Motonosuke, *Agricultural history*, p. 299.

number of varieties does not necessarily represent the area planted, the small number of intermediate and late varieties must have had an important impact on the degree to which they were generally cultivated. As proof of this we may instance the discussion of the growing period of wet-field rice in Suzhou and Songjiang by Yu Ruwei 俞汝為 at the end of the Ming: "By and large, the rice in the wet-fields all relies on water for its nourishment. . . . Irrigation water has to be brought in for the 120 days in which the rice is born, grows, ripens, and bears ears."[93] As it happens, by present-day standards this duration of the growing season makes it an early rice,[94] which thus was still widespread in at least these two important prefectures down to the end of the dynasty. On the other hand, it appears from *Mr. Shen's agricultural encyclopedia* and the *Supplement to the Agricultural Encyclopedia* that in the Huzhou/Jiaxing region the main rice was a late-ripening late variety that was harvested in the tenth lunar month.[95] By the mid-Qing early rice had to all intents and purposes gone from the Jiangnan region, and late-ripening late rice seems mostly to have been grown where cotton and mulberries were comparatively common.[96] If one has regard to the times of transplanting and harvesting, slow-ripening intermediate rice and early-ripening late rice were the main varieties in most places.[97] The generalization of these two varieties was one of the basic conditions

---

[93] Cited in Xu Guangqi, *Complete treatise*, *j*. 16, "Zhejiang shuili."

[94] Amano Motonosuke, *Agricultural history*, p. 292.

[95] See Chen Hengli and Wang Da, *Supplement to the agricultural encyclopedia*, pp. 38–39. According to the "Monthly tasks" section of *Mr. Shen's agricultural encyclopedia* – a late Ming work – the late rice in the eastern part of Huzhou, the main crop in this area, was harvested in the tenth lunar month. The *Supplement to the agricultural encyclopedia*, which is slightly later, says of transplanting in Tongxiang county 桐鄉縣, Jiaxing prefecture, that "it mostly takes place after the summer solstice, being harvested at the end of the autumn," which makes it unquestionably a late rice. The "Monthly tasks" section of *Mr. Shen's agricultural encyclopedia* also describes rice ripening in the ninth lunar month as "early rice," and the "Yun tiandi fa" section also says that "early white rice" (the same variety) is hard to grow, as "it is not easy to apply the fertilizer in a properly balanced way." However, though "the kernels are coarse and hard, it is much used for food, [so] a large quantity should be planted." The principal grain at this time was thus late-ripening late rice, which Shen calls "late rice" or "yellow rice" (*huang dao* 黃稻).

[96] Li Bozhong, "Ming-Qing Jiangnan zhongdao nonghu shengchan nengli chutan" 明清江南種稻農戶生產能力初探 [A preliminary inquiry into the productive capacity of rice farmers in Ming-Qing Jiangnan], *Zhongguo nongshi* 3 (1986).

[97] A rough statistical analysis of local gazetteers shows that from mid-Ming to mid-Qing (and especially in the Qing) transplanting occurred mainly in the fifth lunar month, with the maximum frequency between the solar periods of Grain In Ear and Summer Solstice (approximately June 6 to July 6), and harvesting mainly in the ninth lunar month. See Li Bozhong, "Productive capacity of rice farmers," and *Agriculture in Jiangnan 1622–1850*, ch. 2.2. Seen from a present-day point of view, early, intermediate, and late rice have growing periods of, respectively, 120, 150, and 180 days. See Amano Motonosuke, *Agricultural history*, p. 291. The seedlings take about a month to grow, hence a posttransplanting

for the double-cropping system with over-winter secondary crops (*chunhua* 春花).

I have argued in the past that the quantity of fertilizer per *mu* of rice paddy increased in Ming-Qing Jiangnan, and that a large proportion of this was supplementary fertilizer.[98] There are two peaks in the absorption of nitrogen by single-crop rice, at 20 and 60 days after transplanting;[99] hence the great significance of supplementary fertilizer for yields (especially from intermediate and late rice). It is not, however, easy to determine its specific contribution in isolation from other factors, but as regards nitrogen content, 3 kilograms of soybean cake are broadly equivalent to 1 kilogram of ammonium sulfate.[100] Further, according to the input–output analysis by Dwight Perkins, 1 kilogram of ammonium sulfate will increase grain yield by 6 kilograms in China.[101] In other words, 1 kilogram of soybean cake produces an increase of 2 kilograms of grain. In the Qing period, about 40 *jin* of cake were applied to each *mu* as supplementary fertilizer, which could thus cause an increase of 80 *jin* per *mu* (on the order of 600 kilograms per hectare). These calculations indicate the importance of the effect but take no account of specific conditions of season or locality, and will need therefore to be followed up by determinations based on field investigations.

The two-crops-a-year rotation of wet-field rice with wheat, rape, or beans involved alternating wet-field with dry-field cultivation, which was beneficial to the soil. Zhang Lüxiang observed that growing wheat in a paddy-field would make the soil dry out and increase its porosity, which helped the next crop of rice.[102] Fang Zaihui in modern times has pointed out that the advantage of rotating wet-field rice with barley or wheat, and in particular with rape or broadbeans, is a rational exploitation of the nutritional elements in the soil: a balance is created between the supply and demand of nutrients, which makes the use of fertilizer more effective and hence reduces the quantity needed. It can also influence the humic content of the soil, its total nitrogen content, the unit weight of the arable layer, and the

growing season from, say, the first half of the fifth lunar month to late in the ninth lunar month – implying a total growing season of about $30 + 15 + (3 \times 30) + 15^+ = 150^+$ days – would tend to indicate a slow-ripening intermediate rice or early-ripening late rice.

[98] Li Bozhong, "Raising the intensiveness of cultivation." The increase was due in part to the generalization of the use of supplementary fertilizer, and in part to an increase in the amounts of basic fertilizer applied.

[99] Nanjing nongxue yuan et al., *Crop cultivation*, p. 74.

[100] Beijing nonglin ju, *Nongye changyong shuzi shouce* 农业常用数字手册 [Handbook of numerical values commonly used in agriculture] (Beijing: Nongye CBS, 1980), pp. 186–87, 193.

[101] Dwight Perkins, *Agricultural Development in China, 1368–1968* (Chicago: Aldine Publishing, 1969), p. 73.

[102] *Supplement to the agricultural encyclopedia*, "Bu Nongshu hou," p. 106.

porosity. The result is a more fertile soil with improved plowing characteristics, a possible reduction of toxins, and a lessening of the damage done by
diseases, insects, and weeds.[103] Alternative systems of cultivation, in contrast,
have the defect of leaving the farmland in too humid a condition, which
leads to physiochemical degradation. This is evidently the case for one-
crop-a-year rice, apart from the period in the winter when the field is
drained and the soil turned over and dried, and for double-cropped rice.
Even the rotation of wet-field rice with green manures such as lucerne
(alfalfa) and *Astragalus sinicus* (milk vetch) on a two-crops-a-year basis does
not, however, permit turning and drying the soil in the winter, with the
result that neither crop grows well and yields are low.[104]

Since even more wet-field rice land was transferred to the cultivation of
cotton and mulberry trees in the Ming-Qing period, most of it being of a
kind relatively unsuited for rice growing,[105] the relative quality of the remaining rice land, and its per *mu* yield, ought on the basis of this alone to
have risen. We now look to see if this was so in fact.

THE INCREASED YIELDS OF WET-FIELD RICE PER UNIT OF AREA IN MING-QING JIANGNAN

What was the change in yields per *mu*? Some scholars think that it was
constant, some that it fell, and some again that it went up. In the 1980s this
divergence was very evident, with Yu Yefei 余也非 taking the traditional
position that output per *mu* had remained unchanged through the Yuan,
the Ming, and the Qing.[106] Wu Hui 吴慧 likewise asserts that under the
Qing from 1644 to 1840 yields per *mu* of wet-field rice in Jiangnan were not
greatly different from what they had been in Ming times.[107] Min Zongdian
闵宗殿, however, categorically maintains that there was a falling trend in
yields per *mu* in the Lake Tai region in the Ming-Qing period, and even
regards the Qing level as being no more than 83 percent of that in Ming

[103] Fang Zaihui et al., *Zhejiang farming*, pp. 161–67.
[104] Ibid., pp. 40, 309–10.
[105] Li Bozhong, "Rational utilization of agricultural resources."
[106] Yu Yefei, "Zhongguo lidai liangshi pingjun mou-chanliang kaolüe" 中国历代粮食平均亩产
量考略 [Summary of an inquiry into average yields of food-grain per *mu* through Chinese
history], *Chongqing shifan-xueyuan bao* 重庆师范学院报 3 (1980).
[107] Wu Hui, *Zhongguo lidai liangshi muchan yanjiu* 中国历代粮食亩产研究 [Studies on the per-
mu yields of food grain through Chinese history] (Beijing: Nongye CBS, 1985), pp. 169,
175–77.

times. In contrast to the foregoing three scholars, Wu Chengming 吴承明 is of the opinion that yields went up in the early and mid-Qing.[108] Li Longqian 李龙潜 considers that in such places as Suzhou and Jiaxing in the early and mid-Qing dynasty, wet-rice yields per *mu* were evidently higher than they had been at the end of the Ming.[109]

Before we ask who is wrong and who right as regards this question, several preliminary points need making. (1) There are not many works that focus specifically on Jiangnan, and even fewer that concentrate on the different periods during the Ming and the Qing. (2) The majority of the works that discuss per-*mu* yields of wet-field rice in Jiangnan make their case by means of examples, relying on items taken from collections of documents and relating to this matter. (3) Some scholars regularly use per-*mu* yields from Song times and from modern times (particularly the 1930s and the 1950s) to serve as the basis for evaluating their estimates of Ming and Qing yields in Jiangnan. It is our view that while the above methods are in some respects reasonable, they are also in other respects questionable. First, they do not differentiate the Ming and Qing into distinctive periods for special study, thus having no way of discerning whether or not there were in fact changes. Second, there are large differences between the per-*mu* yields recorded in the historical material on Ming-Qing Jiangnan already in our possession, ranging from *one shi* or less to four *shi* or more, and many of these figures relate to such special circumstances as bumper crops or extremely good-quality land, which makes any judgment about the changes in the average level difficult.[110] Obtainable records of yields are also limited in number and insufficient to support a quantitative analysis of the instances contained in them. Data from the Song and from the present time are valuable reference material when determining Ming-Qing yields, but require us to impose the following conditions: (1) that they be accurate; (2) that attention be paid to the effects of differences in climate and

---

[108] Wu Chengming and Xu Dixin 许涤新, eds., *Zhongguo zibenzhuyi-de mengya – Zhongguo zibenzhuyi fazhan-shi di-yi juan* 中国资本主义的萌芽—中国资本主义发展史第一卷 [The sprouts of capitalism in China – The first chapter in the history of the development of capitalism in China] (Beijing: Renmin CBS, 1985), p. 191.

[109] Li Longqian, *Ming-Qing jingji shi* 明清经济史 [An economic history of the Ming and the Qing] (Guangzhou: Guangdong gaodeng jiaoyu CBS, 1988), p. 407.

[110] You Xiuling has pointed out that at the present time the highest yields are from three to five times the average, and that it takes more than twenty years to raise the level of the large number of average fields to the level of the small number of outstanding ones. See You Xiuling, *Rice cultivation in the Lake Tai area*, pp. 10–41. In Ming and Qing times, with a social organization and techniques of technology transfer inferior to those of the present day, it would have taken longer.

soil conditions in Song and modern times; and (3) that no assumption be made of "linear progress." In other words, these materials serve the function of reference, not of proof. In what follows, a macroscopic analysis of the yields problem is based on the relationship between consumption and production, after which some local records are used to test the conclusions.

As a necessary preliminary we begin with changes in cultivated acreage under wet-field rice, population levels, and rice consumption.

Although there are sizable discrepancies between the official statistics for cultivated land in Ming and Qing times and the reality, among the various important economic regions in China, the figures for Jiangnan's farmland are comparatively close to the truth. Among the statistics for the period prior to 1950, it is generally recognized that those for the 1580s are relatively reliable. Here we conflate the data from the five prefectures of Suzhou, Songjiang, Changshu, Zhenjiang, and Jiangning from *juan* 17 of the Wanli *Da Ming huidian* 萬曆大明會典 [Collected statutes of the Great Ming] and the Wanli land figures given in *juan* 15 of the Kangxi-reign *Zhejiang tongzhi* 浙江通志 [Comprehensive gazetteer for Zhejiang province] for the three prefectures of Hangzhou, Jiaxing, and Huzhou to arrive at an approximate total of 45 million *mu*. This figure is higher than the total obtained by adding together the later totals for individual prefectures and counties, which entitles us to say that concealment must have been low and this figure close to the actual situation.[111]

Because of the expansion of the cultivation of noncereal crops for the market, the area under wet-field rice in Ming-Qing Jiangnan tended continuously to contract. Here, for the sake of simplicity, I shall approximate this for both periods as 90 percent.[112] This is methodologically conservative in that it tends to cause an overestimation of productivity in Ming times, in the sense that it works against the thesis that I should like to establish here,

---

[111] Although the figures of the Wanli survey were not able to escape from those factors indicated by He Bingdi 何炳棣 [Pingti Ho] as making for the official overestimation and underestimation of land throughout Chinese history, in comparison with other regions in China these were of slight effect in Jiangnan, at least since Southern Song times. See He Bingdi, "Nan Song zhi jin tudi shuzi-de kaoshi he pingjia" 南宋至今土地數字的考釋和評價 [An investigation into and an evaluation of figures for cultivated land from the Southern Song to the present day], *Zhongguo shehui-kexue* 3 (1985). The Wanli survey began in Jiangnan and was most conscientiously carried out in that region. Furthermore, the opening up of new lowland farmland ("extensive development") had basically drawn to its close in Jiangnan by this time, and later fluctuations would not have changed its magnitude to any great extent. That Wanli official figures for farmland were basically used throughout the Qing dynasty was mainly due to these reasons, and not necessarily to a purely conservative retention of the original numbers or negligence in investigating.

[112] For a detailed discussion, see Li Bozhong, *Agriculture in Jiangnan, 1620–1850*, ch.2.2.

namely that productivity was rising; thus, once this rise is even so shown to have occurred, it makes the conclusion all the more certainly correct.

Thus the Ming-Qing wet-rice cropping area in Jiangnan may be estimated as 4.05×10^7 *mu*.

The population of Jiangnan in Ming and Qing times is a thorny question. On the basis of my work on demographic change in Jiangnan it is possible to make a rough investigation.[113] By following the method adopted by Wang Yejian 王業鍵,[114] but using the population figures for 1820 established by Liang Fangzhong 梁方仲,[115] and the figures in the Board of Revenue's acreage and tax registers for 1850, it can be determined that the total population in Jiangnan for this latter year was about 36 million. Although G. W. Skinner has pointed out that the official population figures for many places in China in 1850 are too high,[116] it is not possible to obtain better ones, and so they are used here.

There are no usable population figures for the late Ming, so we are obliged to calculate the average annual growth rate from the reliable data for 1393 in the early Ming to 1850. For 1393, the Wanli *Collected statutes of the Great Ming, juan* 19, and the Kangxi *Comprehensive gazetteer for Zhejiang, juan* 15, give us a total population in Jiangnan at this time of 8.7 million people. This implies an average annual growth rate of 0.31 percent. The population in 1620, before the onset of the late Ming socio-economic crisis, would therefore have been 17.6 million. Since the growth rate of the population in Jiangnan in Ming times may have been slightly higher than it was in Qing times, the true total may have been nearer to 20 million.[117]

Consumption of wet-field rice mainly comprised three categories, namely food, seeds, and the raw material for the production of alcohol. Although the payment of tax in grain is not strictly speaking "consumption," attention must also be paid to this aspect. To simplify the analysis, we shall set aside the use of grain for seeds, tax, and alcohol, although the

---

[113] Li Bozhong, "Kongzhi zengzhang yi bao fuyu: Qingdai qian-zhongqi Jiangnan-de renkou xingwei" 控制增長以保富裕—清代前中期江南的人口行為 [Preserving prosperity by controlling (population) growth: demographic behavior in early- and mid-Qing Jiangnan], *Xin shixue* (Taipei) 3.3 (1994).

[114] Yeh-chien Wang [Wang Yejian], "The Impact of the Taiping Rebellion on Population in Southern Kiangsu," (Harvard) *Papers on China* 19 (1965).

[115] Liang Fangzhong, *Zhongguo lidai renkou, tiandi, tianfu tongji* 中国历代人口，田地、田赋统计 [Statistics on population, cultivated land, and land taxes throughout Chinese history] (Shanghai: Shanghai renmin CBS, 1980), pp. 273–79.

[116] G. W. Skinner, "Sichuan's Population Data in the Nineteenth Century: Lessons from Disaggregated Data," *Late Imperial China* 8.1 (1987).

[117] See Li Bozhong, "Preserving prosperity."

amounts were of some significance, and the proportion used for alcohol in Qing times was far above that in Ming times.[118]

A number of authors have discussed rice consumption in Jiangnan, of whom the deepest and most reliable is Shiba Yoshinobu.[119] In his view the annual consumption per person in Ming-Qing Jiangnan was about 3.6 market *shi* 石 (roughly equivalent to Ming or Qing *shi*). Bearing in mind the much-increased production and interprovincial import of wheat in Qing times, and more numerous records of wheat consumption in this latter dynasty, here we provisionally take Bao Shichen's estimate of 3 *shi* of rice per person per year, which leaves 0.6 *shi* over for wheat. For the Ming dynasty we take the average rice consumption per person per year as 3.3 *shi*, which leaves 0.3 *shi* for the wheat component.

On the basis of the foregoing figures it can be calculated that the total consumption of rice in Jiangnan was 6.6×10^7 *shi* in 1620 (that is, $3.3 \times 2 \times 10^7$), and 10.8×10^7 *shi* in 1850 (that is, $3.0 \times 3.6 \times 10^7$). The interprovincial imports must, however, be taken into account. I have estimated that annual interprovincial imports of rice into Jiangnan in the middle of the nineteenth century were about 1.5×10^7 *shi*, on the basis of studies by Quan Hansheng 全汉升 and Wang Yejian, Wu Chengming, and Wang Yejian and Huang Guoshu 黄国枢.[120] Thus 9.3×10^7 *shi* were grown in Jiangnan at this latter date.

---

[118] The alcohol industry made wine, vinegar, soysauce, and brewer's yeast (*qu* 麯), which latter, apart from being used for the production of wine, was also employed in the making of vinegar, soysauce, dyes for foodstuffs, and traditional Chinese medicines. See Hong Guangzhu 洪光柱, *Zhongguo shipin ke-ji shigao* 中国食品科技史稿 [Draft history of the science and technology of Chinese foodstuffs] (Beijing: Zhongguo shangye CBS, 1984), pp. 76–88. Jiangnan people had long been drinkers of rice wine, especially "yellow wine" (*huang jiu* 黄酒), so the quantity would have been substantial. Bao Shichen states that in Suzhou around the beginning of the nineteenth century, the quantity of rice used each year for wine amounted to more than several million *shi* 石. See *Four techniques for the governance of the common people*, *j.* 2, Nong er. He also observes that in Suzhou at this time, "Five or six *jin* of yellow wine was not a large quantity for someone to drink." Zhang Lüxiang said of the early Qing that "It is normal for a man to drink several *sheng* 升 a day [1 *sheng* = 0.01 *shi*]. As for heavy drinkers, there is no counting their consumption." See Chen Hengli and Wang Da, *Supplement to the agricultural encyclopedia*, p. 160. Even assuming no change in the level of per capita consumption of wine in Jiangnan between the Ming and the Qing, the quantity of rice used for making alcohol would have roughly doubled by mid-Qing in contrast with late Ming. See Li Bozhong, *Qing economic history*, ch. 4, sec. 2.1.

[119] Shiba Yoshinobu, "Sōdai no shōhi, seisan suijun shitan" [Tentative inquiry into levels of consumption and production under the Song], *Chūgoku bunka* 1.1 (1991).

[120] Quan Hansheng and Wang Yejian, "Qing Yongzheng-nianjian-de mi-jia" 清雍正年間的米價 [Rice prices during the Yongzheng reign of the Qing dynasty], *Zhongyang yanjiuyuan lishiyuyan yanjiusuo jikan* 30 (1959); Wu Chengming, "Lun Qingdai qianqi woguo guonei shichang" 论清代前期我国国内市场 [On the internal market in the first part of the Qing dynasty], in Wu chengming, *Zhongguo zibenzhuyi yu guonei shichang* [Capitalism in China and

These figures show that in the early seventeenth century the productivity of wet-field rice land was on the order of 1.63 *shi* per *mu* (i.e., 6.6/4.05), and in the mid-nineteenth century of 2.3 *shi* per *mu* (i.e., 9.3/4.05). This was an increase of 0.67 *shi* per *mu* or of 41 percent (i.e., 0.67/1.63). Given the bias toward selecting larger estimates for the Ming where we had a choice, this represents a *minimum* increase.

We now look at the documentation from the two prefectures for which it is densest, namely Suzhou and Songjiang, to see if the above conclusion about the trend is supported.

Perkins has collected 17 figures on per-*mu* productivity of wet-field rice in Suzhou and Songjiang covering the sixteenth to the eighteenth century: 11 of these relate to the sixteenth and seventeenth centuries and range from 2.0 to 6.0 *shi* of unhusked grain, which may be converted to half these values for husked rice. The mean is 3.0, or 1.5 *shi* of husked rice. Six items are from the eighteenth century: they range from 1.0 to 7.2, with the mean being 3.8 *shi* (i.e., 1.9 husked).[121] The increase is 0.8 *shi* per *mu* or 26.6 percent. Wu Chengming has collected 26 figures for the Jiangnan region covering the period 1621 to 1850, excluding double-cropped rice, some 8 of which are explicitly for Suzhou or Songjiang. From 1621 to 1644 productivity was from 1.0 to 3.0 *shi* per *mu*; from 1644 to 1720 it was from 1.0 to 2.0 *shi* per *mu*; and from 1796 to 1850 from 2.0 to 3.0 *shi* per *mu*, exclusively for Suzhou.[122] There would seem to have been a rise overall. In addition to these data, Min Zongdian 闵宗殿 has 6 figures for Suzhou, Songjiang, Jiaxing, and Huzhou from 1488 to 1644: they range from 1.5 *shi* per *mu* to 3.0 *shi*. For the Qing period down to 1850 he has 10 figures for the same area: these range from 1.5 to 3.6.[123] Min finds the Ming average to be 2.3 *shi* and that of the Qing to be 2.0. If, however, we remove the figures for the Guangxu reign (1875–1907) and figures for Jiangxi that Min has mistakenly assigned to Jiangnan, then the mean for the Qing down to 1850 is 2.7 *shi* of husked rice per *mu*, up 0.4 *shi* from Ming times, some 17

domestic markets] (Beijing: Zhongguo shehui kexue CBS, 1985), pp. 257–58; and Wang Yejian and Huang Guoshu, "Shiba-shiji Zhongguo liangshi gong-xu-de kaocha" 十八世纪中國糧食供需的考察 [An investigation into the supply and demand for food grain in eighteenth-century China], in Zhongyang yanjiuyuan jindai-shi yanjiusuo, *Jindai Zhongguo nongcun jingji-shi lunwen-ji* 近代中國農村經濟史論文集 [Anthology of essays on village economy in modern China] (Taipei: Zhongyang yanjiuyuan jindai-shi yanjiusuo, 1989). The estimate is in Li Bozhong, *Qing economic history*, ch. 4, sec. 2.

[121] D. Perkins, *Agricultural development*, pp. 318–19, table G4.
[122] Wu Chengming and Xu Dixin, ed., *Sprouts of capitalism*, pp. 40–41 and 190–91.
[123] Min Zongdian, "Song-Ming-Qing shiqi Taihu diqu shuidao muchanliang-de tantao" 宋明清时期太湖地区水稻亩产量的探讨 [An inquiry into the productivity per *mu* of wet-field rice in Song Ming, and Qing times around Lake Tai], in *Zhongguo nongshi* 3 (1984).

percent. Wu Chengming's figures for parts of Jiangnan other than Suzhou and Songjiang also show a continuous rise in productivity.

There may of course have been variations in productivity in the first two centuries of Qing rule. Liu Yongcheng 刘永成 has analyzed the rent records for 1747–55 in the *Shenyu-tang zubu* 慎餘堂租簿 [Rent books from the Shenyu hall] by a Shen family 沈氏 of Suzhou, and nine cases in the archives of the Board of Punishments relating to rents for farmland in Wujin, Yixing, Jiangyin, Fengxian, Taicang, Jingui, and Huating during the Kangxi, Qianlong, and Jiaqing reigns (1662–1820). He found that the per-*mu* output of wet-field rice was clearly higher in the first two of these reigns than in the third one. Thus in 1722 the figure for Wujin was 5.2 *shi* of husked rice, between 1745 and 1755 the average for Suzhou was 4.12 *shi*, and from 1745 to 1784 six departments or counties averaged 4.16 *shi*; but between 1798 and 1801 Huating and another county produced only 1.86 *shi*.[124] However, the data on per-*mu* output collected by Guo Songyi 郭松义 from fifteen counties in Jiangnan show an average for the Qianlong reign of 2.14 *shi*, and for the Jiaqing and Daoguang reigns of 2.15 *shi* (with the Daoguang level at 2.45),[125] which does not show any clear decline. Since the weather in the early part of the nineteenth century was somewhat worse than it had been in the eighteenth, it is possible that some areas in Jiangnan, and especially those where yields had been particularly high, should manifest some reduction. Overall, though, there does not seem to have been a drop.[126] Although these sparse data cannot provide a satisfac

---

[124] Liu Yongcheng, "Cong zuce, Xingdang kan Qingdai Jiangsu diqu-de liangshi mu-chanliang" 丛租册刑档看清代江苏地区的粮食亩产量 [Looking at the per-*mu* productivity of food-grain output in Jiangsu province on the basis of rent registers and the archives of the Board of Punishments], paper presented to the Zhongguo jingji-shixuehui second annual conference proceedings (Hu'nan: Zhangjiajie, 1993).

[125] Guo Songyi, "Liangshi shengchan-de fazhan" 粮食生产的发展 [The development of food-grain production] in the *Qingdai jingji shi* [Qing economic history] (Beijing: Zhongguo shehui kexue CBS, forthcoming).

[126] There are reasons that probably explain this situation. The weather was not too bad in the twenty or thirty years before 1850 (see Yeh-chien Wang, "Secular trends of Rice Prices in the Yangtze Delta, 1632–1935," in T. Rawski and L. Li, eds., *Chinese History in Economic Perspective* (Berkeley: University of California Press, 1992)) and would have had a limited adverse effect on wet-field rice production. There was, on the other hand, a great increase in the interprovincial import of fertilizer, in the form of beancakes, and the effect of this should not be underestimated. The sheer hard work of the Jiangnan people clearly also had an effect. In Huang Ang's 黃卬 *Xi-Jin zhi xiao lu* 錫金識小錄 [Records of small matters in Wuxi and Jingui] (eighteenth century), j. 1, "Bei can shang," he says: "[The peasants'] diligence in working the farmland was not equaled in earlier times. When they met with droughts or floods they previously used to be in dread of the difficulties and stopped midway [in their efforts to resist]. Today they exert themselves to the utmost to undertake rescue operations." Although this refers to the region of Wuxi and Jingui during the Qianlong reign, there is no reason to think that this was not also the case with many parts of Jiangnan after this time.

tory answer to the problem, when taken together with the preceding quantitative analysis, they provide grounds for believing that there was in fact a significant increase in productivity per *mu* in Jiangnan wet-rice farming during the Ming-Qing period in Jiangnan.

If, *per contra*, it is argued that there was no increase, then the two following questions have to be answered: (1) What factors then prevented the changes described in the earlier part of this chapter from causing a rise in per-*mu* productivity? (2) How was the large consumption deficit that mid-Qing Jiangnan would still have faced, even after allowing for the interprovincial import of grain, resolved? We have not yet seen any credible answers to these questions.

As regards using either Song-dynasty or modern figures for productivity in Jiangnan in order to deny any increase in Ming-Qing productivity, even harder questions have to be met. Both the natural and the socioeconomic conditions were different, or very different, in all three periods. This makes simple comparisons impermissible; and they explain nothing. Shiba has also pointed out that previous Song estimates are biased toward the high side.[127] Chen Hengli and Wang Da, for their part, indicated as long ago as 1958 that the per-*mu* productivity of the main farm crops in Jiaxing and Huzhou in the 1930s was clearly less than it had been in the late Ming.[128] We are therefore inclined to think that traditional wet-rice farming in Jiangnan (i.e., prior to about 1955) reached its peak in the mid-Qing. It is worth noting that this increase was not accompanied by a clearly marked increase in the input of labor,[129] which means that it is hard to explain it in

---

[127] Shiba Yoshinobu, *Jiangnan economy under the Song*, pp. 137–65.

[128] Chen Hengli and Wang Da, *Supplement to the agricultural encyclopedia*, ch. 2 and pp. 26–34, 146–47, 164, 181–84, 189–90, 250.

[129] My 1984 analysis in Li Bozhong, "Intensification of cultivation," did not take into account the labor involved in the application of fertilizer or in pumping water. Their inclusion should raise Qing labor-inputs above the Ming level. In normal years, however, the requirement of rice for water is a constant, so that changes in double-cropping apart, the input of labor per *mu* could not have varied greatly. (See also, however, the comments on pp. 455–6 above.) Labor input for mid-Qing times may be affirmed to have been greater than in Ming. On the other hand, when beancakes were used in the place of other fertilizers, the *Supplement to the Agricultural Encyclopedia* states that there were "economies both in labor and in the amount of fertilizer," and the use of beancakes spread widely in Qing (especially mid-Qing) times. Thus the increase of labor-inputs for fertilizing would not have increased commensurately with the increase in the use of fertilizer.

Furthermore, according to the *Report on agriculture in the Huangpu and Mao [lake] region*, the combined labor requirement for weeding and the application of (supplementary) fertilizer in the rice-paddies in the western part of Songjiang during the Daoguang reign was only one working day (per crop) per *mu*. And the labor required for pumping in the rice-paddies of Songjiang, according to calculations based on records in Shen Jingxian's 沈鏡賢 *Mao-dong caotang biji* 泖東草堂筆記 [Jottings from the Thatched Hall east of the Mao Lake], on which see Wei Jinyu 魏金玉, "Guanyu Zhongguo nongye zibenzhuyi mengya-de

theoretical terms as "involution" (*neijuan-hua* 內卷化). Wang Yejian has argued for a close correlation between changes in the weather and changes in rice prices,[130] which happens to fit with the foregoing conclusions. In the first half of the nineteenth century, the population of Jiangnan had already reached its pre-1950 maximum, and was mainly fed, in spite of considerable interprovincial imports of grain, from locally produced rice. Although there were other important factors involved, such as changes in the velocity of the circulation of money, this increase in unit-area productivity in wet-rice cultivation, which nonetheless did not fall into the trap of "involution," was the main reason why Jiangnan rice prices did fall over a long period. It would, however, also seem that this increased productivity and the resulting economic benefits were in large measure due to changes in the natural environment.

I would like to conclude by emphasizing that the links between farming on the one hand and changes in the natural environment and in human activities on the other are at one and the same time important and complex. The above analysis is only a preliminary inquiry. Though I have expended considerable effort on it, and received the advice and help of a number of colleagues, it is only a beginning. Many important aspects have not been touched on; examples include the changes that occurred in the social system governing agriculture and in the organization of farming, and the impact of various sorts of changes that took place outside the farming sector. I will look both more widely and more deeply in future work.

(*Translated by Mark Elvin*)

jige wenti" 关于中国农业资本主义萌芽的几个问题 [Some questions relating to the "sprouts of capitalism" in Chinese agriculture] in Nanjing da-xue lishixi Ming-Qing-shi yanjiushi ed., *Zhongguo zibenzhuyi mengya wenti lunwenji* 中国资本主义萌芽问题论文集 [A collection of essays on the "sprouts of capitalism" in China] (Nanjing: Jiangsu renmin chubanshe, 1983), was less than 2.5 labor-days per *mu* (per crop). This was less than a quarter of the 10 labor-days needed for "plowing levelling, weeding, and harvesting." There would thus appear to have been limits on the quantity of extra labor spent on the application of extra fertilizer and pumping even by the mid-Qing. Thus any increase is unlikely to have been great when compared with late Ming times.

[130] Wang Yejian [Yeh-chien Wang], "Secular trends."

Diseases

13

Cholera in China, 1820–1930

AN ASPECT OF THE INTERNATIONALIZATION OF INFECTIOUS DISEASE

KERRIE L. MacPHERSON

OVERVIEW

By the 1930s, most Chinese and foreign medical authorities agreed that 1820 marked the year when true Asiatic cholera was introduced to China via the sea route from the Indian subcontinent. Its manifestation was so virulent and so markedly different from previous infections classified in the historical and medical literature as *huoluan* 霍亂, or what was believed to be *cholera asiatica*, that it was thought by many to be an entirely different disease. This chapter will investigate the historical controversies surrounding the identification of cholera, particularly debates over whether the disease was endemic to China prior to 1820 or an "imported" infection. Such conflicting views were determinants affecting the steps taken to arrest the disease and to mitigate its effects. We will also examine the various factors, both human and environmental, that may have influenced its pernicious effects and tenacious presence from the 1820s to the 1930s, when a vaccine conferring limited immunity was widely disseminated in conjunction with ambitious public health measures.

INTRODUCTION

Cholera, the most deadly of the diarrheal diseases, with a mortality averaging approximately half of its incidence before the advent of modern therapies, became pandemic in the nineteenth century, attacking virtually every major country in the world.[1] Emerging from a presumed homeland in the

---

[1] The classic in the field is R. Pollitzer, *Cholera* (Geneva, 1959). See also Oscar Felsenfeld, *The Cholera Problem* (St. Louis, 1967); World Health Organization, *Principles and Practice of*

487

deltas of the Ganges and Brahmaputra rivers in 1817, six pandemics were identified by the third decade of the twentieth century. The disease then receded to its endemic centers in southern and southeast Asia, where it continues to pose a serious health threat. As of 1993, the Centers for Disease Control and Prevention have reclassified cholera as an "emerging infectious disease."[2]

Although watched with keen interest wherever it has prevailed since 1817, its westward diffusions into a susceptible Europe (1830) have attracted the most attention, obscuring its eastward advances. This bias partly explains why authorities disagree on the chronology of the six pandemics that swept the world, and in the case of Chinese researchers even the number of pandemics between 1817 and 1925 (see Table 13.1).[3]

But this is not the sum of the matter. In 1961–70, the United Nations World Health Organization (WHO) identified a seventh pandemic spreading from a focus in Indonesia in 1961 and reaching Korea, China (unconfirmed), Macao, Hong Kong, Taiwan, and the Philippines.[4] From 1964–66 it extended westward to West Pakistan, Afghanistan, Iran, the southern USSR, and Iraq. This last pandemic was not caused by the same classic cholera bacillus, but by a hemolytic (El Tor) biotype of *Vibrio cholerae*, first isolated by Gotschlich in 1905 at the El Tor quarantine station in Egypt.

Cholera Control (Geneva, 1970); and Dhiman Barua and William Burrows, *Cholera* (Philadelphia, 1974). For the Western experience, see Norman Longmate, *King Cholera: The Biography of a Disease* (London, 1966); M. Pelling, *Cholera, Fever, and English Medicine* (Oxford, 1978); C. Rosenberg, *The Cholera Years in the United States in 1832, 1849 and 1866* (Chicago, 1962); and, especially, W. E. van Heyningen and John R. Seal, *Cholera: The American Scientific Experience, 1947–1980* (Boulder, 1983). There is no history of cholera in China except for a score of articles scattered in various journals and Wu Lien-teh, J. W. H. Chun, R. Pollitzer, and C. Y. Yu, *Cholera: A Handbook for the Medical Profession in China* (Shanghai, 1934), which is badly in need of replacement.

[2] Asia and Latin America are the foci. The term refers to disease of infectious origin whose incidence in humans has either increased within the past two decades or threatens to increase in the near future. See *Mortality and Morbidity Weekly Report (MMWR)* 43, no, R.R.5 (April 15, 1994), p. 2. I am indebted to Ken Shortridge for calling my attention to this report and for discussions on recent microbiological thinking on cholera.

[3] See also Kenneth F. Kiple, ed., *The Cambridge World History of Human Disease* (Cambridge, 1993), pp. 642–48.

[4] See B. Barua and B. Cvjetanovi, "Cholera during the Period 1961–1970," in WHO, *Principles and Practice of Cholera Control*, pp. 15–22. The rates of infection in China during the Cultural Revolution from the El Tor pandemic were rumored to be high. In 1961, the outbreak of cholera in Hong Kong and Macao was preceded by an outbreak in China signaled by the number of individuals presenting cholera immunization certificates at the border. The first cases were traced to Mainland origin. The authorities in Guangzhou denied this and all requests for information by the Hong Kong Medical and Health Service were refused. See D. J. M. MacKenzie, *Report on the Outbreak of Cholera in Hong Kong Covering the Period 11th August to 12th October, 1961* (Hong Kong, 1961), pp. 1, 35.

Table 13.1. *Comparative chronology of cholera pandemics*

Haeser (1882)		Hirsch (1883)		Sticker (1912)		Wu (1934)		Pollitzer (1959)		Felsenfeld (1967)	
No.	Period	No.	Period	No.	Period	No.	Period	No.	Period	No.	Period
1(a)	1816–23	1	1817–23	1	1817–38	1	1817–23	1	1817–26	1	1817–26
(b)	1826–37										
2	1840–50	2	1826–37	2	1840–64	2	1826–37	2	1829–52	2	1829–1952(?)
3	1852–60	3	1846–63	3	1863–75	3	1846–62	3	1852–63	3	1852–63
4	1863–73	4	1865–75	4	1881–96	4	1864–75	4	1863–75	4	1863–75
5		5		5	1899–	5	1883–87	5	1881–93	5	1881–96
6		6		6		6	1892–95	6	1899–1923	6	1898–1923
						7	1910–25	7	1961–		

Sources. For Haeser, Hirsch, Sticker, and Pollitzer, see Pollitzer, *Cholera*. See also Felsenfeld, *Cholera Problem*; and Wu Lien-teh et al., *Cholera: A Handbook.*

This biotype was called "paracholera" or "enteritis choleriformis El Tor" and was not identified with *V. cholerae* by the World Health Assembly until 1962, although treatment of patients and control of the epidemic were essentially the same. There are also marked epidemiological differences between El Tor and classical cholera, the consequences of which we will explore later in this essay.

Notwithstanding the violence and high mortality of the nineteenth-century pandemics that followed the rapid increase and expansion of trade and traffic throughout the world, it must be borne in mind that the endemic foci in Asia contain more than half the total world population, with 25 percent of the world's total population residing in China alone. Crowded into massive urban agglomerations with inadequate sanitation and suspect water supplies, an enormous population continues to exist at potential risk from the ravages of cholera, for the only natural reservoir of infection is the human species. Transmission is sustained in a vicious cycle between the vibrio excreter and the environment, with sources of water playing a primary role.

THE *VIBRIO CHOLERAE*

The bacterial cause for classic cholera is the *Vibrio cholerae* or vibrio comma bacillus, discovered by Pacini in 1854 and demonstrated conclusively by Snow to be waterborne. It was isolated by Robert Koch in 1883; his findings were formally reported to the German government in 1884. Although Koch's findings were not universally accepted, they were fundamentally correct and laid the empirical foundations for controlling the disease.[5] From that date, the laboratory became the arena in which an attempt was made to isolate and identify with some precision true cholera vibrios (serogroup 1:0), and choleralike vibrios (non-o:1 serogroup) responsible for causing a wide variety of gastrointestinal disease.[6]

[5] Van Heyningen and Seal, *Cholera: The American Scientific Experience*, pp. 25–27. Indeed, in the following year it was positively identified in Shanghai in the stool smears of a cholera patient in hospital by Drs. Milles and Mcleod, fully two years before laboratory analysis was successfully used in New York. See K. L. MacPherson, *A Wilderness of Marshes: The Origins of Public Health in Shanghai, 1843–93* (London: Oxford University Press, 1987).

[6] See, Pollitzer, *Cholera*, p. 101. Since the outbreaks and rapid spread of 0139 (non-serogroup 01) strain of *V. cholerae* in Madras, India, and southern Bengalesh in 1992, recent investigations suggest that the genetic structure and virulence factors of 0139 strains are closely related to El Tor 01 strains of *V. cholerae*. According to Waldor and Mekalanos, "The notion that only strains in the 01 serogroup of *V. cholerae* can give rise to epidemic and pandemic cholera has been firmly contradicted by the rapid spread of the 0139 cholera epidemic

Although only laboratory tests can confirm the presence of *V. cholerae*, particularly in mild or asymptomatic cases, the disease has striking clinical characteristics. "The disease that begins by killing the patient"[7] commences with the abrupt onset of effortless vomiting and watery diarrhea that assumes a "rice water" appearance. This is due to the multiplication of the organisms in the small bowel and the subsequent production of toxins that cause the mucosal cells of the intestine to secrete isotonic fluid. This is followed by thirst, suppression of urine, and later by cramps of the muscles of the extremities. The patient's voice becomes hoarse and collapse soon follows – a progression of symptoms occurring within 5–12 hours. The patient exhibits a classic cholera physiognomy of a sunken, cadaverous face, bluish-tinged fingernails and shriveled fingers, flat neck veins and a cold, coated tongue. The patient also exudes a characteristic odor of a sweet, fishy type (not at all fecal in character), owing to the soiling of the clothes by the rice-water stool. Without treatment by intravenous fluid replacement, the patient dies from circulatory failure or acute acidosis with failure of the renal functions.[8]

The vibrio is ingested, usually by contaminated water, but also through food, flies, contact with infected persons, and, as more recently established, contact with carriers of the disease. Fomites, such as paper currency, coins, silk, cotton, and tobacco, have only a very circumscribed role to play in the transmission of infection.[9]

Koch described two types of epidemics. In the explosive type, there is an easily identified common source (usually a polluted water supply) in which a large number of cases appear over a short period of time (from one to five days). In a protracted epidemic, the source is not easily identified and fewer

originating in southeastern India." Mathew K. Waldor and John J. Mekalanos, "Emergence of a New Cholera Pandemic: Molecular Analysis of Virulence Determinants in *Vibrio cholerae* 0139 and Development of a Live Vaccine Prototype," *Journal of Infectious Diseases* 170 (1994), pp. 278–82.

[7] Comment made by Dr. James Henderson at the Shandong Road Hospital for Chinese, Shanghai. See Alexander Jamieson "Report on the Health of Shanghai for the Half-year Ended 31st March 1879," *Customs Gazette, Medical Reports* 17 (1879), p. 26.

[8] The universal fear of cholera noted in the literature comes from the corpselike visage of the victims. See A. Mondal and R. B. Sack, "The Clinical Picture of Cholera," in WHO, *Principles and Practice of Cholera Control*, pp. 57–60.

[9] See W. H. Mosley, "Epidemiology of cholera," in WHO, *Principles and Practice of Cholera Control*, pp. 23–27. For the survival of the vibrios on fomites, specifically paper banknotes that were rumored to be a source of infection in Republican China, see H. M. Jettmar, "Investigations on the Vitality of Vibrio Cholerae on Chinese Paper Money," in Wu Lien-teh, ed., *Manchurian Plague Prevention Service, Memorial Volume, 1912–1932* (Shanghai, 1934), pp. 301–06. For a recent discussion, see D. Barua, "Survival of Cholera Vibrios in Food, Water and Fomites," in WHO, *Principles and Practice of Cholera Control*, pp. 29–32.

cases appear over a longer period (several weeks). In the nineteenth and early twentieth centuries the effects of partial immunity in endemic communities and the role of asymptomatic vibrio excreters was not well understood, though often suggested in the literature. Furthermore, the full spectrum of diarrheal diseases caused by the vibrios, including the more numerous mild cases, is only now recognized. There was the eruption of a seventh pandemic in 1961 from Sulawesi, Indonesia, of what was called paracholera (El Tor), which previously had shown no epidemic tendencies, although four prior outbreaks were documented there in the years 1937–38, 1939–40, 1944, and 1957–58. The *Vibrio eltor* is more resistant to various environmental factors and to antibiotics; it causes more mild and asymptomatic infection than the classic vibrio, and a few chronic carriers have been found.[10]

CHOLERA IN ITS HOME

The annals of cholera began in India over 2,000 years ago. Evidence of this extraordinary malady can be found in the literary records, and was described by European explorers, traders, and travelers by the sixteenth century.[11] A dense population, a large surface area of water where the temperature exceeds 17 °C and the humidity exceeds 40 percent for long periods of the year, poor or nonexistent sanitation, and religious practices involving water (and often the disposal of the dead) made cholera a permanent guest. Yet, it is not known why in the second decade of the nineteenth century the disease suddenly became epidemic outside of its historic geographical limits. As Creighton stated in 1894, "the antecedents and circumstances . . . for its diffusiveness far beyond India, constitute one of the greatest problems in epidemiology."[12] Discounting the sanitary habits of the communities affected as a *new* factor, he suggested from his perspective as

[10] Felsenfeld, *Cholera Problem*, pp. 11–17. See also Barua and Burrows, *Cholera*, pp. 367–79, for a lengthy discussion on the role of cholera carriers. During a recrudescence of cholera (El Tor) in Hong Kong in 1963, a restaurant in northwest Kowloon was thought to be the source of infection, and subsequent investigation showed 34% of the staff were excreting vibrios asymptomatically. Five cases were identified as being a direct result of eating in the restaurant, while twelve others occurred as a result of indirect spread. Contaminated food and cooking utensils by carriers was believed to be the source of infection (p. 377).

[11] R. Pollitzer, after reviewing the evidence and the debates over the presence of true Asiatic cholera in India prior to the sixteenth century, concludes that it was probable. See Pollitzer, *Cholera*, pp. 11–13.

[12] C. Creighton, *A History of Epidemics in Britain* (Cambridge, 1894), vol. 2, p. 860.

a follower of Pettenkorfer (Koch's opponent) that the gradual change in the beds of rivers, altering the amount of surface and subsurface water flow, coupled with denser cultivation under British colonial rule, nurtured the cholera vibrio.[13]

Investigations of the influence of climate on the etiology and incidence of disease were pervasive. Eighteenth- and nineteenth-century medical climatologists ascertained that cholera, like other infectious diseases, has a characteristic seasonal pattern, but they also understood that this pattern varied geographically. The inherent difficulty of too much imprecision limited climatology; this method of observation thus gave way by the second half of the nineteenth century to the more promising germ theory of the transmission of disease, which to a great extent owes its formulation to the deadly harvests of epidemic cholera.[14]

Reviving this older medical perspective, a recent thesis suggested that climatic factors such as the world disturbance of weather patterns due to volcanic activity in this period played a role in "facilitating" the first pandemic of cholera. Lowered temperatures and rainfall during the temperate season and drought during the monsoon season reduced grain yields and thus lowered the nutritional status of the population to dangerous levels throughout the eastern portions of India where the first outbreaks of epidemic cholera were recorded. Yet the prevailing season and lowered temperature did have an impact on the disease in another connection. After summarizing the extensive bacteriological studies on the influence of water on the epidemiology of the disease, Pollitzer concluded that "provided conditions for the subsistence of *V. cholerae* do exist, the temperature of the water, which in turn depends upon the prevailing season, is one of the main factors, perhaps the principal factor, determining the length of survival of the organisms."[15]

Another explanation of historic rather than epidemiological significance was the fortuitous intersection of an evolving scientific method and

[13] Ibid.
[14] For China in this connection , see K. L. MacPherson, *Wilderness of Marshes*, pp. 15–48.
[15] See H. Stommel and E. Stommel, "The Year Without a Summer," *Scientific American*, 240 (June 1979), pp. 134–40, who draw on the ideas of John D. Ford, "A Study in Meteorological and Trade Cycle History: The Economic Crisis Following the Napoleonic Wars," *Journal of Economic History* 34.2 (June 1974), p. 332; and Pollitzer, *Cholera*, p. 186. A preliminary survey of unusual climatological factors, i.e., extreme cold, typhoons, drought, flooding, and famine, juxtaposed against recorded epidemics (seventeenth century to nineteenth century) for Guangdong province shows some correlation, but the evidence is incomplete. See Qiao Chengxi 乔盛西 and Tang Wenya 唐文雅, eds., *Guangzhou diqu jiuzhi qihou shiliao huibian yu yenjiu* 广州地区旧志气候史料汇编与研究 [Research and compilation of historical records on climate from old geographical records of Guangzhou] (Guangzhou, 1993), pp. 668–704.

the advent of British colonial administration in India. Incidences of cholera were now recorded with some precision, and by 1872, a well-known authority on Indian cholera, John MacPherson, could note with some confidence that cholera was "one of the oldest diseases whereof a distinct description exists."[16] With deadly accuracy, the British India Reports showed that following an extremely dry, hot summer in 1816, heavy rainfalls causing flooding and harvest failures (a climatic pattern often observed with the outbreak of infection) stimulated an epidemic of cholera in Bengal in 1817. Subsequently the disease traversed the subcontinent along with the masses of religious pilgrims who came to partake of the waters of the Ganges; it was then exported to the regions contiguous with India by soldiers and commercial travelers, then moved throughout southeast Asia, China, the Middle East, and Russia, ending the first pandemic period on record in 1826. Subsequent pandemics with regional variation affected the entire world, and seemed to be preceded by "an outbreak in India of marked and unusual violence."[17]

The speed of transmission also increased as the lines of communication improved throughout the nineteenth century. Thus the sixth pandemic, which followed its well-known land route from India to the southern Asiatic provinces of Russia in 1892 (with a mortality estimated as 220,000 victims) and then on to Western Europe, was disseminated rapidly along improved railway links. This deadly visitor had traveled a similar path in 1826–31 – a five-year period; it now covered the same ground in five months.[18]

Even if some authorities opined that "the disease prefers a land route to a sea route," transmission by sea was an influential factor in the diffusion of cholera as well as in the history of public medicine.[19] In fact it was in direct response to this "dreadful scourge" that in 1851 the major powers agreed upon the International Sanitary Convention, endeavoring to protect themselves from the importation of disease by constructing a strict system of quarantine. Nonetheless, the system's weaknesses seemed obvious to doctors among others; and to critics, it was "utterly powerless to arrest the progress of epidemic disease." This was tantamount, they continued,

---

[16] See John MacPherson, *Annals of Cholera from the Earliest Periods to the Year 1817* (London, 1872) and *Cholera in its Home, with a Sketch of the Pathology and Treatment of the Disease* (London, 1865), for evidence referring to the presence of the disease from 1503 to 1817.

[17] Pollitzer, *Cholera*, pp. 17–21; and Wu Lien-teh et al., *Cholera: A Handbook*, pp. 2–7.

[18] Wu Lien-teh et al., *Cholera: A Handbook*, pp. 5–6.

[19] Ibid., p. 4; and B. Cvjetanovic, "Cholera as an International Health Problem," in WHO, *Principles and Practice of Cholera Control*, p. 9.

to the exploits "of that gallant man who thought to pound up the crows by shutting his park gate."[20] As predicted, such efforts failed to contain infection, but they did help to shift the focus of medical opinion away from a strict quarantine mentality toward preventive medicine and the implementation of a system of public health. And, after Snow's implication of a tainted water supply at the Broad Street pump in London as the source of an epidemic of cholera in 1854, sanitary measures and the provision of abundant supplies of pure water increasingly became the goals of both private and governmental exertions in their war against epidemic diseases.[21] Thus, as Pollitizer states in his classic study of the disease, "it was through cholera, and the fear to which its pandemic sweeps gave rise, that international solidarity in matters of health was born."[22]

HUOLUAN AS CHOLERA

Because of the fears associated with cholera, particularly since its pandemic manifestation in 1817, medical controversy naturally swirled around the work of investigators, both foreign and Chinese, who attempted to answer questions as to whether the infection was endemic to China as was understood to be the case in India or was an imported "foreign" disease, whether the historical annals could yield evidence of its existence, and whether the term *huoluan*, or "sudden disturbance" of the bowels and stomach, in use for over three millennia, was a name for true cholera. If medical opinions divided over these questions, they were not merely academic disquisitions. The answers produced their own controversies, affecting decisions as to the most expedient course of action to mitigate the effects of disease. And like other questions regarding the "public" health, they generated political, social, and economic questions of their own.[23]

Authoritative investigations into this question were conducted in 1933 by two members of the National Quarantine Service of China, its director, Dr. Wu Lien-teh (Wu Liande) 伍連德, and Sung Chih-ai (Song Zhi'ai) 宋志

[20] Great Britain, *General Board of Health Report on Quarantine* (presented to both Houses of Parliament by command of Her Majesty, London, 1849), pp. 405–08.

[21] John Snow, *On the Mode of Communication of Cholera*, republished in *Snow on Cholera* (New York, 1936) pp. 75–78. See also John Duffy, *A History of Public Health in New York* (New York, 1968); and R. A. Lewis, *Edwin Chadwick and the Public Health Movement, 1832–54* (London, 1952).

[22] Pollitizer, *Cholera*, p. 7.

[23] Wu Lien-teh et al., *Cholera: A Handbook*, pp. ix–xv; and K. L. MacPherson, *Wilderness of Marshes*, passim.

愛. Using the ancient term without committing themselves as to its equivalency in the past with true cholera, and acknowledging the nosological conundrums involved in any translation of traditional Chinese medical thinking into modern form, they attempted to answer the question, What could the *huoluan* of the ancients have been?[24]

They commenced with an analysis of the oldest known medical treatise, the *Nei jing* 內經, basically a Han-dynasty work but attributed to the semimythical Yellow Emperor, Huangdi (2697–2597 B.C.). The *Su wen* 素問 section describes a diarrheal disease with symptoms of vomiting and gastric pain (from uncleanliness or stagnation of food in the stomach) that came when the "crops were stunted" due to dry, hot weather. The *Ling shu* 靈樞 section describes symptoms that were clearly a disorder of the stomach and intestines. Some inkling of the connection between climate, including seasonal patterns and gastrointestinal diseases, was clearly recognized by these ancient observers.[25]

In 1929, Chen Bangxian 陳邦賢 (1889–1976), head of the Jiangsu Medical Academy, in his work on medicine in China, collated data regarding subsequent knowledge of *huoluan* from 1134 B.C.:[26]

Zhou and Qin Dynasties (1134–206 B.C.)

In the *Chunqiu kao* 春秋考 it was stated that Xiang Gong 襄公 once made a visit to Jing 荊 [comprising He'nan, Hebei, Guangxi, and parts of Sichuan, Guizhou and Guangdong] and found many soldiers stationed there suffering from *huoluan*, due to misery, rain, heat, and damp.

Han Dynasty (202 B.C.– A.D. 220)

In the *Shanghan lun* 傷寒論 [Essay on typhoid], a disease with vomiting and diarrhea was called *huoluan*.

In the *Han shu* 漢書, many cases of *huoluan* were reported to have occurred in Guangdong.

Jin and Sui Dynasties (265–618)

Huoluan was mentioned as being caused by the intake of raw food and cold drink, wearing of wet shoes, and exposure to wind and cold, and as far back as 610, Zhao Yuanfang 巢元方, in his *Bing yuan* 病源 [Sources of disease], considered *huoluan* to be due to the faulty ingestion of food. He also mentioned, among contributory causes, alcohol drinking, irregular lifestyle, and partak-

---

[24] Wu Lien-teh and Sung Chih-ai, "Huo-luan: A Study of this Syndrome and its Relation to Cholera Asiatica," *National Quarantine Service Reports, Series 4* (1933), pp. 1–16.

[25] Ibid., pp. 2–3; and Wu Lien-teh et al., *Cholera: A Handbook*, pp. 7–8.

[26] For background on Chen, see Xu Shenqu 俞慎初, *Zhongguo yixue jianshi* 中国医学简史 [A brief history of Chinese medicine] (Fuzhou, 1983), pp. 481–82.

ing of excessive raw and cold food. Zhao also referred to the presence of muscular cramps which he assigned to the entry of cold air into the tendons.

Tang Dynasty (618–907)

Huoluan was recorded in 816 and according to Liu Zihou 柳子厚, vomiting and diarrhoea should not be induced.

Song Dynasty (960–1279)

According to Chen Wuze 陳無澤, *huoluan* is a disease with severe pain in the heart region and abdomen, vomiting, diarrhea, chill, fever, headache, and dizziness. Vomiting appears first if pain in the epigastrium occurs early; diarrhea first if abdominal pain comes early; and vomiting and diarrhea appear together if pains in both regions occur at the same time. The patient dies if cramp spreads into the abdomen.

Yuan Dynasty (1279–1368)

According to Zhang Jiegu 張潔古, when the trouble is in the middle *jiao* 中焦 (epigastric region), there will be *huoluan* with cramp, vomiting, and diarrhea. When *yin* and *yang* [female and male] principles are not in harmony, the disease will be an acute one with pain. In cases of this sort rice water should not be taken.

Ming Dynasty (1368–1644)

According to Wang Kentang 王肯堂 "heat" is the commonest cause of *huoluan*, which frequently occurs in autumn.

Qing Dynasty (1644–1912)

Literally, *huoluan* means "sudden confusion." It occurred in China every year during the summer and autumn. It is called wet cholera (*shi huoluan* 濕霍亂) in *Wan bing hui chun* 萬病回春 [Treatment of diseases]; melon-pulp infection 瓜瓤瘟 in [Infectious diseases 瘟疫論, 1642]; *fansha* 番痧 in [Zhang's medicine 張氏醫通, 1695]; toxic diarrhea in [Medicine: a critique 醫林改錯, 1838]. Nowadays it is called cramp of *huoluan* 霍亂轉筋; infection of the calf muscle cramp 弔腳痧; and infection of the finger pulp shrinkage 癟螺痧.

After the introduction of Western medicine, it is called *Cholera asiatica* 亞細亞霍亂; true cholera 真霍亂; choleraic vomiting and diarrhea 霍亂吐寫; or colic with gripe 犴腸痧. The Japanese transliterate it as "cholera" 虎列拉 [i.e., *korerra*]. The disease was prevalent during the time of Qianlong (1736–95) and Jiaqing (1796–1820). The biggest outbreak before the Republic (1911) occurred in 1902.[27]

---

[27] Chen Bangxian, *Zhongguo yixue shi* 中國醫學史 [A history of Chinese medicine] (1929. Reprinted, Taipei, 1956), pp. 11a–b, 25a, 35b, 45a–b, 53b–54a, 65a–b, 81a–b, 109b; and the summary in Wu Lien-teh and Sung Chih-ai, "Huo-Luan: A Study, pp. 3–4.

To Chen's data, Wu and Sung added other terms given to the infection, such as "tiger-wolf sickness" 虎狼病.[28]

Imura Kōzen, in a series of articles on epidemics in China drawn from local gazetteers, written for a Japanese medical journal in 1936–37, listed ten probable premodern names for cholera. In addition to those previously cited, they included: *zhuanjin* 轉筋 (twisting of the tendons); *jiaochangsha* 絞腸痧 (twisting of the intestines infection), also written as *jiaochangsha* 攪腸痧; *wenluosha* 瘟螺痧 (the snail pestilence); *wenduli* 瘟毒痢 (pestilence of poisonous diarrhea); and *douchangsha* 疛腸痧. Many of the terms accurately denoted the sequelae and infectious nature of the disease.[29]

A fourth source for the history of *huoluan* was written in 1838 by Wang Shixiong 王士雄 (Mengying 孟英), a native of Haichang 海昌, Zhejiang province, where he practiced as a traditional medical specialist on bowel diseases. The two-volume monograph, called *Huoluan lun* 霍亂論 [Essay on cholera], was destroyed during the Taiping Rebellion (as were many other books and medical treatises), but the author brought out an improved edition in Shanghai in 1862.[30] By that time, Wang had the benefit of immediate experience with three of the world pandemics that affected China. He was also familiar with Western medical perspectives and therapeutics, an acquaintance probably gained from medical missionaries and doctors in the Treaty Ports. The monograph was written as a handbook for practitioners, with emphasis on diagnostic and therapeutic techniques.

Wu and Sung, though praising Wang for his efforts at "rational therapy" and for taking great pains to distinguish between what he designated as authentic *huoluan* – which to Wang clearly meant true Asiatic cholera – and other similar maladies, discount his assumption that the *huoluan* of the

---

[28] Wu Lien-teh et al., *Cholera: A Handbook*, p. 9. J. Needham suggested that the "melon pulp fever" of the seventeenth century was polio cerebral-spinal fever; see H. Dunstan, "The Late Ming Epidemics: A Preliminary Survey," *Ch'ing shih went-t'i* 3 (1975), p. 22. Chinese authorities identified it as *huoluan*.

[29] Imura Kōzen 井村哮全, "Chihōshi ni kisaiseraretaru Chūgoku ekirei ryakkō" 地方志に記載せられたる中國疫癘略考 [A short treatise on epidemics in China from local gazetteers] *Chūgai Iji Shinpō* 中國醫事新報 1,238 (1936), p. 551. According to Macgowan, *wenluosha* was a name given to cholera at Suzhou because "medicine proving inert, recourse was at last had to snails (with which the shrivelled fingers were tipped)," Daniel J. Macgowan, "Dr. D. J. MacGowan's Report on the Health of Wenchow for the Half-year Ended 31st March 1884," *Customs Gazette Medical Reports* 27 (1884), p. 2.

[30] Wang Shixiong, *Huoluan lun* 霍亂論 [Essay on cholera] (Shanghai, 1862), reprinted in Cao Bingzhang 曹炳章, ed., *Zhongguo yixue dacheng* 中國醫學大成 [Complete works of Chinese medical science] (Taipei, 1944), vol. 3, pp. 1015–16. Wang apparently was from a family of medical practitioners and had great success with his treatment of cholera in Shanghai. See Xu Shenqu, *Brief history of Chinese medicine*, p. 379.

classics was the same disease "which in his day was certainly more conspicuous than any co-existing cases of sporadic choleraic or cholera-like ailments." "Cholera," in their view, was rather "one of the several diseases covered by the generic term *huoluan*." They concluded:

> After reviewing this subject in the light of our present-day knowledge, we feel that most of the ancient writers on *huo-luan* did not and could not describe true cholera. For that dangerous infection, though possibly not entirely absent from old China, was evidently much rarer than, and not so widespread as, in the nineteenth and twentieth centuries.[31]

Wu and Sung were not alone in their estimations. An eminent member of the Shanghai medical community, who was an adviser to the Shanghai municipal government Board of Health, president of the Shanghai branch of the Pharmaceutical Association, editor of the *Shehui yibao* (*Medical Society Journal*), as well as a medical activist, Dr. Yu Yunxiu 余雲岫, stoutly denied the existence of *Cholera asiatica* in China before its importation from India by land route in 1817.[32] For Yu, the deciding factor before that critical date was that writers had failed to allude to the epidemic nature of the disease. He could well have echoed the medical purist Xu Zimo 徐子默 (a contemporary of Wang's), who insisted that "in ancient times there was no such sickness as 'contracting the tendons of the legs disease.' It suddenly appeared between summer and autumn of the *xin si* 辛巳 year (1821)."[33]

If a trace of nationalism could be found in Dr. Yu's denial of the existence of true cholera in China in ancient times, his conclusions were also supported by the numerous researches conducted since the opening of the Treaty Ports in 1842 by foreign medical doctors and medical missionaries such as David Manson and Daniel J. Macgowan. Drawn from societies deeply worried about the devastating effects of epidemic disease, primarily cholera, these doctors were intensely interested in discovering its source or sources and arresting it there. Manson, serving as a surgeon to the Chinese

---

[31] Wu and Sung, "Huo Luan: A Study," p. 16. Wu did accept that cholera was present in China before the nineteenth century, "though rare." Wu Lien-teh et al., *Cholera: A Handbook*, p. 15.

[32] Wu Lien-teh et al., *Cholera: A Handbook*, p. 10. Although Yu was one of the most respected scholars of Chinese medicine, he was known as an opponent of traditional Chinese medical practice, attempting to regulate and control, through licensing, traditional practitioners in Shanghai. See, Xu Shenqu, *Brief history of Chinese medicine*, p. 396.

[33] Xu Zimo, *Diaojiaosha fanglun* 弔腳痧方論 [Essay on *diaojiaosha*], original 1860. Reprinted in Min Changle 閔長樂 and Chen Xiuyuan 陳修園, eds., *Chen Xiuyuan yi shu qishier zhong* 陳修園醫書七十二種 [Chen Xiuyuan's collection of Seventy-two medical books] (Taipei, 1964), vol. 3, p. 1. See also Yu Yunxiu, "Xinyi yu shehui, huoluan bing yange shuolüe" 新醫與社會，霍亂病沿革說略 [The new medicine and society, a summary of the successive changes of the disease *huoluan*], *Shishi xinbao* 時事新報 (autumn 1926).

Imperial Maritime Customs, concluded from his investigations into the Fujian provincial gazetteers that there was no evidence to show that the epidemics noted in these chronicles were of cholera. The first clear record of the disease dated from August and September of the first year of Daoguang (1821): "An epidemic spread over the whole province (全省) of Fujian, vomiting and purging came on very suddenly and countless numbers died, being men in the morning and spirits at night."[34]

Daniel J. Macgowan, customs surgeon in Wenzhou in 1884, was also skeptical of the endemicity of cholera in China. But he revised his opinion after the severe epidemic of 1883, which prompted him to make a deeper investigation of the subject, particularly Chinese therapeutics. He argued that it must be a new disease for the following reasons:

> Indian cholera in China differs from the common cholera of the country only in its epidemic character, the former being migratory, the latter stationary. In its marches from region to region it is as irregular here as in its Gangetic home, leaping over certain districts, sometimes to return, and at others not. Instead of moving as though air-borne or conveyed by persons, it rises here and there as if it had been awaiting the concurrence of certain telluric and atmospheric conditions for its development – conditions that exist in one district but are absent in a contiguous locality, and that are wholly absent sometimes for successive years. Its history indicates either that a specific germ was conveyed from abroad or that there suddenly arose successively from south to north a series of conditions which favoured the development of a virulent form of endemic cholera which became epidemic.[35]

Almost one hundred years later, in 1977, Selwyn also argued (contrary to established opinion) in the *Proceedings of the Royal Society of Medicine* that a "subtle genetic change must have occurred in a member of the vibrio genus," giving birth to a new disease that became pandemic in 1817.[36]

To the Western-trained medical doctor Huang Kuan 黃寬 (Wong Fun), investigating the frequency of cholera at Guangzhou in 1873,

[34] Chen Shouqi 陳壽祺, comp., *Fujian tongzhi* 福建通志 [Gazetteer of Fujian province] (1831. Reprinted, Taipei, 1968), j. 272, p. 5182. See also D. Manson, "Dr. Manson's Report on the Health of Amoy for the Half-year Ended 30th September 1877," *Customs Gazette, Medical Reports* 14, p. 33.

[35] Daniel J. Macgowan, "Dr. D. J. Macgowan's Report on the Health of Wenchow for the Half-year ended 31st March 1884," *Customs Gazette, Medical Reports* 27, p. 11.

[36] S. Selwyn, "Cholera Old and New," *Proceedings of the Royal Society of Medicine* 70 (1977), p. 301. Darwinian ecologists would argue that antigenic diversity of microparasites coupled with specific host immunity plays a key role in "regulation and convolution of microparasites and their hosts." See D. James Nokes, "Microparasites: Viruses and Bacteria," in Michael J. Crawley, ed., *Natural Enemies: The Population Biology of Predators, Parasites and Diseases* (London, 1992), p. 374.

The term *huo-luan*, commonly used to signify cholera, seems to answer more to the English than to the Asiatic form of the disease. It is a general term, including colic, English, and sometimes Asiatic cholera. When the disease takes on the epidemic form, it goes by the name *wen-yi* 瘟疫, not *huo-luan*, though *wen-yi* properly means pestilence. Even to a Chinese physician the term *huo-luan* suggests none of the dreadful ideas associated with epidemic cholera in the mind of an European, which seems to show that *huo-luan* does not mean epidemic cholera.[37]

Macgowan completed the picture by stating that a disease called dry cholera (*cholera sicca* or *siderans?*) was quite common in the south and occurred during hot weather.[38] It went under the term *sha* 痧 and included colic, sunstroke heat apoplexy, and so on. It was prevalent in Guangzhou: "the Cantonese affirm that *sha* has prevailed among them from time immemorial, which may explain their belief that they always had Asiatic cholera among them."[39]

Who then was responsible for the confusion? According to Chen Shengkun 陈胜昆, the muddle began with Wang Shixiong. Marshaling impressive documentary evidence, Chen concluded that the disease was imported to China via the sea route from India and spread from south (Guangdong and Fujian) to north with a speed and intensity unlike outbreaks of *huoluan* recorded in the classic medical texts. Furthermore, it was called by the entirely new name of *diaojiaosha* 吊脚痧 (contracting-the-leg-tendons disease). Thus Chen agreed with Xu Zimo, whom he considered a "hero" for first recognizing the difference, and excoriated Wang Shixiong, who had insisted that this was not a new disease but a form of *huoluan* and named it *huoluan zhuanjin*.[40]

Opponents of the belief that true cholera was endemic to China based their assertions primarily on three major points: the difficulties of historical and modern terminology; the problem of constructing a comparable nosology between Chinese and Western medicine; and the failure of past records to acknowledge the infection's epidemic form, the latter point in particular leading to the conclusion that in 1820–21 a new disease ap-

---

[37] Wong Fun, "Dr. Wong Fun's Report on the Health of Canton for the Half-year Ended 30th September 1873," *Customs Gazette, Medical Reports* 6 (1879), p. 49.

[38] *Cholera sicca*, or more correctly *siderans*, seems to be a clinical (though rare) syndrome of cholera that is rapidly fatal with the absence of diarrhea and vomiting. It was observed by Koch in 1884 and in India, China, and Europe. See Pollitzer, *Cholera*, pp. 687, 733–35.

[39] Daniel J. Macgowan, "Dr. D. J. Macgowan's Report on the Health of Wenchow for the Half-year Ended 30th September 1881," *Customs Gazette, Medical Reports* 22 (1881), p. 27. Wang Shixiong agreed; see *Essay on cholera*, p. 1023.

[40] Chen Shengkun, *Zhongguo jibing shi* 中国疾病史 [History of the diseases of China] (1980), pp. 30–31.

peared. There were others, however, who stressed contrary conclusions. Like Wang Shixiong, Drs. Lockhart (1862), Dudgeon (1872), and Thomson (1890), after a careful reading of the records, felt that *huoluan* was indeed cholera and it had existed in China "from time immemorial." The clinical description of the disease in the medical classics, for them, was overwhelmingly conclusive even if the epidemic nature of the disease was not mentioned. Further proof as to the true nature of *huoluan*, they asserted, could be found in the obvious care that Chinese medical practitioners had taken since ancient times in providing abundant remedies and recommending treatments for the disease. These cures proved to be, if not helpful, at least worthy of further investigation (and often were similar to their own therapies).[41]

Those interested in mapping comparative medical nosologies pointed to important environmental differences between India and China that may have accounted for the absence of true cholera in the Chinese past. Simmons, in his 1879 monograph "Cholera Epidemics in Japan," argued that "in countries [China and Japan] so rich in historic records as are the two remotest empires of the Orient . . . there is good ground for the belief that lack of evidence of numerous visits of the evil is fair negative proof of the infrequency of its appearance." If China possessed all the conditions eminently necessary to propagate the disease – "the habits of the people" and the "condition of the walled towns in which many of them are crowded" – Simmons asked, can this exemption from cholera "be real or is it only apparent?"

For Simmons the answers could be found in the fact of "the utter insignificance of the flow of life eastward from India" in the past compared with the "more frequent and rapid communication that now exists" between cholera's "Indian home and lands nearer to the rising sun." Thus:

> The Western advantages of steam transport conferred upon their peoples have probably been for something in the transport of the seed of the great zymotic destroyer, in a fructifying state, by way of intervening islands and peninsulas, to the shores of China and this still more distant empire.

Simmons dated that first visitation of Asiatic cholera in the year 1669 from Malacca by sea; its second known appearance was recorded by "Gentil, in

---

[41] See, e.g., J. Dudgeon, "John Dudgeon's Report on the Physical Conditions of Peking, and Habits of the Pekingese as Bearing on Health," *Customs Gazette, Medical Reports* 4 (1872), p. 39; and J. C. Thomson, "Native Practice and Practitioners," *China Medical Missionary Journal* 4.3 (1890), pp. 181–84. For case studies and treatment, see Wang Shixiong, *Essay on cholera,* pp. 1031–53.

his *Voyage aux Indes Orientales*" (presumably the *Voyage dans les mers de l'Inde*), as being in 1761 (southeast Asia), reaching China in 1769.[42]

As for the "apparent predisposing inducements" to the introduction and spread of cholera Simmons argued that *compared to India* the habits and customs of China helped to mitigate these factors. First, drinking water, though derived from wells, springs, and rivers in both places, was usually boiled before consumption in China. Also the Chinese lacked religious pilgrimages and rites such as bathing in and drinking untreated river water as in India. Second, nightsoil, which the Chinese considered a valuable fertilizer, was hoarded and returned to the soil, reducing "the danger of contamination" to "a minimum."[43]

Yet for others, the ultimate test of the salubrity of China lay in the quality of its water and the general health of the communities using the water. Were its rivers merely great cloacae freighted with disease and death? And to what extent was the handling, disposal, and preparation of nightsoil for agricultural purposes of such a large population managed with any proficiency, rendering it harmless?[44] If cholera, like many other infectious diseases, was a "malady of filth," were the conditions prevailing in the cities, towns, and villages (reckoned by foreign doctors to be even worse than their own filthy cities) conducive to fostering the disease?[45] If cholera was not endemic, could the introduction of the infection in 1820–21, if the environment was favorable, have made it thereafter a permanent and deadly resident?

THE 1821 EPIDEMIC

In the first year of Daoguang [1821], on the first day of the fourth month, the sun and the moon came together and the five planets were joined like a

---

[42] D. B. Simmons, "Cholera Epidemics in Japan," *Customs Gazette, Medical Reports Special Series* 2 (1879), pp. 1–2. However, Pollitzer (*Cholera*, p. 15) could not verify in Gentil's volume that cholera was imported into China in the eighteenth century.

[43] The operative comparison is with India, where the sanitary conditions prevailing almost defy description; see Simmons, "Cholera Epidemics in Japan," p. 26.

[44] On the medical dangers of nightsoil use in China in the nineteenth and early twentieth centuries, see K. L. MacPherson, *Wilderness of Marshes*, pp. 49–122; J. Maxwell and W. H. Jeffreys, *The Diseases of China* (London, 1911), p. 168; and J. C. Scott, *Health and Agriculture in China* (London, 1952), who advocated the use of stringent, scientific management of nightsoil fertilizer in lieu of traditional methods to eliminate the devastating effects of fecal-related diseases still suffered in China.

[45] See J. Dudgeon, *The Diseases of China* (Glasgow, 1877), pp. 7–15; and Wang Shixiong, *Essay on cholera*, p. 1020.

string of pearls. By the seventh month convulsions due to *huoluan* broke out and became epidemic, lasting until the ninth month, with uncountable deaths.[46]

This account from an 1884 gazetteer of Beijing exemplifies the brief but poignant records found in many local chronicles of pandemic cholera in 1821. Supernatural or extraordinary physical events often marked the onset of the epidemic – a "black ether" moving across the sky from southeast to southwest and then northwest was said to have caused the autumn epidemic.[47] An "epidemic prevailing everywhere" in 1821 in Guangdong is tersely recorded, and the blunt "Daoguang yuan nian da yi" [1821, great pestilence].[48]

Local records were often of unspecified epidemics, related only by proximity in time and space. Undaunted by these methodological enigmas, and correctly assuming that the Chinese compilers understood the meaning of an epidemic, that is, "when everyone is suffering from the same illness, this is what is meant by an epidemic" (眾人同病：即疫也),[49] Imura Kōzen surveyed more than 600 local gazetteers to map the incidence of presumed cholera during the years 1820–22. Accepting the inherent risks in using the same methodology and surveying approximately 530 mostly county-level gazetteers (in all provinces of the Qing empire), we can supplement Imura's record at the provincial level but more specifically at the county level for the years 1820–22 (see Map 13.1). For example, in 1820, Imura indicated five provinces affected by epidemic cholera: Guangdong, Jiangsu, Jiangxi, Shandong, and Zhejiang – to which we can add Hu'nan and Yunnan.[50] For 1821, Imura showed six provinces affected: Fujian, He'nan, Hu'nan, Jiangsu, Shandong, and Zhejiang – but Guangdong, Guangxi, and

---

[46] Li Hongzhang 李鴻章 and Zhang Zhidong 張之洞 et al., eds., *Guangxu Shuntian fuzhi* 光緒 順天府志 [Guangxu gazetteer of Shuntian prefecture] (1889. Reprinted, Taipei, 1965), vol. 8, p. 4388.

[47] Wang Qigan 王其淦, ed., *Yanghu xianzhi* 陽湖縣志 [Gazetteer of Yanghu county (Jiangsu)] (1880. Reprinted, Taipei, 1968), vol. 8, *j*. 29, pp. 2995–96.

[48] Yang Kaidi 楊開第 and Yao Guangfa 姚光發, eds., *Huating xianzhi* 華亭縣志 (1879. Reprinted, Taipei, 1970), vol. 3, *j*. 23, p. 1771; Zhao Ersun, ed., *Qing shi gao* 清史稿 [Draft history of the Qing] (1928. Reprinted, Taipei, 1976), vol. 6, *j*. 40, pp. 1530–31.

[49] I am indebted to Mark Elvin for the quotation and for many expert but unacknowledged suggestions. See Imura, *Short treatise*, no. 1,238, p. 552. The quote is from Wang Shixiong, *Essay on cholera*, p. 1019.

[50] Imura, *Short treatise*, no. 1,239, p. 31. For Hu'nan in 1820, see, e.g., Lei Feipeng 雷飛鵬 et al., eds., *Lanshan xian tu zhi* 藍山縣圖志 [Gazetteer of Lanshan county] (1933. Reprinted, Taipei, 1974), vol. 7, p. 433; and Liu Huabang 劉華邦, ed., *Guidong xianzhi* 桂東縣 志 [Gazetteer of Guidong county] (1866. Reprinted, Taipei, 1975), vol. 11. p. 676. For Yunnan, see, e.g., Wang Wenshao 王文韶, ed., *Xu Yunnan tongzhi gao* 續雲南通志稿 [Draft supplementary annals of Yunnan Province] (1894. Reprinted, Taipei, 1966), vol. 2, p. 576.

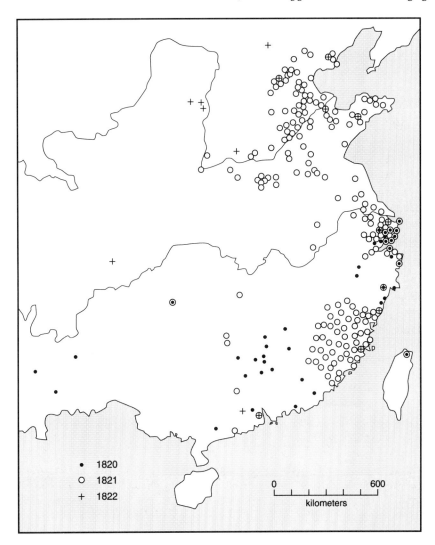

Map 13.1. Cholera epidemics of the years 1820, 1821, and 1822.

Zhili (comprising modern Hebei province with part of Liaoning and Inner Mongolia) also experienced epidemics.[51] For 1822, Imura recorded epidemics in eight provinces: Fujian, Guangdong, Hebei, He'nan, Shaanxi,

[51] Imura, *Short treatise*, no. 1,239, pp. 31–33. For 1821 see, e.g., Li Shijin 厲式金, ed., *Xiangshan xianzhi* [Gazetteer of Xiangshan county], for Guangdong; Zhou Zanyuan 周贊元, et al., eds., *Huaiji xianzhi* 懷集縣志 [Gazetteer of Huaiji county] (1916. Reprinted, Taipei, 1975), vol. 8, p. 580, for Guangxi. For one county in Hebei missed by Imura, see Li Xingzhuo 李興焯, ed., *Pinghu xianzhi* [Gazetteer of Pinghu county] (1934. Reprinted, Taipei, 1969), vol. 13, p. 322, where the epidemic is specified as *huoluan*.

Shandong, Jiangsu, and Zhejiang – but Sichuan, Hu'nan, Zhili, and Shanxi also recorded pestilence.[52] We were also able to map the 1821 epidemic by showing seasonal variation (see Map 13.2). Map 13.2 lends credence to the obiter dicta that the disease's "peculiar feature" of "leaping over whole districts and even departments" was characteristic of the 1821 epidemic.[53] However inconclusive and incomplete the data, what emerges is evidence of three years of extraordinary epidemic activity that supports the contention that the disease was "imported." Clearly, by 1820–21, the infection was moving from the coastal areas to the interior along major riverine and other transportation routes.[54]

Imura believed the first pandemic of cholera came to China by sea through the Straits of Malacca in 1819, then moved northward from Wenzhou and Ningbo. Alternatively, it was recorded that the disease invaded Siam (Thailand) from the Straits in 1819, 1822, and again in 1849, coming from Penang, crossing the Malay Peninsula to Ligore, and finally reaching Bangkok with great mortality before continuing to China.[55] Yu Yunxiu surmised that the epidemic reached China by overland route, as did Dr. Livingstone writing in 1824, twenty miles distant from Guangzhou:

> I am pretty certain the Cholera Morbus, in an epidemic form had not been seen in this part of China within thirty years, till sometime after it appeared in Bengal. It seems to have appeared first in Tartary, afterwards in the N.W. of China. It appears to have made its progress southward by irregular leaps, destroying full half the number it seized. It committed dreadful ravages here two and three years ago.[56]

---

[52] Imura, *Short treatise*, no. 1,239, p. 33. For Sichuan in 1822 see He Huayuan 何華元 et al., eds., *Ziyang xianzhi* 資陽縣志 [Gazetteer of Ziyang county] (1861. Reprinted, Taipei, 1971), vol. 14, p. 639. For Shanxi, see Lai Changqi 賴昌期 et al., eds., *Yangcheng xianzhi* 陽城縣志 [Gazetteer of Yangcheng county] (1874. Reprinted, Taipei, 1976), vol. 18, p. 1140. For Hu'nan, see Ji Youqing 嵇有慶, ed., *Ling xianzhi* 零縣志 [Gazetteer of Ling county] (1875. Reprinted, Taipei, 1975), vol. 12, p. 1153.

[53] The remarks were made by Chinese informants interviewed by the Rev. Milne in Ningbo; see W. C. Milne, "Notices of Asiatic Cholera in China," *Chinese Repository* 12 (1843), p. 489. For further discussions of the propagation of the disease by "shorter or longer relay stages," see Pollitzer, *Cholera*, pp. 878–80.

[54] I am indebted to Yeung Wingyu for assistance with data collection and to Dr. James Wang and H. K. Kwan of the Department of Geography, University of Hong Kong, for assistance with the execution of the maps.

[55] *Chinese Repository* 18 (1849), pp. 503–04; and House of Representatives, *The Cholera Epidemic of 1873 in the United States* (Washington, 1875), p. 537. The later source reports that English ships were reputed to have carried the disease to Bangkok in July 1819, causing forty thousand deaths.

[56] J. Livingstone, "Observations on the Epidemic Cholera as it appeared in China," *Transactions, Medical and Physical Society, Calcutta* 1 (1825), p. 205.

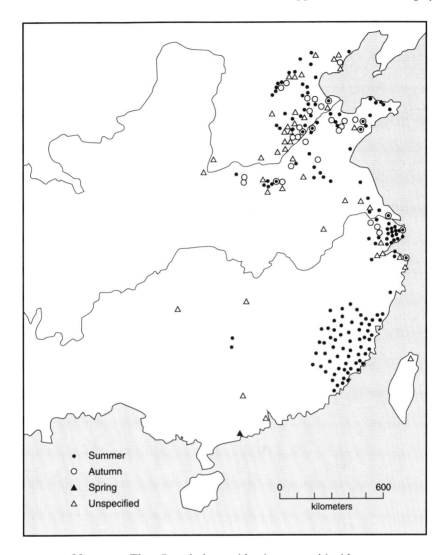

Map 13.2. The 1821 cholera epidemic: seasonal incidence.

Yet most authorities agreed that it came by land and sea. Simmons constructed a map (see Map 13.3) showing the routes the disease might have taken from India to China by both land and sea:

The epidemic of 1817, which had its origin in Bengal, extended up the Ganges as far as Allahabad; and up the Bramapootra from Dacca, north-east to Ringpore, whence it travelled to the borders of Thibet and South-western China. In 1820 it again appeared in the latter country – first in Canton. This

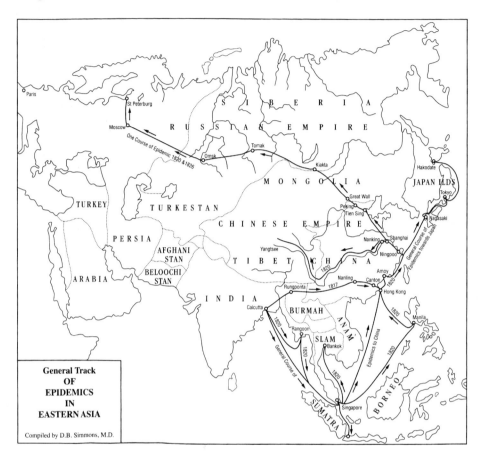

Map 13.3. D. B. Simmons's map of the routes taken by cholera epidemics in the nineteenth century (up to 1879).

particular epidemic originated on the eastern coast of Hindustan; thence it was carried by English troops to Burmah, during the war with that nation; thence from Bangkok and Canton, from which foci it penetrated into the interior of China by direct route. Again radiating to Ningpo, and following the course of the Yangtze, it travelled by this track also into the very heart of the empire. In 1821 it reached Peking, where it reproduced itself in 1822 and 1823, and formed the centre of infection in Northern Asia.[57]

---

[57] Simmons, "Cholera Epidemics in Japan," p. 2. There was also a well-established direct junk trade between China and India that could account for the spread of the infection. See James L. Maxwell, "The History of Cholera in China," *China Medical Journal* 41.7 (July 1927), p. 597.

Simmons continued his account of what later was identified as the second pandemic wave to reach China:

> In 1826, it was again borne from India to China. It once more reached Peking, whence, steadily advancing, it crossed the Chinese wall, swept through Mongolia, and eventually travelled to Moscow. In 1840 the Government of India despatched a combined European and native army to China in the interest of the opium trade. This force carried with it the seeds of cholera, which not only arrived at Peking, but followed the track of the caravans westward as far as Russia.[58]

In 1842, due to an outbreak of "the severest form of cholera" among the British transports "that lay abreast of Nanking and Chinkiang fu" as well as among the Chinese living "within the west gate" of Dinghai (chief town of Zhoushan island, Zhejiang), the Rev. W. C. Milne in Ningbo was asked by the British military and naval authorities to investigate whether Asiatic cholera had visited China, "especially in the northern parts of the country."[59]

Milne used his contacts among the Chinese medical practitioners in Ningbo and Dinghai to answer a "list of queries" given to him by the British military. After a lengthy discussion of the disease "commonly known" as *huoluan*, he pointed out that "there is a species of cholera, which is spoken of by the natives of those provinces which it has visited, in terms that betoken their horror at it, while they regard it as entirely *sui generis* and utterly incurable." The symptoms, for Milne, suggested that this was true Asiatic cholera.[60]

Relying on the testimony of an "aged resident" of Ningbo, Doctor Chang, "an acupuncturist of long standing" who had traveled "not a little in his own country," Milne reported:

> that this severe type of cholera broke out first in the third month of the first year of the reigning emperor, A.D. 1820,[61] and that it had been transmitted by a Fukien trading junk from Siam to Fukien, from which province it travelled into Canton, and thence into Kiangsi and Chekiang, taking a northerly direction, until it reached the province of Chihli, where it, however, did not commit extensive ravages. The two provinces of Kiangsi and Chekiang are said to have suffered the most from its devastations.[62]

---

[58] Simmons, "Cholera Epidemics in Japan," pp. 2–3.

[59] W. C. Milne, "Notices of Asiatic Cholera," p. 485.

[60] Ibid., p. 486.

[61] Milne is of course writing during the reign of Daoguang (1821–50), who ascended the throne in 1820 but decreed that the following year would be styled the first of his reign.

[62] Ibid., p. 487. For example, a great epidemic was recorded in four cities of Ganzhou prefecture in Jiangxi; see Wei Ying 魏瀛 et al., comps., *Ganzhou fuzhi* 贛州府志 [Gazetteer of

In its progress through Zhejiang province, reaching the city of Ningbo in May of 1821, he continued, "it is calculated that, in that department alone, – two thousand individuals fell victim to its rage, during the first outbreak of the disease."[63] Confirming Dr. Chang's account was a merchant (Mr. Hu) who was in the city at that time: "while he walked the streets on his usual routine of business – he daily saw people suddenly drop down under its overwhelming attack."[64]

It appeared again in the following two years. "but with redoubled violence, and during the summers of these three years, 1820–21–22, (for it made its appearance always during the hot weather), ten thousand people are supposed to have been carried off in the city and department of Ningpo."[65]

Milne's teacher, a native of Hangzhou, informed him that from June to August of 1821 and 1822, "people died like sheep." Another medical practitioner ("at the east gate of the city of Ningpo") corroborated these accounts and added that the first victim "to the cholera" had been the emperor Jiaqing, father of Daoguang. Milne decided this was merely a rumor; after "minuter inquiries" it appeared that the emperor had died of "a stroke, apoplexy or paralysis."[66] Leaving no stone unturned in his inquest, he interviewed a local official and "head of the police establishment" who informed him "that species of cholera raged furiously" during the same period in Shandong, his native province.[67] In September of 1821 it was rumored that in Dongchang, Dezhou, and Jiningzhou people were cheated out of their money because of the epidemic.[68]

Wang Shixiong, who witnessed this epidemic in Shanghai, wrote in his *Essay on cholera* that the number of deaths was so great that there were not enough coffins to bury the dead. The poor who died were so numerous that the government paid out over 100,000 taels of silver for coffins in just a few months. Besides silver, medical supplies were sent to many areas and the

---

Ganzhou prefecture] (1873. Reprinted, Taipei, 1970), vol. 22, p. 435. Of six counties reporting epidemics in Zhejiang, Cixi county specifies *huoluan* and *diaojiaosha* as the causes. See Feng Keyong 馮可鏞, ed., *Cixi xian zhi* 慈谿縣志 [Gazetteer of Cixi county] (1899. Reprinted, Taipei, 1975), vol. 55, p. 1201.

[63] Milne, "Notices of Asiatic Cholera," p. 487.

[64] Ibid., p. 488.

[65] Ibid., p. 487.

[66] Ibid., p. 488.

[67] Ibid. Out of fifty-two county-level gazetteers we surveyed for Shandong province, thirty counties reported epidemics with high mortality, only two counties specifying *huoluan*.

[68] *Qing shilu, Daoguang chao* 清實錄，道光朝 [Veritable records of the Qing dynasty, Daoguang reign] (Reprinted, Taipei, 1964), *j.* 2, pp. 29–30b.

county examinations were delayed until October.[69] Milne's informants stressed that the poor suffered the most, and they added that the victims were mostly under seventy years of age, predominately male, and of no particular class of laborers – this could also be said of the victims of the same pandemic in other places in the world.[70]

Of some interest, Wang mentioned a popular idea circulating in Shanghai during the epidemic that eating watermelon could prevent death, which proved subsequently to be false, though he felt that there was something therapeutic in watermelon juice.[71] Interestingly enough, watermelons, which were (and still are) consumed in great numbers in Shanghai during the summer months, were implicated in spreading the disease, through improper handling by hawkers with contaminated water (sprinkled on the slices to keep them moist) and exposure to flies.[72] Experiments were even made in 1923 by the Shanghai municipal government's Pathological Laboratory to see how long cholera vibrios could live on cut watermelons (up to twenty-four hours) and in watermelon juice.[73]

Over half of Wang's volume is devoted to cures and remedies of the disease, since, in his words, although cholera was a constant visitor, the mortality rate was swelled by misdiagnosis and wrongly prescribed medicines.[74] To that end he investigated Western medicine and practices extant in Shanghai from a comparative perspective. Although he retained his traditional perspective, the results of this investigation can be seen in his advocacy of sanitation, ventilation, strict personal hygiene, careful diet, and most importantly the use of pure water, as if he had been trained in the same medical schools as his Western counterparts in Shanghai.[75]

[69] Wang Shixiong, *Essay on cholera*, p. 1019. See also Wang Xianqian 王先謙 and Zhu Shouming 朱壽明, eds., *Donghua lu* 東華錄 [Records of the Eastern Gate] (Taipei, 1963), *j.* 1, p. 20a.

[70] Milne, "Notices of Asiatic Cholera," p. 486. See also J. Watson, "Dr. James Watson's Report on the Health of Newchwang for the Half-year ended 31st March 1878," *Customs Gazette, Medical Reports* 15 (1878), p. 30, where he states that in 1862, large numbers of homeless and destitute refugees from Shandong swelled the mortality rate.

[71] Wang Shixiong, *Essay on cholera*, p. 1019.

[72] The problem of unlicensed hawkers selling contaminated food was a longstanding one. In 1912 the Japanese authorities declared a quarantine against ships coming from Shanghai because passengers were becoming ill after disembarking. The source was hawkers selling contaminated food at the wharves. See *Shanghai Municipal Gazette*, March 13, 1913. See also Mark Elvin, "The Gentry Democracy in Shanghai, 1905–1914," Ph. D. dissertation, Cambridge University (1967–68), pp. 118–19, for a discussion of public health provisions made by the Chinese city council governing Nanshi after 1905 that banned the sale of sliced watermelon and other foods such as ice creams, iced lemonade, and flavored ices made with unboiled water.

[73] *Shanghai Municipal Council Health Report for 1923*, p. 19.

[74] Wang Shixiong, *Essay on cholera*, p. 1037.

[75] Ibid., p. 1059.

The epidemics also encouraged eclecticism. During the 1883 epidemic, for example, a survey by the *Shenbao* newspaper is revealing. Cholera outbreaks were reported to be due to overcrowding, polluted water, and improper disposal of nightsoil,[76] but the villagers of the Pingshan region (Sichuan) believed that the disease could be expunged by sacrificing their livestock when any became infected, with the result that almost the entire animal population of the area was eliminated.[77] In Yingkou the epidemic was thought to be due to the consumption of fruit;[78] congee (rice gruel, a staple food of the South) was also implicated.[79] Thus science, religion, and local customs and beliefs formed an arsenal of knowledge in the fight against the disease.[80]

But one aspect of Western medicine, the postmortem examination, was not generally practiced by Chinese doctors.[81] When Milne's informant, Dr. Chang, was asked if he had conducted such an exam, he "confessed that, so far from looking at the corpse, he was so frightened that at last he declined attending upon even the living." As in Europe and other parts of the world visited by cholera, fear of the scourge in China was palpable. Sadly, Milne reported, "every person to whom I spoke on the subject . . . answered in language most strongly expressive of their dislike and dread, as if in recollection of past horrors, and in despair of meeting any antidote."[82]

THE CHOLERA YEARS

Since the first pandemic of cholera reached China in 1820 and records were first kept, there were forty-six invasions of varying intensity until 1932. According to Wu Lien-teh's report on the 1932 cholera epidemic in China, of the forty-six invasions, ten materializing in the years 1822–24, 1826–27,

[76] *Shenbao* 申報, June 1, 1883.
[77] Ibid., June 16, 1883.
[78] Ibid., August 4, 1883.
[79] Ibid., July 21, 1883. Sticker showed in 1912 that rice gruel and other cereals "if kept under suitable temperatures, form a favourable substance for the growth of *V. cholerae*"; Pollitzer, *Cholera*, p. 178.
[80] Wang Shixiong (*Essay on cholera*, p. 1030) explained the increase of idol worshiping during epidemics as due to the fact that priests and nuns seemed to survive the outbreaks. He attributed this to their diet and their avoidance of fresh seafood. Numerous outbreaks of cholera, particularly of the El Tor biotype, were attributed to contaminated seafood; see Pollitzer, *Cholera*, pp. 258–862, and for a recent outbreak in Hong Kong, see *South China Morning Post*, July 4, 10, 1994. A detailed anthropological examination of a Yunnan community's reactions to a cholera epidemic at a later date was made by Francis L. K. Hsu, *Religion, Science and Human Crises* (London, 1952).
[81] James Henderson, *Memorials of James Henderson, M.D., Medical Missionary to China* (London, 1870), p. 104.
[82] Milne, "Notices of Asiatic Cholera," p. 489.

1840, 1862, 1883, 1902, 1909, 1919, 1926, and 1932 spread northward into Manchuria, southward as far as Guangzhou, and westward as far as Hu'nan, Hubei, and Sichuan. There was no year when the disease was entirely absent. In 1932, cholera invaded 23 provinces and 312 large cities, with 100,000 reported cases and 34,000 deaths.[83]

From 1842 until the turn of the century, China came under the scrutiny of foreign medical doctors and sanitarians attempting to formulate general laws affecting health and disease in China. They first tried to understand the environment from a climatological point of view, then in the 1870s turned to the refinement of topographies – attempts to map local diseases by place, by population, by incidence, by standardized types and effects, and by etiology, connecting China with an international medical circuit. Like evolving concepts of public medicine and public health in the West, these ideas resulted in the establishment of a system of public health in the foreign concessions and settlements in the Treaty Ports. And, by the early twentieth century, with the growing numbers of Western-trained Chinese medical personnel, public health systems were slowly implanted throughout the cities, towns, villages, and to a lesser degree rural areas of China.[84] "The crowning feat of public health activities" for Wu Lien-teh and others who had labored for decades in the medical field was the creation during the period 1928–36 of the National Ministry of Health.[85]

But in the early years, investigations into the nature of cholera in China were also years of fighting the invasions. Statistics of incidence and mortality had to be compiled in the face of imperfect or nonexistent statistics from Chinese records. In 1862 (a particularly bad year for cholera) it was estimated that between Shanghai and Songjiang (a distance of forty miles) one-eighth of the population died from the disease.[86] In 1863, a British Army Medical Report stated that between the middle of June until July 15–16 (three weeks), "the mortality among the Chinese was very great – seven-eight-nine-ten-eleven-twelve-hundred daily, and on the 14th July the mortality reached 1,500 in 24 hours."[87] During the same summer in

---

[83] Wu Lien-teh, "The 1932 Cholera Epidemic in China with Special Reference to Shanghai," *National Quarantine Reports*, series, 3 (1932), p. 9.

[84] For the nineteenth century, see, K. L. MacPherson, *Wilderness of Marshes*, pp. 259–75. See also Ka-che Yip, "Health and society in China: Public Health Education for the Community, 1912–37," *Social Science and Medicine* 16 (1982), pp. 1197–1205.

[85] Wu Lien-teh and K. C. Wong, *The History of Chinese Medicine* (Tientsin, 1932) p. 719; Li Tingan 李廷安, *Zhongwai yixue shi* 中外醫學史 (Shanghai, 1946), pp. 38–51; and L. M. Chen, "Public Health in National Reconstruction," *Bulletin, Council of International Affairs* 3.3 (1937), pp. 51–82.

[86] Wu Lien-teh et al., *Cholera: A Handbook*, p. 17.

[87] R. A. Jamieson, "Dr. Alexander Jamieson's Report on the Health of Shanghai for the Half-year Ended 30th September, 1877," *Customs Gazette Medical Reports* 14 (1877), p. 41.

Beijing, for two months the death rate was estimated at 15,000 (the population was thought to be around 1.5 million) or 1 percent of the population.[88] In 1878 in Niuzhuang, cholera claimed 50–200 victims a day from a population of 50,000, and "whole trades ceased their business, deserted the town and went home to their adjacent villages," thus spreading the disease.[89] In 1888, between Tianjin and Beijing whole villages were reported depopulated. In 1892 in Chongqing, a "well-drained" city that had not experienced an epidemic for six years, upwards of 13,000 died, or 5 percent of the population.[90]

Information was at a premium. Routes of the epidemics were tracked – and naturally they coincided with the main riverine transportation systems.[91] The disease was spread by soldiers, refugees from famine, or local conflicts, as well as by itinerant merchants, and farmers traveling through China's "formicatious system" of market towns and village fairs.[92] The disease, as in India, often broke out after a dry season ending in heavy rains.[93] The reason for this was surmised to be the prevalent system of surface drainage found in Chinese cities and towns, unmaintained from one season to the next and often (because of the lack of public latrines) the receptacle of nightsoil. A dry season led to the accumulation of refuse and choked the drains until rain flushed them out. Heavy rains and flooding spread the contents of these drains over a wide area, contaminating sources of water and in the rural districts flushing the nightsoil from the fields into the villages. Although drinking water was usually boiled, water for washing foods, vessels, and clothing and for personal hygiene was not.[94]

[88] Dudgeon, *Diseases of China*, p. 45.

[89] Watson, "Report on the Health of Newchwang," p. 29.

[90] See A. P. Peck, "Notes on Cholera in North China," p. 163. Depopulation of villages was also reported in Guangdong: see "Correspondence," *China Medical Missionary Journal* 2 (1888), p. 174; "Correspondence," *China Medical Missionary Journal* 6 (1892), p. 205. In Chengdu, fifty miles from Chongqing, "200–600 coffins were carried out of the gates daily." *China Medical Missionary Journal* 6 (1892), p. 216.

[91] Dudgeon, *Diseases of China*, p. 45; A. P. Peck, "Notes on Cholera in North China," pp. 163–64.

[92] A. P. Peck, "Notes on cholera in North China," pp. 164–65. Macgowan reported in 1851 that the rural areas between Shanghai and Ningbo suffered the most, "affording another evidence that in this part of China at least, the cities are the most healthy portions of the land." See *Chinese Repository* 20 (1851), p. 533–34.

[93] Zuo Huichun 左輝春, ed., *Xuzeng Gaoyou zhouzhi* 續增高郵州志 [Continuation of the Gaoyou department gazetteer] (1844. Reprinted, Taipei, 1974), vol. 6, p. 731. See also C. F. Mills, "Report on the Health of Ningpo for the Period 1st April 1907 to 31st May, 1909," *China Medical Journal* 24 (1910), p. 58.

[94] Wang Shixiong, *Essay on cholera*, p. 1059; R. A. Jamieson, "Dr. Alexander Jamieson's Report on the Health of Shanghai for the Half-year Ended 30th September 1871," *Customs Gazette, Medical Report* 2 (1871), p. 34; and Watson, "Report on the Health of Newchwang," p. 28.

The stark record of mortality focused attention on the sanitary conditions and water supplies of China's cities as the chief culprits in the spread of disease. But not everyone agreed, at least not until more substantial and uncontrovertible evidence was forthcoming. Did sanitary measures, especially the supply of "perfectly pure water," limit disease in populous cities? As the medical influences of water were better understood, the answer for an increasing number of doctors, both Western and Chinese, was yes.[95]

The emplacement of the medical and sanitary infrastructures of Chinese cities in the nineteenth and twentieth centuries was to a great extent prompted by "ordinary and extraordinary epidemics" such as cholera.[96] By the 1920s, coupled with technological advances, the accepted concepts and practices of public health were becoming established. The environmental approach to the disease was now supplemented by a deeper biological and chemical understanding of the vibrio as well as by control and management of the disease through effective treatments and immunization.[97] A chapter in the history of medicine that has yet to be written is the application of intravenous saline treatment of cholera in China.[98]

CONCLUSION

The first pandemic of cholera to reach China in 1820–21 exposed important issues in the understanding of the etiology of the disease, as well as in the history of epidemiology. The debates over whether the disease was "imported" or endemic to China played a role in the understanding of the interrelationship of infectious diseases and the environment. Though

[95] For a discussion of the first modern waterworks in Asia, see K. L. MacPherson, *Wilderness of Marshes*, ch. 5, pp. 83–122. By 1932, the Chinese municipal authorities were making regular laboratory analyses of water supplies, showing in Nanjing, e.g., that twelve wells were infected with cholera vibrios; see Wu Lien-teh, "The 1932 Cholera Epidemic in China with Special Reference to Shanghai," p. 5.

[96] For an interesting account of this development in Fuzhou, see W. W. Peter, "The Field and Methods of Public Health Work in the Missionary Enterprise," *China Medical Journal* 11.3 (1926), pp. 185–239.

[97] See Li T'ingan, *A Report on the Bureau of Public Health, City Government of Greater Shanghai* (Shanghai, 1934), pp. 1–20; *China Medical Journal* 27 (1913), pp. 107–17; "Kaolin in the Treatment of Cholera," *China Medical Journal* 33 (1919), pp. 396–97; and L. H. Braafladt, "Asiatic Cholera: A Study of 100 Cases," *China Medical Journal* 34 (1920), pp. 243–51.

[98] See Charles C. J. Carpenter, "Treatment of Cholera – Tradition and Authority versus Science, Reason, and Humanity," *Johns Hopkins Medical Journal* 139 (1976), pp. 153–62, showing the "erratic nature of the evolution of therapy in this field" (p. 153). For the debates over the use of intervenous therapy in China, see G. D. Whyte, "The Treatment of an Epidemic of Cholera by Roger's Method," *China Medical Journal* 27 (1913), pp. 107–17.

many investigators believed that true cholera was introduced from India, once planted in what proved to be the receptive soil of China, the disease took root. Others, often studying the medical classics of China, were persuaded that they were observing not, a "new" disease, but one that had transformed itself to assume epidemic form. The discovery (not necessarily the origin) of the El Tor vibrio in 1905, only twenty-one years after Koch's laboratory identification of the *Vibrio cholerae,* and the medical establishment's refusal to identify it with *V. cholerae* until 1962, encourages some speculation on this point.

The El Tor biotype did not assume pandemic form until 1961, and compared with classical cholera the infection-to-case ratio is higher[99] and the vibrios are hardier, surviving longer in the environment. There are also on record cases of convalescent carriers of the El Tor biotype that excreted vibrios intermittently for relatively prolonged periods – in one case in the Philippines up to ten years. After extensive epidemiological studies on carriers in 1962–67, the WHO Expert Committee on Cholera, in its second report in 1967, concluded that the role of the carrier in the transmission of cholera El Tor is very important. Furthermore, a few chronic carriers of *V. cholerae* have all been infected with the El Tor biotype. In 1971, an outbreak in West Bengal of both Ogawa and Inaba serotypes of El Tor and *V. cholerae* was recorded, but the classical biotype did not spread westward (its usual pattern), bearing out observations made in India that in the long run the El Tor biotype replaces the classical vibrio wherever they co-occur. As Barua concluded, "Could one surmise that the classical *V. cholerae* has lost its pandemic quality?"[100]

Paul Ewald, in his study *Evolution of Infectious Disease,* argues that "the traditional characterization of cholera as an extremely severe waterborne pathogen was largely accurate for the classical type but not for the el tor type." For Ewald the improvement of water supplies is a significant factor in favoring the slower-spreading, environmentally competitive El Tor vibrio.[101] The ratio of cases of two serologically cross-reacting biotypes competing for survival in the same population of susceptible hosts, as in West Bengal for example, could also be explained by the level of relative immunity present in the community to either biotype based on previous infections – the so-called waxing and waning of epidemics over time.

Ewald also believes that the conditions favoring enhanced toxin produc-

---

[99] During the El Tor outbreak in 1961–63 in Hong Kong, the estimated infection-to-case ratio was 100:1, indicating a very large reservoir of symptomless vibrio excreters. See Barua, *Cholera,* p. 383.

[100] Ibid., pp. 368, 11.

[101] Paul Ewald, *Evolution of Infectious Disease* (Oxford, 1994), p. 83.

tion by the vibrios, and therefore virulence, were likely present in South Asia four thousand years ago, leading to "the evolution of an illness indistinguishable from cholera." The thesis of the recent origin of cholera adduces as evidence the "absence of cholera in Europe prior to the early eighteenth century in spite of prior contact from medieval crusades, trade caravans, or boat routes"; Ewald proposes an alternative explanation:

> The cultural vectors hypothesis, however, explains how cholera could remain limited to South Asia even under these conditions: highly virulent *V. cholerae* can be maintained only if the waterborne cultural vector is present in a fairly large population. On overland trade routes or among small crews on long voyages, this kind of transmission is unlikely; the populations of highly virulent *V. cholerae* in such groups would die out much as other virulent pathogens die out in small population.[102]

The waterborne cultural vector hypothesis has merit in explaining the sudden virulence of the 1817 outbreak in Bengal in India. The unusually heavy rains noted in the records, coupled with copious atmospheric volcanic dust that lowered temperatures throughout the world, particularly water temperatures, enhanced the survival and replication of the cholera vibrios, and as Ewald points out, increased the virulence of the disease. Poor sanitation would have fostered its spread and malnutrition would have limited herd immunity if extant. In addition, the accelerated reproduction of the vibrios would have favored antigenic activity, leading to what many commentaries describe as the advent of a new or "transformed" disease.

But why did *V. cholerae* suddenly spread in 1817 from its Gangetic homeland? As we have seen, sea and land routes were the modes of transmission consistent with the geographical location of the afflicted areas. The evidence adduced above in the case of China, 1820–21, clearly supports this view, although our evidence of the observed land connection is sketchy, with some unspecified epidemics recorded in 1817, 1818, and 1819 in the interior. Discounting improvements in communications as the key element in the first pandemic period, other factors in addition to the "waterborne cultural vector" must have favored the spread of the disease.

The role of asymptomatic carriers (not as well documented in the case of *V. cholerae* as El Tor, given the timing of the pandemics and the then-current scientific knowledge), the level of immunity in the infected communities, along with demographic, behavioral, and social structures, no matter how difficult to assess historically, were also influential factors. If, for example, as Simmons assented in 1879, the use of boiled drinking water

---

[102] Ibid., p. 80.

and the removal of nightsoil from the populous cities, towns, and villages of China, *compared to India*, had a mitigating effect on the spread of disease, other observations stressed conflicting data: poor or nonexistent sanitation and the use of untreated water for washing, food preparation, and personal hygiene. Nevertheless, the chronology and routing of the six pandemics of *V. cholerae* and their virulence outside of India, in regions of South Asia including China that were even thought to have harbored the infection "from time immemorial," supports the thesis first suggested by Xu Zimo that an entirely new disease was imported into China in 1820–21.

Yet, as we have seen, evidence to the contrary poses an intriguing question. Wang Shixiong was convinced that the disease he was treating was the same or a modified form of the ancient infection *huoluan*. Could the El Tor vibrio actually be the nonpandemic source of what historically in China (and perhaps India) was called *huoluan*? What we know of the biological strategy of the El Tor biotype – its slower replication, its relative nondependence on waterborne transmission, its higher asymptomatic carrier incidence (the silent epidemic), and so on – fits the historical descriptions of pre-1820 *huoluan* discussed in this essay. Could the *V. cholerae* of India perhaps have been a newer, more virulent form of the disease that became epidemic and then pandemic in 1817? *V. cholerae* might then have become less virulent as public health systems emerged and water supplies became purer, until the 1960s when El Tor, for reasons we have reviewed, became ascendant. Unlike the *V. cholerae* that became the primary focus of intensive medical investigation after 1817 when it became pandemic, leading to its isolation in 1883, it was only after the El Tor biotype (isolated in 1902) became pandemic in the 1960s that the medical establishment identified it with *V. cholerae* in 1962. Perhaps the two medical opponents, Wang Shixiong and Xu Zimo, were both prescient in their acute observations of cholera in China.

An alternative speculation, drawing on Selwyn's analysis and later elaborated by McNichol and Doetsch (1983)[103] and others, is that the sudden appearance of *V. cholerae*, like El Tor, was the result of genetic changes in the vibrios over time. The newly emerging 0139 strain of *V. cholerae* in Asia supports this evolutionary view, although definitive research into the evolutionary tree of *V. cholerae* has yet to be concluded.[104] This could explain the

---

[103] L. A. McNicholl and R. N. Doetsch, "A Hypothesis Accounting for the Origin of Pandemic Cholera: A Retrograde Analysis," *Perspectives on Biology and Medicine* 26 (1983), pp. 547–52.

[104] See, *MMWR*, p. 2. New research into the cholera bacteria's evolution and life cycle reports that the gene that codes for the cholera toxin that causes the life-threatening diarrhea of the disease is carried by a bacteriophage – a virus that infects *V. cholerae*. Waldor and

references in the historical literature of diseases like *huoluan* with clinical manifestations very similar to cholera.

Speculation aside, what is clear is the link between the disease and the environment and human vulnerability to microorganisms. Poor sanitation, polluted water supplies, poverty, and ignorance are the conditions in which cholera survives. The history of cholera in China forms an important benchmark in our understanding of an international problem that merits further investigation.

Mekalanos believe that "the CTX virus must have infiltrated a once-harmless strain of *V. cholerae* to create the strain responsible for the first great cholera pandemic of 1817. Another, separate infiltration by the same virus probably created the El Tor strain that began the more recent pandemic in 1961." See Pyllida Brown, "Cholera's Deadly Hitchhiker," *Science* 272 (June 28, 1996), p. 2037; Nigel Williams; "Page Transfer: A New Player Turns Up in Cholera Infection," *Science* 272 (June 28, 1996), pp. 1869–70; and Mathew K. Waldor and John J. Mekalanos, "Lysogenic Conversion by Filamentous Phage Encoding Cholera Toxin," *Science* 272 (June 28, 1996), pp. 1910–14.

14

Environment and Tuberculosis in Modern China

ZHANG YIXIA AND MARK ELVIN

OVERVIEW

Tuberculosis was the greatest single cause of death worldwide in the last century and in the early part of this century. The influence of environmental conditions on the prevalence of tuberculosis has been investigated for some countries, but the case of China has been relatively neglected. In this chapter, we first use both new and previously neglected data to outline the probable general correlation between epidemic tuberculosis and the overall course of modern Chinese history on the basis of long-term tuberculosis mortality changes in Shanghai, Beijing, and Tianjin. We then focus on the relations between epidemic tuberculosis and environmental conditions in China both at work and away from the workplace. The results show that tuberculosis was a disease of indoor life. The percentage of people suffering from tuberculosis was primarily associated with their occupations and the time spent indoors. In particular, wherever there was a dense local indoor concentration of population, with poor ventilation, or the environment has a high density of airborne particles, there was an increased probability that workers would develop tuberculosis. Residential overcrowding also proved a major contributory cause of the spread of tuberculosis among Chinese. Eating habits and widespread spitting were probably also implicated, though this cannot be shown from the statistical information presented here. Finally, we analyze fourteen tuberculosis outbreaks in present-day China and point out the continuing importance of improvement in the environment for the control of tuberculosis in China.

INTRODUCTION

Tuberculosis is an infectious disease usually caused by the common human tubercle bacillus (*Mycobacterium tuberculosis*). The disease can affect almost any part of the body, but the most common form of the disease is pulmonary tuberculosis. The tubercle bacillus contains a large amount of lipids in the cell wall, hence it is more resistant than most bacteria to heat and other environmental influences. It can live in dried sputum in a room without sunlight for six to eight months. When mixed with dust suspended in the air, the bacillus can even maintain infectivity for eight to ten months. The infection is easily transferred by breathing infected droplets exhaled from persons with tuberculosis. The risk of developing the disease depends in part on the quantity of bacilli to which the individual is exposed, and thus the bacilli are most likely to infect people in dark, damp, ill-ventilated and overcrowded houses or workplaces. In general, the progress of tuberculosis is slow, since the bacillus reproduces slowly. People with tuberculosis can maintain a regular life for years with or without showing symptoms. Some of them develop the active form of the disease without knowing it is tuberculosis, continually exhaling tubercle bacilli into their surroundings, and so become a source of infection. The chronic character of tuberculosis makes it ultimately more harmful to public health than acute infectious diseases.

HISTORY

Tuberculosis probably existed in China at least two thousand years ago.[1] It was first described by the name of *xulao bing* 虛癆病 (weak consumptive disease) in the *Huangdi neijing* 黃帝內經 [The Yellow Emperor's manual of corporeal medicine] in the Western Han dynasty (202 B.C. – A.D.). The symptoms of *xulao bing*, namely coughing, abnormal appearance, fever, a weak and fast pulse (*ke* 咳, *tuoxing* 脱形, *shenre* 身熱, *mai xiao yiji* 脈小以疾),[2] a blocked chest and shortage of breath (*xiongzhong qiman, chuanxi*

---

[1] Tuberculosis scars were found in the lung of a woman's mummified body dating from the Western Han period (202 B.C. – A.D. 9) excavated in Hu'nan province in 1973, *National Geographic* 145 (May 1974), p. 663. See also the letter from Drs. A. Freedman and A. J. Proust in *Medical Journal of Australia* 1978 (April), p. 392, mentioning "two small calcified tuberculous foci in the apex of the left lung" of this cadaver.

[2] *Huangdi neijing, lingshu* 黃帝内经灵枢 [The Yellow Emperor's manual of corporeal medicine, the vital axis] (Reprinted, Beijing: Renmin Weisheng CBS 人民卫生出版社 [People's Health

bubian 胸中气滿 喘息不便),[3] were very close to the symptoms of tuberculosis today. More symptoms that resemble those of tuberculosis were described under the different names of *lao ji* 勞祭 (exhausted sacrifice), *gu zheng* 骨蒸 (bone-phthisis), *shi zhu* 尸疰 (corpse infection), *chong zhu* 蟲疰 (parasite infection), *gui zhu* 鬼疰 (ghost infection), *wugu* 無辜 (innocence), *luoli* 瘰癧 (scrofula), and so on, in later dynasties.[4,5] The infectiousness of tuberculosis was first realized by Ge Hong 葛洪 (A.D. 281–361) in the Jin dynasty. He called the disease *shi zhu* 尸注 (corpse infection) and pointed out that the disease could be passed from a dead person to other members of the family and could cause the extermination of the entire family.[6] There is a custom handed down from generation to generation in some areas of China until the present: when a person dies of a lung disease, his nose and mouth will be covered by a piece of silk wadding[7] (Zhejiang province) or a piece of dough (Shanxi province) to prevent the "consumptive parasite" from coming out. It is not clear when this custom began, but it is likely that the realization of the infectious character of tuberculosis by the ancient Chinese had some influence on it.

Human tuberculosis is commonly believed to be derived from bovine tuberculosis in domestic cattle, as *Mycobacterium bovis* also infects humans whereas *M. tuberculosis* (the specifically human form of tuberculosis) does not infect cattle. However, the finding of tuberculosis traces on the ribs of skeletons from hunting and gathering populations in the New World before Columbus, when no domestic cattle were present, suggests other sources of human tuberculosis.[8] In ancient China the bird population was

Press], 1957), p. 98; and Lu Kuisheng 陸奎生, *Zhongguo yixueshi shang zhi feibing zhiji* 中國醫學史上之肺病治蹟 [The development of therapy for tuberculosis in Chinese medical history], *Guoyi Baodao* 國醫報導 [National Medical Report] 3.3 (1941).

[3] *Huangdi neijing suwen* 黃帝内经素问 [The Yellow Emperor's manual of corporeal medicine, the plain questions (and answers)], (Reprinted, Beijing: Renmin Weisheng CBS 人民卫生出版社 [People's Health Press], 1962), p. 46.

[4] Fan Bingzhe 范秉哲 et al., "Feijiehe Zhongyi zhiliao gaiyao" 肺结核中医治疗概要 [Outline of Chinese medical therapy for pulmonary tuberculosis], in Fan Bingzhe, ed., *Jiehebing Xue* 结核病学 [Tuberculosis] (Beijing: Renmin Weisheng CBS, 1964), pp. 303–04.

[5] Wang Qiming 王启明, "Feijiehe 肺结核" [Pulmonary tuberculosis], in Wang Qiming, ed., *Zhong-Xi-yi jiehe zhiliao jiehebing* 中西医结合治疗结核病 [The therapy of tuberculosis by combining Chinese and Western medicine] (Chongqing: Sichuan Kexue CBS 四川科学技术出版社 [Sichuan Science Press], 1983), p. 79.

[6] Ge Hong 葛洪, *Zhou hou bei ji fang* 肘后备急方 [Handbook of medicines for emergencies] (Reprinted, Beijing: Renmin Weisheng CBS, 1956), p. 20: "*sihou fuchuan zhi pangzen, naizhi miemen* 死後復傳之旁人，乃至滅門."

[7] Lu Kuisheng, *Development of therapy for tuberculosis*, pp. 14–18.

[8] M. J. Allison et al., "Documentation of a Case of Tuberculosis in Pre-Columbian America," *American Review of Respiratory Disease* 107 (1973), pp. 985–91; Marc Kelley and Marc Micozzi, "Rib Lesions in Chronic Pulmonary Tuberculosis," *American Journal of Physical Anthropology* 65 (1984), pp. 381–86.

suspected of being the source of human tuberculosis. Thus Chao Yuanfang 巢元方 of the Sui dynasty analyzed the origins of children's tuberculosis – *wugu bing* 無辜病 (the innocent's disease) – in his book *Zhubing yuanhou zonglun* 諸病源候總論 [General discussion of the etiology of diseases] (A.D. 610) as follows: "There is a bird called the 'Innocent,' which sleeps during the day and roams about at night. If you wash the clothes and bedding of small children and leave them out overnight, and this bird thereupon flies over them, and you then give the clothes to the children to wear, or fold the mats over for them to sleep on, then this will cause the children to break out in this disease."[9] It is known that the Chinese have almost certainly had no habit of drinking milk (as opposed to eating milk-derived products at certain times in the past.)[10] There are not many cases of human tuberculosis that are caused by *M. bovis* (typically, less than 10 percent). Therefore, human tuberculosis, at least in China, is not likely to have originated from *M. bovis*. Although cases of *M. avium* causing human tuberculosis are rare at present, bearing in mind the possibility that the mycobacterium may have evolved over the long history of tuberculosis, it is possible at least to entertain the idea that birds may have played a part in the origins of human tuberculosis.

PRESENT TIMES

In recent times tuberculosis has been the most harmful infectious disease and the leading single cause of all deaths in China. In the 1920s, more than 850,000 people died of TB each year, equal to about a hundred every hour. Most of the people who died of TB were between twenty and thirty-five years old, when they were still strong members of the labor force. It has been calculated that, in this age group, one person died of TB out of every three who died of any kind of disease. In the 1930s, Dr. Wu Liande reported that 1.2 million people died of TB in the whole of China each year. More than 10 million people were estimated to have an active form of the disease.[11] Sixty-five percent of the children under ten

[9] Chao Yuanfang 巢元方 et al., *Zhubing yuanhou zonglun* 諸病源候總論 [Etiology of disease] (Reprinted, Beijing: Renmin Weisheng CBS, 1955), p. 259. See also Xiao Shuxuan 蕭叔軒, "Jiehebing zai Zhongguo yixueshi shang de fazhan" 結核病在中國醫學史上的發展 [The development of tuberculosis in Chinese medical history], *Zhonghua yishi zazhi* 中華醫史雜誌 [Journal of Chinese medical history], 3.1 (1951), pp. 25–33; 3.2, pp. 28–40; 3.3, pp. 20–30; 3.4, pp. 13–22.

[10] Shi Shenghan 石聲漢, *A Preliminary Survey of the Book "Ch'i min yao shu," an Agricultural Encyclopaedia of the 6th Century* (Beijing: Science Press 科學出版社, 1958), p. 89.

[11] Wu Liande 伍連德, "Jiehebing" 結核病 [Tuberculosis], *Zhonghu Yixue Zazhi* 中華醫學雜誌 [Chinese Medical Journal] 20.1 (1934), pp. 84–115.

years,[12] and almost all of those (more than 90 percent) around twenty years of age in urban areas were infected.[13] After the 1950s, TB mortality dropped quickly, but, compared to developed countries, TB is still a problem in the PRC today.

The history of tuberculosis among an ancient people constituting a fifth to a quarter of the world's population should be, in itself, of interest from any point of view. However, it is a subject concerning which there are only the most meager and fragmentary data. It is difficult to say exactly when China's tuberculosis epidemic began. There were, strictly speaking, no TB mortality statistics for any city predating 1949. The only continuing first-hand information on the prevalence of TB is from the handful of Western-trained medical men working in the missionary hospitals located in the concessions of Shanghai and reported by the health officer of Shanghai Municipal Council (whose jurisdiction covered only the International Settlement [*gonggong zujie* 公共租界], and not the parts of the city under Chinese rule) in its annual reports from 1901 to 1936. Though these statistics were limited to the International Settlement,[14] to some extent they must reflect the prevalence of tuberculosis in cities in the early part of the twentieth century in China. However, China is a vast country with a huge population. The Shanghai International Settlement was only a small part of it and cannot represent even the cities completely, let alone the whole country.

Epidemic tuberculosis is influenced by many social and economic factors, such as housing conditions, poverty, overwork, anxiety, and more recently (after the 1950s) medical circumstances (for example, BCG vaccination, chemotherapy, and government control programs). The curves of TB mortality in Shanghai from 1901 to 1990 (Tables 14.1 and 14.2 and Fig. 14.1), in Beijing from 1926 to 1991 (Fig. 14.2), and in Tianjin from 1950 to 1990 (Fig. 14.3) presumably show these influences on epidemic TB in China.

The great change in TB mortality from 1901 to 1902 shown in Figure 14.1 is unlikely to reflect the true story; it is probably due to the use of different statistical methods.

---

[12] Chinese years of age (age one at birth and a year older at each New Year).

[13] Cai Rusheng 蔡如昇, "Jiehebing de liuxingbing xue" 結核病的流行病學 [Etiology of tuberculosis], *Zhonghua yixue zazhi* 中華醫學雜誌 [Chinese Medical Journal] 8 (1955), pp. 710–14.

[14] The Chinese population of the "foreign settlement" (it is not clear if this includes the French Concession) was about 0.5 million in 1910 and 1.0 million by the middle of the 1930s. See R. Murphey, *Shanghai: Key to Modern China* (Cambridge, Mass.: Harvard University Press, 1953), p. 22.

Table 14.1. *Tuberculosis mortality among the Chinese in the pre-war Shanghai Concessions*

Year	Estimated population	No. of TB deaths	Mortality per 100,000
1901	350,000	1,097	313.43
1902	350,000	2,000	571.43
1903	375,000	1,976	526.93
1904	385,000	1,827	474.55
1905	452,716	1,414	312.3
1906	475,000	1,000	210.53
1907	510,000	960	188.24
1908	530,000	938	176.98
1909	550,000	828	150.55
1910	488.005	618	126.64
1911	492,000	789	160.37
1912	500,000	1,096	219.20
1913	510,000	1,008	197.65
1914	520,000	1,051	202.12
1915	620,401	1,024	165.05
1916	630,510	1,034	163.99
1917	644,580	1,111	172.36
1918	659,000	1,237	187.71
1919	673,000	1,063	157.95
1920	759,839	1,070	140.82
1921	780,000	879	112.69
1922	814,000	870	106.88
1923	830,000	822	99.04
1924	835,000	867	103.83
1925	798,810	871	109.04
1926	802,700	1,127	140.40
1927	812,075	975	120.06
1928	821,400	871	106.04
1929	830,760	966	116.28
1930	971,397	855	88.02
1931	987,397	956	96.82
1932	1,030,554	746	72.39
1933	1,065,554	873	81.93
1934	1,100,496	987	89.69
1936	1,141,727	735	64.38

Source: Shanghai Municipal Council Reports.

Table 14.2. *Tuberculosis mortality in Shanghai under the PRC*

Year	No. of TB deaths	Mortality per 100,000
1951	10,949	208.0
1956	5,317	89.2
1961	3,516	54.5
1965	2,000	31.1
1966	1,904	29.8
1971	1,499	26.0
1976	1,086	19.6
1978	786	14.1
1981	525	8.6
1986	176	6.06
1990	334	4.28

Source: Shanghai TB Prevention Institute. The mortality rate for 1965 is from Sun Zhongliang 孙中亮, "Shanghai jiehebing fangzhi jinkuang yu jidian yijian" 上海结核病防治近况与几点意见 [The present tuberculosis prevention situation in Shanghai and a few suggestions], *Zhongguo fanglao tongxun* 中国防痨通讯 [Bulletin of the Chinese Antituberculosis Association] 1 (1981) pp. 4–7. The number of TB deaths for 1978 is calculated from population figures given in Guojia tongjiju chengshi shehui jingji diaocha zongdui 国家统计局城市社会经济调查总队 [Urban Social and Economic Survey Organization of the State Statistical Bureau, the People's Republic of China], *Zhongguo chengshi sishi nian* 中国城市四十年 [Forty years of China's cities] (Beijing and Hong Kong: China Statistical and Consultancy Service Center and the International Center for the Advancement of Science and Technology, 1990), pp. 86–7.

The intermittent increases in TB mortality in the following years may have reflected (at least in part) such factors as wars, political and social upheaval, economic stresses, and natural disasters. A possible example is the rise following the 1911 revolution.

At the beginning of the twentieth century, tuberculosis headed the list of fatal diseases among the Chinese, being responsible for one in four or five of all deaths, many more than any other disease. Western doctors believed that most cases of pulmonary tuberculosis were contracted by breathing the infected droplets ejected by infected persons during coughing, sneezing, and speaking, and that therefore spitting and insufficient air space were the

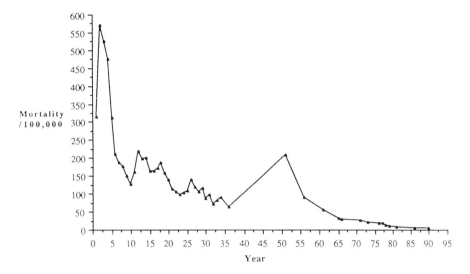

Figure 14.1. Shanghai TB mortality, 1901–90.

chief secondary causes. They introduced knowledge about tuberculosis, and distributed Tuberculosis Prevention Notices widely among the Chinese. The drop of the number of TB deaths during this period may have owed something to their efforts, though the general history of epidemiology before the effective treatments of very recent times offers warnings against attributing too much to therapy or to such interventions.[15]

During the period of the Chinese Republic, TB mortality kept decreasing in Shanghai, in spite of the massive inmigration and outmigration and massive local unemployment.[16] Even in the 1920s and 1930s, prior to the Japanese invasion of northern China, Shanghai relied primarily on local supplies of rice (defined as coming from within a radius of less than 120 kilometers), with rice imported from other provinces and abroad mainly as only a stabilizing factor in years of bad local harvests. The vulnerable point of food supplies was the disruption of local water transport by civil war and floods, which is what happened in 1926, with a rise both in TB mortality and in imports of foreign rice (300 million pounds as contrasted with 0.2

---

[15] Notably the work of T. McKeown, *The Modern Rise of Population* (London: Arnold, 1976), esp. pp. 92–93.

[16] M. Elvin, "Introduction" to M. Elvin and G. W. Skinner, eds., *The Chinese City Between Two Worlds* (Stanford, Calif.: Stanford University Press, 1974), pp. 11–12, documents estimated unemployment in the early 1930s as over 9% of total urban population (not of labor force), and a ratio of migrants (those entering or leaving within a given year) to population that often exceeded 200/1,000.

million in 1924, the lowest year). The summer of 1926 was exceptionally hot and humid, and the rainfall heavy. Refugees from ravaged districts came in an almost continuous stream to Shanghai to seek safety. They filled the railway stations, the principal wharves, the hotels, and the lodging houses. It was difficult ever to estimate their number. As the result of natural disasters and refugee inmigration, cholera became epidemic and the number of tuberculosis deaths increased. Rather similar events occurred in 1931, with imports of 200 million pounds of foreign rice, when floods in the lower Yangzi had disrupted inland shipping, and again in 1932, the year of the Japanese attack on the city.[17] Some 60,000–70,000 refugees poured into the International Settlement, plus 100,000 refugees from the Yangzi River region, with the result that the concession became very crowded. Cholera and smallpox were prevalent,[18] but – surprisingly – the recorded TB mortality fell. This may have been the consequence of inadequate statistical coverage of the refugee population, or the "masking" effect of the more acute diseases, but if so, we have to ask why this did not also occur in 1926. This problem is beyond our present data to resolve, but in general we may speculate that the stability of the city's food supplies, based on its exceptionally effective transport network, helped to underpin the gradual decline in TB mortality in spite of many adverse factors. There was also, of course, the continued introduction of knowledge about tuberculosis from Western countries; more and more Chinese doctors paid attention to TB prevention, with government support.

No statistical reports are available for the period of the civil wars (1937–45 and 1946–49). However, it seems certain that TB mortality increased during these years, judging by the data for before and after this period.[19]

Eight years of war against the Japanese indirectly caused the birth of the People's Republic of China in 1949 and also caused some danger to this new life. Tuberculosis at this time was killing more people per year than the war had done (at least by direct action).

After the establishment of the People's Republic of China, TB mortality decreased rapidly, for the following reasons: (1) general socioeconomic conditions were improved; (2) an antituberculosis network was established

---

[17] Murphey, *Shanghai: Key to Modern China*, pp. 140–52.
[18] Yang Shangchi 杨上池 *Sanshi niandai de Quanguo Haigang Jianyi Guanlichu yu Wu Liande Boshi* 三十年代的全国海港检疫管理处与伍连德博士 [The National Seaport Quarantine Administrative Office of the 1930s and Dr. Wu Liande], *Zhonghua Yishi Zazhi* 中华医史杂志 [Journal of Chinese Medical History] 18.1 (1988), pp. 29–32.
[19] It should be recalled that in England TB mortality rose during both world wars. See H. Coovadia and S. Benatar, eds., *A Century of Tuberculosis: A South African Perspective* (Cape Town: Oxford University Press, 1991), p. 17.

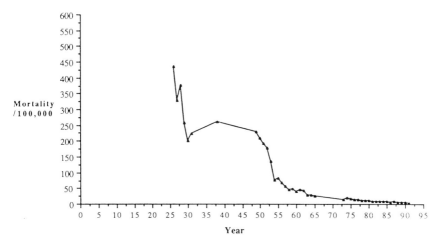

Figure 14.2. Beijing TB mortality, 1926–91. *Source*: Data (1926–38) for the First Health Area of Beiping from Hsu Hsuyu, "The Fight against Tuberculosis in China in the Last 100 Years and the Present Situation," *Bulletin of the International Union Against Tuberculosis and Lung Disease* 62.4 (1987), pp. 11–15. Data (1949–91) for Beijing urban area from the Beijing TB Prevention Institute.

in cities; (3) BCG vaccination was supplied throughout the country; and (4) effective chemotherapy began to be applied.

Even given the above protection, economics still showed its influence on the tuberculosis epidemic. From the curves of TB mortality in Beijing and Tianjin shown in Figures 14.2 and 14.3, we can see that TB mortality increased from 1960 to 1962, when national economic stress was severe, especially as regards food supplies, this being a period when the grain output per head in He'nan and Hebei provinces fell by 44 percent and 24 percent respectively as compared to the average for the period 1952–57.[20]

The history of tuberculosis in China is thus a long one, and the recent epidemic of the disease seems to have been influenced by rather more factors and to be perhaps somewhat more complex than those in the developed countries. In the main part of this chapter, we concentrate on the relation between tuberculosis and environmental conditions, including both the working environment and housing. It should constantly be remembered, however, when reading the sections that follow, that there is invariably some ambiguity about the meaning in practice of the concept of

[20] K. R. Walker, *Food Grain Procurement and Consumption in China* (Cambridge: Cambridge University Press, 1984), p. 159.

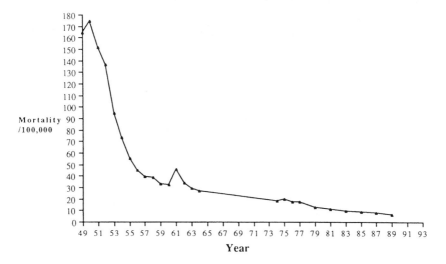

Figure 14.3. Tianjin TB mortality, 1949–89. *Source*: Tianjin Tuberculosis Institute.

"infection" as it relates to TB. The disease may be entirely quiescent, contained by the host's immune system, and only detected by the old lesions in lung tissues visible in X-rays, or by the response to a Mantoux test, both subject to some interpretative uncertainty. Or it may be active, clinically evident, and infectious. Even so, only in a small percentage of such cases will laboratory testing have put the diagnosis beyond reasonable doubt.

THE WORKING ENVIRONMENT

OCCUPATION

Dr. Oldt investigated the records and case histories of more than fifteen thousand in-patients in a number of hospitals of Guangdong and tried to find what kind of people were the most likely to suffer from tuberculosis, and whether the percentage of TB patients out of the total patients admitted was related to age, sex, income level, or occupation.[21] He classified the patients basically according to their economic condition, as shown in Table

---

[21] F. Oldt, "Tuberculosis in Kwangtung According to Age, Sex, Occupation and Economic Condition," *Chinese Medical Journal* 47 (1933), pp. 111–27.

Table 14.3. *Tuberculosis according to occupation (Guangdong, 1933)*

Occupation	Total patients	TB patients	TB patients as a % of total
Professional and "better" class			
Leisured class	202	24	11.9
Preacher	86	9	10.5
Teacher	179	15	8.4
Medical	160	10	6.3
Secretary	53	3	5.7
"Single" groups			
Student	954	106	11.1
Business	1,149	97	8.4
Children	3,340	279	8.4
Housewife	2,342	155	6.6
Semiprofessionals			
Actor	17	1	5.9
Soldier	2,376	46	1.9
Police	57	1	1.8
Engineer fireman	23	0	0
Artisan class			
Printer	20	4	20.0
Paper-objects maker	18	3	16.7
Seamstress/tailor	239	31	13.0
Weaver	215	25	11.6
Jeweler/silversmith	26	3	11.5
Servant	385	41	10.6
Barber	19	2	10.5
Firecracker maker	10	1	10.0
Carpenter	88	8	9.1
Bamboo worker	23	2	8.7
Filature worker	119	9	7.6
Mechanic/electrician	50	4	6.6
Shoemaker	47	2	4.3
Mason	46	1	2.2
Laboring class			
Farmer	1,590	109	6.8
Laborer	1,322	62	4.6
Boatman	231	10	4.3
Peddler	122	4	3.3
Sailor	83	2	2.4
Fisherman	10	0	0.0

Source: Oldt, "Tuberculosis in Kwangtung."

14.3. Note that we have omitted those groups containing less than ten cases.

From Table 14.4 we can see that the percentage of TB patients had no correlation with the patients' economic status. The poorer class did not necessarily show a higher percentage than the "better" class. The laboring class had a lower income than did the artisan class, though it was generally supposed to have a higher probability of suffering from TB. In fact, the percentage of patients with TB from a laboring-class background was only half of that of the artisan class. The semiprofessional class containing soldiers and police was considered poorer than the professional "better" class, which contained medical personnel and leisured people, though better off than the laboring and artisan classes. Yet, regardless of its economic status, the semiprofessional class showed the lowest percentage of TB patients among all classes.

The percentage of TB patients was, however, closely related to the patient's working environment. The people who were working indoors, such as members of the artisan class and professional people, were more likely to be suffering from tuberculosis (10.42 percent and 9.0 percent respectively) than those who had an outdoor life such as the laboring class (5.6 percent) and soldiers, police, and other semiprofessionals (1.9 percent). Even within the artisan class, we can see this difference. Paper-object makers and printers led an indoor life and also worked in an environment with a high density of fibers (as paper was made from fibrous materials), and this was particularly so for the printers, who worked with volatile printing ink that caused a suffocating and unhealthy atmosphere. As the result of these poor working conditions the paper-object makers and the printers presented a high percentage of TB patients (16.7 percent and 20 percent respectively). At the opposite end of the range, the masons in the artisan class only showed 2.2 percent of patients suffering from TB, because they spent most of their time outdoors, although presumably they generated some rock powder as they worked. Business people and housewives also had a higher percentage of TB, primarily because they spent most of their time indoors. As regards children and students, they had a relatively high TB percentage among patients, no doubt because they were at the age of high susceptibility, but perhaps also because they spent substantial time indoors studying.

It should be said that although the percentage of patients infected with TB had no relation to the group's income level, the mortality may have had such a relation, since a better economic status probably offered better chances to escape death from the disease.

Table 14.4. *Summary of TB incidence by class (Guangdong, 1933)*

Occupation	Total patients	TB patients	TB patients as a % of total
Students	954	106	11.1
Artisan class	1,305	136	10.4
Professional and "better" class	680	61	9.0
Businessmen	1,149	97	8.4
Children	3,340	279	8.4
Housewives	2,342	155	6.6
Laboring class	3,358	187	5.6
Semiprofessionals	2,473	48	1.9

Source: Table 14.3.

It is well known that TB was prevalent throughout at least urban China in the 1930s. Eighty percent of urban dwellers over fifteen years old were infected by the tubercle bacillus. However, the authorities fixed their attention on other infectious diseases, such as cholera, malaria, plague, and leprosy, perhaps because of the more visibly epidemic character of these diseases, and also because they were on the whole more amenable to control than tuberculosis. Professor Qiu Zuyuan 裘祖源, one of the pioneers of Chinese TB epidemiology and antituberculosis campaigns, established China's first tuberculosis clinic in Beiping (as it was then) in 1935. The clinic aimed at the early diagnosis of tuberculosis and at preventing the spread of tuberculosis among the population. The clinic also provided practice for medical students where they could learn more about TB prevention and put into effect what they had learned. Professor Qiu extended their work into the social domain when he started the study of the epidemiology of TB in China. He and his colleagues X-rayed more than thirty thousand people from factories, universities and schools, government offices, and the catering and service trades (see Table 14.5). It was found that hairdressing had the highest TB prevalence rate (19.2 percent) among all occupations. This was particularly the case for barbers working in public bathhouses, nearly three out of ten of whom were suffering from tuberculosis (27.3 percent). The cutting room in China was usually very small and with poor ventilation. It was obvious that cutting hair for customers obliged the hairdresser or barber to come into close contact with customers who were TB sufferers, and that the limited space made it easy for the infection to be transmitted. Nonbarber staff working in the public bathhouses had a

Table 14.5. *TB prevalence rate and occupations (Beiping, 1939)*

Occupation	No. of subjects	No. of sufferers	Prevalence rate %
Factory workers	23,582	1,113	4.7
Undergraduates	4,367	221	5.1
Catering trade	1,733	103	5.9
Administrative staff	5,807	441	7.6
Hairdressers	604	116	19.2
Public bathroom barbers	66	18	27.3
Public bathroom nonbarber staff	492	41	8.3

Source: Beijing TB Prevention Institute, ed., *TB Prevention* (Beijing, 1976).

lower prevalence rate than barbers, but higher than that for administrative staff, and for catering-trade and factory workers.

Overcrowding has always been a problem in Beijing. It was common at this time for several persons to sleep in the same room. It was usually impossible to have a bathroom in residential quarters. The public bathhouse was the only place where people could wash themselves. No showers were available at that time and customers all bathed in the same pool. It is needless to point out how easily the bacillus could be transmitted from the sick to the healthy. The requirement that the bathhouse be kept warm also made for poor internal ventilation. It was difficult for people who were working in this environment to escape from infection. Compared to bathhouse staff, administrative staff had a much lower prevalence rate (7.6 percent). Although administrative staff spent most of their time indoors, they had a better environment, or at least better ventilation. Catering-trade and factory workers had relatively lower prevalence rates, which were presumably associated with the nature of their working spaces and working environment.

People who worked in different factories had different probabilities of suffering from tuberculosis. Mines and factories such as cement plants and textile mills, where the environment had a high density of dust, made it easy for the workers to develop lung diseases, in particular tuberculosis. An investigation conducted in He'nan province in 1990 examined 364 workers from a cement plant and 982 workers from a pharmaceutical factory by radiography. The result showed a significant difference in the tuberculosis prevalence rates between these two groups ($p < 0.01$). The TB prevalence rate among cement plant workers was 1.6 percent, while the prevalence rate among pharmaceutical factory workers was 0.2 percent. The significant difference between these two groups was that the workers in the cement plant worked in an environment with a high density of cement dust, which is one of the substances that can weaken the immune system and thus increase the probability of developing tuberculosis.

Even in the same textile mill, workers with different types of work had different prevalence rates. X-ray chest examination of 333,303 workers from textile mills in Shandong province showed that people who worked in an environment with a high density of cotton fibers, metals, and mixed dust particles had a higher TB prevalence rate (224 per 100,000) than those who worked in a cleaner atmosphere (140 per 100,000).[22]

Factories with a bad atmospheric environment not only cause high TB prevalence rates among their employees, but also influence the inhabitants in the surrounding areas. Mentougou and Fangshan, for example, are two present-day counties in the Beijing area. They have similar situations, and even the average wages of the inhabitants are comparable (1,751 and 1,727 yuan per person per year in 1988). But they differ in TB prevalence rates (91.2 per 100,000 vs. 41.3 per 100,000) and in TB mortality rates (10.6 per 100,000 vs. 6.3 per 100,000). The reason for the difference is probably that Mentougou contains several coalmines whereas Fangshan contains only factories producing foods such as fruit jam.

CROWDED WORKING SPACE

A crowded working space is another factor promoting the spread of TB. Since the 1980s, the Chinese government has encouraged the development of industries in small towns. Most of these factories have not had adequate funds for the proper construction of premises at the beginning of their operations. Usually the buildings are simple and crude. There is a clothing factory in Nanhui county, in the Shanghai area, that is an example of this phenomenon. The workshop is small and crowded, and the employees toil at an assembly line where adjacent positions are less than one meter apart. The products are processed and then passed on by hand. The factory is located by the sea and the wind is strong in all seasons. To keep the interior warm, the doors and windows are always shut, and heavy curtains are added in winter. It is easy to imagine how bad the ventilation is. One worker here contracted TB in 1980, but still kept working. As the result of this spreading the tubercle bacillus in these poorly ventilated conditions for

[22] Shandong sheng fangzhi xitong jiehebing feibu jibing yanjiusuo 山东省纺织系统结核病肺部疾病研究所 [The Tuberculosis and Pulmonary Diseases Research Institute for the Shandong Textile System], ed., *Zhongguo fanglao zazhi* 中国防痨杂志 [The Chinese Antituberculosis Journal] 13.3 (1991), p. 109.

Table 14.6. *TB Deaths in the Shanghai prison*
(1912–21)

Year	Total deaths	Deaths from TB	% TB
1912	21	6	29
1913	26	19	73
1914	56	31	55
1915	55	28	51
1916	76	59	78
1917	117	62	53
1918	129	105	81
1919	123	101	82
1920	119	97	82
1921	83	74	89
Totals	805	582	72

Source: Annual Report of the Shanghai Municipal
Council, 1922.

four years, forty-seven of this colleagues contracted the disease. In contrast,
among the leaders, who worked in offices far removed from the work floor,
no one became infected.[23]

Tuberculosis is still a public health problem in China. The lack of
attention paid to the working environment plays an important role in this
situation.

THE SHANGHAI PRISON

We have said that TB is essentially a disease of indoor life. In the early years
of the twentieth century, it was noticed that tuberculosis was the greatest
single medical problem in the prison of Shanghai's International Settlement. Observations on TB in the prison were maintained for ten years,
from 1912 to 1921. It was found that 72 percent of the total deaths of
convicts were due to tuberculosis. This was much higher than the rate for
people who lived outside the prison. The figures in Table 14.6 are extracted from the Annual Reports of the Commissioner of Public Health.

---

[23] Huang Jiansheng 黄建生 et al., *Xiangzhen fuzhuangchang jiehebing baofa liuxing lianxu guancha baogao* 乡镇服装厂结核病暴发流行连续观察报告 [Report of a continued investigation into the outbreak of tuberculosis in a clothing factory in a small town], *Zhongguo fanglao tongxun* 中国防痨通讯 [Bulletin of the Chinese Antituberculosis Association] 8.2 (1986), pp. 15–17.

The health officer suspected that the lack of fat, salt, and total energy value in the diet was the reason for these TB deaths, because he believed that other influencing factors such as sanitation, cleanliness, and ventilation in the prison were better than those to which the great majority of the convicts were accustomed outside. The fact was, though, that TB deaths remained at the same level after improvements in the prison diet. It is obvious that the convicts lived in a confined space and had few outdoor activities. In light of the correlation between the rate of TB infection and occupation that was demonstrated earlier, we have reason to conclude that the lack of outdoor life was probably the real reason for the relatively higher TB death rate among convicts.

THE HOUSING ENVIRONMENT

TUBERCULOSIS AS A CITY DISEASE

As early as 1916, a Chinese doctor pointed out the importance of the effect of housing conditions on epidemic tuberculosis. He wrote in the *Zhonghua yixue zazhi* 中華醫學雜誌 (Chinese Medical Journal): "Several diseases can develop as the result of poor housing conditions. Whenever these diseases are more prevalent in the places where the poor live, tuberculosis appears as the most distinctive illness and is out of control at present. For the purpose of attracting more attention to the prevention of this disease, it would be better if it were called a 'housing disease' than an infectious disease."[24]

Tuberculosis was called the housing disease for two reasons. One was refugee inmigration and spatial concentration, and the other was that industrialization attracted ever more laborers to the city, and together these caused residential and workplace overcrowding. By the early part of the twentieth century, as a result of civil disturbances and natural disasters, numerous refugees and poor peasants come into the city and their numbers continued to grow. They inhabited the slums, where the houses were generally very small, with low ceilings, moist and dark, and overoccupied. The habit of indiscriminate spitting made the situation worse. The bacilli mixed with the dust suspended in the atmosphere of rooms inhabited under such bad conditions undoubtedly contributed to a high frequency of tubercular disease.

---

[24] Zhoukui Zhongheng 周逵仲衡, "Yibao Cuoyao" 醫報撮要 [Outline of Medical Reports], *Zhonghua yixue zazhi* 中華醫學雜誌 [Chinese Medical Journal] 2.2. (1916), p. 47.

At the beginning of Chinese industrialization, the number of cotton mills grew quickly in Shanghai. In Japanese-owned mills after about 1925[25] and more generally during the 1930s, most of the workers were indentured laborers – increasingly females and children – who had been bought in from the countryside. Wages and conditions varied significantly from one factory to another, with complex systems of grading within the work force. In a sense, those on contracts could be seen as the temporary serfs of their labor contractors, who appropriated a large part of their earnings. Other, ordinary female workers could often be distinguished from those under contract by their elegant makeup and the relatively good quality of their clothes (though it should be noted that in some Japanese factories dirty clothing could lead to dismissal). Wages for cotton-spinning were the third lowest (higher only than those in match factories and silk-reeling establishments). The labor contractors, often linked with the underworld (who sometimes would escort the girls to and from work), forced these women to work exhausting hours under severe physical discipline, often limited their right to leave the premises, and by various devices minimized the earnings the workers got to spend. Groups of contract workers (most of whom would be girls) might sleep in a room that might also be used as their dining room during the day and their toilet at night. As regards food, meat and fish were only regularly obtainable in some factories (the usual right to take a lunch hour outside the factory often being denied), and in some factories ordinary workers were not allowed to bring in meals with them from home. Thus these girls labored in surroundings full of airborne cotton fibers and dust as well as heat and noise, usually alternating on a weekly or fortnightly basis between a day shift and a night shift, each of somewhat more than eleven hours. Tuberculosis was, not surprisingly, prevalent among them.[26]

Crowded living caused epidemic TB in the cities. The countryside was relatively isolated at that time and country people had less chance to be

---

[25] The contract system for female workers, who were kept in quasi-prison conditions for the duration of their period of obligation, may have been influenced by practices in Japan. See Sung Jae Koh, *Stages of Industrial Development in Asia: A Comparative History of the Cotton Industry in Japan, India, China, and Korea* (Philadelphia: University of Pennsylvania Press, 1966), esp. pp. 62–74. In 1896–97 84% of the mostly female workers in the cotton-spinning industry were reported to have (unspecified) diseases "incurred in the line of work"; later, the prevalence of tuberculosis in the 1930s was described as "terrible" by a foreign observer (p. 71).

[26] Alain Roux, *Le Shanghai ouvrier des années trente: coolies, gangsters et syndicalistes* (Paris: l'Harmattan, 1993), esp. ch. 1. Roux notes on p. 65 that in 1930, of 800 cotton workers in a factory examined by doctors, there was an incidence of tuberculosis among the men of 6%, among the women of 14%, and among the children of 22%.

exposed to the bacillus (although migrants took the disease back to the countryside). Therefore, TB at this time, and until quite recently, was primarily a city disease. Several reports have shown the difference between cities and villages. Among the children who lived in the Tianjin city area in the 1950s, for example, 86.7 percent were infected, while among the children who lived in the countryside, the TB infection rate was only 48.7 percent.[27] For the inhabitants of Shanghai city in 1957, the TB prevalence rate was 42.0 percent (on the basis of the tuberculin test), but for the villagers in the surrounding countryside the TB prevalence rate was 23.4 percent.[28] If we compare cities and villages in different provinces (see Fig. 14.4), it is apparent that the highest infection rate was among the people who lived in the city area of Beijing, and that the infection rate of the countryside near Beijing (Hebei province) was lower than in the city but higher than in the countryside far away (in the case shown, Qinghai province).[29]

The TB epidemic was gradually controlled in the cities after the 1950s, as BCG vaccination and chemotherapy started to be applied. However, in the countryside, declines in TB mortality and the prevalence rate have been slow. This is due to poor nutrition, poor health care, and lack of knowledge about preventative measures in the countryside. Once people who live in the countryside have been infected, they are more likely to develop a serious condition. At present, TB is no longer a city disease. It is now more prevalent in villages than in cities. The national TB epidemiology investigation of 1984–85 shows that TB mortality is 8 per 100,000 in cities (181,210 persons examined), 21 per 100,000 in towns (71,578 persons examined), and 37 per 100,000 in the villages (922,639 persons examined).[30] The transmutation of TB from a city disease into a village disease has been influenced by many factors, and the mechanism is rather complex.

LIFESTYLE

Epidemic tuberculosis is also related to lifestyle. The United States Census showed the mortality from TB among the Chinese living in the United

---

[27] Geng Guanyi 耿贯一, "Jiehebing" 结核病 [Tuberculosis], in Liuxingbing xue 流行病学 [Epidemiology] (Beijing: Renmin Weisheng CBS, 1979), pp. 489–504.

[28] See Sun Zhongliang, "Present TB prevention situation in Shanghai."

[29] See Geng Guanyi, "Tuberculosis."

[30] Zhonghua Renmin Gongheguo Weishengbu 中华人民共和国卫生部 [Health Department of the People's Republic of China], 1984/1985 Quanguo jiehebing liuxingbingxue chouyang diaocha ziliao huibian 一九八四/一九八五全国结核病流行病学抽样调查资料汇编 [Compilation of materials from the nationwide tuberculosis sample-based epidemiological investigation] (Beijing: Health Department of the People's Republic of China, 1988).

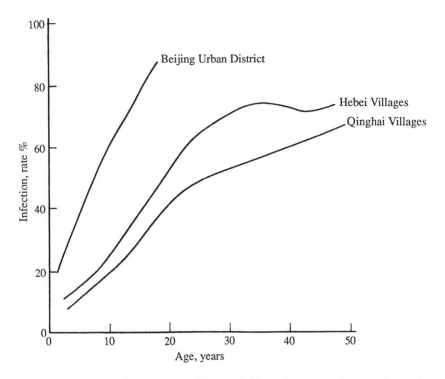

Figure 14.4. TB infection rates in Beijing and villages in two provinces, prior to the 1970s. *Source*: Geng Guangyi, "Tuberculosis."

States was 658.5 per 100,000 living in 1900, nearly four times that of the general white population.[31] It was the main cause of death among overseas Chinese. Data collected from the inhabitants of Chinatowns in various cities in the United States showed a frightening percentage of TB deaths relative to all deaths (see Table 14.7).[32]

In New York City, the TB death rate among Chinese reached 50 percent of all deaths, as shown in Table 14.8.

In the Chinatowns of Portland and San Francisco, mortality was more than double that in the surrounding white population. The high TB death rate among these overseas Chinese was very likely due to their manner of living, crowded in rooms that few white people could endure for a single night. The habit of eating from the same dishes may have also contributed

---

[31] W. H. Chun, "On the Comparative Frequency of Non-pulmonary Tuberculosis in North China," *National Medical Journal of China* 14 (1928), pp. 245–51.

[32] W. W. Cadbury, "Suggestions for an Anti-Tuberculosis Crusade in Canton, China," *China Medical Journal* 25.2 (1911), pp. 80–87.

Table 14.7. *Deaths due to TB as a percentage of all deaths of males in the United States by attributed ethnic category, 1900*

Chinese	White	Negro	Amerindian
36	13.6	19.7	30

Table 14.8. *TB mortality as a percentage of all deaths in New York City by attributed ethnic category, 1902*

Chinese	Irish	Negroes	Scots	French	Germans	Scandinavians	Austrians	U.S.	Canadians	Russians	Italians
50.0	42.0	41.6	38.3	34.0	32.4	30.3	30.1	30.1	29.2	29.1	21.9

to the high mortality among Chinese. When healthy people and people with the disease sit around the same table, with chopsticks and spoons going in and out of the same dishes and soups, opportunities are afforded to the bacillus to transfer from the sick to the healthy. Occupation should also be considered. Most of the overseas Chinese at that time worked in sweatshops, laundries, or restaurants, and this may have been another cause of their high TB mortality.

TB OUTBREAKS IN PRESENT-DAY CHINA

Epidemic tuberculosis has been effectively controlled only since 1949. However, in recent years, the situation has improved only slowly. During the ten years from 1975 to 1985, TB mortality remained around 35 per 100,000 for the whole country.[33] According to the results of the National Tuberculosis Epidemiology Investigations conducted in 1990, TB preva-

---

[33] Wang Zhongren 王中仁, Shijie jiehebing-de liuxing qushi gei women de qishi 世界结核病的流行趋势给我们的启示 [Enlightenment from the trend of tuberculosis prevalence world-wide], *Zhonghua jiehe he huxi zazhi* 中华结核和呼吸杂志 [Chinese Journal of Tuberculosis and Respiratory Disease] 14.6 (1991), pp. 323–24.

lence rates were even increasing in six provinces: Sichuan, Hebei, Guizhou, Hubei, Liaoning, and Shanxi.[34]

Fourteen TB outbreaks were reported during 1979–84.[35] Twelve cases occurred in schools and two in the army. All the victims lived in dormitories where inmates were very crowded, for example in the Agriculture School of Zunyi, where eleven students lived in a room 3.5 by 6.5 meters (22.75 square meters) containing six bunk-beds. First one student contracted TB; then, after several months, all the students in this room were discovered to be infected, and seven of them developed an active form of the disease.[36] Nine outbreaks happened during the winter in northeastern and north-western China, which are very cold in winter. People who live there have to close windows and doors tightly to keep rooms warm. Some of the rooms are often closed for nine hours at night during this period, in such a way that no fresh air comes in at all. An analysis of these outbreaks leads to the conclusion that overcrowding is still playing an important role in TB epidemics in China.

We may end by speculating that if the built environment is of such importance as it evidently is for this one particular – and terrible – disease, how many other significant dimensions may it not have, not only medical but social, psychological, even spiritual, much less accessible to observation?

---

[34] Zhonghua Renmin Gongheguo Weishengbu 中华人民共和国卫生部 [Health Department of the People's Republic of China], *1990 Quanguo jiehebing liuxingbingxue chouyang diaocha ziliao huibian* 一九九〇全国结核病流行病学抽样调查资料汇编 [Compilation of materials from the nationwide tuberculosis sample-based epidemiological investigations] (Beijing: Health Department of the People's Republic of China, 1992).

[35] Bulletin of the Chinese Antituberculosis Association, ed., *Shisiqi jiehebing baofa liuxing fenxi* 十四起结核病暴发流行分析 [Analysis of 14 Tuberculosis Outbreaks], *Zhongguo Fanglao Tongxun* 中国防痨通讯 [Bulletin of the Chinese Antituberculosis Association] 7.3 (1985), pp. 124–27.

[36] Yan Dexiang 严德祥等 et al., *Zunyi nongxiao jiehebing baofa liuxing-de diaocha baogao* 遵义农校结核病暴发流行的调查报告 [A report on the investigation of the outbreak of tuberculosis in Zunyi Agricultural School], *Zhonghua jiehe he huxi zazhi* 中华结核和呼吸杂志 [Chinese Journal of Tuberculosis and Respiratory Disease] 4.2 (1981), pp. 65–68.

Representations of the Environment – The Official Mind

15

From the Yellow River to the Huai

NEW REPRESENTATIONS OF A RIVER NETWORK AND THE HYDRAULIC CRISIS OF 1128

CHRISTIAN LAMOUROUX

INTRODUCTION[1]

In the course of the winter of 1128, Du Chong 杜充 (?–1141), the governor of Kaifeng 開封, seeing the threat that the Jurchen cavalry were once again bringing to bear on the capital of the empire of the Northern Song (960–1127), decided to open breaches in the dikes of the Yellow River close to eighty kilometers north of the city, so causing a flood that he hoped would prove sufficient to break the enemy's attacks.[2] Although this desperate measure does not seem to have had any great military effect, it was nonetheless the origin of an important diversion of the Yellow River: as its waters flowed south they invaded the bed of the Qing 清河 River, before reaching the Huai 淮河, whose lower course they were to take over in its entirety after the end of the twelfth century. The mouth of the Yellow River was thus to remain south of the Shandong Peninsula until the middle of the nineteenth century, while the Huai, robbed of its exit to the sea, was progres-

Abbreviations used in the notes: *QSW Quan Song wen* [Complete Song prose]; *SHY Song huiyao jigao* [Draft of important Song documents]; *SS Songshi* [History of the Song]; *XNYL Jianyan yilai xinian yaolu* [Important affairs since the Jianyan period]; *XZCB Xu zizhi tongjian changbian* [Continuation of the *Comprehensive Mirror to Assist Government*]. For bibliographical details, see footnotes 2, 6, 7, and 12.

[1] I should like to thank Mark Elvin, whose suggestions as a translator have allowed me to simplify and clarify more than one point, and Bernard Lepetit, whose readings of my text, by stripping away what was not essential, have given more coherence and force to my thinking.

[2] Tuo Tuo, *Songshi* [History of the Song; hereafter *SS*], *j.* 25 *Gaozong* 2 (Beijing: Zhonghua shuju, 1977), vol. 2, p. 459; Li Xinyuan, *Jianyan yilai xinian yaolu* [A record of important affairs since the Jianyan period; hereafter *XNYL*], Qinding siku quanshu (Shanghai: Shanghai guji CBS), *j.* 18, p. 19a.

sively to flood the swamps and lakes of its old lower course, so forming the great Hongze 洪澤 Lake (see Map 15.1).

This event in 1128, which was decisive for the future of the imperial capital and of importance in the war between the Jin 金 (1115–1234) and the Song dynasties, was no more than an anecdote compared to the ecological catastrophe that it unloosed. From this point of view it even seems that the historian today should, like the chronicler of times past, limit himself to recording the episode as a fact. To the extent that the history of the environment is today constructed on the basis of a refusal to separate culture and nature, bringing its analyses to bear on the cultural elements that permit a society to integrate natural factors into its practice and its discourse, it may nonetheless be useful to attempt a sociopolitical approach to the ecological upheavals that ruined the Huai valley after 1128.

Given that the technical forms with which each society equips itself to achieve a material authority over nature vary across time and space, the historian for his part is called upon to bring to light the systems of values whose evolution makes possible new relationships between nature and society. In order to do this, the history of nature has to be conceived of from the point of view of levels of analysis that are proper to the social sciences, linking the short-term time of politics, and indeed of certain economic and social mutations, with the evolution of nature across long-term time. The events of 1128 seem to lend themselves particularly well to this undertaking. It is of course true that water had been part of the military arsenal since antiquity,[3] but the sacrifice by a dynasty of its own hydraulic installations, whose erection and maintenance were the expression of its concern for good government, brings into play just that relationship between technology and ideology about which we have been speaking. The decision to destroy the dikes rested in fact on the conviction that the Yellow River was a natural barrier that could shelter the south of China from assailants moving down upon it from the north, water continuing in some fashion to play the role that it had played since the peace concluded in 1005 with the Liao 遼 dynasty (915–1123). Hydraulic action was the ultimate recourse against enemy superiority, and more than a mere military option: it was necessary to keep the Yellow River within the empire, since it was a strategic resource that the Song had been developing for more than a century to defend itself against external attack. As it happened, nature put this pro-

---

[3] Examples of the use of hydraulics as a weapon, a question to which we shall return later, are attested in the *Zuozhuan*, Zhaogong 30th year (512 B.C.) (cf. James Legge, *The Chinese Classics*, vol. 2, p. 733), and in the *Hanshu*, j. 29, *Gouxu zhi* 9 (Beijing: Zhonghua shuju, 1975), vol. 6, p. 1692. It should, however, be noted that on each occasion it was a question of disrupting the hydraulic system of the enemy.

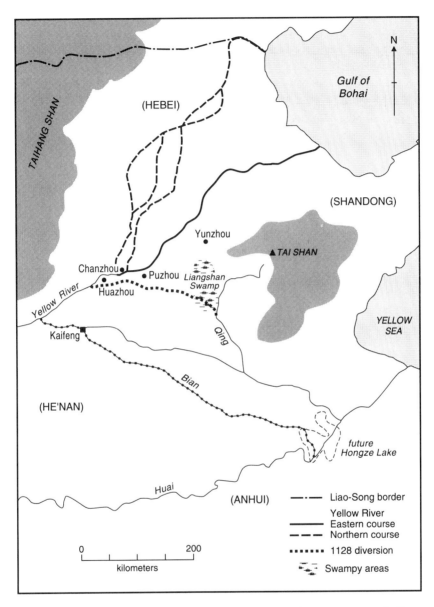

Map 15.1. Lower basin of the Yellow River from the tenth century to 1128. *Source*:
Zou Yilin, "Huanghe xiayou hedao bianqian jiqi yingxiang gaishu," in Tan Qixiang,
Huanghe shi luncong (Shanghai: Fudan daxue CBS, 1986), p. 230.

gram of defense into effect, in that it was precisely the waters of the Yellow River that, having captured the lower course of the Huai, were to serve as the new official frontier between the state of the Jin and that of the Song once this latter had fallen back southward.

If the action of Du Chong, who was soon to be entrusted with the highest military responsibilities,[4] is to be fully intelligible, it needs to be set in a new perspective. The problem is to discover how the ideological developments that dominated the development of the resources available for defense to the Northern Song gave water, and in particular the Yellow River, an essential role. Insofar as the system of values attached to this river touched upon every domain of practice and representation, whether social, economic, political, military, symbolic, or religious, it would be impossible to undertake an inquiry of this scale in the present context. We shall therefore content ourselves with making evident a few elements that may contribute to a social history of the environment, taking as our point of departure the concatenation of tensions, conflicts, and decisions whose logic the political debates allow us to discover.

THE SEARCH FOR A STATUS QUO IN UNSTABLE SURROUNDINGS

From the beginning the Song had to mobilize their soldiers to confront a continuous series of breaches in the dikes on the Yellow River, principally between Hua 滑州, Chan 澶州, and Pu 濮州,[5] to the northeast of their capital. It would appear that the authorities had no strategic program of

---

[4] In slightly more than six months he obtained five promotions. The last of these, in the intercalary eighth month of 1129, made him vice-president of the Right of the Department of the Affairs of State and administrator in charge of the Grand Secretariat (*Shangshu youpuye tong pingzhangshi* 尚書右僕射同平章事), as well as commissioner of imperial defense (*Yuying shi* 御營使). On these promotions cf. *XNYL, j.* 20, p. 23b; *j.* 21, p. 21b; *j.* 24, p. 1a; *j.* 25, p. 17b; and *j.* 27, p. 6b. It should be remembered that Du went over to the enemy in the tenth month of 1129.

[5] Yao Hanyuan gives two chronological tables of breaks in the dikes, for the periods 880–959 and 960–1048 respectively. Cf. Yao Hanyuan, *Zhongguo shuili shi gangyao* [Outline of the history of water control in China] (Beijing: Shuili dianli CBS, 1987), table 5-4, pp. 162–69, and table 5-5, pp. 174–84. Except where otherwise indicated, our description of hydraulic history at the beginning of the Song dynasty is based on this work and that of Zheng Zhaojing, *Zhongguo shuili shi* [History of water control in China] (Reprinted, Taipei: Shangwu yinshuguan, 1970). Both provide a systematic compilation of the events recorded in the various sources, mainly the Qing geographical book *Xingshui jinjian* 行水金鑑 [The golden mirror of the moving waters], whose *juan* 9–14 detail Song policy regarding the changes in the course of the Yellow River.

conservancy at this time; they were above all concerned with filling in breaches as and when these occurred. Thus in 967 a system of annual labor service was created in the prefectures along the river's banks to take care of maintenance and repairs; and incumbent magistrates were given the title of River Levee Commissioner (*He di shi* 河隄使) and made responsible for the quality of the work done.

The first site of works aimed at the improvement of the river's course was only established in 993–94, in response to the proposal of a military palace bureaucrat, Liang Rui 梁睿 (no date), who was serving as an inspector of watercourses (*Xunhe gongfeng guan* 巡河供奉官). He had a diversionary canal of about twenty kilometers in length excavated in Hua prefecture, where the dikes seemed to him to be particularly vulnerable, and thus associated himself with the hydraulic policy that emphasized "dividing the force of the current" (*fen shuishi* 分水勢). The layout was completed the same year by another channel of from six to seven kilometers in length that ran from the wooden protective revetment at Hancun 韓村 in the western part of the prefecture. Rather than an amelioration of the river, however, this was a once-off action that, in the last analysis, merely had the effect of displacing the breaches downstream to between Chan and Yun 澶州、鄆州.

Faced with a new series of catastrophes, the authorities seem to have stressed an intensified surveillance: in 1004 the direct responsibility of the prefects holding office was supplemented by that of a central bureaucrat, whose task it was to draw up a report on the condition of the dikes that he had to inspect by a personal visit to the places concerned.[6] The promotion of the local magistrates depended on the success of their hydraulic works and, according to an edict of 1005, on their ability to save labor services and materials, the total of which was submitted for audit in connection with the spring-season levies. In some special cases, moreover, like that of Huazhou in 1020, an edict could authorize a magistrate to commute the taxes and labor services due as fall-season levies to the materials needed for the maintenance of the dikes.[7] These institutional measures indicate, in their own way, a new certainty, namely that the authorities were more and more aware of the permanent nature of the problems presented by the river. Even if the emperor Zhenzong 真宗 (968 [reigned 997]–1022) sent out an official to make a sacrifice whenever an important work site had finished its

[6] Xu Song, *Song huiyao jigao* [Draft of Song important documents; hereafter *SHY*] (Beiping: Beiping tushuguan, 1936. Reprinted, Taipei: Xin wenfeng chuban gongsi, 1976), "Fangyu [Zhi He]," 14/4.

[7] Ibid., 14/9; Li Tao, *Xu Zizhi tongjian changbian* [Long draft for the continuation of the *Comprehensive Mirror to Assist Government*; hereafter *XZCB*] (Reprinted, Beijing: Zhonghua shuju, 1979), *j.* 96, month 7, vol. 7, p. 2204.

job,[8] he knew, as did his bureaucracy, that the success of these undertakings did not depend only on the virtue of his conduct. Technical means, that is, human and material resources, were in a state of constant mobilization; and several bureaucrats, of whom the best known was without doubt Chen Yaozuo 陳堯佐 (963–1044), the fiscal vice-intendant of the Liang-Zhe and later intendent of Jingxi before becoming the prefect of Hua,[9] grew famous as a consequence of the hydraulic works done under their direction, or, more simply, thanks to their plans for river improvement.

During the entire earlier part of the eleventh century, the authorities had, as it happened, to choose between two main options: to cut diversion channels to reduce the force of the current by dividing it, as Chen Yaozuo again proposed in 1015,[10] or, on the other hand, to maintain and improve the systems of dikes. These systems underwent a considerable development thanks to the use of "set-back dikes" (yaodi 遙隄), which were built up on the basis of the alluvium deposited by major floods, and to "sawteeth" (juya 鋸牙) and "horse-heads" (matou 馬頭), stone jetties placed across the direction of the current to break its force.[11] Lastly, fascines (sao 埽), which were huge rolls of vegetable material intended to protect the most exposed banks and to fill in breaches, seem to have been a Song invention, perhaps in part the offspring of Southern know-how: It was a certain Liu Ji 劉吉 (n.d.), a bureaucrat who came from Jiangnan and was thus, as the Song huiyao 宋會要 emphasizes, "experienced in hydraulic matters," who was the first to be mentioned in the sources as having had recourse to fascines.[12] Their creation and emplacement was an important part of the bureaucratic

---

[8] This occurred in 1004, 1010, 1011, 1020, and 1022. Cf. SHY, "Fangyu," 14/4, 14/5, 14/8, 14/9, 14/10.

[9] See his biography in SS, j. 284 (vol. 27, pp. 9582–83), and Ouyang Xiu's encomium on his hydraulic skills in the inscription he wrote for his funerary stela. See Ouyang Xiu, Ouyang Xiu quanji [Complete works of Ouyang Xiu] (Taipei: Shijie shuju, 1983], j. 20, "Ju shu ji," "Chen-gong shendao bei ming – bing xu," vol. 1, pp. 142–43.

[10] SHY, "Fangyu," 14/6.

[11] On these technical developments see Yoshioka Yoshinobu, Sōdai Kōga-shi kenkyū [Studies on the history of the Yellow River] (Tokyo: Ochanomizu shobō, 1978), pp. 12–36.

[12] SHY, "Fangyu," 14/2–3; and XZCB, j. 23, month 7 (3/523). It should be noted that in 1012, when Chen Yaozuo had observed that the gabions (bamboo mats in which stones were wrapped) used to build the dikes of the Qiantang River hardly offered any resistance to the attacks of the tide, he proposed using wood and earth, the materials specific to fascines. To judge from his request that specialized workers (saojiang 埽匠) be sent from the capital, he was unable so easily to find any such near to where he was. See Ouyang Xiu, Quanji, "Chen-gong," p. 143, and the "Qiantang-jiang di shi zou," a passage from the Haitang lu [Record of the seawalls] in the Quan Song wen [Complete Song prose; hereafter QSW] (Reprinted, Chengdu: Ba-Shu shushe, 1989), vol. 5, p. 378. Fascines and the problems of their emplacement are described in SS, j. 99, "Hequ" 1 (7/2265–66), and in XZCB, j. 100, month 1 (8/2312). See likewise the description given by J. Needham on the basis of Shen Gua's Mengqi bitan in Science and Civilisation in China, vol. 4, part 3, Civil Engineering and Nautics (Cambridge: Cambridge University Press, 1971), pp. 341–43.

system for the conservancy of the river to the extent that it was necessary to gather large quantities of materials, to store them where they were safe from fire,[13] and to mobilize the conscripted workers whose duty it was to make them and install them. In 1027 there were altogether forty-six such stores, of which almost half were at Chan and Hua.

Overall, however, the same men did not hesitate to use both options, no doubt as circumstances required. Thus it was that Chen Yaozuo, the prefect of Hua in 1021, put an end to the catastrophe provoked by the opening of breaches in the dikes in his prefecture since 1019, one that had caused more than thirty cities to be damaged by the waters which went as far south as the great marsh of Liangshan and, beyond that, to the Huai itself. Chen had a canal opened and a large dike built at the same time, with several fascines being put in place by means of a "wooden dragon" (*mulong* 木龍), a structure floating in the water that protected the dike and an innovation destined to be more widely used later.

Our sources mention the first hydraulic treatises as coming from this period, but none of them have survived. These works no doubt proposed solutions that matched the scale of the challenge, an example being the *Dao He xingsheng shu* 導河形勝書 [Documents on the strategic advantage of directing the Yellow River], in three chapters with illustrations (*tu* 圖), presented to the court in 1012 following the several breaches during the preceding year, its compiler being a certain Li Chui 李垂 (965–1033), a simple assistant staff author and revising editor of the Institutes and Archives (*Zhuzuo zuolang guange jiaoli* 著作佐郎館閣校理).[14] This project for improving the lower course of the Yellow River was rejected, so inadequate did the response that it proposed appear, while its ambition and cost also seemed excessive to the commission of inquiry that was ordered by the emperor to take a decision on the matter.[15]

What Li Chui was proposing did in fact exceed all the projects to which we have so far alluded. To be sure, he also started from the principle of dividing the current, but the multiplication of distributary channels that he supported would have allowed the river to return, at least in part, to its ancient channels (see Map 15.2).[16] Li's program was well and truly one of improvement in that he was not only not content with reorganizing the

---

[13] In 989 fire destroyed "1.7 million [items consisting of?] bamboos, trees, poles, and bunches of straw." Cf. *SHY*, "Fangyu," 14/3.

[14] *SS, j*. 91, "He qu" 1 (7/2261–62). The *XZCB, j*. 77, month 1 (6/1752–54), speaks of the *Dao He xingshi shu* 導河形勢書 [Documents on the configurations (involved) in directing the Yellow River] of which it provides a slightly more complete summary.

[15] *XZCB, j*. 77, month 1 (6/1754).

[16] Tan Qixiang, "Haihe shuixi-de xingcheng yu fazhan" [The formation and development of the hydrologic system of the Haihe], *Lishi dili* 4 (1986), pp. 1–27.

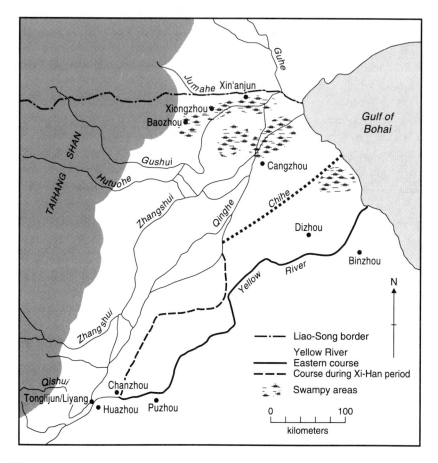

Map 15.2. Reconstruction of the ancient courses of the Yellow River and the formation of the Haihe River network. *Source*: Tan Qixiang, "Haihe shuixi de xingcheng yu fazhan," *Lishi dili* 4 (1986), p. 8.

lower course of the river in such a way as to put an end to floods, but likewise developed the idea that the configuration of the course was the only natural obstacle that could block the incursions of the Qidan (Khitan) cavalry into the great plain. That, he took pains to make clear, was a new problem.[17]

The infiltration of hydraulic concerns into military preoccupations was not a new figure in the rhetoric about the river. We see here once again the conviction that its waves could block the enemy's cavalry, evident in the

---

[17] *XZCB, j.* 77, month 1 (7/1754), and *SS, j.* 91 (7/2262).

recent history of the Five Dynasties. On the order of the ruler of the Later Liang (907–23), General Duan Ning 段凝 (n.d.) had broken the dikes below Suanzao 酸棗, west of Hua prefecture. Even if a century and a half later Duan was depicted as a soldier who was "neither clear-headed nor courageous," and owing his command solely to palace intrigues,[18] his military action does not seem to deserve such condemnation. Sima Guang 司馬光 (1019–86) does not attribute the decision to break the dikes to Duan, but only mentions the ruler's command; and in his account of an analogous decision,[19] leaves it to be understood that the only solution that was realistic and militarily effective was the water that had already flooded the same prefectures of Cao 曹州 and Pu.

Above all, at the end of the tenth century, when several resounding defeats had persuaded the dynasty to abandon its urge toward going on the offensive and to adopt a defensive strategy toward the Liao state, the Yellow River and water were associated with the stabilization of the frontier. In 991, He Chengju 何承矩 (946–1006), the prefect of Xiong 雄州, stressed to the court the defensive opportunities represented by the complex of pools and lakes to the west of what is today Tianjin.[20] Strengthened by the initial success of his colonies implanted ten years previously, He Chengju had the intention in 1003 of reorganizing the hydrography to benefit the rice fields. The emperor, however, estimated that the local population would find it difficult to bear the implementation of this program, and refused to authorize the improvement of the lower course of the Yellow River where it passed through the prefectures of Bin 濱州 and Di 棣州,[21] stressing moreover that proposals to divert the waters of the river at that point toward the Chihe 赤河 (see Map 15.2)[22] and the sea had been put forward "many times" before the project of the venturesome prefect – something of which hardly any traces have survived.

For all that He Chengju and Li Chui were moved by different preoccupations, they grounded their pleas on partly analogous arguments. They both gave priority to the same northern hydrographic network, though Li Chui wished to use it at the exact point at which the Yellow River enters the great plain, while He Chengju was concerned to organize it in the region

---

[18] Sima Guang, *Zizhi tongjian* [Comprehensive mirror to assist government] (Beijing: Zhonghua shuju, 1987), j. 272, vol. 19, pp. 8890–91.

[19] Ibid., j. 270, vol. 19, pp. 8824.

[20] He Chengju, "Shang Taizong lun tangpo tuntian zhi li" [A discussion of the advantages of barrage-and-lake systems and of military colonies submitted to the Emperor Taizong], *QSW* 3/348.

[21] *SHY*, "Fangyu," 14/4.

[22] For an attempted reconstruction of the course of the Chihe see Li Xiaocong, "Chihe kao" [An inquiry into the Chihe], *Lishi dili* 4 (1986), pp. 138–44.

around its debouchment into the sea. Now, this coincidence between
hydraulic geography and military rhetoric in fact permits us another way of
reading the priorities supported by the authorities at the dawn of the
eleventh century. Behind the anxiety to defend themselves from the river
and the mighty Qidan, the court had to take upon itself a political decision;
and, as is known, after the treaty of Chanyuan 澶淵, which was signed in the
first month of 1005, political conditions limited the margin of maneuver
enjoyed by the Song. This treaty provided that "the walls and moats of the
two states may be preserved as in the past. The dredging and repair of the
moats can be done in the customary fashion. It will, however, be forbidden
to build new walls and moats, or to move any watercourse."[23] It would
appear that the prefect of Xiong had perfectly anticipated the new hand of
cards to be played, but Li Chui's project of 1012 ran up against the status
quo solemnly imposed by the treaty. The rejection of his proposals was no
doubt motivated by financial considerations, and even more by the concern
to lighten the burden of those liable for labor conscription, but it is also to
be explained, at this time, by a care not to touch the strategic rivers, the
Zhanghe 漳河 and the Hutuohe 滹沱河, both of which were referred to in
the grounds set forward for judgment by the commission of inquiry.[24]

The arguments that were exchanged make clear, as it were in three
dimensions, the hesitations that beset those holding responsibility at the
time, and allow us to glimpse the tensions and political splits between them
that were to become ever more evident from the time when the lower
course of the Yellow River was physically disrupted. It was true that the
frequency of high discharges and of floods inevitably inserted the management of the river into the organization of taxes and labor services, so
bringing bureaucratic responsibility into play. It was true that works were
regularly undertaken both to maintain and to open up new watercourses.
Nonetheless, improvements worthy of the name remained rare. A number
of burcaucrats sought above all else the status quo in a hydraulic space that
appeared to them perhaps more destabilized than intrinsically unstable.
The philosophy that guided their action with respect to the Yellow River fed
upon the political principle of stability (*anjing* 安靜), a principle that was
also required by the frontiers of the empire, still under military threat.
When the emperor asked Ding Wei 丁謂 (962–1033), the intendant of
Kuizhou 夔州, to explain to him why calm reigned on the distant southwestern frontier, the latter, who was a declared enemy of both Li Chui and
Chen Yaozuo, replied in his memorial:

[23] *XZCB, j.* 58, month 12 (5/1299).
[24] *XZCB, j.* 77, month 1 (6/1754).

The public servant, entrusted [by the emperor] with his job, does not look for exploits to perform. He does not stir up affairs, and regards stability as success. In all that he builds, he forever conforms to the texts of past and present edicts. It is thus certain that the barbarian hordes will not dare to attempt any adventure, or to engage in any unconsidered action [that may bring down upon them] the punishment of Heaven.[25]

It was, however, necessary to choose between two difficult positions, the filling in of the beds of the rivers (confined between dikes) or their unimpeded opening (by not closing breaches), since the water was hardly able to search for and thus find a solution on its own account. After the twenties of the eleventh century, breaches in the dikes continued to occur, again mostly in Chan prefecture. Downstream, at Henglong 橫隴, one of the fascines gave way in 1034, causing the division of the river into several streams, all oriented toward the north, the waters joining those of the Chihe, the You 游, and the Jin 金水, to the east of Daming 大名, the northern capital (see Map 15.3).[26] Now, divided in this fashion, "the course of the river slowed down (*chi* 遲), stagnated (*zhu* 貯), and deposited its suspended sediment (*yu* 淤)," a rule well known to the hydraulics experts, who had formulated it in Han times.[27] Since that time the river has always raised its riverbed higher and higher and been obliged to find new courses, this being the mechanism that explains the wanderings of the lower course. In 1048 the Yellow River opened a northern path from the fascine at Shanghu 商胡 in Chan prefecture, but throughout the second half of the eleventh century there were in effect several courses, essentially two northern ones and one eastern one, which were opened, abandoned, or reactivated (see Map 15.1).[28]

Nature had decided and imposed its choice on the authorities, who were obliged on this occasion to improve the river in a systematic fashion. Thus

---

[25] *XZCB, j.* 55, month 11 (5/1221).
[26] Zou Yilin, "Songdai Huanghe xiayou Henglong bei liu zhu dao kao" [An investigation into the main northern courses on the lower reaches of the Yellow River from Henglong in Song times], in Tan Qixiang, ed., *Huanghe shi luncong* (Shanghai: Fudan daxue CBS, 1986), pp. 132–33.
[27] The formula is from Zhang Rong 張戎, at the time of Wang Mang 王莽 (reigned 9–23), cited by Zheng, *History of water control*, p. 10.
[28] Yoshioka, *Yellow River*, pp. 423–25, gives a table of changes of course for the Yellow River and references to the polemics that they provoked. Hypotheses on the lines of the lower northern course of the river, which sometimes made use of several channels at the same time, are set forth in Zou Yilin, "Lower reaches of the Yellow River," pp. 134–45, and mapped in Tan Qixiang, *Zhongguo lishi ditu ji* [Historical atlas of China] (Shanghai: Ditu CBS, 1982) vol. 6, maps 16–17. The eastern course was used from 1061 to 1081, and again from 1089 to 1099. The two northern courses were active, one from 1048 to 1089, and the other from 1081 to 1093 and again from 1099 to 1127.

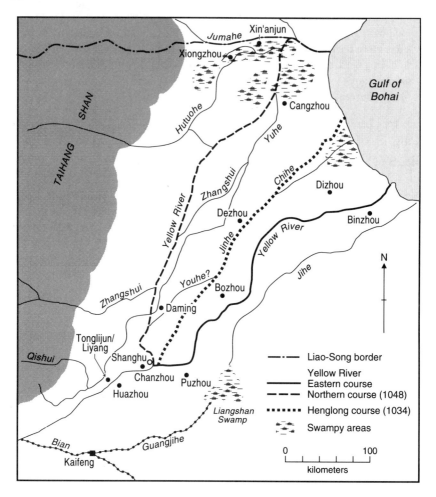

Map 15.3. Courses of the Yellow River in Hebei from 1034 to 1048. *Source*: Yao Hanyuan, *Zhongguo shuili shi gangyao* (Beijing: Shuili dianli cbs, 1987), p. 185.

the polemics were to continue, until the end of the dynasty, between the partisans of a reestablishment of the old course and those who defended a northern course. These conflicting pleas, aimed at winning the support of the bureaucratic hierarchies or of the emperor himself, developed their technical arguments within the framework of a rhetoric of river improvement, and it is here that their entire value resides, for these texts refer directly to the implicit geography of the would-be improvers, who found themselves obliged to crystallize their vision of the territory and hence their political program. In order to be convincing, the technical options proferred had to link themselves, whatever their effectiveness may have been, with the major themes of policy: the stability and defense of the state, the constraints on the budget, and financial organization. If the improvement of the Yellow River had become an important political stake in the factional struggle in the course of the eleventh century, it was through these polemics that its image was progressively altered, and it is thus appropriate to turn our attention to these debates.

THE HYDRAULIC CRISIS AND YELLOW RIVER CONSERVANCY

Let us begin by recalling the chronology of these events in summary fashion. The Yellow River, having broken the fascine at Henglong in 1034, then that at Shanghu in 1048, entered a phase of great instability. The debates were particularly intense between 1048 and 1056, prior to the attempt to use levees to force the river to resume its eastern course into the bed of the River of Six Pagodas (Liuta he 六塔河), which lasted for only one day, in the fourth month of the first year of the Jiayou 嘉祐 reign-period (1056). After this disaster, the authorities seem to have resigned themselves for a time to the northern course – or, more exactly, to the northern courses, since in 1060 a new distributary formed below Daming called the Ergu 二股. Discussion then resumed around projects of improvement aimed at orienting this new channel toward the east, with the reformers, who were in power at this time, showing themselves very much in favor of these operations. In 1072, however, these improvements provoked a new crisis and the appearance of another northern course. From this moment on, the emperor Shenzong 神宗 (1048 [reigned 1067]–1085) showed himself skeptical with respect to the hydraulic activism of his advisers, and it was he who was to insist upon respect being shown to the natural course of the river (shun shui 順水), once the Ergu had vanished in 1077, and all the projects directed at reestablishing an eastern course had been abandoned. If we except the brief period between 1093 and 1099, when there was a revival of the controversy over the restoration of an eastern course on the basis of the former Ergu, the main thrust of government action hereafter was aimed at constructing and consolidating the dikes, which were ranked according to their strategic importance until the waters of the Yellow River encroached upon the bed of the Huai after 1128, soon clearing for themselves several ways to the south. They were to abandon the eastern part of the great North China plain from the thirteenth to the middle of the nineteenth century.

In the seventh month of the new reign-period of Brilliant Celestial Help (1034), the Yellow River opened up several channels below the fascine at Henglong, and these began to settle into a permanent pattern of shifting about across the whole expanse of Hebei. The order was given to fill in the breach that was at the origin of the floods that were ravaging Dezhou 德州 and Bozhou 博州, much further north, but this undertaking was soon judged to be unfeasible by the high bureaucrats who had been sent in haste to the site.[29] In spite of several cash bonuses to the soldiers who were carrying out the works, and in spite of tax exemptions for all those who delivered on the spot the construction materials that the authorities required,[30] the building of levees that would allow the Yellow River to return to its former channel appeared less and less realistic. In 1036 a certain Wang Guo 王果 (n.d.) proposed abandoning the work-site, stressing that the nature of the topography in Hebei was "a basin in which banks form by the accumulation of sediments."[31] It is, however, known that not until 1041 did an imperial edict officially put an end to the work-site opened at Henglong six years previously. For Li Di 李迪 (971–1047), whose pleas carried the day with the emperor, the technical argument – which gave pride of place to the division of the flow and the renovation of the dikes at Jin, in the environs of Daming – linked naturally with the budgetary argument.[32]

There was nothing new in the bureaucracy's desire to make savings in the upkeep and reconstruction of the banks along the river, that is, in the war against waste. The figures in a memorial by Wen Ji 文洎 (n.d.) in 1036 show, however, the scale of the management problems presented at this time by the protection of the banks and levee building.[33] Wen, who was the intendant of exchange for the passes of Sanmen and Baibo (*Sanmen Baibo fayun shi* 三門白波發運使) demanded the revision of the quotas fixed ten or so years before, in order to make regular provision to the riverine prefectures of the materials needed for the fascines. As he saw it, these materials were becoming scarce because of the exorbitant demand for them. The number of wooden stakes (*shao* 梢) made of willow or acacia had risen from one or two million to close to four million the previous year, and had

---

[29] *XZCB, j.* 115, month 10 (9/2703).

[30] There are several examples from 1035 in ibid., *j.* 116 (9/2732 and 2735) and *j.* 117 (9/2745).

[31] Ibid., *j.* 118, month 5 (9/2785).

[32] Ibid., *j.* 131, month 2 (10/3109).

[33] *SHY*, "Fangyu," 14/14–16, gives a full text of this memorial but dates it to the eighth month of the eighth year of the Tiansheng reign-period (July 1030). The *Xu zizhi tongjian changbian, j.* 115 (9/2709), gives the date as the twelfth month of the second year of the Jingyou reign-period (January 1036).

reached nearly eight million in 1035, while the quantity of bamboos had doubled. Some 25 million *cheng* 稱 (or over 221,000 tonnes)[34] of materials had been delivered during the year for all the fascines on the Yellow River. Now this mass of matériel, part of which had rotted without being used, could have been reduced by 30 percent to 50 percent without the slightest shortage being occasioned, as several trials of this type were said to have made clear. On the other side, costs never stopped expanding, since in addition to the maintenance of the conscripted laborers – some hundred thousand men who had to cover more than a thousand *li* on the round trip to and from the work-sites – the administration had to pay 35,000 people whom it had employed (*gu* 顧) this year alone, at the rate of three to five strings of cash each. In sum, Wen Ji noted that, as the nature of the works had changed, it was now a question of handling the improvement of the river's course itself and not merely of maintaining the levees and the fascines; they had likewise changed in scale. The work-sites took on an unprecedented magnitude both in their duration and in the resources in men and materials that were mobilized.[35] All improvements had henceforth to be debated at the highest level of the state, as involving not only the career of a local official but the credit of the imperial government, and this despite the fact that these operations still depended on routine procedures.

These new tensions became apparent to contemporaries after 1048 when the court regularly debated the actions to be taken in response to the new shifts of course by the river. The clearest manifestation of this awareness was institutional: in 1051 the Bureau of Rivers and Canals (*He-qu an* 河渠案), which was subordinate to the Finance Commission (*San si* 三司), was replaced by the new Office of Rivers and Canals (*He-qu si* 河渠司), responsible for supervising the labor force and materials destined for the improvement of the Yellow River and the Bian Canal 汴河.[36] This reform of the central organs stemmed first of all from the fact that handling the river was no longer a simple matter of administrative routine carried on between the powerful central institution of the Finance Commission and the fiscal intendants (*zhuanyun shi* 轉運使) who were its representatives in the various northern circuits. The centralization of the management of the resources destined for the handling of the river was shown to be indispensable once

---

[34] According to Wu Chengluo, *Zhongguo du-liang-heng shi* [History of weights and measures in China] (Beijing: Shanghai shudian, 1984), p. 236, 1 *cheng* was 15 *jin*. Since the Tang, 1 *jin* has had several different values. Here we use 1 *jin* = 590 grams.

[35] Yoshioka, *Yellow River*, p. 169, has tried to draw up a table on the basis of reckoning in men and in units of labor (*gong*), notwithstanding the heterogeneity of the units of measurement.

[36] *SHY*, "Zhiguan," 5/42.

hydraulic operations, whose costs could no longer be borne at the local level, appeared as a new charge in the budgets controlled by the central administration.

Budget rhetoric at this time took two main forms. One was that of memorials evaluating the cost of operations discussed at court. The other was that of memorials that were intended to show the advantages or the disadvantages of a given solution with respect to public finances. Wen Ji's text of 1036 is a good example of the first type of document. The sources thus indicate quantified evaluations, often without giving any more details than the names of the bureaucrats responsible, but one may assume that they were accompanied by more circumstantial reports. At least in the eyes of the chroniclers, however, the very dryness of these estimations was also a form of eloquence: "Since the breach opened at Shanghu is 557 paces across, filling it in will require 10,426,800 standardized work units (*gong* 工), or in other words the labor of 14,260 soldiers and conscripted laborers for 100 days."[37]

This administrative accounting, which was henceforth practiced by the bureaucrats sent out by the central administrations to serve on the spot, continued the methods of calculation earlier perfected by local officials. It was these latter who had elaborated a unit of measure to evaluate the importance of a work-site, namely the *gong*,[38] and it seems likely that they had still to play their part in collaboration with the former, at least until the use of this unit became standard. A second type of document developed a different rhetoric:

> For the court, the north (*shuofang* 朔方) forms the territorial base that permits it to resist the barbarians and defend itself against them. Only [the prefectures of] Cang 滄州, Di, Bin, and Qi 齊州 are sufficiently rich for the court to draw the goods from them that are needed to supply its troops. After the dikes broke at Henglong, revenues were reduced by half, and following

---

[37] *SHY*, "Fangyu," 14/17. The figures of 10,416,800 and 14,160 are to be found in the *XZCB*, *j*. 165, month 8 (12/3965).

[38] Yoshioka devotes a chapter of his *Yellow River* to the *gong* (pp. 160–81), a concept already used in the Han mathematical treatise *Jiuzhang suanjing* 九章算經. He notes on p. 170 that the *gong* had been defined in Tang times as a unit of agricultural work, equal to the daily task assigned to a man on public lands or colony lands. Under the Song, the *gong* as used in public works represented a fixed multiple of the quantity of earth extracted and the linear displacement of this weight, e.g., kg.km = c (see the table on p. 171). Thus in 1023 the *gong* designated the removal of a carrying-pole load of 36 kg of earth a distance of 15 km, plus the return journey with an empty load, while the *tugong* 土工 was defined as the extraction of 30 kg of earth and its removal a distance of 20 paces. This second measure was readopted by Ouyang Xiu in the second memorial that he devoted to the handling of the Yellow River (p. 168).

the disaster at Shanghu losses have reached 80 to 90 percent. Furthermore our dynasty relies on the Yellow River to provide a reinforcement for its capital with respect to internal [disorders], and an obstacle to the barbarians' cavalry with respect to the exterior. These were the reasons our forebears paid such attention to the strictness of the rules relating to the protection of the Yellow River.[39]

The jeopardy was twofold. It was budgetary, to the extent that the richest prefectures had been ruined and their population put to flight by the floods; and it was military, to the extent that the defense system (as already described by He Chengju and Li Chui) had been destabilized. The matter was important, and following this memorial, which was unspecific about costs, an evaluation procedure was set in motion. The emperor dispatched a group of officials as a commission of inquiry, and they returned a favorable report, calculating the projected canal of "263 *li* 里 and 180 paces" as "needing 44,194,960 *gong*." We must be somewhat skeptical of these figures, but such precision – even when it was so fanciful that it at times provoked sarcastic comments – was apparently necessary to allow the dossier to proceed on its way through the bureaucratic hierarchy. But the memorial from Jia Changchao 賈昌朝 (998–1065), just cited, had recourse to arguments that were not those of a prefect reporting a breach in a dike. His discourse tended in effect to set his propositions in a strategic perspective where financial concerns, which were well and truly present in the form of the losses logged up in the best-off prefectures of Hebei, were linked with the policy of frontier defense against the Liao, the conclusion of the argument largely resting on the natural barrier constituted by the Yellow River. In other words, he was dealing with the problem of the Yellow River and how it should be handled not as an administrator but as a statesman.

Most of the officials who debated the handling of the river after this time adopted this tone of voice, and the argument relating to defense was put forward so regularly that it became a commonplace in discourse about the Yellow River and Hebei. The geostrategic situation is perhaps best put into perspective in a text from Hu Su 胡宿 (996–1067):

> Your servant has learned that the land forever preserves its strategic points, whereas states hardly have any permanent territory. Today as in the past this is what distinguishes the conditions of success from those of failure. In times past the passes of Lulong 盧龍 and Baitan 白檀 marked the line of division between the north and the south, and their control enabled the Middle Kingdom to stop short the enemy from the north. Today, on the contrary, these two obstacles are in the hands of the enemy, and the topography of

[39] *XZCB, j.* 165, month 12 (12/3977).

Hebei hardly presents any strategic point that is suitable for defense. From either the north or the south of the Yellow River one goes as far as Chanyuan across a plain of two thousand *li*.... Ever since the Yellow River broke its dikes at [Shang]hu and abandoned its former channel at Henglong, the Middle Kingdom has lost the barrier constituted by the great river; and if the barbarians take advantage of the gap to ravage Cang and Jing 滄州、景州, then Shandong will be under threat.[40]

Thus it was that in 1055, when Ouyang Xiu 歐陽修 (1007–72) addressed three memorials to the throne, his voice sounded discordant, however prophetic it may later have appeared to historians, who have for this reason been inclined to give him an important place. In his second memorial Ouyang based his argument on geographical considerations, demonstrating the contradiction that remained between the deposition of alluvium, which raised the bed of the channel, and the hydrology that determined the drainage in terms of the line of the maximum slope.[41] He discredited those who defined budgets without taking into account such physical realities such as the slope or the quantity of flow. In spite of his pressing insistence, Ouyang was barely listened to, and this was in proportion – it seems to me – to his effort to adhere solely to hydraulic facts. Whereas forty years earlier, the strategic project of Li Chui had appeared as quite out of the ordinary and unrealistic, hydraulic discourse had now become unacceptable because it lacked a strategic perspective.

The handling of the Yellow River was thus no longer seen solely as a response to natural phenomena. It depended first and foremost upon the strategic aims of the statesmen who formulated the dynasty's policy. In their eyes, the Yellow River and its network constituted essential elements in the means for defending the empire against enemies from the north, and the handling of Hebei had a decisive weight in the state's budget, both on account of the damage done there by floods and the enormous requirements of the military apparatus. Because the handling of the Yellow River was inserted directly into the budget managed at the central level by the Finance Commission, it began to compete or interact with the other items on which the dynasty had to make choices, and this precisely at a period when political struggles over budgets were becoming acute.

[40] Hu Su, "Lun Hebei bian bei shi yi zou" [Memorial on the organization of the defense of the Hebei frontier], in "Wen-gong ji," in *QSW* (11/405–06). In another text, which probably dates from the 1060s, Hu Su repeats this description word for word (*QSW*, 11/409).

[41] *SS, j.* 91, "Hequ" 1 (7/2270–71).

TENSIONS OVER BUDGETS AND
POLITICAL STRUGGLES

In the fifth month of the new reign-period of Brilliant Celestial Help (1034), a mere few weeks before the catastrophe at Henglong, the financial commissioner (*Sansi shi* 三司使) Cheng Lin 程琳 (988–1056) came to the conclusion that there were too many soldiers along the northern frontiers and that the financial burden was crushing.[42] The deficits, so far from diminishing, were to grow deeper, and several contemporaries diagnosed them as the sickness that was weakening the dynasty and would end by destroying it. Under these conditions it is hardly surprising that the massive assistance from the central administration was opposed by certain of the highest members of the Finance Commission. The commission was meant to control the totality of the financial power of the regular administration once the officials in charge of public finances had all been placed under its authority, and the financial autonomy of the prefectures had been officially abolished in the commission's favor in 973, while an accounting agency (*yingzai si* 應在司) that was directly under its tutelage was established at the prefectural level in 994.[43] It was, moreover, from this angle that the Bureau of Rivers and Canals, one of the twenty-four departments of the commission, was able to exercise its control over the hydraulic enterprises of the local administrators. It is clear enough, however, that other financial networks remained strong enough to exercise pressure on the commission. The Imperial Treasury (*Neizang* 內藏), which was under the control of the palace eunuchs, not only received any budget surpluses when these occurred, but, when the wars of unification had come to an end, also profited from the casting of coinage and levies of silk goods. Local administrations also had a certain financial latitude thanks to the effects of tax exemptions, commutations, and – above all – the stocks in the Ever-Normal granaries (*changping cang* 常平倉).[44]

---

[42] *XZCB, j.* 114, month 5 (9/2675–76).

[43] Wang Shengduo, "Songchao licai tizhi you Sansi dao Hubu-de bianqian" [The change from the Finance Commission to the Ministry of Finance in Song financial institutions], in *Song-Liao-Jin shi luncong* [Collected essays on Song, Jin, and Liao history] (Beijing: Zhonghua shuju, 1991), pp. 135–36, and Wang Shengduo, *Liang–Song caizheng shi* [History of public finance under the Northern and Southern Song] (Beijing: Zhonghua shuju, 1995), p. 532.

[44] Cheng Minsheng ("Lun Bei-Song caizheng-de tedian yu jipin-de jiaxiang" [On the particular characteristics of the financial administration of the Northern Song and its alleged impoverishment], *Zhongguo shi yanjiu* (1984), vol. 3, pp. 27–44) has suggested that the analysis of these multiple financial circuits would without doubt allow a new approach to the Song dynasty's deficits.

If, under circumstances such as these, Cheng Lin thought that reducing the means at the disposal of the imperial army and recruiting local troops would ease the strain on the Imperial Treasury, his plea does not seem to have been aimed simply at resolving financial tensions, but at defending the interests of his powerful institution. As is evident from Figure 15.1 and the numerical evidence given in Table 15.1, at the moment when Cheng was deploring these deficits, the commission was no longer alone in benefiting from the transfer payments made from the treasury. More precisely, this assistance, which had been given to it on a priority basis before the 1030s, was hereafter to become episodic, and then to disappear almost completely, just at the time when direct aid allocated by the treasury to the two circuits of Hebei and Shaanxi in the form of precious metals, silks, and cash was becoming more and more frequent. The direct assistance granted by the treasury to the regional administrations in the frontier circuits was to the detriment of the financial resources on which the commission had established its authority.

In 1034, exactly at the time when the local administrations were no longer in a position to deal with the management of the Yellow River, the Finance Commission, upon which these administrations directly depended for funding, was weakened by the reorientation of the aid given by the Imperial Treasury, now accorded to the regional authorities for purchases intended for the troops. Hydraulic developments and the imperatives of defense thus combined to reduce the authority of the principal financial organ of the empire, which is well known to have been the object at this period of intense criticisms.[45] Overall, the linkage between the political struggle, administrative reorganization, and the management of the Yellow River had already seemed plausible to us on account of the suppression in 1051 of the Bureau of Rivers and Canals: this was the first real attack on the institutional monopoly of finances exercised by the commission.

The sequence of institutional developments confirms this initial diagnosis: in 1058, two years after the failure of the hydraulic work-site of the Six Pagodas, the commission was stripped of all competence in hydraulic affairs by the setting up of the Inspectorate-General of Waters (Dushui jian 都水監). This new administration became entirely independent, thanks to the direct attachment of the local inspectorates (wai 外) to the central department (nei 內).

---

[45] On the rivalry between financial administrations, see the articles of Cheng Minsheng and Wang Shengduo, and also Umehara Kaoru, "Songdai-de neizang yu zuozang" [The Imperial Treasury and the Treasury of the Left under the Song; this is the Chinese translation of his "Sōdai no naisō to sasō," published in 1971], Shihuo yuekan 6.1–2 (1976), pp. 34–66; and Robert Hartwell, "The Imperial Treasuries: Finance and Power in Song China," Bulletin of Song-Yuan Studies 20 (1988), pp. 18–89.

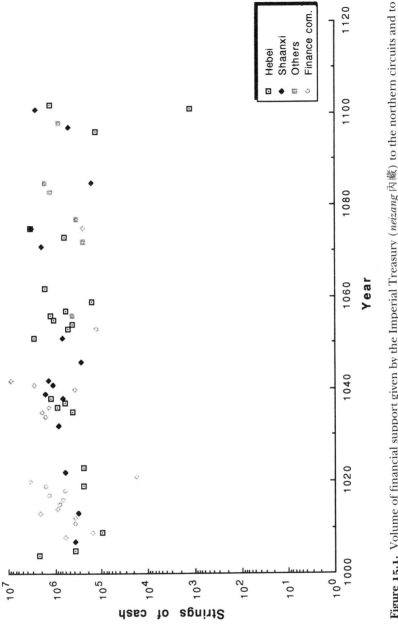

Figure 15.1. Volume of financial support given by the Imperial Treasury (*neizang* 內藏) to the northern circuits and to the Finance Commission during the eleventh century. *Source:* Umehara, "Song imperial treasury," pp. 39–41.

Table 15.1. *Valuation (in thousands of strings of cash) of the financial support provided by the Imperial Treasury to the northern circuits and the Finance Commission during the eleventh century*

Year	To the Finance Commission	To Hebei	To Shaanxi	To other provinces
1003	1,800	0	0	0
1004	300	0	0	0
1006	0	300	0	0
1007	0	0	0	50
1008	80	0	0	130
1010	0	0	0	300
1011	0	0	0	300
1012	0	250	0	1,650
1013	0	0	0	73
1014	0	0	0	650
1015	0	0	0	550
1016	0	0	0	1,100
1017	0	0	0	500
1018	200	0	0	1,300
1019	0	0	0	2,800
1020	0	0	0	14
1021	0	500	0	0
1022	200	0	0	0
1031	0	660	0	0
1033	0	0	0	1,300
1034	330	0	0	1,500
1035	700	0	0	1,100
1036	500	0	0	0
1037	975	550	0	0
1038	0	1,300	0	0
1039	0	0	0	300
1040	0	900	0	2,200
1041	0	1,100	0	6,800
1045	0	220	0	0
1050	2,160	550	0	0
1052	410	0	0	100
1053	330	0	0	0
1054	850	0	0	0
1055	1,000	0	330	0
1056	460	0	0	0
1058	130	0	0	0
1061	1,260	0	0	0
1070	0	1,500	0	0
1071	0	0	200	0
1072	500	0	0	0

Table 15.1. *(cont.)*

Year	To the Finance Commission	To Hebei	To Shaanxi	To other provinces
1074	2,600	2,500	0	200
1076	0	0	275	0
1082	0	0	1,000	0
1084	0	130	1,300	0
1095	100	0	0	0
1096	0	400	0	0
1097	0	650	650	0
1100	1	2,000	0	0
1101	1,000	0	0	0

Source: This table is based on the information gathered by Umehara Kaoru, primarily from the *Song huiyao* and the *Xu Zizhi tongjian changbian*. See his "Songdai de neizang yu zuozang" [The Imperial Treasury and the Treasury of the Left under the Song], a Chinese translation of his "Sōdai no naisō to sasō" of 1971, *Shihuo yuekan* 6.1–2 (1976), pp. 39–41, to which a figure has been added for 1045 on the basis of the *Songshi, j.* 198, *Bing* 12 (14/4934).

The difficulty has been to find a common unit of account into which all the products paid into the treasury – silks, precious metal (silver), and other moneys – may be converted. We have chosen to use the string of cash, since we have in hand the official exchange rates of the string for an ounce of silver and for silk in the eleventh century. Angela Yu-Yun Sheng, in her unpublished doctoral thesis, "Textile use, technology, and change in rural textile production in Song China (1960–1279)" (University of Pennsylvania, 1990), table 6, p. 216, has compiled a table that presents the prices that may be obtained from the Song sources. Although these only represent particular moments in time, she argues that they suffice to show the fluctuations in the price of silk. We therefore give here the mean prices per length:

960–1030	1,000 copper cash = 1 string
1031–55	1,100
1056–69	1,300
1070–81	1,500
1082–95	1,300
1096–1100	1,000

It was after 1038, the year when the military clashes that were to culminate in the war of 1042–44 between the Xixia 西夏 and the Song began, that the decisive changes occurred. At this period the civil and military administration of the northern circuits was regularly entrusted to a high civilian official, namely the military superintendent (*Jinglüe shi* 經略使 or *Jinglüe anfu shi* 經略安撫使), who had the ascendancy over the fiscal intendant, a functionary who in principle answered to the Finance Commission.[46] These superintendents, who were able to count on the assistance of the Imperial Treasury, were powerful men at this time, and capable in practice of defining the immediate priorities.

From this date on, the essential problem of military logistics was intermixed with that of the independence of the regional administrators with respect to the central financial organs, an eminently political problem. If they were to have no financial elbow room in the midst of a military crisis, the superintendents of the frontier regions would be threatened with asphyxia and their troops with listlessness or defeatism; but if they were too independent, these superintendencies menaced the centralized structure that the Song had made such an effort to build, being haunted by the fear of perpetuating the centrifugal tendencies that had undermined and ruined the empire of the Tang. Now the physical link between these regional powers in full expansion and the capital was guaranteed by the waterways of the hydrographic network of the Yellow River. In the eyes of the superintendents and their political friends, the management of the Yellow River had to become part of a military rhetoric that assigned a double function to these waterways: they formed a natural obstacle without which any defensive system remained fragile; and they constituted the logistical framework that made it possible to maintain a human Great Wall confronting the barbarians:

> Complete reliance was not previously placed on the deliveries (*ru zhong* 入 中) made along the frontiers. The border prefectures likewise planned purchases of cereals that were transported in official convoys along the imperial canal (*Yuhe* 御河). The army's reserves were thus assured without any interruption. Now the imperial canal has recently been left abandoned, and since there are no more transport vessels to move the cargo, reliance is placed wholly on the deliveries.[47]

This report was drawn up by Ouyang Xiu, one of the architects of the first reform. It goes on to touch on a point that is crucial, in that it unveils the political tensions with which we have been concerned here, while explaining the contradictions that were undermining the supplying of the troops on the frontier:

> It has emerged, after inquiry, that the sixteen frontier districts were originally outside the zone where official purchases were made in cash (*xianqian bian di*

---

[46] These transformations in the regional administration have been studied by Michael McGrath in his unpublished doctoral dissertation. "Military and Regional Administration in Northern Sung China (960–1126)," Princeton University (1982), esp. ch. 5, "The military intendant," pp. 189–270.

[47] Ouyang Xiu, "Qi zhi Yuhe cui gang" [Request for setting up government shipping on the Imperial Canal], in *Complete works*, vol. 2, "Hebei feng shi zoucao," *j.* 1, pp. 948–49.

見錢便糴), and that the seven border districts of Daming prefecture have recently authorized merchants to carry out their deliveries according to the principles of the Three Clauses (*sanshuo ruzhong* 三説入中). Now, the two systems cannot be applied simultaneously. If, as between these two areas, the price obtainable for bonds [granted under the Three Clauses] is not a competitive rate for the difficulties [of deliveries on the frontiers], the merchants will only go to the border districts to effect their deliveries. If high prices at the frontiers [enable merchants to] procure profits [by going there], then merchants prepared to make deliveries to the border districts will become scarce.

The contradiction between the system of official purchases based on credit backed by cash and that of deliveries at the frontiers returns us directly to the political and administrative confrontation between the regional authorities and the Finance Commission. The official purchases were made possible by the direct assistance of the Imperial Treasury, and controlled by the administration then in charge of the military superintendents, whereas the system of deliveries was founded on the circulation of bonds guaranteed by the accounts office of monopolies at the capital, and, in consequence of this, was placed directly under the authority of the Finance Commission. The disorganization of the transport network, for which Ouyang held the fiscal intendants responsible, was in fact a general phenomenon in this period, and also criticized by Fan Zhongyan (989–1052),[48] but the interest again lies in the mode of argument developed. The competition between different parts of the administration that was suggested by the budgetary considerations raised by Cheng Lin in 1034 had clearly evolved into a contradiction in the memorial of Ouyang Xiu.

The sharpness of the antagonism was confirmed in two responses made in 1047 to the personal commands of the emperor by the financial commissioner Zhang Fangping 張方平 (1007–91), in which he unequivocally threatened the military superintendencies,[49] and then denounced the extreme independence of Hebei:

Your servant has already expressed his disapproval of the way in which our dynasty is exhausting the life forces of the universe in order to maintain an excessive number of soldiers, who are, what is more, the instigators of serious

---

[48] Fan Zhongyan, "Zou qi mian Guanzhong zhiyi lianghsui que qi yu cibian ruzhong hudou" [Memorial requesting the abolition of the double-tax transfer in Guanzhong, and requesting deliveries of food grain in the rear-border areas], QSW, vol. 9, pp. 548–49.

[49] Zhang Fangping, "Dui shouzhao yi dao" [Reply to the autograph imperial edict], "Lequan ji," j. 18 (QSW, 19/13–14). The XZCB, j. 163 (12/3923–30), dates both texts to the third month of 1048.

disorders. Now, of all the regions of the empire, it is Hebei that is the most affected by this situation. Why is this? Ever since the rebellion of An [Lushan 安祿山] and Shi [Siming 史思明] during the Tianbao 天寶 reign-period [742–56] under the Tang, and later under the Five Dynasties, with the Later Tang or Later Zhou, Hebei has been inherited by this succession of dynasties as their private property, as it was taken to be by the Wei [in former times], and thus it is that the Hebei army is naturally inclined to arrogance and violence. Furthermore, since [Hebei] is in contact with the barbarians to the north, our dynasty has given it particularly favorable treatment. So it is that, in spite of a lasting peace, it has hardly abandoned this arrogance, which makes the solution of the problems very difficult.[50]

The commissioner regarded Hebei at the end of 1040s as a state within a state, a situation that it was appropriate to rectify if the court's plan was truly to restore good order to public finances. The real or supposed autonomy of Hebei seemed all the more dangerous to him in that his own administration was increasingly becoming too weak to be able to play a role in this region. The decline in its financial means had progressively reduced its capacity to intervene in two essential domains, the purchase of grain on the frontiers and the hydraulic management of the Yellow River. After 1051 the control of this sector slipped entirely from its grasp.

It is obviously necessary to stress that events did not develop in the linear fashion that the above sketch might seem to suggest. It has already been indicated that Fan Zhongyan called for the abandoning of fiscal transfers in favor of frontier deliveries, a system controlled by the commission to which he himself answered in his capacity as a fiscal intendant.[51] It is known that he was to recommend for the key post of intendant of exchange (fayun shi 發運使) a man whose experience had been in the accounting office of state monopolies, Xu Yuan 許元 (989–1057). It is also known that other officials saw little if any contradiction between deliveries on the frontiers and purchases, calling for an increase in the former while stipulating that the latter should be used "when timely."[52] The first reform, that of 1043–44, was, however, also an occasion for a hardening of positions, which gave ideas a certain coherence and a programmatic character that contemporaries had

---

[50] Zhang Fangping, "Zai dui yuzha yi dao" [Second reply to the imperial order], "Lequan ji," j. 18 (QSW, 19/19).

[51] Fan Zhongyan, "Double-tax transfer," QSW, vol. 9, pp. 548–49.

[52] Bao Zheng, "Qing yu Huai Wei di mi xiu Yuhe chuan yun zou" [Memorial requesting the mending of the boats of the Imperial Canal for the shipment of the "harmoniously purchased" rice from the prefectures of the Huai and Wei areas], "Qing Hebei jishi jizhi hudou zou" [Memorial requesting a seasonable policy on food grain in Hebei], and "Qing tian Hebei ruzhong liangcao zou" [Memorial requesting an increase in the deliveries of food grain and fodder to Hebei] in QSW, vol. 13, pp. 425–26.

no hesitation in seeing as an indication of the formation of "cliques" (*pengdang* 朋黨).

While it is not appropriate to develop further here the theme of differences between the central administration and the growing power of the local authorities in Hebei, it remains to be discovered in what respects the reorganization of public finances that resulted from these political struggles was able to contribute to making of Hebei and its waterways a unique space, something that is confirmed by the type of discourse current on the eve of the great flood of 1048.

FINANCIAL SPACES AND PROJECTS OF HYDRAULIC MANAGEMENT AND IMPROVEMENT

In 1038, once the court had become aware that the supply of grains to the capital was encountering difficulties, it reestablished the post of superintendent of exchange for Huainan, Jiang–Zhe, and Jing–Hu (*Huainan Jiang–Zhe Jing–Hu zhizhi fayun shi* 淮南江浙荊湖制置發運使) which had been abolished four years earlier.[53] Once war against the Xixia had started in 1042, the situation – already critical because of brigandage – hardly grew any better. In 1043, Fan Zhongyan, who was then in charge in order to implement his plan of reform, therefore recommended a financial specialist, Xu Yuan, to be the Exchange Intendancy supervisory official for Jiang–Huai (*Jiang–Huai fayun panguan* 江淮發運判官);[54] Xu Yuan was soon to become exchange intendant for the six southeastern circuits, and to hold this post for close to twelve years.[55] It was Xu who, working under the administration of Fan in Shaanxi, proposed a change in the rules governing the state salt monopoly in the southeast in order to reactivate the delivery of cereals to the northwestern frontier.[56] It was he who was to organize, thanks to the commutation into monetary form of the tax in circuits that

[53] *XZCB, j.* 115 (9/2710).

[54] The author translates this title as "assistant aux approvisionnements," that is, "assistant for supplies."

[55] For the history of the post of exchange intendent see Aoyama Sadao, *Tō-Sō jidai no kōtsū to chishi chizu no kenkyū* [Studies on transport and local gazetteers and maps under the Tang and Song] (Tokyo: Yoshikawa kobunkan, 1963), ch. 9, "Sōdai ni okeru sōun no hattatsu," pp. 354–60, 368–74, where the policies of Xu Yuan and Xue Xiang are described. There is a summary of this article in Françoise Aubin, *Études Song* 1 (1976), fasc. 3, pp. 281–96.

[56] The action taken by Xu in the framework of the salt monopoly is presented by Guo Zhengzhong, *Songdai yanye jingli shi* [Economic history of the salt industry under the Song] (Beijing: Renmin CBS, 1990], pp. 751–52.

had deficits in grain,[57] the transfers of funds needed for the "harmonious purchases" (*hedi* 和糴) in circuits with a surplus, a procedure that allowed the tribute quotas once again to be filled. The accumulation of grains, which would always be considered a priority, was thus effected not only through taxation but also by means of these purchases and interregional transfers, which were soon made to assume a quasi-fiscal form as obligatory transfers (*yipei* 抑配). This type of purchase had been foreseen since quotas had been fixed at the beginning of the century, and it occupied an important place in the structure of the tribute, namely between a third and a half of its anticipated 6 million *shi* 石 (i.e., about 4 million hectoliters).[58]

Since the quality of these transfers depended on good circulation of traffic, the upkeep and the development of the waterways once more became matters at issue in the fiscal domain, as had been the case at the beginning of the dynasty. Xu Yuan therefore reorganized the convoys on the Bian River by recruiting private boatmen; and he had a new canal cut between Chuzhou 楚州 and the Bian.[59] The policy that he followed was explicitly modeled on that of the great financiers of the Tang dynasty, Pei Yaoqing 裴耀卿 (681–743) and Liu Yan 劉晏 (715–80). This fiscal and financial reorganization very clearly rested on a territorial reality that the forms of discourse brought to the forefront, namely the riches of the south. In 1040, Fu Bi 富弼 (1004–83), in the formulation of a strategy aimed at mobilizing the whole empire in its confrontation with the Xixia – a strategy that was to be rejected by the court – had already stressed the role of background support on a large scale that should be played by the southeast,[60] and in 1044 Li Gou 李覯 (1009–59) summed up these territorial equilibria as follows: "Today our empire rests on the Jiang–Huai region. Without the Jiang–Huai region it could not meet its needs, whereas the Jiang–Huai region could, on its own and without the empire, constitute a state."[61] The stabilization of these systems of purchases thus depended on the capacity of the administration to apply simultaneously the two aspects

---

[57] This commutation is attested even before the nomination of Xu by Zhang Fanping, who spoke of this practice from 1040 onward. See Zhang Fangping, "Lun Jingshi jun chu shi zou" [Memorial on stocks held for troops in the Capital area], *QSW*, "Lequan ji," j. 23 (*QSW* 19/118).

[58] This is the equivalent suggested by Shimasue Kazuyasu, "Sōdai Jōkyobei to kin' yuhō" [Provincially remitted grain and the law governing tribute distribution under the Song], in *Sōdai no seiji to shakai* [Politics and society under the Song] (Tokyo: Sōdai-shi kenkyū-kai, 1988), p. 10. See likewise pp. 4–5, where Shimasue makes clear the importance of harmonious purchase following the setting of the quotas in 1007.

[59] *SS, j.* 96, "Hequ" 6 (7/2381).

[60] *XZCB, j.* 128, month 8 (10/3034).

[61] Li Gou, "Ji shang Fu shumi shu" [Letter to Fu (Bi), commissioner for military affairs], *QSW* 21/322.

of the policy put in place by Xu: to assemble the funds needed for the transactions and to guarantee the uninterrupted circulation of products.

It will be recalled that it was exactly during the years when Xu Yuan took the administration of transport in hand that the Imperial Treasury reoriented its financial aid in the direction of the three frontier circuits of the north. The gifts, or advances, agreed to by the center had to cover the cost of the purchases from the merchants at the frontiers, but it is known that this type of transaction did not satisfy the merchants, who, *per contra*, preferred deliveries made on credit in return for state monopoly goods. Between 1041 and 1054 the deliveries to Hebei are said to have reached a total of between three and four million *shi* per annum, and that in the single year 1055 the central administration had to absorb deliveries of six million *shi*, the equivalent of a year's official quota of tribute grain from the southeast.[62] Enormous financial means were thus required to put an end to the perversions of the delivery system, which was in its turn denounced in 1055, and then again in 1056, by Xue Xiang 薛向 (1016–81) when he was on a mission of inspection concerning official purchases on credit of grains and fodder in Hebei (*Hebei tiju liang-cao di bian* 河北提舉糧草羅便):

> In the seventeen districts that together make up the frontiers (*bingbian* 並邊), one can reckon up a yearly total of 1.8 million *shi* of grain [close to 1.2 million hectoliters], which represent 1.6 million strings of cash, as well as 0.65 million *shi* of soybeans [over 0.4 million hectoliters] and 3.7 million bales of fodder. Over the whole of the frontier, the annual fiscal revenues in grains, beans, and fodder may attain 0.5 million [strings?]; all the rest is delivered (*ru zhong*) by merchants. I would request the abolition of these deliveries of grain everywhere on the frontier, and the transfer from the capital to Hebei of cash and silk goods to be dedicated to "harmonious purchases" in cash.[63]

Insofar as the system of deliveries and smuggling, inherent in the state monopolies, brought about the collapse of the revenues derived from salt and tea, contributing in large measure to the ruin of the finances of the Finance Commission, this latter was now more inclined than previously to decentralize payments through establishing a partnership with the merchants.[64] This was why the logic of covering the costs of purchases became increasingly different in the six southern circuits under the intendent of transports – a number that rose to nine after 1069, under the authority of

---

[62] Shiba Yoshinobu, "Sōdai shiteki seido no enkaku" [The evolution of the system of grain procurement through public purchase under the Song], in *Aoyama Hakushi koki kinen Sōdaishi ronsō* [Anthology on Song history for the seventieth anniversary of Dr. Aoyama] (Tokyo: shōshin shobō, 1974), p. 133.

[63] *SS, j.* 184, "Shihuo xia" 6 (13/4493).

[64] It should be recalled that the tea monopoly was abolished in 1059, and the farming out of the salt monopoly (*pumai fa* 扑買法) began in the southeast in the 1060s.

Xue Xiang – and the three northern circuits. The former relied on the transfer of local resources, and the latter on the payments made by the Imperial Treasury. In effect, even if all these purchases depended, on account of their volume, on financing that only the treasury was in a position to guarantee, the mechanisms were noticeably different. In the north, where the market was controlled by large merchants, the authorities made their payments in money, precious metals, and silk goods, once again complying with the demands of their commercial partners who wanted to return to the system of negotiable bonds valued in cash or in tea, even during the period of the reforms of Wang Anshi 王安石 (1021–86).[65] In the south the purchasing procedures worked out by Xu Yuan and developed by Xue Xiang rested largely on the tribute grain itself. Shimasue Kazuyasu has shown that after 1069, the date when the "rules for equitable deliveries" (*junshu fa* 均輸法) were established, the percentage of grain that was actually transported to the capital essentially consisted of purchases, while the percentage that was missing represented the loan made by the treasury for these purchases. In other words, even if the treasury at times supported purchases in the southern circuits,[66] this was first and foremost an accounting game that permitted the authorities to provide regular financing for the supply of grains to the capital.

Henceforth waterborne traffic had additionally to be organized as a function of the financial spaces, which signified that certain waterways fell and others rose in the importance attributed to them. Toward the end of the 1040s, six years after Ouyang Xiu had deplored, as we have seen, the condition of the Imperial Canal and the contradictions in official policy, Bao Zheng 包拯 (999–1062) wrote a series of memorials, composed between the spring and the summer of 1049, in which he returned to the difficulties of supplying Hebei and the importance of the waterways.[67] He stressed the interest that the authorities had in redefining the local military regions so as to rely on the richest prefectures in He'nan, a circuit that he

---

[65] Shiba Yoshinobu, "System of grain procurement through public purchase," p. 133.

[66] Shimasue Kazuyasu gives several instances of money payments made to the account of the south in his article "Sōdai jōkyobei": in 1069 (p. 18) this was done to establish the rules for "equitable deliveries," and again in 1076 and 1079 (p. 21).

[67] Bao Zheng, "Feng zhao Hebei jizhi hudou ri shang dian zou" [Memorial transmitted to the palace in the ordinary way in accordance with the imperial edict on food grain in Hebei], "Qing zhibo Bianhe lianggang wang Hebei zou" [Memorial requesting the requisitioning of the Bian-river food-grain convoys for Hebei], "Qing yu Huai – Wei di mi xiu Yuhe chuan you zou" [Memorial requesting the mending of the boats of the Imperial Canal . . .], "Qing Hebei jishi jizhi hudou zou" [Memorial requesting a seasonable policy on food grain in Hebei], and "Qing tian Hebei ruzhong liangcao zou" [Memorial requesting an increase in the deliveries of food grain and fodder to Hebei], in QSW, "Bao Zheng ji," *j.* 10 (13/423–26).

represented as a major back-up zone precisely because of the communications axis provided by the Imperial Canal.[68] Even so, since the object of his reports was to draw attention to an urgent situation, Bao exhorted the administration to have recourse to all possible means to obtain grain supplies: purchases, deliveries by merchants, and even the mobilization of the goods brought from the southeast along the Bian Canal.[69]

Bao moreover sharpened his ideas by systematizing them. He proposed a plan for transport to Hebei, conceiving of a northern network that would be symmetric with that in the south, having its axis of symmetry through the center at Kaifeng:

> Your servant is of the opinion that the greatest of all advantages is that grains are transported along the imperial Canal (*Yuhe*) upstream from Huai (zhou) 懷州, Wei (zhou) 衛州, and Tonglijun 通利軍, and then downstream to the frontier prefectures. . . . The frontier prefectures are only suffering from a lack of boats. If we had available two or three hundred boats, they could circulate back and forth without interruption, there would no longer be any worry about shortages in the frontier reserves, and we should also avoid deliveries at high prices and thus the wasting of public funds.[70]

These texts call for several remarks. The first is factual: the boats on the Yuhe, whose poor condition and shortage of crews had also been deplored by Ouyang Xiu around 1044,[71] were still as few in number, which leads us to think that the traffic – or at least the administration convoys – had hardly increased. The second remark concerns what we are obliged to consider as the administrative utopia of Bao: in a few phrases he summons up a vision of boats going north from the capital as far as Wei or Tonglijun, counterparts of Sizhou 泗州, Chuzhou, or Zhenzhou 真州 to the south of Kaifeng. In these cities the grain would be unloaded and then forwarded on by the Yuhe to be distributed on the frontiers, in a mirror image of the process of collection that had made it possible to gather it together in the prefectures of the south. Bao was patently desirous of seeing the systems unified, and so much so that the component parts already seemed to him as it were inscribed in the hydrographic network.

---

[68] Bao Zheng, "Qing nuoyi Hebei bing ma shi zou" [Memorial requesting the removal of troops and horses from Hebei], *QSW*, "Bao Zheng ji," *j*. 8 (13/402–04).

[69] Bao Zheng, "Memorial requesting the requisitioning of the Bian-river food-grain convoys for Hebei," *QSW*, "Bao Zheng ji," *j*. 10 (13/424).

[70] Bao Zheng "Memorial requesting the mending of the boats," *QSW*, "Bao Zheng ji," *j*. 10 (13/I.425).

[71] Ouyang Xiu, *Complete works*, "Qi zhi Yuhe cui gang" [Request for the establishment of government shipping on the Imperial Canal], p. 948, recalls that of the 1800 boats of the Yuhe fleet listed by the ancient registers, only 300 remained.

Some years later, in 1057, Zhang Fangping returned to the Finance Commission, where he had held a position twelve years earlier. In a long memorial he set himself to drawing up the balance sheet of the policy of stocking grain at the capital since 1045, and tried to express the reasons that, in his view, explained the low level of the reserves in grain, which had declined by three-fifths according to his inquiry. An adversary of the policy elaborated by Xu Yuan and pursued by Xue Xiang, he deplored the practice, generalized after 1040, of commuting grains for money, and set himself to presenting the situation regarding the moving of the grain, network by network:

> As to the Yellow River, I have examined the edict of the second year of Jingde 景德 (1005) that fixes the annual contribution to be made by the fiscal intendent of Shaanxi to the capital at 0.3 million *shi* of fodder; the least quantity over and above this in any grain to be transferred. . . . I have checked that over the last few years not a single boat has been sent, that not a single transport has been made in the direction of the capital. . . . In recent times the frontier has been calm and the Guanzhong 關中 area [the earlier metropolitan area "within the passes"] has enjoyed several years of good harvests, and thus this circuit is not short of resources. Up to the present the court has every year supplied it with large quantities of provisions and silks, and the old quota of 0.3 million *shi* of fodder is [simply] for calculation in the total estimation of the tribute. I would request that a special edict be issued ordering the Fiscal Intendancy of Shaanxi and the Exchange Intendancy of Sanmen and Bai-Bo to conform completely with the old directives from the autumn of the second year of the Jiayou reign-period (1057).[72]

Two years later, it has been said, the tribute grain carried on the Yellow River was to be suppressed and in 1060 the Exchange Intendancy of Sanmen and Bai-Bo removed! The failure of Zhang's proposals cannot simply be explained by the defects in the administration that he himself had brought to attention. The disappearance of the tribute grain brings us – at last – to the complexity of the decisions that were made about the Yellow River at the end of the 1050s. It is particularly striking to note that Zhang, for all that he was preoccupied with the improvement of waterways, said nothing about the Yellow River in the columns of writing that he devoted to the upkeep of the waterways. The devastating setback at the work-site of the Six Pagodas was only a year previous, it is true, and no doubt imposed a certain reserve on the subject. But there was more to it than that, as may be intuited from the passage devoted to canals:

[72] Zhang Fangping, "Lun Jingshi jun chu shi zou" [Memorial on stocks held for troops in the Capital area], *QSW*, vol. 19, pp. 119–20.

Before the Tiansheng 天聖 reign-period (1023–31), [the Bian River] was dredged and maintained every year, and the households that lived along the watercourse each of them kept the tools needed for dredging, which were extremely varied in nature. Thus it was unknown for the riverbed to be obstructed. At the beginning of the Tiansheng reign-period [the start of the reign of the emperor Renzong 仁宗], Zhang Junping 張君平 held out the prospects of the advantage to be had from doing away with the conscript labor services of the spring season, an abolition that was first put into effect at this time; the administration thus adopted the wretched project of a person lacking in any perception and taking pleasure in the profits to be derived from the reduction of the costs of the labor services, in order to be credited with some sort of success. The result of this was the deposition of alluvium, which obstructed the channel bed and hindered the passage of the convoys. As to the Huimin [Canal 惠民河] and the Guangji [Canal 廣濟河], along which came the supplies from the four quarters that were gathered together at the capital, thanks to the all-but-endless succession of boats provisioning the collectivity and individuals, they have both of them been blocked for some years past.[73]

The whole of Zhang's case was aimed at restoring the movement of grain to the capital; he said nothing about the sharing out of the resources of the empire. Above all, as has been noted above, he did not accept the priority given to those practices that attempted to make the tribute grain a tool allowing the government to regulate the flow of grains in the empire, under the heading of subsidies, assistance, or loans; he refused to regard the capital as anything other than the grand center where grain was stockpiled, whereas the Imperial Treasury was already seeking to organize and redistribute resources by serving as an organ that loaned grain and controlled its movements. Now, whether for Zhang or his adversaries, the movements along the Bian Canal were essential: in the first place, they supplied the capital; and in the second, they made it possible to refill the coffers of the treasury, which fed the administrations of the frontier zones. It is this point in common between the reformers and their adversaries that has to be elucidated insofar as the higher value accorded to the canal entailed the downgrading of the Yellow River.

The hydraulic reality was that of a network in which the Bian had to be made a branch of the Yellow River, since without the water of the Yellow the level of the canal would not have been adequate for navigation (see Map 15.4). With its waters, however, the Yellow River brought alluvium that it spread on the bed of this derivative waterway. The men of the time there-

---

[73] Zhang Fangping, "Stocks held for troops," *QSW*, vol. 19, p. 121.

fore devoted themselves to defining several policies to deal with this problem: dredging the bed, at the cost of imposing heavy labor services; scouring the channel with the water of nearby rivers; and displacing the point at which the canal articulated with the Yellow River.[74] What was more, as the result of ice and low winter water levels, the entry from the Yellow River into the Bian Canal was closed each year by the authorities, who cleared it each spring. This gave the traffic a seasonal nature that was in contradiction with the political desire to develop exchanges based on waterways. Hydraulic activism directed at the navigability of the canals therefore increased, with the proclaimed objective of assuring permanent traffic along the Bian.

Although a yearly corvée for the care of the channel bed was reinstated after 1050,[75] it probably remained subject to the accidents of the availability of budgetary means, as Zhang Fangping's memorial suggests. It was above all with the start of the years of reform that the major work-sites were inaugurated. Now, although some of the attempts to resolve the contradictions that have been described above only ended in transitory implementations – such as the new junction with the river that was opened in 1071 but only for three years – others were veritably demiurgic enterprises, as for example the improvement of the Baigou 白溝 or, above all, the diversion of the waters of the Luo 洛河. In 1073 Wang Anshi showed himself well disposed to the development of the project of scouring the Bian with the water of the Baigou: it seemed as if it would be possible using this river, to which the waters of the Jing and the Suo would be joined, and thanks to a system of barrages (*bei* 陂) and locks (*zha* 閘), to open a new canal that would be navigable all year round, and that might be able to replace the Bian itself.[76] Zhang Fangping set himself against this project: "The Bian river comes up to the walls of our capital and is the foundation on which our dynasty is built. It is thus not to be compared to small canals and hydraulic systems."[77]

---

[74] For a presentation of the problems and for the policies adopted to master the canal during the reform period, see Furubayashi Morihiro, "Hoku-Sō Kinei, Genpō nenkan ni okeru Benga no suiro kōji" [Waterway engineering on the Bian River in the Xining and Yuanfeng reign-periods (1068–83) of the Northern Song], in Chūgoku suiri-shi kenkyū-kai, ed., *Satō Hakushi taikan kinen Chūgoku suiri-shi ronsō* [A collection of essays on the history of water control in China to mark the retirement of Dr. Satō Taketoshi] (Tokyo: kokusho kankōsha, 1984], pp. 153–82. The hydraulic problems of the network constituted by the Yellow River, the Bian, and the Huai are presented in Christian Lamouroux, "Les contradictions d'un réseau hydraulique: l'exemple du bassin de la Huai sous les Song du Nord," *T'oung Pao* 75 (1989), pp. 127–62.

[75] For a list of the works done on the Bian, see Yao Hanyuan, *History of water control in China*, tables 5–11, pp. 255–58.

[76] *SHY*, "Shihuo," 61/101.

[77] Zhang Fangping, "Lun Bianhe lihai shi" [On the advantageous and disadvantageous aspects of the Bian River], "Lequan ji," *j.* 27 (*QSW* 19/192).

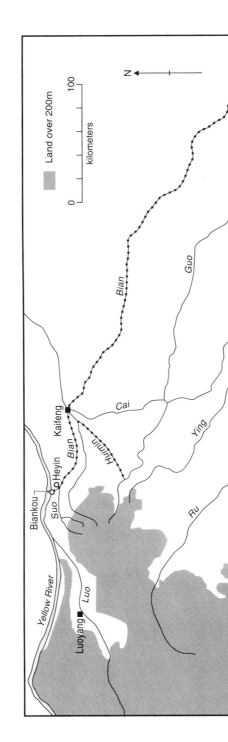

Map 15.4. The juncture of the Bian River canal with the Yellow River. *Source:* Huang Shengzhang, *Lishi dili lunji* (Beijing: Renmin CBS, 1982), p. 186; and Yao Hanyuan, *Zhongguo shuili shi gangyao* (Beijing: Shuili dianli CBS, 1987), p. 261.

Zhang had scarcely given up the arguments that had been his some fifteen years earlier, as always connecting the defense of the Bian to that of public finances. The irony of the passing of time, however, was that it was for precisely the same motives as those of the old commissioner that the Bian was being threatened: since it was not navigable round the year, it caused disorder in the movement of provisions to the capital. As events turned out, the project was to come to nothing, but the idea of maintaining a permanent traffic on the Bian remained the primary objective since another proposal – one that completed that for the opening of the Baigou – was made to solve the problem by joining the Huimin Canal and the Bian.[78] Even after the departure of the reformers, the authorities were looking for a solution, and this solution, once found, was to save the Bian while condemning the Yellow River.

Between 1075 and 1076 a new debate was launched over the question of a work-site for the scouring of the canal that would make the "Bian limpidly clear" (qing Bian 清汴). It was a matter of diverting toward the Bian from reservoirs to the west of the capital waters that had only a slight load of suspended sediment. In 1078, when the Yellow River took a more northerly course, this project, which had been temporarily abandoned, was reactivated and approved, and the work was done in forty-five days – at the very beginning of 1079. A canal was opened on the Luo above its juncture with the Yellow River and its course ran south of this latter in such a way that it joined the Bian at a point downstream of Biankou 汴口, where each year this canal was relinked with the Yellow River.[79] In the course of these debates, Fan Ziyuan 范子淵 (n.d.) submitted a memorial of ten points, the first eight of which emphasized the advantages to putting an end to the supplying of the waters of the Bian from the Yellow River. The yearly work at Biankou to establish or suppress the junction would be saved. So would the outlays for the hydraulic protection of the capital. There would be less damage to the dikes of the Bian. There would be reduced danger for navigation. There would be permanent traffic all through the year. The Bian would be connected to the network of the Jing 金水 and the Luo, allowing the movement of southeastern products to the region west of the capital. And the permanent problem of maintaining the same level in the waters of the canal and the Yellow River would end.[80]

---

[78] Feng Jing's 馮京 project. See SHY, "Shihuo," 61/101.

[79] On the story of the junction between the Luo and the Bian see Furubayashi, "Waterway engineering on the Bian River," pp. 163–70.

[80] XZCB, j. 297, month 3 (21/7224).

The most convinced supporters of this project thus put forward arguments that presented the Yellow River as a scourge. It seems that this was the right sort of rhetoric, since criticisms of a technical nature that underlined the strictly geographical difficulties of the undertaking were hardly paid any attention. Thus An Tao 安燾 (n.d.) pointed out without effect that the Suo 索河, whose bed was lower than that of the Bian over a distance of twenty kilometers, could not supply the canal as claimed, which indicated that there was a major risk of inadequate water supply; he added that since the filtering basins for the waters (*shen shui tang* 滲水塘) were joined to the Yellow River they remained threatened by the deposition of sediment and by peak discharges, and that, on account of the topography, the locks could only control the outflow in an imperfect fashion.[81] Notwithstanding these facts, the joining of the Bian and the Luo was to stay at the center of political and hydraulic debates until the end of the dynasty. While discussions about abandoning this junction began again in 1089 and ended in the return of the waters of the Yellow River into the Bian in 1090, this was because there was a threat from the peak discharges of the Yellow River and the administration was struggling to face up to the crisis. It was not because it believed that there was any positive advantage for the Bian in changing the system by which it was being fed. On the contrary, it seems that after 1094 the benefits of a "limpidly clear Bian" were returned to the primary place, and that this led in 1097 to the implementation of a new connection with the Luo and the closing of Biankou.[82] The waters of the Yellow River were thus barred from any outlet to the south until the decision of Du Chong in 1128.

The Yellow River – a watercourse not utilized for the transport of the tribute grain since 1059; a massive consumer of labor power and matériel, especially after 1048; an obstacle, on account of its heavy deposition of sediment, to the regular transport of the supplies that were, after the end of the 1060s, a new financial imperative – was now no more than a liquid and capricious frontier, fit only to serve as the rampart that certain opponents of the reforms, distrustful of the military authorities in Hebei, had, ever since 1048, wanted to see it become. Some weeks before the great flood at Shanghu, and at a time when, at his suggestion and that of Cheng Lin, the administration was undertaking a redivision of the military regions of Hebei, Xia Song 夏竦 (985–1051) stressed the danger of the army possessing too much power. In his eyes, the mass of the water made it possible to limit the role played by the military commanders, and hence

---

[81] Ibid., month 3 (21/7224–25).
[82] Yao Hanyuan, *History of water control in China*, p. 259.

their arrogance, since it was capable in and of itself of accomplishing the mission of defending the territory against enemies.[83] If I may be permitted so to express it, the defensive program of 1128 had thus been determined eighty years before being put into effect by Du Chong.

On balance, the strategic decisions that guided the birth of the Southern Song dynasty (1127–1279) confirmed that the concept of a river frontier had imposed itself in the manner suggested. Those in command were scarred by the repeated raids of enemy cavalry forces, and many of them saw the Yangzi as the new line of defense for the empire; few were inclined to preach a return to the northern plain. Even to those who judged it to be essential for the court to be north of the Huai, establishing it again at Kaifeng seemed hardly to deserve consideration, for it appeared evident to everyone that a natural barrier was a necessary condition for the protection of the capital, and hence the stabilization of the situation. Thus it was that Zong Ze 宗澤 (1060–1128), Du Chong's predecessor as governor of Kaifeng, at least initially wanted to found a new capital at Chang'an 長安 after the sack of Kaifeng. He was of the opinion that from the great northwestern city the dynasty would have been able to regain the allegiance of the rebel commanders in the great plain and recover the two sovereigns held prisoner by the enemy, who was incapable of deploying his forces westward.[84] As is well known, several victorious attacks led from the Yangzi, and equally, no doubt, the prudence of the Jin, who found themselves in difficulties when far removed from their bases, led to a compromise that made the Huai the new northern frontier of the Southern Song. From this time on, physiographical reality and military and diplomatic strategy combined to make a part of this river a new branch of the Yellow River, and geography made this frontier in a certain sense into a natural one. In order for this convergence between nature and sociopolitical factors to happen, however, it had been necessary for the values attached to the Yellow River to be redefined throughout the course of the eleventh century.

Our intention has been to show how political and financial history was able to determine as much as it did the decisions to be made with respect to the environment, and we have sought to discover indications of the downgrading of the Yellow River from political memorials, which offer materials in abundance. It is self-evident that this is not the only path, and that it would be appropriate to look in literature for themes that make clear

---

[83] *XZCB, j.* 164 (12/3947–48).

[84] Zong Ze, "Qi du Chang'an shu" [Request to establish the Capital at Chang'an], *Zong Ze ji* [Collected works of Zong Ze] (Hangzhou: Zhejiang guji CBS, 1984), pp. 10–11.

the new images of the Yellow River. Yoshioka has tried to do this, using the poems of Ouyang Xiu as his point of departure.[85] Far from the literati-officials, however, there are other domains awaiting exploration, beginning with that of religious practices that were developed around water and the river. The importance has been noted of the sacrifices intended to conse-crate the dikes restored under the emperor Zhenzong, and Su Che 蘇轍 (1039–1112) himself spoke of the significance of the Daoist rituals that accompanied the great programs of work in 1089 designed to improve the Ergu.[86] These beliefs and practices, which created the very order of the world, without question determined the support that a project could at-tract, or its absence; they influenced the ability of the authorities to mobi-lize the population; and they obliged the emperor himself – the emperor more than anyone else – to conceive of the policy of improving the Yellow River within the vast context of the mutations of the world with which his action or his refusal to act were interlinked.

In 1050 the emperor felt astonishment at a commentary on the hexa-gram *Wuwang* 無妄 – symbolizing the absence of causes, or calamities – and asked, "How can one say that for disasters associated with the hexagram *Wuwang* the absence of medicine has a happy outcome?" Yang An'guo 楊安 國 (n.d.) thereupon replied with an example:

> Today the Yellow River has broken through its dikes. For fifty years soldiers and civilian population have been on the registers for labor services. The expenditures that sap the resources of the empire have hardly ever ceased, yet the Great River has still not regained its [old] bed. . . . Your servant is of the view that the misfortunes [inherent] in the Yellow River and the barbarians go back to ancient times, and it is thus fitting that, just as Yao and Shun exerted themselves to conform with the aspirations of their people, [Your Majesty] should practice the perfecting of virtue at the appropriate moment, and the catastrophe will disappear of itself. It is for this reason that an absence of medicine has a happy outcome.[87]

Such a text points to both change and to the perception of change. It reminds us to how great an extent the people of that time paid attention not only to developments but, one might say, to the nature of these devel-opments. Catastrophes and disfunctions of the environment were so many

---

[85] Yoshioka, *Yellow River*, pp. 371–89.

[86] Su Che, "Beijing nan kai Erguhe daochang qingci" [Green petition for the Daoist ceremony to be held in celebration of the opening of the Ergu River south of the Northern Capital], *Luancheng ji* [Collected works of Luancheng], *j.* 34 (Shanghai: Shanghai guji CBS, 1987), vol. 2, p. 750.

[87] *XZCB, j.* 169, month 11 (12/4064).

negative signs for the holder of power; but it would seem that the political and economic mutations that modified this power were imagined in this selfsame framework of thought, and obeyed the same values. It was not solely because the river had overflowed its banks that contemporaries perceived the existence of a crisis; it was doubtless also because it was thanks to this breakpoint that it was possible to read most exactly the change in behavior and in values of a power that had been called upon to reorganize itself to meet the unending challenges of the world.

(Translated by Mark Elvin)

16

Official Thinking on Environmental Issues and the State's Environmental Roles in Eighteenth-Century China

HELEN DUNSTAN

INTRODUCTION

Let us begin with a snapshot – a moment from routine local government decision making caught in a bureaucratic document. This document shows how in 1727 at least three levels of the Zhejiang provincial hierarchy considered a petition from some local "fishing households" proposing a scheme for biological control of the waterweed that repeatedly obstructed the important irrigation functions of Hangzhou's West Lake.

The idea of the "fishing households" was both simple and self-interested. To obviate the need for laborious human interventions to remove the waterweed, they proposed to stock the lake with "weed fish," which would eat the first shoots of the weed as they appeared. To fund this undertaking, "advantageous both to public and to private interests," the petitioners requested an official loan. The recommendation of the local and regional authorities, recorded in our document, was that the petitioners be lent 300 taels, on the following understandings: first, that the loan would be repaid when the grown fish were sold; second, that the petitioners would reinvest a portion of their profit in maintaining the fish stock; third, that the petitioners would be liable to punishment if they failed to keep the lake waterweed-free; and fourth, that they should pay an annual rent for using

The archival material used in this essay was obtained during a 1993 research visit to China funded by grants from the U.S. National Endowment for the Humanities, an independent federal agency. I thank both the Endowment and the staff of the First Historical Archives in Beijing. Thanks are due also to the Shanxi Prosperous Chemical Industries Group Ltd. (Yuncheng, Shanxi) for permitting me access to its records room; and to Mark Elvin, Shiba Yoshinobu, and other Hong Kong conference participants for valuable comments on an earlier version of this essay.

the lake waters. A problem arose, however, out of the "public" status of West Lake. Reserving fishing rights in the lake for the petitioners would have meant depriving the general public of its accustomed access, thereby creating anger and endless disputes. A fish weir was therefore to be established in the inner section of the lake for the "weed fish," while the area near the shores would be left open to the public.[1]

Prima facie, the above snapshot shows the Zhejiang regional bureaucracy in what might now be considered quite a favorable light, close both to the people and to nature. Quickly recognizing a private business initiative for what it was, the authorities proposed both to cooperate with the petitioners and to back their scheme financially, while paying due regard to the claims of the broader public. More relevant to the topic of this chapter, the authorities were supporting a business venture whose ostensible purpose was to control the growth of harmful weeds without recourse to toxic substances. Here indeed was "appropriate technology," and a weed killer innocent of silent springs.

It would be premature, on the basis of one document, to hail the eco-friendly eighteenth-century Chinese official as a role model for contemporary bureaucrats. Still less should we draw overoptimistic inferences from the general perception that traditional Chinese government was essentially a matter of philosophically trained administrators (administrators trained, that is to say, in a rational humanistic doctrine which yet recognized the limitations of man's place in the cosmos) presiding over what was, in an obvious if naive sense, a nature-based economy. The modest purpose of this chapter is not to construct a single image of the eighteenth-century Chinese (or Manchu) administrator in his environmental aspect; nor, even, is it to assemble all the evidence that can be found of environmental insight on the part of Qing officials. Rather, it is to view some eighteenth-century official thought and action at close quarters, so as to formulate a nuanced, and therefore, one hopes, realistic provisional evaluation. If the present chapter is ambivalent about the degree of environmental wisdom shown by Qing officialdom, this no doubt reflects in part the specific characteristics of the period under examination: a period of rapid population growth in which the moral imperative for officialdom seemed to be to lead the people in providing for their own subsistence. The limits of expansion, although clearly sensed, were only gradually becoming manifest.

---

[1] Wang Jun, "Memorandum *re* clearing *feng* 葑 weed from West Lake," in He Changling 賀長齡, comp., *Huangchao jingshi wenbian* 皇朝經世文編 [A statecraft anthology of our august dynasty], hereafter *Statecraft anthology*, 8 vols. (1873 edition. Preface dated 1826. Reprinted, Taipei, 1964), *j.* 116, p. 23a–b.

16.1. OFFICIAL ATTITUDES

It goes without saying that there was no word in the late traditional Confucian-trained administrator's lexicon directly corresponding to the modern word "environment." In a broad sense, and to confine ourselves for the moment to the orthodox view, the environment within which the Confucian-trained administrator knew he operated was the quite literally anthropocentric, gendered cosmos – Heaven (male) above, Earth (female) below, mankind (male-dominated) in the middle. The governing power in this triad was Heaven, which not only was the creative (generative) force, but also had an effective will, and fundamentally benevolent intentions toward mankind (or indeed life in general, but in the event of interspecies clashes of interest, it was human life that counted). Earth's role was to bring forth what Heaven generated, and to support and nourish; while the possibility of Earth's having an independent will was never, to my knowledge, raised, Earth was often represented as sharing in Heaven's benevolence toward living beings (meaning especially man). Explicit references to the division of labor between Heaven and Earth, and to their commonality of sentiment, occur frequently in later traditional bureaucratic documents; "Heaven generates and Earth brings to completion" (*Tian sheng di cheng* 天生地成) and "Heaven and Earth love life" (*Tian Di ai sheng* 天地愛生) are representative clichés.

In particular, however, Earth was possessed of *li* 利 (literally, benefits or profits), as in the phrase *dili* 地利, best understood as referring to the productive potential of the physical earth, intended for man's benefit. Granted (where relevant) the necessary climatic conditions, sent by Heaven, it was up to man to invest toil and ingenuity in realizing Earth's potential, thereby bringing forth the means of mankind's sustenance, and creating an admirable material civilization fit to awe barbarians. The state justified its existence by supposedly leading society in this endeavor, and considerable vigor was indeed expected at least of the Qing administrator in "enriching [his people] as a prerequisite to teaching them [morality]" (*xian fu hou jiao* 先富後教).[2] The state, however, also had its own claims on resources, and exploited some of them in its own interests.

Earth's potential classically took vegetable form (above all crops, but also forest products, food for edible or otherwise useful fauna, and so on), and

[2] For the expression *xian fu hou jiao*, an allusion to *Lunyu* 論語 [The Analects of Confucius] 13.9, see Yang Chun, "Life of His Honor Mr. Yang, prefect of Quzhou," in *Statecraft anthology*, *j.* 115, p. 3a.

the never-ending cycle of productive and nonproductive phases characteristic of plant life provided a model which could be applied to the mineral
kingdom also. Mineral resources, from salt to silver, were not necessarily
conceived as having been (to all intents and purposes) created once and
for all, and therefore as being nonrenewable. While the common sense of
official copper mine administrators was that the exhaustion of the ores at a
particular site meant the end of a story, one Manchu governor-general was
still capable of writing, in 1734, that "copper, zinc, the precious metals, and
tin are all produced by congelation of Earth's ethers (*di qi ning cheng* 地氣
凝成). When this one falls into decline, that one is rising into fullness; when
that one falls into decline, this one is rising into fullness. If one exploits
them turn and turn about, one can truly avoid lack and the exhaustion [of
the stock of any given metal]."[3]

It was common knowledge that in this broad cosmological scheme of
things, mankind could cause temporary impairments in the conditions
which normally sustained its welfare. Just as a descent group's ancestors
were basically on its side but might still punish if offended, so Heaven and
Earth were basically on mankind's side, but did not hesitate to send down
punishments and warnings. These were typically climatic aberrations, such
as droughts, and could result in vast populations suffering for the presumed transgressions of Heaven's son (the emperor), or one of his representatives within the hierarchy of regional administration. In addition to
these orthodox assumptions, pervasive elite and "popular" quasi-scientific
or religious belief systems (notably geomancy) no doubt disposed many an
individual administrator to trace specific environmental misfortunes to
invisible processes set off by human offenses or defaults.

The knowledge that there could be cosmological or religious explanations for certain adverse climatic or other environmental phenomena
formed part of the cognitive framework within which official life was lived,
but absolutely did not dominate the everyday consciousness of territorial
administrators. When remedial rituals were required, they performed
them, yet ritual action can have consumed only a very small proportion of
the average local or regional official's time. For no one has it been truer
that "the proper study of mankind is man" than for the Confucian scholar-
official. For the rest of the chapter I shall be concerned with perceptible
man–environment interactions brought about by desires on the part of
both state and society to exploit Earth's potential to the best possible
advantage. Even here, one senses that official expertise lay far more in the

---

[3] Emida, "Memorial asking leave to open mines and extract ore for minting," in *Statecraft
anthology*, j. 52, pp. 16b–17a.

management of human affairs than in even indigenous environmental sciences.

It is true that one finds plenty of references to natural structures and forces, and to the ecological chain reactions set off by human activity, in official texts discussing practical economic and environmental problems. For example, He'nan was once said to be particularly rich in grain production because it "lies in the center of the [Chinese] world, and has level and extensive arable, while the veins of its soil (*tumai* 土脈) are deep and rich." Explaining the propensity to drought of the Wei valley in Shaanxi, and, therefore, the poverty of the region's agricultural economy, Bi Yuan wrote that "in Shaanxi the earth is thick while the waters run deep. The *qi* 氣 (ethers, vital forces) of mountains and marshes do not interpenetrate, [and so] there is ever the calamity of unbroken sunshine." A directive by Chen Hongmou 陳宏謀 reflects the widespread contemporary belief in an association between locust plagues and waterlogged terrain – along with the less than scientific explanation for the putative phenomenon that was common in Qing China:

> In He'nan last year the [Yellow] River rose unusually high, and there was widespread inundation. Fish and suchlike creatures deposited their spawn in all low-lying and waterlogged locations, and wherever water plants grew thickly, or rushes and reeds were dense. Meanwhile, the winter snows have not fallen everywhere, and once the springtime thaw has come, [the spawn] will turn into locust grubs. If the grubs are not exterminated promptly, they will eventually emerge and jump about, and then grow wings and turn into locusts.

Finally, some notion of the role of using moisture in soil salinization may conceivably be reflected in the following comment by the magistrate of a southern He'nan county that was prone to flooding. "Much of the Ruyang 汝陽 arable is poor and saline. It is in the course of things that when water is ascendant, soil suffers."[4]

---

[4] *Gongzhong zhupi zouzhe, Caizheng, Cangchu* 宮中硃批奏摺、財政、倉儲 [Imperially rescripted palace memorials: fiscal affairs, granary reserves], hereafter *Memorials: granary reserves*, First Historical Archives (Beijing) Ya'ertu, Qianlong (QL) 6(1741)/4/29; Bi Yuan, "Memorial on agriculture, irrigation, and animal husbandry in Shaanxi" (1782), in *Statecraft anthology*, j. 36, p. 4a; Chen Hongmou, "Directive on precautionary action regarding locust grubs" (1752), in Chen Hongmou, 培遠堂偶存稿：文檄 *Peiyuan tang oucun gao: wenxi* [Chance Survivals from the Peiyuan Hall: directives], hereafter *Chance survivals* (n.d.), j. 31, p. 8a; and 1690 *Ruyang xianzhi* 汝陽縣志 [Gazetteer of Ruyang county], j. 4, p. 1b. For poetic evidence of the widespread nature of the belief about aquatic fauna, waterlogged or reed-covered terrain, and the genesis of locusts, see Zhang Yingchang 張應昌, comp., 清詩鐸 *Qing shiduo* [The bell of poetry: Qing dynasty], 2 vols. (Beijing, 1960), vol. 2, pp. 517, 519, 520, and 522. I owe the references to the *Qing shiduo* to Mark Elvin.

Examples of official consciousness of interactions between man and nature are well represented in the contributions to the present volume by Osborne (Chapter 7) and Vermeer (Chapter 8), as well as previous scholarship. Three additional examples, two of them from North China, will suffice. In 1736, the famous antiquarian Fang Bao 方苞 expressed concern that widespread tobacco cultivation was ruining prime land. Grain crops or vegetables planted on land that had been used to grow tobacco turned out bitter and inedible, he claimed. In 1792, the Shanxi governor wrote that reeds had ceased to grow on the southern margin of the great Xiezhou 解州 salt lake when extension of the area allotted for preparing brine caused "penetration by the salty ethers" (*luqi ziqin* 滷氣滋侵). By 1761, this same region's crucial runoff drainage channel was said to be silting up twice as quickly as in former years because, the local soil being "loose and easily detached," the extension of cultivation all over the hillsides was causing abnormally large quantities of soil and mud to be swept into the channel by its mountain tributaries after heavy rainfall. On the more constructive side, a sense of the need for environmental responsibility on officialdom's part is conveyed as follows in the preamble to one Qing conservationist report discussed below: "The ultimate true way of managing the countryside[5] is a sound method for both shewing loving-kindness to the folk and cherishing the things around them (*renmin aiwu* 仁民愛物)."[6]

Finally, as an example of a more extensive account of nature's workings, here is an eighteenth-century description of the role of the so-called Black River on the south side of the Xiezhou salt lake in generating brine ready for drawing into the "plots" into which the salt lake was divided, there to await crystallization:

It is on the Black River that the salt lake plots (*xidi* 畦地) depend for [their supply of brine for the technique known as] induction and exposure [to the sun] (*jiaoshai* 澆曬). The [river's] water is deep, and the mud by nature is pure black, hence the name "Black River." Suspended within the black mud are nitrous boards (*xiaoban* 硝板), the salty ethers (*luqi*) [given off by which]

[5] *Jingye*, from the phrase *tiguo jingye* 體國經野 at the beginning of the *Zhouli* [Rites of Zhou]. In its original context, this phrase appears to mean "dividing up the royal capital, and laying out the countryside." See William T. de Bary, *Waiting for the Dawn: A Plan for the Prince. Huang Tsung-hsi's "Ming-i-tai-fang lu"* (New York, 1993), pp. 128 and 222–23, n. 3.

[6] Fang Bao, *Fang Bao ji* 方苞集 [Collected works of Fang Bao], 2 vols. (Shanghai, 1983), vol. 2, p. 532; *Gongzhong zhupi zouzhe, Caizheng, Yanwu* 鹽物 [Imperially rescripted palace memorials: fiscal affairs, salt; hereafter *Memorials: salt*], First Historical Archives (Beijing), Feng Guangxiong QL 57 (1792)/1/12, and Sahadai QL 26 (1761)/10/25; Niu Yunzhen, "Report containing proposals for restricting access to the mountain forests," in *Statecraft anthology*, *j.* 38, p. 10a.

are very strong. These [boards] are the source of the salt industry.[7] The taste is both bitter and salty. Whenever rain has fallen, the water collects within the black mud, soaking until it has matured, at which point it is led into the plots. This is [the start of] the induction and exposure salt-production [process], and it takes very little effort. If [the Black River] becomes silted, the black mud is submerged by loess, and the salt ethers (*yanqi* 鹽氣) cannot rise. Even if there is some depth of water, its taste will be insipid and its nature weak.[8]

This last account comes from a salt administration gazetteer. Its length reflects the detailed knowledge necessary in a specialized administrative agency devoted to managing a large and valuable natural resource – and in any case, the 1776 memorial from which it seems to have been plagiarized acknowledges that the information was provided by the salt-plot owners and elderly local residents.[9] The role of local people in creating environmental consciousness emerges strikingly through Anne Osborne's splendid examples of articulated local elite understanding of the relationship between excessive reclamation and erosion in the Lower Yangzi highlands.[10] Of course, individuals who acquired such consciousness as resident members of agricultural communities, or even as paternalist absentees, presumably took it with them if they left their native county as officials. Yet my impression is that the more fragmentary articulations quoted above are more typical for eighteenth-century bureaucratic documents than rich and extensive expositions. Their undeveloped nature surely reflects the fact that Qing officials generally did their systematic thinking rather about human, and particularly administrative, problems. Discussions of how to collect the land tax both successfully and with maximum sensitivity to peasant interests can be detailed, logical, perceptive, and exhaustive. Environmental thinking was commonly attenuated by contrast.

---

[7] Literally, "the mother of the salt production." This account is remarkably close to the mark, given that it is uninformed by modern chemistry. *Xiaoban* (硝砭 or 板) is now recognized as being the popular name for the salt lake's underlying stratum of bloedite ($Na_2Mg(SO_4)_2 \cdot 4H_2O$, i.e., hydrous sodium magnesium sulfate). Depending on the seasonal temperature, mirabilite (hydrous sodium sulfate), thenardite (anhydrous sodium sulfate), or (in summer) magnesium sulfate and rich sodium chloride brine form above the bloedite stratum. See Li Zhulin 李竹林 and Huang Xuqun 黃徐羣, "Cong yanye dao huagong chanpin – jian'guo hou Yuncheng yanchi de juda bianhua" [From salt production to the products of chemical industry: great changes at the Yuncheng Salt Lake since the foundation of the People's Republic], *Shanxi wenshi ziliao* 山西文史資料 [Materials on the History and Culture of Shanxi] 82 (1992), p. 154. Today the salt lake is used almost exclusively for the production of mirabilite.

[8] Bo Nongqi 白農起, comp., *Hedong yanfa tiaoji ji* 河東鹽法調劑紀 [Record of adjustments in the Hedong salt administration] (1784), j. 2, p. 2a.

[9] *Memorials: salt*, Bayansan and Chang Ling QL 41/10/18.

[10] See Chapter 7 of the present volume.

Confucian humanism (or anthropocentrism) was all in favor of the
flourishing and propagation of the human species. For a region to be
"prosperous and teeming" was a positive phenomenon. However, while
consciousness of regional overcrowding can be traced back at least to the
Sui dynasty (A.D. 589–618),[11] it is well known that already by the 1740s, half
a century before the famous essay of "the Chinese Malthus" Hong Liangji 洪
亮吉 (1746–1809), growing population pressure, signaled by rising grain
prices, had come to be perceived as a *national* problem.[12] The potential
tension between population and resources was quite clearly seen: "population is becoming daily more abundant" was possibly the commonest cliché
of eighteenth-century official economic discourse, yet juxtaposed with it
one regularly finds some indication of awareness that the productive
capacity of the natural environment is ultimately limited. In the eighteenth
century, however, propensity to recognize the problem was not matched by
preparedness to see it as susceptible to radical remedial action by the state.
As far as I am aware, it was not until Wang Shiduo's 汪士鐸 diary entries for
1855–56 that any member of the Qing intelligentsia proposed systematic
measures to halt the growth of population.[13]

Officialdom certainly knew that poor (and even not-so-poor) families
sought to limit their numbers by infanticide or abandonment of neonates,
but such actions, being violations of basic Confucian values, had to
be counteracted by official prohibition, suasion, or officially sponsored
philanthropy, and could not be condoned.[14] Even popular customs
which tended to reduce the birth rate were not necessarily immune to
official disapproval. Thus in the nineteenth-century Canton delta, officials
actively attempted to suppress a local tradition that they perceived as

[11] I refer to the introduction of the category of "restricted localities": areas in which, owing to
land shortage, each able-bodied male's standard allocation under the "equal holdings
system" was reduced. See Denis Twitchett, *Financial Administration under the T'ang Dynasty*,
2d ed. (Cambridge, 1970), pp. 4 and 9.

[12] See, e.g., *Memorials: granary reserves*, Zhu Lunhan QL 6 (1741)/7/20 and Yang Xifu QL 13
(1748)/3/?, and the citations of one or both documents by Quan Hansheng 全漢昇,
Zhongguo jingji shi luncong 中國經濟史論叢 [Collected papers on Chinese economic history],
2 vols. (Hong Kong, 1972), vol. 2, pp. 496–97; and Madeleine Zelin, *The Magistrate's Tael:
Rationalizing Fiscal Reform in Eighteenth-Century Ch'ing China* (Berkeley, 1984), pp. 294–97.

[13] Wang's proposed measures included the death penalty for persons marrying under the age
of twenty-five (males) or twenty (females), as well as for a wide range of offenders, from
gamblers to students of Song Neo-Confucianism; the introduction of a tax incentive for
infanticide of second daughters; a limit of two sons per family; compulsory abortion; and
the creation of special institutions for the chaste. See Frank Dikötter, "The Limits of
Benevolence: Wang Shiduo (1802–1889) and Population Control," *Bulletin of the School of
Oriental and African Studies* 55.1 (1992), pp. 110–14.

[14] See, e.g., Zhao Hong'en 趙宏恩, *Yuhua tang Liang-Jiang pi'an* [Replies by the Liang-Jiang
governor-general to his subordinates, from the Yuhua Hall], pp. 1a–b, in Zhao Hong'en,

female resistance to marriage, but which in most cases involved only postponement of cohabitation and of the initiation of full conjugal relations.[15] Transgressions against the cosmological order had to be opposed; it was a rare Confucian-educated writer who glimpsed that the forces of population pressure were greater than this human construct, and threatened to overturn assumptions of the continuity of the familiar. Such an exceptional literatus had been Chen Qide 陳其德, who wrote a vivid eyewitness description of the natural disasters of the last years of the Ming dynasty (early 1640s). Overwhelmed by the spectacle of a calamity that had engulfed not only his native Zhejiang, but also much of northern and central China, he exclaimed, "Surely it cannot be that creation has multiplied too greatly, [so that] the present cruel blaze is being spread; or that the people's prodigality has reached the extreme, and the Supreme Lord's heart, grown weary of them, has cast them off to this extent!"[16]

And Wang Taiyue 王太岳, who served as Yunnan provincial administration commissioner in the 1770s, wrote a poem about the state-sponsored copper mines which provides an interesting parallel to some of Pierre-Étienne Will's material in its depiction of miners enduring denaturing conditions as they engaged in operations that (as we would say) nature had not intended.[17] After lamenting the loss of life caused by cave-ins resulting from desperate speculative digging as the tolerably accessible ores down the existing shafts became depleted, Wang observes:

> When the mountains and seas gestate wealth,
> The purpose, surely, is not to bring down disaster upon
> teeming life.
> *Yin* and *Yang* in-gather and give forth by turns,
> In every breath performing their role of creation.
> To take all that is made, without the sense to show
> restraint,
> Will be enough to wear out Heaven and Earth.[18]

Yuhua ji 玉華集 (1734); Angela Leung, "L'accueil des enfants abandonnés dans la Chine du bas-Yangzi aux XVIIe et XVIIIe siècles," *Études Chinoises* 4.1 (1985), pp. 16–29; and T'ien Ju-k'ang, *Male Anxiety and Female Chastity: A Comparative Study of Chinese Ethical Values in Ming-Ch'ing Times* (Leiden, 1988), pp. 28–31.

[15] Janice E. Stockard, *Daughters of the Canton Delta: Marriage Patterns and Economic Strategies in South China, 1860–1930* (Stanford, Calif., 1989), pp. 12–19 and 105–10.

[16] Chen Qide, "Zai huang jishi" [Record of calamity and famine], in 1882 *Tongxiang xianzhi* 桐鄉縣志 [Gazetteer of Tongxiang county], *j.* 20, p. 9a.

[17] See Chapter 9 of this volume.

[18] Wang Taiyue, "A copper mine lament," in Zhang Yingchang, comp., *Bell of poetry*, vol. 2, pp. 927–28 (translation with apologies to Mark Elvin, to whom I owe the reference).

In general, however, the big "what if . . ." and "what happens when . . ." questions seem not to have been pressed, at least in writing. Many eighteenth-century authors were capable of assuming that, for the span of future time that it made sense to think about, Heaven and Earth had in fact provided adequately for expanding humankind. Local administrators simply had to intensify their ingenuity and diligence in urging the people on to harder work while finding new sources of livelihood for them, and (where feasible) removing social impediments to the maximal realization of Earth's productive potential. Hu Baoquan 胡寶瑝 a probationary investigating censor in the 1740s, used arithmetic to show that the present situation was still perfectly manageable. Inasmuch as the Han dynasty population had peaked at some 59 million, and the Ming in its glory had had only about 65 million, whereas the present count stood at about 144 million, it did indeed appear that the contemporary population was double that of yore. But given that the empire's arable was about 8.5 million *qing*, and assuming that the least skillful farmer could achieve productivity adequate to nourish thirty people from one *qing*,[19] there was still the means to provide for up to 250 million people. Even if one subtracted 20 percent of the estimated output to allow for harvest failures, there would still be more than ample for the present population, even without imports from Vietnam and Siam. Later in the memorial that presents this calculation, Hu lists the policy initiatives that provincial chief administrators should consider as including "encouraging diligence in agriculture, promoting irrigation, instructing lazy farmers to till energetically, [so that] the annual harvest can be doubled; [and] turning barren soil into fertile land [so that] the Earth's potential is still richer."[20]

It is difficult to believe that provincial administrators, confronted with the concrete realities of specific regions, were always quite as simply optimistic, yet they too were more likely to embark on what Will felicitously calls "productivist adventures"[21] than to analyze the long-term problem. Provincial governor Bi Yuan's 畢沅 1782 blueprint for expansion in Shaanxi (a text mentioned also by Will) may serve to represent a very substantial genre of eighteenth-century official writing.[22]

[19] I.e., one person from every 3.3 *mu* – a realistic estimate for China's wet-rice regions, but surely overoptimistic as a national average! I am indebted to Eduard Vermeer for this interpretation of the passage.
[20] *Memorials: granary reserves*, Hu Baoquan QL 8 (1743)/6/28.
[21] Will, Chapter 9 of this volume.
[22] Ibid. As Will's account implies, there is nothing in this particular document to suggest a retreat from productivism. For a rich analysis of the whole genre, see Pierre-Étienne Will, "Développement quantitatif et développement qualitatif en Chine à la fin de l'époque impériale," in *Annales: Histoire, Sciences Sociales* 4 (1994), pp. 863–902.

Bi proposed a threefold program to help Shaanxi play its part in grappling with the nation's population problem. This would be done by "drawing on the full strength of the people in accordance with what suits the land, so as to reap the natural benefits." In the first place, Bi envisaged an official survey of the southern Shaanxi highlands so that their settlement could be put on a more systematic basis. This settlement, he implied, had previously been a spontaneous process of reclamation by rootless inmigrants from the central and upper Yangzi regions, Gansu, and He'nan, but the provincial administration had gained its first taste of implementing managed settlement at the time of the central Yangzi famine of 1778–79. At that time the Shaanxi authorities had settled over a hundred thousand people in the southern highlands; there was scope for them to settle many more.

Second, emboldened by the success of the recent restoration of the Longdong (Zheng-Bai) irrigation system,[23] Bi proposed to undertake a systematic, quantified survey of the potential for the restoration or creation of such systems throughout at least central Shaanxi. He enumerated those of the province's "great streams" that fed into the Yellow River (the Wei 渭 and its tributaries; the obliquely north–south Luo 洛); commented on their length; and suggested that there was no reason why – if only officialdom would be more public-spirited – they could not all be used to supply similar water distribution networks. When this was done, not only would "barren soil be transformed into good arable, and the farmers naturally reap the benefit of doubled yields"; the diversion of so much water into reservoirs and irrigation channels might also serve slightly to diminish the force of the water entering the Yellow River, thus indirectly benefiting the regions downstream.

Finally, having personally observed that the northern border grasslands still appeared perfectly lush, Bi planned an elaborate state-sponsored scheme to restore northwestern China's defunct stock-rearing industry of its ancient and celebrated glory. First – yet again – there was to be an official survey to determine the number of "camels, horses, oxen, and sheep" to be acquired for each county; then allocation of official "idle monies" to purchase the animals and hire skilled pastoralists to teach the people how to care for them; then "experimental" rearing of the animals by individual households, under the supervision of specially assigned petty officials; then division of the first year's offspring to provide, on one hand, for the repayment of the public funds, and on the other, for the permanent stock of each participant; and finally, a self-sustaining industry in which the

---

[23] See Will, Chapter 9 of this volume.

people would be free to sell the animals they raised, except for those necessary to maintain the stock, and for a tax of one beast in fifteen (one in ten for sheep). Once this scheme had proved its worth by enriching the economies of border region households, it was to be gradually extended first to the historical pasture lands of the interior, and finally to certain militarized zones, where it would strengthen the army's economic base.[24] While some features of Bi's stock-rearing plan are familiar from other contexts, it is perhaps unusual in its ambition and indifference to major economic risk.

Among the positive things that might be said about Bi's blueprint, and many others like it, are that they are bold, ingenious, and resourceful. Before mentioning the less happy aspects, it is necessary to point out two common characteristics of eighteenth-century Sino-Manchu developmental planning. These characteristics are probably limitations from an economic point of view, but potential saving graces from an environmentalist perspective.

In the first place, while the documents do not make an explicit conceptual distinction between expansion and growth, it is probably correct to say that overall it was more the former that their authors were pursuing. That is to say: it is not difficult to illustrate that eighteenth-century officials could recognize the desirability of increasing yields from given quantities of land; that the concept of output per capita was not completely alien to them; that the desirability of increasing output per capita was implicitly recognized; and that eighteenth-century officials were far from averse to increases in per capita income. Thus the consciousness of at least some regional administrators matched the existence of "pockets of growth" in the later traditional Chinese economy.[25] In certain specific and/or regional contexts, their objective was *growth*, sometimes of a crude and simple kind (output per capita will rise if idlers exert more muscle power), but sometimes based on ideas about using resources, including labor, to improved advantage. However, the central driving force behind all their discussions – consciousness of population pressure – was not such as to create perception of the need for more output *per person* as the central problem (even though, as Mark Elvin has illustrated, when technological means of raising output per person were to hand, they could win the acclamation of the literati).[26] It was

[24] Bi Yuan, "Memorial on agriculture," in *Statecraft anthology, j.* 36, pp. 4a–5a.
[25] Cf. Madeleine Zelin, "Capital Accumulation and Investment Strategies in Early Modern China: The Case of the Furong Salt Yard," *Late Imperial China* 9.1 (1988), p. 117. For a fuller exploration than can be given here of the expansion vs. growth issue in late-imperial China, see Will, "Développement quantitatif."
[26] Mark Elvin, "Skills and Resources in Late Traditional China," in Dwight H. Perkins, ed., *China's Modern Economy in Historical Perspective* (Stanford, Calif., 1975), pp. 102–03.

land, not labor, that was in short supply, and therefore had to be induced to yield more per unit. Overall, the deliberators were trapped into the pursuit of what might be called defensive expansion: producing more in order to supply a swollen population. The vision of a globally enriched society was a Confucian piety but not a realistic goal.

Secondly and concomitantly, while contemporary growth strategies rely heavily on encouraging the mass consumption of products that are not strictly necessary for sustaining human life, there existed among Qing administrators the opposite tendency of perceiving unnecessary popular consumption as wasteful, and of wishing to restrict if not eliminate it. This attitude, although both readily explicable by the circumstances and often motivated by the best paternalist intentions, ran counter to the drive to increase the sources of livelihood. It is not that Qing officialdom had no conception of the economic case for unnecessary consumption. To the contrary, diversified regional development plans could reflect an implicit acceptance that unnecessary products (sugar, for example) would be consumed, to the benefit of those producing them and, thereby, of society at large.[27] However, it came at least equally naturally to many a Qing administrator to adopt the attitude exemplified by one Manchu provincial governor in 1741. In the preamble to a memorial discussing how to promote the "community granary" system in He'nan as a way of saving grain against bad harvests, he deplored the tendency of He'nan peasants to celebrate good harvests by turning wheat into yeast for liquor preparation, selling grain "as they like," building extensions to their homes, renovating temples, and holding religious festivals. All these, he indicated, were wasteful uses of the harvest, and "devoid of benefit." Part of the activity to which he objected was no doubt simply a matter of peasants directly consuming extra grain; but also condemned by implication was a certain potential for income supplementation and seasonal or year-round livelihood in food-processing (including North China's substantial liquor industry), construction, the manufacture of religious goods, and the supplying of materials for these activities.[28] As Amartya Sen might have seen it, preoccupation with the red herring of "food availability" in famine years could thus distract administrators from the more important task of boosting the "exchange entitlements" of society's more vulnerable households.[29] However one may judge the anti-waste approach as anti-famine strategy, the perception that assuring basic needs must override society's instincts for diversified consumption is cer-

[27] See, e.g., *Memorials: granary reserves*, Tuoyong QL 7 (1742)/11/9.
[28] *Memorials: granary reserves*, Ya'ertu QL 6/4/29.
[29] Amartya Sen, *Poverty and Famines: An Essay on Entitlement and Deprivation* (Oxford, 1982).

tainly at odds with the modern Western pattern of industrial development, with its advantages and curses.

In 1739, a certain investigating censor advocated that the chief administrators of all provinces whose regional products included such ideal famine foods as the Fujian sweet potato or Guizhou dryland rice should take steps to disseminate seeds and cultivation information to other provinces, so as to "share the potential with the rest of the empire." He concluded with the words: "It will be possible to bring all wasteland under cultivation, and to have all substances that save from famine at [the people's] disposal; it would seem that this will benefit the people's livelihood and do it no harm."[30] In fact, as everybody knows, reclamation of hillside "wasteland" with imported miracle crops during the eighteenth century did untold environmental damage in the Yangzi and Han River drainages, through soil erosion and the consequent silting of riverbeds. Similarly, blanket orders to undertake innovative irrigation projects, such as those envisaged for Shaanxi by Bi Yuan, led to soil salinization and reduced yield in the Great Leap Forward (1958–60).[31] Lush pasture can likewise be ruined by overgrazing. Section 16.2 of this chapter will further explore the environmental sensitivity or insensitivity of selected Qing official development initiatives. But it will also cast the net a little wider.

16.2 FROM ATTITUDES TO ACTIONS

A full typology of interactions in the state–society–environment triangle would have to include a large number of possibilities. The state might provide leadership to society in (a) preserving or restoring the environmental conditions necessary for accustomed levels of production; and (b) making the environment yield extra sustenance, thereby inducing environmental change. Society might (and, indeed, more commonly did) spontaneously induce change in the environment by intensifying or expanding cultivation or other forms of exploitation, or by altering the manner of its exploitation; the state would be left to make (or fail to make) a conservationist response. The state itself might exploit, and therefore influence, both society and environment in its own economic interests. Features of the

---

[30] *Memorials: granary reserves*, Liu Fang'ai QL 4/4/29.
[31] Ho Ping-ti, *Studies on the Population of China, 1368–1953* (Cambridge, Mass., 1959), pp. 145–51, 188, and 273; Nicholas R. Lardy, "The Chinese Economy under Stress, 1958–1965," in Roderick MacFarquhar and John K. Fairbank, eds., *The Cambridge History of China*, vol. 14 (Cambridge, 1987), p. 370.

environment might change, apparently spontaneously, leaving both state and society with the problem of response. Finally, groups within society might take their own measures to conserve or restore their own environment for their own uses; depending on the context, the state might ignore, encourage, assist, or repress such grass-roots efforts.

It is also necessary to recognize that official measures that would have served to protect sections of the natural environment were not always inspired by conservationist concerns. It is conceivable that, all in all, measures whose motivation was the maintenance of law and order or even frontier defense did more environmental good (or at least had the potential for it) than those born of environmental consciousness. Of course, security and defense considerations could also lead to the adoption of environmentally destructive measures. In one situation, military concerns could inspire afforestation plans; in another, the burning down of forests.[32] To ignore the environmental impact of non-environmental and non-economic policies would leave us with a partial view of the late-imperial state in its environmental roles. It would also deprive us of an opportunity to watch officials grappling with an apparent conflict of policy objectives (social order vs. defensive economic expansion) that is itself relevant to understanding the priorities of Qing administration.

Unfortunately, space does not permit even a superficial exploration of all the above possibilities. My approach will rather be to scrutinize a small number of documents that show officials thinking in environmentally relevant ways; these documents correspond to three of the above forms of interaction. We shall, so to speak, quiz two regional officials about the environmental sensitivity of their development programs; watch one county magistrate responding to the threat posed by society to local forests; and notice, again, Hu Baoquan, somewhat later on in life, urging that, in the interests of security, public exploitation of a certain tract of wilderness should be forbidden. Such an approach will not provide us with a secure foundation for generalizing about the environmental consciousness of late-imperial officials. It is, however, one possible answer to the problem of combining depth and breadth: a searching look at a few documents is perhaps better preparation for sound evaluation than generalization based on scanning many.

[32] For a late Ming example of border defense concerns inspiring proposals for tree planting, see Dong Qichang 董其昌, comp., *Shenmiao liuzhong zoushu huiyao* 神廟留中奏疏彙要 [Collection of the most important memorials retained within the palace during Shenzong's reign] (1624. Reprinted, Beijing, 1937), "Bingbu" [Board of Military Affairs], *j.* 2, pp. 9b–10a. For examples of the military destruction of forest cover, see section 16.2.2 below; and Osborne, Chapter 7 of this volume.

16.2.1. ENVIRONMENTALLY SENSITIVE
STATE DEVELOPMENT PROGRAMS?

I have selected for examination two development programs that, prima facie, would earn green stars because their authors seek to promote reforestation and are concerned about soil quality or conservation. Both authors recognize that the environment is vulnerable; they seem, indeed, more sensitive toward the environment than they are toward the local populations, whose compliance is to be more or less coerced through penalties. Yet in each case the specifically environmental thinking is unsystematic, while the systematic nature of the second program creates an environmental hazard which its author fails to address.

Yu Sen 俞森, from Zhejiang, was He'nan province's assistant surveillance commissioner with special responsibility for watercourses during 1687–90.[33] It was presumably while in this post that he devised a socio-economically utterly unrealistic scheme by which He'nan's recovery from the devastation of the late Ming rebellions would be enhanced by a mass afforestation program. The main purpose of this afforestation would be to provide individual households with important economic assets. It would therefore, in Yu's opinion, *have* to be done on a mass basis, since otherwise,

> When the Master of Works is looking for great trees,[34] and throughout the kingdom there are none to be found, save for one family that has them, this is the beginning of disaster [for that family]. . . . When the whole neighborhood is overgrown yet ripe fruits are a-dangling, even a fenced garden plot with broken willows[35] will become a target at which all take aim. ... If within one village there is but one family that grows trees, or if within one county there is but one village growing them, the benefit is small and the risk great, [so that] one cannot but pay heed to it. If the whole county is growing trees, the benefit will be extensive; if the whole prefecture is growing them, the benefit will be still more extensive; if the entire province grows them, the benefit will be broadest of all, and what worry need there be about disaster being concentrated upon any individual [community or family]?

In other words, any family or village which was alone in owning trees risked attracting the aggression of rapacious state or wretched neighbors; best,

---

[33] 1735 *He'nan tongzhi* 河南通志 [Gazetter of He'nan province] (1882 ed.), *j.* 35, p. 16a.
[34] An allusion to *Mengzi* 孟子 [The Book of Mencius] IB:9, referring to the search for timber for palace construction.
[35] There are successive allusions here to *Shi* 詩 [The Book of Odes], Odes nos. 174 and 100.

therefore, to spread the burden of the state's cupidity while eliminating envy by promoting universal ownership.

To achieve his vision, Yu wanted every household, irrespective of status, to be ordered to plant thirty jujube trees, thirty persimmons, and one hundred each of elms and willows. Penalties would be inflicted "without mercy" on households which failed to comply; households which exceeded these quotas or which "broadly planted miscellaneous trees" would be rewarded with an honorific banner. In view of the grave land-shortage in late-imperial China, such a scheme could only have been thinkable in the aftermath of the severe depopulation mentioned in Yu's preamble.[36] His discussion, with its literary flavor, is nonetheless akin to the typical utopian musing of the late seventeenth-century out-of-office would-be practical administrator; Yu himself recognized that he did not have the authority to carry out his plan. His discussion merits our attention chiefly because three of Yu's "eight advantages of growing trees" are environmentalist by implication, although their content remains limited and not very scientific.

As Yu perceived it, the main case for growing trees was economic and, in a broad sense, cultural. To summarize five of his eight "advantages": trees produced far higher yields (by volume – he failed to specify of what) per unit area than cereal crops; the fruits and nuts brought trading profits in good years and might still be available as famine foods when the agricultural staples failed; the availability of timber made possible superior dwellings; afforestation would provide an ample supply of wood for coffins and utensils; and finally, there were the special benefits of growing mulberries. Obvious as some of these points may be, it was important to Yu to spell them out. More interesting, however, is what the remaining three points disclose about Yu's own environmental consciousness, or, to be more specific, the extent of his concern about erosion.

First, in pointing out that afforestation would solve the fuel problem, Yu mentioned that the poor were driven by their lack of fuel to "pick up horse droppings and dig grass out by its roots." He did not, unfortunately, explain why this was a bad thing. An environmentalist would say that widespread reliance on animal manure and whole grass plants for fuel in a once-wooded area both reflects an advanced stage of environmental degradation and contributes to further deterioration. It is most probable that Yu knew both that the manure could have been used to conserve soil fertility and

---

[36] Did He'nan still seem depopulated as late as the late 1680s? Cultivated acreage figures from one southern He'nan county suggest that it could well have. Ordinary registered cultivated acreage in Ruyang was about 5,901 *qing* in 1608. Officially cut to about 576 *qing* in 1646, it had recovered to only about 3,057 by 1690. 1690 *Gazetteer of Ruyang, j.* 4, pp. 7b, 10b, 13b.

that destruction of the remaining vegetation was speeding erosion; but he did not articulate this understanding. He possibly intended no more than to convey the seriousness of the fuel shortage. This passage could, therefore, be read as an example of a Chinese official noticing an environmental problem without any clear awareness of the principles involved.

Second, however, Yu's appreciation of the usefulness of the willow in hydraulic engineering reflects direct concern with controlling soil erosion in one specific context. "The soil of He'nan is not firm," he wrote, "and river banks are liable to become eroded. If one plants rows of willow trees, the roots will intertwine, [so that] the protective dike is solid. At what point will it be possible for [it] to be washed away?"[37]

If this observation seems a little narrow, Yu's final comment transcends the bounds of physical environmentalism. He took as his starting point the traditional belief that there were two possible principles determining how the cosmological "five phases" (wood, fire, soil, metal, and water) succeeded to each other: the "generation" principle (wood generates fire, fire generates soil, etc.), and the "conquest" principle (water conquers fire, fire conquers metal, etc.).[38] He deduced from his understanding of the interrelation of the two principles the general proposition, environmentally unexceptionable, that there is a positive correlation between lack of tree cover and susceptibility of the soil to wind erosion; but this was only a step toward his final claim, which was that there is a positive correlation between wind erosion and a decline in civilized behavior. He wrote:

> The functioning of the five phases [is such that] failure to conquer means failure to generate. If now trees are scarce, wood will not conquer soil, and the nature of the soil will be light and easily blown away, while the human character will become crude and fierce. If trees are plentiful, the soil will not fly up, and men will revert to refinement and good order.

This might seem quaint, until we remember that Yu had quite possibly read or heard descriptions of He'nan in the last years of the Ming associating drought-parched soil, dust storms, and marauding rebel armies. His environmentalist social psychology is thus not necessarily without representational value. It would, however, have been more solidly grounded had he

---

[37] For Ming examples of the practice of planting willow trees on dikes, see Helen Dunstan, *The Ho-tung Salt Administration in Ming Times*, Ph.D. dissertation, Cambridge University (1980), p. 62; and Morita Akira, "Water Control in Zhehdong during the Late Mirng," translated by Mark Elvin and Tamura Keiko, in *East Asian History* 2 (1991), p. 60. In the latter example, which comes from southern China, camphor laurels and catalpas are recommended along with willows.

[38] On the origin and significance of these and related beliefs, see Angus Graham, *Disputers of the Tao: Philosophical Argument in Ancient China* (La Salle, Ill., 1989), pp. 325–56.

been able to set out the physical mechanisms linking deforestation with drought and wind erosion, and these with breakdown of the social order. He was on the right lines, but not demonstrably for the right reasons.[39]

Chen Hongmou, as Yunnan provincial administration commissioner in 1737, had special reason to plan for the expansion of food production in his jurisdiction. On one hand, he was confronted with mountainous territory whose original, non-Han population was unaccustomed to the intensive agricultural land-use standard in other parts of China; at the same time, the rapid development of Yunnan's mining industry, especially after 1726, was generating a sizable nonagricultural population that had somehow to be fed. Chen took the positive, one is tempted almost to say voluntarist, approach. The physical problem was real, but a solution was at hand in greater effort by society (meaning, in this case, the hapless farmers).

> Yunnan has enjoyed protracted peace, and population is expanding mightily. In addition to this, there are mineshafts everywhere, and one person's tillage fails to provide sufficient food for several people. It is not entirely that the earth's strength has already been exhausted; [the problem] arises rather from a failure of diligence up till now in [the application of] human effort.[40]

A major thrust of Chen's agricultural improvement program was expansion of Yunnan's cultivated acreage through crop diversification. Chen had complained in 1734 that "In years when rain and shine come at their proper time, [the people] only know enough to cultivate the fertile, irrigated arable. As for the poorer land, they invariably leave it abandoned without a second thought." The neglect of the unirrigable, often higher land continued in years of adverse climatic conditions, the people "suffering hunger with their arms folded" rather than taking the initiative to plant the poorer land in crops other than rice. Since the 1734 harvest was threatened by late rains, Chen launched a drive to urge "the scholars, commoners, and Miao and Guo [tribesmen]" to cultivate their hillsides with a range of dryland crops, including beans and squashes.[41]

Under the more systematic plan devised by Chen in 1737, officialdom was to take an active, not to say aggressive, role. Local magistrates, personally touring the rural areas, were to quiz the local people whenever they encountered an untilled patch of land. "They should ask why it has hitherto been left uncultivated, and investigate what crops could well be planted on it." They were to develop irrigation, promote wet-rice agriculture where

---

[39] Yu Sen, "On the growing of trees," in *Statecraft anthology, j.* 37, p. 11a–b.
[40] Chen Hongmou, *Chance survivals, j.* 4, p. 44a–b.
[41] Ibid., *j.* 2, pp. 25a–26a.

possible, encourage the adoption of "miscellaneous dryland crops" and vegetables where not, and help the people to acquire seeds.[42] A scheme for indirect but real state supervision with a long history in Chinese administrative writing was to be transplanted. Headmen and senior members of local communities were to "exhort morn and night," rewarding the diligent and punishing the lazy. They themselves would be punished or rewarded at the end of the year according to the extent of cultivation realized by their community. Chen was as heedless as any European colonist of the possibility that the indigenous peoples might have concepts of the relationship between man and land other than those of individual possession and the duty to exploit:

> In the case of land that has an owner, let it be cultivated by him; in the case of ownerless land, it should be permitted for [him who comes forward] to become its [recognized] cultivator. Once the land is cultivated, [the local authorities] should periodically inspect it, and not let it go out of cultivation. Severe punishment should be imposed for obstruction and theft.[43]

In certain circumstances, and assuming that the state's rewards and punishments could be as influential as Chen thought, such a program might be a recipe for ecological disaster. Its potential for environmental harm was mitigated, however, by two additional themes: the importance of teaching the local people how to "brew" animal manure; and the desirability of reversing the existing trend toward deforestation. Chen does not weave these themes into any broader ecological discussion. The role of the animal manure was simply to make it possible to raise crops every year from Yunnan's poorer soil (which was impossible as long as "the folk do not know how to accumulate manure, but let their pigs and oxen roam over the countryside"). Tree cover was basically for firewood – although Chen's language was probably intended also to evoke a general feeling, informed by every Chinese scholar's childhood study of *Mencius*, that "denuded hills" (*tongshan* 童山) were a sad thing.[44]

[42] The food plants Chen enumerates include the following: winter- and spring-sown buckwheat, oats, wheat, broad beans, soybeans, "rat beans," *qingke* 青稞 barley, yams and other root vegetables, and wild food plants. He does not mention maize. Ibid., *j.* 4, p. 44b.

[43] Ibid., p. 46a; cf. William Cronon, *Changes in the Land: Indians, Colonists, and the Ecology of New England* (New York, 1983), ch. 4. What most saliently distinguishes Chen's approach from that which seventeenth-century English settlers imposed in New England is (a) that with Chen the assumption of the state's right to insist on cultivation replaces the concept (later elaborated by Locke) of the individual's right to land in which he was the first to invest labor; and (b) that Chen does not articulate the doctrine that a people which fails to "improve" land may justifiably be dispossessed by one disposed and qualified to do so.

[44] *Chance survivals, j.* 2, p. 43b; *Mengzi* VIA:8.

It is always refreshing to see a highly educated Confucian official taking a detailed interest in manure. In the case under discussion, Chen's knowledge was at second hand, being drawn from what became a pilot project in Luoci 羅次 county. He cited a 1734 plan by the former Luoci magistrate to provide seeds and oxen and hire laborers to till land left uncultivated by the local people, who "do not know how to grow dryland crops." The plan, whose purpose was to provide the local people with a model, had included the idea of building pens for pigs, oxen, hens, and ducks, "to demonstrate the technique of brewing manure." In authorizing the plan, Chen had added some refinements, not all of them environmentally sound:

> This apart, such things as mountain clods (*shanling tupi* 山嶺土坯), which combine grass and soil, when dried, burned, and blended into the manure, can all serve as fertilizer. Then again, if one dug small ditches beside major thoroughfares, placed various grasses and the bark of trees inside them, and [let them] daily collect the water where oxen and horses have been, not only would this be a convenience for travelers, but, more importantly, it would permit the accumulation of manure. One could proceed similarly in hillside bamboo forests and mountain hollows, and on the vacant land by villages. As for places where oxen and horses used for transport are left grazing, one could dig a small pit to the side and sweep in the droppings.[45]

By early 1737, the new Luoci incumbent had reported favorably on his predecessor's efforts, which he said he had continued. The result was that "in Luoci there is gradually coming to be no dry land left waste, while the farmers leave out nothing as they accumulate manure, and all the poor land, once cultivated, yields harvests." This encouraged Chen to seek the governor's approval for a provincewide manure accumulation drive as part of his broader program.

On reforestation, Chen had this to say:

> In mountainous Yunnan there were [originally] endless bamboo forests covering the serried hills, while trees and grasses grew luxuriantly, and ample firewood was there for the taking. However, because the salt-works require wood, and mines and mints require charcoal, there has been daily cutting, resulting in denuded hills almost as far as the eye can see. Firewood and charcoal have gradually become dear and hard to come by; even the roots of grass and bark of trees are almost rarities. . . . Yunnan, being mountainous in all directions, has land on which grain crops cannot be grown, but it has absolutely no place in which trees cannot be planted. Besides, [since the province] was originally wooded with tall forests and dense bamboo thickets

---

[45] Chen Hongmou, *Chance survivals*, j. 4, p. 43a–b, and j. 2, pp. 43b–44a.

which have only now been felled almost to the last tree, reforestation should indeed be altogether feasible.

Chen concluded by pointing out that if the present short-sighted failure to replant continued, the scarcity of firewood would be progressively exacerbated. The warning was timely, but the ecological analysis seems shallow. Chen wanted information about tree-planting methods to be disseminated along with exhortations to accumulate manure. Such proposals were of course both worthy and potentially beneficial, but they were not well integrated into his overall development plan, which reflects no awareness either of the dangers of erosion or of the means by which it can be controlled.[46]

16.2.2. PROTECTING THE ENVIRONMENT FROM EXPLOITATIVE SOCIETY

In fact, consciousness of the relationship between erosion and the clearing of hillsides can be traced, in China, at least as far back as the Southern Song (1127–1279).[47] Rich evidence of such consciousness in the eighteenth and nineteenth centuries has been presented by Ho and, in the present volume, Osborne and Vermeer, while Elvin has shown that, in the first half of the nineteenth century, Bao Shichen 包世臣 took serious account of the risk of erosion in his detailed instructions for reclaiming hillsides.[48] Thus the problem is not to demonstrate that consciousness, sometimes fairly sophisticated, of such problems existed; rather, as the previous section suggests, it is to determine how far it influenced the mass of officials as they designed, implemented, or, conceivably, decided not to implement "productivist" schemes.

However, if for the moment we confine ourselves to illustrating official conservationism at its most developed, a document that commends itself to our attention is the "Report proposing measures for restricting access to the mountain forests," by Niu Yunzhen 牛運震, a Gansu county magistrate in

---

[46] The above account is based on Chen Hongmou, *Chance survivals, j.* 4, pp. 43a–46b, except where otherwise stated.

[47] See Vermeer, Chapter 8 of this volume.

[48] Ho, *Studies on the Population of China*, pp. 148–51; Osborne, Chapter 7 of this volume; Vermeer, Chapter 8 of this volume; and Elvin, "Skills and Resources," pp. 93–94. Equally important is Perdue's demonstration that, from the 1740s on, officialdom was well aware that excessive lowland reclamation could aggravate the risk of flooding, if it meant depriving seasonally swollen rivers of their overspill catchment areas. See Peter C. Perdue, *Exhausting the Earth: State and Peasant in Hunan, 1500–1850* (Cambridge, Mass., 1987), pp. 219–33.

the 1740s – or, to use the richer subtitle, "Findings on protecting the mountain forests to provide shade for the springs and to conserve the snows (*yin quan hu xue* 蔭泉護雪), thereby nourishing the veins of Earth (*pei dimai* 培地脈) and improving the success of farming." Niu's jurisdiction, whose population included a substantial non-Han element, lay at a high altitude, and apparently had extensive forest cover. Its cold winds created an intense local demand for charcoal. Niu had been provoked by an increase in the price of charcoal to request authorization for a plan for managing the county's forest resources by controlling public access. The present document is a follow-up report required by the provincial governor.

The document's chief significance is its clear exposition of the relationship between forest cover and water conservation – an awareness shaped in part by information from the local non-Han leader. While the report further shows Niu making the distinction, still familiar today, between local users of forest resources and the more environmentally destructive outside business capital, he does not consider local users harmless: forests could need protection from the grass-roots users too.

Niu proposed a different level of protection for each of five forest zones within the county. His general principle was that forests whose water-conservation functions were important for human purposes must basically be protected, while the others could be basically left open to the public. Thus deserving of "perpetual closure" were the thick forests in the eastern part of the county. This area, said Niu, had no rivers and few springs, and the water supply of the local population came entirely from reservoirs. Letting the forests grow even denser would permit the accumulation of snow to greater depths; the extra snow, on melting, would enrich the water supply as well as contributing to soil moisture (*runze tugao* 潤澤土膏). Alternative fuel sources were readily available in the area in the form of coal and grasses (thus use of fossil fuel was to help protect live trees).

Snow accumulation was also the primary consideration behind the "closure as appropriate" that Niu recommended for some of the county's northern forests. These forests had been deliberately set on fire in a military campaign, and nothing now remained except small clusters of under-sized trees. The rivers and irrigation channels that watered the adjacent agricultural areas depended on "the winter snow being deep and thick, [so that] the springtime water may flow freely." The forest cover should be spared while it regenerated, Niu opined, because the irrigation of crop land depended on it.

Some forests in the western sector of the county, inhabited by non-Han people and under the jurisdiction of an Aboriginal Office, were similarly important for conserving snow either for irrigation or for drinking water. Niu had asked the Aboriginal Office head to send him proposals for managing these forests, and he cites the latter's report as stating that the people of the area where drinking water was in short supply "rely on the water flowing down from the accumulated snow [around] the pine roots." Presumably out of sensitivity to his own people's needs and habits, the Aboriginal Office head proposed not complete closure of these forests, but rather that closure be the norm, with fixed periods of public access. Niu endorsed this.

To be left open to the public for controlled exploitation were some extensive areas of dense forest in the grassy uplands in the northwest of the county. The significance of these forests in Niu's eyes had nothing to do with agriculture or water conservation; his proposals treated them simply as sources of wood for charcoal or timber, which must be allowed to last. He distinguished two categories of user: the local people, whose economy was based on grazing, woodcutting, and charcoal burning; and capitalistic outside merchants, who used hired labor to make charcoal and fell trees for timber. Niu thought that the local people could be left to cut wood as they chose, but that the outside merchants should be made to acquire permits specifying the number of trees that they might fell and the length of time for which they were allowed to operate. There was thus hope of avoiding denudation, he opined.

Finally, in accordance with the request of the Aboriginal Office head, Niu envisaged no controls at all on woodcutting and charcoal burning in some adjacent areas of mixed Han and non-Han settlement where the water-conservation function of the forests had no agricultural significance. Presumably, the threat of outside capital had not yet reached these areas.[49]

This is an impressive document, but it still has its limitations. The author presents his ideas less systematically than I present them here (or at least, he arranges his material according to other principles), and his motivation remains anthropocentric. Correspondingly, there is a somewhat one-dimensional feel to the document. Niu has one ecological insight, and takes action on it; the document does not reflect the mind of a naturalist, activated by curiosity about the whole rich range of ecological relationships represented by the forest.

What of official sensitivity toward the environmental impact of manufacturing and mining (whether private, state-run, or something in between)? A stone inscription tells of one occasion on which industrial pollution came

---

[49] *Statecraft anthology, j.* 38, p. 10a–b.

to the attention of local officialdom: in 1737, 108 local residents (mainly farmers, but including two members of the monastic community), submitted a petition complaining that dyeing workshops in the scenic Huqiu 虎丘 hill district near Suzhou 蘇州 were polluting the water supply. They believed that use of the polluted irrigation water was harmful to the crops; they were also concerned about the ability of the many local tea booths to serve drinkable tea, about the general health risk, and about the outrage of this celebrated religious beauty spot being treated with such disrespect. The reponse of the authorities was to reassert an earlier (1724) proscription of dyeing in the area, and to have the prohibition carved in stone.[50]

As for mining, any official sufficiently well educated to have studied the *Hanshu* might recall a strident and lengthy protest against creeping commercialization and monetization by the conservative statesman Gong Yu 貢禹 (fl. 44 B.C.). This, among other complaints, posited a relationship between mining, deforestation, and the incidence of natural disasters:

> Digging some thousands of feet into the ground [results in] dissipating the quintessence of the *yin qi* 陰氣. Earth's stores are left depleted, so that [it] is unable to retain the *qi* and send forth clouds. The felling of forests knows no seasonal restraints. One cannot be certain that the calamities of flood and drought do not arise from this.[51]

In the Qing dynasty, Chen Hongmou, as we have seen, deplored the deforestation that arose from mining, but did not express fear of the consequences beyond a fuel shortage whose severity must have been common knowledge. Tan Cui 檀萃, a slightly later advocate of silver mining, went so far as to reassure his readers about Gong Yu's concerns. These concerns, he hinted, might have been reasonable in Gong's day, because at that time official pressure to exploit mineral resources had been felt throughout the empire. Now, however, the mining was all concentrated in distant Guizhou and Yunnan, and whatever its climatic effects might be, they could not affect the rest of the empire. "The damage remains hazy."[52]

Ni Shui 倪蛻, a man of Kunming (Yunnan), disagreed. In about 1730 he wrote a letter to some unnamed official to express his opposition to silver

[50] Suzhou Lishi Bowuguan, Jiangsu Shifan Xueyuan Lishi Xi, and Nanjing Daxue Ming Qing Shi Yanjiushi, comps., *Ming Qing Suzhou gongshangye beike ji* 明清蘇州工商業碑刻集 [Stelae inscriptions relating to industry and commerce from Ming and Qing Suzhou] (Jiangsu, 1981), pp. 71–73. Many characters are missing from the inscription on which this account is based; a twenty-five-character lacuna immediately after the mention of the tea booths renders the interpretation uncertain at this point.

[51] Ban Gu, *Hanshu* 漢書 [A history of the (Former) Han dynasty], 12 vols. (Beijing, 1975), vol. 10, *j.* 72, p. 3075.

[52] Tan Cui, "A record of mines," in *Statecraft anthology*, *j.* 52, p. 13b.

mining in the province. Near the end, he listed a number of ways in which, he claimed, mining was injurious to the local population. Three of these were environmental. First, the smoke from smelting and refining made pulse crops wither; second, the water of the streams in which ore had been washed was harmful to young rice plants; and finally, again, hills in the vicinity of mines became denuded (like Chen, Ni mentioned the disappearance of grasses as well as trees). Unfortunately, Ni did not pause to explain *exactly* why denudation of the hills was a bad thing; he was too interested in his next theme, which was the alleged adverse social consequences of mining development. On this, he waxed eloquent:

> Fugitives are concealed and rebels harbored, with no inquiries as to whence they hail; great malefactors and heinous wrongdoers take advantage [of the mines] to hide their tracks, and this again is to the population's injury. Men leave their proper occupations and hasten to the mines, where they engage in wrongdoing: they gamble and cut purses, cheating and swindling fearlessly, and this again is to the population's injury. Vagabonds are daily gathering in greater numbers, outlaws daily multiplying; robbing and murdering, they band together, attaching themselves to the law-abiding to gain protection, and this again is to the population's injury.[53]

The contrast between this diatribe and Ni's brief statements on environmental damage reminds us of the way in which preoccupation with the world of man repeatedly impeded late-imperial Chinese writers from developing their environmental observations into systematic study. This is, however, the moment to address the theme of nonenvironmentalist concerns inspiring official decisions whose effect would have been conservationist. Fear of the social consequences that Ni so vividly portrays could provoke officialdom into the view that certain resources were best left unexploited, no matter what their benefits. Nature reserves would be created because of social fears.

16.2.3. UNINTENTIONAL ENVIRONMENTAL PROTECTION

Although in fact the eighteenth century saw an unprecedented mining boom in China's southwestern provinces, the conventional early Qing suspicion of mining communities may conceivably have saved some mountain forests and probably resulted in reprieves for many more. But it was not

---

[53] Ni Shui, "Letter to the authorities discussing mine affairs," in *Statecraft anthology, j.* 52, p. 14b.

only potential mining sites whose exploitation might be forbidden because of law-and-order fears. Wild mountain areas, especially those straddling provincial boundaries, were conventionally seen as natural lairs for men of desperate character; it was thought to follow that their economic potential, whether agricultural or mineral, might be best left unexploited. Public access would be officially prohibited by "sealing off" the hills.

The 1827 *Huangchao jingshi wenbian* 皇朝經世文編 (a famous anthology of administrative documents and essays on government) conveniently juxtaposes two memorials by eighteenth-century Jiangxi governors arguing that one particular range of hills should (in the first case) or should not (in the second) be opened to the public for cultivation or other forms of exploitation. Besides recommending opposite courses of action, the two reports conjure up quite different images of the terrain itself. Assuming, for now, that both governors were describing the same extent of territory viewed at the same time of year, this is a timely reminder that Qing bureaucrats, like others, were capable of slanting their representations of reality to suit their policy preferences, or, at least, letting their policy preferences shape their perceptions.

The Tongtang 銅塘 hills occupied an area some few hundred *li* in circumference in northeastern Jiangxi, near the Zhejiang and Fujian borders. They had been sealed off since the second quarter of the fifteenth century, when they had harbored "evil-hearted bandits." Early in Qing times, the authorities had again had trouble with a bandit infestation of these hills, and by the 1740s there were "official troops on guard at every point of access."[54] The first of our two memorials, written by Chen Hongmou in 1744, was the latest of a series of abortive proposals that the ban be lifted. It was inspired partly by a recent edict calling for broader exploitation of "the potential of mountains and marshes," partly by Chen's sense of the intensity of population pressure in Jiangxi, and partly, one suspects, by doubt about the advisability of retaining a ban that was slowly becoming a dead letter. According to Chen, cultivation on the perimeter had already caused considerable shrinkage in the area of the restricted zone. Not only were villages of cultivators gradually forming, but "the markers now established to delimit the forbidden zone contain a smaller area than those of former times; the old broadness and vastness are no more."

---

[54] Cai Shiying, "Memorial on the sealed hills" (c. 1655), in 1875 *Guangfeng xianzhi* 廣豐縣志 [Gazetteer of Guangfeng county], *j.* 9, part 2, pp. 8b–9a; Chen Hongmou, "Memorial requesting the opening of the sealed hills and the Yushan lead mines of Guangxin prefecture" (1744), in *Statecraft anthology*, *j.* 34, pp. 16b–17a.

Chen painted a rosy picture of the developmental potential of the Tongtang hills. He had sent a team of officials to inspect the area, and reported their findings as follows:

> Inside the sealed-off area, grasses and trees grow wild and thick, and paths are steep and winding; the hilly depths are broad and vast, while valley waters turn and twist. Within, there still remain some marked-out plots of land, just fit to be converted into arable. On the remaining ground one could grow hemp or indigo, vegetables or fruit. Although there are no quality woods such as the cryptomeria or cedar, there is an extremely rich profusion of mixed trees and bamboos. The mountain streams and gullies flow downstream out of the hills, all providing water transport to a major river.

This depiction of the wilderness stressed natural richness, which needed only to be domesticated by a throng of farmers. Chen's vision was a happy one: an "untold number" of the poor would "leap" to mark out the parcels they proposed to cultivate, fell the bamboo and trees, and create irrigated or unirrigated fields according to the availability of water. The security problem, which was not so very serious to begin with, could be addressed through a judicious combination of measures, including an appropriate military presence. One would depart from the unfortunate status quo, in which "land fit for plowing, well-digging, and pasturage has all been grazing-ground for weasels, deer, and squirrels." For indeed,

> Deep mountains, great ravines like these are found in every province; in this present period of splendor when reclamation progresses everywhere along the distant frontiers and in Miao tribal territories, to leave this single nook of the interior perpetually sealed off, abandoned as wasteland, has really something in it of refusing food through fear of choking.[55]

Chen's rhetoric was sufficient to inspire orders for a reconsideration, but after the Zhejiang and Fujian authorities had been consulted, his plea was rejected. Nonetheless, proposals that the ban be lifted continued to be made. Eventually Hu Baoquan, governor during 1755–57 and part of 1761, decided on a personal inspection. The forbidden zone described in his memorial was altogether inhospitable:

> Moving inward from the boundary, all is towering peaks and piling crags, sheer scars and hanging precipices. . . . Here and there one finds scattered patches of level ground, but none of them amounts to much. Among the trees there is no decent timber: their bloated trunks weave into sinuous shapes, densely cloaking the steep faces and the deep ravines. The lower slopes,

---

[55] *Statecraft anthology, j.* 34, pp. 16b–17a.

meanwhile, jumble up together, often separated by a mountain stream. When the water rises, these become impassible. The mountain paths are almost vertical: only by hanging on to creepers and pulling oneself up by [the branches of] the trees can one advance. All along the perilous way [the path] twists every few feet, so that one loses sight at once of where one has just been. The soil, moreover, is all sand and stone, so that unless one takes provisions with one, there is nothing on which to subsist.

Hu argued that, so far from having the economic potential of which the advocates of exploitation spoke, the Tongtang range offered "nothing but ruggedness and steepness." He concluded that there could be no more doubt but that, on grounds of social order, the ban should be retained, and made detailed proposals for tightening the guard system.[56]

It is certainly appropriate to question the real value of official protection to this area and others like it. We have seen that Chen believed the forbidden zone to have shrunk considerably by his day. The difference between his account of it and Hu's cannot be completely explained by the supposition that it had shrunk still further by Hu's day, because a mid-seventeenth-century gubernatorial report described the territory in terms quite similar to Hu's.[57] Nonetheless, it is suggestive that Hu distinguished between the whole hilly area, whose circumference he estimated at "some three hundred *li*," and the actual forbidden zone, whose circumference did not, he thought, exceed one hundred, and whose boundaries were between twenty and forty *li* in from the guard posts. He also mentioned that some cultivators, mainly Fujianese, had built shacks within the zone and settled down to live in them.

It is reasonable to assume that the power of the Qing state to keep land-hungry peasants out of "sealed hills" was ultimately limited.[58] Presumably, the exploitation bans fulfilled a deterrent or delaying function, rather than permanently saving areas of wilderness. Meanwhile, what we have seen of Chen Hongmou may serve to symbolize two of China's major problems in the last few hundred years. The concern for forests that he showed while in Yunnan, having only a shallow and anthropocentric grounding, could not withstand the dual pressures of (a) land-hunger in Jiangxi, and (b) the advisability of showing oneself eager to comply with policy directions laid down in the nation's capital.

---

[56] Hu Baoquan, "Memorial requesting the continued sealing of the Tongtang hills," in *Statecraft anthology, j.* 34, pp. 17a–18a; or *Gazetteer of Guangfeng, j.* 9, part 2, pp. 9b–11a.

[57] Cai Shiying, "Memorial on the sealed hills," in *Gazetteer of Guangfeng, j.* 9, part 2, pp. 8a–9b.

[58] Cf. the frank admission of defeat in Zhu Gui, "Report discussing reclamation on the Nantian hills," in *Statecraft Anthology, j.* 34, pp. 18a–19b. See also Vermeer, Chapter 8 of this volume.

CONCLUSION

There was certainly plenty of potential for eighteenth-century Chinese administrators to be environmentally responsible. Much fragmentary environmental knowledge was available, while the concern with agriculture expected of most of them, the background of many in landowning families still personally interested in the management of their estates, and even literary and artistic sensibilities, could, arguably, have combined to encourage a positive orientation toward the world of growing things. There were also potential influences from Daoism: the respect for "naturalness" invoked by Will,[59] and the refusal of real Zhuangzi Daoism to privilege the human point of view at all. And yet the material presented in this chapter does not show eighteenth-century officialdom completely realizing the level of environmental sensitivity that might have been attainable, given these various advantages.

It is at least as reasonable to celebrate some eighteenth-century officials for what they glimpsed and what they tried to do as it is to point out their shortcomings. More to the point, the shortcomings are easily explicable. Not only, as others have demonstrated, did population pressure (and the greed of powerful members of society) pose formidable obstacles to official conservationism; the need to show that one was an effective conduit for "Heaven and Earth's love for [human] life" could also provoke ecologically blind official drives to help the growing population solve its subsistence problems. There were also institutional impediments. Too much elite intellectual energy was consumed in bureaucratic tasks to leave much spare for carrying out systematic ecological investigations. Meanwhile, ecological concerns were only one among a number of considerations that territorial administrators had to take into account. The price of environmental irresponsibility would usually be paid long after any given official had moved on; the problems which claimed his urgent attention concerned the management of human society, including the extraction of revenue for the state. While the human-centeredness of Confucianism did not cause this bias, it did nothing to challenge it; Zhuangzi's challenge went unheeded, as one would expect.

[59] See Chapter 9 of this volume.

Representations of the Environment – Literary and Popular Sensibility

17

Ecologism versus Moralism

CONCEPTIONS OF NATURE IN SOME LITERARY TEXTS OF MING-QING TIMES

PAOLO SANTANGELO

"The scenery beyond the seas is the same as it ever was," said Duo the Ninth, "but the circumstances in which individuals find themselves are different. The only delight of Tang Ao in days past was to ramble and divert himself, being entirely free of any attachments: he just enjoyed leisure without restraint, and whatever he heard and whatever he saw belonged all to a happy atmosphere. . . . Now Miss Tang's sole concern is searching for her father. Her heart-mind is full of limitless attachments. Anxiety fills her breast, and sorrowful cares her stomach. Thus everything she sees or hears, either prompts a sense of separation from him, or grief that her father has passed beyond the bounds of this world. However many scenic vistas open before her, they are transformed into a domain of unrestricted bitterness. . . . Thus, while contemplating one's environment may be a means of engendering feelings, it may also be that one's surroundings arise from what one is feeling. Nothing there is that is not made so by the heart-mind, nor can in any degree be forced to be otherwise."[1]

This chapter presents some ways in which nature is described, felt, or in general presented in some Ming-Qing literary works, to help us obtain a better understanding of the mentality of this period.

We have identified two ways of interpreting nature and – in a sense – making use of it: (1) as a metaphor that expresses emotions; and (2) as an opportunity for aesthetic and/or religious contemplation.

It would be arbitrary to try to oppose the two concepts since they are

This essay is the result of work carried out in the framework of the C. N. R. research on ethical concepts in Ming-Qing China. I would like to thank the conference participants for their comments, and I am especially grateful to Mark Elvin for his helpful suggestions.

[1] Li Ruzhen 李汝珍, *Jinghua yuan* 鏡花緣 [The destinies of the flowers in the mirror] (1828. Reprinted, Taipei: Sanmin shuju, 1979), *h.* 43, p. 210. Basically Mark Elvin's translation.

complementary; but their identification is clearly useful for our purposes. The point rather is that the focus will be at one time on the contemplation of nature itself, and at another on the emotions and symbolic, or meta-phorical, associations generated by natural images.[2] Both such perspectives are, however, unified by a deep religious-moral sense that is based on the concept of the unity of the whole universe and on the search for a personal perfection.

The Ming and Qing period also inherited the concept of "wilderness," the hostile perception of a nature that the late-imperial Chinese found frightening and repulsive, like their ancestors in the "Great Summons."[3] In such a case the "artificial" is seen as a positive product of human civilization, which modifies nature from an adversary to a friend of humankind, as it is clearly seen in the passage quoted elsewhere in the present volume by Liu Ts'ui-jung: "The vapors of mountains and rivers have accumulated to be-come miasma; once subjected to management by man, these vapors will leak away, and the compactness [they now possess] will be opened up gradually; this is the common rule of nature." Thus, as far as a "natural-artificial" polarization is concerned, the interrelation of the two concepts is quite complex, and it is hard to try to simplify it. The Chinese of course had a clear distinction between "artificial" as it applied to manufactured arti-cles, and "natural" as applied to flora and fauna.[4] If we want to schematize

---

[2] Somewhat similar is Wang Guowei's distinction between the poems "seen as through a veil or mist (*ge* 隔)" and poems "experienced directly with no intervening wall or partition between" (*buge* 不隔). Adele Austin Rickett explains that a poem is *ge* "when it sets out to accomplish one thing and ends up accomplishing something else. For example, if a poet's intention is to describe lotus blossoms, he should stick to that theme and do all possible to bring the flowers to life for the reader. If, however, he keeps intruding his own feelings into his description and uses the theme of the lotus to relieve his own frustration and unhappi-ness, he may succeed in conveying those feelings but he fails to present the 'soul' of the lotus." Adele Austin Rickett, *Wang Kuo-wei's Jen-chien Tz'u-hua: A Study in Chinese Literary Criticism* (Hong Kong: Hong Kong University Press, 1977), p. 28.

[3] Cf. the eastern "great sea," southern beasts and monsters, western dangers, and northern frost, expressionistically described in the *Dazhao*, in the *Chuci* 楚辭 [*Songs of the South*] (Reprinted, Beijing: Renmin wenxue CBS, 1953), pp. 13b–14b. See David Hawkes's transla-tion in *Ch'u Tz'u: The Songs of the South* (Oxford: Clarendon Press, 1959), p. 110. See also his translation of the "Summons for a Gentleman Who Became a Recluse," in Cyril Birch, ed., *Anthology of Chinese Literature from Early Times to the Fourteenth Century* (New York: Grove, 1965), vol. 1, pp. 79–80. Other common examples can be found in poetic laments from frontier lands. It should be noticed, however, that some desolate descriptions, like the "Summons of the Soul" and the above-mentioned "Great Summons," were also literary devices used to hasten the soul's return, as Zhu Xi admits in his preface. Cf. Li Chi, "Chu Hsi the Poet," *T'oung Pao* 58 (1972), p. 106.

[4] "This distinction between the uninterfered with and the interfered with" – says C. S. Lewis, dealing with the concept of "natural" (*Studies in Words* [Cambridge: Cambridge University Press, 1975], pp. 45–46) – "may be held to enshrine a very primitive, and almost magical or

a different evaluation of the above dichotomy, we could say that it depends on where the emphasis is laid: either on the Daoist simplicity that is contrasted with any external affect or servitude, or on the anthropocentric Confucian concept of culture that is contrasted with rudeness and a lack of elegance or fair social behavior.[5] The Chinese, however, do not only conceive of human artifacts as having a character opposed to what is "spontaneously produced by nature." We may single out a third category, that of "artificial nature," that is to say the manipulated natural world, whose common examples range from the art of gardens to that of floriculture. In these cases, unlike in other arts, illusions and artifices are less easily distinguished from reality itself because the material and tools are nature itself.[6] An illustration is the cult of the positive power of "wilderness" that has boosted the fabrication of artificial mountains and forests, as in the case of Zhang Lun's 張倫 garden in Luoyang, in the sixth century.[7] The above category might also have a broader meaning. In the *Honglou meng* [The dream of the red chamber], when Baoyu and his father are doing the rounds of the Garden of the Broad Vision, the father asks his son what he thinks of an imitation village.

> I have never really understood – Baoyu replied promptly – what it was the ancients *meant* by "natural" (*tianran* 天然). . . .

---

animistic, conception of causality. . . . If ants had a language they would, no doubt, call their anthill an artifact and describe the brick wall in its neighbourhood as a *natural* object."

[5] The roots of a Daoist literary concept of nature can be traced back to *Zhuangzi*. If the "genuine" is stressed, then the elegance and refined sense belong to it, as Jiang Zong 江總 (519–94) contrasted it with the complexities of the human world (cf. Obi Kōichi 小尾郊 一, *Chūgoku bungaku ni arawareta shizen to shizenkan* 中國文學に現われた自然と自然觀 [Nature and the conception of nature as expressed in Chinese literature] (Tokyo, 1964), p. 48). For a more complex and syncretic vision see Liu Xie's 劉勰 (465–522) *Wenxin diaolong* 文心雕龍 [The Literary Mind and the Carving of Dragons]. For instance, Liu Xie contrasts of *ziran* with *waishi* 外飾, "external adornment," but, at the same time, traces the origin of literature to nature (pp. 12–21 of the excellent Vincent Yu-chung Shih's bilingual version, Hong Kong: Chinese University Press, 1983).

[6] Cf., e.g., some examples (including Li Yu's and Shen Fu's views) mentioned by Johnston R. Stewart, *Scholar Gardens of China: A Study and Analysis of the Spatial Design of the Chinese Private Garden* (Cambridge: Cambridge University Press, 1991), pp. 16, 48–54.

[7] "He built up – it is reported – a mountain called Jingyang as if it were a work of Nature, with piled-up peaks and multiple ranges rising in steep succession, with deep ravines and caverns and gullies tortuously linked. So lofty were the forests, so gigantic the trees that sun and moon could not penetrate their shadowed obscurity; so luxuriant were the vines and creepers in their festooning as to control the passage of wind and mist. Here the [Daoist] adepts, the lovers of mountains and wilderness, might have roamed until they quite forgot to return to their heaven." Michael Sullivan, *The Birth of Landscape Painting in China* (London: Routledge and Kegan Paul, 1962), p. 197. On Zhang Lun's biography see *Weishu* [The official history of Wei] (Beijing: Zhonghua, 1974), *j.* 24, pp. 617–19.

"Natural" is that which is spontaneously produced by nature as opposed to that which is produced by human artifice 天然者天之自成不是人力之所為. A farm set down in the middle of a place like this is obviously the product of human artifice. . . . It does not look even a particularly remarkable view. How could it attain to the pattern of naturalness of the other places we have just been looking at? Or their natural flavour? The bamboos in those other places may have been planted by human hand and the streams diverted out of their natural courses, but there was no *appearance* of artifice. That's why, when the ancients use the term "natural" I have my doubts about what they really meant. For example, when they speak of a "natural painting," I can't help wondering if they are not referring to precisely that forcible interference with the landscape to which I object: putting hills where they are not meant to be, and that sort of thing. However great the skill with which this is done, the results are not in the end appropriate. . . .[8]

This case can be also considered as belonging to "artificial nature" because the imitation village is a part of the Garden, that is, part of the scenic environment.[9] This manipulation of nature might be considered aesthetically congruous or incongruous according to personal taste and values. Just before this passage, Baoyu's father says that "although the scenery is made by human artifice, its sight is moving, awakening the desire to get back to rural life."[10] Here it is clear that the divergent positions of the father and the son depend on whether the moral evocation (for the father the sight of the village is moving because it awakens the desire for rural simplicity) or the aesthetic sense (does the whole thing look as if it had happened without human aid, or is human intervention noticed?) is stressed. For the orthodox Confucianist, the moral meaning and conven-

---

[8] *Honglou meng* 紅樓夢 [Dream of the red chamber] (1791. Reprinted, Beijing: Renmin wenxue CBS, 1957), *h.* 17, pp. 191–92. Hawkes's translation (Cao Xueqin, *The Story of the Stone, also known as the Dream of the Red Chamber* [Harmondsworth, 1973], vol. 1, pp. 336–37) with small changes. It is worth noting the distinction elaborated by Li Zhi 李贄 in his *Miscellanea* (*Zashuo* 雜説), where he compares the *Baiyueting ji* 拜月亭記 [Pavilion of the shining moon] and the *Xixiangji* 西廂記 [Western chamber] with the *Pipaji* 琵琶記 [Lute]. He contrasts the "product by transformation" (*huagong* 化工) and the "product by painting" (*huagong* 畫工): the former is the masterpiece that has been composed in a natural way; the latter is the work that is the result of technical artifice. What is called the product of art – Li Zhi explains – is the imitation by the author of nature's transformative work; but in reality nature does not need any artifice, and thus what is natural is superior to any craft. Cf. *Fenshu* 焚書 [The book to be burnt], *j.* 3, pp. 96–98, and J.-F. Billeter's translation (1979), pp. 258–62. And again, the shift from the beauty of nature to the dramatic performance and its reversal in Zhang Dai efface any boundary between nature and art. Cf. Wai-yee Li, *Enchantment and Disenchantment: Love and Illusion in Chinese Literature* (Princeton: Princeton University Press, 1993), pp. 47–48.

[9] The topic of gardens is dealt with in section 17.3.

[10] *Dream of the red chamber, h.* 17, p. 190.

tional allusion are preeminent, while for Cao Xueqin's Daoistic sensibility, when the manipulation of nature is in some way forced by humans, the result is a failure. Even in the case of out-of-season flowers, intervention is generally perceived as a negative action, an infraction of natural rules and order.[11]

Furthermore, in many Confucian currents nature was supposed to be affected by human morality, and therefore it was strictly associated with the retributive concept of destiny, as well as with political legitimation theory. In particular, the historical conception of Heaven's Mandate (*Tianming* 天命) is strictly concerned with the observation of nature and environmental reactions. On the other side, criticism against the doctrines of interaction between Heaven and humanity can be summarized in the following proposition: Conceiving nature in the ambit of an anthropocentric morality is like saying that man was created in order to satisfy mosquitoes' need of blood sucking. Hence in the history of Chinese thought we can sum up two main tendencies: the unitary view (*Tianren heyi* 天人合一 or *Tianren ganying* 天人感應), which envisages continuous interaction and reciprocity between Heaven and humanity; and the opposite view (*Tianren zhi fen* 天人之分), which sees no relation between nature and humanity, between destiny and human behavior.[12]

[11] I am indebted to Mark Elvin for the following references. Xie Zhaozhe 謝肇淛, in his *Wuzazu* 五雜組 [Fivefold miscellany] in "Biji xiaoshuo daguan" (Taipei: Xinxing shuju, 1960–86), 8th collection, p. 3997; j. 10, p. 32, blames the expensive practice of producing flowers out of season by heating earthen cellars containing the plants: "These are products really out of season, against the universal order" (其實不時之物 非天地之正也). Furthermore, at the start of the *Destinies of the flowers in the mirror*, the forced blooming of all the flowers out of season is treated by the celestial authorities as a crime against the proper hierarchy. See Elvin's acute comments on the above novel: "The Inner World of 1830," *Daedalus* 120.2 (spring 1991), pp. 35–36, 43. For analogous criticism against unnecessary interference with nature in ancient Rome, see Seneca (c. 4 B.C.–A.D. 65), *Epistolae morales* [Moral letters], trans. R. M. Gummere (Cambridge, Mass., 1959), p. 122, quoted by J. Goody, *The Culture of Flowers* (Cambridge: Cambridge University Press, 1993), p. 64, n. 140. On the other side, if a plant blooms out of time, the event is considered a presage, as in the case of the begonia that flowers in November in the *Dream of the Red Chamber*. The forced production of flowers and the growing of out-of-season plants have been practiced in China since the Han dynasty, especially on the occasion of the New Year (see J. Goody, *Culture of Flowers*, pp. 407–08).
[12] Cf. Jiang Guozhu 姜国柱, *Zhongguo renshi lun shi* 中国认识论史 [History of Chinese philosophical concepts] (Zhengzhou: He'nan renmin, 1989), p. 20. However, an intermediate position is Xunzi's idea of interference within distinction: "Instead of magnifying Heaven and contemplating it, why not domesticate and curb it?" Burton Watson, *Hsün-tzu: Basic Writings* (New York, Columbia University, 1963), j. 17, p. 44. In actual fact, the situation is far more complex, since the Chinese terms *Ming* (Mandate, destiny) and *Tian* (Heaven) often retain strong moral overtones, similar to those of the Christian term "Providence," while the ideas of fortune, fate, and destiny do not necessarily have any ethical implications in the West. However, the supple concept of *Tianming* kept a realistic attitude, as it took into

17.1. SOME PROBLEMS OF DEFINITION

Tang Xianzu 湯顯祖 (1550–1616), stressing the independence of personal expression and the absolute inadequacy of imitation in literature, says:

> the miraculous (*miao* 妙) qualities of prose do not result from following another's example and becoming exactly like him. Rather, they come naturally in an unconscious flash of spiritual inspiration (*ziran lingqi huanghu er lai busi er zhi* 自然靈氣恍惚而來 不思而來).... When Su Zizhan [Su Shi] painted withered trunks, bamboos, and rocks, he broke completely with painters of both the past and his present, and the style of his paintings became all the more marvelous.[13]

In Tang's words, concepts concerning "nature" thus appear two times: first, as *ziran*, spontaneity and the genuine expression of the individual self, and as the content of a painting: trunks, bamboos, and rocks. The concept of nature is itself ambiguous and is used in a variety of meanings. In the European languages the word comes from the Latin *natus*, past participle of *nascor*, "I am born."[14] The corresponding Greek term, *physis* (birth, nature), refers to the general concept of creation as well as the principle inherent in every being. In Chinese, the term closest to having a similar etymology is *xing* 性. Absent in the Shang inscriptions and rarely found in works from the early Zhou period, in the literary documents that can reasonably be considered prior to Confucius, the character *xing* was probably homophonous and synonymous to *sheng* 生 (to be born, to generate, to live). In later literature, *xing* was used to indicate "nature" as the essence of the human and of every other being, and the proper course of development for each living thing. In this meaning, *ziran* is the quality (self-so-ness, being so-of-

---

account the element of "consensus," as well as those of efficiency and organization, which interacted with environmental conditions (water control, grain-price stabilization, state assistance in case of calamities, etc.). But this topic deserves a specific study that differentiates the rational and irrational, realistic and mythological elements of this doctrine. As far as human responsibility in natural disasters and the influence of human action on the environment are concerned, they have already been exhaustively examined by Pierre-Étienne Will, Eduard Vermeer, and Peter Perdue.

[13] In *Zhongguo meixue shi ziliao xuanbian* 中國美學史資料選編 (下) [Collection of materials concerning the history of Chinese aesthetics] (Taipei: Fuxin), 1984, pp. 473–74; R. J. Lynn, "Alternative Routes to Self-Realization in Ming Theories of Poetry," in Susan Bush and Christian Murck, eds., *Theories of the Arts in China* (Princeton: Princeton University Press, 1983), pp. 335–36.

[14] Cf. B. Karlgren, *Grammatica Serica Recensa* (Stockholm: Museum of Far Eastern Antiquities, 1972), p. 214 n. 812 a–d (*sheng*), n. 812 q–r (*xing*); D. Munro, *The Concept of Man in Early China* (Stanford, Calif.: Stanford University Press, 1969), pp. 65–85, 210, 212–16.

itself) of *xing* (one's inner nature-constitution). In a recent contribution,[15] Roger Ames emphasizes the historical, cultural, and social aspects of *xing*, rather than a pure static endowment that cannot be changed through human action (in Graham's words, "the process of becoming human"). Ames thus argues the inadequacy of the translation "human nature," as this latter is influenced by the cosmogonic idea (of an antecedent creative principle), while *xing* requires a term able to express its meaning of ongoing poietic process, the retrospective definition based on growing and refinement (especially in the human context).

According to *Webster's*, "nature" can be defined as the "essential character of a thing," as well as "vital functions," and "any or all of the instincts, desires, appetites, drives, etc. of a person or animal," or even "what is regarded as normal or acceptable behavior."

When speaking of nature in the West we basically have at least a double meaning on two different levels, depending on whether it is understood as being within or outside humankind:

(1) Within humankind: (a) that which is normal or correct in that it corresponds to the general order and to the particular human order; or (b) that which is instinctive and therefore in opposition to what is considered superior – reason, free will, or the supernatural.

(2) Outside humankind: (a) a unity that humans are part of, including both their creative and destructive tendencies; or (b) nature as set against man the artificer (*homo faber*).

It is obvious how from these various answers to the question of "what is natural" arise empirical attitudes and theoretical conceptions that are quite distinct, if not opposed. An exemplary contradiction is found in its utmost clarity in the Romantic paradox of Rousseau's *Émile*, where man, product of nature, deceives it and turns against it. With Oscar Wilde we may remind ourselves that "To be natural is such a difficult pose to keep up." Not too far from this paradox, *mutatis mutandis*, are the different interpretations given in China to the meanings of spontaneity and artificiality.

Nature can therefore mean, in Liu Xie's words, "Spring and autumn rolling around, succeeding one another, and the *yin* and *yang* principles

---

[15] R. Ames, "The Mencian Conception of *Ren xing*: Does it Mean 'Human Nature'?," in Henry Rosemont, Jr., ed., *Chinese Texts and Philosophical Contexts: Essays Dedicated to Angus Graham* (La Salle, Ill.: Open Court, 1991), pp. 143–175. Ames stresses the dynamic character of the concept, its "achievement" rather than "a priori" aspect, its tendential rather than fixed and unchanging endowment; quoting Mencius's concept of the *xing* of the mountain, he points out its cultural character, which goes beyond basic conditions: "The forests which once covered the mountain are natural to it, not as an essential endowment, but as a refinement that takes place over its history" (p. 146).

alternatingly darkening and brightening."[16] This is the sum total of all things (*wanwu* 萬物) in time and space, the universe (*tiandi* 天地, *yuzhou* 宇宙); *Yuzhou* literally means "time-space": the place and moment where interaction takes place. In popular religion, *fengshui* 風水 theory and practice explain the world as a product of delicately balanced forces, a living system in which everything is connected by shared rhythms and resonances, in analogy with modern ecology in the West. This feeling is very deeply and broadly spread among the Chinese.[17] Nature also signifies natural scenery, including the plants and animals that are part of it (close to the idea of "environment," *huanjing* 環境).[18] It is expressed by the term *jing* 景, or *fengjing* 風景, "wind and light," that is, "what can be seen in the open air."[19] As the physical world it is often referred to as "objects and colors," *wuse* 物色,[20] that is, the world of all phenomena and images (*wanxiang* 萬象). This term seems to suggest nature as being in some way one's sensation of it, and implies a big question that cannot be properly dealt with here, but that constantly lies at the back of our reflections: the relation between reality and subjective representation, in other words the interaction between the inner and the external world.[21]

If we examine the main classes into which Chinese painting has been divided, we can see that most of them belong to the broad meaning of nature: "landscape" (*shanshui* 山水), "birds and flowers" (*lingmao huahui* 翎毛花卉), "plants and insects" (*cao chong* 草蟲), and even "men and other beings" (*ren wu* 人物) are often conceived as just parts of the landscape.[22]

---

[16] Liu Xie, *The Literary Mind*, trans. V. Y.-C. Shih, pp. 476–77: 春秋代序陰陽慘舒.

[17] Cf. Daniel Overmeyer, *Religions of China: The World as a Living System* (New York: Harper & Row, 1986), pp. 12–16. This is not in contradiction with praise of pollution in big cities, as a sign of industrialization.

[18] On this subject, see the famous scholar Zhu Guangqian 朱光潛, *Wenyi xinlixue* 文藝心理學 [The psychology of art and literature] (Shanghai: Kaiming shudian, 1936) p. 132. See also M. Sabattini's translation in *The Aesthetic Thought of Zhu Guangqian* (Rome: Istituto Italiano per il Medio ed Estremo Oriente, 1984), p. 153: "Nowadays, people usually consider nature to be the non-human things facing man. Such things as the sky, the earth, the stars, the mountains, rivers, vegetation, birds, wild animals, insects, fish, etc., are all grouped under the heading "nature." Sometimes "natural" is contrasted with "artificial" – while man belongs to nature, all the things he makes are not "nature." This meaning is not completely accurate – a natural landscape can also contain cities and palaces."

[19] See Ogawa Tamaki's article on the development of the perception of landscape among the Six Dynasties poets, "Rikuchō shijin no fūkei kan" 六朝詩人の風景觀 [Landscape as viewed by the Six Dynasties poets], *Shūkan Tōyōgaku 50* (1983), pp. 25–33.

[20] See, e.g., the *Literary Mind*'s definition "When objects and colors in the physical world change, our heart-minds are also affected" (pp. 476–77; cf. also pp. 482–83).

[21] Such an analysis should start from an examination of the Daoist concept of knowledge and reality and the Buddhist perception of phenomena. A few aspects will be dealt with in the paragraph on nature and emotions.

[22] In the ten-subjects classification of *Xuanhe huapu* 宣和畫譜 [Catalogue of paintings in Emperor Huizong's collection] (1120), only the first four items are not directly related to

While landscape offers the fullest possible expression of the unity of the Dao and harmony of the universe, flowers, plants, and animals express some specific aspects of the same Dao.[23]

Nature thus may correspond to the modern Chinese *ziran* (from *ran*, whose basic meaning is "to be so" or "so-of-itself"). The term that appears in controversial passages of the *Daodejing* (chs. 25 and 17) is equivalent to "being so of oneself," "self-so," "caused from within," thus meaning "nature, natural." When, however, "nature" acquires a metaphysical value, and corresponds in English to the capitalized written term "Nature,"[24] it resembles the concept *Tian* 天, Heaven/sky = natural + moral universal order, *Dao* 道, the Way, the ultimate, independent and immanent source of universal order.

If a generalization is allowed, stress should be placed on the relative absence, in various Chinese notions, of any idea of an external creative *archē*, an original creator and organizer that *transcends* nature. Compared with Western thought, in China the universe was generally seen as a ceaseless cosmic creative process without a temporal beginning or an external agent: that is, an autonomous organism whose parts spontaneously interact and above which there exists no creative principle, antecedent and preordained, that lies in the origin of the natural and/or moral order.[25] The

nature (Daoist and Buddhist scenes, human figures, palaces and vehicles, frontier tribes). Cf. E. Balázs and Y. Hervouet, eds., *A Sung Bibliography* (Hong Kong: Local Printing Press, 1978), p. 273.

[23] Cf. Sze Mai-mai, *The Way of Chinese Painting: Its Ideas and Technique with Selections from the Seventeenth Century Mustard Seed Garden Manual of Painting* (Taipei: Caves Books, 1982), p. 99.

[24] See, for instance, A. C. Graham, "Mysticism and the Question of Private Access," in M. I. Bockover, ed., *Rules, Rituals, and Responsibility: Essays Dedicated to Herbert Fingarette* (La Salle, Ill.: Open Court, 1991), pp. 165, 168.

[25] Cf. Joseph Needham, *Science and Civilisation in China*, vol. 2, *History of Chinese Scientific Thought* (Cambridge: Cambridge University Press, 1956), pp. 33–583; Frederick W. Mote, "The Cosmological Gulf between China and the West," in D. Buxbaum and F. Mote, eds., *Transition and Permanence in Chinese History and Culture* (Hong Kong: Cathay Press, 1972), pp. 3–21. However, as Mark Elvin has demonstrated in his "Was there a Transcendental Breakthrough in China?," in S. N. Eisenstadt, ed., *The Origins and Diversity of the Axial Age* (Albany: SUNY Press, 1986), pp. 343–44, there are some "creationist" hints in ancient Chinese literature. See also Réal Roy, "Cosmologie du *Huainan zi*: science ou philosophie" and Rémi Mathieu, "Une création du monde," in Charles Le Blanc and Rémi Mathieu, eds., *Mythe et philosophie à l'aube de la Chine impériale: études sur le Huainan zi* (Montréal: Les Presses de l'Université de Montréal, 1992), pp. 49–67, 69–87, and esp. 78–79 and p. 81 n. 5. Of course such elements, including tendencies toward some kind of transcendent source or creative principle or an administration over nature by the celestial bureaucracy, do not lessen the holistic and organicist character of the Chinese conception if it is compared with Western cosmologies. Cf. also Alison Harley Black's essay, *Man and Nature in the Philosophical Thought of Wang Fu-chih* (Seattle: University of Washington Press, 1989), esp. pp. 3–53, which contrasts the so-called Chinese "expressionism" with Western "creationism."

Greek concept of the fatality of an implacable destiny is missing, as is the need for a natural law that is external or transcendent. Therefore culture and art become the realization of the Dao, unlike the traditional Western opposition between nature and culture, on which the concept of *mimesis*[26] is based. While for Aristotle the imitative tendency is innate in humans and the *object* of imitation is external, for Chinese thinkers the human capability of expression is nothing but the continuation, the transmission, and the interpretation of nature, a modeling on the basis of nature (thus "spontaneity"). Neither do the *li* 理, that is, the heavenly principles, have a character comparable to Plato's ideas or beauty, or to the Christian God, not to mention the Hellenistic concept of God's creation *ex nihilo* ("out of nothing" other than the Creator, as distinguished from the thing created). Furthermore, the Greek conception of an inert passive matter composed of indestructible particles is opposed by the Chinese conception in which the bipolarity of the opposites is complementary, like the interaction existing between Heaven and Earth through valleys and mountains, or the upward motion of fire and the downward motion of rain in the creative process of reciprocal penetration (*gantong* 感通).[27] Nature in Chinese culture, as is clear in the term *ziran*, is self-generative, and implies, among other things, the absence of the conception of the absolute necessity of a "natural law," external or transcendent. Nature contains its *archē*, it relies on nothing other than itself; *Tian* and *Dao* indicate the absolute and independent character of nature.[28] Ever since the beginning of ethical-cosmological speculation,[29] the polysemous notion of *wen* has been based on an analogical and parallel relation between the processes of *Tianwen* and *renwen*, and finds further developments in the critical elaboration of Liu Xie.[30] The

---

[26] J. Liu, *Chinese Theories of Literature* (Chicago: University of Chicago Press, 1975), pp. 47–57; F. Jullien, "L'oeuvre et l'univers: imitation ou déploiement (limites à une conception mimétique de la création littéraire dans la tradition chinoise)," *Extrême-orient Extrême-occident* 3 (1983), pp. 69–80; M. Gálik, "The Concept of Creative Personality in Traditional Chinese Literary Criticism," *Oriens Extremus* (1980), pp. 186–202.

[27] Cf. François Jullien, "La conception du monde naturel, en Chine et en Occident, selon Tang Junyi," in *Extrême-orient Extrême-occident* 3 (1983), p. 122.

[28] Richard Van Houten, "Nature and *ziran* in Early Chinese Philosophical Literature," *Journal of Chinese Philosophy* 15 (1988), pp. 33–49, esp. 36–37.

[29] Cf. the *bi* hexagram in the *Yijing*: "We look at the ornamental figures of the sky, and thereby ascertain the changes of the seasons. We look at the ornamental observances of society, and understand how the processes of transformation are accomplished all under heaven." James Legge, trans., *The I Ching: The Book of Changes* (1899. Reprinted, New York: Dover, 1963), p. 231. Cf. also Jullien, "L'oeuvre et l'univers," pp. 52–58; Gálik, "Concept of Creative Personality, pp. 183–87.

[30] Cf. F. Jullien, "L'oeuvre et l'univers," pp. 59–66; Gálik, "Concept of Creative Personality," pp. 186–87.

metaphysical reflection derives therefore from this conception of nature, moving dialectically between the two opposite and complementary poles of positive and negative, active and receptive, that follow on by turn (*yin* and *yang*, *qian* 乾 and *kun* 坤).[31] However, this conception is based on interactive relations (*jiaogan* 交感) rather than on deterministic ones.

Summing up, among the various concepts, nuances, and emphases on nature, what we are examining here is the Chinese perception of the visible world, in its aspects of the aesthetic environment and a means of understanding a deeper reality and self-perfection.

17.2. THE METAPHOR OF NATURE AS AN EXPRESSION OF ONE'S EMOTIONS

Since antiquity, recourse has been had to descriptions of nature (*yongwu* 詠物) to express a series of allegories through a rich symbolic repertory of allusions and mythological archetypes: animals and plants as moral qualities.[32] There are frequent descriptions of the moods and sentiments of the author, or even of attitudes such as detachment, or a sense of the vanity of things, through the presentation of the objects of nature.

First of all, love and suffering are some of the favorite themes of Chinese writers, and not only in poetry. In the West, classic Greek literature presented motifs such as love, the naïveté of rustic life, and spontaneous contact with nature. In the Attic comedy shepherd and peasant characters were opposed to city-dweller types. And in Hellenistic times pastoral verse arose with its idealization of the life in the fields as the object of happiness. Theocritus's poetry was to find a creative imitator in Virgil, who was echoed later with the affirmation of the inclination for imitation of the classical style and for bucolic themes. The medieval poets sang their loves celebrating the spring, the month of May, the flowers, the singing of birds, expressing their own feeling through nature. The French poets of the Pléiade, on

---

[31] Cf. Hattori Takeshi 服部武, "Chūgoku ni okeru shizen kan" 中國における自然觀 [The view of nature in China], *Tōyō gakujutsu kenkyū* 6.5 (1967), pp. 161–63.

[32] For instance, solitary birds like the crane represent the man of superior virtue. Cf. James Hightower, *The Poetry of T'ao Ch'ien* (Oxford: Clarendon Press, 1970), pp. 15, 40, 84, 89, 95–96, 129, 130, 133–34, 146, 203–04, on the bird symbol; pp. 113–15, 136, 178, 202, for the pine tree symbol; Pauline Yu, "Metaphor and Chinese Poetry," *Chinese Literature: Essays, Articles, Reviews* 3 (1981). See also Wong Shileen, *Kung Tzu-chen* (Boston: Twayne Publishers, Hall & Co., 1975), pp. 130–46, 166; and Maggie Keswick with Charles Jencks, *The Chinese Garden: History, Art and Architecture* (London: Academy Editions, 1978), pp. 176–78. For the symbolism of other plants and flowers cf. J. Goody, *The Culture of Flowers*, pp. 360–70.

the model of the Latin elegiac poets, imagined their love in wild places, and saw their beloved mirrored in the reflection of the water or in the shapes of the clouds; they confided in nature, searching for its benevolence, and found in it the remembrance of happy times. For them, love was a cosmic power, orderer of chaos and creator of all things, so that nature was not just an ornament or an environment. In Europe after the sixteenth century, nature began to be interpreted as an object of specifically aesthetic enjoyment, to which the development of pastoral music contributed, from the Renaissance to the Baroque, and even until Romanticism. With the Romantic age the idyllic element changed into a true feeling for nature.

In China, however, already in the fourth century nature has assumed an aesthetic aspect through poetic resorts to empathy (the fusion of feelings and images), and therefore accompanied the development of painting as the highest art, a process that reached its acme with the "painting of the literati" in the Song and Yuan epoch.[33] This style blended the external expression with the sentiment, stressing the expression of a mood rather than a passive representation of how objects are perceived. In *wenren* painting, the artist's work not only expressed but was identified with the process of self-cultivation influenced by Daoist and Chan practices. "Writing of

---

[33] An excellent example of the attribution of sentiment to objects and nature, thus reflecting the narcissistic emotions of the author, is the sixth-century anthology *Yutai xinyong* 玉臺新詠 [New songs from a jade terrace]. Zhu Guangqian distinguished between three phases in the evolution of the relation between the feeling and image of nature in Chinese poetry: up to and during the Han dynasty emotion prevails over image and nature serves simply as a background to human events; between the Han and Wei dynasties there is a blending of feelings and images; later, the feeling of nature prevails. See Zhu, *Psychology of art and literature*, p. 133. See also Sabattini's translation, *The Aesthetic Thought*, pp. 154, 165: "The use of the natural landscape as a subject for art seems to have occurred at a very early date in China, but a real love for nature began to appear as a widely felt mood only during the Tao Qian and Xie Lingyun epoch. The poems in the *Classic of Poetry*, like antique painting, made use of nature simply as background or foil. For this reason, they mainly belong to the *xing* form [one of the six principles of poetry, according to the *Shijing*: it refers to the welling up of emotions aroused by contact with the scenery]. This form implied that observations of nature gave rise to emotions relating to human affairs. From the Jin and Tang dynasties, the praising of nature became the prevailing practice, under the influence of the poets, painters and Buddhist monks. In the West we rarely find descriptions of natural landscapes in the works of antiquity, and it is possible to say that a love for nature began with Rousseau. The Romantic writers then enthusiastically gave impetus to this sentiment, such that the call to 'return to nature' became stronger day by day. . . . According to Rousseau, nature was originally completely good and beautiful. With the coming of man, came also society and culture; with the coming of society and culture, there came, in consequence, evil and ugliness." In his reflections on the Chinese view of nature, Hattori Takeshi, "Chūgoku ni okeru," pp. 154–63, points out that, starting from the medieval period, the new aesthetic attitude toward nature was influenced by the southern environment, while the traditional moral veneration of Heaven was more indebted to the monotonous and desolate landscape of the Yellow River.

one's intentions" (*xieyi* 寫意)[34] was a technique that aimed at grasping the essence of things instead of merely describing nature: the inner world was reflected in the scenery of Wu Zhen's mountains and rivers, or in Ni Zan's austere bamboos. Painters lived in close communion with nature, penetrating her various moods by the long discipline of meditation. Like poets, they aimed at conveying a spiritual and natural atmosphere. Thus nature was not only the scenery of objective forms and phenomena, but above all the same reality that existed within themselves. As Cheng Te-k'un says, "The ever-changing elements of the artist's consciousness played a great part in shaping the nature that he recollected and reproduced. The composition revealed something of his own inner self, glimpses of the great breath or consciousness that enlivens every form or entity in nature. . . . Man and other creatures in nature became equals. In the eyes of the artist everything in the universe is a living thing possessing the capacity of passion, sympathy, anger and poignant feeling."[35]

In Ming and Qing literature, which was the heir to the semantic and rhetorical legacy of medieval elaboration, the spring thus becomes an ode to love and life, the autumn a lament for decadence and old age, a nostalgia for past youth and bygone love;[36] the changing of the seasons represents the vanity of every sentiment and passion.

A beautiful page in which love is blended with the perception of nature and spring is this description of the reawakening to love of Liniang, the heroine of the *Mudan ting* 牡丹亭 [The Peony Pavilion]:

> Ah spring, now that you and I have formed so strong an attachment, what shall I find to fill my days when you are past? . . . They were all telling the truth, those poems and ballads I read that spoke of girls of ancient times in springtime moved to passion (*chun ganqing* 春感情), in autumn to regret.

---

[34] In Liu Xie's *Literary Mind* (pp. 376–79), this concept of nature as a metaphor that expresses the emotions is prefigured in the chapter *bixing* 比興, where *bi* is "a description of a thing used to embody an intention" (寫物以附意) and *xing* is a sort of parable drawn from the natural world.

[35] Cheng Te-k'un, "Chinese Nature Painting," *Renditions* (spring 1978), p. 14. Furthermore, in plays like *Xixiangji* 西廂記 [The western chamber], "nature, existing as image, metaphor or scenic description – quoting Christina Shu-Hwa Yao – is assimilated in human form, not as nature untouched. It is presented as the reflection of both the inner world of the characters and the outward action of the play. The world presented in our play, therefore, is human in perspective. A "persistent personalization" is found in the play. Man projects himself into the non-human world and therefore animates the inanimate. Objective nature echoes and mirrors the human world." Cf. Christina Shu-hwa Yao, "The Design within the Symbolic Structure in Hsi-Hsiang-Chi," in *Études d'histoire et de littérature chinoises offertes au Professeur Jaroslav Prusek* (Paris, 1976), p. 322.

[36] What is meant here is not that all poems on autumn follow the convention of "grief in autumn," *beiqiu* 悲秋, but that the general trend was in that direction.

Here am I at the "double eight," my sixteenth year, yet no fine "scholar to break the cassia bough" has come my way.[37]

Liniang falls asleep, and in her dream she meets the student Liu Mengmei. During their union, the Flower Spirit states that between them there exists a predestined marriage that must some day be fulfilled.[38] Here nature, and specifically the garden of the Peony Pavilion, becomes the catalyzer of the genuine emotion of the protagonists.

Concerning the opposite season, during the Song dynasty, Zhu Xi (1130–1200), commenting on a poem attributed to Song Yu that dealt with melancholy induced by the desolation of autumn, wrote that

> Autumn, with each year, is the time when prosperity gives place to decline. The season resembles a dynasty in its final years or a nation on the verge of collapse. . . . Therefore, loyal officials and noble-minded persons banished because of slanders feel especially grieved when touched by the scene of desolation, coldness and dreariness. During their trips far from home, they gaze at the distant mountains or bemoan the passage of time by the riverside where they see off those returning home. Because of their separation from home and homesickness, their grief is all the more acute.[39]

Zhu Xi's comments offer some useful indications. First of all we may notice that he follows the traditional "moral" interpretation of art; thus he educates and domesticates the sentiment of melancholy, and in so doing he covers up its "petty" or "unconscious" motivations by supplying it with civil and political ideals. Next, it is worth noting the close connection between autumn and sad feelings – "autumnal mind" (qiuxin 秋心), "the mind filled with sorrow," as these feelings were called by Gong Zizhen 龔自珍 (1792–1841)[40] – which in Chinese tradition are so closely associated that they

---

[37] Tang Xianzu 湯顯祖, Tang Xianzu ji 湯顯祖集 [collected works of Tang Xianzu] (Reprinted, Shanghai: Renmin CBS, 1973), Mudanting, chu 齣 10, p. 1846, translation by Cyril Birch, Tang Xianzu, The Peony Pavilion (Mudan ting) (Bloomington: Indiana University Press, 1980), p. 46. The literary references come from the Shijing.

[38] Tang Xianzu ji, Mudanting, chu 10, p. 1849; cf. also Birch, tr., Peony Pavilion, p. 49.

[39] Chuci jizhu 楚辭集註 [Collected comments on the Songs from the South], quoted and translated in Zhao Minli, "Autumn, Lovesickness and Homesickness – A Major Theme in Chinese Literature," Social Sciences in China 4 (1991), pp. 163–64. Zhu Xi, who was himself a good poet and was poetically inclined by temperament, regarded poetry writing as peripheral if compared with self-cultivation; however, his love for nature and solitude is clearly manifested in his poems on the cool autumnal air. Cf. Li Chi, "Chu Hsi the Poet," pp. 55–119 (on the Chinese attitude toward nature see pp. 92–119).

[40] Gong Zizhen, Gong Zizhen quanji 龔自珍全集 [Gong Zizhen's complete works] (Shanghai: Shanghai renmin, 1975), ji 輯 9, p. 479; cf. also "the resonance of autumn struck jades," ibid., ji 1, p. 89. Cf. also the term qiuqing 秋情, the sad feeling inspired by an autumn landscape; see, e.g., Daiyu's poem in ch. 45 of the Honglou meng.

became one of the major themes in Chinese lyric literature.[41] Even when people believe they live a solitary and secluded life, according to Gong Zizhen, their mind is not actually free from passions. On the contrary, they become a prey to the sentiment of melancholy, owing to their loneliness. Through inner analysis, one can discover that such an unsatisfied mood is a sickness, a kind of nostalgia due to a lack of present affection and to a remembrance of past emotions. Art, especially poetry, has an important role in this process. This sentiment is a deep feeling, where the self is felt to be floating and dispersed, like an autumn leaf swept by the first cold winds.[42]

Although a premonition of death and a sense of the passing of things may overshadow the pleasure of contemplating nature, this feeling does not arouse desperation. In addition to the effect of the "inner imitation" due to the empathy arising from the contemplation of nature, separation or death are perceived, in practical Chinese fashion, as elements of the same reality: each and every thing has its time, and the awareness of this truth should not distract us from our current activities.[43]

In Chinese literature there appears a recurring *topos* relative to those particular events and objects capable of evoking a situation or a sentiment felt in the past, or a person from a long time ago. This is represented by the

---

[41] Zhao Minli ("Autumn, Lovesickness," pp. 149–73) demonstrates how in Chinese literature the works expressing sad sentiments associated with autumn not only are a natural response to the sense of brevity of human life but have always an obvious indissoluble bond with the themes of lovesickness and homesickness.

[42] Gong Zizhen, *Complete works*, *ji* 1, pp. 89–90.

[43] Two works, one a play, one prose fiction, the *Pipa ji* and the *Jin ping mei*, contain the same poem describing nature after a spring shower: "It is evening. The storm has passed over the south pavilion, red petals float on the surface of the pond. Slowly the distant rumbling thunder moves off, the rain stops and the clouds dissolve. . . . In the shadow of the willow, a young cicada takes up his song. . . . Let us arise and take one another by the hand, let us dress one another's hair. The moon shines on the silk curtains: yet no loving couple lies there. The audacious mandarin duck moves acrobatically amongst the lotus leaves on the water which laps just enough to scatter drops like pearls; they send out inebriating scents. A fragrant breeze moves lightly along the flower beds by the summer pavilion. How could our souls be anything but consoled? Why should we yearn for the Island of the Blessed or the Land of the Fairies? Afterwards, when the West wind blows once more, autumn will come. Perhaps we do not notice, but the seasons and years pass all the same." This passage is quoted by Gao Ming 高明, *Pipa ji* 琵琶記 [The lute] (Taipei: Jinfeng, 1987), j. 21, p. 180. See *Jin ping mei* 金瓶梅 [Plum in a golden vase], crit. ed. Chongzhen (Xinke xiuxiang piping) (Taipei: Xiaoyuan, 1990), h. 27, pp. 352–53; *Jin ping mei cihua*, abridged ed. (Hong Kong: China Books Press, 1986), h. 27, pp. 329–30. Cf. André Lévy, tr. and ed., *Fleur en Fiole d'Or (Jin Ping Mei cihua)* (Paris: Gallimard, 1985). These last lines express such an awareness, and yet within them there is no lack of the joy of living; indeed, the poem could be interpreted as a sophisticated and delicate allusion to the sexual union of a couple of lovers. (Note the allusions to clouds and rain, the shade of the willow and mandarin ducks.)

expressions *chujing shengqing* 觸景生情 (in recalling a sentiment)[44] and *dujing siren* 賭景思人 (when it is a person or being called to mind). This *topos* in some cases expresses the sense of regret or guilt of the transgressor, sometimes it rekindles the feeling of love. Thus peonies can remind an adulteress or an abducted bride of her husband, as in the fifth story of *Huanxi yuanjia* 歡喜冤家 [Adversaries in love]: here it is the peonies that, after miraculously blooming for a second time in autumn, had been the indirect cause of a couple's separation, and now induce the young woman to seek out her husband.[45] And again, in the seventh short story from the same collection, "The Tricks of Chen Zhimei," the inauspicious presentiments deriving from the guilty feelings of the protagonists are stirred by scenes of nature: the story speaks of the adultery committed by Mrs. You with the merchant Chen Cai (Zhimei), who marries her after killing her husband, but after many years of passionate life together, they feel compelled to confess their crime and accuse each other. In one episode, Mrs. You, after making love with Chen by a pond, frightens two mandarin ducks in heat by striking the water with a stick. This reaction, in itself insignificant, induces Chen to recite several verses on the misfortune that would come from disturbing the coupling ducks. The woman is surprised by Chen's ability to recite poetry and tries to persuade him to recite another poem, striking a frog in the pond. The sight of the dead amphibian floating in the water reminds Chen of the image of the body of You's husband, which he had thrown in a river eighteen years before. At first, he does not want to recite the verses that emerge in his mind so as not to vex You, but, in the end, at her insistence, he writes them on a piece of paper, which will later become the evidence that she will use against him in court.[46]

In this "humanization" process of nature, not only animals but also plants participate in human emotions. Worth noting is the tradition that identifies the perpetuity of "true love" with the growth of certain trees and the appearance of a couple of birds. The prototype of such a plant is the "tree of mutual love," *xiangsishu* 相思樹, also called the tree of immortal love.[47] It is mentioned in the story of Han Ping 韓憑 (with the variants *Feng*

---

[44] Cf. the expression "looking at phenomena excites emotions" 賭物興情, in *The Literary Mind*, pp. 94–95.

[45] Cf. *Huanxi yuanjia* 歡喜冤家 [Antagonists in love] (1640. Reprinted, Shenyang: Chunfeng wenyi, 1989), *h.* 5, pp. 87–107, and *Tanhuanbao* 貪歡報 [Retribution for the lecherous, 1640], *h.* 5, pp. 1–20, quoted in Robert Keith McMahon, *Causality and Containment in Seventeenth-Century Chinese Fiction* (Leiden: Brill, 1988), p. 94. See esp. *Antagonists, h.* 5, p. 98; and *Retribution, h.* 5, p. 12a.

[46] Cf. *Antagonists, h.* 7, pp. 123–33, and *Retribution, h.* 7, pp. 1–11, quoted in McMahon, *Causality and Containment*, pp. 94–95.

[47] I am indebted to Anne Osborne for pointing out a similar image in Western tradition: the union of trees after the death of the two lovers in the "Ballad of Barbara Allen."

馮 or *Peng* 朋) of the *Soushenji* 搜紳記 [In search of marvels], a collection of stories compiled originally in the fourth century, but whose present text comes from a Ming edition.[48] The most important elements of the legend are:

(1) Han Ping, minister of the king Kang of Song (in the period of the Warring States), marries a beautiful woman, Miss He.

(2) The king likes the young lady. He therefore kidnaps her, and casts Han Ping into prison.

(3) Lady He sends a secret, ambiguous message to her husband, which is discovered by the king.

(4) Han Ping then commits suicide.

(5) When Lady He learns of this, she contrives to throw herself down from a high tower, leaving behind a letter in which she asks to be buried together with her husband.

(6) The king, enraged at her suicide, orders the corpse of Lady He to be buried in a grave far from the tomb of her husband.

(7) Later, a great catalpa tree (*zimu* 梓木) with two trunks grows from the two coffins; its branches and roots intertwine.

(8) A pair of mandarin ducks (*yuanyang* 鴛鴦)[49] nest on this tree, attracting the attention of local inhabitants with their sad singing.

(9) Thus the story ends, with the comment that the tree was called the tree of mutual love and that the term "mutual love" comes from here.

Leaving out the problem of whether the feeling celebrated here is "love" itself or conjugal devotion, the consolatory function of the legend is clear: an unlucky but constant love is embodied by the miraculous tree that unites that which has been divided against man's will, and the two lovers, or husband and wife, are changed into a pair of birds. The motif of the plant representing the immortalization of the feeling of love and devotion surely comes from before the fourth century, as it can be found, for instance, in the famous ballad (*yuefu*) of the Han dynasty *Kongque dongnan fei* 孔雀東南飛 [Southeast fly the peacocks]. It celebrates conjugal love and ends with the image of the two trees of a pine (*songbo* 松柏) and a *Firmiana* (*wutong* 梧桐) intertwining their branches and leaves, with the presence of a pair of birds, above the common grave of the husband and wife.[50]

---

[48] *Soushenji* 搜神記 [Seeking the spirits] (1603), *j.* 11, pp. 915–16 (Biji xiaoshuo daguan, Taipei: Xinxing shuju, 1978): *Gujin tushu jicheng* 古今圖書集成 [Completed collection of illustrations and writings of ancient and modern times], *Bowu huibian, Caomu dian* 240 (Chengdu: Zhonghua shuju, 1985), vol. 56, pp. 67119–20.

[49] See allusions to the tree of mutual love and to the story of Han Ping in the paragraph on mandarin ducks in the encyclopedia *Gujin tushu jicheng, Bowu huibian, Qinchong dian* 47 (1985), vol. 51, pp. 63474–75. See also the metamorphosis of Han Peng into a bird in the paragraph on various birds, ibid., p. 63521.

[50] Cf. Sawada Mizuho 澤田瑞穗, *Ren ri ji* 連理樹 [The tree of eternal love], in *Chūgoku bungaku kenkyū* 6 (1980), p. 8.

Variants on the same theme go back to the *Soushenji*, like "The Song of Han Peng,"[51] "Han Peng" in the *Taiping guangji* 太平廣記 [Extensive gleanings of the Taiping period],[52] and in *Taiping yulan* 太平御覽 [Imperial digest of the Taiping period].[53] Worth noting – because they represent different paragons of love and some of them are preserved in Ming fiction – are three other cases that share the general aspiration to the immortality of true love. We find all of them in *Taiping guangji*. In the story of Lu Dongmei 陸東美, under the same *topos* of the "twin catalpa tree" and the pair of birds a new, atypical element is introduced: for "mutual love" (*xiang'ai* 相愛) not only the wife but the husband also is ready to die. Lu Dongmei and his wife love each other so passionately that they cannot be separated even for a short time. But one day she dies. In dispair, Dongmei lets himself die of starvation, and both are buried together.[54]

The other case of mutual love, *Panzhang* 潘章, is extended to homosexual love: it describes the story of the love between the king of Chu, Zhongguang 仲光, and Panzhang. They are buried together, and the double tree that grows on their grave and whose branches are intertwined is called "the Common Pillow Tree" (*Gongzhenshu* 共枕樹).[55]

---

[51] *Han Peng fu* 韓朋賦, discovered in Dunhuang Caves. Among the new elements, see Han Peng's departure and his prolonged absence beyond the term he promised for his return (this element will be important in the love literature, as in the first story of *Gujin xiaoshuo*); the miraculous union of the two corpses; the two white stones on the graves; the retributive morality that explicitly links the bad behavior of the king and the end of Song rule; and that, instead of the twin catalpas, the trees growing from the two graves are a *cassia* (*gui* 桂) and a *Firmiana* (*wutong* 梧桐). Cf. Wang Liqi 王利器, "Dunhuang wenxue zhong de Han Peng fu" 敦煌文學中的韓朋賦 [The *fu* of Han Peng in Dunhuang literature], *Wenxue yichan zengkan* 1 (1955) (Beijing: Zuojia CBS); and Sawada Mizuho's essay, *Ren ri ju* (1980), pp. 1–20. See also Takahashi Minoru 高橋稔, "Rikuchō shikai ni okeru ai to shi" 六朝志怪における愛と死 [The motifs of love and death in the Six Dynasties' genre "describing anomalies"], *Chūgoku bungaku kenkyū* 4 (1966), pp. 21–35.

[52] *Taiping guangji* 太平廣記 [Extensive gleanings from the reign of the Great Tranquillity] (981. Reprinted in *Biji xiaoshuo daguan*, reprinted, Yangzhou: Jiangsu Guangling guji keyin, 1983), vol. 2, pp. 281–82, *j.* 463, pp. 43–44, *Qinniao* 禽鳥 4. Cf. also *Gujin tushu jicheng, Bowu huibian, Caomu dian* 309, pp. 67762–63.

[53] *Taiping yulan* 太平御覽 [Imperial digest of the reign of the Great Tranquillity] (Reprinted, Shanghai: Zhonghua shuju, 1960], *j.* 559, p. 2527, *Liyibu* 38, *zhongmu* 3 禮儀部. 塚墓.

[54] *Taiping guangji, j.* 389, p. 40.

[55] *Taiping guangji, j.* 389, p. 40. The case of the "Homosexual Tree" (literally the "tree of the southern wind mode"; *Nan* 南 means "south," but it is a homonym of the term "male" 男; thus, homosexuality is called "southern wind mode" 南風) is also presented by Li Yu in his *Silent Operas*: "The practice is prevalent in all parts of the country, but especially in Fujian. From Jianning and Shaowu onward, every prefecture and county is worse than the one before. And not only are the men fond of it, even such insentient creatures as plants and trees have become infected and take delight in it. Deep in the mountains grows the banyan tree (*rongshu* 榕樹), also known as the Southern Mode tree. If there is a sapling nearby, the banyan will actually lean over and try to seduce it. Eventually, when it has succeeded, its

In the third case, the "mutual love tree" grows on the grave of the wife who has died waiting for her husband's return. This time, the branches and leaves of the plant turn toward where the husband is.[56] Here the legend of the tree of eternal love is applied to the more common motif of female dedication, lending to it a supernatural dignity.

In the Ming dynasty, Feng Menglong 馮夢龍 included the stories of Han Ping and of Lu Dongmei in his collection of love stories.[57] The romantic image of two trees that intertwine their branches above the tombs of a couple separated by the perfidy of men is to be found in a delicate story by Li Zhen 李禎 (Changqi 昌祺, 1376–1452).[58]

Another two examples of the employment of nature are dealt with in

---

branches will be clutching the sapling in a tight embrace, as it folds the young tree into its bosom. The two will then form a single tree which is impossible to separate with knife, saw, axe or chisel. That is why the banyan is known as the Southern Mode tree.

"Not long ago a certain licentiate heard about the tree but was sceptical. Not until he arrived in Fujian and saw it with his own eyes did he realize that there are many strange things in the world and that not everything in oral legend or popular romance is necessarily false. In a chastened mood, he wrote the following quatrain:

> The double lotus, the branches entwined –
> Who would deny love to plant and tree?
> It's true that there exists a Southern Mode;
> You won't believe until you come and see.

Gentle reader, does it not stand to reason that, if plants and trees behave in this manner, a similar obsession is to be expected among men?" Li Yu, *Li Yu quanji* 李漁全集 [Li Yu's complete works], ed., Helmut Martin, *Wushengxi* 無聲戲 [Silent operas] (Taipei: 1970), j. 6, pp. 5385–86; translation by Hanan, *Silent Operas* (Hong Kong: Renditions, Chinese University of Hong Kong, 1990), p. 101. Cf. also Lanselle Rainier, ed. and tr., *Le poisson de jade et l'épingle au phénix: douze contes chinois du XVII siècle* (Paris: Gallimard, 1987), pp. 309–10.

[56] *Taiping guangji*, j. 389, p. 37. Cf. also j. 408, p. 25, *xiangsicao* 相思草 (j. 408, p. 25).

[57] Cf. *Lianzhizi shuangyuanyang* 連枝梓雙鴛鴦, and *Shuangzi shuanghong* 雙梓雙鴻 in his *Qingshi* 情史 [Anatomy of love] (1629–32. Reprinted, Shenyang: Chunfeng wenyi), j. 19, pp. 313–14. See also for the pear tree, the bamboo, the mutual-love grass, and the love tree, j. 23, pp. 790–92 (*li* 梨, *zhu* 竹, *xiangsicao* 相思草, *youqingshu* 有情樹).

[58] A young man of letters, Cui, after many trials, married Penglai 蓬萊; but three years after their wedding, some bandits killed the husband and their leader spared the young woman to keep her as a concubine. She, however, devised a stratagem to be brought next to Cui's corpse and killed herself there. Then the bandit had the bodies buried twenty paces from each other. Years later, an administrator of the secretariat sent several people to investigate and perform the due funeral honors. On their return they revealed that on each grave a tree had grown, both leaning toward one another, their branches interwined in such a way that it was impossible to separate them. (至則兩墓之上，各生一樹相向，枝連柯抱，妝糾結不可解) *Jiandeng yuhua* 剪燈餘話 [More stories written while trimming the wick] (Taipei: Shijie shuju, 1978), j. 2, pp. 26–27; *Jiandeng xinhua* 剪燈新話 [New stories written while trimming the wick] (Shanghai: Shanghai guji, 1981), j. 2, pp. 163–69. Cf. Jacques Dars, tr., *En mouchant la chandelle: nouvelles chinoises des Ming* (Paris, 1986), pp. 162–70. The same story is also included, in an abridged version, in Feng Menglong's *Qingshi*, j. 19, pp. 315–18, "Lianlishu" 連理樹 [The tree of eternal love].

Xiyoubu 西遊補 [The dream of the Monkey], a short novel that draws inspiration from the well-known *Journey to the West* and is attributed to Dong Yue 董説 (1620–86). They are worth noting because they constitute another way of representing nature. In these passages sarcasm blends with symbolism in an abstract and metaphysical atmosphere. The first passage at the beginning of the novel presents a dispute between Monkey and the monk Xuanzang about the color of what appear when seen from afar to be some peonies, but which will later reveal themselves to be groups of young girls and youths:

> So the Monkey said: "Master, those peonies are red."
> And the monk: "No! They are not red."
> So the Monkey retorted: "I think that your eyes are blinded by the brightness of the spring sun if you still insist that these peonies, that are so red, are not red. Why do not you dismount your horse and sit down while I call on the Bodhisattva king of medicine so that you may cure your sight? Do not try to proceed while your sight is so dimmed by this illness. If you take the wrong road, do not blame the rest of us."
> The monk: "Vile Monkey, it is you who does not see well! And instead you accuse me of poor sight."
> "If your sight is not dimmed, Master, then why do you state that the peonies are not red?"
> "I did not say that the peonies are not red, I only said that the red is not of the peonies."
> "Master, if the red is not of the peonies, I think it is due to the reflection of the sun on the flowers that they are so red."
> At these words, the monk decided that his disciple was farther yet from reality: "You idiot of a monkey – he raged – you yourself are red and you attribute the color now to the peonies, now to the sun. What nonsense!"
> "You want to joke, Master! The fur that covers my body is fairish, the tiger skin I wear is spotted, and my cape is iridescent. Where do you see red in me?"
> "I did not say that your body is red, I meant to say that you are red inside. Wukong, listen to my *gatha*." And still on his horse, he recited:

> > The peonies are red.
> > Red is the mind of the disciple.
> > When the peonies are all fallen
> > It is if they have not yet bloomed.[59]

In these lines, somewhat absurd and at least a bit surreal, the image of the spring flowers gives way, in a humorous tone, to a reflection on the

---

[59] Dong Yue, *Xiyou bu* (Taipei: Shijie shuju, 1983), *h.* 1, pp. 2–3. Cf. Shuen-fu Lin and Larry Schulz, tr., *The Tower of Myriad Mirrors, a supplement to* Journey to the West *by Tung Yüeh (1620–1686)* (Berkeley: Asian Humanities Press, 1988), pp. 24–25.

subjectivity of images and the attraction for that which we consider beautiful. At the end we understand in what way the monk, even in his pedantry, was right: the appearance that surrounds us is nothing but a projection of our thoughts, desires, and aspirations. The logic of the passage brings to mind, *per contra*, Wang Yangming's well-known statement inspired by the sight of a tree in blossom on a hill:

> The Teacher was roaming in Nanzhen. A friend pointed to flowering trees on a cliff and said, "[You say] there is nothing under heaven external to the mind. These flowering trees on the high mountain blossom and drop their blossoms of themselves. What have they to do with my mind?"
>
> The Teacher said, "Before you look at these flowers, they and your mind are in the state of silent vacancy. As you come to look at them, their colors at once show up clearly. From this you can know that these flowers are not external to your mind."[60]

The second passage describes the scenery, in part realistic and in part imaginary, that the Monkey, guided by a Daoist wizard, sees during a pilgrimage in the mountains.

> So the two, joking as if they were old friends, set out. After passing a stone ladder, before them lay a cave out of which a brook flowed.
>
> "Have we reached your house?" asked the Monkey.
>
> "Not yet – said the old man – This place is called *Imitation of the Ancient Evening Scenery.*"
>
> The Monkey admired the scenery, which was truly splendid. To the left there was a grassy expanse on which some rocks were scattered randomly, and a dozen sumac trees with twisted branches surrounded a straw hut. In front of the door there was a great red pine and numerous Liquidambar trees enveloped by the fog, forming a complete landscape with the forest and the mountain, the wind and the rain. On the side of the forest one could glimpse half a bamboo fence from which two or three kinds of field flowers peeped out. . . .
>
> Suddenly they reached another enchanted cave.
>
> "Neither is this my home, – explained the old man – it is called *Imitation of the Taikun Pond.*"
>
> All around they were surrounded by green summits, some of which

---

[60] Wang Yangming, *Yangming quanshu* 陽明全集 [Wang Yamgming's complete works] (Sibu beiyao. Reprinted, Taipei: Taiwan Zhonghua shuju, 1979), *j.* 3, p. 14. Translation by Chan Wing-tsit, *Instructions for Practical Living and other Neo-Confucian Writings by Wang Yang-ming* (New York: Columbia University Press, 1963), p. 222. As Wang Yangming explains in another passage, the master of the body is the mind, and intentions all emanate from the same mind. Objects are the directions of intentions, like serving one's parents or loving people, or seeing, speaking, and so on. This is the reason why neither principles nor objects are outside the mind. *Yangming quanshu, j.* 1, p. 4a.

seemed to look up at the sky, others seemed to bow down to drink water; one summit seemed as if it were running, another sleeping, still another as if it were whistling; and there were summits that were sitting, faced each other like Confucians, summits that were about to take flight, summits resembling rejoicing spirits, or that looked like oxen, horses, or goats.

The Monkey, laughing, commented: "All of these stone men and stone horses are all perfectly sculpted but there are no tombstones to be seen; maybe there is no one capable of sculpting inscriptions."

"Young monk, – said the old man – do not speak in jest, rather look at the water."

The Monkey bowed down his head and looked carefully, and saw upside down in the water all the surrounding green summits. The rippling surface of the lake looked like paintings of mountains and forests.[61]

The first observation concerns nature: the scenery that appears before the Monkey's eyes is marvelous because it *looks natural*, but in reality it is *artificial* inasmuch as it is an imitation of famous landscapes. This enjoyable ambiguity is mastered by Chinese painters and especially garden architects: gardens' rocks and hills are based on those represented in paintings, as well as pictures of gardens that are themselves illustrations of paintings. Like the constituent materials used in the ancient arts of gardens and bonsai,[62] rocks and grass, bamboo and trees with twisted branches, caves and brooks, are wisely combined. All these natural statues manifest the traditional Chinese worship for stones and rocks, considered as a concentration of the creative forces of the Dao. In this enchanted place even the mountains seem alive: what amazes the onlooker rather is that these natural sculptures are not accompanied by tombstones, expected by the Chinese eye. The rain and wind are also present, and the people encountered are part of the scenery. The mountain lake, lastly, is nothing but a mirror, and like every mirror, it gives a reflection of the protagonist's inner self, by now undisturbed by the excitement of the passions that drove him to wander anxiously through the World of Illusions, and the Worlds of the Past and Future, and to lose sight of the monk Xuanzang and his mission. The subtle ripples that still veil the lake's surface mean that the Monkey is not yet completely ready to regain his place in the pilgrimage to the West.

Nature – "natural" or "artificial" nature – therefore represents or evokes not only feelings and passions, but also moods, states of the mind, and its moral journey. Echoing Guo Xi's (c. 1020–90) lesson on the interaction

[61] Dong Yue, *Xiyoubu, j.* 13, pp. 4–5. Cf. Shuen-fu Lin and Larry Schulz, tr., *The Tower of Myriad Mirrors*, pp. 158–160.
[62] Cf. Rolf A. Stein, *Le monde en petit* (Paris: Flammarion, 1987).

between moods and nature,[63] Duo the Ninth says in *The Destinies of the Flowers in the Mirror* that "while contemplating one's environment may be a means of engendering feelings, it may also be that one's surroundings arise from what one is feeling."[64] It seems that Li Ruzhen here distinguishes two different cases: in the former the emotion is induced by the mind's reaction to the external environment; in the latter the contemplation of the scenery is influenced by personal moods. The first case would appear as subjectivity coming from objectivity, when – in Baoyu's father's words – the sight of a place moves the mind (入目動心).[65] In fact, in both cases everything starts from the subject's mind: as Duo the Ninth goes on, "Nothing there is that is not made so by the heart-mind 莫不由於心造, nor can in any degree be forced to be otherwise."[66] A landscape is either sad or joyful according to cultural convention, or because of one's mood; the flux between the inside and outside worlds starts from man reaching scenery and then from the scenery comes back to man. From everyone's experience, we know that on the emotional level, the object becomes relevant only with respect to the extent and in the way that it is subjectively perceived. Were the peonies red or was the Monkey's mind red? From the *Dream of the Monkey* it was rather clear that the color was coming from Monkey's inner attitude. And Wang Yangming stated that the flowers seen on a cliff were inside the mind. The description of a landscape, plant, or other thing, thus cannot exist without a particular subjective feeling on the part of the person who observes it at the moment of perception. This was the case for Tao Yuanming contemplating the Southern Mountain, cited by Zhu Guangqian, as he reflected upon the aesthetic concept of beauty:

> When we feel that nature is beautiful, nature has already become an image expressing a feeling. . . . The old pine, once it has become the object of our appreciation, is no longer unexpressive matter, but has definitively changed into an image or form that expresses a particular feeling. . . . The old pine is like a dictionary. Each person chooses from it the words necessary to express his own particular feelings.[67]

---

[63] In the two-way relationship, emotions are aroused by the sight of nature and the artist's mood is so projected onto nature that his perception of nature changes following his emotions. Cf. Sakanishi's translation, *An Essay on Landscape Painting* (London 1935), pp. 38–39, quoted in Laurence Sickman and Alexander Soper, *The Art and Architecture of China* (Harmondsworth: Penguin Books, 1978), p. 219.

[64] Li Ruzhen, *Destinies of the flowers*, *h.* 43, p. 210.

[65] *Dream of the red chamber*, *h.* 17, p. 190: the sight of that place, thus, awakens some idea, intention, or desire. Liu Xie, anyway, had written that "when objects and colors in the physical word change, our heart-minds are also affected" 物色之動心亦搖焉 (*Literary Mind*, pp. 476–77).

[66] Li Ruzhen, *Destinies of the flowers*.

[67] Zhu Guangqian, *Psychology of art*, p. 156; Sabattini, *Aesthetic Thought*, p. 176.

17.3. GARDENS AND FLOWERS

In the examples that follow, the writer introduces scenery and plants in order to create in the reader the same mood as is in himself, and to share with the reader the emotion the scene has stirred in him. We have several such examples in the major novels of the period, among which I have examined the *Dream of the red chamber, Plum in a golden vase,* and the *Unofficial history of the literati.* Of the 21 passages which have been selected and examined (10 from *Plum in a golden vase,* 6 from the *Unofficial history,* and 5 from the *Dream of the red chamber*), 16 treat traditional scenery, that is, gardens, plants, and rural panoramas, while 2 concern pictorial representations and 3 deal with performances that could not be included at all among natural sights: firework displays and decorations for urban festivities. Their comparison allows us to see similar attitudes as well as some differences, which, however, go beyond the present study. What is worth noting now is that of the 16 representations of enjoyment of natural scenery, 3 supply a more or less detailed description of private gardens,[68] one also includes an appreciation of the vases rather than the flowers,[69] another includes the sight of paintings and poems,[70] and the last also contains listening to music.[71]

Anyway, the perception of natural beauty is mostly attained through the eyes. The most common expressions concerning the act of observing and admiring are *yanchou* 眼瞅, "looking";[72] *shangwan* 賞玩, "enjoying or appreciating the sight";[73] *guan, kan, kanjian,* 觀，看，看見, "observing";[74] *siguyiwang* 四顧一望, "looking around";[75] and *qiao, jian* 瞧, 見 "seeing."[76] If visual contemplation is the main function, what are its meanings and objects?

In the following passage, for instance, Baoyu is enchanted by the brilliance and contrast of the colors in the snowy garden:

---

[68] *Dream of the red chamber, h.* 17, pp. 185–97; *Plum in a golden vase, h.* 19, pp. 233–34; *h.* 54, p. 705.

[69] *Plum in a golden vase, h.* 61, p. 812.

[70] *Unofficial history, h.* 11, p. 118.

[71] Ibid., *h.* 29, pp. 289–90.

[72] *Dream of the red chamber, h.* 11, pp. 129–30.

[73] *Plum in a golden vase, h.* 19, p. 233–34; cf. also *shangxue* 賞雪, "enjoy the sight of the snow," ibid., *h.* 67, p. 903.

[74] *Dream of the red chamber, h.* 11, pp. 130–31 (*kan yuanzhongjing* 看園中景, "to admire the scenery inside the garden"); *Plum in a golden vase, h.* 19, pp. 233–34; *h.* 21, p. 273; *h.* 61, p. 812; *h.* 98, pp. 1384–85; *Unofficial history, h.* 1, p. 5; *h.* 8, pp. 88–89; *h.* 48, p. 474.

[75] *Dream of the red chamber, h.* 49, pp. 606.

[76] Ibid., *h.* 40, pp. 480–81; *Plum in a golden vase, h.* 54, p. 705.

Once outside the courtyard gate, the Garden stretched out on every hand in uniform whiteness, uninterrupted except for the dark green of a pine-tree or the lighter green of some bamboos here and there in the distance. He felt as if he was standing in the middle of a great glittering crystal bowl. Proceeding on his way, he had just turned a spur in the miniature mountain whose foot he was skirting, when his senses were suddenly ravished by a delicate cold fragrance.[77]

First, we notice that gardens are well-delimited places (of the type called a *hortus conclusus*, i.e., an enclosed garden), which are separated from the surrounding area by a wall: the *Daguanyuan* (大觀園), or Baoyu's ideal Garden of the Broad Vision, is a kind of protective fortress, however ephemeral it is. Also in European medieval literature gardens were represented as, and often were, unreachable, well-protected, and walled places.[78] Gardens thus seem a "concentration" of nature, but are not only nature, as they reflect "social and personal reality."[79] Exemplary is the description of Sima Guang's urban garden, the "Garden of Enjoying [Music] by Yourself Alone" (*Dule yuan* 獨樂園).[80] After presenting all the main elements of his garden (library, pavilions, streams, island, terrace, trees, and flowers), Sima Guang explains that there are gathered together, in front of one's eyes, all the principles of phenomena and beings, before their formation and extending in every direction.[81] Like a landscape painting, gardens should give

---

[77] *Dream of the red chamber*, h. 49, p. 606. David Hawkes, *Story of the Stone*, vol. 2, pp. 481–82.

[78] It is not by chance that "paradise," in both its Hebrew and Greek forms (*pardes, paradeisos*), comes from the ancient Iranian *pairidaeza*, "enclosure, park, garden." For nature as inner reflection of jealous love, see, e.g., *Guigemar*, in Giovanna Angeli, ed., *Lais* (Parma: Pratiche, 1992), pp. 64–65, 141a, 219–22: "in a garden, under the tower,/all around there was an enclosure;/the wall was of green marble,/very high and thick!" ("En un vergier, suz le dongun,/La out un clos tut envirun;/De vert marbre fu li muralz,/Mult par esteit espés e halz!").

[79] Cf. Mara Miller, *Garden as an Art*, p. 177.

[80] The term comes from *Mencius* 1, 2, 1, and expresses the true joy Sima Guang could find there. Earlier description of an ideal garden can be found in the *Songs of the South (Chuci)*, in a poem of perhaps the 4th century B.C. Cf. "The Summons of the Soul," translated by David Hawkes, in Cyril Birch, ed., *Anthology of Chinese Literature*, pp. 75–76. In the Han period several writers, Sima Xiangru among them, described the Imperial Park, symbol of the imperial power and territory and an imitation of the paradise of immortality. Taking their style from the imperial parks, the first elaborate private gardens were built by princes and great merchants of the Han dynasty – like the fantastic garden of Yuan Guanghan on the outskirts of the capital, with its artificial mountain.

[81] "Sima Guang usually spent a great part of his time in the Studio reading books: he learned from the great sages as his teachers and discussed with the worthies as if they were his friends; he inquired into the origins of humanity and righteousness, and investigated the sources of the rites and music. All principles of phenomena and beings, before their formation and extending in every direction, gathered together in front of his eyes. . . . Under moonlight and with a clear breeze he walked as he liked: all his senses and

a view of the total universe in a small size: *juti erwei* 具體而微, and reveal the
beauty and essence of all beings according to the heart-mind.[82] Although
their beauty basically lies in natural landscapes, they contain pavilions,
houses, and many products of human artifice; some of them pretend even
to offer the Confucian simplicity of the farming life. Often framed inside
the geometric square of urban centers, their apparent irregularity is harmo-
nized with the symmetry of pavilions, study rooms, galleries, bridges, and
halls that are built inside; even natural elements like trees, stones, water,
and hills are arranged as artificially as are components of any work of art:
the art of building mountains, as Li Yu said, was similar to writing an essay.
Their structure obeys a complex architectonic plan, which not only follows
the ideological purpose of creating a microcosm of the universe,[83] but at
the same time resorts to ingenious artifices and devices in order to offer
artistic sceneries, surprising and unexpected sights, and various and extraordinary perspectives. Therefore the evaluation of reactions to the contemplation of gardens and of their descriptions offers much more
information on the cultural elements of a certain society than merely their
attitude toward nature.

　　In the introduction, after the quotation of a passage from *Dream of the red
chamber*[84] in which Baoyu criticizes the imitation village of Daoxiang 稻香村
in the Garden of the Broad Vision, we are presented with the new category
of "artificial nature": it arises in the case of gardens where nature is obviously manipulated by human artifice. This manipulation of nature might
be considered aesthetically positive or negative, and the dispute between
two different aesthetic concepts implies different philosophical and moral
views, and different perceptions of the "natural." According to Baoyu's
father, the Garden of the Broad Vision has turned out well: it accomplishes
its own functions of self-cultivation, and throughout its mysteries it leads to

---

　　feelings were totally his very own." Cf. *Sima Wengong wenji* 司馬温公文集, *Dule yuan* 獨樂園
[Collected works of Sima Guang], *j.* 13, p. 304. Zhu Xi also speaks of his delight in the
plants of his garden and the miniature landscapes that he prepared with basins, incense
burners, and strange rocks, so that he could enjoy the taste of the universe with rivers,
mountains, and clouds. Cf. Li Chi, "Chu Hsi the Poet" p. 115.

[82] For aesthetic conception relating to painting, see, e.g., Shitao, as in *Les Propos sur la
peinture du moine Citrouille-amère*, tr. Pierre Ryckmans (Paris: Hermann, 1984), pp. 139–40,
9–10.

[83] Cf. Andrew Plaks, *Archetype and Allegory in the "Dream of the Red Chamber"* (Princeton:
Princeton University Press, 1976), p. 146. One might say that the Chinese garden is both
the timeless and spaceless place that transcends the social rhythm and order, and at the
same time is functionally related to them. On the influence of dream visions and the
building of gardens in the Ming dynasty, see Jan Stuart, "A Scholar's Garden in Ming China:
Dream and Reality," *Asian Art* 3.4 (1990), pp. 31–51.

[84] *Dream of the red chamber*, *h.* 17, pp. 191–92.

the search for simplicity and purity.[85] This means not only that the garden has an aesthetic function, but that its contemplation induces moral values. In fact, the domestication and manipulation of nature in gardens and their *inclusion in an urban context* can be understood as a conscious or unconscious attempt to solve dialectically the old contradiction between civil engagement and retreat to countryside. The solution of the garden was in some way the solution to the contrast between urban and official life on the one hand and rural and free life on the other, parallel to the contrast between the artificial and the natural. From the ideological point of view, the aesthetic contemplation of nature was included in a Neo-Confucian frame, and the official did not need to leave his engagement in order to concentrate himself in meditation and in the search for sagehood: he could any time become a free hermit whenever he visited his garden. If this hypothesis is correct, Baoyu's critical words sound really subversive. Blaming the aesthetic incongruity of the little imitation village, he seems – at least partially – to reject the compromising Neo-Confucian solution and to prefer a radical reversion back to Tao Yuanming's seclusion. In other words, although he does not reject convention (and human culture) as a means of representing authentic reality, he emphasizes the ideal of the creative and vital spirit rather than the value of simple rusticity. It is also true that for Baoyu the contemplation of nature means self-perfection, but this depends more on the *form* than on the moral *contents*: on whether the components are well assorted or not.

In the passages from the three novels concerning the contemplation of scenery, we may note, first of all, the concurrence of all the senses – sight above all – in the contemplative process, then the evocation of a feeling of nostalgia, and the close relation between nature and art. The beauty of rural scenery is often associated with the beauty of paintings and poetic verses; the garden is not just a copy of the universe, but it is itself a universe: the landscape architect must be skillful enough to be as "natural" as the brush and the ink of the painter, which "correspond to the naturalness of heaven and earth" (以筆墨之自然合乎天地之自然).[86] What is admired is natural beauty such as that of the snow,[87] the blossoming of plants, the yellowing and fading of the leaves; and it is indeed this kind of beauty that one attempts to immortalize, even if rarely successfully, in paintings:

---

[85] Ibid., *h.* 17, pp. 186, 190. Jia Zheng says, e.g., that "although the scenery is made by human artifice, its sight is moving, awakening the desire to get back to rural life."

[86] This phrase is Tangdai's 唐岱, a landscape painter of Manchu origin, and a disciple of Wang Yuanqi 王原祁 (1642–1715).

[87] Ibid., *h.* 49, p. 606; *Plum in a golden vase, h.* 21, p. 273, *h.* 67, p. 903.

"You know, we country folk like to get a picture at the New Year that we can stick up on the wall. Every year just before New Year the farmers come into town to buy one. Many's the time of an evening when the day's work was done we've sat and looked at the picture on our wall and wished we could get inside it and walk around, never imagining that such beautiful places could really be. Yet now I look at this Garden here, and it's ten times better than any picture I ever saw. If only I could get someone to make a painting of it all, just the way it is, that I could take back to show the others, I do believe I should die content!"[88]

In fact, both gardens in *Plum in a golden vase* and *Dream of the red chamber* are nothing but mediated projections of the mind of Ximen Qing and Baoyu. The Garden of the Broad Vision – whose centrality as a *locus amoenus* has been pointed out by Andrew Plaks and Yu Yingshi[89] – is the utopia of a purely juvenile and feminine domain, free from the social restrictions, responsibilities, authority, and hierarchy of everyday life, an island where sentiments are unrestrained and spontaneously expressed.[90] Similarly, Ximen's garden is the mirror of his lustful mind, which reflects his greedy and sensual desires, his yearning for immoral pleasures.

These gardens, therefore, have a strong character of ambiguity, and cannot be seen just as positive paradises or negative hells of temptation. The Garden of the Broad Vision is illusory, like a dream or the "World of Illusions of the Great Void," but it is real like our affective world, which gives colors to our perceptions. It is thus the world of passions and desires (*qing*),[91] and at the same time the celebration of ideal beauty: "All beautiful

---

[88] Cf. *Dream of the red chamber*, h. 40, pp. 480–81. On the *succedaneous function* of paintings for real landscapes, see Zhu Xi, *Zhuzi daquan* 朱子大全 [Great compendium of Master Zhu], Sibu beiyao (Reprinted, Taipei: Taiwan Zhonghua, 1933), vol. 45, c. 78: "But now really I have no leisure time for this place, and for the moment I just think back to that beautiful landscape in this way, and write poems about it. I will ask a painter to draw its picture, and every time I look at it, I will console myself" 顧今誠有所未暇姑記其山水之勝如此並為之詩將 使畫者圖之時覽觀以自慰也. See also Li Chi, "Chu Hsi the Poet," p. 108. Also for Yuan Hongdao 袁宏道 (1568–1610) the enjoyment of flowers was just a substitute for people living in the cities who were bereaved of the natural scenery.

[89] Cf. A. Plaks, "Allegory in *Hsi-yu chi* and *Hung-lou meng*," in A. Plaks, ed., *Chinese Narrative: Critical and Theoretical Essays* (Princeton: Princeton University Press, 1977), p. 197. Plaks, however, notices the different significance of the allegorical garden in Europe and in China: "the Western concern with distinguishing the true from the false paradise or properly ordering the totality of created Nature to the uncreated Grace of its First Cause, as opposed to the Chinese notion of the interfusion of universality and particularity in the self-contained ground of existence." See Yu Yingshi 余英時, *Hongloumeng-de liangge shijie* 紅樓夢 的兩個世界 [The two worlds of the *Honglou meng*] (Taipei: Lianjing, 1978).

[90] Or better, as Yu Yingshi notices in his penetrating analysis (*The two worlds*, pp. 41–143, on the Garden of the Broad Vision), the utopian world of the Garden has its own order, hierarchy, and values. Yu Yingshi points out the difference between these two worlds as a key to understanding the novel.

[91] Cf. Yu Yingshi, *The two worlds*, p. 54.

sceneries of heaven and earth are here assembled."[92] As M. E. Scott points out, "like the garden in *Jin Ping Mei*, *Daguanyuan* is a playground of desire, but in *Honglou meng* desire is defined more broadly than in *Jin Ping Mei*, for it includes not only ordinary lust and greed, which aim to possess and thereby annihilate their objects, but also that inattainably perfect love which one finds only in dreams, when both the self and the object of desire are free of all social constraints and obligations."[93] Furthermore, the Garden of the Broad Vision, as well as the garden in the medieval Western *Romance of the Rose*, is deeply concerned with natural beauty, but is invaded at the end by the forces of evil, and the beauty becomes corrupted, decays, and collapses. The *Daguanyuan*'s impending decadence is no less dramatic: from its origin – the garden originated in the combination of the two older gardens of the Ning and Rong Mansions, both to some degree contaminated by previous lustful practices – its purity is threatened by dirty and sordid elements.[94] The causes of such corruption are anyway quite different in European and Chinese literature. In fact, the Chinese garden is the refuge for solitary meditation as well as the place for parties with friends and social relations, without a clear distinction between self-cultivation and leisure; it may be a space for the eremitic life or for any kind of mundane pleasure. The garden being a microcosm of the universe as well as an objectivation of the human mind, it shows not only a kaleidoscope of environments and a ceaseless alternation of styles and vistas, but also the owner's complex life and character, his deep contradictory tendencies.

Unlike medieval Western gardens – whose landscape was part divine gift and *part human penance*[95] – the Chinese literary gardens, in spite of their ambiguity, are not marked by the stain of the original sin. This is quite obvious, as original sin depends on Christian tradition, but it is an important difference in character that clearly entails consequences for the perception of nature. In their cosmic completeness, the gardens of *Plum in a golden vase* and *Dream of the red chamber* attempt to present the characteristics of every season and the aspects of every different kind of environment. Chapter 19 of *Plum in a golden vase*[96] provides a synthetic description of the marvels of Ximen's garden. There is no season without flowers: "Each of

---

[92] *Dream of the red chamber*, h. 18, p. 206. Compare this sentence with the more philosophical statement of Sima Guang quoted previously.

[93] Cf. Mary Elizabeth Scott, *Azure from Indigo: "Hong lou meng"'s Debt to "Jin Ping Mei*," Ph.D. dissertation, Princeton University (1989), p. 216.

[94] In the famous episode of the flower burial, Daiyu says to Baoyu: "The water that you see here is clean, but farther on, once it flows out, it will be polluted by impurities from people's houses." *Dream of the red chamber*, h. 23, p. 268.

[95] See the interesting book on Western traditional landscape and garden by D. Pearsall and E. Salter, *Landscapes and Seasons of the Medieval World* (London: Elek, 1973), p. 127. My italics.

[96] Cf. *Plum in a golden vase*, h. 19, pp. 233–34.

the four seasons provides scenes for the delight of people," says the long poem before describing some of the plants and flowers (peach, lotus, water lily, chrysanthemum, plum, willow, cherry, apricot, rose, pine, pear, peony, pine, bamboo, palm, sunflower, etc.). *Dream of the red chamber* describes details of the Garden of the Broad Vision in its chapters 17 and 18: plants, flowers, buildings, waters, and rocks, corners for enjoying the moon, gleams of lantern light, faint sounds of music. After visiting the garden, Jia Zheng comments: "although the scenery is made by human artifice, its sight is moving, awakening the desire to get back to rural life."[97]

Furthermore, in the description of the garden we find several buildings and artificial works, including lakes, mounds, isles, and rivers. This beauty is natural because it derives from the changing of the seasons and the employment of the effects that nature itself produces, but at the same time that which allows us to appreciate it is human artifice, the technique and taste that make possible the exaltation of the contrast of colors, and the creation of original and strange images through a wise combination of flowers and plants of every kind with these buildings, hills, and artificial waterways: "'Without this hill,'[98] Jia Zheng observed visiting the new garden, 'the whole garden would be visible as one entered, and all its mystery would be lost.'"[99]

This makes clear the admiration for the "artificial and miniature mountains, caves, lakes, and gold-fish ponds,"[100] windows shaped like the moon, and caverns of snow; halls of the wind, and halls of the waters, walls of pine-trees and passages of bamboos;[101] or for "white rocks in all kinds of grotesque and monstrous shapes, rising course above course up one of its sides, some recumbent, some upright or leaning at angles, their surfaces streaked and spotted with moss and lichen or half concealed by creepers, and with a narrow, zig-zag path only barely discernible to the eye winding up between them. . . . Pavilions nestled on mounds. . . .";[102] "painted and carved pavilions built from the slopes on either side, their lower halves concealed amidst the trees, their tops reaching into the blue, . . . below the well, row

---

[97] Cf. *Dream of the red chamber*, h. 17, pp. 185–97. Spring scenes are presented in chs. 18–25 of *Dream*, summer scenes in chs. 26–36, while autumn and winter scenes are respectively described in chs. 37–47 and 48–53.

[98] For the tradition of the "artificial mountains" (*jiashan* 假山) in the miniaturized gardens, see Rolf Stein, *Le monde en petit* (Paris: Flammarion, 1987); Italian translation: *Il mondo in piccolo* (Milano: Il Saggiatore, 1987), pp. 37–48.

[99] Cf. *Dream of the red chamber*, h. 17, p. 186.

[100] Cf. ibid., h. 11, pp. 130–31; h. 17, pp. 185–97. Cf. *Plum in a golden vase*, h. 19, pp. 233–34; h. 54, p. 705. Cf also the quoted passage from *Xiyoubu*.

[101] Cf. *Plum in a golden vase*, h. 19, pp. 233–34.

[102] Cf. ibid.

upon row of miniature fields full of healthy-looking vegetables and flowers."[103] And again, it is the skill of the builder that creates surroundings that recall a Daoist paradise and islands of happiness.[104] This does not mean, however, the conception of an ideal aesthetic value of which the artist is creator. There is no metaphysical contradiction between the "natural" and the "artificial," although the two terms are in continuous dialectical opposition: the conceiver of the garden has done nothing but translate "spontaneously" the beauty of nature, without adding anything – as we have already noticed in the scenes from the *Dream of the Monkey*. However, not only the "artificial" may be functional with respect to the "natural," but even the "conventional" may be functional with respect to the "spontaneous": landscapes, pavilions, bridges, ponds, bamboos, birds, and flowers. It does not matter if the individual elements may appear conventional, even hackneyed. The suggestiveness comes from the whole combination, which borrows the artificial and the conventional in order to hint at feelings and revelations.[105] From the quotation of the passage from the *Dream of the Monkey* we have seen how what *looks natural* in reality may be *artificial* and vice versa. The conventional way of representing the famous landscapes influences the perception itself of landscapes so that paintings and gardens play on the ambiguity between transfigured and real nature, as in Li Gonglin's 李公麟 famous picture of the Western Garden (about 1080), where the "artificial" rocks inside the garden interact with the "natural" mountains visible in the background beyond the garden.[106]

The close relation between the scenery in paintings and the art of construction of a garden, did not relate only to the effort of balancing shadow and light, water, wood, stone, flowers, and so on, but also to constant literary and historical allusions. Moreover, the construction of a private garden was much more than this, because it was the demonstration of the owner's creativity and wealth. But there was more to it: especially from the end of the Ming dynasty, the tendency, which had started in Song times, of building private gardens among the literati, developed into a more personal and emotional art, thanks also to the patronage of rich

---

[103] Cf. *Dream of the red chamber*, h. 11, pp. 130–31, h. 17, pp. 185–97.

[104] Cf. *Plum in a golden vase*, h. 54, p. 705.

[105] As Michael Sullivan writes of painters, "the Chinese scholar-painter, as a philosopher, seeks to distill the essence of nature and to see beyond the visible forms to the reality that lies behind them." "Chinese Art and Its Impact on the West," in Paul Ropp, ed., *Heritage of China: Contemporary Perspectives on Chinese Civilization* (Berkeley: University of California Press, 1990), p. 279.

[106] Maggie Keswick contrasts "false" with "real" mountains. See *Chinese Garden*, p. 101, illustration p. 103 no. 94. Cf. also Johnston R. Stewart, *Scholar Gardens of China*, p. 38.

merchants.[107] By virtue of the popularity reached by some novels and plays, the garden was seen also as a representation of the inner world of the owner and his or her visitors. The cult of the emotions and the cult of characters like Liniang, Baoyu, or Daiyu could not but have consequences for the perception of gardens in the late-imperial age.

And lastly, building a garden is – from the ideological point of view – like collecting all the elements of the universe and concentrating them in this microcosm. This aggregation, moreover, is not just a *static* collection, like a museum, or a botanical or zoological garden. It is a "natural" reproduction, in a limited space, of the *dynamic* flow of the universe. Thus the garden is the place where every season is enjoyed; but it is also the whole cosmos, and thus the place of contemplation and meditation; it helps humans to merge harmoniously into their environment, by discovering the same harmony within themselves.

Generally speaking, the development of a contemplative attitude in this period can be explained by the search for a serene and uncontaminated life, in a time of social crisis and political turmoil. The rediscovery of the ideal of the "recluse," furthermore, broadened the field of personal sensibilities, promoting private aspirations of a refined and aesthetic life. Thus, in the paintings of landscapes, where the "vital energy of mountains and forests" (*shanlinqi* 山林氣) is captured with detached tranquillity, the harmony with nature's grandeur expresses the painter's inner world.[108] The reproduction of the macrocosm (nature/universe) in a microcosm

---

[107] Concerning the ever more expensive demand for elaborate urban gardens, one impoverished poet wrote: "A cooling breeze and a shining moon. Of course these are priceless. Alas that they have brought but forty thousand cash!" (quoted in Maggie Keswick, *The Chinese Garden*, p. 76, caption 73). Allusion is made to the proverb: "The pure wind and the bright moon are in essence beyond any price" 清風明月本無價.

[108] One should not be surprised if even the "negative" characters of *Plum in a golden vase* enjoy the sublime and cathartic experience of the contemplation of nature. First of all, the characters in *Plum* are very complex, and in everyone we can find vices blended with humanity. Furthermore it is possible that the ambiguous and sarcastic attitude of the author of *Plum* allows such sacrilegious contradiction, an example of which is the way Ximen pursues his lustful ends through the use of the Confucian cardinal relations. As M. E. Scott, in *Azure from Indigo*, pp. 200–04, has noticed, Ximen's new garden is a portrait of Ximen's dissolute nature since its beginning, because its history comes from an adultery with overtones of incest. The park was made by annexing the existing garden of Ximen's sworn brother Hua Zixu's house next door, and the money he spent on it came from the store of wealth that Li Ping'er, Hua's wife, had secretly transferred to her lover Ximen, who climbed the garden wall at night to meet her. Moreover, this garden, instead of serving as a refuge of retreat from worldly affairs – as was considered appropriate in traditional China – became a place to transact political business, to accept bribes, to trade political favors and practice corruption. However, even Baoyu's Garden of the Broad Vision had a shady origin, as its site was a combination of the sites of two previous gardens described as the dirtiest places in the world. Cf. Yu Yingshi, *Two worlds*, pp. 48–50, 97–105.

(bonsai, garden, or painting) and its contemplation are a means to the intellectual process of investigating things; at the same time they allow the metaphysical exercise of understanding the *true* reality as well as aesthetic cultivation.

No less intense than the obsession with stones was the cult of flowers. Cultivation of flowers and ornamental plants – as well as the building of real or miniaturized gardens – has a long history in China. Especially in the Song dynasty, flora played an essential role in Chinese culture and literature. It was, however, at the end of the Ming dynasty that the practice of "loving flowers" (*aihua* 愛花) became more and more popular not only among literati, but also among the common people. Zhang Dai 張岱 (1597–1689), in his *Tao'an mengyi* 陶庵夢憶 [Dream remembrances], describes the maniacal passion of a certain Jin Rusheng 金乳生 in caring for his innumerable flowers and in struggling against the plant parasites.[109] Zhang Dafu 張大復 (1554–1630) shows an unsuspected aspect of the personality of a high official, Wang Xijue 王錫爵 (1534–1611), well known for his courage and strictness of principles:[110] the ingenuousness and freshness of his soul in the ambit of his passion for chrysanthemums.[111]

Among many literati, Chen Jiru 陳繼儒 (1558–1639) and Shen Fu 沈復 (1763–?) called such a passion a "sickness for flowers" (*huapi* 花癖).[112] No

[109] *Tao'an mengyi* [Dream remembrances] (Taipei: Taiwan Kaiming shudian, 1978), *j.* 1, pp. 4–5. This passage has been translated into Japanese by Gōyama Kiwamu 合山究 in his essay on the "lovers of flowers" of Ming and Qing dynasties, "Min Shin jidai ni okeru aikasha no keifu" 明清時代における愛花者の系譜 [The lineage of the "flower lovers" in Ming and Qing periods], *Bungaku ronshū* 28 (1982), pp. 95–123; he gives several examples taken from the "notes" and fiction of the period.

[110] Wang Xijue had to resign from his office owing to his opposition to the all-powerful minister Zhang Juzheng; after Zhang's death, Wang pursued a policy of great rigor. Cf. Goodrich and Fang, eds., *Dictionary of Ming Biography, 1368/1644* (New York: Columbia University Press, 1976), pp. 1376–79.

[111] "Wang Wensu (Xijue) had a passion for chrysanthemums and cultivated any kind of them. Once, Du Xingtao came. Seeing a 'white scissors' chrysanthemum, he unwittingly entered the flowerbed without exchanging a word. 'Your passion,' Wang laughingly exclaimed, 'thus is not inferior to mine. I will present you one of these chrysanthemums.'" *Meihua caotang bitan* 梅花草堂筆談 [Notes from the Plum-Flowers retreat] (Reprinted, Shanghai: Shanghai guji CBS, 1986), *j.* 8, p. 534.

[112] Chen Jiru, *Huashi ti ji* 花石題記, in Zhu Jianxin 朱建新, ed., *Wan Ming xiaopin xuanzhu* (Taipei: Shangwu, 1984), p. 100. Cf. also Gōyama Kiwamu 合山究, "Lineage of the flower lovers," 1982, p. 97. In several Chinese novels, from the *Plum in a golden vase* to the Shen Fu's *Six Chapters of a Floating Life* we find passages where the characters enjoy the beauty of flowers and have parties in their honor (see for instance Shen Fu, *Fusheng liuji* 浮生六記 [Six chapters of a floating life], Taipei: Jinfeng CBS, 1986, *j.* 1, p. 28, on chrysanthemums, *j.* 2, p. 37, on orchids and azaleas). Shen Fu says that "his love for flowers became a sickness" (ibid., *j.* 2, p. 37. Among the many passages dedicated to plants, stones and gardens, almost the whole of *juan* two is dedicated to such subjects).

less enthusiatic was Wu Zhuang 吳莊, a scholar of the early Qing period, whose various nicknames included "Besotted on Orchids" (lanchi 蘭癡), "Companion of Chrysanthemums" (julü 菊侶), and "Friend of Lotus Flowers" (lianchou 蓮儔); he was proud of his taste for observing orchids, chrysanthemums, peonies, plums, and any kind of plants.[113] Gao Qi 高啟 (1336–74) celebrated his aspiration for solitude and self-perfection on the one side, and love for beautiful women on the other, describing plum flowers under the bright moonlight.[114] Chen Jiru considered the cultivation of flowers as one of the noblest activities; Zhang Dafu appreciated such a passion even in its excesses (including the case of an official and orthodox Confucianist); and Wu Zhuang expressed his enthusiasm with pseudonyms alluding to the floral world. Beyond its botanic-scientific interest, we may single out in this development of the aesthetic sense toward flowers the aspects that we noticed at the beginning of this chapter. On the one side it meant the cultivation of the pure aesthetic pleasure coming from the contemplation of the beauty of flowers, the colors of their petals and leaves, the shape of stems and stalks, and the perception of their perfume;[115] on the other side, it implied the subtle intellectual association with symbols and metaphors: such a sense not only expressed feelings and emotions but also found its moral justification in the more general metaphor of the flower, symbol of the pure and uncorrupted life, and of the superiority of the choice of a hermitlike existence in order to avoid the vulgarity and turbidity of common life. If the lotus was for Buddhists the symbol of purity growing from the mud, the plum flower represented, from the Song period, faithfulness and honesty. The cult of the plum flower had religious nuances that can be seen in the desire to die under such a tree or to have it planted on one's tomb.[116] Consequently, gardens – from the Imperial Huamingdian 華明殿 of Xuanzong[117] 玄宗 to the chrysanthemums of Tao Yuanming 陶淵明 – are considered as islands of retreat from the world. On the other hand flowers were ambiguously symbols of love for beauties.[118]

---

[113] Cf. Gōyama Kiwamu, "Lineage of the 'flower lovers,'" pp. 98–99.

[114] For the text and translation of the poem, see Huang Yung-wu, "Four Symbolic Plants in Chinese Poetry," *Renditions* (spring 1978), pp. 72–73.

[115] Cf., e.g., *Dream of the red chamber, h.* 80, p. 1035, where the flowers' fragrance is mentioned as a source of enjoyment for the spirit of man (清香也是令人心神爽快的). See also the four episodes in praise of orchids, in *Renditions* (autumn 1977), pp. 92–95, 153–54 (Chin Chun-ming, "In Praise of the Orchid," trans. Yuan Heh-hsiang).

[116] Cf. Gōyama Kiwamu, "Lineage of the 'flower lovers,'" pp. 106–08.

[117] For a brief account on Xuanzong's and other imperial gardens, see Keswick, *Chinese Garden*, pp. 50–72.

[118] The garden as the *locus* of erotic desires and the flowers as personification of women's seduction can easily be seen in the drama *Peony Pavilion* mentioned above, with the key role

The contemplation of natural and rural scenes is usually accompanied by the aesthetic pleasure that the scene provokes in the onlooker, as in the *Plum in a golden vase*. On the contrary, in *Dream of the red chamber* and *Unofficial history of the literati* the contemplation of the scenery sometimes brings with it the nostalgic remembrance of some event or the surfacing of a sad thought.[119] As we have already mentioned, such an attitude is similar whether it results from the sight of an actual natural scene or from a pictorial representation. What is different, however, is the observation of an urban spectacle during a festivity, such as fireworks or the display of lanterns. In these cases, present especially in the *Plum in a golden vase*,[120] the sense of well-being derives mostly from the excitement and collective participation with friends and relatives, rather than from a sense of unity with the entire universe and from the projection of one's self into some of its fragments. A certain contrast between the bustle of urban life and the peacefulness of rural life, even if expressed in rather Arcadian Daoist terms, is found in the *Dream*[121] and in the *Unofficial history*,[122] while it does not appear in the *Plum*, where, as the passage from chapter 89 demonstrates,[123] the movement from everyday activities to rural surroundings is a natural transition. It is doubtless true, moreover, that the different temperaments of the authors are reflected in their respective perceptions of nature:

being played by the Flower Spirit: it should be noted that the spring dream and the consequent love were aroused in Du Liniang's mind by her stroll in the flowering garden. The Spirits of Flowers are metaphors for beauties and love in several Ming and Qing stories, like Pu Songling's "Goddess of Flowers" 花神 or a Ming collection of tales, *Yijian shangxin* 一見賞心 [Love at first sight]. Even a late Ming manual for dream interpretation, He Dongru's 何棟如 (1527–1637) *Menglin xuanjie* 夢林玄解 [Mysterious explanations of the forest of dreams] (1636), deals with the erotic nature of the dreams about gardens; one of the stories recorded there strongly reminds the reader of the love of the two characters of *Peony Pavilion* (*j.* 3, p. 41a). Worth noting is the explicit comment by Zhang Chao 張潮 (seventeenth century), in his notes on Wang Zhuo's 王晫 writings, where he decodes the love messages in literature: owing to the traditional topic of predestined loves between flower spirits and scholars, love for flowers was immediately perceived as love for beautiful maids 以愛花之心愛美人. See *Kanhua shuyi ji* [A strange experience viewing flowers] 看花述異記, in *Yu Chu xinzhi* 虞初新誌 [The new magician's report] (1700. Reprinted in *Biji xiaoshuo daguan*, Yangzhou: Jiangsu Guangling guji keyinshe, 1983), *j.* 12, p. 9b. Cf. also Judith Zeitlin, *Historian of the Strange: Pu Songling and the Chinese Classical Table* (Stanford, Calif.: Stanford University Press, 1993), pp. 132–35.

[119] *Dream of the red chamber*, *h.* 11, pp. 129–30; *h.* 11, pp. 130–31; *Plum in a golden vase*, *h.* 54, p. 705. This attitude reminds us of the famous poem by Li Bai in which he looks at the scenery illuminated by the moonlight in front of his bed, and nostalgically remembers his native place.

[120] *Plum in a golden vase*, *h.* 15, pp. 186–87; *h.* 42, p. 544; *h.* 46, p. 583; and partially *h.* 89, p. 1265.

[121] *Dream of the red chamber*, *h.* 17, pp. 186–97.

[122] *Unofficial history*, *h.* 8, pp. 88–89.

[123] See the description of flowers and nature outside the city in *juan* 89, pp. 1265–66 of *Plum in a golden vase*.

intimate for Cao Xueqin, aesthetic for Wu Jingzi, and as a refined background for a hedonistic life in the *Plum*.

17.4. THE CONTEMPLATION OF NATURE

The examples presented in the previous sections predominantly display the relation between the representation of nature and the manifestation of sentiments (and that one finds in artistic criticism in the ancient debate on the binomial *qing/jing* 情景 – loosely, "feelings" and "scenery").[124] Naturally this does not exclude an attitude of aesthetic contemplation, from which, furthermore, according to art critics and Chinese thinkers, some sentiments are derived, whether they are to be understood as emotional reactions to external stimuli, as in the case of Lu Ji 陸機 (261–303), or are taken as an intuitive identification with the cosmic Dao, as in the case of the so-called Metaphysicians.[125]

As a general trend, notwithstanding the prevailing humanistic perception of the universe, nature in China maintains a preeminent role in painting as well as in poetry. The humanization of nature, however, deeply influences its perception so that it is often identified with one's sensation or image of it. From the fourth century on, nature takes on an aesthetic aspect through poetic and artistic resorts to empathy. Scenery often becomes

---

[124] In the immense literature on the subject, worth noting is the position of Wang Fuzhi on the fusion of *qing* and *jing*, far from the common opinion that tends to see the reflection of one's subjective mood onto natural surroundings. He does not believe that the emotions expressed in a poem should be reinforced by natural scenes customarily associated with that emotion. On the contrary, he argues that "to convey the feeling of sorrow in a scene of joy, or to convey the feeling of joy in a scene of sorrow, doubly increases the joy or the sorrow (以樂景寫哀 以哀景寫樂 一倍增其哀樂). . . . Those who use their *qing* well do not hoard up the youth or decay of things in nature to enhance their own sorrow or joy. Are things so predictable? When I am sad, must there be things to meet me with their sorrow? When I am happy, must there be things to welcome me with their own joy? Men of little understanding are quick to seize any support for their private feelings. . . . As for those who are not reduced to helplessness by *qing*, they recognize that when they are sad, things can still be happy, but this does not alter the fact that they are themselves sad; when they are happy, things can still be sad, but this does not alter the fact that they are themselves happy. Such men contemplate the world with a large heart: they are never rushed along in one direction by passion, and so their thoughts are never impeded, their words never dry up; and they know peace and harmony in mind." Siu-kit Wong's translation in "*Ch'ing* and *ching* in the Critical Writings of Wang Fu-chih," Adele Austin Rickett, ed., *Chinese Approaches to Literature from Confucius to Liang Ch'i-ch'ao* (Princeton: Princeton University Press, 1978), pp. 127–29.

[125] In the latter case, the mind would be in harmony, and its feelings would be moderate and balanced. See James Liu, *Chinese Theories of Literature* (Chicago: University of Chicago Press, 1975), p. 72; Siu-kit Wong, "*Ch'ing* and *ching*," pp. 121–50.

primarily the expression of a mood rather than a description of how objects are perceived, and is so identified with an inner reality; at the same time the contrast "natural–artificial" reflects the search for a refined and free life. After the Sui and Tang unification, a change seems to take place concerning this contrast: the prominence of southern culture privileges the cult of natural scenery, but it is carried out in the ambit of a reconciliation between Daoist ideals and the Confucian values. Nature and its contemplation are incorporated in a Confucian perspective, as gardens are built and included in the great urban centers: according to the compromise of the new official orthodoxy, civil engagements, exams, and official duties and honors are no more contrasted with reclusion and eremitic life. Thus, grasping the essence of things through aesthetic contemplation is not far removed from the self-cultivation process, no matter whether according to Daoist or Chan or Neo-Confucian practices. This ideological trend favors the broadening of a new sensibility toward the contemplation of nature. In a more and more urbanized society (in the most advanced areas and leading cultural centers) the "wild" seems to lose some of the feared magic power recognized by earlier writers, and to become the object of a more aesthetic cult, the focus of a cultured taste for nature in strange, fantastic, and odd forms. This shift is confirmed by a similar subtle change in the art of gardens; they maintain the character of a magical space, but in which what is emphasized is more an aesthetic attitude rather than the mysterious power of the universe.

Besides that, Ming and Qing literature seems to continue the semantic and rhetorical heritage of medieval and Tang-Song elaborations. In Ming and Qing representations of nature several elements are borrowed from previous times; in the *Peony Pavilion*, for instance, or in the Qing poet Gong Zizhen, nature is a metaphor for a sentiment, a passion, or a desire. We also find the moral domestication of subconscious impulses, supplying them with civil and political ideals. In the former case the author or the protagonist responds to the emotional impact of landscape upon him, and the evocation of sentiments follows the ancient formula of "expressing one's thoughts by lodging them in objects" (*jiwu chensi* 寄物陳思),[126] while in the latter case it is morality that prevails and embodies the sentiment itself. Very common also is the concept of the unity of the whole universe and the search for personal perfection. Shitao 石濤 (1662–1706), in his masterpiece of aesthetic theory, maintains "the possibility of embracing the form

---

[126] I am grateful to Mark Elvin for the opportunity to read his unpublished notes on Obi Kōichi's book, *Nature and the conception of nature*, on the idea of nature in Chinese literature up to the Tang dynasty.

and spirit of mountains and rivers 能貫山川之形神. . . . Thus, mountains and rivers and all beings reveal their magic soul 薦靈 to man because of his creative power."[127]

The "humanization" process of nature is also evident in several stories where animals and plants manifest human emotions: the constance of the "true love" is often combined with the theme of the two trees intertwining their branches and/or roots (as in the "tree of mutual love," *xiangsishu* 相思樹) or that of the pair of mandarin ducks, *yuanyang* 鴛鴦). Nature is also involved in particular events and objects capable of evoking a situation or a sentiment felt in the past, or a person from a long time ago, nourishing sometimes the sense of regret, and sometimes the feeling of love. The image of the spring peonies brings in somewhat absurd and at least to some degree surreal elements to the *Dream of the Monkey*, and presents, in a humorous tone, a reflection on the deceitful projection of our desires and aspirations. But a similar image allows Wang Yangming to explain his concept of the identity of mind, will, and action.

Nature is also present in the microcosm of the garden, where the aesthetic and philosophical tradition offer the opportunity to combine the contemplation of beauty with the representation of inner world, and/or the utopia of the *locus amoenus*. Here the Daoist paradise is balanced with the urban Confucian civil engagement, and the result is a dialectic interaction between the "natural" and the "artificial." In the passages on gardens and flowers the aesthetic enjoyment of contemplation often overrides the more directly passionate sentiments that are also involved. The same "spirit of mountains and forests" is perceived in the Alpine scenery of another passage of the *Dream of the Monkey*: it is marvelous because it *looks natural*, but in reality it is *artificial* inasmuch as it is an imitation of famous landscapes, as in gardens and bonsai. It mirrors the protagonist's inner self on its moral journey. What is worthy of note is that nature as a landscape – in the garden as well as in a painting or a bonsai – is not just an object to be admired or a representation of something else: it is the spectator himself, who is absorbed by it.

Empathy, the ability to project oneself beyond one's ego and identify oneself with the *other*, goes beyond the aesthetic phenomenon, as was clearly demonstrated for China by Zhu Guangqian,[128] and it enters into the psychological, religious, and moral fields. It is the ability to "enter into the

---

[127] *Huayulu*, part 8, in Shitao, *Les Propos sur la peinture*, pp. 155, 69, 148–49, 47–48.

[128] Cf. Zhu Guangqian, *Psychology of art*, pp. 33–52; Sabattini, *The Aesthetic Thought*, pp. 45–65.

role of another at a *practical* level,"[129] that is, to identify oneself with another person to the point of grasping his thoughts and moods, or to transfer in imagination our feelings to inanimate beings (*yiqing* 移情). It is the specific ability of poets, artists, and mystics to reach union with the universe, to knock down the barriers between man and nature, or between the ego and the others, between the subject and the object, and to step out of the finite into the infinite. "[Scenes and emotions] fuse with one another as one climbs high and looks afar" (*heyu dengtiao* 合於登眺), writes the poet Xie Zhen 謝榛 (1495–1575), stressing the identification of subjective consciousness with objective reality by means of intuition (神) during the contemplation of nature.[130] Contemplation of nature becomes the opportunity of catharsis, a therapy of "dissolving my heart in mountains and waters" *sanhuai shanshui* 散懷山水.[131] But love for natural scenery may be so strong that one can fall ill and die. This is the case of the lady whose heart was transformed into a sort of agate, symbol of the determination and endurance of her profound *qing*. When her heart was cut into slices, each of them was found to be like a fine painting, bearing images of the landscapes with mountains, rivers, and trees that she had contemplated during her short life.[132] Empathy is also the innate morality of every man, that is, the tension of sympathy and compassion that does not allow us to bear others' suffering, and that finds in humaneness (*ren* 仁) the Confucian virtue par excellence. Just think of the apologue of the Hill of the Oxen in which Mencius's ecological concern is identified with a moral anxiety for the cultivation of the natural goodness characteristic of humankind, a concern we also find in later authors like Wang Chong.[133]

Into the holistic and Neo-Confucian mystic trend that runs from Zhang Zai (1020–77) to Gao Panlong (1562–1626), even the *Dream of the red chamber* with its unconventional conceptions can be inserted; it takes up the Buddhist issue of the "salvation" of all beings, including plants, and at the

---

[129] Cf. G. H. Mead, *Mente, Sé e società* (Firenze: Barbera 1966), Italian trans. of *Mind, Self and Society* (1934).

[130] Cf. James Liu, *Chinese Theories of Literature*, pp. 41–42.

[131] Quoted in the above-mentioned notes by Mark Elvin.

[132] *Qingshi* (1986), *j.* 11, p. 312. This short story appears at the end of the main tale *Xin jian jin shi* 心堅金石 [A heart strong like gold and stone], in the chapter dedicated to "metamorphosis for love" (情化). Worth noting are the editor's final comments, talking of a sort of correspondence of sentiments between the inanimate things of the natural scenery and the individual's spirit that has been fixed on them.

[133] He writes in *Lunheng, Shujie* (quoted in *Materials concerning the history of Chinese aesthetics* [see fn. 13], vol. 1, p. 126): "A mountain without forests is a bare mountain, . . . a man without culture is nothing but a rustic."

same time also takes on the different heritage of the cult of sentiments that developed in China especially among intellectual circles of Jiangnan in the late Ming period.[134] In this way, the religious sensitivity of the author is reinforced, on the one hand, by the dominant ideology of the *sanjiao* (the "three doctrines"), and, on the other, by the traditional lyric vision of Chinese fiction.[135] Nature allows a reflective and lyric approach to reality.[136]

> [Baoyu said,] "The crab-apple tree in the courtyard here: only one half of it budded this year; the other side seems to have died. I knew at the time that something awful must be going to happen; now I can see that it must have been a portent of her death."
>
> Aroma laughed out loud. "Forgive me, but I just can't help myself. You really are an old woman! And you supposed to be so educated! How can what happens to trees and plants have anything to do with human beings?"
>
> Baoyu sighed. "What do you know about it? Not only plants and trees, but all things that live and grow have feelings. And like us, they are most responsive to those who most appreciate them. There are plenty of examples from history: the juniper tree in front of the temple of Confucius, the milfoil that grows beside his tomb, the cypress in front of Zhuge Liang's shrine, the pinetree that grows in front of Yue Fei's grave: all those paragons of the vegetable world, mightily endowed with vital essence and able to withstand the ravages of the centuries, have withered and dried up in times of disorder, only to flourish once more when times were prosperous. In the course of a thousand or more years all of them have died and come to life again several times over. If those are not portents, what are they? On a somewhat less exalted level there are the peonies beside Yang Guifei's Aloeswood Pavilion, the rhododendrons of the Duanchenglou and the evergreen grass on Lady Bright's grave. Surely you can't deny that all these are instances of sympathy between plants and humans? I see no reason to doubt that our crab-apple tree too was reacting to a human situation."[137]

[134] By "cult of sentiments" I mean the new intellectual trend that can be noticed especially at the end of Ming dynasty. Its main characteristics can be summed up as: reevaluation of emotions; identification of some sentiments with virtues; supremacy of some passions, provided that they are within the requirements of society; a more important role played by women in literary works; a new concept of heroes; perseverance of the "true" sentiments, which overcome even death; and positive evaluation of some kinds of obsessions (癖, 狂).

[135] Wong Kam-ming, "Point of View, Norms and Structure: Hung-lou Meng and Lyrical Fiction," and Yu-kung Kao, "Lyric Vision in Chinese Narrative: A Reading of Hung-lou Meng and Ju-lin Wai-shih," in A. H. Plaks, ed., *Chinese Narrative: Critical and Theoretical Essays* (Princeton: Princeton University Press, 1977), pp. 203–26 and 227–43 respectively.

[136] On lyricism in traditional Chinese literature, see Gálik, "Concept of Creative Personality," pp. 192–96.

[137] *Dream of the red chamber*, h. 77, pp. 999–1000; David Hawkes, *Story of the Stone*, pp. 540–41. Cf. also the debate in *Jinghua yuan*, h. 71, p. 343, and Mark Elvin's comments in "The Inner World of 1830," *Daedalus* 120.2 (1991), p. 40. On the Buddhist debate concerning the Buddha Nature and sensibility of plants and weeds, cf. W. R. LaFleur, "Saigyō and the Buddhist value of nature," *History of Religions* 13.2–3 (1973–74).

18

Water, Love, and Labor

ASPECTS OF A GENDERED ENVIRONMENT

ANTONIA FINNANE

The Nanling 南嶺 Mountains wander through the southeastern corner of China, rising above the hills of Guangdong and overlooking those of Hu'nan. They impede easy communication, and so make an obvious site for the administrative border that divides these two provinces. They also form a climatic boundary: on the Guangdong side the summers are long, warm, and wet, while on the Hu'nan side they are cooler and dryer. These differences in climate signify differences in agriculture as well, so that the mountains mark a boundary between a double-cropping rice cultivation area and a rice-tea cultivation area.[1] Finally, in Skinnerian geography, these mountains mark a macroregional boundary, dividing Lingnan from the middle Yangzi region.[2]

Li Zongren 李宗仁, marching from Guangdong to Hu'nan across the Nanling range in 1916, was indifferent to most of these differentiating features. His keen eye observed instead another interesting phenomenon: there were differences in the condition of women on either side of the mountains. As he later recalled:

> The women of Kwangtung worked as hard as the men. There were practically no women with bound feet south of P'ingshih 坪石. But after we passed that town, we saw that all the women's feet were bound. Their bound feet were sometimes as small and as slender as bamboo shoots. . . . [T]he women in Hu'nan were thus physically handicapped and could not do a man's job.

---

[1] John Lossing Buck, *Land Utilization in China* (1937. Reprinted, New York: Paragon, 1968), p. 38.

[2] G. W. Skinner, "Regional Urbanization in Nineteenth-Century China," in G. W. Skinner, ed., *The City in Late Imperial China* (Stanford, Calif.: Stanford University Press, 1977), p. 212ff.

They could, as he goes on to show, do a woman's job. Alongside busy roads in the Xiang River 湘江 valley were numerous inns.

> To attract passing travellers, the inn operators usually hired beautiful girls to sit in the doorways doing their sewing. These girls were beautifully made-up and were young and attractive, with very tiny feet. But the fact was that they were daughters of neighbouring farmers, hired by the inn owners as window dressing. After sunset they picked up their sewing and went home.[3]

Li Zongren was neither an anthropologist nor a human geographer, but his impressions are perhaps the more striking for being untutored. In effect his account is a social description of the environment through which he is moving. Although this environment has physical and economic features (the streams are narrow, the water is clear, the people are working), it is mostly for Li a social environment. So when he remembers an old Chinese saying that "the plum flowers of the southern slopes of the Nanling Mountains bloom much earlier than those on the north," it is not as oral information on the cycle of seasons that he recalls it but rather as an illustration of differences in "customs and habits of people on two sides of the mountain."[4] The land for him is mediated by human actors, and the primacy of the social in his description of his environs is notable for coming from a country boy who was himself used to working the land.

This passage is interesting on another count as well. The "customs and habits" on which it dwells are evident to Li primarily through the appearance and behavior of women. Male members of the local society are only tangentially present in his descriptions: they are those beside whom the women work in Guangdong, or for whom they work in Hu'nan. Like the land itself, they are taken for granted, indicated indirectly through reference to their womenfolk. But since this obliqueness or near-silence by no means obscures their presence, the prominence accorded to women in Li's description produces a gendered landscape, in which women are a significant variable.

The actual details of the "customs and habits" recorded by Li reveal how dynamic this variable was. These details include first and foremost the difference in patterns of women's labor north and south of the mountains. Li's interest is primarily in the cultural implications of this phenomenon, but the economic implications are clear. What he observed was in keeping with an analysis of rural women's labor later made by Ester Boserup: that is,

---

[3] Tong Te-Kong and Li Tsung-jen, *The Memoirs of Li Tsung-jen* (Boulder, Col.: Westview Press, 1979), p. 49.
[4] Ibid.

in regions of plow cultivation, women do relatively little farm work and sometimes none at all, the double-cropping rice area of China being a major exception to the rule.[5]

Coupled with the differences in the patterns of labor are differences in the appearance of the women. The main distinction noted is that Hunanese women bind their feet, whereas Cantonese women do not; but in recording the return journey from Hu'nan to Guangdong, Li has more to say. At the very border, the elegant, leisured women of Hu'nan gave way to the sweating, laboring, sunburnt women of Guangdong. "Comparing them with the light complexions, delicate skins and elegant manners of the women of Hu'nan, we found them strange and unattractive at first," recalled Li, who then added thoughtfully: "This experience taught me how social customs and even concepts of beauty differ from place to place."[6]

He was still in Guangdong, stationed in the prosperous city of Zhaoqing 肇慶, when yet another manifestation of local culture caught his attention. Startled one day by a commotion in the streets, he rushed out of his office in time to witness a battle being waged between two families over the daughter of one who was promised as a bride to the other. It ended with the bride being secured for the groom, everyone smiling, and the wedding festivities following in due course. He was astonished to discover that "'bride capture' was an old local custom, handed down for thousands of years."[7] With this item, unfortunately, his ethnography comes to an end, as matters of war and politics begin to dominate the memoirs to the exclusion of all else.

Given the importance of the nature of women's labor to the wealth of some regions and the poverty or dependence of others, gender has received surprisingly little attention in work on spatial differentiation in China. Skinner did indeed take the number and ranking of brothels into account in constructing his hierarchy of urban places; by and large gender remains an issue to be addressed in this context.[8] The entire macroregional system is perhaps most easily envisaged in terms of the dispersal and activities of males. To imagine a large central place in the late-imperial period is to imagine powerful officials and merchants, boatmen, and hawkers coming and going with merchandise, bankers and clerks,

---

[5] Ester Boserup, *Women in Economic Development* (London: Earthscan, 1989), pp. 15–35.

[6] Tong and Li, *Memoirs of Li Tsung-jen*, p. 57.

[7] Ibid., pp. 61–62.

[8] There are of course local studies that focus specifically on the nature of women's labor and/ or on patterns of gender relations, the most notable in recent years being Janice Stockard, *Daughters of the Canton Delta: Marriage Patterns and Economic Strategies in South China, 1860–1930* (Stanford, Calif.: Stanford University Press, 1989).

native-place organizations offering help and hospitality to sojourners from afar. The periphery, of course, is characterized merely by the rarity or dearth of such activities.

It is clear that spatial organization in China had other markers. From Li Zongren's memoir of his travels between Guangdong and Hu'nan emerge boundaries marked out by sexuality, aesthetics, and work. Both in his representation of the differences between Hu'nan and Guangdong and in the detail by which he effects this representation, he draws attention especially to sexual difference as a variable in the experience, perception, and making of place. In the present chapter, I consider the potential significance of this variable in what I think of as a contribution to a social history of the environment.

The place I explore is that part of Jiangsu lying north of the Yangzi River and south of the Huai. This is a place in search of a name, as Jeffrey Kinkley once remarked of western Hu'nan.[9] In Qing documents it is referred to on the basis of different geographical and bureaucratic criteria as Jiang-Huai 江淮, Huainan 淮南 (particularly with reference to the salt industry), Huai-Yang 淮揚, or even Huai-Yang-Tong 淮揚通, the two last-mentioned deriving from the designation of circuits. It is now commonly known as "Subei" 蘇北, at least in mandarin,[10] but this term, which means northern Jiangsu, can be used to refer to the far north of the province as well as the central portion with which I am concerned here. It will serve present purposes to refer to it simply as "Jiangbei" 江北, which means "north of the [Yangzi] river" and can be used to differentiate this central part of Jiangsu province from Huaibei 淮北, the land "north of the Huai." "Jiangbei" itself is a rather vague term but is, generally speaking, appropriate to the historical period with which I am here concerned: the three centuries or so between the beginning of Manchu rule in the seventeenth century and the Japanese occupation of China in the twentieth. (See Map 18.1.)

Jiangbei has been fixed in the Jiangnan world view as a poor and backward place. People from Jiangbei who live in Jiangnan – particularly in Shanghai – are subject to the expression of a prejudice that in the 1930s was likened by John Lossing Buck to that between whites and blacks in the

---

[9] Jeffrey Kinkley, *The Odyssey of Shen Congwen* (Stanford, Calif.: Stanford University Press, 1987), p. 9.

[10] In Shanghai dialect "Jiangbei" appears still to be the common rendering. This may be true also for Cantonese. In any event, it is the characters for "Jiangbei" rather than for "Subei" that appear in an article in a contemporary Hong Kong magazine. See Liu Jin 劉金, "Yuanlao Chen Yun jiyu zhichi – Jiang Zemin de qingyun lu (san)" [Party elder Chen Yun gives his support – Jiang Zemin's road to the top (3)], *Jiushi niandai yuekan* 12 (December, 1990), pp. 72–74.

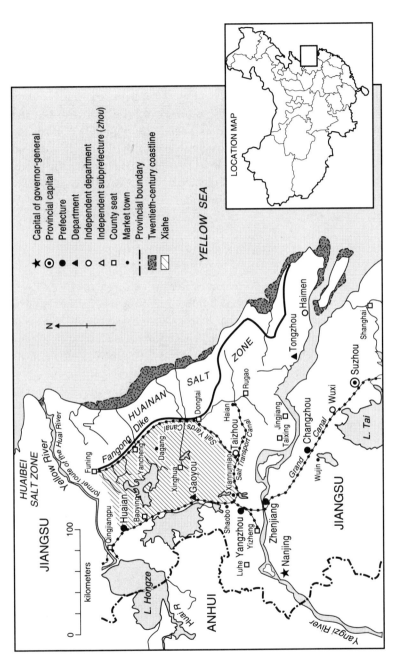

Map 18.1. The Jiangbei region (central Jiangsu province) in the nineteenth and twentieth centuries.

United States. But Jiangbei itself was differentiated between richer and poorer, urban and rural, northern and southern. The poverty of twentieth-century Jiangbei is generally attributed to environmental problems arising in the latter half of the nineteenth century, after the shift of the Yellow River back to its northern route.[11] These problems are imagined, not without good reason, as lying in the domain of water control, but there were other facets to environmental management in Jiangbei, particularly from the time of the Yellow River's move north, and not all areas were subject to severe flooding. Jiangbei in its late-imperial form was the product of an environmental history that had yielded a highly differentiated landscape not at all predictable from antiquity.

THE MAKING OF JIANGBEI

The exploitation of this region began rather prematurely in the early sixth century B.C., when the first canal linking the Yangzi and the Huai – a forerunner of this section of the later Grand Canal – was built. Reportedly during the Han dynasty, a second canal was constructed, running eastward from the newly established city of Guangling 廣陵 (the ancient and now literary name for Yangzhou) for the purpose of transporting salt being produced on the coast. Within the framework thus provided these developed the complex network of waterways that was to become the dominant feature of the Huai-Yang area.

In the Han dynasty, the distance between Guangling and the coast was not great. The center of salt production was Taizhou 泰州, now well and truly an inland city but then known as Hailing 海陵 (Hill-by-the-sea). To this day houses in the rural area east of Taizhou feature prominent prow-shaped gable-ends, attributed to the cultural influence of seafaring on domestic architecture.[12] Sea floods were a problem in this flat, low-lying area, and in the eighth century a dike was built to protect the fields. This

---

[11] Emily Honig, *Creating Chinese Ethnicity: Subei People in Contemporary Shanghai, 1850–1980* (New Haven, Conn.: Yale University Press, 1992); Fei Hsiao Tung, "Small Towns in Northern Jiangsu," in Fei Hsiao Tung et al., eds., *Small Towns in China: Functions, Problems and Prospects* (Beijing: New World Press, 1986), p. 90; Du Wenzhen 杜問貞, *Zhongguo renkou: Jiangsusheng fence* [The population of China: Jiangsu] (Beijing: Zhongguo zaizheng jingji CBS, 1987), p. 10ff.

[12] Yang Shu 樣叔, "Qimiao de wuji" [Strange gables], in Cao Yongsen 曹永森, ed., *Yangzhou fengqing* [The atmosphere of Yangzhou] (Nanjing?, 1991), pp. 58–62. For comparison, see Ronald G. Knapp, *China's Traditional Rural Architecture: A Cultural Geography of the Common House* (Honolulu: University of Hawaii Press, 1986). The Taizhou style is not included in the large variety of gables and eaves depicted.

was subsequently extended and in its final form ran almost the full length of the central Jiangsu coast.[13] East of the dike coastal tides deposited layers of silt that helped elevate the coastal area relative to that inland.

A second diking project of significance to the region was that in the northwest, near to the present city of Huaian 淮安. Here the Huai River occasionally overran its banks, and the waters began to accumulate in marshes and lakes to the south.[14] From the Han dynasty onward, diking was employed to contain these floods. With the bifurcation of the Yellow River into a northern and a southern stream in the following century, the drainage of the Huai began to cause increased difficulty, and in 1415 a dike was constructed to contain the growing body of water that had formed from the river's southward overflow. After the full diversion of the Yellow River to a southern course in 1495, Jiangbei's destiny as an environmental problem par excellence was sealed. The Huai River, unable to compete with the Yellow River, turned back on itself to form the vast Hongze Lake 洪澤湖. Despite elaborate control mechanisms, the silt-laden water of the Yellow River regularly entered the lake and thence the Grand Canal, which the lake now fed. The beds of both lake and canal gradually rose, necessitating a steady elevation of dikes and creating a situation of extreme and often-repeated peril for the farming lands east of the Grand Canal, especially the low-lying area known as Xiahe 下河, now termed Lixiahe 裡下河.

A massive overhaul of the system over the turn of the seventeenth century succeeded in reducing floods to manageable levels for the century from 1705 and 1805. Thereafter, steady deterioration in the whole system finally resulted in the Yellow River shifting back to a northern course, which removed from the vicinity a very unwelcome neighbor but at the same time resulted in a steady diminution of government interest in Jiangbei.[15] The Yellow River left behind two reminders of its sojourn in the south. One was the existence of Hongze Lake, which continued to drain the Huai River's waters with an inefficiency reflected in continued although now rather less frequent floods in Jiangbei. The other was that its copious deposits of silt had gradually extended the landmass along the coast. In this way, the hills

---

[13] See Ji Chao 稽超, "Fan-gong ti de xingzhu ji qi zuoyong" [The construction and uses of the Fan Gong Dike], *Fudan xuebao* 8 (1980), pp. 59–61.

[14] Christian Lamouroux, "Les contradictions d'un système hydraulique: l'exemple du bassin de la Huai sous les Song du Nord" *T'oung Pao* 75.1–3 (1989), pp. 127–62.

[15] Antonia Finnane, "The Origins of Prejudice: The Malintegration of Subei in Late Imperial China," *Comparative Studies in Society and History* 35.2 (April 1993). See also D. Gandar, *Le Canal Impérial: Étude historique et descriptive, Variétés Sinologiques* 4 (Shanghai: Tucewei Press, 1894); Harold Hinton *The Grain Tribute System of China (1845–1911)* (Cambridge, Mass., 1956); Piero Corradini, "L'abbandono del 'canale imperiale' (yün-ho) come via di navigazione," *Rivista degli studi orientali* 37 (1962), pp. 115–22.

of Shaanxi, to the extent that they contributed to the silt content of the Yellow River, contributed also to the making of Jiangbei.

The Yangzi had its own contribution to make to the formation of Jiangbei. Between Guazhou 瓜州 in the west, where the Grand Canal entered the Yangzi, and Lujing Harbor 蘆涇港 south of Tongzhou, and then again from Lujing Harbor eastward to Haimen, the northern bank consisted of a series of shoals. This feature, like the mudflats on the coast, signified an absence of port facilities, which appears to have inhibited healthy levels of traffic across the Yangzi. Thus despite its riverine location, Rugao 如皋 county in the early twentieth century was a poor, isolated place.[16] At the turn of the century, Lujing Harbor, some four miles south of the city of Tongzhou, was used as an anchorage port by paddle steamers, but the narrow, shallow, tortuous waterways leading north meant that there was no easy access inland by water except by small boats. At Tongzhou itself there were "neither fishing boats nor merchant boats, only small boats from the inland waterways."[17]

The Yangzi River in this area is also rather unstable, with shifting currents altering the disposition of sand banks in such a way as to confound Captain Sherard Osborne when, passing south of Tongzhou in 1858, he found that the depth of six fathoms sounded by Captains Collinson and Kellet eighteen years before had shrunk to one. Eventually he reckoned that the river might have moved, so retracing his course, he took his vessel north of a shoal that had previously been connected to the northern bank.[18] The county of Jingjiang 靖江 was in its entirety the product of this instability. Emerging from the waters as a sandy island during the Three Kingdoms period, it was at one stage close to the southern bank and was populated by people from Jiangnan. In the Ming it was still "surrounded with water" but the gradual silting up of the riverbed on its north side finally made it the neighbor of Taixing 泰興 and Rugao. The district of Qidong 啟東, now the southeastern promontory of Jiangbei, was similarly formed.[19]

[16] See Lenore Barkan, "Nationalists, Communists and Rural Leaders: Political Dynamics in a Chinese County, 1927–1937," Ph.D. dissertation, University of Washington, Seattle (1983).

[17] *Jiangsu yanhai tuzhi* [Gazetteer of the Jiangsu coast in maps], comp. Zhu Zhengyuan 朱正元 (1899. Reprinted in Chengwen gazetteer series, Zhongguo fangzhi congshu, Huazhong 151, Jiangsu province, Taipei, 1974), pp. 32a–33a.

[18] Laurence Oliphant, "Notes of a Voyage up the Yang-tze or Ta-kiang, from Wusung to Hankow," *Journal of the Royal Geographical Society of London* 30 (1860), pp. 79–93. The earlier voyage is reported in Lord Colchester and Captain Collinson, "On the Yang-tze-kiang," *Journal of the Royal Geographical Society of London* 17 (1847), pp. 130–45.

[19] Li Changchuan 李長傳, *Jiangsusheng dizhi* [Gazetteer of Jiangsu province] (Shanghai, 1936. Reprinted in Chengwen gazetteer series, Zhongguo fangzhi congshu, Huazhong, 473, Jiangsu province, Taipei, 1983), pp. 345, 347.

Jiangbei thus featured a highly textured landscape produced by the natural or manipulated movement of waters. In brief, the Grand Canal served to divide the relatively elevated lakes area of the western part of Jiangbei from the lowlands of the east, while the Salt Transport Canal demarcated the higher south from the lower north of eastern Jiangbei, the Lixiahe area. The Fan Gong Dike 范公堤, running almost the full length of the coast, divided the higher coast from the lower inland region. These canals and dikes also demarcated types of land use and livelihood. Dry-weather crops, including cotton, could be grown on the northern bank of the Yangzi, but only as far north as the Salt Transport Canal, beyond which paddy rice reigned supreme. East of the Fangong Dike the land was originally reserved for salt production and the cultivation of rushes for fuel, but in the early twentieth century it was reclaimed, largely for agriculture, including cotton. West of the Grand Canal there was little dry land. The lakes that bordered the canal were exploited for fishing, duck breeding, and the harvesting of water lilies and water chestnuts. The region as a whole was fairly discrete, at least as long as the Yellow River flowed south. The high dikes and treacherous waters of the Yellow River in its lower reaches inhibited easy communication between the Jiangbei and Huaibei sections of Jiangsu province. The Yangzi was an almost equally substantial barrier separating Jiangbei from the Jiangnan section of Jiangsu. To the west, Jiangbei was divided from Anhui province by the Grand Canal and the lakes bordering it, while to the east lay an unfriendly sea (see Map 18.1).

A GENDERED ENVIRONMENT?

I think it probable that the diversity of local conditions prevailing during this environmental history – high and low, wet and dry, coastal and inland, Yangzi and Huai side – could be mapped in terms of a variation of rites of passage and the terms of reference in popular culture that both informed and reflected the pattern of gender relations in Jiangbei; that is to say, that environmental differences correlated to some extent with cultural differences.

How can this correlation be described as other than pure contingency? Alfred Kroeber commenced his exposition of this problem with the assumption "that on the one hand culture can be understood primarily only in terms of cultural factors, but that on the other hand no culture is wholly intelligible without reference to the noncultural or so-called environmental factors with which it is in relation and which condition it."[20] The distinction between culture and environment is slightly problematic in circumstances where the environment has itself been partly shaped by culture: politics, wars, technology, and trade all had their part to play in the formation of Jiangbei.[21] And if this narrows the gap between the categories of environment and culture, the relationship between the two on the other hand becomes attentuated when we consider in the case of Jiangbei how different the environmental circumstances there were from those which originally nurtured sedentary agriculture, the Chinese script, Confucianism, Buddhism, the bureaucracy, and other aspects of the cultural world into which every new little Jiangbei baby was born. In brief, the environmental history of a local culture in China is by no means entirely a local history.

The preserved or salvaged elements of local cultures in Jiangbei nonetheless show how the environment both mediated and contributed to cultural particularism. The local environment provided a prism through which life was viewed. Thus in folk song, the environment and gender relations are mutually metaphorized with reference to specific environmental features. In Gaoyou 高邮, lying north of Yangzhou and on the banks of the Grand Canal, peasants sang as they planted their rice:

Sun shining down all over the land
Which lad and lass aren't hand in hand?
If the lad and the lass aren't hand in hand
The Yangzi and the Grand Canal will flood the land.[22]

This song probably postdates the southward shift of the Yellow River, when the Yangzi began to compete with the Huai as a major source of floods in the southwest of Jiangbei. The balance of the waters is equated in its lines with the balance of sexual relations.

In Funing 阜宁, on the northern coast, different environmental features were drawn upon. Funing was far from the Yangzi but was near the Yellow River until its mouth moved north. A song, mourning the fate of a little daughter-in-law, retains the memory of the Yellow River as a symbol of death and destruction:

Little red weed leaning on a tree,
A daughter-in-law at seven was she.

[20] Alfred Kroeber, "Relations of Environmental and Cultural Factors," in Andrew P. Vayda, ed., *Environment and Cultural Behaviour* (Garden City, N.Y.: New York Natural History Press, 1968), p. 350.
[21] See Finnane, "Origins of Prejudice," p. 218ff.
[22] Ding Jiatong, Zhou Weiguo et al., eds., *Yangzhou geyao yanyu ji* [Collected songs and sayings of Yangzhou] (Beijing: Zhongguo minjian wenyi CBS, 1989), p. 43.

Beaten by the master, cursed by his wife.
In the Yellow River she took her life.[23]

Similar strategies are used in reference to the urban hierarchy in Jiangbei. A narrative song recorded in Baoying 寶應 but possibly originating in Taizhou begins with a girl throwing stones at a boy, with such accuracy as to make his head bleed. He threatens to go to Yangzhou, the administrative center, and sue her. She pleads with him not to do so:

My family has three fine roan horses,
With bridles of silver and hooves of gold;
Why don't you take one and go on a trip?
Xuzhou, Suzhou, Hangzhou, Huizhou.
Ride right through the city of Yangzhou,
Turn around again and come to Taizhou.
Be a good fellow and take a horse.
You don't have to sue me in Yangzhou.[24]

After he refuses the horse and numerous other bribes, the girl finally offers him herself, and he settles down with her in Taizhou, far from the Yangzhou yamen. This song places the Jiangbei cities of Taizhou and Yangzhou in a larger urban network and regional context. Suzhou and Hangzhou represent Jiangnan, the golden land across the Yangzi. Xuzhou represents Huaibei, the area neighboring Jiangbei on the north side. As for Huizhou, the route between this southern Anhui city and Yangzhou was particularly well worn, for from Huizhou came the salt merchants who dominated Yangzhou through much of the late-imperial period.

Apart from identifying the network of regional urban centers, this song differentiates the administrative center (in this case Yangzhou) from the "home place" or "ancestral village" (*guxiang* 故鄉), that place where people had home, hearth, parents, and children. The distinction between Yangzhou and the place called home is made again in a children's song that traces a journey from the city back to a village where the little traveler's maternal grandmother lives. In both this and the preceding song, the idea of home is presented through reference to a female presence: that of the bride in the former case and that of the maternal grandmother in the latter, calling to mind the "uterine family" posited by Margery Wolf.[25]

---

[23] Zhu Jiefan 朱介凡, comp., *Zhongguo geyao lun* [On Chinese songs] (Taipei, 1974), p. 512.

[24] Ding et al., eds., *Songs of Yangzhou*, p. 61. Recorded in 1987 as sung by Cai Jiamin, seventy-three years old, of Baoying.

[25] Margery Wolf, *Women and the Family in Rural Taiwan* (Stanford, Calif.: Stanford University Press, 1972).

Row, row, row, row
The boat turns its bow,
I row to Wantou.
Can't sleep at Wantou,
I row to Shaobo;
Don't stay at Shaobo,
I row to Gaoyou.
Flowers in bloom at Gaoyou,
I row to Xinghua;
I meet a fine lad at Xinghua,
He helps me row to Taizhou;
I meet a fine lass at Taizhou,
She helps us row,
Row, row, row, row,
Row to the bridge where Ma's ma lives.[26]

This appears to be the song of a rural migrant, a not uncommon phenomenon in Yangzhou. Refugees came periodically to the city in flight from flood and famine, seeking food and employment. The detail of the journey is such that we may well imagine for Jiangbei a sort of songline such as Bruce Chatwin discovered in Australia.[27]

What would Li Zongren have observed if he had followed such a songline? As in Zhaoqing, he would have observed peculiar local customs at weddings, making each district more or less culturally specific. The standard Six Rites of marriage observed among Han Chinese[28] had in most cases been reduced to three or four by the late-imperial period thoughout China, but they were supplemented by a range of other practices, some of which were widespread – as in the "depraved practice" (*louxi* 陋習) of teasing the bride (*nao fang* 鬧房), while others were strictly local or regional. In Huaian prefecture, for example, levirate marriage was known, and among the very poor there was even a practice of "renting a wife" (*zu qi* 租妻): in this case, the woman would live with the man for payment for a couple of years and leave him any child born of the period of cohabitation.[29] The practice of

---

[26] Ding et al., eds., *Songs of Yangzhou*, p. 142. Song recorded in 1988 by two men in their seventies.

[27] Bruce Chatwin, *The Songlines* (London: Cape, 1987).

[28] See Vermier Chiu, *Marriage Laws and Customs of China* (Hong Kong: Chinese University, Institute of Advanced Chinese Studies and Research, 1966), pp. 4–7; Ma Zhixiao, *Zhongguo-de hunsu* [The marriage customs of China] (Taipei: Jinshi shuju, 1981), pp. 7–14.

[29] Lou Zikuang 婁子匡, *Hun su zhi* [Gazetteer of marriage customs] (Taipei: Shangwu, 1975), pp. 111–12.

raising a little daughter-in-law, documented by Wolf and Huang in northern Taiwan,[30] was also known both in Huaian prefecture and – in the late nineteenth century at least – in Yangzhou.[31]

Some variations in marriage rites seem only fortuitously linked to location. A widespread though not canonical practice in China was for the bride to fast for three days before the wedding. In Jiangbei, this was preceded by several months' observance of a restricted diet, the period of complete fast ranging from three to five days before the wedding.[32] The purpose of the pre-wedding fast was apparently to eliminate the need for the girl to relieve herself between departure from her home and consummation of the marriage. As though to make this clear, in Yangzhou the bride's trousseau included a large brass chamber pot in which was placed a smaller chamber pot containing various sweetmeats and ritual objects.[33] In the southeastern city of Tongzhou, however, the bride actually broke her fast just before leaving for her new home, when her mother would – and still does – serve her poached eggs in sweetened water (*tang shui gun dan* 糖水滾蛋) to sustain her on her journey.[34] This ritual is explained by a local legend according to which a girl actually dropped dead from weakness on arrival at the groom's house.[35]

In other cases a direct relationship between culture and ecology is apparent. The so-called duck rites of Gaoyou show the same use of nature-for-culture metaphors that appear in song, local produce providing people with their ritual materials. Gaoyou lies within Lixiahe to the east of the Grand Canal but the district stretches across the canal to the lakes on the western side, and in this watery domain duck breeding is a major economic activity. Gaoyou ducks, it is said, compare poorly with Shaoxing ducks for

---

[30] Arthur Wolf and Chieh-shan Huang, *Marriage and Adoption in China, 1845–1945* (Stanford: Stanford University Press, 1980), pp. 230–41.

[31] Geraldine Guiness, *In the Far East: Letters from Geraldine Guiness in China* (Melbourne: M.L. Hutchinson, 1901), pp. 50–2. The report is of an attempted opium suicide by a little daughter-in-law. The practice of taking a little daughter-in-law was reported to me by the Women's Federation in Yancheng, but was noted as having been not very common. Interview, December 1992.

[32] Lou Zikuang, *Marriage customs*, (Taipei, 1975), p. 111.

[33] Zhao Xueli and Cao Yongquan, "Tan Yangzhou hunsu" [On the marriage customs of Yangzhou], in Cao Yongsen, ed., *Yangzhou fengqing* [The atmosphere of Yangzhou] (Nanjing: Jiangsu wenyi CBS, 1991), p. 68.

[34] Ling Na, "Tangshui gundan" [Boiled eggs in sweetened water], in *Zhongguo minjian gushi quanji* [Complete collection of Chinese folktales], vol. 23, *Jiangsu minjian gushiji* [Collected folktales of Jiangsu] (Taipei: Yuanliu chuban shiye gufen youxian gongsi, 1989), pp. 124–26.

[35] Ibid.

fertility but are incomparable in quality.[36] In Gaoyou people tend ducks, eat ducks, sell ducks, and give ducks, especially in the observance of family rituals. The exchange of ducks during marriage rites begins at the time of betrothal (*xiading* 下訂), when the man's side sends a pair of fattened ducks to the woman's side, to demonstrate the family's ability to provide, and the promise of a life of plenty. At the time of setting the date, the man's side sends a pair of "necking ducks" (*jiaobo ya* 交脖鴨): these are in a bamboo basket enclosed at the top with webbing that allows only the ducks' necks and heads to protrude. Thus confined, the ducks inadvertently twist their necks around each other, representing to the woman's family that the time of marriage is approaching. On the marriage day itself, the bride is accompanied on her journey by a pair of ducks in the same bamboo basket, but this time the ducks' necks are tied together with hair from her own head, a transfer to the ducks of the practice of knotting together the hair of the bride and groom.

The completion of marriage rites by no means signals an end to sending ducks. After the new bride has been installed in her husband's home, her family will take advantage of the first festival to go and see her: they take with them a present of two plucked ducks, the beak of each bound with a piece of red silk. This is a message to the young couple not to fight and a sign of the distaff side's desire that their daughter bring peace and harmony to her new family. When their daughter becomes pregnant, the parents send along a male duckling, in congratulations at the beginning of the new generation and to express a wish that the child might be a boy. Near to the time of confinement, they send along a fat, tender duck, to express the hope that the confinement may go well, with no injury to their daughter's health. At the child's first birthday, they send a pair of wild ducks, expressing the hope that the child may grow up safely like a duck in the wild, and also the wish that the first child will be followed by a second. Finally, when the child starts school, the distaff side will often send along a duck with the beak stuffed full of spring onions (*cong* 蔥), in Chinese a homonym for the word "clever" (as in *congming* 聰明).[37]

Environmental conditions determined other aspects of marriage rituals. Fetching the bride, once undertaken in sedan chairs, is now more commonly undertaken using a bicycle or truck. In Lixiahe, however, fetching

[36] Shu Lin 樹林, Wen Shi 聞史, and Qing Sen 慶森, "Gaoyou maya yu shuanghuang dan" [Gaoyou's hemp ducks and double-yolk eggs], in *Yangzhou chuantong mingyou chanpin shi* [A history of Yangzhou's widely famed traditional products], *Yangzhou wenshi ziliao* 9 (Yangzhou, 1990), p. 33.

[37] Dong Shiwu 童適吾, "Gaoyou yali" [The duck rites of Gaoyou], in Cao Yongsen, ed., *Atmosphere of Yangzhou*, pp. 42–43.

the bride takes place on a boat, a practice that may be accorded some antiquity. The decorated sedan chair is placed on a boat and proceeds to the bride's home. Wealthy families use three boats, the first carrying musicians, the second the sedan chair, the bridegroom, and his companions, and the third empty on the forward journey but laden with the trousseau on the return. Families of lesser means need use only one boat, but because the sedan chair is placed on the boat, the groom can with propriety travel on the same vessel. In the 1930s Fei Xiaotong observed a similar practice in the Lake Tai area, where the many canals also allow widespread use of small craft for transport. The practice continues to be observed in this area, even in cases where bride and groom are effectively neighbors and have to take a roundabout route in order to give some substance to the journey.[38]

Further differentiations in rites distinguish those who live on the land and those who live on the water. Both the wetlands of Lixiahe and the uplands of the coast have generated social differentiation by occupation between the farmers and the fishers. But the fishers of the wetlands, unlike those of the coast, are boat people: they live on their boats, are distinguished by their dress, and marry among themselves according to their own rituals.[39] Living cheek by jowl with the farmers but rarely mixing with them, they occupy a particular place in the culture of Lixiahe. In the 1920s it was reported that among Xinghua peasants, the fisher people held the key to problems of infertility among their neighbors. If a woman were barren, someone wishing to do her a good turn would steal a boat pole from a fisher family's boat and present it to her at New Year, thus ensuring that she would bear a child in the course of the year. But if the theft was espied by the fisher family, this would be quite inefficacious.[40] The marriage practices of the fisher people are conventional but mediated by their material conditions. The gift from the man's family to the woman's takes the form of a box of eggs and a boat box, the latter meant to signify that the man's boat has a stable mooring place. The wedding takes place on boats, as the fishers

[38] Fei Hsiao-t'ung, *Peasant Life in China: A Field Study of Country Life in the Yangtze Valley* (London: Routledge and Kegan Paul, 1939), pp. 44–45; "Sunan shuixiang hunsu lu" [Account of the marriage customs of the waterside villages in southern Jiangsu], in Yang Zidong 樣子東, Chang Zhou 常舟 et al., eds., *Zhonghua minsu fengqing daguan* [Overview of folk customs in China] (Xi'an, 1993), p. 184.

[39] In many respects they seem comparable to the boat people of Canton. See Lin Mu 林木, "Shuixiang funü fushi tan" [On the costume and accessories of women in the waterside localities], in Cao Yongsen, ed., *Atmosphere of Yangzhou*, pp. 11–14; and "Danhu funü shenghuo" [The life of Dan women], in Lü He 綠荷, ed., *Zhongguo funü shenghuo* [The life of Chinese women] (Shanghai: Shanghai wenyi CBS, 1991), pp. 38–40.

[40] *Zhonghua quanguo fengsu zhi* [Gazetteer of the customs of all China], comp. Hu Puan 胡樸 安 (1992. Reprinted, Taipei, 1966), pt. 2, j. 2, p. 108.

have no *pied à terre*. On the wedding night the boats of the two families draw alongside the shore, the woman's ahead of the man's. Subsequently the man's boat draws level with the woman's, and she crosses to join him. The man's boat then draws ahead, before mooring for the night. The festivities are held the next day, one boat being devoted to the preparation of the food, which is delivered to the guests by a small canoe. The following day again, the young couple visit the woman's family, who also honor the occasion with a feast.[41]

Marriage rites seem to be a sort of language, and like languages they bear their history in themselves. This history was at least in part an environmental history, as clearly illustrated in the example of the county of Jingjiang. Jingjiang was a Wu-speaking area, having originally been an island close to the south bank of the Yangzi River. I have heard it said that there is a bridge on the border of Jingjiang and Taixing, and if you cross the bridge, you have to speak another language. In the nineteenth century Jingjiang was distinguished from Jiangnan by the lie and productivity of its land, which reportedly made Jingjiang people rather niggardly and necessitated that they be hardworking and enduring. But Jingjiang people clung tenaciously to their southern heritage. Thus it was written: "Jingjiang belongs to Wu. Its rites, festivals, and customs are still broadly the same as in all the districts of Jiangnan."[42]

Just as in the case of language, so too, and perhaps with greater refinement, did marriage rituals serve as communal boundary markers in Jiangbei. This is clear from evidence of the practice of *qinying* 親迎 (the husband going in person to fetch the bride). *Qinying*, one of the six ritual steps of marriage, was once held to be so important that if the husband did not himself come to fetch the bride, the bride's family would not let her go.[43] From the middle of the Ming period the practice has been found to have been on the wane throughout China.[44] This can be corroborated for Jiangbei. In the sixteenth century it could be explicity stated that in the low-lying, waterside department of Gaoyou "there is still *qinying*," implying that elsewhere this practice was becoming relatively rare. From a survey of the

[41] Interview with Ran Lingxiu 冉玲秀, Xinghua, December 1992.

[42] *Jingjiang xianzhi* [Jingjiang county gazetteer], ed. Ye Zisen 葉滋森 et al., comp. Zhu Xiang et al. (1879. Reprinted in Chengwen gazetteer series, Zhongguo fangzhi congshu, Huazhong, 464, Jiangsu province, Taipei, 1983), *j.* 5, p. 14a.

[43] Li Zhongxiang 李仲祥 and Zhang Faling 張發嶺, *Zhongguo gudai Hanzu hun sang fengsu* [Marriage and funeral customs among the Han in ancient China], (Beijing: Zhonggong Zhongyang dangxiao CBS, 1991), p. 34.

[44] Hang Long 行龍, "Qingmo Minchu hunyin shenghuo zhong de xinchao" (New fashions in married life in the late Qing–early Republican period), *Jindaishi yanjiu* [Studies in modern history] 3.68 (1991), p. 175.

other local gazetteers of Jiangbei, it is clear that the practice was disappearing in one area after another during the late-imperial period. Among the people living in the salt-producing region on the coast, observance of *qinying* in the late seventeenth century was restricted to the four salt yards around Dongtai. In the southeastern department of Tongzhou, it was occasionally being performed by common people in villages and towns, but not by the great families. In Yangzhou prefecture around the same time it was observed only in the waterside districts of Baoying and Xinghua. In the northern prefecture of Huaian it was revived among the gentry in the late eighteenth century, only to disappear again in the nineteenth. (See Table 18.1.)

The significance of *qinying* and of its widespread abandonment in the late-imperial period, together with the variables governing its retention, abandonment and recent revival, are topics deserving further investigation.[45] In both the Tongzhou and the Huaian cases, the relationship between *qinying* and social status is clear: in the former, great families did not observe the practice and in the latter they attempted to revive it. What can be said of variations in the practice between districts, as opposed to between social strata? In the middle of the nineteenth century, Xinghua, in the middle of the watery domain of Lixiahe, was declared to be the last bastion of *qinying*. The 1852 edition of the local gazetteer notes: "Other counties do not have *qinying*, only in Xinghua is it [still practiced]."[46] This, to be sure, was exaggerating the case. In Yancheng 鹽城, which belonged to Huaian prefecture but lay next to the Yangzhou counties of Xinghua and Dongtai, *qinying* was generally observed in the mid-eighteenth century, when it appears to have been rare elsewhere in the prefecture. In Funing, next to Yancheng, *qinying* is described as conventional in the 1930s. In Baoying, neighboring Xinghua, *qinying* is noted for the 1840s and is unlikely to have disappeared by the 1850s.

These references suggest that the *qinying* area, plausibly with Xinghua as the core area, stretched beyond the county boundaries into other parts of the Lixiahe area. The retention of *qinying* in Xinghua is consistent with this

---

[45] Maurice Freedman, in an analysis directed at defining the commonalities in rather than the differences between marriage rituals in China, notes casually that the "husband may have gone to fetch [the bride] or waited at home to receive her." Freedman, "Rites and Duties, or Chinese Marriage," in *The Study of Chinese Society: Essays by Maurice Freedman*, selected and introduced by G. W. Skinner (Stanford: Stanford University Press, 1979), p. 267. Ma Zhixiao makes the same general statement with reference to marriage rites within Jiangsu province: Ma Zhixiao, *Marriage customs of China*, p. 337.

[46] *Chongxiu Xinghua xianzhi* [County gazetteer of Xinghua, revised], ed. Liang Yuandi 梁園棣 (1852. Reprinted in Chengwen gazetteer series, Zhongguo fangzhi congshu, Huazhong, 28. Jiangsu province, Taipei, 1970), part 4, *j.* 1, p. 1a.

Table 18.1. *Documented observance of* qinying *(the groom going in person to fetch the bride) in Jiangbei*

Year	Place	Record
1572	Gaoyou	Most observe *qinying*.
1673	Taizhou	*Qinying* in Dongtai, Dingxi, Caoyan, & Heduo salt yards.
1733	Yangzhou prefecture	*Qinying* only in Baoying and Xinghua.
1742	Yancheng	"Son-in-law must go in person to meet the bride."
1743	Jiangdu (Yangzhou)	No *qinying*.
1755	Tongzhou	*Qinying* occasionally observed by commoners, not by great families.
1748	Huaian prefecture	Gentry revival of *qinying*.
1808	Rugao	No *qinying*.[a]
1840	Baoying	Stress on *qinying*.
1852	Xinghua	"Other districts do not have *qinying*, only Xinghua."
1817	Dongtai	*Qinying* rare.
1873	Shanyang (Huaian)	No *qinying*.
1879	Jingjiang	No *qinying*.
1886	Taixing	*Qinying* rare.
1935	Funing	*Qinying* observed.[b]

[a] The source states that of the orthodox rites, only "asking the name" (*wen ming* 問名) is observed.

[b] The source describes the groom being accompanied by a male affine going to meet the bride, and names the practice as *ling qin* 領親 guiding the relative – i.e., back to her new home), but adds, "this is the old *qinying*."

Sources: See "Sources for Local History" at the end of this chapter.

county's reputation as a conservative and superstitious place. Hu Puan observed that "the people of Xinghua are very hidebound," and proceeded to tell two quaint tales of their "most laughable" superstitious practices, both related to fertility.[47] Doré, who was stationed in Rugao and had quite a good knowledge of the differences in cultural practices between Jiangnan and Jiangbei, noted the practice of small boys wearing a silver dog's collar, which he quoted Lixiahe people as saying "hemmed the child's spirit in." He also describes – though without reference to place – the practice of

---

[47] Hu Puan, *Gazetteer of Customs*, pt. 2, *j.* 2, p. 108.

boys' wearing an earring in the left ear, to fool evil spirits into thinking that they were girls.[48] This, along with the more widespread custom of wearing a plait, is again widely prevalent in Xinghua.

Such superstitions may reflect the sheer tenuousness of life in this poor and flood-prone area, but the geography of *qinying* also suggests that communication routes had a part to play in the transformation or retention of ritual practices: the more accessible the county, the less likely was it to have retained *qinying*. It is true that the capital of Baoying was situated on the Grand Canal: that it should have been highly conservative in its social practices despite being on a major communication route surprised observers, who noted the paradox.[49] The differences between Gaoyou and Baoying in the observance of *qinying* may have been due to Gaoyou's proximity to the Yangzhou metropolitan area. In the case of Xinghua, neither the county capital nor any of the local market towns was on a main thoroughfare. Xinghua was the lowest of the counties below the canal, its fields broken up by canals and lakes, its villages located in islands, its county capital surrounded by water. It was on the way only to Yancheng. Few went there for a purpose and few passed it by chance.

As for Yancheng and Funing, these counties – like Xinghua itself – encompassed both wetlands and uplands, paddy farming and salt-producing land. They shared Xinghua's relative inaccessibility and poverty. Their standing in the hierarchy of localities in Jiangbei is illustrated in Emily Honig's findings on people from Jiangbei in Shanghai. Yangzhou people had a higher place in the occupational hierarchy in Shanghai than migrants from Xinghua, Yancheng, and Funing, and the Yangzi jurisdictions of Haimen, Nantong, and Rugao also supplied Shanghai with relatively successful migrants, answering for the majority of Jiangbei businessmen in Republican-era Shanghai.[50]

The wealth and accessibility of Yangzhou stands in sharp contrast to that of the *qinying* counties. A curious variation of marriage in Jiangbei was to be found in Yangzhou, although Li Zongren would have been too late to see it in operation.[51] This was the selection of a secondary wife or concubine

---

[48] Henri Doré, *Researches into Chinese Superstitions*, part 1: *Superstitious Practices*, trans. M. Kennelly, S. J. (Shanghai, 1914. Reprinted, Taipei: Chengwen, 1966), vol. 1, pp. 14–15.

[49] *Chongxiu Baoying xianzhi* [Gazetteer of Baoying county, revised], ed. Meng Yulan 孟毓蘭, with Cheng Guanxuan et al., (1840. Reprinted in Chengwen gazetteer series, Zhongguo fangzhi congshu, Huazhong, 406, Jiangsu province, Taipei, 1983), *j.* 9, 11a.

[50] Honig, *Creating Chinese Ethnicity*, p. 70.

[51] It is possible that the practice long continued in diminished form. In 1992 I interviewed an elderly Yangzhou man, Mr Chen Feng 陳方, who was born in 1910. He was the youngest son of a woman activist, Guo Jianren 郭鹽忍, who was closely acquainted with the minor warlord Xu Baoshan, governor of Yangzhou after the 1911 Revolution. According to Mr. Chen, Xu

through a private market in young girls who were procured in childhood from their parents, instructed in the fine arts, and then sold off to the highest bidder. The practice appears to have emerged in the late sixteenth century and lasted at least until the middle of the nineteenth.[52] If in Xinghua and on the coast the preservation of *qinying* may be tentatively related to the isolation of those areas, in Yangzhou the market in "thin horses," as the hapless girls were called, was certainly for the contrary reason. Situated close to the junction of the Grand Canal and the Yangzi River, Yangzhou was a busy entrepôt for waterborne traffic and in addition the center of the Lianghuai salt monopoly. Wealth, communications, and a large population of sojourners destined it to be a place of high demand for women. A Hubei folksong tells it all:

> Little watermelon, smooth and round,
> Me and my rice are Yangzhou bound,
> Everyone in Yangzhou loves my rice,
> But I think Yangzhou girls are nice.
> Feet so tiny, shoes so narrow,
> Can't even walk up to a fellow.
> Three years older I won't have,
> Three years younger is the one I'll love.[53]

Finally, there were women in Jiangbei who did not get married at all. Marriage resistance has been described in an explicitly environmental context by Marjorie Topley and Janice Stockard. In the silk-producing districts of the Guangdong delta, women's work made possible their economic independence, and social structures were in place to enable them to avoid or skirt the problem of marriage. Were there other environments that might have encouraged marriage avoidance? In the middle of the nineteenth century, Jesuit missionaries in the poor, coastal county of Haimen, east of Tongzhou, found fertile ground for the recruitment of nuns. Unlike in Jiangnan, these young women, typically sixteen to eighteen years of age, would not live in a congregation. Rather, reported Father Théobald Werner:

> Almost all live in isolation with their families, surrounded by corrupt and corrupting pagans. From the outside, nothing distinguishes them from other women. . . . Except for a handful, all are poor and earn their living through

had purchased his wife from an establishment in Yangzhou. Xu was later assassinated, allegedly at the hands of Chen Qimei, on whom see Mark Elvin, "The Revolution of 1911 in Shanghai," *Papers on Far Eastern History* 29 (March 1984), pp. 119–61.

[52] Wei Minghua, "Yangzhou shouma" [The thin horses of Yangzhou], *Dushu* [Reading] 3 (1983), pp. 103–07.

[53] Zhu Jiefan, *On Chinese songs*, p. 388.

constant and often extremely wearisome labor. In Haimen, only one or two families in a hundred enjoy comfortable circumstances. A virgin who is poor, living thus together with the mass of people, passes the day reeling her bobbin and weaving her cotton. Often also will she sacrifice her sleep and work well into the night to make up for time consecrated to prayer or charitable works. Her task accomplished, she gives one piece of cloth to her parents and takes the rest to sell, buying household necessities with the profits.[54]

The poverty and piety of these young women is commented on in almost equal measure. Werner notes also that when taking her vows, the girl would be accompanied by her parents. If this was so, then the support given by the parents to the girl's adoption of a celibate life suggests the family's dependence on her labor for the household economy. Poor as it was, Haimen district's dry, sandy soil was favorable to the production of cotton, which provided women with quite different economic opportunities from those found in Yangzhou.

The "thin horses of Yangzhou" and the nuns of Haimen together draw attention to other variables in gender relations in Jiangbei. Female labor and related footbinding practices both varied in some sort of relationship to environmental conditions in this region. There were no mountains in Jiangbei, but there were borders that demarcated footbinding practices and women's work almost as clearly as did the Nanling Mountains between Hu'nan and Guangdong. Yangzhou was renowned for its small-footed women.[55] This may be attributed in part to the intensively urban culture developed within this wealthy city in the late-imperial period. It was linked also to the prominence Yangzhou enjoyed as a marketplace for concubines,[56] and hence to the economic opportunities for women in this locality. In the eighteenth century the practice of poor families selling off their daughters to be raised for sale as concubines or courtesans in Yangzhou was attributable to the fact that women here otherwise had no gainful employment,[57] a fact that one young woman was still bitterly complaining of in the 1930s.[58]

[54] J. De La Servière, S. J., *Histoire de la mission du Kiang-nan* [History of the Jiangnan mission] (Zi-ka-wei, 1914), vol. 1, p. 237.

[55] Li Youning 李又寧 and Zhang Yufa 張玉法, *Jindai Zhongguo nüquan yundong shiliao 1842–1911* [Documents on the feminist movement in modern China, 1842–1911], 2 vols. (Taipei: Biographical Literature Publishing Company, 1975), vol. 2, p. 895.

[56] See Zhang Dai 張岱, "The Thin Horses of Yangzhou," trans. David Pollard and Soh Yong Kian, *Renditions* 33 and 34 (spring and autumn 1990), pp. 160–62.

[57] *Chongxiu Yangzhou fuzhi* [Gazetteer of Yangzhou prefecture, revised edition], ed. and comp. Akedanga 阿克當阿 and Yao Wentian 姚文田 (1810. Reprinted in Chengwen gazetteer series, Zhongguo fangzhi congshu, Huazhong, 145, Jiangsu province, Taipei, 1974), *j.* 60, pp. 11b–12a.

[58] Wu Lie 吳烈, "Suowei 'Shenghuo ban'" [The so-called life class], *Funü shenghuo* [Women's Life] 3.11 (December 16, 1936), pp. 20–21.

Out in the countryside, women were not much busier, for "the custom down in the country is for women to stay in the house apart from during the busy farming season."[59] Here, however, it would seem that bound feet were a less common phenomenon. So it is that in *Tides of Guangling*, the fictional Mama Huang says, "We're country people; we don't need small feet to look good."[60] Northeast, along the canals and lake waters leading to Xinghua, the numbers of women with bound feet steadily diminished. In Lixiahe, where the growing season was often short because of the threat of floods and the winter task of dredging and diking was heavy, women's labor was urgently needed on the land. Bound feet and working in water do not go together, as the peasant women of Guangdong well knew.[61] And among the fisher families of Lixiahe, too, bound feet were unknown. Living as they did on small, unstable boats, the fishwives were in need of all their agility to manage their daily lives. When they hawked their catch in the markets along the Grand Canal, their hardy bare feet marked them off from the townswoman. The distinction is well illustrated in a nineteenth-century woodblock print that depicts street stalls and hawkers around Yangzhou: one shows a fishwife, with large bare feet; another a towns-woman with child in tow, small feet protruding from her trouser cuffs (see Fig. 18.1).[62]

Farther east again, however, the lakes and marshes gave way to higher, drier land. The Fan Gong Dike marked the border between the wetlands and the uplands, and to the east of the dike, where the people were poor but the land was dry, the women bound their feet. Women's work in Yancheng in the pre-Communist period is retrospectively summed up by the saying "wok and stove, shoes and feet, needle and thread," a reference to purely domestic work and the labor of footbinding.[63] It is a summary borne out by observations of Jiangbei women in the 1930s that their place

---

[59] Li Hanqiu 李涵秋, *Guangling chao* [Tides of Guangling] (1909–20. Reprinted, Tianjin: Baihua wenyi CBS, 1985), p. 1.

[60] Ibid., p. 185.

[61] Ran Lingxiu, head of the Women's Federation in Xinghua, observed that she had worked in the countryside for ten years between 1968 and 1978 and had come across no women with bound feet. Interview, December 1992. In Yangzhou, on the other hand, even today it is possible to see very old women with bound feet, despite Yi Junzuo's observation to the contrary (see below). It seems probable that in the 1930s, when Yi was in Yangzhou, bound-footed women still kept very much indoors.

[62] Zhu Xi 朱熙 and Lin Fengshu 林風書, "Shenxiang zhong-de jiaomai shen" [The sound of hawkers in the alleyways], in Cao Yongsen, ed., *Atmosphere of Yangzhou*, pp. 105–06.

[63] Interview with the Women's Federation, Yancheng, December 1992. In both Dongtai and Yancheng, I was told that the Fan Gong Dike marked a border between small-foot and big-foot areas.

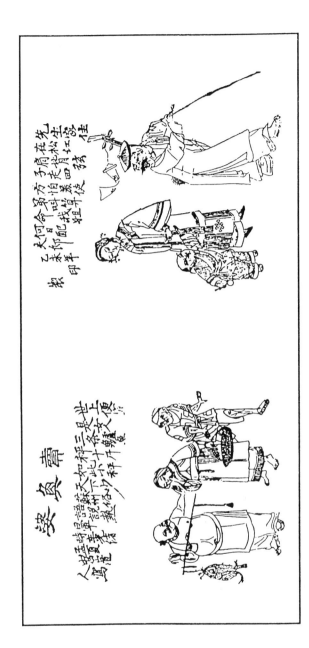

Figure 18.1. Fishwife and townswoman in nineteenth-century Yangzhou. *Source* Cao Yongsen, ed., *Atmosphere of Yangzhou*, pp. 105–06.

was held to be in the home,[64] and by a much earlier jaundiced description of gender differentiation in Yancheng: "the men are hard-working, the women are indolent; each inch of silk, each foot of cloth is purchased at the market."[65]

Small feet were probably the rule all the way down the coast to Nantong (Tongzhou), because in the 1920s Nantong people used to jeer at Haimen people for their big-footed women.[66] Many Haimen people were not really Jiangbei people at all, but migrants from the culturally southern but poor district of Chongming island, who imported big-footed practices into a small-foot area.[67] Generally, however, the foot-binding distinction between Jiangnan and Jiangbei is held to have been in the reverse direction, with binding more common south of the river. Alicia Little reported that at an anti-footbinding meeting held in Chongqing, the approving response of a Nanjing woman to the comment that women from northern Jiangsu do not bind their feet was, "Yes, yes! . . . they don't bind there! And they are strong – very!"[68] Yi Junzuo was clearly surprised in 1932 that all the women he saw in Yangzhou had big feet, but since he also observes that these "Yangzhou" women were actually, nine out of ten, migrants from the greater Yangzhou administrative area, that is, from other parts of Jiangbei, it might be concluded that the reputation of Jiangbei women as natural-footed had some substance.[69] This might also explain the strong emphasis on footbinding in Yangzhou in earlier times, as Yangzhou people liked to distinguish themselves from the Jiangbei *hoi polloi*.

Bound feet made labor on the land difficult and, as far as farm labor was concerned, can be correlated with differences between dry and wet environments, as also with those between urban and rural ones. Less obvious to the eye of the traveler passing by would have been the extent of household production of cloth, an economic activity not incompatible with

---

[64] "Jiangbei funü shenghuo" [The life of Jiangbei women], in Lü He, ed., *Life of Chinese Women*, pp. 68–69.

[65] *Yancheng xianzhi* [Gazetteer of Yangcheng county], ed. Liu Chongzhao 劉崇照, comp. Long Jidong (1899. Reprinted in Xuesheng shuju gazetteer series, Jiangsu fangzhi, 9, Taipei, 1968), j. 2, p. 29b.

[66] *Nantong fangzhi gongren geyao xuan* [Collected songs of the Nantong textile workers], ed. Zhang Mulin 張慕林 (Nanjing: Jiangsu renmin CBS, 1982), pp. 87–88.

[67] Ibid.

[68] Alicia Little, *Land of the Blue Gown* (New York: Brentano, 1902), p. 151.

[69] Yi Junzuo 易君左, *Xianhua Yangzhou* [Idle talk on Yangzhou] (Shanghai: Zhonghua shuju, 1934), pp. 15, 17. Yi Junzuo's observation stands in sharp contrast to that of Sidney Gamble, who in 1929 found bound feet to be an almost universal phenomenon for women over forty years of age in Dingxian in northeast China, the proportion decreasing only slightly for those over thirty. Sidney D. Gamble, *Ting Hsien* (1954. Reprinted, Stanford, Col.: Stanford University Press, 1968), p. 46.

footbinding. The statement that in Yangzhou "women have no employment" highlights a significant feature of the gender division of labor in Jiangbei implicit in the low level of commercial household production. In the case of rural people in the Yangzhou area, the division of labor was described not by the classic formula "he plows, she weaves" (*nan geng nü zhi* 男耕女織) but by "he plows, she weeds" (*nan geng nü chu* 男耕女鋤).[70] References to women's labor elsewhere in Jiangbei are few and far between, a silence bespeaking the absence of developed household industry in late-imperial times through to the twentieth century.

This is corroborated by such references as there are. In the eighteenth century Zheng Banqiao 鄭板橋, a native of Xinghua, observed in a letter to his cousin that "the women of our town cannot weave coarse silk or cotton, but they can still cook and sew and do their part nobly."[71] In the neighboring county of Baoying, women did embroidery and sewing in their spare time.[72] In the coastal county of Dongtai women bred silkworms as a leisure activity, but the market for the silk produced was very small.[73] In Huaian in the middle of the eighteenth century, a prefect complained that no one in his jurisdiction knew even how to grow cotton, let along how to process it.[74] In the late nineteenth century, virtually the same observation is made concerning sericulture: "Few people [in Huaian] know about [sericulture] and those who do know about it are unwilling to undertake it, so very few mulberry trees are planted." Part of the problem, in his opinion, was the women, who "are lazy and just like having a good time."[75] Zheng Banqiao, critical of women in Xinghua for playing mahjong, was clearly of the same opinion.

In brief, spinning and weaving as commercial enterprises were virtually unknown along the entire length of the Grand Canal area from Yangzhou in the south to Huaian in the north, throughout Xiahe and on the greater

---

[70] Li Hanqiu, *Tides of Guangling*, p. 1.

[71] I have used the translation from Lin Yutang, "Family Letters of a Chinese Poet," in *Chinese Wit and Wisdom*, ed. and trans. Lin Yutang (London: Michael Joseph, 1960), p. 492. Lin omits five of the collection of sixteen letters originally published by Zheng, along with portions of two more. For a full translation of the letters into French, with an introduction and detailed notes, see J. P. Diény, *Les "Lettres familiales" de Tcheng Pan-kiao*, Mélanges publiés par l'institut des hautes études chinoises, vol. 2 (Paris: Presses universitaires de France, 1960). My thanks to M. Diény for supplying me with a copy of his work.

[72] *Gazetteer of Yangzhou* (1810), *j.* 61, pp. 2b–3a.

[73] *Gazetteer of Dongtai, j.* 19, p. 7b.

[74] *Daqing lichao shilu* [Veritable records of the Qing dynasty] (1937. Reprinted, Taipei: Huawen shuju, 1965), Qianlong section, *j.* 437, pp. 16b–17a.

[75] *Huaian fuzhi* [Gazetteer of Huaian prefecture], ed. Sun Yunjin 孫雲錦, comp. Wu Kuntian (1884. Reprinted in Chengwen gazetteer series, Zhongguo fangzhi congshu, Huazhong, 398, Jiangsu province, Taipei, 1983), *j.* 2, pp. 6b–7a.

part of the coast. The Yangzi districts east of Yangzhou have in this respect to be distinguished from the rest of Jiangbei. Silk was produced in Taixing during the late Ming, although again on no very large scale. More important was the development of a cotton industry in Tongzhou and Haimen. In Haimen during the eighteenth century "three hands [thus] engaged were enough to support eight people."[76] In nineteenth-century Jingjiang good-quality cloth was also produced, although "not as good as in Jiangnan." There was a marginal northward extension of cotton growing into the elevated areas of Dongtai, but it seems that during the late-imperial period secondary production did not extend beyond the eastern riverine districts.

If the women were not spinning and weaving, then neither were the men trucking and bartering. The dearth of household industry correlates with the observed low level of commercial enterprise in Jiangbei throughout the late-imperial period up into the twentieth century. In Yangzhou during the eighteenth century there were of course plenty of merchants, but they came from elsewhere.[77] Once the salt monopoly collapsed, the merchants disappeared. A mixture of cultural and environmental explanations were offered for the absence of enterprise elsewhere. Thus in Huaian, "the people do not like venturing far afield. They hand over goods to outside merchants to dispose of. One does not hear of anyone dealing in things other than rice, millet, wheat, beans, garden vegetables, and aquatic products. The profits from salt all accrue to sojourners of means, who take [the money] and go."[78] Baoying is "a lowly little place, surrounded by canals and lakes. [The people] living by the water are of passive disposition. The scholars read the *Poetry* and *History* classics. The people quietly till and dredge. They do not admire trade and commerce."[79] In Xinghua, "the land is low, the soil poor and the floods many. [Local] products are basically very few."[80]

Between lazy women, scholarly men, and many floods, Jiangbei society seemed ill equipped for the challenge of economic modernization that the twentieth century brought. The environment as a factor determining the limits of household production in Jiangbei, however, was not that of

---

[76] *Tongzhou zhilizhouzhi* [Gazetteer of the independent department of Tongzhou] (Reprinted in Chengwen gazetteer series, Zhongguo fangzhi congshu, Huazhong section, 151, Jiangsu province, Taipei, 1974), *j.* 1, p. 33b.

[77] *Gazetteer of Yangzhou, j.* 60, p. 3b.

[78] *Gazetteer of Huaian,* ed. Wei Zhezhi 衞哲治, *j.* 15, p. 7a.

[79] *Baoying xianzhi* [Gazetteer of Baoying county], ed. Dai Bangzhen 戴邦楨, comp. Zhao Feng (1932. Reprinted in Chengwen gazetteer series, Zhongguo fangzhi congshu, Huazhong section, 31, Jiangsu province, Taipei, 1970), *j.* 1, p. 30a–b.

[80] *Gazetteer of Xinghua, j.* 3, p. 1a.

Jiangbei alone, for Jiangnan had stolen the march on Jiangbei in commercial production of cloth. In the later eighteenth century, Wuxi merchants sold "no less than several tens of millions" of cloth pieces to "Huaian, Yangzhou, Gaoyou, Baoying and other places,"[81] and in the twentieth century, Jiangbei industry was consistently undercut by the more efficient and aggressive production, marketing, and financing strategies of the southerners.[82]

ENVIRONMENT AND CULTURE: A DYNAMIC RELATIONSHIP?

What I have described in the preceding pages is perhaps best placed under the heading of a geography of culture. The variations in practices and perceptions from one part of Jiangbei to the next are comprehensible in light of geographical variations defined by environmental features. Considered as history rather than simply as circumstance, however, the environment also provides a context for examining cultural change. Did cultural history keep pace with environmental history, show its dynamism, share its vicissitudes?

It is clear from the example of *qinying* what might anyway be supposed: first, that culture does not stand still, and second that a cultural practice has a spatial and an environmental context. The precise relationship between a changing environment and a changing culture is not so obvious. In the case of the old salt-production zone, mutually influential changes in environment and society followed the intervention of the modernizing Zhang Jian. The coast offered conditions congenial to the cultivation of cotton and dry-weather crops. In land newly emerging from the sea, levels of salination were of course too high for the planting of crops. Peasants watched for what weeds were growing before venturing to plant anything. Once the level dropped below 0.45 percent, salt-resistant crops could be grown. Below 0.26 percent, the land became genuinely productive.[83]

Of crucial importance to the underdevelopment of the coast, then, was the alienation of land to the salt monopoly, the profits from which largely went out of Jiangbei. Most of the coastal area was given over to the production of rushes for fuel for the salt furnaces. These would only grow in

---

[81] Zheng Zhanggan 鄭昌淦, *Ming Qing nongcun shangpin jingji* [The rural commodity economy of the Ming-Qing period] (Beijing: Zhongguo renmin daxue CBS, 1989), p. 150.

[82] Finnane, "Origins of Prejudice," p. 229.

[83] Sun Jiashan 孫家山, *Subei yanken shi chugao* [Preliminary history of the salt reclaimed lands in Subei] (Beijing: Nongye CBS, 1984), p. 12.

conditions of low salinity (below 0.26 percent) but covered a vast acreage. It has been calculated that from 1820 to the early twentieth century, when the quantity of salt being produced from the Huainan salt yards never exceeded 3,320,000 buckets (400 *jin*), the rushlands accounted for 6 million *mu* of land, sufficient for the production of 12 million buckets of salt. As late as 1914, Zhang Jian observed that salt production in Juegang salt yard (near Tongzhou) was steadily declining, and begged that of the 510,000 *mu* of rushlands in this yard, 410,000 *mu* be released for more productive purposes.[84]

With land reclamation under way, much of the coast was in fact turned over to cotton production. Land reclamation on the coast, allowing the expansion of the cotton industry, led in the Nantong-Haimen area to a decline in the size of landholdings and to increased household reliance on spinning and weaving, activities in which men increasingly participated. This was accompanied by what Kathy Walker refers to as "the feminization of agriculture," with women forming an ever-growing proportion of the agricultural labor force, mostly concentrated in the cotton fields.[85]

The industrialization of the southeast simultaneously gave rise to new prescriptions for social status and different although still gendered modes of declaring communal boundaries. The cotton mills offered economic opportunities to Nantong and Haimen people, but they were not opportunities that they necessarily wanted for their daughters. So they sang a song bewailing their own fate:

> A good man should not a soldier be.
> A good woman no factory worker she.
> Weeping for her mother at every step,
> Factory work is her bitter fate.[86]

The factory floor indeed provided conditions for sexual dalliance over which parents had little control, and girls' eyes now met boys' over the machines instead of across the waterways. Songs were sung about this, also.[87] And factories brought Nantong women, speaking their idiosyncratic dialect, into daily contact with Wu speakers from Chongming and Haimen. The latter teased the former for their accents, and the former jeered at the latter for their big feet.[88]

---

[84] Ibid., pp. 23–24.
[85] Kathy Le Mons Walker, "Economic Growth, Peasant Marginalization, and the Sexual Division of Labour in Early Twentieth-Century China: Women's Work in Nantong County," *Modern China* 19.3 (July 1993), pp. 369ff.
[86] *Collected songs of the Nantong textile workers*, p. 5.
[87] Ibid., pp. 86–87.
[88] Ibid., pp. 87–88.

At the same time, past patterns of land use and economic activity served to limit the effects of social change on the coast. In Tongzhou and Haimen women had long been employed in spinning and weaving, and when salt-yard lands were freed for the extension of cotton production, "nine out of ten households" echoed to the sound of the spinning wheel.[89] Tongzhou's early advantage in household production allowed it to move quickly into a position of dominance over the northern coastal districts. In autumn each year, after the annual cotton harvest, Funing's major market town was swamped by merchants from Tongzhou and Haimen buying up the raw product.[90] Efforts to establish spinning and weaving enterprises in imitation of the southeast failed. In Funing in the 1930s, the major handicraft noted for women was the weaving of rush mats and baskets.[91] Environmental change along the Jiangsu coast in the early twentieth century, a conse-quence of land reclamation for the production of cotton, thus did nothing to alter the favorable economic position in which Tongzhou had earlier stood relative to Funing.

Elsewhere in Jiangbei, the social effects of environmental change were even less obvious. For Yangzhou, the major environmental event in the late-imperial period was the shift of the Yellow River and the associated decline of the Grand Canal as a transport route. The rise of Nantong spelled the decline of Yangzhou, but it was a long time before Yangzhou people real-ized this. The head of the Jiangsu educational commission, Yi Junzuo, clearly felt as if he were stepping into a time-warp when he visited Yangzhou in 1932. Men still visited the teahouses in the morning and the bathhouses in the afternoon, leisurely wending their way past the crumbling ruins of old salt-merchant mansions just as if these were still splendid. The women, indeed, were notable for the absence among them of bound feet, a sign perhaps of the number of them who came from outside the city limits. But they too were leading lives of a past era. There was no motorized transport in Yangzhou, and no railway joined it to anywhere else, so the boats that came and went from the city wharves allowed people the illusion that the Grand Canal was still the vital artery leading from the heart of the empire in Jiangnan to its nerve center in Beijing. Yangzhou was like Minas Velhas, the Brazilian town that Braudel found intriguing for its survival "after the failure of the gold-mines . . . as an old-time town, with poor revenues and a mediocre population," but telling in its survival of the past from which it

---

[89] Luo Qiong 羅瓊, "Jiangsu beibu nongcun-de laodong funü" [The working women of the northern part of Jiangsu], *Dongfang zazhi* [Eastern miscellany] 32.14 (1935), p. 108.

[90] *Funingxian xinzhi* [New gazetteer of Funing county] (1935. Reprinted in Chengwen gazet-teer series, Zhongguo fangzhi congshu, Huazhong, 166, Jiangsu province, Taipei, 1975), *j.* 14, p. 1b.

[91] Ibid., *j.* 13, p. 1b.

ANTONIA FINNANE

has survived; perpetuating from generation to generation the mechanisms by which it had operated in those earlier, grander times.[92]

In Jingjiang, by contrast, the memory of Jiangnan origins encouraged people to a certain consciousness of what was happening on the south bank of the Yangzi. Like the rest of Jiangbei, Jingjiang was isolated from the economic development of southern Jiangsu in the twentieth century, so that in the 1930s someone wanting to buy a packet of biscuits would have to cross the river to Jiangyin, a distance of three or four *li*. Far away as it now was from its ancient home, and disadvantaged moreover by poor communications, Jingjiang showed to the occasional visitor evidence of a modern turn of life that was at that time hardly evident in Yangzhou. Zhu Ziqing's son recalls that when his father remarried and brought his new wife back to Yangzhou in 1932, she caused quite a sensation on account of her dress, high heels, and glasses. "At that time in Yangzhou," he writes, "very few women in Yangzhou wore high heels, and in the beginning I harbored feelings only of strangeness and alarm toward this new mother."[93] In Jingjiang, however, "women with curled hair, wearing eyebrow liner, lipstick, and short-sleeved cheongsams, [were] often to be found in the parks or on the streets" of Jingjiang. "And high-heeled shoes," adds the informant, "were another thing I quite frequently saw."[94] In this respect, the people of Jingjiang were behaving in a way consistent not so much with the imperative of modernization as with their own past, which dictated that they should remain forever different from their neighbors.

Finally, in the heart of Jiangbei, where the dry lands and the wetlands confronted each other across the Fan Gong Dike, the collapse of the salt industry on the east side of the dike and its replacement by a meager agriculture had by no means reduced the significance of the dike as a social boundary. This had been described in the eighteenth century:

> The people of the villages in the western part are all farmers, and with the incessant floods and droughts very few were able to put aside anything. They had no choice but to live simply. The salt workers in the yards drew their livelihood from boiling up the seawater. They had permanent employment but were not always working. They liked to shirk and hated engaging in trade. They thought nothing of wandering away elsewhere, drinking and eating, and

[92] Fernand Braudel, "In Bahia, Brazil," in *On History*, trans. Sarah Matthews (London: Weidenfeld and Nicolson, 1980), pp. 165–76.

[93] Zhu Runsheng 朱闰生, "Run'er de mianhuai – yi fuqin Zhu Ziqing" [Son Run's fond memories: remembering my father Zhu Ziqing], *Yangzhou wenxue* 18–19 (1990), pp. 17–20.

[94] "Jingjiang funü shenghuo" [The life of Jingjiang women], in Lü He, ed., *Life of Chinese Women*, p. 71.

wearing out each other's hospitality. At the gateways and in the main thoroughfares of the town were teahouses, taverns, and bathhouses, and in the city it was even more thus.[95]

More than a century later, the wealth had gone but the cultural contrasts remained the same. The farming people of the west spoke of the former salters to the east with contumely, a prejudice echoed in the observations of officials who found the farmers poor and frugal and the salters "lazy, quarrelsome and vicious."[96]

It is, then, only in part that changes in cultural practice provide us with a social history of the environment. Continuity of practice contributes a steady counterpoint. This can be seen in Yangzhou, where people still assumed that the canal was grand; in Jingjiang, where people steadily resisted the logically compelling conclusion that they lived in Jiangbei; and on the coast, where time-honored distinctions between farmers and salters outlasted the blurring between the two occupational categories. This seems entirely attributable to these people clinging to the remnants of the material circumstances that had in the first instance nurtured the local societies into which they were born. These circumstances often continued to define the sense of self and community that they expressed in their songs, rites of passage, and in general the "combination of manipulation and enjoyment" that de Certeau has nicely described as serving to refashion "even the field of misfortune."[97]

CONCLUSION

The women's domain is a fruitful field for indices to and insights into other historical processes. Differentiation in the nature of women's labor, for example, allows us retrospectively to predict the alteration in the urban hierarchy within Jiangbei as the level of government interest and intervention in the region diminished in the later nineteenth century. Within Jiangbei, Yangzhou, where the women had no employment, had unquestionably been the largest and wealthiest city, so that the term "a little Yangzhou" was used to describe other places – Huaian, Gaoyou, Dongtai – when they were enjoying comparative prosperity. The relatively favorable

---

[95] *Gazetteer of Dongtai*, j. 15, p. 8a.
[96] Helen R. Chauncey, *Schoolhouse Politicians: Locality and State During the Chinese Republic* (Honolulu: University of Hawaii Press, 1992), p. 36.
[97] Michel de Certeau, *The Practice of Everyday Life*, trans. Steven Rendall (Berkeley: University of California Press, 1984), p. 18.

placement of Yangzhou with respect to the natural environment and communications is not in question. In the 1930s, Yi Junzuo noted these characteristics as conferring the ease of life that made Yangzhou people lazy, to which fact he attributed, in turn, the city's lack of economic vitality.[98] Tongzhou, where the women spun and wove, had by this time long since taken over Yangzhou as the most significant urban center in Jiangbei.[99] The decline of Yangzhou is usually put down to the decline of the Grand Canal, a consequence in turn of the shift of the Yellow River, but this only exposed the weakness of the local economy. In a place where "women had no employment," Yangzhou had nothing to fall back upon after the departure of the salt merchants. The collapse of the Lianghuai salt monopoly, which had linked and subordinated Tongzhou to Yangzhou, effectively sundered the relationship between these two cities; thereafter Tongzhou entered increasingly into the orbit of Shanghai. Yangzhou furthermore lost its sway over the northern coastal districts, and was replaced by Tongzhou. Put in another way, land had replaced water as the most significant economic factor in Jiangbei, with the sea and the Grand Canal declining in favor of the cotton fields.

Differentiation in the patterns of women's labor and perhaps of footbinding further helps explain the occupational structure in Jiangnan in the early twentieth century. In Jiangyin, where women were suffering unemployment because of the collapse of the market for locally woven cloth, Jiangbei women successfully competed with them for the well-paid work of rice threshing.[100] This was attributed to their greater physical strength and powers of endurance, which they might well have possessed relative to the spinning and weaving women of Jiangyin. Women from Yangzhou, however, had a different heritage to draw upon. In the Shanghai demimonde, Hershatter has shown, Yangzhou women had a much more favorable niche in the market than women from other parts of Jiangbei.[101] This might have been due to links with the bathhouses that Yangzhou men ran in Shanghai,

[98] Yi Junzuo, *Idle talk on Yangzhou*, p. 21.

[99] Bureau of Foreign Trade, *China Industrial Handbooks: Kiangsu* (Shanghai, 1933. Reprinted Taipei: Chengwen, 1973), pp. 122–24, 329–30.

[100] Ding Fengjia 丁逢甲, "Wo suo jian zhi bendi funü shenghuo xianzhuang" [My observations of the present situation of the lives of women in this district], *Funü zazhi* [Women's Magazine] 1.9 (1915), p. 2; "Wo suo jian zhi wailai funü shenghuo xianzhuang" [My observations of the present situation of the lives of women who have migrated here], *Funü zazhi* 1.9 (1915), p. 1.

[101] Gail Hershatter, "Prostitution and the Market in Women in Early Twentieth-century Shanghai," in Rubie S. Watson and Patricia Buckley Ebrey, eds., *Marriage and Inequality in Chinese Society* (Berkeley: University of California Press, 1990), pp. 256–85.

but it also owed something to the survival of the idea that Yangzhou produced beautiful women.[102]

A history of the environment particularly asks us to consider the place of land, water, and other resources in human society. Without the link to human society, this would become merely natural history. In these pages I have been concerned to show not only how the life experiences of women in different parts of Jiangbei were conditioned by the environment but also how the environment was interpreted through their lives. Environmental differences and change over time in Jiangbei were eloquently represented by the large-footed women working the Xinghua paddy-fields, the small-footed, idle women in Yangzhou city, the small-footed women spinning in Tongzhou and cooking and sewing in Yancheng, the lazy women in Huaian, the short-haired women of Jingjiang walking around in their high heels, all getting married or being sold off in ways according to custom or necessity, bearing and rearing their children, and sometimes disposing of them.

Overall, my research into gender relations in Jiangbei has done little to qualify the idea of the Jiangbei environment as essentially harsh, though not entirely for self-generating environmental causes. This environment provided some correspondingly harsh similes in popular sayings about women. In Yancheng they say, "women are like rushes: beat them as much as you like";[103] in Xinghua, to console those who have a daughter rather than a son, "if you don't have rice, darnels are good enough";[104] and in Taixing, "a man without a wife can't have a family; a woman without a husband runs wild as hemp."[105] Comparable sayings from elsewhere are often used to represent women in China as cruelly abused by a society that valued men and belittled women. But there was another side to gender relations in China and less terrible ways in which the environment was drawn upon to represent them. Thus in Gaoyou, home to so many ducks. the following song was once sung:

> Boy and girl and a river in between,
> The boy sends a duck and the girl sends a goose.
> The duck sees the goose and says "quack, quack."

---

[102] See Zhu Ziqing 朱自清, "Shuo Yangzhou" [Speaking of Yangzhou], *Renjian shi* [This human world] 16 (1934), p. 35.

[103] Cited by members of the Women's Federation, Yancheng, at an interview in December 1992.

[104] Darnels (*beizi* 稗子) are a sort of weed that grows alongside the crop. Cited by Ran Lingxiu in an interview, December 1992.

[105] Ding et al., eds., *Songs of Yangzhou*, p. 196.

The goose sees the duck and says "honk, honk,"
Says "honk, honk."
The duck calls the girl and the goose calls the boy.

Boy and girl and a river in between,
The boy sends a duck and the girl sends a goose.
The boy sends the duck across as quick as he can,
The girl calls the goose to cross the stream,
Cross the stream.
The boy loves the girl and she loves him.[106]

SOURCES FOR LOCAL HISTORY

Reprints of Huazhong prefectural, departmental, and county gazetteers.

(A) Chengwen, Taipei, with original and reprint dates and serial numbers, followed by *juan* and page references:
Baoying. Revised. 1840/1983. 406: 9.11a.
Shanyang. Revised. 1873/1983. 414: 1.6a.
Xinghua. Revised. 1852/1970. 28: 1.pt. 4, 1a.
Yangzhou. Revised. 1810/1974. 145: 60.7a.
Dongtai. 1817/1970. 27: 15.2b.
Gaoyou. Revised. 1813, 1845/1970. 29: 6.16a.
Huaian. 1884/1983. 398: 2.6b-7a.
Huaian. 1748/1983. 397: 15.5a.
Jingjiang. 1879/1983. 464: 5.15ab.

(B) Xuesheng shuju reprints, Taipei, with Jiangsu gazetteers serial number, followed by *juan* and page:
Rugao. 1808/1968. 1: 8.3a.
Taixing. 1886/1968. 7: 3.4a.

(C) Rare gazetteers series, Yangzhou, no serial number, but with *juan* and page:
Yancheng. 1742/n.d. 4.33a.

---

[106] Ibid., p. 142. This is one of a group of songs collected in Gaoyou in the years 1956–57.

The Environment and Early Modern Economic Growth in Taiwan and Japan

19

Nonreclamation Deforestation in Taiwan, c. 1600–1976

KUO-TUNG CH'EN

INTRODUCTION

Taiwan was incorporated into China in 1683, when the grandson of Koxinga surrendered the island to the Qing. This inaugurated a long phase of Chinese rule with incessant Han Chinese inmigration until 1895, when Taiwan and adjacent islands were ceded to Japan. Under Qing rule, it witnessed the rapid growth of population on account of both inmigration and natural multiplication. The increased population created a strong demand for cultivable lands. In consequence, forests were cleared and trees were felled in massive quantities. After the land had been developed, the inhabitants began to have to procure some forest produce outside the cities, towns, and cultivated areas. This led to the lumbering activities of the Qing period. Owing to particular conditions to be discussed later, these tree-cutting activities were, however, confined to a rather small scale, apart from reclamation purposes. The first purpose of this chapter is to inquire into the problem of how far Taiwan's mountain areas were deforested during the influx of inmigration and land reclamation. Very little scholarship has been dedicated to this subject, and there are no statistics to be referred to. To study Qing forest issues, the basic facts have first to be reconstructed. Section 19.1 is therefore longer than the other parts of this chapter.

Toward the end of the nineteenth century, the use of forests in Taiwan underwent a significant change. Modern economic development required the inhabitants to entract more wood from the forests than they had been used to doing, and technically speaking, they were now more capable of doing so than before. Thus the mode of deforestation became diverted from its traditional ways. Section 19.2 is consequently discussion of the lumbering industry under Japanese colonial rule.

Japanese colonial rule over Taiwan lasted only until the defeat of Japan in World War II. After Taiwan had been retroceded to China, civil war broke out on the Chinese mainland, which at length led to the evacuation of the Nationalist government to Taiwan in 1949. In order to raise funds for the provision of the army and civil servants, as well as for industrialization projects, the Nationalists sought sources in the forests, besides other sectors of the economy, and an age of hyperdeforestation was ushered in during the third quarter of the twentieth century. We will establish the features of this deforestation in section 19.3.

19.1. FOREST PROBLEMS UNDER THE QING (1683–1895): DEFORESTATION OR PRESERVATION?

Taiwan was an island with a wonderful cover of vegetation. According to legend, that was why it was named "Formosa," or the beautiful island, by the first Portuguese passers-by. Even in 1968, when it was undergoing hyperdeforestation, the area covered with forests still amounted to 2,224,472 hectares, 55 percent of the whole island. At that time, out of the total forested area, 20 percent was conifers, 3 percent was mixed with both conifers and hardwoods, and the rest (77 percent) was hardwoods and bamboo. The different types of forest were distributed according to the altitudes of land. The forested area under 600 meters formed 25.8 percent of the total, 600 to 1,200 meters 23 percent, 1,200 to 2,000 meters 27 percent, 2,000 to 3,000 meters 21.6 percent, and 2.6 percent was located above 3,000 meters.[1] The excellent structure of forests provides Taiwan with a good variety of potential resources. (See Map 19.1.)

Although before Qing rule there were aborigines and no want of short-time occupiers (such as the Dutch, the Spaniards, the Japanese, and of course the Han Chinese), most of the area of the island was left with its wonderful cover of trees, except for the part under grassland in southwestern Taiwan. Even to the end of the seventeenth century, most of the plains area was not yet inhabited by the Han Chinese, and the forests were left intact. Therefore, as we can see from the journal kept by Yu Yonghe 郁永河, who came to Taiwan to procure sulfur for the Fuzhou arsenal in 1697, bushes and jungle were spread throughout the island apart from the Anping 安平 area (Tainan).[2]

[1] Hu Hung-yu 胡宏渝, *Taiwan nongdi liyong tuji* 台灣農地利用圖集 [Atlas of agricultural land use in Taiwan] (Taichung: Provincial Government of Taiwan, 1970), p. 285.
[2] Yu Yonghe 郁永河, *Bihai jiyou* 裨海紀遊 [Records of a trip over a small sea] (Taipei: Provincial Government of Taiwan, 1950), pp. 13a and 20a.

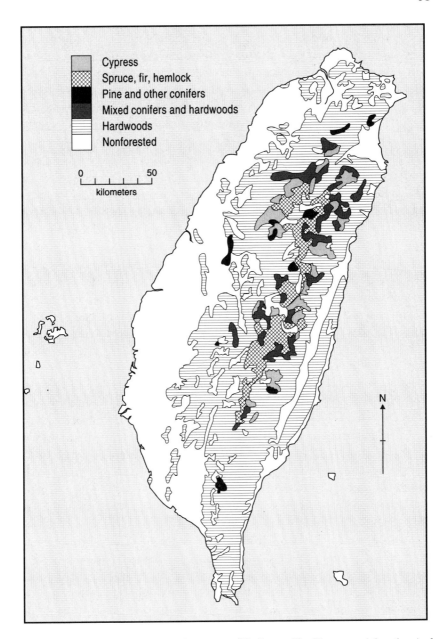

Map 19.1. Types of forests in Taiwan, c. 1968. *Source*: Hu Hung-yu, *Atlas of agricultural land use in Taiwan*, map 20-1.

From the beginning of the eighteenth century, however, the Han Chinese started to flood in, and land was developed quickly. Two centuries later, statistics derived from the scientific cadastral investigation conducted by the Japanese colonial government reveal that in 1905 the cultivated area of Taiwan occupied 624,501 hectares, 17.35 percent of the total area of the island.[3] Our data for the cultivated area around the 1680s indicate only 17,898 hectares.[4] Hence we can assume that about 606,603 hectares, 16.85 percent of the whole island, were developed under the Qing and immediately after. These figures show that a vast area had been cleared for agricultural purposes. In addition to this, cities and towns grew along with population and the economy. Land clearance was inevitably accelerated. Therefore, the original bushes, jungles, and other forms of woodland must have been destroyed in the course of land reclamation. But such activities mostly took place in the areas at lower altitudes, primarily in the plains, basins, and river valleys. The reclamation movement did not touch the heart of the forest. In this chapter, we will not deal with the problem of the development of cultivated land and the growth of settlements, for which readers are requested to refer to Chapter 6, by Professor Liu Ts'ui-jung.

As our concern is mainly with nonreclamation lumbering activities, our focus inevitably centers on the higher-altitude areas that were, broadly speaking, hills and mountains, occupied by the aborigines. The Qing authorities considered Han Chinese activities in the forested area as troublesome, for they always brought about conflict between their subjects and the native inhabitants. Moreover, the standing army of the Qing was not strong enough to round up rebels or outlaws once they had taken refuge in the mountains. Therefore, the government was averse to allowing people to go into the mountains, and a ban against settling there was promulgated at the beginning of Qing rule. However, it was not until the outbreak of the Zhu Yigui 朱一貴 Rebellion in 1721 and its suppression in the next year that the regulations came to be strongly enforced. Thereafter, a policy of segregating the Han Chinese and the aborigines was adopted. Before long, a demarcation line, called the *fanjie* 番界 (aborigines' frontier), was gradually defined in the first half of the eighteenth century. This line lay between the plains and the mountains, usually several miles from the foot of the mountains. The authorities ordered earthen mounds (*tuniu* 土牛) to be built, and

---

[3] Joint Commission on Rural Reconstruction (JCRR), *Taiwan Agricultural Statistics, 1901–1955* (Taipei: JCRR, 1956), p. 11.

[4] Ch'en Cheng-hsiang 陳正祥, *Taiwan tudi liyong* 台灣土地利用 [Land utilization in Taiwan] (Taipei, 1950), p. 51.

ditches (*tuniugou* 土牛溝) to be dug adjacent to it along the demarcation line. The line was completed in 1761, and formed an artificial boundary between the Han Chinese settlements and those of the aborigines.[5] It was not very effective, however, in keeping away Han Chinese land seekers. By way of peaceful arrangements with the aborigines or by means of military colonization, it was still possible for them to develop land within the zone of the aborigines. Finally, a second (new) demarcation line was drawn, extending the boundary of the zone of the Han Chinese and the "civilized aborigines" (*shoufan* 熟番) further eastward, "either to the foot of mountains, or by the riverbanks" (*huo di shangen, huo bang kengkan* 或抵山根, 或傍坑崁). Beyond the old demarcation line was the territory of the "uncivilized aborigines" (*shengfan* 生番). The zone between the two lines was originally designated as a reserve land for the civilized aborigines, but in practice it was shared by them and the Han Chinese.[6]

Although the old demarcation line has been considered to have been ineffective in preventing the Han Chinese from entering into the frontier areas set aside for the aborigines, it was in some sense quite efficacious in discouraging people from using the forests there, for the Qing authorities had special agents to carry out their segregation policy.

In the eighteenth century Taiwan had a standing navy equipped with some ninety-eight war junks. Originally, their construction and repair was carried out mostly on the mainland, but in 1725, four years after the Zhu Yigui Rebellion, the emperor decided to set up a shipyard in Taiwanfu (Tainan) for these vessels. Then, in 1777, the shipyard was rebuilt with offices, storehouses, and a *Tianhougong* 天后宮 (temple of the Goddess of the Seafarers), along with work yards and docks. To supply building materials, a group of military lumberjack chiefs (*jungong jiangshou* 軍工匠首) was appointed to contract for camphor wood, while other items were imported from the mainland.[7] The work is depicted in Figure 19.1.

The lumberjack chiefs were never paid sufficient remuneration for sup-

[5] A map of Taiwan with the (old) demarcation line (in red ink) was drawn in or about 1761. It is now deposited in the library of the Institute of History and Philology, Academia Sinica. A color reproduction and a short note on it are available in Shi Tianfu 施添福, "Qing Qianlong zhongye Taiwan fanjietu Yilan" 清乾隆中葉台灣番界圖一覽 [A glimpse of the map of the Fanjie in Taiwan during the mid-Qianlong period under the Qing], in *Taiwanshi tianyeyanjiu tongxun* 台灣史田野研究通訊 [Newsletter of Taiwan History Field Research] 19 (1991), pp. 46–50.

[6] Shi Tianfu, "Qingdai Taiwan Zhuqian diqu-de tuniugou he quyu fazhan," 清代台灣竹塹地區的土牛溝和區域發展 [The Earthen-mound ditches in the Zhuqian area in Qing Taiwan], *Taiwan fengwu* 台灣風物 [Taiwan Folkways] 40.4 (1990), pp. 1–68.

[7] Jiang Yuanshu 蔣元樞, *Chongxiu Taijun gejianzhu tushuo* 重修台郡各建築圖說 [An illustrated introduction to the reconstructed architecture and public works of Taiwan prefecture] (Taipei: Bank of Taiwan, 1970), pp. 41–42.

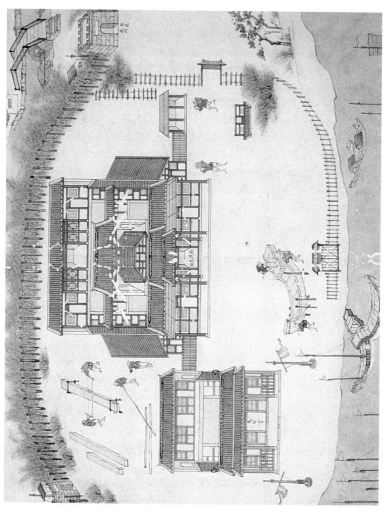

Figure 19.1. The naval shipyard at Taiwanfu being rebuilt in 1777. *Source*: Jiang Yuanshu, *Illustrated introduction to the reconstructed architecture of Taiwan prefecture* (original watercolor on pith paper in the National Palace Museum, Taipei).

plying camphor wood. However, in order to reimburse them, they were given the monopoly of some particular types of forest products, such as distilled camphor, camphor wood, and rattan. Not only were the materials from within the aboriginal zone to be first sold by the lumberjack chiefs, but all camphor and rattan, if produced legally in other locales (such as within the proprietary domain of any reclamation project authorized by the government), had also to be sold to the lumberjack chiefs before being put on the market. Therefore, in order to safeguard their monopoly, the chiefs always kept an eye on activities affecting the use of forest resources. This caused the prohibitory decree to be more efficiently enforced.[8]

In 1722, after the suppression of the Zhu Yigui Rebellion, the authorities reinforced the law against trespassing on aboriginal land, making it punishable by the penalty of flagellation with 100 strokes (*zhang yibai* 杖一百). However, if the intruder meant to exploit forest resources, that is, to gather rattans, to entrap deer, to fell trees, or to collect coir palms (*chouteng* 抽藤, *diaolu* 釣鹿, *famu* 伐木, *caizong* 採椶), then an additional penalty of three years in prison (*tu sannian* 徒三年) was to be inflicted.[9] Such a heavy punishment also helped to fend off the nonfranchised users of the forests.

Common civilians were thus kept away from the mountains, as far as the forestry was concerned. The military lumberjack chiefs and the dependent lumberers hired by them were a small privileged group that was legally allowed to use the forests in the forbidden areas. Occasionally, other camphor distillers could also go into the mountains to make camphor under their cover. But where were the legal lumberers working? How many people were involved in deforesting activities? How much of the woods was rooted up? No statistics are available for our analysis. Notwithstanding this, we will try to address these questions, though some guesswork may be necessary.

First, concerning the locales of lumbering, my efforts have resulted in the identification of thirteen places (see Map 19.2). Details are given in my article on the Qing lumberjacks.[10] Here is a summary of my findings. In the southern part of Taiwan, lumberjacks worked in the vicinity of Checheng 車

[8] Lian Heng 連横, *Taiwan tongshi* 台灣通史 [A general history of Taiwan] (Taipei: Bank of Taiwan, 1962), pp. 381 and 504; Chen Shengshao 陳盛韶, *Wensu Lu* 問俗錄 [Records on customs and manners] (Beijing: Shumu Wenxian CBS, 1983), pp. 136–37; A. Frater, "Report on the Foreign Trade at Tamsui and Kelung during the Year 1876," *British Parliamentary Papers* (Belfast: Irish University Press, 1971), vol. 11, p. 98.

[9] Lian Heng, *General history*, p. 445; Shen Baozhen 沈葆楨, *Shen Wensu-gong zhengshu* 沈文肅公政書 [Political writings of Shen Baozhen] (Taipei: Zhonghua Shuju, 1971), p. 2261.

[10] Kuo-tung Ch'en, "Jungong jiangshou yu Qingling shiqi Taiwan-de famu wenti" 軍工匠首與清領時期台灣的伐木問題 [Naval lumberjacks and tree-felling activities in Taiwan under the Qing, 1863–1875], *Journal of Social Sciences and Philosophy* 7.1 (March 1995), pp. 123–58.

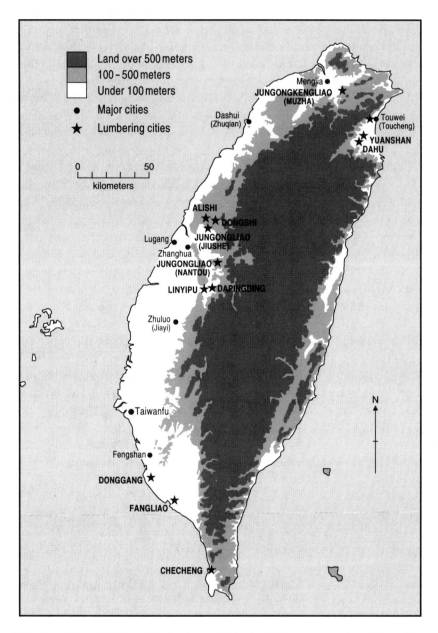

Map 19.2. Sites of military lumbering activities in Taiwan, 1725–1875. *Source*: Kuo-tung Ch'en, "Naval Lumberjacks," Map 1. See footnote 10.

城, Fangliao 枋寮, and Donggang 東港, places close to the seashore. However, as observed by an early nineteenth-century official, Yao Ying 姚瑩, the production of camphor wood in those areas was rather small. Most of the camphor wood came from the part of Taiwan north of Jiayi 嘉義 (called Zhuluo 諸羅 prior to 1787).[11] In northern Taiwan, three areas formed the major lumbering grounds. They are the borders of what are today the Taichung (Taizhong) Basin, Taipei (Taibei) Basin, and Ilan 宜蘭 Plain.

Surrounding the Taichung Basin, six locales have been identified. These are Dongshi 東勢 (altitude: 320–60 meters above sea level), Alishi 阿里史, Jiushe Jungongliao 舊社軍功寮 (both 130–40 meters), Nantou Jungongliao 南投軍功寮 (90 meters), Dapingding 大坪頂 (with a peak of 409 meters), and Linyipu 林圯埔. The locale of Linyipu is between 109 and 1,830 meters; that is to say, it is located in an intermediate position between the plain and the mountains.[12]

In the vicinity of the Taipei Basin, only one locale is identified: in present-day Muzha 木柵. The place itself is now called Jungongkengliao 軍工坑寮, having a peak with an altitude of 112 meters.

As for the Ilan area, which was called Gemalan 噶瑪蘭 during the Qing, there were three locales having lumbering grounds. They are Toucheng 頭城, Yuanshan 員山, and Dahu 大湖, all under 400 meters.

The thirteen places mentioned above have been identified from contemporary records, gazetteers, and land deeds, as well as unpublished papers that originally belonged to one large, but now extinct, aboriginal community (the *Anli wenshu* 岸裡文書). (The last collection has been well studied by my colleague Ch'en Ch'iu-k'un 陳秋坤, in terms of the loss of land to the Han Chinese by those aborigines.)[13] Though the investigation was not exhaustive, I believe it was quite comprehensive. It covered all possible lumbering grounds and included lumbering activities between 1758 and 1824, a fairly long period of observation. At least we can accept the findings as representative as regards the military lumberjacks' activities. Those activi-

[11] Yao Ying 姚瑩, *Dongcha jilüe* 東槎紀略 [Concise records of an eastbound voyage] (Taipei: Bank of Taiwan, 1957), pp. 112–13.
[12] Chuang Ying-chang 莊英章, *Linyipu: yige Taiwan shizhen-de shehui jingji fazhanshi* 林圯埔：一個台灣市鎮的社會經濟發展史 [Lin Yi Pu: the social and economic history of a Chinese township in Taiwan] (Taipei: Academia Sinica, 1977), p. 7.
[13] Ch'en Ch'iu-k'un 陳秋坤, "Taiwan tuzhu siyou diquan yanjiu" 台灣土著私有地權研究 [A study on the private landownership of the aborigines] (manuscript). I would like to thank Dr. Ch'en for offering me a copy of this work. The following citations from the *Anli wenshu* are adapted from his research. Dr. Ch'en's work is now published under the title *Qingdai Taiwan tuzhu diquan* 清代台灣土著地權 [Taiwan's aboriginal property rights in the Qing period] (Taipei: Academia Sinica, 1994).

ties were as a rule conducted in places with a low elevation (with the exception of Linyipu, where the lumbering ground may have been higher). All these areas were domains of bamboo and hardwoods (see Map 19.1). This is understandable, because the lumberjacks' target was camphor trees only; they did not have to go up any higher.

The second question, then, is what was the scale of lumbering activities? This is a very difficult question to answer. What we can conjecture is that the scale must have been limited. Why? Because the duty of the lumberjack chiefs was to provide camphor wood for the naval shipyard, which was in charge of the repairs and replacement of no more than one hundred junks. These came into docks in rotation: all the war junks would not go through the process of repairs and replacement until several years had elapsed. (How long a cycle took depended on administrative efficiency. Usually, it was more than six years.) Therefore, only some ten to twenty junks went into the docks each year. Furthermore, most of the materials required for the junk repairs or reconstruction came from the Chinese mainland; "what is needed in Taiwan is camphor wood only," said a circuit intendent who was concurrently in charge of the shipyard in 1849.[14] The camphor wood was used for minor parts only. Therefore, the demand for camphor wood was not very large, as far as the government was concerned. One document of the *Anli wenshu* shows that, in 1769, when thirteen junks were awaiting repairs and reconstruction, fifty "large or medium" pieces of camphor wood were ordered by the circuit intendent to be provided by the lumberjack chiefs.[15] We can therefore infer that, even if all the junks had needed work in the same year, the demand could not have been for more than 400 pieces of wood. As one camphor tree could produce at least one piece of wood, no more than 400 trees should have been felled in a whole year!

Another source reveals that between 1810 and 1820, the Gemalan area supplied the shipyard with "four shipments per annum, 120 pieces for each shipment" (*meinian sizai, meizai yibaiersijian* 每年四載, 每載一百二十件).[16] The total shipment was thus 480 pieces per year. In 1824, we also find lumbering activities in the Linyipu area; that is to say, around the 1820s,[17] the government shipyard could have had a supply of more than 480 pieces of

---

[14] Xu Zonggan 徐宗幹, *Siweixinzhai wenbian* 斯未信齊文編 [Collected essays of the Siweixin study] (Taipei: Bank of Taiwan, 1960), p. 77.

[15] *Anli Wenshu* 岸裏文書 [Documents from Anli community] (Taipei: National Taiwan University), G112, pp. 102–03.

[16] Yao Ying, *Eastbound voyage*, p. 113.

[17] Lin Wenlong 林文龍, "Taiwan zhongbu gubei xushi" 台灣中部古碑續拾 [Further collections of old stela inscriptions found in central Taiwan], *Taiwan Fengwu* 40.4 (1990), p. 125.

camphor wood. This quantity was far larger than what was needed by the shipyard. The officers in charge, in fact, enjoyed a handsome surplus and as a rule sold off the extra wood for making up the contingent costs incurred by their mission, for the government's budget was constantly tight and they were never sufficiently funded.[18] In short, the real demand from the government was very low, and contributed little to the deforestation.

However, as we mentioned above, the lumberjacks were not adequately reimbursed. To compensate, they were invested with the monopoly of certain forest products. It seems that the government did not set a maximum amount for what they could get from the forests; therefore, they would of course work for their own benefit. They would extract as much wood or other items as possible, and sell the surplus through the market. The records regarding Gemalan's lumbering activities show that, around 1821, there were seven places with lumberers. Some of them consisted of ten or so lodges (*liao* 寮), some of four or five lodges. Each lodge accommodated from ten to forty lumberers.[19] If we take the median for estimation, there would have been ten lodges, each containing twenty-five lumberers, in each of the lumbering grounds. The total is thus likely to have been approximately 1,750 men. Given so large a labor force, suppose that three camphor trees were felled per lumberer per annum: the annual production could then have exceeded 5,000 pieces a year. All the forest resources of Gemalan were under the lumberjack chief of Mengjia 艋舺. Deducting the 480 pieces required by the authorities, the lumberjack chief still had plenty to sell on the market. After defraying all the costs contingent, it still could make him a good fortune!

However, the scale of lumbering could not have been too large. There was the problem of the transportation needed to get the timbers out of the felling sites. In localities where rivers or creeks were close to hand, the lumberers would have made use of them. But even so, to steer the logs down to the seaports was a demanding task, for the streams were not always smooth or straight. There were rocks and other hindrances along the way. Some lumberers therefore tried to use artificial canals to float them down, which gave rise to troubles with the proprietors of those canals.[20] If water routes were absent, the lumberjacks were obliged to resort to overland transportation. The *Anli wenshu* also reveals that in 1771, the Anli aborigi-

---

[18] Xu Zonggan, *Siweixin study*, p. 74; Chen Peigui 陳培桂, *Danshuiting zhi* 淡水廳志 [Gazetteer of Danshui subprefecture] (Taipei: Bank of Taiwan, 1963), p. 188; Chen Shengshao, *Customs and manners*, pp. 136–37.

[19] Yao Ying, *Eastbound voyage*, pp. 112–13.

[20] Lin Wenlong, "Old stela inscriptions," p. 125.

nes were ordered to supply corvée laborers to help move camphor planks
by ox-carts from Jiushe Jungongliao to Shuili 水裡 harbor, in the estuary of
the Dadu 大肚 River.[21] After the logs had reached one of the harbors along
the coast, there were additional difficulties. Offshore shipping was underdeveloped, and the junks employed for coasting were usually too small to
take the logs on board. Therefore, in order to bring camphor planks from
Danshui 淡水 (northern Taiwan) to the shipyard in Taiwanfu in the early
eighteenth century, they were first shipped to Amoy (Xiamen) on board
cross-channel junks, then transshipped back by other routes to their final
destination.[22] The difficulties in transportation therefore strongly discour-
aged the lumberjacks from getting much more wood than was needed for
their commission and for supporting their livelihood.

Difficulties in transportation apart, going up to the mountains for felling
trees in itself obliged the lumberjacks to risk their lives. As Lien-sheng
Yang's study of lumbering activities in other parts of China shows, casualties
were high for the lumberers. Yang copies a Sichuan saying cited by Lü Kun
呂坤 (1536–1618): "Of one thousand workers entering the mountains [for
timber], only five hundred may come out [intact]" (*rushan yiqian, chushan
wubai* 入山一千, 出山五百),[23] because of attacks by wild beasts or other
mishaps, in addition to the difficulty of travel. In Taiwan, the case was even
worse, for the mountains were occupied by aborigines. The military
lumberers were allowed to pass over the aboriginal boundary, and camphor
trees were abundant in the aborigines' land. If the lumberers formed a
large enough group, the aborigines might stay away from them, or even
approach them to lend a hand.[24] Through the grease of gift giving, the
lumberers might seek acquiescence or even cooperation from the aborigines. But this was not always the case; quarrels and conflicts became inevitable, and homicides occurred on some occasions.[25] On account of the
danger of attacks by beasts or by uncivilized aborigines, the civilized aborigines were sometimes asked to send guards to escort the lumberers to the

[21] *Anli Wenshu*, G111, p. 4.

[22] Fan Xian 范咸, *Chongxiu Taiwanfu zhi* 重修台灣府志 [Revised edition of the gazetteer of
Taiwan prefecture] (Taipei: Bank of Taiwan, 1961), p. 90

[23] Lien-sheng Yang, "Economic Aspects of Public Works in Imperial China," *Excursions in
Sinology* (Cambridge, Mass.: Harvard University Press, 1969), p. 217.

[24] Zhu Shijie 朱仕玠, *Xiaoliuqiu manzhi* 小琉球漫誌 [Miscellaneous notes on Taiwan] (Taipei:
Bank of Taiwan, 1957), p. 74; Wu Zhenchen 吳桭臣, "Minyou ouji" 閩遊偶記 [Occasional
notes taken during a trip to Fujian], in *Taiwan yudi huichao* 台灣輿地彙鈔 [An anthology of
geographical writings related to Taiwan] (Taipei: Bank of Taiwan, 1965), p. 22.

[25] *Qingdai Taiwan dazu diaochashu* 清代台灣大租調查書 [Collected documents for the investigation of principal tenancy in Taiwan under the Qing] (Taipei: Bank of Taiwan, 1962), pp.
769–70.

grounds. In addition, although the relationship between the civilized aborigines and the Han Chinese was generally cordial, the lumbering activities drove away animals from the felling sites, and hence caused a dearth of game for the aborigines. To make things worse, some conscienceless lumberers even induced Han Chinese to move into the aborigines' land to make charcoal or to till the land. Through such infamous methods, much of the land was transferred into the hands of the Han Chinese. All these troubles caused bitter resentment in the aborigines, who also misbehaved toward the authorities.[26]

The difficulties of transportation, the danger of working in the mountain forests, and the quarrels and conflicts aroused between the lumberers and the aborigines combined to make it unlikely that lumbering activities were engaged in on a large scale. No serious deforestation was incurred on the lumberjacks' account, especially since their target was only the bigger camphor trees, not all the plants in the woods; and thus the trees could naturally grow back one decade or two after having been removed.

The ban on Chinese entering the aboriginal areas was repealed by a decree from Shen Baozhen, the imperial commissioner, who came to Taiwan in 1875 to handle the problems that had resulted from the Mudanshe 牡丹社 Incident. The lumberjack chiefs' monopoly of forest resources was revoked at the same time.[27] During the two decades thereafter, people enjoyed better opportunities to use the forests, although in ensuing decrees, the government reserved *Tongcao* 通草 (*Tetrapanax papyriferus* [Hook.] K. Koch.) and rattans to be the aborigines' exclusive right, and the trade in camphor was kept in government monopoly off and on. By paying a fee, however, the populace could enjoy the right of appropriating forest resources.[28]

Up to now, we have dwelt upon the tree-felling activities of the military

---

[26] Ch'en Ch'iu-k'un, "Private landownership."

[27] Shen Baozhen, *Political writings*, pp. 2261–62; Frater, "Report on Foreign Trade," p. 98. In order to publicize his decision, Shen's decree for the opening of the mountains and revocation of the lumberjacks' monopoly was inscribed in stelae, which then were erected at strategic points on routes to the mountains. One of these stelae was installed in Lugu 鹿谷, which is located just outside of the old demarcation line, and quite close to the military lumbering ground of Dapingding. For the stela inscription, see Liu Zhiwan 劉枝萬, ed., *Taiwan zhongbu beiwen jicheng* 台灣中部碑文集成 [Collected inscriptions of central Taiwan] (Taipei: Bank of Taiwan, 1962), p. 114.

[28] *Liu Mingchuan fu-Tai qianhou dang'an* 劉銘傳撫臺前後檔案 [Archives of the period around Liu Mingchuan's governorship in Taiwan] (Taipei: Bank of Taiwan, 1969), pp. 39–60; *Dan-Xin dang'an xuanlu xingzhengbian chuji* 淡新檔案選錄行政編初集 [Selected administrative documents from the Danshui-Xinzhu archives, first series] (Taipei: Bank of Taiwan, 1971), pp. 369–70; Tang Zangun 唐贊袞, *Taiyang jianwen lu* 台陽見聞錄 [Observations on southern Taiwan] (Taipei: Bank of Taiwan, 1958), pp. 23–24.

lumberers. We have mentioned that they suppled their extra camphor planks to the market. But was that sufficient for civil use, and was there any other demand for forest products during the Qing? We should discuss these questions to some extent before ending this section.

The Chinese inmigration and reclamation movement started to become phenomenal from the early eighteenth century onward. As the Chinese inmigrants were all from the mainland, the ways forests were used by their compatriots in their places of origin provides a means of understanding the ways adopted in Taiwan. Let us cite some findings by the geographer Yi-fu Tuan to make a checklist of probable usage by the Han Chinese in Taiwan.

Tuan finds that as a general rule for all people, burning down wood-lands was the common means of clearing land. After burning and clearing the land where trees used to grow, the land was then used as a pasture for grazing or as a paddy-field. However, extensive animal husbandry was not popular in China. The most common purpose for clearing land China was for reclamation. In addition, the Chinese people were also in the habit of burning woodland or forest to drive off wild animals, manifestly for the security of the nearby settlements. In the process of clearing a piece of land, people might gather some wood, which could be used for shipbuilding or for constructing dwellings. However, Tuan argues, in history, the shipbuild-ing industry was smaller in China than it was in the Western world, and hence consumed less wood. In addition to ships and houses, Chinese people also used wood to manufacture pith paper, ink sticks, and similar items. But probably the most important use of wood was for fuel. All settlements experienced a constant demand for firewood or other forms of fuel for cooking and heating.[29]

According to the findings by Yi-fu Tuan, in traditional China, in addition to land reclamation, people cut down trees for fuel, for the construction of houses and junks, and for making furniture, stationery, and agricultural tools. What was the situation in Taiwan during the Qing period?

Let us start with shipbuilding. It may perhaps have been the case gener-ally, as asserted by Tuan, that the shipping industry was small in China, but this may not have been so for Taiwan. Taiwan is surrounded by open water, and junks were vital to its communication with the mainland. Moreover, the development of Taiwan's economy, seen with hindsight, strongly de-pended on its trade with the mainland. Therefore, during the Qing period, a merchant fleet of considerable size was maintained. In their heyday, the

---

[29] Yi-fu Tuan, *China*, vol. 1 of *The World's Landscape*, ed. J. M. Houston (London, 1970), pp. 37–41.

number of junks plying the strait was as many as 500 or more, their cargo capacity ranging from several hundred to 6,000 or 7,000 piculs. Taking the usually quoted average cargo capacity of 2,000 piculs (120 tonnes) for convenience of calculation, the fleet was able at any one time to carry cargoes of as much as 60,000 tonnes.[30] As these junks also constantly served as interport carriers for Taiwan's western coastline, their presence reduced the demand for shipping by locally made junks. But there were in any case small junks for local use, especially for fishing. In short, Taiwan's demand for shipping was fairly strong. But all the merchant junks were built in Fujian, and even the major repair work was done over there.[31] As a consequence, shipbuilding was less developed in Taiwan than on the mainland. Only two local civilian shipyards can be found in the records. One was in the Zhuqian 竹塹 (today's Xinzhu 新竹) area; the other was next to the naval shipyard in Tainan.[32] Moreover, as revealed in the *Danshui-Xinzhu Archives* (Dan-Xin Dang'an 淡新檔案), the principal materials for constructing local junks were also imported from abroad.[33] It is very likely that what was demanded from local supply was camphor wood only. Moreover, bamboo rafts were more frequently used for cross-river and offshore transportation than wooden junks.[34] This further limited the demand for camphor wood.

After shipbuilding, how much wood was needed for the construction of dwellings? In the early Qing dynasty, most Chinese dwellings in Taiwan were cottages made of wood and thatched with straw or couch grasses. The frameworks of these cottages were principally made of wood from a kind of

[30] Ch'en Kuo-tung 陳國棟, "Qingdai zhongye Xiamen-de haishang maoyi, 1727–1833" 清代中葉廈門的海上貿易 [Maritime trade of Amoy during the mid-Qing period, 1727–1833], in Zhang Bincun 張彬村, ed., *Zhongguo haiyang fazhanshi lunwenji* 中國海洋發展史論文集 [Works on the maritime development of China], vol. 4 (Taipei: Academia Sinica, 1991), p. 81. For further details, see Ch'en Kuo-tung, "Qingdai zhongye Taiwan yu dalu zhijian-de fanchuan maoyi: yi chuanbo wei zhongxin de shuliang guji" 清代中葉中臺灣與大陸之間的帆船貿易：以船舶為中心的數量估計 [Junk trade between Taiwan and the Chinese mainland during the mid-Qing period: an estimation of the shipping capacity], *Researches in Taiwanese History* 1.1 (June 1994), pp. 55–96.

[31] Ding Yuejian 丁曰健, *Zhi-Tai bigao lu* 治台必告錄 [Indispensable references for the administration of Taiwan] (Taipei: Bank of Taiwan, 1958), p. 169.

[32] Wu Xueming 吳學明, *Jinguangfu ken'ai yu Xinzhu dongnan shanqu-de kaifa, 1834–1895* 金廣福墾隘與新竹東南山區的開發 [The Jinguangfu land reclamation organization and the development of the mountainous area of southeastern Xinzhu, 1834–1895] (Taipei: National Taiwan Normal University, 1986), pp. 220–21; *Anpingxian zaji* 安平縣雜記 [Miscellaneous notes on Anping county] (Taipei: Bank of Taiwan, 1959), pp. 80–90.

[33] *Documents from the Danshui-Xinzhu archives*, pp. 331–39.

[34] Xu Xueji 許雪姬, "Zhufa zai Taiwan jiaotongshi-shang-de gongxian" 竹筏在台灣交通史上的貢獻 [On the contribution of bamboo rafts in the history of Taiwan's transportation], *Taiwan Fengwu* 33.3 (1983), pp. 1–9.

tree called *jiuqiong* 九芎 (*Lagerstroemia subcostata*) or some other trees found at low altitudes. Starting from the early eighteenth century, and flourishing from the end of this same century, a fashion of "replacing straw with tile" (*yimao-yiwa* 易茅以瓦) prevailed in the island. It finally led well-to-do house-holds to building dwellings with bricks and tiles.[35] Wood of better quality was required for these brick houses, but such kinds of wood were all imported from the mainland. The gazetteer of Hengchun 恒春 describes the materials for house construction at the end of the nineteenth century as follows:

> No cedar (*shan* 杉, *Cunninghamia sinensis*) wood is produced locally in Tainan [county]. Moreover, [local products of] stone, tile, and brick are not as durable as those from the mainland. In the old days [i.e., prior to the cession of Taiwan to Japan], all materials were purchased and shipped to Hengchun by the Bureau of Fujian Shipyards. Artisans also came here by crossing the seas. Beams, pillars, rafters, posts and handles, etc., were readily prepared in advance [before shipping]. What had to be done on the spot was nothing but to tenon and to mortise, that is, to put the parts together.[36]

This was, however, not just the local situation of Tainan. Similar practices were also prevalent throughout the island. The famous historian Lian Heng 連橫 wrote in his *Taiwan Tongshi* 台灣通史 [A general history of Taiwan] that "Though timber is produced in Taiwan, cedar wood for constructing houses is frequently procured from the upper river valleys of Fujian, while bricks and tiles are taken from Zhangzhou 漳州 and Quanzhou 泉州."[37] While the well-to-do used imported materials to build their residences, the countryfolk and the city dwellers with lesser means still lived in thatched cottages. In terms of house construction, therefore, the demand for local production was concentrated on low-quality trees such as the *jiuqiong*.

What was the situation, then, regarding furniture? Rattans were popular for making beds, chairs, cases, and so on.[38] They were available locally, but free trade in the material was not allowed. Before 1875, the military lumber-jack chiefs enjoyed a commercial monopoly. Consumers were obliged to purchase them through government-authorized "rattan shops" (*tenghang* 藤

---

[35] Fang Hao 方豪, "Taiwanshi-shang-de yimao-yiwa" 台灣史上的易茅以瓦 [On "replacing straw with tile" in the history of Taiwan], in *Fang Hao liushi zidinggao* 方豪六十自訂稿 [The collected works of Father Maurus Fang Hao, revised and edited by the author on his sixtieth birthday] (Taipei: Xuesheng shuju, 1969), vol. 1, pp. 738–43.

[36] Tu Jishan 屠繼善, *Hengchunxian zhi* 恒春縣志 [Gazetteer of Hengchun county] (Taipei: Bank of Taiwan, 1960), p. 45.

[37] Lian Heng, *General history*, p. 602.

[38] John Phipps, *A Practical Treatise on the China and Eastern Trade* (Calcutta, 1835), pp. 327–28.

行).[39] The monopoly of these rattan shops was revoked after this date, but, as mentioned above, only the aborigines could be the original providers if the canes had been produced on their land. However, as rattan was an article that could easily be brought out from the forests without being noticed, there apparently existed a clandestine trade. There was no shortage of reports throughout the Qing of the "vagabonds" (illegal wood seekers) who cut rattans deep in the woods.[40] Regardless of whether they were handled through the monopoly or the illicit trade, rattans were only a forest by-product, and taking out rattans from the forest did not cause deforestation.

Like rattans, bamboo was also very likely to have been used for making furniture. It was widely available in the vicinity of settlements, and there was no need to get it in the mountains. If it had been produced only in the mountains, shipping it out would have encountered difficulties in transportation similar to those in the case of camphor wood. A ruling of 1824 by the Zhanghua 彰化 magistrate shows that during shipment of bamboo from Linyipu, some irrigation canals were adversely affected, and the parties concerned had to ask for compensation.[41] Furthermore, around 1800, because the China Seas were infested with pirates, the government enforced a regulation to check all the bamboo that passed through any seaports. (The officials believed the pirates would be thus deprived of materials for their sails, which were frequently made of bamboo.) It gave the officers a chance to ask for bribes, and reduced the profit margin of bamboo trading.[42] Free passage of bamboo was not given to the populace until Shen Baozhen's decree. Under such unfavorable circumstances, the bamboo trade was nothing more than a local, small-scale business. In addition, bamboo was mainly a product from low-altitude areas, and hence its cutting did not cause much deforestation.

As for furniture of the better quality, the work of the craftsmen who made it in Tainan in the late nineteenth century was called "making minor woodwork" (zuoxiaomu 做小木), while house construction was called "making major woodwork" (zuodamu 做大木).[43] The materials for "minor wood-

---

[39] Liu Zhiwan, ed., *Collected inscriptions*, p. 114; Chen Shengshao, *Customs and manners*, pp. 136–37.

[40] For example, see *Dan-Xin dang'an* 淡新檔案 [Unpublished Danshui-Xinzhu archives], photocopies deposited in the Institute of History and Philology, Academia Sinica, #22407-7. Wu Sha 吳沙, the famous pioneer in the development of the Gemalan area, is also said to have led a gang of vagabonds collecting rattans in the Sandiao 三貂 (San Diego) aboriginal communities during the late eighteenth century. Cf. Lian Heng, *General history*, p. 853.

[41] Lin Wenlong, "Old stela inscriptions," pp. 125–26.

[42] Shen Baozhen, *Political writings*, p. 2262; Yao Ying, *Zhongfutang xuanji* 中復堂選集 [Selected works of the Zhongfu study] (Taipei: Bank of Taiwan, 1960), pp. 122–26.

[43] *Notes on Anping*, p. 80.

work" were most likely, as in the case of the pillars and beams for brick houses, to have been imported from the mainland.

After furniture, let us turn to agricultural tools. These were basically made locally. Yao Ying once mentioned that people went to the vicinity of Gemalan to get wood for such tools.[44] But the principal parts of the tools were made of iron, which had to be imported from the mainland, and was, again, under some sort of government control.[45] Its importation was limited. Agricultural tools were therefore produced only for local use, not for export. High-quality wood was not needed; hardwoods available in the neighborhood of the farmers were suitable. In addition, we may mention that the principal overland transportation vehicle, the ox-cart, was also made of hardwood.[46]

The only stationery produced in Taiwan was paper. But the industry started fairly late. *Tongcao* is grown in Taiwan, and *chushu* 楮樹 (also known as *goushu* 構樹 or *luzaicaoshu* 鹿仔草樹, *Broussonetia papyrifera*), the traditional source for papermaking, is also widely available throughout the island. Bamboo was also used for manufacturing paper. Even with so rich a natural endowment, however, there was no papermaking industry, at least prior to 1741, at the time the revised edition of the *Gazetteer of Taiwan* was being compiled.[47] Our earliest information about the production of paper is from the diary kept by the circuit intendent Xu Zonggan 徐宗幹 in 1853, when he made use of some local paper (*jipizhi* 雞皮紙, "chicken-skin-like paper") to bind his manuscripts. The quality of this product was low.[48] However, progress was made, and in the 1860s, we begin to notice a small export of paper made in Taiwan.[49] At the same time, Taiwan kept importing a great amount of coarse paper to make "joss paper" (paper to be burned for worshiping deities).[50] The fact suggests that paper production in Taiwan did not consume much of local forest resources.

---

[44] Yao Ying, *Eastbound voyage*, p. 113.

[45] Chen Bin 陳璸, *Chen Qingduan-gong wenxuan* 陳清端公文選 [Selected works of Chen Bin] (Taipei: Bank of Taiwan, 1961), p. 12; Chen Shengshao, *Customs and manners*, pp. 136–37.

[46] Chen Hanguang 陳漢光, "Taiwan banlun niuche-zhi jinxi" 台灣板輪牛車之今昔 [Past and present of Taiwan's wooden-wheel ox-cart], *Taiwan wenxian* 台灣文獻 [Taiwanese History Studies] 11.4 (1960), pp. 14–32.

[47] Liu Liangbi 劉良璧, *Chongxiu Fujian Taiwanfu zhi* 重修福建台灣府志 [Gazetteer of Taiwan prefecture, Fujian province], rev. ed. (Taipei: Bank of Taiwan, 1961), p. 114.

[48] Xu Zonggan, *Siweixinzhai zalu* 斯未信齋雜錄 [Miscellaneous records of the Siweixin study] (Taipei: Bank of Taiwan, 1960), p. 96.

[49] William Gregory (Vice-Consul), "Exports at the Port of Tamsuy (including Kelung)," *British Parliamentary Papers*, vol. 9, p. 87.

[50] Wu Yisheng 吳逸生, "Mengjia guhanghao gaishu" 艋舺古行號概述 [A short account of the old commercial houses of Mengjia], *Taibei Wenwu* 台北文物 [Taipei History] 9.1 (1960), p. 11.

The forest-derived materials used most extensively by the Chinese, according to Tuan, were brushwood and charcoal. The more the settlements increased in number and the larger they grew in size, the greater the demand for fuelwood became. G. William Skinner has a similar observation. Skinner finds that the Chinese usually made the city the center for their economic activities. The city, as the core of economic development, tended to cause deforestation in its vicinity. When the trees in the adjacent area were felled, it was possible for the city to expand. It would usually happen that the city dwellers would then begin to search for wood in more distant areas, and this exacerbated the problem of deforestation.[51] In sum, deforestation has been closely related to the making and maintenance of settlements in China, especially to the provision of fuel.

Fuel was needed because everybody has to cook, and sometimes to heat their houses, even on that semitropical island, during the winter. Fuelwood was used in two different ways: in the form of the dried raw material and as charcoal. For the former, one could just pick up the dried branches of a tree or the trunk of a dead one to satisfy one's own needs. But for the latter, living trees had to be felled. Figures showing the comparative use of these two forms of fuelwood during the Qing are not available. But even as late as in 1953, 81.8 percent of fuelwood still came from dried branches of a living tree, or the whole body of a dead tree, the rest being from charcoal.[52] It seems likely that the unprocessed wood was consumed mainly by country dwellers, while the charcoal was used by people who lived in cities or citylike settlements. The country dwellers, mostly peasants, had access to the woods and bushes in their vicinity, and hence got firewood without difficulty. But it could be quite difficult for the city dwellers to do so. They had to depend on commercialized fuel sources, of both raw wood and charcoal.

Firewood and charcoal were massive in volume and low in unit price, hence not profitable if imported. They were therefore entirely locally produced. As these were necessities for the populace, the government was not opposed to letting its subjects pick up firewood or make charcoal, so long as these activities took place on personally owned or public land. Sometimes, officials even took measures to protect the civil right of free wood picking, as exemplified in a 1778 document. According to this source, Zhang Suoshou 張所受, the magistrate of Zhuluo county, explicitly opened a hill in the vicinity of today's Xinying 新營 in 1765 and declared

---

[51] G. William. Skinner, "Cities and the Hierarchy of Local Systems," in G. W. Skinner, ed., *The City in Late Imperial China* (Stanford, Calif.: Stanford University Press, 1977), p. 287.

[52] Guo Baozhang 郭寶章, "Taiwan-zhi xintan" 台灣之薪炭 [Brushwood and charcoal in Taiwan], in *Taiwan-zhi mucai wenti* 台灣之木材問題 [Wood issues in Taiwan] (Taipei: Bank of Taiwan, 1967), p. 163.

that all residents were entitled "to pick up firewood, to inter their deceased relatives, and to feed their cattle" there (*qiaocai* 樵採, *yingzang* 塋葬, *muyang* 牧養).[53]

Collecting fuel materials was very common, and took place everywhere. Some particular features deserve mention. First, although people were not supposed to pick up firewood or make charcoal on aboriginal land, they sometimes did so with the tacit consent of the aborigines.[54] Second, as the population and number of settlements grew larger and larger, the commercial fuel business became even more thriving. Shops selling firewood and charcoal appeared in Taiwanfu, Mengjia (Taipei), and other major cities in the eighteenth century.[55] In addition, periodic markets for transactions in these materials also existed in the countryside prior to the Japanese occupation.[56] The commercially traded materials were mostly supplied from within the Han Chinese boundary. Though some military lumberjack chiefs might have covered up for illicit charcoal makers, and some aborigines might have been willing to connive with Han Chinese to get fuel materials in the aboriginal zone, the effect of this on deforestation should not be overestimated. The major sources for charcoal during the Qing were the longan tree (probably *shanlongyan* 山龍眼, *Helicia formosana*) or *jiuqiong* and other lower-quality hardwoods. *Xiangsishu* 相思樹 (*Acacia confusa*) popular for making charcoal in the twentieth century, was not yet in great use in those days.[57] In short, the fuel materials all derived from low-altitude trees. Their use did not cause much deforestation.

---

[53] Huang Dianquan 黃典權, ed., *Taiwan nanbu beiwen jicheng* 台灣南部碑文集成 [Collected inscriptions of southern Taiwan] (Taipei: Bank of Taiwan, 1965), pp. 409–10.

[54] For examples see Tu Jishan, *Gazetteer of Hengchun*, p. 253; Lu Dejia 盧德嘉, *Fengshanxian caifangce* 鳳山縣採訪冊 [Oral histories of Fengshan county] (Taipei: Bank of Taiwan, 1960), pp. 37–38.

[55] In the early days, peasants picked up brushwood and brought it to sell in the cities during the off-season of farm work. See Chen Wenda 陳文達, *Taiwanxian zhi* 台灣縣志 [Gazetteer of Taiwan county] (Taipei: Bank of Taiwan, 1961), p. 57. But when the demand increased, permanent shops were opened in the cities for the convenience of the inhabitants. The first charcoal shop in Mengjia was started at the beginning of the nineteenth century. As Taipei Basin was developed later than the southern and central areas, we can assume that charcoal shops probably made their appearance in other major cities as early as the eighteenth century. Cf. *Taibeishi zhigao* 台北市志稿 [Draft gazetteer of Taipei municipality] (Taipei: Municipal Government of Taipei, 1962), p. 96; *Taibeishi zhi* 台北市志 [Gazetteer of Taipei municipality] (Taipei: Municipal Government of Taipei, 1980), p. 137.

[56] Such periodic markets existed, for example, in Beipu 北埔 (in Xinzhu). See Zheng Yunpeng 鄭雲鵬 and Zeng Fengchen 曾逢辰, *Xinzhuxian zhi chugao* 新竹縣志初稿 [First draft of the gazetteer of Xinzhu county] (Taipei: Bank of Taiwan, 1959), pp. 21–22; Chen Chaolong 陳 朝龍, *Xinzhuxian caifangce* 新竹縣採訪冊 [Oral histories of Xinzhu county] (Taipei: Bank of Taiwan, 1962), p. 103.

[57] Zhu Shijie, *Notes on Taiwan*, p. 6; Chen Wenda, *Gazetteer of Taiwan*, p. 31.

All the wood in demand on the civilian side, as discussed above, could be supplied by the military lumberers, by importation, by the land reclaimers in the course of clearing land, or just picked up in the neighborhood of the settlers' communities. That meant that local residents could have sufficient forest produce for their own daily use. Under such circumstances, the illegal use of forests, though it existed, was uncommon. A document dated 1800 reveals that prior to that date, a few woodcutters picked up rattans and collected timber in Nanshikeng 南勢坑, Wuniulan 烏牛欄, Dongshijiao 東勢角, and Toubiaopu 投標埔, places east of the Taichung Basin.[58] However, such an illegal activity could not have been on a large scale.

In addition to Yi-fu Tuan's checklist, there was still one important economic activity that had much to do with deforestation. This was the camphor-distilling industry. As early as the early 1600s, camphor was produced and used for medicinal purposes; it continued to be exported to the Chinese mainland throughout the Qing.[59] Prior to the 1860s, when treaty ports were opened to foreign traders in Taiwan, the amount exported remained limited. However, after the opening of these treaty ports, the military lumberjack chiefs' monopoly on the sale of camphor was strongly challenged by foreign traders, and large amounts were shipped to Europe. The lifting of the ban on entering the aborigines' land in 1875 also encouraged daring people to make more camphor for foreign markets. Between 1860 and 1894, the average exportation was in the neighborhood of 10,000 piculs (600 tonnes).[60] As the distillation of camphor never halted, camphor-tree grounds in the lower-altitude areas were in due course exhausted. Camphor makers were forced to move up into the mountains. Here, their activities occasionally aroused troubles with the uncivilized aborigines. Moreover, most of the tree grounds, after depletion of the camphor wood, were turned into cultivated land. Deforestation thus ensued. The British vice-consul Robert Swinhoe observed in 1864:

> The Taoutae [i.e., circuit intendant], on behalf of the Government, lays claims to all the timber of the island adapted for naval purposes, or, in other words, the camphor wood only; for no steps are taken to prevent the settlers in the bush from cutting down other wood for domestic use, or for charring into charcoal. Were the injunctions issued with a view to preserve the wood, which is daily being cut away without any attempts to replant it for future use, the measure might be applauded as a beneficial one, . . . but it refers unquestionably to camphor alone. The fine camphor trees thus destroyed it will take

---

[58] *Documents on principal tenancy*, pp. 769–70.
[59] Lian Heng, *General history*, p. 504.
[60] Lin Man-hung 林滿紅, *Cha, tang, zhangnao yu wan-Qing Taiwan* 茶、糖、樟腦與晚清台灣 [Tea, sugar, camphor, and late-Qing Taiwan] (Taipei: Bank of Taiwan, 1978), pp. 22–23.

scores of years to replace, and as, from the peculiar character of their large outspreading growth, they only occur at widely-scattered intervals, the time may not be distant when the chief source of profit from this neighbourhood will be reckoned as one of the things of the past. As it now stands, I presume the Government have the title over all the jungly land of the Colony, and they may be right in restricting the privilege of demolishing the finest timber to one party for a valuable equivalent. A great deal of secret destruction of timber is always going on, and were it not for the vigilance of the mandarins and of the parties concerned, the annihilation of the tree on these hills would be, doubtless, brought about in a speedier manner. The tree, according to accounts, appears only to flourish in this island and the Komolan Department [i.e, the Gemalan subprefecture], it having some time since disappeared from mountains of the southern departments accessible to the Chinese settler.[61]

A similar statement is found in acting vice-consul E. Colborne Baber's report of 1873:

Camphor – The trees which produce this valuable article are not found within the district marked on maps of Formosa as Chinese Territory. They occur only within the country of aborigines, or upon the immediate border. The manufacture of camphor necessitates the destruction of the trees, which are never replanted; as the country becomes denuded the aborigines recede, and the Chinese effect a corresponding encroachment. As a consequence the border-country is in a continual state of disturbance, and fearful outrages are committed by both sides on every opportunity.[62]

From these statements, we may conclude that the camphor industry did exert a strong effect upon deforestation. Luckily, camphor also grew at lower altitudes. (That is why the tree grounds could be turned into cultivated land after being deforested.) Furthermore, deforestation was a cumulative effect of camphor making, which did not grow very large until the Japanese occupation. After the Japanese came to Taiwan, the annual production of camphor and camphor oil rose to the level of 30,000 piculs (1,800 tonnes).[63] The consequent deforestation was then greatly augmented.

---

[61] "Commercial Reports from Her Majesty's Consuls in China" (from Robert Swinhoe to Sir F. Bruce), *British Parliamentary Papers*, vol. 6, p. 7.

[62] E. Colborne Baber (Acting Vice-Consul), "Report on Foreign Trade at Tamsuy (including Kelung) for the Year 1872," *British Parliamentary Papers*, vol. 10, p. 197.

[63] Taiwansheng Xinzhengzhangguan Gongshu Tongjishi 台灣省行政長官公署統計室 [Department of Statistics, Office of the Governor of Taiwan], *Taiwansheng wushiyinianlai tongjitiyao* 台灣省五十一年來統計提要 [Taiwan province: statistical summary of the past 51 years] (Taipei: Provincial Government of Taiwan, 1946), p. 1027.

To sum up the foregoing observations, we conclude that non-reclamation deforestation was not very serious in the mountainous areas. This was partly because the inhabitants of Taiwan only sought lower-altitude trees and forest by-products, and partly because their ability to go up and fell trees in the high mountains was limited. The forest was in consequence rather well preserved, though unintentionally. On account of the low utilization of forest resources, the Qing people's knowledge of Taiwan's forests was very poor. Everywhere authors or compilers of books or gazetteers declared that the only useful wood produced in Taiwan was the camphor. They also believed, mistakenly, that no pinewood and no cedarwood were produced in Taiwan.[64] They never had the chance to penetrate into the core of Taiwan's forest resources. This had to wait until the next stage.

19.2. THE LUMBERING INDUSTRY UNDER JAPANESE RULE, 1895–1945

In 1895, Taiwan was ceded to Japan. This ushered in a new stage of systematic investigation and deforestation of Taiwan's forests.

According to the interpretation of Yanaihara Tadao 矢內原忠雄, the purpose of woodland investigation was to pave the way for the transformation of Taiwan's economy into a capitalist system. The goal was the same as that of the farmland investigation, that is, to delimit the boundaries of property and to make it suitable for real-estate transactions.[65] The investigations brought the lion's share of the woodland under the control of the government.

After the Japanese takeover of Taiwan in 1895, the colonial government published an administrative ruling called the *kan'yū rin'ya torishimari kisoku* 官有林野取締規則 (rules and regulations regarding the management of the state-owned forests and fields). The purpose of these rules was to assent government ownership of all lands for which no one could produce any document to testify to their being privately owned. As a result, except for the paddy-fields under cultivation, almost all the land, especially the woodland, came into the hands of the colonial administration. This was because, though the inhabitants might have used the woodland for one or another

[64] Yao Ying, *Eastbound voyage*, p. 113; Yao Ying, *Works of the Zhongfu study*, pp. 66 and 178; Tu Jishan, *Gazetteer of Hengchun*, p. 45; Ding Yuejian, *Indispensable references*, p. 302.
[65] Yanaihara Tadao 矢內原忠雄 (translated into Chinese by Zhou Xianwen 周憲文), *Riben diguozhuyi-xia-zhi Taiwan* 日本帝國主義下之台灣 [Taiwan under Japanese imperialism] (Taipei: Pamir, 1985), pp. 19–20.

purpose during the Qing, the Chinese government had as a rule never issued a deed to the users. At this time, however, the colonial authorities did not launch any project to investigate the acreage and situation of these woodlands.[66]

Several years later, the government commenced a land investigation project. Between 1898 and 1904, under the administration of the *rinji tochi chōsa kyoku* 臨時土地調查局 (extraordinary bureau for land survey), a land investigation was conducted on a fairly large scale. About 21 percent of the land was brought under the scope of this project, but only a small proportion of the woodland was included. A complete investigation of the forests was carried out between 1910 and 1914. In this investigation, owing to the difficulty of transportation, Taitung and Hualien were for the time being excluded. A subsequent survey was carried out between 1914 and 1925. Finally, in 1934, the total acreage of the forests was ascertained: 2,444,236.26 hectares, or 67.97 percent of the whole island. Out of this total, state-owned woodland amounted to 2,182,863.73 hectares, while 261,372.53 hectares belonged to private owners.[67] The confirmation of forest land ownership was therefore not completely concluded until toward the end of the Japanese occupation. Thus Yanaihara Tadao's argument about transforming Taiwan's economy into a capitalist system should be slightly modified. Doubtlessly, the general purpose of land survey (both of the fields and of the forest) had the implicit aim of settling the ownership of land in order to facilitate the capitalist transformation of Taiwan's agricultural economy, but it took a long time to complete the project.

Soon after the commencement of the land survey, the Japanese authorities became involved in the lumbering industry. It started with the Alishan 阿里山. In 1899, an exploration of that mountain area was launched by a technician of the Tainan county government, and its rich endowment of Chinese cypress (*hongkuai* 紅檜, *Chamaecyparis formosensis*) was discovered.[68] In 1906, the Japanese commercial group Fujita Gumi 藤田組 was authorized by the colonial government to explore the resources of the Alishan. This group started to build a railroad and to prepare all the necessary equipment for felling and hauling out trees from the mountains. Unfortunately for the group, it ran short of working capital and was forced to renounce its privilege in 1908. The colonial government then took the project in hand itself. An operation station was formally established in April

---

[66] Zhou Zhen 周楨, *Taiwan-zhi senlin jingli* 台灣之森林經理 [The management of Taiwan's forestry] (Taipei: Bank of Taiwan, 1972), pp. 3–6.

[67] Ibid., p. 20.

[68] Zhou Zhen, *Taiwan-zhi famu shiye* 台灣之伐木事業 [The lumbering industry in Taiwan] (Taipei: Bank of Taiwan, 1958), pp. 51–52.

1910.[69] Two years later, a Ledgerwood cableway skidder for bringing out timber arrived from the United States and lumbering commenced. In September of the same year, part of the railroad was completed, and wood from Alishan began to be transported to the market.[70]

The Alishan operation station turned out to be very successful, and its scale was gradually enlarged. Consequently, a bureau in charge of the management of forestry and lumbering was installed in the colonial government's headquarters in Taihoku 台北 (i.e., Taipei) in 1915 to replace the operation station in the mountains. With the successful case of the Alishan as a model, the colonial government became much interested in developing the forest business. Two outposts were set up in the following year in Yuanshan (in the Ilan area) and Tuniu 土牛 (in Shigang 石岡 of Taichung county, close to Dongshi) with the purpose of developing the lumbering industry in the neighboring forests. (Both Yuanshan and Dongshi were Qing military lumbering grounds.) Later on, in 1924 and 1926, in order to manage their business better, the two outposts were moved to Luodong 羅東 and Fengyuan 豐原, two towns more accessible to markets. The Luodong outpost was responsible for the lumbering ground called the Taipingshan 太平山 ground after 1945, and that of Fengyuan for Baxianshan 八仙山. Alishan, Taipingshan, and Baxianshan were the three major tree grounds for Taiwan's lumbering activities, and they were all operated by the government.[71]

As the government owned most of the woodland of the island, and it was almost the only institution that possessed sufficient capital to develop the lumbering industry, it was a matter of course that the industry was mainly maintained by the government. However, after the outbreak of the war in the Pacific in 1942, the situation changed, and the privatization of the lumbering industry commenced. In fact, the Japanese had already been involved in protracted warfare with the Chinese on the mainland since 1937, and had diverted much of their resources to the battlefields. The government had subsequently found itself caught in dire need of capital to operate the lumbering industry. In the meantime, the war required the colonial government to supply more and more wood for military purposes. Under such circumstances, the colonial government adopted the policy of reorganizing the industry. The government-managed lumbering activities were transferred to business corporations, which allowed private persons to

[69] Zheng Yueqiao 鄭月樵, "Taiwan mucai-zhi chanxiao" 台灣木材之產銷 [On the production and marketing of Taiwan's timber], in *Wood Issues in Taiwan*, p. 108.
[70] Zhou Zhen, *Lumbering industry in Taiwan*, p. 53.
[71] Zheng Yueqiao, "Production and marketing," p. 108.

Table 19.1. *Lumbering activities on the major grounds in Taiwan, 1912–45*

Year	Alishan		Taipingshan		Baxianshan		Lintianshan	
	Area (ha)	Wood produced (m³)	Area (ha)	Wood produced (m³)	Area (ha)	Wood produced (m³)	Area (ha)	Wood produced (m³)
1912	43	29,063						
1913	108	49,214						
1914	74	45,936						
1915	144	117,332	49.58	22,448.55	14.58	12,764		
1916	124	105,586	89.25	25,126.12	49.50	19,499		
1917	116	89,933	44.62	21,125.55	34.69	12,443		
1918	132	142,606	64.46	31,399.08	34.69	14,615		
1919	122	167,688	79.33	34,141.51	24.79	13,295		
1920	117	87,317	72.39	31,254.38	9.90	4,153		
1921	115	104,555	109.09	39,476.00	19.80	7,634		
1922	145	112,484	92.10	61,130.25	14.85	10,286		
1923	112	83,532	99.13	41,329.50	13.06	11,600		
1924	130	78,752	118.47	37,708.85	19.31	13,076		
1925	164	76,871	125.45	56,219.06	32.69	19,246		
1926	108	69,236	143.13	51,796.32	31.98	21,427		
1927	208	91,072	148.76	62,513.38	54.41	27,323		
1928	168	80,668	138.84	72,012.32	111.03	42,878		
1929	199	102,602	129.69	72,377.03	112.06	46,656		
1930	201	78,703	128.92	67,247.00	82.17	35,139		
1931	209	97,347	134.00	66,457.15	149.75	46,567		
1932	260	88,070	248.70	82,637.95	92.00	39,228		
1933	475	120,664	252.05	79,681.14	98.05	51,225		
1934	520	114,798	393.39	86,105.40	196.39	61,395		
1935	558	119,031	273.94	73,608.22	148.37	53,516		
1936	551	110,274	253.74	76,563.27	161.80	46,910	50	
1937	769	129,535	244.32	76,889.13	142.79	44,547		1,824
1938	479	83,524	138.50	61,146.24	179.00	69,888		228
1939	552	133,126	231.01	128,870.46	235.00	84,502	120	750
1940	660	169,374	220.89	109,990.77	215.00	77,711	130	1,035
1941	654	167,137	230.60	92,890.19	406.00	111,052	190	18,120
1942	360	137,469	301.01	98,396.63	432.00	10,733	200	24,680
1943	665	160,411	242.94	119,278.24	276.00	63,868		43,740
1944	445	107,483	175.54	104,610.30	23.30	55,461		32,100
1945	86	18,437	63.23	25,548.80	207.00	21,596		5,450
Total	9,773	3,469,830	5,037.07	2,009,978.79	3,621.96	1,150,233	690	127,927

Source: Zhou Zhen. *Lumbering industry in Taiwan*, pp. 60-62, 80-81, 93-94 and 135.

buy their stocks or to own an entire enterprise. As a consequence, the lumbering industries were privatized.[72]

The average annual production of timber under the Japanese was about 160,000 to 170,000 cubic meters between 1912 and 1934. Thereafter, on account of the contingent demand for timber occasioned by the war, it increased to some degree.[73] For timber production statistics for this period, see Table 19.1.

Basing ourselves on Table 19.1, we find that the annual production of wood in Taiwan was still on a rather small scale. The output could hardly

[72] Zhou Zhen, *Lumbering industry in Taiwan*, p. 4.
[73] Cf. Zheng Yueqiao, "Production and marketing," p. 111.

Table 19.2. *Importation and exportation of wood in Taiwan, 1912–45*

Year	Importation (A)		Exportation (B)		Balance (A–B)	
	Quantity (m³)	Value (yen)	Quantity (m³)	Value (yen)	Quantity (m³)	Value (yen)
1912		4,175,569		93,841		
1913		3,635,317		134,664		
1914		2,502,682		191,615		
1915		2,183,174		230,546		
1916		2,111,048	19,682	732,847		
1917		3,188,879	17,907	846,125		
1918	411	4,158,040	6,850	697,106		
1919	13,829	6,747,113	16,366	604,939		
1920 [a]	21,275	10,334,473	12,846	1,488,667		
1921	122,597	6,648,553	9,956	629,273	112,641	6,019,280
1922	476,457	5,041,580	25,124	1,820,147	451,333	3,221,433
1923		4,003,170	39,268	3,468,176		534,994
1924	347,226	3,784,334	16,662	2,276,130	330,564	1,508,204
1925		5,382,978	15,963	2,961,170		2,421,808
1926	208,027	5,728,637	14,909	3,259,488	193,118	2,469,149
1927	244,145	6,736,842	18,218	2,918,464	225,927	3,818,378
1928	302,406	9,820,898	20,179	3,395,595	282,227	6,425,303
1929	355,531	11,024,974	23,269	2,255,504	332,262	8,769,470
1930	300,243	7,757,142	20,208	1,379,194	280,035	6,377,948
1931	296,503	6,865,832	21,401	1,202,125	275,102	5,663,707
1932	320,734	7,343,733	28,662	1,803,736	292,072	5,539,997
1933	301,342	7,601,577	40,470	2,384,294	260,872	5,217,283
1934	330,772	8,870,884	63,984	2,407,342	266,788	6,463,542
1935	459,148	12,498,385	29,154	1,514,033	429,994	10,984,352
1936	543,107	14,852,979	33,390	2,175,843	509,717	12,677,136
1937	516,295	15,085,875	28,651	2,239,144	487,644	12,846,731
1938	464,260	19,031,222	39,791	3,395,595	424,469	15,635,627
1939	484,027	21,318,558	56,133	4,859,590	427,894	16,458,968
1940	555,311	1,710,455	9,020		546,291	
1941	221,410	1,425,605	4,403		217,007	
1942	95,507	2,430,931	886		94,621	
1943	6,601	2,312,942				
1944						
1945						

[a] Figures for the years prior to 1921 are not reliable; hence the calculation of balances for those years is here omitted.

Source: Zheng Yueqiao, "Production and marketing," in *Wood issues in Taiwan*, pp. 128-29.

have met the domestic demand of local markets. Therefore, most of the forest products should have been consumed locally. A small part of the forest produce was, however, exported to other countries. As far as the entire Japanese colonial period is concerned, the balance of trade in timber and wood products was unfavorable to Taiwan, both in terms of value and of quantity (see Table 19.2). The local wood products were usually of better quality and fetched better prices. From Table 19.3, one

Table 19.3. *Timber imports and exports with average prices, 1921–39*

Year	Importation			Exportation		
	Quantity (m³)	Value (yen)	Average price	Quantity (m³)	Value (yen)	Average price
1921	122,597	6,648,553	54	9,956	629,273	63
1922	476,457	5,041,580	11	25,124	1,820,147	72
1923		4,003,170		39,268	3,468,176	88
1924	347,226	3,784,334	11	16,662	2,276,130	137
1925		5,382,978		15,963	2,961,170	186
1926	208,027	5,728,637	28	14,909	3,259,488	219
1927	244,145	6,736,842	28	18,218	2,918,464	160
1928	302,406	9,820,898	32	20,179	3,395,595	168
1929	355,531	11,024,974	31	23,269	2,255,504	97
1930	300,243	7,757,142	29	20,208	1,379,194	68
1931	296,503	6,865,832	23	21,401	1,202,125	56
1932	320,734	7,343,733	23	28,662	1,803,736	63
1933	301,342	7,601,577	25	40,470	2,384,294	59
1934	330,772	8,870,884	27	63,984	2,407,342	38
1935	459,148	12,498,385	27	29,154	1,514,033	51
1936	543,107	14,852,979	27	33,390	2,175,843	65
1937	516,295	15,085,875	29	28,651	2,239,144	78
1938	464,260	19,031,222	41	39,791	3,395,595	85
1939	484,027	21,318,558	44	56,133	4,859,590	87

Note: Average prices are expressed in yen per cubic meter. Figures rounded.

Source: Table 19.2

can see that the unit prices for imported timber ranged from 11 to 54 Japanese yen, but those for exported timber ranged from 38 to 219 yen! Hence by exporting a given quantity of timber, money could be earned to ship back to Taiwan a much greater quantity of wood products to fill the gap that the local products were unable to satisfy.[74] This means that during the fifty-one years of Japanese rule, Taiwan did not fell as many trees as the local economy demanded. Moreover, in terms of value, exports still ran short of the imports. The unfavorable balance had to be met with resources from other sectors of the economy. Hence the other sectors paid for the preservation of the forests by means of importing timber and wood products. Such an arrangement, though not purposely designed, in effect contributed to the better preservation of Taiwan's forest resources.

Efforts at reforestation also occurred during the Japanese colonial period. But the acreage of reforestation fell short of that of deforestation. Those lumbering grounds for which statistics are available, Alishan, Taipingshan, and Baxianshan, together with two other minor lumbering

[74] Ibid.

Table 19.4. *Deforestation and reforestation in Taiwan, 1895–1945*

Place	Area lumbered (ha)	Area replanted (ha)	Area deforested (ha)
Alishan	9,771.13	3,100.00	6,671.13
Taipingshan	5,037.07	2,537.02	2,500.05
Baxianshan	3,621.96	868.18	2,753.78
Tailuge	104.32	154.06	-49.74
Lintianshan	690.00	52.60	637.40
Total	19,224.48	6,711.86	12,512.62

Source: Zhou Zhen, *Lumbering industry in Taiwan*, p. 150.
Note: "Deforested" is defined as "Lumbered – replanted."

locales, Tailuge 太魯閣 (in Hualien) and Lintianshan 林田山 (also in Hualien), had an aggregate deforested area of 19,224.48 hectares before 1945, while only 6,711.86 hectares were reforested. This means that only 34.91 percent of the deforested area had been reforested (see Table 19.4). An area of 12,512.62 hectares was left barren after its trees had been felled. This is the equivalent of 0.51 percent of Taiwan's woodland, or 0.355 percent of the total area of the whole island. The figures are small. We can therefore conclude that, because the scale of lumbering industry was still limited, deforestation was not serious during the Japanese period.

19.3 HYPERDEFORESTATION IN THE THIRD QUARTER OF THE TWENTIETH CENTURY

The second half of the twentieth century, on the contrary, saw the most serious deforestation in Taiwan, especially during the third quarter of the century, when trees were felled on a comparatively large scale. From 1964 onward, annual lumbering activities affected more than 10,000 hectares! That is to say, within two years, they produced effects more than equivalent to what had been caused during the entire Japanese period! Between 1958 and 1976, the annual production of timber in every year exceeded 1,000,000 cubic meters (see Table 19.5). The period of hyperdeforestation coincides with the period between the two aerial surveys of Taiwan's forest resources (1954 and 1972). During that period, Taiwan was in dire need of

Table 19.5. *Lumbering activities in Taiwan, 1946–76*

Year	Wood produced (m³)	Index[a]	Year	Wood produced (m³)	Index
1946	102,203	19.74	1962	1,332,977	257.46
1947	677,659	130.88	1963	1,472,689	284.44
1948	494,372	95.49	1964	1,613,753	311.69
1949	436,136	84.24	1965	1,663,296	321.26
1950	517,743	100.00	1966	1,430,446	276.28
1951	745,137	143.92	1967	1,577,731	304.73
1952	886,527	171.23	1968	1,557,321	300.79
1953	763,036	174.38	1969	1,475,586	285.00
1954	914,950	176.72	1970	1,554,589	300.26
1955	806,644	155.80	1971	1,762,006	340.32
1956	775,054	149.70	1972	1,790,163	345.76
1957	981,105	189.50	1973	1,714,469	331.14
1958	1,103,417	213.12	1974	1,533,907	296.27
1959	1,251,874	241.79	1975	1,110,260	214.44
1960	1,221,492	235.93	1976	1,101,481	212.76
1961	1,333,251	257.51			

Note: The total quantity of wood produced during 1957-76 was 28,581,813 cubic meters.

[a] Index: 1950 = 100.

Source: Calculated from Taiwan Forestry Bureau, comp., *Taiwan Forestry Statistics*, annual publication, in series.

foreign exchange to finance its industrialization projects. Moreover, the evacuation of the Nationalist government from the mainland had brought a large population to Taiwan, which, when added to the natural increase of population, greatly augmented the demand for wood. As a result, though Taiwan produced more timber than before, much of the demand still had to be met by importation. In terms of quantity, throughout the period between 1950 and 1976, imports remained larger than exports. But in terms of value, that of exports started to exceed the value of imports from 1958 onward (see Table 19.6). By this time the export of timber was not just designed to offset the import of lesser-quality timber for domestic use. It also aimed at procuring surplus foreign exchange for the financing of local industrialization. In this sense, contrary to the case under Japanese

Table 19.6. *Importation and exportation of wood in Taiwan, 1950–76*

Year	Importation (A) Quantity (m³)	Importation (A) Value (NT yuan)	Exportation (B) Quantity (m³)	Exportation (B) Value (NT yuan)	Balance (A−B) Quantity (m³)	Balance (A−B) Value (NT yuan)
1950	34,715			1,299,842		
1951	21,689	11,727,696	698	702,038	20,991	11,025,658
1952	26,364	11,389,746	400	3,788,673	25,964	7,601,073
1953	50,698	24,022,994	1,275	4,662,690	49,423	19,360,304
1954	113,773	58,109,289	1,624	11,522,137	112,149	46,587,152
1955	65,096	37,440,003	6,353	18,979,084	58,743	18,406,919
1956	101,511	90,942,965	6,931	20,794,818	94,580	70,148,147
1957	163,364	117,982,059	6,869	81,310,867	156,495	36,671,192
1958	107,739	78,448,260	41,399	189,328,706	66,340	−110,880,446
1959	169,827	153,306,989	55,425	199,746,192	114,402	−46,439,203
1960	169,013	139,512,422	51,932	397,959,771	117,081	−258,447,349
1961	169,628	173,344,008	89,671	623,799,347	79,957	−450,455,339
1962	278,412	318,495,914	133,217	623,799,347	145,195	−305,303,433
1963	447,617	553,389,925	201,049	980,557,582	246,568	−427,167,657
1964	565,916	676,553,441	328,068	1,512,083,896	237,848	−835,503,455
1965	626,175	700,237,841	415,406	1,656,975,389	210,769	−956,737,548
1966	694,591	835,969,363	418,929	2,030,378,124	275,662	−1,194,408,761
1967	745,345	919,252,374	431,659	2,240,121,996	313,686	−1,320,869,622
1968	1,098,018	1,389,162,334	435,736	3,388,880,657	662,282	−1,999,718,323
1969	1,193,671	1,545,635,792	523,524	4,369,093,658	670,147	−2,823,457,866
1970	1,500,845	1,974,088,779	595,727	5,377,976,884	905,118	−3,403,888,105
1971	2,233,535	2,850,404,777	722,656	6,692,388,255	1,510,879	−3,841,983,478
1972	3,685,916	4,754,043,000	1,175,437	10,635,532,000	2,510,479	−5,881,489,000
1973	3,909,995	7,213,586,000	1,309,450	14,618,272,000	2,600,545	−7,404,686,000
1974	3,682,806	8,968,305,000	935,963	12,556,768,000	2,746,843	−3,588,463,000
1975	3,768,728	8,899,938,000	1,010,092	10,477,257,000	2,758,636	−1,577,319,000
1976	4,144,202	9,710,685,000	1,331,706	20,945,180,000	2,812,496	−11,234,495,000

Source: Calculated from Taiwan Forestry Bureau, comp., *Taiwan Forestry Statistics*, annual publication, in series.

Table 19.7. *Timber imports and exports with average prices, 1950–76*

Year	Importation			Exportation		
	Quantity (m³)	Value (NT yuan)	Average price	Quantity (m³)	Value (NT yuan)	Average price
1950	34,715				1,299,842	
1951	21,689	11,727,696	541	698	702,038	1,006
1952	26,364	11,389,746	432	400	3,788,673	9,472
1953	50,698	24,022,994	474	1,275	4,662,690	3,657
1954	113,773	58,109,289	511	1,624	11,522,137	7,095
1955	65,096	37,440,003	575	6,353	18,979,084	2,987
1956	101,511	90,942,965	896	6,931	20,794,818	3,000
1957	163,364	117,982,059	722	6,869	81,310,867	11,837
1958	107,739	78,448,260	728	41,399	189,328,706	4,573
1959	169,827	153,306,989	903	55,425	199,746,192	3,604
1960	169,013	139,512,422	825	51,932	397,959,771	7,663
1961	169,628	173,344,008	1,022	89,671	623,799,347	6,957
1962	278,412	318,495,914	1,144	133,217	623,799,347	4,683
1963	447,617	553,389,925	1,236	201,049	980,557,582	4,877
1964	565,916	676,553,441	1,196	328,068	1,512,083,896	4,609
1965	626,175	700,237,841	1,118	415,406	1,656,975,389	3,989
1966	694,591	835,969,363	1,204	418,929	2,030,378,124	4,847
1967	745,345	919,252,374	1,233	431,659	2,240,121,996	5,190
1968	1,098,018	1,389,162,334	1,265	435,736	3,388,880,657	7,777
1969	1,193,671	1,545,635,792	1,294	523,524	4,369,093,658	8,346
1970	1,500,845	1,974,088,779	1,315	595,727	5,377,976,884	9,028
1971	2,233,535	2,850,404,777	1,276	722,656	6,692,388,255	9,261
1972	3,685,916	4,754,043,000	1,290	1,175,437	10,635,532,000	9,048
1973	3,909,956	7,213,586,000	1,845	1,309,450	14,618,272,000	11,164
1974	3,682,067	8,968,305,000	2,436	935,963	12,556,768,000	13,416
1975	3,768,728	8,899,938,000	2,362	1,010,092	10,477,257,000	10,373
1976	4,144,202	9,710,685,000	2,343	1,331,706	20,945,180,000	15,728

Note: Average prices are expressed in NT yuan per cubic meter. Figures rounded.
Source: Calculated from Taiwan Forestry Bureau, comp., *Taiwan Forestry Statistics*, annual publication, in series.

rule, the forests of Taiwan paid for the other sectors of the economy. The staples of exportation were still primarily the treasured woods, such as Chinese cypress (*hongkuai*), Chinese cedar (*xiangshan* 香杉 or *luandashan* 巒大杉, *Cunninghamia konishii*), and Japan cypress (*bianbo* 扁柏, *Chamaecyparis obtusa formosana*, or *C. taiwanensis*). The new situation was reflected in the unit prices of the imported and exported timber. The prices for a cubic meter of imported timber ranged from 432 to 2,435 NT yuan, but those for the exported woods ran from 1,006 to 15,728 NT yuan (see Table 19.7)! Chinese cypress was especially important. It comprised 56.33 percent of the total quantity of timber exported, and produced 60.98 percent of the total

Table 19.8. *Exportation of cypress wood from Taiwan, 1961–72*

Year	Quantity of cypress exported (m³)	Percentage of all wood exports	Value of cypress exported (NT yuan)	Percentage of value of all wood exports
1961	23,960	58.44	33,665,000	40.87
1962	69,099	95.48	87,895,000	51.00
1963	65,611	95.73	210,395,000	71.68
1964	83,160	44.57	267,256,000	58.45
1965	86,526	56.64	255,441,000	52.76
1966	115,072	72.28	591,946,000	85.69
1967	38,457	28.73	290,323,000	41.83
1968	41,485	32.30	360,427,000	51.81
1969	59,400	40.14	535,570,000	57.11
1970	89,427	62.37	975,766,000	83.91
1971	60,957	42.06	766,975,000	76.81
1972	31,915	47.26	454,200,000	59.78
Total	365,069		4,829,858,000	
Average		56.33		60.98

Source: Calculated from Inspectorate General of Customs, Statistical Department, comp., *The Trade of China [Taiwan District]*, annual publication, in series.

value generated by wood exports between 1961 and 1972 (see Table 19.8).[75]

Deforestation on a large scale was made possible during this period by the improvement in tools and machines, and even more by the advanced progress of transportation. During the Japanese colonial period, timber was brought out from the forests mainly by railway. The construction of a mountain railroad requires a large sum of money and takes a fairly long time to complete. Moreover, the railroad could only reach those areas that had comparatively gentle gradients. Under these limiting conditions, the lumbering industry was confined to a small scale. But the commencement of business by the Daxueshan Lumbering Company (Daxueshan Linye Gongsi 大雪山林業公司) brought a drastic change to this situation. From

[75] Basic facts for this period are derived from Zhou Zhen, *Lumbering industry in Taiwan* and *Management of Taiwan's forestry*; and Li Gang 李剛, *Beiqi-de Senlin* 悲泣的森林 [The wailing forests] (Taipei: Commercial Press, 1988). Information provided in the annual forestry statistics reports, published by the authorities, is also referred to. For sources, please see Tables 19.1–19.8.

1958–59 on, the company introduced the trail system and employed trucks to bring out trees from the forests. The trucks could enter most places to collect felled trees, and the lumbering grounds were consequently extended deep into the forests. The forest trails were also easily opened; this caused a serious problem of soil preservation on the previously forested ground.

Of course, there was reforestation after 1945. The authorities even claim that the reforestation area is larger than that of deforestation. But this cannot be very close to the truth. First, the rate of survival of the newly planted saplings has never been scientifically surveyed, and it is likely that a major part of the young trees can not have lived very long. Second, it takes several decades for a young sapling to grow into a big tree comparable to one that has been felled. Until that day is reached, there is still a problem of deforestation. It is not surprising, therefore, that the two aerial surveys unreservedly reveal that between 1954 and 1972, the forests of Taiwan did encounter a great loss of acreage. In 1954, the total area of woodland stood at 2,412,100 hectares (which is quite close to the number derived from the 1934 survey, namely, 2,444,236.26 hectares), out of which 1,969,500 hectares belonged to forests. But the 1972 survey found that the forests had been reduced to 1,864,700 hectares. Thus 104,800 hectares had been deforested during the eighteen years between the surveys. The loss of forests consisted of 3 percent of the total acreage of the island, or 5.32 percent of where it stood in 1954.

The deforestation was serious in the third quarter of our century. It caused 3 percent of the island to become barren. But if we take into consideration what kind of trees were felled, the problem appears even more severe. The treasured woods were cut down first! Even though there were reforestation projects, as a rule, a less useful tree, *liushan* 柳杉 (*Cryptomeria japonica*), was replanted.

Sometime around 1972, the scale of lumbering began to diminish. This was partly because the increasing cost of production has acted as a disincentive to the lumbermen; it was also because economic development had seen its fruition and had relieved the forest of the burden of supplying capital for industrialization. Anyway, hyperdeforestation began to subside after 1972. Though the area annually deforested was still above 10,000 hectares for a few years, between 1977 and 1983 only 43,760 hectares were deforested in all (on average, 6,251 hectares each year). The total volume of timber brought out from the mountains was 5,680,980 cubic meters and so still resulted in some deforestation during this period (on average, 811,569 cubic meters per year). A declining trend has appeared, however, and continues.

CONCLUSION

Located in a semitropical region and surrounded by the China Seas and the Pacific Ocean, Taiwan is an island where trees grow easily. Before it was developed, it was well covered with forests, bushes, and grasslands.

From the sixteenth century onward, the island began to receive inmigrants from the Chinese mainland. These newcomers rapidly deforested the plains areas during the eighteenth and nineteenth centuries. But as far as nonreclamation deforestation is concerned, the people under the Qing did not denude any great area of trees. Their demand for forest produce was limited, and their skill in felling trees was primitive. Moreover, their knowledge about Taiwan's forest resources was poor.

During the Japanese colonial period, the rich endowment of Taiwan's forest resources began to be known, and a modern lumbering industry was introduced. But during this period, Taiwan imported more timber and wood products than it exported, both in quantity and in value. Such an import–export structure entailed that local forestry produced only a part of the timber required by the domestic market. Forest resources were hence better preserved than they would otherwise have been.

After Taiwan reverted to the Nationalist government, and especially after local industrialization had started, a hyperdeforestation occurred in the island. Trees were felled at high speed. A policy of exporting timber of better quality in exchange for lower-quality timber was followed, and the value of exports was far larger than that of the imports. Forestry, during the third quarter of this century, paid in part for the financing of industrialization. On account of its linkages with the other sectors of the economy, more timber was demanded, and lumbering was carried out on a considerable scale. Between 1954 and 1972, Taiwan saw a period of hyperdeforestation.

Luckily, this trend has come to a halt since the late 1970s. Industrialization has produced sufficient capital to finance itself, and no longer relies on support from forestry. In consideration of the need to preserve forest resources, lumbering activities are now in principle stopped. All the old lumbering grounds have been made into recreation parks. The nightmare seems to have ended.

20

Hydroelectricity and
Industrialization

THE ECONOMIC, SOCIAL, AND
ENVIRONMENTAL IMPACTS
OF THE SUN MOON LAKE
POWER PLANTS

AN-CHI TUNG

HYDROPOWER AND INDUSTRIALIZATION

Hydraulic power was first utilized in electricity production at the end of the nineteenth century.[1] Since hydroelectricity is cheap to produce, it soon became an important source of energy. Although hydropower generation is subject to hydraulic cycles, the use of reservoirs greatly enhanced production stability. As reservoir hydroelectricity offers cheap and abundant power, the world is building more and larger reservoirs for development purposes. Famous examples include Egypt's Aswan Dam and China's Three Gorges Reservoir (on which construction has just started), both of which facilitate and promote industrialization.

Taiwan's first electricity reservoir was built at Sun Moon Lake 日月潭 (henceforth SML) in 1934. Although hydroelectricity as a whole is relatively insignificant today, the SML electricity played a crucial role in the industrialization of Taiwan. The completion of the reservoir plant tripled the electricity capacity of the island. As more and cheaper electricity became available, the colonial government was able to put up a modern industrial sector to serve Japan's inflating military ambition. The economy entered a different development regime after the war, but the SML plants remained important. In 1950, 93.5 percent of total generated electricity

---

[1] The world's first hydropower plant was built in 1882 in Appleton, Wisconsin. It was a small direct-current plant, not yet equipped for long-distance transmission. The first large-scale hydropower plant was the Niagara Falls plant, established in 1895.

was hydroelectricity, and half of this was produced in the two SML plants. The ample supply of energy made possible postwar recovery and subsequent economic takeoff. In other words, SML electricity has contributed to the economic welfare of Taiwan.

Besides economic effects, a hydropower reservoir often has noneconomic impacts as well. It may serve irrigation, recreation, flood control, and other functions. It may also dislocate a large population,[2] induce earthquakes,[3] alter the climate pattern,[4] and sterilize the soil.[5] These effects are often overlooked for political reasons, or simply because they do not show up in the short run. Yet some effects can be so detrimental as to make a seemingly blissful project totally unjustifiable.[6] The relation between a hydropower project and economic welfare must be examined in a broader context and in a longer time frame.

The SML project does affect the social and ecological environments of Taiwan, though these impacts have not yet attracted much attention. One reason is that the SML reservoir was constructed under Japanese rule, and the colonizers were insensitive to social and environmental results. Adverse impacts have not been studied in recent times either, for hydropower is gradually being replaced by thermal and nuclear power and does not appear to matter much. Despite this, our study finds that there are costs hidden behind the obvious economic benefits of the SML project, such as the extinction of certain species and unequal income distribution. It demonstrates how an economic activity affects our natural and social environments intentionally and unintentionally.

This chapter looks into the economic and noneconomic aspects of the SML hydropower reservoir. After this introduction, section 20.1 deals with the construction of the SML hydropower plant. Section 20.2 analyzes the economic consequences. The following two sections look into the social and environmental impacts. Finally, section 20.5 concludes the chapter.

---

[2] Forced outmigrants may amount to 1.2 million along the Yangzi River near the Three Gorges Dam.

[3] Seismic frequency increases substantially near the reservoirs in the Sudan.

[4] The rainy season near Lake Volta in Ghana shifted from October to July or August after dam construction.

[5] The Aswan Dam impedes much of the waterborne nutrients that feed downstream soils. This and the above examples are drawn from L. Votruba and V. Broza, *Water Management in Reservoirs* (Amsterdam: Elsevier, 1989), pp. 406–26.

[6] For example, a cross-border hydroelectricity project on the Danube was suspended due to environmental concerns. See J. Mortar and A. Poole, "Hydropower and Its Constraints," in T. Johansson, H. Kelly, A. Reddy and R. Williams, eds., *Renewable Energy: Sources for Fuels and Electricity* (London: Earthscan Publications, 1993), p. 92.

20.1. CONSTRUCTION OF THE
SML PROJECT

Before the introduction of electricity, the major sources of energy on the
island were coal, charcoal, and other types of primary energy. When Taiwan
began to produce electricity in the twentieth century, total energy supply
increased tremendously. Most of the electricity generated was hydroelectricity in early days. This section first looks into the life cycle of hydroelectricity in Taiwan, then explores the construction of SML project, which was
the most important project before the war.

20.1.1. ELECTRICITY TECHNOLOGY

Taiwan's first hydroelectric plant was established in Guishan 龜山 on the
Xindianqi 新店溪 River in 1905.[7] Hydroelectricity dominated other types of
electricity thereafter. By 1953, hydropower contributed 94 percent of total
electricity. But the share declined to 6.1 percent by 1991, while thermal
power composed 56.1 percent and nuclear power 37.8 percent (see Fig.
20.1).

   The decline in the importance of hydroelectricity has to do with faster
technological progress in thermal and nuclear electricity technologies in
the postwar period. First, the generating motor of thermal power was no
longer restricted to short operating hours. Second, oil, which was inexpen-
sive and abundant, began to be applied to the production of thermal
electricity. Moreover, nuclear plants started to produce cheap electricity in
larger volume with more stability, despite the high cost of building these
plants. Therefore, the composition of electricity changed over time away
from hydropower.

20.1.2. WATER RESOURCE ENDOWMENT

Resource endowment also explains the rise and decline of hydropower
generation. Most advanced economies began with thermal technologies.[8]

---

[7] Governor Liu Mingchuan 劉銘傳 set up the first electricity generator in 1888 in Taipei. Coal
   was the fuel. See Taipower Company, 台灣電力公司, *Taiwan dianli chuangye bai zhounian* 台
   灣電力創業百週年 [One hundred years of Taiwan's electricity since its start] (Taipei:
   Taipower, 1988), pp. 18–20.
[8] Before long-distance transmission of electricity became economically feasible, thermal electricity was far more favorable than hydropower, since thermal plants could be built near city
   centers while hydropower plants had to be located near rivers or lakes. Despite hydropower

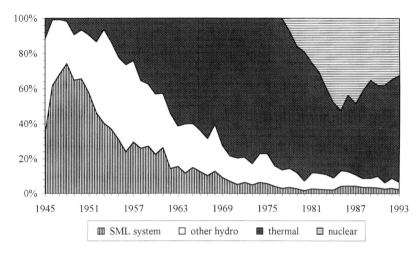

Figure 20.1. Electricity production in Taiwan (1945–93). *Source*: Taipower Company 台灣電力公司, *Taidian tongji nianbao* 台電統計年報 [Taipower statistical yearbook], various years.

Instead, Taiwan relied on hydropower from the very start. This can be attributed to its abundant water resources. Annual precipitation (2,510 mm) in Taiwan is more than twice the world average on land and ocean (1,130 mm).[9] Although most rivers are short, they are steep and contain vast potential energy.[10] These conditions are favorable for the exploitation of hydroelectricity. According to one estimate in the 1960s, the density of water resources in the island is higher than that in Norway,[11] which has up to the present relied almost entirely on water resources for

being cheaper to produce, in the United States, the share of hydroelectricity in total installed capacity was only raised from 13 percent to 22.7 percent between 1900 and 1950. Dai Zhijun 戴之焌, trans., "Yibai nian lai de shuili 一百年來的水力 [Hydroelectricity in the last one hundred years]," *Taidian gongcheng yue kan* 台電工程月刊 [Taipower Engineering Monthly] 54 (1953), pp. 3–6.

[9] Zhang Yutian 張玉田, *Shui ziyuan kaifa yu hechuan shuiwen xue* 水資源開發與河川水文學 [Water resource development and river hydrology] (Taipei: Hsü's Foundation, 1987), p. 7; Mortar and Poole, "Hydroelectricity and its constraints," p. 75.

[10] The steepness of a river is measured by its gradient, i.e., the ratio of river length to elevation of stream head; the lower this ratio, the steeper the river. The gradient of the Rhône, the steepest river in Europe, is 2,200 to 1; but the gradient of the Zengwenqi 曾文溪, a rather gentle river in Taiwan, is 820 to 1, and the gradient of the Dajiaqi 大甲溪 is 39 to 1.

[11] Ke Wende 柯文德 and Lu Chengzong 盧承宗, "Rizhi shidai Taiwan zhi dianye 日治時代台灣之電業 [Taiwan's electricity under Japanese rule]," *Taiwan zhi dianli wenti* 台灣之電力問題 [Issues of Taiwan's electricity], *Taiwan Research Monograph*, 16 (Taipei: Bank of Taiwan, 1952), p. 163.

power generation. Map 20.1 shows the distribution of potential hydroelectricity in Taiwan in 1993.

Yet not all water resources are technically usable, and fewer are economically suitable. To begin with, annual precipitation is unevenly distributed over seasons and across regions. The rain in southern Taiwan concentrates in summer months, while minimum river discharge is close to zero in dry months. In central Taiwan, discharges of the Zhuoshuiqi 濁水溪 vary from 0.1 cubic meter per second in winter to 2,200 cubic meters per second in summer. Production of hydropower is therefore quite unstable, especially in plants without flow regulation. Second, most river basins are rather fragile in geological structure. Weathering and erosion take place very often, which speed up sedimentation in the river. Floods, earthquakes, and deforestation in upstream areas further exacerbate the problem.[12] As a result, hydropower facilities tend to have a shorter service life than would be reasonably expected.[13]

Despite these disadvantages, the potential of the island's hydropower production was rather good, as implied by relatively low development cost, which is the major part of the total cost of hydropower production. In the 1940s, the development cost of a hydropower plant was between 500 and 1,000 yen per kilowatt (henceforth kw) in Japan proper, but was only 400–600 yen in Taiwan.[14]

Other fuels were not effective substitutes for water resources for electricity generation, at least in early times. Taiwan used to export coal. But the quality was low and the cost of thermal power derived from it was high.[15] Therefore, thermal electricity was only produced for peak-hour demand or in dry seasons as a supplement to hydroelectricity. As more and more water resources were put into use, it became harder to find new hydropower resources. While fossil and nuclear fuels can easily be supplemented by

[12] One salient example is the Wulai 烏來 hydropower plants. The civic engineering work was completed in 1947, but a flood in 1948 soaked the generator room and blocked the tailrace. Due to the premature siltation, it took an additional year before the generating motor could be installed. See Zhu Shulin 朱書麟, "Taiwan zhi dianyuan 台灣之電源 [Taiwan's electricity sources]," Issues of Taiwan's electricity, pp. 39–44.

[13] At the Tiansongpi 天送埤 plant, rotors of the water turbine could be worn out after the astonishingly short period of seven to twelve months. See Gu Daxiang 古達祥 and Zhao Naiji 趙迺冀, "Taiwan dianli zhi jishu wenti 台灣電力之技術問題 [Technical problems in Taiwan's electricity]," Issues of Taiwan's electricity, p. 126.

[14] Huang Hui 黃輝, "Taiwan zhi dianye 台灣之電業 [Taiwan's electricity industry]," Issues of Taiwan's electricity, p. 17.

[15] In 1985, the average operating cost of hydropower was 0.477 NT yuan per kwh (kilowatt-hour), 0.7449 NT yuan for nuclear power, and 1.7408 NT yuan for thermal power. Taipower Company 台灣電力公司, Taidian gongcheng yue kan 台電工程月刊 [Taipower engineering monthly] 434 (1984), inner front cover.

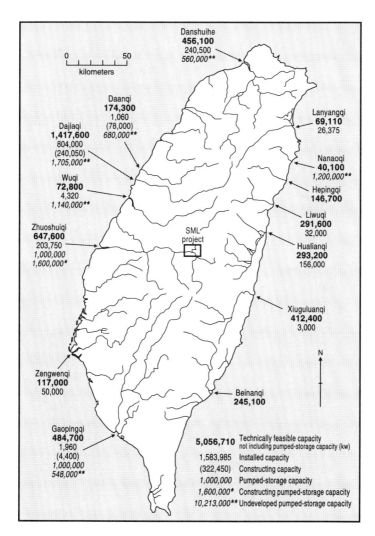

Map 20.1. Potential hydroelectricity in Taiwan (1993). *Source*: Taipower Company, *Taidian tongji nianbao* 台電統計年報 [Taipower statistical yearbook] (1993), pp. 144–45.

imports, water resources in general cannot. Therefore, hydroelectricity was bound to grow more slowly than other types of electricity. The same story occurred in Japan and the world as a whole,[16] though the changes were more dramatic in Taiwan.

---

[16] G. Allen, *A Short Economic History of Modern Japan* (London: Macmillan, 1981), p. 266.; D. Landes, *The Unbound Prometheus* (Cambridge: Cambridge University Press, 1969), p. 287; Mortar and Poole, "Hydropower and Its Constraints," p. 73.

Table 20.1. *Installed electricity capacity in Taiwan*
(1919–89)

Year	Total (1,000 kw)	Hydro (%)	Thermal (%)	Nuclear (%)
1919	11	79.3	21.3	
1924	24	74.5	25.5	
1929	29	68.0	32.0	
1934	150	83.5	16.5	
1939	225	75.8	24.2	
1944	321	83.1	16.9	
1949	259[a]	82.6[a]	17.4	
1954	392	84.3	15.7	
1959	706	70.7	29.3	
1964	1,209	55.6	44.4	
1969	2,375	32.1	67.9	
1974	4,537	31.3	68.7	
1979	8,723	17.0	67.4	15.5
1984	13,884	11.4	56.2	32.4
1989	17,926	15.4	53.6	31.0
1994	20,983	17.4	58.1	24.5

[a] Actual capacity after war damage.
Sources: Ke Wende 柯文德 and Yang Shaoxun 楊紹勳, "Taiwan-zhi dianli (tongji)" 台灣之電力（統計）[Taiwan's electricity (statistics)], *Taiwan zhi dianli wenti* 臺灣之電力問題 [Issues of Taiwan's electricity], *Taiwan Research Monograph* 16 (Taipei: Bank of Taiwan, 1952), pp. 204, 206, 207; Taipower Company 台灣電力公司, *Taidian tongji nian bao* 台電統計年報 [Taipower statistical yearbook] (Taipei: Taipower, 1968), p. 97; Council for Economic Planning and Development, *Taiwan Statistical Data Book* (Taipei: Council for Economic Planning and Development, 1995), p. 93.

Hydropower's share of total installed capacity decreased to below 50 percent in the late 1960s. Until then, hydropower was always the dominant source of electricity, with the exception of a few years immediately before the completion of the SML plant. We now turn to an analysis of the SML project.

20.1.3. THE RIVER AND THE LAKE

The SML project utilizes the water of the Zhuoshuiqi, which is the longest river (178.6 kilometers) in Taiwan. The river flows westward through central Taiwan and empties into the Pacific Ocean. The upstream area is geologically fragile and is quite vulnerable to erosion and landslide. "Zhuoshuiqi" literally means "turbid water river," its silt content being higher than other rivers.[17] In the lower reaches, the plains of Yunlin 雲林 and Jiayi 嘉義 are parts of the main agricultural region of Taiwan. The river is steep (with a gradient of 55 to 1) and contains high hydraulic potential, but the water flow is highly variable in different seasons, and needs to be regulated by dams and reservoirs. The SML reservoir was the first attempt to tap this rich resource.

Sun Moon Lake is a natural lake surrounded by high mountains. It is near the geographical center of Taiwan. Before the power plant was built, the lake was about 5 meters deep, 726.8 meters above sea level, and measured less than 5 square kilometers in size. It was formed about 15,000 years ago. Other lakes of the same age in nearby Toushe 頭社 and Puli 埔里 dried out and turned into fertile basin plains. SML is not yet cut through by any river because it is on a higher level. With little water inflow or outflow, SML has remained a lake until today.[18]

The lake is some distance away from the Zhuoshuiqi. Water has to be diverted from Wujie 武界, which is farther up on the main stream. Wujie is one of the major "knickpoints" on the Zhuoshuiqi, where the flow velocity increases because of the steepening of the riverbed. It is therefore a suitable site for dams.[19] The concrete gravity dam at Wujie was 48.5 meters high (raised to 57.6 meters later) and 90.9 meters long. Average discharge near Wujie is 43 tonnes per second, but maximum intake is only 40 tonnes per second (annual average 25 tonnes), so there are often overflows from the Wujie dam. There are six sluicegates at the crest of the dam and five additional gates in the spillway. These gates help to raise water level and to settle silt. The water inflow then travels 15 kilometers through tunnels and canals to reach the lake-reservoir.[20]

Dams at Toushe, Shuishe 水社, and Dishan 地山 made a reservoir out of the lake. The level of the lake was elevated by about 18 meters (21 meters

---

[17] In Jiji 集集 near Sun Moon Lake, average annual silt content is 14.7 kilograms per cubic meter. This figure is lower than the representative figures for the Yellow River (37.6 kg/m³) and the Colorado River (16.5 kg/m³), but is considerably higher than that of the Nile (1.6 kg/m³) and the Yangzi (0.4 kg/m³). See Mortar and Poole, "Hydropower and Its Constraints," p. 103.

[18] Wang Zhiheng 王志恆, *Sun Moon Lake feng guang* 日月潭風光 [Scenes of Sun Moon Lake] (Taipei: Wang Zhiheng, 1960), pp. 18–19.

[19] Some rivers have irregularities in their long profiles because of changes in the base level to which they have to cut down. Thus a knickpoint is formed.

[20] Although 15 kilometers is a short distance, this was a difficult engineering work and took nine years to complete.

later), with an effective storage volume of 126 million cubic meters (148 million cubic meters later). The scale is rather unimpressive by world standards today (see Table 20.2). Nevertheless, the SML-Wujie complex was the only reservoir in prewar Taiwan, and was one of the major reservoirs in the entire Japanese colonial empire.

The lake water is then led through pressure tunnels to the power plant on the Shuiliqi 水里溪, a tributary of the Zhuoshuiqi, with an effective water head of 320.5 meters. Initially, the installed capacity of the first SML plant (renamed Daguan 大觀 after the war) was 100,000 kw, with a stable generating capacity of 58,600 kw. Through transmission and distribution networks, its output helped to relieve power shortages in both the northern and southern parts of Taiwan.[21]

20.1.4. PROGRESS OF THE PROJECT

Most electricity enterprises in the world are operated or regulated by the public sector, for power generation is a social infrastructure that requires high capital and intensive technology. In Taiwan, public operation was the principle until the construction of the SML plant, which was built and run by a private firm.

In 1919, the colonial government reorganized the public Taiwan Sōtokufu Denki Sagyōsho 台灣總督府電氣作業所 (Taiwan Government-General Electricity Operation Institute) into a private enterprise, Taiwan Denryoku Kabushikikaisha 台灣電力株式會社 (Taiwan Electricity Company, henceforth TEC). The privatization was necessary to finance the SML project, since the Japanese Diet had rejected the Government-General's previous proposal of issuing government bonds. The Government-General owned 40 percent of the shares of TEC, whose total capital stock amounted to 30 million yen; it paid for its shares in fixed assets rather than cash. Private shareholders paid 18 million yen (60 percent of total shares), which became part of the SML project fund. Since the total expense of the SML project was estimated to be 48 million yen, the rest of the fund (30 million yen) was raised by issuing corporate bonds. The construction work began right after the establishment of the TEC in 1919.

It is to be noted that TEC behaved as if it were a public enterprise, despite the majority private ownership. This was not only because the Government-General was the single largest shareholder, but also because it

[21] At the completion of the plant, 60% of its electricity output was sent to the south and 40% to the north. Transmission stations were constructed in Taipei, Wufeng 霧峯, Jiayi, and Kaoshiung 高雄.

Table 20.2. *Comparison of dams*

Dam	River (country)	Year completed	Dam height (m)	Max. reservoir volume ($10^6 \, \mathrm{m}^3$)	Current installed electricity capacity ($10^3 \, \mathrm{kw}$)
Buffalo Bill	Shoshone (USA)	1910	99	519	–
Hoover	Colorado (USA)	1936	221	36,703	1,036
Grande Dixence	Dixence (Switzerland)	1961	285	400	685
Sanmenxia	Yellow River (China)	1962	107	65,005	1,000
Akosombo	Volta (Ghana)	1965	141	148,000	
Guri	Caroni (Venezuela)	1968	106	17,700	10,300
Aswan High	Nile (Egypt)	1970	111	164,000	
Dams in Taiwan					
Wujie	Zhuoshuiqi	1934	57.6	0.055	
SML (Shuishe)	Zhuoshuiqi	1934	30	168	110
SML (Jugong)	Zhuoshuiqi	1937	27	0.0516	43.5
Wanda	Zhuoshuiqi	1943	13	–	15.3
Wushe	Zhuoshuiqi	1959	114	150	20.7
Shimen	Danshuihe	1964	133	316	90
Dajian (Deji)	Dajiaqi	1973	180	232	234
Zengwen	Zengwenqi	1973	133	708	50
Feicui	Danshuihe	1986	120	406	71
Minghu	Zhuoshuiqi	1986	58	9	1,000
Mingtan	Zhuoshuiqi	1992	63	14	1,068

Sources: E. Goldsmith and N. Hildyard, eds., *The Social and Environmental Effects of Large Dams*, vol. 1: *Overview* (Camelford, England: Wadebridge Ecological Centre, 1984), appendix 1; J. Mortar and A. Poole, "Hydropower and Its Constraints," T. Johansson, H. Kelly, A. Reddy and R. Williams, eds., *Renewable Energy: Sources for Fuels and Electricity*, (London: Earthscan, 1993), p. 80; Taipower Company, "Ba yu shuiku yi lanbiao" 壩與水庫一覽表 [A table of dams and reservoirs], *Taidian gongcheng yue kan* 台電工程月刊 [Taipower engineering monthly] 434 (1984) and 435 (1984), inner front cover; Xu Yansun 許硯蓀 and Zhang Shaozeng 張紹曾, "Taiwan hechuan yu shuiku jianshe 台灣河川與水庫建設 [Taiwan's rivers and reservoir construction]," Taiwan yinhang jingji yanjiu shi" 台灣銀行經濟研究室, ed., *Taiwan-de hechuan* 台灣的河川 [Taiwan's rivers], *Taiwan Research Monograph* 84 (Taipei: Bank of Taiwan, 1966), pp. 138, 167; Taipower Company, *Taiwan dianli fazhan shi* 台灣電力發展史 [History of the development of electricity in Taiwan] (Taipei: Taipower, 1989), part 3, p. 8.

held tight control over personnel and management.[22] TEC functioned as an important tool of the colonial government, while the latter was quite supportive when TEC needed its help.

The SML work was projected to finish by 1924. In 1921, a substantial part of the peripheral work was done. However, design errors and inflation problems raised the total budget to 77.8 million yen. Part of the construction work had to be frozen in 1922. To solve the problem, the Government-General arranged a loan from Japan in 1923. The loan was not realized because a serious earthquake occurred in the Kantō 關東 area of Japan in September. The SML project had to be halted in 1926, locking in the 28.2 million yen that was spent already.

Electricity demand continued to grow despite the delay of the SML project. To cope with the supply shortage, TEC built two thermal plants with the help of the Government-General.[23] In the meantime, it sought continuously to revive the SML project. In 1929, TEC decided to resume the project on a smaller scale by means of government investment and foreign borrowing.[24] In the same year, TEC acquired the private Taiwan Denki Kōgyō Kabushikikaisha 台灣電氣興業株式會社 (Taiwan Electric Industrializing Company).[25] TEC's total capital increased by 4.495 million yen; investment by the state was no longer needed. In 1931, TEC issued U.S.-dollar-denominated bonds in New York and raised 41.31 million yen, which exceeded the original target (39.47 million yen). The SML project was able to resume after a halt of five years. Although there was an exchange rate

[22] Taiwan Sōtokufu 台灣總督府, *Taiwan denryoku kabushikikaisha setsuritsusho* 台灣電力株式會社 設立書 [Memorandum of the establishment of Taiwan Electricity Company] (Taipei: Taiwan Government-General, 1919), pp. 1–4.

[23] The Government-General acquired from the TEC the railway between Ershui 二水 and Waichecheng 外車埕, which was originally built for transportation of the building materials of the SML project. With this added income, the TEC was able to construct thermal plants in Songshan 松山 and Kaoshiung, each with 10,000 kw capacity. See Huang, "Taiwan's electricity," p. 4. According to Yanaihara Masao 矢內原忠雄, this is an example of how economic speculation is protected by political forces. See Yanaihara Masao (Zhou Xianwen 周憲文, trans.), *Riben diguozhuyi-xia-de Taiwan* 日本帝國主義下之台灣 [Taiwan under imperialist Japan] (Taipei: Pamir, 1985), p. 15.

[24] In 1928, an American consulting firm, Stone and Webster, suggested rationalizing and scaling down the original scheme. Estimated costs were reduced from 49.6 million yen to 42 million yen.

[25] The main purpose of the TEC was to improve the efficiency of supply of electricity in the island. This was done by setting up the SML plant and by consolidating the many private electricity firms. By 1934, there were only five electricity utilities left including the TEC, but the TEC alone accounted for 96.25% of total installed capacity. In 1944, the TEC became the only electricity enterprise in Taiwan.

crisis in 1931–32,[26] TEC managed to finish the project in 1934 by economizing the budget and through open-market financial maneuvers.

Altogether, it took fifteen years for the completion of the SML project. Total cost amounted to 68.5 million yen, and total labor was 2.53 million man-days. It was a major work at its time, and exerted long and extensive impacts on the Taiwan economy.

20.1.5. A SYSTEM OF RESERVOIRS

There are other reservoirs on the Zhuoshuiqi that operate within the SML reservoir system. Map 20.2 shows the locations of the dams and plants. There are obviously great advantages in the operation of a series of plants on the same stream system.

The second SML plant (named Jugong 鉅工 after the war) was completed in 1939. It is located on the Tongguiqi 銃櫃溪, another tributary of the Zhuoshuiqi. Because it makes use of the first SML plant's tailwater, there is a great saving in construction cost. The installed capacity is 43,500 kw, which is 43.5 percent of that of the first SML plant, but total construction expenses were only 9 percent of the first plant.[27] Its tailwater is then led through the Tongguiqi back to the Shuiliqi.

Farther upstream are two dams at Wanda 萬大 and Wushe 霧社.[28] They are both part of the Ten-Year Two-Million-Kilowatt Electricity Development Plan of the 1940s, though only the Wanda dam was completed before the war ended.[29] The Wanda dam, completed in 1943, is located on the Wandaqi 萬大溪. It is a suitable dam site, because there is a knickpoint in the riverbed, and the effective water head (275 meters) is fairly high. But the stable generating capacity of the Wanda power plant was only 30 percent of its total installed capacity (15,200 kw) due to extreme geological fragility. A major restoration in 1950–51 enabled Wanda to double and stabilize its annual production since 1954.

[26] The net proceeds of the bond issue (U.S.$20.45 million) were deposited in Japan in the form of yen (41.31 million yen) in 1931. At the end of the year, gold export was suddenly prohibited by the Japanese Finance Ministry. Yen exchange rates plunged from 1 yen for 0.495 U.S. dollar to 0.3525 dollar, then to 0.20 dollar. The TEC's interest burden thus more than doubled. Ke and Lu, "Electricity under Japanese rule," pp. 158–60.
[27] Construction costs were 64.297 million yen for Daguan and 5.989 million yen for Jugong.
[28] The location of the Wanda dam is now named Aowanda 奧萬大. The Wushe dam, Wushe plant, and Wanda plant are located at a site now named Wanda.
[29] With the outbreak of the Pacific war in 1941, the Government-General started to plan for new electricity sources. This development plan was to prepare Taiwan as the base for Japan's southward expansion. See Ke and Lu, "Electricity under Japanese rule," pp. 172–77.

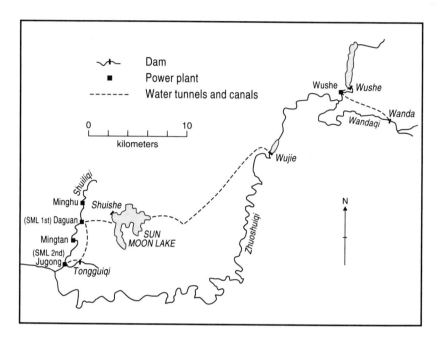

Map 20.2. The Sun Moon Lake system of reservoirs, dams, and hydroelectric power plants, central Taiwan. *Source*: Pan Qifen 潘其芬 and Chen Xiaoyong 陳孝墉, "Lun Wushe shuiku yu Sun Moon Lake shuiku-zhi yingyong" 論霧社水庫與日月潭水庫之 運用 [On utilizing Wushe reservoir and Sun Moon Lake reservoir], *Taidian gongcheng yuekan* 台電工程月刊 [Taipower engineering monthly] 80 (1955), p. 1.

The Wushe dam is 18 kilometers upstream from Wujie on the Wusheqi 霧社溪. The construction began in colonial times, but was finished much later in 1957 with the help of U.S. aid. A high dam (97 meters in height, raised to 114 meters later) was built to create a reservoir. The effective volume of the reservoir is quite large (128.6 million cubic meters), but since electricity is only a side product, the installed capacity of the generating motors, which are located on the same site as the Wanda plant, is small (20,000 kw). Rather, its main function is to control sediment and to regulate water flows into SML. More specifically, the reservoir helps to increase the flow to Wujie during the dry seasons,[30] and thus raised the output of the

[30] The Wushe dam effectively raised the May–October share in total annual runoff from 22% to 41%. It helped to average out water flows across the months. See Xu Hongxi 須洪熙 and Kuang Dielun 鄺疊倫, *Zhuoshuiqi liuyu shui ziyuan youxiao liyong zhi yanjiu* 濁水溪流域水資源 有效利用之研究 [Effective utilization of water resources in Zhuoshuiqi area] (Taipei: Ministry of Economic Affairs, 1978), table 4-2.

Table 20.3. *SML electricity production (1943–90)*

Year	SML (10⁶ kwh)	Share of total production	SML system[a] (10⁶ kwh)	Share of total production	Hydro (10⁶ kwh)	Share of total production	Total (10⁶ kwh)
1943					1,074	89.9%	1,195
1944					1,022	97.1%	1,053
1945	84	23.6%	122	34.0%	315	88.2%	357
1946	267	56.6%	292	61.9%	468	99.2%	472
1947	291	50.5%	394	68.4%	572	99.3%	576
1948	449	53.3%	626	74.3%	829	98.3%	843
1949	385	45.1%	553	64.8%	774	90.6%	854
1950	462	44.4%	682	65.6%	972	93.5%	1,040
1960	455	12.5%	812	22.4%	2,065	56.9%	3,628
1970	530	4.0%	915	6.9%	2,846	21.5%	13,213
1980	345	0.8%	604	1.5%	2,095	5.1%	40,813
1990	515	0.6%	2,730	3.3%	8,167	9.9%	82,350

[a] SML system includes the first and second SML plants (Daguan and Jugong), Wanda 萬大, and Wushe 霧社, and (after 1985) the Minghu 明湖 plant.
Sources: Taipower Company, *Taiwan dianli fazhan shi* 台灣電力發展史 [History of the development of electricity in Taiwan] (Taipei: Taipower, 1989), tables 5.1.2-2 and 5.3.5-1; Taipower Company, *Taidian tongji nian bao* 台電統計年報 [Taipower statistical yearbook] (Taipei: Taipower, 1993), pp. 26–27; Taipower Company, *Taiwan dianli gongsu guangfu shi nian tongji huibao: zi Minguo sanshisi-nian zhi sishisi-nian* 台灣電力公司光復十年統計彙報：自民國三十四年至四十四年 [Postwar statistics of Taipower Company: 1945–55] (Taipei: Taipower, 1956), p. 24.

two SML plants by 11 percent in 1951. Moreover, it helps to reduce the maintenance cost of the Wujie dam by U.S. $10,000 each year.[31]

More recently, two pumped-storage power plants were constructed on the Zhuoshuiqi, both using SML as the upper pond. Water is pumped to the upper pond during off-peak hours so that it can generate electricity in the conventional way during peak hours. The recursive use of water enables large-scale power generation. The installed capacity at Minghu 明湖 (completed in 1986) is 1 million kw, and the capacity of Mingtan (明潭, completed in 1994) will be 1.6 million kw when fully installed. These giant plants raise the hydropower capacity of the Zhuoshuiqi from 0.6 million kw to a total of 3.2 million kw. This number far exceeds the total of realized and under-construction capacity on the Dajiaqi (1.4 million kw), although the latter river is the best endowed with resources by conventional calculations.[32]

[31] Zhu, "Taiwan's electricity sources," pp. 50–51.
[32] Taipower Company, *Taidian tongji nianbao* 台電統計年報 [Taipower statistical yearbook] (Taipei: Taipower, 1993), pp. 144–45.

These reservoirs and dams are functionally integrated and their effects are cumulative. Their output forms a substantial part of total hydroelectricity. In 1948, their combined production was 75.5 percent of total hydropower generated. The figure declined to 19.5 percent in 1983. With the addition of pumped-storage electricity, it rose again to 42.3 percent in 1991, though hydroelectricity as a whole was relatively unimportant in the 1980s and 1990s (see Table 20.3).

Clearly, these plants on the Zhuoshiqi interact with each other. Some of their effects will be discussed in later sections. We now concentrate on the SML project itself.

20.2. THE ECONOMIC EFFECTS OF THE SML PROJECT

The SML project was constructed for development purposes in the colonial period. It helped with postwar reconstruction and economic development, too. This section looks into the economic effects of the project, and, in particular, its industrializing effects.

20.2.1. PREPARATION FOR INDUSTRIALIZATION

Taiwan was an agricultural appendage of Japan in the early colonial days. The production structure of the economy leaned disproportionately toward rice and sugar. Among the industrial sectors, 86.3 percent of total industrial production was in the food-processing sector alone in 1914.[33] Most other manufacturing goods had to be imported from Japan.

Local industry was given a chance to grow after the outbreak of World War I, as Japanese suppliers of industrial goods were busy expanding into other Asian markets. Between 1914 and 1917, the total value of Taiwan's industrial production rose from 53 million yen to 167 million yen. Modern industries, such as textile, metal, nonmetal, and chemicals, emerged and expanded (see Table 20.4).

Expecting the boom in industries to continue, the Government-General began to lay out a plan for the 100,000 kw power plant at SML. The project was ambitious, considering that it would construct the largest plant in the

---

[33] Zhang Zonghan 張宗漢, *Guangfu qian Taiwan zhi gongye hua* 光復前台灣之工業化 [Prewar Taiwan's industrialization] (Taipei: Linking Publishing Co., 1980), p. 27.

Table 20.4. *Economic sectors and their shares of total production (1905–40)*

	Economic activity (%)				Industrial sector (%)									
Year	Agriculture	Industry	Forestry, fishery, mining	Total	Food	Chemical	Nonmetal	Machinery	Wood	Metal	Textile	Printing	Other	Total
1905	74.9	19.6	5.6	100.0										
1915	54.2	38.7	7.0	100.0										
1920[a]	47.8	44.8	7.4	100.0	73.7	6.8	5.1	3.3	3.3	2.6	1.3	1.2	3.3	100.0
1925	55.1	37.1	7.8	100.0	71.7	9.7	3.2	1.9	3.0	1.7	2.0	1.2	5.4	100.0
1930	47.1	44.9	8.0	100.0	76.4	6.7	3.3	2.3	3.1	1.8	1.0	1.4	4.0	100.0
1935[b]	50.9	41.4	7.7	100.0	71.5	9.1	3.0	2.3	4.5	3.0	1.2	1.5	4.0	100.0
1940[b]	41.2	48.0	10.9	100.0	65.1	11.9	2.6	4.2	1.4	5.0	1.8	1.4	6.5	100.0

[a] Calculation of industrial sectors for 1920 is based on 1921 figures.

[b] Monopoly commodity is excluded.

Sources: Zhang Zonghan 張宗漢, *Guangfu-qian Taiwan-zhi gongyehua* 光復前台灣之工業化 [Prewar Taiwan's industrialization] (Taipei: Linking Publishing Co., 1980), table 7, pp. 15–16; Taiwan Administrative Headquarters 台灣省行政長官公署, *Taiwan-sheng wushiyi-nian-lai tongji tiyao: 1895–1945* 台灣省五十一年來統計提要 [Fifty-one years of statistics of Taiwan: 1895–1945] (Taipei: Taiwan Administrative Headquarters, 1946), tables 269–77.

entire Japanese empire,[34] and that the anticipated electricity capacity was nine times the installed capacity in Taiwan in 1919. The colonial government was confident of the engineering technology, and they had plans for the absorption of the new electricity. Ideally, the increase in electricity would be used in new industries (fertilizers, textiles, base metal, paper, for instance).[35] As these industries expanded, their production would not only replace imports, but also provide exports to southeast Asian markets.

In actuality, Taiwan's economic role to Japan did not change much in the 1920s, and the colonial industrial policy was limited to the food-processing sector. Although agriculture's share in total production dropped from 74.9 percent in 1905 to 47.1 percent in 1930, and industry's share rose from 19.65 percent to 44.9 percent, food processing remained the dominant industry, contributing at least 70 percent of total industrial production.

When the SML project came to a stop in 1926, the development prospects of the new industries that were energy-intensive became dimmer.

20.2.2. ABSORPTION OF SML ELECTRICITY AFTER 1934

The political and economic needs of Japan gradually altered in the 1930s with the aggrandizement of her colonial ambitions. Taiwan's new role was to serve as an industrial extension of Japan, while southeast Asia was to provide agricultural products. To industrialize the island, the projected SML electricity became indispensable. In this new situation, the SML work resumed in 1931 and was completed three years later.

After the resumption of the project, the promotion of strategic industries was no longer the sole concern of TEC. To bail itself out from the foreign exchange losses in 1931–32, TEC made careful plans with respect to finance, production, and sales. According to their estimate, 8,000 kw of electricity would be lost in transmission and transportation, 23,000 kw would replace thermal production and purchased electricity,[36] and

---

[34] At that time, the Inawashiroko 猪苗代 plant was the largest hydropower plant in Japan, completed in 1914 with a capacity of 37,500 kw. Taiwan Sōtokufu, *Memorandum of Taiwan Electricity Company*, pp. 27–29.

[35] Taiwan Sōtokufu 台灣總督府, *Denki jyuyō no kenkyō to kongo zōshin no sūsei* 電氣需要の現況と今後增進の趨勢 [Present condition of electricity demand and its trend of increase] (Taipei: Taiwan Government-General, 1918).

[36] TEC used to purchase electricity from other private firms and from certain industries for their surplus. The amount was not much, as TEC's share in total installed capacity was already 88.33% in 1933 and 96.25% in 1934. See Ke Wende 柯文德 and Yang Shaoxun 楊紹勳, "Taiwan zhi dianli (tongji) 台灣之電力（統計） [Taiwan's electricity (statistics)]," *Issues of Taiwan's electricity*, p. 204.

22,000 kw would meet natural increase in demand during 1934–38. Maximal and average net increase in electricity capacity would then be 47,000 kw and 28,000 kw, respectively. TEC designed sales schemes to utilize this additional electricity.

For household use, the electricity tariff was reduced by 20 percent, and new customers were offered special rates. Household power consumption almost doubled in quantity during 1934–41,[37] along with an expansion into suburban and rural areas. Although household use decreased after 1941 due to wartime control, the 1944 figure was still one-third higher than that in 1934.

It was the industrial sector that absorbed most of the new SML electricity (see Fig. 20.2). The ratio of industrial use to household use rose from 51:49 in 1935 to 81:19 in 1941, and to 83:17 in 1944. As the use of electricity intensified in the industrial sector, industrial production increased rapidly. By 1940, the value of industrial production exceeded that of agricultural production. More specifically, heavy and chemical industries grew at a faster pace than the food-processing industry did. TEC successfully promoted the new industries.

20.2.3. GROWTH OF THE NEW INDUSTRIES

Aluminum, steel, and fertilizers absorbed most of the SML electricity. In 1940, TEC's contract capacity with the Nihon Aluminum Kabushikikaisha 日本鋁業株式會社 (Japan Aluminum Company) and the Taiwan Denka Kabushikikaisha 台灣電化株式會社 (Taiwan Electrification Company) totaled 53,000–56,000 kw. This quantity was about a quarter of TEC's total contract capacity (225,000 kw) in 1940, and was higher than the total capacity (38,919 kw) in the first half of 1934.[38] Without the SML project, these new enterprises would not have been possible.

These power-consuming industries were introduced into Taiwan by the deliberate efforts of the colonial government. TEC helped to reduce their costs by offering cheap electricity; TEC also invested in these new ventures to reduce their financial risks. Japan Aluminum Company is a clear example. The company was established in 1935 in Kaohsiung. It adopted the rather advanced technology of electrolysis, which was new to Japan itself, too. As a shareholder (6.8 percent) of Japan Aluminum Company, TEC

[37] Calculated from Ke and Yang, "Statistics," pp. 211–13.
[38] Contract capacity is in general higher than actual capacity utilized. Liu Deyu 柳德玉 and Yan Zhengqian 顏鄭潛, "Taiwan zhi dianye yu jingji" 台灣之電業與經濟 [Taiwan's electricity and economy], *Issues of Taiwan's electricity*, p. 75.

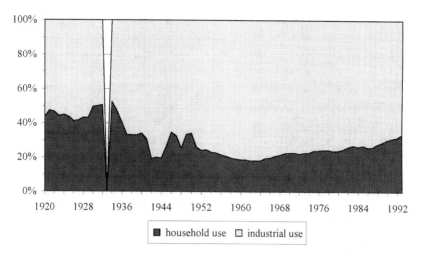

Figure 20.2. Electricity consumption in Taiwan (1920–92). *Source*: Taipower Company, *Taidian tongji nianbao* 台電統計年報 [Taipower statistical yearbook], various years.

agreed to lower the basic rate for the company while charging a variable rate proportional to the company's profits. Between 1938 and 1943, the average rate Japan Aluminum Company paid to TEC was 0.008–0.0135 yen per kwh, compared to a standard meter price of 0.023–0.05 yen per kwh in 1937. As a result of the heavy subsidy, Japan Aluminum Company was able to supply half of Japan's annual demand.

A second example is the Taiwan Electrification Company, also established in 1935. The company produced chemicals and steel that were not produced in the island before. TEC held 10 percent of its shares. The electricity rate it paid was only 0.0079–0.0083 yen per kwh in 1940–44.[39] Low electricity costs must have helped the company to be competitive in the export markets in Japan and Europe.

The fast growth of the new industries soon used up SML's surplus electricity and called for more electricity generation. The second SML plant was completed in 1937, and there were plans for further development in Dajiaqi and eastern Taiwan. The success of SML electricity in promoting Taiwan's prewar industrialization is obvious.

---

[39] Ke and Lu, "Electricity under Japanese rule," p. 194; Zhang, *Prewar Taiwan's Industrialization*, p. 80.

20.2.4. POSTWAR ECONOMIC DEVELOPMENT

The two SML plants and other power plants and facilities were severely damaged during the war. Typhoons and floods did more harm. Immediately before the end of the war, actual generating capacity was reduced to only 33,000 kw in the whole island.[40]

Because of its importance, the electricity industry was given the top priority during the postwar reconstruction, along with fertilizer and textile industries. The SML plants were the first to be repaired. By 1951, total electricity generation (1.285×10^9 kwh) had exceeded the maximal level in prewar times (1.195×10^9 kwh in 1943). The first SML plant alone produced 56.5 percent of total electricity in 1946. In 1948, the two SML plants and the Wanda plant produced 74.3 percent of total electricity; in 1952, they provided 46.3 percent of total electricity.

Sufficient power supply enabled the rapid growth of textile, fertilizers, and other industrial sectors.[41] These industries helped to replace imports and then provided goods for export markets. Through forward and backward linkage effects, the economy grew rapidly at an annual average of 9.75 percent in real terms during 1961–80. In this successful period of development, hydroelectricity not only was indispensable in the early reconstruction but also contributed to the steady growth later on. SML electricity had a crucial role in it.

20.2.5. COSTS AND BENEFITS OF INDUSTRIALIZATION

Postwar industrialization was clearly beneficial to the people of Taiwan in economic terms. Yet prewar industrialization was more to the benefit of the colonizers. This can be seen from two aspects. First of all, the new electricity was primarily utilized by industries that were related to Japan's colonial and military needs. Their outputs were mostly exported to Japan. Growth of nonmilitary industries was limited. Textiles, for example, formed only 1.8 percent of total manufacturing production in value terms in 1940. Growth of household use of electricity was limited, too, especially after the war in the Pacific broke out in 1941. Household electricity use declined to only 20

---

[40] Taipower Company, *Taiwan dianli fazhan shi* 台灣電力發展史 [History of the development of electricity in Taiwan] (Taipei: Taipower, 1989), p. 2–37.

[41] C.-Y. Lin, *Industrialization in Taiwan, 1946–72: Trade and Import-Substitution Policies for Developing Countries* (New York: Praeger, 1973), pp. 78, 98–99.

percent of total power generation, while aluminum refining alone used 38 percent of all electricity in 1943. Evidently, the tilted allocation of electricity consumption was designed to benefit the rulers rather than the ruled.

Second, the sustainability of modern industries was dependent on TEC's heavy subsidy, and was at the expense of the local Taiwanese. TEC charged the household sector an average rate more than ten times the rate paid by favored industries.[42] These new industries were mostly owned by Japanese business groups.[43] It was the Taiwanese users in traditional sectors and the household sector that paid for the subsidy. The economic benefits of industrialization brought about by the SML project have to be discounted for the distributional effects.

20.3. ENVIRONMENTAL EFFECTS OF THE SML PROJECT

The impact of the SML project can be evaluated in a broader sense. The construction work enlarged the shallow lake and submerged a considerable area of land. The inflow of Zhuoshuiqi water also affected the quality of the lake. These conditions brought about further changes in the social and natural environment of the watercourse and the surrounding regions. Influences like these go to work before the commencement of construction, and they last for many decades after the retirement of the project. These impacts of the SML project are examined here.

20.3.1. CHANGES IN THE NATURAL LANDSCAPE

The scenic beauty of SML has long been recognized and was once considered the major attraction of Taiwan. Dam construction made quite a few permanent changes. The first visible change was the physical merging of Sun Lake and Moon Lake. Originally, they were two separate but connected lakes, Sun Lake in the north and Moon Lake in the south. The former had a sun shape and was reddish in color, while the latter had a crescent shape with a greenish tint. In 1934, as the water surface was raised by 18 meters (21 meters later), the two lakes lost their individual

---

[42] In 1937, TEC charged the favored enterprises 0.0079–0.0135 yen per kwh. The regular meter rate for industrial use was 0.023–0.05 yen per kwh, and household use was 0.08–0.18 yen per kwh.

[43] For example, the major owners of the Japan Aluminum Company were Mitsui, Mitsubishi, and TEC; and the Taiwan Electrification Company was set up by the Mitsui group.

shapes and united to form one lake. But the name, Sun Moon Lake, stayed on.

Some lands, including the major part of Pearl Island 珠嶼 (also called Pearl Hill 珠仔山, and Guanghuadao 光華島 after the war), were lost to the water as the lake expanded from 4.55 square kilometers to 7.73 square kilometers in area. Pearl Island had always been the main charm of the lake district, and was likened to a fairyland in many poems.[44] It was located where the two lakes met, 26 meters above lake level and 8 hectares in area. There once were farms, a school, a shrine, and so on. Residents relied on canoes for transportation to the outside world. After 1934, the island was only 5 meters above water level and only one hectare in size. Most of the rice paddy and many poetic scenes were submerged.

To the east of Pearl Island was a huge rock shaped like a name seal, and thus named "Stone Seal," or Shiyin 石印. The aboriginal settlement on and near Pearl Island was named after this landmark. Since the rock was just one meter above water level, it disappeared forever into the water along with other historical and geographical attractions in 1934.

20.3.2. CHANGES IN FAUNA AND FLORA

As Sun Moon Lake turned from a shallow lake (5 meters in depth) into a deep reservoir (26 meters in depth), the living environment was altered for the plants and fish. Many plants in and around the lake were deliberately removed to avoid blocking the inflow and outflow of the reservoir water. For example, most of the water lilies 蓮 and water caltrop 菱 disappeared after 1934. These plants had been abundant in the shallow parts of the lake;[45] one of the "eight tourist charms" of SML was the overlapping leaves of the water lilies – not visible nowadays, of course.

The "floating islands," or feng 葑, also vanished. These were clumps of intertwining grass and soil, some of them large and strong enough to support two people. Probably because there were trees and plants growing on top, they were mistaken as "floating rice paddy" 浮田 in earlier times, and were recorded as a marvel of SML. Quite numerous in Moon Lake, they often drifted into the lake center under the southwest wind. After the com-

[44] See the poems quoted in Lin Hengdao 林衡道, "Sun Moon Lake zhi jin-xi" 日明潭之今昔 [The present and past of Sun Moon Lake], *Taiwan mingsheng guji diaocha* 台灣名勝古蹟調查 [Survey of scenic and historic sites in Taiwan] (Taichung: Historical Research Commission of Taiwan Province, 1978), p. 106; and the poem by Gōtō Shinpei 後藤新平 in Taiwan Sōtokufu 台灣總督府, *Taiwan jijō* 台灣事情 [Annual reports on Formosa] (Taipei: Taiwan Government-General, 1921), p. 33.

[45] Deng Chuan'an 鄧傳安, "You Shuilishe ji" 遊水裏社 [Journey to Shuilishe], *Li ce hui chao* 蠡測彙鈔 [Collections of my observations] (1823. Reprinted, Shanghai: Shangwu, 1937).

pletion of the SML project, all but one floating island were dragged ashore. The only one left was fixed in position so as not to block water flows.[46]

The removal of the floating islands affected the breeding of a small fish called the *qili* 奇力魚 (*Cultriculus kneri*), which laid its eggs alongside them. The aboriginal Thao people 邵族 were known as good fishermen, and fishing was their main source of income besides agriculture before 1934. The Thao used to place special containers along the floating islands to catch the *qili*. After the elimination of the floating islands, the Thao constructed artificial ones by planting soil and grass on bamboo rafts. These artificial islands remain important to fishing in SML, although the fish catch has clearly declined over the years.

20.3.3. WATER QUALITIES AND SILTATION

Eutrophication has been a problem plaguing many lakes and reservoirs, including Deji 德基 reservoir on the Dajiaqi and Feicui 翡翠 reservoir on the Danshuihe 淡水河.[47] Eutrophication refers to the enrichment of waters during the aging of a lake or a reservoir. Human activities along the shoreline accelerate this process, as large quantities of sewage or fertilizer are released into the lake, increasing nitrogen and phosphorus concentrations in the water. The increase of nutrient content leads to the development of certain bacteria and then to the growth of algae. Water quality deteriorates. The deterioration then brings about the degradation of natural beauty, the reduction of fish catch, and other undesirable effects.

According to earlier records, the water in SML was so clear that even the sand on the bottom was visible.[48] The inflow of Zhuoshuiqi water in 1934 surely brought changes to the physical, chemical, and biological characteristics of the lake water. Fortunately, overall water quality is not too bad at present. A 1985 study indicated that the water quality was fine, and eutrophication was not yet a problem.[49] Another investigation by the Environment Bureau further predicts that the quality will even improve with the

[46] Li Yih-Yüan 李亦園, "Thaozu-de jingji shenghuo" 邵族的經濟生活 [Economic life of the Thao, Sun Moon Lake], *Kaogu renlei xuekan* 考古人類學刊 [Reviews of archaeology and anthropology] 9.10 (1958), p. 61.
[47] Lü Guangyang 呂光洋, "Shuiku shuiba dui xiliu shengtai-xi-de yingxiang ji qi duice" 水庫水壩對溪流生態系的影響及其對策 [The impacts of reservoir construction on stream ecosystems and techniques for habitat improvements], *Gongcheng huanjing hui kan* 工程環境會刊 [Journal of engineering the environment] 10 (1988), p. 36.
[48] Deng, *You Shuilishe ji*.
[49] Luo Renjun 羅仁鈞 and Ouyang Jiaohui 歐陽嶠暉, "Sun Moon Lake shuiku shuizhi texing" 日月潭水庫水質特性 [Characteristics of the water quality in Sun Moon Lake reservoir], *Gongcheng* 工程 [Engineering monthly] 58 (1985), pp. 23–36.

use of the two pumped-storage power stations, for the operation of these plants should increase water circulation and prevent the growth of undesirable algae.[50]

Related to water quality is the process of siltation, which reduces the storage volume and shortens the reservoir's service life. The Zhuoshuiqi is notorious for its high sediment transportation. Yet the effective storage volume of the SML reservoir changed little after the inflow of Zhuoshuiqi water. The maximum storage volume declined from 147.18 million cubic meters in 1950 to 145.29 million cubic meters 1964.[51] Calculated from these figures, average annual loss of volume was only 0.09 percent. Although a reservoir stops functioning before it is fully silted up, we can reasonably expect a long service life for SML.[52]

Some factors help to keep the SML system functioning satisfactorily. First, SML is a diversion reservoir, that is, it is not located directly on the main stream. Most of the sedimentation occurs in Wujie before reaching the lake. Wujie itself suffers much from sedimentation and needs frequent maintenance. Second, upstream dams help to reduce the sediment content in SML. After the construction of five upstream dams, it was estimated that the service life of Lake Mead behind Hoover Dam in the United States was extended from 144 years to 233 years.[53] The Wushe dam serves a similar function to the SML reservoir. In fact, the Wushe reservoir is losing its capacity much faster than the SML, at an average annual rate of 0.9 percent between 1958 and 1966.[54]

To sum up, the construction of the SML project did not result in serious quality deterioration of the lake. However, the project is not without costs. Some natural scenery was lost, for example. These negative results were downplayed by the colonial government,[55] but they cannot be ignored in a comprehensive analysis.

[50] Lin Wan'er 林莞爾, "Qian tan mingtan chouxu shuili fadian jihua shigong guihua" 淺談明潭抽蓄水力發電計劃施工規劃 [About the planning of the construction of Mingtan pumped-storage project], *Taidian gongcheng yue kan* 台電工程月刊 [Taipower engineering monthly] 457 (1986), pp. 1–10.

[51] Zhou Jiahui 周嘉會 and Ye Minsong 葉民松, "Wushe Sun Moon Lake liang shuiku zhushui dianneng-zhi yantao" 霧社、日月潭兩水庫貯水電能之研討 [A study of the storage capacity of the Wushe and Sun Moon Lake reservoirs], *Taidian gongcheng yue kan* 台電工程月刊 [Taipower engineering monthly] 238 (1968), pp. 7–13.

[52] Reservoirs in other countries can expect 250 to 300 years of service life. See Votruba and Broza, *Water Management in Reservoirs*, p. 411.

[53] C. Davis, ed., *Handbook of Applied Hydraulics* (New York: 1952), p. 19.

[54] In September 1958, effective reservoir storage volume was 148.6 million cubic meters; in April 1966, it was 138.22 million cubic meters. Zhou and Ye, "Wushe and SML," pp. 7–8. However, this rate is low compared to Feicui reservoir on the Xindianqi, whose service life, estimated to be less than 50 years, will terminate in the year 2030.

[55] See, e.g., the discussions in Taiwan Sōtokufu, *Taiwan jijō* (1921), p. 33, and *Taiwan jijō* (1938), p. 685.

20.4. SOCIAL AND ECONOMIC EFFECTS
OF THE SML PROJECT

The SML project also affects the social and economic environment in the surrounding area. There were public health problems during the construction period, and the completion of the reservoir made fundamental changes in the economic life of the Thao residents.

20.4.1. PUBLIC HEALTH CONCERNS

A construction project often creates conditions that favor the transmission of certain epidemics or diseases. As Wujie and the SML were both surrounded by mountains, public health problems could hardly be avoided. The influx of two to four thousand workers in 1931–34, which almost doubled the population of the SML area, further aggravated the situation. Malaria, *tsutsugamushi* river fever 恙蟲病, and other diseases plagued the workers and residents to various degrees.

Malaria had been an islandwide disease, carried by infected mosquitoes. In the 1930s, malaria incidence expanded geographically along with the progress of the engineering work.[56] The three parties – TEC, the construction companies, and the government – collaborated to extend preventive and treatment services. In the latter half of 1933, the number of malaria patients declined substantially. But the disease was not totally eliminated until after the war.[57]

As for *tsutsugamushi* river fever, it is most serious in river areas, especially after a flood. There was a sudden outburst in 1932 near Wujie, which had an obvious connection with the SML project. TEC's preventive measures against the *tsutsugamushi* mite were effective and the disease did not plague residents for very long.[58]

---

[56] There had been few cases of malaria in Mujilan 木屐蘭 before the SML project. The number of patients increased as the construction entered the area (Ke and Lu, "Electricity under Japanese rule," p. 169).

[57] By the 1950s, 80% of SML residents still suffered from malaria. A complete extinction was announced by the World Health Organization in 1965. See Department of Health, The Executive Yuan, Republic of China, *Public Health in Taiwan Area, Republic of China* (Taipei: Department of Health, 1991), pp. 44–45; Chen Xueming 陳學明, *Alishan Sun Moon Lake han Jianan dajun* 阿里山日月潭和嘉南大圳 [Alishan, Sun Moon Lake and Jianan Conduit] (Taipei: New Century Publishing Co., 1950), p. 29.

[58] Morishita Kaoru 森下薫, "Taiwan no tsutsugamushibyō" 台灣の恙蟲病 [Tsutsugamushi Disease in Taiwan], *Taiwan shipō* 台灣時報 [Taiwan Times] 11 (1933), p. 55.

20.4.2. INVOLUNTARY OUTMIGRATION

The loss of land necessitated population resettlement. One to two hundred hectares of land were lost to the water after 1934.[59] This submerged land included Shiyin, formerly the major settlement of the Thao. TEC bought up inundated residential lands and cultivated fields that were 24 meters above the original water level, although the water rose by about 21 meters at most. TEC moved most of the people who lost their lands to Bujishe (卜吉社, named Dehuashe 德化社 after the war) on the southeast bank, which was at that time a Han 漢 settlement.

The scale of outmigration in 1934 was small, as the Thao population had already been on a declining trend for a century. In 1847, there were 861 Thao people in Shuishe, Toushe, Maolan 貓蘭, and Yuchi 魚池. In Shuilishe alone, there were 434 Thao people. Rice cultivation and fishing were their main economic activities. By 1896, the population had declined to less than 400 due to a number of epidemics that probably killed 500 people. Since aggressive Han inmigrants took over quite a few Thao lands, forced departures and settlement consolidation caused some other deaths.

During the colonial period, more outmigration took place. The Shuishe people were merged into Shiyin, and the Toushe residents moved farther away to Dapinglin 大平林 in the southwest. The first national survey in 1920 indicated that there were 289 Thao residing in Shuishe, Toushe and Maolan. In 1930, another survey recorded only about 150 Thao, and 86 of them resided in Shiyin (Shuishe). A 1955 investigation reported 185 Thao in Bujishe (Shuishe) and 60 in Toushe. As the Toushe settlement was not affected by the SML construction, the number of people forced to leave Shuishe in 1934 should have been between 86 and 185.[60] But according to the memory of Yuchi villagers, 200 households were affected.[61] In all, at least 1,000 people were forced to leave.

---

[59] Total land loss was estimated to be 160 *jia* 甲 (*Taiwan jijō* [1933], p. 597), or as 200-plus *jia*. Wang, *Sun Moon Lake Scenes*, p. 15. One *jia* is equal to 0.97 hectare.

[60] Chen Qilu 陳奇祿, "Sun Moon Lake de Thaozu shehui" 日月潭的邵族社會 [Thao society, Sun Moon Lake], *Kaogu renlei xuekan* 考古人類學刊 [Reviews of archaeology and anthropology] 9.10 (1958), pp. 1–40.

[61] Taiwan-sheng wenxian hui 台灣省文獻會, ed., "Yuchi-xiang qilao koushu lishi zuotan-hui jilu 魚池鄉耆老口述歷史座談會記錄 [Records of the panel discussion of the oral history of the Yuchi villagers]," *Nantou-xian xiangtu shiliao* 南投縣鄉土史料 [Documents of Nantou prefecture's local history] (Taichung: Historical Research Commission of Taiwan Province, 1993), p. 336.

20.4.3. LAND COMPENSATION AND TOURISM

Those who moved to Bujishe were not adequately compensated. Although
they were entitled to cultivate and to live on TEC land by paying rent in
kind, they lost landownership. During the Qing dynasty, the Thao used to
grow crops on their own land or on state-owned "station land" 屯田.[62] They
also had the right to lands that were leased to Han people.[63] There were
some changes after the Japanese came. The "station land" system was
canceled, and leased lands were mostly sold to the Han people. Nevertheless, the Thao still owned a substantial amount of land in their own names
before 1934. With the construction of the SML project, they were turned
into semitenants. These migrants lost not only their homes, but also their
livelihood.

As the prospect of further agricultural development on the rented land
was dismal, Thao people gradually turned to tourism for a living. Before
1931, the Government-General invested in road construction to facilitate
the development of the surrounding area.[64] After the war, new facilities
were added. Lake cruises, traditional song-and-dance shows, and photography in Thao costumes became the new attractions. Although agricultural
activities continued, the younger generation tended to shift to new occupations. A field study in 1955 shows that those families that derived a higher
proportion of their income from tourism were richer than those that
participated less in tourism.[65]

The domestic and economic activities of the Thao are no longer the
same after the SML project. As the Thao form a small ethnic and cultural
minority, these changes have accelerated their melting into the dominant
Han society. Some problems persist. First, most of the tourism income goes
into the pockets of Han residents. Thao people have benefited relatively

[62] The "station land" system began in 1788 after the Qing government put down the revolt led
by Lin Shuangwen 林爽文 in 1787. By arranging militia labor to develop the land, the state
had better control of the local people. Shuilishe and Pulishe together owned more than one
hundred *jia* of land in 1788, while Thao people owned a similar area. See Yao Ying 姚瑩,
Pulishe ji lüe 埔裏社紀略 [Notes on Pulishe] in Wang Xiqi, ed., 王錫祺, *Xiao fang hu zhai yudi
cong chao* 小方壺齊輿地叢鈔 [Xiaofanghu Study collections of geographical writings] (1838.
Reprinted, Taipei: Guangwen Book Co., 1962).

[63] Han people were prohibited by law from cultivating lands in aboriginal areas before 1850.
Yet the development went on despite the law. In 1850, the Qing government accepted the
proposal of the Thao people to legalize the cultivating rights of the Han, but to make the
cultivators pay rents to the Thao. Li, "Economic Life of the Thao," p. 50.

[64] Liu Zhiwan 劉枝萬, "Nantou-xian mingsheng guji" 南投縣名勝古蹟 [Scenic and historic
sites in Nantou], *Nantou wenxian congji* 南投文獻叢輯 [Nantou Documents Series], vol. 2
(Nantou: Historical Research Commission of Nantou prefecture, 1954), p. 51.

[65] Li, "Economic Life of the Thao," p. 53.

less. Second, the introduction of a monetary economy has resulted in income inequality and has thus created social problems. Third, the disappearance of the traditional Thao culture has been a loss to both Thao and Han people.

To conclude, the number of people affected during and after the construction of the SML project was rather small. In comparison, the Three Gorges Dam will affect several thousand times as many residents as in the SML case, while the electricity generation will be only about 200 times as much. The social disturbance of SML was relatively minor. But exactly because the Thao people are few in number, their living rights were easy to overlook.

20.5. NONECONOMIC EFFECTS OF ECONOMIC ACTIVITIES

To sum up our findings, hydroelectricity was once crucial in initiating Taiwan's industrialization. Due to technical and natural constraints, however, hydropower became less and less relevant over time, and is rather insignificant today. Although the importance of SML electricity is declining, its role in Taiwan's economic development remains indispensable.

Seen in a broader context, the SML project involves several interesting results. First, although it brought about industrialization, the benefits were distributed unequally in favor of the colonizers. Second, the construction of the reservoir had certain environmental costs, though they were not very serious ones. Third, the public health problem was quickly controlled during the construction period, yet the Thao people experienced longer-term changes. They lost not only their homes but also their livelihoods, and the compensation was limited.

SML does not seem to have created any calamity yet, either because it is small in scale or because it is in essence a worthy project. But the various disadvantages mentioned in the text remind us of its multidimensionality. One lesson can be drawn here. Since we eventually bear all the economic and noneconomic consequences of our activities, we probably make better decisions when we learn to take these effects into account in advance.

Environmental Problems and Perceptions in Early Industrial Japan

TESSA MORRIS-SUZUKI

During the 1980s the growing global environmental crisis evoked world-wide concern and encouraged concerted efforts to find international solutions to a problem that knows no frontiers. Environmental issues came to be part of the repertoire of contemporary political and social debate throughout the world. In China, from 1978 onward, senior scientists began to publish warnings of impending environmental crisis, and during the early 1980s leading newspapers published numerous letters from readers complaining of pollution problems. One result was a growing official awareness of the environmental aspects of economic development.[1] But although such concerns have become international, the language and imagery in which they are articulated is not necessarily universal. Understandings of environmental problems are shaped not just by the nature of the present crisis, but also by preexisting treasuries of ideas about the relationship between humans and nature.

As Leo Marx has shown, for example, environmental ideas in the United States are strongly influenced by images of a pastoral ideal inscribed in classics like Washington Irving's "Legend of Sleepy Hollow" and Henry David Thoreau's *Walden*.[2] Similarly, the imagery of European environmentalism is difficult to understand without some reference to a vision of wilderness whose origins go back at least to the Romantic movement of the

I am indebted to Professor Miyamoto Kenichi of Ritsumeikan University and to Mr. T. Tamai and Mr. K. Hosoda of the Kanagawa Prefecture Kawasaki Library for their kind assistance in obtaining the material on which this chapter is based.

[1] See Vaclav Smil, *The Bad Earth: Environmental Degradation in China* (New York: M. E. Sharpe, 1984), pp. 169–72.

[2] Leo Marx, *The Machine in the Garden: Technology and the Pastoral Ideal in America* (Oxford: Oxford University Press, 1964).

late eighteenth century. The rhetoric of U.S. and European environmental-ism, therefore, does not always strike a responsive chord in other parts of the world. Though problems may be shared, the language in which they are described and the perspective from which they are analyzed may vary widely. The heritage of ideas does not, of course, constitute a rigid cultural mold, predetermining the nature of environmental debate in particular countries; but it does provide the raw material with which environmental-ists consciously or unconsciously work as they struggle to address the prob-lems of their own day.

This chapter focuses on perceptions of environmental disruption in Japan. The story of Japan's early environmental protests has particular relevance to the modern Chinese experience for two reasons. On the one hand, Japan, as an early and rapid industrializer, has long since been forced to confront problems of industrial pollution very like those that have emerged very recently as topics of controversy in China. To take just one example, the cadmium pollution recently documented by Hong Zhiyong and others around a major copper smelter in Daye county is reminiscent of the severe problems experienced around Mitsui Mining's copper and zinc mine at Kamioka since about 1910.[3] On the other hand, the repertoire of ideas that Japanese farmers, factory workers, and intellectuals brought to bear on environmental problems, particularly in the early stages of industri-alization, was powerfully influenced by Chinese thought. As in most areas of the Japanese intellectual tradition, fundamental concepts such as notions of the relationship between heaven (*ten* 天) and earth (*chi* 地), spirit (*ki* 気) and regulating principle (*ri* 理), were imported from China, but were then adapted and reworked to suit changing local circumstances. Compari-sons between China and Japan, therefore, shed particularly interesting light upon the various ways in which this shared heritage of concepts has been adapted and combined with Western modes of thought in addressing common problems of industrialization and its environmental conse-quences. This chapter will not attempt explicit comparisons of this sort, but will, I hope, provide some implicit suggestions of similarity and contrast with the pictures painted elsewhere in this volume.

When I first visited Japan in 1973, at the height of the "first wave" of contemporary environmentalism, I was conscious of a slight sense of per-plexity, whose origins I would, at that time, have found hard to put into words. Grass-roots environmental movements were very active both in Ja-

---

[3] Z. Hong et al., *Cadmium Exposure in Daye County, China*, University of Queensland Depart-ment of Economics Discussion Paper no. 58 (1991); N. Huddle et al., *Island of Dreams: Environmental Crisis in Japan* (New York, 1975), pp. 186–88.

pan and in Britain (where I had come from), and the issues they addressed – photochemical smog, water pollution, urban blight, and so on – were broadly similar. And yet in some way perceptions of these issues seemed unexpectedly different. The most obvious sign of difference was perhaps that Japanese environmental debates were generally constructed around the concept of *kōgai* 公害 (generally translated as "public harm" or "destruction of the public domain"), a term that focused attention on the social context and the human costs of pollution. The implications of *kōgai* are, I think, well conveyed by a recent study of pollution in Japan that begins by stating that

> The problems of industrialisation-induced environmental pollution are fundamentally life-threatening and as such can and must be avoided. The severe problems brought on by environmental destruction can never be completely rectified because the culpable industrial organisations, the victims of environmental pollution, and the negatively affected society as a whole can never be fully freed from the deleterious affects of such intrusions. . . . [P]ollution problems manifest themselves as ruined health in specific populations or as the overall destruction of specific ecosystems. Just as the driver of an automobile benefits from the motion provided by the combustion of fuel, so also does he become, at the same time, a victim of the exhaust gases thereby generated. The use of chemical fertilisers and insecticides by farmers more often than not also kills fresh-water fish, which are a primary protein source for those same farmers.[4]

In Britain, by contrast, the construction of pollution problems seems better represented by the opening passages of Richard Mabey's *Pollution Handbook*, published in 1974. Mabey begins with graphic details of the disappearance of peregrine falcons from the Scottish highlands, and goes on to say:

> We are living at a time when our towns and countryside are being destroyed on a scale that would be more usual in time of war. Historical buildings are being demolished (often illegally), hedges and woods torn up by the roots, industrial chemicals flushed into the rivers that supply our drinking water, toxic fumes poured out of power stations and the exhausts of the juggernaut lorries choke our high streets. Very few people escape pollution in some form. You will probably know yourself of a favourite pond that has been ruined by refuse dumping, or seen washing blackened by smoke from a nearby factory.[5]

[4] T. Hayashi, "Foreword," in J. Ui, ed., *Industrial Pollution in Japan* (Tokyo: United Nations University Press, 1992), p. vii.
[5] R. Mabey, *The Pollution Handbook* (London: Penguin Education, 1974), p. 7.

The anger here, I would suggest, is provoked less by a life-threatening "destruction of the public domain" than by the betrayal of an aesthetic of wilderness or of pastoral beauty. These contrasts, of course, stemmed partly from differences in the scale and nature of environmental damage in Britain and Japan, but they also seem to reflect more subtle differences in the location of environmental ideas within a wider framework of social and political discourse in the two countries.

ANTIPOLLUTION MOVEMENTS IN EARLY INDUSTRIAL JAPAN

In this chapter I hope to explore the development of Japanese discourse on the environment by focusing particularly on the social and ideological context of antipollution movements in the early industrial period (from the late nineteenth century to World War II). This is a period of special interest because it marks a crucial phase of transition. Looking at the rhetoric of environmental ideas in these decades enables us to see the ways in which various forms of preindustrial "tradition" were adapted to the circumstances of the industrial age, and also helps to provide a more historically based understanding of the nature of environmental debate in postwar Japan. Of course, the philosophies of recent environmental movements do not simply draw on their prewar counterparts, but are also influenced by ideas from other parts of the world and from other aspects of political and social debate within Japan. The story of prewar antipollution movements can, however, shed some interesting light on enduring and significant features of modern Japanese social thought.

These prewar environmental movements are also of interest because they are relatively unknown, both in Japan and elsewhere. Between the 1890s and the late 1930s protests against industrial pollution in Japan were numerous and widespread: accurate statistics are of course hard to come by, but by 1931 the government was so concerned about the problem that it began to include a regular section on industrial pollution in the yearly reports of its factory inspectors. According to the figures given in these reports, the annual number of disputes over factory pollution rose from 69 in 1931 to 84 in 1933 and to 105 in 1935. Although highly industrialized areas like Hyōgo predictably recorded the highest number of disputes, relatively rural prefectures such as Gifu also figure prominently in the reports (see Table 21.1 for 1935). The most common cause of complaint (accounting for more than half of all cases in 1935) was emission of waste water from factories, though smoke and dust from factory chimneys also

Table 21.1. *Pollution-related disputes by prefecture in Japan, 1935*

Hokkaido	–
Tokyo	7
Kyoto	2
Osaka	12
Kanagawa	8
Hyōgo	12
Nagasaki	–
Niigata	–
Saitama	5
Gunma	3
Chiba	–
Ibaraki	3
Tochigi	1
Nara	–
Mie	2
Aichi	2
Shizuoka	3
Yamanashi	–
Shiga	3
Gifu	9
Nagano	–
Miyagi	–
Fukushima	4
Iwate	–
Aomori	–
Yamagata	1
Akita	–
Fukui	1
Ishikawa	1
Toyama	3
Tottori	–
Shimane	–
Okayama	1
Hiroshima	3
Yamaguchi	6
Wakayama	1
Tokushima	–
Kagawa	–
Ehime	–
Kōchi	–
Fukuoka	4
Ōita	3
Saga	1
Kumamoto	4

Table 21.1. *(Cont.)*

Miyazaki	–
Kagoshima	–
Okinawa	–
Total	105

Source: Shakaikyoku Rōdōbu, *Annual report of the Factory Inspectorate*, 1935, pp. 497–99.

provoked a substantial number of disputes; the most persistent offenders were the chemicals and dyestuffs industries, which between them were involved in some 77 percent of incidents recorded for 1935.[6]

Rather oddly, considering the interest in more recent Japanese environmental problems, the prewar protests have attracted relatively little attention. With one exception – the case of the Ashio copper mine dispute[7] – most English-language works on Japan's modern history ignore them. Even in Japan, many of these early cases of environmental action are largely forgotten (Ashio again being the exception). Recent works by scholars like Miyamoto Kenichi and Ui Jun are helping to unearth the historical roots of modern environmental consciousness,[8] but in general, I think, there is still an assumption that prewar Japanese society (whether because of innate social harmony or a repressive political system) was exceptionally unresistant to the official ideology of industrialization.

SOCIAL CONTEXT AND ANTIPOLLUTION PROTEST IN PREWAR JAPAN: THE CASE OF THE ASHIO DISPUTE

A closer look at the prewar environmental disputes casts a very different light on the matter. It suggests that quite important sections of the Japanese population were unhappy at the social costs imposed by rapid industrial

---

[6] Shakai Kyoku Rōdō Bu 社會局労働部, *Kōjō kantoku nempō* 工場監督年俸 [Annual report of the Factory Inspectorate], (1935), pp. 493 and 499.

[7] On the Ashio dispute, see K. Shoji and M. Sugai, "The Ashio Copper Mine Pollution Case: The Origins of Environmental Destruction," in Ui, ed., *Industrial Pollution*, pp. 18–63; K. Strong, *Ox Against the Storm: The Biography of Tanaka Shozo, Japan's Conservationist Pioneer*, (Tenterden: Norbury, 1977).

[8] See for example Ui, ed., *Industrial Pollution*; K. Miyamoto 宮本憲一, *Kankyō to kaihatsu* 環境と開発 [Environment and development] (Tokyo: Iwanami Shoten, 1992), pp. 124–62.

growth, and that even in the remote villages of rural Japan, there were those who were able to weave these generalized discontents into a fairly coherent critique of the political and economic structure. To understand the nature of these criticisms, we need to begin by looking at the social context of the prewar protests and identifying the social background of the chief participants. I shall try to do that here by outlining a few major cases of antipollution protest from the first half of the twentieth century.

The Ashio copper mine dispute is so well known that it is perhaps not necessary to describe it in detail. It is, however, worth some discussion because it was a particularly influential incident that provoked widespread public debate about environmental issues. The copper deposits at Ashio in northeastern Japan were first worked in the early seventeenth century, but the mine was abandoned in the 1790s, in part at least because of protests from local farmers. In the 1870s the Ashio mine was acquired by the entrepreneur Furukawa Ichibei, who proceeded to develop it on a large scale. Furukawa's expansion plans caused havoc in the surrounding countryside. Mountainsides were denuded of trees to provide fuel for the copper smelters, resulting in serious flooding and soil erosion. Fumes from the smelters damaged local crops, and, most seriously of all, toxic tailings from the mine were dumped into the neighboring Watarase River, and were then spread over downstream rice fields when the river flooded.

The extent of the disaster began to become evident in the late 1880s, when crops in areas along the Watarase River failed. Farmers from the district petitioned their prefectural government and the Ministry of Agriculture and Commerce, and in the 1890s staged large-scale demonstrations in their own prefecture and in Tokyo. An important element in the dispute was the leadership provided by the local Parliamentary representative, Tanaka Shōzō, son of a prosperous peasant and village head from a community on the banks of the Watarase River. Tanaka's irascible, eccentric, and indomitable personality was to earn him an almost mythical status in Japanese history.[9] Not only did he pursue the cause of the farmers in the Diet, he also succeeded in winning the support of an improbable array of prominent Japanese citizens including the Women's Christian Temperance Movement, Christian reformers such as Uchimura Kanzō, a number of conservative politicians including Katsu Kaishu (the founder of the Japanese Navy), several student groups, and the young anarcho-socialist Arahata Kanson (who, in old age, was to play a leading role in the antipollution movements of the 1960s).[10] In addition, the protests also received

[9] See Strong, *Ox Against the Storm.*
[10] Ibid., pp. 89 and 138; Huddle et al., *Island of Dreams*, p. 32.

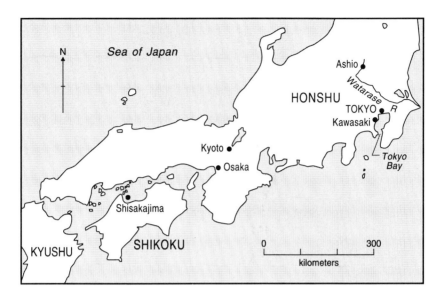

Map 21.1. Sites of antipollution disputes in early industrial Japan.

assistance from some sections of the press and from a handful of academic scientists, who helped to establish the link between pollution from the Ashio mine and the failure of crops along the Watarase River.[11]

In response to the protests, the government eventually forced Furukawa to carry out pollution control measures, including the building of sedimentation tanks for waste water. These, however, proved inadequate to the task. In 1904, after further protests and violent clashes with police, a new plan was put forward by the prefectural government to construct a large reservoir to trap polluted floodwaters from the river, in the process submerging the small and severely polluted village of Yanaka. Tanaka Shōzō bitterly opposed this plan, not only because it sacrificed the interests of the farmers of Yanaka village, but also because he believed it to be a technically inappropriate solution to the problem. From 1904 until his death in 1913, supported by a dwindling band of villagers, he waged a battle with the authorities first to save Yanaka from destruction and later to win compensation for the displaced villagers. In the event, the Yanaka "reservoir" turned into a toxic swamp, and pollution continued to plague the area even after the closure of the Ashio mine in 1973.[12]

The coalition of protesters brought together under Tanaka's leadership

[11] Strong, *Ox Against the Storm*, pp. 71–74.
[12] Huddle et al., *Island of Dreams*, p. 33.

helped to draw nationwide attention to the problem, and produced some results, including the payment of some compensation to affected farmers and to the villagers removed from Yanaka. In a sense, however, the very scale of the pollution problem, and of the sympathy that it elicited, made it difficult to hold the protest movement together. The company became adept at using compensation and outright bribery as means of pitting one community or group of farmers against another, and in the end there were few who possessed the stamina to pursue the defense of Yanaka village to the bitter end.

A COMMUNITY UNITED:
THE SHISAKAJIMA SMELTER CASE

Although it was by far the most famous, the Ashio dispute was by no means the only instance of protest against mining activities in early industrial Japan. As the Ashio protests reached their height, a somewhat smaller but still significant and well-documented dispute was beginning at the opposite end of the country in the Iyo district of Shikoku. Here the target of complaint was the Sumitomo company, which had been mining copper in the mountains of Shikoku since the late seventeenth century. Even before the Meiji Restoration, Sumitomo's Besshi mines had caused such severe water pollution to the surrounding area that the local Domain, which reaped substantial benefits from the mine, had been obliged to reduce the amount of rice tax payable by Besshi farmers.[13] The problem was greatly magnified, however, after 1883, when Sumitomo constructed a large copper smelter using imported technology near the coastal town of Niihama. By the early 1890s, crop yields from the farms around Niihama were showing drastic decline, which local residents attributed to emissions of smoke and gas from the smelter chimney. At first Sumitomo denied responsibility for the problem, but after widespread protests by farmers, and studies by their own technicians and by government scientists, it became obvious that sulfur dioxide fumes from the smelter were causing serious damage to the environment.[14]

---

[13] Yonemaru Chūtarō 米丸忠太郎, *Shisakajima seirenjo engai mondai no keika to engaichi ni shosuru nōkō ni tsuite* 四坂島製錬所煙害問題の経過と煙害地に処する農耕に就いて [Concerning the development of smoke pollution problems at the Shisakajima smelter and agriculture in the polluted area] (Shisakajima Engai Jogai Kisei Dōmeikai, 1930), p. 102.

[14] Yonemaru, *Concerning the development of smoke pollution*, pp. 2–5; Sumitomo Kinzoku Kōzan Kabushiki Kaisha 住友金屬鉱山株式會社, *Sumitomo Besshi Kōzanshi* 住友別子鉱山史 [A history of the Sumitomo Besshi Mine], vol. 2 (Tokyo: Sumitomo Kinzoku Kōzan Kabushiki Kaisha, 1991), pp. 13–14.

As a response to the problem Sumitomo was persuaded to move its smelting operations offshore to Shisakajima, a little group of islands in the Seto Inland Sea. Land was reclaimed to link the islands together, and work began on port facilities and a new smelter incorporating the latest imported technology.[15] The Shisakajima smelter started operations in 1905, at the height of the Russo-Japanese War, and it almost at once became obvious that the pollution problem had been aggravated, not solved.

The Eastern Iyo region to the immediate south and east of Shisakajima is a rich farming area that, at the beginning of the century, produced large crops of rice and some wheat. The coastal plain stretches flat for a dozen or so kilometers inland, until it reaches the sharp escarpment of the rugged Shikoku mountains. When Sumitomo moved its smelter to Shisakajima, the company had failed to calculate that the prevailing winds would carry the fumes from the chimneys directly onto the coastal plain, where, trapped by the mountains, the noxious gases would wreak enormous damage. Within a few months of the opening of the smelter, the leaves of plants on the coastal plain were beginning to turn an unhealthy gray.[16] A British journalist who visited the area during World War I described how the road along which he traveled had once been lined with cherry trees, planted "so that the traveller might enjoy the beauty of their blossoms in spring and their foliage and outlines the rest of the year. The trees had attained noble proportions when the refinery started work and very soon killed most of them. They looked as though they had been struck by lightning."[17]

At first the story followed a pattern not unlike that of the Ashio incident. Farmers in the affected area organized themselves and lodged protests with Sumitomo and the prefectural authorities. The company initially disclaimed all responsibility for the damage and the prefecture seemed inclined to ignore the problem, but in 1908 a mass meeting of some two thousand farmers persuaded the prefectural governor to send in scientists from the local research laboratory to investigate the damage. The governor in turn petitioned the Ministry of Agriculture and Commerce, which dispatched its own scientists and inspectors to the region.[18] By now, the issue had also begun to be taken up by local representatives in the Diet, and by

---

[15] Sumitomo Kinzoku Kōzan Kabushiki Kaisha, *History of Sumitomo Besshi Mine*, vol. 2, pp. 15–18.

[16] Isshiki Kōhei 一色耕平, ed., *Ehime Ken Tōyo engai shi* 愛媛県東予煙害史 [A history of smoke pollution in Tōyo, Ehime prefecture] (Tōyo Shi, 1926), pp. 14–15; Tōyo Shishi Hensan Iinkai 東予市誌編さん委員会, ed., *Tōyo shishi* 東予市誌 [A history of Tōyo City] (Tōyo Shi: Gyōsei, 1988), pp. 614–15.

[17] J. W. Robertson Scott, *The Foundations of Japan* (London: John Murray, 1992), pp. 226–27.

[18] Tōyo Shishi Hensan Iinkai, ed., *History of Tōyo City*, p. 617.

August of that year, Sumitomo headquarters in Osaka recognized the need to send a technician to investigate the situation. He arrived to be greeted by a large group of protesting farmers, whose numbers quickly grew to around five thousand, and the police had to be called in to rescue him and the local Sumitomo branch managers from possible injury. The farmers then organized themselves in almost military fashion and marched to the Niihama branch office of Sumitomo, where they demanded direct negotiations with the company.[19]

The negotiations proved to be a long-drawn-out affair, but the results, from the point of view of the farmers, were surprisingly satisfactory. In 1910, Sumitomo was persuaded to sign a "contract" with the local residents, which not only provided substantial compensation for damage to crops, but also imposed limits on the level of production at the smelter and stated that production was to cease altogether for forty days at the height of the rice-growing season. The contract ran for three years, during which time Sumitomo was to make efforts to find a technical solution to the pollution problem at the smelter.[20] In the event, this 1910 contract proved to be only the first of many. Further agreements were signed in 1913, 1916, 1919, 1923, 1925, 1928, 1930, 1933, 1937, and 1939, providing between them a total of over 2 million yen in compensation to the farmers. In addition to these funds, which were administered by the local village authorities and used to improve fertilization and irrigation, Sumitomo also paid another 2 million-odd yen to a special Agricultural and Forestry Promotion Fund, part of which was used to support the prefecture's agricultural development policies. A particularly intriguing element in the compensation was the further 1.78 million yen paid into funds for "protecting scenic beauty" and for "thought improvement" (shisō zendō 思想善導). The latter was used to establish a local middle school, expand and improve other schools in the area, and support the activities of youth groups, women's groups, Buddhist associations, and so forth.[21] Perhaps the most important outcome of the compensation payments, however, was that they put financial pressure on Sumitomo to introduce pollution control technologies. With the help of the German-designed Petersen system, the company succeeded in reducing sulfur dioxide emissions from 10,000 parts per million (ppm) in 1916 to 1,900 ppm in 1934.[22]

[19] Ibid., pp. 619–20; Isshiki, ed., History of smoke pollution in Tōyo, pp. 25–28; Sumitomo Kinzoku Kōzan Kabushiki Kaisha, History of Sumitomo Besshi Mine, pp. 22–27.
[20] Tōyo Shishi Hensan Iinkai, History of Tōyo City, pp. 622–25.
[21] See Kaida Atsushi 戒田淳, Niihama to Sumitomo 新居浜と住友 [Niihama and Sumitomo] (Niihama: Ehime Chihōshi Kenkyūkai, 1972), p. 107.
[22] Miyamoto, Environment and development, pp. 131–32.

An important explanation for the farmers' success appears to lie in the social background to their protest. The Eastern Iyo district was an overwhelmingly agricultural area, with little industry other than some small-scale textile production and the Sumitomo smelter itself. The main social divisions were between landlords and tenant farmers. Pollution from the Shisakajima smelter did in fact serve to exacerbate the tensions between landlord and tenant that started to appear throughout the region around the beginning of the Taishō period. Tenants in affected areas demanded that their rents be reduced; landlords resisted.[23] In the end, however, neither landlord nor tenant had anything very much to gain from the presence of the Shisakajima smelter, and both had a great deal to lose from pollution. So, while tenant and small-scale farmers protested at the village level, landlords lent support at the level of the Prefectural Assembly and even of the national government.

The leadership for the protest movement seems to have come mainly from the middle stratum of relatively prosperous small farmers: the sort of people who typically served as village or town heads (*sonchō* 村長 and *chōchō* 町長).[24] The most prominent activist, indeed, was a man whose background was very similar to that of Tanaka Shōzō, although his career was not quite as dramatic or as illustrious as Tanaka's. Isshiki Kōhei, the headman of Nyūgawa town, was (like Tanaka) a largely self-educated "improving farmer." His schooling consisted only of a few years at the local temple school, but he had read widely and even taught himself some English, and his ability to grasp new knowledge is evident from the confidence with which he handled the scientific and technical details of the antipollution case. Isshiki was not only prominent in the conflict with Sumitomo. He also served several terms as town head and was elected to the Prefectural Assembly, where he supported the cause of tenant farmers in their disputes with landlords. His particular interests were education and improvements in farm technology, and we can be confident that the schemes to use compensation funds for building schools owed much to Isshiki's inspiration.[25]

Although the Shisakajima dispute failed to win widespread national attention, the Iyo farmers (like their counterparts at Ashio) did receive some support and encouragement from individuals who might loosely be termed "outside intellectuals." In the Shisakajima dispute, the most important of these outsiders were government scientists commissioned by the

[23] See Yonemaru, *Concerning the development of smoke pollution*, pp. 127–29.

[24] Tōyo Shishi Hensan Iinkai, *History of Tōyo City*, p. 636.

[25] On Isshiki Kōhei, see Ehime Kenshi Hensan Iinkai 愛媛県史編さん委員會, ed., *Ehime Kenshi: Jinbutsu* 愛媛県史—人物 [A history of Ehime prefective: biographies) (Matsuyama: Seki Kabushiki Kaisha, 1990), pp. 68–69; Tōyo Shishi Hensan Iinkai, *History of Tōyo City*, p. 619.

Prefectural Research Laboratory and the Ministry of Agriculture and Commerce to study the effects of pollution in the district. A number of these experts not only provided evidence to support the farmers' case, but also seem to have developed a quite strong identification with their cause. For example, Yonemaru Chūtarō, a scientist sent to the region by the Ministry of Agriculture and Commerce, wrote a highly sympathetic report that was published by the farmers' antipollution organization in 1930.[26] Such sympathy for antipollution movements among the lower to middle ranks of the bureaucracy was not unusual. Another well-known instance is the story of Yanagita Kunio – later to become Japan's most famous ethnographer – who wrote several critical accounts of industrial and mining pollution when he was employed by the Ministry of Agriculture and Commerce in the early twentieth century.

A COMMUNITY DIVIDED: AJINOMOTO AND THE CITIZENS OF KAWASAKI

It is important to notice, though, that support for antipollution movements varied considerably from one part of the country to another. In rural areas like Eastern Iyo it was relatively easy to unite the local population behind such movements, but in small towns and villages close to the major cities, landlords and large farmers were likely to have a financial stake in commerce or manufacturing, and were therefore less eager to support their less prosperous neighbors' complaints about pollution. A good illustration of this social split can be seen by looking at environmental protests in the Kawasaki area, between the mushrooming metropolises of Tokyo and Yokohama. In 1913, for example, the Suzuki trading company, which manufactured monosodium glutamate (MSG) under the trade name Ajinomoto, decided to move its factory from Abiko on the outskirts of Tokyo to the Kawasaki district. The production process used by Ajinomoto involved the creation of large amounts of chemically polluted waste starch, and the emission of hydrochloric acid gas: indeed, the decision to move from Abiko was prompted by complaints about pollution from a number of aristocratic families who had summer villas in the area.[27] Initially, a village just across the Tama River from Kawasaki was chosen for the new factory, but news of the planned construction evoked loud protests from local

---

[26] Yonemaru, *Concerning the development of smoke pollution.*
[27] Urayama Jotarō, *Suzuki Saburōsuke* (Tokyo: Suzuki Saburōsuke Denki Hensankai, 1932), p. 94.

farmers, who were concerned at the possible effects of pollution on their orchards. On the other side of the river in the town of Kawasaki itself, however, the leading figures on the local council were only too eager to welcome the Ajinomoto factory. In return, Suzuki assured the residents that it would be introducing a new MSG process using sulfuric acid, which would reduce the level of gas emissions.[28] The Kawasaki factory was opened in 1914, but because of practical problems with the sulfuric acid technology, Suzuki was forced to revert to the older technique, and air pollution soon became a major problem.

In 1916, Suzuki Shōten began to receive complaints of damage to orchards from surrounding farmers, and the following year the company conducted an investigation of the extent of the pollution problem.[29] On the basis of this study, compensation payments of varying amounts were made from 1921 onward. In 1924, for example, local farmers received 16,000 yen from the company. By the mid-1920s, however, technical improvements were reducing the emissions of gas, and by the end of the decade air pollution from the factory was no longer a serious concern.[30]

This, however, is not the end of the story. The Ajinomoto factory was still dumping large amounts of chemically treated starch into the Tama River, where it was carried downstream toward Tokyo Bay. In 1928, after heavy rain, the river flooded and polluted water poured onto the neighboring orchards, damaging the trees. The company argued that the weather rather than their effluent was to blame, but eventually a settlement involving the payment of a small sum of "consolation money" was reached through the mediation of the local police chief.[31] It is perhaps worth noting at this point that police chiefs played a pivotal role in many pollution disputes, not only as mediators, but also in some cases by organizing forums on pollution problems for company managers.[32]

The main victims of the water pollution, however, were the residents of Taiji, a small farming and fishing community on the shore of Tokyo Bay, whose major products included shellfish and seaweed. In 1918 members of the fishing cooperatives of Taiji and neighboring villages lodged a com-

---

[28] Kanagawa Kenritsu Toshokan 神奈川県立図書館, *Keihin Kōgyō chitai kōgaishi shiryōshū* 京浜工業地帯公害史資料集 [Collected documents on the history of pollution in the Keihin industrial area] (Kawasaki: Kanagawa Kenritsu Kawasaki Toshokan, 1972), pp. 56–57.

[29] Ibid., p. 57; Nempyō Henshū Iinkai 年表編集委員會, ed., *Kōgai oyobi rōdō saigai nempyō* 公害および労働災害年表 [Chronology of pollution and industrial accidents] (Tokyo: Kōgai Taisaku Gijutsu Doyūkai, 1970), p. 10.

[30] Kanagawa Kenritsu Kawasaki Toshokan, *Collected documents*, p. 57.

[31] Suzuki Rokurō 鈴木六郎, ed., *Ajinomoto enkakushi* 味の素沿革史 [A History of Ajinomoto] (Tokyo: Ajinomoto Kabushiki Kaisha, 1941), pp. 75–76.

[32] See, e.g., *Annual report of the factory inspectorate*, 1935, p. 447.

plaint with Suzuki Shōten, claiming that their seaweed beds were being destroyed by water pollution. In 1924, some three hundred fishermen marched on the company to demand compensation. The management responded by obtaining weather data from the prefectural meteorological station, which (the company claimed) proved that unusual climatic conditions rather than pollution was the cause of the problem.[33] But the consciences of management were perhaps not entirely easy, for in 1923, while still denying responsibility, they had made *ex gratia* payments of 40,000 yen to the fishermen's cooperatives "to prevent misunderstanding."[34] The fishermen were not so easily persuaded. In 1932, two hundred of them staged a waterborne protest on the Tama River, and eventually the company was forced to seek arbitration from outside experts, in the form of scientists from the government's Fisheries Education Center. Tests of river water near the Ajinomoto factory found some evidence of pollution with sulfuric acid and other substances, but the government scientists were unable to prove a connection between these and damage to the seaweed beds. Nevertheless, the company was persuaded to pay a further 30,000 yen in compensation. By this time the shellfish at the mouth of the Tama River were also dying, and claims began to be lodged with the company by fishermen of the Taiji Shellfish Farming company, the main cooperative involved. Even as late as July 1942, with the Pacific War at a crucial turning point, the fishermen of Taiji were still doggedly lodging complaints about pollution with Ajinomoto, only to be told that they had failed to produce sufficient evidence.[35]

Although the farmers and fishermen of the Kawasaki area gained some modest compensation from the Ajinomoto factory, and although their protests undoubtedly encouraged the introduction of less polluting technologies, the settlement of their claims was far less comprehensive than the concession that the Shikoku farmers won from Sumitomo. To understand why this was so we need to look more closely at the social context of the Kawasaki dispute.

The town of Kawasaki had been an important staging post on the Tōkaidō (the main road between Edo and Kyoto) before the coming of the railway. As a result it had a relatively diversified economy.[36] Many of the

[33] Suzuki, *History of Ajinomoto*, p. 126.

[34] Ibid., p. 126.

[35] Kanagawa Kenritsu Kawasaki Toshokan, *Collected documents*, pp. 58–59; Suzuki, *History of Ajinomoto*, pp. 171–75.

[36] Hitotsubashi Daigaku Kōgai Mondai Kenkyūkai 一橋大學公害問題研究會, *Kawasaki no kōgyō hatten to kōgai hantai undō* 川崎の工業発展と公害反対運動 [Industrial development and the antipollution movement in Kawasaki] (Tokyo: Histotsubashi Daigaku Kōgai Mondai Kenkyūkai, n.d.), p. 39.

leading landowners in the district had nonagricultural interests as restaurant owners, merchants, and the like, and it was these people who dominated the local affairs of the town. From the beginning of the Taishō period (1912–26) a group of local notables including Ishii Taisuke, the son of a landowner and timber merchant who served several terms as town head, and Tanaka Kamenosuke, a prosperous restaurant owner, developed an energetic policy of attracting industry to their area.[37] In doing this they were undoubtedly furthering their own commercial interests, but also, as they were at pains to point out, they were rescuing the region from the decline into which it had seemed likely to fall after the coming of the railway.[38] The Ajinomoto factory was just one of many attracted to the area between 1900 and 1920. Others included Asano Cement, Tokyo Electric, Nippon Kōkan, Fuji Gas, and Meiji Sugar Refineries, some of which in turn became the center of pollution disputes that, for reasons of space, I shall not discuss here.[39] The coalition of interests between small farmers and powerful landlords that formed in Eastern Iyo was therefore missing in Kawasaki. Instead, the farmers and fishermen, who constituted a steadily shrinking proportion of the population, found themselves confronting, not only the might of large corporations, but also the power of the leading citizens in their own region.

Fishing and farming cooperatives still provided a ready-made framework for organizing antipollution activities, and in some less industrialized towns like Taiji the town council might support the complaints of the local fishermen, but in larger towns like Kawasaki and in the arena of prefectural politics, antipollution movements found themselves at odds with a local policy that saw the advance of "industrial culture" as the one route to prosperity.[40]

THE IDEOLOGY OF
PREWAR ENVIRONMENTAL PROTEST

Environmental protests in prewar Japan, then, were not simply a matter of city versus countryside, but reflected a rather more complex division of

[37] For information on Ishii Taisuke and Tanaka Kamenosuke, see Kanagawa Ken 神奈川県, *Kanagawa Kenshi, Betsuhen 1: Jinbutsu* 神奈川県史別編1－人物 [A history of Kanagawa prefective, Appendix I: Biographies] (Yokohama: Kanagawa Ken, 1983), pp. 56 and 472.

[38] See, e.g., Kanagawa Kenritsu Kawasaki Toshokan, *Collected documents*, p. 59.

[39] For a full list of factories in the area by 1916, see Kanagawa Ken 神奈川県, "Kawasaki hōmen no kōgyō" 神奈川方面の工業 [Industry in the Kawasaki area], reprinted in *Keizai to bōeki* 経済と貿易 [Economy and trade] 88 (January 1966), p. 43.

[40] See Ishii Taisuke, Introduction to Yamada Sōtarō 山田蔵太郎, *Kawasaki Shikō* 川崎誌考 [Reflections on the Kawasaki Annals] (Kawasaki: Ishii Bunko, 1926), p. 5.

interests. Farmers and fishermen, whether large or small, seem to have been likely to join the protests where their exposure to pollution put their livelihoods at risk. The most active participants in the protests, however, were often medium-sized farmers, though where there were substantial opportunities for commercial investment, large landlords might opt to support industrial development rather than to protect farming.

On the other hand, environmental protests in prewar Japan also received important support from sections of the urban middle classes: social reformers, journalists, scientists, and middle-ranking officials appear from time to time among the dramatis personae of these conflicts. (Even the unfortunate protesters of the Kawasaki area received vocal support from one anonymous journalist on the local *Yokohama Trade News*.) Needless to say, this varied group of antipollution activists did not speak with one voice. For many of the farmers and fishermen involved, the issue at stake was a simple matter of survival, and one that they may never have attempted to place into any wider moral or political framework. And yet, in the writings left behind not just by prominent figures like Tanaka Shōzō and Uchimura Kanzō but also by the forgotten activists of Shisakajima, Kawasaki, and elsewhere, certain common themes seem to recur.

To understand these repeated refrains it is important, I think, to say something about the intellectual heritage on which the prewar protesters could draw. In recent years, a number of writers have argued that "traditional" Japanese thought was founded on a concept of harmony between human beings and nature: humanity, we are told, was seen "as an integral part of nature"; preindustrial Japan had no concept of "human beings as subject and nature as object."[41] These arguments are often developed through references to Zen Buddhism, with its negation of barriers between the human self and its surrounding environment, and to Shintō, with its powerful sense of nature as imbued with divine spirit. I have suggested elsewhere, however, that these were not the only traditions that influenced the early modern Japanese visions of nature.[42] Another powerful influence was the Confucian notion of the benign ruler whose responsibility was to relieve the sufferings of his subjects. This implied, among other things, the harnessing of nature to serve human needs.

Confucian concepts of nature were developed in various ways during the two centuries before the beginning of Japanese industrialization. The

---

[41] See E. Olson, "Man and Nature: East and West," *Asian Profile* (December 1975), p. 643; Tomiyama Kazuko 富山和子, *Mizu to midori to tsuchi* 水と緑と土 [Water, plants, and earth] (Tokyo: Iwanami Shinsho, 1971), p. 102.

[42] See T. Morris-Suzuki, "Concepts of Nature and Technology in Pre-Industrial Japan," *East Asian History* 1 (June 1991).

seventeenth-century scholar Kumazawa Banzan (1619–91) elaborated a philosophy in which human morality and the preservation of nature were integrally connected. On the one hand, immoral conduct by the ruler was the cause of natural disaster; on the other, human prosperity and abundance was best assured by the careful management and conservation of water and forest resources (*chisan chisui* 治山治水 – literally the management of mountains and waters).[43] During the eighteenth century, however, as craft industry developed and as some Japanese scholars acquired a degree of familiarity with Western scientific writings, the Confucian vision of the benign ruler began to be reworked by certain philosophers into much more overtly interventionist ideas of the human role in nature. One key concept in this lineage of ideas was the notion of *kaibutsu* 開物 – the "opening up of things" – which was used by the agrarian philosopher Satō Nobuhiro (1769–1850) to justify a utopian vision of an authoritarian and developmentalist state. Another (whose origins, like the origins of the term *kaibutsu*, lie in the Chinese classics) was the vision of humans as *yūsei no saireibutsu* 有生の最靈物 or *banbutsu no reichō* 萬物の靈長, literally meaning the "supreme spirit of all creatures." Although the overtones of domination are not quite as harsh here as they are in the European notion of humans as "lords of creation," the phrase nevertheless conveys a strong sense of humanity as the most active, potent, creative force in a numinous natural order. (It is relevant to note that the expression *banbutsu no reichō* gave rise in modern Japanese to the word *reichōrui* 靈長類, which is used to translate the term "primate" in its zoological sense.) Tamura Ransui, one of the leading eighteenth-century scholars of natural history, for example, saw human beings as "the image of the universe, the possessors of the five virtues and the supreme spirits amongst living things (*yūsei no saireibutsu*), who therefore use nature to sustain themselves. Humans in turn sustain nature, and it is through humans that nature becomes potent."[44]

Though some Japanese writers (like Satō Nobuhiro) linked their vision of nature to authoritarian political philosophy, others tried to devise a philosophy that would offer a more careful balance between the demands

[43] See I. J. McMullen, "Kumazawa Banzan and Jitsugaku: Towards Pragmatic Action," in W. T. de Bary and I. Bloom, eds., *Principle and Practicality: Essays in Neo-Confucian and Practical Learning* (New York: Columbia University Press, 1979); also *Nihon shisō taikei* 日本思想大系 [An outline of Japanese thought], vol. 30 (Tokyo: Iwanami Shoten, 1971).

[44] Bitō Masahide 尾藤正英, "Edo jidai chūki ni okeru honzōgaku: Kindai kagaku no seisei to kanren suru men yori" 江戸時代中期における本草學－近代科學の生成と關連する面より [Medical biology in the mid-Edo period: in relation to the establishment of modern science], *Tokyo Daigaku kyōikubu jinbun kagaku kiyō* 東京大學教育部人文科學紀要 [Tokyo University Education Faculty Bulletin of Human Sciences], part 11, History and Culture 2, Historical Research Report 5 (1956), p. 63.

of nature and humanity, of ruler and ruled. A key figure in this context was the agrarian sage Ninomiya Sontoku (1787–1856), who supported his vision of rural harmony with an eclectic mixture of ideas borrowed from Daoism, Buddhism, Confucianism, and other sources. On the one hand, Ninomiya argued that all creatures are "gods and Buddhas"; on the other, that "Human beings are at the head (*chō* 長) of all creation, so that man is called the spirit of all living things (*banbutsu no rei* 萬物の靈). The proof is that he rules over the beasts, birds, insects and plants and may kill or keep them alive without being condemned therefor."[45]

His solution to this paradox was to draw a distinction between the "Way of Heaven" and the "Way of Humanity." In terms of the Way of Heaven, all beings were part of the single great circle of creation, in which there was no distinction between high and low, good and bad, crops and weeds. With the coming of humanity, however, the Human Way came to be added to the Way of Heaven. This Human Way inescapably involved judgments about good and bad, and just as inescapably demanded that humans should intervene in nature to make it "good" and fertile in their own terms. The Human Way, however, was not wholly separate from or antagonistic to the laws of the natural world, but related to them as a water wheel relates to the river which turns it, revolving "by partly yielding to, and partly resisting the force of the current. If it is entirely put into the water, it will not revolve but will be carried away by the current. . . . On the other hand, if it is kept apart from the water it will never revolve."[46]

Ninomiya's ideas had a profound impact on some of the leading antipollution activists in prewar Japan, including Tanaka Shōzō and his ally in the Ashio dispute, Uchimura Kanzō. This influence is most clearly reflected in the way in which both perceived the connection between moral, social, and environmental issues. Like Ninomiya Sontoku, both Tanaka and Uchimura believed that a balanced relationship between human beings and nature was inextricably linked to a proper balance in social relationships, and to correct ethical conduct by the individual. The use of nature by human beings was not in itself seen as being something wrong: on the contrary, it was a positive virtue. Tanaka's most impassioned argument against the flooding of Yanaka village was that it would prevent the land from serving its intended purpose as a source of food:

---

[45] See *An outline of Japanese thought*, vol. 52, p. 197; the English translation is adapted from T. Ishiguro, ed., *Ninomiya Sontoku: His Life and "Evening Talks"* (Tokyo; Kenkyūsha, 1955), pp. 95–96.

[46] Ishiguro, ed., *Ninomiya Sontoku*, p. 103.

If, in their disgust at the people of Yanaka, the bureaucrats do not want them to cultivate its land, all right – let somebody else till its fields: Japanese, American, Chinese, anyone. That the soil should be tilled is the law of heaven. It doesn't matter if the Yanaka folk don't eat what's grown there. Let the birds eat the crops – the deer, the wild boar. Heaven's laws would still be observed. Let thieves come, even, and steal the rice! That men and animals should eat the fruits of the earth is Heaven's law. God would have none of them starve.[47]

Development, in the sense of opening up the land, is an essential part of morality. It is when development becomes distorted by ignorance and greed that things go wrong. The correct course of development, according to Tanaka, involved working with rather than against the flow of nature: working with a genuine empathy, rather than a calculating eye on profit:

No men love mountains and rivers now. When trees are planted on the hillsides, it is not done from love, but from greed, for what the timber will fetch. Who plants a tree in his garden and thinks of nothing but the fuel it will give him? The gardener loves his trees. Planting in the mountains and in the garden may look the same, but the spirit is different. Forestry is based on greed, not love; even when trees are planted as they should be, where rivers rise, it is not done with love, it is not the Way of forestry.[48]

In a similar vein Uchimura Kanzō, explicitly paraphrasing Ninomiya Sontoku, wrote, "he that is in league with Nature hastes not; neither does he plan work for the present alone. He places himself in Nature's current, as it were, and helps and enhances it, and is himself helped and forwarded thereby."[49] It is particularly interesting to see the ways in which both Uchimura and Tanaka sought to reconcile these essentially Sino-Japanese ideas of a benign Way of Heaven with the principles of Christianity, to which Tanaka too became a somewhat eccentric convert in his later years. In Uchimura's case, this process of reconciliation involved reworking the more "environmentally sound" sections of the Bible in a peculiarly Confucian way. Thus in criticizing contemporary industrial morality he complained:

Instead of saying: the earth is the Lord's and the fullness thereof, Modernism says: the earth is man's and [the] fullness thereof. It exhausts one source of resources after another, and never gives thanks to the Creator; and in its

---

[47] Quoted in Strong, *Ox Against the Storm*, p. 183.
[48] Quoted in ibid., p. 224.
[49] K. Uchimura, "Ninomiya Sontoku: A Peasant Saint," in Ishiguro, ed., *Ninomiya Sontoky*, p. 44.

eagerness to enjoy present life, it pays no attention to the welfare of the future generations.[50]

For both Tanaka and Uchimura it was the "modern" belief in the unfettered pursuit of individual profit that destroyed the balance, both *between* humans and nature and *within* the human community itself. Despite their similarities, however, there are distinct differences between Tanaka's and Uchimura's reworkings of tradition. Tanaka was always more insistent in his emphasis on nature as something precious in its own right. His philosophy of loving care for the mountains and rivers drew on the earlier ideas of Kumazawa Banzan, who had indeed been responsible for designing one of the major dikes protecting the Watarase River.[51] As he grew disillusioned with humanity in his old age, so Tanaka tended to put increasing stress on the need for humans to purify their fallible spirits by immersing themselves in nature. In one of his later writings, he specifically rejected the vision of humanity as "the supreme spirit of nature" (*banbutsu no reichō*), arguing that

> Humans should not be the lords of creation; they should rather be the slaves of creation (*banbutsu no dorei* 萬物の奴隷), its servants and its messengers. . . . They should dwell in the midst of nature and become its reflection, living at peace rather than in conflict with other creatures, correcting their own faults and nurturing their own energy, never cutting themselves off in solitude. . . . Thus they may grow close to the Spirit.[52]

Uchimura, on the other hand, was inclined to place greater emphasis on the ideal of humanity working with nature to create a socially benign form of development. His alternative to the dominant ideology of industrialization was not so much one in which the individual became immersed in nature, but rather one where development was based on the indigenous potential of the rural community. As he put it in his laudatory paraphrase of Ninomiya Sontoku's ideas,

> *the wilderness must be opened by its own resources, and poverty must be made to rescue itself.* . . . In this way alone was this our fruitful Nippon opened to cultivation in the days of the gods. All was wilderness then; and without any help, by their own efforts, with the land's own resources, they made fields, gardens, roads, and cities as we see them today.[53]

---

[50] Uchimura Kanzō 内村鑑三, *Uchimura Kanzō chosakushū* 内村鑑三著作集 [The collected works of Uchimura Kanzō] vol. 7 (Tokyo: Iwanami Shoten, 1953), pp. 121–22.

[51] See Strong, *Ox Against the Storm*, p. 150.

[52] Quoted in Amamiya Gijin 雨宮義人, *Tanaka Shōzō no hito to shōgai* 田中正造の人と生涯 [The personality and life of Tanaka Shōzō] (Tokyo: Meikeidō, 1954), p. 329.

[53] Uchimura, "Ninomiya Sontoku," p. 16.

It is Uchimura's approach that seems to be closer to the mainstream thinking behind the grass-roots antipollution movements of his day. No other prewar antipollution struggle generated such a wealth of philosophical speculation as the Ashio incident, but a few less famous movements did leave a record of their aims and motives, and from these we can obtain some sense of an implicit philosophy of the human–nature relationship. The opponents of the Sumitomo smelter in Shikoku, under the energetic leadership of Isshiki Kōhei, used part of their compensation money to publish a detailed record of their struggles, and also sponsored other publications related to their cause. From these it seems that their leaders at least espoused ideals not dissimilar to Uchimura Kanzō's. Isshiki Kōhei himself was clearly no revolutionary, nor did his views necessarily coincide with those of present-day environmentalism. He had a firm belief in economic development and the use of modern technology, and argued that ultimately mining, "which creates wealth by unearthing hidden riches," and farming, "which provides food for the people," must progress together.[54] The main task was to ensure that technology was used not simply to enrich the factory owners, but also to solve the problems of pollution that industry created.[55] In the documents submitted to the Diet by Isshiki and his fellow protest leaders, a central theme was that the balance between the various parts of society was being destroyed, and that the result was a collision between the interests of mining and industry on the one hand and agriculture on the other.

Despite the farmers' insistence that some compensation be used for preserving the appearance of natural scenic areas, these documents contain few direct references to the conservation of nature as such, but many to the sufferings of ordinary rural people, and many to the need for a form of development that would be of greater immediate benefit to them. It is interesting that one of the chief complaints against Sumitomo was that pollution from the smelter had disheartened farmers and so set back local programs to encourage the greater use of fertilizers and pest control in farming:

> In recent times farming has experienced the most remarkable development. The main reason for this is the gradual spread of the application of science (*gakuri ōyō* 學理應用) brought about by various forms of agricultural promotion funds. But since the air pollution problems have begun to work immeasurable damage on crops, many people have started to regard the application of science as a wasted effort, and to lose their faith in the possibility of

[54] Isshiki, ed., *History of smoke pollution in Toyo*, p. 478.
[55] See, e.g., ibid., pp. 274–76.

progress. Moreover, they have come to view the local authority's scientists and their extension work with hostility, and will hardly pay any attention to educational meetings and other forms of agricultural improvement activity.[56]

Pollution was also evil because it created social discord, both between industry and agriculture and between landlord and tenant.[57] Above all, it undermined that independent "self-awareness" (*jikaku* 自覺) which made the farmer the backbone of the nation.[58] The solution, then, lay not in abandoning industrial development, but in pursuing a path of "balanced development," where technology and careful location would be used to prevent industry from harming agriculture, while education, research , and government assistance would be used to increase farm productivity.

In the case of the Ajinomoto dispute in Kawasaki, the protesters left no organized record of their motives and emotions, but the language used in their appeals to the company and to local government seems to suggest an ideological framework not unlike that of their counterparts in Shikoku. The Kawasaki protesters were particularly eager to point out the social and economic value of their own particular occupations: to demonstrate, in short, that the fishing village, as much as the giant industrial factory, had a valuable part to play in the prosperity of the national community.

> Our town of Taiji [stated an appeal from the Fishermen's Association to the prefectural governor] has produced seaweed since ancient times. Our seaweed is famous throughout the nation. The variety known as "Imperial Asakusa seaweed" comes largely from our area. Its quality knows no equal, and production runs to some 1 million yen per year. Therefore, the prosperity or failure of production is not just a matter of the profits of producers, but also has a very great effect on the various merchants who provide links to consumers and on the whole economy of the town.[59]

This sense of the village, with its special skills and resources, as a place to be valued and sustained contrasted with an official ideology in which the destruction of the village was seen as an inevitable (if regrettable) social cost of progress. In the words of a report by the strongly developmentalist Kawasaki prefectural authorities:

> It is a fact common to all countries that, with the advance of culture, the part of the population employed in agriculture should decline and the part em-

[56] Yonemaru, *Concerning the development of smoke pollution*, pp. 125–26.
[57] Ibid., pp. 127–28.
[58] Isshiki, ed., *History of smoke pollution in Toyo*, p. 479.
[59] *Yokohama Bōeki Shimbun* 横浜貿易新聞 [Yokohama Trade Newspaper] (Feb. 4, 1923); reproduced in Kanagawa Kenritsu Kawasaki Toshokan, *Collected documents*, p. 63.

ployed in commerce and industry should increase, and in our country it must also be so. . . . Gloomy scholars of agriculture and zealous theorists of regional improvement may bemoan the fact, but everywhere throughout the world this is the steppingstone to industrial progress.[60]

CONCLUSIONS

While the conventional picture of preindustrial Japanese culture emphasizes the theme of harmony between humans and nature, the conventional picture of modern Japanese culture tends paradoxically to emphasize the theme of unresisting acquiescence in the destruction of nature. It has been argued that Japan's "cosmos of meaning" created a society in which modern industrial technology was simply "affirmed, approved, and accepted from the viewpoint of secular usefulness."[61] The stories we have looked at here, however, serve as reminders of the fact that concern about the environmental costs of industrialization have a long history in Japan. These stories suggest, indeed, that the "cosmos of meaning" was a rather complex entity, capable of reinterpretation in ways that challenged, as well as ways that supported, the dominant policies of industrialization. While notions of the "opening up" of nature fed the stream of ideas that flowed into the official ideology of *fukoku kyōhei* 富國強兵 (enriching the nation and strengthening the army), concepts of a balance between "the Way of Heaven" and "the Way of Humanity" provided material for the construction of alternative visions of development. Even among the ranks of the antipollution activists themselves, the existing heritage of ideas was reworked in a variety of different ways in order to give meaning to the social and environmental disruptions caused by rapid economic change.

Within this diversity, though, some broad common elements are evident. For one thing there is a recurring vocabulary: terms like "the Way of Heaven" and "the supreme spirit of living things" are constantly re-echoed and given new meanings in changing social and political contexts. For another, the sense of the interweaving of human society and morality with the very structure of nature itself gives a particular flavor to environmental debates in prewar Japan. Nature was identified not so much (as in the European tradition) with wilderness and freedom from social constraint, but rather with the very basis and origin of social order. These elements can

---

[60] Kanagawa Ken, "Industry in the Kawasaki area," p. 54.
[61] J. Kyogoku, "'Modernisation' and Japan," in N. Hagihara et al., eds., *Experiencing the Twentieth Century* (Tokyo: University of Tokyo Press, 1985), p. 268.

help us to understand the rhetoric and the action, the strengths and the weaknesses of environmental action in early industrial Japan.

As industrialization spreads throughout Asia, replicating Japan's experiences of environmental destruction on a far wider scale, so it becomes increasingly important to understand how common environmental problems are interpreted in differing social and intellectual settings. Japan provides one useful example of the way in which varied elements of "tradition" can be reinterpreted to deal with new problems. In this sense, the study of Japan's history may play some role in creating a deeper international understanding of the many possible approaches to a global problem.

Contributors

Kuo-tung Ch'en
Institute of Economics
Academia Sinica
Nankang
Taipei, Taiwan, ROC 11529
e-mail:
ktchen@ieas.econ.sinica.edu.tw

Helen Dunstan
The School of Asian Studies
University of Sydney
Sydney
Australia 2006
e-mail:
helen.dunstan@asia.su.
    edu.au

Mark Elvin
Division of Pacific and Asian
    History
Research School of Pacific and
    Asian Studies
Institute of Advanced Study
Australian National University
Canberra, ACT
Australia 0200
e-mail:
mde402@coombs.anu.edu.au

Antonia Finnane
Department of History
University of Melbourne
Parksville, Victoria
Australia 3052

Wolfgang Holzner
Institut für Botanik
Universität für Bodenkultur
Gregor Mendel-Str. 33
A-1180 Wien
Austria

Monika Kriechbaum
Institut für Botanik
Universität für Bodenkultur
Gregor Mendel-Str. 33
A-1180 Wien
Austria

Christian Lamouroux
École française d'Extrême-Orient
22, Avenue du Président Wilson
75116 Paris
France

Li Bozhong
Institute of Economics
Academy of the Social Sciences
2 Yuetan, Beixiaojie
Beijing
People's Republic of China
100836

Liu Ts'ui-jung
Institute of Economics
Academia Sinica
Nankang
Taipei, Taiwan, ROC 11529
e-mail: ectjliu@sinica.edu.tw

Kerrie L. MacPherson
Department of History
University of Hong Kong
Pokfulam Road
Hong Kong
e-mail: klmacp@hkucc.hku.hk

Robert B. Marks
Department of History
Whittier College
Whittier, CA 90608
USA
e-mail: rmarks@whittier.edu

J. R. McNeill
Department of History
Georgetown University
Washington, DC 20057
USA
e-mail: mcneillj@
  guvax.acc.georgetown.edu

Nicholas K. Menzies
The Ford Foundation
PO Box 41081
Nairobi
Kenya
e-mail: n.menzies@fordfound.org

Tessa Morris-Suzuki
Division of Pacific and Asian
  History
Research School of Pacific and
  Asian Studies
Australian National University
Canberra, ACT
Australia 0200
e-mail: tms@coombs.anu.edu.au

Anne Osborne
Department of History
Rider College
2083 Lawrenceville Road
Lawrenceville, NJ 08648
USA
e-mail:
osborne@enigma.rider.edu

Paolo Santangelo
Istituto Universitario Orientale
Dipartimento di Studi Asiatici
Piazza Domenico Maggiore, 12
80134 Napoli
Italy
e-mail: p.santangelo@iol.it

Shiba Yoshinobu
International Christian University
10-2, Osawa 3-chome
Mitaka-shi, Tokyo 181
Japan

Su Ninghu
Manaaki Whenua/
Landcare Research NZ, Ltd.
Private Bag 3127
Hamilton
New Zealand
e-mail: sun@landcare.cri.nz

An-Chi Tung
Institute of Economics
Academia Sinica
Nankang
Taipei, Taiwan, ROC 11529
email:
actung@ieas.econ.sinica.edu.tw

Eduard B. Vermeer
Sinologisch Instituut
Leiden University
Arsenaalstraat 1
2311 Leiden
The Netherlands
e-mail:
ebvermeer@rullet.leidenuniv.nl

Pierre-Étienne Will
Collège de France
11, Place Marcelin-Berthelot
75231 Paris Cedex 05
France
e-mail: will@idf.ext.jussieu.fr

Zhang Yixia
The Flinders University
PO Box 10242
Gouger Street
Adelaide, South Australia
Australia 5001

Index

Subjects have been aggregated here into general categories, with subcategories. Levels of division are (1) **BOLD** general category, (2) *italicized* subcategory, (3) Capitalized entry (with colon separating entry and page numbers), (4) lowercased subentry (with comma separating subentry and page numbers), (5) lowercased sub-subentry (with no punctuation separating sub-subentry and page numbers).

Chinese is ordered by syllables: thus "Shanxian" precedes "Shangyu". "(J)" indicates, where not otherwise obvious, that an entry applies to Japan. "(E)" in similar fashion indicates Europe.

Users may find it helpful to glance first through the category headings, and see what is listed under each, if they intend to use the index systematically or frequently. Note in particular that personal names appear under **INDIVIDUALS**, and that **PLACES** (with **LAKES**, **MOUNTAINS**, **RIVERS**, and **SEAS**) in effect constitutes a gazetteer.

ANIMALS

Antelope: 87; Camels: 595; Cattle: 57, 120, 121, 122, 129, 167, 168, 193, 241, 242, 248, 373, 376, 395n, 595, 712; Crocodiles: 227; Deer: 167, 171–3, 187, 612, 699; Dogs: 6; Donkeys: 121; Dragons: 129; Earthworms: 172; Elk: 171; Gazelles: 87; Goats: 57, 105, 114, 248; Horses (and cavalry): 17, 34, 121, 256, 395n, 545, 561, 582, 595, 605; Jackals: 92; Kyang (wild donkeys): 87; Leopards: 129;

Monkeys: 114; Mules: 250; Oxen: 122, 170, 250, 256, 257, 595, 604, 605, 704; earth oxen (*tuniu*) as frontier markers, 175–6, 188, 696; pottery oxen conferring supernatural protection, 390; Pigs: 35, 120, 121, 122, 129, 256, 257, 422, 604, 605; wild, 130; Pikas: 92; Rats: 17; Sables: 10; Sheep: 57, 105, 256, 257, 376, 595; wild, 87; Snails: 6; Snakes: 172, 197; adders, 172; Squirrels: 612; Tigers: 227; Turtles: 208, 227; Water buffalo: 422; Weasels: 612; "Wild beasts": attacks by, 704; Wolves: 92; Yaks: wild, 87

Selected aspects

Animal husbandry: 712; extensive, not popular in China, 706; Burning to drive off: 706; Extinctions: 729; Grazing pressure: 78, 88–95, 101–4, 598; Impact of hydropower schemes on: 749–50; Loss of wildlife: 260; Scared away from logging sites: 705

BIRDS

Chickens: 257, 422; Domestic fowl: 35; Ducks: 605, 665; ritual use of, 669–70; Falcons: peregrine, 758; Geese: 689–90; Raptors: 92; Songs of: 171; Waterfowl: 264

BUILDING/CONSTRUCTION

Boats: as homes, 671, 678; Bridges: 332n; Built environment (living environment): 198–9; and tuberculosis, ch.

Floods: as impact on harvest, 426; Frost: 412n, 421, 422, 428, 433, 461; Growing seasons: 413, 420, 471 (rice), 472n (rice); busy farming, 678; Hydropower schemes: effects of on, 729; Ice: effect on water flow into Bian, 578; Ice ages: 348; little, 451–2; Insolation (and solar radiation): 413, 419, 450, 468, 470, 589; per cm^2, 452; hours of, 452 (annual), 454; Long-term trends: 366; global nature of, 415–6; improvement in 18th c., 268; worsening in 19th c., 178; possible periodicities, 366; Maladjustment of migrants to: 193, 196; Mediterranean type: 60; Microclimates: 237; and vegetation change, 40–1; Monsoon rains: 273, 360; Monsoon regime: 285, 348, 419, 422, 453; disrupted, 431; North Pacific subtropical high: 422, 431; Periodicities: floods and droughts, 418; Periodization: from 1400 to 1900, 451, 452; Precipitation (mainly rainfall): 328, 348, 364, 366, 417–9, 431, 443, 450; annual, 452; Himalayan, 65, 76; "plum rains," 348, 470; in S. China, 413–4; seasonal maxima, 285; in Taiwan, 731, 732; variability, 323; Raindrops, effect of impact: 218–9, 272–3; Rainstorms: 216–7, 299, 322, 327; as cause of floods in Jiangnan, 453; hurt harvest, 603; Shaanxi: 325; Snow: 65n, 70, 411, 412n, 421 (spring), 422, 589; accumulation of, 607–8; Snowmelt: 364; crucial for irrigation systems, 607; South China: subtropical, 413; Sunshine: see Insolation; Taiwanese: 171; Techniques for the historical study of: 43; Temperature: 450; accumulated, 471–2; annual mean, 348, 350, 452 (in Jiangnan), 471; effects on soils, 465; monthly mean in S. China, 413, 414–7; N. hemisphere trends, 411n, 416–7; trends in S. China, 445; winter (S. China), 414, 415; Volcanic eruptions: cause cooling, 415, 419n, 431; Warming: brings rain in S. China, 432; Warmth: total annual, 452; Weather: from 1820 to 1850, 482n; Wind: carries pollution, 765 (J); cold, creates need for fuel, 607; erosion by, 602, 603; uses of for rice, 469

COMMODITIES (*see also* **TECHNOLOGIES TRADE**)

Ajinomoto: *see* Monosodium glutamate; Alcohol: 479–80, 597; Aquatic products: 682; Bark: 258; Baskets: bamboo, 670; Beans: 682; Beds: 708; Biscuits: 686; Camphor: oil, 699, 713–4; wood, 697, 699, 701, 702, 703, 704, 706, 707; Chairs: 708; Chamber pots: 669; Charcoal: price of, 250; Cheongsams (short-sleeved): 686; Cloth: 683; Coffins: 601; Concubines: 676, 677; Deerskin: 167, 172–4; Dyes (for food): 480; Eyebrow liner: 686; Firewood: 167; high price of, 217; Flowers: 213; Fruits: 601; Fungi: 258; Furniture: 706, 708, 709 (bamboo); Glasses (optical): 686; Hides: 239; High-heeled shoes: 686; Ink sticks: 706; Iron: for tools, 710; Knives: 213; Lipstick: 686; Medicines: 480; Millet: 682; Monosodium glutamate: 768–71 (J); Nuts: 601; Paper: 213, 710; "joss paper," 710; pith paper, 706; Religious goods: 597; Rice: 682; Scissors: 213; Seaweed (J): 778; Silk: prices of, 567; Soysauce: 480; Sugar: 507; Sulfur: 170, 171, 694; Timber: ch. 19; 249, 601; impediments to commercial growing of, 252; prices of, 209, 210, 251; shortage of, 216, 278; source of merchant capital, 220; used for, carts 710, everday objects 706, ships 702–3, 706, sleepers (ties) 254; tools 706, 710; Umbrellas: 213; Utensils: 601; Varnish: 213; Vegetables: 682; Venison: 167, 172; Vinegar: 480n; Wheat: 682; Wine: 480n; Yeast: 480, 597

CONFLICTS OVER ENVIRONMENTAL ISSUES, ch. 21

Aborigines versus government: 705; Ajinomoto (Suzuki Shōten/Kawasaki) dispute (J): 768–71, 778; arbitrated, 770; Anti-pollution protests against mines and factories (J): ch. 21; success or failure linked to involvement/non-involvement of local leaders, 767 (J), 771–2 (J); statistics

IDEAS *(cont.)*

467; wilderness, 13, 14, 171; Yellow R., ideology relating to, 548; *yin* and *yang*, 197, 497, 593, 623, 627; Cholera: new virulence perhaps due to genetic change, 500, 518; whether indigenous or not to China, debate over, 495–503; Defensive expansion: 597; Diseases: environmental factors in, ch. 13, 493; germ theory of, 493; Double cropping: postulated change in from Song to Ming, 464–5; Ecological complementarity: 35; Economic speculation protected by political forces: 738n; Environment: effect of on human character, 686–8; Environment and culture (and customs): covariance of, 665–6, 675, 683–7; Environmental crisis: current Chinese awareness of, 756; Environmental damage: perceptions of, European 758–9, Japanese ch. 21; Environmental decisions affected by politics and finance: 582; Environmental history: 5–8, 14–18, 48–9; Environmental threshold: 230; "Expansion" contrasted with "growth": 596; Geography of culture: 683; Geomancy (*fengshui*): 218, 588, 624; God: 626; Harvest ratings: 427, 436*f*; Hydraulic society interpreted: bureaucratic model versus community (collectivity) model, 337–8; Hydrology: modern theories on carrying capacity of a flow, 401–2;

Japanese concepts (late-traditional and early modern): authoritarian elements in, 773; balance between humans and nature, 774; balance between Way of Heaven (cosmic parity of beings) and Way of Humanity (hierarchical and moral), 774, 779; barriers between self and nature unreal, 772; benign ruler helps people by economic development, 772; Christianity, incorporation of elements of, 775; Confucianism, 772; development (*kaibutsu*) seen as positive, 773; disasters caused by ruler's bad conduct, 773; divine spirit in nature, 772; farming/mining symbiosis, 777; human/nature harmony, an oversimple formula, 772, 779;

human/nature reciprocity, 775; humans, are supreme among creatures 773, 779, should be "slaves of nature" 776, sustain nature 773; ideology of environmental protest, 771–9; *kōgai*, 758; loss of proper empathy with nature, 775; modern acquiescence in destruction of nature – an oversimple formula, 779; morality and preservation of nature linked, 773, 779; natural moral basis of farming, 775; Nippon golden age, 776; official developmentalist creed, 778–9; pollution a cause of social discord, 778; primates, term for, 773; public harm, 758; reinterpretation of traditional ideas, 780; resources consumed without thought for the future, 775–6; rural community model for fruitful collaboration with nature, 776; science, beneficial 777–8, misuse creates loss of faith in 777–8; Shintô, 772; technology should serve welfare of all, 777; villages as valuable as factories, 778; Zen, 772;

King's law: 439–41; Limits: of premodern intensified economic exploitation reached, 222; of premodern lowland productivity reached, 205, 209; Long-term unsustainability of highland economy: 229–30; Low impact of ideas on actions: 39; Macroregional cycles: 445–6; *Malthusian theory*: 131; Marxist and Nationalist views of: ecological destruction, 253–4; "sprouts of capitalism," 449; Nature and society: 546; Non-linearity of change: 131; Religion: Buddhism, 105, 655, 666; Christianity, 121, 676–7; Daoism, 583; emperor's religious function, 583; environmental behavior, religion not a good predictor of, 105; Hinduism, 94, 105; Islam, 94, 105; Rice yields in Ming-Qing: mainland debate on, 476–7; Science: in environmental disputes, 763 (J), 765 (J), 770 (J) (*see also* Chinese concepts: hydrology, experiments); Statistical techniques: for price data, 436n, 440–1; Subsistence crisis theory: 430, 444–5; Technological progress: invention, innovation, diffusion, 459; Technol-

INSECTS and ARTHROPODS, etc., 197, 476

INSTITUTIONS and CUSTOMS (*see also* **POLITICS; WAR**)